GENETICS

ETHICS, LAW AND POLICY

Fourth Edition

■　■　■

by

Lori B. Andrews
Distinguished Professor of Law
Chicago–Kent College of Law
Illinois Institute of Technology

Maxwell J. Mehlman
Distinguished University Professor
Arthur E. Petersilge Professor of Law
Case Western Reserve University

Mark A. Rothstein
Herbert F. Boehl Chair of Law and Medicine
University of Louisville

AMERICAN CASEBOOK SERIES®

American Casebook Series is a trademark registered in the U.S. Patent and Trademark Office.

© West, a Thomson business, 2002, 2006
© 2010 Thomson Reuters
© 2015 LEG, Inc. d/b/a West Academic
    444 Cedar Street, Suite 700
    St. Paul, MN 55101
    1-877-888-1330

West, West Academic Publishing, and West Academic are trademarks of West Publishing Corporation, used under license.

Printed in the United States of America

ISBN: 978-1-63459-157-7

For Christopher, Rory, Gabe, Julia, Lisa and Rachel

PREFACE TO THE FOURTH EDITION

Genetics is entering all aspects of our lives. People use genetic genealogy to discover distant relatives. Hospitals apply cutting-edge genetic technologies to diagnose and treat. Television shows feature the latest in forensic DNA, and courts use those techniques to convict or exonerate people. Legislators, courts and even the President weigh in on how to best take advantage of new genetic technologies. Government agencies such as the Food and Drug Administration and U.S. Patent and Trademark Office struggle with how to regulate genetic technologies. And certain technologies raise profound moral questions of life and death—and of how to define "human."

Every day thousands of people face individual choices about genetics. At the same time, hundreds of policy decisions are made about genetics—such as whether a particular test should be offered, what information should be provided to a patient in advance of a genetic test, and who should have access to the results. Doctors determine whether to test patients for a newly-discovered genetic mutation. Health insurers analyze whether to reimburse for such a test. The Food and Drug Administration struggles with the question of whether university laboratories offering genetic tests should be regulated. State lawmakers debate whether an insurer should be able to deny an individual life insurance because his or her sibling or parent has a genetic disorder.

Developments in genetics touch us as individuals and as members of society. They raise important questions for health care providers, economists, public health officials, corporations, insurers, and employers. They also raise issues for lawyers, judges, and legislators that encompass all areas of law—from tort law to constitutional law, from intellectual property law to employment law, from family law to criminal law.

To introduce the legal, ethical, economic, and social implications of genetics, we have included a wide variety of materials in this book. It contains relevant judicial opinions drawn from the federal and state courts. The book also contains statutes, administrative regulations, medical professional guidelines, and international treaties. It details the actual practices governing genetic research, diagnosis, treatment, and product development. The book deals only with human genetics and does not cover genetically-modified plants or animals. It is designed for use by not only law students, but students of health sciences, public health, sociology, public policy, bioethics, and various other disciplines. In law schools, the casebook serves an additional function. Courses using Genetics: Ethics, Law and Policy can act as a capstone to the law school education, providing a context for students to apply the knowledge they learned in tort, constitutional, medical, family, criminal, insurance, employment, and intellectual property law.

The casebook is divided into four major sections. The first section (Chapters 1 and 2) provides an introduction to the context in which decisions about genetics have been made. It details the scientific basis for genetic technology and the historical use of genetic ideas.

The second section (Chapters 3 through 5) covers genetic research, including issues related to federal and international regulations and intellectual property rights. It also includes an analysis of the application of genetics to racial and ethnic groups.

The third section (Chapters 6 through 10) deals with medical applications of genetics, including preimplantation screening, prenatal testing, newborn screening, the testing of children, cancer testing, pharmacogenomics, and gene therapy. It includes information about federal, state and professional oversight of the quality of genetic services, as well as judicial opinions about liability in the provision of genetic services.

The fourth section (Chapters 11 through 17) addresses the non-medical application of genetics, including paternity testing. The major focus of this section is on the use of genetic technologies by social institutions—such as law enforcement officials, courts, insurers, employers and schools.

To our readers, please note that we use both of the terms "genetics" and "genomics" in this casebook. We use the term "genetics" to refer both to the entire field generally and to single-gene, Mendelian scientific approaches. We use the term "genomics" to refer specifically to next-generation science such as whole genome sequencing. For example, with pharmacogenetics, the starting point is a human population with a genetic disease, and the task is to identify the genes that are associated with the disease. With pharmacogenomics, the starting point is the genome, the sequence of human DNA, and the task is to identify the diseases that are associated with differences in the genome, or polymorphisms.

This edition of the casebook has been updated to address several pivotal developments—the enactment of the Affordable Care Act, the U.S. Supreme Court's decision invalidating patents on human genes, the Court's decision on the constitutionality of entering DNA profiles of arrestees into a forensic DNA database, the expansion of personalized medicine (sometimes called precision medicine), and the regulation of genetic tests (including direct-to-consumer tests).

We are grateful to our many talented colleagues from law, social sciences, molecular biology, clinical genetics, philosophy, bioethics, economics, genetic counseling, and public health whose ideas and interactions with us have helped shape this book.

LORI ANDREWS
MAXWELL MEHLMAN
MARK ROTHSTEIN

ACKNOWLEDGMENTS

Allen, Anita L., Genetic Privacy: Emerging Concepts and Values, in Genetic Secrets: Protecting Privacy and Confidentiality in the Genetic Era, 31, 33–34 (Mark A. Rothstein, ed. 1997). Copyright © 1997 by Yale University. Reprinted by permission.

American Academy of Pediatrics, Newborn Screening: A Blueprint for the Future; A Call for a National Agenda on State Newborn Screening Programs, Report of the Task Force on Newborn Screening excerpted from Birth to the Medical Home; Pediatrics, volume 106: 389–390 (2000), used with permission of the American Academy of Pediatrics. Copyright © August 2000 American Academy of Pediatrics.

American Medical Association, Code of Medical Ethics, Opinion 2.11: Gene Therapy (1996). Copyright © 1996 American Medical Association. Reprinted with permission from the American Medical Association.

American Society for Reproductive Medicine, Minimum Genetic Testing for Gamete and Embryo Donors, 99 Fertility and Sterility, 2013, No. 1. Reprinted by permission from the American Society for Reproductive Medicine (Fertility and Sterility, 2013, Vol. 99, 45).

American Society of Human Genetics, Points to Consider: Ethical, Legal, and Psychosocial Implications of Genetic Testing in Children and Adolescents, in American Journal of Human Genetics, volume 57, 1233 (1995). Reprinted with permission of the University of Chicago Press excerpts from the American Society of Human Genetics and American College of Medical Genetics, Copyright © (1995) by the American Society of Human Genetics. All rights reserved.

American Society of Human Genetics, Social Issues Committee and American College of Medical Genetics, Social, Ethical, and Legal Issues Committee, Genetic Testing in Adoption, American Journal of Human Genetics, volume 66, 761–767 (2000). Copyright © 2000. Reprinted with permission of the American Society of Human Genetics.

American Society of Human Genetics, Statement on Informed Consent for Genetic Research, American Journal of Human Genetics 1996; volume 59, 471–473. Copyright © 1996, the American Society of Human Genetics. Reprinted with permission of the University of Chicago Press.

Andrews, Lori B. et al., Assessing Genetic Risks: Implications for Health and Social Policy, 40–41 (1994). Copyright © 1994. Reprinted with the permission of National Academy Press, Washington, D.C.

Andrews, Lori B., Future Perfect: Confronting Decisions About Genetics, 56–62 (2001). Copyright © 2001, Lori B. Andrews. Columbia University Press. Reprinted with the permission of the publisher.

Andrews, Lori B., Is There a Right to Clone? Constitutional Challenges to Bans on Human Cloning, 11 Harv. J.L. & Tech. 643, 647–648, 661–667 (Summer, 1998). Copyright © 1998, the President & Fellows of Harvard College. Reprinted with the permission of the Harvard Journal of Law and Technology.

Andrews, Lori B., Predicting and Punishing Antisocial Acts: How the Criminal Justice System Might Use Behavioral Genetics, in Behavioral Genetics: The Clash of Culture and Biology, 120–122 (Ronald A. Carson and Mark A. Rothstein eds., 1999). Copyright © 1999 Johns Hopkins University Press. Reprinted with the permission of Johns Hopkins University Press.

Andrews, Lori B., Prenatal Screening and the Culture of Motherhood, 47 Hastings L.J. 967, 970–971, 994–1000 (April 1996). Copyright © 1996, the University of California, Hastings College of the Law. Reprinted from 47 Hastings Law Journal (1996), with permission.

Andrews, Lori B., The Clone Age: Adventures in the New World of Reproductive Technology, 142–144 (2001). Copyright © 1999 by Lori B. Andrews. Reprinted by arrangement with Henry Holt & Company, LLC.

Andrews, Lori and Dorothy Nelkin, Body Bazaar: The Market For Human Tissue in the Biotechnology Age, 60–62, 102–103 (2001). Copyright © 2001, Random House Inc. Reprinted with permission of Random House.

Avise, John, The Genetic Gods: Evolution and Belief in Human Affairs, 50 (1998). Copyright © 1998 by the President and Fellows of Harvard College. Reprinted by permission of the publisher, Harvard University Press.

Baily, Mary Ann and Thomas H. Murray, Ethics, Evidence, and Cost in Newborn Screening, 38 Hastings Center Report 23, 27–28 (May/June 2008). Used with permission.

Berg, P. et al., Letter: Potential Biohazards of Recombinant DNA Molecules, Science, volume 185, 303 (1974). Reprinted with permission.

Bloch, Maurice et al, Predictive Testing for HD in Canada: The Experience of Those Receiving an Increased Risk, American Journal of Medical Genetics, volume 42, 499–507 (1992). Reprinted with permission of Wiley-Liss, Inc. a subsidiary of John Wiley & Sons, Inc. Copyright © 1992.

Bok, Sissela, Secrets: On the Ethics of Concealment and Revelation, 20 (1983). Copyright © 1982 by Sissela Bok. Used by permission of Pantheon Books, a division of Random House, Inc.

Bowser, Rene, Race as a Proxy for Drug Response: The Dangers and Challenges of Ethnic Drugs, 53 DePaul Law Review 1111 (2004). Reprinted with permission.

Brock, Dan W., Allen Buchanan, Norman Daniels, and Dan Wikler (eds.), From Chance to Choice: Genetics and Justice, 27–28 (2000). Reprinted with the permission of Cambridge University Press. Copyright © 2000 Cambridge University Press.

Brothers, Kyle B. & Mark A. Rothstein, Ethical, Legal, and Social Implications of Incorporating Personalized Medicine into Healthcare, 12 Personalized Med. 43 (2015). Copyright © Future Medicine, Ltd. Reprinted by permission.

Cavalli-Sforza, Luigi Luca, Remarks Upon Being Awarded the Balzan Prize for the Science of Human Origins (1999). Reprinted by permission.

Churchill, L.R. et al., Genetic Research as Therapy: Implication of 'Gene Therapy' for Informed Consent, 26 Journal of Law, Medicine, & Ethics 38 (Spring 1998). Copyright © 1998, Reprinted with the permission of the American Society of Law, Medicine & Ethics. All rights reserved.

Faden, Ruth R., Neil A. Holtzman, Judith A. Chwalow, Parental Rights, Child Welfare, and Public Health: The Case of PKU Screening, American Journal of Public Health, volume 72, 1396, 1397–1398 (1982). Reprinted with permission of the American Public Health Association. Copyright © 1982, the American Public Health Association.

Collins, Francis S., Shattuck Lecture—Medical and Societal Consequence of the Human Genome Project, New England Journal of Medicine, volume 341, 31–33 (1999). Copyright © 1999 Massachusetts Medical Society. Reprinted with permission. All rights reserved.

Duster, Troy, Behavioral Genetics and Explanations of the Link Between Crime, Violence, and Race, in Wrestling with Behavioral Genetics: Science, Ethics, and Public Conversations, 154–156 (Erik Parens, Audrey R. Chapman, and Nancy Press eds.)(2006). Copyright © 2006 Johns Hopkins University Press. Reprinted with permission of Johns Hopkins University Press.

Epstein, Richard A., The Legal Regulation of Genetic Discrimination: Old Responses to New Technology 74 B.U. L. Rev. 1, 12–13 (1994). Copyright © 1994 by the Trustees of Boston University; Richard A. Epstein. Reprinted by permission.

Fost, Norman, Genetic Diagnosis & Treatment Ethical Considerations, American Journal of Disease of Children, volume/edition 147, 1190 (1993). Copyright © 1993 American Medical Association. Reproduced with permission of American Medical Association in the format Textbook via Copyright Clearance Center.

Foster, et al. Excerpts from Foster et al., A Model Agreement for Genetic Research in Socially Identifiable Populations, American Journal of Human Genetics, volume 63, 696–702 (1998). Copyright © 1998. Reprinted with the permission of the University of Chicago Press.

Fukuyama, Francis, Our Posthuman Future: Consequences of the Biotechnology Revolution, 204 (2002), © 2002 by the author. Reprinted by permission.

Garraway, Levi A., Genomics Driven Oncology: Framework for an Emerging Paradigm, 31 J. Clinical Oncology 1806, 1806–1813 (2013). Copyright © 2013 American Society of Clinical Oncology. Reprinted by permission.

Goldstein, Norm, Owner of 'Genius' Sperm Bank Pleased by Results, The New York Times, December 11, 1984, A17. Reprinted with permission of the Associated Press. Copyright © 1984 the Associated Press.

Greely, Henry T., The Control of Genetic Research: Involving the "Groups Between," 33 Hous. L. Rev. 1397, 1399–1402 (1997). Copyright © 1997, Houston Law Review. Reprinted with permission of the University of Houston Law Review.

Hall, Mark A., Legal Rules and Industry Norms: The Impact of Laws Restricting Health Insurers' Use of Genetic Information 40 Jurimetrics 93, 94–99, 122 (1999). Copyright © 1999 American Bar Association; Mark A. Hall. Reprinted by permission.

Harris, Cailin, Statutory Prohibitions on Wrongful Birth Claims & Their Dangerous Effects on Parents, 34 Boston College J. L. & Soc. Just. 365 (2014). Reprinted with permission.

Harsanyi, Zsolt and Richard Hutton, Genetic Prophecy: Beyond the Double Helix, 187–188 (1981). Copyright © 1981. Reprinted with permission of the authors.

Hoffman, Sharona and Mark Rothstein, Genetic Testing, Genetic Medicine and Managed Care, Wake Forest Law Review, volume 34, 849, 875–876 (1999). Reprinted with permission of the Wake Forest Law Review.

Hyman, Steven E., Using Genetics to Understand Human Behavior: Promises and Risks in Wrestling With Behavioral Genetics: Science, Ethics, and Public Conversation, 113–116 (Erik Parens, Audrey R.

Chapman, & Nancy Press eds. 2006) Copyright © Johns Hopkins University Press. Reprinted with permission of Johns Hopkins University Press.

Imwinkelried, Edward and D. H. Kaye, DNA Typing: Emerging or Neglected Issues, 76 Wash. L. Rev. 413, 416–440 (2001). Copyright © 2001 Washington Law Review Association. Reprinted with permission of the authors.

Juengst, Eric T., The Perils of Genetic Genealogy, 10 CenterViews 1 (Winter 1996). Copyright © 1996. Reprinted with permission of the author.

Kaiser, Jocelyn, A Plan to Capture Human Diversity in 1000 Genomes. Excerpted with permission from Science, volume 319, 395 (2008). Copyright © 2008 American Association for the Advancement of Science.

Kerouac, James D., The Regulation of Home Diagnostic Tests for Genetic Disorders: Can the FDA Deny Premarket Application on the Basis of the Devices, 5 Journal of Biolaw & Business 34–43 (2002). Reprinted with permission.

Khan, Zeshan Q., Colonialism Revisited: Insights into the Human Genome Diversity Project, 3 J.L. & Soc. Challenges 89, 89–115 (1999). Copyright © 1999. Reprinted with permission.

Khoury, Muin J., et al., Will Genomics Widen or Help Heal the Schism Between Medicine and Public Health?, 33 Am. J. Prev. Med. 310, 313 (2007). Copyright © 2007 Elsevier. Reprinted by permission.

Krimsky, Sheldon, The Profit of Scientific Discovery and Its Normative Implications, 75 Chicago–Kent L. Rev. 15, 21–22, 28–37 (1999). Copyright © 1999, IIT Chicago–Kent College of Law. Reprinted with permission of Chicago–Kent Law Review.

Lacy, James V. et al., Technology Transfer Laws Governing Federally Funded Research and Development, 19 Pepp. L. Rev. 1, 9–11, 13–14 (1991). Copyright © 1991. Reprinted with the permission of the Pepperdine Law Review.

Lander, E.S. Scientific Commentary: The Scientific Foundations and Medical and Social Prospects of the Human Genome, 26 Journal of Law, Medicine & Ethics 184, 184–185 (1998). Copyright © 1998, Reprinted with the permission of the American Society of Law, Medicine & Ethics. All rights reserved.

Lander, Eric, DNA Fingerprinting: Science, Law, and the Ultimate Identifier, in The Code of Codes, 191–210 (Daniel J. Kevles and Leroy Hood, eds., 1992). Reprinted by permission of the publisher from in The Code Of Codes: Scientific and Social Issues in the Human Genome

Project, edited by Daniel J. Kevles and Leroy Hood, Cambridge, Mass.: Harvard University Press, Copyright © 1992 by Daniel J. Kevles and Leroy Hood.

Ledley, Fred, A Consumer Charter for Genomic Services, 20 Nature Biotechnology 767 (2002). Reprinted with permission.

Lewin, Tamar, Boom in Genetic Testing Raises Questions on Sharing Results, The New York Times, July 21, 2000, A1. Reprinted with permission from The New York Times Agency. Copyright © 2000, The New York Times Agency.

Lewis, C.S., The Abolition of Man, 70–71 (1947). Copyright © C.S. Lewis Pte. Ltd. 1943, 1946, 1978. Extract reprinted by permission.

Lombardo, Paul A., Three Generations, No Imbeciles: New Light on Buck v. Bell, in the New York University Law Review, volume 60, 30, 50–61 (1985). Reprinted with permission from the New York University Law Review.

Lowden, J. Alexander, Genetic Risks and Mortality Rates, in Genetics and Life Insurance: Medical Underwriting and Social Policy, 95–98 (Mark A. Rothstein ed. 2004). Copyright © 2004, MIT Press. Reprinted with permission.

Malinowski, Michael J., Dealing with the Realities of Race and Ethnicity: A Bioethics–Centered Argument in Favor of Race–Based Genetics Research, 45 Hous. L. Rev. 1415, 1433–1436 (2009). Reprinted by permission of the Houston Law Review.

Marchant, Gary E., Genetic Susceptibility and Biomarkers in Toxic Injury Litigation, 41 Jurimetrics 67, 87 (2000). Copyright © 2000 by American Bar Association, Gary E. Marchant. Reprinted by permission.

Marchant, Gary E., Toxicogenomics and Environmental Regulation, in Genomics and Environmental Regulation: Science, Ethics, and Law, 11–14 (Richard R. Sharp, Gary E. Marchant, and Jamie A. Grodsky eds. 2008). Copyright © Johns Hopkins University Press. Reprinted with permission of Johns Hopkins University Press.

Marshall, Eliot, Tapping Iceland's DNA. Excerpted with permission from Science, volume 278, 566 (1997). Copyright © 1997, American Association for the Advancement of Science.

Matthews, Anne L., Genetic Counseling, in the Encyclopedia of Ethical, Legal & Policy Issues in Biotechnology, volume 1, 349–350 (T.H. Murray and M.J. Mehlman, eds., 2000). Reprinted with permission of John Wiley & Sons, Inc. Copyright © 2000.

McGuire, Amy L., Rebecca Fisher, Paul Cuseman, Kathy Hudson, Mark A. Rothstein, Deven McGraw, Stephen Matterson, John Glasser, and Douglas Henley, Confidentiality, Privacy, and Security

Considerations for the Storage of Genetic and Genomic Test Information in Electronic Health Records: Points to Consider, 10 Genetics in Med., 495, 495–499, (2009). Reprinted by permission.

Mehlman, Maxwell J., Access to the Genome and Federal Entitlement Programs, in The Human Genome Project and the Future of Health Care, 119–123. (T.H. Murray and M.J. Mehlman, R.F. Murray, Jr., eds., 1996). Reprinted with permission of Indiana University Press. Copyright © 1996 from Access to the Genome and Federal Entitlement Programs.

Mehlman, Maxwell J., Modern Eugenics and the Law, in A Century of Eugenics in America: From the "Indiana Experiment" to the Human Genome Era, Paul A. Lombardo, Ed. (Indiana University Press, Forthcoming 2010). Used with permission.

Mehlman, Maxwell J., Jessica W. Berg, Eric T. Juengst, and Eric Kodish, Ethical and Legal Issues in Enhancement Research on Human Subjects, 20 Cambridge Q. of Healthcare Ethics 30, 32–34 (2011). Used with permission.

Morse, Stephen J., Genetics and Criminal Responsibility, 15 Trends in Cognitive Sciences 378, 379 (2011). Copyright © 2011 Elsevier. Reprinted by permission.

Murray, Thomas H., Genetic Exceptionalism and "Future Diaries": Is Genetic Information Different from Other Medical Information?, in Genetic Secrets: Protecting Privacy and Confidentiality in the Genetic Era, 60, 71 (Mark A. Rothstein, ed. 1997). Copyright © 1997 by Yale University. Reprinted by permission.

National Research Council, Applications of Toxicogenomic Technologies to Predictive Toxicology and Risk Assessment, 173, 186–189 (2007). Reprinted with permission by the National Academy of Sciences, Courtesy of the National Academies Press, Washington, DC.

National Research Council, The Evaluation of Forensic DNA Evidence, 171–173 (1996). Copyright © 1996, National Academy Press. Reprinted with permission of the National Academy of Sciences.

Obasogie, Osagie K., Playing the Gene Card? A Report on Race and Human Biotechnology (Center for Genetics and Society 2009). Used with permission.

Orentlicher, David, Genetic Privacy in the Patient-Physician Relationship, in Genetic Secrets: Protecting Privacy and Confidentiality in the Genetic Era 77, 78–81 (Mark A. Rothstein, ed. 1997). Copyright © 1997 by Yale University. Reprinted by permission.

Owen, James, Future Humans: Four Ways We May, or May Not Evolve, National Geographic News, Nov. 24, 2009. Copyright © 2009 National Geographic. Reprinted by permission.

Parens, Erik, Authenticity and Ambivalence: Toward Understanding the Enhancement Debate, 35 Hastings Center Report 34, 37–38 (2005). Reprinted with permission.

Parens, Erik and Eric Juengst, Inadvertently Crossing the Germ Line, Science, volume 292, 397 (2001). Reprinted with permission of the American Association for the Advancement of Science. Copyright © 2001 American Association for the Advancement of Science.

Plomin, Robert et al., Behavioral Genetics, in Behavioral Genetics in the Postgenomic Era, 10–14 (Robert Plomin et al. eds., 2003). Copyright © 2003 by the American Psychological Association. Reprinted with permission.

Pollack, Andrew, Patient's DNA May Be Signal to Tailor Drugs, The New York Times, Dec. 30, 2008, at A1. Reprinted with permission.

Rebouché, Rachel and Karen Rothenberg, Mixed Messages: The Intersection of Prenatal Genetic Testing and Abortion, 55 How. L. J. 983, 993–996. Reprinted with permission.

Reilly, Philip R., Eugenics, Ethics, Sterilization Law, in 1 Encyclopedia of Ethical, Legal & Policy Issues in Biotechnology, 204–208. (T.H. Murray and M.J. Mehlman, eds., 2000). Reprinted with permission of John Wiley & Sons, Inc. Copyright © 2000.

Ridley, Matt, Genome: The Autobiography of a Species in 23 Chapters 43–46 (1999). Copyright 1999 by Matt Ridley, reprinted by permission of HarperCollins Publishers, Inc.

Ridley, Matt, Nature Via Nurture: Genes, Experience, and What Makes Us Human 260–262 (2003). Copyright © 2003 by Matt Ridley, reprinted by permission of HarperCollins Publishers, Inc.

Roberts, Jessica L., Preempting Discrimination: Lessons from the Genetic Information Nondiscrimination Act, 63 Vand. L. Rev. 439, 440–441 (2010). Reprinted by permission.

Roses, Allen D., Pharmacogenetics and the Practice of Medicine, Nature, volume 405, 857–865 (2000). Reprinted with permission from Pharmacogenetics and the Practice of Medicine, Nature, volume 405, 857–865 (2000). Copyright © 2000 Macmillan Magazines, Ltd.

Rothman, Barbara Katz, Genetic Maps and Human Imaginations: The Limits of Science in Understanding Who We Are, 18, 247–248 (1998). Copyright © 1998 by Barbara Katz Rothman. Reprinted by permission of W.W. Norton & Company, Inc.

Rothstein, Laura F., Genetic Information in Schools, in Genetic Secrets: Protecting Privacy and Confidentiality in the Genetic Era, 317–320 (Mark A. Rothstein ed., 1997). Copyright © 1997 by Yale University. Reprinted by permission.

Rothstein, Mark A., Behavioral Genetic Determinism: Its Effects on Culture and Law, in Behavioral Genetics: The Clash of Culture and Biology, 89–96 (Ronald A. Carson and Mark A. Rothstein eds., 1999). Copyright © 1999 Johns Hopkins University Press. Reprinted by permission of the Johns Hopkins University Press.

Rothstein, Mark A., Expanding the Ethical Analysis of Biobanks, 33 J.L. Med. & Ethics 89–91 (Spring 2005). Reprinted with permission of the American Society of Law, Medicine & Ethics.

Rothstein, Mark A., Genetic Exceptionalism and Legislative Pragmatism, 35 Hastings Center Report No. 4, 27–33 (2005). Copyright © 2005. Reprinted with permission of the Hastings Center.

Rothstein, Mark A., Genetic Stalking and Voyeurism: A New Challenge to Privacy, 57 Kansas Law Review (2009) 539, 546–548. Reprinted by permission.

Rothstein, Mark A., Genetics and the Work Force of the Next Hundred Years, 2000 Colum. Bus. L. Rev. 371, 371–372 (2000). Copyright © 2000 Columbia Business Law Review; Mark A. Rothstein. Reprinted by permission.

Rothstein, Mark A., GINA's Beauty Is Only Skin Deep, 22 GeneWatch No. 2, 9–10 (2009), Reprinted with the permission of GeneWatch, the magazine of the Council for Responsible Genetics. May not be reproduced for any political purpose, including use in candidate campaigns or for legislative lobbying.

Rothstein, Mark A., Legal Conceptions of Equality in the Genomic Age, 25 Journal of Law & Inequality: A Journal of Theory & Practice 429, 455–460, (2007). Reprinted with permission.

Rothstein, Mark A., Occupational Health and Discrimination Issues Raised by Toxicogenomics in the Workplace, Genomics and Environmental Regulation 184–188 (Richard R. Sharp, Gary E. Marchant, & Jamie Grodsky, eds., 2008). Copyright © Johns Hopkins University Press. Reprinted with permission of Johns Hopkins University Press.

Rothstein, Mark A., Policy Recommendations, in Genetics and Life Insurance: Medical Underwriting and Social Policy, 252–261 (Mark A. Rothstein, ed. 2004). Copyright © 2004, MIT Press. Reprinted by permission.

Rothstein, Mark A., Predictive Genetic Testing for Alzheimer's Disease in Long–Term Care Insurance, 35 Ga. L. Rev. 707, 716–731 (2001). Copyright © 2001 Georgia Law Review Association, Inc.; Mark A. Rothstein. Reprinted by permission.

Rothstein, Mark A., Preventing the Discovery of Plaintiff Genetic Profiles by Defendants Seeking to Limit Damages in Personal Injury Litigation, 71 Ind. L.J. 877, 878–891 (1996). Copyright © 1996 by the Trustees of Indiana University; Mark A. Rothstein. Reprinted by permission.

Rothstein, Mark A., GINA, the ADA, and Genetic Discrimination in Employment, 35 J.L. Med. & Ethics 837–839 (2008). Copyright © 2008. Reprinted with permission of the American Society of Law, Medicine & Ethics. May not be reproduced without express written consent.

Rothstein, Mark A. and Mary R. Anderlik, What is Genetic Discrimination and When and How Can it Be Prevented? 3 Genetics in Med. 354, 354–355 (2001). Reprinted by permission.

Rothstein, Mark A., Yu Cai, and Gary E. Marchant, Ethical Implications of Epigenetics Research, 10 Nature Reviews Genetics 224 (2009). Copyright © 2009 Nature Publishing Group. Reprinted by permission.

Rothstein, Mark A. and Sandra Carnahan, Legal and Policy Issues in Expanding the Scope of Law Enforcement DNA Data Banks, 67 Brook. L. Rev. 127 (2001). Copyright © 2001. Reprinted with the permission of the Brooklyn Law Review.

Rothstein, Mark A. and Phyllis Griffin Epps, Ethical and Legal Implications of Pharmacogenomics, 2 Nature Reviews Genetics 228–230 (2001). Copyright © 2001, Macmillan Magazines, Ltd.

Rothstein, Mark A. and Yann Joly, Genetic Information and Insurance Underwriting: Contemporary Issues and Approaches in the Global Economy in Handbook of Genetics and Society, 130–132 (Paul Atkinson, Peter Glasner, & Margaret Lock, eds., 2009). Copyright © 2009. Reprinted with author permission.

Rothstein, Mark A. and Meghan K. Talbott, Compelled Disclosure of Health Information: Protecting Against the Greatest Potential Threat to Privacy, JAMA 295(24) 2882–2885 (2006). Copyright © 2006 American Medical Association All rights reserved. Reprinted with permission.

Sandel, Michael, The Case Against Perfection: What's Wrong with Designer Children, Bionic Athletes, and Genetic Engineering, Atlantic Monthly (April 2004). Reprinted with permission.

Stock, Gregory, Redesigning Humans: Our Inevitable Genetic Future, 1–5 (2002). Reprinted with permission.

Stolberg, S., The Biotech Death of Jesse Gelsinger, The New York Times Sunday Magazine, November 28, 1999, 137. Reprinted with permission, The New York Times Agency. Copyright © 1999, The New York Times Agency.

Trefethen, Amanda, The Emerging Tort of Wrongful Adoption, 11 J. Contemp. Legal Issues 620, 620–624 (2000). Copyright © 2000, Journal of Contemporary Legal Issues. Reprinted with the permission of the Journal of Contemporary Legal Issues.

Vogelstein, Bert, et al., Cancer Genome Landscapes, 339 Science 1546 (2013). Copyright © 2013 American Association for the Advancement of Science. Reprinted with permission.

Willing, Richard, DNA and Daddy, USA Today, July 29, 1999, 1A. Copyright © 1999, USA Today. Reprinted with permission.

Winker, Margaret A., Race and Ethnicity in Medical Research: Requirements Meet Reality, 34 J. Law, Med., & Ethics 520, 520–522 (2006). Reprinted with permission of the Journal of Law, Medicine, and Ethics.

Wood, Alastair J.J., Racial Differences in the Response to Drugs— Pointers to Genetic Disorders, 344 New England Journal of Medicine 1393, 1395 (2001). Reprinted with permission.

Wright Clayton, Ellen, Screening and Treatment of Newborns, 29 Houston Law Review, 85, 103–134 (1992). Reprinted with permission from the Houston Law Review, Copyright © 1992.

Zick, Cathleen D. et al., Genetic Testing, Adverse Selection, and the Demand for Life Insurance, 93 Am. J. Med. Genetics 29, 29–32, 35–38 (2000). Copyright © 2000 by Wiley–Liss, Inc. Reprinted by permission of Wiley–Liss, Inc., a subsidiary of John Wiley & Sons, Inc.

Zick, Cathleen D. et al., Genetic Testing for Alzheimer's Disease and Its Impact on Insurance Purchasing Behavior, 24 Health Affairs 483, 484–488 (2005). Copyright © 2005, by Project HOPE—The People-to-People Foundation, Inc. Reprinted by permission.

Zimmerman, B.K., Human Germ Line Therapy: The Case for its Development and Use, Journal of Medicine and Philosophy, volume 16, 593 (1991). Copyright © 1991 by Swets & Zeitlinger, Publishers. Reprinted with permission.

PHOTO ACKNOWLEDGMENTS

Leja, Darryl Henrietta Lacks (HeLa) Timeline. National Human Genome Research Institute, www.genome.gov.

Rosalind Franklin's Original DNA Radiograph. Photo. Reprinted with permission of King's College London.

Photograph of Carrie Buck and Mother. Arthur Estabrook Papers, M.E. Grenander Department of Special Collections & Archives, University at Albany, SUNY.

Photograph of John Moore. Reprinted with permission.

Photograph of Watson and Crick, Photo Researchers, Inc., 307 Fifth Avenue, 3rd Floor, New York, NY 10016. With permission.

Photograph of White House announcement of completion of the Human Genome Project with the permission of the Associated Press.

President Obama signing the Patient Protection and Affordable Care Act on March 23, 2010. Photo credit: Pete Souza. Photo was altered to black and white. Reprinted under CC by 2.0, http://creativecommons.org/licenses/by/2.0/.

SUMMARY OF CONTENTS

PREFACE TO THE FOURTH EDITION V

ACKNOWLEDGMENTS IX

PHOTO ACKNOWLEDGMENTS XXI

TABLE OF CASES XLIII

Chapter 1. Introduction 1
I.   Genes and the Past 2
II.   Genes and the Future 6
III.   Genes and the Present 12
IV.   The ELSI Program 17

Chapter 2. Scientific and Historical Overview 21
I.   Introduction 21
II.   History of Genetic Science 21
III.   Structure of DNA 23
IV.   Cells and Chromosomes 26
V.   Genes and Proteins 27
VI.   Genetic Differences Among Individuals 29
VII.   Cell Division 29
VIII. Patterns of Inheritance 31
IX.   The Human Genome Project 35
X.   Historical Overview: Eugenics 43

Chapter 3. Genetic Research 83
I.   Introduction 83
II.   Regulation of Research 85
III.   Research on Tissue Samples 102
IV.   Research on Human Embryos 117
V.   Liability in the Research Context 122

Chapter 4. Commercialization of Genetic Research: Property, Patents, and Conflicts of Interest 129
I.   Introduction 129
II.   The Patent System 131
III.   Policy Arguments Related to Patenting of Genetic Materials 134
IV.   Case Law on Patentable Subject Matter 137
V.   International Aspects of Biotech Patents 149
VI.   Technology Transfer Laws and Commercialization 151
VII.   Patients: The Sources of Genes and Cell Lines 158

Chapter 5. Race and Ethnicity 179
I.   Introduction 179

II.   Is There a Genetic Basis for Race?.. 179
III.   Genetics and African Americans.. 186
IV.   Genetics and Ethnicity 200

Chapter 6. Genetics and Reproduction.. **215**
I.   Introduction.. 215
II.   Prenatal Screening... 216
III.   Reproductive Technology and Genetics 247
IV.   Paternity and Assisted Reproduction 260
V.   The Genetic Frontier: Human Cloning................................. 280
VI.   Use of Genetics and Reproductive Technologies for Non-Medical
        Purposes... 285

Chapter 7. Clinical Applications of Genetics in Diagnostics............ **297**
I.   Introduction.. 297
II.   Genetic Testing Technology.. 299
III.   Regulation of Genetic Testing Products and Services 303
IV.   Clinical Genetic Screening and Testing................................ 310
V.   Cancer Genomics.. 348
VI.   Direct-to-Consumer Genetic Testing 351

Chapter 8. Clinical Applications of Genetics in Treatment.............. **369**
I.   Introduction.. 369
II.   Pharmacogenomics.. 369
III.   Gene Therapy 394

Chapter 9. Public Health **445**
I.   Introduction.. 445
II.   Public Health Genetics 445
III.   Public Health Emergencies and Genomics............................ 450
IV.   Newborn Screening Programs.. 451

Chapter 10. Genetic Enhancement.. **481**
I.   Introduction.. 481
II.   Procedures 481

Chapter 11. Parentage and Family Law **515**
I.   Introduction.. 515
II.   Reassessing Traditional Presumptions of Paternity in the DNA
        Era.. 517
III.   Genetics and Switched Babies.. 532
IV.   Genetics and Immigration 533
V.   Genetics, Adoption, and Disability....................................... 536

Chapter 12. Forensics: Genetic Testing for Identification................ **553**
I.   Introduction.. 553
II.   Admissibility of DNA Evidence in Criminal Cases............... 554
III.   DNA Banks.. 591

IV.   DNA Identification Outside the Criminal Setting 620

Chapter 13. Mental and Behavioral Genetics **627**
I.   Introduction 627
II.   History of Mental and Behavioral Genetics 629
III.   Scientific Issues 632
IV.   Criminal Law 637
V.   Education 657
VI.   Tort Law 668

Chapter 14. Privacy and Confidentiality **671**
I.   Introduction 671
II.   Genetic Privacy and Confidentiality 673
III.   Legal Protections for Medical and Genetic Privacy 683
IV.   Dealing With Genetic Differences 702

Chapter 15. Insurance **709**
I.   Introduction 709
II.   Health Insurance 711
III.   Life Insurance 735
IV.   Disability Insurance 751
V.   Long-Term Care Insurance 754

Chapter 16. Employment Discrimination **761**
I.   Introduction 761
II.   Genetic Discrimination Under the Americans With Disabilities Act
       (ADA) 771
III.   Genetic Nondiscrimination Laws 776

**Chapter 17. Environmental and Occupational Regulation and
Personal Injury Cases** **793**
I.   Introduction 793
II.   Regulation 794
III.   Litigation 808

INDEX 823

TABLE OF CONTENTS

PREFACE TO THE FOURTH EDITION V

ACKNOWLEDGMENTS IX

PHOTO ACKNOWLEDGMENTS XXI

TABLE OF CASES XLIII

Chapter 1. Introduction 1
I.   Genes and the Past 2
        John Avise, The Genetic Gods: Evolution and Belief in Human
              Affairs... 2
        Luigi Luca Cavalli-Sforza, Remarks Upon Being Awarded the Balzan
              Prize for the Science of Human Origins.. 3
        Note.. 4
        Matt Ridley, Genome: The Autobiography of a Species in 23
              Chapters... 4
        Notes and Questions 6
II.   Genes and the Future 6
        Mark A. Rothstein, Genetics and the Work Force of the Next
              Hundred Years 7
        James Owen, Future Humans: Four Ways We May, or May Not
              Evolve.. 7
        C.S. Lewis, The Abolition of Man.. 10
        Notes and Questions 11
III.   Genes and the Present... 12
        Kyle B. Brothers & Mark A. Rothstein, Ethical, Legal, and Social
              Implications of Incorporating Personalized Medicine into
              Healthcare... 12
        Barbara Katz Rothman, Genetic Maps and Human Imaginations:
              The Limits of Science in Understanding Who We Are 15
        Notes and Questions 16
IV.   The ELSI Program 17
        Francis Fukuyama, Our Posthuman Future: Consequences of the
              Biotechnology Revolution... 19
        Note... 19

Chapter 2. Scientific and Historical Overview 21
I.   Introduction 21
II.   History of Genetic Science 21
        Eric S. Lander, Scientific Commentary: The Scientific Foundations
              and Medical and Social Prospects of the Human Genome
              Project 21
III.   Structure of DNA 23

IV.   Cells and Chromosomes.. 26
V.   Genes and Proteins 27
VI.   Genetic Differences Among Individuals 29
VII.   Cell Division 29
VIII.   Patterns of Inheritance... 31
IX.   The Human Genome Project 35
       National Human Genome Research Institute, NIH Understanding
           Our Genetic Inheritance: The U.S. Human Genome Project the
           First Five Years: Fiscal Years 1991–1995 35
       Notes 35
       Remarks by the President, Prime Minister Tony Blair of England,
           Dr. Francis Collins, Director of the National Human Genome
           Research Institute, & Dr. Craig Venter, President and Chief
           Officer, Celera Genomics Corporation, on the Completion of
           the First Survey of the Entire Human Genome Project 37
       Notes and Questions 40
       National Human Genome Research Institute, International
           HapMap Project Overview.. 42
       Notes and Questions 43
X.   Historical Overview: Eugenics 43
       Allen Buchanan et al., From Chance to Choice: Genetics and
           Justice 44
       Philip R. Reilly, Eugenics, Ethics, Sterilization Laws, In 1
           Encyclopedia of Ethical, Legal, and Policy Issues in
           Biotechnology.. 45
       Buck v. Bell.. 48
       Paul A. Lombardo, Three Generations, No Imbeciles: New Light on
           Buck v. Bell... 50
       Notes and Questions 54
       Poe v. Lynchburg Training School & Hospital 59
       Notes 62
       Skinner v. Oklahoma 63
       Notes and Questions 69
       Taylor v. Kurapati... 70
       Notes 74
       Maxwell J. Mehlman, Modern Eugenics and the Law, in A Century
           of Eugenics: From the Indiana Experiment to the Human
           Genome Era 76
       Questions 81

Chapter 3. Genetic Research 83
I.   Introduction... 83
II.   Regulation of Research 85
     A. Types of Genetic Research 85
     B. The Federal Approach... 88
       Henry T. Greely, The Control of Genetic Research: Involving the
           "Groups Between".. 88

Federal Research Regulations 89
 C. Special Concerns About Genetic Research 94
  U.S. Dept. of Health and Human Services, Office of Protection
   From Research Risks (OPRR) Protecting Human Research
   Subjects: Institutional Review Board Guidebook 94
  Zsolt Harsanyi & Richard Hutton, Genetic Prophecy: Beyond
   the Double Helix 98
  Notes and Questions 99
 D. State Regulation of Research 101
III. Research on Tissue Samples 102
 A. The Nature of the Research 102
  National Bioethics Advisory Commission (NBAC), Research
   Involving Human Biological Materials: Ethical Issues and
   Policy Guidance 102
 B. Biobanks 103
  Mark A. Rothstein, Expanding the Ethical Analysis of
   Biobanks 103
  Notes and Questions 106
 C. Medical Organization Guidance About Research on Tissue
   Samples 109
  American Society of Human Genetics, Statement on Informed
   Consent for Genetic Research 109
 D. Case Study of Research on Existing Samples 112
  Centers for Disease Control and Prevention, "National Health
   and Nutrition Examination Survey" 112
  Notes and Questions 115
IV. Research on Human Embryos 117
 A. The Purpose of Embryo Research 117
 B. Constitutional Concerns in Embryo Research 118
  Lifchez v. Hartigan 118
  Notes and Questions 121
V. Liability in the Research Context 122
  Ande v. Rock 122
  Note 127

Chapter 4. Commercialization of Genetic Research: Property,
Patents, and Conflicts of Interest **129**
I. Introduction 129
II. The Patent System 131
 A. Requirements for a Patent 131
  Lori Andrews, The "Progress Clause": An Empirical Analysis
   Based on the Constitutional Foundation of Patent Law 131
 B. Statutory Authority 133
  Patent Code 35 U.S.C. §§ 101–103 133
III. Policy Arguments Related to Patenting of Genetic Materials 134
  Lila Feisee, Are Biotechnology Patents Important? Yes! 134

      U.S. Department of Energy Office of Science, Office of Biological
          and Environmental Research, Human Genome Program 135
      Notes and Questions 136
IV.   Case Law on Patentable Subject Matter 137
      Diamond v. Chakrabarty 137
      Association for Molecular Pathology v. Myriad Genetics, Inc. 140
      Harvard College v. Canada (Commissioner of Patents) 145
      Question 148
V.   International Aspects of Biotech Patents 149
      Directive 98/44/EC of the European Parliament and of the Council
          of 6 July 1998 on the Legal Protection of Biotechnological
          Inventions 149
      Agreement on Trade-Related Aspects of Intellectual Property
          Rights (TRIPS) 151
VI.   Technology Transfer Laws and Commercialization 151
      James V. Lacy et al., Technology Transfer Laws Governing
          Federally Funded Research and Development 151
      Sheldon Krimsky, The Profit of Scientific Discovery and Its
          Normative Implications 153
      Lori Andrews & Dorothy Nelkin, Body Bazaar: The Market for
          Human Tissue in the Biotechnology Age 156
      Notes and Questions 157
VII. Patients: The Sources of Genes and Cell Lines 158
      Moore v. Regents of the University of California 158
      Greenberg v. Miami Children's Hospital Research Institute, Inc. 168
      American Medical Association, Council on Ethical and Judicial
          Affairs, Code of Medical Ethics: Current Opinions With
          Annotations, 2012–2013 ed. 175
      Notes and Questions 175

Chapter 5. Race and Ethnicity **179**
I.   Introduction 179
II.   Is There a Genetic Basis for Race? 179
      Osagie K. Obasogie, Playing the Gene Card? A Report on Race and
          Human Biotechnology 180
      Michael J. Malinowski, Dealing With the Realities of Race and
          Ethnicity: A Bioethics-Centered Argument in Favor of Race-
          Based Genetics Research 181
      Margaret A. Winker, Race and Ethnicity in Medical Research:
          Requirements Meet Reality 183
      Notes and Questions 185
III.   Genetics and African Americans 186
      A. Eugenics 186
      B. Sickle Cell Screening 188
          Lori Andrews et al., Assessing Genetic Risks: Implications for
          Health and Social Policy 188
          Notes and Questions 189

C. Race-Based Drugs.. 190

Food and Drug Administration, FDA Approves BiDil Heart
Failure Drug for Black Patients 190

Alastair J.J. Wood, Racial Differences in the Response to
Drugs—Pointers to Genetic Differences 191

Rene Bowser, Race as a Proxy for Drug Response: The Dangers
and Challenges of Ethnic Drugs 194

Notes and Questions 198

IV. Genetics and Ethnicity 200

A. Research on Isolated Populations 200

Henry T. Greely, The Control of Genetic Research: Involving the
"Groups Between" 200

Zeshan Q. Khan, Colonialism Revisited: Insights into the Human
Genome Diversity Project 201

Jocelyn Kaiser, A Plan to Capture Human Diversity in 1000
Genomes 204

Notes and Questions 205

B. Concerns About "Group" Harms... 208

Eric T. Juengst, The Perils of Genetic Genealogy......................... 208

Morris W. Foster et al., A Model Agreement for Genetic Research
in Socially Identifiable Populations... 210

Lori Andrews, Havasupai Tribe Sues Genetic Researchers 212

Notes and Questions 214

Chapter 6. Genetics and Reproduction... **215**

I. Introduction 215

II. Prenatal Screening... 216

A. Prenatal Screening Techniques... 216

Lori B. Andrews, Future Perfect: Confronting Decisions About
Genetics... 216

Notes and Questions 219

B. Liability for Malpractice in Prenatal Screening............................... 220

Cailin Harris, Statutory Prohibitions on Wrongful Birth Claims
& Their Dangerous Effects on Parents 220

Keel v. Banach... 221

Molloy v. Meier 225

Notes and Questions 232

Curlender v. Bio-Science Laboratories.. 236

Doolan v. IVF America (MA) Inc. 240

Notes and Questions 242

C. Mandatory Prenatal Screening 243

Lori B. Andrews, Prenatal Screening and the Culture of
Motherhood 243

Notes and Questions 247

III. Reproductive Technology and Genetics.. 247

A. Procedures... 247

B. Genetic Screening in the Context of Assisted Reproduction 248

Minimum Genetic Screening for Gamete Donors, Approved by
 the Board of Directors of the American Society for
 Reproductive Medicine 248
 C. Liability in Reproductive Technology 250
 Johnson v. Superior Court of Los Angeles County 250
 Harnicher v. University of Utah Medical Center 255
 Notes and Questions 258
IV.   Paternity and Assisted Reproduction 260
 People v. Sorensen 260
 Jhordan C. v. Mary K. 263
 Soos v. Superior Court in and for County of Maricopa 268
 Perry-Rogers v. Fasano 272
 Note on Embryo Mix-Ups 276
 Notes and Questions 278
V.   The Genetic Frontier: Human Cloning 280
 Lori B. Andrews, Is There a Right to Clone? Constitutional
 Challenges to Bans on Human Cloning 280
 Notes and Questions 283
VI.   Use of Genetics and Reproductive Technologies for Non-Medical
 Purposes 285
 A. Sex Selection 285
 Lori B. Andrews, The Clone Age: Adventures in the New World
 of Reproductive Technology 285
 The American Society for Reproductive Medicine's Position on
 Gender Selection 286
 Notes and Questions 287
 B. Conceiving a Sibling to Be a Donor 289
 Ferrell v. Rosenbaum 290
 Notes and Questions 295

Chapter 7. Clinical Applications of Genetics in Diagnostics 297
I.   Introduction 297
II.   Genetic Testing Technology 299
III.   Regulation of Genetic Testing Products and Services 303
 Secretary's Advisory Committee on Genetics, Health, and Society,
 U.S. System of Oversight of Genetic Testing: A Response to
 the Charge of the Secretary of Health and Human Services 303
 Notes and Questions 309
IV.   Clinical Genetic Screening and Testing 310
 Maurice Bloch et al., Predictive Testing for Huntington Disease in
 Canada: The Experience of Those Receiving an Increased
 Risk 310
 Notes and Questions 313
 Tamar Lewin, Boom in Genetic Testing Raises Questions on
 Sharing Results 315
 Notes and Questions 317
 A. Liability Issues 318

Pate v. Threlkel 318
Safer v. Pack 321
Notes and Questions 325
B. Genetic Counseling... 329
    Anne L. Matthews, Genetic Counseling, in Encyclopedia of
        Ethical, Legal, and Policy Issues in Biotechnology 329
    Notes and Questions 330
C. Genetic Testing of Children and Adolescents..................... 331
    American Society of Human Genetics and American College of
        Medical Genetics, Points to Consider: Ethical, Legal, and
        Psychosocial Implications of Genetic Testing in Children
        and Adolescents 331
    Notes and Questions 334
D. Access to Genetic Services 334
    Maxwell J. Mehlman, Access to the Genome and Federal
        Entitlement Programs, in The Human Genome Project and
        the Future of Health Care... 335
    Mark A. Rothstein & Sharona Hoffman, Genetic Testing,
        Genetic Medicine, and Managed Care.................................... 340
    Rachel Rebouché & Karen Rothenberg, Mixed Messages: The
        Intersection of Prenatal Genetic Testing and Abortion 340
    Notes and Questions 342
E. Incidental Findings 342
    Presidential Commission for the Study of Bioethical Issues,
        Anticipate and Communicate: Ethical Management of
        Incidental and Secondary Findings in the Clinical,
        Research, and Direct-to-Consumer Contexts........................ 342
    ACMG Policy Statement: Updated Recommendations Regarding
        Analysis and Reporting of Secondary Findings in Clinical
        Genome-Scale Sequencing 344
    Notes and Questions 346
V.   Cancer Genomics... 348
    Levi A. Garraway, Genomics Driven Oncology: Framework for an
        Emerging Paradigm 348
    Bert Vogelstein et al., Cancer Genome Landscapes 349
    Note and Questions... 350
VI. Direct-to-Consumer Genetic Testing 351
    Maxwell J. Mehlman, Direct-to-Consumer Genetic Testing............... 351
    James D. Kerouac, The Regulation of Home Diagnostic Tests for
        Genetic Disorders: Can the FDA Deny Premarket Application
        on the Basis of the Device's Social Impacts? 357
    Letter to Ann Wojcicki, CEO of 23andMe, Inc., From Food and
        Drug Administration.. 363
    Fred Ledley, A Consumer Charter for Genomic Services................... 367
    Notes and Questions 367

Chapter 8. Clinical Applications of Genetics in Treatment.............. 369
I.   Introduction 369
II.   Pharmacogenomics... 369
       Allen D. Roses, Pharmacogenetics and the Practice of Medicine 369
       Food and Drug Administration, Guidance for Industry:
              Pharmacogenomic Data Submissions 376
       Notes and Questions 381
       Mark A. Rothstein & Phyllis Griffin Epps, Ethical and Legal
              Implications of Pharmacogenomics 385
       Notes and Questions 392
III.   Gene Therapy 394
       A. History of Gene Therapy.. 394
       B. Science of Gene Therapy 402
       C. Regulation of Gene Therapy 404
              1.   The Recombinant DNA Advisory Committee (RAC).............. 404
                    Paul Berg et al., Letter.. 404
                    Notes and Questions... 407
                    American Medical Association Council on Ethical and
                           Judicial Affairs.. 407
                    Questions.. 408
                    Department of Health and Human Services, Recombinant
                           DNA Research: Request for Public Comment on "Points
                           to Consider in the Design and Submission of Human
                           Somatic-Cell Gene Therapy Protocols"............................ 410
                    Notes and Questions... 415
              2.   Food and Drug Administration... 418
                    Food and Drug Administration, Statement of Policy for
                           Regulating Biotechnology Products................................ 418
                    Notes and Questions... 424
              3.   Protecting Human Subjects 429
                    Larry R. Churchill et al., Genetic Research as Therapy:
                           Implications of "Gene Therapy" for Informed
                           Consent.. 429
                    Notes and Questions... 433
       D. Germline Therapy 434
       Notes and Questions 440
       Burke K. Zimmerman, Human Germ-Line Therapy: The Case
              for Its Development and Use 441
       Notes and Questions 444

Chapter 9. Public Health 445
I.   Introduction... 445
II.   Public Health Genetics 445
       Muin J. Khoury et al., Will Genomics Widen or Help Heal the
              Schism Between Medicine and Public Health? 445

Wayne D. Hall, Rebecca Mathews & Katherine I. Morley, Being
    More Realistic about the Public Health Impact of Genomic
    Medicine 446
Mark A. Rothstein, Privacy Issues in Public Health Genomics, in
    Genomics and Public Health: Legal and Socio-Ethical
    Perspectives 448
Notes and Questions 449
III.   Public Health Emergencies and Genomics 450
IV.   Newborn Screening Programs 451
American Academy of Pediatrics, Report of the Task Force on
    Newborn Screening, Published as a Call for a National
    Agenda on State Newborn Screening Programs 451
Ellen Wright Clayton, Screening and Treatment of Newborns 454
Notes and Questions 460
Mary Ann Baily and Thomas H. Murray, Ethics, Evidence, and
    Cost in Newborn Screening 463
Ruth R. Faden et al., Parental Rights, Child Welfare, and Public
    Health: The Case of PKU Screening 465
Norman Fost, Genetic Diagnosis and Treatment: Ethical
    Considerations 467
Notes and Questions 469
Douglas County v. Anaya 469
Notes and Questions 476
American Academy of Pediatrics, Report of the Task Force on
    Newborn Screening (Published as a Call for a National
    Agenda on State Newborn Screening Programs) 477
Notes and Questions 479

Chapter 10. Genetic Enhancement 481
I.   Introduction 481
II.   Procedures 481
Jon W. Gordon, Genetic Enhancement in Humans 485
Notes and Questions 489
Maxwell J. Mehlman et al., Ethical and Legal Issues in
    Enhancement Research on Human Subjects 490
Notes and Questions 493
Michael Sandel, The Case Against Perfection: What's Wrong With
    Designer Children, Bionic Athletes, and Genetic
    Engineering 497
Gregory Stock, Redesigning Humans: Our Inevitable Genetic
    Future 500
Erik Parens, Authenticity and Ambivalence: Toward
    Understanding the Enhancement Debate 503
Notes and Questions 506
Maxwell J. Mehlman, The Law of Above Averages: Leveling the
    New Genetic Enhancement Playing Field 507
Notes and Questions 511

Chapter 11. Parentage and Family Law 515
I.   Introduction 515
II.   Reassessing Traditional Presumptions of Paternity in the DNA
       Era 517
       Michael H. v. Gerald D. 517
       Richard Willing, DNA and Daddy 521
       Lach v. Welch 526
       Notes and Questions 528
III.   Genetics and Switched Babies 532
       Mays v. Twigg 532
       Question 532
IV.   Genetics and Immigration 533
       Notes and Questions 534
V.   Genetics, Adoption, and Disability 536
       Amanda Trefethen, The Emerging Tort of Wrongful Adoption 536
       Meracle v. Children's Service Society of Wisconsin 539
       American Society of Human Genetics Social Issues Committee and
           American College of Medical Genetics Social, Ethical, and
           Legal Issues Committee, Genetic Testing in Adoption 544
       In re Marriage of Carney 546
       Notes and Questions 551

Chapter 12. Forensics: Genetic Testing for Identification 553
I.   Introduction 553
II.   Admissibility of DNA Evidence in Criminal Cases 554
       A. The Science of Forensic DNA Testing 554
           The National Commission on the Future of DNA Evidence,
               The Future of Forensic DNA Testing: Predictions of the
               Research and Development Working Group 554
           Notes and Questions 557
           Emerging Technologies: YSTR, Low Copy Numbers and SNPs 558
           Notes and Questions 559
       B. The Legal Standards for Admissibility 560
           National Research Council (NRC), The Evaluation of Forensic
               DNA Evidence 560
       C. Assessing the Reliability of DNA Evidence 561
           Eric E. Lander, DNA Fingerprinting: Science, Law, and the
               Ultimate Identifier in The Code of Codes: Scientific and
               Social Issues in the Human Genome Project 561
       D. Concerns About DNA Evidence 563
       E. Admission of DNA Evidence Through Expert Testimony 564
           Williams v. Illinois 564
           Notes and Questions 568
       F. Obtaining DNA Samples for a Match 572
           Lori Andrews & Dorothy Nelkin, Body Bazaar: The Market for
               Human Tissue in the Biotechnology Age 572

Edward Imwinkelried & D. H. Kaye, DNA Typing: Emerging
or Neglected Issues 573
Notes and Questions 577
G. Post-Conviction DNA Testing 581
Seth Axelrad & Juliana Russo, Survey of Post-Conviction
DNA Testing Statutes 581
Notes and Questions 584
District Attorney's Office for the Third Judicial District v.
Osborne 584
Notes and Questions 590
III. DNA Banks 591
A. Constitutionality of Forensic DNA Banks 591
Jones v. Murray 591
Maryland v. King 598
State v. Medina 603
Kaemmerling v. Lappin 607
B. Policy Issues in Forensic DNA Banks 611
Mark A. Rothstein & Sandra Carnahan, Legal and Policy
Issues in Expanding the Scope of Law Enforcement
DNA Data Banks 611
Seth Axelrad, Use of Forensic DNA Database Information for
Medical or Genetic Research 613
Notes and Questions 614
IV. DNA Identification Outside the Criminal Setting 620
Mayfield v. Dalton 620
Notes and Questions 625

Chapter 13. Mental and Behavioral Genetics 627
I. Introduction 627
II. History of Mental and Behavioral Genetics 629
Mark A. Rothstein, Behavioral Genetic Determinism: Its Effects on
Culture and Law in Behavioral Genetics: The Clash of Culture
and Biology 629
III. Scientific Issues 632
Steven E. Hyman, Using Genetics to Understand Human Behavior:
Promises and Risks in Wrestling With Behavioral Genetics:
Science, Ethics, and Public Conversation 632
Robert Plomin, John C. DeFries, Ian W. Craig & Peter McGuffin,
Behavioral Genetics in Behavioral Genetics in the
Postgenomic Era 634
Notes and Questions 636
IV. Criminal Law 637
A. Overview 637
Troy Duster, Behavioral Genetics and Explanations of the Link
Between Crime, Violence, and Race in Wrestling With
Behavioral Genetics: Science, Ethics, and Public
Conversation 637

Mark A. Rothstein, Applications of Behavioural Genetics:
Outpacing the Science? 639
B. Culpability 641
Lori B. Andrews, Predicting and Punishing Antisocial Acts:
How the Criminal Justice System Might Use Behavioral
Genetics in Behavioral Genetics: The Clash of Culture
and Biology 641
Stephen J. Morse, Genetics and Criminal Responsibility 643
Millard v. Maryland 644
Notes and Questions 648
C. Sentencing 650
Hill v. Ozmint 650
Notes and Questions 651
D. Commitment Proceedings 653
Kansas v. Crane 653
Notes and Questions 656
V.   Education 657
Mark A. Rothstein, Genetics and the Work Force of the Next
Hundred Years 657
Gary E. Marchant & Jason S. Robert, Genetic Testing for Autism
Predisposition: Ethical, Legal and Social Challenges 658
Emily Chang, In China, DNA Tests on Kids ID Genetic Gifts,
Careers 659
Laura F. Rothstein, Genetic Information in Schools in Genetic
Secrets: Protecting Privacy and Confidentiality in the Genetic
Era 661
Doe v. Knox County Board of Education 663
Notes and Questions 667
VI.   Tort Law 668
Carlsen v. Wackenhut Corp. 668
Notes and Questions 669

Chapter 14. Privacy and Confidentiality **671**
I.   Introduction 671
Sissela Bok, Secrets: On the Ethics of Concealment and
Revelation 671
Notes and Questions 672
II.   Genetic Privacy and Confidentiality 673
A. Analytical Framework 673
Anita L. Allen, Genetic Privacy: Emerging Concepts and Values
in Genetic Secrets: Protecting Privacy and Confidentiality
in the Genetic Era 673
David Orentlicher, Genetic Privacy in the Patient-Physician
Relationship in Genetic Secrets: Protecting Privacy and
Confidentiality in the Genetic Era 674
Notes and Questions 675

Lori B. Andrews, Future Perfect: Confronting Decisions About Genetics 677

Notes and Questions 678

B. Applications 679

1. Electronic Health Records and Networks 679

Amy L. McGuire et al., Confidentiality, Privacy, and Security of Genetic and Genomic Test Information in Electronic Health Records: Points to Consider 679

Notes and Questions 680

2. Compelled Disclosures 681

Mark A. Rothstein & Meghan K. Talbott, Compelled Disclosure of Health Information: Protecting Against the Greatest Potential Threat to Privacy 681

Notes and Questions 682

III. Legal Protections for Medical and Genetic Privacy 683

A. Constitutional Law 683

NASA v. Nelson 683

Notes and Questions 687

B. Legislation 689

1. Genetic Exceptionalism 689

Thomas H. Murray, Genetic Exceptionalism and "Future Diaries": Is Genetic Information Different From Other Medical Information? In Genetic Secrets: Protecting Privacy and Confidentiality in the Genetic Era 689

Note 689

Mark A. Rothstein, Genetic Exceptionalism and Legislative Pragmatism 690

2. State Legislation 693

New Mexico Genetic Information Privacy Act 693

Notes and Questions 695

3. Health Insurance Portability and Accountability Act (HIPAA) 695

Office for Civil Rights, Department of Health and Human Services, Summary of the HIPAA Privacy Rule 696

Note 700

C. Common Law 700

Mark A. Rothstein, Genetic Stalking and Voyeurism: A New Challenge to Privacy 700

Notes and Questions 702

IV. Dealing With Genetic Differences 702

Mark A. Rothstein, Legal Conceptions of Equality in the Genomic Age 702

Notes and Questions 703

Mark A. Rothstein, Genetic Stalking and Voyeurism: A New Challenge to Privacy 704

Notes and Questions 707

Chapter 15. Insurance **709**
I.   Introduction 709
II.   Health Insurance.. 711
     A. Background 711
     B. State Laws 712
         Kan. Stat. Ann. § 40–2259 713
         Notes and Questions 714
         Mark A. Hall, Legal Rules and Industry Norms: The Impact of
             Laws Restricting Health Insurers' Use of Genetic
             Information 714
         Notes and Questions 716
     C. Federal Laws 718
         Health Insurance Portability and Accountability Act 718
         Notes... 720
         Genetic Information Nondiscrimination Act (GINA) 720
         Mark A. Rothstein, GINA's Beauty is Only Skin Deep.................. 723
         Notes and Questions 724
         Affordable Care Act of 2010.. 725
         Notes and Questions 729
     D. Coverage Decisions... 729
         Katskee v. Blue Cross/Blue Shield.................................... 729
         Notes and Questions 733
III.   Life Insurance.. 735
     Mark A. Rothstein & Yann Joly, Genetic Information and Insurance
         Underwriting: Contemporary Issues and Approaches in the
         Global Economy in Handbook of Genetics and Society:
         Mapping the New Genomic Era 735
     J. Alexander Lowden, Genetic Risks and Mortality Rates, in
         Genetics and Life Insurance: Medical Underwriting and
         Social Policy 736
     Notes and Questions 738
     Vermont. Stat. Ann. Tit. 18, Ch. 217 739
     Notes and Questions 740
     Chabner v. United of Omaha Life Insurance Co..................... 741
     Notes and Questions 747
     Mark A. Rothstein, Policy Recommendations, Genetics and Life
         Insurance: Medical Underwriting and Social Policy.................... 747
     Notes and Questions 751
IV.   Disability Insurance... 751
     Susan M. Wolf & Jeffrey P. Kahn, Genetic Testing and the Future
         of Disability Insurance: Ethics, Law, and Policy........................ 752
     Notes and Questions 753
V.   Long-Term Care Insurance 754
     Mark A. Rothstein, Predictive Genetic Testing for Alzheimer's
         Disease in Long-Term Care Insurance 754
     Cathleen D. Zick et al., Genetic Testing for Alzheimer's Disease
         and Its Impact on Insurance Purchasing Behavior 756

Notes and Questions 758

Chapter 16. Employment Discrimination **761**
I.   Introduction 761
     A. What is Genetic Discrimination? 763
        Matt Ridley, Nature Via Nurture 763
        Mark A. Rothstein & Mary R. Anderlik, What Is Genetic
             Discrimination and When and How Can It Be Prevented? ... 764
        Notes and Questions 766
        Richard A. Epstein, The Legal Regulation of Genetic
             Discrimination: Old Responses to New Technology 767
        Notes and Questions 768
     B. The Why and How of Employer Access to Genetic Information.... 769
        Note on Employer Access to Employee Health Information.......... 769
        Notes and Questions 771
II. Genetic Discrimination Under the Americans With Disabilities Act
     (ADA) 771
     A. Coverage 771
     B. Medical Examinations 773
        Americans With Disabilities Act 773
        Notes and Questions 775
        Other Laws Applicable to Genetic Discrimination in
             Employment 775
III. Genetic Nondiscrimination Laws 776
     A. State Laws 776
     B. Federal Laws 777
        Overview of the Genetic Information Nondiscrimination Act of
             2008 (GINA) 777
        Genetic Information Nondiscrimination Act of 2008 (GINA) 778
        Jessica L. Roberts, Preempting Discrimination: Lessons From
             the Genetic Information Nondiscrimination Act 785
        Notes and Questions 786
        Mark A. Rothstein, GINA, The ADA, and Genetic Discrimination
             in Employment 787
        Notes and Questions 788
        Poore v. Peterbilt of Virginia, LLC 789
        Notes and Questions 791

**Chapter 17. Environmental and Occupational Regulation and
     Personal Injury Cases** **793**
I.   Introduction 793
II. Regulation 794
     A. Environmental 794
        National Research Council, Applications of Toxicogenomic
             Technologies to Predictive Toxicology and Risk
             Assessment 794

Gary E. Marchant, Toxicogenomics and Environmental Regulation, in Genomics and Environmental Regulation: Science, Ethics, and Law 796
Notes and Questions 798
Mark A. Rothstein, Yu Cai & Gary E. Marchant, Ethical Implications of Epigenetics Research 799
Notes and Questions 800
B. Occupational 801
Mark A. Rothstein, Occupational Health and Discrimination Issues Raised by Toxicogenomics in the Workplace in Genomics and Environmental Regulation: Science, Ethics, and Law 801
Notes and Questions 803
Mark A. Rothstein, Genetics and the Work Force of the Next Hundred Years 804
Notes and Questions 805
Genetic Testing for Susceptibility to Carpal Tunnel Syndrome ... 806
III. Litigation 808
A. Injury 808
Bryson v. Pillsbury Co. 808
Notes and Questions 811
B. Causation 812
Wintz v. Northrop Corp. 812
Notes and Questions 816
C. Damages 816
Mark A. Rothstein, Preventing the Discovery of Plaintiff Genetic Profiles by Defendants Seeking to Limit Damages in Personal Injury Litigation 816
Notes and Questions 820

INDEX 823

TABLE OF CASES

The principal cases are in bold type.

A.C., In re.. 246
American Textile Mfrs. Institute, Inc.
  v. Donovan.................................... 804
Ande v. Rock................................ **122**
Anderson v. HMO Nebraska,
  Inc.. 734
Anne R. v. Estate of Francis C........ 530
Antony B., In re 552
Appeal in Maricopa County Juvenile
  Action Numbers JV–512600 and
  JV–512797, Matter of 618
Art Goebel, Inc. v. North Suburban
  Agencies, Inc. 228
Association for Molecular
  Pathology v. Myriad Genetics,
  Inc.... **140**
Azzolino v. Dingfelder 232
B.K.F., Interest of........................... 552
B.S., Juvenile, In re........................ 552
Baby Boy Doe, In re........................ 246
Baby M, Matter of........................... 278
Bain Peanut Co. v. Pinson 66
Baker v. State Bar of California 652
Baker v. United States 427
Banks v. United States 618
Basten v. United States 233
Bearder v. State.............................. 479
Bell v. Wolfish................................. 596
Bergy, In re 138
Boone v. Boozman.................. 472, 474
Borello v. U.S. Oil Co....................... 540
Boutilier v. Immigration &
  Naturalization Service................ 535
Bradshaw v. Daniel 326
Brady v. Maryland........................... 586
Brim v. State.................................... 563
Brothers Seed Co. v. Kalo Inoculant
  Co..................................... 139, 144
Brown v. Dibbell 327, 734
Brown v. Hot, Sexy and Safer
  Productions, Inc. 474
Brown v. Regents of Univ. of
  California 178
Bryson v. Pillsbury Co. **808**
Buck v. Bell.......... 48, 65, 68, 69, 636
Bullcoming v. New Mexico 567
Burr v. Bd. of County Com'rs........ 537
Buzzanca, In re Marriage of.......... 278
Cairl v. State.................................... 229
Caldwell v. State............................. 649
California v. Collins......................... 562

California v. Greenwood 576
Carlsen v. Wackenhut Corp. **668**
Carney, In re Marriage of.......... **546**
Cassidy v. SmithKline Beecham 393
Chabner v. United of Omaha Life
  Insurance Co.............................. **741**
Champion v. Knasiak 815
Chaney v. Heckler............................ 425
Chischilly, United States v............. 569
Church of Lukumi Babalu Aye, Inc. v.
  Hialeah 471, 475
Clark v. Children's Memorial
  Hospital 233
Collins v. Harker Heights............... 587
Comstock, United States v. 656
Connolly v. Nicollet Hotel.............. 231
Cornerstone Bible Church v. City of
  Hastings...................................... 475
Crawford v. Washington................. 564
Curlender v. Bio-Science
  Laboratories.............................. **236**
D.W. v. State Department of Human
  Resources.................................... 552
Daniels v. Hadley Mem'l Hosp. 294
Daubert v. Merrell Dow
  Pharmaceuticals................. 560, 815
Davis v. Mississippi 574
Department of Human Res. v.
  Smith 471,
  475
Diamond v. Chakrabarty 130,
  137, 143, 147, 166
District Attorney's Office for the
  Third Judicial District v.
  Osborne...................................... **584**
Doe v. City of Chicago..................... 775
Doe v. Hamburg 279
Doe v. Knox County Board of
  Education **663**
Doe v. Roe....................................... 820
Doe v. Southeastern Pennsylvania
  Transp. Auth. (SEPTA)............. 688
Doolan v. IVF America (MA)
  Inc.... **240**
Douglas County v. Anaya........... **469**
Employers Mut. Cas. Co. v. A.C.C.T.,
  Inc.. 228
Evelyn H. v. David H. 529
Ewaniszyk, In re 652
Ferguson v. City of Charleston....... 611
Ferrell v. Rosenbaum **290**

Ford v. Schering-Plough Corp........ 743
Friedman v. Boucher.............. 617, 618
Frye v. United States 560
Funchess v. Cecil Newman Corp. .. 228
Garrett v. City of New Berlin........ 541
Gideon v. Wainwright 590
Goss, State v. 578
Gradjelick v. Hance 228
Greenberg v. Miami Children's Hospital Research Institute, Inc. **168**
Greenholtz v. Inmates of Nebraska Penal & Correctional Complex... 652
Hamdi v. Rumsfeld...................... 588
Harnicher v. University of Utah Medical Center **255**
Harris v. Mutual of Omaha Companies.................................... 734
Harvard College v. Canada (Commissioner of Patents) **145**
Harvey v. Horan 588
Hill v. Ozmint **650**
Hoffpauir, Estate of v. Sudwisher 528
Holder v. Prudential Insurance Co. of Am. 734
Hudson v. Palmer 596
Identigene, Inc. v. Goff 528
Indianapolis, City of v. Edmond 611
International Union, UAW v. Johnson Controls, Inc............................... 804
Jacobson v. Massachusetts 50, 55
Jhordan C. v. Mary K. **263**
Johnson v. Calvert.......................... 275
Johnson v. Superior Court of Los Angeles County **250**
Jones v. Murray **591**
Juvenile 2006-833, In re................. 552
Kaemmerling v. Lappin **607**
Kansas v. Crane **653**
Kansas v. Hendricks....................... 653
Karen P. v. Christopher J.B. 530
Katskee v. Blue Cross/Blue Shield **729**
Katz v. United States 577
Keel v. Banach **221**
Kekis v. Blue Cross and Blue Shield of Utica-Watertown, Inc. 734
Killingbeck v. Killingbeck 530
Kissinger v. Board of Trustees...... 473, 475
Kizer v. Sulnick 252
Kyllo v. United States 578
La Fleur v. Mosher 541
Lach v. Welch **526**
LaGuerre, People v. 579
Lee, United States v. 472
Lehr v. Robertson 271, 516
Levias v. United Airlines 702

Lifchez v. Hartigan......118, 218, 282
Lininger v. Eisenbaum 229
Lundgren v. Fultz 229
Malone ex rel. Randolph v. Barnhart...................................... 530
Martinez v. Long Island Jewish Hillside Medical Center 235
Martinez, People v. 572
Maryland v. King **598**, 603
Matson v. Bd. of Educ.................... 688
Mayfield v. Dalton **620**
Mays v. Twigg **532**
McAllister v. Ha 235
McIntosh v. Milano 323
Medina, State v. **603**
Melendez-Diaz v. Massachusetts ... 567
Meracle v. Children's Service Society of Wisconsin **539**
Michael H. v. Gerald D. **517**
Michael J. v. Los Angeles County Department of Adoptions............ 543
Michelman v. Erlich 234
Michigan Dep't of State Police v. Sitz... 593
Millard v. Maryland **644**
Miller v. Reed 472
Missouri v. McNeely 599
Mobley v. Head................................ 651
Mobley v. State................................ 651
Molloy v. Meier............................. **225**
Moore v. Regents of the University of California.............................. **158**
Moss v. Moss 529
Murray v. State................................ 568
NASA v. Nelson............................. **683**
Nasert, In re Estate of 531
National Treasury Employees Union v. Von Raab................. 592, 600, 622
Nixon v. Administrator of General Services.. 683
Norman-Bloodsaw v. Lawrence Berkeley Laboratory 775, 807
Pallozzi v. Allstate Life Insurance Co. 747
Palsgraf v. Long Island R. Co. 231
Parker v. Metropolitan Life Ins. Co. 743
Parker v. Wellman 812
Pate v. Threlkel............230, **318**, 322
Paternity of Cheryl, In re 529
Pennsylvania v. Ritchie 586
Perez v. Wyeth Laboratories, Inc. 393
Perry-Rogers v. Fasano.............**272**
Pierce v. Society of Sisters............. 473
Pioneer Hi-Bred v. Holden Foundation 173
Planned Parenthood v. Casey........ 246

Poe v. Lynchburg Training School & Hospital **59**
Poore v. Peterbilt of Virginia, LLC **789**
Powell v. Alabama 589
Powell v. Texas 656
Prince v. Massachusetts 473, 474
Quiroz v. Neelly 535
Reed, State v. 580
Relf v. Weinberger 62
Reno v. Flores 587, 589
Rezulin Products Liability Litigation, In re 812
Richard P. v. Vista Del Mar Child Care Service 543
Rieck v. Medical Protective Co. 542
Roberts, State v. 649
Robinson v. California 656
Roe v. Wade 232, 246
Roper v. Simmons 652
Rushford v. Caines 529
Safer v. Pack **321**
Salerno, United States v. 652
San Antonio Independent School Dist. v. Rodriguez 597
San Jose Christian College v. Morgan Hill 475
Schenebeck v. Sterling Drug, Inc. 393
Schlagenhauf v. Holder 819
Schmerber v. California 573, 599, 621
Schroeder v. Perkel 229, 319
Shabazz v. State 558
Skillings v. Allen 229
Skinner v. Oklahoma **63**
Skinner v. Railway Labor Executives' Ass'n 575, 592, 596, 599, 622
Slansky v. Nebraska State Patrol 475
Slayton, In re Marriage of 529
Soos v. Superior Court in and for County of Maricopa **268**
Sorensen, People v. **260**
Speck v. Finegold 237
Stiver v. Parker 260
Stone v. Daviess County Div. of Children & Family Services 552
Sudwischer v. Estate of Hoffpauir 528
Sutton v. United Air Lines, Inc. 773
Swanson, Swanson By and Through v. Guthrie ISD I–L 472
Tanner, People v. 649
Tarasoff v. Regents of Univ. of Cal. 323, 325
Taylor v. Kurapati **70**
Torrance P., In re 552
Troxel v. Granville 474

Tuan Anh Nguyen v. Immigration & Naturalization Service 533
Turpin v. Mobley 651
Turpin v. Sortini 234
Urbaniak v. Newton 702
Washington University v. Catalona, et al. 107, 108
Weikert, United States v. 618
Werlein v. United States 809
Weyer v. Twentieth Century Fox Film Corp 742, 744
Whalen v. Roe 683
Wilkinson v. Austin 588
Williams v. Illinois **564**
Wilson v. Group Hospitalization & Medical Services, Inc. 734
Wintz v. Northrop Corp. **812**
Wisconsin v. Dabney 572
Wisconsin v. Yoder 473
Wise v. Fryar 530
Wood v. University of Utah Medical Center 234
Yukl, People v. 649
Zepeda v. Zepeda 234

GENETICS
ETHICS, LAW AND POLICY

Fourth Edition

CHAPTER 1

INTRODUCTION

■ ■ ■

For all of recorded human history—and undoubtedly long before—humans have been fascinated by parentage and familial relationships, as well as the inheritance of physical, mental, and behavioral traits. Until the last century, however, our knowledge of human inheritance was limited to observing the associations of expressed factors. Inherited afflictions were seemingly caused by the indecipherable and unpredictable hand of fate. Humans lacked the ability to predict or explain the inter-generational transmission of any of these characteristics.

It is only since the turn of the twentieth century that human genetics has emerged as a rigorous science. Building on the work of Charles Darwin and Gregor Mendel in the nineteenth century, Thomas Hunt Morgan, James Watson, Francis Crick, Sydney Brenner, Frederick Sanger and numerous other scientists began to unravel the mysteries inside the nucleus of the cell. By the start of the twenty-first century, a draft sequence of the entire three billion letters of human DNA had been completed.

Gregor Mendel

Although the role of genes in human life is still vigorously debated in scientific, political, and theological circles, the impact of genetics goes well beyond understanding modes of inheritance and predisposition to illness. Genetics raises exciting possibilities for disease prevention, treatment, and cures. As scientists learn that virtually all health conditions are affected to some degree by genetic factors, genetics will become an increasingly essential part of primary care and all medical specialties. In the health care setting, genetics implicates important issues of privacy, confidentiality, informed consent, the physician-patient relationship, access to health care, public health, and myriad other issues. Beyond health care, genetics is becoming a more common issue in criminal and civil litigation, forensics, employment, insurance, family law, intellectual property, and other areas.

This chapter puts genetics in the broadest perspective, by viewing the past, future, and present of human life through the lens of genetics.

I.   GENES AND THE PAST

The study of genetics requires the widest possible perspective, beginning with evolution of life on earth, the emergence and migration of humans, and the nineteenth century discovery of natural selection and the basic principles of heredity.

JOHN AVISE, THE GENETIC GODS: EVOLUTION AND BELIEF IN HUMAN AFFAIRS
50 (1998).

Physicists and astronomers who subscribe to the big bang theory of the origin of the universe tell us that it took place roughly 15 billion years ago. If we compress these 15 billion years into one year, the big bang occurs on January 1. The earth comes into existence on approximately September 12, and the first known forms of life appear about October 7. Eukaryotic organisms begin to flourish by mid-November, and by December 17 diverse invertebrate life roams the planet. The first mammals appear on December 26, the first primates on December 29, and the first hominoids on December 30. It is not until late in the final day of our calendar year, December 31 at about 10:30 P.M., that the earliest human creatures amble onto the evolutionary stage. By 11:46 P.M., humans domesticate fire. Thirteen minutes later they are drawing extensive cave paintings, inventing agriculture, and beginning to cluster into the first large towns. Jesus is born four seconds before the present, at 11:59:56 P.M. Within the last second of the cosmic calendar, Europeans discovered the western hemisphere, many countries become mechanized and industrialized, and, perhaps most germane to the current discussion, the experimental method of science, which provides an objective and empirical illumination of the biotic geneses, emerged.

These scientific perspectives are sobering. No longer can we rationally see ourselves as the focal point of creation, either in space or time. We are dwarfed by the immensity of our surroundings, and by the vastness of time within which we participate for so brief an instant.

By measuring the degree of variation in DNA, scientists can determine the degree of relatedness of individual species of plants and animals. They also can estimate when any two lines of living things diverged to form separate branches of the evolutionary tree.

Humans are a young species and therefore have comparatively little intra-species genetic variation. Using new techniques, however, scientists can identify patterns of slight differences in human DNA. This information has been used to help write the history of our species, including migration patterns, the development of various language groups, and the genetic basis for differences in human appearance.

The following excerpt is from a speech given by Dr. Luigi Luca Cavalli-Sforza, a leading population geneticist, upon being awarded the Balzan Prize for his research.

LUIGI LUCA CAVALLI-SFORZA, REMARKS UPON BEING AWARDED THE BALZAN PRIZE FOR THE SCIENCE OF HUMAN ORIGINS
(1999).

The first approach I tried for reconstructing the history of human evolution was the use of evolutionary trees. Their application relies on the principle that the longer the separation of two populations, the greater is, in probability, the magnitude of the genetic difference between them. This requires [us] to measure a quantity we have called genetic distance. When one examines the genetic distance between species which have been separated for very long times, tens or hundreds of millions of years, one usually examines one individual per species, and finds species differ for many single genetic differences. The proportion of units of DNA which is different in two species is related in a simple way to their evolutionary time separation. But human populations have been separated for a comparatively very short time. Archeology shows that modern humans appeared only a little more than [one] hundred thousand years ago, in Africa, and spread first to Asia, between 100,000 and 50,000 years ago, and from S.E. Asia first to Oceania between 60,000 and 40,000 years ago. Europe was reached about 40,000 years ago from both West Asia and North Africa, and America from Siberia beginning 15,000 years ago.

Mutation first appears in one individual, and then it spreads to other individuals only in successive generations, when the individual carrying the mutated type has several progeny carrying the mutation, either because mutants are favored by selection and survive easily or have more children, or they are favored by chance. It usually takes a great number of generations before the mutation is found in many individuals, and even more for it to replace completely the original type. Thus between the first appearance of a mutation and the replacement of the original type there will usually elapse a very long time. During that period the mutant type is "polymorphic," i.e. there coexist in the population both the original (ancestral) type and the mutant one. It is extremely rare that a mutation has reached 100% in humans living in one part of the world and is absent in other parts. In fact, we find that any population, however small, has enormous genetic variation; on average, one finds 85% of the total human variation is within populations, and only 15% between.

* * *

I don't like the word "race" because it corresponds to old subdivisions that are inconsistent with genetic reality and unjustifiable by a rational classification. Moreover, there is no real use of such classifications and, what is worse, there is always an associated racist flavor. Darwin had already recognized the difficulty of a rational classification of races in what is almost a perfect continuum, and noted the futility of racial classifications, given the enormous variety of numbers and definitions of races which different taxonomists have traditionally offered, from two to more than one hundred. The current trend to increased admixture can only make races even less clear.

NOTE

For a further discussion, see Luigi Luca Cavalli-Sforza & Marcus W. Feldman, The Application of Molecular Genetic Approaches to the Study of Human Evolution, 33 Nature Genetics 266 (2003).

MATT RIDLEY, GENOME: THE AUTOBIOGRAPHY OF A SPECIES IN 23 CHAPTERS
43–46 (1999).

Darwin was not a little nervous on the subject. He had recently come under attack from a fierce Scottish professor of engineering, strangely named Fleeming Jenkin, who had pointed out the simple and unassailable fact that natural selection and blending inheritance did not mix. If heredity consisted of blended fluids, then Darwin's theory probably would not work, because each new and advantageous change would be lost in the general dilution of descent. Jenkin illustrated his point with the story of a white man attempting to convert an island of black people to whiteness merely by breeding with them. His white blood would soon be diluted to insignificance. In his heart

Charles Darwin

Darwin knew Jenkin was right, and even the usually ferocious Thomas Henry Huxley was silenced by Jenkin's argument, but Darwin also knew that his own theory was right. He could not square the two. If only he had read Mendel.

Many things are obvious in retrospect, but still take a flash of genius to become plain. Mendel's achievement was to reveal that the only reason most inheritance *seems* to be a blend is because it involves more than one particle. In the early nineteenth century John Dalton had proved that water was actually made up of billions of hard, irreducible little things called atoms and had defeated the rival continuity theorists. So now Mendel had proved the atomic theory of biology. The atoms of biology might have been called all sorts of things: among the names used in the first years of this century were factor, gemmule, plastidule, pangene, biophor, id and idant. But it was 'gene' that stuck.

* * *

Yet even in his lifetime Mendel came tantalizingly close to full recognition. Charles Darwin, normally so diligent at gleaning ideas from the work of others, even recommended to a friend a book, by W.O. Focke, that contained fourteen different references to Mendel's paper. Yet he seems not to have noticed them himself. Mendel's fate was to be rediscovered, in 1900, long after his own and Darwin's deaths. It happened almost simultaneously in three different places. Each of his rediscoverers—Hugo de Vries, Carl Correns and Erich von Tschermak, all botanists—had laboriously duplicated Mendel's work on different species before he found Mendel's paper.

* * *

But the very fact that the dreaded [William] Bateson was Mendelism's champion led European evolutionists to be suspicious of it. In Britain, the bitter feud between Mendelians and 'biometricians' persisted for twenty years. As much as anything this passed the torch to the United States where the argument was less polarized. In 1903 an American geneticist called Walter Sutton noticed that chromosomes behave just like Mendelian factors: they come in pairs, one from each parent. Thomas Hunt Morgan, the father of American genetics, promptly became a late convert to Mendelism, so Bateson, who disliked Morgan, gave up being right and fought against the chromosomal theory. By such petty feuds is the history of science often decided. Bateson sank into obscurity while Morgan went on to great things as the founder of a productive school of genetics and the man who lent his name to the unit of genetic distance: the centimorgan. In Britain, it was not until the sharp, mathematical mind of Ronald Fisher was brought to bear upon the matter in 1918 that Darwinism and Mendelism were at last reconciled: far from contradicting Darwin, Mendel had brilliantly vindicated him. 'Mendelism', said Fisher, 'supplied the missing parts of the structure erected by Darwin.'

NOTES AND QUESTIONS

1.   New discoveries in genetics are helping to write the history of our species and our relationship with other species. For example, humans and chimpanzees are 98%–99% alike genetically. The Human Genome Project has also confirmed the fundamental genetic homogeneity of our species. Any two individuals are 99.9% identical from a genetic standpoint. Genetics also helps to explain the relationships of groups of individuals, including ancient migration patterns and the development of language and culture. For example, population genetics demonstrates clearly that "race" is a social rather than a biological construct. Thus, new discoveries in genetics have had and will continue to have great importance in numerous fields of the natural and social sciences, as well as in the attitudes and ideals of ordinary citizens.

2.   The astounding pace of genetic discovery needs to be put into perspective. Mendel's work was only rediscovered at the turn of the twentieth century; it has been only 60 years since the correct number of chromosomes in humans and the double helical structure of DNA were discovered; it was not until the 1990s that the loci of a substantial number of genes associated with debilitating diseases were determined; and it was not until the spring of 2001 that scientists were able to revise the approximation of the number of genes in humans from 80,000–100,000 to 32,000. By 2005, the estimate of the number of human genes was 20,000–25,000—the same number as for the spotted green puffer fish.

3.   In 2009, researchers announced that they had reconstructed the genome of Neanderthals, a human species that became extinct 30,000 years ago. The Neanderthal genome has been used to trace the human lineage as it evolved over millions of years. Scientists also have disclosed that some Neanderthal genes have been preserved in modern humans, thereby confirming that there was interbreeding. See Svante Pääbo, Neanderthal Man: In Search of Lost Genomes (2014).

4.   There are numerous excellent and accessible books about evolution and genetics. Among the best recent ones are Daniel J. Fairbanks, Relics of Eden: The Powerful Evidence of Evolution in Human DNA (2007); John Quackenbush, Curiosity Guides: The Human Genome (2011).

II.   GENES AND THE FUTURE

Genetic engineering is destined to play a role in the future of humans, although the nature and extent of the effects are subject to extensive debate.

MARK A. ROTHSTEIN, GENETICS AND THE WORK FORCE OF THE NEXT HUNDRED YEARS

2000 Colum. Bus. L. Rev. 371, 371–72 (2000).

The December 5, 1999 issue of The New York Times Magazine is a special issue devoted to describing the efforts of The New York Times to create a time capsule to be opened in the year 3000. A panel of experts from various fields provided their opinions on, among other things, the location, architecture, contents, and style of the capsule. Besides these immediate issues, some of the experts observe that other likely events of the next thousand years would complicate any long-range planning for the year 3000, including the following: (1) the tectonic plates holding the American and European continents will drift apart by as much as sixty feet; (2) the sea level will rise by about eight feet; (3) the United States will cease to exist as a country by then; and (4) the language spoken by the inhabitants of New York City will be totally different from today's English—even today's English as spoken by the inhabitants of New York City.

Interestingly, the discussion of the New York City of the distant future failed to mention the biology of the inhabitants in the year 3000. When one thinks of the inhabitants of the Earth in one thousand years, one is easily drawn into a science fiction world of humans with unlimited lifespans, robots, cyborgs, chimeras, clones, and extraterrestrials. Even without such dramatic changes in the population of the planet, advances in our understanding of and ability to manipulate human biology are taking place at a rate much faster than the continental drift, and the consequences of at least some of the changes will be realized in our lifetimes.

JAMES OWEN, FUTURE HUMANS: FOUR WAYS WE MAY, OR MAY NOT EVOLVE

National Geographic News, Nov. 24, 2009,
http://news.nationalgeographic.com/news/pf/78656051.html.

But where is evolution taking us? Will our descendants hurtle through space as relatively unchanged as the humans on the starship Enterprise? Will they be muscle-bound cyborgs? Or will they choose to digitize their consciousnesses—becoming electronic immortals?

And as odd as the possibilities may seem, it's worth remembering that, 150 years ago, the ape-to-human scenario in On the Origin of Species struck many as nothing so much as monkey business.

PREDICTION ONE

Human Evolution Is Dead

"Because we have evolved, it's natural to imagine we will continue to do so, but I think that's wrong," anthropologist Ian Tattersall of New York's American Museum of Natural History said in an email.

"Everything we know about evolutionary change suggests that genetic innovations are only likely to become fixed in small, isolated populations," he said. For example, Darwin's famous Galápagos finches each evolved from their mainland ancestor to fit a unique habitat on the isolated islands in the Pacific.

Natural selection, as outlined in *On the Origin of Species*, occurs when a genetic mutation—say, resulting in a spine suited to upright walking—is passed down through generations, because it affords some benefit. Eventually the mutation becomes the norm.

But if populations aren't isolated, crossbreeding makes it much less likely for potentially significant mutations to become established in the gene pool—and that's exactly where we are now, Tattersall said.

"Since the advent of settled life, human populations have expanded enormously. *Homo sapiens* is densely packed across the Earth, and individuals are unprecedentedly mobile.

"In this situation, the fixation of any meaningful evolutionary novelties in the human population is highly improbable." Tattersall said. "Human beings are just going to have to learn to live with themselves as they are."

Steve Jones, a genetics professor at University College London, put forward a similar scenario during a recent lecture series marking the bicentenary of Darwin's birth and the 150th anniversary of *On the Origin of Species* at the University of Cambridge.

The human population will become more alike as races merge, he said, but "Darwin's machine has lost its power."

That's because natural selection—Darwin's "survival of the fittest" concept—is being sidelined in humans, according to Jones.

The fittest will no longer spearhead evolutionary change, because, thanks to medical advances, the weakest also live on and pass down their genes.

When *On the Origin of Species* was published in 1859, only about half of British children survived to 21. Today that number has swelled to 99 percent.

In developed countries, "the fact that everybody stays alive, at least until they're sexually mature, means ['survival of the fittest' has] got nothing to work with," Jones said. "That part of the Darwinian fuel has gone."

PREDICTION TWO

Humans Will Continue to Evolve

Other scientists see plenty of evidence that human evolution is far from over.

* * *

Geoffrey Miller, an evolutionary psychologist at the University of New Mexico, believes Darwinian evolution in humans is actually speeding up. He highlighted sexual selection through mate choice as one key driver.

"You still have powerful mate choice shaping mental traits particularly . . . traits that are needed to succeed economically and in raising kids," Miller said.

"We're also going to get stronger sexual selection, because the more advanced the technology gets, the greater an effect general intelligence will have on each individual's economic and social success, because as technology gets more complex, you need more intelligence to master it," he said.

"That intelligence results in higher earnings, social status, and sexual attractiveness."

Miller added that artificial selection using genetic technologies will likely accentuate these changes in the future.

* * *

PREDICTION THREE

Humans to Achieve Electronic Immortality

A philosophy known as transhumanism sees humans taking charge of their evolution and transcending their biological limitations via technology.

In essence, the old-fashioned evolution of *On the Origin of Species* may be beside the point: The future may belong to unnatural selection.

Nick Bostrom, director of the Future of Humanity Institute at the University of Oxford, said Darwinian evolution "is happening on a very slow time scale now relative to other things that are leading to changes in the human condition"—cloning, genetic enhancement, robotics, artificial intelligence, and nanotechnology, for starters.

Transhumanism raises a spectacular array of possibilities, from supersoldiers and new breeds of athletes to immortal beings who, having had their brains scanned atom by atom, transfer their minds to computers.

* * *

Whereas the current human generational cycle takes some 20 years, a digitalized individual could replicate themselves in seconds or minutes, Bostrom said.

Of course copying yourself isn't without complications, Bostrom acknowledges.

"Which one of them is you?" he writes. "Who owns your property? Who is married to your spouse?"

PREDICTION FOUR

New Era of Evolution Awaits on Off-World Colonies?

"Some major new isolating mechanism" would be needed for a new human species to arise, according to John Hawks, an anthropologist at the University of Wisconsin-Madison.

Despite up to 30,000 years of partial isolation among populations in places such as Australia and Papua New Guinea, human speciation did not occur, he noted.

But if, in the far distant future, habitable planets beyond our solar system were colonized by Earth migrants, that could provide the necessary isolation for new human species to evolve.

"If we had spacefaring people who went on one-way voyages to distant stars, that might be enough to trigger speciation," Hawks said.

But, he added, "if you think about it, a small group of people went on a one-way voyage to [the Americas] 14,000 years ago, and then when new people [Europeans] showed up 500 years ago, they were still the same species."

C.S. Lewis, The Abolition of Man
70–71 (1947).

In reality, of course, if any one age really attains, by eugenics and scientific education, the power to make its descendants what it pleases, all men who live after it are the patients of that power. They are weaker, not stronger: for though we may have put wonderful machines in their hands we have pre-ordained how they are to use them. And if, as is almost certain, the age which had thus attained maximum power over posterity were also the age most emancipated from tradition, it would be engaged in reducing the power of its predecessors almost as drastically as that of its successors. And we must also remember that, quite apart from this, the later a generation comes—the nearer it lives to that date at which the species becomes extinct—the less power it will have in the forward direction, because its subjects will be so few. There is therefore no question of a power vested in the race as a whole steadily growing as long as the race survives. The last men, far from being the heirs of power, will be of all men most subject to the dead hand of the great planners and conditions and will themselves exercise least power upon the future. The real picture is that of one dominant age—let us suppose the hundredth century A.D.—which resists all previous ages most successfully and dominates all subsequent ages most irresistibly, and thus is the real master of the human species. But even within this master generation (itself an infinitesimal minority of the species) the power will be exercised by a minority smaller still. Man's conquest of Nature, if the dreams of some scientific planners are realized, means the rule of a few hundreds of men over billions upon billions of men. There neither is nor can be any simple increase of power on Man's side. Each new power won by man is a power over man as well. Each advance leaves him weaker as well as stronger. In every victory, besides being the general who triumphs, he is also the prisoner who follows the triumphal car.

NOTES AND QUESTIONS

1.   Germ-line gene therapy, genetic enhancement, xenobiotics, and similar measures raise the issue of our genetic stewardship for future generations. A compelling argument could be made that scientists should not manipulate the gene pool until the consequences of such interventions are known with absolute certainty, and even then certain alterations of germlines should be impermissible. On the other hand, it also may be asserted that germline interventions in a small number of individuals are unlikely to affect the genetic heritage of a species with seven billion people; countless other technological discoveries over thousands of years—from fire to agriculture to sanitation—have affected the gene pool to a much greater degree; and in an age of international scientific research there is very little that can be done to prevent scientists from performing virtually any research somewhere. For another view of the future, see Lee M. Silver, Remaking Eden: How Genetic Engineering and Cloning Will Transform the American Family (1998).

2.   Is it possible to say no to science? Could we, as a society or world community, say that some measures have too much risk to be undertaken or that the consequences of some interventions undermine the fundamental characteristics of humans? Are there some activities that can truly be said to be "playing God"? See John H. Evans, Playing God? Genetic Engineering and the Rationalization of Public Bioethical Debate (2002).

3.   And who is to decide about possible alterations of the human germline?

> We recognize ourselves, measured against such goals and ideals, to be imperfect creatures. We wish to be more generous, more mathematically able, more musical, more athletic—less like brutes and more like gods, or demigods at least. Yet as noble as our aspirations for shedding our failings might be, our history also suggests that, being flawed as we are, we can never blindly trust our own aspirations to reshape ourselves.

Celeste M. Condit, The Meanings of the Gene: Public Debates About Human Heredity 245 (1999).

III. GENES AND THE PRESENT

Although it is enlightening and humbling to study the evolutionary past, and tantalizing and provocative to contemplate the distant future, we cannot ignore the present. In genetics, the present always includes the near future.

To many researchers and clinicians, modern medicine is embarking on the great age of personalized medicine. Using genomic information and environmental exposure data it will be possible to calculate an individual's risk of numerous diseases and to formulate an individually-based prevention or treatment strategy. In some areas of medicine, such as oncology, personalized approaches are quickly becoming the standard of care. For other disorders, personalized medicine is moving more slowly. The following article considers some of the ethical, legal, and social implications of personalized medicine.

KYLE B. BROTHERS & MARK A. ROTHSTEIN, ETHICAL, LEGAL, AND SOCIAL IMPLICATIONS OF INCORPORATING PERSONALIZED MEDICINE INTO HEALTHCARE
12 Personalized Med. 43, 45, 47 (2015).

In the last ten years, as the technology and evidence bases of personalized medicine were developing, bioethics scholars began contemplating the ethical, legal, and social implications of the initial applications of this approach to medicine, forming the field of investigation known as ELSI scholarship. Some of the foundational issues considered were safety and efficacy, informed consent, access, and reimbursement. In recent years, technologies such as next-generation sequencers and gene expression assays have become less expense and more suitable for clinical application, and as a result personalized medicine has become established in a growing number of clinical areas. With these clinical applications, however, the implications of personalized medicine have expanded in scope and complexity. This trend is likely to continue in coming years, with wider adoption throughout the healthcare system creating a need to broaden the focus of work in this area.

* * *

Personalized medicine is likely to have major effects on the physician-patient relationship. In the pre-genomic era, the diagnosis and treatment of genetic disorders was the exclusive province of clinical geneticists, pediatricians, neurologists, oncologists, and a few other specialists. In the era of personalized medicine, the focus is shifting from rare monogenic disorders to common chronic diseases, and the responsibility for treating patients with asthma, hypertension, diabetes, and similar disorders belongs to primary care physicians and a wide range of specialists. The first issue is whether these physicians have adequate training to provide the essential services of personalized medicine, such as interpretation of whole genome sequencing results, formulating prevention and treatment strategies based on genomic information, and applying pharmacogenomic principles and products in prescribing.

Besides a lack of training on the part of physicians, another problem is the lack of time. Because personalized medicine will often involve the use of genome sequencing or other complex laboratory tests, it is likely to increase the time needed for a number of clinical tasks. For example, before a genetic test is performed, pretest genetic counseling is necessary to determine whether the patient understands the implications of the test on his or her health care as well as the possible social implications of test results. After receiving test results, the physician must interpret the information and apply genomic insights in designing a treatment plan. Widely varying health literacy among patients means that some patients will need much more time for explanations. All of these steps are time consuming, yet the trend in health care is not to increase, but to decrease the amount of time for clinical encounters.

It is not clear what effects personalized medicine will have on time-pressured clinical encounters. One possibility is that providers will make trade-offs, spending less time on some patient complaints or conditions in order to spend more time on others. This might lead to an unsatisfactory physician-patient relationship as well as the possibility that subtle sentinel events will be overlooked until they develop into more persistent medical problems. Another possibility is that nurses or other allied health care providers will be given greater responsibility in counseling or follow-up, despite a similar lack of training. Still another possibility is that patients will need to assume a larger role in their own health management. In any event, it is quite likely that personalized medicine will lead to changes in the physician-patient relationship.

* * *

In addition to the goals already mentioned, leaders in this field have hoped that personalized medicine will contribute to the elimination of health disparities. One proposed mechanism for attaining this goal is that the overrepresentation of particular phenotypes in certain racial or ethnic groups may serve as an indicator of underlying genotype-phenotype associations, which might then allow for the development of targeted therapies. Similarly, there is hope that pharmacogenomics researchers may identify the genetic variants that contribute to recognized differences in drug responses among racial and ethnic groups.

This account of the potential for personalized medicine to address health disparities has raised controversy. In particular, a number of critics have argued that work to explain race-based health disparities within the framework of genomics has tended to reinforce the mistaken belief that racial categories can be mapped directly onto biological realities. Others have argued that by highlighting genetics as an important avenue for addressing health disparities we may obscure the importance of social, cultural, and economic factors in perpetuating disparities.

* * *

Another set of challenges that threaten to exacerbate health disparities in the coming decade are economic barriers that both limit access to healthcare and reduce the benefit patients are able to derive from that care. This characteristic is common to many new healthcare technologies: if patients are unable to access a new technology, then they are also unable to enjoy benefits from that technology.

In the case of personalized medicine, the laboratory tests that inform personalization, such as next-generation sequencing, are likely to be quite expensive at first, despite optimism that the $1000 genome has arrived. Such milestones do not account for labor costs, analytical costs, or commercial mark-up. An additional source of increased cost will be the interventions that are recommended in light of these laboratory test results. For example, pharmacogenomic testing may have the potential to decrease overall costs at the level of the healthcare system. At the level of individual patients, however, many are still likely to end up taking medications with higher direct costs compared with the standard therapy.

The costs of personalized therapeutics and the tests that inform their use are unlikely to cause difficulty for patients already well-served in the healthcare system. In countries with private insurance systems, patients with comprehensive health insurance coverage or the ability to cover such costs out-of-pocket will be able to undergo new tests and receive the benefits of individualized treatments despite their cost. Patients with no insurance, as well as patients with insurance designed to provide only urgent care, are unlikely to benefit from these advances.

BARBARA KATZ ROTHMAN, GENETIC MAPS AND HUMAN
IMAGINATIONS: THE LIMITS OF SCIENCE IN
UNDERSTANDING WHO WE ARE
18, 247–248 (1998).

Genetics isn't just a science; it is a way of thinking. Ruth Hubbard, professor emerita at Harvard and herself a biologist, points out that scientists are not detached observers of nature. They are constantly making decisions about what they will consider significant, and these choices are not merely individual or idiosyncratic, but reflect the society in which the scientists live and work. Genetic thinking, genetics as our society is developing it, genetics as we use it and think it and speak it, genetics as an ideology for our time, is about seeds. Genetics is the most obvious and direct scientific descendent of this traditional, father-based worldview, an attempt to understand the very meaning of life by understanding genes, bits of DNA, the updated version of seeds.

* * *

People map what they value, what they think is important. We are choosing to map the human genome. A map is a guide: it tells you what is there, but it also tells you how to get places. The genome map, as we have seen, may end up taking us places we don't want to go. What with slippery slopes, camels at the tent, and the way one thing leads to another, the world that we're creating with this map may not be a world in which we'd want to live. But how can anyone argue against mapping, against exploration? How can we stand here, of all places, in the "new world," and wring our hands and fret about exploration? Yet maybe exactly here, the land that native people lost to explorers, the land where the language blends the words of the British colonizers with the rhythms of the African slaves, maybe here in this unmeltable pot, we're best placed to think about maps, where they take us and where they lead.

Why are we spending our precious dollars on this map? What are we looking for? If our concern is with preventing disability and disease, with extending the life span, with lowering infant mortality, with making smarter people, there are better places to spend money. They want to find the genetic contribution to intelligence? Appreciate each baby with wonder and awe at its developing mind, nurture that intelligence in a rich and stimulating and safe environment, offer schools that inspire as well as instruct, and then get back to me on the question of individual—or racial—variation in intellectual potential. Don't start with schools that warehouse kids, televisions that stupefy them, and parents who are overburdened and overstressed, and then look for the genes for intelligence.

Cars, violence, lead and other poisons in the air and water, all kinds of things are destroying our children, their bodies and their minds, at higher rates than our genes. A mother's zip code is still the best predictor of infant mortality. Deal with poverty, and then get back to me on genetics research.

NOTES AND QUESTIONS

1. Among other things, Brothers and Rothstein are concerned about the possibility that new advances in personalized medicine have the potential to increase health inequality. Couldn't the same criticism be leveled against any new technology? What would Rothman say? Is there a way to have both new technologies and more health equality? For a further discussion of the policy issues raised by personalized medicine, see Geoffrey S. Ginsburg & Huntington F. Willard, Genomic and Personalized Medicine: Foundations and Applications, 154 Translational Research 277 (2009).

2. Rothman's book was written in the midst of the Human Genome Project, and it focused on genome research. To what extent do her insights apply to the personalized medicine era? The Rothman excerpt raises the issue of whether science is really value neutral. According to the National Research Council:

> One myth about scientific research is that science is value neutral—that new scientific understandings await discovery, that these discoveries have no independent moral significance, and that they take on moral significance only when individuals and groups of individuals assign weight to scientific findings. One flaw in this argument is that there are seemingly limitless areas for scientific inquiry, yet there are finite numbers of scientists and limited resources to pursue research. Therefore, scientists and society must set priorities for research, and those priorities are a function of societal values. Even though scientists often make adventitious discoveries, they generally discover what they are looking for, and what they are looking for are the things that science and society value discovering.

Committee on Applications of Toxicogenomic Technologies to Predictive Toxicology, National Research Council, Applications of Toxicogenomic Technologies to Predictive Toxicology and Risk Assessment 173 (2007). Do you agree?

3. Fundamental discoveries in science have the potential to effect drastic social change. What are the moral implications of these advances? Harold Shapiro, Former President of Princeton University and Chair of the National Bioethics Advisory Commission, stated: "We may or may not need new moral philosophies, but we are more likely to get to the moral high ground if scientists and others work together to help shape the uses of new knowledge. The fact that the moral context of scientific discoveries is defined by the objectives and applications of this new knowledge gives all of us additional responsibilities and inevitably new anxieties." Harold T. Shapiro,

Reflections on the Interface of Bioethics, Public Policy, and Science, 9 Kennedy Inst. Ethics J. 209, 222 (1999).

4.   The effect on society of advances in science and technology is a familiar theme. Thoreau said: "We do not ride on the railroad; it rides upon us." Henry David Thoreau, Walden and Other Writings 83 (Random House ed. 1950). His concern, of course, was that we are not the masters, but the servants of technology. The railroads opened up vast expanses of our country in the nineteenth century and greatly improved commerce and transportation. But the railroads literally carved a swath through cities, towns, and forests; belched smoke and sparks and noise; and forced people to live by its scheduled arrivals and departures.

To paraphrase Thoreau in the genetics context: We do not probe the gene; it probes us. New advances in genetics are forcing us to reassess the value systems and political assumptions on which our society is based. We now must probe what it means to be human, what it means to be normal, what we mean by equality and discrimination, what the social consequences are of individual and group genetic variability, what it means to be healthy, who should have access to health care, what property rights to biological discoveries should be recognized, what obligations exist among family members, what the contours are of the physician-patient relationship, what tradeoffs exist between using DNA for identification and civil liberties, and how privacy and confidentiality can be protected without sacrificing other interests. These and numerous other foundational questions are sometimes framed as legal issues, but often they are combinations of ethics, law, policy, and other disciplines. That is why this book is called Genetics: Ethics, Law and Policy.

5.   Beyond its obvious influence on health law, genetics will affect numerous other areas of the law, including criminal law, constitutional law, forensics, intellectual property, family law, civil rights law, insurance law, employment law, and tort law. This book deals with the legal issues raised by genetics, as well as the scientific, ethical, and social context in which they arise.

IV.   THE ELSI PROGRAM

The experience with eugenics in the early twentieth century, as well as other controversial programs such as the sickle cell screening effort in the early 1970s (see the discussion in Chapter 5), created concern about the potential abuses of the scientific advances made possible by the Human Genome Project. The response was to establish a special program within the Human Genome Project, called the Ethical, Legal and Social Implications or ELSI program, to focus on the project's ethical, legal, and social implications. The ELSI program was conceived by the first director of the Human Genome Project at the National Institutes of Health (NIH),

James Watson, who, along with Francis Crick, had discovered the structure of the DNA molecule.

Watson himself gives the following account of the origin of the ELSI program:

> In putting ethics so soon into the genome agenda, I was responding to my own personal fear that all too soon critics of the Genome Project would point out that I was a representative of the Cold Spring Harbor Laboratory that once housed the controversial Eugenics Record Office. My not forming a genome ethics program quickly might be falsely used as evidence that I was a closet eugenicist, having as my real long-term purpose the unambiguous identification of genes that lead to social and occupational stratification as well as genes justifying racial discrimination. So I saw the need to be proactive in making ELSI's major purpose clear from its start—to devise better ways to combat the social injustice that has at its roots bad draws of the genetic dice.

James Watson, A Passion for DNA: Genes, Genomes & Society 202 (2000).

Watson insisted that between 3 and 5 percent of the federal budget for the Human Genome Project be devoted to ELSI-sponsored studies by researchers outside of the government. Administration of the ELSI program was shared by the NIH, which created an ELSI Branch within what became the National Center for Human Genome Research, and the Department of Energy, which was interested in the Human Genome Project as a result of its effort to measure the biological effects of atomic radiation. For a history of the Department of Energy's involvement in the inception of the Human Genome Project, see Robert M. Cook-Deegan, The Gene Wars: Science, Politics, and the Human Genome (1994).

The ELSI program was unprecedented as an attempt to shape US science policy, and it has had its share of critics. As reported by Eric Juengst, the first chief of the ELSI Branch at NIH, one senior NIH official complained: "I still don't understand why you want to spend all this money subsidizing the vacuous pronouncements of self-styled 'ethicists'!" Watson replied that, for better or worse, "the cat was out of the bag." The official retorted: "But why inflate the cat? Why put the cat on TV?" Juengst adds:

> Pro-genomicists, like the NIH official quoted above, saw it as at best a waste of (increasingly scarce) NIH research dollars, and at worst an overblown hand-waving that could backfire badly on the scientific community if it actually succeeded in getting the public's attention. Anti-genomicists suspected that the program was, at best, a clever attempt to create a screen of ethical smoke

behind which the [Human Genome Project's] juggernaut could build up speed, and, at worst, an attempt to buy off the very critics who might otherwise make trouble for the scientists.

Eric Juengst, Self-Critical Federal Science? The Ethics Experiment Within the U.S. Human Genome Project, 13 Social Philosophy & Policy 63, 66–67 (1996). Another criticism, voiced by George Annas and Sherman Elias, was that the one policy issue that received no attention from ELSI was whether the Human Genome Project should proceed in the first place. From its inception in 1990 to 2014, the ELSI program at NIH has sponsored more than 480 projects at a total cost of $317 million.

FRANCIS FUKUYAMA, OUR POSTHUMAN FUTURE: CONSEQUENCES OF THE BIOTECHNOLOGY REVOLUTION
204 (2002).

The community of bioethicists that has grown up in tandem with the biotech industry is in many respects a double-edged sword. On the one hand, it has played an extremely useful function by raising doubts and questions about the wisdom and morality of certain technological innovations. On the other hand, many bioethicists have become nothing more than sophisticated (and sophistic) justifiers of whatever it is the scientific community wants to do, having enough knowledge of Catholic theology or Kantian metaphysics to beat back criticisms by anyone coming out of these traditions who might object more strenuously. The Human Genome Project from the beginning devoted 3 percent of its budget to studying the Ethical, Social, and Legal Implications of genetic research. This can be regarded as commendable concern for the ethical dimensions of scientific research, or else as a kind of protection money the scientists have to pay to keep the true ethicists off their backs. In any discussion of cloning, stem cell research, germline engineering, and the like, it is usually the professional bioethicist who can be relied on to take the most permissive position of anyone in the room.* But if the ethicist isn't going to tell you that you can't do something, who will?

NOTE

As you read through this book you should be alert to the tone and emphasis of the bioethics commentary. Are the authors objectively evaluating the facts and policy implications? Are they being too gentle or too harsh with

---

* This phenomenon is a common one and is known as regulatory "capture," whereby the group that is supposed to be overseeing the activities of an industry becomes and agent for the industry. This happens for many reasons, including the dependence of the regulators on the regulatees for money and information. In addition, there are the career incentives that most professional bioethicists face. Scientists do not usually have to worry about winning the respect of ethicists, particularly if they are Nobel Prize winners in molecular biology or physiology. On the other hand, ethicists face an uphill struggle winning respect of the scientists they must deal with, and are hardly likely to do so if they tell them they are morally wrong or if they depart significantly from the materialist worldview that the scientists hold dear.

their criticisms of the research, clinical, or applied use of new genetic knowledge?

CHAPTER 2

SCIENTIFIC AND HISTORICAL OVERVIEW

■ ■ ■

I. INTRODUCTION

This chapter is designed for the reader who does not have a background in the science and history of human genetics. It provides an overview of the science pertaining to cells, chromosomes, genes, proteins, genetic differences among individuals, patterns of inheritance, a brief description of mapping and sequencing the human genome, and an overview of the history of genetic science, including the history of eugenics. It is intended to provide a scientific and historical overview to assist in understanding the material in the remainder of the book. It also identifies some of the key legal and ethical issues that are raised by scientific developments.

II. HISTORY OF GENETIC SCIENCE

ERIC S. LANDER, SCIENTIFIC COMMENTARY: THE SCIENTIFIC FOUNDATIONS AND MEDICAL AND SOCIAL PROSPECTS OF THE HUMAN GENOME PROJECT
26 J.L. Med. & Ethics 184, 184–185 (1998).

* * *

Genetics is a remarkable discipline, because it offers a generic approach that enables scientists to pursue any disease-related question, from inflammatory bowel disease to schizophrenia. How is this possible? The foundations of this story, as almost everything in genetics, go back to the fundamental insight of Gregor Mendel in 1865.

Mendel noted that hereditary traits in the pea plant could be explained by the action of certain invisible but predictable "factors" (the word *gene* was coined only at the beginning of the twentieth century). Mendel noted that each individual inherited two copies of each factor— one from each parent. And, each individual passed on one copy to its offspring. For example, when a pure-breeding green plant is mated with a pure-breeding yellow plant, the offspring will inherit one color gene from the green parent and one from the yellow parent. Finally, when the resulting plant is crossed with itself, the genes reassort: offspring of different types reemerge in the next generation.

Mendel's extraordinarily important and simple concept—that discrete factors control inheritance—was not regarded as earthshaking in its time, probably because it was so abstract. Mendel did not know the identity of the factors. He simply inferred their existence to explain the results of his pea experiments. About thirty-five years passed before cell biologists studying the division of cells noticed strange structures that appear red when cells underwent division. When cells underwent meiosis to make gametes (sperm or eggs), the structures lined up in pairs, and one copy of each pair would be transmitted. When two gametes fused to give rise to an offspring, each parent thus contributed one copy of each such structure.

This strange choreography—pairs splitting, sending one to the offspring, and then rejoining—behaved just as Mendel's abstract factors had behaved. The cell biologists did not know what these objects were, but, because they stained them with certain dyes, they named them chromosomes—a Latinate term meaning *colored things*. These chromosomes seemed likely to hold the secret of inheritance.

Soon after this discovery, scientists set out to understand how chromosomes controlled inheritance. By about 1911, a student at Columbia University named Alfred Sturtevant made a key observation: by following the inheritance patterns of genes, it was possible to infer whether genes were nearby one another on a chromosome. Nearby genes would tend to be transmitted together, whereas distant genes would tend to be separated by recombination events (that is, exchanges of genetic material). In other words, one could measure the location of genes on chromosomes by how frequently they were transmitted together. Sturtevant began building genetic maps, showing the locations of genes that controlled various traits in the fruit fly, such as body color and eye color. He was teasing apart the secrets of inheritance patterns that controlled traits, without knowing anything about the actual DNA that encoded them.

The idea that one could trace inheritance in this fashion was applied widely to flies, corn, and many other organisms. Moreover, it soon became clear that, in principle, the same basic ideas applied to the human being. However, one could not set up human matings to study inheritance, as in the fly or in corn. Also, one did not have simple, single-gene traits with which to trace inheritance patterns (with a few exceptions, such as a blood group). Thus, for most of this century, our understanding of human genetics was largely theoretical, not operational. Seventy years of scientific progress were required before human geneticists could do what Sturtevant was doing in 1911. The DNA revolution offered the key.

Rosalind Franklin's original DNA radiograph. *Photo Credit: King's College, London*

[Eds.—By the 1950s, many scientists around the world were attempting to discover the structure of DNA. Rosalind Franklin, a chemist and X-ray crystallographer at King's College, London, took an X-ray diffraction image of DNA. That image led to the discovery of the double-helix structure of DNA. After viewing Franklin's image, James Watson and Francis Crick performed their seminal work to understand the structure of DNA and how its double-helical properties enabled it to encode information, to divide apart, and to pass the information on to daughter cells.] * * * Work conducted in the 1960s showed how DNA actually encodes information in the language of the genetic code, which specifies the instructions for making proteins. Finally, the tools of recombinant DNA, developed during the 1970s, allowed molecular biologists to copy (or clone) and read the sequence of individual pieces of DNA. After all of that work—from 1910 to 1980—it was finally possible to apply Sturtevant's techniques of genetic mapping to humans. To trace inheritance, one could not use curly wings and white eyes as with *Drosophila*. However, one could use simply the spelling differences in DNA.

The discoverers of the structure of DNA, James Watson at left and Francis Crick, seen with their model of part of a DNA molecule in 1953.
A Barrington Brown/Science Source.

III. STRUCTURE OF DNA

DNA (short for *deoxyribonucleic acid*) is a molecule consisting of a string of chemicals called *nucleotides*. Each nucleotide is composed of a sugar, a phosphate, and a base. To understand the structure of DNA, first think of a ladder cut in half down the middle of the rungs. The sugars and phosphates of the nucleotides are connected to one another to form a long strip like the side of the ladder. The half rungs of the ladder consist of the bases, sticking out from the side. The bases are the important part of the DNA molecule: their order, or *sequence*, forms the genetic code of the organism.

There are four nucleotide bases: adenine, guanine, cytosine, and thymine, known by their initials A, G, C and T. These bases attach or bond to one another according to a strict set of rules: A only bonds with T and vice versa, while G only bonds with C and vice versa.

In humans and other higher organisms, the DNA molecule actually is two strands of DNA, as if you reunited the two halves of the ladder. Each of the sides of the ladder is a strip of sugars and phosphates. The rungs are the bases that stick out and that are connected together in pairs according to the bonding rules: A with T, G with C. This double-stranded DNA molecule is twisted around the mid-point of the rungs to give it its famous "double-helix" appearance. See Figure 2–1.

Figure 2–1

DNA Molecule

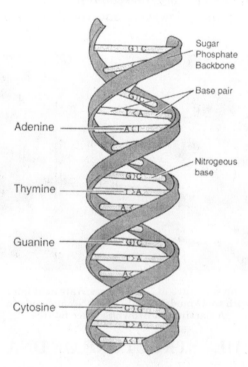

In human DNA, there are about three billion rungs of the ladder, or pairs of nucleotide bases. The DNA of the bacterium *E. coli* has about four million base pairs, and yeast has about 15 million.

Triggered by cellular enzymes, DNA duplicates or *replicates*. It does this first by unwinding from its twisted double-helix shape and breaking apart at the bonds between the base pairs, like unzipping a zipper. This produces two separate strands of DNA, like the two halves of our ladder. In the nucleus of the cell where replication takes place are many unattached nucleotides. When the double strand unzips, these free-standing bases bind to the exposed bases of the DNA strands according to the binding rules. This produces a complementary copy of the strand. Suppose, for example, that at one point on the original double helix DNA molecule, there was an A attached to a T, followed by a G attached to a C. After the molecule unzips into two separate strands, the exposed A on one of the single strands binds with a free-standing T, the exposed G binds with a free-standing C, and so on. The same thing happens with the other single strand: the T binds with a free-standing A, the C to a G, and so on. The result is two new double-helix-shaped, double-stranded DNA molecules each of which reproduces the sequence of base pairs in the original double-stranded molecule. See Figure 2–2.

Figure 2–2

DNA Replication

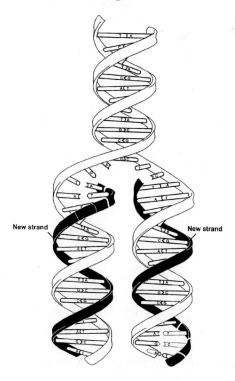

DNA replication occurs when cells divide, as described below.

IV.   CELLS AND CHROMOSOMES

Most human DNA is found in cell nuclei. Each cell nucleus contains chromosomes—physically-distinct, microscopic structures composed of double strands of DNA folded and twisted so they can fit into the confined space. (If the DNA in the chromosomes of a single cell nucleus were unwound and laid end-to-end, it would stretch more than five feet.) There are a total of 24 different chromosomes. Two of the chromosomes determine sex, and are called "X" and "Y." A normal female has two X chromosomes; a male has one X and one Y. The remaining 22 chromosomes, referred to by number, are called *autosomes*.

Most normal cell nuclei contain two sets of 23 chromosomes, or a total of 46. Each set is comprised of the 22 autosomes and a sex chromosome. One set of chromosomes derives from the person's mother and one set from the father. This fact helps explain why children have characteristics that cannot be found in either parent. See Figure 2–3 for a photograph image of a microscopic view of an individual's chromosomes, called a *karyotype*.

Figure 2–3

Karyotype of Human Chromosomes

Some genetic diseases result from chromosomal abnormalities. For example, Down syndrome occurs when an individual inherits an extra copy of chromosome 21. For this reason, it is also known as "Trisomy (meaning three copies) 21." Some males have an extra Y sex chromosome. As described in Chapter 13, some people believed that this made them more aggressive and prone to engage in violent criminal behavior.

A small amount of human DNA is found outside the cell nucleus, in cell structures called *mitochondria*. This enables researchers to trace a population's pattern of genetic descent, and has implications for certain infertility treatments that involve inserting one person's nuclear DNA into another person's egg cell from which the nucleus has been removed.

V.   GENES AND PROTEINS

Along certain stretches of DNA, the sequences of nucleotide bases contain instructions for making proteins. Proteins form the structural components of cells and tissue and the enzymes that control biochemical reactions, including the functioning of the genes themselves. The stretches of DNA containing protein instructions are called *genes,* and genes are said to *code for* specific proteins. Initially, the non-gene stretches of DNA were referred to as "junk DNA" on the assumption that they had no important function. It turns out that these non-protein coding regions of DNA are indeed important, for they contain instructions for turning genes on and off, and non-coding portions of human DNA have been associated with risks for prostate, breast, and colon cancer, and heart attacks.

Proteins consist of long, complex chains of twenty different types of amino acids. Within the gene stretches of DNA, there are sequences of bases called *exons* that code for specific amino acids. Each of these sequences, called *codons* or *triplets*, is only three bases long. Other stretches of sequences within genes, called *introns*, do not code for amino acids. Thus, there appear to be large amounts of DNA, including both non-coding stretches between the genes and introns within the genes, that do not code for proteins.

The instructions for making proteins contained in genes are decoded via two processes called *transcription* and *translation*. In transcription, the portion of the double strand of DNA containing a gene first unwinds and breaks apart. But then, instead of making a copy of the DNA with free-standing nucleotides like during DNA replication, different enzymes—still following the binding rules—construct a different type of complementary strand using three of the four DNA nucleotides (A, G, and C), a fourth nucleotide called uracil that binds with A the same as T, and a different type of sugar, ribose. Hence the name of this material: RNA (*ribonucleic acid*). This form of RNA contains not only the triplets, which code for amino acids, but also the introns, so enzymes strip out the intron sequences, producing a strand that only contains amino-acid coding sequences. This is called *messenger RNA (mRNA)*. It is the result or product of transcription.

So far this process has taken place inside the cell nucleus. But now the messenger RNA exits the cell nucleus and enters the cytoplasm, where it encounters a structure called a *ribosome*. In the process called translation, the ribosome reads the sequence in the messenger RNA and puts together a chain of amino acids which becomes a protein.

The number of DNA bases that are required to produce a protein varies from only 100 to a couple of million, depending on how complex a protein it codes for and how many of its bases are introns. The longest gene is 2.4 million bases long, and codes for the protein that malfunctions in muscular dystrophy.

Until recently, geneticists believed that a single human gene coded for a single protein. Since there are about 100,000 proteins, this meant that there should be about 100,000 human genes. It now appears that there are only around 20,000 to 25,000 human genes. This means the some genes can code for more than one protein, depending on how the amino acids are arranged and how the protein is shaped or folded. This has several implications. First, it shows that the greater complexity of a human, compared to other organisms such as the small flowering plant *Arabidopsis thaliana*, with about the same number of genes, is not due to the difference in the number of genes. Second, the more complex relationship between genes and proteins is likely to complicate the task of linking genes to specific diseases or traits and of finding effective treatments.

In 2003, the National Human Genome Research Institute at NIH established a research program called the Encyclopedia of DNA Elements (ENCODE) to identify all the functional elements of the human genome, not just the genes themselves. In 2007, researchers announced that a pilot project that had examined 1 percent of the genome had found that, while the protein-coding components of genes account for only about 2 percent of human DNA, 93 percent of the DNA is functionally active, in that it is transcribed into RNA. The non-protein-coding gene elements include genes that do not code for proteins, regulatory elements that control the transcription process, and elements that maintain the structure of chromosomes and mediate their replication. In addition, the ENCODE results showed that genes were not strings of nucleotides like beads along the DNA molecule, as had long been assumed, but instead, that many genes overlap one another and share stretches of DNA. In short, the ways in which DNA functions are far more complex than previously thought.

VI. GENETIC DIFFERENCES AMONG INDIVIDUALS

The exact sequence of genes differs among people. For example, all humans have a gene that codes for the protein huntingtin. But the sequence of nucleotide bases of that gene can differ from one person to another. One stretch of the gene consists of a repeat of three bases, C, A, and G. Most people have 26 or fewer repeats. But some people have a lot more CAG repeats. The extra repeats interfere with the production of the huntingtin protein; as a result, these people will get Huntington disease, the fatal, neurological disorder that killed folksinger Woody Guthrie. We tend to say that these individuals "have the gene for Huntington disease." Since we all have the gene for the protein huntingtin, it is more accurate to say that affected individuals have a gene with the variation or *mutation*—an extra number of CAG repeats—that causes the disease.

Another example is cystic fibrosis. Everyone has a certain gene, called the CFTR gene, that affects the transport of chloride in the body. In the most common form of cystic fibrosis, there is a mutation on this gene: three bases, CTT, that code for the amino acid phenylalanine, are missing from a certain location, known as position 508.

Another term used to describe the different versions of the same gene among different individuals is *allele*. We say that people with 26 or fewer CAG repeats and people with a lot more repeats on the huntingtin gene, or people with and without the CTT sequence at position 508 of the CFTR gene, have different *alleles* of the same gene. These differences in alleles produce genetic disease. They also account for much of the variety in human observable characteristics—why some people have blue eyes and some brown, and so on. Put another way, these differences in genetic make-up, or *genotype*, produce differences in observable characteristics, or *phenotype*.

Most genetic sequences are the same from one person to the next; only about 0.1 percent differ. But these differences are the basis for genetic testing to diagnose and predict susceptibility to genetic diseases, discussed in Chapters 7 and 8; to inform reproductive decision-making, discussed in Chapter 6; to establish paternity, described in Chapter 11; and to distinguish individuals for identification purposes on the basis of samples of their DNA, which is covered in Chapter 12.

VII. CELL DIVISION

There are two types of human cell division processes, *meiosis*, in which certain specialized cells form reproductive cells (eggs or sperm), and *mitosis*, which occurs when *somatic* or non-reproductive cells divide.

In mitosis, an enzyme in the cell nucleus first causes duplicates to be made of the chromosomes. This creates 92 chromosomes (two sets of the original 46, itself composed of two sets of the 23 different chromosomes, one from each parent, with each chromosome consisting of a double-strand of DNA). The chromosomes arrange themselves in pairs joined near their centers and line up along the midline of the nucleus. The sets of pairs then split apart and are pulled toward the opposite sides of the nucleus. The cell itself pinches in two, creating two new cells, each with a full set of 46 chromosomes. These chromosomes are essentially identical to the original 46, except for alterations or mutations that occur by duplication error or that are introduced by environmental factors or through deliberate manipulation. (It is important to note that these alterations in somatic cell DNA will not be passed on to an individual's offspring. If the alterations occur early enough in human development, such as in an early-stage fetus, or if they affect enough of a person's somatic cells, they can have significant effects on the person's phenotype, including causing genetic disease. But the disease will not be inherited by the person's children.)

Meiosis is the process by which reproductive cells—eggs or sperm—are fashioned. It takes place either in the ovaries or the testes.

The first step in meiosis is the same as in mitosis: in a specialized cell, the 46 chromosomes (comprising two sets of 23, one of which was inherited from each parent) duplicate to form 92. The duplicated pairs of paternal and maternal chromosomes fuse together near their centers, and the pairs arrange themselves along the midline of the cell nucleus, with each paternal pair lining up across from its corresponding maternal pair (i.e., paternal chromosome 4 across from maternal chromosome 4, and so on). But the paternal and maternal pairs can line up on different sides of this midline independently of one another, so that the paternal pair of chromosome 4's may be lined up across from a maternal pair of 4's, but next to a maternal pair of 5's, which is across from a paternal pair of 5's, and so on. In addition, in an apparently random fashion, enzymes cut out pieces of the chromosomes and exchange them across the midline, so that one paternal chromosome 4 may now have a piece of maternal chromosome 4 and vice versa. This is called *crossing over* or *recombination*. See Figure 2–4.

Figure 2–4

Crossing Over or Recombination

Now the cell begins to pull apart and eventually pinches off to form two new cells, each with 46 chromosomes. But note that these chromosomes are not duplicates of the original 46. Instead, they consist of a different mixture of maternal and paternal chromosomes, and each chromosome may contain DNA from the other parent. These cells then divide again, but without any duplicating of DNA, to yield four new cells, each with 23 chromosomes. Again, some of these chromosomes will be maternal and some paternal in origin, and their maternal and paternal DNA will be mixed up because of recombination.

In the case of eggs, three of the four new cells are discarded and the fourth becomes an egg. All of this takes place while the female fetus is in the womb: a woman is born with her full compliment of reproductive cells. In the case of sperm, each of the four cells becomes a sperm, and males continue to produce sperm through meiosis throughout their reproductive lifetimes. (This has an impact on, among other things, the techniques by which deliberate changes might be made in the DNA of reproductive cells, for example, to prevent offspring from inheriting a genetic disease.)

Genetic variation between parents and children results from three factors: the fact that the child inherits one set of chromosomes from each parent; the fact that the DNA gets mixed up in the process of meiosis; and the occurrence of spontaneous mutations, due either to errors that take place when cells divide, or to environmental factors such as X-rays. Someday, perhaps, variation may also result from intentional manipulation.

VIII. PATTERNS OF INHERITANCE

The simplest rules of inheritance apply to gender. Every egg that a woman produces will only have a copy of the X sex chromosome (since a person with a Y chromosome would be male). Since males have one X and one Y chromosome, a sperm has a 50/50 chance of containing either one. Therefore, when a sperm fertilizes an egg, if the sperm contains an X chromosome, the child will be female (since it will inherit an X from each parent). On the other hand, if the sperm contains a Y chromosome, the child will be male (since it will inherit an X chromosome from the mother and a Y from the father).

Characteristics other than gender can result from environmental factors, from genes, or from the interaction of environmental factors and genes. Genetic effects may result either from a single gene or from a number of genes interacting with one another, in which case it is called a *multigene* or *multifactorial* effect. Finally, genetic effects can either be *dominant* or *recessive*.

To understand the difference between dominant and recessive, remember that an individual inherits two sets of genes, one from the mother and one from the father. The sequences of the bases on those genes can be essentially identical (although there may be minor differences), in which case the individual is said to be *homozygous* for that gene, or the sequences of the bases of the two genes can be different in significant respects, in which case the individual is *heterozygous* for the gene. If the individual is homozygous for a gene that codes for a single-gene characteristic, for example, eye-color, then the phenotype will reflect the gene. Thus, a person who inherits two genes for blue eyes will have blue eyes, and a person who inherits two genes for brown eyes will be brown-eyed. But if the individual is heterozygous, the effect on the phenotype (here, eye color) will depend on which genetic characteristic is dominant and which is recessive. In terms of eye color, brown is a dominant characteristic, while blue is recessive. In a person who is heterozygous for eye color and who has one brown-eyed gene and one blue-eyed gene, the dominant brown-eyed gene will trump the recessive blue-eyed gene, and the person will have brown eyes. In order for the phenotype to exhibit a recessive genetic characteristic like blue eyes, the person must have two copies of the recessive gene, one from each parent.

Patterns of inheritance become especially complicated when we try to figure out whether children will display a particular phenotype based on their genetic inheritance from their parents. Parents who are both homozygous for the same eye color, for example, will have children all of whom have the same eye color as the parents. But suppose one parent has blue eyes and the other brown eyes. In order for the one parent's eyes to be blue, both copies of the eye-color gene have to be blue-eyed, since blue is recessive. The brown-eyed parent may be homozygous for brown eyes, or may be heterozygous; in either case, the parent's eyes will be brown because brown is dominant. If the brown-eyed parent is homozygous, then all the couple's children will have brown eyes, since each child will inherit one brown-eyed gene from the brown-eyed parent, and brown is dominant so it will override the blue-eyed gene from the other parent. If the brown-eyed parent is heterozygous, however, each child has a 50/50 chance of inheriting that parent's brown-eyed gene and a 50/50 chance of inheriting the parent's blue-eyed gene. So each child will have a 50/50 chance of having two blue-eyed genes (which will give them blue eyes) or one blue-and one brown-eyed gene, which, since brown is dominant, will give them brown eyes.

What if both parents have brown eyes, and both parents are heterozygous, each having a recessive blue-eyed and a dominant brown-eyed gene? Each child has a 50/50 chance of inheriting either one of either parent's eye-color genes, and this will average out to 1 in 4 children inheriting two blue-eyed genes and therefore being blue-eyed; 1 in 4 children inheriting two brown-eyed genes and therefore being brown-eyed; and 2 out of 4 children inheriting one of each gene, but still being brown-eyed because brown is dominant. Each child of these parents thus has a 25 percent chance of being blue-eyed and a 75 percent chance of being brown-eyed.

One final concept: The children in the foregoing example who inherit one dominant brown-eyed gene and one recessive blue-eyed gene will be brown-eyed, but they will be *carriers* for the blue-eyed trait. This means that they can pass the blue-eyed gene on to their children. This is why brown-eyed parents with brown-eyed children can have a blue-eyed grandchild. The grandchild can inherit two blue-eyed genes from brown-eyed parents who are carriers of the recessive blue-eyed trait.

So far we have been focusing on single-gene characteristics. These include Huntington disease, achondroplasia (a type of dwarfism), and the ability to roll your tongue into the shape of a "U." These three phenotypes happen to also be dominant: a person only needs to inherit one copy of the huntingtin gene with too many CAG repeats, for example, to get Huntington disease. (What is the chance that the child of a person with Huntington disease will also have the disease?) Other single-gene characteristics are recessive; a person must inherit copies of the gene from both parents to manifest the characteristic. Recessive single-gene characteristics include albinism, cystic fibrosis, sickle cell disease, and Tay-Sachs disease.

All of these phenotypes happen to be not only single-gene but *autosomal*. This means that the single gene that is associated with the characteristic is located on one of the 22 pairs of chromosomes that do not determine gender. As a result, a person can inherit the gene from either parent. There are other single-gene characteristics that are *sex-linked*, meaning that the gene is located on a sex chromosome, usually the X chromosome. A few of these *X-linked* characteristics are dominant; each child of a mother with a dominant X-linked characteristic has a 50/50 chance of inheriting the characteristic, and if the parent with the gene is the father, then only daughters can inherit the characteristic (since males must have inherited the father's Y chromosome, and a child who inherits the father's Y chromosome will not inherit a trait linked to the X chromosome). Most X-linked characteristics, such as color blindness, are recessive. (The children of a normal mother and a color-blind father will all be normal, but female children will be carriers; 1 in 4 of the children of a normal father and a mother who is a carrier will be a normal female, 1 in 4 will be a normal male, 1 in 4 will be a female carrier, and 1 in 4 will be a color-blind male.)

To add to the complexity, remember that so far we are only discussing single-gene characteristics. Many characteristics, however, result from the interaction of more than one gene. (Imagine the complexity of the patterns of inheritance for these multifactorial traits.)

Furthermore, genetic characteristics vary in terms of their *penetrance* and *expressivity*, and sometimes also in terms of their *age of onset*.

Penetrance refers to whether or not a gene will give rise to a phenotype. Some genes, like the gene for Huntington disease, are *completely penetrant*: if a person has too many CAG repeats, he or she invariably will exhibit symptoms of the disease at some point in their lives. Other genes, such as the gene for the disease retinoblastoma, are not completely penetrant; a person may have the gene and not get the disease.

Expressivity refers to the degree of the phenotypic effect—in the case of a genetic disease, the severity of the symptoms. Some genes are highly expressive: the gene will produce significant effects on the phenotype, and persons with a highly expressive genetic disease will have severe symptoms. Other genes have *variable expressivity*, meaning that there can be a range of symptoms. For example, the gene for a disease called neurofibromatosis produces multiple tumors and other serious conditions in some individuals, but others with the same gene merely have a few skin discolorations or a few tumors.

Some genes produce effects in people at different ages, depending on the sequence of bases. A person who has more than 40 CAG repeats on the huntingtin gene will definitely develop Huntington disease by the time he or she is 50 years old, but the greater the number of repeats beyond 40, the earlier the age of onset of symptoms, and people with as many as 60 repeats often develop symptoms in adolescence.

Finally, it is crucial to continue to bear in mind the influence of environmental factors. Consider the following statement by Ruth Hubbard and Richard Lewontin:

* * * [E]ven in the case of so-called simple mendelian variations, the relation between the DNA sequence of a gene and the corresponding phenotype is far from simple. When we move from the relatively rare conditions whose patterns of inheritance follow Mendel's laws (such as cystic fibrosis, phenylketonuria, and Huntington's disease) to the more prevalent and usually late-onset conditions that sometimes have familial components (such as diabetes, coronary heart disease, Alzheimer's disease, and certain cancers), the situation becomes even more complicated. In these diseases, the patterns of transmission are unpredictable and seem to depend on various other factors, be they social, economic, psychological, or biologic.

Ruth Hubbard and Richard Lewontin, Sounding Board: Pitfalls of Genetic Testing, 334 New Eng. J. Med. 1192, 1193 (1996).

IX. THE HUMAN GENOME PROJECT

NATIONAL HUMAN GENOME RESEARCH INSTITUTE, NIH
UNDERSTANDING OUR GENETIC INHERITANCE: THE U.S.
HUMAN GENOME PROJECT THE FIRST FIVE YEARS:
FISCAL YEARS 1991–1995
(1990).

The Human Genome Initiative is a worldwide research effort that has the goal of analyzing the structure of human DNA and determining the location of all human genes. In parallel with this effort, the DNA of a set of model organisms will be studied to provide the comparative information necessary for understanding the functioning of the human genome. The information generated by the human genome project is expected to be the source book for biomedical science in the 21st century. It will have a profound impact on and expedite progress in a variety of biological fields, including those such as developmental biology and neurobiology, where scientists are just beginning to understand the underlying molecular mechanisms. The analysis and interpretation of the information will occupy scientists for many years to come. Thus, the maximal benefit of the human genome project will only be achieved if it is surrounded by research efforts that are focused on understanding and taking advantage of the human genetic information.

NOTES

The first phase of the Human Genome Project (HGP) involved *mapping* the human genome. The goal was to locate all human genes on their chromosomes. There are basically two kinds of maps, referred to by the confusing names *genetic* or *genetic linkage*, and *physical*.

Genetic or genetic linkage maps identify *genetic markers* on chromosomes. A genetic marker is a stretch of nucleotide bases that is physically located in the same region of DNA as a gene. The marker may actually include all or part of the gene, or it may consist of bases in the stretches between genes. To be useful, a marker must be close enough to a gene that the marker is likely to be inherited along with the gene. Because DNA is somewhat chopped up during cell division, the physically farther away one stretch of DNA is from another, the less likely that the two stretches will be inherited together. The bases that comprise the marker also must be known to be *polymorphic*, that is, to differ among individuals, or at least among the members of a family, depending, for example, on whether or not they have a genetic mutation.

Markers enable genetic information about individuals to be determined without knowing the exact location of genes or the sequences of their nucleotide bases. Suppose a person wants to know if he or she has inherited a certain genetic mutation, say one that causes disease. Geneticists test that person's DNA, as well as the DNA of members of that person's family. They are searching for a marker or set of markers that is present in the DNA of family members who have the mutation and that is not present in the family members who do not have the mutation. If the person has the marker, then it is likely that he or she also has inherited the mutation, and vice versa. The process of identifying markers by testing members of a family is called *linkage analysis*. Hence the term "genetic linkage map." In this manner, geneticists were able to test for a number of genetic diseases, including cystic fibrosis, sickle cell disease, and Tay-Sachs disease, before the actual genes for these diseases were identified or their sequences were decoded.

Gradually, researchers built up genetic linkage maps that tended to be associated with various inherited diseases. By studying the frequency with which specific markers were associated with specific genetic mutations, moreover, they calculated the probability that the marker would be inherited along with the mutation. A genetic or genetic linkage map expresses the results in units called *centimorgans*. A marker and a gene are one centimorgan apart when there is a one percent chance that they will not be inherited together. Currently, over 2,200 disorders have been tied to specific genes.

Physical maps reflect actual physical distances between stretches of DNA, as opposed to the statistical calculations represented by the centimorgans on a genetic or genetic linkage map. Physical maps come with varying degrees of detail or resolution, ranging from the distance between regions on chromosomes observable by staining, to maps of fragments of DNA arranged in order along the chromosomes, to the ultimate physical map: the sequence of base pairs.

REMARKS BY THE PRESIDENT, PRIME MINISTER TONY BLAIR OF ENGLAND, DR. FRANCIS COLLINS, DIRECTOR OF THE NATIONAL HUMAN GENOME RESEARCH INSTITUTE, & DR. CRAIG VENTER, PRESIDENT AND CHIEF OFFICER, CELERA GENOMICS CORPORATION, ON THE COMPLETION OF THE FIRST SURVEY OF THE ENTIRE HUMAN GENOME PROJECT

June 26, 2000.

THE EAST ROOM

The President [William Clinton]: Good morning.

* * *

Nearly two centuries ago, in this room, on this floor, Thomas Jefferson and a trusted aide spread out a magnificent map—a map Jefferson had long prayed he would get to see in his lifetime. The aide was Meriwether Lewis and the map was the product of his courageous expedition across the American frontier, all the way to the Pacific. It was a map that defined the contours and forever expanded the frontiers of our continent and our imagination.

Today, the world is joining us here in the East Room to behold a map of even greater significance. We are here to celebrate the completion of the first survey of the entire human genome. Without a doubt, this is the most important, most wondrous map ever produced by humankind.

The moment we are here to witness was brought about through brilliant and painstaking work of scientists all over the world, including many men and women here today. It was not even 50 years ago that a young Englishman named Crick and a brash even younger American named Watson, first discovered the elegant structure of our genetic code. Dr. Watson, the way you announced your discovery in the journal "Nature," was one of the great understatements of all time. "This structure has novel features, which are of considerable biological interest."

How far we have come since that day. In the intervening years, we have pooled the combined wisdom of biology, chemistry, physics, engineering, mathematics and computer science; tapped the great strengths and insights of the public and private sectors. More than 1,000 researchers across six nations have revealed nearly all three billion letters of our miraculous genetic code. I congratulate all of you on this stunning and humbling achievement.

Today's announcement represents more than just an epic-making triumph of science and reason. After all, when Galileo discovered he could use the tools of mathematics and mechanics to understand the motion of celestial bodies, he felt, in the words of one eminent researcher, "that he had learned the language in which God created the universe."

Today, we are learning the language in which God created life. We are gaining ever more awe for the complexity, the beauty, the wonder of God's most divine and sacred gift. With this profound new knowledge, humankind is on the verge of gaining immense, new power to heal. Genome science will have a real impact on all our lives—and even more, on the lives of our children. It will revolutionize the diagnosis, prevention and treatment of most, if not all, human diseases.

In coming years, doctors increasingly will be able to cure diseases like Alzheimer's, Parkinson's, diabetes and cancer by attacking their genetic roots. Just to offer one example, patients with some forms of leukemia and breast cancer already are being treated in clinical trials with sophisticated new drugs that precisely target the faulty genes and cancer cells, with little or no risk to healthy cells. In fact, it is now conceivable that our children's children will know the term cancer only as a constellation of stars.

But today's historic achievement is only a starting point. There is much hard work yet to be done. That is why I'm so pleased to announce that from this moment forward, the robust and healthy competition that has led us to this day and that always is essential to the progress of science, will be coupled with enhanced public-private cooperation.

Public and private research teams are committed to publishing their genomic data simultaneously later this year, for the benefit of researchers in every corner of the globe. And after publication, both sets of teams will join together for an historic sequence analysis conference. Together, they will examine what scientific insights have been gleaned from both efforts, and how we can most judiciously proceed toward the next majestic horizons.

What are those next horizons? Well, first, we will complete a virtually error-free final draft of the human genome before the 50th anniversary of the discovery of the double helix, less than three years from now. Second, through sustained and vigorous support for public and private research, we must sort through this trove of genomic data to identify every human gene. We must discover the function of these genes and their protein products, and then we must rapidly convert that knowledge into treatments that can lengthen and enrich lives.

I want to emphasize that biotechnology companies are absolutely essential in this endeavor. For it is they who will bring to the market the life-enhancing applications of the information from the human genome. And for that reason, this administration is committed to helping them to make the kind of long-term investments that will change the face of medicine forever.

The third horizon that lies before us is one that science cannot approach alone. It is the horizon that represents the ethical, moral and spiritual dimension of the power we now possess. We must not shrink from exploring that far frontier of science. But as we consider how to use new discovery, we must also not retreat from our oldest and most cherished human values. We must ensure that new genome science and its benefits will be directed toward making life better for all citizens of the world, never just a privileged few.

As we unlock the secrets of the human genome, we must work simultaneously to ensure that new discoveries never pry open the doors of privacy. And we must guarantee that genetic information cannot be used to stigmatize or discriminate against any individual or group.

Increasing knowledge of the human genome must never change the basic belief on which our ethics, our government, our society are founded. All of us are created equal, entitled to equal treatment under the law. After all, I believe one of the great truths to emerge from this triumphant expedition inside the human genome is that in genetic terms, all human beings, regardless of race, are more than 99.9 percent the same.

What that means is that modern science has confirmed what we first learned from ancient fates. The most important fact of life on this Earth is our common humanity. My greatest wish on this day for the ages is that this incandescent truth will always guide our actions as we continue to march forth in this, the greatest age of discovery ever known.

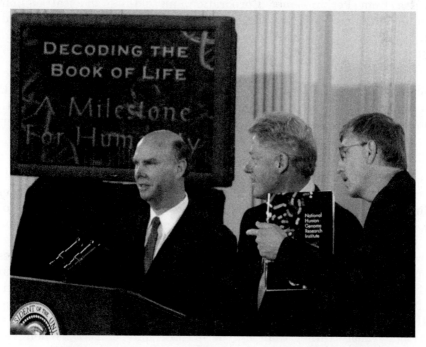

White House announcement of completion of the Human Genome Project, Craig Venter left, Francis Collins right. AP Photo/Ron Edmonds

NOTES AND QUESTIONS

1.   The term "Human Genome Project" (HGP) technically refers to the publicly-sponsored effort to map and sequence the human genome. The HGP originally expected to complete its sequencing of the human genome by 2005, at a cost of approximately $3 billion. In the U.S., funding was provided by Congress to the National Institutes of Health (NIH) and, to a much smaller extent, the Department of Energy (which had an interest in genetics as a result of its concern about the effects of atomic radiation). The NIH in turn channeled the funds to a consortium of nine research establishments, with most of the funds going to Washington University at St. Louis, Baylor College of Medicine, and the Whitehead Institute in Cambridge, Massachusetts. At the NIH, the HGP initially was overseen by an "Office of Human Genome Research," created in 1988, and headed by James Watson. In 1990, the "office" was transformed into a free-standing "center," and in 1997, the center finally achieved the status of a full-fledged "institute." In the U.K., the Wellcome Trust sponsored research at the Sanger Center. Additional public efforts were made in other countries under a loose affiliation called HUGO (for "Human Genome Organization").

Compared to publicly-funded efforts, only a small amount of mapping and sequencing initially took place in the private sector. This changed in 1998 with the formation of a company called Celera Genomics. Celera grew out of the development of faster sequencing machines. With $200 million in funding from Perkin-Elmer Corporation, an old-line medical equipment manufacturer, and with a scientist named Craig Venter as its president, Celera set out from scratch to complete its own sequence map by 2001 by running 200 of the machines around the clock.

The sequencing technique Celera used, called a "shotgun" approach, differed from the HGP approach. The HGP identified specific regions of DNA and proceeded to sequence them. Celera sequenced chunks of DNA without knowing where they were located, and then relied on computers to identify overlapping sequences at the ends of the chunks to piece them together.

At first the two programs regarded each other with antagonism. This was due in part to the high historical and scientific stakes and to the impact of success and failure on personal reputations, but also to a fundamental difference in regard to the intended use of results. As a public-funded project, the HGP was committed to making its sequencing immediately available to the public for free, while Celera, a private, for-profit company, intended to extract commercial value from its research efforts. (For more discussion about the intellectual property aspects of the HGP, see Chapter 4.) Francis Collins, the director of the National Human Genome Research Institute (NHGRI) at NIH, responded to Celera's challenge by vowing to speed up the HGP and complete a "rough draft" of the human genome by 2000 and a final version by 2003, rather than by the original date of 2005. When Venter scoffed that the HGP would not meet this timetable, some HGP scientists raised concerns about whether Celera could reassemble its fragments into an accurate map of the entire genome. Both sides seemed vindicated when the HGP began cranking out large portions of sequences in keeping with its new schedule, and Celera published an accurate sequence of the genome of the fruit fly, *Drosophila*. The race heated up.

Ultimately, Ari Patrinos, the head of the Human Genome Project at the Department of Energy, invited Collins and Venter to his home for pizza and beer and, after several more meetings, the two rivals agreed to cooperate in issuing a joint statement with President Clinton at the White House announcing the completion of their sequencing efforts, excerpts of which appear above. The HGP subsequently published its sequence map in the journal *Nature* while Celera published its map in *Science*.

Ironically, at the time of the June 26, 2000, announcement, neither sequencing effort was complete. The HGP had only finished a "working draft," with 97 percent of the human genome sequenced and only 85 percent placed in the proper order. Venter stated that Celera had sequenced 99 percent of the genome, but that its supercomputers (which comprised the largest private supercomputing capacity in the world) were still piecing the fragments together.

On April 14, 2003, the International Human Genome Sequencing Consortium announced that it had really finished the sequencing of the human genome. But even then, the sequencing was not quite complete. It was not until May 2006 that researchers announced that they had completed the sequencing of the last chromosome, chromosome 1.

2.   Whose genome was sequenced? The NHGRI report said that the DNA came from a number of sources. But most of the DNA sequenced by the public consortium came from one man, although there were segments from eleven other people from different backgrounds. Celera sequenced DNA from three females and two males. The males were Caucasians; there was one African-American woman, one Hispanic woman, and one woman of Asian descent. Craig Venter has said that he was one of the two males. What are the scientific and policy consequences?

3.   Having announced that they had finished sequencing the human genome, the scientists working on the Human Genome Project debated what they should do next. Some of them continued to work on sequencing the DNA of other organisms, successfully sequencing rice (2002), plague (2001), malaria (2002), and the mouse (2002). The genomes of a number of organisms are being sequenced by the large-scale sequencing capacity developed by the Human Genome Project. These include the dog, the rat, the chicken, the honey bee, two fruit flies, the sea urchin, two puffer fish, two sea squirts, two roundworms, several fungi, baker's yeast and many prokaryotes (bacteria and archaea) including *Escherichia coli*. Additional organisms already in the NHGRI sequencing pipeline are: the macaque, the orangutan, the kangaroo, the cow, the gray short-tailed opossum, the platypus, the red flour beetle, the domestic cat, the flatworm *Schimdtea mediterranea*, more species of fruit fly and several species of fungi.

4.   The cost of DNA sequencing has continued to decline. The Human Genome Project originally estimated a cost of $1 per nucleotide base pair. (Given the estimated three billion base pairs in the entire human genome, this cost was the basis for the original estimate that the project would cost $3 billion.) By 2005, the cost had dropped to less than 1/10th of a cent.

———————

Meanwhile, other researchers embarked on a new mega-project: creating a haplotype map of the human genome.

NATIONAL HUMAN GENOME RESEARCH INSTITUTE, INTERNATIONAL HAPMAP PROJECT OVERVIEW
Sept. 2005.

The DNA sequence of any two people is 99.9 percent identical. The variations, however, may greatly affect an individual's disease risk. Sites in the DNA sequence where individuals differ at a single DNA base are called single nucleotide polymorphisms (SNPs). Sets of nearby SNPs on the same chromosome are inherited in blocks. This pattern of SNPs on a block is a haplotype. Blocks may contain a large number of SNPs, but a few SNPs are enough to uniquely identify the haplotypes in a block. The HapMap is a map of these haplotype blocks and the specific SNPs that identify the haplotypes are called tag SNPs.

The HapMap should be valuable by reducing the number of SNPs required to examine the entire genome for association with a phenotype from the 10 million SNPs that exist to roughly 500,000 tag SNPs. This will make genome scan approaches to finding regions with genes that affect diseases much more efficient and comprehensive, since effort will not be wasted typing more SNPs than necessary and all regions of the genome can be included.

In addition to its use in studying genetic associations with disease, the HapMap should be a powerful resource for studying the genetic factors contributing to variation in response to environmental factors, in susceptibility to infection, and in the effectiveness of and adverse responses to drugs and vaccines. All such studies will be based on the expectation that there will be higher frequencies of the contributing genetic components in a group of people with a disease or particular response to a drug, vaccine, pathogen, or environmental factor than in a group of similar people without the disease or response. Using just the tag SNPs, researchers should be able to find chromosome regions that have different haplotype distributions in the two groups of people, those with a disease or response and those without. Each region would then be studied in more detail to discover which variants in which genes in the region contribute to the disease or response, leading to more effective interventions. This should also allow the development of tests to predict which drugs or vaccines would be most effective in individuals with particular genotypes for genes affecting drug metabolism.

NOTES AND QUESTIONS

1.   The haplotype mapping project, called the International HapMap Project, or simply, HapMap, began as a three-year program in 2002 with pledges of $100 million from six nations (Canada, China, Japan, Nigeria, the United Kingdom and the United States). By February 2005, the project had reached its initial goal of mapping one million SNPs. Currently over 10 million SNPs have been identified.

2.   HapMap began analyzing blood samples from donors from five populations: Han Chinese in Beijing, Japanese in Tokyo, Yoruba in Ibadan, Nigerians, and Utah residents with ancestry from northern and western Europe. No medical or personal identifying information was obtained from the 270 donors. However, the samples are identified by the population from which they were collected. What ethical, legal, and social issues does this raise?

3.   In 2002, Craig Venter resigned as head of Celera and started a foundation called The J. Craig Venter Institute.

4.   Studies that take advantage of new high-speed sequencing technologies (discussed in Chapter 4) have accelerated the search for SNPs associated with disease. These studies, referred to as whole genome or genome-wide association studies (GWAS), search for SNPs by comparing the entire genome of large numbers of individuals with particular diseases to the genomes of control groups without the diseases.

5.   Another post-Human Genome Project research program is the 1000 Genomes Project, an international research consortium formed to sequence the genomes of approximately 1,200 people from around the world to provide medically useful information on human genetic variation. The project was funded by the Wellcome Trust Sanger Institute in England, the Beijing Genomics Institute Shenzhen in China, and the National Human Genome Research Institute at the National Institutes of Health. The results of the project were made public in January 2009.

6.   In 2007, the NIH initiated the Human Microbiome Project. The goal of this project is to use DNA sequencing to obtain a better understanding of the microbial communities that inhabit the human digestive system. These microorganisms are essential for human metabolism, and their cells outnumber human cells by a factor of ten to one.

X.   HISTORICAL OVERVIEW: EUGENICS

Current ethical, legal, and policy developments concerning human genetics cannot be understood without reference to the historical background. Part of this background, the history of the science of human genetics, was described earlier in this chapter and will be supplemented in later chapters in discussions of specific scientific applications, such as gene therapy. This section covers a different aspect of the historical setting—the eugenics movement that flourished during the first half of the twentieth century. It is safe to say that no phenomenon has done more to shape the ethical, legal, and policy attitudes toward human genetics than the philosophy of eugenics and the actions that it inspired.

This section begins with an explanation of the term "eugenics" and a historical description of the movement that bears its name. The section then explores the reaction of American law, and discusses the ways in which eugenic thinking continues to be reflected in public attitudes and policy.

ALLEN BUCHANAN ET AL., FROM CHANCE TO CHOICE: GENETICS AND JUSTICE
27–28 (2000).

The current revolution in molecular biology is not the first but the second large-scale attempt to modify the pattern of human heredity for the better. The eugenics movement of 1870–1950 came first. These large-scale social movements, originating in England but ultimately involving public advocates and membership organizations from Brazil to Russia, located the source of social problems in the genes of individuals and sought to alter the pattern by which these genes would be transmitted to future generations. In the United States, the movement received substantial funding from the great family fortunes, including Carnegie and the Rockefellers, and it was endorsed, with varying degrees of enthusiasm, by most scientists working in the field of human genetics. Indeed, eugenics was the motivation for much of the early scientific research in this field.

Nevertheless, the history of eugenics is not a proud one. It is largely remembered for its shoddy science, the blatant race and class biases of many of its leading advocates, and its cruel program of segregation and, later, sterilization of hundreds of thousands of vulnerable people who were judged to have substandard genes. Even worse, eugenics, in the form of "racial hygiene," formed part of the core of Nazi doctrine. Hitler endorses it in *Mein Kampf,* and once in power expanded both eugenic research and, borrowing from U.S. models, a program of sterilization that became the first step toward the murder of handicapped "Aryans" and ultimately millions of victims of the Holocaust.

PHILIP R. REILLY, EUGENICS, ETHICS, STERILIZATION LAWS,
IN 1 ENCYCLOPEDIA OF ETHICAL, LEGAL, AND POLICY
ISSUES IN BIOTECHNOLOGY

204, 204–208 (Thomas H. Murray & Maxwell J. Mehlman eds. 2000).

ORIGINS AND RISE OF THE EUGENICS MOVEMENT

Although speculations about the perfectibility of humankind date at least as far back as the flowering of philosophy among the ancient Greek city states, the first serious social policy proposal to improve the gene pool of our species that was tied to scientific claims arose in England in the second half of the nineteenth century. Francis Galton, a Victorian polymath who was probably influenced by the revolutionary impact of *The Origin of Species* published in 1859 by his cousin, Charles Darwin, began investigating the inheritance of talent among eminent English families about 1864. He coined the term eugenics (from the Greek, fusing words for good and birth) in 1883 in *Inquiries into Human Faculty and its Development*. Public interest in the notion that success and failure in life might be closely tied to the germ plasm that one inherited grew rapidly, especially in England and the United States, and the new word enjoyed a certain vogue. * * *

In the United States eugenic policies, which flowered in the early twentieth century, germinated in the climate of progressive reform that took root in the last quarter of the nineteenth century. From 1850 to 1880, the states had built many prisons, hospitals, insane asylums, and colonies for the mentally retarded. Initial enthusiasm faded as funding problems arose and conditions declined. Richard Dugdale, a well-to-do Englishman who made New York City home, was an ardent social reformer and one of many who sought to improve such facilities. It was while inspecting prisons in upstate New York that he discovered a large family many of whose members seemed to be inhabiting one state facility or another. His book, *The Jukes,* based on an exhaustive study of the family, detailed the cost to taxpayers of their incarceration and support. He also championed two ideas that would become core beliefs among many Americans within a decade: that feeblemindedness, epilepsy, drunkenness, criminality, and insanity had strong hereditary influences, and that affected individuals tended to produce larger than average numbers of offspring.

Interest in eugenics was widespread in the United States just as biologists rediscovered the laws of inheritance that Gregor Mendel had postulated in 1865, but which had been reported in an obscure local scientific journal and been little noticed. Charles Davenport, a talented young biology professor, played an instrumental role in propagating "mendelism" in the United States. He was quick to apply the theory to problems of human heredity and about 1905 he secured a large gift from

Mrs. E.H. Harriman (the wife of the railroad magnate) to develop and sustain a eugenics research facility at Cold Spring Harbor on Long Island, an entity which operated independently of the Station for Experimental Evolution that he had founded there a couple of years earlier. One of his most important decisions was to recruit a midwestern high school teacher named Harry Hamilton Laughlin to direct the Eugenics Record Office. In so doing, Davenport, a highly respected biologist who would become a member of the National Academy of Sciences, tied human genetics to eugenics and provided eugenics with a cloak of scientific legitimacy that it wore for more than three decades.

* * * Between 1910 and 1920 eugenicists working in association with the Eugenics Record Office and sometimes assisted by Laughlin's field-workers published a number of lengthy monographs with colorful names, such as *The Hill Folk: Report of a Rural Community of Hereditary Defectives*. These monographs reinforced the eugenic ideas propounded in *The Jukes* and the equally famous *The Kallikaks* (1912), written by Henry Herbert Goddard, a prominent psychologist who worked at the Vineland Training School in New Jersey and who imported IQ testing from France about 1905.

* * *

During the 1920s Laughlin also spent an immense amount of time drafting and lobbying for the enactment of laws to permit state officials to sterilize institutionalized retarded persons without their consent. He helped propagate the second wave of such laws that swept through America in the 1920s, and he provided an important deposition in the lower court proceedings that led to *Buck v. Bell*, in which the United States Supreme Court ultimately upheld the constitutionality of a law he helped to craft. This opinion removed lingering doubts in many state legislatures and made possible the enactment of about a dozen new laws (discussed below) in the ensuing five years.

* * *

FIRST STERILIZATION LAWS

The nation's first sterilization bill was introduced in the Michigan legislature in 1897, but did not come to floor vote. In 1905 the Pennsylvania House of Representatives became the first legislative body to pass a bill proposing involuntary sterilization of certain institutionalized persons, but the governor vetoed it. On April 9, 1907, Indiana governor J. Frank Hanly, a month after a sizable majority of both houses had voted favorably, signed the nation's first eugenic sterilization law. The statute authorized the compulsory sterilization of "confirmed criminals, idiots, imbeciles and rapists" residing in a state institution if, after appropriate review, a panel of one physician and two surgeons concluded that it was "inadvisable" that the individual procreate and that there was "no probability of improvement." * * *

In 1909 the legislatures in California, Connecticut, Oregon, and Washington passed similar laws. Despite overwhelming support in the legislature, the governor of Oregon vetoed the bill sent to him; the other three governors promptly signed their bills into law. In the ensuing four years (1910–1913), ten states (Iowa, New Jersey, Nevada, New York, North Dakota, Michigan, Kansas, Wisconsin, Vermont, and Nebraska) passed sterilization laws. In general, there was little opposition and most votes were lopsided. Only in the state where the vote was close (96–82 in the House), Vermont, did a governor cast a veto.

* * *

By 1913 involuntary sterilization programs were active in 14 states. There were significant differences in their scope and pace, partly because in a number of the states opponents of eugenics attacked the constitutionality of the enabling laws. In every instance (Indiana, Iowa, Michigan, Nevada, New Jersey, New York, and Washington) in which the constitutionality was put at issue, the courts invalidated the laws, usually on the grounds that they violated the requirements of the Due Process Clause of the Fourteenth Amendment. Laws that targeted prisoners were held to violate the Eighth Amendment prohibiting cruel and unusual punishments. In Oregon the sterilization law, which also was challenged on constitutional grounds, was repealed by public referendum only months after the governor signed it. [The grounds for reversal were, in one state, that the law violated the prohibition against cruel and unusual punishment; and in other states, that these laws violated equal protection because they only applied to institutionalized persons, or that they violated due process by not providing adequate procedural safeguards.—Eds.] * * *

RESURGENCE OF STERILIZATION LAWS

Eugenic Thinking in the 1920s

During the 1920s the eugenics movement, which prior to the World War had begun to decline, grew and prospered. * * * Especially in the midwest, interest in positive eugenics (the search for methods to have genetically superior children) captured the imagination. County fairs sponsored "fitter family" contests in which people, not unlike the prize hogs or cattle they showed, competed for blue ribbons based on their pedigree, physical examinations, and their children's report cards.

At the Eugenics Record Office, Laughlin, stung by the constitutional defeats suffered by the involuntary sterilization laws between 1913 and 1918, produced a massive tome on the societal benefits of eugenic sterilization. He carefully analyzed the laws that the courts had found flawed, and then drafted and circulated a model sterilization law that he hoped would satisfy the constitutional concerns. In the early 1920s his work was widely used by legislators who wanted to sponsor such bills. His polemics on sterilization found their way to Nazi Germany where Laughlin was held in such high regard that he was awarded an honorary degree by the University of Heidelberg in 1934.

Beginning in 1923 there was a major resurgence of sterilization laws. After five years of legislative inactivity, new laws were enacted in Delaware, Michigan, Montana, and Oregon. Virginia adopted a law in 1924, and governors signed seven of the nine bills that were passed in 1925. By January 1926 eugenic sterilization laws were on the books of 17 states and small bands of pro-sterilization lobbyists were urging many others to follow suit. In some states directors of state institutions permitted involuntary eugenical sterilizations to occur despite the absence of enabling laws.

In mid-1925 the Michigan Supreme Court upheld the constitutionality of the new law which it held was "justified by the findings of Biological Science," and was a "proper and reasonable exercise of the police power of the state." This greatly encouraged other legislatures, but many still wondered how such laws would fare before the United States Supreme Court. In a bold move, pro-sterilization forces in Virginia decided to find out. The resulting decision, *Buck v. Bell*, was the single most important event in the history of the sterilization laws in the United States.

BUCK V. BELL
274 U.S. 200 (1927).

MR. JUSTICE HOLMES delivered the opinion of the Court.

This is a writ of error to review a judgment of the Supreme Court of Appeals of the state of Virginia, affirming a judgment of the Circuit Court of Amherst County, by which the defendant in error, the superintendent of the State Colony for Epileptics and Feeble Minded, was ordered to perform the operation of salpingectomy upon Carrie Buck, the plaintiff in error, for the purpose of making her sterile. The case comes here upon the contention that the statute authorizing the judgment is void under the Fourteenth Amendment as

Carrie Buck and her mother.

denying to the plaintiff in error due process of law and the equal protection of the laws.

Carrie Buck is a feeble minded white woman who was committed to the State Colony above mentioned in due form. She is the daughter of a feeble minded mother in the same institution, and the mother of an illegitimate feeble minded child. She was eighteen years old at the time of the trial of her case in the Circuit Court, in the latter part of 1924. An Act of Virginia, approved March 20, 1924, recites that the health of the patient and the welfare of society may be promoted in certain cases by the sterilization of mental defectives, under careful safeguard, etc.; that the sterilization may be effected in males by vasectomy and in females by salpingectomy, without serious pain or substantial danger to life; that the Commonwealth is supporting in various institutions many defective persons who if now discharged would become a menace but if incapable of procreating might be discharged with safety and become self-supporting with benefit to themselves and to society; and that experience has shown that heredity plays an important part in the transmission of insanity, imbecility, etc. The statute then enacts that whenever the superintendent of certain institutions including the above named State Colony shall be of opinion that it is for the best interests of the patients and of society that an inmate under his care should be sexually sterilized, he may have the operation performed upon any patient afflicted with hereditary forms of insanity, imbecility, etc., on complying with the very careful provisions by which the act protects the patients from possible abuse.

The superintendent first presents a petition to the special board of directors of his hospital or colony, stating the facts and the grounds for his opinion, verified by affidavit. Notice of the petition and of the time and place of the hearing in the institution is to be served upon the inmate, and also upon his guardian, and if there is no guardian the superintendent is to apply to the Circuit Court of the County to appoint one. If the inmate is a minor notice also is to be given to his parents if any with a copy of the petition. The board is to see to it that the inmate may attend the hearings if desired by him or his guardian. The evidence is all to be reduced to writing, and after the board has made its order for or against the operation, the superintendent, or the inmate, or his guardian, may appeal to the Circuit Court of the County. The Circuit Court may consider the record of the board and the evidence before it and such other admissible evidence as may be offered, and may affirm, revise, or reverse the order of the board and enter such order as it deems just. Finally any party may apply to the Supreme Court of Appeals, which, if it grants the appeal, is to hear the case upon the record of the trial in the Circuit Court and may enter such order as it thinks the Circuit Court should have entered. There can be no doubt that so far as procedure is concerned the rights of the patient are most carefully considered, and as every step in this case was taken in scrupulous compliance with the statute and after months of observation, there is no doubt that in that respect the plaintiff in error has had due process of law.

The attack is not upon the procedure but upon the substantive law. It seems to be contended that in no circumstances could such an order be justified. It certainly is contended that the order cannot be justified upon the existing grounds. The judgment finds the facts that have been recited and that Carrie Buck "is the probable potential parent of socially inadequate offspring, likewise afflicted, that she may be sexually sterilized without detriment to her general health and that her welfare and that of society will be promoted by her sterilization," and thereupon makes the order. In view of the general declarations of the legislature and the specific findings of the Court, obviously we cannot say as matter of law that the grounds do not exist, and if they exist they justify the result. We have seen more than once that the public welfare may call upon the best citizens for their lives. It would be strange if it could not call upon those who already sap the strength of the State for these lesser sacrifices, often not felt to be such by those concerned, in order to prevent our being swamped with incompetence. It is better for all the world, if instead of waiting to execute degenerate offspring for crime, or to let them starve for their imbecility, society can prevent those who are manifestly unfit from continuing their kind. The principle that sustains compulsory vaccination is broad enough to cover cutting the Fallopian tubes. Jacobson v. Massachusetts, 197 U.S. 11. Three generations of imbeciles are enough.

But, it is said, however it might be if this reasoning were applied generally, it fails when it is confined to the small number who are in the institutions named and is not applied to the multitudes outside. It is the usual last resort of constitutional arguments to point out shortcomings of this sort. But the answer is that the law does all that is needed when it does all that it can, indicates a policy, applies it to all within the lines, and seeks to bring within the lines all similarly situated so far and so fast as its means allow. Of course so far as the operations enable those who otherwise must be kept confined to be returned to the world, and thus open the asylum to others, the equality aimed at will be more nearly reached.

Judgment affirmed.

MR. JUSTICE BUTLER dissents.

PAUL A. LOMBARDO, THREE GENERATIONS, NO IMBECILES: NEW LIGHT ON BUCK V. BELL
60 N.Y.U.L. Rev. 30, 50–62 (1985).

The trial of Buck v. Bell took place November 18, 1924. Strode [counsel for the superintendent of the state institution] presented eight witnesses from the area near Carrie's home in an attempt to prove her "social inadequacy." Additionally, Strode introduced a lengthy deposition from a eugenical expert from New York and had another eugenicist testify at the trial, both of whom informed the court about Carrie's feeblemindedness in light of eugenical theory. He also put two Virginia physicians on the stand to bolster the case in favor of the sterilization law.

In contrast, Whitehead [counsel for Buck] called no witnesses to dispute the specific allegations against Carrie or to cast doubt on the "scientific" theories about which Strode's four "experts" had testified. Moreover, Whitehead's cross-examination of the witnesses for the State was so weak that it was often unclear which side he was representing. * * * A cursory review of the trial transcript readily supports this view; a more thorough analysis of the case Whitehead could have presented suggests a deliberate decision not to defend Carrie.

Among the allegations Whitehead chose not to dispute were several assertions about Carrie's background. For example, famed eugenicist Harry Laughlin never examined Carrie, but drew firm "scientific conclusions" from very sketchy information supplied by Priddy [id.][superintendent of the state institution], compelling one commentator to label Laughlin's analysis as "near-psychic." Laughlin's deposition relied on Priddy's "facts" as proof not only of Carrie's alleged feeblemindedness, but also of her generally undesirable character. She had, said Priddy, a "record during life of immorality, prostitution, and untruthfulness; [had] never been self-sustaining; [and] has had one illegitimate child * * * supposed to be mental defective." Her mother, Emma Buck, "was maritally unworthy; having been divorced from her husband on account of infidelity * * * [and] has had one illegitimate child and probably two others inclusive of Carrie Buck * * *." With regard to the Buck family generally, he concluded, "[t]hese people belong to the shiftless, ignorant, and worthless class of anti-social whites of the South * * * [about whom] it is impossible to get intelligent and satisfactory data * * *."

Most of these comments, left unchallenged by Whitehead, were not only of questionable relevance, but untrue. Had Whitehead chosen to investigate Carrie's background he easily could have collected evidence to refute most of Priddy's charges. For example, on the question of her illegitimacy, he could have found that her parents, Frank and Emma Buck, were married in 1896. The available records indicate that when Carrie was born in 1906, her parents were still married. A common law presumption effective in Virginia at that time would have established Carrie's legitimacy. Was Carrie feebleminded? This was the purported justification for her commitment to the Colony, yet the majority of witnesses called by Strode had no firsthand knowledge of Carrie. Seven of the eleven witnesses either had never met Carrie or refused to offer any conclusion about her mental condition. Several of Carrie's own teachers could have attested, with supporting documentation, that Carrie was not mentally deficient. School records indicate that Carrie was a normal child: In the five years that she attended school, she was promoted to the sixth grade. In fact, the year before she left school, her teacher entered the comment "very good—deportment and lessons" and recommended her for promotion. That teacher and her records would have contradicted the testimony of the single witness who claimed that Carrie was "anti-social" because she had written notes to boys in school.

Was Carrie immoral? Apart from how ridiculous this charge sounds today, broadly defined character traits such as immorality were at issue in the trial. Priddy linked Carrie's supposed predisposition to "anti-social" behavior to the same characteristics he had observed in her mother and the "generally accepted theory of the laws of heredity." Whitehead easily could have questioned the charge of "immorality" by calling witnesses of his own. Carrie had attended church and church school and had been a member of two church choirs in her hometown. Such testimony would have, at the least, posed doubts about the accuracy of the investigation into her character.

The eugenical basis of the Virginia sterilization law required that Carrie's inadequacies be hereditary—that she be the "probable potential parent of socially inadequate offspring." To show this hereditary link, Strode elicited testimony that Carrie's mother, Emma, was a feebleminded patient at the Colony, that Carrie had exhibited "peculiarities" since childhood, that supposed members of Carrie's family were "peculiar," and that Carrie's child was slow. Strode's evidence was weak, yet Whitehead's cross-examination, when it took place at all, failed to attack the evidence.

Why, given the weakness of Strode's evidence, was Carrie chosen as the perfect candidate for sterilization? The answer to this question clarifies the unstated purpose of the sterilization policy: she had delivered a child, but was unmarried. Poor, and born of a disgraced mother herself, Carrie was likely to be the parent of more of the "shiftless, ignorant and worthless class of anti-social whites" from which she came. The single fact of her unwed motherhood was Priddy's proof of her deficiency.

However, strong evidence existed to mitigate Carrie's responsibility for her bastard child. The circumstances of her commitment and the contradictions in the testimony of her foster parents would have alerted any conscientious attorney to probe further. As Carrie's commitment papers show, the foster parents [the Dobbses] with whom she lived for fourteen years were very anxious to have her put away.

* * *

What the trial did not reveal was that, despite all the discussion of her immoral behavior, Carrie was pregnant because she had been raped.

Mrs. Dobbs was away "on account of some illness," in the summer of 1923. During her absence Carrie was raped by Mrs. Dobbs's nephew. Commitment to the Colony would hide Carrie's shame; more importantly for Mr. and Mrs. Dobbs, it would save the family reputation.

* * *

Whitehead neither called the Dobbses as witnesses nor challenged Priddy by introducing readily available data on Carrie's parents, her church attendance, or her school record—data Priddy (and presumably Whitehead) had considered "impossible to get." Whitehead failed as Carrie's attorney not because he was incompetent, underpaid, or merely ineffectual. He failed because he intended to fail.

Whitehead had long been associated with Strode and Priddy. He helped Strode with his election campaign and helped him obtain an Army commission. As a member of the Colony Board, Whitehead authorized Priddy's sterilization requests. A building named in Whitehead's honor was opened at the Colony just two months before Carrie's arrival. Strode, in turn, recommended Whitehead for a government position only six days before Carrie Buck's trial. Proof that Whitehead intended to lose Carrie Buck's case does not, however, rely primarily on the evidence of these close, personal associations. Whitehead's role and intent are amply documented in the minutes of the Colony Board.

* * *

In 1930 Doctor Bell reported that after her sterilization, Carrie Buck "was immediately returned to society and made good." That evaluation was only partially true. Although she was paroled as a domestic helper to a family in Bland, Virginia, she remained under the control of the Colony. Her discharge, like that of all sterilized Colony women, was conditioned on an annual visit to Doctor Bell for a physical examination. Had there been any complaints of ill behavior, she could have been returned to the Colony at once.

After Carrie left the Colony, she married and became a member of the Methodist Church in Bland where she sang in the choir as she had as a teenager in Charlottesville. After twenty-four years of marriage, her husband died and she traveled to Front Royal, Virginia, where she met and later married Charles Detamore. He took work in farms and orchards and Carrie assisted a local family in caring for an elderly relative.

In 1970, with Carrie suffering from ill health, the couple returned to Carrie's hometown. They moved into a single-room cinder block shed with no plumbing, which the owner allowed them to inhabit rent-free. They lived there ten years in abject poverty, until in 1980 Carrie was hospitalized for exposure and malnutrition. After she recovered partially, she and her husband were taken to a state-operated nursing home outside Waynesboro, Virginia. She died there on January 28, 1983, at the age of seventy-six. Her body was returned to Charlottesville, where she was buried only a few steps from the graves of her daughter, Vivian, and her foster parents, Mr. and Mrs. Dobbs.

Throughout Carrie's adult life she regularly displayed intelligence and kindness that belied the "feeblemindedness" and "immorality" that were used as an excuse to sterilize her. She was an avid reader, and even in her last weeks was able to converse lucidly, recalling events from her childhood. Branded by Holmes as a second generation imbecile, Carrie provided no support for his glib epithet throughout her life.

Carrie's daughter Vivian, like her mother, was wrongly accused. On the basis of a nurse's comment that she was "not quite normal," Vivian Buck was used to prove her mother's hereditary "defects." Although she lived barely eight years, she too disproved Holmes's epigram. In her two years of schooling, she performed quite well, at one point earning a spot on the school "Honor Roll."

Of the three generations, the least is known about Emma Buck. She died at the Colony, leaving few records of her life. She was, at worst, the "moron" that Priddy claimed; no one but Holmes charged her with imbecility. Her true shortcomings probably stemmed from poverty and perhaps promiscuity.

NOTES AND QUESTIONS

1.   The decision in *Buck* was generally considered to be a progressive result. Brandeis, Stone, and Taft joined in Holmes' majority opinion. Only Justice Butler, the Court's only Catholic, dissented (without opinion). (Many Catholics at the time were troubled by eugenics, which some people thought should authorize non-treatment of "defective" newborns.) The outcome in *Buck* was embraced by such progressives of the time as Clarence Darrow, Helen Keller, and Margaret Sanger, who founded Planned Parenthood.

2.   Note the elaborate procedural protections provided for in the statute pursuant to which Carrie Buck was sterilized. Are there any additional protections that might have been provided? Given the scope of the existing protections, how can the outcome in her case be explained? Does this suggest anything about the usefulness of procedural protections to prevent abuses?

3.   Is Justice Holmes correct in analogizing sterilization to "call[ing] upon the best citizens for their lives" to promote "the public welfare"? When is the government permitted to require someone to die for the public welfare? Could the state kill someone to prevent the spread of an infectious disease?

4.   A recurrent theme in this book is the degree to which the government should be permitted to control human reproductive behavior.

What does the *Buck* case suggest are the limits on the power of the state to restrict reproduction? Are there any circumstances in which the state would be justified in sterilizing people against their will? Does the answer turn on whether only certain types of individuals, such as those considered "defective," are being singled out? In the mid-1970s, one Indian state adopted a policy of sterilizing women after their third child. See Note, India's Compulsory Sterilization Laws: The Human Rights of Family Planning, 8 Cal. W. Int'l L. J. 342 (1978). Is population control a sufficiently important social purpose to justify forced sterilization?

5.   Justice Holmes stated that "[t]he principle that sustains compulsory vaccination is broad enough to cover cutting the Fallopian tubes," and cited Jacobson v. Massachusetts, 197 U.S. 11 (1905). That case upheld a Massachusetts requirement of smallpox vaccinations against a challenge that they infringed personal liberty. In his opinion, Justice Harlan observed:

> According to settled principles the police power of a State must be held to embrace, at least, such reasonable regulations established directly by legislative enactment as will protect the public health and the public safety.

* * *

> [I]n every well-ordered society charged with the duty of conserving the safety of its members the rights of the individual in respect of his liberty may at times, under the pressure of great dangers, be subjected to such restraint, to be enforced by reasonable regulations, as the safety of the general public may demand.

* * *

> [T]he means prescribed by the State to that end [must have a] real and substantial relation to the protection of the public health and safety.

197 U.S. at 25, 29, 31. Does the statute at issue in *Buck* meet these standards?

6.   Beyond compulsory vaccination, "[g]overnment engages in a broad range of restrictions of the person to reduce the spread of infection—civil confinement (isolation, quarantine, and compulsory hospitalization), mandatory treatment, and criminal penalties for knowing or willful exposure to disease." Lawrence O. Gostin, Public Health Law: Power, Duty, Restraint 203 (2000). To what extent does a genetic disease resemble a communicable disease? Is a genetic disease sufficiently "communicable" that the government is entitled to invoke its public health authority to prevent the disease from being "spread"? If so, what public health measures would be appropriate? For example, could the government, under its power to protect the public health, require someone to undergo genetic testing to determine if a fetus was affected with a genetic abnormality or disorder? Would the answer depend on whether or not the condition was treatable? See the discussion of mandatory screening programs in Chapter 9.

7.   Following *Buck*, a total of 28 states had enacted compulsory sterilization laws by 1931. In California, the number of reported sterilizations rose from 322 in 1925 to 2,362 over the course of 1928 and 1929. Nationally, approximately 3,000 operations were reported annually prior to the Second World War. More occurred that were not reported. For more complete information, see Phillip R. Reilly, Eugenics, Ethics, Sterilization Laws, in 1 Encyclopedia of Ethical, Legal, and Policy Issues in Biotechnology 204 (Thomas H. Murray & Maxwell J. Mehlman eds. 2000).

8.   Eugenics theories also were seized upon by the descendants of early, Northern European immigrants to preserve their political power in the face of later waves of immigration. As Celeste Condit writes in her book, The Meanings of the Gene (1999), at 35:

> The turn of the century was an anxious era for the relatively well-to-do Americans whose ancestors had come from Europe and who had dominated the continent for 200 years. Massive migration from rural areas to cities was occurring. From 1800 to 1920 the population in the United States shifted from overwhelmingly rural (75 percent) to majority urban (51 percent). This migration was creating and amplifying what we now know to be the standard problems of urban poverty in industrializing areas. However, the scope and scale of these problems were probably both new and shocking to the members of the society. While absolute numbers of those involved in crime and poverty might not have increased, the proximity to crime, poverty, prostitution, and other social ills that accompanies life in a city environment was nonetheless capable of creating distress. The shock was exacerbated by the immigration of a variety of different ethnic groups with a vast array of languages, cultural values, and cultural practices different from those preferred by the people derived from Northern European ancestry and culture. As Diane Paul has noted, a third of the population in 1920 consisted of immigrants and their children, and the proportions were higher in cities. The descendants of the Northern Europeans who had gained dominance by displacing the native population 200 years earlier were now faced with losing that dominance in turn.

9.   World War II marked a watershed in the eugenics movement because of the association between eugenics and the Nazis. As described by Buchanan et al.:

> Eugenics was central to the entire Nazi enterprise, joined with romantic nativist and racist myths of the purebred Nordic. The emphasis on "blood" called for a purifying of the nation's gene pool so that Germans could regain the nobility and greatness of their genetically pure forebears.

> As Robert Proctor and other historians have shown, the subsequent programs of sterilization, euthanasia of the unfit (a program that took the lives of tens of thousands of "Aryans," mostly young

children), and eventually the Holocaust itself were part of the unfolding of this central idea. The sterilization and "euthanasia" programs, which did not initially target Jews and other minorities, were an exercise in negative eugenics designed to improve the native German stock from its degenerated condition. Legislation barring sexual relations between Jews and "Aryans," and ultimately the Holocaust were intended to prevent further adulteration of the "pure" German nation with inferior genes. Jews and others who contributed "evil" genes were the disease afflicting the German nation, which Hitler, the physician, would cure.

Allen Buchanan et al., From Chance to Choice: Genetics and Justice 37 (2000).

The Nazi sterilization program, although much larger in scope, employed many of the same legal mechanisms as the Americans:

A comprehensive German eugenic sterilization law was enacted on July 14, 1933. Pursuant to it, the nation set up a network of Hereditary Health Courts empowered to sterilize persons about whom, in "the experience of medical science, it may be expected with great probability that their offspring may suffer severe physical damage." At first persons with any one of nine conditions were targeted: inborn feeblemindedness, schizophrenia, manicdepressive [sic] insanity, hereditary epilepsy, Huntington's chorea, hereditary blindness, hereditary deafness, severe hereditary physical deformity, and severe habitual drunkenness. Each special court had three members: a district judge, a local public health official, and a physician deemed to be expert in making the evaluations of the individuals thought to be at risk.

The scale of the eugenic sterilization program in Nazi Germany dwarfed those in all other nations, including the United States. In 1934 more than 200 courts received 84,500 petitions to sterilize. These were sometimes filed by doctors or local public health officials, but often they were filed by one family member about another. In one of the more extreme examples of patriotism, substantial numbers of deaf persons volunteered to be sterilized as a show of support for the "fatherland." Of the 64,499 petitions that were heard, the courts decided for sterilization in 56,244 for a eugenic conviction rate of 87 percent. By 1935 more than 150,000 sterilizations had been approved, many based on judicial proceedings that must have taken under an hour.

Over the ensuing years the scope of the law was broadened. For example, in 1934 it was amended to apply to non-Germans living in Germany. During the 1940s people were often sterilized on the weakest of pretenses, such as being half-Jewish. In 1951, the Central Association of Sterilized People in West Germany estimated that the Nazi programs had sterilized 3,500,000 persons, although it is not possible to document the claim.

Philip R. Reilly, Eugenics, Ethics, Sterilization Laws, in 1 Encyclopedia of Ethical, Legal, and Policy Issues in Biotechnology 210 (Thomas H. Murray & Maxwell J. Mehlman eds. 2000).

10. The American eugenics movement was a major influence on the Nazis. Hitler was in jail and working on *Mein Kampf* in 1924 when he read about the Virginia sterilization statute, and a sterilization provision was the first law the Reichstag enacted after he gained power. Hitler's intent originally was to use sterilization to eliminate inferior populations, but once the war started and he needed hospital beds for wounded soldiers, he decided to empty the mental wards by killing the patients. This policy then grew to encompass the extermination of other undesirables, including Jews and Gypsies.

11. The German sterilization law was based on a "prototypical Model Sterilization Law" drafted by Harry Laughlin, the director of the Eugenics Record Office at Cold Spring Harbor, Long Island. As noted in the Reilly excerpt, Laughlin was held in such high regard by the Nazis that he received an honorary degree from the University of Heidelberg in 1934.

12. Although eugenics-based sterilization in the United States declined markedly after World War II, it did not disappear altogether. As Reilly reports, between 1948 and 1955, approximately 186 women were sterilized in North Carolina. In 1958, Georgia, North Carolina and Virginia reported 574 sterilizations, 76 percent of the national total. At one South Carolina facility for the incurably mentally ill, 104 inmates, 102 of whom were black, were sterilized between 1949 and 1960. From 1970 to 1974, 23 sterilizations were performed in North Carolina state institutions, although most often at the request of relatives concerned that an inmate would become pregnant against her will.

13. For more historical information about the eugenics movement in America, see Paul A. Lombardo, Three Generations, No Imbeciles: Eugenics, the Supreme Court, and Buck v. Bell (2008); Paul A. Lombardo, 'The American Breed': Nazi Eugenics and the Origins of the Pioneer Fund, 65 Albany L. Rev. 743–830 (2002), Paul A. Lombardo, Taking Eugenics Seriously: Three Generations of ??? are Enough?, 30 Fla. St. U. L. Rev. 191–218 (Winter 2003), and Michael J. Malinowski, Choosing the Genetic Makeup of Children: Our Eugenics Past-Present, and Future?. 36 Conn. L. Rev. 125–224 (2003).

POE V. LYNCHBURG TRAINING SCHOOL & HOSPITAL
518 F.Supp. 789 (W.D.Va.1981).

TURK, J.

This case is filed as an individual and class action suit challenging the involuntary sterilization of a number of men and women by Virginia state officials acting pursuant to a statute enacted in 1924 by the Commonwealth of Virginia. The complaint also challenges the constitutionality of the purported refusal of appropriate Virginia state officials to notify all those persons who received such surgery as to their medical status and medical alternatives. In short, plaintiffs allege that many of those who were involuntarily sterilized are still unaware of the reason for their infertility as well as the medical ramifications of the procedure.

* * *

In 1924, the Commonwealth enacted legislation providing for the sexual sterilization of "mental defectives" in certain cases. 1924 Acts of Assembly, Chap. 394. As set forth in defendants' memorandum in support of the motion to dismiss, the statute specifically prescribed certain preliminary procedural steps including notification to the individual, or his or her parent, guardian, or committee as might be appropriate. Shortly after enactment of the statute, the constitutionality of the entire practice was tested in court, and the controversy eventually reached the United States Supreme Court. In Buck v. Bell (1927), the United States Supreme Court held that the statute was not violative of any constitutionally guaranteed rights. However, in 1974, the involuntary sterilization statute was repealed. 1974 Acts of Assembly, Chap. 296. The parties agree that the Commonwealth has no statutory procedures permitting involuntary sterilization at the current time.

Several of the individual plaintiffs in this case underwent involuntary sterilization pursuant to the statute. These plaintiffs also purport to sue on behalf of all persons who have been involuntarily sterilized at governmental institutions in Virginia under color of state law.

* * *

Plaintiffs' prayer for relief essentially tracks the contentions set forth in their complaint. Stated briefly, plaintiffs seek as follows:

1.   Entry of a judgment declaring that:

(a)   the forced surgical sterilization of the sterilized class by Virginia state officials and agencies violated the Fourteenth Amendment, 42 U.S.C. § 1983, and the common law of Virginia; and

(b) defendants' subsequent failure to notify and prevent further harm to members of the sterilized class violates the Fourteenth Amendment, 42 U.S.C. § 1983, the Developmentally Disabled Assistance and Bill of Rights Act, and the common law of Virginia.

2.   Entry of an Order enjoining defendants from authorizing or conducting any surgical sterilization without prior informed consent; and

3.   Entry of an Order requiring defendants to provide adequate notice to all members of the sterilized class of the facts and circumstances of their involuntary surgical sterilization, including the effects and possible reversibility of the operations, and to provide such medical, surgical, and psychological assistance as is necessary to prevent further harm to members of the sterilized class, including operations to reverse the sterilization where possible.

Plaintiffs also seek compensation for costs, attorneys' fees, and other relief as may prove appropriate.

Defendants' motion to dismiss for failure to state a claim is based on the assertions that the requested relief is barred by virtue of the Eleventh Amendment; that the complaint does not allege an actual case or controversy; and that the action is barred by virtue of the applicable statute of limitations.

* * *

The court has reached the conclusion that the motion must be granted in part and denied in part. Specifically, as to the different forms of relief sought by the complaint and as enumerated above, the court will enter an order granting the motion as to sections 1(a) and 2 of the prayer, and denying the motion as to sections 1(b) and 3.

* * *

Regardless of whatever philosophical and sociological valuation may be made regarding involuntary sterilizations in terms of current mores and social thought, the fact remains that the general practice and procedure under the old Virginia statute were upheld by the highest court in the land in Buck v. Bell, supra. It is no answer for the plaintiff to allude to changing patterns of social and constitutional thought as a ground for reopening the inquiry. Since 1974, well before the filing of the instant action, Virginia has had no involuntary sterilization statute. In short, this court has neither the authority nor the occasion to undertake an evaluation as to the constitutionality of the old Virginia statute permitting forced sterilizations. * * *[1]

Given the repeal of the involuntary sterilization statute, it is also apparent that plaintiffs are not entitled to an order, as sought in section 2 of the prayer, enjoining defendants from authorizing or conducting any surgical sterilization without prior informed consent. The complaint gives absolutely no indication that any of the defendants are likely to undertake such action in the future.

* * *

The court now directs its attention to those portions of plaintiffs' complaint and prayer dealing with defendants' alleged failure to notify plaintiffs of the fact of their sterilization and to otherwise provide information and assistance as might be appropriate. As suggested above, the old Virginia statute contained provisions which insured, at least in theory, that persons considered for involuntary sterilization, and their representatives, would be well advised prior to the surgery as to its purpose.

Plaintiffs have alleged facts which indicate that in at least some instances, such notification was not provided and that potential candidates were affirmatively misled as to the purpose of the surgery. Plaintiffs contend that many such persons who were inadequately or inaccurately informed have suffered and continue to suffer medical, emotional, and mental problems, arising in large part from unsuccessful and uninformed attempts to deal with their infertility. Plaintiffs contend that defendants continue to refuse to notify and inform all those affected persons despite the fact that defendants now have reason to believe that some involuntarily sterilized persons were not properly notified at the time of their hospitalization. In short, plaintiffs contend that, in actual practice, the notification provisions of the statute were often not honored and that state officials have continued to perpetrate the deprivation through their subsequent refusal to notify all involuntarily sterilized

---

[1]   The court recognizes that in making these arguments, and in attempting to distinguish Buck v. Bell, supra, plaintiffs have relied primarily on what they perceive as a constitutional deficiency in the procedural aspects of the old Virginia statute. The court also recognizes that *Buck* dealt with an attack to the statute's substance rather than its procedure. Nevertheless, in delivering the court's opinion in *Buck*, Justice Holmes specifically noted that " . . . there is no doubt that . . . plaintiff in error has had due process of law." 274 U.S. at 207, 47 S. Ct. at 584. The court notes that plaintiffs have also alleged a deviation between the stated procedure and the actual procedure under the statute. While these allegations will be considered in more detail in the context of the contention of a "continuing deprivation" due to failure to notify, the court notes for purposes of this argument that, at the most, plaintiffs might establish that on some occasions, certain officials acted inconsistently with the procedural requirements of the statute. Such a circumstance certainly would not justify entry of a declaration holding all sterilizations under the statute to be illegal as per plaintiffs' prayer. Moreover, an allegation of such past deviations, standing alone, does not remotely suggest the existence of a present case and controversy, absent a viable demand for monetary damages and absent identification of any parties defendant who could now be held answerable for such damages.

persons as to their status. To the extent that the complaint sets forth such allegations, and to the extent of sections 1(b) and 3 of the prayer for relief, the court must conclude that the complaint states a claim.

NOTES

1.   The *Poe* case was settled in 1983 when state officials agreed to attempt to locate all surviving victims and provide a small amount of compensation.

2.   In 1977, a federal court invalidated regulations issued by the Department of Health Education and Welfare [now Health and Human Services] that authorized the sterilization of adults, minors, and mental incompetents by federally-funded family planning programs on the ground that the sterilizations were not voluntary. Relf v. Weinberger, 372 F.Supp. 1196 (D.D.C. 1974), vacated as moot, 565 F.2d 722 (D.C. Cir. 1977). Judge Gerhard Gesell noted that "minors and other incompetents have been sterilized with federal funds and that an indefinite number of poor people have been improperly coerced into accepting a sterilization operation under the threat that various federally supported welfare benefits would be withdrawn unless they submitted to irreversible sterilization. Patients receiving Medicaid assistance at childbirth are evidently the most frequent targets of this pressure, as the experiences of plaintiffs Waters and Walker illustrate. Mrs. Waters was actually refused medical assistance by her attending physician unless she submitted to a tubal ligation after the birth. Other examples were documented." The court ruled that the sterilizations were not authorized by applicable federal laws. The court's opinion observed that "since these conclusions are based on statutory rather than constitutional grounds, the Court need not reach the question of whether involuntary sterilization could be funded by Congress." The case ultimately was vacated after the Department of Health and Human Services adopted regulations conforming to the district court's order. Relf v. Weinberger, 565 F.2d 722 (D.C. Cir.1977).

3.   The minors sterilized with federal funds that Judge Gesell referred to in *Relf* included Mary Alice and Minnie Lee Relf, black children aged 12 and 14 respectively, who were sterilized without their knowledge or consent by authorities in Montgomery, Alabama. An older sister, Katie, 17, avoided surgery only by physically resisting. The children's mother, who was unable to read, had placed an "X" on the consent document without knowing what it said. She assumed, she explained later, that she was merely authorizing continued use of Depo-Provera injections, which the girls had been receiving as an experimental contraceptive. For more details on the Relfs and similar cases, see Donna Franklin, Beyond the Tuskegee Apology, Washington Post, May 29, 1997, at A23. How do the protections mandated by the court in *Relf* prevent this from happening again?

As the administration of Depo-Provera to the Relf children suggests, compulsory contraception is a eugenic alternative to compulsory sterilization.

After the FDA approved Norplant, a surgically-implanted, long-lasting contraceptive, legislators in a number of states proposed linking Norplant use to eligibility for welfare benefits. Although no such requirement has been adopted, Norplant has been covered under all state Medicaid programs.

4.   The United States and Germany are not the only countries to have engaged in eugenics-based sterilizations. Between 1935 and 1976, approximately 60,000 people, mostly women, were sterilized in Sweden. They were typically poor, had learning disabilities, or were non-Nordic, and were labeled as genetically or racially "inferior." One of the major justifications for this sterilization program was that it would reduce the cost of the Swedish welfare state by reducing the number of people who would have to be supported. One woman is reported to have been sterilized because she could not master her confirmation studies well enough to satisfy her priest. Another was judged to be mentally slow as a child because she could not read the blackboard; it later turned out that she merely needed glasses. For a fuller account of the Swedish program, see Dan Balz, Sweden Sterilized Thousands of "Useless" Citizens for Decades, Washington Post, Aug. 29, 1997, at A1. In 1999, the Swedish government agreed to pay $20,780 to each surviving person who had been sterilized.

5.   In 1994, the Chinese national legislature passed a law entitled "Law of the People's Republic of China on Maternal and Infant Health Care." The statute requires every couple to undergo a premarital medical examination, and where this shows "genetic disease of a serious nature which is considered to be inappropriate for child bearing from a medical point of view, the two may be married only if both sides agree to take long term contraceptive precautions or to take ligation operation for sterility." Moreover, termination of pregnancy must be advised when a fetus has a "defect of a serious nature" or a "genetic disease of a serious nature." "Relevant mental diseases" include schizophrenia and manic depressive psychosis. The Chinese legislation is described in an editorial by Martin Bobrow, head of the genetics department at Cambridge University, Redrafted Chinese Law Remains Eugenic, 32 J. Med. Genetics 409 (1995).

A related use of compulsory sterilization is to punish the commission of a crime. The Supreme Court had occasion to consider the constitutionality of such an approach in the following case.

SKINNER V. OKLAHOMA
316 U.S. 535 (1942).

MR. JUSTICE DOUGLAS delivered the opinion of the Court.

This case touches a sensitive and important area of human rights. Oklahoma deprives certain individuals of a right which is basic to the perpetuation of a race—the right to have offspring. Oklahoma has decreed the enforcement of its law against petitioner, overruling his claim that it violated the Fourteenth Amendment. Because that decision raised grave and substantial constitutional questions, we granted the petition for certiorari.

The statute involved is Oklahoma's Habitual Criminal Sterilization Act. Okla. Stat. Ann. Tit. 57, §§ 171, et seq.; L. 1935, pp. 94 et seq. That Act defines an "habitual criminal" as a person who, having been convicted two or more times for crimes "amounting to felonies involving moral turpitude," either in an Oklahoma court or in a court of any other State, is thereafter convicted of such a felony in Oklahoma and is sentenced to a term of imprisonment in an Oklahoma penal institution. Machinery is provided for the institution by the Attorney General of a proceeding against such a person in the Oklahoma courts for a judgment that such person shall be rendered sexually sterile. §§ 176, 177. Notice, an opportunity to be heard, and the right to a jury trial are provided. §§ 177–181. The issues triable in such a proceeding are narrow and confined. If the court or jury finds that the defendant is an "habitual criminal" and that he "may be rendered sexually sterile without detriment to his or her general health," then the court "shall render judgment to the effect that said defendant be rendered sexually sterile" (§ 182) by the operation of vasectomy in case of a male, and of salpingectomy in case of a female. § 174. Only one other provision of the Act is material here, and that is § 195, which provides that "offenses arising out of the violation of the prohibitory laws, revenue acts, embezzlement, or political offenses, shall not come or be considered within the terms of this Act."

Petitioner was convicted in 1926 of the crime of stealing chickens, and was sentenced to the Oklahoma State Reformatory. In 1929 he was convicted of the crime of robbery with firearms, and was sentenced to the reformatory. In 1934 he was convicted again of robbery with firearms, and was sentenced to the penitentiary. He was confined there in 1935 when the Act was passed. In 1936 the Attorney General instituted proceedings against him. Petitioner in his answer challenged the Act as unconstitutional by reason of the Fourteenth Amendment. A jury trial was had. The court instructed the jury that the crimes of which petitioner had been convicted were felonies involving moral turpitude, and that the only question for the jury was whether the operation of vasectomy could be performed on petitioner without detriment to his general health. The jury found that it could be. A judgment directing that the operation of vasectomy be performed on petitioner was affirmed by the Supreme Court of Oklahoma by a five to four decision.

Several objections to the constitutionality of the Act have been pressed upon us. It is urged that the Act cannot be sustained as an exercise of the police power, in view of the state of scientific authorities respecting inheritability of criminal traits. It is argued that due process is lacking because, under this Act, unlike the Act upheld in Buck v. Bell, 274 U.S. 200, the defendant is given no opportunity to be heard on the issue as to whether he is the probable potential parent of socially undesirable offspring. It is also suggested that the Act is penal in character and that the sterilization provided for is cruel and unusual punishment and violative of the Fourteenth Amendment. We pass those points without intimating an opinion on them, for there is a feature of the Act which clearly condemns it. That is, its failure to meet the requirements of the equal protection clause of the Fourteenth Amendment. We do not stop to point out all of the inequalities in this Act. A few examples will suffice. In Oklahoma, grand larceny is a felony. Okla. Stats. Ann. Tit. 21, §§ 1705, 5. Larceny is grand larceny when the property taken exceeds $20 in value. Id. § 1704. Embezzlement is punishable "in the manner prescribed for feloniously stealing property of the value of that embezzled." Id. § 1462. Hence, he who embezzles property worth more than $20 is guilty of a felony. A clerk who appropriates over $20 from his employer's till (id. § 1456) and a stranger who steals the same amount are thus both guilty of felonies. If the latter repeats his act and is convicted three times, he may be sterilized. But the clerk is not subject to the pains and penalties of the Act no matter how large his embezzlements nor how frequent his convictions. A person who enters a chicken coop and steals chickens commits a felony (id. § 1719); and he may be sterilized if he is thrice convicted. If, however, he is a bailee of the property and fraudulently appropriates it, he is an embezzler. Id. § 1455. Hence, no matter how habitual his proclivities for embezzlement are and no matter how often his conviction, he may not be sterilized. Thus, the nature of the two crimes is intrinsically the same and they are punishable in the same manner. Furthermore, the line between them follows close distinctions—distinctions comparable to those highly technical ones which shaped the common law as to "trespass" or "taking." There may be larceny by fraud rather than embezzlement even where the owner of the personal property delivers it to the defendant, if the latter has at that time "a fraudulent intention to make use of the possession as a means of converting such property to his own use, and does so convert it." If the fraudulent intent occurs later and the defendant converts the property, he is guilty of embezzlement. Whether a particular act is larceny by fraud or embezzlement thus turns not on the intrinsic quality of the act but on when the felonious intent arose—a question for the jury under appropriate instructions.

It was stated in Buck v. Bell, that the claim that state legislation violates the equal protection clause of the Fourteenth Amendment is "the usual last resort of constitutional arguments." Under our constitutional system the States in determining the reach and scope of particular legislation need not provide "abstract symmetry." They may mark and set apart the classes and types of problems according to the needs and as dictated or suggested by experience. It was in that connection that Mr. Justice Holmes, speaking for the Court in Bain Peanut Co. v. Pinson, 282 U.S. 499, 501, stated, "We must remember that the machinery of government would not work if it were not allowed a little play in its joints." Only recently we reaffirmed the view that the equal protection clause does not prevent the legislature from recognizing "degrees of evil" by our ruling in Tigner v. Texas, 310 U.S. 141, 147, that "the Constitution does not require things which are different in fact or opinion to be treated in law as though they were the same." Thus, if we had here only a question as to a State's classification of crimes, such as embezzlement or larceny, no substantial federal question would be raised. For a State is not constrained in the exercise of its police power to ignore experience which marks a class of offenders or a family of offenses for special treatment. Nor is it prevented by the equal protection clause from confining "its restrictions to those classes of cases where the need is deemed to be clearest." As stated in Buck v. Bell, " . . . the law does all that is needed when it does all that it can, indicates a policy, applies it to all within the lines, and seeks to bring within the lines all similarly situated so far and so fast as its means allow."

But the instant legislation runs afoul of the equal protection clause, though we give Oklahoma that large deference which the rule of the foregoing cases requires. We are dealing here with legislation which involves one of the basic civil rights of man. Marriage and procreation are fundamental to the very existence and survival of the race. The power to sterilize, if exercised, may have subtle, far-reaching and devastating effects. In evil or reckless hands it can cause races or types which are inimical to the dominant group to wither and disappear. There is no redemption for the individual whom the law touches. Any experiment which the State conducts is to his irreparable injury. He is forever deprived of a basic liberty. We mention these matters not to reexamine the scope of the police power of the States. We advert to them merely in emphasis of our view that strict scrutiny of the classification which a State makes in a sterilization law is essential, lest unwittingly, or otherwise, invidious discriminations are made against groups or types of individuals in violation of the constitutional guaranty of just and equal laws. The guaranty of "equal protection of the laws is a pledge of the protection of equal laws." When the law lays an unequal hand on those who have committed intrinsically the same quality of offense and sterilizes one and not the other, it has made as invidious a discrimination as if it had selected a particular race or nationality for oppressive treatment. Sterilization of those who have thrice committed grand larceny, with immunity for those who are embezzlers, is a clear, pointed, unmistakable discrimination. Oklahoma makes no attempt to say that he who commits larceny by trespass or trick or fraud has biologically inheritable traits which he who commits embezzlement lacks. Oklahoma's line between larceny by fraud and embezzlement is determined, as we have noted, "with reference to the time when the fraudulent intent to convert the property to the taker's own use" arises. We have not the slightest basis for inferring that that line has any significance in eugenics, nor that the inheritability of criminal traits follows the neat legal distinctions which the law has marked between those two offenses. In terms of fines and imprisonment, the crimes of larceny and embezzlement rate the same under the Oklahoma code. Only when it comes to sterilization are the pains and penalties of the law different. The equal protection clause would indeed be a formula of empty words if such conspicuously artificial lines could be drawn. In Buck v. Bell, the Virginia statute was upheld though it applied only to feeble-minded persons in institutions of the State. But it was pointed out that "so far as the operations enable those who otherwise must be kept confined to be returned to the world, and thus open the asylum to others, the equality aimed at will be more nearly reached." Here there is no such saving feature. Embezzlers are forever free. Those who steal or take in other ways are not. If such a classification were permitted, the technical common law concept of a "trespass" based on distinctions which are "very largely dependent upon history for explanation" could readily become a rule of human genetics.

* * *

Reversed.

MR. CHIEF JUSTICE STONE, concurring:

I concur in the result, but I am not persuaded that we are aided in reaching it by recourse to the equal protection clause. If Oklahoma may resort generally to the sterilization of criminals on the assumption that their propensities are transmissible to future generations by inheritance, I seriously doubt that the equal protection clause requires it to apply the measure to all criminals in the first instance, or to none.

Moreover, if we must presume that the legislature knows—what science has been unable to ascertain—that the criminal tendencies of any class of habitual offenders are transmissible regardless of the varying mental characteristics of its individuals, I should suppose that we must likewise presume that the legislature, in its wisdom, knows that the criminal tendencies of some classes of offenders are more likely to be transmitted than those of others. And so I think the real question we have to consider is not one of equal protection, but whether the wholesale condemnation of a class to such an invasion of personal liberty, without opportunity to any individual to show that his is not the type of case which would justify resort to it, satisfies the demands of due process.

There are limits to the extent to which the presumption of constitutionality can be pressed, especially where the liberty of the person is concerned and there the presumption is resorted to only to dispense with a procedure which the ordinary dictates of prudence would seem to demand for the protection of the individual from arbitrary action. Although petitioner here was given a hearing to ascertain whether sterilization would be detrimental to his health, he was given none to discover whether his criminal tendencies are of an inheritable type. Undoubtedly a state may, after appropriate inquiry, constitutionally interfere with the personal liberty of the individual to prevent the transmission by inheritance of his socially injurious tendencies. Buck v. Bell, 274 U.S. 200. But until now we have not been called upon to say that it may do so without giving him a hearing and opportunity to challenge the existence as to him of the only facts which could justify so drastic a measure.

Science has found and the law has recognized that there are certain types of mental deficiency associated with delinquency which are inheritable. But the State does not contend—nor can there be any pretense—that either common knowledge or experience, or scientific investigation, has given assurance that the criminal tendencies of any class of habitual offenders are universally or even generally inheritable. In such circumstances, inquiry whether such is the fact in the case of any particular individual cannot rightly be dispensed with. Whether the procedure by which a statute carries its mandate into execution satisfies due process is a matter of judicial cognizance. A law which condemns, without hearing, all the individuals of a class to so harsh a measure as the present because some or even many merit condemnation, is lacking in the first principles of due process. And so, while the state may protect itself from the demonstrably inheritable tendencies of the individual which are injurious to society, the most elementary notions of due process would seem to require it to take appropriate steps to safeguard the liberty of the individual by affording him, before he is condemned to an irreparable injury in his person, some opportunity to show that he is without such inheritable tendencies. The state is called on to sacrifice no permissible end when it is required to reach its objective by a reasonable and just procedure adequate to safeguard rights of the individual which concededly the Constitution protects.

MR. JUSTICE JACKSON concurring:

I join the CHIEF JUSTICE in holding that the hearings provided are too limited in the context of the present Act to afford due process of law. I also agree with the opinion of MR. JUSTICE DOUGLAS that the scheme of classification set forth in the Act denies equal protection of the law. I disagree with the opinion of each in so far as it rejects or minimizes the grounds taken by the other.

Perhaps to employ a broad and loose scheme of classification would be permissible if accompanied by the individual hearings indicated by the CHIEF JUSTICE. On the other hand, narrow classification with reference to the end to be accomplished by the Act might justify limiting individual hearings to the issue whether the individual belonged to a class so defined. Since this Act does not present these questions, I reserve judgment on them.

I also think the present plan to sterilize the individual in pursuit of a eugenic plan to eliminate from the race characteristics that are only vaguely identified and which in our present state of knowledge are uncertain as to transmissibility presents other constitutional questions of gravity. This Court has sustained such an experiment with respect to an imbecile, a person with definite and observable characteristics, where the condition had persisted through three generations and afforded grounds for the belief that it was transmissible and would continue to manifest itself in generations to come. Buck v. Bell, 274 U.S. 200.

There are limits to the extent to which a legislatively represented majority may conduct biological experiments at the expense of the dignity and personality and natural powers of a minority—even those who have been guilty of what the majority define as crimes. But this Act falls down before reaching this problem, which I mention only to avoid the implication that such a question may not exist because not discussed. On it I would also reserve judgment.

NOTES AND QUESTIONS

1.   Under *Skinner,* what sorts of sterilization laws, if any, would survive constitutional challenge? What other governmental interventions involving genetics and the regulation of human reproduction would the decision in *Skinner* support? What interventions would be prohibited?

2.   Compare *Skinner* with Buck v. Bell. Does *Skinner* overrule *Buck*? What language in *Skinner* can you cite to support your position?

3.   Was the Oklahoma statute at issue in *Skinner* drafted to use sterilization as a punishment and deterrent for crimes or a eugenic strategy for reducing crimes in future generations?

4.   Which constitutional theory, equal protection or due process, do you think provides the most appropriate basis for striking down the statute?

5.   Why do you think thieves but not embezzlers were covered by the statute?

6.   Although *Skinner* is often cited as a great anti-eugenics decision, note how the Douglas and Stone opinions incorporate eugenic language and rationale.

7. Justice Jackson's concurrence, in which he questioned the legitimacy of "biological experiments," is ironic. After World War II, Justice Jackson was appointed chief prosecutor for the Nuremberg trials.

8. In contrast to *Skinner,* where state law authorized sterilization as a punishment for committing a crime, sterilization and other restrictions on reproduction may also be employed to deter the commission of future crimes. For example, in 1996 California enacted a law authorizing voluntary chemical or surgical castration for the first offense of child molesting and mandating castration as a condition of parole for repeat offenders. Cal. Penal Code § 645. Georgia, Florida, and Montana have adopted similar statutes. Chemical castration involves the use of Depo-Provera, a synthetic progesterone that decreases testosterone, causing a reduction in sex drive and an improved ability to control sexual fantasizing. For more on chemical castration, see Avital Stadler, Comment, California Injects New Life Into an Old Idea: Taking a Shot at Recidivism, Chemical Castration, and the Constitution, 46 Emory L. J. 1285 (1997). One judge conditioned parole for a convicted child abuser on surgical implantation of the contraceptive Norplant. The defendant challenged the requirement, but the case was dismissed as moot after other parole violations occurred.

9. Are there other current examples of eugenics programs in the United States? What about government maternal and prenatal health care programs? What about the use of the courts to collect wrongful birth damages from health care professionals whose negligent failure to provide appropriate genetic counseling or testing results in the birth of a child with genetic diseases or abnormalities?

TAYLOR V. KURAPATI
600 N.W.2d 670 (Mich. App. 1999).

WHITBECK, J.

Plaintiffs Brandy and Brian Taylor, individually, and Brandy Taylor as next friend and mother of Shelby Taylor, a minor, appeal as of right the trial court's order granting summary disposition in favor of defendants Surender Kurapati, M.D., and Annapolis Hospital with respect to their wrongful birth and negligent infliction of emotional distress claims.

* * *

The Taylors filed their complaint in August 1996. The Taylors alleged that Brandy Taylor had a doctor-patient relationship with Kurapati, a specialist in radiology, and Annapolis. On April 19, 1994, Brandy Taylor gave birth to the couple's daughter, Shelby Taylor. Throughout her pregnancy, Brandy Taylor had been treated by Dr. Leela Suruli. Suruli had ordered that a routine ultrasound be performed in Brandy Taylor's second trimester. The ultrasound was conducted on

December 4, 1993, and interpreted by Kurapati, an agent of Annapolis. Kurapati concluded that the pregnancy was seventeen weeks along, plus or minus two weeks, and that there were no visible abnormalities with the fetus. A second ultrasound was conducted on March 16, 1994, and interpreted by another physician, Dr. M.B. Cash. Cash indicated that the baby's femurs could not be adequately identified and believed that a high resolution ultrasound could be helpful for further investigation. Suruli told Brandy Taylor that the baby had short femur bones and would merely be shorter than average. Brandy Taylor decided not to have another ultrasound. Shelby Taylor was born on April 19, 1994, with "gross anatomical deformities including missing right shoulder, fusion of left elbow, missing digits on left hand, missing femur on left leg and short femur on right." A study at the University of Michigan Hospital suggested that Shelby Taylor had femur-fibula-ulna syndrome.

In their complaint, the Taylors alleged that the standard of care in performing the initial ultrasound had been breached by Kurapati when he failed to locate all four limbs at the time of the ultrasound. The Taylors alleged that the ultrasound should have shown Shelby Taylor's disabilities and that the failure to reveal the disabilities deprived the Taylors of their right to make a reproductive decision regarding the pregnancy. In addition to their claim of medical malpractice, the Taylors also alleged that, because of defendants' negligence, they suffered emotional distress at witnessing the birth of their child.

* * *

This review of the elements of tort liability points up the extraordinary nature of the trial court's holding that the plaintiffs were entitled to no recovery as a matter of law. We have here a negligent, wrongful act by the defendant, which act directly and proximately caused injury to the plaintiffs. What we must decide is whether there is justification here for a departure from generally applicable, well-established principles of law:

* * *

At its intellectual core, the wrongful birth tort this Court created in Eisbrenner relies on the benefits rule this Court adopted in Troppi. To say the very least, continued reliance on this rule has some far-reaching, and profoundly disturbing, consequences. This rule invites the jury in wrongful birth cases to weigh the costs to the parents of a disabled child of bearing and raising that child against the benefits to the parents of the life of that child. This rule thus asks the jury to quantify the unquantifiable with respect to the benefits side of the equation. Further, to posit a specific question: how does a jury measure the benefits to the parents of the whole life of the disabled child, when the potential of that child is unknown at the time of suit? How, for example, would a hypothetical Grecian jury, operating under Michigan jurisprudence, measure the benefits to the parents of the whole life of Homer, the blind singer of songs who created the Iliad and the Odyssey? Absent the ability to foretell the future and to quantify the value of the spoken and then the written word, how, exactly, would the jury do that?

Further, the use of the benefits rule in wrongful birth cases can slide ever so quickly into applied eugenics. The very phrase "wrongful birth" suggests that the birth of the disabled child was wrong and should have been prevented. If one accepts the premise that the birth of one "defective" child should have been prevented, then it is but a short step to accepting the premise that the births of classes of "defective" children should be similarly prevented, not just for the benefit of the parents but also for the benefit of society as a whole through the protection of the "public welfare." This is the operating principle of eugenics. James E. Bowman provides a dark, single sentence description of eugenics: "Eugenics espouses the reproduction of the 'fit' over the 'unfit' (positive eugenics) and discourages the birth of the 'unfit' (negative eugenics)." Paul A. Lombardo more broadly, and more charitably, defines eugenics as the idea that the human race can be gradually improved and social ills simultaneously eliminated through a program of selective procreation and describes its most enthusiastic American advocates:

> Francis Galton, Karl Pearson, and others who called themselves eugenicists believed in improving the human condition through the use of science. They understood their field as the marriage of the biological sciences, including medical genetics, with the then new discipline of biostatistics. The most passionate of American eugenicists, such as Charles Davenport and Harry Laughlin, wished to develop a taxonomy of human traits and to categorize individuals as "healthy" or "unhealthy," and "normal" or "abnormal," within their classification scheme. Working under the presumption that most, if not all, human traits are transmitted genetically, the eugenicists encouraged educated, resourceful, and self-sufficient citizens to mate and produce "wellborn" eugenic children. In contrast, the dysgenic were discouraged from reproducing. Harry Laughlin called dysgenic groups "socially inadequate" and defined them to include: the feebleminded, the insane, the criminalistic, the epileptic, the inebriated or the drug addicted, the diseased— regardless of etiology, the blind, the deaf, the deformed, and dependents (an extraordinarily expansive term that embraced orphans, "ne'er-do-wells," tramps, the homeless and paupers.)

To our eyes, this concept appears simultaneously cruel and laughable, but we should remember that the concept, and the values, of eugenics had a profound effect on American society. We should also recall that the courts were not above the use of this type of rhetoric. One of the most respected jurists in American history, Justice Oliver Wendell Holmes, wrote the decision in Buck v. Bell.

* * *

Finally, we should not forget the influence that the Third Reich's experiments with sterilization had on the American eugenics movement. As Lombardo notes, Dr. Joseph DeJarnette, who testified as an expert witness in the Buck trial, made the following comments about those experiments:

> No person unable to support himself on account of his inherited mental condition has a right to be born. . . . In Germany the sterilization law embraces chronic alcoholics, certain hereditary physical diseases, the hereditarily blind and deaf, the criminally insane, feebleminded and epileptic. By December 31, 1934 Germany had sterilized 56,224 [persons].

Lombardo notes that Dr. DeJarnette continued to express his admiration for Hitler's campaign in the good doctor's last official comment regarding sterilization in 1938:

> Germany in six years has sterilized about 80,000 of her unfit while the United States with approximately twice the population has sterilized about 27,869 to January 1, 1938, in the past 20 years. The death rates in Virginia from sterilization is [sic] negligible—not over one in a thousand. . . . The fact that there are 12,000,000 defectives in the United States should arouse our best endeavors to push this procedure to the maximum.

To our ears, at the close of the twentieth century, this talk of the "unfit" and of "defectives" has a decidedly jarring ring; we are, after all, above such lethal nonsense. But are we? We know now that we all have at least five recessive genes but, according to Bowman, when scientists map the human genome, they will unveil many more potentially harmful genes in each of us. Bowman states that "psychoses, hypertension, diabetes, early-and late-appearing cancers, degenerative disorders, susceptibility genes for communicable diseases, genes for various mental deficiencies, aging genes, and other variations and disorders will be ascertained." Will we then see the tort of wrongful birth extended to physicians who neglect or misinterpret genetic evidence and thereby fail to extend the option of a eugenic abortion to the unsuspecting parents of a genetically "unfit" and "defective" child? Our current acceptance of the wrongful birth tort would require the answer to this question in Michigan to be: yes. We further note that it is but another short half step from the concept of preventing the birth of an "unfit" or "defective" child to proposing, for the benefit of the child's overburdened parents and of the society as a whole, that the existence of the child should not be allowed to continue. Again, this sounds preposterous, but is it? As described by Bowman:

> Daniel Callahan, the former President and Founder of the Hastings Center, the preeminent center for bioethics in the United States, has proposed age-based rationing of health care for elderly persons to alleviate escalating health care costs. Pain relief would be in order, but not life-saving measures, including nutrition. In short, aged individuals past their late seventies or early eighties should go quietly into the night in order that the generation to follow would have access to health care—in their early years.

If the elderly have a duty to die—indeed, to be starved to death—then why not the disabled child? After all, if that child never should have been born, then that child has no real right to go on living, thereby imposing the costs of the child's continued existence on the parents and society. This, we conclude, is the logical end of the slippery slope inherent in the application of the benefits rule through the wrongful birth tort.

CONCLUSION

We conclude that this intermediate appellate court should not continue to recognize the wrongful birth tort without the slightest hint of approval from the Michigan Supreme Court or our Legislature.

NOTES

1.   See the discussion of wrongful birth actions in Chapter 6.

2.   The *Buck* case dealt primarily with what is called "negative eugenics"—the use of state power to prevent the birth of "undesirable" offspring. Another form of eugenics is "positive eugenics," which encourages the birth of children with "desirable" traits.

The father of modern eugenics, Francis Galton, influenced by the views of Malthus, was appalled by his observation that "inferior" people were reproducing at great rates while the best and the brightest had small families. Positive eugenics captured the popular imagination during the 1920s, when state fairs hosted "Fitter Families Exhibits" and "Perfect Baby Competitions"; livestock was judged in one barn, human lineage in another. Students on field trips who obtained a good eugenics evaluation might win a "Goodly Heritage" medal. The American Eugenics Society also sponsored awards for church sermons extolling marriages of "the best" with "the best."

An extreme example of positive eugenics was the Nazi's "Lebensborn" program, where public health officials selected Aryan women to breed with SS soldiers and raised the resulting children in special foster families. At the same time, in a program promoted by the Army Air Corps in the United States, the Pioneer Fund, created by a group of wealthy conservatives, offered military pilots and crews who had three children $4,000 (about

$45,000 today) to help educate a fourth. (For a description of what happened to the twelve children who were born under the program, see Douglas A. Blackmon, A Breed Apart: A Long-Ago Effort to Better the Species Yields Ordinary Folks, The Wall Street Journal, Aug. 17, 1999, at A1.)

Are there any examples of positive eugenics programs in the United States today? Consider the following:

ASSOCIATED PRESS, OWNER OF "GENIUS" SPERM BANK PLEASED BY RESULTS

The New York Times, Dec. 11, 1984, at A17.

Robert Graham still gets some negative reaction to his sperm bank, but his list of genius donors is slowly growing and 15 children have been born to women chosen as recipients.

Mr. Graham vigorously denied that he was trying to create a super race through his Repository for Germinal Choice, popularly known as the Nobel Prize sperm bank, but he says he envisions a better society populated by smarter children born to parents who meet his standards for health and emotional stability.

"We are, I would think, selective," Mr. Graham said in a recent interview at his downtown office. "But we're not racist. We'll accept excellence in any race. What we're really trying to do is optimize the conditions for having children."

Most of the women who receive the semen, which is kept in a frozen state, are in their mid-to late 30's. Many have tried unsuccessfully for years to bear children with their husbands. Occasionally, the recipient's husband has a hereditary problem that he does not want to pass on.

* * *

Secrecy shrouds most of the names involved with the repository, started in 1979. Only William B. Shockley, who shared a Nobel Prize for the invention of the transistor and who says blacks as a group are intellectually inferior to whites for genetic reasons, has made his donations public.

Nine other men, all possessing an I.Q. of at least 140, are regular donors, Mr. Graham said.

Women who inquire about insemination through the repository are given a booklet showing the characteristics of the donors, who are not identified by name.

Sperm is given to the women free except for a $50 application fee, $10 a month for liquid nitrogen for storage and shipping costs. The women are required to be married and to prove it.

* * *

Mr. Graham, 78 years old, does not pay any fee to the repository's donors, but sends someone to pick up their donations.

"These are men who would never be on call to a doctor," Mr. Graham said. "And they don't do this because they need the money."

But running the nonprofit repository and paying its four employees costs Mr. Graham several hundred thousand dollars annually. He said money was no problem because he made a fortune by inventing shatterproof eyeglasses.

HE NOW SEEKS ATHLETES

Since the repository's founding, Mr. Graham has been primarily interested in attracting men whose area of excellence is sciences or the arts. Since the 1984 Olympics in Los Angeles, he also has been looking for donors who are outstanding athletes and have high intelligence.

"We have an interview with a gold medal winner in a week or two," Mr. Graham said. "Our present donors are all geniuses. Now we're also emphasizing outstanding bodies."

* * *

MAXWELL J. MEHLMAN, MODERN EUGENICS AND THE LAW, IN A CENTURY OF EUGENICS: FROM THE INDIANA EXPERIMENT TO THE HUMAN GENOME ERA
(2010).

* * *

Commentators often distinguish between "state-sponsored" and "private" reproductive decisions, suggesting that only the former can be considered to be eugenics. [Troy] Duster states, for example: "[I]t is imperative to distinguish between state-sanctioned eugenics programs on the one hand, and private, individualized, *personal* decisions that are socially patterned on the other." But the exercise of state power, and the dividing line between state-sponsored and private decision-making, are less clear-cut than Duster implies. At one extreme, the state can prohibit a eugenic practice. In Skinner v. Oklahoma, for example, the Supreme Court held that it was unconstitutional for a state to require certain habitual criminals to be sterilized but not others. * * *

At the other extreme, the state may compel a eugenic practice, such as Indiana did when it enacted [the nation's first] involuntary sterilization law [in 1907]. Between these two extremes, however, there are a number of gradations. For example, the government can provide financial inducements for eugenic practices, such as tax breaks and welfare penalties for having desirable or undesirable children, or damages awarded by the judicial system to families whose physicians failed to prevent the birth of children with disabilities. Even when the government merely refrains from limiting or prohibiting eugenic practices, it might be said to be sanctioning them implicitly. Duster might regard reproductive decisions by parents as "personal," but the government arguably collaborates when it turns a blind eye.

In short, when the law influences reproductive decision-making in such a way as to encourage or discourage the birth of specifically types of desirable or undesirable individuals, this is at least suggestive of a eugenics objective. The more overt this objective, or the greater the impact of the law on individual reproductive decisions, the more frankly eugenic the law can be considered. This is not meant to imply that forced sterilization is on a par with government inaction in the face of private behavior. Yet * * * society has employed indirect as well as direct means to control reproductive behavior in order to achieve eugenic goals. The memory of the victims of the Indiana law and its successors would be dishonored if we examined the current state of affairs using too narrow a view of this history.

A.   LEGALLY TOLERATED PRACTICES.

A number of practices typically are thought of as private because they result from private rather than public decision-making. But the fact that the law permits them to take place indicates a measure of public acquiescence, if not approval.

This category includes attempts to achieve what might be considered positive neoeugenic objectives. One example is selective breeding to produce a "better" genetic lineage. This has long taken place with animals, but it also takes place in humans. The most notorious recent case is the Chinese basketball player Yao Ming, whose parents were mated by the Chinese government because of their height and athletic prowess and who was forced to play basketball at an early age. Private forms of selective breeding are rampant in the United States, including mating within certain social circles, such as "coming out" at debutant balls, arranged marriages and semi-arranged marriages in which the couple is brought together by the parents, and most recently, computerized dating services in which participants select one another according to desirable traits. One such service, eHarmony.com, provides information about 29 personal characteristics, including appearance, intellect, industriousness, ambition, family background, education, and character. Those who avail themselves of these dating services can compress investigations that used to take a number of "dates" into the click of a button.

Some of the most glaring selective breeding practices are associated with gamete donation. The Genetics & IVF Institute, for example, provides the following information about egg donors: adult photos, childhood photos, audio interviews, blood type, ethnic background of donor's mother and father, height, weight, whether pregnancies have been achieved, body build, eye color, hair color and texture, years of education and major areas of study, occupation, Scholastic Aptitude Test (SAT) scores and grade point averages, special interests, family medical history, essays by donors, and personality typing based on the Keirsey test, which uses a Jungian approach to classify temperaments into 12 categories, such as "rational and reserved" or "artisan and introspective." The California Cryobank, Inc. provides purchasers of donor sperm with a 26-page donor profile. A company called Fertility Alternatives pays a premium to "exceptional" egg donors. To qualify, the donor must have graduated from a major university, or be currently attending one, preferably Ivy League; have a GPA of 3.0 +; SAT scores of 1350+ or ACT scores of 30+; and have a documented high IQ.

The degree to which the law accommodates these assisted reproductive practices is striking. Although health care is one of the most heavily regulated industries in the country, the only federal law specifically governing in vitro fertilization (IVF) services is the Fertility Clinic Success Rate and Certification Act of 1992, which merely requires infertility clinics to report success rates in a standardized fashion. State regulation is minimal. The criticisms leveled at the recent IVF-assisted birth of octuplets to an unmarried, unemployed woman illustrate this regulatory lacuna.

Conceivably, state law might encourage selective breeding by permitting parents to sue infertility clinics for negligence in failing properly to screen gamete donors. The leading case is Harnicher v. University of Utah Medical Center. [See Chapter 6]

* * *

While the parents in the *Harnicher* case used selective breeding in the hopes of achieving a positive neoeugenic goal, the law also countenances a number of practices that might be deemed negative neoeugenics. One obvious example is fetal testing followed by aborting the fetus for reasons that do not relate to the mother's health. Another is preimplantation genetic diagnosis (PGD) of fertilized embryos in the course of IVF, where only those embryos with the best genetic endowment are implanted in the uterus and allowed to gestate. The law leaves IVF services essentially unregulated. A third technique is community-based genetic testing for matchmaking purposes, such as screening programs for Tay-Sachs and other recessive genetic diseases prevalent in Jews of Ashkenazi descent. The pioneer program is Chevra Dor Yeshurim ("Association of the Upright Generation"), which screens Orthodox Jewish adolescents in New York and does not allow a matchmaker to arrange a marriage between two individuals who both carry a recessive mutation.

Finally, there are private family planning initiatives. One is Project Prevention (formerly "CRACK"). This was started in California in 1997 by a woman who wanted to punish the drug-addicted mother who had given birth to 4 children she had adopted. When she failed to persuade the state legislature to criminalize drug-addicted mothers, she created CRACK, which gives drug addicts $200 if they undergo sterilization or use long-term birth control. In 2003, the organization claimed to have 23 chapters nationwide and had paid 907 persons, including 361 who had tubal ligations. African Americans and Hispanics accounted for 401 of the participants. At present, there is no state or federal law that would interfere with this project.

B.   LEGALLY FACILITATED PRACTICES.

In some instances, the law goes farther than turning a blind eye; it actually aids the practice of neoeugenics. One example is the ability of parents to bring so-called "wrongful birth" actions. [See Chapter 6]

* * *

Another method by which the government involves itself in what might be considered neoeugenics is providing public funding for family-planning programs aimed at preventing the birth of children to poor mothers. According to the Alan Guttmacher Institute, the government in 2001 spent $1.26 billion on reversible contraceptive services and $95 million on sterilization services. These funds are distributed through several programs: Medicaid, Title X, Title V (Maternal Child Block Grants), Social Services Block Grants, and TANF (Temporary Assistance for Needy Families). These programs would not be particularly neoeugenic if they provided family-planning assistance to all socio-economic groups, but virtually all of these funds are earmarked for the poor. * * *

Organizations that provide these federally-funded family planning services are typically non-profits, and therefore another way that the government facilitates their activities in by giving them a subsidy in the form of exempting them from federal and state taxes. * * *

Another government tax policy that might be considered neoeugenic is federal child tax credits. Until statutory limits are reached, the more children the taxpaying family has, the larger the number of credits that it can claim. The policy might be regarded as eugenic in that, since only families with enough income to pay taxes benefit from the credit, the policy creates an incentive for better-off families to have more children.

Contrast child tax credits with so-called family caps under state welfare programs. Unlike child tax credits that encourage taxpaying families to produce more offspring, family caps apply to families on welfare, discouraging them from becoming larger by halting increases in welfare benefits once there are more than a certain number of children. Currently 24 states have some version of this policy. Dorothy Roberts observes that "[l]ike birth control programs and reproductive punishments, contemporary welfare policies share features of eugenic thinking. * * * Of course, the current welfare family caps are not premised on notions of recipients' genetic inferiority. But, like eugenic programs of the past, they are seen as a way of ridding America of the burden poor people pose."

In Dandridge v. Williams, the Supreme Court upheld family caps in the face of constitutional challenge. The Court ruled that the state of Maryland did not violate the Equal Protection Clause of the Fourteenth Amendment because it had a reasonable basis for the policy, namely, "the state's legitimate interest in encouraging employment and in avoiding discrimination between welfare families and the families of the working poor." Interestingly, the state itself had articulated an additional goal— "providing incentives for family planning"—on which, without comment, the Court apparently declined to rely.

C.   LEGALLY MANDATED PRACTICES.

So far we have considered government toleration or subsidization of practices that can be considered neoeugenic. Additionally, there are some practices that the government currently mandates by law. All of them are in aid of negative eugenics objectives in that they discourage reproduction by undesirable segments of the population. One example is sterilization and other restrictions on reproduction employed ostensibly to deter the commission of future crimes. For example, California in 1996 enacted a law authorizing voluntary chemical or surgical castration for the first offense of child molesting and mandating castration as a condition of parole for repeat offenders. * * * Although the intent of these laws arguably is to prevent child molestation, they are eugenic in that they decrease the likelihood that child molesters will reproduce.

The criminal justice system deters reproduction not only by sex offenders but by all incarcerated criminals. In a broader sense, then, the entire criminal system is a negative neoeugenic program. Only five states (California, Mississippi, New Mexico, New York, and Washington) permit prisoners to have conjugal visits with their spouses, despite some evidence that such visits reduce the incidence of prison rape.

In the early 20th century, eugenic goals fueled restrictive immigration laws. Similar objectives arguably are associated with current efforts to limit immigration, including the plan to construct a fence along the border with Mexico. * * *

* * *

The state-mandated initiative that most overtly raises eugenics concerns, however, is newborn screening for nontreatable disorders. [See Chapters 6 and 9] * * *

The development of faster and cheaper technologies such as tandem mass spectrometry and microchip arrays enable programs to screen for far greater numbers of disorders, including many for which no readily effective treatments presently exist. Screening for these nontreatable disorders can be beneficial, in that it could spare families years of uncertainty once symptoms emerged; alert them to be on the watch for new discoveries that could provide their children with treatment; provide children with adjunctive if not curative interventions; and facilitate participation of the children in research on their disorders. Yet some public health advocates offer an additional rationale for screening for nontreatable disorders: that it can serve as a valuable tool in family planning. One recent article explains, for example: "Arguments for considering broader benefits from the early diagnosis that only newborn screening can provide include . . . knowledge on which to base reproductive decision-making years before a disease would be diagnosed for the affected child. . . ."

Moreover, as noted above, newborn screening is mandatory. * * *

* * * Newborn screening for treatable disorders is laudable. Screening for nontreatable disorders, however, is another matter. The screening is mandated by the state, and is imposed on parents over their objection. Nontreatable disorders would be included in part in order to discourage parents from giving birth to additional children with those disorders. This will prevent these children from inheriting genes that will make them a burden on society. Viewed in this manner, the resemblance between this program and classic eugenic practices, especially on this, the centennial of the first eugenic law, is, at least, disconcerting.

QUESTIONS

1. To what extent should the programs and practices described by Mehlman count as eugenics?

2. In what ways do they rekindle or avoid the concerns raised by the efforts of the eugenics movement in the 20th century?

CHAPTER 3

GENETIC RESEARCH

■ ■ ■

I.   INTRODUCTION

Each year, more genetic mechanisms that underlie diseases are uncovered, new diagnostic tests to pinpoint genetic disorders are introduced into clinical practice, and experimental therapies to treat genetic diseases are developed. Since so many traits, conditions, diseases, and defects have a genetic basis, almost everyone is a potential subject of genetic research. Potential genetic research subjects range widely in age, including embryos, fetuses, newborns, children, and adults. They differ in condition—healthy, mentally disabled, physically ill. The experimental procedures and products range in the level of risk they pose to the subject. The methodology of the research varies widely as well, ranging from pedigree studies to whole genome sequencing to determine the nuances of a person's genes that correlate with disease or that increase the likelihood that a certain treatment will succeed.

Experimentation with human subjects has existed since the beginning of the science of medicine. However, it was not until the early twentieth century that ethical and legal considerations regarding such research came to the fore. The atrocities committed by Nazi physicians in experiments (some done in the name of genetics or, more properly stated, eugenics) led to the development of certain principles and guidelines that affect research on humans today. In the trials of those physicians, the court set forth standards that should be complied with both before and during research. These standards, subsequently adopted by the United Nations General Assembly, are known as the Nuremberg Code. The tenets of the code significantly influenced later state laws and federal regulations in the United States dealing with research.

The Nuremberg Code provides guidance for assuring that participation in research is voluntary and that the risks of research are minimized. The code requires that certain basic scientific research and animal research must be done before human research is undertaken, that the human research must be well-designed and undertaken only by scientifically qualified individuals, that the potential results justify the level of risk involved in the performance of the research, and that those results are not procurable by other means of study. The central tenet of the Nuremberg Code is that participation in research must be voluntary, informed, and uncoerced, and that the subject has the right to bring the experiment to an end. The code also requires the minimization of research risks through the appropriate design and conduct of the research as well as through adequate preparation and facilities. Research is forbidden if there is an *a priori* reason to believe death or disabling injury will occur (although the Nuremberg Code does allow for a potential exception if the researchers also serve as subjects) and on-going research must be stopped if there is reason to believe that its continuation will lead to the injury, disability, or death of the subject.

Subsequent societal discussion of research in the decades since the adoption of the Nuremberg Code has highlighted some additional ethical concerns. One concern is that subjects for research must be selected equitably; for example, a particular class or race of subjects should not serve as subjects for research that primarily benefits people of another class or race. With respect to potential genetics research on fetuses, there is concern that a disproportionate share of the fetal research burden might fall upon people of color. Since African-American infants have a higher morbidity and mortality rate than do Caucasian infants, it might be argued that they stand to benefit more from fetal research. However, it can conversely be argued that research on infants from minority or poor families will more likely be used to benefit wealthier white mothers and infants who have better access to new medical technologies.

There has also been a move toward requiring that research proposals be reviewed in advance by groups unrelated to the research project itself. This has led to the formation of Institutional Review Boards (IRBs), committees designed to approve, disapprove, review, and monitor biomedical research involving human subjects. The purpose of IRB review is to assure that proper steps are taken to protect the rights and welfare of human research subjects.

Federal regulations, adopted in 1975 to regulate federally-funded research, focus on avoiding unnecessary physical risks to the subject, assuring informed consent and confidentiality, and assessing the merits of the proposed research in advance. Genetics research, however, raises ethical and legal concerns not necessarily addressed by the federal regulations. Much genetics research is conducted with private funds (for example, by biotechnology companies) and thus is not covered by the federal regulations protecting human subjects, although if it will result in a marketable product it will be regulated by the Food and Drug Administration. Genetics research presents risks beyond physical risks—such as psychological risks and risks of discrimination. In addition, genetics research raises risks of stigmatization not only to the individual participating in the research, but to relatives or members of the ethnic group who share some of his or her genes. This has led to consideration about whether group consent, in addition to individual consent, should be required before certain types of genetic research are undertaken. Also of concern has been the question, as discussed in Chapter 5, of how to operationalize consent and otherwise protect human subjects in the international setting as researchers seek DNA from members of indigenous groups.

While the law has focused on protection of people from risks in their interactions with researchers, new concerns have been raised about genetic research undertaken on previously-collected tissue samples. All of us have DNA on file someplace. Since the late 1960s, virtually every newborn in the United States has undergone public health department testing for certain genetic diseases; many laboratories have saved those blood samples. After blood tests or biopsies are undertaken in hospitals, the samples are saved and often made available for further research without the individual's knowledge or consent. A major policy question has arisen about whether the person whose blood or other tissue sample is used for genetic research should have the chance to either consent or refuse to participate in such research.

II.   REGULATION OF RESEARCH

A.   TYPES OF GENETIC RESEARCH

Genetic sequencing research involves determining the chemical make-up of the genome, which consists of three billion base pairs of the nucleotides adenine, guanine, cytosine, and thymine. In 2001, scientists announced the completion of a rough draft of a model human genome sequence. Far from signaling the end of genomic research, scientists are now working with human subjects to make use of this information. Research is being undertaken to determine whether individuals with a certain genetic profile are also more likely to develop certain diseases than those with a different make-up. There are also studies underway to investigate the varying manifestations of each particular genetic profile, to understand the role of proteins created by genes, and to target drugs and therapies more precisely based on genetic information. In 2015, President Obama launched a $215 million genetics research effort, the Precision Medicine Initiative. The research will involve sequencing the genomes of a million Americans and combining that data with their health information, environmental and lifestyle data, and personal device and sensor data. The goal is to determine how to more precisely prevent and treat each individual patient's disease. www.whitehouse.gov/the-press-office/2015/01/30/fact-sheet-president-obama-s-precision-medicine-initiative.

Genome-Wide Association Studies

Currently, genome-wide association studies (GWAS) are the most prevalent type of clinical genetics research conducted. Medical researchers are no longer limited to the study of a few diseases with simple genetic causes. The research field has expanded to cover diseases caused by the interactions between multiple genes as well as interactions between genes and the environment. Researchers employ GWAS to uncover these interactions.

GWAS depend upon variation in the human genome to uncover interactions. The most common variations are single nucleotide polymorphisms (SNPs). A SNP is a single change in the nucleotide sequence of a gene. For example, one person might have an AATGGCA genotype for a trait and another person might have an AATGTCA genotype. The human genome is estimated to contain 10 million SNPs.

GWAS analyze the distribution of SNPs in hundreds or thousands of individuals to determine which SNPs are associated with a particular disease. GWAS generally consist of two groups: a group of individuals known not to have a particular disease, and a group of individuals who are known to have a particular disease. The genetic information of these two groups is compared and the SNPs that occur in statistically significant amounts in the population known to carry the disease, which are also generally absent in the population known not to carry the disease, are said to be associated with the target disease. Once the GWAS identify the genes that are likely associated with increased risk of disease, further studies are free to focus on these genes and tease apart their interactions with each other and the environment. GWAS themselves do not directly lead to medical products that reach the public but rather pave the way for research that eventually will.

GWAS have proved to be an effective tool for studying linkages between genetic variation and disease. For example, in 2005, three independent research groups identified a link between age-related macular degeneration and a variation in a gene involved in creating a protein that regulates inflammation. Other studies have found links between genetic variation and increased or decreased risk for such diseases as Crohn disease, Parkinson disease, type 2 diabetes, and others. See www.genome.gov/20019523 for more information.

However, GWAS also have limitations. The common genetic variations that they target equate to only a fraction of the total amount of variation in the genome. Additionally, many of these variations have low to moderate effects in explaining gene expression and protein function. It may be the case that an inordinately large number of such genetic variations is required to explain any sizeable percentage of variation in observable expression or function in relation to any given disease. Some believe that analyzing rarer genetic variations will lead to the discovery of more manageable genetic pathways that account for a larger portion of disease risk and have greater effect on gene expression and protein function. Scientists are ill-equipped to detect these rare variations. See David B. Goldstein, Common Genetic Variation and Human Traits, 360 New Eng. J. Med. 1696 (2009).

Geno-Phenobanks

An emerging trend is that of genetic research conducted through the use of geno-phenobanks. Geno-phenobanks link medical records and personal information with genomic information. Using geno-phenobanks, genomic information can be linked with electronic health information in an attempt to uncover any correlations between a given phenotype and a particular genetic sequence. Maxwell J. Mehlman, Ethical, Legal, Social, and Policy Issues in the Use of Genomic Technology by the U.S. Military, J. of Law and the Biosciences (2014). This type of research has been referred to as "medical-sequencing research," and has already been implemented in several research initiatives. Morris W. Foster & Richard R. Sharp, Ethical Issues in Medical-Sequencing Research: Implications of Genotype-Phenotype Studies for Individuals and Populations, 15 Human Molecular Genetics R45 (2006). For instance, Vanderbilt University and Northwestern University have linked their BioVU and NUgene biobanks, respectively, to electronic health records to uncover genotype-phenotype associations. Marylyn D. Ritchie et al., Robust Replication of Genotype-Phenotype Associations Across Multiple Diseases in an Electronic Medical Record, 86 American J. of Human Genetics 560 (2010). Both universities are affiliated with the Electronic Medical Records and Genomics (eMERGE) Network, a consortium developed by the National Human Genome Research Institute that combines DNA biorepositories with electronic health records. See https://emerge.mc.vanderbilt.edu/ for more information. Similarly, the National Institutes of Health's (NIH) database of Genotypes and Phenotypes (dbGaP) is an archive of genotype-phenotype association research that is largely available to the public. See www.ncbi.nlm.nih.gov/gap for more information. NIH also offers a Phenotype-Genotype Integrator (PheGenI) for researchers, available at www.ncbi.nlm.nih.gov/gap/phegeni.

Beyond analyzing inherited genes, genetics research can involve epigenetics, which focuses on chemical changes to DNA that modify gene activity without altering the genetic sequence itself. Epigenetic signals, such as methylation, may help guide stem cells as they develop into other types of cells. Researchers believe that the presence of a methyl group near the start of a gene marks the gene as turned off and blocks its activity. Epigenetic signals, which are established in the early embryo, can be influenced by environmental factors and random mutations throughout a person's life, and some signal patterns may be related to diseases such as cancer. Scientists suspect that differences in epigenetic signals due to environmental factors could account for why identical twins do not look exactly alike despite sharing the same genetic sequence. See Tina Hesman Saey, Epigenetics: From Islands to the Shores, 175 Science News 5 (Feb. 14, 2009).

Once the connection between a particular genetic trait and an illness or characteristic is understood, clinical research can be undertaken, including DNA diagnostic studies (to develop techniques for determining the presence of specific DNA mutations) and gene therapy research (to develop treatments for genetic disease at the DNA level). See Chapters 7 and 8.

B. THE FEDERAL APPROACH

HENRY T. GREELY, THE CONTROL OF GENETIC RESEARCH: INVOLVING THE "GROUPS BETWEEN"
33 Hous. L. Rev. 1397, 1399–1402 (1997).

* * *

Existing regulation of biomedical research in the United States works at two levels. At one level, federal law in effect requires researchers to submit proposals for studies of human subjects to expert panels, which must judge those proposals based on their adherence to federal regulations for the protection of human subjects. Those regulations, bolstered by both international declarations and trends in United States domestic law, also enshrine the second level of control: the requirement that individual research subjects be fully informed about the nature, scope, and risks of the research and agree formally to participate in it.

Substantial federal regulation of biomedical research began in the aftermath of the disclosure of research that abused human subjects, notably the notorious Tuskegee syphilis study. This regulation is indirect but overpowering. First, any research funded by the federal government—and any research institution that receives federal funds—is required by regulation to take certain steps to protect human research subjects. These regulations may be promulgated separately by federal agencies that fund research, but they are largely identical. Substantively, the rules demand that the research risks to subjects be justified by the potential benefits of the research, that broad informed consent be provided, and that special protections be applied to particularly vulnerable populations. Procedurally, the regulations force all such research to be approved by IRBs [institutional review boards], which determine whether the research meets federal standards.

Second, any research to be used in supporting applications to the Food and Drug Administration (FDA) must also satisfy regulations for protecting subjects. The regulations are largely similar to those of the funding agencies, but they expand the reach of those provisions to research performed by institutions that do not receive federal grants: notably pharmaceutical and biotechnology companies. Importantly, these regulations apply not only to companies from the United States and those doing research in the United States, but to companies from any country doing biomedical research anywhere that plan to use the research in support of an application to the FDA. Those firms must also have their relevant research approved by IRBs.

Thus, the federal government effectively regulates biomedical research, not by asserting its direct governmental power to require that research follow certain rules, but by withholding federal benefits—research funding or regulatory approval—from institutions that have not met federal rules.

FEDERAL RESEARCH REGULATIONS
45 C.F.R. § 46.101 et seq.

PART 46—PROTECTION OF HUMAN SUBJECTS

SUBPART A—BASIC HHS POLICY FOR PROTECTION OF HUMAN RESEARCH SUBJECTS

§ 46.101 To what does this policy apply?

* * *

(b) Unless otherwise required by department or agency heads, research activities in which the only involvement of human subjects will be in one or more of the following categories are exempt from this policy:

* * *

(4) Research, involving the collection or study of existing data, documents, records, pathological specimens, or diagnostic specimens, if these sources are publicly available or if the information is recorded by the investigator in such a manner that subjects cannot be identified, directly or through identifiers linked to the subjects.

* * *

(e) Compliance with this policy requires compliance with pertinent federal laws or regulations which provide additional protections for human subjects.

(f) This policy does not affect any state or local laws or regulations which may otherwise be applicable and which provide additional protections for human subjects.

* * *

§ 46.102 Definitions.

* * *

(d) *Research* means a systematic investigation, including research development, testing and evaluation, designed to develop or contribute to generalizable knowledge. Activities which meet this definition constitute research for purposes of this policy, whether or not they are conducted or supported under a program which is considered research for other purposes. For example, some demonstration and service programs may include research activities.

* * *

(f) *Human subject* means a living individual about whom an investigator (whether professional or student) conducting research obtains

> (1) Data through intervention or interaction with the individual, or

> (2) Identifiable private information.

Intervention includes both physical procedures by which data are gathered (for example, venipuncture) and manipulations of the subject or the subject's environment that are performed for research purposes. Interaction includes communication or interpersonal contact between investigator and subject. *Private information* includes information about behavior that occurs in a context in which an individual can reasonably expect that no observation or recording is taking place, and information which has been provided for specific purposes by an individual and which the individual can reasonably expect will not be made public (for example, a medical record). Private information must be individually identifiable (i.e., the identity of the subject is or may readily be ascertained by the investigator or associated with the information) in order for obtaining the information to constitute research involving human subjects.

* * *

§ 46.107 IRB membership.

(a) Each IRB shall have at least five members, with varying backgrounds to promote complete and adequate review of research activities commonly conducted by the institution. The IRB shall be sufficiently qualified through the experience and expertise of its members, and the diversity of the members, including consideration of race, gender, and cultural backgrounds and sensitivity to such issues as community attitudes, to promote respect for its advice and counsel in safeguarding the rights and welfare of human subjects. In addition to possessing the professional competence necessary to review specific research activities, the IRB shall be able to ascertain the acceptability of proposed research in terms of institutional commitments and regulations, applicable law, and standards of professional conduct and practice. The IRB shall therefore include persons knowledgeable in these areas. If an IRB regularly reviews research that involves a vulnerable category of subjects, such as children, prisoners, pregnant women, or handicapped or mentally disabled persons, consideration shall be given to the inclusion of one or more individuals who are knowledgeable about and experienced in working with these subjects.

(b) Every nondiscriminatory effort will be made to ensure that no IRB consists entirely of men or entirely of women, including the institution's consideration of qualified persons of both sexes, so long as no selection is made to the IRB on the basis of gender. No IRB may consist entirely of members of one profession.

(c) Each IRB shall include at least one member whose primary concerns are in scientific areas and at least one member whose primary concerns are in nonscientific areas.

(d) Each IRB shall include at least one member who is not otherwise affiliated with the institution and who is not part of the immediate family of a person who is affiliated with the institution.

(e) No IRB may have a member participate in the IRB's initial or continuing review of any project in which the member has a conflicting interest, except to provide information requested by the IRB.

(f) An IRB may, in its discretion, invite individuals with competence in special areas to assist in the review of issues which require expertise beyond or in addition to that available on the IRB. These individuals may not vote with the IRB.

* * *

§ 46.111 Criteria for IRB approval of research.

(a) In order to approve research covered by this policy the IRB shall determine that all of the following requirements are satisfied:

(1) Risks to subjects are minimized: (i) By using procedures which are consistent with sound research design and which do not unnecessarily expose subjects to risk, and (ii) whenever appropriate, by using procedures already being performed on the subjects for diagnostic or treatment purposes.

(2) Risks to subjects are reasonable in relation to anticipated benefits, if any, to subjects, and the importance of the knowledge that may reasonably be expected to result. In evaluating risks and benefits, the IRB should consider only those risks and benefits that may result from the research (as distinguished from risks and benefits of therapies subjects would receive even if not participating in the research). The IRB should not consider possible long-range effects of applying knowledge gained in the research (for example, the possible effects of the research on public policy) as among those research risks that fall within the purview of its responsibility.

(3) Selection of subjects is equitable. In making this assessment the IRB should take into account the purposes of the research and the setting in which the research will be conducted and should be particularly cognizant of the special problems of research involving vulnerable populations, such as children, prisoners, pregnant women, mentally disabled persons, or economically or educationally disadvantaged persons.

(4) Informed consent will be sought from each prospective subject or the subject's legally authorized representative, in accordance with, and to the extent required by § 46.116.

(5) Informed consent will be appropriately documented, in accordance with, and to the extent required by § 46.117.

(6) When appropriate, the research plan makes adequate provision for monitoring the data collected to ensure the safety of subjects.

(7) When appropriate, there are adequate provisions to protect the privacy of subjects and to maintain the confidentiality of data.

(b) When some or all of the subjects are likely to be vulnerable to coercion or undue influence, such as children, prisoners, pregnant women, mentally disabled persons, or economically or educationally disadvantaged persons, additional safeguards have been included in the study to protect the rights and welfare of these subjects.

* * *

§ 46.116 General requirement of informed consent

* * *

(d) An IRB may approve a consent procedure which does not include, or which alters, some or all of the elements of informed consent set forth in this section, or waive the requirements to obtain informed consent provided the IRB finds and documents that:

(1) The research involves no more than minimal risk to the subjects;

(2) The waiver or alteration will not adversely affect the rights and welfare of the subjects;

(3) The research could not practicably be carried out without the waiver or alteration; and

(4) Whenever appropriate, the subjects will be provided with additional pertinent information after participation.

(e) The informed consent requirements in this policy are not intended to preempt any applicable federal, state, or local laws which require additional information to be disclosed in order for informed consent to be legally effective.

C. SPECIAL CONCERNS ABOUT GENETIC RESEARCH

U.S. DEPT. OF HEALTH AND HUMAN SERVICES, OFFICE OF
PROTECTION FROM RESEARCH RISKS (OPRR) PROTECTING
HUMAN RESEARCH SUBJECTS: INSTITUTIONAL
REVIEW BOARD GUIDEBOOK

5-42 to 5-51 (1993), www.genome.gov/10001752.

HUMAN GENETIC RESEARCH

Human genetic research involves the study of inherited human
traits. Much of this research is aimed at identifying DNA mutations that
can help cause specific health problems. The identification of genetic
mutations enables clinicians to predict the likelihood that persons will
develop a given health problem in the future or pass on a health risk to
their children. For many disorders, however, there will be a considerable
time lag between the ability to determine the likelihood of disease and the
ability to treat the disease.

Efforts to isolate DNA mutations involved in disease in order to
understand the origins of the pathophysiological process are becoming
increasingly common across the broad sweep of biomedical research, from
cardiology to oncology to psychiatry. IRBs [Institutional Review Boards]
should expect to see more of these kinds of studies in the future. * * *

* * *

Unlike the risks presented by many biomedical research protocols
considered by IRBs, the primary risk involved in the first three types of
genetic research [family linkage studies, identification of genes, and DNA
diagnostic studies] are risks of social and psychological harm, rather than
risks of physical injury. Genetic studies that generate information about
subjects' personal health risks can provoke anxiety and confusion,
damage familial relationships, and compromise the subjects' insurability
and employment opportunities. [See Chapters 15 and 16 for a discussion
of the legal issues raised by genetic discrimination.] For many genetic
research protocols, these psychosocial risks can be significant enough to
warrant careful IRB review and discussion. The fact that genetic studies
are often limited to the collection of family history information and blood
drawing should not, therefore, automatically classify them as "minimal
risk" studies qualifying for expedited IRB review.

* * *

Subject Recruitment and Retention. The familial nature of the
research cohorts involved in pedigree studies can pose challenges for
ensuring that recruitment procedures are free of elements that unduly
influence decisions to participate. The very nature of the research exerts

pressure on family members to take part, because the more complete the pedigree, the more reliable the resulting information will be. For example, revealing who else in the family has agreed to participate may act as an undue influence on an individual's decision, as may recruiting individuals in the presence of other family members. (Both would also constitute a breach of confidentiality * * *.)

Recruitment plans, some of which are described here, can attempt to address these problems; each approach has its own strengths and weaknesses. One strategy is to use the proband as the point of contact for recruiting. [The proband is the person whose case serves as the stimulus for the study of other members of the family.] This approach insulates families from pressure by the investigator, but presents the risk that the proband may be personally interested in the research findings and exert undue pressure on relatives to enroll in the study. Furthermore, the proband may not want to act as a recruiter for fear that other family members will then know that he or she is affected by the disease. Another approach is direct recruitment by the investigator through letters or telephone calls to individuals whose identity is supplied by the proband. Direct recruitment by the investigator may, however, be seen as an invasion of privacy by family members * * *. A third approach is to recruit participants through support groups or lay organizations. Adopting this strategy requires investigator and IRB confidence that these organizations will be as scrupulous in their own efforts to protect subjects as the investigator would be. A fourth possibility is to contact individuals through their personal physicians. Prospective subjects contacted by their physician may, however, feel that their health care will be compromised if they do not agree to participate. In the end, the IRB must ensure that the recruitment plan minimizes the possibility of coercion or undue influence.

In contrast to inappropriate pressure placed on prospective participants to join the study is the possibility that a subject may agree to participate out of a misguided effort to obtain therapy. The purposes of the research and how subjects will or will not benefit by participation must be clearly explained.

* * *

Defining Risks and Benefits. Potential risks and benefits should be discussed thoroughly with prospective subjects. In genetic research, the primary risks, outside of gene therapy, are psychological and social (referred to generally as "psychosocial") rather than physical. IRBs should review genetic research with such risks in mind.

Psychological risk includes the risk of harm from learning genetic information about oneself (*e.g.*, that one is affected by a genetic disorder that has not yet manifested itself). Complicating the communication of genetic information is that often the information is limited to probabilities. Furthermore, the development of genetic data carries with it a margin of error; some information communicated to subjects will, in the end, prove to be wrong. In either event, participants are subjected to the stress of receiving such information. For example, researchers involved in developing presymptomatic tests for Huntington Disease (HD) have been concerned that the emotional impact of learning the results may lead some subjects to attempt suicide. They have therefore asked whether prospective participants should be screened for emotional stability prior to acceptance into a research protocol.

Note that these same disclosures of information can also be beneficial. One of the primary benefits of participation in genetic research is that the receipt of genetic information, however imperfect, can reduce uncertainty about whether participants will likely develop a disease that runs in their family (and possibly whether they have passed the gene along to their children). Where subjects learn that they will likely develop or pass along the disease, they might better plan for the future.

To minimize the psychological harms presented by pedigree research, IRBs should make sure that investigators will provide for adequate counseling to subjects on the meaning of the genetic information they receive. Genetic counseling is not a simple matter and must be done by persons qualified and experienced in communicating the meaning of genetic information to persons participating in genetic research or persons who seek genetic testing.

Debate about the social policy implications of genetic information is vitally important and is occurring on a national and international level, but is not literally a concern for IRBs. The IRB's concern is, first, to ensure that these risks will be disclosed to subjects, and, second, to protect subjects against unwarranted disclosures of information.

* * *

Privacy and Confidentiality Protections. Special privacy and confidentiality concerns arise in genetic family studies because of the special relationship between the participants. IRBs should keep in mind that within families, each person is an individual who deserves to have information about him-or herself kept confidential. Family members are not entitled to each other's diagnoses. Before revealing medical or personal information about individuals to other family members, investigators must obtain the consent of the individual.

Data must be stored in such a manner that does not directly identify individuals. In general, except where directly authorized by individual subjects, data may not be released to anyone other than the subject. An exception to requiring explicit authorization for the release of data may be secondary research use of the data, where the data are not especially sensitive and where confidentiality can be assured. IRBs should exercise their discretion in reviewing protocols that call for the secondary use of genetic data. Furthermore, when reviewing a consent document, IRBs should note agreements made by investigators not to release information without the express consent of subjects. Subsequent requests for access to the data are subject to agreements made in the consent process. For studies involving socially sensitive traits or conditions, investigators might also consider requesting a certificate of confidentiality.

* * *

Publication Practices. One final issue involving consent is the publication of research data. The publication of pedigrees can easily result in the identification of study participants. Where a risk of identification exists, participants must consent, in writing, to the release of personal information. Various authors have noted the problem of obtaining consent for the publication of identifying data, and have recommended that consent to the publication be obtained immediately prior to the publication, rather than as part of the consent to treatment or participation in research. It is worth noting, however, that to address this concern, IRBs must also resolve the following questions: Who determines the risk of identification, and on what grounds? Who are defined as participants (is it everyone listed in the pedigree, some of whom have been contacted by investigators, some of whom have had information about them provided by a family member)?

While IRBs must be careful to avoid inappropriate restrictions on investigators' research publications, some evaluation of publication plans is important as part of the IRB's overall interest in preserving the confidentiality of research subjects. One approach for investigators to use in evaluating their publication plans might be to work in a step-wise fashion: First, is publication of the pedigree essential? If publication of the pedigree or other identifying data (*e.g.*, case histories, photographs, or radiographs) is essential, can some identifying data be omitted without changing the scientific message? (The practice of altering data—such as changing the birth order and gender—is controversial, and no clear professional consensus yet exists as to whether this is an appropriate practice.) Finally, if the pedigree must be published, and if identifying data cannot be omitted in an appropriate manner without changing the scientific message, subjects must give their permission for publication of data that may reveal their identity.

ZSOLT HARSANYI & RICHARD HUTTON, GENETIC PROPHECY:
BEYOND THE DOUBLE HELIX
187–188 (1981).

THE EXTRA Y: A CRIMINAL CHROMOSOME?

On July 13, 1966, a tall loner with "Born to Raise Hell" tattooed on his arm brutally murdered eight Chicago nurses in their residence. Soon after, Richard Speck was captured, tried, and imprisoned. Journalists covering the case had a field day. Several self-appointed genetic experts speculated loosely about his genes. They noted his height and his criminal record and suggested that he might belong to a class of criminals that had been discovered just the year before: a group of unusually tall men who carried an extra Y chromosome in addition to the normal male set of XY sex chromosomes.

High rates of XYY carriers in mental-penal institutions had been discovered in Edinburgh, Scotland. Subsequent studies confirmed the initial findings: The incidence of XYY chromosome carriers in the general population is about one in a thousand; but in institutions, it was found to be about two in a hundred. That difference was considered significant. Scientists and journalists alike theorized that the abnormality was a marker for criminal behavior; several lawyers tried to defend their XYY clients by pleading insanity based solely on the presence of the extra Y.

Richard Speck turned out to have the normal complement of chromosomes, and the furor surrounding the journalists' suspicions soon died out. But once questions about the criminal tendencies of those with XYY chromosomes had been raised, they had to be answered. In 1968, two Boston-based scientists, Stanley Walzer, a psychiatrist, and Park Gerald, a geneticist, decided to survey all male offspring born in Boston's Children's Medical Center, typing them for their sex chromosomes and following those who turned out to have more than the usual complement.

The project began quietly enough. But by 1973 it had aroused a storm of controversy around the Boston area. In an ideal world, the project might have been a fine bit of scientific investigation; but in a world that had managed to tag carriers of XYY as holders of the legacy of Richard Speck, it seemed dangerous.

Those who opposed the research raised serious questions both about its value and about its impact on its young subjects:

1. Had the devastating publicity given the XYY type crippled the Walzer study even before it began because of the "criminal" label that would be applied to anyone with the chromosomal abnormality?

2. Did the scientists' methodology, which involved informing the parents of the abnormality, render the study useless by

changing parental behavior toward the offspring and affecting the critical issue of the environment?

3.   Was the study endangering children who might otherwise grow up to be normal, leading to a kind of self-fulfilling prophecy?

NOTES AND QUESTIONS

1.   If you were on an IRB evaluating the proposed XYY study, would you have voted for it to go forward? What alternative design might you use to determine if an XYY chromosomal complement was linked to a higher level of aggression? Ultimately, researchers in Denmark concluded that XYY men were less likely to be aggressive than their XY counterparts.

> The investigators examined the chromosomes of thousands of tall Danes (since those with the abnormality are, on the average, six inches taller than the general population) so that they could study a group of XYYs chosen from among ordinary citizens, rather than from among inmates of an institution. Then they took case histories to find out whether those in the sample had been convicted of crimes, evaluated the types of crimes, and examined their findings in the light of three possible explanations: that XYYs were, in fact, more aggressive and antisocial than the rest of the population; that the intellectual impairment known to be brought on by the extra Y chromosome made XYYs easier to catch; and that their added height made aggression easier and caused others to perceive them as more dangerous * * *.

> The Danish group found that about 42 percent of the XYYs they uncovered (five out of twelve) had criminal records, much more than the 9 percent who turned up among the controls. But except for one man who badly beat his wife while he was drunk, the crimes were neither aggressive nor violent. And some of the convictions were directly tied to crimes that someone with normal intelligence and impulses would never have been caught doing * * *.

Zsolt Harsanyi & Richard Hutton, Genetic Prophecy: Beyond the Double Helix 188–189 (1981). The issue of XYY karyotype is also discussed in Chapter 13, Mental and Behavioral Genetics.

2.   Most Institutional Review Board assessments of research focus on the physical risks of participation in the research. If the research only involves a blood test, it might be viewed as a study presenting "minimal risks." In what ways do the federal research regulations allow less scrutiny for a study with minimal risks? Why does the Office for Human Research Protections (formerly the Office for Protection from Research Risks (OPRR)) think genetic research presents more than minimal risks?

3.   How, if at all, would the federal research regulations apply to the following research protocols:

a)   A biotechnology company, using venture capital, institutes a project to identify genes associated with asthma.

b)   Researchers propose to test Abraham Lincoln's blood from the cloak Mary Todd Lincoln wore on the night of the assassination to see if the president had a genetic predisposition to Marfan syndrome, a connective tissue disorder. See Robert Kurson, In Old Blood, Chicago Magazine, Mar. 2001, at 24. See also Philip R. Reilly, Abraham Lincoln's DNA and Other Adventures in Genetics (2000). For proposed guidelines regarding testing DNA from historic figures, see Lori Andrews et al., Constructing Ethical Guidelines for Biohistory, 304 Science 215–216 (2004).

c)   A genetic researcher with a grant from the National Institutes of Health undertakes a study of the Huntington disease gene in a large family. The participants do not wish to know if they have inherited the mutated form of the gene. After he completes the study, he proposes to publish a family tree—without identifiers—to identify which family members have the mutation. By looking at the tree, a 19-year-old family member will realize he has the mutation. Would anything in the federal regulations prohibit the publication of the family tree? In The Ethics of Prediction: Genetic Risk and the Physician-Patient Relationship, 1 Genome Sci. & Tech. 21 (1995), Eric Juengst points to an actual study in which genetic information about misattributed paternity was revealed to participants in this manner. Should the researcher avoid a potential confidentiality breach by "disguising" the family tree by changing the number of siblings or the sex of certain family members? How would such a change affect the research utility of the family tree?

d)   A state university with a federal grant appoints the following people from its faculty and administration as the only members of its Institutional Review Board: a female pathologist, a female geneticist, a female law professor, and the female head of the university tech transfer office. Is this IRB properly constituted? If not, why not?

4.   Should researchers inform participants of incidental findings that concern the participant's health, even if those findings are not the subject of the research project? For example, if a participant's genetic sample indicated that he was highly likely to develop Huntington disease in the future, is the researcher obligated to inform the participant? What if the study was meant to determine the genetic basis for baldness? What if the researcher who analyzed the sample was not a medical doctor? For an analysis of incidental findings in research involving biobanks, see Susan M. Wolf et al., Managing Incidental Findings and Research Results in Genomic Research Involving Biobanks and Archived Data Sets, 14 Genetics in Medicine 361 (2012). For

guidelines about disclosure about both primary and secondary findings see Lisa Eckstein et al., A Framework for Analyzing the Ethics of Disclosing Genetics Research Findings, 42 Journal of Law, Medicine and Ethics 190 (2014). For issues raised about the disclosure of incidental findings in clinical settings see Chapter 7.

5.   As GWAS become more powerful, researchers will likely be able to link increasing amounts of genetic variation with susceptibility to disease. What if certain racial or ethnic groups are found to be more vulnerable to certain diseases than others? Should that information be made public? Should we develop medications that are specifically approved for different races and ethnic groups?

6.   The federal Department of Health and Human Services proposed that changes be adopted to the federal research regulations. Human Subjects Research Protections: Enhancing Protections for Research Subjects and Reducing Burden, Delay, and Ambiguity for Investigators, 76 Fed. Reg. 44512 (proposed July 26, 2011). For a comparison of the key provisions of the existing and proposed regulations, see the chart created by the U.S. Department of Health and Human Services. Regulatory Changes in ANPRAM, Comparison of Existing Rules with Some of the Changes Being Considered (Table), HHS.gov, www.hhs.gov/ohrp/humansubjects/anprm changetable.html.

D. STATE REGULATION OF RESEARCH

The federal research regulations specifically do not preempt state or local laws or regulations that provide additional protections for human subjects. Only a handful of states, such as Virginia, have adopted comprehensive laws governing human research. See Va. Code Ann. §§ 32.1–162.16–.20. Many states, however, have adopted laws governing research on certain vulnerable populations, such as children or people with mental disabilities. See Elyn R. Saks et al., Proxy Consent to Research: The Legal Landscape, 8 Yale Journal of Health Policy, Law, and Ethics Issue 2, 37 (2013). States have also adopted restrictive laws governing research on embryos and fetuses. The state laws on research are particularly important because, unlike the federal research regulations, they apply to research no matter what the source of funding.

Starting in the mid-1990s, a new trend in state laws emerged. Some states adopted laws forbidding genetic testing without an individual's written informed consent. Yet most of those laws created exceptions that allowed researchers to undertake certain types of genetic testing without informed consent. The Massachusetts law, Mass. Stat. Ann. 111 § 70G, for example, allows investigators undertaking pharmacological or clinical research to undertake genetic testing on a person's anonymized DNA without his or her consent if the research has been approved by an IRB.

Other states exempt any researcher from having to comply with the informed consent provision, without even requiring IRB approval.

III. RESEARCH ON TISSUE SAMPLES

A. THE NATURE OF THE RESEARCH

NATIONAL BIOETHICS ADVISORY COMMISSION (NBAC),
RESEARCH INVOLVING HUMAN BIOLOGICAL MATERIALS:
ETHICAL ISSUES AND POLICY GUIDANCE
1–14 (1999).

Biomedical researchers have long studied human biological materials—such as cells collected in research projects, biopsy specimens obtained for diagnostic purposes, and organs and tissues removed during surgery—to increase knowledge about human diseases and to develop better means of preventing, diagnosing, and treating these diseases. Today, new technologies and advances in biology provide even more effective tools for using such resources to improve medicine's diagnostic and therapeutic potential. Yet, the very power of these new technologies raises a number of important ethical issues.

Is it appropriate to use stored biological materials in ways that originally were not contemplated either by the people from whom the materials came or by those who collected the materials? Does such use harm anyone's interest? Does it matter whether the material is identified, or identifiable, as to its source, or is linked, or linkable, to other medical or personal data regarding the source?

* * *

Although protection of human subjects in research is of primary concern in the U.S. biomedical research system, research that uses biological materials—materials that often are distanced in time and space from the persons from whom they were obtained—raises unique challenges regarding the appropriate protection of research subjects.

* * *

Policies and guidelines governing human subjects research should permit investigators—under certain circumstances and with the informed, voluntary consent of sample sources—to have access to identifying information sufficient to enable them to gather necessary data regarding the subjects. Provided that adequate protections exist (which usually, but not always, include informed consent), such information gathering could include ongoing collection of medical records data and even requests for individuals to undergo tests to provide additional research information. In some cases, it even will be acceptable for investigators to convey information about research results to the persons whose samples have been studied. Where identifying information exists, however, a well-developed system of protections must be implemented to ensure that risks are minimized and that the interests of sample sources are protected.

* * *

How well does the existing Federal Policy for the Protection of Human Subjects (the so-called Common Rule, codified at 45 C.F.R. Part 46) meet these objectives? Specifically, does it provide clear direction to research sponsors, investigators, IRBs, and others regarding the conduct of research using human biological materials in an ethical manner? NBAC finds that it does not adequately do so. In some cases, present regulatory language provides ambiguous guidance for research using human biological materials. For example, confusion about the intended meaning of terms such as "human subject," "publicly available," and "minimal risk" has stymied investigators and IRB members. Beyond these ambiguities, certain parts of current regulations are inadequate to ensure the ethical use of human biological materials in research and require some modification.

B. BIOBANKS

MARK A. ROTHSTEIN, EXPANDING THE ETHICAL
ANALYSIS OF BIOBANKS
33 J.L. Med. & Ethics 89–91 (2005).

Biobanks are repositories of human biological materials collected for biomedical research. There are over 300 million stored specimens in the United States, and the number grows by 20 million per year. In the post-genome world of high throughput gene sequencing and computational biology, biobanks hold the promise of facilitating large-scale research studies. New organizational and operational models of research repositories also raise complex issues of big science, big business, and big ethical concerns.

Biobanks represent a new paradigm for biomedical research. Traditional research with biological specimens generally involves: (1) a single researcher or an established group of researchers; (2) obtaining and using the samples in defined ways to research in discrete areas; and (3) obtaining informed consent from each research subject to use his or her sample and, where appropriate, an authorization to obtain, use, and disclose the subject's health information. By contrast, with biobanks: (1) the individual or entity obtaining the sample may not be engaged in research, but may be only a broker or intermediary supplying specimens to other researchers; (2) the purpose of a biobank is to develop a repository that can be used for many research protocols, often in numerous scientific areas; (3) a biobank contemplates future research activities, including research by investigators who cannot be specified at the time of the sample collection; and (4) research using biobanks seeks to move beyond the one study/one informed consent model to a format of obtaining general (or blanket) consent to participate in the research activities of the biobank.

Some of the uncertainty surrounding the ethical and legal rules relating to biobanks can be traced to the fact that many developers and administrators of biobanks, researchers, regulators, and research subjects have viewed biobanks within the context of the traditional research paradigm.

* * *

It has been widely observed that the nature and degree of risk of biobank research depends on (1) the identifiability of the sample and any linked health information, and (2) whether the samples are extant or to be collected prospectively. Furthermore, just as the benefits of research go beyond the researchers and their affiliated institutions and entities to the public, the risks of research go beyond the individual human subjects to population groups with which the subject is associated as well as the general public. Therefore, societal interests appear on both the benefit and risk side of research.

The use of biobanks in research may be considered to raise the risks of both intrinsic harms and consequential harms, both of which may be manifested at the individual, group, or societal levels.

INTRINSIC HARMS

Research with identifiable samples raises the risk that there will be an invasion of the sample donor's privacy through disclosure of sensitive information. Research with unidentifiable samples raises the risk that the subject's sample will be used for research of which the sample donor does not approve (e.g., behavioral genetics) or otherwise violates the sample donor's strongly held beliefs (e.g., by failing to return bodily tissues in violation of religious precepts).

Even where direct personal identifiers have been removed, labels on biological samples and linked medical records may contain demographic data, such as gender, race, and ethnicity. Research findings indicating that members of certain subpopulations are more likely to have a genotype conferring an increased risk of disease or other traits could lead to stigma or discrimination against members of specific population groups. Thus, some forms of research may carry social risks beyond the donors of biological specimens. Another example of group intrinsic harm would be where a religious group opposed to abortion, such as Mormons in Utah, was concerned that its population database was being used in genetic research that might lead to more abortions (e.g., research on a gene linked to the likelihood of non-lethal birth defects).

CONSEQUENTIAL HARMS

Research with identifiable samples raises the risk of genetic discrimination by disclosure of individual research findings to third parties through clinical records or compelled disclosures.* * * Sometimes, harms may be considered both intrinsic and consequential. The ethical conduct of research exemplifies a society's respect for persons. Ethical lapses undermine public trust in the research enterprise and may result in widespread and long-lasting consequences, including reduced public funding for research, unwillingness of individuals or groups to participate in research, and distrust of the medical establishment that may extend to the clinical setting.

INFORMED CONSENT AND AUTHORIZATION

Informed consent has been variously defined as a legal doctrine, an ethical precept, and a system of shared decision making. Regardless of the specific meaning used, informed consent is a central tenet of biomedical research. The Nuremberg Code in 1947 established that the touchstone of ethical research is informed consent. The voluntary consent of the human subject is absolutely essential * * *. The primacy of informed consent is now codified in the federal Protection of Human Subjects Rule, also known as the Common Rule.

To some extent, the current research regulations are based on a narrow view of the research enterprise. The rules implicitly contemplate *individual* consent for particular research projects, *individual* risks and benefits, and largely *individual* consequences of the research. Under the current research rules, informed consent is an integral part of research, and it is obtained only after the specific elements of the research have been conceptualized and approved by an institutional review board (IRB). At present, IRBs attempting to protect group or societal interests in research are left without clear direction by the Common Rule.

Biobanks give rise to new relationships and ethical issues distinct from traditional concerns about the subjects of research. Biobanks frequently involve a separation of the sample collection process (and thus the informed consent process) from the actual research on the sample. The research may be undertaken years after the sample collection and may involve hypotheses and methods that could not have been contemplated at the time of the sample collection. With most sample collection, there are de minimis or no physical risks to the research subjects; the common risks are dignitary (e.g., use of specimens without consent in violation of religious or personal values). The social risks (e.g., stigmatization or discrimination) are often group-based (e.g., race/ethnicity) and implicate research subjects and non-subjects alike. The benefits of the research are often more diffuse and involve broader societal concerns about advancing scientific knowledge as well as the prevention, diagnosis, and treatment of disease. If informed consent is based on promoting autonomy and the rights of individuals, what ethical paradigm should govern the fundamentally social enterprise of biobank research?

There is considerable scholarly and professional debate on the necessity or nature of informed consent for biobank research. There are two main issues. First, informed consent is broadly required when samples will be collected, stored, or released in an individually identifiable form. Identifiability, however, is quite complicated. The literature is strewn with terms of indecipherable distinctions: anonymous, anonymized, linked, unlinked, coded, key-coded, double coded, masked, encrypted, identified, and deidentified. It is clear that a standard nomenclature is needed, but there are numerous proposed taxonomies that only seem to make matters more confusing.

Second, informed consent depends on whether the samples are extant or prospective. Nearly all proposals relax the rules on informed consent for archival samples, especially those that are not identifiable. The effect of applying contemporary informed consent criteria to samples collected many years ago would be to render these resources largely unavailable to researchers. For prospective samples, however, informed consent should be required, regardless of the identifiability or anonymity of the sample. Simply stated, research ethics and respect for persons do not permit investigators to appropriate an individual's specimen without permission. Moreover, as discussed earlier, group-based harms do not require individually-identifiable specimens.

NOTES AND QUESTIONS

1. The Precision Medicine Initiative launched in 2015 will involve combining genome sequence information from one million volunteers with medical record data, environmental and lifestyle data, and personal device and sensor data. President Obama said, "We're going to make sure that protecting patient privacy is built into our efforts from day one. * * * It's not going to be an afterthought. [Patient rights advocates will] help us design this initiative from the ground up, making sure that we harness new technologies and opportunities in a responsible way." www.whitehouse.gov/the-press-office/2015/01/30/remarks-president-precision-medicine.

What controversies would such a population-based biobank create? What legal protections might be necessary? For a discussion of the legal questions raised by biobanks, see the symposium issue "Regulation of Biobanks" (edited by Mark A. Rothstein & Bartha Maria Knoppers), 33 J. L. Med. & Ethics 1–188 (2005).

2. Since the early 1980s, Dr. William Catalona, a prostate cancer surgeon, has asked his patients if they were willing to let him use the tissue removed during their surgery, blood, and other tissue for research. Over the years he amassed over 30,000 tissue samples and an enviable set of research results. Thanks to Dr. Catalona's research, men now routinely use a simple blood test to screen for prostate cancer. When Dr. Catalona decided to leave his job at Washington University to take a new position at Northwestern, he intended to take the tissue samples with him to continue his research. He sought permission from the research subjects to move the samples and over 6,000 people asked that their samples be transferred to Northwestern University.

Washington University sought to prevent the transfers by asking a federal court to declare that the university was the legal owner of the samples. The patients were eventually added as necessary parties to the matter; they argued that they owned their samples and could thus transfer them. Washington University argued that the patients had no ownership rights to tissue that had been donated for research purposes. The patients and Dr. Catalona disputed that depiction, claiming that the tissue samples had not been donated or gifted to the university, but were instead provided to Dr. Catalona for a particular use—research on prostate cancer. The patients also claimed that, under the research informed consent forms, they had retained rights to control what happened to their tissue samples, including the right to withdraw samples from research and in some cases to have samples destroyed, and as such there could not have been a gift of their tissue samples to the university. In April 2006, the district court ruled that the informed consent form under which the patients retained rights was "inconsequential" and held that the samples were the property of Washington University. Washington University v. Catalona, et al., 437 F.Supp.2d 985 (E.D. Mo.2006). The court stated that the patients released their samples to Washington University as *inter vivos* gifts, finding all the elements of a gift were present on the facts: (1) present donative intent, (2) delivery of the gift, and (3) acceptance of the gift.

The Court of Appeals for the Eighth Circuit affirmed the judgment of the district court. In addressing the issue of whether the patients' limited rights to withdraw their tissue from research prevented them from making an *inter vivos* gift, the appellate court noted that under Missouri law, an individual can give a charitable donation as a valid gift, even if the donation is subject to a condition of revocation. In this case, the condition of revocation would be the patients' rights to withdraw from research. Thus, according to the court, the patients made valid *inter vivos* gifts to Washington University under Missouri law.

Additionally, the appellate court clarified what it meant if the patients withdrew from research. The district court had indicated that federal regulations permitted Washington University to use a patient's tissue for research if it removed all donor-identifying information, even if the patient expressed a desire to withdraw from the research process. In contrast, the Eighth Circuit stated that patients have the right to withdraw from research by (1) prohibiting future research of any kind on their samples, (2) refusing to donate more samples, and (3) refusing to answer additional questions.

By deciding that tissue can be given as a gift and acknowledging that patients can retain rights to their tissue, the appellate court's decision implicitly recognizes that people have property interests in their tissue. See Washington University v. Catalona, 490 F.3d 667, 673–676 (8th Cir. 2007), cert. denied, 552 U.S. 1166 (2008). Should the courts formally recognize a property interest in excised tissue? If so, how extensive should this interest be? Should individuals retain control of their samples even after donating them to research? Should relatives of donors be able to control the use of the donor's sample after the donor's death?

3.   The limits of genome research are illustrated by a 2015 study by Stanford researchers and their colleagues across the globe. Their study tested sets of twins' immune system markers and found nearly 60% of the immune system differences were based on the environment rather than genes. See Petter Brodin et al., Variation in the Human Immune System Is Largely Driven by Non-Heritable Influences, 160 Cell 37 (Jan. 15, 2015).

4.   At a cost of several million dollars, the National Institutes of Health collected tissue samples, including spinal fluid, from individuals afflicted with Alzheimer disease and also from healthy individuals, for use in future studies conducted by the National Institute for Mental Health (NIMH). When a researcher attempted to gain access to some of these samples for use in a new study, she was told by Dr. Pearson ("Trey") Sunderland III, the head of Geriatric Psychiatry at NIMH, that a freezer malfunction had destroyed 95% of the samples. However, Dr. Sunderland was unable to substantiate his claims and a Congressional investigation was launched to determine what happened to the samples.

The investigators discovered that Dr. Sunderland had provided over 3,000 tissue samples and associated clinical data to the pharmaceutical company Pfizer. The samples came from 538 patients over a 15-year period. Staff of H. Comm. on Energy and Commerce, 109th Cong., A Staff Report: For the Use of the Subcommittee on Oversight and Investigations In Preparation for Its Hearing, Human Tissue Samples: NIH Research Policies and Practices, June 13–14, 2006. The investigators also uncovered a previously undisclosed financial relationship between Dr. Sunderland and Pfizer. Pfizer paid Dr. Sunderland as a consultant at the same time that Pfizer was entering into official research partnerships with NIMH. As a result, Dr. Sunderland was often paid simultaneously by NIMH and Pfizer for the same work. Dr. Sunderland received hundreds of thousands of dollars from Pfizer for his consultations, but did not disclose this information or seek approval to act as a consultant for Pfizer as required by federal regulation.

Dr. Sunderland was ultimately charged with violations of a federal law which acts to prevent conflicts of interest—18 U.S.C. § 208(a)—which carried with it a potential 5-year prison sentence under 18 U.S.C. § 216(a)(2) if his actions were willful.

Dr. Sunderland was allowed to plead guilty to a misdemeanor charge with two years of probation and 400 hours of community service at a geriatric psychology service. He also agreed to pay the government $300,000.

Paul W. Lewis, one of the research participants who provided tissue samples for the Alzheimer studies, stated that he felt Dr. Sunderland received little more than "a slap on the wrist," and stated that he would attempt to retrieve his sample from the NIH. David Willman, NIH Researcher is Ordered to Forfeit Pfizer Payments, Los Angeles Times, Dec. 23, 2006, at A22. Did Dr. Sunderland do anything wrong? If so, do you think that he should have received a harsher punishment? What might be the legal basis for Paul Lewis to sue the NIH?

C. MEDICAL ORGANIZATION GUIDANCE ABOUT RESEARCH ON TISSUE SAMPLES

AMERICAN SOCIETY OF HUMAN GENETICS, STATEMENT ON INFORMED CONSENT FOR GENETIC RESEARCH
59 Am. J. Human Genetics 471–474 (1996).

* * *

RESEARCH USING PROSPECTIVELY COLLECTED SAMPLES

In genetic studies that are designed to collect new biological samples from individuals, the investigators generally have the opportunity to communicate with potential subjects in advance and involve them in the research by obtaining their informed consent. This should be encouraged, except for the prospective studies in which samples are collected anonymously, or have been "anonymized."

Studies that maintain identified or identifiable specimens must maintain subjects' confidentiality * * *. To ensure maximum privacy, it is strongly recommended that investigators apply to the Department of Health and Human Services for a Certificate of Confidentiality. Investigators should indicate to the subject that they cannot guarantee absolute confidentiality.

Research results or samples should not be given to any of the subject's family members by the investigator without the explicit, written permission of the subject, except under extraordinary circumstances. Within the limits of the law, the results must not be shared with employers, insurance companies, or other parties without the written permission of the subject.

CONSENT DISCLOSURES

Subjects providing consent to prospective studies should be told about the types of information that could result from genetic research. Subjects must be given sufficient information to understand the implications and the limitations of research. Individuals should be told the purpose, limitations, possible outcomes, and means of communicating results and maintaining confidentiality. They should be informed of what information may reasonably be expected to result from the genetic study. Importantly, subjects should also understand that unexpected findings, including identification of medical risk, carrier status, or risk to offspring affected by genetic disease, may arise.

During the course of molecular genetic diagnosis, the results may indicate that the child is not the offspring of one or both the presumed parents. The investigator therefore should consider including in the consent form a statement that misidentified parentage will not be disclosed. Another example of unforeseen outcome is genetic heterogeneity in which disorders which were initially thought to be due to defects in a single allele or locus are associated with new ones.

Additional risks that should be disclosed to subjects of certain genetic research studies include the possibility of adverse psychological sequelae, disruption of family dynamics, and social stigmatization and discrimination. All genetic research studies involving identified or identifiable samples in which disclosure of results is planned should have medical geneticists and/or genetic counselors involved to ensure that the results are communicated to the subjects accurately and appropriately. The consent form should not promise significant breakthroughs in diagnosis, treatment or outcome to entice participation. Also, careful attention by all parties involved in genetic research should be given to avoiding actions that could be coercive to potential subjects.

DISPOSITION OF SAMPLES AND RESULTS

Depending on the study, subjects may be given the opportunity to determine if they want to be informed of the results of their testing. Subjects should be informed if the sample will be stored for later study, but they also need to be told that there is always the possibility of storage failure. Decisions related to disposition of results or samples after the subject's death should be specified by the subject.

In some studies researchers may wish to disclose results to subjects. If so, it is the obligation of the subjects to keep the investigator informed of how they may be contacted. Investigators should indicate to study subjects that certain results may not allow definite answers until an analysis of the entire study has been completed (and, sometimes, not even then). Under such circumstances, results cannot be communicated expeditiously.

Subjects involved in studies where the samples are identified or identifiable should indicate if their sample should be used exclusively in the study under consideration. If the sample is to be used more generally, subjects should be given options regarding the scope of the subsequent investigations, such as whether the sample can be used only for a specific disease under investigation, or for other unrelated conditions. It is inappropriate to ask a subject to grant blanket consent for all future unspecified genetic research projects on any disease or in any area if the samples are identifiable in those subsequent studies.

Subjects involved in studies in which the samples are identified or identifiable should indicate if unused portions of the samples may be shared with other researchers. If the subject is willing to have the sample shared with other researchers, it is the responsibility of the principal investigator to distribute the sample, so as to ensure that the agreement embodied in the informed consent is upheld. Finally, subjects should decide if subsequent researchers may receive their samples as anonymous or identifiable specimens.

RETROSPECTIVE STUDIES OF EXISTING SAMPLES

We endorse the use of anonymous samples for genetic research. Importantly, in retrospective research proposing to use samples collected anonymously or anonymized, there is no possibility, or need, to obtain consent.

For many studies, there may be benefits to making identifiable samples anonymous, because this effectively protects subjects from some of the risks of genetic research. Importantly, making samples anonymous will eliminate the need for recontact to obtain informed consent. This will also reduce the chance of introducing bias due to inability to recontact some, or the possible refusal of others to participate. On the other hand, investigators should consider the appropriateness of anonymizing samples, especially when there is available medical intervention for the disorder being tested.

For research involving identifiable samples, the investigator should be required to recontact the subjects to obtain consent for new studies. However, an investigator may seek a waiver based on the following criteria of 45 CFR 46.116:

1.   The research involves no more than minimal risk to the subjects;

2.   The waiver or alteration will not adversely affect the rights and welfare of the subjects;

3.   The research could not practicably be carried out without the waiver or alteration; and

4.   Whenever appropriate, the subjects will be provided with additional pertinent information after participation.

For research involving samples that retain identifiers, consent should be obtained. Waivers may be granted, although the waivers will be difficult to justify by the above criteria if identifiers are retained.

D.   CASE STUDY OF RESEARCH ON EXISTING SAMPLES

The following is the text of a brochure distributed by the Centers for Disease Control and Prevention (CDC) for a study of Americans' health. In the course of the study CDC researchers conducted blood tests on tens of thousands of people, took their health histories, and undertook certain other procedures such as X-rays. After this was done, researchers wanted access to the blood samples to conduct genetic research. Officials at the CDC convened a panel of experts to determine whether there was anything in the federal regulations or the brochure itself that would preclude using the blood samples for genetic research without asking the people who provided the blood initially for consent for that new use.

CENTERS FOR DISEASE CONTROL AND PREVENTION, "NATIONAL HEALTH AND NUTRITION EXAMINATION SURVEY"

Department of Health and Human Services, Centers for Disease Control brochure.

More than 70,000 persons have participated in the National Health and Nutrition Examination Surveys (NHANES).

It is the willingness of the people that makes this survey work. Since the early 1960's, NHANES has identified many health problems that affect all of us. Through continued research, health promotion and disease prevention, such health problems as heart disease have declined.

The third National Health and Nutrition Examination Survey (NHANES III) will be used to track the progress of combating disease in this country. Tracking our progress helps to prevent future disease. As a result, NHANES information that has been very valuable to our health in the recent past promises to be even more so in the future.

* * *

NHANES III Is Different From Other Surveys

NHANES III is different because it is the only national survey in which physical examinations are performed to measure a person's health. We are studying how current health habits and practices relate to future health. After several years, we will check back with you to note any changes in your health. A small sample of your blood will be kept in long-term storage for future testing. The examinations are conducted by a medical doctor and a highly trained medical staff in modern specially designed mobile units.

* * *

We Need Your Help

You were especially selected to be a part of NHANES III. You will represent hundreds of persons like yourself.

To show our appreciation for your participation, we provide:

Health Examinations

The data are collected through physical measurements, laboratory testing, and health interviews. There are no internal examinations given in this survey. Depending on your age you may be in the Examination Center for up to 3½ hours. You will have the opportunity to learn about your health along with contributing to knowledge of the health needs of other Americans.

Your Examinations May Include:

Health Measurements

- Blood pressure
- Height, weight, and body fat
- Allergy test
- Lung capacity test
- Electrocardiogram
- Arthritis test (x rays of knees and hands)
- Bone density measurement (x rays of the hip)
- Ultrasound test for gallstones
- Dental check up

Laboratory Tests

Blood

- Cholesterol
- Anemia
- Kidney
- Liver
- Diabetes
- Lead
- Acquired immunodeficiency Syndrome (AIDS)
- Thyroid

Urine

- Drug use
- Kidney

Private Health Interviews

- Nutrition
- Reproductive health
- Sexual experience
- Physical activity
- Mental health
- Health habits

Q. What are the benefits for me?

A. • The opportunity to make an important contribution to the health of the nation

- Valuable health tests
- Cash payment for participating in the survey.

Q. Will I receive the results of my AIDS test?

A. No. The AIDS testing is being done in the NHANES III survey so we can determine how many people in the United States are infected with the AIDS virus. In order to make extra sure that the results are kept private, no information that would allow us to identify you will be attached to the blood specimens tested for AIDS virus. Therefore, your test results will be anonymous. If you would like to have an AIDS test and receive the results in a confidential manner, our staff can give you the name of a clinic in your area where you can go.

Q. How will I receive the results of my examination?

A. The results of your examination will be sent to you in about 12–16 weeks. Of course, if we should find something important to your health before that time, you will be notified.

* * *

Health information collected in the NHANES III is kept in strictest confidence. Without your approval our staff is not allowed to discuss your participation in this study with anyone under penalty of Federal law. Section 308(d) of the Public Health Service Act (42 USC 242m) and the Privacy Act of 1974 (5 USC 552A). However, in the case of children we will refer clear evidence of physical abuse to the responsible state agency for possible follow-up.

Notice—Information contained on this form which would permit identification of any individual or establishment has been collected with a guarantee that it will be held in strict confidence, will be used only for purposes stated for this study, and will not be disclosed or released to others without the consent of the individual or the establishment in accordance with section 308(d) of the Public Health Service Act (42 USC 242m).

NOTES AND QUESTIONS

1.   How should an institutional review board assess a proposal to use the existing NHANES samples for new types of genetic research? Can such research go forward without consent? Would it fall within the exception of 45 C.F.R. § 46.101(b)(4)? Would it violate any provisions of the brochure, which participants signed as an informed consent form? Would the results of the new genetic tests have to be disclosed to people? Would identifiers have to be removed from the samples before they were analyzed?

For a discussion of how one interdisciplinary advisory workshop resolved these questions, see Ellen Wright Clayton et al., Informed Consent for Genetic Research on Stored Tissue Samples, 274 JAMA 1786 (1995). For alternative recommendations on research involving previously-collected tissue samples, see National Bioethics Advisory Commission, Research Involving Human Biological Materials: Ethical Issues and Policy Guidance (1999).

2.   Clayton et al. suggest the following guidelines:

People should have the opportunity to decide whether their samples will be used for research. This option should be presented when samples are collected for whatever reason if it is likely that the samples will also be used for research. In addition, the possibility of future research should generally be discussed whenever tissue samples are collected for any research project.

If people agree to such use, they should then be offered the following options:

1.   Whether they are willing to have their samples used in identifiable or linked research. To make this complex decision, potential subjects must be informed about (a) the risks and benefits of participation; (b) the extent to which confidentiality realistically will be maintained. Investigators are strongly encouraged to seek certificates of confidentiality; (c) under what circumstances, if any, they will be recontacted. If recontact may occur, subjects must be offered the opportunity to refuse to participate. Even if specific information will not be made available, researchers could offer to send a periodic newsletter to participants so that they can be aware of new findings and can seek them through their health care provider if they are interested. The circumstances under which the researcher will decline to provide preliminary results either in individual contacts or in the newsletters should also be defined; and (d) their ability to withdraw from the project in the future. In general, a decision to withdraw should allow the individual to stop

any further personal involvement and to withdraw any samples or data that contain identifiers from use in research that occurs after the date of withdrawal.

Because of the complexity of the issues that individuals must consider in deciding whether to participate in such research, the workshop participants believe that it is not desirable to ask sources to sign statements in which they agree to the use of their identifiable samples for research without being informed about the scope and potential consequences of the projects.

2.   Whether they wish or are willing to have their samples stripped of identifiers for use in research. Individuals should be told that when their samples are used anonymously, they cannot be given specific information about findings related to their samples.

Whether people permit researchers to use identifiable or anonymous samples, they should be informed of the extent to which the researcher may be motivated by interests other than those of the source. People should be told whether they will share in the profits of any commercial products that might be developed based on findings from the research.

In addition, many at the workshop urged that people who provide tissue samples, particularly for use in identified or linkable research, should also be given the following choices:

1.   Whether they are willing to have their samples shared with other investigators either inside or outside the institution in which they are collected. Individuals may wish to permit their samples to be used only by investigators at academic institutions and not by those involved with commercial enterprises, although the distinctions between these two groups are increasingly difficult to define. In any event, samples should be shared with investigators who were not involved in the research project to which the subjects agreed only after identifiers have been removed.

2.   Whether they wish their samples to be used only to study certain disorders. Some individuals may wish to limit the use of their samples to specific diseases in which they are interested, such as breast cancer or cystic fibrosis. Others may wish to specify that their samples not be used to study certain classes of disorders, such as behavior-related diseases, disorders that are currently untreatable, diseases that are particularly stigmatizing to members of a group, or those for which prenatal diagnosis is the primary option.

Ellen Wright Clayton et al., Informed Consent for Genetic Research on Stored Tissue Samples, 274 JAMA 1786, 1791 (1995). What are the likely impacts of these suggestions on protecting human subjects? How will each of these suggestions affect the research effort itself?

3.   In July 2010, the HHS proposed changes to the HIPAA privacy rules intended to streamline the process for obtaining informed consent for clinical trial participation and authorization for use of protected patient data and biological materials. Modifications to the HIPAA Privacy, Security, and Enforcement Rules Under the HITECH Act; Proposed Rule, 75 Fed. Reg. 40,868 (proposed July 14, 2010). The changes would allow the use of a single informed consent document for both enrollment in a clinical trial and future research use of patient data and human tissue. *Id.* at 40,892–40,893. Under the proposed rule, HIPAA-covered entities could combine both conditioned and unconditioned authorizations, as long as the document clearly states that it is the individual's choice whether to opt in to the unconditioned research activities. *Id.* Similarly, the Secretary's Advisory Committee on Human Research Protections (SACHRP) and the Institute of Medicine (IOM) have both recommended that HHS allow researchers to seek consent for future research if there is enough description of possible future uses in the document to allow for informed consent. Medical Research Law & Policy Report, HIPAA Proposes Rule Change to Streamline Informed Consent, Authorization for Research, 9 MRLR 441 (July 21, 2010).

4.   Do the ASHG's recommended guidelines for informed consent meet all the concerns raised in the Institutional Review Board Guidebook?

5.   Since at least the time of adoption of the Nuremberg Code, research subjects have had the right to withdraw from a research project at any time. George Annas has suggested that, with respect to genetic research, this means that subjects should be able to order their DNA samples destroyed at any time. Annas also suggests that in order for the right of withdrawal to be meaningful, researchers should inform the people who provided DNA of their research agenda. George J. Annas, Rules for Research on Human Genetic Variation—Lessons from Iceland, 342 New Eng. J. Med. 1830, 1832 (2000). How solid is the legal basis for such a right? What are the practical implications of such a right?

IV.   RESEARCH ON HUMAN EMBRYOS

A. THE PURPOSE OF EMBRYO RESEARCH

In a society deeply divided over the moral and legal status of embryos, any scientific or medical project using tissue or cells from embryos is bound to raise serious philosophical and social concerns. Because varying viewpoints regarding the legal protection of embryos and fetuses have been enacted into law in different states, it is often difficult for researchers and physicians to determine which laws cover their work. Indeed, statutory and court precedents dealing with embryo and fetal research, abortion, organ transplant, and payment for body tissue all have ramifications for genetic research involving embryo stem cells. Yet no two states have identical laws covering these procedures. Federal law and regulations, too, limit the type of experimentation that may be undertaken with human embryos.

In the genetics realm, three types of embryo research are being pursued extensively. The first is research in which the embryo is intended to be used to create a child. This includes research to diagnose or treat genetic diseases in the embryo. Because of the link between some forms of embryo research and reproductive decisions, bans on embryo research of this type have been challenged as unconstitutional.

The second type of research involves embryos created in the process of in vitro fertilization but not implanted. These embryos are often frozen for a period of time and then destroyed. The third type of embryo research involves embryos created specifically for research purposes. The latter two types of research are intended to benefit other individuals, such as through the use of embryo stem cells to create potential therapeutic cell lines. Some state laws limit research on embryos. For example, Louisiana prohibits research on in vitro fertilized embryos. La. Rev. Stat. Ann. § 9:122. And because federal law bans research which destroys embryos, a controversial question has arisen about the circumstances under which federally-funded researchers can undertake embryo stem cell research.

B. CONSTITUTIONAL CONCERNS IN EMBRYO RESEARCH

LIFCHEZ V. HARTIGAN
735 F.Supp. 1361 (N.D. Ill. 1990).

Memorandum Opinion and Order

WILLIAMS, J.

Dr. Lifchez represents a class of plaintiff physicians who challenged an Illinois statute that banned research on fetuses and embryos in a way that appeared to prohibit certain novel reproductive technologies and experimental genetic testing.

* * *

VAGUENESS

Section 6(7) of the Illinois Abortion Law provides as follows:

(7) No person shall sell or experiment upon a fetus produced by the fertilization of a human ovum by a human sperm unless such experimentation is therapeutic to the fetus thereby produced. Intentional violation of this section is a Class A misdemeanor. Nothing in this subsection (7) is intended to prohibit the performance of in vitro fertilization.

Ill. Rev. Stat., Ch. 38 & 81–26, § 6(7) (1989). Dr. Lifchez claims that the Illinois legislature's failure to define the terms "experimentation" and "therapeutic" renders the statute vague, thus violating his due process rights under the Fourteenth Amendment. The court agrees.

Vague laws—especially criminal laws—violate due process in three ways. First, they fail to give adequate notice of precisely what conduct is being prohibited. Without such notice, it is impossible for people to regulate their conduct within legal bounds * * *. The second problem with vague statutes is that, by failing to explicitly define what conduct is unlawful, they invite arbitrary and discriminatory enforcement by the police, judges, and juries * * *.

Last, vague standards of unlawful conduct, coupled with the prospect of arbitrary enforcement, will inevitably cause people to "steer far wider of the unlawful zone * * * than if the boundaries of the forbidden areas were clearly marked." * * * This is an especially dangerous consequence of vague statutes that encroach upon constitutional rights * * *. It is a fundamental principle of due process that persons " 'of common intelligence' not be forced to guess at the meaning of the criminal law."

* * *

A.   *Experiment or Routine Test?*

The Illinois legislature's failure to define "experimentation" and "therapeutic" in § 6(7) means that persons of common intelligence will be forced to guess at whether or not their conduct is unlawful. As Dr. Lifchez points out in his briefs, there is no single accepted definition of "experimentation" in the scientific and medical communities. Dr. Lifchez identifies four referents for the term. One meaning of experiment is pure research, where there is no direct benefit to the subject being experimented on, and the only goal of the research is to increase the researcher's knowledge * * *. This definition describes the defendants' "Orwellian nightmare" of laying out fetuses in a laboratory and exposing them to various harmful agents "just for the scientific thrill" of it * * *. A second meaning of experiment includes any procedure that has not yet been sufficiently tested so that the outcome is predictable, or a procedure that departs from present-day practice. This is the kind of definition adhered to by insurance companies, which often deny coverage for procedures whose effectiveness is not generally recognized * * *. Dr. Lifchez also cites to the definition of experiment by the American Fertility Society, which includes as "experimental" even standard techniques when those techniques are performed by a practitioner or clinic for the first time * * *. Finally, any medical therapy where the practitioner applies what he learns from one patient to another, could be described as an "experiment." * * * This definition of experiment is in line with that apparently contemplated by the federal regulations on protection of human research subjects: "Research means a systematic investigation designed to develop or contribute to generalizable knowledge." 45 C.F.R. § 46.102(e) (1989).

* * *

It is difficult to know where along this broad spectrum of possible meanings for "experiment" to fit the medical procedures performed by Dr. Lifchez and his colleagues. These procedures can be roughly divided into three kinds: diagnostic, in vitro fertilization and related technologies, and procedures performed exclusively for the benefit of the pregnant woman. The statute's vagueness affects all three kinds of procedures, but in different ways.

DIAGNOSTIC PROCEDURES

One of the more common procedures performed by reproductive endocrinologists is amniocentesis. Amniocentesis involves withdrawing a portion of the amniotic fluid in order to test it for genetic anomalies. It is performed on women considered to be at risk for bearing children with serious defects * * *. The purpose of the procedure is to provide information about the developing fetus; this information is often used by women in deciding whether or not to have an abortion. Although now routinely performed, amniocentesis could be considered experimental under at least two of Dr. Lifchez' definitions: it could be classified as pure research, since there is no benefit to the fetus, the subject being "experimented" on; it could also be experimental (as defined by the American Fertility Society) if the particular practitioner or clinic were doing it for the first time.

Amniocentesis illustrates well the problem of deciding at what point a procedure graduates from "experimental" to routine. Does this occur the fifth time a procedure is performed? the fiftieth? the five hundredth? the five thousandth?

* * *

B. *Therapeutic Intent*

The defendants claim that the scienter requirement in § 6(7), "Intentional violation of this section is a Class A misdemeanor," saves it from being unconstitutionally vague. It is true that a scienter requirement can do this for a statute * * *. However, a scienter requirement cannot save a statute such as § 6(7) that has no core of meaning to begin with.

* * *

[T]he legality of diagnostic or screening procedures such as amniocentesis and chorionic villi sampling will depend on whether they are "tests" or "experiments." If a practitioner is unable to tell whether a procedure he is about to perform is an experiment or a test, grafting on a requirement that he intend it to be one or the other does not mitigate the vagueness of what is being forbidden. In other words, while the physician may take comfort in the fact that he is administering a test in good faith, he still does not know which tests are tests and which are experiments. To the extent that amniocentesis and chorionic villi sampling (or attempts to improve them) may be experimental, they are almost certainly illegal under § 6(7). They are designed to give information about fetal development, and often aid women in making a decision about whether or not to have an abortion. Considering in addition the risk factor of spontaneous abortion from these procedures, they can hardly be called therapeutic to the fetus, no matter the practitioner's intent.

* * *

REPRODUCTIVE PRIVACY

Section 6(7) of the Illinois Abortion Law is also unconstitutional because it impermissibly restricts a woman's fundamental right of privacy, in particular, her right to make reproductive choices free of governmental interference with those choices * * *. Section 6(7) intrudes upon this "cluster of constitutionally protected choices." * * *

It takes no great leap of logic to see that within the cluster of constitutionally protected choices that includes the right to have access to contraceptives, there must be included within that cluster the right to submit to a medical procedure that may bring about, rather than prevent, pregnancy. Chorionic villi sampling is similarly protected. The cluster of constitutional choices that includes the right to abort a fetus within the first trimester must also include the right to submit to a procedure designed to give information about that fetus which can then lead to a decision to abort. Since there is no compelling state interest sufficient to prevent a woman from terminating her pregnancy during the first trimester, * * * there can be no such interest sufficient to intrude upon these other protected activities during the first trimester. By encroaching upon this protected zone of privacy, § 6(7) is unconstitutional.

NOTES AND QUESTIONS

1. One of the reasons that the Illinois ban on embryo and fetal research was unconstitutional was that it was vague. Would the following, more specific laws be upheld as constitutional under the *Lifchez* logic?

a. A law banning genetic testing for sex selection purposes.

b. A law banning the use of human embryos to create stem cells to make heart cells for people who have had heart attacks.

c. A law banning the creation of children through human cloning.

2. What concerns about informed consent should be raised when embryo stem cell research is undertaken? A 2007 study at nine infertility clinics found that donors preferred to donate embryos to research rather than donate embryos to another couple or thaw embryos and discard them. Additionally, according to the study, the decision to donate embryos was affected by the type of research proposed. For example, 62% of respondents stated that they would be somewhat or very likely to donate embryos to stem cell research aimed at understanding and treating human disease or injury, whereas only 28% stated that they would be somewhat or very likely to donate embryos to improve cloning techniques. Anne Drapkin Lyerly & Ruth R. Faden, Willingness to Donate Frozen Embryos for Stem Cell Research, 317 Science 46 (2007). Is the informed consent requirement under the federal rules met by asking the couple for consent to do research? Or must the couple be told the details of each specific study?

3. A study reported in the *New England Journal of Medicine* showed that as often as 71% of the time couples change their minds about what they would like to do with excess embryos created during the in vitro fertilization process. See Susan C. Klock, Sandra Sheinin & Ralph R. Kazer, The Disposition of Unused Frozen Embryos, 345 New Eng. J. Med. 69 (2001)(letter to the editor). How should researchers approach informed consent in light of this study? Should the couple be recontacted before specific research is undertaken?

4. For a further discussion of the constitutionality of human reproductive cloning, see Chapter 6.

V. LIABILITY IN THE RESEARCH CONTEXT

ANDE V. ROCK

647 N.W.2d 265 (Wis. App. 2002).

BACKGROUND

ROGGENSACK, J.

C.E.A. was born to Linda and Charles Ande on July 13, 1993. There was then ongoing a cystic fibrosis research project which had begun in 1985. Philip Farrell and Norman Fost were the co-investigators. To test for the presence of factors indicative of cystic fibrosis, the study used excess blood that had been drawn from all newborns to conduct statutorily required tests for the presence of other congenital and metabolic disorders. The research protocol required that the parents of half of the newborns in the study were told if their child tested positive for cystic fibrosis. A nutritional plan was made available to them immediately, as it was the researchers' theory that treating the nutritional needs of children with cystic fibrosis before they became symptomatic would result in a less vigorous development of the disease with fewer impairments to overall health. The other half of the children who were tested were placed in the "blinded control" group. Their parents and their treating physicians were not told if they had tested positive for factors indicative of cystic fibrosis. C.E.A. was placed in the blinded group, and therefore, her parents and her primary physician, Dr. Amy Plumb, were not told that she had tested positive.

Prior to testing the blood of newborns for cystic fibrosis, a pamphlet was prepared that told about the different tests that were required to be completed on newborns' blood. It also told of the cystic fibrosis test that would be run as part of a research project. It described the dangers of cystic fibrosis and stated that cystic fibrosis was an inherited disorder. The pamphlet also arguably implied that positive test results would be reported to the infant's physician, and a phone number was listed for parents who wanted additional information about the test.[3] There is no assertion that the Andes were asked for or gave specific, written consent to have the cystic fibrosis test run on C.E.A. or to have the results of that test go unreported to them. Subsequent to birth, C.E.A. had difficulties thriving. On June 23, 1995, when C.E.A. was almost two years old, she was diagnosed with cystic fibrosis. At the time that the Andes learned that C.E.A. had cystic fibrosis, Linda Ande was pregnant with a second child. The Andes' second child, C.L.A., is also afflicted with cystic fibrosis.

In this lawsuit, the Andes' allegations may be summarized into the assertion that the defendants committed three wrongful acts that give rise to the Andes' various claims: (1) The cystic fibrosis test was run without their informed consent; (2) treatment was withheld from C.E.A. when the investigators had knowledge that nutritional treatment would reduce the severity of her cystic fibrosis; and (3) C.E.A.'s test results were withheld from them. They allege to have been harmed by these acts in two ways: (1) If they had been given the test results, they would have accepted treatment for C.E.A. to lessen the severity of the progression of her illness; and (2) if they had been given the test results, they would not have conceived C.L.A. They do not identify any harm they suffered from the alleged lack of informed consent to run the test in the first instance.

In response, the defendants assert that they did not test C.E.A.'s blood without the Andes' knowledge and consent. They also contend that although all the children in the blinded control group were tested as newborns, no one reviewed the test results for the control group, some of

---

[3]   The brochure was revised numerous times, with differing disclosures listed in each version. The edition that plaintiffs' attorneys aver was presented to the Andes states:

One-half of the blood samples are tested for CF before the babies are one month old. The remaining blood samples are partially tested at this time. Testing on these blood samples is completed when the children are 4 years old. Positive test results are reported to your child's doctor.

If the CF research test is done, you may contact your doctor, certified nurse-midwife, or the CF specialist at (608) 263-8555 for the result.

which were negative and some of which were positive for factors indicative of cystic fibrosis. Therefore, the defendants contend they did not withhold information from the Andes. The defendants also raised many affirmative defenses, including failure to state a claim and qualified immunity.

* * *

MEDICAL MALPRACTICE

[E]ven if we were to assume arguendo that the researchers had a duty to obtain informed consent from the Andes, that the pamphlet that was provided was insufficient to do so, and that the researchers had a duty to share what information was available to them with the Andes, there is no allegation in the complaint of any relationships between the Andes and any of the researchers from which one could conclude that such duties arose from a physician-patient relationship, rather than from ordinary negligence principles.

FEDERAL CLAIMS

The Andes' federal claims invoke 42 U.S.C. § 1983 (1994).[8] They claim a due process violation because the defendants deprived them of their liberty and property interests by arbitrarily placing C.E.A. in the blinded control group of the cystic fibrosis study and by withholding her test results from them for almost two years, during which time beneficial treatment was withheld from C.E.A. and the Andes conceived another child who also has cystic fibrosis. The respondents contend that the Andes' claims may not proceed because they are protected by qualified immunity.

1.   42 U.S.C. § 1983 overview

Section 1983, in and of itself, does not create substantive rights; rather, it provides a remedy for the deprivation of rights that are established elsewhere. In a § 1983 claim that alleges a violation of either procedural or substantive due process, a plaintiff must show a deprivation of an interest in life, liberty or property that is protected by the Constitution. Although the Andes allege the deprivation of substantive rights, based on what they characterize as the withholding of medical information about C.E.A., they are not clear about whether their due process claims implicate a property interest or a liberty interest. We will examine each interest in turn.

---

[8]   *42 U.S.C. § 1983* (1994) provides in relevant part:

Every person who, under color of any statute, ordinance, regulation, custom, or usage, of any State or Territory or the District of Columbia, subjects, or causes to be subjected, any citizen of the United States or other person within the jurisdiction thereof to the deprivation of any rights, privileges, or immunities secured by the Constitution and laws, shall be liable to the party injured in an action at law, suit in equity, or other proper proceeding for redress.

* * *

3.   *Violation of a clearly established right*

   a.   Property interest

* * *

* * * The Andes have cited no Wisconsin case to us which holds that they had a property interest in the test results of the cystic fibrosis study, nor have they cited any cases which are closely analogous. Additionally, our research has uncovered no such Wisconsin case that predates the disclosure of the information to the Andes in 1995. * * * Accordingly, the Andes have failed to establish the first step necessary to a due process claim based on the deprivation of a clearly established property right and therefore, their claim in this regard was properly dismissed.

   b.   Liberty interest

   The Andes also allege a constitutional violation of a liberty interest based on the failure to obtain informed consent for the testing that was done, as well as on the alleged failure to disclose information. Liberty interests may arise under either state or federal law. For example, the Fourteenth Amendment of the United States Constitution protects an "individual interest in avoiding disclosure of personal matters." This personal liberty interest arises from a "guarantee" under federal law of certain zones of privacy. The Supreme Court has also recognized that there is a constitutionally protected liberty interest in bodily integrity and in the right to determine what medical treatment shall be accepted or refused, and that parents have a constitutionally protected right to obtain needed medical treatment for their child so long as the child's rights are protected by the process employed. While neither the Wisconsin Supreme Court nor the United States Supreme Court has yet addressed whether there is a constitutionally protected liberty interest in receiving information from a research project relative to one's genetic predisposition to give birth to a child with a genetically transmitted disorder or in receiving information from a research project that would assist a parent in making informed health care choices for his or her child, we cannot say with certainty that the withholding of the results of C.E.A.'s test did not implicate a liberty interest in either the parents or C.E.A. Therefore, for purposes of our discussion we shall assume, without deciding, that a liberty interest could be established if this case were to go to trial.

   Once a liberty interest has been established, it may not be denied without a constitutionally acceptable amount of procedural due process. In regard to the alleged failure to obtain informed consent before the cystic fibrosis test was run in the first instance, the Andes base none of their claimed injuries on an unauthorized disclosure of private information, as they might if the researchers had disclosed C.E.A.'s condition to third parties. And they identify no harm that they suffered by not giving consent to the test in the first instance. For example, they do not allege that they would not have permitted the test if they had known it was being conducted. Instead, all of their alleged injuries flow from not having the results of the test at or near the time it was conducted. Therefore, we will not address their claims in regard to an alleged lack of informed consent further.

We now turn to the alleged failure to timely disclose the results of C.E.A.'s cystic fibrosis test. The closest the Andes come in making an argument that the alleged failure to disclose was a clear violation of their rights is to contend that one of the defendants, Richard Aronson, as the Medical Director for the Wisconsin Newborn Screening Program conducted under the direction of the Wisconsin Department of Health and Family Services, had a statutory duty under Wis. Stat. § 253.13(5) to disclose the results of the testing for congenital disorders. Section 253.13(5) stated in relevant part:

> The department shall disseminate information to families whose children suffer from congenital disorders and to women of child-bearing age with a history of congenital disorders concerning the need for and availability of follow-up counseling and special dietary treatment and the necessity for testing infants. The department shall also refer families of children who suffer from congenital disorders to available health and family services programs and shall coordinate the provision of these programs. The department shall periodically consult appropriate experts in reviewing and evaluating the state's infant screening programs.

In 1993, the year C.E.A. was born, Wis. Admin. Code § HSS 115.04 (1993) set out the tests to be done and for which information was required to be provided under § 253.13. Cystic fibrosis was not then a required test under § HSS 115.04.

* * *

The Andes also allege a "general" violation of substantive due process, claiming that the actions of the defendants were arbitrary and capricious in the way in which they selected C.E.A for the control group and failed to disseminate the information they had about her. Substantive due process protects individuals from arbitrary, wrongful, governmental actions regardless of the process afforded prior to the deprivation. The Supreme Court has repeatedly explained that the touchstone of substantive due process is the protection of the individual against arbitrary action of government. Substantive due process against governmental actors who engage in conduct that "shocks the conscience" or conduct that interferes with rights "implicit in the concept of ordered liberty." However, even so generalized a claim of protection still requires the identification of a clearly protected interest that the actor's conduct violates. Due process claims are not a substitute for general tort claims. The Andes have failed to identify any Wisconsin or federal case law clearly establishing such an interest. Therefore, we conclude that qualified immunity bars all their federal claims.

CONCLUSION

Because we conclude that plaintiffs have made no showing of a physician-patient relationship with any remaining defendant, which relationship is necessary to support a medical malpractice claim, and that plaintiffs have made no showing of a clearly established state property right or a clearly established state or federal liberty interest that any named defendant's conduct violated, we affirm the judgment and order of the circuit court.

By the Court.—Judgment and order affirmed.

NOTE

1.   The need for large numbers of research subjects has led to the proliferation of genomic biobanks from which researchers can draw samples. Do the researchers who use this data have an ethical duty to inform participants of their individual results? Consider different results that may be available to the participants: identification of a variant related to a treatable condition, identification of an environmental factor related to a treatable condition, identification of a variant that is related to an untreatable condition, or identification of a variant of unknown significance. What if the variant has unknown significance at the time of the study, but researchers later are able to determine some significance, should a continuing duty exist? Who should cover the costs of informing the individual? A study of 141 adults found a strong desire to be able to access individual results, as well as the ability to change their preferences over time. The study participants viewed access to results as a valuable incentive for participating in the biobank. Juli Murphy et al., Public Expectations for Return of Results from Large-Cohort Genetic Research, 8 American Journal of Bioethics 36 (2008).

CHAPTER 4

COMMERCIALIZATION OF GENETIC RESEARCH: PROPERTY, PATENTS, AND CONFLICTS OF INTEREST

■ ■ ■

I.   INTRODUCTION

Genetic research is undertaken at universities, government laboratories, and private companies, with funding from public, corporate and philanthropic sources. But at some point, the discoveries need to be turned into tangible products, such as diagnostics and treatments. This chapter explores the incentives for product development and technology transfer in the genetics realm and analyzes the issues raised by the commercialization of genes and cell lines.

The framers of the U.S. Constitution realized that it was important to create incentives for technological innovation. The U.S. Constitution, Art. 1, § 8, cl. 8 provides that Congress shall have the power "To promote the Progress of Science and useful Arts, by securing for limited Times to Authors and Inventors the exclusive Right to their respective Writings and Discoveries."

This constitutional clause provides the foundation for the federal patent statute, which rewards inventors with a 20-year period of exclusivity that allows them to forbid anyone else from making, using, selling, or offering to sell their invention in order to make sure that novel, useful, and nonobvious technologies get developed that otherwise might not have been created.

For nearly two decades, policy questions were raised about whether patents were appropriate for genetic sequences. Was a gene an "invention" or was it an unpatentable product of nature? Was the incentive of a patent necessary to encourage the discovery of genes or were other motivations and incentives (such as federal funding) sufficient?

Scientists were searching for and finding genes long before patents were available. They did so for a number of reasons, including a desire to help humankind, win a Nobel Prize, achieve academic advancement, and gain professional status. When the Human Genome Project was undertaken to spend billions of dollars of taxpayer money to locate and sequence all human genes, key researchers in the field warned about the risks of giving intellectual property rights over genes. They said that if scientists were allowed to "own" genes and reap financial rewards by having exclusive rights to any diagnostic or treatment technologies developed with the gene they found, they would be less likely to share copies of the genes they discovered or even share information about those genes. And, in fact, these dangers came to pass once patents were issued on human genes.

The ascendancy of patents as a means of encouraging innovation in the life sciences became clear in courts and Congress in the early 1980s. The Supreme Court in Diamond v. Chakrabarty, 447 U.S. 303 (1980), held that patents could issue on genetically-engineered organisms. Congress adopted a series of technology transfer laws that allowed federally-funded researchers, including those at federal laboratories and at universities, to patent and gain a commercial interest in inventions that they created with taxpayer money—something that was previously considered to be a criminal usurpation of public funds.

Concerns have been raised about the increasing focus on patenting and commercializing genetic discoveries within university and government molecular biology laboratories. Researchers with commercial interests—who are now the majority in the genetics field—sometimes protect their interests in ways that are fundamentally changing the nature of science. They keep information confidential that they once readily shared. There is also evidence that the sharing of research materials is decreasing. Scientists with access to biological materials from patients are now less likely to give samples of those materials to other researchers. This is true even with genes and cell lines, where replication techniques can create millions of copies of the genes or cells and thus sharing does not diminish the first scientist's ability to carry out research. Other researchers have reported difficulty in accessing research tools—such as gene segments—developed through taxpayer-funded research at the National Institutes of Health. There are questions about whether this approach will best serve society in the long run.

The zeal over patents led scientists and the biotech companies to patent the genes they were discovering. By the time the issue reached the U.S. Supreme Court in 2013, 41% of human genes had been patented. The Court held that the patents on two isolated human breast cancer genes were invalid since genes were products of nature, not inventions of man.

This does not mean that patents are inappropriate for all genetic inventions. Patents are proper for diagnostic kits, pharmaceutical-like gene therapies, and other inventions. But questions will still arise about where to draw the line. If a scientist creates a super insulin gene to help people with diabetes, for example, how different does it have to be from the "natural" gene to be patentable? And what are the appropriate technology transfer laws to make sure that scientific discoveries are translated into health care products?

Elsewhere in the world, there are differences in patent law that deserve attention. Should there be a broad research exemption in the United States as exists in many other technologically-developed countries? Should limits on what can be patented that are in force elsewhere be considered in the United States, such as restrictions on patents on embryo cell lines or animals that have been genetically engineered with human cancer genes?

The genetic gold rush that resulted from the possibility of biotech patents profoundly changed the relationship between patients and physicians. Some patients, such as John Moore, began to feel that they were being harvested by their doctors, who were making deals with biotech companies to sell patients' tissue, genes, cell lines, and other body parts. Courts and medical organizations began to deal with questions of the duties owed to patients when their tissue was commercialized. Biotechnology is unlike other industries since much of the raw material for the research (the "bio" in biotechnology, such as the genes in genetic diagnostics) comes from people. Without the trust of the people whose tissue is used, there will be no tissue available to provide the foundation for the biotech industry. The policies created in the seemingly obscure area of patent and tech transfer law thus have life and death implications for all of us.

This chapter details the legal requirements for obtaining a patent, discusses technology transfer laws, and analyzes the rights of individuals whose bodies are the sources of patented genes and cell lines.

II.   THE PATENT SYSTEM

A.   REQUIREMENTS FOR A PATENT

LORI ANDREWS, THE "PROGRESS CLAUSE": AN EMPIRICAL
ANALYSIS BASED ON THE CONSTITUTIONAL
FOUNDATION OF PATENT LAW
15 N.C. J. L. & Tech. 537, 537–546 (2014).

When the Founding Fathers were drafting the U.S. Constitution, they thought about how best to encourage innovation in their new nation. The result was the Progress Clause of the U.S. Constitution, Article I, Section 8, Clause 8. The Progress Clause provides that Congress shall have the power "[t]o promote the Progress of Science and useful Arts, by securing for limited Times to Authors and Inventors the exclusive Right to their respective Writings and Discoveries. . . ." This clause, designed to reward the creation and sharing of new knowledge, is the constitutional basis for the intellectual property system in existence today.

* * *

Patents are not granted for all useful products or processes that result from human ingenuity. For instance, mental processes and abstract ideas are not patentable because "they are . . . basic tools of scientific and technological work." Patenting other raw materials of scientific and technological work, such as laws of nature or products of nature, similarly raises the danger of inhibiting future innovation and "foreclose[ing] more future invention than the underlying discovery could reasonably justify."

In a series of cases over the past 150 years, the Supreme Court has held that one cannot patent abstract ideas, laws of nature, products of nature, or materials isolated from products of nature if those materials behave in the same way they would in nature.

* * *

The mechanism by which Congress chose to encourage innovation was to grant an inventor a patent—a monopoly on any use of the patented invention in exchange for a disclosure in the patent application of how the invention can be made. This is thought to encourage innovation by stimulating people to invent in the first place, often by making a better, cheaper, more interesting, and more effective alternative to an existing invention. Thus, if a person patents a mousetrap made of wood, when the patent application later becomes public (a condition of the patent grant), other inventors can read about how the inventor made the mousetrap and can create variations using significantly different materials or processes.

Under the Patent Act, a patent is a limited legal monopoly given to an inventor who meets certain constitutional and statutory requirements. The invention must be novel, non-obvious, and useful.

* * *

For twenty years from the date of the filing of the patent application, a patent holder controls any use of its invention and can prevent anyone else from using, making, selling, or importing the invention. The patent holder can keep an invention away from the public altogether. The inventor can decide that he will be the only one to sell the invention and charge as much as he wants for the invention. Or the inventor can, for royalty fees, grant exclusive rights to a single licensee to use the invention or make the invention available for royalty fees in a non-exclusive fashion to all comers.

Unlike in copyright law, there is no patent law exception for fair use. Unlike patent law in other countries, there is no general statutory research exception in the United States. * * * Under American patent law, an inventor can refuse to make the invention and forbid others from making it. In contrast, under American trademark law, a person can lose the mark if he does not use it for three years. And in Europe, patent holders are required to "work" the patent and make the invention available or else their rights are constricted.

The American patent system is a three-way give-and-take among the U.S. Patent and Trademark Office ("USPTO"), the courts, and Congress. All three have active roles in assuring that the goals of the patent system are met and that the monopoly granted is not too broad. Often this means that Congress and the courts winnow back patents erroneously granted by the USPTO. Between 25% and 75% of litigated patents are found invalid during litigation, sometimes because their scope is so broad that they cover unpatentable subject matter such as abstract ideas, laws of nature, or products of nature. Sometimes the director of the USPTO has had to review and invalidate provisions of improperly granted patents—this has happened, for example, with patents on certain computer programs. In other instances, Congress has stepped in—for example, by exempting doctors from patent infringement liability if they use a patented medical or surgical procedure.

B. STATUTORY AUTHORITY

PATENT CODE
35 U.S.C. §§ 101–103

§ 101.   Inventions patentable

Whoever invents or discovers any new and useful process, machine, manufacture, or composition of matter, or any new and useful improvement thereof, may obtain a patent therefore, subject to the conditions and requirements of this title.

§ 102.   Conditions for patentability; novelty

    (a) Novelty; prior art.—A person shall be entitled to a patent unless—

        (1) the claimed invention was patented, described in a printed publication, or in public use, on sale, or otherwise available to the public before the effective filing date of the claimed invention; or

        (2) the claimed invention was described in a patent * * * or in an application for patent published or deemed published * * * in which the patent or application, as the case may

be, names another inventor and was effectively filed before the effective filing date of the claimed invention.

* * *

§ 103.   Conditions for patentability; non-obvious subject matter

A patent for a claimed invention may not be obtained, notwithstanding that the claimed invention is not identically disclosed as set forth in section 102, if the differences between the claimed invention and the prior art are such that the claimed invention as a whole would have been obvious before the effective filing date of the claimed invention to a person having ordinary skill in the art to which the claimed invention pertains. Patentability shall not be negated by the manner in which the invention was made.

III. POLICY ARGUMENTS RELATED TO PATENTING OF GENETIC MATERIALS

LILA FEISEE, ARE BIOTECHNOLOGY PATENTS IMPORTANT? YES!
1 PTO TODAY 9, 9–12, (2000).

Biotechnology is one of the most research intensive and innovative industries in the global economy today. While the promise of new discovery is great, this does not come without cost. It takes hundreds of millions of dollars to bring a new pharmaceutical to the marketplace. Without patent protection for biotechnological research, there would be little incentive for investors to risk their capital and many of the potential benefits of biotechnology would not come to fruition. By rewarding inventors for their discoveries for a limited time, the patent system supports innovation while, at the same time, dedicating these discoveries to the public. Thus, both the private sector and the public benefit.

Patent protection in the area of biotechnology also serves the larger economy by providing a forum that encourages both innovation and investment. It also benefits society by providing the means to reduce disease and suffering for both humans and animals. Such results promote and enhance the dignity and quality of life * * *. Biotechnology patents allow for the dissemination of potentially valuable scientific information. The availability of the information disclosed in biotechnology patents enables others in the field of science to build on earlier discoveries. Not only can other researchers use the information in a patent, but by disclosing cutting edge scientific information, the patent system avoids expensive duplication of research efforts. It is only with the patenting of biotechnology that some companies, particularly small companies, can raise capital to bring beneficial products to the market place or fund further research.

In addition, this capital provides jobs that represent an immediate public benefit independent of the technological benefits. Continuing employment opportunities represent a national resource for the future because they encourage the youth of today to become the scientists and inventors of tomorrow. Thus, the patent system not only fosters benefits to our society today, but ensures our future ability to innovate and grow.

U.S. DEPARTMENT OF ENERGY OFFICE OF SCIENCE, OFFICE OF BIOLOGICAL AND ENVIRONMENTAL RESEARCH, HUMAN GENOME PROGRAM
http://web.archive.org/web/20101003085133/
http://www.ornl.gov/sci/techresources/Human_Genome/elsi/patents.shtml

GENETICS AND PATENTING

* * *

What are some of the potential arguments for gene patenting?

- Researchers are rewarded for their discoveries and can use monies gained from patenting to further their research.
- The investment of resources is encouraged by providing a monopoly to the inventor and prohibiting competitors from making, using, or selling the invention without a license.
- Wasteful duplication of effort is prevented.
- Research is forced into new, unexplored areas.
- Secrecy is reduced and all researchers are ensured access to the new invention.

What are some of the potential arguments against gene patenting?

- Patents of partial and uncharacterized cDNA sequences will reward those who make routine discoveries but penalize those who determine biological function or application (inappropriate reward given to easiest step in the process).
- Patents could impede the development of diagnostics and therapeutics by third parties because of the costs associated with using patented research data.
- Patent stacking (allowing a single genomic sequence to be patented in several ways such as an EST, a gene, and a SNP) may discourage product development because of high royalty costs owed to all patent owners of that sequence; these are costs that will likely be passed on to the consumer.

* * *

- Costs increase not only for paying for patent licensing but also for determining what patents apply and who has rights to downstream products.

- Patent holders are being allowed to patent a part of nature—a basic constituent of life; this allows one organism to own all or part of another organism.

- Private biotechs who own certain patents can monopolize certain gene test markets.

- Patent filings are replacing journal articles as places for public disclosure—reducing the body of knowledge in the literature.

NOTES AND QUESTIONS

1.   A 2013 study found that 41% of all human genes were explicitly claimed in United States patents. Jeffrey Rosenfeld & Christopher E. Mason, Pervasive Sequence Patents Cover the Entire Human Genome, 5 Genome Med. 27 (2013).

2.   How might a trade secret approach to genetic discoveries differ from that of a gene patenting approach? What is the likely impact of each on research? What is the likely impact of each on the development of gene therapies?

3.   About one-quarter of gene patent holders did not allow any other physician or laboratory to test for "their" patented gene. The company holding the patent on a gene associated with Alzheimer disease, for example, would not let any laboratory except its own perform the test. Doctors and labs across the country faced a lawsuit if they tried to determine whether one of their patients has the genetic form of Alzheimer disease even though testing could easily be done by anyone who knows the gene sequence without using any product or device made by the patent holder.

This exclusivity impeded research to improve diagnosis. Various mutations in the same gene can cause a particular disease. But companies that do not let anyone else test for "their" gene make it more difficult to find mutations than if other labs were also testing the same gene. In countries where the Alzheimer gene and hemochromatosis gene were *not* patented, researchers found previously unknown mutations. These mutations could be used to diagnose people who would not otherwise be diagnosed.

4.   Most drugs only work on a percentage of patients who use them. Genetic testing can help distinguish those patients for whom a drug will work from those for whom it will not. But such tests will also limit the market for drugs. A pharmaceutical company filed for a patent on a genetic test to determine the effectiveness of one of its asthma drugs. But the company said it would not develop the test—or let anyone else develop it. Geeta Anand, Big Drug Makers Try to Postpone Custom Regimens, The Wall Street Journal, June 18, 2001, at B1. Should a company lose its patent in a case like this,

where the company is not developing the invention? There is a concept in trademark law, under 15 U.S.C. § 1127, whereby the owner can lose a trademark he or she does not use for three consecutive years (since part of the requirement for trademark protection is use in commerce).

Would your opinion change if the patent owner had reasons other than financial ones for wanting to prevent the creation or use of the patented invention? Some scientists have suggested creating a chimera, mixing human and chimp DNA to produce a subhuman species to do menial tasks. Biologist Stuart Newman filed a patent application on that technology. He planned to use the patent to prevent anyone from making such a creation for the 20-year period that he controlled the patent. His patent was denied on the grounds that the chimera "includes within its scope a human being" and people are not patentable. John Travis, Patently Unpatentable, 156 Science News 127 (1999).

IV.   CASE LAW ON PATENTABLE SUBJECT MATTER

DIAMOND V. CHAKRABARTY
447 U.S. 303 (1980).

BURGER, J.

We granted certiorari to determine whether a live, human-made micro-organism is patentable subject matter under 35 U.S.C. § 101.

I.

In 1972, respondent Chakrabarty, a microbiologist, filed a patent application, assigned to the General Electric Co. The application asserted 36 claims related to Chakrabarty's invention of "a bacterium from the genus *Pseudomonas* containing therein at least two stable energy-generating plasmids, each of said plasmids providing a separate hydrocarbon degradative pathway." This human-made, genetically engineered bacterium is capable of breaking down multiple components of crude oil. Because of this property, which is possessed by no naturally occurring bacteria, Chakrabarty's invention is believed to have significant value for the treatment of oil spills.

* * *

The patent examiner * * * rejected claims for the bacteria. His decision rested on two grounds: (1) that micro-organisms are "products of nature," and (2) that as living things they are not patentable subject matter under 35 U.S.C. § 101.

Chakrabarty appealed the rejection of these claims to the Patent Office Board of Appeals, and the Board affirmed the Examiner on the second ground. Relying on the legislative history of the 1930 Plant Patent Act, in which Congress extended patent protection to certain asexually reproduced plants, the Board concluded that § 101 was not intended to cover living things such as these laboratory created micro-organisms.

The Court of Customs and Patent Appeals, by a divided vote, reversed on the authority of its prior decision in In re Bergy, 563 F.2d 1031, 1038 (1977), which held that "the fact that microorganisms * * * are alive * * * [is] without legal significance" for purposes of the patent law.

* * *

II.

The Constitution grants Congress broad power to legislate to "promote the Progress of Science and useful Arts, by securing for limited Times to Authors and Inventors the exclusive Right to their respective Writings and Discoveries." Art. I, § 8, cl. 8. The patent laws promote this progress by offering inventors exclusive rights for a limited period as an incentive for their inventiveness and research efforts.

* * *

The question before us in this case is a narrow one of statutory interpretation requiring us to construe 35 U.S.C. § 101, which provides:

> Whoever invents or discovers any new and useful process, machine, manufacture, or composition of matter, or any new and useful improvement thereof, may obtain a patent therefor, subject to the conditions and requirements of this title.

Specifically, we must determine whether respondent's micro-organism constitutes a "manufacture" or "composition of matter" within the meaning of the statute.

III.

* * *

"[C]omposition of matter" has been construed consistent with its common usage to include "all compositions of two or more substances and * * * all composite articles, whether they be the results of chemical union, or of mechanical mixture, or whether they be gases, fluids, powders or solids." * * *

The relevant legislative history also supports a broad construction. The Patent Act of 1793, authored by Thomas Jefferson, defined statutory subject matter as "any new and useful art, machine, manufacture, or composition of matter, or any new or useful improvement [thereof]." The Committee Reports accompanying the 1952 Act inform us that Congress intended statutory subject matter to "include anything under the sun that is made by man."

This is not to suggest that § 101 has no limits or that it embraces every discovery. The laws of nature, physical phenomena, and abstract ideas have been held not patentable. Thus, a new mineral discovered in the earth or a new plant found in the wild is not patentable subject matter. Likewise, Einstein could not patent his celebrated law that $E=mc^2$; nor could Newton have patented the law of gravity. Such discoveries are "manifestations of * * * nature, free to all men and reserved exclusively to none."

Judged in this light, respondent's micro-organism plainly qualifies as patentable subject matter. His claim is not to a hitherto unknown natural phenomenon, but to a nonnaturally occurring manufacture or composition of matter—a product of human ingenuity "having a distinctive name, character [and] use." The point is underscored dramatically by comparison of the invention here with that in Funk [Brothers Seed Co. v. Kalo Inoculant Co., 333 U.S. 127 (1948)]. There, the patentee had discovered that there existed in nature certain species of root-nodule bacteria which did not exert a mutually inhibitive effect on each other. He used that discovery to produce a mixed culture capable of inoculating the seeds of leguminous plants. Concluding that the patentee had discovered "only some of the handiwork of nature," the Court ruled the product nonpatentable.

* * *

Here, by contrast, the patentee has produced a new bacterium with markedly different characteristics from any found in nature and one having the potential for significant utility. His discovery is not nature's handiwork, but his own; accordingly it is patentable subject matter under § 101.

* * *

Congress is free to amend § 101 so as to exclude from patent protection organisms produced by genetic engineering. Cf. 42 U.S.C. § 2181(a), exempting from patent protection inventions "useful solely in the utilization of special nuclear material or atomic energy in an atomic weapon." Or it may choose to craft a statute specifically designed for such living things. But, until Congress takes such action, this Court must construe the language of § 101 as it is.

* * *

BRENNAN, J., WHITE, J., MARSHALL, J., and POWELL, J. join, dissenting.

* * *

The sweeping language of the Patent Act of 1793, as re-enacted in 1952, is not the last pronouncement Congress has made in this area. In

1930 Congress enacted the Plant Patent Act affording patent protection to developers of certain asexually reproduced plants. In 1970 Congress enacted the Plant Variety Protection Act to extend protection to certain new plant varieties capable of sexual reproduction. Thus, we are not dealing—as the Court would have it—with the routine problem of "unanticipated inventions." In these two Acts Congress has addressed the general problem of patenting animate inventions and has chosen carefully limited language granting protection to some kinds of discoveries, but specifically excluding others. These Acts strongly evidence a congressional limitation that excludes bacteria from patentability.

First, the Acts evidence Congress' understanding, at least since 1930, that § 101 does not include living organisms. If newly developed living organisms not naturally occurring had been patentable under § 101, the plants included in the scope of the 1930 and 1970 Acts could have been patented without new legislation. Those plants, like the bacteria involved in this case, were new varieties not naturally occurring.

* * *

Congress plainly has legislated in the belief that § 101 does not encompass living organisms. It is the role of Congress, not this Court, to broaden or narrow the reach of the patent laws. This is especially true where, as here, the composition sought to be patented uniquely implicates matters of public concern.

ASSOCIATION FOR MOLECULAR PATHOLOGY V. MYRIAD GENETICS, INC.

569 U.S. ___, 133 S. Ct. 2107, 186 L.Ed.2d 124 (2013).

THOMAS, J.

Respondent Myriad Genetics, Inc. (Myriad), discovered the precise location and sequence of two human genes, mutations of which can substantially increase the risks of breast and ovarian cancer. Myriad obtained a number of patents based upon its discovery. This case involves claims from three of them and requires us to resolve whether a naturally occurring segment of deoxyribonucleic acid (DNA) is patent eligible under 35 U.S.C. § 101 by virtue of its isolation from the rest of the human genome. We also address the patent eligibility of synthetically created DNA known as complementary DNA (cDNA), which contains the same protein-coding information found in a segment of natural DNA but omits portions within the DNA segment that do not code for proteins. For the reasons that follow, we hold that a naturally occurring DNA segment is a product of nature and not patent eligible merely because it has been isolated, but that cDNA is patent eligible because it is not naturally occurring. We, therefore, affirm in part and reverse in part the decision of the United States Court of Appeals for the Federal Circuit.

* * *

Scientists can * * * extract DNA from cells using well known laboratory methods. These methods allow scientists to isolate specific segments of DNA—for instance, a particular gene or part of a gene—which can then be further studied, manipulated, or used. It is also possible to create DNA synthetically through processes similarly well known in the field of genetics. One such method begins with an mRNA molecule and uses the natural bonding properties of nucleotides to create a new, synthetic DNA molecule. The result is the inverse of the mRNA's inverse image of the original DNA, with one important distinction: Because the natural creation of mRNA involves splicing that removes introns, the synthetic DNA created from mRNA also contains only the exon sequences. This synthetic DNA created in the laboratory from mRNA is known as complementary DNA (cDNA).

Changes in the genetic sequence are called mutations. Mutations can be as small as the alteration of a single nucleotide—a change affecting only one letter in the genetic code. Such small-scale changes can produce an entirely different amino acid or can end protein production altogether. Large changes, involving the deletion, rearrangement, or duplication of hundreds or even millions of nucleotides, can result in the elimination, misplacement, or duplication of entire genes. Some mutations are harmless, but others can cause disease or increase the risk of disease. As a result, the study of genetics can lead to valuable medical breakthroughs.

* * *

Myriad discovered the precise location and sequence of what are now known as the BRCA1 and BRCA2 genes. * * * Before Myriad's discovery of the BRCA1 and BRCA2 genes, scientists knew that heredity played a role in establishing a woman's risk of developing breast and ovarian cancer, but they did not know which genes were associated with those cancers.

* * *

Once it found the location and sequence of the BRCA1 and BRCA2 genes, Myriad sought and obtained a number of patents. Nine composition claims from three of those patents are at issue in this case. Claims 1, 2, 5, and 6 from the '282 patent are representative. The first claim asserts a patent on "[a]n isolated DNA coding for a BRCA1 polypeptide," which has "the amino acid sequence set forth in SEQ ID NO:2." SEQ ID NO:2 sets forth a list of 1,863 amino acids that the typical

BRCA1 gene encodes. Put differently, claim 1 asserts a patent claim on the DNA code that tells a cell to produce the string of BRCA1 amino acids listed in SEQ ID NO:2.

Claim 2 of the '282 patent operates similarly. It claims "[t]he isolated DNA of claim 1, wherein said DNA has the nucleotide sequence set forth in SEQ ID NO:1." Like SEQ ID NO:2, SEQ ID NO:1 sets forth a long list of data, in this instance the sequence of cDNA that codes for the BRCA1 amino acids listed in claim 1. Importantly, SEQ ID NO:1 lists only the cDNA exons in the BRCA1 gene, rather than a full DNA sequence containing both exons and introns. As a result, the Federal Circuit recognized that claim 2 asserts a patent on the cDNA nucleotide sequence listed in SEQ ID NO:1, which codes for the typical BRCA1 gene.

Claim 5 of the '282 patent claims a subset of the data in claim 1. In particular, it claims "[a]n isolated DNA having at least 15 nucleotides of the DNA of claim 1." The practical effect of claim 5 is to assert a patent on any series of 15 nucleotides that exist in the typical BRCA1 gene. Because the BRCA1 gene is thousands of nucleotides long, even BRCA1 genes with substantial mutations are likely to contain at least one segment of 15 nucleotides that correspond to the typical BRCA1 gene. Similarly, claim 6 of the '282 patent claims "[a]n isolated DNA having at least 15 nucleotides of the DNA of claim 2." This claim operates similarly to claim 5, except that it references the cDNA-based claim 2. The remaining claims at issue are similar, though several list common mutations rather than typical BRCA1 and BRCA2 sequences.

Myriad's patents would, if valid, give it the exclusive right to isolate an individual's BRCA1 and BRCA2 genes (or any strand of 15 or more nucleotides within the genes) by breaking the covalent bonds that connect the DNA to the rest of the individual's genome. The patents would also give Myriad the exclusive right to synthetically create BRCA cDNA. In Myriad's view, manipulating BRCA DNA in either of these fashions triggers its "right to exclude others from making" its patented composition of matter under the Patent Act.

But isolation is necessary to conduct genetic testing, and Myriad was not the only entity to offer BRCA testing after it discovered the genes. The University of Pennsylvania's Genetic Diagnostic Laboratory (GDL) and others provided genetic testing services to women. Petitioner Dr. Harry Ostrer, then a researcher at New York University School of Medicine, routinely sent his patients' DNA samples to GDL for testing. After learning of GDL's testing and Ostrer's activities, Myriad sent letters to them asserting that the genetic testing infringed Myriad's patents. App. 94–95 (Ostrer letter). In response, GDL agreed to stop testing and informed Ostrer that it would no longer accept patient samples. Myriad also filed patent infringement suits against other entities that performed

BRCA testing, resulting in settlements in which the defendants agreed to cease all allegedly infringing activity. Myriad, thus, solidified its position as the only entity providing BRCA testing.

* * *

Section 101 of the Patent Act provides:

"Whoever invents or discovers any new and useful . . . composition of matter, or any new and useful improvement thereof, may obtain a patent therefor, subject to the conditions and requirements of this title." 35 U.S.C. § 101.

We have "long held that this provision contains an important implicit exception. Laws of nature, natural phenomena, and abstract ideas are not patentable." Rather, " 'they are the basic tools of scientific and technological work' " that lie beyond the domain of patent protection. As the Court has explained, without this exception, there would be considerable danger that the grant of patents would "tie up" the use of such tools and thereby "inhibit future innovation premised upon them." This would be at odds with the very point of patents, which exist to promote creation.

The rule against patents on naturally occurring things is not without limits, however, for "all inventions at some level embody, use, reflect, rest upon, or apply laws of nature, natural phenomena, or abstract ideas," and "too broad an interpretation of this exclusionary principle could eviscerate patent law." As we have recognized before, patent protection strikes a delicate balance between creating "incentives that lead to creation, invention, and discovery" and "imped[ing] the flow of information that might permit, indeed spur, invention." We must apply this well-established standard to determine whether Myriad's patents claim any "new and useful . . . composition of matter, § 101, or instead claim naturally occurring phenomena."

It is undisputed that Myriad did not create or alter any of the genetic information encoded in the BRCA1 and BRCA2 genes. The location and order of the nucleotides existed in nature before Myriad found them. Nor did Myriad create or alter the genetic structure of DNA. Instead, Myriad's principal contribution was uncovering the precise location and genetic sequence of the BRCA1 and BRCA2 genes within chromosomes 17 and 13. The question is whether this renders the genes patentable.

Myriad recognizes that our decision in [Diamond v.] Chakrabarty, 447 U.S. 303 (1980) is central to this inquiry. In *Chakrabarty,* * * * [t]he Court held that [a] modified bacterium was patentable [because] the patent claim was "not to a hitherto unknown natural phenomenon, but to a nonnaturally occurring manufacture or composition of matter—a product of human ingenuity 'having a distinctive name, character [and] use.'" * * * In this case, by contrast, Myriad did not create anything. To be sure, it found an important and useful gene, but separating that gene from its surrounding genetic material is not an act of invention.

Groundbreaking, innovative, or even brilliant discovery does not by itself satisfy the § 101 inquiry. In Funk Brothers Seed Co. v. Kalo Inoculant Co., 333 U.S. 127 (1948), this Court considered a composition patent that claimed a mixture of naturally occurring strains of bacteria that helped leguminous plants take nitrogen from the air and fix it in the soil. * * * The Court held that the composition was not patent eligible because the patent holder did not alter the bacteria in any way. His patent claim thus fell squarely within the law of nature exception. So do Myriad's. Myriad found the location of the BRCA1 and BRCA2 genes, but that discovery, by itself, does not render the BRCA genes "new . . . composition[s] of matter," § 101, that are patent eligible.

* * * Myriad's patent descriptions simply detail the "iterative process" of discovery by which Myriad narrowed the possible locations for the gene sequences that it sought. Myriad seeks to import these extensive research efforts into the § 101 patent-eligibility inquiry. But extensive effort alone is insufficient to satisfy the demands of § 101.

Nor are Myriad's claims saved by the fact that isolating DNA from the human genome severs chemical bonds and thereby creates a nonnaturally occurring molecule. * * * If the patents depended upon the creation of a unique molecule, then a would-be infringer could arguably avoid at least Myriad's patent claims on entire genes (such as claims 1 and 2 of the '282 patent) by isolating a DNA sequence that included both the BRCA1 or BRCA2 gene and one additional nucleotide pair. Such a molecule would not be chemically identical to the molecule "invented" by Myriad. But Myriad obviously would resist that outcome because its claim is concerned primarily with the information contained in the genetic *sequence,* not with the specific chemical composition of a particular molecule.

* * *

Further undercutting the PTO's practice, the United States argued in the Federal Circuit and in this Court that isolated DNA was *not* patent eligible under § 101, and that the PTO's practice was not "a sufficient reason to hold that isolated DNA is patent-eligible." These concessions weigh against deferring to the PTO's determination.

cDNA does not present the same obstacles to patentability as naturally occurring, isolated DNA segments. As already explained, creation of a cDNA sequence from mRNA results in an exons-only molecule that is not naturally occurring. Petitioners concede that cDNA differs from natural DNA in that "the non-coding regions have been removed." They nevertheless argue that cDNA is not patent eligible because "[t]he nucleotide sequence of cDNA is dictated by nature, not by the lab technician." That may be so, but the lab technician unquestionably creates something new when cDNA is made. cDNA retains the naturally occurring exons of DNA, but it is distinct from the DNA from which it was derived. As a result, cDNA is not a "product of nature" and is patent eligible under § 101, except insofar as very short series of DNA may have no intervening introns to remove when creating cDNA. In that situation, a short strand of cDNA may be indistinguishable from natural DNA.

HARVARD COLLEGE V. CANADA (COMMISSIONER OF PATENTS)

[2002] 4 S.C.R. 45.

* * *

BASTARACHE, J.

I.   INTRODUCTION

118 This appeal raises the issue of the patentability of higher life forms within the context of the *Patent Act*, R.S.C. 1985, c. P-4. The respondent, the President and Fellows of Harvard College, seeks to patent a mouse that has been genetically altered to increase its susceptibility to cancer, which makes it useful for cancer research. The patent claims also extend to all non-human mammals which have been similarly altered.

119 The Commissioner of Patents upheld the Patent Examiner's refusal to grant the patent. This decision was in turn upheld by the Federal Court, Trial Division, but was overturned by a majority of the Federal Court of Appeal. * * *

120 * * * [T]he sole question is whether Parliament intended the definition of "invention", and more particularly the words "manufacture" or "composition of matter", within the context of the *Patent Act*, to encompass higher life forms such as the oncomouse. In my opinion, Parliament did not intend higher life forms to be patentable. Had Parliament intended every conceivable subject matter to be patentable, it would not have chosen to adopt an exhaustive definition that limits invention to any "art, process, machine, manufacture or composition of matter". In addition, the phrases "manufacture" and "composition of matter" do not correspond to common understandings of animal and plant life. Even accepting that the words of the definition can support a broad interpretation, they must be interpreted in light of the scheme of the Act and the relevant context. The Act in its current form fails to address many of the unique concerns that are raised by the patenting of higher life forms, a factor which indicates that Parliament never intended the

definition of "invention" to extend to this type of subject matter. Given the unique concerns associated with the grant of a monopoly right over higher life forms, it is my view that Parliament would not likely choose the *Patent Act* as it currently exists as the appropriate vehicle to protect the rights of inventors of this type of subject matter.

II. FACTUAL BACKGROUND

121 On June 21, 1985, the respondent, the President and Fellows of Harvard College ("Harvard"), applied for a patent on an invention entitled "transgenic animals". The invention aims to produce animals with a susceptibility to cancer for purposes of animal carcinogenic studies. * * *

122 The technology by which a cancer-prone mouse ("oncomouse") is produced is described in the patent application disclosure. * * *

123 In its patent application, the respondent seeks to protect both the process by which the oncomice are produced and the end product of the process, i.e. the founder mice and the offspring whose cells are affected by the oncogene. The process and product claims also extend to all non-human mammals. In March 1993, by Final Action, a Patent Examiner rejected the product claims (claims 1 to 12) as being outside the scope of the definition of "invention" in s. 2 of the *Patent Act*, but allowed the process claims (claims 13 to 26). In August 1995, * * * the Commissioner confirmed the refusal to grant a patent for claims 1 to 12. The Federal Court, Trial Division dismissed the respondent's appeal from the decision of the Commissioner. The respondent's further appeal to the Federal Court of Appeal was allowed by a majority of the court, Isaac J.A. dissenting. The Commissioner of Patents appeals from that decision.

III. RELEVANT STATUTORY PROVISIONS

124 Patent Act, R.S.C. 1985, c. P–4

> 2. In this Act, except as otherwise provided,
>
> "invention" means any new and useful art, process, machine, manufacture or composition of matter, or any new and useful improvement in any art, process, machine, manufacture or composition of matter;

* * *

V. ANALYSIS

* * *

B. *The Definition of "Invention": Whether a Higher Life Form Is a "Manufacture" or a "Composition of Matter"*

* * *

155 Having considered the relevant factors, I conclude that Parliament did not intend to include higher life forms within the definition of "invention" found in the *Patent Act*. In their grammatical and ordinary sense alone, the words "manufacture" and "composition of matter" are somewhat imprecise and ambiguous. However, it is my view that the best reading of the words of the Act supports the conclusion that higher life forms are not patentable. As I discuss below, I do not believe that a higher life form such as the oncomouse is easily understood as either a "manufacture" or a "composition of matter". For this reason, I am not satisfied that the definition of "invention" in the *Patent Act* is sufficiently broad to include higher life forms. This conclusion is supported by the fact that the patenting of higher life forms raises unique concerns which do not arise in respect of non-living inventions and which are not addressed by the scheme of the Act. Even if a higher life form could, scientifically, be regarded as a "composition of matter", the scheme of the Act indicates that the patentability of higher life forms was not contemplated by Parliament. Owing to the fact that the patenting of higher life forms is a highly contentious and complex matter that raises serious practical, ethical and environmental concerns that the Act does not contemplate, I conclude that the Commissioner was correct to reject the patent application. This is a policy issue that raises questions of great significance and importance and that would appear to require a dramatic expansion of the traditional patent regime. Absent explicit legislative direction, the Court should not order the Commissioner to grant a patent on a higher life form.

* * *

In [Diamond v.] Chakrabarty, [447 U.S. 303,] 308 [(1980)], "manufacture" was defined as

> the production of articles for use from raw or prepared materials by giving to these materials new forms, qualities, properties, or combinations, whether by hand-labor or by machinery.

These definitions use the terminology of "article", "material", and *"objet technique"*. Is a mouse an "article", "material", or an *"objet technique"*? In my view, while a mouse may be analogized to a "manufacture" when it is produced in an industrial setting, the word in its vernacular sense does not include a higher life form. * * * In my opinion, a complex life form such as a mouse or a chimpanzee cannot easily be characterized as "something made by the hands of man".

160 As regards the meaning of the words "composition of matter", I believe that they must be defined more narrowly than was the case in *Chakrabarty*, namely "all compositions of two or more substances and ... all composite articles". If the words "composition of matter" are understood this broadly, then the other listed categories of invention, including "machine" and "manufacture", become redundant. This implies that "composition of matter" must be limited in some way. Although I do not express an opinion as to where the line should be drawn, I conclude that "composition of matter" does not include a higher life form such as the oncomouse.

* * *

164 Lastly, I wish also to address Rothstein J.A.'s assertion that "[t]he language of patent law is broad and general and is to be given wide scope because inventions are, necessarily, unanticipated and unforeseeable" (para. 116). In my view, it does not thereby follow that all proposed inventions are patentable. * * * Although Parliament would not have foreseen the genetically altered mouse and the process of genetic engineering used to produce it, Parliament was well aware of animal husbandry or breeding. * * * Yet Parliament chose to define the categories of invention using language that does not, in common usage, refer to higher life forms. * * *

* * *

166 Patenting higher life forms would involve a radical departure from the traditional patent regime. Moreover, the patentability of such life forms is a highly contentious matter that raises a number of extremely complex issues. If higher life forms are to be patentable, it must be under the clear and unequivocal direction of Parliament. For the reasons discussed above, I conclude that the current Act does not clearly indicate that higher life forms are patentable. * * * [T]he Act supports the opposite conclusion—that higher life forms such as the oncomouse are not currently patentable in Canada.

* * *

VI. CONCLUSION

207 For the reasons given above, the appeal is allowed. No order as to costs will be given in light of the Commissioner's oral submissions.

QUESTION

1.   The United States and Canada have taken different positions on the patentability of the Harvard oncomouse. A patent on the oncomouse was granted by the USPTO (U.S. Patent No. 4,736,866) on April 12, 1988, and has not been subject to a challenge of its validity. How might the United States

Supreme Court have ruled if the oncomouse patent was challenged under 35 U.S.C. § 101 for being a non-patentable subject matter?

V. INTERNATIONAL ASPECTS OF BIOTECH PATENTS

DIRECTIVE 98/44/EC OF THE EUROPEAN PARLIAMENT AND OF THE COUNCIL OF 6 JULY 1998 ON THE LEGAL PROTECTION OF BIOTECHNOLOGICAL INVENTIONS

Official Journal of the European Communities L 213, 30/07/1998 P.0013–0021.

CHAPTER I.   PATENTABILITY

Article 1

1.   Member States shall protect biotechnological inventions under national patent law. They shall, if necessary, adjust their national patent law to take account of the provisions of this Directive.

* * *

Article 2

1.   For the purposes of this Directive,

(a) "biological material" means any material containing genetic information and capable of reproducing itself or being reproduced in a biological system;

(b) "microbiological process" means any process involving or performed upon or resulting in microbiological material.

* * *

Article 3

1.   For the purposes of this Directive, inventions which are new, which involve an inventive step and which are susceptible of industrial application shall be patentable even if they concern a product consisting of or containing biological material or a process by means of which biological material is produced, processed or used.

2.   Biological material which is isolated from its natural environment or produced by means of a technical process may be the subject of an invention even if it previously occurred in nature.

Article 4

1.   The following shall not be patentable:

(a) plant and animal varieties;

(b) essentially biological processes for the production of plants or animals.

2.   Inventions which concern plants or animals shall be patentable if the technical feasibility of the invention is not confined to a particular plant or animal variety.

3.   Paragraph 1(b) shall be without prejudice to the patentability of inventions which concern a microbiological or other technical process or a product obtained by means of such a process.

Article 5

1.   The human body, at the various stages of its formation and development, and the simple discovery of one of its elements, including the sequence or partial sequence of a gene, cannot constitute patentable inventions.

2.   An element isolated from the human body or otherwise produced by means of a technical process, including the sequence or partial sequence of a gene, may constitute a patentable invention, even if the structure of that element is identical to that of a natural element.

3.   The industrial application of a sequence or a partial sequence of a gene must be disclosed in the patent application.

Article 6

1.   Inventions shall be considered unpatentable where their commercial exploitation would be contrary to *ordre public* or morality; however, exploitation shall not be deemed to be so contrary merely because it is prohibited by law or regulation.

2.   On the basis of paragraph 1, the following, in particular, shall be considered unpatentable:

(a)   processes for cloning human beings;

(b)   processes for modifying the germ line genetic identity of human beings;

(c)   uses of human embryos for industrial or commercial purposes;

(d)   processes for modifying the genetic identity of animals which are likely to cause them suffering without any substantial medical benefit to man or animal, and also animals resulting from such processes.

AGREEMENT ON TRADE-RELATED ASPECTS OF INTELLECTUAL PROPERTY RIGHTS (TRIPS)

www.wto.org/english/docs_e/legal_e/27-trips.pdf.

Section 5: Patents

Article 27 Patentable Subject Matter

1. Subject to the provisions of paragraphs 2 and 3 below, patents shall be available for any inventions, whether products or processes, in all fields of technology, provided that they are new, involve an inventive step and are capable of industrial application * * *. [P]atents shall be available and patent rights enjoyable without discrimination as to the place of invention, the field of technology and whether products are imported or locally produced.

2. Members may exclude from patentability inventions, the prevention within their territory of the commercial exploitation of which is necessary to protect *ordre public* or morality, including to protect human, animal or plant life or health or to avoid serious prejudice to the environment, provided that such exclusion is not made merely because the exploitation is prohibited by domestic law.

3. Members may also exclude from patentability:

    (a) diagnostic, therapeutic and surgical methods for the treatment of humans or animals;

    (b) plants and animals other than microorganisms, and essentially biological processes for the production of plants or animals other than non-biological and microbiological processes. However, Members shall provide for the protection of plant varieties either by patents or by an effective *sui generis* system or by any combination thereof. The provisions of this subparagraph shall be reviewed four years after the date of entry into force of the WTO [World Trade Organization] Agreement.

VI. TECHNOLOGY TRANSFER LAWS AND COMMERCIALIZATION

JAMES V. LACY ET AL., TECHNOLOGY TRANSFER LAWS
GOVERNING FEDERALLY FUNDED RESEARCH
AND DEVELOPMENT
19 Pepp. L. Rev. 1, 9–11, 13–14 (1991).

Economists have long realized that innovation affects demand and is thus one of the key forces that drives capitalism. A robust economy requires investment in research and development, as technological change most often results in production shifts, which can form the cornerstone of economic development and expansion. Technological innovation, however, can only be economically meaningful when it impacts the market. Therefore, a good idea which is never commercialized simply remains only a good idea.

The absence of a federal technology transfer policy prior to 1980 resulted in an enormous investment of money in R & D, which yielded a great deal of government-owned, but unlicensed, patents. Technological, bureaucratic, legal and communications problems, as well as a lack of basic incentives, prevented the transfer of this technology to American industry.

* * *

The commercialization of federal technology is a complicated problem. Historically, there were no incentives for institutions or individuals who performed government research to produce commercially viable technology. A major stumbling block was the lack of a statutory basis for royalty sharing. Without such explicit authority, it was unlikely that inventors in the public sector would be motivated by salary alone.

* * *

An economic parable states: "Lease a man a garden and in time he will leave you a patch of sand. Make a man a full owner of a patch of sand and he will grow there a garden on the sand." This parable highlights one of the basic problems with federal patent policy and technology transfer prior to 1980. There was no incentive for government inventors or institutions to create commercially viable technology because there was no legal basis to gain a piece of the resulting monetary rewards. As a result, commercially viable technology was not being created, and the wealth of federal inventions that were available for licensing were not being transferred for use in the private sector.

* * *

As a result of this concern, Congress enacted a series of bipartisan initiatives in the 1980s. These initiatives were aimed at revising government patent policy, reducing legal and bureaucratic barriers, and creating incentives to improve federal technology transfer to the private sector.

* * *

In short, recipients of government contracts, grants and cooperative agreements for the performance of experimental, developmental or research work funded in whole or in part by the federal government may now elect to retain title to any subject invention made in the course of that work.

* * *

[T]he government by statute must retain certain residual rights to the invention, including a government-use license to practice the invention, the right to limit exclusive licenses into which the funding recipient may wish to enter, and so-called "march-in" rights.

The government-use license that the Bayh-Dole Act imposes on contractors and grantees must provide the federal government with, at a minimum, "a nonexclusive, nontransferable, irrevocable, paid-up license to practice or have practiced for or on behalf of the United States any subject invention throughout the world." The statute also provides that the license may provide for such additional rights in favor of the government as are determined to be necessary by the government agency entering into grant, contract or cooperative agreement.

* * *

Finally, the government retains so-called "march-in" rights to inventions made with full or partial government funding. The government is provided the right to "march-in" and retake title to inventions in those cases where: (1) "action is necessary because the contractor or assignee has not taken, or is not expected to take within a reasonable time, effective steps to achieve practical application of the subject invention;" or (2) "action is necessary to alleviate health or safety needs which are not reasonably satisfied" by the contractor or grantee; or (3) "action is necessary to meet requirements for public use specified by Federal regulations and such requirements are not reasonably satisfied" by the contractor or grantee; or (4) the contractor or grantee has granted an exclusive license in violation of the "Preference for United States Industry."

SHELDON KRIMSKY, THE PROFIT OF SCIENTIFIC DISCOVERY AND ITS NORMATIVE IMPLICATIONS
75 Chi.–Kent L. Rev. 15, 21–22, 28–37 (1999).

[S]everal pieces of legislation were enacted in 1980 to create more cooperation between industries and universities. The Stevenson-Wydler Technology Transfer Act of 1980 encouraged interaction and cooperation among government laboratories, universities, big industries and small businesses. In the same year, Congress passed the Bayh-Dole Patent and Trademark Laws Amendment, which gave intellectual property rights to research findings to institutions that had received federal grants. Discoveries and inventions from public funds could be patented and licensed, initially to small businesses, with exclusive rights of royalties given to the grantee * * *. In 1983, by executive order, President Reagan extended the Bayh-Dole Act to all industry. To close the circle of research partnerships among industry, universities and government, Congress passed the Federal Technology Transfer Act of 1986, which expanded science-industry collaboration to laboratories run by the federal government. Governmental standards for keeping an arm's length from industry were being turned on their head. Through this act, a government scientist could form a "Cooperative Research and Development Agreement" ("CRADA") with a company as a route to commercializing discoveries made in a federal laboratory. Government scientists could accept royalty income up to a given amount [$150,000], fifteen percent of the National Institutes of Health (the "NIH") share, to supplement their salaries. At the time this policy was enacted, there was virtually no public discussion about the blatant conflicts of interest that this would introduce. The CRADA required government scientists to keep company data confidential and impeded the sharing of information in government laboratories.

* * *

By the mid-1980s, genetic technology had spawned hundreds of new companies, many with academic scientists as officers, board members or consultants. Small venture capital companies colonized the faculty of prestigious universities for building their intellectual capital. Major corporations that had sector interests in drugs, therapeutics, and agriculture invested large sums into multi-year contracts with universities.

* * *

A number of studies published in the early 1990s began to shed some light on the extent to which the burgeoning field of biotechnology had begun to impact universities.

* * *

* * * [T]hese new arrangements * * * impeded the "free, rapid, and unbiased dissemination of research results." Biotechnology faculty with industry support were four times as likely as other biotechnology faculty to report that trade secrets had resulted from their research. The vast majority of the faculty without industry support viewed the commercial relationships as undermining intellectual exchange and cooperation within departments. The surveys also revealed that faculty believed the new relationships were responsible for skewing the research agenda in biology toward applied research.

* * *

[T]wo concerns flowing from the intense commercialization of science that could not be resolved by ethical standards established within universities were conflicts of interest and scientific bias * * *. Of the 789 articles and 1105 Massachusetts authors reviewed in * * * [a] study, thirty-four percent of the papers met one or more of the criteria for possessing a financial interest. Furthermore, none of the articles revealed the authors' financial interests.

* * *

[A] study which appeared in the Journal of General Internal Medicine reported that clinical trials sponsored by pharmaceutical companies were much more likely to favor new drugs (an outcome beneficial to the sponsoring companies in this case) than studies not supported by the companies.

A recent study [found] that * * * those authors who were supportive of the obesity drugs were significantly more likely than the authors who were neutral or critical of the drugs to have a financial agreement with a manufacturer of a calcium channel blocker (ninety-six percent, sixty percent and thirty-seven percent respectively).

* * *

Because every biomedical discovery has potential monetary value, the new culture of science will seek to protect that discovery from becoming part of the "knowledge commons." * * * Scientists, instead of sharing their discoveries in a timely fashion, are protecting them as trade secrets. This has resulted in wasteful duplication of research, not for the sake of verifying results, but rather for establishing the unpublished data needed to secure intellectual property rights over the discovery. Writing in Science, Eliot Marshall noted, "[w]hile some duplication is normal in research, experts say it is getting out of hand in microbe sequencing. Tuberculosis, like Staph aureus and H. pylori will be sequenced many times over in part because sequencers aren't sharing data, whether for business reasons or because of interlab rivalries."

* * *

Companies have taken out patents on disease causing bacteria and viruses, sometimes keeping confidential parts of the sequenced genome. This may inhibit two companies competing in the search for a cure or treatment for a disease. Why should anyone own the natural sequence of a natural microorganism? Pharmaceutical companies can now exercise property ownership over both the drug to treat a disease and the microorganism that causes it. The intense privatization of biomedical knowledge that has evolved since the 1980s threatens the entire edifice of public health medicine.

LORI ANDREWS & DOROTHY NELKIN, BODY BAZAAR: THE
MARKET FOR HUMAN TISSUE IN THE BIOTECHNOLOGY AGE
60–62 (2001).

Nowhere are these fundamental changes in scientific research more evident than at the National Institutes of Health, where scientists who are paid with taxpayer dollars can patent their research and pad their salaries with royalties. Allowing publicly-funded researchers to gain commercially, however, means that government-funded laboratories are experiencing some of the same problems with secrecy and conflicts of interest as industry-funded academic laboratories.

When government scientists enter joint ventures with business, their lips must be sealed concerning their data. Cooperative research and development agreements (CRADAs) restrict free access of information in NIH labs because of the requirement that company data be kept confidential. Anthony S. Fauci, the director of the National Institute of Allergy and Infectious Diseases, is worried about the effect of "CRADA fever." For the first time in his several decades at NIH, he says, scientists are reluctant to share information.

Leslie Roberts, writing in Science, points out, "The obvious concern is that some investigators might use the resources developed with public funds for their own proprietary interest. Yet another question is how will the genome project receive impartial advice when nearly everyone has a financial stake in it?"

People increasingly feel they are paying twice for research—once to the government to fund the research, and then again to the biotech companies who sell them products developed from taxpayer-funded research. In the pharmaceutical field, patents are generally thought to be necessary in order to encourage the discovery of drugs, and to fund the testing of these drugs on animals and humans. But genetic discoveries are very different from drug development. The public pays for the research that yields discoveries of genetic associations with disease. Genetic testing can be applied to humans as soon as the gene is accurately identified, without costly clinical trials. Financial compensation is thus less warranted.

The high costs of genetic tests and treatments seems ludicrous, given that taxpayers have provided much of the funding for their discovery. The NIH paid $4.6 million toward discovery of a gene predisposing women to breast cancer.

This situation—in which private companies [such as Myriad, which holds the patent on the BRCA1 gene and the BRCA2 gene predisposing to cancer] get a boost from taxpayer-funded research—occurs daily. Sixty-three percent of gene patents are based on research funded with federal money. The same thing occurs with funding for drug research. A Boston Globe investigative report revealed "a billion-dollar taxpayers' subsidy for pharmaceutical companies already awash in profits." Of the 50 top-selling drugs, 48 benefited from federal research money in their development or testing phases. A kidney cancer drug, Proleukin, benefited from $46 million in research funds. Patients nevertheless pay up to $20,000 per treatment. Taxcol, a breast and ovarian cancer treatment, received a $27 million federal subsidy; the treatment cost—$5,500.

Federal subsidies could have a much different impact on drug prices. The federal research handout could come with a requirement that the drug company lower prices to the consumer.

* * *

Protests against federal subsidies of pharmaceutical companies erupted in the 1980s around the drug AZT, which was developed through taxpayer-funded research at the National Cancer Institute. Studies in 1986 determined that AZT could be used to treat AIDS, and the FDA rapidly approved the drug. Burroughs-Wellcome received the exclusive right to market the drug and charged $10,000 to $12,000 for a year's supply. AIDS activists questioned the high price, given that the drug's development had been subsidized by the federal government. In response, Burroughs-Wellcome lowered the price to $2,500 and in 1989 the NIH responded by imposing a "reasonable pricing clause" in its subsequent contracts with companies. The reasonable pricing clause required companies to which the NIH licensed its products to prove that there was "a reasonable relationship between the pricing of license product, the public investment in the product, and health and safety needs of the public." This approach made good sense, but in April 1995 NIH Director Harold Varmus unilaterally decided to eliminate the reasonable pricing clause. A federal bill to reinstate it has been introduced in Congress, but at this writing it is languishing in committee. U.S. Representative Bernard Sanders of Vermont suggests a more direct approach: cutting the prices of drugs that are developed with public funds.

NOTES AND QUESTIONS

1.   What was the purpose of the technology transfer laws?

2.   Should products such as genetic tests or gene therapies that are developed with substantial amounts of public funds be priced or marketed differently than privately developed tests and therapies?

3.   When a researcher has a financial interest in the gene or drug that he or she studies, should that fact be disclosed in publications? Since the publication of the Krimsky article, the journal Nature has changed its policy and now requires disclosures of conflicts of interest.

4. If you wanted to design a study to determine if the technology transfer laws have been effective, how would you do it? How would you define and measure "success"? The number of patents obtained by government employees and federally-funded researchers has increased since the laws' passage. Is that a sufficient indicator of success?

VII. PATIENTS: THE SOURCES OF GENES AND CELL LINES

Patent on John Moore's cells   John Moore

MOORE V. REGENTS OF THE UNIVERSITY OF CALIFORNIA
793 P.2d 479 (Cal. 1990).

PANELLI, J.

We granted review in this case to determine whether plaintiff has stated a cause of action against his physician and other defendants for using his cells in potentially lucrative medical research without his permission. Plaintiff alleges that his physician failed to disclose preexisting research and economic interests in the cells before obtaining consent to the medical procedures by which they were extracted.

* * *

The plaintiff is John Moore (Moore), who underwent treatment for hairy-cell leukemia at the Medical Center of the University of California at Los Angeles (UCLA Medical Center). The five defendants are: (1) Dr. David W. Golde (Golde), a physician who attended Moore at UCLA Medical Center; (2) the Regents of the University of California (Regents), who own and operate the university; (3) Shirley G. Quan, a researcher employed by the Regents; (4) Genetics Institute, Inc. (Genetics Institute); and (5) Sandoz Pharmaceuticals Corporation and related entities (collectively Sandoz).

Moore first visited UCLA Medical Center on October 5, 1976, shortly after he learned that he had hairy-cell leukemia. After hospitalizing Moore and "withdr[awing] extensive amounts of blood, bone marrow aspirate, and other bodily substances," Golde confirmed that diagnosis. At this time all defendants, including Golde, were aware that "certain blood products and blood components were of great value in a number of commercial and scientific efforts" and that access to a patient whose blood contained these substances would provide "competitive, commercial, and scientific advantages."

On October 8, 1976, Golde recommended that Moore's spleen be removed. Golde informed Moore "that he had reason to fear for his life, and that the proposed splenectomy operation . . . was necessary to slow down the progress of his disease." Based upon Golde's representations, Moore signed a written consent form authorizing the splenectomy.

Before the operation, Golde and Quan "formed the intent and made arrangements to obtain portions of [Moore's] spleen following its removal" and to take them to a separate research unit. Golde gave written instructions to this effect on October 18 and 19, 1976. These research activities "were not intended to have . . . any relation to [Moore's] medical . . . care." However, neither Golde nor Quan informed Moore of their plans to conduct this research or requested his permission. Surgeons at UCLA Medical Center, whom the complaint does not name as defendants, removed Moore's spleen on October 20, 1976.

Moore returned to the UCLA Medical Center several times between November 1976 and September 1983. He did so at Golde's direction and based upon representations "that such visits were necessary and required for his health and well-being, and based upon the trust inherent in and by virtue of the physician-patient relationship. . . ." On each of these visits Golde withdrew additional samples of "blood, blood serum, skin, bone marrow aspirate, and sperm." On each occasion Moore travelled to the UCLA Medical Center from his home in Seattle because he had been told that the procedures were to be performed only there and only under Golde's direction.

"In fact, [however,] throughout the period of time that [Moore] was under [Golde's] care and treatment, . . . the defendants were actively involved in a number of activities which they concealed from [Moore]. . . ." Specifically, defendants were conducting research on Moore's cells and planned to "benefit financially and competitively . . . [by exploiting the cells] and [their] exclusive access to [the cells] by virtue of [Golde's] on-going physician-patient relationship. . . ."

Sometime before August 1979, Golde established a cell line from Moore's T-lymphocytes.[2] On January 30, 1981, the Regents applied for a patent on the cell line, listing Golde and Quan as inventors. "[B]y virtue of an established policy . . ., [the] Regents, Golde, and Quan would share in any royalties or profits . . . arising out of [the] patent." The patent issued on March 20, 1984, naming Golde and Quan as the inventors of the cell line and the Regents as the assignee of the patent. (U.S. Patent No. 4,438,032 (Mar. 20, 1984).)

The Regent's patent also covers various methods for using the cell line to produce lymphokines. Moore admits in his complaint that "the true clinical potential of each of the lymphokines . . . [is] difficult to predict, [but] . . . competing commercial firms in these relevant fields have published reports in biotechnology industry periodicals predicting a potential market of approximately $3.01 Billion Dollars by the year 1990 for a whole range of [such lymphokines]. . . ."

* * *

Based upon these allegations, Moore attempted to state 13 causes of action. [These were: (1) conversion; (2) lack of informed consent; (3) breach of fiduciary duty; (4) fraud and deceit; (5) unjust enrichment; (6) quasi-contract; (7) bad faith breach of the implied covenant of good faith and fair dealing; (8) intentional infliction of emotional distress; (9) negligent misrepresentation; (10) intentional interference with prospective advantageous economic relationships; (11) slander of title; (12) accounting; and (13) declaratory relief.] Each defendant demurred to each purported cause of action. The superior court, however, expressly

---

[2] A T-lymphocyte is a type of white blood cell. T-lymphocytes produce lymphokines, or proteins that regulate the immune system. Some lymphokines have potential therapeutic value. If the genetic material responsible for producing a particular lymphokine can be identified, it can sometimes be used to manufacture large quantities of the lymphokine through the techniques of recombinant DNA. (See generally U.S. Congress, Office of Technology Assessment, *New Developments in Biotechnology: Ownership of Human Tissues and Cells* (1987) at pp. 31–46 (hereafter OTA Report)) * * *.

While the genetic code for lymphokines does not vary from individual to individual, it can nevertheless be quite difficult to locate the gene responsible for a particular lymphokine. Because T-lymphocytes produce many different lymphokines, the relevant gene is often like a needle in a haystack. (OTA Rep., supra, p. 42.) Moore's T-lymphocytes were interesting to the defendants because they overproduced certain lymphokines, thus making the corresponding genetic material easier to identify. (In published research papers, defendants and other researchers have shown that the overproduction was caused by a virus, and that normal T-lymphocytes infected by the virus will also overproduce * * *.)

Cells taken directly from the body (primary cells) are not very useful for these purposes. Primary cells typically reproduce a few times and then die. One can, however, sometimes continue to use cells for an extended period of time by developing them into a "cell line," a culture capable of reproducing indefinitely. This is not, however, always an easy task. "Long-term growth of human cells and tissues is difficult, often an art," and the probability of succeeding with any given cell sample is low, except for a few types of cells not involved in this case.

considered the validity of only the first cause of action, conversion [and rejected it] * * *.

[T]he Court of Appeal reversed, holding that the complaint did state a cause of action for conversion * * *.

A.   BREACH OF FIDUCIARY DUTY AND LACK OF INFORMED CONSENT

Moore repeatedly alleges that Golde failed to disclose the extent of his research and economic interests in Moore's cells before obtaining consent to the medical procedures by which the cells were extracted. These allegations, in our view, state a cause of action against Golde for invading a legally protected interest of his patient. This cause of action can properly be characterized either as the breach of a fiduciary duty to disclose facts material to the patient's consent or, alternatively, as the performance of medical procedures without first having obtained the patient's informed consent.

Our analysis begins with three well-established principles. First, "a person of adult years and in sound mind has the right, in the exercise of control over his own body, to determine whether or not to submit to lawful medical treatment." Second, "the patient's consent to treatment, to be effective, must be an informed consent." Third, in soliciting the patient's consent, a physician has a fiduciary duty to disclose all information material to the patient's decision.

These principles lead to the following conclusions: (1) a physician must disclose personal interests unrelated to the patient's health, whether research or economic, that may affect the physician's professional judgment; and (2) a physician's failure to disclose such interests may give rise to a cause of action for performing medical procedures without informed consent or breach of fiduciary duty.

* * *

Indeed, the law already recognizes that a reasonable patient would want to know whether a physician has an economic interest that might affect the physician's professional judgment. As the Court of Appeal has said, "[c]ertainly a sick patient deserves to be free of any reasonable suspicion that his doctor's judgment is influenced by a profit motive." The desire to protect patients from possible conflicts of interest has also motivated legislative enactments. Among these is Business and Professions Code section 654.2. Under that section, a physician may not charge a patient on behalf of, or refer a patient to, any organization in which the physician has a "significant beneficial interest, unless [the physician] first discloses in writing to the patient, that there is such an interest and advises the patient that the patient may choose any organization for the purposes of obtaining the services ordered or requested by [the physician]." Similarly, under Health and Safety Code section 24173, a physician who plans to conduct a medical experiment on a patient must, among other things, inform the patient of "[t]he name of the sponsor or funding source, if any, . . . and the organization, if any, under whose general aegis the experiment is being conducted."

* * *

Yet a physician who treats a patient in whom he also has a research interest has potentially conflicting loyalties. This is because medical treatment decisions are made on the basis of proportionality—weighing the benefits *to the patient* against the risks *to the patient*. * * * A physician who adds his own research interests to this balance may be tempted to order a scientifically useful procedure or test that offers marginal, or no, benefits to the patient. The possibility that an interest extraneous to the patient's health has affected the physician's judgment is something that a reasonable patient would want to know in deciding whether to consent to a proposed course of treatment. It is material to the patient's decision and, thus, a prerequisite to informed consent.

* * *

B.   CONVERSION

Moore also attempts to characterize the invasion of his rights as a conversion—a tort that protects against interference with possessory and ownership interests in personal property. He theorizes that he continued to own his cells following their removal from his body, at least for the purpose of directing their use, and that he never consented to their use in potentially lucrative medical research. Thus, to complete Moore's argument, defendants' unauthorized use of his cells constitutes a conversion. As a result of the alleged conversion, Moore claims a proprietary interest in each of the products that any of the defendants might ever create from his cells or the patented cell line.

* * *

Since Moore clearly did not expect to retain possession of his cells following their removal, to sue for their conversion he must have retained an ownership interest in them. But there are several reasons to doubt that he did retain any such interest. First, no reported judicial decision supports Moore's claim, either directly or by close analogy. Second, California statutory law drastically limits any continuing interest of a patient in excised cells. Third, the subject matters of the Regents' patent—the patented cell line and the products derived from it—cannot be Moore's property.

Neither the Court of Appeal's opinion, the parties' briefs, nor our research discloses a case holding that a person retains a sufficient interest in excised cells to support a cause of action for conversion. We do not find this surprising, since the laws governing such things as human tissues, transplantable organs, blood, fetuses, pituitary glands, corneal tissue, and dead bodies deal with human biological materials as objects sui generis, regulating their disposition to achieve policy goals rather than abandoning them to the general law of personal property. It is these specialized statutes, not the law of conversion, to which courts ordinarily should and do look for guidance on the disposition of human biological materials.

* * *

Moore, adopting the analogy originally advanced by the Court of Appeal, argues that "[i]f the courts have found a sufficient proprietary interest in one's persona, how could one not have a right in one's own genetic material, something far more profoundly the essence of one's human uniqueness than a name or a face?" However, as the defendants' patent makes clear—and the complaint, too, if read with an understanding of the scientific terms which it has borrowed from the patent—the goal and result of defendants' efforts has been to manufacture lymphokines. Lymphokines, unlike a name or a face, have the same molecular structure in every human being and the same, important functions in every human being's immune system. Moreover, the particular genetic material which is responsible for the natural production of lymphokines, and which defendants use to manufacture lymphokines in the laboratory, is also the same in every person; it is no more unique to Moore than the number of vertebrae in the spine or the chemical formula of hemoglobin.

Another privacy case offered by analogy to support Moore's claim establishes only that patients have a right to refuse medical treatment * * *. Yet one may earnestly wish to protect privacy and dignity without accepting the extremely problematic conclusion that interference with those interests amounts to a conversion of personal property. Nor is it necessary to force the round pegs of "privacy" and "dignity" into the square hole of "property" in order to protect the patient, since the fiduciary-duty and informed-consent theories protect these interests directly by requiring full disclosure.

* * *

The extension of conversion law into this area will hinder research by restricting access to the necessary raw materials. Thousands of human cell lines already exist in tissue repositories, such as the American Type Culture Collection and those operated by the National Institutes of Health and the American Cancer Society. These repositories respond to tens of thousands of requests for samples annually. Since the patent office requires the holders of patents on cell lines to make samples available to anyone, many patent holders place their cell lines in repositories to avoid the administrative burden of responding to requests. At present, human cell lines are routinely copied and distributed to other researchers for experimental purposes, usually free of charge. This exchange of scientific materials, which still is relatively free and efficient, will surely be compromised if each cell sample becomes the potential subject matter of a lawsuit.

* * *

For these reasons, we hold that the allegations of Moore's third amended complaint state a cause of action for breach of fiduciary duty or lack of informed consent, but not conversion.

* * *

BROUSSARD, J., concurring and dissenting.

* * *

With respect to the conversion cause of action, I dissent from the majority's conclusion that the facts alleged in this case do not state a cause of action for conversion * * *. [T]he pertinent inquiry is not whether a patient generally retains an ownership interest in a body part after its removal from his body, but rather whether a patient has a right to determine, before a body part is removed, the use to which the part will be put after removal. Although the majority opinion suggests that there are "reasons to doubt" that a patient retains "any" ownership interest in his organs or cells after removal, the opinion fails to identify any statutory provision or common law authority that indicates that a patient does not generally have the right, before a body part is removed, to choose among the permissible uses to which the part may be put after removal. On the contrary, the most closely related statutory scheme—the Uniform Anatomical Gift Act—is quite clear that a patient does have this right.

* * *

One of the majority's principal policy concerns is that "[t]he extension of conversion law into this area will hinder research by restricting access to the necessary raw materials"—the thousands of cell lines and tissues already in cell and tissue repositories. The majority suggests that the "exchange of scientific materials, which still is relatively free and efficient, will surely be compromised if each cell sample becomes the potential subject matter of a lawsuit."

This policy argument is flawed in a number of respects * * *. For example, if a patient donated his removed cells to a medical center, reserving the right to approve or disapprove the research projects for which the cells would be used, and if another medical center or a drug manufacturer stole the cells after removal and used them in an unauthorized manner for its own economic gain, no breach-of-fiduciary-duty cause of action would be available and a conversion action would be necessary to vindicate the patient's rights. Under the majority's holding, however, the patient would have no right to bring a conversion action, even against such a thief. As this hypothetical illustrates, even if there were compelling policy reasons to limit the potential liability of innocent researchers who use cells obtained from an existing cell bank, those policy considerations would not justify the majority's broad abrogation of *all* conversion liability for the unauthorized use of body parts.

* * *

Because potential liability under a conversion theory will exist in only the exceedingly rare instance in which a doctor knowingly concealed from the patient the value of his body part or the patient's specific directive with regard to the use of the body part was disregarded, there is no reason to think that application of settled conversion law will have any negative effect on the primary conduct of medical researchers who use tissue and cell banks.

* * *

Under established conversion law, a "subsequent innocent converter" does not forfeit the proceeds of his own creative efforts, but rather "is entitled to the benefit of any work or labor that he has expended on the [property]."

* * *

Finally, the majority's analysis of the relevant policy considerations tellingly omits a most pertinent consideration. In identifying the interests of the patient that are implicated by the decision whether to recognize a conversion cause of action, the opinion speaks only of the "patient's right to make autonomous medical decisions" * * * and fails even to mention the patient's interest in obtaining the economic value, if any, that may adhere in the subsequent use of his own body parts. Although such economic value may constitute a fortuitous "windfall" to the patient * * *, the fortuitous nature of the economic value does not justify the creation of a novel exception from conversion liability which sanctions the intentional misappropriation of that value from the patient.

* * *

It is certainly arguable that, as a matter of policy or morality, it would be wiser to prohibit any private individual or entity from profiting from the fortuitous value that adheres in a part of a human body, and instead to require all valuable excised body parts to be deposited in a public repository which would make such materials freely available to all scientists for the betterment of society as a whole * * *. But the majority's rejection of plaintiff's conversion cause of action does not mean that body parts may not be bought or sold for research or commercial purposes or that no private individual or entity may benefit economically from the fortuitous value of plaintiff's diseased cells. Far from elevating these biological materials above the marketplace, the majority's holding simply bars *plaintiff*, the source of the cells, from obtaining the benefit of the cells' value, but permits *defendants*, who allegedly obtained the cells from plaintiff by improper means, to retain and exploit the full economic value of their ill-gotten gains free of their ordinary common law liability for conversion.

* * *

MOSK, J., dissenting.

* * *

[T]he majority conclude that the patent somehow cut off all Moore's rights—past, present, and future—to share in the proceeds of defendants' commercial exploitation of the cell line derived from his own body tissue. The majority cite no authority for this unfair result, and I cannot believe it is compelled by the general law of patents: a patent is not a license to defraud. Perhaps the answer lies in an analogy to the concept of "joint inventor." I am aware that "patients and research subjects who contribute cells to research will not be considered inventors." Nor is such a person strictly speaking a "joint inventor" within the meaning of the term in federal law. (35 U.S.C. § 116.) But he does fall within the spirit of that law: "The joint invention provision guarantees that all who contribute in a substantial way to a product's development benefit from the reward that the product brings. Thus, the protection of joint inventors encourages scientists to cooperate with each other and ensures that each contributor is rewarded fairly."

* * *

The majority begin their analysis by stressing the obvious facts that research on human cells plays an increasingly important role in the progress of medicine, and that the manipulation of those cells by the methods of biotechnology has resulted in numerous beneficial products and treatments. Yet it does not necessarily follow that, as the majority claim, application of the law of conversion to this area "will hinder research by restricting access to the necessary raw materials," i.e., to cells, cell cultures, and cell lines.

* * *

To begin with, if the relevant exchange of scientific materials was ever "free and efficient," it is much less so today. Since biological products of genetic engineering became patentable in 1980 (Diamond v. Chakrabarty, 447 U.S. 303 (1980)), human cell lines have been amenable to patent protection and, as the Court of Appeal observed in its opinion below, "The rush to patent for exclusive use has been rampant." * * * Thus defendants herein recited in their patent specification, "At no time has the Mo cell line been available to other than the investigators involved with its initial discovery and only the conditioned medium from the cell line has been made available to a limited number of investigators for collaborative work with the original discoverers of the Mo cell line."

* * *

"Record keeping would not be overly burdensome because researchers generally keep accurate records of tissue sources for other reasons: to trace anomalies to the medical history of the patient, to maintain title for other researchers and for themselves, and to insure reproducibility of the experiment."

* * *

In any event, in my view whatever merit the majority's single policy consideration may have is outweighed by two contrary considerations, i.e., policies that are promoted by recognizing that every individual has a legally protectible property interest in his own body and its products. First, our society acknowledges a profound ethical imperative to respect the human body as the physical and temporal expression of the unique human persona. One manifestation of that respect is our prohibition against direct abuse of the body by torture or other forms of cruel or unusual punishment. Another is our prohibition against indirect abuse of the body by its economic exploitation for the sole benefit of another person. The most abhorrent form of such exploitation, of course, was the institution of slavery. Lesser forms, such as indentured servitude or even debtor's prison, have also disappeared. Yet their specter haunts the laboratories and boardrooms of today's biotechnological research-industrial complex. It arises wherever scientists or industrialists claim, as defendants claim here, the right to appropriate and exploit a patient's tissue for their sole economic benefit—the right, in other words, to freely mine or harvest valuable physical properties of the patient's body.

* * *

The majority's final reason for refusing to recognize a conversion cause of action on these facts is that "there is no pressing need" to do so because the complaint also states another cause of action that is assertedly adequate to the task; that cause of action is "the breach of a fiduciary duty to disclose facts material to the patient's consent or, alternatively, . . . the performance of medical procedures without first having obtained the patient's informed consent".

* * *

The remedy is largely illusory * * *. Few if any judges or juries are likely to believe that disclosure of such a possibility of research or development would dissuade a reasonably prudent person from consenting to the treatment. For example, in the case at bar no trier of fact is likely to believe that if defendants had disclosed their plans for using Moore's cells, no reasonably prudent person in Moore's position— i.e., a leukemia patient suffering from a grossly enlarged spleen—would have consented to the routine operation that saved or at least prolonged his life.

* * *

The second reason why the nondisclosure cause of action is inadequate for the task that the majority assign to it is that it fails to solve half the problem before us: it gives the patient only the right to *refuse* consent, i.e., the right to prohibit the commercialization of his tissue; it does not give him the right to *grant* consent to that commercialization on the condition that he share in its proceeds.

* * *

In sum, the nondisclosure cause of action (1) is unlikely to be successful in most cases, (2) fails to protect patients' rights to share in the proceeds of the commercial exploitation of their tissue, and (3) may allow the true exploiters to escape liability. It is thus not an adequate substitute, in my view, for the conversion cause of action.

GREENBERG V. MIAMI CHILDREN'S HOSPITAL RESEARCH INSTITUTE, INC.

264 F.Supp.2d 1064 (S.D. Fla. 2003).

MORENO, J.

Plaintiffs Daniel Greenberg ("Greenberg"), Fern Kupfer ("Kupfer"), Frieda Eisen ("Eisen"), David Green ("Green"), Canavan Foundation, Dor Yeshorim, and National Tay-Sachs and Allied Diseases Association, Inc. (collectively "Plaintiffs") brought this diversity action for damages and equitable and injunctive relief to redress Defendants' alleged breach of informed consent, breach of fiduciary duty, unjust enrichment, fraudulent concealment, conversion, and misappropriation of trade secrets. The individual plaintiffs Greenberg, Kupfer, Eisen, and Green are parents of children who were afflicted with Canavan disease. The other Plaintiffs are non-profit organizations that provided funding and information to Defendants to research and discover the Canavan disease gene. Defendants are the physician-researcher, Dr. Reuben Matalon ("Matalon"), Variety Children's Hospital d/b/a Miami Children's Hospital ("MCH"), and the hospital's research affiliate, Miami Children's Hospital Research Institute ("MCHRI").

The Complaint alleges a tale of a successful research collaboration gone sour. In 1987, Canavan disease still remained a mystery—there was no way to identify who was a carrier of the disease, nor was there a way to identify a fetus with Canavan disease. Plaintiff Greenberg approached

Dr. Matalon, a research physician * * * [and] requested Matalon's involvement in discovering the genes that were ostensibly responsible for this fatal disease, so that tests could be administered to determine carriers and allow for prenatal testing for the disease.

Greenberg and the Chicago Chapter of the National Tay-Sachs and Allied Disease Association, Inc. ("NTSAD") located other Canavan families and convinced them to provide tissue (such as blood, urine, and autopsy samples), financial support, and aid in identifying the location of Canavan families internationally.

* * *

The individual Plaintiffs allege that they provided Matalon with these samples and confidential information "with the understanding and expectations that such samples and information would be used for the specific purpose of researching Canavan disease and identifying mutations in the Canavan disease which could lead to carrier detection within their families and benefit the population at large." Plaintiffs further allege that it was their "understanding that any carrier and prenatal testing developed in connection with the research for which they were providing essential support would be provided on an affordable and accessible basis, and that Matalon's research would remain in the public domain to promote the discovery of more effective prevention techniques and treatments and, eventually, to effectuate a cure for Canavan disease." This understanding stemmed from their "experience in community testing for Tay-Sachs disease, another deadly genetic disease that occurs most frequently in families of Ashkenazi Jewish descent."

Using Plaintiffs' blood and tissue samples, familial pedigree information, contacts, and financial support, Matalon and his research team successfully isolated the gene responsible for Canavan disease. * * * [U]nbeknownst to Plaintiffs, a patent application was submitted for the genetic sequence that Defendants had identified. This application was granted in October 1997. * * * Through patenting, Defendants acquired the ability to restrict any activity related to the Canavan disease gene, including without limitation: carrier and prenatal testing, gene therapy and other treatments for Canavan disease and research involving the gene and its mutations.

Plaintiffs allege that they did not learn of [the patent] until November 1998, when MCH revealed their intention to limit Canavan disease testing through a campaign of restrictive licensing of the Patent.

* * *

Based on these facts, Plaintiffs filed a six-count complaint on October 30, 2000, against Defendants asserting the following causes of action: (1) lack of informed consent; (2) breach of fiduciary duty; (3) unjust enrichment; (4) fraudulent concealment; (5) conversion; and (6) misappropriation of trade secrets. Plaintiffs generally seek a permanent injunction restraining Defendants from enforcing their patent rights, damages in the form of all royalties Defendants have received on the Patent as well as all financial contributions Plaintiffs made to benefit Defendants' research. Plaintiffs allege that Defendants have earned significant royalties from Canavan disease testing in excess of $75,000 through enforcement of their gene patent, and that Dr. Matalon has personally profited by receiving a recent substantial federal grant to undertake further research on the gene patent.

* * *

A.   LACK OF INFORMED CONSENT

Plaintiffs * * * claim that Defendants breached this duty [of informed consent] * * * when they did not disclose the intent to patent and enforce for their own economic benefit the Canavan disease gene. The duty was also breached by the misrepresentation of the research purpose that Matalon had included on the written consent forms. Finally, the Plaintiffs allege that if they had known that the Defendants would "commercialize" the results of their contributions, they would not have made the contributions.

* * *

The question of informed consent in the context of medical research, however, is a relatively novel one in Florida. Medical consent law does not apply to medical researchers. Florida Statute § 760.40 does require, however, that a person's informed consent must be obtained when any genetic analysis is undertaken on his or her tissue.

* * *

Since the law regarding a duty of informed consent for research subjects is unsettled and fact-specific and further, Defendants conceded at oral argument that a duty does attach at some point in the relationship, the Court finds that in certain circumstances a medical researcher does have a duty of informed consent. Nevertheless, without clear guidance from Florida jurisprudence, the Court must consider whether this duty of informed consent in medical research can be extended to disclosure of a researcher's economic interests.

* * *

Defendants assert that extending a possible informed consent duty to disclosing economic interests has no support in established law, and more ominously, this requirement would have pernicious effects over medical research, as it would give each donor complete control over how medical research is used and who benefits from that research. The Court agrees and declines to extend the duty of informed consent to cover a researcher's economic interests in this case.

* * *

In declining to extend the duty of informed consent to cover economic interests, the Court takes note of the practical implications of retroactively imposing a duty of this nature. First, imposing a duty of the character that Plaintiffs seek would be unworkable and would chill medical research as it would mandate that researchers constantly evaluate whether a discloseable event has occurred. Second, this extra duty would give rise to a type of dead-hand control that research subjects could hold because they would be able to dictate how medical research progresses. Finally, the Plaintiffs are more accurately portrayed as donors rather than objects of human experimentation, and thus the voluntary nature of their submissions warrants different treatment. Accordingly, the Court finds that Plaintiffs have failed to state a claim upon which relief may be granted, and this count is DISMISSED.

B.   BREACH OF FIDUCIARY DUTY

The individual Plaintiffs allege in Count II of the Complaint that all the Defendants were in a fiduciary relationship with them, and as such, they should have disclosed all material information relating to the Canavan disease research they were conducting, including any economic interests of the Defendants relating to that research.

* * *

Defendants assert that the Complaint does not allege any facts that show that the trust was recognized and accepted. Plaintiffs allege, however, that Defendants accepted the trust by undertaking research that they represented as being for the benefit of the Plaintiffs. * * * Taking all the facts alleged as true, the Court finds that Plaintiffs have not sufficiently alleged the second element of acceptance of trust by Defendants and therefore have failed to state a claim. There is no automatic fiduciary relationship that attaches when a researcher accepts medical donations and the acceptance of trust, the second constitutive element of finding a fiduciary duty, cannot be assumed once a donation is given. Accordingly, this claim is DISMISSED.

C.   UNJUST ENRICHMENT

In Count III of the Complaint, Plaintiffs allege that MCH is being unjustly enriched by collecting license fees under the Patent. * * * The Court finds that Plaintiffs have sufficiently alleged the elements of a claim for unjust enrichment to survive Defendants' motion to dismiss.

* * *

[T]he facts paint a picture of a continuing research collaboration that involved Plaintiffs also investing time and significant resources in the race to isolate the Canavan gene. Therefore, given the facts as alleged, the Court finds that Plaintiffs have sufficiently pled the requisite elements of an unjust enrichment claim and the motion to dismiss for failure to state a claim is DENIED as to this count.

D.   FRAUDULENT CONCEALMENT

Count IV of the Complaint alleges that MCH fraudulently concealed from the Plaintiffs that (1) the Hospital would economically benefit from Canavan research; (2) it would patent the Canavan gene mutation; and (3) it would license the testing under the Patent.

* * *

[T]here was no duty of disclosure to the Plaintiffs. Allegations of fraudulent concealment by silence must be accompanied by allegations of a special relationship that gives rise to a duty to speak. * * * [T]he facts asserted as fraudulently concealed were accessible to the Plaintiffs. A patent becomes public knowledge when issued and Plaintiffs could have undertaken due diligence to uncover the facts surrounding the patent application. Plaintiffs' allegations that they were prevented from making reasonable inquiries because they had no reason to believe that patenting would occur is unavailing because if they were so concerned about a possible intent to patent then a simple phone inquiry to the Defendants would have uncovered this fact.

* * *

Plaintiffs contend that, but for the fraudulent non-disclosure, they would have acted differently. Nevertheless, fraud must be specially pled, and the Complaint does not adequately allege a claim based on a special relationship or of injury nor does it allege more specifics about efforts at concealment or about any representations made by Matalon as to what he would do with the test results. Therefore, the Court finds that the Complaint lacks the specificity required by Fed.R.Civ.P. 9(b). Accordingly, the fraudulent concealment claim is DISMISSED.

E.   CONVERSION

The Plaintiffs allege in Count V of their Complaint that they had a property interest in their body tissue and genetic information, and that they owned the Canavan registry in Illinois which contained contact information, pedigree information and family information for Canavan families worldwide. They claim that MCH and Matalon converted the names on the register and the genetic information by utilizing them for the hospitals' "exclusive economic benefit." The Court disagrees and declines to find a property interest for the body tissue and genetic information voluntarily given to Defendants. These were donations to research without any contemporaneous expectations of return of the body tissue and genetic samples, and thus conversion does not lie as a cause of action.

In Florida, the tort of "conversion is an unauthorized act which deprives another of his property permanently or for an indefinite time." Using property given for one purpose for another purpose constitutes conversion.

First, Plaintiffs have no cognizable property interest in body tissue and genetic matter donated for research under a theory of conversion. This case is similar to Moore v. Regents of the University of California, where the Court declined to extend liability under a theory of conversion to misuse of a person's excised biological materials. 51 Cal.3d 120 (Cal.1990). The plaintiff in Moore alleged that he had retained a property right in excised bodily material used in research, and therefore retained some control over the results of that research. The California Supreme Court, however, disagreed and held that the use of the results of medical research inconsistent with the wishes of the donor was not conversion, because the donor had no property interest at stake after the donation was made. The Court also recognized that the patented result of research is "both factually and legally distinct" from excised material used in the research.

Second, limits to the property rights that attach to body tissue have been recognized in Florida state courts * * * Similarly, the property right in blood and tissue samples also evaporates once the sample is voluntarily given to a third party.

Plaintiffs rely on Pioneer Hi-Bred v. Holden Foundation, 1987 WL 341211 (S.D.Iowa, Oct.30, 1987), aff'd, 35 F.3d 1226 (8th Cir.1994), for their assertion that genetic information itself can constitute property for the purposes of the tort of conversion. In that case, the Court held that a corn seed's property interest in the genetic message contained in a corn seed variety is property protected by the laws of conversion. Plaintiffs argue that giving permission for one purpose (gene discovery) does not mean they agreed to other uses (gene patenting and commercialization). Yet, the Pioneer court recognized that, "where information is gathered and arranged at some cost and sold as a commodity on the market, it is properly protected as property." This seemingly provides more support for property rights inherent in Defendants' research rather than the donations of Plaintiffs' DNA. * * *

Plaintiffs have not cited any case that interprets the statute [Fla. Stat. § 760.40 which provides that the results of DNA analysis "are the exclusive property of the person tested"] as applying to an analogous factual situation, and this Court's investigation did not find any relevant case either. Moreover, even assuming, arguendo, that the statute does create a property right in genetic material donated for medical research purposes, it is unclear whether this confers a property right for conversion, a common law cause of action.

Finally, although the Complaint sets out that Plaintiff Greenberg owned the Canavan Registry, the facts alleged do not sufficiently allege the elements of a prima facie case of conversion, as the Plaintiffs have not alleged how the Defendants' use of the Registry in their research was an expressly unauthorized act. The Complaint only alleges that the Defendants "utilized the information and contacts for their exclusive economic benefit." There is no further allegation of the circumstances or conditions that were attached to the Defendants' use of the Canavan Registry. Nor are there any allegations about any of the Plaintiffs' entitlement to possess the Registry.

The Court finds that Florida statutory and common law do not provide a remedy for Plaintiffs' donations of body tissue and blood samples under a theory of conversion liability. Indeed, the Complaint does not allege that the Defendants used the genetic material for any purpose but medical research. Plaintiffs claim that the fruits of the research, namely the patented material, was commercialized. This is an important distinction and another step in the chain of attenuation that renders conversion liability inapplicable to the facts as alleged. If adopted, the expansive theory championed by Plaintiffs would cripple medical research as it would bestow a continuing right for donors to possess the results of any research conducted by the hospital. At the core, these were donations to research without any contemporaneous expectations of return. Consequently, the Plaintiffs have failed to state a claim upon which relief may be granted on this issue. Accordingly, this claim is DISMISSED.

F.   MISAPPROPRIATION OF TRADE SECRETS

The Canavan Registry was not misappropriated by MCH because there is no allegation that MCH knew or should have known that the Canavan Registry was a confidential trade secret guarded by Plaintiffs, and furthermore, that Matalon had acquired through improper means. Plaintiffs cannot donate information that they prepared for fighting a disease and then retroactively claim that it was a protected secret. * * * This claim is therefore DISMISSED.

AMERICAN MEDICAL ASSOCIATION, COUNCIL ON ETHICAL AND JUDICIAL AFFAIRS, CODE OF MEDICAL ETHICS: CURRENT OPINIONS WITH ANNOTATIONS, 2012–2013 ED.

(2013).

2.08 Commercial Use of Human Tissue

The rapid growth of the biotechnology industry has resulted in the commercial availability of numerous therapeutic and other products developed from human tissue. Physicians contemplating the commercial use of human tissue should abide by the following guidelines:

(1) Informed consent must be obtained from patients for the use of organs or tissues in clinical research.

(2) Potential commercial applications must be disclosed to the patient before a profit is realized on products developed from biological materials.

(3) Human tissue and its products may not be used for commercial purposes without the informed consent of the patient who provided the original cellular material.

(4) Profits from the commercial use of human tissue and its products may be shared with patients, in accordance with lawful contractual agreements.

(5) The diagnostic and therapeutic alternatives offered to patients by their physicians should conform to standards of good medical practice and should not be influenced in any way by the commercial potential of the patient's tissue.

Issued June 1994 based on the report Who Should Profit from the Economic Value of Human Tissue? An Ethical Analysis, adopted June 1990.

NOTES AND QUESTIONS

1.   On what legal grounds does the patient have a right to be informed of a physician's research interests and commercial interests?

2.   Why does Justice Mosk believe that the nondisclosure causes of action are inadequate?

3.   Is it likely that granting Moore a property interest in his tissue would have hampered research? How?

4.   Are there situations in which an individual should have a property interest in his or her tissue or genes?

5.   Would allowing a person to have a property right in his or her genes "commodify" individuals? If selling genes is permitted, what about other

parts of people like organs? What about selling people as a whole—i.e., slavery?

It is important to note that just because something is legally considered to be property does not preclude limiting its sale or use. Justice Mosk in his *Moore* dissent points out, "For a variety of policy reasons, the law limits or even forbids the exercise of certain rights over certain forms of property. For example, both law and contract may limit the right of an owner of real property to use his parcel as he sees fit. Owners of various forms of personal property may likewise be subject to restrictions on the time, place, and manner of their use. Limitations on the disposition of real property, while less common, may also be imposed. Finally, some types of personal property may be sold but not given away, while others may be given away but not sold, and still others may neither be given away nor sold." What restrictions, if any, are appropriate for genes?

6.   Justice Broussard suggests an alternative to patenting: making cell lines and genes available to all scientists through a public repository. What are the pros and cons of this more communitarian alternative instead of allowing either the patients or the scientists to have a property right in cells or genes?

7.   The majority in *Moore* makes much of the fact that California statutes (such as public health laws on the disposal of human tissue) limit patients' control over their cells. Justice Mosk, in dissent, notes that the statutory law also "does not authorize the principal use that defendants claim the right to make of Moore's tissue, i.e., its commercial exploitation." Do the existing statutes shed light on the question of whether patients should have a property right in their tissue or genes?

8.   The court in *Greenberg* notes in its discussion of conversion that Florida law limits the property rights a person has in body tissue. What if such a law did not exist? Would the court have come to the same conclusion with only the decision in *Moore* to rely on?

The court also states that any property rights that might exist in body tissues evaporate once the body tissues are voluntarily given to a third party. What would happen, however, if some property rights were retained? If the person providing the body tissues to the third party retained the right to have the tissues removed from the research being undertaken, or retained the right to have the tissues destroyed, would the outcome be the same?

9.   A company, DNA Copyright Institute of San Francisco, offers to copyright celebrities' DNA for $1,500 by filing their DNA code with the U.S. copyright office. The company's founder says copyrighting DNA will protect against unauthorized cloning of celebrities. Although codes in general are protectible by copyright, some copyright experts argue that such a procedure is inappropriate for the genetic code, since individuals are not the "author" of their DNA. Philip Cohen, Born to Make You Happy, New Scientist, April 25, 2001, at 12.

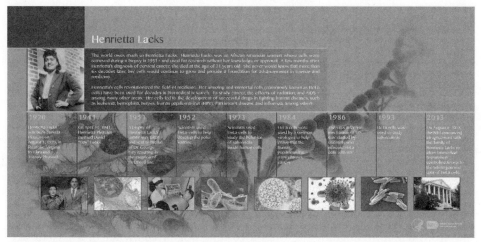

This timeline includes events from 1920 (when Lacks was born) to 2013 (when NIH announced an agreement with the Lacks family to allow biomedical researchers controlled access to the whole genome data of HeLa cells).

Credit: Darryl Leja, National Human Genome Research Institute, www.genome.gov

10. Although much attention has been paid to the John Moore case, he is not the first person whose cell lines were made commercially available. In 1951, a 31-year-old African-American woman, Henrietta Lacks, was dying of cervical cancer. Dr. George Otto Gey, a cell biologist at Johns Hopkins University at the time, used her cancerous tissue to create the first immortalized human cell line, the HeLa cell line, which could grow continuously in vitro. The HeLa cells have been used by generations of scientists for research. In an interview, her husband said, "As far as them selling my wife's cells without my knowledge and making a profit—I don't like it at all. They are exploiting us both." Harriet A. Washington, Henrietta Lacks—An Unsung Hero, Emerge, Oct. 1994, at 29; Rebecca Skloot, The Immortal Life of Henrietta Lacks (2010).

11. Patients' tissue samples are now a commercial resource for hospitals. Duke University Medical Center entered into a commercial agreement with Ardais, granting the start-up genomics company access to Duke's patients' tissue. Harvard Beth Israel Deaconess Medical Center entered into a similar arrangement. Should patients whose tissue is part of these deals be informed of the arrangements? Should they receive compensation? For information about the agreements, see Deborah Josefsen, Human Tissue for Sale: What Are the Costs?, 173 Western J. Med. 302 (2000).

12. In the *Moore* case, Justice Mosk suggested that patients or research subjects who were the source of genes or cell lines could be listed as co-inventors on the patent. A decade later, in 2000, the patient group PXE International followed that approach. The patients suffered from pseudoxanthoma elasticum, a genetic disorder that causes connective tissue in the skin, eyes, and arteries to calcify. Because PXE had been an under-

researched disease, PXE International took the initiative to set up a tissue bank of families afflicted with the disease. Before researchers gained access to the tissue bank, they had to sign a contract saying that they would share with PXE International the ownership and profits from research using those samples. When University of Hawaii pathobiologist Charles Boyd found the PXE gene in 2000, he filed a patent application listing Sharon Terry, the founder of PXE International and the mother of two children with the disorder, as a co-inventor on the patent. PXE International will split royalties gained from the patent equally with the university, and will have control over licensing arrangements for the gene patent. Matt Fleisher, Seeking Rights to Crucial Genes, Nat'l L. J., June 25, 2001, at C 1.

If you were representing a patient group, what provisions might you want to put into an agreement with researchers?

13. When arrangements to be a co-inventor or co-owner of a patent are not made in advance, the people whose DNA was used to find a particular gene may not be able to assert a claim to be recognized on the patent. Eric Fuchs realized he had been repeatedly exposed to HIV infection without becoming symptomatic. He suggested to researchers that they search his blood for the unique factor that appeared to make him immune. When researchers at the Aaron Diamond AIDS Research Center found it, they patented it. Fuchs believes that his role in the research should be recognized via co-ownership of the patent.

In an analogous case, a non-scientist who conceived of a particular type of research was not granted any rights to share in the proceeds of the resulting patent. Marlo Brown, a veterinary hospital manager who maintained a shelter for sick, stray, and abandoned cats, brought detailed observations and records of her cats' illnesses to a well-known animal virologist at U.C. Davis School of Veterinary Medicine. Brown provided the cats' histories and blood samples, as well as her belief that the cats were infected with a virus similar to the human AIDS virus. After extensive lab work, the virologist and a colleague received a patent based on their isolation and substantial purification of the virus. Though the doctors widely and publicly credited Brown for her role in the discovery of the new virus, "FIV," the court ruled that she was not a joint inventor under patent law. The court reasoned, "she at most played a substantial role in the discovery of FIV * * * regardless of the value of her research leads, she cannot be deemed to have contributed to the conception of the inventions covered by the patents." Brown v. Regents of Univ. of California, 866 F.Supp. 439 (N.D.Cal.1994).

CHAPTER 5

RACE AND ETHNICITY

■ ■ ■

I.   INTRODUCTION

The relationship between genomic science and concepts of race and ethnicity has generated considerable controversy. The chapter begins by exploring the scientific dispute over whether there is a genetic basis for racial categorization. The materials that follow focus on African Americans. They explain that, in addition to focusing on individuals such as persons with disabilities regardless of their racial or ethnic background, the eugenics movement in the U.S. specifically targeted African Americans. The chapter then describes the sickle cell screening program, the first population-specific genetic screening initiative in the U.S., and its adverse effects on African Americans. The section concludes with the current controversy over researching and marketing drugs for use specifically by African Americans.

Modern genetics affects additional groups besides African Americans, and the chapter next explores issues raised by research on the DNA of indigenous populations, including objections to certain research projects by Native Americans. The chapter concludes with a discussion of efforts to identify and reduce the risk of group harms.

II.   IS THERE A GENETIC BASIS FOR RACE?

The recent discovery that there are only about 25,000 human genes—far fewer than previously thought—underscores the fact that the genetic variation between individuals is extremely small. This is also true for genetic differences between specific populations, including racial and ethnic minorities. For the most part, members of racial and ethnic minorities have the same distribution of genetic sequences as the majority. In some cases, however, members of minority and ethnic groups will have a different distribution of alleles. This raises questions about therapeutic testing for diseases that occur with varying frequencies in different populations. As Herbert Nickens points out:

> There is potential for discrimination and stigma in both circumstances. There is potential for differential treatment for minorities with "defective genes," even for those traits for which minorities have a similar distribution of variation as that for

179

majority populations; and certainly there is potential for stigma for those negative traits or diseases which are strongly associated with minorities.

Herbert Nickens, The Genome Project and Health Services for Minority Populations 59, in The Human Genome Project and the Future of Health Care (Thomas H. Murray et al. eds. 1996). (As discussed in Chapter 6, problems also arise with genetic testing of minorities and ethnic groups for reproductive purposes.)

OSAGIE K. OBASOGIE, PLAYING THE GENE CARD? A REPORT ON RACE AND HUMAN BIOTECHNOLOGY

Center for Genetics and Society 2009, www.thegenecard.org.

What does it mean to say that race is not biologically significant? Researchers in the social and life sciences have argued that race is not a meaningful biological category, that it is a "social construction" rather than a scientific fact.

But what does this mean? These phrases are typically used to convey the ideas that

- the importance placed on the outward physical distinctions that societies traditionally use to draw racial boundaries vary substantially over time and place,
- these physical distinctions do not reflect any inherent meanings, abilities, or disabilities, and
- racial differences in social and health outcomes do not correlate meaningfully with underlying biological or genetic mechanisms.

In short, as University of California, Berkeley Law Professor Ian Haney Lopez argues, the constructionist view "rejects the most widely accepted understanding of race . . . [which holds that] there exist natural, physical, divisions among humans that are hereditary, reflected in morphology, and roughly captured by terms like Black, White, and Asian."

There are certainly biological components to race and health outcomes, though often only because of the way certain groups are treated in relation to how they are perceived. A key example of this phenomenon was demonstrated by Johns Hopkins epidemiologist Michael Klag, who found that rates of hypertension among Black Americans correspond to skin complexion; those with darker skin have higher rates. Klag showed that this is not simply a genetic or biological phenomenon, but rather a health outcome linked to skin tone discrimination and the higher degree of stress experienced by dark-skinned Blacks. While the effect was biological, the cause was largely social.

Of course, genes (along with other biological and environmental factors) shape human variation and outward physical appearance, and many of these characteristics are heritable. Evolutionary dynamics have conferred some different phenotypic traits and genetic signatures to geographically separated groups that may loosely resemble social categories of race. Thus, as Francis Collins notes, the ability to identify genetic variations that provide "reasonably accurate" yet "blurry" estimates of portions of an individual's ancestry suggest that "it is not strictly true that race or ethnicity has no biological connection."

But it is important to put even loose correlations between race and genes or genetic predispositions in an appropriate context. An early and enduring finding in human genetic studies is that there is typically more genetic variation within socially defined racial groups than between them. Another consistent finding is that for any observable "racial" trait, there are no corresponding genetic boundaries between population groups. They are discordant—that is, the collection of observable physical cues that society often uses to create the idea of discrete racial groups are not mirrored by corresponding genetic boundaries. Instead, biologists find graded variations in the percentages of groups with each characteristic.

In other words, the sharp delineations that society makes with regards to racial categories are not meaningfully reflected in our genes. That is why scientists such as Yale geneticist Kenneth Kidd conclude that "there's no such thing as race in *Homo sapiens*. . . . There's no place [in our genes] where you can draw a line and say there's a major difference on one side of the line from what's on the other side." To say that race is a social construction is to emphasize that in most cases, racial categories based upon phenotype (physical appearance) ultimately provide a poor way to proxy individual genotype, or genetic variations that may be exclusive to certain populations.

MICHAEL J. MALINOWSKI, DEALING WITH THE REALITIES OF RACE AND ETHNICITY: A BIOETHICS-CENTERED ARGUMENT IN FAVOR OF RACE-BASED GENETICS RESEARCH
45 Hous. L. Rev. 1415, 1433–1436 (2009).

Those in the scientific and medical communities opposed to research based on race and ethnicity emphasize that these groupings are inconsistent with the scientific reality of human genetics. They draw from the ample body of literature by Professors Cavalli-Sforza, Lewontin, and their contemporaries, and also reference recent findings that bolster the argument that race and ethnicity are more social constructs than genetic realities. Opponents assert that a preferred methodology for population genetics is research centered on diseases or at least specific and more reliable genetic particulars. They argue this approach will help avoid wasting resources, forcing outcomes, and chancing the affirmation of racial and ethnic groupings and social stereotypes. According to bioethicist and Ph.D. scientist Mildred Cho, the race and ethnicity categories are unworkable: "Because social perceptions of the meaning of race and ethnicity are extremely fluid, basing research findings on these categories or applying scientific findings based on perceived race or ethnicity is fraught with problems. Thus, attempts to better define [the racial and ethnic] structure [of drug response] will be futile."

Sociologist Troy Duster and many other opponents raise concerns about biologic determinism, meaning that genetic protocols crafted around race and ethnicity will become self-fulfilling prophecies. They emphasize the genetic commonality in any group due to the youth of the human species and its overwhelming genetic sameness. Professor Duster also addresses the broader social implications of underscoring lines traditionally drawn around groups based upon race and ethnicity through genetics research protocols that suggest their validity. He warns that singling out these groups further affirms prejudices and increases their vulnerability to discrimination, exploitation, and health inequality. According to Professor Duster, the scientific community has shifted from "genetic sameness" as the mantra for mapping the human genome to a mantra of "genetic differentiation" through ongoing efforts to make medical sense out of the genome map, including population genetics, pharmacogenomics, and identification of SNPs.

A number of law academics have entered the debate and argued against the perpetuation of race in the biomedical context with cautions about the weighty social and legal implications involved. In fact, there is a discernible majority opinion among law academics that race-based genomics research is undesirable on multiple levels and perhaps even illegal. The literature includes articles by Professors Erik Lillquist and Charles Sullivan, Professor Sharona Hoffman, Professor Jonathan Kahn, and a University of Minnesota symposium chaired by Professor Wolf, which includes an article by Professor Dorothy Roberts.

Proposals have been made to distinguish basic, clinical, epidemiological, and other forms of research, and to introduce legal restraints on the use of race and ethnicity in a manner tailored to each research specialty. The general consensus among law opponents is that the use of race and ethnicity in biomedical research always warrants caution and legal restraints, but there is a continuum: use of race in clinical research is least acceptable; use in epidemiological research, such as research on the correlation between race and health disparities, is most acceptable; and other types of research place between the two. Also, the general consensus is that the use of race in research and medicine runs contrary to U.S. law and policy that broadly proscribes it. Lillquist & Sullivan conclude that the use of race in research and medicine should be severely circumscribed, if not prohibited almost entirely. Their proposed standard for using race in medical treatment is extremely restrictive. They would require a scientific basis to establish not simply that the use of race is helpful in diagnosis and treatment, but that it is the best known method at the time. Professor Hoffman declares that " 'race-based' medicine is an inappropriate and perilous approach" and proposes regulatory reforms to heavily restrain, if not entirely eliminate, both race-based research and medicine. She proposes "attributes-based" identification as a race-neutral alternative.

Collectively, legal academics generally approach race-based research from the standpoint of U.S. jurisprudence and public policy against discrimination and associated social and ethical concerns. Their analysis of potential legal constraints on race-centered research begins with restrictions on intentional disparate treatment based on race by government entities under the Equal Protection Clause of the Fourteenth Amendment and the Due Process Clause of the Fifth Amendment. They emphasize that government use of racial classifications triggers strict scrutiny, but recognize that government actions, including programs thoughtfully crafted to promote affirmative action, survive such scrutiny where there is a compelling government interest and the use of race is narrowly tailored to promote that interest. They generally concede that, under established jurisprudence, government sponsorship of responsible race-based genetics research is likely to survive such challenges, though the present Court recently questioned Seattle and Louisville school diversity policies and subjected them to further inquiry.

MARGARET A. WINKER, RACE AND ETHNICITY IN MEDICAL RESEARCH: REQUIREMENTS MEET REALITY
34 J. L. Med. & Ethics 520, 520–522 (2006).

In medical research the assumption that race is an important factor is widespread. This may derive from the use of race as a patient descriptor throughout medical training. Medical students traditionally learned that patients' histories begin with "this is a [insert patient's age, presumed race, sex] who presents with a chief complaint of. . . ." In medical editing, peer reviewers sometimes ask that race be reported and analyzed even when originally omitted. However, medicine is hardly unique in its preoccupation with race. Reporting and analyzing medical studies by race may reflect the significant role, both real and perceived, that race plays in the broader society. * * *

Scientific research must be reported accurately to allow interpretation and replication. However, the terms used to describe race and ethnicity often have been inaccurate and inappropriate. The terms "Latino/Hispanic," "Asian," and "white" or "Caucasian" have all been criticized for inaccuracy and ambiguity. The problem is compounded when observers such as researchers or clinicians classify individuals by race based on skin color and appearances, but even self-classification raises issues. In some areas of the United States, fully one-quarter of individuals checked more than one box indicating race/ethnicity in the 2000 census. In addition, translating descriptions of race/ethnicity from the native language in which a survey was administered can lead to additional measurement error.

Despite the many difficulties posed by categorizing race, in some instances it can be important to assess race and ethnicity. First, reporting race can suggest whether the populations studied reflect the diversity of the population to whom the results might be applied. Clinicians, in particular, may need to know whether the characteristics of the study population are comparable to the population the clinician treats. For example, major cardiovascular risk factors were first defined in the middle-class white population of Framingham, Massachusetts, but it was unclear whether these risk factors were applicable to more diverse populations. In fact, the risk factors do predict cardiovascular disease in more diverse populations, but the relative importance of specific risk factors varies by the racial and ethnic background of the population. For similar reasons, the National Institutes of Health (NIH) requires that race and ethnicity be measured and reported in funded research, in part to ensure that traditionally understudied non-white populations are included.

Race also may be used as one of several parameters to determine whether randomization has been successful. This assessment may be useful to readers as one description of the population of research participants, but the existence of the variable tempts the researcher or reviewer to request results by race whether or not such analysis is appropriate. If such analyses are conducted without considering other contributing factors such as socioeconomic differences, the results may lead to incorrect interpretation and implications.

The third reason to assess race and ethnicity is that racial disparities in risk factors, treatment, and outcomes are common in the United States and race must be measured if reasons for the disparities are to be studied. Racial disparities often persist after controlling for socioeconomic measures such as income and education. However, the reasons underlying disparities are more complex than differential treatment or racism by clinicians. In a 2004 study, Elizabeth Bradley and colleagues found that when both admitting hospital and race were assessed, health care disparities varied primarily by hospital rather than by race; the association of disparities with race was a result of blacks being cared for in hospitals with worse process of care. Another 2004 study, by Peter Bach and colleagues, found that physicians treating black patients were less likely to be board-certified and had less access to high-quality specialists, diagnostic imaging, and ancillary services. These studies suggest that interventions to reduce health disparities will need to address more than socioeconomic differences. Eliminating disparities will require a nuanced understanding of patient care, quality of care, and behavior of clinicians and patients.

* * *

A fourth reason for assessing race is related to the tenuous connection between race and genetics. Genetic factors associated with drug metabolism can enhance or reduce a drug's effectiveness or adverse effects. In some cases, some of these genetic tendencies may be associated with a particular race. However, when race is used as a proxy for what presumably is a genetic marker for susceptibility to a given drug's effects, some members of the population who may benefit from the drug will be excluded from treatment and some members of the population targeted for the drug will not benefit. A statistical difference in drug response between different racial or ethnic groups should be the starting point for genetic studies, not the final conclusion resulting in different drug indications by race.

* * *

Given that some legitimate reasons to assess race exist in medical research, the measurement and reporting of race should be as accurate and transparent as possible.

NOTES AND QUESTIONS

1.   The scientific consensus seems to support the lack of a genetic basis for racial categorizations. See Ian Tattersall & Rob DeSalle, Race?: Debunking a Scientific Myth (2011) and Race and the Genetic Revolution: Science, Myth, and Culture (Sheldon Krimsky & Kathleen Sloan eds. 2011). In that case, what is the proper role of the concept of race in genetic research, health care research, and policy more generally? See, e.g., Sharona Hoffman, Is There a Place for "Race" as a Legal Concept? 36 Ariz. St. L. J. 1093 (2004). Nicholas Wade's 2014 book, A Troublesome Inheritance: Genes, Race, and Human History, discussed further in the notes following section IIIB below, argues that there is a definite genetic basis for race and that the refusal to acknowledge this is due to efforts by social scientists such as Franz Boas to combat racism.

2.   What policy measures might be taken to reduce the risk of discrimination or stigma when members of minority and ethnic groups obtain therapeutic genetic testing?

3.   The Obasogie excerpt gives an example of how differences in hypertension based on skin complexion can lead to erroneous assumptions about racial determinants of health status. Another example was a finding

that African-American steel workers have higher lung cancer rates compared with whites. It turned out that blacks were given the dirtiest, most dangerous jobs, such as standing on top of coke ovens, which exposed them to a higher risk of disease. See Elaine Draper, Risky Business: Genetic Testing and Exclusionary Practices in the Hazardous Workplace 65–96 (1991).

III. GENETICS AND AFRICAN AMERICANS

A. EUGENICS

The eugenics movement in the United States, described in Chapter 2 specifically targeted African Americans. In his book, Inheriting Shame: The Story of Eugenics and Racism in America (1999), Stephen Selden describes how a prominent eugenics organization called the Galton Society was founded in 1918 to promote the notion of genetic differences among races. Meetings discussed purported findings from the new IQ tests about differences in intelligence between Caucasians and African Americans and the need to curb intermarriage between the races. In 1928, for example, Charles Davenport, who founded the Eugenics Record Office described in Chapter 2, gave a talk on "The Evidence of Disharmony in Negro-White Crosses." In a 1913 book, Davenport had listed as undesirable characteristics of African Americans "a strong sex instinct, without corresponding self-control; a lack of appreciation for property distinction (a capacity for which an African origin would hardly have contributed); a certain lack of genuineness—a tendency to pass off clever veneer for the real thing, due to inability or unwillingness to master fundamentals; [and] a premature cessation of intellectual development." Davenport went on to recommend that African Americans who were unable to control their sexual urges or who were uneducable should be prevented from reproducing, if necessary, via sterilization. Note that African Americans were among the plaintiffs who challenged a federal sterilization program in Relf v. Weinberger, discussed in Chapter 2.

Proceedings of the International Congress of Eugenics, including one held at the American Museum of Natural History in 1921, focused on differences in racial worth. One exhibit at the 1921 conference, for example, compared African-American and white fetuses and concluded that the latter had larger brains. Eugenics newsletters such as the Eugenical News published articles complaining that "the worst thing to happen to the . . . United States was the bringing of large numbers of Negroes, nearly the lowest of races, to our shores" and arguing that it was time for the host "to destroy its parasite" by repatriating African Americans "of breeding age" to Africa.

Selden also describes how eugenicists pushed for laws restricting racial intermarriage, such as a 1913 Maryland law that called it an "infamous crime" to be "forever prohibited and void."

The racist theme that African Americans inherit less favorable genomes than others persists. One of the most well-known modern proponents of this view is Charles Murray, coauthor of the 1994 book, The Bell Curve: Intelligence and Class Structure in American Life. But as Paul Lombardo explains, his views on genes, race, and intelligence are rooted in the American eugenics movement. Paul A. Lombardo, "The American Breed": Nazi Eugenics and the Origins of the Pioneer Fund, 65 Alb. L. Rev. 743 (2002).

In 2014, the topic surfaced again with the publication of a book entitled A Troublesome Inheritance: Genes, Race, and Human History, by Nicholas Wade, who was then science editor at the New York Times. Wade did not directly claim that African Americans have less desirable genomes than other races, but summarized his thesis by maintaining that "there is a genetic component to human social behavior; that this component, so critical to human survival, is subject to evolutionary change and has indeed evolved over time; that the evolution in social behavior has necessarily proceeded independently in the five major races and others; and that slight evolutionary differences in social behavior underlie the differences in social institutions prevalent among the major races." Elsewhere he stated: "Several social behaviors that economists have identified as obstacles to progress are ones that could well have a genetic basis. One is the radius of trust, which can extend to strangers in modern economies but is confined to family or tribe in premodern ones." He then quoted an economist from Cameroon who describes African societies as being like a football team in which "one player will not pass the ball to another out of fear that the latter might score a goal." Wade's book was heavily criticized. A review in The New York Times Sunday Book Review, for example, described it as "a deeply flawed, deceptive and dangerous book." David Dobbs, Sunday Book Review: The Fault in Our DNA "A Troublesome Inheritance" and "Inheritance," July 10, 2014, www.nytimes.com/2014/07/13/books/review/a-troublesome-inheritance-and-inheritance.html?_r=0.

Some prominent African Americans were themselves advocates of eugenics. Gregory Michael Dorr and Angela Logan describe what they call "assimilationist eugenics" perspectives of W.E.B. DuBois and others. See Gregory Michael Dorr & Angela Logan, "Quality, Not Mere Quantity, Counts": Black Eugenics and the NAACP Baby Contests, in A Century of Eugenics: From the "Indiana Experiment" to the Human Genome Era 68–92 (Paul A. Lombardo ed. 2011). DuBois stated that "the Negro . . . must begin to train and breed for brains, for efficiency, for beauty." He conceived of a segment of ten percent of the African American population which he called "the Talented Tenth," and, state Dorr and Logan, believed that "long-term African American advance depended on the prolific reproduction of the Talented Tenth." In addition, the NAACP conducted its own "fitter families" contests, a positive eugenics practice described in Chapter 2, in part to raise funds for the organization's anti-lynching campaign, but also, state Dorr and Logan, to "sensitize participants to the need for (and benefits of) rational eugenic procreation."

B. SICKLE CELL SCREENING

LORI ANDREWS ET AL., ASSESSING GENETIC RISKS: IMPLICATIONS FOR HEALTH AND SOCIAL POLICY
40–41 (1994).

A serious set of errors was made in the establishment of sickle cell screening programs in the African-American community in the early 1970s. Some of these screening programs were established without adequate consultation and education of the affected communities. A test then in common use failed to distinguish individuals with the disease from those who were only carriers. No treatment was available or on the horizon. The only benefit of early detection for infants with the disease was to ensure that children would receive medical care promptly when they became sick, yet improved access to medical care was not usually part of the programs. Nor was prenatal diagnosis available at that time; the only way parents could avoid having affected children was not to have children at all or to avoid mating with another carrier.

Since 8 percent of African Americans are carriers of the sickle cell trait, many carriers were detected in screening programs. However, knowledge of having the trait was appropriate only for reproductive purposes since there is a 1 in 4 risk of having an infant with sickle cell anemia if both parents carry the trait. However, confusion about the significance of carrying the common sickle cell trait (about 1 in 12 African Americans) and the rare sickle cell anemia (with a frequency of about 1 in 600) often led to stigmatization and discrimination.

In the early 1970s, seven states passed mandatory laws requiring sickle cell screening, while ten others had voluntary laws. Some laws called for newborn screening. Others erroneously regarded sickle cell anemia as an infectious disease and called for screening before a child could enter school. Others required it as a condition of obtaining a marriage license. In at least one state law, as well as in the National Sickle Cell Anemia Control act of 1972, it was evident that legislators had confused the frequency of the trait (about 1 in 12 African Americans) with the frequency of the disease of about 1 in 600. The national act required programs supported with federal funds to be voluntary, not mandatory.

Nevertheless, even in the late 1970s, some screening in at least one state was done without informed consent.

The experiences in the sickle cell screening programs of the early 1970s reinforce the need for education before screening and for counseling after screening. Enthusiasm turned to suspicion as many African-Americans concluded that the intent was to eradicate the sickle cell gene by preventing carriers from reproducing—thereby reducing the birth rate in the black community. These genetic testing programs were perceived by some as genocidal in intent.

Considerable time, effort, and money have been required to overcome these early mistakes. To promote research and develop high-quality programs of screening and counseling, the National Heart, Lung, and Blood Institute provided funding in the 1970s under the national act to establish 10 centers for sickle cell disease research and 25 clinics to carry out education, screening, and counseling in high-risk populations. Under these auspices, protocols for more effective education, screening, and counseling were developed and the criteria for appropriate management of sickle cell anemia were developed. Early studies by the Centers for Disease Control (CDC) found that the laboratories providing tests often made technical errors and were sometimes doing primary screening with a test that did not distinguish sickle cell trait from the disease. Federal support through the CDC proficiency testing and assistance program helped laboratories to improve the quality of testing. Similarly, federal support for community-based sickle cell programs included education of providers and consumers, improving the understanding of both groups. It was not until 1978 that sickle cell anemia could be diagnosed in amniotic fluid cells obtained by amniocentesis. Prior to that time, diagnosis was possible on fetal blood, although obtaining it carried much greater risks to the fetus than amniocentesis. And not until 1986, as the result of a collaborative nationwide randomized control trial, was it established that penicillin prophylaxis reduced infant and childhood mortality from sickle cell anemia, thereby providing a therapeutic rationale for screening newborns for sickle cell anemia. Although 42 states now screen newborns for sickle cell disease, not all infants with the disease receive treatment.

NOTES AND QUESTIONS

1.   In her book *Killing the Black Body*, Dorothy Roberts explains that "what began as a strategy to improve the health of Blacks soon turned into an instrument of medical abuse. Because screening programs often provided no counseling, there was rampant confusion between carriers of the trait and those who had the disease. Many people who had only sickle-cell trait were mistakenly convinced that their health was in jeopardy. Even the preamble of the federal law stated erroneously that 2 million Americans had sickle-cell *disease* rather than the *trait*." Dorothy Roberts, Killing the Black Body: Race,

Reproduction, and the Meaning of Liberty 257-258 (1997). Roberts notes that 14 states required sickle-cell screening in order for Blacks to attend public school and obtain a marriage license; Blacks were denied admission to the Air Force Academy; most of the commercial airlines fired or grounded Black pilots; and Blacks had problems obtaining insurance. Roberts also describes efforts to prevent Blacks from having children. Carriers for the trait were often counseled to avoid reproducing, and in 1971 members of the Department of Obstetrics and Gynecology at Tennessee College of Medicine published an article recommending sterilization for women with the disease.

2.   For additional background on the sickle cell screening program, see Keith Wailoo, Dying in the City of the Blues: Sickle Cell Anemia and the Politics of Race and Health 165–196 (2001).

3.   Nobel laureate Linus Pauling, who did pioneering work in the late 1940s on the molecular basis for sickle cell disease, urged that all carriers of the sickle cell trait be tattooed with an "S" on their foreheads so that they could avoid reproducing with another carrier. Linus Pauling, Reflections on the New Biology, 15 UCLA Law Rev. 269 (1968).

4.   As described in Chapter 2, Orthodox Jewish communities have instituted successful programs to prevent the marriage of two people who carry the mutation for Tay-Sachs disease. Could a similarly community-based effort be employed in the case of sickle cell? What would such a program look like and what legal obstacles might it encounter?

C. RACE-BASED DRUGS

FOOD AND DRUG ADMINISTRATION, FDA APPROVES BiDIL HEART FAILURE DRUG FOR BLACK PATIENTS
June 23, 2005,
www.fda.gov/NewsEvents/Newsroom/PressAnnouncements/2005/ucm108445.htm.

The Food and Drug Administration (FDA) approved BiDil (bye-DILL), a drug for the treatment of heart failure in self-identified black patients, representing a step toward the promise of personalized medicine.

Heart failure is a condition in which the heart is weakened and does not pump enough blood. It can be caused by a variety of damage to the heart, including heart attacks, high blood pressure, and infections.

The approval of BiDil was based in part on the results of the African-American Heart Failure Trial (A-HeFT). The study, which involved 1,050 self-identified black patients with severe heart failure who had already been treated with the best available therapy, was conducted because two previous trials in the general population of severe heart failure patients found no benefit, but suggested a benefit of BiDil in black patients. Patients on BiDil experienced a 43% reduction in death and a 39%

decrease in hospitalization for heart failure compared to placebo, and a decrease of their symptoms of heart failure.

"Today's approval of a drug to treat severe heart failure in self-identified black population is a striking example of how a treatment can benefit some patients even if it does not help all patients," said Dr. Robert Temple, FDA Associate Director of Medical Policy. "The information presented to the FDA clearly showed that blacks suffering from heart failure will now have an additional safe and effective option for treating their condition. In the future, we hope to discover characteristics that identify people of any race who might be helped by Bidil."

BiDil is a combination of two older drugs, neither approved for heart failure—hydralazine and isosorbide dinitrate.

As an anti-hypertensive agent, hydralazine relaxes the arteries, and decreases the work of the heart. The anti-anginal agent, isosorbide dinitrate, relaxes the veins as well as the arteries. Isosorbide seems to work by releasing nitric oxide at the blood vessel wall, but its effect usually wears off after half a day. Hydralazine may prevent this loss of effect. But how the two drugs work together is not fully known.

ALASTAIR J.J. WOOD, RACIAL DIFFERENCES IN THE RESPONSE TO DRUGS—POINTERS TO GENETIC DIFFERENCES
344 New Eng. J. Med. 1393, 1395 (2001).

* * *

Why do patients have different responses to a given drug, and more specifically, why do patients of different racial and ethnic groups have different responses? In the past, our understanding was relatively simplistic and included the recognition that such differences were fundamentally determined by variability in the concentrations of a drug (pharmacokinetic variability) or by variability in the responses to a drug at a given concentration (pharmacodynamic variability). Racial and ethnic differences in drug responses have now been well described for a range of drugs and reflect genetic differences, environmental differences (including shared cultural and dietary habits), and fundamental differences in the pathogenesis of diseases.

Genetic differences among racial and ethnic groups usually reflect differences in the distribution of polymorphic traits, which occur at different frequencies in different populations, rather than a trait unique to a particular racial or ethnic group. The underlying genetic determinants of the response to a drug and, specifically, racial and ethnic differences in that response are beginning to be unraveled and do indeed appear to be based on the varying distributions of polymorphisms in drug receptors or drug-metabolizing enzymes among different racial and ethnic groups. Persons whose genes encode drug-metabolizing enzymes that lack normal activity have impaired metabolism of the drug substrates of the affected enzyme. Polymorphisms of the enzymes responsible for drug metabolism are distributed differently among different racial and ethnic groups, so the proportion of people with impaired metabolism differs among these groups.

Thus, CYP2D6, the cytochrome P-450 enzyme responsible for the metabolism of drugs such as beta-blockers (including carvedilol) and tricyclic antidepressants, and for the metabolism of codeine to morphine, is functionally absent in 8 percent of whites but fewer than 1 percent of Asians, resulting in different drug concentrations and responses in these racial groups. Black Americans and Africans have a high frequency of a CYP2D6 allele that encodes an enzyme with impaired activity. This allele is virtually absent from white and Asian populations. It is particularly relevant to the study by Yancy et al., because CYP2D6 is responsible for the metabolism of one of the isomers of carvedilol, and stereoselective metabolism would be expected to contribute to differences in the toxicity and efficacy of carvedilol. Patients with the CYP2D6 phenotype of poor metabolism and black patients homozygous for the other CYP2D6 allele encoding impaired metabolism would be at particular risk of excess alpha-adrenergic blockade, perhaps even during the initial period of open-label therapy before randomization. It would therefore be of great interest to extend the study of Yancy et al. to determine whether the CYP2D6 genotype determined either therapeutic responses to carvedilol or its toxic effects.

Recent studies have addressed the role of differing rates of drug metabolism in patients' responses in clinical practice and clinical trials. CYP2C9 is the cytochrome P–450 enzyme responsible for the metabolism of the isomer of warfarin that is principally responsible for the anticoagulant effect of the drug. Two CYP2C9 alleles that produce a phenotype of poor metabolism occur in 11 percent and 8 percent of whites but only 3 percent and 0.8 percent of blacks. Such persons have impaired metabolism of warfarin and thus increased plasma concentrations of the drug. Of more importance to clinical practice, persons with the genotype of impaired metabolism require lower doses of warfarin to achieve an anticoagulant effect similar to that in patients with the normal genotype and are more likely to have an excessive anticoagulant response after the initial dose. In addition, bleeding episodes tend to be more common in persons with the genotype of impaired metabolism.

The proton-pump inhibitor omeprazole is metabolized by CYP2C19, another drug-metabolizing enzyme that exhibits polymorphism with phenotypes of varying distributions among different racial groups. For CYP2C19, in contrast to CYP2D6, the phenotype of poor metabolism is relatively rare in whites (occurring in < 2 percent) but is frequent in

Asians (occurring in 18 to 20 percent). Omeprazole is frequently used as part of a combination regimen to eliminate *Helicobacter pylori* in patients with peptic ulcer disease, and the rate of response is dependent on the CYP2C19 genotype, ranging from 28 percent in patients who are homozygous for the extensive-metabolism allele to 100 percent in those with poor metabolism. Thus, the frequency of genetic polymorphisms of the enzymes responsible for drug metabolism varies among racial groups and contributes to variability in drug response among these groups.

Another genetically determined variable that is responsible for differences in drug response among racial and ethnic groups involves the drug receptors themselves, which also exhibit functionally important genetic polymorphisms. Our understanding of the role of receptor polymorphisms is less advanced than that of drug-metabolism polymorphisms. Polymorphisms of receptors relevant to therapy for heart failure, including β and ¥ adrenergic receptors, endothelial nitric oxide synthase receptors, and angiotensin II type 1 receptors, have all been described and in some cases have been linked to function or therapeutic response in patients with heart failure. The distribution of receptor polymorphisms differs among populations of different racial backgrounds. Such racial differences in receptor polymorphisms may contribute to previously recognized racial differences in the vascular response to adrenergic agonists, a potentially important pathophysiological mechanism in heart failure. There are marked differences among whites, blacks, and Asians in the frequency of polymorphisms of adrenergic receptors, including the β_1-, β_2-, and $¥_1$ adrenergic receptors.

Thus, racial differences in the response to drugs not only have practical importance for the choice and dose of drugs but should also alert physicians to the important underlying genetic determinants of drug response. The logical extension of the studies reported in this issue of the *Journal* will be the identification of the genetic determinants of the reported racial differences, rather than attention to the external phenotypic manifestations of race. The identification of such genetic determinants will make possible better definition of the targets of current and future therapies and will lead to therapies that are more specific. However, an increased specificity of therapies is likely to increase the differences in response among persons of different genetic backgrounds.

RENE BOWSER, RACE AS A PROXY FOR DRUG RESPONSE:
THE DANGERS AND CHALLENGES OF ETHNIC DRUGS
53 DePaul L. Rev. 1111 (2004).

* * *

IV. RACIAL REPACKAGING—THE STORY OF BIDIL

Even though race has not been shown to be a strong proxy for drug metabolism, a drug called BiDil is poised to become the first drug ever approved by the FDA to treat heart failure in African Americans, and only in African Americans. BiDil is a combination of two vasodilators, hydralazine and isosorbide dinitratre (H/I). Vasodilators dilate blood vessels and ease the strain put on the heart in pumping blood. BiDil is thought to have an added benefit of improving levels of nitric oxide in the blood, which is also thought to be of great benefit to individuals suffering from heart failure.

BiDil is an underused drug that has been around for decades; it certainly did not begin as an ethnic drug. This brief review of BiDil's origins demonstrates the centrality of commerce and the exploitation of racial categories in the repackaging of BiDil as a wonder drug for African Americans.

It all begins with the first Vasodilator Heart Failure Trial (V-HeFT I). In this medical trial, which lasted from 1980 to 1985, cardiologists found that the H/I (BiDil) combination appeared to have a beneficial impact in reducing mortality from heart disease. The V-Heft I trial was soon followed by another trial, V-HeFT II, which lasted from 1986 to 1991. This trial compared the efficacy of the H/I (BiDil drugs) against the drug enalapril, an angiotensin-converting enzyme (ACE) inhibitor. The second trial found that enalapril had a more beneficial effect on mortality than the H/I combination. The results of the second trial established ACE inhibitors as the front-line therapy for heart failure. ACE inhibitors have not totally replaced H/I, however, because between 20% and 30% of congestive heart failure patients do not respond well to them. That is roughly 1.5 million patients annually (including members of all racial groups), and current guidelines still recommend the H/I combination for these patients.

The V-HeFT investigators presented the H/I (BiDil drugs) as generally efficacious in the population at large, without regard to race. In 1987, Dr. Jay Cohn, one of the principal investigators in the V-HeFT studies applied for and received a patent on the H/I drugs. In the patent description, Cohn made no mention of race, asserting that H/I substantially and significantly reduces the incidence of mortality in congestive heart patients. Clearly, he believed the BiDil drugs would be used to treat all people suffering from heart failure.

The H/I drugs are generic drugs. Cohn and others combined them into a single pill for easy administration. By 1994, tests were conducted to make sure that the pill form was just as effective as the administration of the drugs separately. They were. Cohn and Medco, which had acquired the intellectual property rights from Cohn, were now ready to approach the FDA for the approval of BiDil for use in the general population.

In 1996, Medco submitted a new drug application (NDA) to the FDA. Jay Cohn optimistically asserted at the time that the BiDil formulation represented a very convenient dosage that, once approved by the FDA, would lead to an increased usage of this therapy in the general population. An industry report estimated a potential market of up to sixty million dollars in annual sales for BiDil.

In an unanticipated move, however, the FDA voted nine to three against approving BiDil, even though extensive findings in peer reviewed journals supported Cohn's claim that the H/I combination substantially and significantly reduced the incidence of mortality in congestive heart failure patients. The agency concluded that while the drug had clinical significance, it failed to meet the biostatistical criteria of probability and efficacy sufficient for the FDA to grant a NDA. In particular, the FDA noted that data from the V-Heft studies contained too many variables specified as endpoints for them to interpret the data with biostatical certainty. The next day, Medco's stock dropped by 25%.

To salvage the drug, the BiDil promoters repackaged it along racial lines. Jay Cohn went back one more time to the V-HeFT data, this time to analyze the differential effects of BiDil and enalapril by race. In 1999, Cohn and others published a paper asserting that the H/I combinations worked better in blacks than ACE inhibitors. Specially, they concluded:

> The H-I combination appears to be particularly effective in prolonging survival in black patients and is as effective as enalapril in this subgroup. In contrast, enalapril shows its more favorable effect in the white population . . . the consistency of observations of a racial difference in response in V-HeFT I and V-HeFT II . . . lend credence to the suggestion that therapy for heart failure might appropriately be racially tailored.

That same year Daniel Dries coauthored a study in the prestigious New England Journal of Medicine suggesting that racial differences exist in the natural progression of congestive heart failure. The implicit conclusion is that heart disease is a different disease in blacks and whites and, therefore, it must be treated with different therapies. This theory of biological difference is consistent with Jay Cohn's claim that the black/white disparity in death rates from heart failure is partly attributable to "a pathophysiology found in black patients that may involve Nitric Oxide (NO) insufficiency arising from either reduced NO production, enhanced NO inactivation or both."

In 1999, NitroMed Inc., a Boston area biotech firm specializing in the development and commercialization of nitric oxide enhanced medicines, acquired the intellectual property rights to BiDil. NitroMed announced its plans to amend the NDA to seek approval for the use of BiDil to treat and prevent mortality associated with heart failure in African-American patients. After a meeting in Washington, the FDA approved the use of BiDil as a drug to treat heart failure in African Americans, pending the successful results of a confirmatory trial. That trial, A-HeFT, the African American Heart Failure Trial, is currently underway.

The FDA's tentative approval represents a significant expansion of the potential BiDil market. NitroMed currently estimates that approximately 750,000 African Americans suffer from heart disease. The implication is that all African Americans suffering from heart disease should be taking BiDil (because it is a different disease), not just those who cannot tolerate or do not respond well to ACE inhibitors. Without doubt, the huge commercial implications of the first ethnic niche market allowed NitroMed to raise over $31.4 million from several private venture capital firms to support the confirmatory trials. Recently, pharmaceutical giant Merck & Co., Inc. formed a multi-year research collaboration with NitroMed, even though BiDil is the company's most advanced product to date.

V.   A NEW THERAPY OR A NEW MARKET FOR AN UNDERUSED DRUG?

BiDil started as a drug for use in the general population but has emerged as a drug for use only in African Americans. A fundamental question is whether significant scientific evidence demonstrates that all African Americans with heart problems should take this drug, or are NitroMed's claims merely a scheme to expand and exploit a potentially lucrative market. As discussed below, substantial evidence raises serious questions about the underpinnings of NitroMed's claims.

First, the study authored by Peter Carson along with Jay Cohn, claiming that blacks respond better to H/I than to ACE inhibitors, retrospectively analyzed data from V-HeFT I and II. It was not prospectively designed to study racial differences in response to treatment, rather, an existing and rather old data set was reanalyzed. There are well documented statistical problems involving randomization and stratification by race in such retrospective studies.

Second, black participants had higher levels of comordid [sic] factors such as diabetes and hypertension. Essentially, the white and black populations were not the same. Few doctors would use monotherapy (a single drug) for cardiovascular disease in patients with concomitant diabetes and hypertension. Therefore, this study may simply confirm what we already know: use of a single ACE inhibitor at a standard dose is not effective for patients who also have diabetes and hypertension, but is effective for patients without these conditions.

Third, the study purports to consider relevant nongenetic environmental influences on the development and progression of heart failure, and includes two such factors—education and "financial distress (yes vs. no) during the past twelve months." While education and experience of financial distress are relevant factors to consider in examining nongenetic environmental influences, the implicit understanding is that they are exhaustive of all such relevant factors.

Vast medical and public health literature shows that a host of deleterious conditions accompany black status in the United States, including differential exposures to environmental toxins, discrimination, residential segregation, and differential political power, both in terms of individual level of control and the allocation of resources. Indeed, a Harvard study shows that the stress of experiencing racism raises blood pressure. It is now well established that physiological processes respond to psychosocial stress. Therefore, the unmeasured variation in environmental exposures could account for the differential response in hospitalization and survival, not differences in drug metabolism.

Fourth, as fortune would have it, one of the strongest critiques has come from one of the coauthors of the original study, Dr. Daniel Dries. In 2002, Dries took issue with the earlier New England Journal of Medicine piece arguing that the ACE inhibitor, enalapril, worked equally well in blacks and whites:

> Despite recent concerns that angiotensin-converting enzyme (ACE) inhibitors may be less efficacious in black patients with [heart failure], the present study demonstrates that enalapril significantly reduced the risk of development of [heart failure] in both blacks and whites * * *. The consistency of results in black and white subjects strengthens the argument that ACE inhibitor-therapy should continue to be used in black patients with [heart failure].

These findings are consistent with the recent African American Study of Kidney Disease and Hypertension that demonstrated a benefit of ACE inhibitor therapy in patients with renal disease.

Finally, NitroMed has relied heavily on the claim that African Americans have twice the risk of dying from heart failure than whites. If this is true, then it is highly plausible that the difference is due to genetic rather than environmental factors. This two-to-one disparity has been floating around uncontested in the scientific literature for decades. Dr. Jonathan Kahn of the University of Minnesota has demonstrated conclusively that the NitroMed claim about the scope of black and white differences is simply untrue. Dr. Kahn traced the citation sources back nearly two decades, and found that the difference between blacks and whites is actually 1.2 to 1. While there is a difference, it is far less than the two-to-one ratio that would warrant special trials for blacks. Thus, "substantial scaffolding of the BiDil clinical trials is based upon incorrect statistical data on racial disparities."

NOTES AND QUESTIONS

1.   For a general discussion of pharmacogenomics, the use of genomic information in pharmaceutical research, development, and marketing, see Chapter 8.

2.   NitroMed sold BiDil to Arbor Pharmaceuticals in October 2008 for $24.5 million.

3.   Does the BiDil case illustrate the problem of racial bias and genetics, discussed earlier? Consider the following:

> The Association of Black Cardiologists, Inc. (ABC), co-sponsor of the landmark African-American Heart Failure Trial (A-HeFT), is pleased that the U.S. Food and Drug Administration (FDA) approved BiDil® (isosorbide dinitrate/hydralazine hydrochloride) for the treatment of heart failure in black patients on [sic] yesterday. A-HeFT was the first clinical trial conducted in an all black heart failure population. BiDil is an orally-administered medicine shown in A-HeFT to improve survival, reduce the rate of first hospitalization for heart failure and improve patient-reported functional status, as an adjunct to current standard heart failure therapy in self-identified black patients.

> "The approval of BiDil is a major step toward eliminating existing cardiovascular-related health disparities affecting African Americans, a population that is disproportionately burdened by heart failure," said B. Waine Kong, Ph.D., J.D., chief executive officer of the Association of Black Cardiologists, Inc. "The ABC is proud to have played an integral role in the African American Heart Failure Trial and we look forward to continued progress in cardiovascular health for African Americans."

Press Release, Association of Black Cardiologists, FDA Approval of BiDil® Brings New Hope to Black Heart Failure Patients (June 24, 2005).

In an article in the Cambridge Quarterly of Healthcare Ethics, Joon-Ho Yu, Sara Goering and Stephanie Fullerton provide an interesting explanation for the support for BiDil among many leaders in the African-American community:

> BiDil's approval has been widely critiqued in academic circles on numerous grounds. Nevertheless, many advocates for African

American health concerns have argued that BiDil is an important step toward reducing disparities in healthcare by creating medical therapies that are responsive to African American needs. Many of these advocates also publicly rejected the notion that BiDil is a race-specific drug, arguing that social race is a poor surrogate for the biological differences that underlie BiDil's efficacy. Thus, competing commitments to reducing health disparities while rejecting a biologically deterministic view of race have placed African American community leaders and health advocates in a state of conflict, both among themselves and with academic scholars of race, with respect to the desirability of BiDil.

In this paper, we offer a sympathetic reading of this response to BiDil by some African American community leaders and aim to show how many of the academic critiques have failed to adequately account for the competing commitments of community stakeholders. We argue that justice involves not only the fair distribution of benefits but also an element of recognition, such that socially marginalized groups have the opportunity to be heard and to participate in decisionmaking. In the case of BiDil, we believe that African American community leaders capitalized on an opportunity to bring attention to African American health issues, even as they risked complicity with an inaccurate portrayal of race as biological. Using Nancy Fraser's bivalent theory of justice (involving both recognition and redistribution), we argue that community leaders can be viewed as strategically affirming the use of race in hopes of ultimately transforming the process of drug development and garnering more careful attention to the problem of health disparities. Given the context of health disparities and statements made by community advocates that explicitly link BiDil to remedying such disparities, we believe this strategy is best understood not simply as a calculated risk assumed for the sake of some consequentialist benefit but rather as a means of asserting a demand for justice.

Joon-Ho Yu, Sara Goering & Stephanie M. Fullerton, Race-Based Medicine and Justice as Recognition: Exploring the Phenomenon of BiDil, 18 Cambridge Q. of Healthcare Ethics 57, 57–58 (2009).

4.   As mentioned in note 3, BiDil initially received widespread support from African-American leaders, including the Congressional Black Caucus, the NAACP, and the Association of Black Cardiologists. Regardless of the genetic or biological basis for BiDil, the drug appeared to offer some promise in improving health outcomes for cardiovascular disease, a particularly serious problem in the African-American population. Nevertheless, BiDil has proved to be a commercial failure. There are two main reasons. First, BiDil was, arguably, a breakthrough of convenience. The standard dosing is two pills, three times a day, for a total of six pills per day. Taking the generic versions of hydralazine and isosorbide dinitrate (nitroglycerin) requires four

pills, four times a day, for a total of 16 pills per day. But, there is a heavy price for this convenience. BiDil costs about $4,000 per year, or about four to seven times more than the generic equivalents. Many health insurance companies have refused to cover BiDil on their formularies. Second, many African-American patients, upon learning that BiDil was approved only for self-identified African Americans, told their physicians that they would rather have the drug prescribed for white patients. Clearly, genetics, drugs, and race remain very complicated issues. For a comprehensive discussion, see Jonathan Kahn, Race in a Bottle (2014).

IV. GENETICS AND ETHNICITY

A. RESEARCH ON ISOLATED POPULATIONS

HENRY T. GREELY, THE CONTROL OF GENETIC RESEARCH: INVOLVING THE "GROUPS BETWEEN"
33 Hous. L. Rev. 1397, 1414–1415 (1997).

The HGDP [Human Genome Diversity Project] intends to collect a representative sample of human genetic variation. It would like to collect DNA from members of about five hundred of the roughly five to ten thousand human populations in the world. This DNA would be stored in repositories and made available to researchers. The samples would all be subjected to analysis under a standard set of markers, and the results would be placed in a database, also generally available to researchers. The result would be a reference library of human genetic diversity, which the HGDP estimates could be completed in about five to seven years, for a cost of about twenty-five to thirty-five million dollars.

Improved information about human genetic diversity can be important for at least four different reasons. First, thus far the vast majority of detailed research into human genetics has been done with Europeans or North Americans of European descent, and thus omits the eighty percent of the world's population that is not of European ancestry. It is fundamentally unfair to the majority of humanity to describe the human genome without including a representative sample of all humans. Second, studying human genetic diversity will help us understand better the workings of evolution in humans, including the ways in which culture influences evolution. Third, greater knowledge of human genetic diversity will improve medicine, both because it will advance the study of those genetic diseases found largely in non-European populations, and because genetic variation is basic to better understanding a host of diseases found in all peoples. Finally, studying human diversity will help us uncover our shared human history. Genetic results, when interpreted along with evidence from anthropology, archaeology, history, linguistics, and other fields, will help map human migrations and expansions in prehistoric times.

ZESHAN Q. KHAN, COLONIALISM REVISITED: INSIGHTS INTO THE HUMAN GENOME DIVERSITY PROJECT
3 J.L. & Soc. Challenges 89, 89–115 (1999).

The HGDP, a Project created by Stanford geneticist Luigi Luca Cavalli-Sforza, intends to obtain DNA samples from between 400 to 722 indigenous groups throughout the world. By obtaining samples from peoples who have remained culturally, geographically and biologically isolated from the rest of the world, the Project hopes to obtain DNA samples from those whose blood has remained relatively consistent for centuries. Western scientists created this project for three primary reasons: (1) the location of genes among indigenous peoples that immunize them from genetic diseases (as well as the location of disease-causing genes); (2) the formation of a family tree that depicts the evolution and migratory patterns of existing humans; and (3) an increased sampling pool for the Human Genome Project.

* * *

Opponents of the HGDP have concerns on many levels. These include problems with the potential benefits depicted by the proponents of the Project, as well as fears that relate to histories of exploitation; the aboriginal people fear that once again, others will exploit them * * *. The primary argument against the Project * * * is that any medical advances associated with genes will not benefit indigenous peoples. Scientific advances may help those who can afford treatment or who live in a society where concerns such as mental disorders or genetic cancers supersede concerns about malaria. However, it is unlikely that such medical advances associated with genes will directly benefit those who provide the "raw materials" for the design of such knowledge. Moreover, if gene therapies were created, it is unlikely that indigenous peoples could afford them. Such a system, by its very nature, is colonialism in its purest form—the appropriation of resources from the colonized to benefit the colonizing people, without proper compensation, as determined by the subject indigenous people.

* * *

There are many examples of profiting from naturally occurring substances at the expense of indigenous peoples. One is the Indian neem tree. A U.S. chemicals company obtained a patent for a natural pesticide extracted by generations of Indian farmers from the seed of the neem tree. The traditional methods, however, were not protected by patent thus the chemical company only had to extract the pesticide and claim it as its own. Because a patent entitles one to control its use by others, Indian farmers must now pay a royalty to the chemical company to use the extract.

Another example of plant appropriation is quinine, the well-known cure for malaria. The drug comes from the bark of the cinchona tree of Peru. Indigenous Andean groups used quinine as a cure for fevers, learning to do so by supposedly watching feverish jaguars eat it. In addition, the rosy periwinkle plant of Madagascar has been found to possess certain cancer-fighting characteristics. Eli Lilly developed two drugs from the plant, resulting in $100 million in annual sales. Madagascar received none of the profits.

In 1990, scientist Sally Fox received a patent for colored cotton. This fabric is highly lucrative since it is environmentally friendly and some of the largest U.S. clothing manufacturers desire such material. The seed for Sally Fox's cotton, however, came from a U.S. Department of Agriculture sample collected from Latin America. The seed is the result of centuries of cultivation and breeding by indigenous peoples. To date, 15,000 indigenous farmers grow the cotton, and over 50,000 indigenous women spin and weave it. These are just a few examples of the profiteering which has occurred over the past twenty-five years.

* * * One could argue that there is a clear difference between plants and human genetic material, however, members of indigenous peoples may not share this view of distinction. Many see themselves, as well as the plant-life around them, as parts of a natural gestaltic whole. The separation of plant-life from human genetic material is seen by some as a cultural imposition upon these people. Distinct ownership of living materials is not a part of their understanding. Notions of exclusive property rights over naturally occurring substances are a violation of the beliefs held by many of the indigenous people. Ownership is often a cultural construct of the colonizing world and its imposition upon indigenous peoples is commonly seen as a form of cultural imperialism.

* * *

[The indigenous groups have raised concerns about the patenting of their DNA.] Since patenting a U.S. citizen's DNA for profit is acceptable, it seems logical that the next target is DNA from other countries. In 1993, the U.S. government filed a patent claim for the cell line of a Guaymi woman from Panama. Although the government withdrew its claims, it has filed two other patent applications on human cell lines of indigenous peoples—one from the Solomon Islands, and the other from Papua New Guinea. Eventually, the government filed papers to forfeit its "rights" to the patent claims with the Patent and Trademark Office (PTO) * * *. The Guaymi tribal president stated that he, "never imagined people would patent plants and animals. It's fundamentally immoral, contrary to the Guaymi view of nature, and our place in it. To patent human material

* * * to take human DNA and patent its products * * * that violates the integrity of life itself, and our deepest sense of morality."

* * *

[The indigenous groups are also concerned that genetic research will be used in an attempt to prove their "inferiority," like research on skull size was used in an earlier era in an attempt to prove the intellectual inferiority of Native Americans.] What many scientists seem to miss is that the scientific data, which to scientists are irreducible truths, are prone to the same socially arbitrary appropriation as already existing tools for racial subordination. Scientists themselves have claimed to discover the lack of a "novelty seeking gene" among Asians that may predispose them to an unchanging and settled lifestyle. Does this mean that "afflicted" Asians are incapable of innovation, and thus cultural evolution? Or have Asians hit an evolutionary plateau?

* * *

[There is also concern that indigenous peoples' samples are being used without their consent.] Janelle Noble [a scientist for a pharmaceutical company who collected tissue samples from people in South America], once questioned the purpose of obtaining informed consent from native peoples who had lived uncomplicated agrarian lifestyles for hundreds of years. According to Noble, "there is no point in telling them [indigenous people] we're going to do HLA typing on their genes since they would not understand what HLA typing is in the first place," and that the subjects of the HGDP "as much as they can understand, they are giving their informed consent." This comment implies that it is a waste of time to properly give these people information so that they can make a truly informed choice. Indeed, many proponents and opponents alike have questioned the ability of native peoples' ability to give truly informed consent. George Annas, bioethicist from Boston University's School of Public Health, claims that if many of these people knew the true purpose of the Project, they would not give their consent since the Project violates essential notions they hold of life. But Noble's condescension precludes the possibility of even remedial knowledge from being offered to these people. Many people have echoed the sentiment asserted by Annas. Upon awareness of the Project's basic agenda and methodology, a group of indigenous people in North and South America created the Declaration of Indigenous Peoples of the Western Hemisphere Regarding the Human Genome Diversity Project, which condemned the Project on many fronts. Seventeen organizations consisting of and representing indigenous people from British Columbia to Bolivia signed the document * * *.

JOCELYN KAISER, A PLAN TO CAPTURE HUMAN
DIVERSITY IN 1000 GENOMES
319 Science 395 (2008).

It's sign of how fast horizons are changing in biology: Researchers who only a few years ago were being asked to justify the cost of sequencing a single human genome are now breezily offering to sequence 1000. And they say they can do it in a flash. Over the next 3 years, an international team plans to create a massive new genome catalog that will serve as "a gold-standard reference set for analysis of human variation," says Richard Durbin of the Sanger Institute in Hinxton, U.K., who proposed the project just last year.

The 1000 Genomes Project, as it's called, will delve much deeper than the sequencing of celebrity genomes, three of which were completed last year. It will help fill out the list of new genetic markers for common diseases that came out in 2007, says Francis Collins, director of the U.S. National Human Genome Research Institute (NHGRI) in Bethesda, Maryland. At the same time, new technologies will be put to the test, and researchers will work out how to handle a growing deluge of data. Such practical advances will be needed a few years from now when sequencing entire genomes will be routine, notes population geneticist Kenneth Weiss of Pennsylvania State University in State College, who is not part of the project. "This seems overall like a next logical step," he says.

The search for disease genes took off last year, building on the first human genome reference sequence in 2003 and the subsequent HapMap. The latter describes how blocks of DNA tagged by common variants, called single-nucleotide polymorphisms (SNPs), vary in different populations. These SNPs have turned up more than 100 new DNA markers associated with common illnesses such as diabetes and heart disease. But the HapMap includes only the most common markers, those present in at least 5% of the population.

To find rarer SNPs that occur at 1% frequency, genome leaders say, they need to sequence about 1000 genomes. According to a plan hammered out by about three dozen experts last year, the project will take advantage of new technologies that have slashed the cost of sequencing. The work will be done by the three U.S. sequencing centers funded by NHGRI, the Sanger Institute, and the Beijing Genomics Institute (BGI) in Shenzhen, China.

Because the technologies are so new, the consortium will start with three pilot projects. One will exhaustively sequence the entire genome of six individuals: two adults and both sets of their parents. DNA in these six genomes will be analyzed repeatedly up to 20 times to ensure almost complete coverage. A second project will sequence 180 individual genomes at light (2x) coverage, leaving gaps. The third project will be to fully sequence (20x coverage) the protein-coding regions of 1000 genes (5% of the total) in about 1000 genomes. The samples, all anonymous and with no clinical information, will mainly be drawn from those collected for the HapMap, which includes people of European, Asian, and African descent.

The pilots should take about a year and will put the new technologies to a "very vigorous test," Collins says. After that, the consortium will decide what coverage to use to sequence the entire set of 1000 genomes. Most of the project's $30 million to $50 million price tag will be paid from the existing sequencing budgets of institutes, organizers say.

The new catalog could help disease gene hunters in several ways. It may allow researchers simply to hunt through an index for a SNP in a particular location that alters a gene product rather than run a time-consuming sequencing project, Collins says. The project will also catalog genes that are sometimes lost or duplicated; such copy-number variants can cause disease. By compiling rarer variants, it should also help resolve a debate about the relative contribution of these mutations to disease risks. "There's no question it's going to be a tremendous resource," says Yale University's Judy Cho, who has used the HapMap to find a new gene for Crohn's disease.

China is also launching its own human genomes project. BGI Shenzhen this month announced that it is seeking 99 volunteers who will help pay to have their genomes sequenced as part of a study of diversity. The 3-year effort, called the Yanhuang Project after the Yan and Huang tribes that are believed to be ancestors of modern Chinese, will overlap with the 1000 Genomes Project. With proper consent, some volunteers' genomes will be sequenced for both efforts, says Wang Jun, director of BGI Hangzhou.

In a parallel effort, J. Craig Venter of the J. Craig Venter Institute in Rockville, Maryland, says his team will sequence up to 10 individuals this year and publish the data along with medical information. Venter—who dismisses the 1000 Genomes Project as "more survey work" because not all genomes will be sequenced to great depth—has even bolder plans. He says he aims for "complete diploid genome sequencing" of 10,000 human genomes in the next decade. Still, he says, "it's great that there's such an expansion of things."

NOTES AND QUESTIONS

1. By 2005, the Human Genome Diversity Project collected over 1,000 cell lines from more than 50 populations all over the world and sent those samples to over 50 research groups globally. Luigi Luca Cavalli-Sforza, The Human Genome Diversity Project: Past, Present, and Future, 6 Nature Reviews Genetics 333 (2005). However, the Human Genome Diversity Project appears not to have moved forward due to a lack of funding; in 2005 the

National Institutes of Health refused to fund the HGDP. See Henry T. Greely, Lessons From The HGDP?, 308 Science 1554 (2005).

2.   The Genographic Project seeks to tell the genetic origin story of humanity, describing in detail the patterns of human migration over the past 150,000 years. It is a privately funded venture, sponsored by National Geographic and funded by the Waitt Family Foundation, as well as other private contributors. Although the general public is welcome to participate in the project by contributing DNA samples, the Genographic Project seeks to collect 100,000 samples from various indigenous and traditional peoples throughout the world to complete its goal. The Genographic Project relies on the genetic information of indigenous and traditional peoples it considers sufficiently isolated from the general population as reference points to determine paths of human migration throughout history. Ultimately, the Project hopes to produce its findings in a database that associates genetic variations in global populations with anthropological information about the cultures involved in the Project—the creators of the Project argue that such anthropological information is necessary to contextualize and understand the genetic data, particularly where globalization threatens to erase traditional cultures around the world. Researchers involved in the Project have already published several scientific papers utilizing the genetic data collected thus far. For more information, visit https://genographic.nationalgeographic.com/faq/about-project/.

The Genographic Project hopes to quash speculation of "bioprospecting"—the appropriation of indigenous and traditional people's genetic material for the research and production of commercial products—by anonymizing genetic samples and requiring informed consent from both individuals and communities of indigenous or traditional descent. Additionally, the Genographic Project does not create cell lines from collected samples and prohibits their use in medical research.

However, the Genographic Project's claim to tell the origin story of humanity is problematic. Some see the Genographic Project as diminishing the personhood of indigenous and traditional people by reinforcing a stereotype that they are primal or primitive by characterizing their genetic heritage as isolated or unique. Additionally, the migration story told by the genetic data may conflict with indigenous peoples' understanding of their origins or could potentially be used against them in the resolution of legal issues such as land ownership conflicts. For a treatment of these issues see Kim TallBear, Narratives of Race and Indigeneity in the Genographic Project, 35 J.L. Med. & Ethics 412 (2007). Are there any situations, political, legal or otherwise, where genetic migration data might be useful or beneficial to indigenous and traditional peoples? For what reasons might indigenous people oppose such research?

3.   The International HapMap Project specifically aims to provide genetic information that medical researchers will later use to predict and treat disease. The project is a publicly and privately funded venture, with

financial support from several countries, including the United States. To accomplish its goal, the project maps common genetic variations and shows where the variations occur in the genome. Additionally, it shows how these variations are distributed within different populations throughout the world. The project also creates and maintains cell lines of its samples for medical researchers, first, to create the map of genetic variation (the HapMap), and second, for use in future medical research. The project has collected genetic material from peoples of African, Asian, and European ancestry, including, but not limited to, indigenous peoples and continuously makes updates available on its website as new data is collected and analyzed. For more information, visit http://hapmap.ncbi.nlm.nih.gov/thehapmap.html.en.

In an attempt to avoid ethical controversy, the International HapMap Project has instituted informed consent procedures for research participants. The project's informed consent materials inform individual participants and their communities that their genetic material may later be used by medical researchers in studying disease. And to obtain informed consent at the communal and individual level, the project attempts to create relationships between researchers and participating communities through a number of devices, including Community Advisory Groups (CAG). CAGs act as intermediaries between communities and researchers and facilitate discussion of the project. As the project continues, updates concerning the status and use of communal samples are sent through CAGs to communities for discussion and interpretation. The informed consent materials also provide that CAGs will help participating communities to understand how future research projects conducted with their samples might affect them. Additionally, all studies that use samples from the International HapMap Project need IRB approval.

However, the individuals and communities who provide samples do not have any direct influence over whether research will be conducted on those samples. Nor are communities able to prevent an organization from patenting future findings based on the study of their samples. What if the IRB approves a project that the study participants do not approve? Whose opinion should control the use of the samples in genetic research? See the discussion of the HapMap in Chapter 2.

4.   The Khan excerpt mentions concerns that the Guaymi tribe raised after cell lines derived from its people were patented. Other indigenous groups have also raised concerns about the benefits promised to them in exchange for donating blood samples. In 1996 a group of researchers visited the Karitiana tribe in Brazil promising medicine if the Karitiana would give blood for research. Eleven years later, the tribe never received medicine but discovered that their blood samples were on sale by a French blood and DNA repository for $85 a sample. The French repository says it provides samples only to scientists who agree not to commercialize their findings or transfer the material to third parties. A major concern with retrieving blood samples from isolated tribes like the Karitiana is that often the tribes have had little to no contact with the outside world at the time of their agreements with

researchers. Do you think it is possible for people "who had lived uncomplicated agrarian lifestyles for hundreds of years" to be capable of giving informed consent? Members of other tribes have also raised religious objections. The Yanomami demanded their blood samples back because they believe a soul cannot rest until all of a person's tissue is cremated. See Larry Rohter, In the Amazon, Giving Blood but Getting Nothing, The New York Times, June 20, 2007, at A1.

B. CONCERNS ABOUT "GROUP" HARMS

ERIC T. JUENGST, THE PERILS OF GENETIC GENEALOGY
10 CenterViews 1 (1996).

Origin stories are powerful. Think of the tenacity with which adoptees can pursue their birth parents' identities, or the pride that families often take in their geographical roots, or the controversies over teaching human evolution to school kids. No matter how new social conventions and technologies allow us to reinvent our identities, our sense of self nonetheless depends heavily on where we came from—that is, on our family tree and our family's travels * * *. Given this, it should have been anticipated that the Human Genome Diversity Project (HGDP) would attract attention.

* * *

First, it risks the appearance of granting biological legitimacy to social categories, inappropriately "naturalizing" the lines among groups and adding the authority of science to the attempt of those—both within and outside particular groups—to set those groups apart from the rest of society. The concept of "race" may be undermined, but in its place the thoroughly respectable concept of a "deme"—as a genetically differentiated subpopulation—can still serve as a scientific foundation for unjust attitudes and practices. If ethnic groups and minority communities are counted as human demes, the local tensions between them can take on the virulence of racism as new species of "demic discrimination."

Second, by identifying 500 populations as "particularly representative of ancestral populations," the project risks reifying these groups in the public's mind as representing the "original pure types" of humanity, reinforcing the idea that human groups can be graded, for better or worse, in terms of their distance from their stock. This could have stigmatizing consequences for either the target groups (if they are seen as "primitive") or for mixed groups (if they are seen as "polluted") depending on the local social context.

Third, even if we could prevent people from misinterpreting the HGDP's basic human taxonomy, what about the stories that would ultimately emerge? The stories that scientists will be able to tell after working with the HGDP's cell banks will be stories about lineage and land tenure: stories about who is most closely related to whom and who got where first. Here is where the power of our origin stories asserts itself. Even where ethnic tensions are not involved, stories about lineage and land tenure have always been humanity's two favorite excuses for claiming social privilege. Any new information that could add scientific credibility to the arguments of those disputing such claims could be easily abused. Would the HGDP archivists police the users and uses of their databank to discourage those seeking to settle political disputes?

Finally, looking for the genomic hallmarks of particular social groups could produce tools for carrying out a program of demic discrimination by making DNA identification tests possible. One can imagine two scenarios: one in which the privileged caste tests for their own definitive DNA hallmarks as inclusion criteria for social opportunities, and one in which a particular group's markers are used to identify them for oppression. At first, there seemed to be some comfort in scientific skepticism that any such unique markers could be found for any human groups larger than extended families. But consider this January 14, 1996 news flash:

> An extremely rare mutation on the Y chromosome may be a genetic marker that is unique to the people who first migrated to the Americas some 30,000 years ago researchers report * * * A group of Stanford University researchers have identified a mutation that in their sample (of 500 DNA samples from populations around the world) exists only in Indian populations in North and South America and in Eskimo groups * * * The Y chromosome mutation occurred in a stretch of DNA that is not related to a gene, but is part of the "junk" DNA that separates the genes.

Would it be fair for an American man to use a positive test for this mutation in supporting a claim to affirmative action benefits? What about native American women and men with maternal lines of descent, who could not show this proof of American Indian ancestry? Would it be right for a South American government to publish the results of this test for all political candidates? The capacity for both uses of this little tidbit from the human origin story is already with us in genotyping labs throughout the hemisphere.

MORRIS W. FOSTER ET AL., A MODEL AGREEMENT FOR
GENETIC RESEARCH IN SOCIALLY IDENTIFIABLE POPULATIONS
63 Am J. Human Genetics 696, 696–702 (1998).

* * *

COMMUNAL DISCOURSE

We used a process of communal discourse to engage the participation of the Apache Tribe of Oklahoma. We began by conducting a health survey through 150 ethnographic interviews (20% of the adult population). The interviews included questions about who was consulted in making health-care decisions. We used the answers to those questions to identify public and private social units that Apaches were accustomed to consult about their well-being. These units were considered by community members to be the most appropriate entities to consult about the collective implications of genetic research. Our definition of "appropriate" is derived from the population's preexisting processes for reaching a communal consensus. Although such processes vary among populations, our procedure for identifying culturally appropriate decision-making units is generally applicable. Anthropology has well-defined methods for the study of collective decision making.

A related problem was the inclusion of a cross-section of appropriate social units sufficient to represent all segments of the Apache population. Here, we relied on a combination of information from the health-survey interviews and advice from Apache elders. Members of the Apache community were themselves very aware of the question of representativeness—a necessary element in reaching any communal consensus—and were able to guide us in including specific social units. In the Apache community, the major public unit is a five-person Apache Business Committee that is elected by tribal members. It is recognized as having public authority to make formal decisions about matters affecting the well-being of the community as a whole. Everyday private life, however, is ordered by five major extended families, which are the private units within which information about such matters as individual health status is confidential. The Apache Business Committee takes care to appoint members from each of the major families to any community panel.

We requested that the Apache Business Committee sponsor a series of public meetings, open to all tribal members, in which we explained our research goals. As a result of this initial dialogue, we modified our goals to take account of communal priorities * * *. [T]he Apache Business Committee * * * appointed a committee to evaluate the research proposal * * *. The Apache Business Committee designated this committee as a "tribal institutional review board" (IRB) but that designation may be somewhat misleading. What the Apaches called a "tribal IRB" functioned in a dual role that is not standard in bioethical practice; that is, it both evaluated the research project for its implications for the Apache community and then explained those implications to and negotiated them with researchers. Typically, an IRB undertakes only the first of these tasks, whereas inclusion of the second might be considered—according to Euro-American ethics—as creating a conflict of interest for the IRB. In the case of the Apache community, however, such a separation of responsibilities was seen by members as impractical. Those persons who were judged most knowledgeable in evaluating the cultural implications of the proposed research also were considered the most appropriate persons to negotiate community-specific concerns with researchers. The same qualities of personal and cultural authority were deemed necessary for both tasks. To avoid confusion with more typical IRBs, we will use the term "community review board," or "CRB," to refer to the Apache committee.

* * *

Apaches discussed implications for the community as issues separate from those for individuals. They recognized that risks of stigmatization and discrimination would apply to all tribal members, not just to those who might volunteer as study participants. They asserted a communal interest even for biological specimens that would be individually anonymous, because of the use of the collective name "Apache." This communal interest was no less for stored materials subject to studies in the future. Nevertheless, despite potential collective risks, Apaches were strongly motivated to participate in research on diabetes mellitus, which they perceived as a major health problem.

[Among the provisions that the Apaches negotiated were the following:]

PUBLICATIONS

All manuscripts that report project findings will be reviewed by the Apache CRB, which will have 60 days to raise objections to use of the tribal name. In that event, investigators either could revise the manuscript to satisfy Apaches' concerns or could publish the results without naming the Apache tribe. Although study populations traditionally have been named in scientific publications, keeping their identities confidential would not necessarily invalidate analyses of genetic factors for disease susceptibility and resistance.

INTELLECTUAL PROPERTY

According to long-established practice, as well as limited legal precedent, individuals who donate biological materials do not have legal claim on the intellectual property derived from them. In our agreement, the owner of any intellectual property is the university, the sponsoring institution. The subcontract, however, recognizes the unique contribution of the participating community in the creation of that intellectual property. The university will deduct 10% of royalties for legal and administrative costs. Of the remainder, the university will retain 30%, the tribe will receive 30%, and investigators will receive 30%. The unassigned 10% will be retained in a reserve fund for liability or litigation. The Apache CRB resolved that any royalties to the tribe be earmarked for the promotion of the health and education of tribal members.

ARCHIVAL STORAGE AND STUDY

At the conclusion of our project, we will negotiate with the tribal CRB the issue of long-term storage of biological specimens. If we are unable to reach an agreement, those materials will be disposed of in a culturally appropriate manner. However, if the tribal CRB permits storage of samples, explicit provisions will be negotiated to define how future research projects would receive community approval.

CULTURAL CONCERNS

We encountered some concerns that are culturally specific to the study population. Apaches have restrictions about physical contact that are specific to gender, family, and age. Thus, the tribal CRB decided that blood samples should be drawn by a non-Apache. Apaches also expressed an interest in what is done with biological materials that are not consumed by laboratory analyses. Those materials still are considered part of the body, so investigators and the tribal CRB will review procedures to ensure that the proper respect is accorded. More generally, each of the other provisions negotiated with the tribe was interpreted from a uniquely Apache cultural perspective. For instance, concerns about adverse affects [sic] from the publication of scientific findings focused on stigmatization of families with a history of diabetes within the community, rather than on discrimination from outside. Similarly, the primary concern about the use of archival specimens was in potential studies comparing the Apache genome with those of other Native peoples. Results from such comparative studies could contradict Apache origin narratives. Both these risks are based on how Apaches culturally construct their own sense of shared identity, not on how others view them.

LORI ANDREWS, HAVASUPAI TRIBE SUES GENETIC RESEARCHERS

4 L. & Bioethics Report 10–11 (2004), reprinted in 31 Privacy J. 5–6 (April 2005).

The foundation of genetics research around the world was built on studies of Drosophila and lab rats. But with the advent of the Human Genome Project, genetics researchers turned increasingly to humans as research subjects. Now researchers are finding that the human subjects have a characteristic that other species do not: their concerns about informed consent, privacy, and fair dealing sometimes lead them to file lawsuits when researchers behave in a way that the subjects find unacceptable.

Litigation pending before Judge Fredrick J. Martone of the U.S. District Court for Arizona could help clarify the duties of genetics researchers toward their subjects. Members of the Havasupai Tribe allege that researchers of Arizona State University ("ASU") and the University of Arizona ("U of A") collected 400 blood samples from them for researching diabetes, but that additional unauthorized research was undertaken on those samples regarding schizophrenia, inbreeding, and population migration. They assert that the research on schizophrenia and inbreeding was stigmatizing to them and that they would not have authorized the migration research because it conflicts with their religious origin story.

The 650-member Havasupai Tribe are descendants of the Hohokam Indians, who migrated north from Mexico around 300 B.C. The Havasupai settled in an isolated and remote location in the Grand Canyon, which is still only accessible by horseback, foot, or helicopter. Such isolation is the reason that the Havasupai Tribe poses a restricted gene pool, in which certain genetic diseases are at higher incidence than in, say, a general urban population. In fact, the Havasupai have one of the highest incidences of type 2 diabetes anywhere in the world. In 1991, 55% of Havasupai women and 38% of the Havasupai men were diabetic.

In 1989, two tribe members approached an ASU faculty member, asking for help to stem the tribe's high incidence of diabetes. They allege that researcher Therese Markow and a colleague originally presented their project to the tribal council as consisting of three elements: (1) "diabetes education," (2) "collecting and testing blood samples from individual members to identify diabetics or persons susceptible to diabetes," and (3) "genetic testing to identify an association between certain gene variants and diabetes among Havasupai people." They allege that Markow did not inform them that she was in the process of, or had previously submitted, a grant application to study schizophrenia among the Havasupai. Nor were they subsequently told that Markow caused her medical assistant to surreptitiously examine their medical charts for schizophrenia after operating hours of the local health clinic. The complaint alleges that the defendants authored 15 publications dealing with schizophrenia, inbreeding, and theories about ancient human population migrations from Asia to North America—secondary uses of the samples to which the Havasupai say they would not have consented.

* * *

In defense of Markow, *Nature* reports that research into interbreeding and migration patterns is "an accepted procedure" for researching the extent to which the studied population is isolated. According to *Nature*, information on the extent to which a studied population is isolated is "important" for the genetic investigation of a disease. However, most research to identify human disease genes has proceeded without inbreeding studies and *Nature* fails to explain how schizophrenia is linked to diabetes research. Moreover, even if such studies were standard procedure, the Havasupai argue that they should have been told of these "accepted procedures" before they were asked whether they were willing to consent to the research.

NOTES AND QUESTIONS

1. In April 2010, Arizona State University settled the case brought by the Havasupai Tribe by agreeing to pay $700,000 to 41 members of the tribe, return the blood samples that had been used for the research, and help tribal members obtain federal funds and scholarships. See Amy Harmon, Tribe Wins Fight to Limit Research of Its DNA, The New York Times, April 22, 2010, at A1. Defending the case cost the university $1.7 million.

2. Various indigenous groups have taken formal stances against certain types of genetic research. In the Declaration of Indigenous Peoples of the Western Hemisphere Regarding the Human Genome Diversity Project, www.ankn.uaf.edu/IKS/declaration.html for example, participating indigenous organizations stated "we particularly oppose the Human Genome Diversity Project which intends to collect, and make available our genetic materials which may be used for commercial, scientific and military purposes."

3. In the 1999–2000 session, the following bill, "An Act Related to DNA Testing and Native Americans" was introduced in the Vermont legislature: "The commissioner shall by rule establish standards and procedures for DNA–HLA testing to determine the identity of an individual as a Native American, at the request and the expense of the individual. The results of such testing shall be conclusive proof of the Native American ancestry of the individual." If such a bill does pass, what use might Native Americans make of DNA testing? Can you envision situations in which such testing might be used to disadvantage Native Americans?

CHAPTER 6

GENETICS AND REPRODUCTION

■ ■ ■

I.   INTRODUCTION

For centuries, parents followed folk myths in attempts to control the characteristics of their children. In earlier generations, people believed that conceiving under certain circumstances (a full moon or with a particular item under the bed) would influence the traits of their offspring. As physicians gained greater knowledge about inheritance, couples began to incorporate into their reproductive decisions information from family histories about the risk of passing on a particular genetic disease to their children.

In recent decades, genetic testing has entered the obstetric realm to provide more precise predictions about inheritable diseases. Couples planning to conceive can be screened to see if they are carriers of genetic diseases. During pregnancy, tests can be undertaken on the embryo or fetus itself. Most pregnant women in the United States now undergo some form of prenatal screening, such as ultrasound, amniocentesis, chorionic villi sampling, or other tests. New technologies are available such as a blood test of the mother to analyze the health status or genetic make-up of the fetus. By testing the woman's blood for a particular gene product from the fetus (known as maternal serum alpha-fetoprotein), a physician can assess whether the child will have a neural tube defect such as spina bifida or anencephaly. Or the physician can analyze cell-free DNA from the fetus which is circulating in the mother's blood to determine whether there are any genetic mutations which would indicate the child will experience Down syndrome, Tay-Sachs, or another genetic disease.

In the wake of the Human Genome Project, the range of genes that can be tested prenatally has grown exponentially. Ethical questions arise about whether fetuses should be tested for diseases that will not manifest until later in life, such as breast cancer, or for traits that do not represent diseases, such as by using the controversial genetic test that purports to indicate homosexuality. Legal questions also abound about which genetic tests health care professionals should offer and the circumstances under which they may be found liable for negligence in testing.

What can people do in response to concerns that they might pass on a genetic disease to their children? A range of responses is available. Some people who are at risk of passing on a gene mutation related to a recessive genetic disorder choose not to marry a person with the same mutation. Other people choose to undergo in vitro fertilization and preimplantation screening in order to implant only embryos that have not inherited the disease. Still others undergo prenatal diagnosis during pregnancy and then decide whether or not to terminate a pregnancy if the fetus is affected.

An additional option for couples at genetic risk is to use an egg donor, sperm donor, or embryo donor to provide a genetic component of the pregnancy. As with an infertile couple's use of third party aid in reproduction, the process raises questions about what type of genetic screening should be done on the donor and how legal parenthood should be determined.

These reproductive technologies are challenging the traditional determination of maternity and paternity. It is now possible for an infertile woman to contract with an egg donor and a surrogate mother to bear a child for her. Which of these three mothers—the genetic one, the gestational one, or the social one, should be considered the legal mother? In such cases, as with sperm donation, assignment of legal parenthood relies less on biology and more on social constructs, looking at the intent of the parties prior to conception to determine in whom rights and responsibilities with respect to the child should vest.

Nearly 40 years ago, the first baby created through in vitro fertilization was born. Over a decade ago, the human genome was sequenced. The combination of those technological advances has led to further attempts to push scientific boundaries. Embryos can now be screened not just for genetic diseases, but for potential behavioral traits, as well as for gender. Babies can be created to serve as donors for siblings who are ill. And the potential exists for a person to create a child by cloning himself or herself. This chapter discusses the legal and ethical issues raised by the use of genetics in the context of reproduction.

II. PRENATAL SCREENING

A. PRENATAL SCREENING TECHNIQUES

LORI B. ANDREWS, FUTURE PERFECT:
CONFRONTING DECISIONS ABOUT GENETICS
56–62 (2001).

Family history has long been used to predict a couple's general chance of giving birth to a child with a particular disorder. Starting thirty years ago with the advent of prenatal diagnosis through amniocentesis, specific genetic information about a particular fetus became available to parents. Today, genetic information related to reproduction is obtainable in numerous ways. One partner may have a mutation associated with Huntington disease or breast cancer, for example, and face a decision about whether the fetus should be tested for that mutation. In other instances, the parents may not know their genetic make-up, but each (or maybe both) may be tested in advance of reproduction (or even during pregnancy) for mutations that are common in their ethnic group—such as cystic fibrosis for Caucasians, sickle cell anemia for African Americans, or Tay-Sachs for Ashkenazi Jews. Or the fetus itself may be tested, which can reveal previously unknown genetic information about the mother, the father, or both. Parents-to-be may learn that both are carriers of a recessive disorder, that one has a mutation associated with a dominant disorder, or that the woman has passed on a mutation associated with an X-linked disorder.

The range of conditions that can be screened for prenatally is growing exponentially each year. More than 500 different conditions can be diagnosed through chorionic villi sampling or amniocentesis. The availability of these tests affects even those people who decide not to have them done. Some women say that friends and relatives have made them feel irresponsible for not having genetic testing; others have felt guilty and responsible if they had a child with a genetic disorder (either after refusing testing or after deciding to carry through the pregnancy of an affected child). Yet, as more and more prenatal genetic tests become available, parents are increasingly feeling that they are put into the position of playing God. Should they have prenatal screening for a disorder that won't affect their child until much later in life—or should they bank on a cure being developed in the child's lifetime? Should they abort a fetus whose disorder is treatable, albeit at some expense? As testing becomes available to tell whether a fetus is at a higher likelihood of suffering from breast cancer, colon cancer, heart disease, diabetes, and Alzheimer disease, should such tests be utilized? What about for alcoholism, violence, and other behavioral traits? In studies with varying degrees of scientific repute, genes have been implicated in shyness, bedwetting, attempted rape, homosexuality, manic-depressive disorder, arson, tendency to tease, traditionalism, tendency to giggle or to use hurtful words, and zest for life. Should testing for such traits be done prenatally? If so, what should be done with the resulting information?

* * *

Many couples who use genetic services in conjunction with reproduction feel that it has offered them an overall benefit by allowing them to make an informed choice about their pregnancies. In fact, couples have sued when they felt deprived of prenatal genetic information. At least one federal court [Lifchez v. Hartigan, 735 F.Supp. 1361, 1377 (N.D. Ill.1990), cert. denied, 498 U.S. 1069 (1991)] has recognized the importance of this choice by indicating that the constitutional protections of the abortion decision logically "must also include the right to submit to a procedure designed to give information about that fetus which can then lead to a decision to abort."

* * *

The Physical Risk of Prenatal Screening

Some forms of prenatal testing present physical risks to the fetus, but others are relatively unintrusive. Sampling blood from the fetus while it is in utero through fetoscopy, one of the first means of prenatal tests developed for fetuses, is associated with a 3 to 6 percent risk of fetal death. Amniocentesis, in which fluid from the amniotic sac is withdrawn and analyzed, causes spontaneous abortions in approximately two to three in every 1,000 pregnancies. [This is 0.3% higher than for pregnant women who do not have amniocentesis.] Chorionic villi sampling (CVS), in which a tissue surrounding the fetus is sampled and analyzed between eight and twelve weeks gestation, is associated with a spontaneous abortion rate of about 3.6 percent. [Because many miscarriages occur naturally in the first semester, the additional risk from CVS is approximately 0.8%.] In addition, CVS in early pregnancy presents a risk of limb deformities in approximately one in 3,000 cases. These procedures entail physical risks to pregnant women as well, particularly risks of infection. Some women have chosen to undergo prenatal screening despite the risks because they intend to terminate a pregnancy if the fetus is diagnosed as having a serious disorder.

The prenatal diagnostic techniques of fetoscopy, amniocentesis, and chorionic villi sampling have generally been limited to women whose fetuses are at greater-than-average risk of having a genetic or chromosomal disorder, such as women over age thirty-five (who are at a greater-than-average risk of giving birth to a child with Down syndrome) or women with family histories of or ethnic-group familiarity with genetic disorders. In many instances, the women being offered such prenatal testing have had some experience with the disorders for which the fetus is being tested. Most women are familiar with Down syndrome. Those who have a family history of a disorder such as cystic fibrosis or sickle cell anemia have an affected relative and thus are likely to have some knowledge about the disorder. And in ethnic groups that have a higher-than-average risk of certain genetic diseases, there is often widespread knowledge among members of the community about the particular disorder.

Now, however, prenatal testing is being developed that is less physically risky to the fetus and to the pregnant woman. Some testing can be performed with a sample of the pregnant woman's blood. Genetic mutations affecting the fetus can be identified through maternal/fetal cell sorting, a technique that can analyze fetal cells circulating in the woman's blood. Since the physical risk has been reduced, women who might not otherwise have sought prenatal testing are being asked to do so. One result is that women who have no personal knowledge or experience with a disease or disorder are faced with having to decide whether they are willing to raise a child with these conditions. This stands in contrast to those in situations in which such disorders are generally understood within the woman's community. The more accessible prenatal testing becomes, the more important it is to adequately inform and educate potential parents about their fetus's condition as well as about the long-term consequences of whatever decisions they make. * * * A survey found that 39 percent of people felt that every pregnant woman should have prenatal testing and 22 percent felt that a woman should be required to abort if the baby has a serious genetic defect.

NOTES AND QUESTIONS

1.   The discovery of cell-free fetal DNA led to the development of non-invasive prenatal testing (NIPT) by analysis of maternal blood, a procedure that could replace invasive prenatal diagnostic tests like amniocentesis and chorionic villus sampling which have been associated with miscarriages. Gary J.W. Liao et al., Non-invasive Prenatal Testing Using Cell-free Fetal DNA in Maternal Circulation, 428 Clinica Chimica Acta 44 (2014). NIPT can be used as early as the first trimester of pregnancy to detect with high accuracy whether a fetus has an abnormal number of chromosomes (aneuploidy) resulting in conditions such as trisomies 13 (Patau syndrome), 18 (Edwards syndrome), and 21 (Down syndrome). NIPT can also be used for sex determination as well as the detection of other conditions such as Huntington disease, achondroplasia, cystic fibrosis, and ß-thalassemia. Meredith Vanstone et al., Non-invasive Prenatal Testing: Ethics and Policy Considerations, 36 J. Obstet. Gynaecol. Can. 514 (2014). What are some of the ethical and legal implications if such technology becomes widely available?

2.   The use of prenatal diagnostic tests is widespread, with a greater number of women desiring genetic analysis of their fetuses now that non-invasive prenatal testing is available. A 2014 study found that most women (95–98%) would have a blood screening test to detect spinal muscular atrophy, cystic fibrosis, phenylketonuria, congenital heart defects, Down syndrome, and Fragile X syndrome in their fetus. The majority of women would undergo amniocentesis to detect these conditions also (ranging from 64% for phenylketonuria to 73% for spinal muscular atrophy). Mary E. Norton et al., Women's Attitudes Regarding Prenatal Testing for a Range of Genetic Disorders of Varying Severity, 3 J. Clin. Med. 144 (2014).

B. LIABILITY FOR MALPRACTICE IN PRENATAL SCREENING

CAILIN HARRIS, STATUTORY PROHIBITIONS ON WRONGFUL
BIRTH CLAIMS & THEIR DANGEROUS EFFECTS ON PARENTS
34 Boston College J. L. & Soc. Just. 365, 368–372 (2014).

The wrongful birth cause of action is part of a group of pregnancy-related medical malpractice claims that have become more prevalent due to advance[s] in genetic testing, as well as the recognition of abortion rights and availability of such procedures. Wrongful birth suits are typically brought by parents who claim they would not have conceived or given birth to a child were it not for the defendant's negligence in performing genetic or prenatal testing, testing that if done correctly could have revealed the risk or presence of a health condition in the fetus.

The wrongful birth cause of action is often compared to and confused with wrongful conception (also known as wrongful pregnancy) and wrongful life causes of action. Parents bring a wrongful conception claim to seek damages for the expenses of an unwanted pregnancy and birth that occurs after a failed sterilization procedure. A wrongful life claim is brought by, or on behalf of, a child seeking compensation for the defendant's failure to properly counsel the child's parents about the child's condition. In contrast, a wrongful birth claim is brought by the parents, who claim that were it not for the defendant's negligence, they would have known about the fetus's condition, and they would have had the opportunity to decide whether or not to abort the fetus.

* * *

Wrongful birth claims can be brought based on the defendant's negligence at multiple points before or during the mother's pregnancy. When a wrongful birth claim is based on negligence before pregnancy, the cause of action may stem from a physician's alleged failure to diagnose a genetic condition or disease in an earlier child, if a later child is born with the same condition. In addition, the cause of action can also be brought based on a physician's negligence in performing or failing to perform genetic testing on the child's parents. Similarly, the cause of action may be brought based on a physician's failure to perform or properly handle a prenatal genetic or diagnostic test on the fetus. Additionally, wrongful birth claims can also be based on negligence during pregnancy when a physician fails to discover and inform parents of non-genetic fetal defects, such as a health condition in the mother that could adversely affect the health of the fetus.

In addition to duty and negligence, plaintiffs bringing wrongful birth claims must establish proximate causation. Notably, a wrongful birth claim does not allege that the defendant's negligence actually caused the child's injury. Instead, the plaintiffs allege that because of the defendant's negligence, they did not know about the fetus's impairments and, therefore, they did not have the opportunity to use that information to evaluate whether to terminate the pregnancy. Thus, parents are not suing for the child's impairment itself, but rather for the loss of their choice not to give birth to the unhealthy child. Courts typically use a subjective standard to determine causation, asking whether the particular plaintiffs were deprived of the chance to "accept or reject a parental relationship." It is not necessary for parents to prove decisively that they would have aborted an unhealthy fetus because the crux of their claim is that the defendant's negligence deprived them of the opportunity to make that choice.

Courts often struggle with how to appropriately award damages in wrongful birth cases. Although most courts are willing to compensate parents for the extraordinary medical costs associated with giving birth to and caring for an unhealthy child, some courts are hesitant to award parents damages covering the total cost of caring for their child. In most wrongful birth cases, the parents desired a child and planned to support their child, which, courts have stated, is the obligation of all parents. Thus, while the costs of raising the child that stem from the child's disability or condition may be recovered, those costs that are inherent in raising any child may not be recovered. Some courts also award parents damages for the emotional distress of giving birth to and caring for an unhealthy or disabled child.

KEEL V. BANACH
624 So.2d 1022 (Ala. 1993).

SHORES, J.

The plaintiffs are Karen and Danny Keel, parents of Justin Keel, who was born on January 18, 1985, with severe multiple congenital abnormalities. Justin died in February 1991, at the age of six. The defendants are Warren Banach, M.D., who was Karen's doctor and who performed the sonographic examinations of the fetus, and his professional corporation. The Keels charged the defendants with medical malpractice in failing to discover several severe, life-threatening fetal abnormalities that, the Keels say, had they been known to them, would have caused them to terminate the pregnancy. Actions such as that filed by the Keels have come to be called actions for "wrongful birth."

* * *

The sole issue on appeal is whether this State recognizes a cause of action for wrongful birth. At the outset, we must emphasize the posture in which this case is now before this Court: The question presented for review is not whether the plaintiffs should ultimately prevail in this litigation, but whether their complaint states a claim upon which relief can be granted.

On October 22, 1984, Karen Keel had her first prenatal visit with Dr. Banach, an obstetrician practicing in Ozark, Alabama. There is conflicting testimony as to the content of the conversations between the physician and his patient pertaining to the couple's medical history. The Keels say that they relayed their concerns regarding this pregnancy because Danny had earlier fathered a stillborn infant with anencephaly, the congenital absence of brain and spinal cord, which is the most severe of spinal cord abnormalities. Spinal cord defects are known to be hereditary, and the Keels contend that they told Dr. Banach that they did not want their child to suffer such a fate.

Dr. Banach did a sonogram on October 26, 1984. He derived a biparietal diameter consistent with 19 weeks' gestation, and a femur length consistent with 22 weeks' gestation. Under "obvious anomalies" he wrote: "none seen." The Keels say that, to alleviate their fears, Dr. Banach moved the transducer around to show them what appeared to be a healthy fetus's head, body, arms, and legs. The sonogram machine produced several photographs of the sonographic images. Two were given to Karen.

Another sonogram was performed on January 4, 1985. Again Dr. Banach marked under "obvious anomalies" "none seen." During this sonogram, Dr. Banach determined that the fetus was a male. As during the first sonogram, the machine produced photographs, and all were retained in the medical records.

Justin was born on January 18, 1985, with severe multiple congenital abnormalities. He had only a two-vessel umbilical cord (as opposed to the normal three-vessel cord), a short cord, ventriculomegaly, absent right leg, imperforate anus, one testicle, one kidney, a vertebrae anomaly in the lumbar sacral region, hydrocephaly, a large fluid-filled sac extending off the right aspect of the sacrum consistent with meningocele (spina bifida). Justin underwent numerous surgeries during his life. A shunt from his brain to his heart channeled fluids, which, for the most part, prevented any brain damage due to the hydrocephaly. Blood clots from the heart, impregnating the lungs, a known but unpreventable risk of the shunt, were the direct cause of Justin's death.

According to Dr. Banach, the fact that Danny had fathered a stillborn with anencephaly was not revealed to him until after Justin was born.

The Keels sued Dr. Banach, alleging that he had failed to meet the standard of prenatal care and that, had he done so, he would have further investigated questionable sonogram findings. The plaintiffs contend that there were discrepancies in the fetus measurements that should have prompted further investigation. They contend that there were images on the sonogram that showed an oblong head with open frontal bones visible (known as a "lemon sign," frequently noted in spina bifida). They contend that the sonogram findings should have prompted an amniocentesis, which, had it been performed, would in all likelihood have diagnosed this fetus's neurotube defect.

As described by the considerable literature and litigation in this area, a "wrongful birth action" refers to a claim for relief by parents who allege they would have avoided conception or would have terminated the pregnancy but for the negligence of those charged with prenatal testing, genetic prognosticating, or counseling parents as to the likelihood of giving birth to a physically or mentally impaired child. The underlying premise is that prudent medical care would have detected the risk of a congenital or hereditary genetic disorder either before conception or during pregnancy. In such an action, the parents allege that as a proximate result of this negligently performed or omitted genetic counseling or prenatal testing they were foreclosed from making an informed decision whether to conceive a potentially handicapped child or, in the event of a pregnancy, to terminate it.

* * *

This case involves an alleged failure by Dr. Banach to properly perform prenatal tests that would have revealed severe multiple congenital abnormalities in the fetus, which, if known to the parents, would have weighed in their decision whether to exercise their constitutional right to terminate the pregnancy.

The defendants make compelling policy arguments for rejecting the plaintiffs' cause of action. These include:

"(1) [T]he tort will be particularly subject to fraudulent claims. The cause of action is dependent entirely upon the retrospective and subjective testimony of the mother that had she known of the defects during the pregnancy, she would have aborted the child.

"(2) [T]he wrongful birth action would place a heavy burden on obstetricians/gynecologists. Appellee claims that with respect to obstetrics and gynecology the wrongful birth action will:

"a. Increase abortions;

"b. Increase abortions of healthy fetuses as a risk management action;

"c. Increase the cost of prenatal care as the result of more prenatal testing and the burden on OB/GYNs to obtain detailed informed consent; and "d. Lead to the reduction of OB/GYNs practicing in the state.

"(3) Another concern is . . . the negative impact the cause of action may have on the child by creating an 'emotional bastard.'

"(4) Since the wrongful birth views nonexistence as being greater than life with a disability, the cause of action would have a negative impact on the disabled. The cause of action cries out that children with disabilities constitute injury to parents. This will lead to a stigmatism and high toll on the self-esteem of persons with disabilities at a time when our state and country are moving forward at great lengths to recognize the rights and privileges of the disabled as ordinary citizens."

* * *

Although the arguments of the defendants set out above are compelling, the great weight of authority to the contrary forces us to agree with the majority of the courts and the legal commentators and to hold that an action for the wrongful birth of a genetically or congenitally defective child may be maintained by the parents of such a child.

The nature of the tort of wrongful birth has nothing to do with whether a defendant caused the injury or harm to the child, but, rather, with whether the defendant's negligence was the proximate cause of the parents' being deprived of the option of avoiding a conception or, in the case of pregnancy, making an informed and meaningful decision either to terminate the pregnancy or to give birth to a potentially defective child. Like most of the other courts that have considered this cause of action, we hold that the parents of a genetically or congenitally defective child may maintain an action for its wrongful birth if the birth was the result of the negligent failure of the attending prenatal physician to discover and inform them of the existence of fetal defects.

* * *

The basic rule of tort compensation is that the plaintiff should be put in the position that he would have been in absent the defendant's negligence * * *. "It is a fundamental tenet of tort law that a negligent tortfeasor is liable for all damages that are the proximate result of his negligence."

We follow the holding of other courts that have considered this issue. "[T]he current trend with respect to damages is to allow the recovery of only the additional costs of treatment and special resources for the child, not the entire cost of rearing the child." * * * The primary element of damages that may be recovered in an action for wrongful birth is the pecuniary loss to the plaintiffs, the child's parents, resulting from the care and treatment of the child. The plaintiffs are entitled to recover for the extraordinary expenses they incur because of the child's unhealthy condition, including: (1) hospital and medical costs, (2) costs of medication, and (3) costs of education and therapy for the child.

It is generally recognized that, in a wrongful birth action, parents may recover the extraordinary costs necessary to treat the birth defect and any additional medical or educational costs attributable to the birth defect during the child's minority.

Emotional distress suffered by the parents of an unhealthy child is compensable in a wrongful birth action. A jury could conclude that the defendants, in failing to inform Mrs. Keel of the possibility of giving birth to a child with severe multiple congenital abnormalities, directly deprived her and, derivatively, her husband, of the option to accept or reject a parental relationship with the child and thus caused them to experience mental and emotional anguish upon their realization that they had given birth to a child afflicted with severe multiple congenital abnormalities.

We conclude that the following items are compensable, if proven: (1) any medical and hospital expenses incurred as a result of a physician's negligence; (2) the physical pain suffered by the wife; (3) loss of consortium; and (4) mental and emotional anguish the parents have suffered.

MOLLOY V. MEIER

679 N.W.2d 711 (Minn. 2004).

MEYER, JUSTICE.

Kimberly Molloy (Molloy) and her husband, Glenn Molloy, brought a medical malpractice action against appellants Dr. Diane Meier, Dr. Reno Backus, and Dr. Kathryn Green, claiming they were negligent in failing to diagnose a genetic disorder in Molloy's daughter and their negligence caused Molloy to conceive another child with the same genetic disorder. The district court denied the appellants' motion for summary judgment and concluded that a physician who performs genetic tests on a child owes a duty to the biological parents of that child; that the action did not accrue until the time of conception and, therefore, was not time-barred; and that the action was not barred by Minn. Stat. § 145.424 (2002), which prohibits causes of action for wrongful birth and wrongful life. The court of appeals answered three certified questions and upheld the denial of summary judgment. We granted review and now affirm the court of appeals.

This case arises out of the medical treatment of S.F., the daughter of Kimberly Molloy and her ex-husband, Robert Flomer. As a young girl, S.F. was treated by appellant Dr. Diane M. Meier at Partners in Pediatrics (formerly Oakdale Pediatrics). When S.F. was three years old,

Dr. Meier noted during a check-up that S.F. was developmentally delayed. Dr. Meier ordered a number of tests, but the results did not reveal the source of S.F.'s difficulties. On May 18, 1992, Dr. Meier met with Molloy, Robert Flomer, and S.F. to discuss the possible causes for S.F.'s developmental delays, including the possibility of a genetic cause. Molloy told Dr. Meier about Molloy's mentally retarded half-brother and asked Dr. Meier to conduct genetic tests on S.F. to determine whether S.F. had inherited any abnormalities from Molloy.

In her notes from the May 18 visit, Dr. Meier wrote "? chromosomes + fragile X," which meant she intended to order chromosomal testing and testing for Fragile X syndrome. In May of 1992, a Fragile X chromosomal test capable of diagnosing the disorder with 70 to 80 percent accuracy was in widespread use. A parent who is a carrier of Fragile X has up to a 50 percent chance of giving birth to a child with the condition. Although physicians can treat the symptoms of Fragile X, the condition itself is incurable. Dr. Meier conceded that "it was appropriate to test [S.F.] for [F]ragile X in keeping with accepted standards of pediatric practice on May 18, 1992." According to Molloy, Dr. Meier told her that if S.F. tested positive for a genetic disorder, Molloy should be tested herself.

On June 17, 1992, the chromosome testing ordered by Dr. Meier was performed at North Memorial Medical Center. On July 18, 1992, North Memorial's laboratory reported normal chromosome testing for S.F. Dr. Meier received the test results, telephoned the Flomers and informed them that the test results were negative; i.e., normal. However, Dr. Meier failed to mention that Fragile X testing had not been performed. The Flomers then informed Molloy that the test results were "normal." Based on the fact that Dr. Meier had mentioned Fragile X in her discussion of chromosomal testing, Molloy assumed that the negative test results included a negative result for Fragile X.

Meanwhile, on June 23, 1992, S.F. was referred by Dr. Meier to the Minneapolis Clinic of Neurology where she was seen by Dr. Reno Backus. Dr. Backus testified in his deposition that his role was to evaluate S.F. and report back to Dr. Meier, the referring physician. Dr. Backus met with S.F., Molloy, and the Flomers, and diagnosed S.F. with a pervasive developmental delay of unknown origin. Molloy inquired about her chances of conceiving another child with S.F.'s defect. According to Molloy, Dr. Backus responded that S.F.'s problems were not genetic in origin and the risk that Molloy might give birth to another child like S.F. was extremely remote, especially with a father other than Robert Flomer. Dr. Backus was aware that chromosomal testing had been done but he made his assessment before the test results were known.

Several years later S.F. was referred to Dr. Kathryn Green, who was an employee of the Minneapolis Clinic of Neurology. When Dr. Green saw

S.F. on April 30, 1996, she had the office chart of Minneapolis Clinic, including Dr. Backus's 1992 report. There were no Fragile X testing results in the chart because the testing had never been done. Dr. Green knew of Molloy's mentally retarded half-brother who had exhibited problems similar to S.F.'s. Despite having this information, Dr. Green did not order or recommend Fragile X testing. Dr. Green testified that she recognized the importance of Fragile X testing in general, but she assumed such tests had already been performed on S.F. and had come back negative, as S.F. had already seen three physicians.

In the meantime, Molloy remarried and gave birth to M.M. on June 30, 1998. M.M. showed signs of the same developmental difficulties as S.F., so his pediatrician, Dr. David Tilstra, ordered Fragile X testing for him. The Fragile X test results were positive; i.e., M.M. carried the Fragile X genetic disorder. When Dr. Tilstra received the positive results, he counseled Kimberly and Glenn Molloy about Fragile X syndrome and recommended that they and other potentially affected family members receive testing. Based on Dr. Tilstra's recommendation, S.F. and Kimberly Molloy were tested for Fragile X, and it was discovered that they both carried the genetic disorder.

Molloy commenced this lawsuit on August 23, 2001, alleging that Drs. Meier, Backus, and Green and their employers were negligent in the care and treatment rendered to S.F., Kimberly Molloy, and Glenn Molloy by failing to order Fragile X testing on S.F., failing to properly read those lab tests that were performed, mistakenly reporting that S.F. had been tested for Fragile X, and failing to provide counseling to Kimberly and Glenn Molloy regarding the risk of passing an inheritable genetic abnormality to future children. Molloy claimed she would not have conceived M.M. if Drs. Meier, Backus, and Green had correctly diagnosed S.F. with Fragile X and informed Molloy of the diagnosis.

Drs. Meier, Backus, and Green and their employers moved for summary judgment, arguing that they did not owe a duty to the family of a patient and that, in any event, Molloy's action was barred by the four-year statute of limitations for medical malpractice claims. In opposition, Molloy presented expert testimony of a pediatrician and a pediatric neurologist who described the prevailing standard of care in the medical community with respect to testing and counseling for genetic disorders. The experts indicated that a patient who exhibits the symptoms of this disorder with a family history of mental retardation should be tested for Fragile X. Further, a physician who identifies the possibility of Fragile X has a responsibility to follow up to confirm that the tests are performed. Finally, the physician of a child with Fragile X has an obligation to provide genetic counseling to the child's family.

* * *

The district court denied summary judgment, concluding that the defendants owed a duty to the biological parents of the child, the cause of action was not barred by the four-year statute of limitations, and a claim for wrongful conception was permitted under Minn. Stat. § 145.424. Subsequently, the district court certified the following questions to the court of appeals as "important and doubtful" under Minn. R. Civ. App. P. 103.03(i).

(a) Does a physician who allegedly fails to test for and diagnose a genetic disorder in an existing child leading to the birth of a subsequent child with that disorder owe a legal duty to the child's parents?

(b) When does the statute of limitations begin to run pursuant to Minn. Stat. § 541.076 (2002) in a parents' medical negligence claim alleging failure to test for and diagnose a genetic disorder in an existing child leading to the birth of a subsequent child with that disorder?

(c) Does Minn. Stat. § 145.424 prohibit parents from bringing an action alleging that they would not have conceived the subsequent child described in question (b)?

The court of appeals answered the first certified question in the affirmative: the appellants owed a legal duty to Molloy because appellants "should have foreseen that negligently rendering care to S.F. or erroneously reporting genetic test results to S.F.'s biological parents could result in the birth of another child with fragile X." *Molloy,* 660 N.W.2d at 452. The court of appeals answered the second certified question by concluding that the statute of limitations began to run at the time of M.M.'s conception, the point at which Molloy could establish damages and a viable cause of action in tort. *Id.* at 455. In answering the third certified question, the court concluded that Molloy's action was not barred by Minn. Stat. § 145.424 because she did not claim that, but for the negligence of the appellants, M.M. would have been aborted.

I.

We begin by addressing the first certified question, whether the appellants owed a duty to Molloy regarding the genetic testing and diagnosis of S.F. for Fragile X syndrome. When we review certified questions arising from the denial of summary judgment, we must decide "whether there are any genuine issues of material fact and whether the lower courts erred in their application of the law." Employers Mut. Cas. Co. v. A.C.C.T., Inc., 580 N.W.2d 490, 493 (Minn.1998) (quoting Art Goebel, Inc. v. North Suburban Agencies, Inc., 567 N.W.2d 511, 515 (Minn.1997)). The existence of a duty in a negligence case is a question of law. Funchess v. Cecil Newman Corp., 632 N.W.2d 666, 672 (Minn.2001). We consider the evidence in the light most favorable to the nonmoving party. Gradjelick v. Hance, 646 N.W.2d 225, 231 (Minn.2002).

Molloy advances two legal theories. She first argues that a physician-patient relationship existed between her and the appellants that gave rise to a legal duty to warn her about the risks of becoming pregnant as a carrier of Fragile X. Additionally, citing Skillings v. Allen, 143 Minn. 323, 173 N.W. 663 (1919), Molloy urges this court to hold that even if a physician-patient relationship cannot be established, a physician's duty to warn others of a patient's genetic disorder arises from the foreseeability of injury.

The appellants argue that their duty is owed only to S.F., the person with whom they had a physician-patient relationship. The appellants claim that they met with S.F. solely for S.F.'s own benefit and not for the benefit of her family. If any duty extended beyond the minor patient, the appellants argue that it should reach only those parties who have a contractual relationship with the physician, in this case the Flomers, S.F.'s custodial parents.

* * *

We begin our analysis by observing that a duty to a third party who is not a patient of the physician has been recognized in only a few Minnesota cases. See Lundgren v. Fultz, 354 N.W.2d 25, 28–29 (Minn.1984) (psychiatrist owed duty to third party where patient threatens foreseeable harm to that party and psychiatrist has the ability to control the risk of harm); Cairl v. State, 323 N.W.2d 20, 25 n. 7, 26 (Minn.1982) (treatment facility may owe duty to warn identifiable third parties of violent propensities of a mentally disabled youth whom it released if that youth poses a specific threat to those parties).

* * *

Only a few other jurisdictions have addressed the question of whether a physician owes a legal duty to the family of a patient who received negligent care in the field of genetics. In a case most analogous to the instant one, the New Jersey Supreme Court held that a physician owes a duty to members of the patient's immediate family who might be injured by the physician's breach of duty to the patient. Schroeder v. Perkel, 87 N.J. 53, 432 A.2d 834, 839 (1981). The court held that liability could extend to the patient's family where a doctor's failure to diagnose a first-born child with cystic fibrosis led to the birth of a second child with that disorder and it was foreseeable that the parents would rely on the diagnosis. Id. at 839–40; cf. Lininger v. Eisenbaum, 764 P.2d 1202, 1205 (Colo.1988) (holding that a physician's failure to diagnose the hereditary nature of a child's blindness that led his parents to conceive a second blind child stated a cause of action).

The Supreme Court of Florida has also held that a duty exists where "the prevailing standard of care creates a duty that is obviously for the benefit of certain identified third parties and the physician knows of the existence of those third parties." Pate v. Threlkel, 661 So.2d 278, 282 (Fla.1995). In *Pate,* the defendant physician diagnosed the plaintiff's mother with medullary thyroid carcinoma, a genetically inheritable disease. *Id.* at 279. When the plaintiff learned that she also carried the disease, she sued, alleging that the defendant should have known of the inheritable nature of the disease and owed a duty to inform her mother that the plaintiff may have carried it as well. *Id.* The plaintiff presented expert testimony that the prevailing standard of care required physicians to inform patients of the genetically transferable nature of their conditions. *Id.* at 281. The Florida Supreme Court noted that the standard of care was developed for the benefit of third parties and therefore held that a physician owes a duty to those third parties of whom the physician has knowledge. *Id.* at 282.

* * *

Our decision today is informed by the practical reality of the field of genetic testing and counseling; genetic testing and diagnosis does not affect only the patient. Both the patient and her family can benefit from accurate testing and diagnosis. And conversely, both the patient and her family can be harmed by negligent testing and diagnosis. Molloy's experts indicate that a physician would have a duty to inform the parents of a child diagnosed with Fragile X disorder. The appellants admit that their practice is to inform parents in such a case. The standard of care thus acknowledges that families rely on physicians to communicate a diagnosis of the genetic disorder to the patient's family. It is foreseeable that a negligent diagnosis of Fragile X will cause harm not only to the patient, but to the family of the patient as well. This is particularly true regarding parents who have consulted the physicians concerning the patient's condition and have been advised of the need for genetic testing.

We therefore hold that a physician's duty regarding genetic testing and diagnosis extends beyond the patient to biological parents who foreseeably may be harmed by a breach of that duty. In this case, the patient suffered from a serious disorder that had a high probability of being genetically transmitted and for which a reliable and accepted test was widely available. The appellants should have foreseen that parents of childbearing years might conceive another child in the absence of knowledge of the genetic disorder. The appellants owed a duty of care regarding genetic testing and diagnosis, and the resulting medical advice, not only to S.F. but also to her parents. In recognizing this duty, we apply the principles of negligence law set forth in *Skillings* and *Togstad* and conclude that the duty arises where it is reasonably foreseeable that the parents would be injured if the advice is negligently given. " '[T]he risk reasonably to be perceived defines the duty to be obeyed, and risk imports relation; it is risk to another or to others within the range of apprehension.'" Connolly v. Nicollet Hotel, 254 Minn. 373, 381, 95 N.W.2d 657, 664 (1959) (quoting Palsgraf v. Long Island R. Co., 248 N.Y. 339, 162 N.E. 99, 100 (1928)).

* * *

The final certified question concerns whether Minn. Stat. § 145.424 prohibits Molloy's cause of action. The statute provides in pertinent part:

Subdivision 1. Wrongful life action prohibited. No person shall maintain a cause of action or receive an award of damages on behalf of that person based on the claim that but for the negligent conduct of another, the person would have been aborted.

Subd. 2. Wrongful birth action prohibited. No person shall maintain a cause of action or receive an award of damages on the claim that but for the negligent conduct of another, a child would have been aborted.

Subd. 3. Failure or refusal to prevent a live birth. Nothing in this section shall be construed to preclude a cause of action * * * [claiming that] but for the negligent conduct of another, tests or treatment would have been provided * * * which would have made possible the prevention, cure, or amelioration of any disease, defect, deficiency, or handicap.

The appellants argue that Molloy's action is essentially a "wrongful birth" action, and therefore prohibited by section 145.424, subdivision 2 (2002). Molloy contends that the statute prohibits only claims that but for the negligent conduct, an abortion would have been sought. Because Molloy claims that she would have sought a tubal ligation, not an abortion, if the appellants had fulfilled their duty to her, she argues that her claim is not prohibited. The district court held that Molloy's wrongful-conception cause was not prohibited by the statute and the court of appeals agreed, concluding that the plain language of Minn. Stat. § 145.424 did not bar the action.

* * *

The plain language of section 145.424 does not support the appellants' contention that Molloy's claim is barred by statute. The statute bars claims that but for the negligence, the pregnancy would have been aborted. Molloy makes no claim that she would have aborted M.M. if she had more accurate information about S.F.'s genetic condition. Rather, Molloy's complaint alleges that "[h]ad [she and her husband] known that [S.F.] had Fragile X, they would not have conceived [M.M.]." This states an action not for wrongful life or birth, but rather for wrongful conception—an action that has been recognized in this state for over a quarter century. *Sherlock,* 260 N.W.2d at 174 (holding that parents may sue physician for damages proximately caused by a negligently performed sterilization procedure). Because Molloy's action is properly characterized as one for wrongful conception rather than wrongful birth, it is not barred by Minn. Stat. § 145.424. We answer this certified question in the negative, and affirm the court of appeals.

NOTES AND QUESTIONS

1.   What are the policy reasons for and against the recognition of wrongful birth cases?

2.   How does the traditional tort analysis of duty, breach, causation and damages apply to wrongful birth causes? Early case law dealing with wrongful birth actions rejected the notion that the failure to warn the parents of a fetus' risk of serious defect was actionable because the physician was not the proximate cause of the defect. However, liability for a missed diagnosis in other areas of medicine is common even though, in such cases, the physician did not cause the illness. Another reason that courts were reluctant to recognize the wrongful birth cause of action was that the post-conception remedy available—abortion—was illegal. This reasoning is no longer valid after Roe v. Wade, 410 U.S. 113 (1973), which upheld a woman's constitutional right to undergo an abortion during the first two trimesters of pregnancy. If abortion became illegal again, what effect would that have on wrongful birth cases?

3.   In Azzolino v. Dingfelder, 337 S.E.2d 528 (N.C. 1985), the court refused to recognize a wrongful birth cause of action. The court was concerned, in part, about its eugenic implications. The court said:

> [S]ince the parents will decide which "defects" would have led them to abort the fetus, other questions will rapidly arise in jurisdictions recognizing wrongful birth claims when determining whether such claims will be permitted in particular cases. When will parents in those jurisdictions be allowed to decide that their child is so "defective" that given a chance they would have aborted it while still a fetus and, as a result, then be allowed to hold their physician civilly liable? When a fetus is only the carrier of a deleterious gene and not itself impaired? When the fetus is of one sex rather than the other? Should such issues be left exclusively to the parents with doctors being found liable for breaching their duty to inform parents of any fetal conditions to which they know or should know the parents may object?

* * *

Inevitably this will place increased pressure upon physicians to take the "safe" course by recommending abortion. This is perhaps best illustrated by a story drawn from a real life situation.

A clinical instructor asks his students to advise an expectant mother on the fate of a fetus whose father has chronic syphilis. Early siblings were born with a collection of defects such as deafness, blindness, and retardation. The usual response of the students is: "Abort!" The teacher then calmly replies: "Congratulations, you have just aborted Beethoven."

4.   In traditional tort cases, the plaintiffs have a duty to mitigate damages. Should parents in wrongful birth cases be required to mitigate damages by putting their child up for adoption?

5.   What types of evidence can be used to establish the standard of care in wrongful birth suits?

6.   The fact that the child in *Molloy* had the Fragile X mutation could be important for other family members. According to the court, does the physician have a duty to inform other family members? Is it sufficient if the physician informs the child's parents? See Mark Hallberg & Teresa Fariss McClain, Note: Recent Developments in Health Care Law: Molloy v. Meier Extends Genetic Counseling Duty of Care to Biological Parents and Establishes That Legal Damages Must Occur Before a Wrongful Conception Action Accrues for Statute of Limitations Purposes, 31 Wm. Mitchell L. Rev. 939, 954 (2005).

7.   What should be the scope of damages in wrongful birth cases? The Illinois Appellate court allowed a couple to plead damages that encompassed the care of their child born with Angelman syndrome after physicians failed to diagnose the disease in his older brother. Clark v. Children's Memorial Hospital, 907 N.E.2d 49 (Ill. App. 1st Dist. 2009), affirmed in part, reversed in part, 955 N.E.2d 1065 (2011) (clarifying that parents could not recover damages for cost of care after child had reached majority). In Basten v. United States, 848 F.Supp. 962 (M.D. Ala. 1994), liability was found for wrongful birth when physicians failed to inform a couple of the availability of prenatal testing that would help diagnose spina bifida. In addition to allowing the parents to recover millions of dollars in damages, the court allowed the healthy sister of the affected child to recover $25,000 for "loss of parental services"—the loss of care, counsel, training and education she would have received were it not for her parents' necessity to devote attention to her seriously ill sibling. The court in a footnote said it was awarding those damages "reluctantly" and was doing so because the parties jointly stipulated that the sister of the affected child should recover damages for loss of parental services. What are the arguments for and against such damages? If the "healthy" child can recover such damages because a child born with a genetic impairment takes an excessive amount of parental time, could a first-born child sue his or her parents for having several additional children, thus reducing the attention the first-born will receive?

8.   If parents can recover for wrongful birth, why not grandparents? A New Jersey appellate court held that a grandfather cannot bring a wrongful birth suit on his behalf to recover emotional distress damages arising from the birth of his grandson. The grandfather alleged that a grandparent is a "filament of family life" and that the birth of a child with Tay-Sachs disease affected the entire family. Thus, he argued, he should also be entitled to recover damages for the emotional distress he had when the defendants

failed to inform the mother of his grandson of fetal abnormalities. The appellate court held that only the parents of the child may recover for pain and suffering resulting from the birth of the child. Michelman v. Erlich, 709 A.2d 281 (N.J. Super. A.D. 1998).

9.   Should wrongful birth actions only be permitted where the disorder at issue is serious? Some courts have considered the severity of the disorder as a factor in assessing the health care professional's liability for failing to provide information about genetic risks. For example, in Turpin v. Sortini, 643 P.2d 954 (Cal. 1982), a wrongful birth case, the California Supreme Court asserted, "[i]n this case, in which the plaintiff's only affliction is deafness, it seems quite unlikely that a jury would ever conclude that life with such a condition is worse than not being born at all." Using the reasoning presented in *Turpin*, a slight disadvantage such as short stature would probably not be sufficient to find liability. In Zepeda v. Zepeda, 190 N.E.2d 849, 859 (Ill. App. 1963), the court refused to allow an illegitimate son to sue his father for wrongful life. The court refused to recognize a cause of action because it felt it was the legislature's job to redress such a far-reaching tort. The court noted:

> Encouragement would extend to all others born into the world under conditions they might regard as adverse. One might seek damages for being born of a certain color, another because of race; one for being born with a hereditary disease, another for inheriting unfortunate family characteristics; one for being born into a large and destitute family, another because a parent has an unsavory reputation.

10. Currently, at least seven states—Arizona, Idaho, Michigan, Minnesota, Missouri, Oklahoma, and South Dakota—have laws that prohibit parents from bringing wrongful birth suits against health care providers. Could such statutes be challenged as a violation of the couple's reproductive liberty by eliminating an incentive for physicians to give parents-to-be information necessary to make procreative decisions? In a Utah case, a couple challenged the constitutionality of a Utah statute which prohibited any cause of action "based on [a] claim that but for the act or omission of another, a person would not have been permitted to have been born alive but would have been aborted." Several genetic tests had been conducted, but the parents alleged that they were never accurately informed about the results of the tests or the risks of the fetus having Down syndrome. The Utah Supreme Court rejected a due process challenge to Utah's prohibition on wrongful birth lawsuits because the court found the law did not place an undue burden on a woman's ability to abort a fetus with a genetic anomaly. It also rejected an equal protection challenge to the law because it held that the class of people who choose to abort a fetus with a genetic anomaly is not a recognized class under the equal protection clause. Wood v. University of Utah Medical Center, 67 P.3d 436 (Utah 2002). Utah subsequently repealed its wrongful birth statute in 2008.

11. The North Carolina Supreme Court allowed the parents of a child born with sickle cell disease to bring a medical malpractice suit against a physician, even though North Carolina statutorily bars wrongful birth and wrongful life actions where the claim is the parents would have aborted. The parents alleged that the physician negligently failed to advise them of their own genetic test results showing they were carriers of sickle cell anemia and thus would have a 25% risk of having a child with sickle cell disease. See McAllister v. Ha, 496 S.E.2d 577, 584 (N.C. 1998). In this case, the couple could have chosen not to procreate (rather than abort). However, the court refused to allow the parents to recover damages for any costs associated with child-rearing (including the extraordinary costs of caring for the child due to illness), but would allow the recovery of costs associated with the pregnancy and severe emotional distress.

12. Most cases alleging negligence in prenatal screening deal with false negatives—situations in which parents are erroneously told that their fetus is not afflicted with a serious genetic disorder. What about false positives, though? A couple might erroneously be told their fetus has a serious genetic disease. Such a case is not a wrongful birth case because the fetus is not brought to term, but may be looked at as a wrongful abortion case. In Martinez v. Long Island Jewish Hillside Medical Center, 512 N.E.2d 538 (N.Y. 1987), defendants negligently advised Carmen Martinez that her baby would be born with the congenital birth defect of microcephaly (small brain) or anencephaly (no brain). Based on the extraordinary circumstances, she submitted to an abortion believing that it would be justified. Because of her religious beliefs, she felt abortion was a sin except under justifiable circumstances such as these. When it was shown that the diagnosis was erroneous and that Ms. Martinez had aborted a healthy fetus, she was allowed to maintain a cause of action for emotional distress.

13. The existence of prenatal screening may alter physicians' ideas of responsible parental behavior. When pregnant women do not undergo available prenatal testing, health care professionals blame them for the resulting genetic condition of their child. Theresa M. Marteau & Harriet Drake, Attributions for Disability: The Influence of Genetic Screening, 40 Soc. Sci. Med. 1127 (1995).

14. Currently, in the Orthodox Jewish community of New York, where arranged marriages are still common, genetic information is increasingly being taken into consideration at the matchmaking stage. People who are of Ashkenazi Jewish descent have a one-in-25 chance of having a Tay-Sachs genetic mutation; if two such carriers marry, each child has a one-in-four chance of having the devastating disease. A child with Tay-Sachs appears normal at birth, but later loses motor functions, suffers massive neurological deterioration and seizures, and generally dies by age three. A program in New York known as Chevra Dor Yeshorim (Association of an Upright Generation) offers Tay-Sachs carrier screening to Orthodox Jewish adolescents. Before a marriage is arranged, the matchmaker calls the program with the identification numbers of the two individuals. If they both

carry the gene for Tay-Sachs, they are not matched for marriage. To preserve medical confidentiality, they are not informed why they are not a good match. The program has generated controversy because it has added screening for other disorders, such as cystic fibrosis, which are not necessarily fatal in childhood.

In the Chevra Dor Yeshorim program, if both individuals are carriers, they are found to be "genetically incompatible," but the program does not disclose information of individual genetic risks. In contrast, the Thalassaemia Screening Program (TSP) in Cyprus does disclose carrier status of individual genetic risks. Another difference between the programs is that Chevra Dor Yeshorim tests for diseases such as Tay-Sachs, which is fatal at a very early age; thalassaemia is treatable but at a high cost. Does premarital genetic testing raise any ethical questions? Do you think there is any danger in labeling a couple "genetically incompatible"? See Barbara Prainsack & Gil Siegal, The Rise of Genetic Couplehood? A Comparative View of Premarital Genetic Testing, 1 BioSocieties 17 (2006).

What if a couple undergoing testing in the Chevra Dor Yeshorim program are told that they both carry the Tay-Sachs mutation—and do not marry as a result. If the information is later found to be erroneous, could they sue? What potential damages would there be for the loss of a chance to marry, particularly if each member of the couple marries someone else?

CURLENDER V. BIO-SCIENCE LABORATORIES
165 Cal.Rptr. 477 (Cal. App. 1980).

JEFFERSON, J.

The appeal presents an issue of first impression in California: What remedy, if any, is available in this state to a severely impaired child— genetically defective—born as the result of defendants' negligence in conducting certain genetic tests of the child's parents—tests which, if properly done, would have disclosed the high probability that the actual, catastrophic result would occur?

* * *

In the first cause of action against the named defendants, plaintiff Shauna alleged that on January 15, 1977, her parents, Phillis and Hyam Curlender, retained defendant laboratories to administer certain tests designed to reveal whether either of the parents were carriers of genes which would result in the conception and birth of a child with Tay-Sachs disease, medically defined as "amaurotic familial idiocy." The tests on plaintiff's parents were performed on January 21, 1977, and, it was alleged, due to defendants' negligence, "incorrect and inaccurate" information was disseminated to plaintiff's parents concerning their status as carriers.

The complaint did not allege the date of plaintiff's birth, so we do not know whether the parents relied upon the test results in conceiving plaintiff, or, as parents-to-be when the tests were made, relied upon the results in failing to avail themselves of amniocentesis and an abortion. In any event, on May 10, 1978, plaintiff's parents were informed that plaintiff had Tay-Sachs disease.

As the result of the disease, plaintiff Shauna suffers from "mental retardation, susceptibility to other diseases, convulsions, sluggishness, apathy, failure to fix objects with her eyes, inability to take an interest in her surroundings, loss of motor reactions, inability to sit up or hold her head up, loss of weight, muscle atrophy, blindness, pseudobulper palsy, inability to feed orally, decerebrate rigidity and gross physical deformity." It was alleged that Shauna's life expectancy is estimated to be four years. The complaint also contained allegations that plaintiff suffers "pain, physical and emotional distress, fear, anxiety, despair, loss of enjoyment of life, and frustration. . . ."

The complaint sought costs of plaintiff's care as damages and also damages for emotional distress and the deprivation of "72.6 years of her life." In addition, punitive damages of three million dollars were sought, on the ground that "[a]t the time that Defendants . . . [tested the parents], Defendants, and each of them, had been expressly informed by the nation's leading authority on Tay-Sachs disease that said test procedures were substantially inaccurate and would likely result is disasterous [sic] and catastrophic consequences to the patients, and Defendants knew that said procedures were improper, inadequate and with insufficient controls and that the results of such testing were likely to be inaccurate and that a false negative result would have disasterous [sic] and catastrophic consequences to the Plaintiff, all in conscious disregard of the health, safety and well-being of Plaintiff. . . ."

* * *

The term "wrongful life" has to date served as an umbrella for causes of action based upon any distinguishable factual situations; this has led to some confusion in its use. For purposes of our discussion, the term "wrongful life" will be confined to those causes of action *brought by the infant* alleging that, due to the negligence of the defendant, birth occurred; * * *.

* * *

The high court in Pennsylvania issued an exhaustive opinion in 1979 concerning the various aspects of the "wrongful-life" problem. The case was Speck v. Finegold, 408 A.2d 496 (Pa. 1979), a malpractice suit by parents and child occasioned by the birth of the child with neurofibromatosis, a seriously crippling condition already evidenced in the child's siblings. Overruling the trial court, *Speck* recognized the parents' cause of action but not that of the infant plaintiff.

We quote at length from the *Speck* court's opinion: "In the instant case, we deny Francine's [infant plaintiff's] claim to be made whole. When we examine Francine's claim, we find regardless of whether her claim is based on 'wrongful life' or otherwise, there is a failure to state a legally cognizable cause of action even though, admittedly, the defendants' actions of negligence were the proximate cause of her defective birth. Her claims to be whole have two fatal weaknesses. First, there is no precedent in appellate judicial pronouncements that holds a child has a fundamental right to be born as a whole, functional human being. Whether it is better to have never been born at all rather than to have been born with serious mental defects is a mystery more properly left to the philosophers and theologians, a mystery which would lead us into the field of metaphysics, beyond the realm of our understanding or ability to solve . . . [This] cause of action . . . demands a calculation of damages dependent on a comparison between Hobson's choice of life in an impaired state and nonexistence. This the law is incapable of doing . . . unfortunately, . . . this is not an action cognizable in law. Thus, the recognized principle, not peculiar to traditional tort law alone, that it would be a denial of justice to deny all relief where a wrong is of such a nature as to preclude certain ascertained damages, is inapposite and inapplicable here."

* * *

The circumstance that the birth and injury have come hand in hand has caused other courts to deal with the problem by barring recovery. The reality of the "wrongful-life" concept is that such a plaintiff both *exists* and *suffers*, due to the negligence of others. It is neither necessary nor just to retreat into meditation on the mysteries of life. We need not be concerned with the fact that had defendants not been negligent, the plaintiff might not have come into existence at all. The certainty of genetic impairment is no longer a mystery. In addition, a reverent appreciation of life compels recognition that plaintiff, however impaired she may be, has come into existence as a living person with certain rights.

One of the fears expressed in the decisional law is that, once it is determined that such infants have rights cognizable at law, nothing would prevent such a plaintiff from bringing suit against its own parents for allowing plaintiff to be born. In our view, the fear is groundless. The "wrongful-life" cause of action with which we are concerned is based upon negligently caused failure by someone under a duty to do so to inform the prospective parents of facts needed by them to make a conscious choice *not* to become parents. If a case arose where, despite due care by the medical profession in transmitting the necessary warnings, parents made a conscious choice to proceed with a pregnancy, with full knowledge that a seriously impaired infant would be born, that conscious choice would provide an intervening act of proximate cause to preclude liability insofar as defendants other than the parents were concerned. Under such circumstances, we see no sound public policy which should protect those parents from being answerable for the pain, suffering and misery which they have wrought upon their offspring.

* * *

The extent of recovery, however, is subject to certain limitations due to the nature of the tort involved. While ordinarily a defendant is liable for all consequences flowing from the injury, it is appropriate in the case before us to tailor the elements of recovery, taking into account particular circumstances involved.

The complaint seeks damages based upon an actuarial life expectancy of plaintiff of more than 70 years—the life expectancy if plaintiff had been born without the Tay-Sachs disease. The complaint sets forth that plaintiff's actual life expectancy, because of the disease, is only four years. We reject as untenable the claim that plaintiff is entitled to damages as if plaintiff had been born without defects and would have had a normal life expectancy. Plaintiff's right to damages must be considered on the basis of plaintiff's mental and physical condition at birth and her expected condition during the short life span (four years according to the complaint) anticipated for one with her impaired condition. In similar fashion, we reject the notion that a "wrongful-life" cause of action involves any attempted evaluation of a claimed right *not* to be born. In essence, we construe the "wrongful-life" cause of action by the defective child as the right of such child to recover damages for the pain and suffering to be endured during the limited life span available to such a child and any special pecuniary loss resulting from the impaired condition.

In California, infants are presumed to experience pain and suffering when injury has been established, even if the infant is unable to testify and describe such pain and suffering * * *.

The complaint sought costs of care as an element of special damages, an appropriate item of recovery in cases where, for one reason or another, there is no suit brought by the parents seeking recovery for this pecuniary loss. We are informed, however, that such a suit is pending by the parents of the plaintiff before us. Upon remand, consideration should be given to consolidating plaintiff's cause of action with those of the parents in the interest of efficient use of trial time and the prevention of duplication of effort, as well as the prevention of possible double recovery. Costs of plaintiff's care may only be awarded once.

Finally, we considered the matter of punitive damages. The complaint makes such a request. Our Civil Code section 3294 allows such damages "where the defendant has been guilty of oppression, fraud, or malice, express or implied"; they are given "for the sake of example and by way of punishing the defendant." We need not speculate on the means by which plaintiff plans to establish facts showing oppression, fraud or malice—as related to either the third cause of action stated in the complaint or the entitlement of plaintiff to punitive damages. Such will be the concern of judge and jury when this matter is tried. For our purposes, we find that plaintiff has adequately pleaded a cause of action for punitive damages. We see no reason in public policy or legal analysis for exempting from liability for punitive damages a defendant who is sued for committing a "wrongful-life" tort.

DOOLAN V. IVF AMERICA (MA) INC.

2000 WL 33170944 (Mass. Super. 2000).

CRATSLEY, J.

Pursuant to the summary judgment record, the undisputed material facts are as follows:

In 1993, plaintiff Laureen Doolan gave birth to her first child, Samantha, who was born afflicted with cystic fibrosis. Laureen and her husband, plaintiff John Doolan, subsequently learned that they were both carriers of a cystic fibrosis gene mutation known as Delta F-508. Mr. and Mrs. Doolan wished to have another child, but they wanted some assurance that their second child would not have cystic fibrosis.

In 1996 Mr. and Mrs. Doolan agreed to participate in a series of procedures conducted jointly by the co-defendants that were designed to provide the Doolans with a degree of certainty that their second child would not be afflicted with cystic fibrosis. In November 1996 defendant Ronald Carson, Ph.D. ("Dr. Carson"), the Scientific and Laboratory Director at defendant MPD, harvested a series of Mrs. Doolan's eggs, fertilized the eggs with Mr. Doolan's sperm in vitro, and prepared the resulting embryos for genetic testing. A cell from each of the resulting ten embryos was then retrieved by MPD, whereupon the cells were sent to defendant Genzyme Corporation ("Genzyme").

In December 1996 Genzyme tested the ten cells to ascertain which embryos were (1) afflicted with, (2) carriers of, or (3) free of the cystic fibrosis gene mutation, Delta F-508. In a letter dated December 23, 1996, defendant Katherine Klinger, Ph.D. ("Dr. Klinger"), the Vice President of Science at Genzyme, advised MPD that Embryo No. 7 was free of the cystic fibrosis gene mutation and suitable for implantation. As a result of this finding, Mr. and Mrs. Doolan decided to have MPD implant Embryo No. 7 into Mrs. Doolan on March 10, 1997.

On November 21, 1997, Mrs. Doolan gave birth to her son, minor plaintiff Thomas Doolan. Shortly after Thomas' birth, it was discovered that he did, in fact, suffer from cystic fibrosis and that his condition was due to the Delta F-508 genetic mutation. All three plaintiffs assert claims arising out of (1) MPD's and Dr. Carson's alleged negligence in implanting an embryo that contained the cystic fibrosis gene mutation, and (2) Genzyme's and Dr. Klinger's alleged negligence in advising MPD that Embryo No. 7 was free of the Delta F-508 gene mutation and therefore was suitable for implantation.

* * *

MINOR PLAINTIFF THOMAS DOOLAN'S NEGLIGENCE CLAIM

The almost universal rule in this country is that a physician is not liable to a child who was born because of the physician's negligence. Courts have generally referred to claims alleging that the physician negligently failed to inform the child's parents of the possibility of their bearing a severely defective child, thereby preventing a parental choice to avoid the child's birth, as "wrongful life" cases. The Massachusetts Supreme Judicial Court (SJC) has reasoned that granting the minor plaintiff a cause of action in wrongful life cases would require a comparison of the relative monetary values of existence and nonexistence, a task that is beyond the competence of the judicial system.

* * *

Perhaps sensing the tenuous nature of his "wrongful life" claim, * * * minor plaintiff Thomas Doolan asserts that his negligence claim against the defendants is not a "wrongful life" claim, but rather it is a pre-conception tort, and as such it is not foreclosed under Massachusetts law. Unlike "wrongful life" claims, * * * the SJC has yet to address the viability of pre-conception tort claims * * *. [But] the essence of Thomas Doolan's claim is not that the alleged negligence of the defendants caused him to be born with cystic fibrosis, but rather that the alleged negligence of the defendants denied his parents the opportunity to choose not to conceive and give birth to him. This is precisely the "fundamental problem of logic" that the SJC sought to avoid when it denied the minor plaintiff a cause of action for "wrongful life" * * *.

JOHN AND LAUREEN DOOLAN'S CLAIMS FOR LOSS OF CONSORTIUM

Plaintiffs John and Laureen Doolan advance two arguments in support of their claims for loss of consortium. The plaintiffs first argue that M.G.L. c. 231, § 85X creates a cause of action for parents seeking to recover for the loss of consortium of a dependent child. Section 85X provides:

> The parents of a minor child or an adult child who is dependent on his parents for support shall have a cause of action for loss of

consortium of the child who has been seriously injured against any person who is legally responsible for causing such injury.

The plain language of the preceding section indicates that the plaintiffs may only recover for the loss of consortium of Thomas Doolan against any person who is legally responsible for causing such injury. Plaintiffs have failed to put forth any evidence suggesting that the defendants are legally responsible for causing Thomas Doolan to be born afflicted with cystic fibrosis. This analysis is similar to that found * * * regarding Thomas Doolan's own negligence claims. Therefore, this Court holds as a matter of law that M.G.L. c. 231, § 85X does not confer a cause of action for loss of consortium on the plaintiffs, John and Laureen Doolan.

The second argument made by the plaintiffs in support of their loss of consortium claims asks this Court to undertake an analysis in the realm of the hypothetical. Mr. and Mrs. Doolan assert that were it not for the alleged negligence of the defendants, they would currently be raising a boy named Thomas, and that this child would not be afflicted with cystic fibrosis. Since this hypothetical "healthy" Thomas Doolan would be more likely to be able to offer society and companionship to his parents for the duration of their lifetimes than would the actual Thomas Doolan, plaintiffs reason that they have a cause of action for loss of consortium.

Plaintiffs' argument fails for two reasons. First, the extent of any loss of consortium damages for a child that was never born would be far too speculative to uphold plaintiffs' cause of action. For example, the jury would have to consider the quality of the relationship plaintiffs might have had with their hypothetical son in assessing Mr. and Mrs. Doolan's loss of consortium damages. Furthermore, plaintiffs' assertion that this hypothetical Thomas Doolan would have been "healthy" discounts the possibility that he might have been afflicted with another type of birth defect or long term illness.

NOTES AND QUESTIONS

1. What are the policy arguments for and against wrongful life actions? How do the policy arguments regarding wrongful life cases compare to those involving wrongful birth cases?

2. Should a child be able to bring a wrongful life cause of action against his or her parents in addition to, or instead of, the negligent health care provider? In *dicta*, the *Curlender* court said:

> If a case arose where, despite due care by the medical profession in transmitting the necessary warnings, parents made a conscious choice to proceed with a pregnancy, with a full knowledge that a seriously impaired infant would be born. * * * Under such circumstances, we see no sound policy which should protect those

parents from being answerable for the pain, suffering and misery which they have wrought upon their offspring.

Subsequently, the California legislature passed the following statute:

Cal. Civ. Code § 43.6

§ 43.6.   Immunity from Liability

(a)   No cause of action arises against a parent of a child based upon the claim that the child should not have been conceived or, if conceived, should not have been allowed to have been born alive.

(b)   The failure or refusal of a parent to prevent the live birth of his or her child shall not be a defense in any action against a third party, nor shall the failure or refusal be considered in awarding damages in any such action.

3.   Examples of genetic diseases commonly tested for by preimplantation genetic diagnosis include Down syndrome, cystic fibrosis, thalassemia, sickle cell anemia, Gaucher disease, and hemophilia. Other heritable traits that have been screened in the clinical setting include a gene that predisposes carriers to deafness and a gene that causes early onset Alzheimer disease. Recently, studies have indicated that embryos have been screened and selected to not have genes correlating with an increased risk of developing colon cancer or breast cancer. A child was born in January 2009 in the United Kingdom who had been screened to be free of BRCA genetic mutations linked to breast cancer. Sarah-Kate Templeton, Gene Parents Plan More Babies, The Sunday Times (London), January 11, 2009, at 3. Note that in Great Britain only 5% of the cases of breast cancer are caused by the BRCA gene mutation.

C. MANDATORY PRENATAL SCREENING

LORI B. ANDREWS, PRENATAL SCREENING AND THE CULTURE OF MOTHERHOOD
47 Hastings L.J. 967, 970–971, 994–1000 (1996).

The range of tests offered is growing continually, due in large measure to concerted efforts by the Human Genome Project, a $3 billion federally funded endeavor to map and sequence the complete set of genes in the human body. Prenatal testing is now possible not just for serious, life-threatening disorders but also for disorders that are treatable after birth, for disorders that do not manifest until later in life, such as breast cancer, and even for conditions not thought to be medical problems, such as homosexuality.

At the same time, a developing technology offers more women the option of prenatal testing. This technology, fetal cell sorting, provides fetal information without creating a physical risk to the fetus or the pregnant woman. A "simple" blood test is performed on the woman. In the laboratory, technicians use complex procedures to capture minute quantities of fetal blood cells circulating in the woman's blood. Prenatal diagnosis is undertaken on those cells, to determine, for example, whether the fetus has Down syndrome, cystic fibrosis, Tay-Sachs disease, or other disorders.

Researchers developing fetal cell sorting have pointed out that it could be used to screen large populations of women. One group of researchers has noted that,

> because the * * * procedure requires sampling of maternal blood rather than amniotic fluid, it could make widespread screening in younger women feasible * * *. Widespread screening is desirable because the relatively large number of pregnancies in women below 35 years old means that they bear the majority of children with chromosomal abnormalities despite the relatively low risk of such abnormalities in pregnancies in this age group.

* * *

[The article then documents how some types of genetic testing have been undertaken on pregnant women without their knowledge or consent. It then discusses the policy issues that would be raised by a public health mandate requiring that pregnant women undergo fetal cell sorting.]

* * *

Various blue ribbon panels of government, ethics organizations, and entities like the Institute of Medicine have already concluded that, due to the various psychological and social risks of genetic testing, genetics services should be voluntary. With respect to prenatal testing, the National Institutes of Health Workshop on Reproductive Genetic Testing: Impact Upon Women has recommended that "[r]eproductive genetic services should be meticulously voluntary." Similarly, the Committee on Assessing Genetic Risks of the Institute of Medicine has recommended that "voluntariness should be the cornerstone of any genetic testing program. The committee [finds] no justification for a state-sponsored mandatory public health program involving genetic testing of adults, or for unconsented-to genetic testing of patients in the clinical setting."

Overriding autonomy by mandating fetal cell sorting clearly has the most impact on women. Women are the people subject to genetic testing on their fetuses' behalf, and the action that the state subtly may be trying to encourage is one that the women would have to take—abortion. Additionally, diagnosis of the fetus more often provides information about the mother than about the father. In the case of a recessive disease, an X-linked disease, and some instances of dominant diseases, the fetus' genetic status will provide information to the mother about her genetic status, thus influencing her self-image, her personal relationships, and her relationships with third-party institutions.

Moreover, the intrusion on autonomy may be especially egregious to women, who, more than men, feel that doctors should keep out of reproductive decisions. A Swedish study assessing the attitudes of women and men towards prenatal diagnosis found that autonomy in the decision-making process was more important to women than to men. In response to the question: "[W]ho should decide about prenatal diagnosis, the couple itself or somebody else?," 82% of women indicated the couple should make the decision, compared to 20% of the male partners.

* * *

Currently, the constitutional protections supporting a woman's right to refuse medical interventions during pregnancy are four-fold: privacy protection of certain personal information; protection against unreasonable searches and seizures; protection of bodily integrity; and protection of reproductive decision-making and decisions regarding child-rearing.

* * *

1.   INFORMATIONAL PRIVACY

Medical information is protected as private, in part because of the psychological, social and financial risks associated with its disclosure. Common law privacy protections exist for certain types of medical information, as do federal constitutional protections. Just as "the sensitive nature of medical information about AIDS makes a compelling argument for keeping this information confidential," so too does the sensitive nature of genetic information. Since mandatory genetic testing would provide medical information about the woman or fetus to third parties (the laboratory personnel, the woman's physician), this could arguably be a breach of privacy. Such testing would violate one's privacy right not to know medical information about oneself and one's right to refuse medical information that is part of the right of informed consent in the health care setting.

2.   FOURTH AMENDMENT PROTECTIONS

A pregnant woman could assert a Fourth Amendment right to refuse the fetal cell sorting test. Mandatory blood testing is considered a search and seizure that must comply with Fourth Amendment standards that balance the nature and quality of the intrusion against the strength of a given state interest. Under such an analysis, for example, mandatory testing of an incarcerated individual for HIV infection absent a warrant has been found unconstitutional under the Fourth Amendment. Similarly, mandatory HIV testing of state employees working with developmentally disabled clients was enjoined as an unreasonable search and seizure under the Fourth Amendment, since the employees' privacy interests outweighed the state's interest in preventing the low risk of clients' contracting AIDS from employees. Such precedents would likewise apply to blood tests to obtain genetic information.

3.   PROTECTION OF BODILY INTEGRITY, REPRODUCTIVE AUTONOMY AND PARENTING DECISIONS

Women could also argue that they have a right to refuse fetal cell sorting based on the common law (and, in some cases, constitutional) protections of an individual's bodily integrity, as well as on constitutional protections of reproductive autonomy. Recent cases have begun to recognize a woman's right to refuse invasive interventions, such as Cesarean sections, during pregnancy. In In re A.C. [573 A.2d 1235 (D.C.1990)], the D.C. Court of Appeals held that the decision about whether a pregnant woman should undergo a Cesarean section should be controlled by the woman's wishes, articulated either through her informed consent or, if she is incompetent, through substituted judgment. A similar result was reached in an Illinois case, In re Baby Boy Doe [632 N.E.2d 326 (Ill.Ct.App.1994)]. In that case, a woman refused a Cesarean section on religious grounds, and the state attorney brought suit to force her to undergo the operation. The court upheld the woman's right to refuse, recognizing her right to privacy and bodily integrity. The court held that a woman has no duty to guarantee the physical and mental health of her child and that a woman may refuse forced interventions even if the refusal would be harmful to the fetus.

Parents also have a liberty interest in the type of children that they conceive and raise. In U.S. Supreme Court cases involving child-rearing decisions, the Court has held that the determination of a child's social traits is a matter for the parents to decide (even if state control arguably could produce a better child). A strong argument similarly could be made that a child's genetic traits should be determined by the parents rather than the state. Similar reasoning was used in dicta in Planned Parenthood v. Casey [505 U.S. 833 (1992)], in which the U.S. Supreme Court said,

> If indeed the woman's interest in deciding whether to bear and beget a child had not been recognized as in Roe [v. Wade, 410 U.S. 113 (1973)], the State might as readily restrict a woman's right to choose to carry a pregnancy to term as to terminate it, to further asserted state interests in population control, or eugenics, for example. Yet Roe has been sensibly relied upon to counter any such suggestions.

NOTES AND QUESTIONS

1.   Some physicians undertake genetic testing on pregnant women without informed consent—and tell them the results of the testing only if it indicates a problem. When questioned about this practice, physicians state that other types of unconsented-to testing (such as for gestational diabetes) is routinely done on pregnant women without their consent. Are genetic tests distinguishable? Standard, nongenetic tests are often done in order to be able to treat the fetus. Genetic testing often reveals that the fetus is untreatable, so the "benefit" is the possibility of abortion. There is a much wider range of moral and personal opinion about the advisability of abortion than about treatment of fetuses or newborns. Some women understandably may not want information about their genetic status or the fetus's genetic status because they do not intend to abort or because they do not want to risk genetic discrimination against themselves or their future child. Standard tests are also generally for transitional, pregnancy-related conditions, whereas the genetic information revealed about a woman or her fetus is permanent and immutable in character.

2.   What effect does mandatory genetic testing have on social expectations for women?

III.   REPRODUCTIVE TECHNOLOGY AND GENETICS

A. PROCEDURES

Technologies designed to aid infertile couples who wish to have children can also be used by couples at risk of passing on a genetic disease to their children. In vitro fertilization is a process by which a woman's egg is fertilized with a man's sperm in a petri dish and then transferred into that woman's body or another woman's body. Before the transfer, preimplantation genetic diagnosis can be undertaken on the embryo to determine its genetic make-up.

Third parties—egg donors, sperm donors, and embryo donors—can be used to substitute for the genetic component of one or both parents. But as more actors get involved in the drama of reproduction, the law is increasingly called in to sort out rights and responsibilities. What sort of genetic screening of potential donors is appropriate? Who is liable if a donor passes on a genetic disease? Who are the legal parents when a donor is involved?

Ethical issues abound as well. Should parents be allowed to screen embryos for traits that are unrelated to diseases, such as eye color or athletic ability? In one study, 12% of potential parents surveyed said they would abort a fetus with a tendency to be fat. Should sperm and egg donors be chosen for traits such as appearance, musical abilities or SAT scores? And when is professional self-regulation versus legal regulation appropriate?

B. GENETIC SCREENING IN THE CONTEXT OF ASSISTED REPRODUCTION

MINIMUM GENETIC SCREENING FOR GAMETE DONORS, APPROVED BY THE BOARD OF DIRECTORS OF THE AMERICAN SOCIETY FOR REPRODUCTIVE MEDICINE
99 Fertility and Sterility 47, 62.e1 (2013).

I.   The donor

A.   Should not have any major Mendelian disorder. Mendelian disorders fall into the following categories:

a.   Autosomal dominant or X-linked disorders. Providers should be aware that some autosomal dominant or X-linked disorders can have variable expressivity (meaning that mutation carriers may not have noticeable symptoms) or have an age of onset that extends beyond the age of the donor (one example is Huntington disease).

b.   Autosomal recessive disorders. Donors who are heterozygous need not necessarily be excluded if the reproductive partner has had appropriate carrier screening. The recipient and reproductive partner (as appropriate) should be counseled about the accuracy of the carrier screening test and the residual risk to be a carrier following a negative test. Counseling regarding residual risk is complex and may be best provided by a genetic counselor.

B.   Should not have (or have had) any major malformation of complex cause (multifactorial/polygenic), such as spina bifida or cardiac malformation. A major malformation is defined as one that carries serious functional or cosmetic handicap. However, the definition of "major" is a matter of judgment.

C.   Should not have any significant familial disease with a major genetic component.

* * *

D.   Should not have a known karyotypic abnormality that may result in chromosomally unbalanced gametes. In the general population, the chance of having a chromosomal rearrangement that could be transmitted in unbalanced form to offspring is small, provided the family history is negative for risk factors. Therefore, routine karyotyping of all donors is optional.

E.   Should undergo general population and ethnicity (ancestry)-based genetic screening. Donors should give informed consent prior to carrier screening. Informed consent should include discussion of the natural history of the condition being screened, carrier frequency in the respective ethnic group, detection rate of the test, residual risk to be a carrier when testing negative, and options for persons testing positive. If a prospective donor is identified as a carrier, genetic counseling for both the donor and recipient is recommended.

The recommended list of tests may change as tests for other disorders are developed. Guidelines regarding ethnicity and population-based genetic screening are published by the American Congress of Obstetricians and Gynecologists (www.acog.org) and the American College of Medical Genetics (www.acmg.net). All gamete donors should be evaluated by the current tests recommended at the time of the donation.

Note: It is not appropriate to screen gamete donors for adult onset conditions (such as cancer predisposition, Huntington disease, etc.) without full consent of the gamete donor, including formal genetic counseling.

F.   Should be generally healthy and young. Advanced maternal age is associated with an increased risk for aneuploidy offspring. Advanced paternal age is associated with a moderately increased risk for new mutations in offspring, and an emerging body of evidence suggests an increased risk for complex disorders, including some congenital anomalies, schizophrenia, autism spectrum disorders, and specific forms of cancer.

II.   The donor's first-degree relatives (parents, siblings, and offspring) should be free of:

A.   Mendelian disorders as described in Section I.A.

B.   Major malformations as described in Section I.B.

C.   Significant familial disease with a major genetic component.

D.   A chromosomal abnormality, unless the donor has a normal karyotype.

E.   Mental retardation of undocumented etiology. If family history reveals a disorder for which definitive testing is available, then it is appropriate to refer the prospective donor for genetic counseling for that specific disorder. Testing without a formal genetic consultation would be inappropriate. Genetic test results may determine the appropriateness of using that donor.

C. LIABILITY IN REPRODUCTIVE TECHNOLOGY

JOHNSON V. SUPERIOR COURT OF LOS ANGELES COUNTY
95 Cal.Rptr.2d 864 (Cal. App. 2000).

MALLANO, J.

Petitioners Diane L. Johnson and Ronald G. Johnson, along with their minor daughter Brittany L. Johnson, filed an action against real parties in interest, California Cryobank, Inc., Cappy M. Rothman, M.D., and Charles A. Sims, M.D., claiming that real parties failed to disclose that the sperm they sold came from a donor with a family history of kidney disease called Autosomal Dominant Polycystic Kidney Disease (ADPKD). That sperm was used to conceive Brittany who has been diagnosed with this serious kidney disease.

* * *

The novel issue presented here is whether parents and their child, conceived by the sperm of an anonymous sperm donor, may compel the donor's deposition and production of documents in order to discover information relevant to their action against the sperm bank for selling sperm that they alleged transmitted ADPKD to the child.

* * *

Petitioners sued Cryobank, as well as its employees, officers, and directors, Doctors Sims and Rothman, for professional negligence, fraud, and breach of contract. In their second amended complaint, petitioners allege as follows. Diane and Ronald Johnson decided to conceive a child through the use of a sperm donor upon the recommendation of their infertility doctors. The Johnsons contacted Cryobank's sperm bank facility in Los Angeles. Ultimately, Cryobank sold the Johnsons frozen sperm specimens donated by donor No. 276. At or near the time of sale, the Johnsons signed Cryobank's form agreement that provided, in relevant part, that "Cryobank shall destroy all information and records which they may have as to the identity of said donor, it being the intention of all parties that the identity of said donor shall be and forever remain anonymous."

At the time of their purchase, Cryobank assured the Johnsons that the anonymous sperm donor had been fully tested and genetically screened. The Johnsons' doctors then implanted the purchased sperm in one of Diane Johnson's fallopian tubes. The procedure was successful and Brittany was born on April 18, 1989. In May 1995, the Johnsons were informed that Brittany was positively diagnosed with ADPKD.

As neither Ronald nor Diane Johnson has ADPKD or a family history of the disease, it was donor No. 276 who genetically transmitted ADPKD to Brittany. At the time donor No. 276 sold his sperm to Cryobank in December 1986, Doctors Sims and Rothman at Cryobank interviewed him and learned that the donor's mother and his mother's sister both suffered from kidney disease and hypertension, and the donor's mother suffered a 30 percent hearing loss before the age of 60. The presence of multiple instances of kidney disease coupled with hypertension and neurological disorders, such as deafness, are red flag indicators of the presence of ADPKD in donor No. 276's family, and thus, Cryobank and Doctors Sims and Rothman knew that donor No. 276's sperm could be at risk of genetically transferring kidney disease.

* * *

During the course of the action, petitioners propounded discovery to Cryobank seeking information regarding donor No. 276, including his name, address, and medical history. Cryobank objected to providing any information regarding donor No. 276, claiming the donor's right to privacy and his physician-patient privilege. Cryobank did, however, produce two donor consent agreements that were in use at the time donor No. 276 sold his sperm. Both of these agreements state that the donor will be compensated for each sperm specimen, that he will not attempt to discover the identity of the persons to whom he is donating his sperm, and that his identity "will be kept in the strictest confidence unless a court orders disclosure for good cause. . . ." Cryobank also produced a document showing that on September 6, 1991, Cryobank informed Diane Johnson that donor No. 276 had been withdrawn from the donor program because "new information on his family members . . . indicates that he is at risk for kidney disease" and that a "few small cysts were found" after performing a "renal ultrasound." Cryobank's responses to interrogatories indicated that donor No. 276 had sold 320 deposits of his semen to Cryobank. Donor No. 276's agreement with Cryobank indicated that he received approximately $35 per semen specimen. Donor No. 276 thus received a total of $11,200 for his sperm.

* * *

THE SCOPE OF DISCOVERY

Code of Civil Procedure section 2017 provides the framework for discovery in civil cases. Unless otherwise limited by court order, "any party may obtain discovery regarding any matter, not privileged, that is relevant to the subject matter involved in the pending action . . . if the matter either is itself admissible in evidence or appears reasonably calculated to lead to the discovery of admissible evidence." This same section further provides that "[d]iscovery may be obtained of the identity and location of persons having knowledge of any discoverable matter, as well as of the existence, description, nature, custody, condition, and location of any document. . . ."

* * *

THE PHYSICIAN-PATIENT PRIVILEGE

In order for a party to invoke the physician-patient privilege under Evidence Code section 994, there must be a patient. A "patient" is defined under section 991 as "a person who consults a physician or submits to an examination by a physician for the purpose of securing a diagnosis or preventative, palliative, or curative treatment of his physical or mental or emotional condition." Therefore, if a person does not consult a physician for diagnosis or treatment of a physical or mental ailment, the privilege does not exist. (Kizer v. Sulnick, [248 Cal. Rptr. 712 (Cal.App.1988)] [persons were not patients when they consulted with a physician as part of a study to determine whether residents shared similar medical complaints to determine further whether the presence of a waste facility was the cause of these symptoms because the purpose was not to obtain a diagnosis]).

Real parties in interest have failed to demonstrate that the physician-patient privilege is applicable in this case. The evidence presented to the trial court revealed that donor No. 276 visited Cryobank for the sole purpose of selling his sperm. That he consulted with Cryobank's physicians and medical personnel as part of the process of donating his sperm does not change the dominant purpose for his visit. There was no evidence presented to the trial court that donor No. 276 visited Cryobank "for the purpose of securing a diagnosis or preventative, palliative, or curative treatment of his physical or mental or emotional condition." Thus, we conclude that the physician-patient privilege has no application here.

JOHN DOE'S STATUS AS THIRD PARTY BENEFICIARY

John Doe next claims that petitioners are not entitled to discover his identity because their contract with Cryobank prohibits it. John Doe argues that petitioners' agreement with Cryobank providing that the sperm donor's identity would never be disclosed was made for his benefit and thus, as a third party beneficiary, he is entitled to keep his identity confidential as the agreement requires. While we agree that John Doe is a third party beneficiary, we disagree that the agreement precludes disclosure of his identity or related information under any circumstance.

* * *

And enforcement under all circumstances of a confidentiality provision such as the one in Cryobank's contract with the Johnsons conflicts with California's compelling interest in the health and welfare of children, including those conceived by artificial insemination. There may be instances under which a child conceived by artificial insemination may need his or her family's genetic and medical history for important medical decisions. For example, such genetic and medical history can lead to an early detection of certain diseases and an increased chance of curing them. In some situations, a person's ability to locate his or her biological relative may be important in considering lifesaving transplant procedures. While in most situations the donor's genetic and medical information may be furnished without the need of disclosing the donor's identity, there may be other situations that require disclosure of the donor's identity in order to obtain the needed information. In either event, a contract that completely forecloses the opportunity of a child conceived by artificial insemination to discover the relevant and needed medical history of his or her genetic father is inconsistent with the best interests of the child.

We conclude that Cryobank's agreement with the Johnsons precluding disclosure of the donor's identity and other information pertaining to the donor under all circumstances is contrary to public policy and therefore unenforceable.

* * *

THE CONSTITUTIONAL RIGHT OF PRIVACY

Finally, real parties in interest contend that petitioners are precluded from deposing John Doe because to do so would violate his constitutional right of privacy under the federal and California Constitutions. We agree with real parties that donor No. 276 has a right of privacy in his medical history and his identity. We disagree, however, that such a right precludes his deposition and the production of the records requested in the deposition subpoena.

The California Constitution expressly provides that all people have the inalienable right to privacy.

* * *

"Legally recognized privacy interests are generally of two classes: (1) interests in precluding the dissemination or misuse of sensitive and confidential information ('informational privacy'); and (2) interests in making intimate personal decisions or conducting personal activities without observation, intrusion, or interference ('autonomy privacy')."

* * *

A person's medical history undoubtedly falls within the recognized zones of privacy.

* * *

We conclude that although donor No. 276 does indeed have a limited privacy interest in his identity as a sperm donor and in his medical history, under the circumstances of this case, it would be unreasonable for donor No. 276 to expect that his genetic and medical history, and possibly even his identity, would never be disclosed.

* * *

Petitioners seek to take John Doe's deposition in order to learn of all relevant facts he disclosed to Cryobank regarding his medical history of kidney disease. Petitioners also seek all of John Doe's records pertaining to "his family's affliction with [ADPKD], . . . secondary health problems diagnosed as being caused or related to ADPKD," and "the history of deponent's medical health as it relates to symptomology of ADPKD. . . ." As a result, what is at stake here is not only the disclosure of John Doe's identity and medical history, but of his family's as well. We conclude that such disclosure would involve an invasion of privacy unless reasonably curtailed.

* * *

Because discovery orders involve state-compelled disclosure, such disclosure is treated as a product of state action. Consequently, whenever the compelled disclosure treads upon the constitutional right of privacy, there must be a compelling state interest.

We conclude that there are compelling state interests in this case. First, the state has a compelling interest in making certain that parties comply with properly served subpoenas and discovery orders in order to disclose relevant information to the fullest extent allowable. Second, the state has an interest in seeking the truth in court proceedings. "The state has enough of an interest in discovering the truth in legal proceedings, that it may compel disclosure of confidential material." This includes medical records. Third, the state has a compelling interest in ensuring that those injured by the actionable conduct of others receive full redress of those injuries. Petitioners have demonstrated a compelling need to depose the only independent percipient witness that apparently can reveal the extent of information donor No. 276 disclosed to Cryobank. Such information is not only directly relevant to petitioners' claims, but is also relevant to Cryobank's affirmative defense of comparative fault. Thus, where, as here, the information sought "is essential to the fair resolution of the lawsuit, a trial court may properly compel such disclosure."

* * *

While donor No. 276 has an interest in maintaining the confidentiality of his identity and medical history, we hold that in the context of the particular facts of this case the state's interests, as well as those of petitioners, outweigh donor No. 276's interests. Accordingly, John Doe must appear at his deposition and answer all questions and produce documents that are relevant to the issues raised in the litigation. But this does not mean that John Doe's identity must automatically be disclosed if he indeed is donor No. 276.

* * *

For example, an order could be fashioned which would allow John Doe's deposition to proceed and documents produced on matters relevant to the issues in the litigation but in a manner which maintains the confidentiality of John Doe's identity and that of his family. Attendance at the deposition could be limited to the parties' counsel and the deposition transcript might refer simply to "John Doe" as the deponent. But we leave it to the trial court to craft the appropriate order.

* * *

We conclude that the trial court abused its discretion in denying petitioners' motion to compel John Doe's deposition and production of documents and in granting real parties' motion to quash. The trial court failed to consider the state and petitioners' countervailing interests that favor disclosure and failed to consider an order with "partial limitations rather than [an] outright denial of discovery." Petitioners are entitled to take John Doe's deposition and inquire whether he is donor No. 276, and if he is, delve into his and his family's health and medical history, and his communications with Cryobank, but only as to those issues which are relevant to the pending litigation. Similarly, we conclude that petitioners are entitled to the production of documents identified in their renotice of John Doe's deposition which are relevant and in the possession, custody, or control of John Doe. But John Doe's identity is to be protected to the fullest extent possible and the identities of his family members are not to be disclosed.

HARNICHER V. UNIVERSITY OF UTAH MEDICAL CENTER
962 P.2d 67 (Utah 1998).

HOWE, J.

Plaintiffs David and Stephanie Harnicher, parents of triplets born after in vitro fertilization using donor sperm, brought this action for medical malpractice alleging negligent infliction of emotional distress against defendant University of Utah Medical Center for using sperm from a donor other than the one that the couple had allegedly selected. The trial court found no evidence of physical injury or illness to support an action for negligent infliction of emotional distress and granted summary judgment in favor of the Medical Center. The Harnichers appeal.

David and Stephanie Harnicher sought treatment for infertility at the University of Utah Medical Center Fertility Clinic. Artificial insemination using David's sperm yielded no results. The Harnichers then contacted Dr. Ronald L. Urry of the Fertility Clinic regarding the possibility of in vitro fertilization. Dr. Urry suggested a procedure known as "micromanipulation" wherein holes are drilled in the mother's harvested ova [eggs] to facilitate fertilization. The ova are then placed in a petri dish with harvested sperm and the fertilized ova are subsequently implanted in the uterine wall, enabling the mother to bear her own child. Dr. Urry recommended using a mixture of the husband's sperm and donor sperm.

The Harnichers agreed. The micromanipulation method increased the chances that Stephanie would bear David's biological child. Additionally, the "mixed sperm" procedure potentially allowed the couple to believe and represent that any child born would be David's because if the donor closely matched David in physical characteristics and blood type, the parents would never be sure which sperm actually fertilized the ovum. Therefore the Harnichers evaluated the donor information provided by the Medical Center on that basis. The Medical Center maintains that the couple narrowed the selection to four donors and signed consent forms acknowledging that their doctor would make the final selection. The Harnichers assert, however, that they specifically and exclusively selected donor #183. Stephanie testified that when clinic employee Doug Carroll informed her that only frozen sperm, which has a lower success rate than fresh, was available from donor #183 and asked her if she still wanted to do the donor backup, she replied, "Only if you can get 183. . . . I'll take my lower chances. Let's just go with 183."

The procedure was performed, and Stephanie gave birth to triplets, two girls and one boy. Shortly after their birth, one of the babies became ill, requiring blood tests. Two of the children's blood type revealed that they could not possibly have been the children of either David or donor #183. A DNA test on one of the children established that the father was actually donor #83, another donor on the Harnichers' list.

Donor #183, like David, had curly dark hair and brown eyes. Donor #83 had straight auburn hair and green eyes. One of the triplets has red hair. The Harnichers maintain that the Medical Center's mistaken use of the wrong donor thwarted their intention of believing and representing that David is the children's biological father. They brought this action against the Medical Center alleging that they have "suffered severe anxiety, depression, grief, and other mental and emotional suffering and distress which has adversely affected their relationship with the children and with each other." However, both David and Stephanie testified in their depositions that they had not experienced any bodily harm as a result of the mistake.

* * *

The Harnichers contend that their disappointment in their children has caused them severe emotional distress to the point of mental illness. They ask us to hold that "diagnosed mental illness," standing alone, is sufficient to support a claim for negligent infliction of emotional distress.

* * *

As a result of their fertility treatment, the Harnichers became the parents of three normal, healthy children whom the couple suggest do not look as much like David as different children might have and whose blood type could not be descended from his. This result thwarted the couple's intention to believe and represent that the triplets are David's biological children. Exposure to the truth about one's own situation cannot be considered an injury and has never been a tort. Therefore, destruction of a fiction cannot be grounds for either malpractice or negligent infliction of emotional distress.

The Harnichers' assertion that David did not want children unless they were biologically his own is belied by the couple's knowing consent to the use of donor sperm. Stephanie testified that she could say "with probability," without ever having seen either donor, that the children of donor #183 would have been better looking than her triplets and that in her mind, she was damaged by that fact.

* * *

Realistically, however, it is impossible to know whether the children of donor #183 would have been superior in any way to the triplets or, indeed, whether the same number of babies or none at all would have resulted from the use of the less effective frozen sperm. The supposition that the road not taken would have led to a better result is a common human fallacy; it cannot support an action for negligent infliction of emotional distress. The Harnichers do not allege that the triplets are unhealthy, deformed, or deficient in any way. Nor do they claim any racial or ethnic mismatch between the triplets and their parents. In fact, the couple has presented no evidence at all that the physiological characteristics of three normal healthy children, which could not have been reliably predicted in any event, present circumstances with which "'a reasonable [person,] normally constituted, would be unable to adequately cope.'"

* * *

DURHAM, J., dissenting.

* * *

The majority appears to be reluctant to view the Harnichers' response to their asserted loss as a damaging one, in view of the fact that they do indeed have three healthy and loved children despite the

University's negligence in performing this procedure. The alleged facts, however, clearly meet the traditional standard for negligence: 1) the existence of a duty on the part of the University to use the donor sperm selected by the Harnichers that would have permitted them to believe the children to be their full biological children; 2) a breach of that duty through the University's mistake in using sperm from the wrong donor; 3) injury consisting of the Harnichers' loss of the opportunity to believe their children to be their full biological offspring; and 4) damages in the form of mental illness requiring treatment, accompanied by physical symptoms. . . .

* * *

In conclusion, I believe that a compensable loss and eligible damages have been asserted by plaintiffs and that they are entitled to have their cause of action tried by a jury. I would reverse.

NOTES AND QUESTIONS

1.   What type of genetic screening of gamete donors is appropriate? Should donors be liable if they knew (or should have known) that they risked passing on a certain genetic disease to the resulting children? Should a donor's confidentiality be protected? Should a blood sample of each donor be kept for later genetic testing? Should a donor be required to update the clinic on subsequently-discovered genetic diseases in his or her family so that the children can be warned?

2.   The Utah Supreme Court justices decided three-to-two that the Harnichers could not recover damages when artificial insemination helped them produce three children who were healthy, but did not resemble the husband. Was the case rightly decided? Does this case seem consistent with, or at odds with, the wrongful birth cases?

The dissenting justices in *Harnicher* suggest that if a couple requests sperm from a certain donor, and are given sperm from another donor, that mistake is actionable. Would such an analysis apply if the couple chose sperm or eggs from a donor whom they chose for certain genetic characteristics (e.g., intelligence or perfect pitch), but instead were given gametes from a donor who was not so gifted?

3.   Should sperm and egg donors be compensated for their genetic material? Such payment is banned in many European countries, but generally not in the United States. Should higher payments be allowed to donors thought to have "better" genes? An ad ran in the Ivy League college newspapers offering $50,000 to an egg donor who was tall, athletic and had scored at least 1400 out of a perfect 1600 SAT score. Kenneth Weiss, The Egg Brokers, Los Angeles Times, May 27, 2001, at A1. Is such an approach reminiscent of eugenics?

4.   Sperm donors are often unmarried medical students who do not yet have children of their own. On occasion, donor insemination produces a child with a rare recessive genetic disorder when the donor did not realize he was a carrier. Should he be told that fact so that he can take it into consideration when making his own reproductive plans? What if, as is often the case, the infertility clinic has told him in advance that they will not let him know if his sperm results in a pregnancy (so that he will not track down any resulting child)? In a study of sperm banks faced with the issue of contacting donors, half tracked down the donor to warn of the genetic risk and half did not.

5.   Should there be a limit on the number of times a sperm donor can provide sperm? A British sperm bank founder created 600 children by acting as a sperm donor for his patients between the 1940s and 1960s. Now, British donors are limited to creating 10 children. More recently, in the United States, a donor, Dr. Kirk Maxey, learned that his sperm had been used to create between 200 and 400 children. Since a single sample from a donor is often split into multiple inseminations and since donors are not told how many live births resulted from their donations, donors don't always realize how many children they've created. Maxey is now seeking regulations to deter incest among children created from donor sperm. Bertold Wiesner, British Biologist, Allegedly Fathered 600 Children Through Sperm Donations at Clinic, Huffington Post, April 9, 2012, www.huffingtonpost.com/2012/04/09/bertold-wiesner-british-man-fathered-600-children-kids-sperm-donations_n_1412849.html.

6.   An article in the *Journal of the American Medical Association* describes the case of a 23-year-old man in good health who donated sperm to a U.S. sperm bank almost a hundred times over a two year period. Barry J. Maron et al., Implications of Hypertrophic Cardiomyopathy Transmitted by Sperm Donation, 302 JAMA 1681 (2009). The sperm bank followed protocols standard in the industry at the time of the donation: doctors gave the donor a comprehensive medical evaluation including a complete personal and family medical history in addition to laboratory testing for communicable diseases. Several years later, a woman inseminated with the donor's sperm gave birth to a child diagnosed with hypertrophic cardiomyopathy (HCM)—a heart disease characterized by the thickening of the heart muscle.

What are the pros and cons of undertaking chromosomal analysis on all sperm and egg donors? Would the cost make these procedures less accessible?

Should other women who conceived children with the donor's sperm be told of the birth of the affected child? Most sperm banks do not have records of which recipients conceived. In the case reported in JAMA, however, the sperm bank notified the donor and all other recipients of his sperm that their children were at risk for HCM. Twenty-two children were born using the donor's sperm in addition to two children born to the donor's wife. Five children showed evidence of HCM including one two-and-a-half-year-old child who died waiting for a heart transplant.

7.　The Sixth Circuit Court of Appeals has held that surrogate brokers, lawyers, doctors and psychologists in infertility settings have a heightened responsibility which "gives rise to affirmative duties to act on the part of the surrogacy broker and program participants in order to reduce the risk of harm to the child and to the surrogate mother and the contracting father." These duties include designing and administering a program that provides appropriate testing for sexually transmitted diseases—in that case, cytomegalovirus. Stiver v. Parker, 975 F.2d 261 (6th Cir. 1992). Could these duties also extend to testing for genetic conditions?

IV.　PATERNITY AND ASSISTED REPRODUCTION

PEOPLE V. SORENSEN
437 P.2d 495 (Cal. 1968).

McCOMB, J.

Defendant appeals from a judgment convicting him of violating section 270 of the Penal Code (willful failure to provide for his minor child), a misdemeanor.

The settled statement of facts recites that seven years after defendant's marriage it was medically determined that he was sterile. His wife desired a child, either by artificial insemination or by adoption, and at first defendant refused to consent. About 15 years after the marriage defendant agreed to the artificial insemination of his wife. Husband and wife, then residents of San Joaquin County, consulted a physician in San Francisco. They signed an agreement, which is on the letterhead of the physician, requesting the physician to inseminate the wife with the sperm of a white male. The semen was to be selected by the physician, and under no circumstances were the parties to demand the name of the donor. The agreement contains a recitation that the physician does not represent that pregnancy will occur. The physician treated Mrs. Sorensen, and she became pregnant. Defendant knew at the time he signed the consent that when his wife took the treatments she could become pregnant and that if a child was born it was to be treated as their child.

A male child was born to defendant's wife in San Joaquin County on October 14, 1960. The information for the birth certificate was given by the mother, who named defendant as the father. Defendant testified that he had not provided the information on the birth certificate and did not recall seeing it before the trial.

For about four years the family had a normal family relationship, defendant having represented to friends that he was the child's father and treated the boy as his son. In 1964, Mrs. Sorensen separated from defendant and moved to Sonoma County with the boy. At separation, Mrs. Sorensen told defendant that she wanted no support for the boy, and she consented that a divorce be granted to defendant. Defendant obtained a decree of divorce, which recites that the court retained "jurisdiction regarding the possible support obligation of plaintiff in regard to a minor child born to defendant."

In the summer of 1966 when Mrs. Sorensen became ill and could not work, she applied for public assistance under the Aid to Needy Children program. The County of Sonoma supplied this aid until Mrs. Sorensen was able to resume work. Defendant paid no support for the child since the separation in 1964, although demand therefore was made by the district attorney. The municipal court found defendant guilty of violating section 270 of the Penal Code and granted him probation for three years on condition that he make payments of $50 per month for support through the district attorney's office.

From the record before us, this case could be disposed of on the ground that defendant has failed to overcome the presumption that "A child of a woman who is or has been married, born during the marriage or within 300 days after the dissolution thereof, is presumed to be a legitimate child of that marriage. This presumption may be disputed only by the people of the State of California in a criminal action brought under Section 270 of the Penal Code or by the husband or wife, or the descendant of one or both of them. In a civil action, this presumption may be rebutted only by clear and convincing proof."

* * *

Under the facts of this case, the term "father" as used in section 270 cannot be limited to the biologic or natural father as those terms are generally understood. The determinative factor is whether the legal relationship of father and child exists. A child conceived through heterologous artificial insemination[2] does not have a "natural father," as that term is commonly used. The anonymous donor of the sperm cannot be considered the "natural father," as he is no more responsible for the use made of his sperm than is the donor of blood or a kidney. Moreover, he could not dispute the presumption that the child is the legitimate issue of Mr. and Mrs. Sorensen, as that presumption "may be disputed only by the people of the State of California or by the husband or wife, or the descendant of one or both of them." With the use of frozen semen, the donor may even be dead at the time the semen is used. Since there is no "natural father," we can only look for a lawful father.

---

[2] There are two types of artificial insemination in common use: (1) artificial insemination with the husband's semen, homologous insemination, commonly termed A.I.H. and (2) artificial insemination with semen of third-party donor, heterologous insemination, commonly termed A.I.D. Only the latter raises legal problems of fatherhood and legitimacy.

It is doubtful that with the enactment of section 270 of the Penal Code and its amendments the Legislature considered the plight of a child conceived through artificial insemination. However, the intent of the Legislature obviously was to include every child, legitimate or illegitimate, born or unborn, and enforce the obligation of support against the person who could be determined to be the lawful parent.

* * *

[A] reasonable man who, because of his inability to procreate, actively participates and consents to his wife's artificial insemination in the hope that a child will be produced whom they will treat as their own, knows that such behavior carries with it the legal responsibilities of fatherhood and criminal responsibility for nonsupport. One who consents to the production of a child cannot create a temporary relation to be assumed and disclaimed at will, but the arrangement must be of such character as to impose an obligation of supporting those for whose existence he is directly responsible. As noted by the trial court, it is safe to assume that without defendant's active participation and consent the child would not have been procreated.

* * *

In the absence of legislation prohibiting artificial insemination, the offspring of defendant's valid marriage to the child's mother was lawfully begotten and was not the product of an illicit or adulterous relationship. Adultery is defined as "the voluntary sexual intercourse of a married person with a person other than the offender's husband or wife." It has been suggested that the doctor and the wife commit adultery by the process of artificial insemination. Since the doctor may be a woman, or the husband himself may administer the insemination by a syringe, this is patently absurd; to consider it an act of adultery with the donor, who at the time of insemination may be a thousand miles away or may even be dead, is equally absurd. Nor are we persuaded that the concept of legitimacy demands that the child be the actual offspring of the husband of the mother and if semen of some other male is utilized the resulting child is illegitimate.

In California, legitimacy is a legal status that may exist despite the fact that the husband is not the natural father of the child. The Legislature has provided for legitimation of a child born before wedlock by the subsequent marriage of its parents, for legitimation by acknowledgment by the father, and for inheritance rights of illegitimates, and since the subject of legitimation as well as that of succession of property is properly one for legislative action, we are not required in this case to do more than decide that, within the meaning of section 270 of the Penal Code, defendant is the lawful father of the child conceived through heterologous artificial insemination and born during his marriage to the child's mother.

The judgment is affirmed.

JHORDAN C. V. MARY K.
224 Cal.Rptr. 530 (Cal. App. 1986).

KING, J.

I.   HOLDING

By statute in California a "donor of semen provided to a licensed physician for use in artificial insemination of a woman other than the donor's wife is treated in law as if he were not the natural father of a child thereby conceived." (Civ. Code, § 7005, subd. (b).) In this case we hold that where impregnation takes place by artificial insemination, and the parties have failed to take advantage of this statutory basis for preclusion of paternity, the donor of semen can be determined to be the father of the child in a paternity action.

Mary K. and Victoria T. appeal from a judgment declaring Jhordan C. to be the legal father of Mary's child, Devin. The child was conceived by artificial insemination with semen donated personally to Mary by Jhordan. We affirm the judgment.

II.   FACTS AND PROCEDURAL HISTORY

In late 1978, Mary decided to bear a child by artificial insemination and to raise the child jointly with Victoria, a close friend who lived in a nearby town.[1] Mary sought a semen donor by talking to friends and acquaintances. This led to three or four potential donors with whom Mary spoke directly. She and Victoria ultimately chose Jhordan after he had one personal interview with Mary and one dinner at Mary's home.

The parties' testimony was in conflict as to what agreement they had concerning the role, if any, Jhordan would play in the child's life. According to Mary, she told Jhordan she did not want a donor who desired ongoing involvement with the child, but she did agree to let him see the child to satisfy his curiosity as to how the child would look. Jhordan, in contrast, asserts they agreed he and Mary would have an ongoing friendship, he would have ongoing contact with the child, and he would care for the child as much as two or three times per week.

None of the parties sought legal advice until long after the child's birth. They were completely unaware of the existence of Civil Code section 7005. They did not attempt to draft a written agreement concerning Jhordan's status.

---

[1]   As many as 20,000 women each year are artificially inseminated in the United States. By one estimate some 1,500 of these women are unmarried.

Jhordan provided semen to Mary on a number of occasions during a six-month period commencing in late January 1979. On each occasion he came to her home, spoke briefly with her, produced the semen, and then left. The record is unclear, but Mary, who is a nurse, apparently performed the insemination by herself or with Victoria.

Contact between Mary and Jhordan continued after she became pregnant. Mary attended a Christmas party at Jhordan's home. Jhordan visited Mary several times at the health center where she worked. He took photographs of her. When he informed Mary by telephone that he had collected a crib, playpen, and high chair for the child, she told him to keep those items at his home. At one point Jhordan told Mary he had started a trust fund for the child and wanted legal guardianship in case she died; Mary vetoed the guardianship idea but did not disapprove the trust fund.

Victoria maintained a close involvement with Mary during the pregnancy. She took Mary to medical appointments, attended birthing classes, and shared information with Mary regarding pregnancy, delivery, and child rearing.

Mary gave birth to Devin on March 30, 1980. Victoria assisted in the delivery. Jhordan was listed as the father on Devin's birth certificate. Mary's roommate telephoned Jhordan that day to inform him of the birth. Jhordan visited Mary and Devin the next day and took photographs of the baby.

Five days later Jhordan telephoned Mary and said he wanted to visit Devin again. Mary initially resisted, but then allowed Jhordan to visit, although she told him she was angry. During the visit Jhordan claimed a right to see Devin, and Mary agreed to monthly visits.

Through August 1980 Jhordan visited Devin approximately five times. Mary then terminated the monthly visits. Jhordan said he would consult an attorney if Mary did not let him see Devin. Mary asked Jhordan to sign a contract indicating he would not seek to be Devin's father, but Jhordan refused.

In December 1980, Jhordan filed an action against Mary to establish paternity and visitation rights. In June 1982, by stipulated judgment in a separate action by the County of Sonoma, he was ordered to reimburse the county for public assistance paid for Devin's support. The judgment ordered him to commence payment, through the district attorney's office, of $900 in arrearages as well as future child support of $50 per month. In November 1982, the court granted Jhordan weekly visitation with Devin at Victoria's home.

* * *

In August 1983, Victoria moved successfully for an order joining her as a party to this litigation. Supported by Mary, she sought joint legal custody (with Mary) and requested specified visitation rights, asserting she was a de facto parent of Devin. Jhordan subsequently requested an award of joint custody to him and Mary.

After trial the court rendered judgment declaring Jhordan to be Devin's legal father. However, the court awarded sole legal and physical custody to Mary, and denied Jhordan any input into decisions regarding Devin's schooling, medical and dental care, and day-to-day maintenance. Jhordan received substantial visitation rights as recommended by a court-appointed psychologist. The court held Victoria was not a de facto parent, but awarded her visitation rights (not to impinge upon Jhordan's visitation schedule), which were also recommended by the psychologist.

Mary and Victoria filed a timely notice of appeal, specifying the portions of the judgment declaring Jhordan to be Devin's legal father and denying Victoria the status of de facto parent.

III. DISCUSSION

We begin with a discussion of Civil Code section 7005, which provides in pertinent part: "(a) If, under the supervision of a licensed physician and with the consent of her husband, a wife is inseminated artificially with semen donated by a man not her husband, the husband is treated in law as if he were the natural father of a child thereby conceived * * *. (b) The donor of semen provided to a licensed physician for use in artificial insemination of a woman other than the donor's wife is treated in law as if he were not the natural father of a child thereby conceived."

Civil Code section 7005 is part of the Uniform Parentage Act (UPA), which was approved in 1973 by the National Conference of Commissioners on Uniform State Laws. The UPA was adopted in California in 1975. Section 7005 is derived almost verbatim from the UPA as originally drafted, with one crucial exception. The original UPA restricts application of the nonpaternity provision of subdivision (b) to a "married woman other than the donor's wife." The word "married" is excluded from subdivision (b) of section 7005, so that in California, subdivision (b) applies to all women, married or not.

Thus, the California Legislature has afforded unmarried as well as married women a statutory vehicle for obtaining semen for artificial insemination without fear that the donor may claim paternity, and has likewise provided men with a statutory vehicle for donating semen to married and unmarried women alike without fear of liability for child support. Subdivision (b) states only one limitation on its application: the semen must be "provided to a licensed physician." Otherwise, whether impregnation occurs through artificial insemination or sexual intercourse, there can be a determination of paternity with the rights, duties and obligations such a determination entails.

A. Interpretation of the Statutory Nonpaternity Provision.

* * *

[T]here are at least two sound justifications upon which the statutory requirement of physician involvement might have been based. One relates to health: a physician can obtain a complete medical history of the donor (which may be of crucial importance to the child during his or her lifetime) and screen the donor for any hereditary or communicable diseases. Indeed, the commissioners' comment to the section of the UPA on artificial insemination cites as a "useful reference" a law review article which argues that health considerations should require the involvement of a physician in statutorily authorized artificial insemination. This suggests that health considerations underlie the decision by the drafters of the UPA to include the physician requirement in the artificial insemination statute.

* * *

It is true that nothing inherent in artificial insemination requires the involvement of a physician. Artificial insemination is, as demonstrated here, a simple procedure easily performed by a woman in her own home. Also, despite the reasons outlined above in favor of physician involvement, there are countervailing considerations against requiring it. A requirement of physician involvement, as Mary argues, might offend a woman's sense of privacy and reproductive autonomy, might result in burdensome costs to some women, and might interfere with a woman's desire to conduct the procedure in a comfortable environment such as her own home or to choose the donor herself.

However, because of the way section 7005 is phrased, a woman (married or unmarried) can perform home artificial insemination or choose her donor and still obtain the benefits of the statute. Subdivision (b) does not require that a physician independently obtain the semen and perform the insemination, but requires only that the semen be "provided" to a physician. Thus, a woman who prefers home artificial insemination or who wishes to choose her donor can still obtain statutory protection from a donor's paternity claim through the relatively simple expedient of obtaining the semen, whether for home insemination or from a chosen donor (or both), through a licensed physician.

* * *

The Legislature's apparent decision to require physician involvement in order to invoke the statute cannot be subject to judicial second-guessing and cannot be disturbed, absent constitutional infirmity.

B.   Constitutional Considerations.

Mary and Victoria next contend that even if section 7005, subdivision (b), by its terms does not apply where semen for artificial insemination has not been provided to a licensed physician, application of the statute to the present case is required by constitutional principles of equal protection and privacy (encompassing rights to family autonomy and procreative choice).

1.   Equal protection.

Mary and Victoria argue the failure to apply section 7005, subdivision (b), to unmarried women who conceive artificially with semen not provided to a licensed physician denies equal protection because the operation of other paternity statutes precludes a donor's assertion of paternity where a *married* woman undergoes artificial insemination with semen not provided to a physician.

* * *

But the statutory provision at issue here—Civil Code section 7005, subdivision (b)—treats married and unmarried women equally. Both are denied application of the statute where semen has not been provided to a licensed physician.

The true question presented is whether a completely different set of paternity statutes—affording protection to husband and wife from any claim of paternity by an outsider (Civ. Code, §§ 7004, 7006; Evid. Code, § 621)—denies equal protection by failing to provide similar protection to an unmarried woman. The simple answer is that, within the context of this question, a married woman and an unmarried woman are not similarly situated for purposes of equal protection analysis. In the case of a married woman, the marital relationship invokes a long-recognized social policy of preserving the integrity of the marriage. No such concerns arise where there is no marriage at all. Equal protection is not violated by providing that certain benefits or legal rights arise only out of the marital relationship.

* * *

3.   Procreative choice.

Mary and Victoria argue that the physician requirement in Civil Code section 7005, subdivision (b), infringes a fundamental right to procreative choice, also encompassed by the constitutional right of privacy.

But the statute imposes no restriction on the right to bear a child. Unlike statutes in other jurisdictions proscribing artificial insemination other than by a physician, subdivision (b) of section 7005 does not forbid self-insemination; nor does the statute preclude personal selection of a donor or in any other way prevent women from artificially conceiving children under circumstances of their own choice. The statute simply addresses the perplexing question of the legal status of the semen donor, and provides a method of avoiding the legal consequences that might otherwise be dictated by traditional notions of paternity.

C. Victoria's Status as a De Facto Parent.

Finally, Mary and Victoria contend that even if the paternity judgment is affirmed Victoria should be declared a de facto parent, based on her day-to-day attention to Devin's needs, in order to guarantee her present visitation rights and ensure her parental status in any future custody or visitation proceedings. Present resolution of the de facto parenthood issue for these purposes would be premature and merely advisory. Victoria's visitation rights have been legally recognized and preserved by court order. If no further custody or visitation proceedings occur, the issue of Victoria's de facto parent status and its legal effect will never arise.

IV. CONCLUSION

We wish to stress that our opinion in this case is not intended to express any judicial preference toward traditional notions of family structure or toward providing a father where a single woman has chosen to bear a child. Public policy in these areas is best determined by the legislative branch of government, not the judicial. Our Legislature has already spoken and has afforded to unmarried women a statutory right to bear children by artificial insemination (as well as a right of men to donate semen) without fear of a paternity claim, through provision of the semen to a licensed physician.

SOOS V. SUPERIOR COURT IN AND FOR COUNTY OF MARICOPA
897 P.2d 1356 (Ariz. App. 1994).

CLABORNE, J.

This is a Petition for Special Action from the trial court's order declaring the surrogate parentage contracts statute unconstitutional and ordering an evidentiary hearing to determine which person would be the better "mother" for the triplets. Petitioner Ronald A. Soos ("the Father") contends that the trial court erred as a matter of law in holding the statute unconstitutional and that she exceeded her jurisdiction and legal authority. We disagree and find that the statute violates the Equal Protection Clause of the United States and Arizona Constitutions. * * *

FACTS AND PROCEDURAL HISTORY

The Father and his then wife, Pamela J. Soos ("the Mother"), entered into a surrogate parentage contract with Debra Ballas ("the Surrogate") because the Mother was unable to have children because of a partial hysterectomy. Eggs were removed from the Mother and fertilized in vitro (in a test tube) by sperm obtained from the Father. Pursuant to a "Host Uterus Program" at the Arizona Institute of Reproductive Medicine, the fertilized eggs were implanted in the Surrogate. The Surrogate became pregnant with triplets.

During the pregnancy of the Surrogate, the Mother filed a petition for dissolution of marriage requesting shared custody of the unborn triplets. The Father responded to the petition, alleging that he was the biological father of the unborn triplets, and that pursuant to A.R.S. [Arizona Revised Statutes] section 25–218 (1991), the Surrogate was the legal mother of the triplets. The Father further alleged that since the Surrogate was the legal mother of the triplets, the Mother had no standing to request custody.

In September of 1993, the Surrogate gave birth to triplets. The Father and the Surrogate filed a request for order of paternity with the Maricopa County Superior Court. An order was entered naming the Father as the natural father of the triplets, and the Father took custody of the triplets.

The Mother responded by filing a motion for appointment of counsel for the triplets, a motion for temporary emergency visitation, and a motion to consolidate the dissolution proceeding with the paternity action. In her motions, the Mother attacked the constitutionality of A.R.S. section 25–218(B) declaring the Surrogate to be the legal mother. The trial court in its minute entry said:

> THE COURT FINDS that there is not a compelling state interest that justifies terminating the substantive due process rights of the genetic mother in such a summary fashion.

> The current law could leave a child without any mother, as a gestational mother may have no desire to do more than she was hired to do, which is to carry and give birth to a child. The current law also ignores the important role that generations of genetics may play in the determination of who a child is and becomes. The current law does not consider what is in the best interest of each individual child.

> THE COURT FINDS A.R.S. § 25–218(B) to be unconstitutional.

An evidentiary hearing was set to determine which mother could better assume the social and legal responsibilities of motherhood. The trial court also ordered that the Mother have visitation rights with the triplets, and that the triplets would remain in the temporary custody of the Father. Following the denial of a motion for reconsideration, the Father filed this Petition for Special Action.

* * *

DISCUSSION

* * *

A.R.S. section 25–218 provides in relevant part:

> A. No person may enter into, induce, arrange, procure or otherwise assist in the formation of a surrogate parentage contract.
>
> B. A surrogate is the legal mother of a child born as a result of a surrogate parentage contract and is entitled to custody of that child.
>
> C. If the mother of a child born as a result of a surrogate contract is married, her husband is presumed to be the legal father of the child. *This presumption is rebuttable.* (Emphasis added.)

This statute was fashioned after the Michigan statute and enacted for the purpose of prohibiting surrogate parentage contracts. The minutes of the House Committee on Human Resources & Aging meeting of February 16, 1989, and the minutes of the House Committee on Judiciary of April 4, 1989, reflect the governmental interests in prohibiting surrogate contracts. The statute was designed to stop "baby brokers" and to stop the trafficking of human beings.

The question before us is whether the State's reasons for enacting the surrogate parentage contracts statute are sufficient to withstand constitutional scrutiny under the due process, equal protection, and privacy rights guaranteed by the United States and Arizona Constitutions. We must keep in mind that we are dealing with a custody issue between the biological mother and biological father and the constitutional issues surrounding their competing interests. This is not a case of the surrogate mother versus the biological mother. We are not dealing with the constitutional questions that arise when the surrogate mother wishes to keep the child she bore. Thus, we limit ourselves to the question of whether the statute withstands constitutional scrutiny when it affords a biological father an opportunity to prove paternity and gain custody, but does not afford a biological mother the same opportunity.

EQUAL PROTECTION

We first address the equal protection argument. The Mother argues that A.R.S. section 25–218 unconstitutionally denies her the right to equal protection of the laws. The Equal Protection Clause of the

Fourteenth Amendment of the United States Constitution denies "to states the power to legislate that different treatment be accorded to persons placed by a statute into different classes on the basis of criteria wholly unrelated to the objective of that statute."

In reviewing the statute, we must determine which of three standards applies. The first standard is a strict scrutiny test. It is applied to statutes that involve a suspect class or impinge on a fundamental right. The second standard of review, the means-end scrutiny, has been limited to classifications involving gender and illegitimacy of birth. The final standard, the rational basis test, is used when the legislation does not involve a suspect classification or a fundamental right.

We are dealing with a statute that affects one of the basic civil rights. The due process clauses of the state and federal constitutions, together with the rights emanating from the guarantees of the Bill of Rights, protect "individual decisions in matters of childbearing from unjustified intrusion by the State." "Marriage and procreation are fundamental to the very existence and survival of the race." A parent's right to the custody and control of one's child is a fundamental interest guaranteed by the United States and Arizona Constitutions. Therefore, although a gender-based distinction is at issue, the statute must be tested against a strict scrutiny analysis. That is, the government can only "justify the abridgment of such a fundamental right by demonstrating that a countervailing compelling state interest is thereby promoted and that the means are closely tailored to the end sought to be achieved."

A.R.S. section 25–218(C) allows a man to rebut the presumption of legal paternity by proving "fatherhood" but does not provide the same opportunity for a woman.[2] A woman who may be genetically related to a child has no opportunity to prove her maternity and is thereby denied the opportunity to develop the parent-child relationship. * * * "By providing dissimilar treatment for men and women who are thus similarly situated," the statute violates the Equal Protection Clause.

The Father responds to this problem by arguing that mere biology alone is not enough to create the parental rights guaranteed by our constitutions. We find this argument inapplicable. Lehr v. Robertson [463 U.S. 248 (1983)] holds that mere existence of a biological link is not enough to give rise to constitutional protections. Before a parent can claim a fundamental right, *a developed parent-child relationship must exist.* However, this rule cannot hold true in the surrogacy context. The biological mother can prove maternity only through her genetic or biological link. Further, since the surrogate statute does not recognize the

---

[2]   A.R.S. section 25–218(C) provides that '[i]f the mother of a child born as a result of a surrogate contract is married, her husband is presumed to be the legal father of the child. *This presumption is rebuttable.*'

biological mother as the "legal mother," she has no opportunity to develop a parent-child relationship. She must rely on her biology to protect her fundamental liberties.

* * *

"A classification must be reasonable, not arbitrary, and must rest upon some ground of difference having a fair and substantial relation to the object of the legislation, so that all persons similarly circumstanced shall be treated alike." The surrogate statute violates this principle. We hold that the State has not shown any compelling interest to justify the dissimilar treatment of men and women similarly situated (the biological mother and father). The statute is unconstitutional on equal protection grounds.

CONCLUSION

We find that the surrogate statute affects a fundamental liberty interest. The surrogate statute as it exists violates the equal protection guarantees of the United States and Arizona Constitutions.

PERRY-ROGERS V. FASANO
276 A.D.2d 67 (N.Y. App. Div. 2000).

SAXE, J.

This appeal concerns a tragic mix-up at a fertility clinic through which a woman became a "gestational mother" to another couple's embryo, when the embryo was mistakenly implanted into the wrong woman's uterus. Since a determination of the issues presented may have far-ranging consequences, we attempt here to ensure that our holding is appropriately limited.

FACTS

In April 1998, plaintiffs Deborah Perry-Rogers and Robert Rogers began an in vitro fertilization and embryo transfer program with the In Vitro Fertility Center of New York. However, in the process, embryos consisting entirely of the Rogerses' genetic material were mistakenly implanted into the uterus of defendant Donna Fasano, along with embryos from Ms. Fasano's and her husband's genetic material. It is undisputed that on May 28, 1998 both couples were notified of the mistake and of the need for DNA and amniocentesis tests. The Rogerses further allege, and the Fasanos do not deny, that the Fasanos were unresponsive to the Rogerses' efforts to contact them.

On December 29, 1998, Donna Fasano gave birth to two male infants, of two different races. One, a white child, is concededly the Fasanos' biological child, named Vincent Fasano. The other, initially named Joseph

Fasano, is a black child, who subsequent tests confirmed to be the Rogerses' biological son, now known as Akeil Richard Rogers.

The Fasanos took no action regarding the clinic's apparent error until the Rogerses, upon discovering that Ms. Fasano had given birth to a child who could be theirs, located and commenced an action against them.

PROCEDURAL HISTORY OF THE LITIGATION

On March 12, 1999, the Rogerses commenced a Supreme Court action against the Fasanos as well as the fertility clinic and its doctors. As against the medical defendants, the complaint alleged medical malpractice and breach of contract; as against the Fasanos, it sought a declaratory judgment declaring the rights, obligations and relationships of the parties concerning Akeil.

On April 1 and April 2, 1999, DNA testing was conducted. The results of the test, issued on April 13, 1999, established that the Rogerses were the genetic parents of Akeil. However, according to Ms. Perry-Rogers, the Fasanos agreed to relinquish custody of Akeil to the Rogerses only upon the execution of a written agreement, which entitled the Fasanos to future visitation with Akeil. Ms. Perry-Rogers states that during the period between Akeil's birth on December 29, 1998 and May 10, 1999, the Fasanos only permitted her two brief visits with Akeil, and that she felt compelled to sign the agreement in order to gain custody of her son. The agreement, executed April 29, 1999, contains a visitation schedule providing for visits one full weekend per month, one weekend day each month, one week each summer, and alternating holidays. The agreement also contained a liquidated damages clause, providing that a violation of the Fasanos' visitation rights under the agreement would entitle them to $200,000.

On May 5, 1999 the Fasanos signed affidavits acknowledging that the Rogerses were the genetic parents of the infant, and consenting to the entry of a final order of custody of the child in favor of the Rogerses and to an amendment of the birth certificate naming the Rogerses as the biological and legal parents of the infant. On May 10, 1999, the Fasanos turned over custody of Akeil to the Rogerses, and the following day, May 11, 1999, counsel for the parties signed a stipulation discontinuing with prejudice the plenary action as against the Fasanos.

Despite the discontinuance, by order to show cause dated May 25, 1999, using the same index number of the plenary action, the Rogerses served a petition seeking a declaratory judgment against the Fasanos, naming the Rogerses as Akeil's legal and biological parents, granting them sole and exclusive custody, and permitting them to amend the birth certificate to reflect Akeil's biological heritage. Their application made no mention of the April 29, 1999 visitation agreement. The Fasanos submitted no opposition to the application, and the court granted the application without opposition in a decision dated June 7, 1999, directing settlement of an order.

The Fasanos then sought vacatur of the June 7, 1999 decision on the grounds that the Rogerses had failed to inform the court of the April 29, 1999 agreement, which they contended was a condition precedent to the signing of an order. The Fasanos proposed, in the alternative, a counterorder which specifically acknowledged the visitation agreement.

Although on July 16, 1999, the motion court signed the Rogerses' proposed order, which made no mention of the April 29, 1999 visitation agreement, at the same time the motion court "So Ordered" those paragraphs in the April 29, 1999 agreement which provided for visitation by the Fasanos.

The Rogerses assert that over the next few months, the IAS [International Adoption Services] Court issued oral "visitation orders" in apparent reliance upon the visitation agreement, and directed that a full forensic psychological evaluation of the parties and their infants be conducted by two sets of mental health experts. On January 14, 2000, the IAS Court granted the Fasanos visitation with the child every other weekend.

The Rogerses now challenge the court's January 14, 2000 visitation order. For their part, the Fasanos appeal from the order of July 16, 1999 giving the Rogerses custody of the child, contending that in view of the discontinuance and the failure to thereafter properly commence a new custody proceeding, the court lacked jurisdiction as well as statutory authority to award custody.

* * *

SUBJECT MATTER JURISDICTION AND STANDING

The Rogerses suggest that the Supreme Court lacks subject matter jurisdiction over this dispute because the Fasanos are "genetic strangers" to Akeil. We decline to dispose of the Fasanos' claim on this basis alone. The Supreme Court of the State of New York has subject matter jurisdiction over petitions for custody and visitation pursuant to both the Domestic Relations Law and the Family Court Act.

This is not to say that the Fasanos necessarily have standing to seek visitation with Akeil. However, on this issue we will not simply adopt the Rogerses' suggestion that no gestational mother may ever claim visitation with the infant she carried, in view of her status as a "genetic stranger" to the infant. In recognition of current reproductive technology, the term "genetic stranger" alone can no longer be enough to end a discussion of this issue. Additional considerations may be relevant for an initial threshold analysis of who is, or may be, a "parent."

In referring to the rights and responsibilities of parents, the laws of this State, as well as the commentaries and case law, often use the term "natural parents," as distinguished from adoptive parents, stepparents, and foster parents. Until recently, there was no question as to who was a child's "natural" mother. It was the woman in whose uterus the child was conceived and borne.

It was only with the recent advent of in vitro fertilization technology that it became possible to divide between two women the functions that traditionally defined a mother, at least prenatally. With this technology, a troublesome legal dilemma has arisen: when one woman's fertilized eggs are implanted in another, which woman is the child's "natural" mother?

Although the technology is still fairly new, several cases have been decided that focus on competing claims to child custody arising out of the use of in vitro fertilization technology. These cases are not dispositive here, since visitation rights rather than custody is at issue. However, they contain analysis that provides important background for the issues raised on this appeal.

[The court then discusses reproductive technology cases such as Johnson v. Calvert (851 P.2d 776 (Cal.1993), cert. denied 510 U.S. 874 (1993)), which rely on pre-conception intent in custody decisions.]

* * *

It is apparent from the foregoing cases that a "gestational mother" may possess enforceable rights under the law, despite her being a "genetic stranger" to the child. Given the complex possibilities in these kinds of circumstances, it is simply inappropriate to render any determination solely as a consequence of genetics.

Parenthetically, it is worth noting that even if the Fasanos had claimed the right to custody of the child, application of the "intent" analysis suggested in Professor Hill's article, and employed in Johnson v. Calvert and McDonald v. McDonald would—in our view—require that custody be awarded to the Rogerses. It was they who purposefully arranged for their genetic material to be taken and used in order to attempt to create their own child, whom they intended to rear.

STANDING TO SEEK VISITATION

* * *

We agree that under the circumstances presented, the Fasanos lack standing under Domestic Relations Law § 70 to seek visitation as the child's parents. However, this is not because we necessarily accept the broad premise that in *any* situation where a parent, possessed of that status by virtue of having borne and given birth to the child, acknowledges another couple's entitlement to the status of parent by virtue of their having provided the genetic materials that created the child, the birth parent automatically gives up all parental rights.

Rather, we recognize that in these rather unique circumstances, where the Rogerses' embryo was implanted in Donna Fasano by mistake, and where the Fasanos knew of the error not long after it occurred, the happenstance of the Fasanos' nominal parenthood over Akeil should have been treated as a mistake to be corrected as soon as possible, *before the development of a parental relationship.* It bears more similarity to a mix-up at the time of a hospital's discharge of two newborn infants, which should simply be corrected at once, than to one where a gestational mother has arguably the same rights to claim parentage as the genetic mother. Under such circumstances, the Fasanos will not be heard to claim the status of parents, entitled to seek an award of visitation.

Additionally, the Fasanos' child, Vincent, is not a sibling "by half or whole blood" with the right to proceed under Domestic Relations Law § 71, since the statute makes no reference to "gestational siblings."

* * *

APPLICABILITY OF A "BEST INTERESTS" APPROACH

* * *

In the present case, any bonding on the part of Akeil to his gestational mother and her family was the direct result of the Fasanos' failure to take timely action upon being informed of the clinic's admitted error. Defendants cannot be permitted to purposefully act in such a way as to create a bond, and then rely upon it for their assertion of rights to which they would not otherwise be entitled.

Nor may the parties' visitation agreement form the basis for a court order of visitation. "[A] voluntary agreement . . . will not of itself confer standing upon a person not related by blood to assert a legal claim to visitation or custody".

Finally, the circumstances presented, tragic as they are, do not form the basis for application of the doctrine of equitable estoppel to prevent the Rogerses from challenging the Fasanos' standing to seek visitation.

NOTE ON EMBRYO MIX-UPS

In 2009, Carolyn Savage and her husband Sean learned that a fertility clinic had mistakenly implanted the wrong embryo in her. The Savages say that their doctor told them that if they did not abort, the law would require her to give the child over to the other couple. Since the couple's moral beliefs precluded abortion, they turned over the child to the genetic parents. For information on the case, see Janet Romaker & Tom Troy, Sylvania Township Mom who Received Wrong Embryo Gives Birth to a Boy, Toledo Blade, September 26, 2009, at A1. Can you think of any legal arguments that would have allowed Carolyn Savage to assert parental rights over the child? Would the *Michael H* case discussed in Chapter 11 provide support for such an argument?

What legal arguments could be made that the Savages should have visitation rights to the child or even joint custody with the genetic parents? Full joint parenting was the legal solution in a California case. Susan Buchweitz, a single woman, sought in vitro using a donated egg and donated sperm. Instead, she was implanted with the embryo of a married couple (created with sperm from a woman's husband and an egg from the same donor used by Buchweitz) who were also undergoing in vitro fertilization. Allegedly, the doctor knew within minutes of the procedure that there had been a mistake but Buchweitz was not informed until the child was ten months old. She was sued by the genetic father for full custody of the child. A California court declared Buchweitz the legal mother of the boy and the married man the legal father. She must send the child to the genetic father's house several days a week. Joan Ryan, Biology, Technology in Conflict, San Francisco Chronicle, April 14, 2005, at B1.

Buchweitz and other women have brought malpractice cases against the infertility clinics that have mixed up their sperm, eggs, or embryos. Buchweitz received one million dollars in damages after giving birth to the married couple's embryo. Chris Ayres, Mother Wins $1 M for IVF Mix-up But May Lose Son, The Times (London), Aug. 5, 2004, at 3. When a Long Island, New York woman thought she was being inseminated with her dead husband's sperm, she instead received a stranger's sperm and gave birth to a child of another race. She won a $400,000 settlement with the doctor and sperm bank. True Parents?, San Jose Mercury News, Aug. 2, 2002.

A scandal at another clinic indicated the problem of embryo mix-ups may be more common than previously thought. In most instances, a mix-up is discovered when a child of a different race than the parents is born. Perhaps many more mix-ups have occurred, but were not noticed because the baby was the same race as the parents. In 2009, a New Orleans hospital suspended operations at its in vitro fertilization center because so many embryos had been mislabeled. Michelle Hunter, Ochsner Shuts Down In Vitro Fertilization Center after Mix-up in Labeling Embryos, The Times-Picayune, September 25, 2009.

Can money damages adequately compensate the people who suffer through these infertility mishaps or should greater oversight be considered as well? As a result of an embryo mix-up in Great Britain, the Government's Chief Medical Officer commissioned an examination of Britain's 90 IVF units, which resulted in the issuance of a 180-page report. Clare Dyer, Human Error and Systems Failure Caused IVF Mix Up, 328 BMJ 1518 (2004). Does the U.S. need a similar close scrutiny of the protocols at in vitro fertilization clinics?

NOTES AND QUESTIONS

1.   What are the advantages and disadvantages of a pre-conception intent approach to determining legal parenthood? In the adoption context, pre-birth agreements cannot be enforced if the biological mother changes her mind within a certain period after the birth. Why should it be any different for surrogate motherhood? What if the surrogate mother's own egg is used to create the child? See In the Matter of Baby M, 537 A.2d 1227 (N.J. 1988).

2.   Should the adoption model be used when neither member of the couple has a genetic or gestational tie to the child? In what ways, if any, does the production of a child through the use of a sperm donor, egg donor, or surrogate differ from the adoption of a child? Would home study and court oversight for adoption be appropriate with in this situation? See In re Marriage of Buzzanca, 72 Cal.Rptr.2d 280 (Cal. App. 1998).

3.   In *Jhordan C.*, the court held that, because the artificial insemination had not been undertaken by a physician, the sperm donor's parental rights were not extinguished. Is it likely that the legislature actually intended the determination of paternity to hinge on whether a doctor was involved in the process? If an unmarried woman uses artificial insemination, should it be permissible for her to choose that the baby has no legal father? If the woman has a female partner (or if two gay men arrange for a surrogate mother to bear a child for them), should the child be legally determined to have two parents of the same sex?

4.   One of the rationales the court gave in *Jhordan C.* for physician involvement in donor insemination is that the physician can undertake testing on the donors to help prevent them from passing on genetic or infectious diseases. Given this concern, what issues are raised by the growing trend of private sperm donation, where men advertise on the internet to provide their sperm for free for use in insemination? "This market includes advertisements on Craigslist, Yahoo Groups, and websites such as Sperm Donors Worldwide. Unlike traditional sperm banks, these matching websites are entirely unregulated, men do not receive compensation for their donations, and donors generally allow potential offspring to contact them." Lauren Gill, Who's Your Daddy? Defining Paternity Rights in the Context of Free, Private Sperm Donation, 54 Wm. & Mary L. Rev. 1715 (2013).

5.   Trent Arsenault calls himself a "donorsexual." The Silicon Valley man says he is a virgin but has provided his sperm free to 46 different recipients. The Food and Drug Administration issued a cease and desist letter to him asserting that he was a firm that distributed semen without meeting safety and recordkeeping standards. He faced a $100,000 fine and a year in jail if he continued to donate sperm without complying with FDA regulations. Arsenault filed a response to the cease and desist order requesting a hearing to provide evidence that he fell within the "sexually intimate partner" exception to 21 C.F.R 1271. Arsenault's request was summarily denied over a year later with no explanation from the FDA commissioner and the cease and desist took full effect. Letter from Karen

Midthun, M.D., Director, Center for Biologics Evaluation and Research, FDA, to Trent C. Arsenault (Nov. 1, 2010), www.fda.gov/BiologicsBloodVaccines/ SafetyAvailability/TissueSafety/ucm232852.htm; Amber D. Abbasi, The Curious Case of Trent Arsenault: Questioning FDA Regulatory Authority Over Private Sperm Donation, 22 Annals Health L. 1, 23–24 (2013). In 2013, a woman wishing to use Arsenault's sperm filed suit against the FDA alleging that she had a constitutional right to use sperm from the donor of her choice. Doe v. Hamburg, No. C-12-3412 EMC, (N.D. Cal. 2013). Her case was dismissed due to lack of standing since the regulations would not fine or jail her for using Arsenault's sperm. The court determined that she could not allege a wrong committed by the government against a third party who was not represented in the proceedings and the judge granted defendant's motion to dismiss due to lack of standing. Doe v. Hamburg, No. C-12-3412 EMC, Order Granting Defendants' Motion to Dismiss (N.D. Cal. 2013).

6. The court in *Soos* refers to the genetic mother as the "biological" mother. Could it be argued, though, that the surrogate mother who gestated the child is a biological mother as well? What might be the implication of her biological connection for purposes of determining legal parenthood?

7. While most states have laws severing sperm donors' legal relationship with the child, far fewer states have statutes providing that an egg donor is not the legal parent of the child created with her egg. What would happen if an undergrad in a state without a statute were paid $100,000 for an egg—but the procedure of egg removal was negligent and left her infertile? Should she be able to sue for parental rights to the child born to the egg recipient? If the donor doesn't realize she is infertile until years later, should she later be able to win visitation rights to the child?

8. What factors should be taken into consideration when determining whether biological parents should have a right to custody, visitation, or information about their biological child who was mistakenly given as an embryo to another couple? Should the situation be handled differently than when babies are switched at birth and the switch is discovered later in life?

9. Should a child born through assisted reproduction have a right to know the identity of his or her biological parents? In January 2009, the Missouri legislature considered, but did not pass, a bill which would allow a child born using ART to obtain identifying information regarding the "biological parent," the sperm or egg donor, which the bill would require to be listed on a birth certificate. H.B. 355, 95th Gen. Assem., First Reg. Sess. (Mo. 2009). Do you find the use of the term "biological parent" to identify the donor troubling?

10. How will the growth of public and private DNA databases affect the anonymity promises made by sperm banks to their donors? A 15-year-old boy conceived using donor sperm succeeded in tracking down his biological father using only a $289 DNA test offered by an online genealogy service, genealogical records, and some internet searches. Alison Motluk, Anonymous Sperm Donor Traced on Internet, New Scientist, Nov. 5, 2005, at 6. The boy's

biological father had never supplied DNA to the genealogy service, but two men from the same paternal line were on file. Because the sperm bank had told his mother the donor's place and date of birth, the boy was able to purchase through another online service the names of everyone that had been born in that place on that day. One man's surname matched the surname of the men from the DNA site, and the boy made contact with the donor.

V.   THE GENETIC FRONTIER: HUMAN CLONING

LORI B. ANDREWS, IS THERE A RIGHT TO CLONE? CONSTITUTIONAL CHALLENGES TO BANS ON HUMAN CLONING
11 Harv. J.L. & Tech. 643, 647–648, 661–667 (1998).

Mammalian "cloning" is the manipulation of a cell from an animal or human in such a way that it grows into a virtual copy of that animal or human with identical nucleic DNA. One way to think about it is that cloning is a way to create later-born twins of an individual who is living or has already lived. Unlike naturally occurring twins, however, the clone will not be one hundred percent genetically identical because it will have mitochondrial DNA from the donor of the enucleated egg. In the case of Dolly the sheep, an adult mammary cell containing a copy of every gene needed to make the lamb was extracted, then starved of its nutrients, forcing the cell into a quiescent state. This cell was then fused with an enucleated egg cell—one in which the nucleus has been extracted—and an electric current was run through the fused cell, activating it and causing it to begin to divide. These active cells were then implanted into a surrogate mother and carried to term.

Cloning may be an attractive means of creating a child to people in a variety of situations. If one or both members of a couple are infertile, cloning presents one viable reproductive option. If one member of the couple has a genetic disorder that the couple does not wish to pass on to a child, they could clone the unaffected member of the couple. If both husband and wife are carriers of a recessive genetic disease and are unwilling to run the twenty-five percent risk of bearing a child with the disorder, they may seek to clone one or the other of them. This may be the only way in which the couple will be willing to have a child that will carry on their genetic line.

* * *

WOULD A BAN ON CLONING INFRINGE UPON A CONSTITUTIONAL RIGHT OF SCIENTIFIC INQUIRY?

If Congress (or a state) were to adopt a ban on human cloning, one possible constitutional challenge would be that the law unduly interferes with a right of scientific inquiry * * *. If the First Amendment protects a marketplace of ideas, it seems likely that it would protect the generation of information that will be included in the marketplace. Indeed, the [Supreme] Court's jurisprudence has protected activity under this theory in a variety of settings, such as the financing of speech and the gathering of news * * *. A federal district court similarly suggested that scholars have a right "to do research and advance the state of man's knowledge."

But what does that "right" consist of? Scientists have a right of access to existing information. For example, that federal court suggested in dicta that obscenity laws could not be applied to prohibit the Kinsey Institute from studying obscene materials. However, courts have held there is no fundamental right of scientific inquiry to undertake experiments—in particular, to conduct research on fetuses.

Cloning is sufficiently analogous to embryo research that restrictions on it should not be considered protected by a right of scientific inquiry. In holding that the right to conduct medical research is not fundamental under the Constitution, a federal court held that a state could regulate experimentation involving the unborn so long as the regulation was rational. The court explained, in words that are particularly applicable to cloning, "[g]iven the dangers of abuse inherent in any rapidly developing field, it is rational for a State to act to protect the health and safety of its citizens."

Even if cloning research on humans were protected by the Constitution, certain restrictions would be permissible. The freedom to pursue knowledge is distinguishable from the right to choose the method for achieving that knowledge, which may permissibly be regulated to some extent. Although the government may not prohibit research in an attempt to prevent the development of new knowledge, it may restrict or prohibit the means used by researchers that threaten interests in which the state has a legitimate concern. Research may be restricted, for example, to protect the subject's right to autonomy and welfare by requiring informed, free and competent consent.

* * *

WOULD A BAN ON CLONING INFRINGE UPON THE RIGHT TO MAKE REPRODUCTIVE DECISIONS?

A variety of personal desires may motivate people to utilize cloning. The NBAC [National Bioethics Advisory Commission] report suggests it would be "understandable, or even, as some have argued desirable," to create a child from one adult if both members of the couple have a lethal recessive gene; from a dying infant if his father is dead and the mother wants an offspring from her late husband; or from a terminally ill child to create a bone marrow donor.

* * *

The right to make decisions about whether or not to bear children is constitutionally protected under the constitutional right to privacy and the constitutional right to liberty. The Supreme Court in 1992 reaffirmed the "recognized protection accorded to liberty relating to intimate relationships, the family, and decisions about whether or not to beget or bear a child." Early decisions protected a married couple's right to privacy to make procreative decisions, but later decisions focused on individuals' rights as well: "If the right of privacy means anything, it is the right of the individual, married or single, to be free from unwarranted governmental intrusion into matters so fundamentally affecting a person as the decision whether to bear or beget a child."

A federal district court has indicated that the right to make procreative decisions encompasses the right of an infertile couple to undergo medically-assisted reproduction, including in vitro fertilization and the use of a donated embryo. Lifchez v. Hartigan [735 F.Supp. 1361 (N.D. Ill. 1990)] held that a ban on research on fetuses was unconstitutional not only because it was impermissibly vague, but also because it impermissibly infringed upon a woman's fundamental right to privacy. Although the Illinois statute banning embryo and fetal research at issue in the case permitted in vitro fertilization, it did not allow embryo donation, embryo freezing, or experimental prenatal diagnostic procedures. The court stated: "It takes no great leap of logic to see that within the cluster of constitutionally protected choices that includes the right to have access to contraceptives, there must be included within that cluster the right to submit to a medical procedure that may bring about, rather than prevent, pregnancy."

* * *

However, cloning is too qualitatively different from normal reproduction and from the types of assisted reproduction protected by the *Lifchez* case to simply assume the same Constitutional protections apply. As George Annas suggests, "[t]his change in kind in the fundamental way in which humans can 'reproduce' represents such a challenge to human dignity and the potential devaluation of human life (even comparing the 'original' to the 'copy' in terms of which is to be more valued) that even the search for an analogy has come up empty handed."

Cloning is not a process of genetic mix, but of genetic duplication. In even the most high-tech reproductive technologies available, a mix of genes occurs to create an individual with a genotype that has never before existed on earth. Even in the case of twins, their futures are unknown and the distinction between the offspring and their parents is acknowledged. In the case of cloning, however, the genotype in question has already existed. Even though it is clear that a clone will develop into a person with different traits because of different social, environmental, and generational influences, there is strong speculation that the fact that he or she has a genotype that already existed will affect how the resulting clone is treated by himself, his family, and social institutions.

Just as in the scientific inquiry context, even if a fundamental constitutional right to clone were recognized, any legislation that would infringe unduly upon this right would be permissible if it were narrowly tailored to further a compelling state interest.

NOTES AND QUESTIONS

1.   What types of compelling interests would be sufficient to uphold a ban on human cloning? What level of physical risks to the child might be enough to justify a ban? In animals, cloning only results in a successful pregnancy three to five percent of the time. Even in those rare instances, many of the resulting offspring suffer. One-third die shortly before or right after birth. Other cloned animals seem perfectly healthy at first and then suffer heart and blood vessel problems, underdeveloped lungs, diabetes, immune system deficiencies, severe growth abnormalities or premature aging.

2.   If research on cloning in animals found ways to make the procedure less physically risky, would it be constitutional to ban the procedure because of psychological risks to the child? Andrews asserts that:

> The unique origins of a clone might create unreasonable expectations about [the clone] * * *. Whether or not genetics actually plays such a large role in human development, parents may raise a clone as if they do. After all, regardless of their belief in genetic determinism, the only reason people want to clone (as opposed to adopting or using an egg or sperm donor in the case of infertility) is to assure that a child has a certain genetic make-up. It seems absurd to think that they would forget about that genetic make-up once the clone was born. We already limit parents' genetic foreknowledge of their children because we believe it will improperly influence their rearing practices. Medical genetics groups often caution parents against having their children tested for late-onset genetic disorders, because a child who tested positive could "grow up in a world of limited horizons and may be psychologically harmed even if treatment is subsequently found for the disorder."

> Cloning could undermine human dignity by threatening the replicant's sense of self and autonomy. A vast body of developmental psychology research has demonstrated children's need to have a sense of an independent self. This might be difficult for the clone of a parent or of a previous child who died. Even if the clone did not believe in genetic determinism, the original's life "would always

haunt the later twin, standing as an undue influence on the latter's life, and shaping it in ways to which others lives are not vulnerable."

Andrews, Is There A Right To Clone?, at 653.

3.   In 2009, researchers at the Max Planck Institute for Evolutionary Anthropology in Liepzig, Germany announced they had sequenced the Neanderthal genome and learned that Neanderthals were 99.9% similar to humans. The Institute, in conjunction with 454 Life Sciences Corporation in Bradford Connecticut, isolated and sequenced nuclear DNA retrieved from three shards of female Neanderthal limb bone found in the Vindija Cave in Croatia. The bone shards are estimated to be at least 38,000 years old.

Based on their genetic profile, researchers think that Neanderthals resembled modern humans in many ways. Physically they are described as having "a stocky muscular body with short forearms and legs; a large head with bony brow ridges; a jutting face with a very big nose; and perhaps reddish hair and fair skin." The University of Barcelona's Carles Lalueza-Fox found a unique Neanderthal variant of a pigmentation gene, mc1r, which can result in pale skin and red hair. Neanderthals had big brains that measured between 1200 to 1600 cubic centimeters, which is slightly larger than modern humans' brains. Their genetic profile indicates that they were capable of speech. A 2007 analysis of a 43,000-year-old Neanderthal bone showed the same FOXP2 gene variant that is related to speech in modern humans, rather than the variant that is found in chimps.

Neanderthals are the closest relatives of humans and lived until about 30,000 years ago. They lived in Europe, where fossils have been discovered from Spain to Southern Siberia. Neanderthals survived for about 15,000 years after modern humans appeared. There is no evidence of warfare between Neanderthals and homo sapiens, and competing theories for Neanderthals' extinction are that homo sapiens outcompeted against Neanderthals for resources, or that Neanderthals did not survive the last ice age. See Elizabeth Pennisi, Tales of a Prehistoric Human Genome, 323 Science 866–871, 866 (2009); Max Planck Society, Neanderthal Genome Completed, February 12, 2009, www.mpg.de/591280/pressRelease200902111?filter_order=L&research_topic=; Michael Balter, A Neandertal Primer, 323 Science 870 (2009); Svante Pääbo, Neanderthal Man: In Search of Lost Genomes (2014).

Some anthropologists have suggested cloning a Neanderthal. Would that activity run afoul of laws banning human cloning? If a Neanderthal was born (a tool-making, speaking, redhead), would the U.S. Constitution protect that individual? On what philosophical or legal grounds would you decide whether to consider a Neanderthal a "human"?

VI. USE OF GENETICS AND REPRODUCTIVE TECHNOLOGIES FOR NON-MEDICAL PURPOSES

A. SEX SELECTION

LORI B. ANDREWS, THE CLONE AGE: ADVENTURES IN THE NEW WORLD OF REPRODUCTIVE TECHNOLOGY
142–144 (2001).

In many parts of the world, technology is making the admission standards for birth tougher and tougher. In India, China, Taiwan, and Bangladesh, technicians with portable ultrasound machines go from village to village scanning pregnant women who are desperate to learn whether they are carrying a boy. Many abort when they fail to see a penis on the tiny out-of-focus screen. In Bombay alone, 258 clinics offered amniocentesis for sex selection. In one study of 8,000 abortions in India, 7,999 were female fetuses, leading human rights activists to protest this clear evidence of "gyne"cide. In China, when the one-child policy was strictly enforced, families so preferred males that the sex ratio changed to 153 males for each 100 females.

At Dr. John Stephens's clinics in California, Washington and New York, Western couples too can have prenatal testing for sex selection. One Australian client actually terminated a pregnancy because she couldn't get to Stephens's clinic in time to learn the sex of the fetus. She carried the next pregnancy to term when Stephens vetted it as a boy. Although most couples want a boy, an Israeli couple went to great lengths to have a girl out of fear of losing a son in a military engagement. They aborted a fetus when they learned it was a boy. In the next pregnancy, the wife was carrying twins, a boy and a girl. She used selective reduction to abort only the boy.

Thirty-four percent of U.S. geneticists said they would perform prenatal diagnosis for a family who want a son, and another 28 percent said they would refer the couple to another doctor who would perform such testing. Dorothy Wertz, the social scientist at the Shriver Center for Mental Retardation in Waltham, Massachusetts, who conducted the study, said the percentage of practitioners willing to respond to sex selection request had increased 10 percent from 1985 to 1995. "Autonomy just runs rampant over any other ethical principle in this country," Wertz says. "And it's only going to increase."

* * *

What if a sexual imbalance occurred in the United States, as is now happening in China and India? Sociologist Amitai Etzoni speculated that since women consume more culture and men commit more crimes, sex selection would create a more frontierlike society—with less art and more violence. Since men are more likely to vote Republican, politically there would be a shift to the right.

The overwhelming tilt toward boys is not as pronounced yet in the United States as it is in other countries, but social psychologist Roberta Steinbacher of Cleveland State University worries about the effect on society if couples were able to predetermine their baby's sex. Twenty-five percent of people say they would use a sex selection technique, with 81 percent of the women and 94 percent of the men desiring to ensure their first-born would be a boy. Since other research reveals firstborns are more successful in their education, income, and achievements than latterborns, Steinbacher worries that "second class citizenship of women would be institutionalized by determining that the firstborn would be a boy."

THE AMERICAN SOCIETY FOR REPRODUCTIVE MEDICINE'S POSITION ON GENDER SELECTION

The ASRM Ethics Committee approves of preimplantation genetic diagnosis for sex selection in the case of several genetic diseases. However, in ethics guidelines, it concludes, "The initiation of IVF with PGD [preimplantation genetic diagnosis] solely for sex selection holds even greater risk of unwarranted gender bias, social harm and the diversion of medical resources from genuine medical need. It therefore should be discouraged."

Sex selection through PGD involves the screening of embryos for gender prior to implantation and may result in the discarding of embryos of the undesired gender. In contrast, preconception gender selection methods attempt to separate sperm cells by whether they have an X or Y chromosome, allowing insemination with sperm cells that will produce offspring of the desired sex. Although ethical concerns such as reinforcing gender discrimination, reinforcing gender stereotypes, and causing societal sex-ratio imbalances exist with preconception gender selection, preconception gender selection does not result in the destruction of embryos and the ASRM has taken a more permissive stance on the use of preconception gender selection than with sex selection through PGD.

The Ethics Committee concluded that, "If flow cytometry or other methods of preconception gender selection are found to be safe and effective, physicians should be free to offer preconception gender selection in clinical settings to couples who are seeking gender variety in their offspring if the couples (1) are fully informed of the risks of failure, (2) affirm that they will fully accept children of the opposite sex if the preconception gender selection fails, (3) are counseled about having unrealistic expectations about the behavior of children of the preferred gender, and (4) are offered the opportunity to participate in research to track and access the safety, efficacy and demographics of preconception gender selection. Practitioners offering assisted reproductive services are under no legal or ethical obligation to provide nonmedically indicated preconception methods of gender selection." Ethics Committee of the American Society of Reproductive Medicine, Sex Selection and Preimplantation Genetic Diagnosis, 82 Fertility and Sterility (Suppl. 1) S245 (2004); Ethics Committee of the American Society of Reproductive Medicine, Preconception Gender Selection for Nonmedical Reasons, 82 Fertility and Sterility (Suppl. 1) S232 (2004).

NOTES AND QUESTIONS

1.   Should prenatal sex selection be permitted? Would it be an unconstitutional infringement on the couple's reproductive liberty to ban it? If a couple seeks to have a boy and the geneticist negligently tells them they are carrying a male fetus, would they be able to sue for wrongful birth if the child turned out to be a girl? What damages could they recover? For example, could they recover the lifetime difference in salary, since women make 21% less than men in the same jobs?

2.   Should there be a legal or ethical difference between sex selection using sperm sorting prior to conception versus preimplantation screening versus amniocentesis? Does it matter if the testing is used to select against male embryos when there is the risk of an X-linked disorder? Does it matter if it is used to select in favor of female embryos when a family already has three boys?

3.   What are the appropriate limits of prenatal testing? In one instance, a woman had two children with celiac disease which made them unable to digest carbohydrates. She wanted help from a physician to conceive a third child with the disease. Because the diet for her two children was so complicated, she did not want a child who required an alternative "normal" diet.

A couple who both had inherited the autosomal-dominant condition achondroplasia (dwarfism) had a 50% chance of having a child with this condition. They called the researcher who had cloned the gene and asked for aid in screening and aborting a fetus who would not have achondroplasia.

Ronald M. Green discusses these cases in Prenatal Autonomy and the Obligation Not to Harm One's Child Genetically, 25 J.L. Med. & Ethics 5, 13 (1997). He advocates the following standard:

> Parents are best suited to understand and shape the lives of their offspring. Their freedom of decision in this area should have presumptive priority in our moral and legal thinking. Only in extreme cases are we warranted as a society in denying them access to the professional services they need to realize their choices or in preventing them from exercising those choices. These extreme cases

are characterized by the following two features: (1) the likelihood that, relative to others in the birth cohort, the child will experience significant pain, disability or limitations in life options as a result of avoidable genetic factors; and (2) the parents' reasons for bringing the child into the world in this condition do not constitute reasonable or compelling grounds for respecting their choice.

4.   A study by Kenneth Offit and colleagues analyzed some of the ethical issues raised by pre-implantation genetic diagnosis (PGD). According to the authors, "[f]ocus group surveys and interviews have found that the U.S. public, as well as users of PGD, emphasized the importance of individual decision making regarding the use of reproductive technologies. Individuals stressed ethical as well as personal considerations, including the nature of the trait being avoided." Moreover, "[t]he emotional burden on mutation carriers, who have to cope with their high risk for cancer and make decisions regarding prevention options, is heightened by the knowledge that they might pass the mutation to their children."

To address some of the concerns associated with PGD, the study authors suggest a framework for deciding whether the procedure should be performed to test for cancer susceptibility. The clinician ordering the test should take into account four considerations. First, does the disease develop at an early age of onset? Second, if a person inherits the genetic mutation, how likely is it that he or she will develop the disease? Third, how severe are the disease's symptoms? Fourth, what options are available for treating the disease or for risk-reducing surgery?

Do you think this framework provides an effective means for evaluating the concerns raised by PGD? What are some of the issues raised by PGD that this framework misses? The authors suggest that PGD also creates the possibility of "genetic selection according to economic means" because PGD is usually only covered by insurance companies in the United States when there is coexisting infertility. However, if the couple "desires PGD solely for the purpose of avoiding the risk of transmitting a cancer causing mutation to their children," insurance companies generally will not cover it. Kenneth Offit et al., Preimplantation Genetic Diagnosis for Cancer Syndromes: A New Challenge for Preventative Medicine, 296 JAMA 2727 (2006).

5.   In a study conducted between July 2006 and February 2007, 999 patients answered a survey question: "If you were planning to have a child (or are having a child), which conditions would you want testing for?" Among the choices were blindness, deafness, cancer, heart disease, athletic ability, dwarfism, superior intelligence, mental retardation, tall stature, longevity, or shortened lifespan (death by five, twenty, forty, or fifty years). A majority of the participants indicated that they would test for each of the following conditions: mental retardation, blindness, deafness, dwarfism, heart disease and cancer. Only 10% of the participants of the study would test for athletic ability and only 12.6% of the participants would test for superior intelligence. While the participants indicated that they may not personally test for

enhancements, 52.2% of the participants said that there are no conditions for which genetic testing should never be offered. On the other hand only 6.4% of participants indicated that there are conditions for which testing should never be offered. Feighanne Hathaway, Esther Burns & Harry Ostrer, Consumers' Desire Towards Current and Prospective Reproductive Genetic Testing, 18 J. Genetic Counseling 137 (2009).

6.   Atlas Sports Genetics offers parents a $149 test which identifies variations in their child's ACTN3 gene it claims is a measure of natural-born athletic ability. Using the test, the company claims it can determine whether a child will be a better football player, sprinter, or distance runner. While the science behind the test is questionable, the availability of the test raises the question of whether parents should be allowed to use preimplantation genetic diagnosis to select for these traits. Juliet Macur, Born to Run? Little Ones Get Test for Sports Gene, The New York Times, Nov. 30, 2008, at A1.

Would the potential of risk from the procedure itself be a sufficient rationale to ban the use of preimplantation screening for non-medical reasons? Genetic imprinting disorders are a rare type of birth defect where only a copy of a gene from the mother or the father is expressed, while the copy from the other parent is suppressed or not present. Three types of imprinting disorders (Beckwith-Wiedemann syndrome, Angelman syndrome and hypomethylation syndrome) have been associated with in vitro fertilization, which is the first step in preimplantation diagnosis. What effect does the possibility of an increase in birth defects have on your analysis? For more information on ACTN3, see Chapter 10.

B. CONCEIVING A SIBLING TO BE A DONOR

When Anissa Ayala was diagnosed with chronic myelogenous leukemia, a disease usually fatal within five years, her best chance of survival was a bone marrow donation from a relative. However, neither her parents nor her brother was a close enough match. A nationwide search was unable to locate a compatible donor.

Anissa's parents decided to conceive another child to serve as a donor. Her father underwent surgery to reverse a vasectomy. Her mother was 42 years old when she conceived Marissa. Genetic testing when the fetus was six months old revealed the new daughter would be an appropriate match. When she was 14 months old, she was anesthetized and doctors inserted long needles into her hip bone to withdraw marrow to donate to her ill older sister. Gina Kolata, More Babies Born to Be Donors of Tissue, The New York Times, June 4, 1991, at A1.

In the years since the Ayala case, over one hundred children have been conceived as prospective donors. Couples get pregnant, have the fetus tested prenatally to see if it is a match, and then abort and try again if the new child cannot serve as a donor. There are no figures on how many fetuses have been aborted under these circumstances. One couple who chose not to abort created three additional children yet none was a suitable match. In another family, a baby was created to be a donor—but the infant turned out to have the same rare metabolic disease as the existing child.

In 2000, a Colorado couple, Lisa and Jack Nash, used in vitro fertilization followed by preimplantation genetic testing to conceive a child to be a tissue donor for his older sister who had a rare genetic disease, Fanconi anemia. Of 15 embryos created, only one was a genetic match. When the sibling was born, cells from his cast-off umbilical cord were transfused into his sister. Peter Gorner, A Child is Born and So Is a Genetic Dilemma, Chicago Tribune, October 8, 2000, at 1C. In another case, when a remarried woman learned that a child from her first marriage needed a bone marrow transplant, she used artificial insemination with sperm from her first husband to conceive a child.

FERRELL V. ROSENBAUM

691 A.2d 641 (D.C. App. 1997).

RUIZ, J.

Susan Ferrell and her daughter, Alexis Ferrell, brought a medical malpractice action against Kenneth N. Rosenbaum, M.D., and Children's National Medical Center ("CNMC") based upon their allegedly negligent failure to diagnose Alexis Ferrell as suffering from Fanconi anemia, a potentially fatal genetic blood disorder. The trial court awarded summary judgment to Dr. Rosenbaum and CNMC and denied the Ferrells' motion for reconsideration.

Alexis Ferrell is a young girl who suffers from Fanconi anemia, a progressive aplastic anemia that prevents the production of red and white blood cells and platelets. The physical signs of Fanconi anemia include thumb and kidney abnormalities, small stature and microcephaly. Without a bone marrow transplant, the odds of survival into adulthood are minimal.

Alexis was born on March 27, 1985, at the George Washington University Medical Center in Washington D.C. ("GWUMC"). Shortly after delivery, Alexis was noted to have hypoplastic thumbs and no external auditory canals. Consequently, Susan Ferrell and her husband, Barron Fento Ferrell, were referred to Dr. Rosenbaum, who was Director of Clinical Genetics at CNMC. The morning after Alexis was born, Dr. Rosenbaum examined Alexis at GWUMC and found that in addition to the hypoplastic thumbs and lack of external auditory canals, she also had a slightly anteriorly placed anus and small ears. A renal sonogram also indicated that Alexis was missing a kidney. At this time, Dr. Rosenbaum indicated to Mrs. Ferrell that he would have various diagnostic tests, including a chromosome test, performed on Alexis.

Two days later, on March 30, 1985, an analysis of Alexis's blood performed at GWUMC showed that Alexis had abnormally elevated mean corpuscular volume ("MCV") and mean corpuscular hemoglobin ("MCH") levels and an abnormally low red blood cell ("RBC") count. However, Dr. Rosenbaum did not review these results. After several follow-up visits, Dr. Rosenbaum misdiagnosed Alexis with having a malformation syndrome referred to as the VATER association. Alexis first went to CNMC approximately two weeks after birth, at which time her deformed left thumb was surgically removed. Thereafter, Alexis was continuously seen by Dr. Rosenbaum at CNMC. When Alexis was approximately thirteen months old, Dr. Rosenbaum noted that Alexis was having trouble gaining weight, that her head was abnormally small, and that he "did not think that these problems could be attributed solely to her malformation syndrome."

Hematological data taken from the tests done at GWUMC three days after Alexis's birth on March 30, 1985, and from further tests conducted at CNMC on October 27, 1985, and April 26, 1986, consistently showed that Alexis had abnormally high MCV and MCH levels and an abnormally low RBC. These abnormal results, which were all indicative of Fanconi anemia, were marked on the laboratory reports with asterisks to alert the physicians of their abnormality. However, neither Dr. Rosenbaum, nor anyone else at CNMC, reviewed the results of the blood tests. Further, Dr. Rosenbaum did not pursue his belief that Alexis's problems could not be attributed solely to the malformation syndrome he believed to be affecting her. Instead, when Dr. Rosenbaum last saw Alexis on April 28, 1987, he noted that Alexis's malformation syndrome was following the expected course, and his only recommendation was to see her in one year for a follow-up visit.

Susan Ferrell and her husband separated in June 1987. Mr. Ferrell moved to California two years later and subsequently has contacted Mrs. Ferrell only twice, by telephone, in October 1989 and in Spring 1991. His whereabouts are currently unknown. During their last conversation, Mr. Ferrell told Mrs. Ferrell he was homeless.

Alexis was admitted to Arlington Hospital in April of 1990 with pneumonia. When she was released, Alexis was referred to a hematologist, Dr. Joseph E. Gootenberg, who informed Mrs. Ferrell that because of her physical deformities and blood count, he strongly suspected that Alexis suffered from Fanconi anemia and that he would need to send blood and bone marrow samples to New York for testing in order to confirm his diagnosis. On October 30, 1990, Dr. Gootenberg informed Mrs. Ferrell that his suspicion was correct: Alexis had tested positive for Fanconi anemia.

The basis for Mrs. Ferrell's claim of injury is that had Alexis been diagnosed properly while under Dr. Rosenbaum's care, the Ferrells would have been informed that a matched bone marrow transplant from a sibling donor was the best treatment for their daughter's condition. Because they were then living together and loved Alexis, they would have taken the opportunity to have another child who could have donated a matched bone marrow for transplantation. However, due to Dr. Rosenbaum's and CNMC's negligence, Alexis was misdiagnosed until October 1990 and, consequently, the Ferrells were not informed of the necessary treatment during the time that Mr. Ferrell was part of the family. Since Mr. Ferrell cannot now be found, Alexis's only chance for a matched sibling donor has been foreclosed. Consequently, as a result of Dr. Rosenbaum's and CNMC's negligence, Alexis's chance to obtain the matched bone marrow transplant donor she needs for survival has been significantly reduced.

* * *

Appellees filed a motion for summary judgment stating that there was no genuine issue as to any material fact and that they were entitled to judgment as a matter of law. Mrs. Ferrell responded by filing a motion for partial summary judgment and opposing appellees' motion for summary judgment. Mrs. Ferrell's motion for partial summary judgment was based on appellees' violation of their specific duty to at least review Alexis's blood data. In support of her opposition, Mrs. Ferrell argued that the record contained "ample evidence to support a finding by a jury that [appellees] violated the applicable standard of care and that the negligence effectively deprived Alexis of her only chance of survival."

The Superior Court denied Mrs. Ferrell's motion for partial summary judgment and granted summary judgment to Dr. Rosenbaum and CNMC. First, the trial court found that there were no disputed issues of material fact. Second, the trial court considered that Mrs. Ferrell had not demonstrated that Dr. Rosenbaum and CNMC departed from the applicable standard of care, and that even if she could so demonstrate, "the undisputed evidence does not suggest that an earlier diagnosis would have provided [Alexis] with a sufficiently substantial chance of survival."

* * *

Applying the summary judgment standard to the record before us, we conclude that there was a genuine dispute over material facts. Further, the record contains sufficient evidence from which a jury could find that Dr. Rosenbaum and CNMC violated the standard of care and that this negligence deprived Alexis of a substantial chance for survival. Therefore, appellees are not entitled to judgment as a matter of law. We reverse and remand the case to the trial court.

* * *

Mrs. Ferrell's last contention is that the trial court's conclusion that "there is no prima facie showing of proximate cause" was erroneously based on a misapprehension of Alexis's alleged injury to be that the missed diagnosis of Fanconi anemia delayed a bone marrow transplant. Instead, the claimed injury is the loss of Alexis's best opportunity to have a transplant by a potential sibling donor.

* * *

In her filings in the trial court, as in this court, Mrs. Ferrell has consistently argued that appellees' misdiagnosis harmed Alexis by depriving her parents from being informed, prior to their separation and estrangement, that a sibling could serve as the best bone marrow donor for Alexis, thereby precluding Alexis from any chance of ever obtaining a matched sibling bone marrow donor. Although Dr. Alter's testimony tends to show that the transplant was not appropriate at the time Alexis was diagnosed as suffering from Fanconi anemia, it does not defeat Mrs. Ferrell's showing of proximate cause * * *. [T]he *possibility* remained that, had the Ferrells known about the Fanconi anemia and its optimum treatment with a matched donor transplant, they would have taken steps to conceive a sibling or siblings who could have provided a compatible bone marrow donor whenever the transplant was appropriate. Because the Ferrells did not know of Alexis's anemia and its best treatment, however, they did not take any of these steps at the time. That lost opportunity has meant that the possibility of a matched donor was permanently foreclosed due to Mr. Ferrell's subsequent estrangement from his family. Therefore, appellees' negligence caused Alexis's loss of the opportunity for the best treatment, a transplant from a compatible sibling donor.

* * *

Proximate cause is divided into cause in fact and policy considerations that limit the liability of persons who have, in fact, caused the injury " 'where the chain of events appears highly extraordinary in retrospect.' " Appellees argue that the alleged negligence was not the cause in fact of Alexis's injury because Mrs. Ferrell was unable to demonstrate that she would have certainly conceived a compatible donor sibling.

In determining whether there has been cause in fact, the plaintiff is not required to prove causation to a certainty. The bare possibility that the Ferrells could have had another child, or children, that could have been a suitable bone marrow donor for Alexis, however, is not sufficient to defeat a motion for summary judgment for failure to show proximate causation. Something more is needed. The proper test is whether the plaintiff can prove, by a preponderance of the evidence, that the asserted negligence was a "substantial factor" in causing the injury.

In Daniels [v. Hadley Mem'l Hosp., 566 F.2d 749 (D.C. 1977)], the court applied the substantial factor test in a medical malpractice case where the plaintiff sought damages for a "lost chance of survival." The substantial factor test "is the appropriate test for causation in cases, such at [sic] this, where the harm appears to have been brought about by two or more concurrent causes." The court, applying District of Columbia law, rejected the claim that a plaintiff must conclusively show that the harm would not still have occurred absent the malpractice.

As the court noted:

> [I]t does not lie in the defendant's mouth to raise conjectures as to the measure of the chances that he has put beyond the possibility of realization. *If there was any substantial possibility of survival and the defendant has destroyed it, he is answerable.* Rarely is it possible to demonstrate to an absolute certainty what would have happened in circumstances that the wrongdoer did not allow to come to pass.

In determining whether the negligence was a substantial factor in causing the harm, the *Daniels* court focused on two questions: a) what chance the plaintiff had to survive if properly diagnosed and treated and b) the extent to which the defendants' negligence reduced this chance.

We conclude that *Daniels'* two-pronged analysis correctly applies District of Columbia law on proximate causation in a case such as this involving negligent treatment of a potentially fatal condition. Applying the analysis to this case, we determine that Mrs. Ferrell made a showing, sufficient for summary judgment purposes, that Dr. Rosenbaum's and CNMC's negligence was a substantial factor in causing Alexis's injury. The first prong of the analysis involves Alexis's chances to survive had she been properly diagnosed and treated. Proper treatment in this case, meant a bone marrow transplant from a suitable matched donor. The record clearly supports a finding that had Dr. Rosenbaum or any other qualified person at CNMC reviewed the blood data, a diagnosis of Fanconi anemia would have resulted in 1985, and the Ferrells would have at least been given the opportunity to conceive a child or children who would be compatible donors for Alexis. Mrs. Ferrell testified that she would have done anything possible to help Alexis, including having another child or children; the record supports an inference that Mr. Ferrell would have been supportive of such efforts.[17] According to the expert testimony, the

---

[17] Appellees contend that the record does not support a finding that Mr. Ferrell would have agreed to attempt to conceive another child even if the Ferrells had known that Alexis had Fanconi anemia when Mr. Ferrell was still part of the family. This argument was not made below; therefore it is not before us for consideration. Even were it properly before us, it is without merit. Alexis was born in March 1985. Mrs. Ferrell testified that Mr. Ferrell was very attentive to Alexis and that Mr. Ferrell would spend a lot of time with his daughter. The Ferrells were separated sometime in 1987, and Mr. Ferrell left for California in September 1989. Therefore,

chances were significant that the Ferrells, had they conceived a child, would have yielded a suitable donor for Alexis. Thus, the evidence showed that had Alexis been properly diagnosed when Mr. Ferrell was in her life, and had Alexis received a transplant from a compatible sibling donor Alexis would have had "an appreciable chance of saving [her] life." Id. at 566 F.2d at 758 (concluding that there was an "appreciable chance" that patient's life would have been saved, after bench trial including testimony that 75–85% of patients survived if given proper treatment).

The second prong, whether the defendants interfered with the plaintiff's chance to avoid the harm is easily met in this case. It is plain from the record that Dr. Rosenbaum's and CNMC's alleged negligence directly interfered with the possibility of Alexis having a transplant from a matched sibling donor. Whatever may be said about the speculative nature of the Ferrells having had a child who could donate bone marrow to Alexis, it is beyond doubt that the alleged negligence eliminated *any* chance that the Ferrells would even consider and implement that course of action. Mrs. Ferrell therefore sufficiently demonstrated that the claimed negligence was a substantial factor in the loss of Alexis's best chance for survival. The trial court's conclusion that Mrs. Ferrell did not make a prima facie showing of proximate cause was erroneous.

NOTES AND QUESTIONS

1.   In some cases, an existing family member is a match for an ill child but does not want to go through the painful procedure of bone marrow extraction. Does it seem fair to create a child and force him or her to do something that an existing sibling, cousin or parent will not do? And where

---

Mr. Ferrell was available for four years after Alexis was born. Mrs. Ferrell testified that during that time Mr. Ferrell wanted a reconciliation, but that she did not.

In her response to appellees' Interrogatory No. 14, Mrs. Ferrell stated that had she known that Alexis had Fanconi anemia she

> would have immediately taken all appropriate steps necessary to assure, to the maximum extent possible, the availability of a bone marrow transplant (BMT) for Alexis when needed, including efforts to become pregnant immediately and have as many children as necessary and possible, in light of her maternal age, to obtain a matching sibling donor.

While appellees could argue to a jury that Mr. Ferrell was unlikely to have agreed to conceive another child or children, the record at this point would support a jury finding that Mr. Ferrell would have helped to save his daughter's life.

Our dissenting colleague states that the fact that "Mr. Ferrell might have been willing to reconcile with his estranged wife prior to June 1987 would not reasonably permit a trier of fact to infer that he might have been interested in doing so after October 1990." This conclusion misses the point of Mrs. Ferrell's argument because it assumes the alleged negligence. Had Dr. Rosenbaum adhered to the standard of care, Alexis would have been properly diagnosed in 1985, not in 1990, two years before her parents separated and four years before Mr. Ferrell left for California. The dissent's conclusion is also flawed because it assumes that a reconciliation would have been required to avert the injury suffered by Alexis as a result of the negligence. In fact, only Mr. Ferrell's willingness to *sire* another child or children is at issue. This would require a donation of sperm, and not necessarily reconciliation with the mother.

should we draw the line? Should parents conceive a second child to be a kidney donor for the first?

2.   There are also questions about access to the technologies for prenatal and preimplantation screening for tissue matching. When a child is diagnosed with a disease that would benefit from matched tissue, should the physician have a duty to tell the parents that they could conceive a sibling for donation? Should insurers reimburse for the procedure? The cost to the Nashes of in vitro fertilization and preimplantation screening was $50,000.

3.   In 2012 alone, there were over 165,000 cycles of in vitro fertilization in the United States which were reported to the Society for Assisted Reproductive Technology. Preimplantation genetic diagnosis procedures were performed on 8,000 of the resulting embryos. See www.sartcorsonline.com/rptCSR_PublicMultYear.aspx?ClinicPKID=0. There is no way of knowing exactly how many attempts were made to create "savior siblings" (siblings conceived to be donors). According to data collected in 2006 from fertility doctors in the United States by the Genetics and Public Policy Center at Johns Hopkins University, approximately one percent of all preimplantation genetic diagnosis cycles are conducted for purposes of creating a sibling to be a donor. Beth Whitehouse, The Match: 'Savior Siblings' and One Family's Battle to Heal Their Daughter, 127 (2010).

CHAPTER 7

CLINICAL APPLICATIONS OF GENETICS IN DIAGNOSTICS

■ ■ ■

I. INTRODUCTION

Earlier chapters describe some of the therapeutic advances made possible by the decoding of the human genome, including genetic testing to diagnose and predict genetic illnesses. As more knowledge is gained about genes and how they function, new therapeutic approaches are becoming possible, such as pharmacogenetics, or the use of genetic information to fashion better drug therapies, and gene therapy, which involves altering defective genes or inserting corrected genes into the patient's body. If genetic alterations affect a person's reproductive cells and therefore are passed on to offspring, the result is what is termed germline gene therapy.

This chapter and the next examine the ethical, legal, and social implications of the use of genetic science in medical treatment. This chapter discusses the use of genetic and genomic testing for diagnostic purposes. It begins with a description of genetic testing techniques and how genetic testing is regulated, followed by a discussion of the impact of diagnostic test results on patients and families. It then discusses liability issues, the role of genetic counselors, diagnostic testing of children and adolescents, and access to testing through public and private health insurance programs. The chapter concludes by discussing the issues raised by information obtained from testing that is outside the purpose of the testing, known as incidental findings, and with a brief discussion of genomic cancer testing.

There is considerable debate over the effects that new discoveries in human genetics will have on the practice of medicine. In an address to the Massachusetts Medical Society in May 1999, Francis S. Collins, then the director of the National Human Genome Research Institute at NIH, described how the isolation of disease genes will provide "the best hope for understanding human disease at its most fundamental level." Francis S. Collins, Shattuck Lecture—Medical and Societal Consequences of the Human Genome Project, 341 New Eng. J. Med. 28, 30 (1999). "Even before a gene's role in disease is fully understood," he went on, "diagnostic applications can be useful in preventing or minimizing the development of health consequences." He noted that "successes in reducing disease through treatment have been achieved for the hereditary disorders hemochromatosis, phenylketonuria, and familial hypercholesterolemia, among others. Risk reduction through early detection and lifestyle changes may be possible in the case of disorders associated with predisposing mutations, such as some cancers. As therapies build on knowledge gained about the molecular basis of disease, increasing numbers of illnesses that are now refractory to treatment may yield to molecular medicine in the future."

Collins also described the manner in which genetic knowledge will facilitate what is called "personalized genomic medicine":

> Identifying human genetic variations will eventually allow clinicians to subclassify diseases and adapt therapies to the individual patient. There may be large differences in the effectiveness of medicines from one person to the next. Toxic reactions can also occur and in many instances are likely to be a consequence of genetically encoded host factors. That basic observation has spawned the burgeoning new field of pharmacogenomics, which attempts to use information about genetic variation to predict responses to drug therapies.

* * *

> Not only will genetic tests predict responsiveness to drugs on the market today, but also genetic approaches to disease prevention and treatment will include an expanding array of gene products for use in developing tomorrow's drug therapies. Since the Food and Drug Administration's approval of recombinant human insulin in 1982, over 50 additional gene-based drugs have become available for clinical use. These include drugs for the treatment of cancer, heart attack, stroke, and diabetes, as well as many vaccines.

> Not all therapeutic advances for gene discovery will be genes or gene products. In other instances, molecular insights into a disorder, derived from gene discovery, will suggest a new treatment.

Id. at 33.

Francis Collins was just as optimistic six years later, when, in an article he wrote with Alan F. Guttmacher, he stressed the continued reduction in the cost of genetic sequencing as hastening the introduction of genomic medicine into clinical practice.

Not everyone agrees with these optimistic predictions about the imminence or significance of new genetic insights for the practice of medicine. In an essay entitled "Will Genetics Revolutionize Medicine?" for example, Neil Holtzman and Theresa Marteau assert that the development of treatments will lag behind the identification of genes that cause inherited disorders, and that only a small proportion of the population suffers from such disorders. Holtzman and Marteau caution against concentrating on genetics rather than the contributions that changes in social structure, lifestyle, and environment can make in improving the public health. For their views, see 343 New Eng. J. Med. 141 (2000). Limited successes in genetic medicine seem to bear out the pessimists' views: "Ten years after President Bill Clinton announced that the first draft of the human genome was complete, medicine has yet to see any large part of the promised benefits. For biologists, the genome has yielded one insightful surprise after another. But the primary goal of the $3 billion Human Genome Project—to ferret out the genetic roots of common diseases like cancer and Alzheimer's and then generate treatments—remains largely elusive. Indeed, after 10 years of effort, geneticists are almost back to square one in knowing where to look for the roots of common disease." Nicholas Wade, A Decade Later, Genetic Map Yields Few New Cures, The New York Times, June 13, 2010, at A1.

II. GENETIC TESTING TECHNOLOGY

Information about an individual's genetic endowment can come from a variety of sources, such as family history, physical appearance, and physical examination (including laboratory tests for levels of cholesterol, blood glucose, and other chemicals that may vary, to some degree, as a result of genes). This chapter focuses on one specific type of laboratory testing: DNA testing.

Until fairly recently, knowledge about an individual's genetic inheritance was based on indirect information, such as observations of the symptoms of genetic disease, detection of gene products (e.g., elevated chloride levels in the sweat of persons with cystic fibrosis), or descriptions of symptoms in other family members. In addition, cell nuclei can be collected and cultured and a visual image obtained of the chromosomes. This permits the detection of chromosomal abnormalities such as Down syndrome, caused by an extra copy of chromosome 21. Cellular material can be obtained prenatally through amniocentesis or chorionic villus sampling, facilitating reproductive decision-making such as whether or not to have an abortion. Originally, the chromosomes were visually inspected under a microscope. More recently, a technique called FISH (for "Fluorescence In Situ Hybridization") employs fluorescence to "paint" the chromosomes.

A more direct type of information about genes can be obtained by linkage analysis. This technique is used when the exact location and sequence of the disease gene (or genes) is not yet known. Linkage analysis relies on the identification of "markers," discussed in Chapter 2 (markers, it will be recalled, are stretches of DNA believed to be near to or containing disease genes)—and on an analysis of DNA from family members. (The analysis of DNA from family members is necessary because markers differ among families.)

In the mid-1980s a young scientist, Kary Mullis, developed a method called polymerase chain reaction or PCR. This technique is used to copy, or amplify, small fragments of DNA within a test tube. For DNA testing, a sample of DNA is mixed with three types of chemicals: a primer, which attaches to the DNA and begins the duplication process; an enzyme that makes copies of the DNA; and the nucleotides that are necessary to form the duplicates. This mixture is put in a machine that increases and reduces the temperature every few minutes, doubling the "target" sequence with each cycle. This results in hundreds of millions of copies in a matter of hours. When the final mixture is run through an electrophoretic gel, the amplified stretch of DNA can be seen visually as a band at a known position on the gel. This technique can be used to copy a specific stretch of the DNA that contains the target mutation. If the target mutation is present, it will be amplified and appear on the gel.

PCR is fast and inexpensive. However, it has some limitations, such as the fact that it does not provide information about the entire sequence of the gene, so that if certain mutations are not known or are not tested for, they can be missed.

The third and most sophisticated technique is called DNA sequencing. In the most common type of sequencing, developed by Fred Sanger, a stretch of DNA is amplified and single strands of it are produced. Again, a primer chemical and enzymes are added which make copies of the DNA, but this time the mixture contains special nucleotides that stop the copying at specific points depending on where they are incorporated into the copied sequence. This produces fragments of different lengths. The reaction is repeated four times, for each of the four nucleotides, and the result is run though an electrophoretic gel which reveals the location of the different nucleotides on the original stretch of DNA. The resulting sequence of bases is then analyzed to reveal mutations. This technique yields the most detailed information compared to the others, but is more expensive and time consuming and requires large quantities of DNA.

Most recently, DNA chips have been developed that speed the analysis by several orders of magnitude. These consist of a small glass plate encased in plastic which is manufactured using a process similar to the one used to make computer microchips. The surface of the glass plate, or chip, contains a number of synthetic, single-stranded DNA sequences corresponding to stretches of bases in a "normal" gene. A sample of the individual's DNA, together with a sample of "normal" DNA, are separated into single strands, cut into more manageable sizes, and labeled with different fluorescent dyes—for example, green for the individual's and red for the normal sample. Both samples are then inserted into the chip. There, they bind with any sequences on the chip that have a complementary set of bases. Both a normal sequence from the individual and the corresponding sequence from the normal sample will bind to the complementary sequence on the chip, creating a position on the chip that is red and green. If the individual's sample has a mutation in that sequence, however, only the normal sample will bind to the chip, leaving a position that is red. The result is then analyzed to reveal which mutations, if any, are present in the patient's DNA. The advantage of chips over conventional methods is that they require smaller DNA samples, and can run tests in parallel to detect large numbers of mutations.

This chapter focuses on genetic testing for clinical purposes, that is, to facilitate the diagnosis, treatment, or prevention of genetic disease. It addresses a number of the ethical, legal, and social issues raised by this form of genetic testing. Specifically, it covers the regulation of genetic testing products and laboratory services, the liability of health care professionals for failing to provide access to genetic testing for therapeutic purposes, and several specific problem areas: unanticipated misattributed paternity and maternity (which occurs when a genetic test performed for therapeutic purposes unintentionally reveals that a parent is not biologically related to a child); access to genetic testing; and genetic testing for minorities and ethnic groups.

One type of therapeutic function for genetic testing is to facilitate a diagnosis or prognosis for a person exhibiting disease symptoms. For example, a person experiencing muscle stiffness may have a genetic disease called myotonic dystrophy, which can be pinpointed by genetic testing.

Genetic testing also can be used to predict the risk of future disease, sometimes enabling steps to be taken to prevent or mitigate the disease. One common genetic disorder which can be detected pre-symptomatically is hereditary hemochromatosis (HH), which occurs in 1 in 200 whites, and which is readily treated with phlebotomy (similar to the discredited technique of "bleeding"). Genetic testing also can reveal HIV infection much earlier than traditional antibody-based tests such as the ELISA test.

One of the major issues with genetic testing is its predictive accuracy. This is especially important when the test results might lead to drastic actions, such as radical preventive measures. A good example is genetic testing to detect the risk for breast cancer. In the mid-1990s, researchers identified mutations in two genes, BRCA1 and BRCA2, that were associated with an elevated risk of breast and ovarian cancer in women who have the mutations. Commercial tests for the mutations were quickly developed. Some women with a positive test result have undergone prophylactic radical mastectomies—the removal of their breasts in an attempt to eliminate the tissue at risk for cancer. The problem is that the predictive value of the genetic tests is limited. In the first place, most forms of breast cancer do not appear to be inherited: only about 5 to 10 percent of the 215,000 women annually diagnosed with breast cancer have an inherited form of the disease. Second, these mutations are incompletely penetrant—that is, some women with the mutations will not develop breast cancer as a result. Even in families with a high risk of breast cancer, based on identified cases in the biologic line, between 10 and 15 percent of women with the BRCA 1 mutation will not develop breast cancer. The predictive value of the genetic tests increases substantially with knowledge about other factors, such as whether there is a family history of both breast and ovarian cancer, and the woman's ethnic group, since much of the initial information came from research on Ashkenazic Jews.

Another problem raised by therapeutic genetic testing is the danger of misinterpreting a negative test result. The concern is that persons with negative test results will conclude that they will not get the disease. This could lead them to reduce their vigilance or refrain from taking preventive measures. A woman with a negative genetic test for breast cancer, for example, might reduce her frequency of mammograms. But a negative result does not mean that the person will not get the disease. As noted, most cases of breast cancer do not appear to be inherited. Even when a test for a mutation known to occur in the individual's family is negative, this only means that the individual did not inherit that particular mutation; she may have other genetic mutations for the disease that the test does not detect. Finally, the person may have had the mutation but the laboratory performing the test may have made an error in interpretation or accidentally switched samples, resulting in a "false negative" test result.

For a good overview of genetic testing, see Wylie Burke, Genetic Testing, 347 New Eng. J. Med. 1867–1875 (2002).

A distinction is usually made between "genetic testing" and "genetic screening" for therapeutic purposes. The actual tests are often the same (although the techniques used to interpret the results may differ). The difference between them lies mainly in the degree of suspicion that the person being tested is at risk for the disease in question. The term "genetic testing" is usually reserved for genetic tests on persons with symptoms of the disease or a known family history. "Genetic screening" is conducted on populations of non-symptomatic individuals regardless of whether or not the individual has a family history of the disease. This chapter addresses genetic testing; the chapter that follows, Chapter 8, discusses genetic screening.

Some genetic testing is conducted for non-therapeutic purposes. Some testing is conducted purely for research purposes, which was discussed in Chapter 4. Another principal non-therapeutic use of genetic testing is for forensic purposes, mainly identification, which is discussed in Chapter 11.

Note that the line between therapeutic and reproductive genetic testing is not always a bright one. Reproductive testing may lead to a decision to prevent a pregnancy or live birth. If this decision is based on a desire to avoid the birth of a person who may suffer from a genetic disease, for some geneticists the decision is preventive.

III. REGULATION OF GENETIC TESTING PRODUCTS AND SERVICES

Genetic testing is a complex industry involving a number of technologies. Clinicians or researchers obtain test samples—usually blood samples—from patients. The test samples are processed by a laboratory. This may be a free-standing commercial laboratory to which the clinician sends the sample, or a laboratory operated by the hospital, clinic, or research facility with which the clinician or researcher is affiliated. The laboratory processes the sample. This involves the use of certain machinery such as DNA sequencers, PCR machines, microscopes, plastic and glassware, as well as the use of certain chemicals, called reagents, to interact with the test sample. The laboratory may develop and use its own reagents in its own testing process (which is called an "in-house" test or "home brew"); purchase the reagents for use in its own testing process; or it may purchase a "test kit" from a commercial manufacturer containing reagents, instructions, and usually some equipment. In addition, some companies that have patented the genetic mutation that the laboratory is testing for operate commercial laboratory services that process the patient samples.

SECRETARY'S ADVISORY COMMITTEE ON GENETICS, HEALTH, AND SOCIETY, U.S. SYSTEM OF OVERSIGHT OF GENETIC TESTING: A RESPONSE TO THE CHARGE OF THE SECRETARY OF HEALTH AND HUMAN SERVICES

(2008).

* * * Depending on the aspect of testing, oversight is provided by Government agencies, health care payers, professional associations, or other groups; voluntarily by certain sectors; or not at all. Some aspects of oversight are quite specific to genetic testing, whereas others are of

broader scope, applying to medical devices or other products or professional activities in general.

At the Federal level, oversight of genetic tests includes activities carried out by the Food and Drug Administration (FDA) and the Centers for Medicare & Medicaid Services (CMS). Currently, there are two main pathways for bringing genetic tests into clinical practice. Some tests are developed by in vitro diagnostic (IVD) test manufacturers for distribution in interstate commerce to multiple laboratories. Other tests, known as laboratory-developed tests (LDTs), are developed for use solely in the test developer's laboratory.

FDA regulates genetic tests that qualify as devices, which includes test kits and analyte-specific reagents (ASRs). ASRs can be antibodies, receptor proteins, nucleic acid sequences, or other biological or chemical reagents used to identify or quantify substances in biological specimens. Until recently, FDA has not exercised its regulatory authority over LDTs; the Clinical Laboratory Improvement Amendments of 1988 (CLIA) are used to regulate the laboratories that develop LDTs.

CLIA, which is overseen by CMS, requires all clinical laboratories, including genetic testing laboratories, to undergo inspections to assess their compliance with established standards. This process includes inspections for personnel qualification and responsibilities, quality control standards, PT [proficiency testing], quality assurance, and recordkeeping. CLIA requires a laboratory to verify and establish the analytical performance characteristics of tests offered by that laboratory. Although CMS provides guidance and resources to help laboratories achieve compliance, current regulations do not specify particular procedures or protocols. Rather, they require laboratories to ensure that their test results are accurate, reliable, timely, and confidential and do not present the risk of harm to patients. Many have called for a closer examination and coordination of the dual regulations of FDA and CLIA. In addition, bills were introduced in the 110th Congress that addressed the oversight of genetic testing.

At the State level, many agencies use CLIA requirements to regulate genetic testing laboratories. The States of New York and Washington, however, independently operate laboratory certification programs, both of which are exempt from CLIA because CMS has deemed them equal to or more stringent than CLIA requirements. The New York State Department of Health has one of the most stringent State-level oversight systems, requiring preapproval prior to offering a genetic test in a clinical setting. As all laboratories that solicit and receive specimens from New York are subject to these clinical laboratory requirements, an estimated 75 percent of all cytogenetic and genetic specimens tested in the United States are subject to this oversight.

Ensuring the analytical and clinical validity of genetic testing is paramount. Analytical validity refers to a test's ability to measure the analyte or genotype of interest accurately and reliably; clinical validity refers to a test's ability to detect or predict the associated disorder (phenotype). Only analytical validity is fully enforced under CLIA, as CMS does not have authority under CLIA to enforce clinical validity. FDA plays a role in assessing the clinical validity of genetic tests insofar as it is charged with assessing "safety and effectiveness." Its evaluation of clinical performance depends on the nature of the test, its intended use, and the amount of existing information about the associations of genetic markers and clinical diagnosis.

Prospective data of a test's clinical validity, however, are often unavailable or incomplete for years after a test is developed, especially for predictive or presymptomatic tests. As such, numerous challenges remain for the demonstration of clinical validity, such as the collection of postmarket data and the sharing of information among laboratories.

There are also questions about the sufficiency of CLIA's requirements for assessing the performance of genetic testing laboratories. While CLIA requires laboratories to have quality assurance programs in place, most genetic testing laboratories are not required by CLIA to perform PT unless they are testing a small subset of established analytes regulated under CLIA, none of which are genetic tests per se.

* * *

Clinical utility, which refers to the net balance of risks and benefits associated with using a test in routine practice, is another critical element for translating genetic testing into clinical practice. With the establishment of analytical and clinical validity as prerequisites, information and data illustrating the potential health benefits and harms of a genetic test are necessary for the effective management of patients, the development of professional guidelines, and coverage decisions. The current evidence base for the clinical utility of genetic testing is limited, and public and private health care payers are increasingly calling for such evidence in order to make coverage decisions.

* * *

In considering how genetic tests and the information they provide might be different from other laboratory tests, it is helpful to think about whether other medical information shares some of the characteristics of genetics. Genetic test results for germline mutations do not change over a person's lifetime; they can provide predictive information about the risks of developing disease in the future; they have implications for family members; and the information can be stigmatizing. Some medical tests that are not considered genetic tests, such as those for cholesterol levels or infectious disease, can also provide information about factors that affect the risk of developing disease and may have implications for family members. Other nongenetic medical information, such as a diagnosis of a mental illness or a sexually transmitted disease, can be stigmatizing.

Another potential difference between genetic tests and other laboratory tests is an incomplete understanding of the clinical validity and clinical utility of many genetic tests. Health professionals may also lack sufficient knowledge of genetics and may not be prepared to use genetic tests appropriately. Although the extent may differ, incomplete understanding and provider knowledge can also be true of other medical tests when they are introduced. Thus genetic tests can be treated similarly to other complex laboratory tests that are expected to meet high standards of accuracy, validity, and utility.

* * *

Federal regulation of testing products. Genetic testing products, with limited exceptions, must pass through FDA's medical device premarket clearance or approval processes. As just noted, FDA's statutory mandate under the FFDCA is to ensure that medical devices are safe and effective. FDA has interpreted this mandate as requiring a prior assessment of analytical and clinical performance of the device. This requirement is claims-driven, meaning the manufacturer must provide data supporting any analytical and clinical claims related to the use and/or effectiveness of a product. These claims are distinct from the payment claims used to seek reimbursement.

* * *

Federal regulation of testing services. CMS has regulatory responsibilities for laboratory testing, including genetic testing, under the Clinical Laboratory Improvement Amendments of 1988 (CLIA). CMS oversees the administration of the many functions of CLIA, including the two main requirements for testing services: registration with the CLIA program and certification by an approved accreditation body or CMS. Certification is intended to ensure that a clinical laboratory meets CLIA established standards for quality assurance (QA), records maintenance, proficiency testing (PT), personnel qualifications and responsibilities, and quality control (QC). CLIA requirements for laboratory certification depend on the complexity of the tests performed; the more complex the test, the more stringent the requirements. FDA has been involved with CLIA since 2000, when it took over the responsibility of categorizing the complexity of certain diagnostic tests. These tests are also subject to relevant FTC regulations for marketing.

CLIA gives CMS the authority to regulate laboratories that use laboratory-developed tests (LDTs), as well as FDA-approved or -cleared tests. Although a laboratory can use its LDTs to provide testing services to the public, it cannot sell its LDTs for use by others.

* * *

Although CMS had indicated that it would issue a Notice of Proposed Rulemaking (NPRM) that would establish a genetic testing specialty under CLIA, the agency announced in September 2006 that it would no longer pursue this path. In explaining this decision, CMS stated that CLIA already certifies genetic testing laboratories under requirements for existing specialties, and since the field is so dynamic, prescriptive standards for genetic testing likely would be outdated before they were published. CMS also expressed the view that a genetic testing specialty would not solve the lack of clinical validation of genetic LDTs or address concerns about the lack of PT for genetic testing laboratories. CMS said there were not sufficient data indicating that genetic testing laboratories experience more problems than laboratories performing other types of tests and noted also that there was no widely accepted definition of a "genetic test." Furthermore, the agency expressed its belief that additional CLIA regulations would not address the ethical, legal, and social issues associated with genetic testing.

* * *

Premarket and postmarket Federal regulation of testing products and services. In addition to having no authority or mechanism for external review of the clinical validity and clinical utility of tests, CMS has no authority to perform postmarket review or adverse event reporting, which are safeguards provided in FDA's medical device regulations. To date, there have been few documented cases in which patients experienced harm because of errors in a CLIA-regulated genetic test. The lack of reports, however, may reflect the absence of a reporting requirement. CLIA provides for biennial inspections of laboratories, but these do not focus on the clinical performance records of the LDTs themselves. The FFDCA provides FDA with recall authority with respect to medical devices (including genetic tests). This authority allows the agency to take action to protect the public if, based on adverse event reports or other data, a test or device proves injurious in clinical use. If there are substantiated concerns about analytical accuracy and the laboratory does not correct them, CLIA does provide for sanctions. These sanctions include requiring the laboratory to cease testing or removing its certificate and Medicare payment when there is risk of harm to patients arising from a potentially faulty test result or in a problem testing area.

FDA has statutory authority to require data demonstrating the safety and effectiveness of LDTs, although this authority has been under debate. Within its enforcement discretion, FDA has declined in recent years to exercise this authority. The agency issued two draft guidances in September 2006, however, that are likely to place these tests under the greater scrutiny of premarket review via the 510(k) or PMA processes.

The first guidance clarifies FDA's oversight of analyte-specific reagents (ASRs), which are the building blocks used by clinical laboratories to develop LDTs. * * * The guidance, which was made final in September 2007, clarifies that a single ASR that is combined or promoted for use with another product such as other ASRs, general purpose reagents, controls, laboratory equipment, or software or that is promoted with specific analytical or clinical performance claims, instructions for use in a particular test, or instructions for validation of a particular test using the ASR is not considered by FDA to be an ASR and thus is not exempt from premarket notification requirements. * * *

The second guidance—first issued in September 2006 and revised in July 2007—explains FDA's proposed oversight for a subset of LDTs known as in vitro diagnostic multivariate index assays (IVDMIAs). These must meet premarket and postmarket device requirements under FFDCA and FDA regulations, including, when applicable, premarket review requirements for class II and III devices. IVDMIAs typically use complex mathematical algorithms, often with the aid of computer software, to interpret large amounts of genetic or protein data to yield results that can be used to guide medical decisionmaking. These tests include some of the complex genetic and proteomic tests, such as gene expression profiles that might predict cancer prognosis and guide the use of chemotherapy. In February 2007, FDA cleared the first IVDMIA, MammaPrint®.

There have been various calls over the past decade to require a more rigorous external prior regulatory review process for LDTs. In 1997, the NIH-DOE Task Force recommended systematic, well-designed studies to assess the safety and effectiveness of genetic tests before they become routinely available and after they undergo significant modifications. Three years later, the Secretary's Advisory Committee on Genetic Testing (SACGT) called for FDA to assume responsibility for premarket review, approval, and labeling of all new genetic tests that have moved beyond the basic research stage.

* * *

State regulation of testing services. At the State level, statutory regulation plays an important role in genetic testing. Twenty-six States have some degree of statutory authority for oversight of the practice of clinical laboratory medicine. New York and Washington are the only States that have CLIA-exempt status because their standards have been reviewed by CMS and approved to be at least equivalent to or more stringent than CLIA in accordance with the CLIA statute and regulations. New York State has specific standards for genetic testing, but Washington State does not—although it does review the clinical validity of certain tests. Through its Genetics Disease Branch and newborn screening and prenatal screening program, California has rigorous review of those types of assays, but its oversight does not generally extend to other genetic testing. New Jersey applies some personnel standards of the American Board of Medical Genetics to laboratories that perform genetic testing. With the exception of New York, no State requires review of validation data for individual assays, other than in the context of a physical onsite inspection, which for most State programs does not involve peer review. The Washington State program, however, does evaluate the clinical validity of tests.

* * *

According to data submitted voluntarily to an online directory of genetic tests and the laboratories that offer them, tests for more than 1,500 genetic diseases are offered currently in 1,254 clinical laboratories. FDA has cleared or approved several dozen genetic tests to date (e.g., tests for factor V Leiden/factor II, cystic fibrosis, UGT1A1, cytochrome P450 (CYP450) genes CYP2D6 and CYP2C19, breast cancer prognosis gene expression test, bladder cancer fluorescence in situ hybridization (FISH), prenatal aneuploidy FISH, and HER2 FISH.) This figure refers to molecular genetic tests; when biochemical assays for genetic conditions (mainly for newborn screening) are added, the total approaches 100. Most genetic tests in use today are LDTs and have not been reviewed by FDA. For example, although BRCA tests are widely used to predict patients' future risk of breast and ovarian cancer, no BRCA test has been approved by FDA. A 2003 survey of U.S. molecular diagnostics laboratories found that genetic testing for inherited diseases was the second-largest diagnostic testing activity, representing 15 percent of the total volume of tests performed. Among the laboratories surveyed, 85 percent reported using at least one LDT.

NOTES AND QUESTIONS

1. What are the relative merits of federal, state, and voluntary industry regulation? Which approach makes the most sense for regulating genetic testing?

2. Does the regulatory distinction between genetic testing products and laboratory services make sense? Should genetic testing be regulated by a single entity? If so, which one?

3. Some commentators argue that the FDA should regulate both test products and widely marketed tests offered as a service. See, e.g., Anny Huang, Genetic Information, Legal, FDA Regulation of Genetic Testing, Encyclopedia of Ethical, Legal, and Policy Issues in Biotechnology 441 (Thomas H. Murray and Maxwell J. Mehlman eds. 2000). The latter would

include commercial testing services that analyze samples sent to them by clinicians, and that have patented the genetic mutation in question so that independent laboratories seeking to offer a similar service would have to pay royalties. Myriad Genetics, for example, provides a testing service for the BRCA1 and BRCA2 mutations for breast cancer. Its laboratory is certified by CMS under CLIA, but it has not submitted its tests to the government for a complexity rating (by default, they would be regarded as "high complexity"), and since they are not sold as kits or reagents, neither the FDA nor any other federal agency has evaluated the accuracy and reliability of the tests themselves.

One problem with giving the FDA regulatory authority over laboratory services is that the agency traditionally has been deemed to lack the authority to regulate the practice of medicine. Is a laboratory service the practice of medicine? What if it is provided by a non-physician, for example, a Ph.D.?

IV. CLINICAL GENETIC SCREENING AND TESTING

MAURICE BLOCH ET AL., PREDICTIVE TESTING FOR
HUNTINGTON DISEASE IN CANADA: THE EXPERIENCE OF
THOSE RECEIVING AN INCREASED RISK
42 Am. J. Med. Genetics 499, 499–507 (1992).

Candidates who have received increased risk results are considered to be at high risk for emotional difficulties. Our clinical experience with these individuals in interviews and support groups suggest that all of them undergo a difficult immediate period of adjustment, while some experience a prolonged period of significant emotional distress. During the early follow-up period, a few candidates have expressed regret at taking the test. However, most have reiterated their commitment to the process and stated that it has been helpful and that given the choice they would do it again. It should be appreciated that this program has been carried out in the context of the availability of continued support.

* * *

The stringent protocol of precounselling and assessment used in our program has made it possible to assess the psychosocial status of each candidate, to develop rapport with the candidate and to identify those candidates who require further assessment and possibly treatment before proceeding in the predictive testing program. The development of good rapport is important to allow the candidate to fully engage in the precounselling process of exploring motivation for taking the test and actively preparing to take the test so that individuals who are uncertain do not prematurely participate in predictive testing. Furthermore, with the establishment of open communication the candidate is more likely to seek professional support, if needed, in the follow-up phase.

Our protocol requires that candidates who are either incapable of an informed decision or considered a current suicidal risk should have the delivery of results postponed until these concerns have been resolved. Four candidates have been referred for further assessment based on psychosocial concerns. Of those only one has had testing postponed and this was due to active suicidal risk. The decision to postpone testing can never be taken lightly. The stress of *undergoing testing,* receiving a result, and *adjusting to* the new risk status must be weighed against the stress and uncertainty of living at risk for HD, the blow to the candidate's self-respect by being denied testing, and the possible sense of humiliation and helplessness by having one's autonomy undermined. For example, the first candidate was able to cope with both divorce and job change in the follow-up period. The third candidate had mild depressive symptoms but strongly resisted any suggestion of postponement of testing. The candidate in the fourth case report went through divorce and entered a new relationship. *No candidate who has received an increased risk result in our program has yet made a suicide attempt or required psychiatric hospitalization.* The candidate who had the process postponed due to suicidal risk later resolved some of her personal issues and decided that she did not wish to proceed with predictive testing at that time. At the present time, based on our experience, only a small number of candidates will have testing postponed for psychosocial reasons.

In the second case report we described some of the ramifications of testing for other relatives. The decision to take the test or not must ultimately be made by the person at risk. However, the effects of this decision are not isolated but have a ripple effect throughout the family. The nontested spouse receives information about his/her partner as well as a change in the risk of his/her children and possibly grandchildren. It is this spouse who may later be the primary caregiver for this at risk individual and this person's hopes for the future may also be drastically affected by the test result. Similarly the children of the candidate are simultaneously receiving an alteration in their risk status. Counseling should also be available for relatives as part of any predictive testing program to alleviate some of these potential adverse events.

* * *

In general, open communication is encouraged for candidates in the predictive testing program as it tends to facilitate intimacy, support, and understanding. However, the risks of open communication need also be discussed. It might leave the candidate more vulnerable to rejection, to discriminating policies by employers who may, for example, deny a high risk candidate a deserved promotion. In addition, the candidate may have to deal with the emotional distress of others.

Candidates vary considerably in the defensive postures they adopt in order to live with HD and to prepare and deal with the predictive test results. Although, during precounselling and preparation for results we have strategies to assist candidates to prepare for the impact of the results, their attitudes are usually related to entrenched personality characteristics and are often not fully recognized and dealt with during that phase of the program. The third candidate had convinced herself that she would get an increased risk result and she felt prepared to receive this and thought that she could cope. Nevertheless she experienced considerable distress and prolonged difficulty coping with results. It became apparent in discussion that she had held a deep, powerful, and inadmissible belief that she would receive a decreased risk result. Exploration in the precounselling phase of the candidates beliefs about HD and the expected outcome of predictive testing may allow counseling strategies to deal with this before test results are given.

The fourth candidate, on the other hand, convinced himself that he would get a low risk result. The juvenile onset in one sibling and an early onset in another supported this bias. Neither of these candidates was able to project themselves effectively into both the low-risk and high-risk positions and, therefore, may have failed to effectively acknowledge their *full* range of hopes and fears which may be crucial in the process of psychologically preparing for results. This inability to prepare for both possible outcomes has been an impediment to successful assimilation of decreased risk results as well. The third and fourth case reports illustrate the possible distress that arises in part from not fully preparing for an adverse test result. The precounselling, using discussion, visual imagery, rehearsal, and other techniques has proven helpful for candidates to prepare more *fully* for the eventuality of any outcome.

* * *

Two issues emerged from our experience with the second candidate and his sibling participating concurrently in the program. He indicated at the results session that he did not intend to tell his brother his results at that time. His right to confidential treatment of this information has been clearly established. However, it did impose a challenge upon the counseling team not to let any of his information be disclosed to his brother, as he had told his brother that delivery had been postponed due to laboratory problems. However, some weeks later the candidate did disclose his results to his brother. This reinforced our belief that the candidate is, in most instances, best able to pace him or herself with respect to crucial decisions such as whether and when to take the test, to disclose information about HD or the test, and to join the support group.

This experience also reinforced the importance of addressing the needs of each candidate individually even if more than one family member has requested testing concurrently.

Thus far there have been no catastrophic responses to increased risk results in the Canadian program. The candidates, in general, appear to be coping fairly well, although all have experienced some difficult episodes. Symptoms of depression and anxiety are most common and occur most frequently shortly after receiving results, which is clearly a period when persons are more vulnerable. However, in the longer term, candidates generally become more present-centered in their awareness with a heightened perception of the here and now, but have increased difficulty in planning for the future.

Longitudinal evaluation over the ensuing years will provide much needed information about the long term impact of living at increased risk for Huntington's disease, particularly as the candidates get close to the expected age of manifestation. These evaluations will have relevance for similar testing programs which may be developed for other late onset genetic disorders.

NOTES AND QUESTIONS

1.   Under the protocol employed by the Canadian Huntington disease testing program, counselors evaluated candidates to determine whether they were suitable for testing. In one case, for example, the candidate was found to be experiencing significant emotional distress and to be moderately depressed. However, "[a]s she did not appear to be a suicidal risk, had a stable marriage and sound social supports, was motivated to seek additional individual psychotherapy outside the program, and was able to make an informed decision, we proceeded with predictive testing." Block et al. at 504. Is it appropriate to withhold testing because of these concerns? Is the Canadian protocol consistent with general principles governing informed consent to health care? To what extent, for example, is it appropriate to withhold testing because of fears that the results may emotionally upset the patient? See generally Jessica Berg et al., Informed Consent: Legal Theory and Clinical Practice 79–85 (2001).

2.   The Canadian study also found that approximately 10 percent of those persons receiving a negative result from the test for Huntington disease experienced psychological difficulties, including "survivor guilt," stress from having made irreversible personal and financial decisions based on an expectation that they were affected, and depression once the realization sets in that many problems in their lives remain unchanged. See Marlene Huggins et al., Predictive Testing for Huntington Disease in Canada: Adverse Effects and Unexpected Results in Those Receiving a Decreased Risk, 42 Am. J. Med. Genetics 508 (1992).

3.   Other researchers have studied the impact of genetic testing for breast cancer. A worldwide study of 1,499 women found that 86% of BRCA1-positive subjects and 71% of BRCA2-positive subjects had their ovaries surgically removed by the age of 50. In the same study, 46% of both BRCA1- and BRCA2-positive subjects underwent risk-reducing mastectomy by the age of 70. Xinglei Chai et al., Use of Risk-Reducing Surgeries in a Prospective Cohort of 1,499 BRCA1 and BRCA2 Mutation Carriers, 148 Breast Cancer Res. Treat. 397 (2014).

4.   In 1993, researchers announced that they had discovered a gene, APOE, that is associated with Alzheimer disease. In 1995, a working group of the American College of Medical Genetics and the American Society of Human Genetics issued a consensus statement that clinicians should not offer predictive testing, even to members of high-risk families. See Statement on the Use of Apolipoprotein E Testing for Alzheimer Disease, 274 JAMA 1627 (1995). The group noted uncertainties about the predictive value of test results (including that 35 to 50 percent of patients with Alzheimer disease do not have the mutation), and took the position that predictive testing "may be valuable only if prevention can be affected by lifestyle changes or early drug intervention," which was not the case with Alzheimer disease. Is this an appropriate stance? Should the decision be left up to the individuals seeking testing? What standards should be used to determine if a genetic test is predictive enough to be suitable for clinical use? Who should establish these standards? In a 2004 article, researchers studying attitudes toward genetic testing for an inherited form of amyotrophic lateral sclerosis (Lou Gehrig disease) recommended that individuals considering being tested be informed that the purpose of the testing is for research rather than disclosure of individual results. See Joanna H. Fanos, Deborah F. Gelinas & Robert G. Miller, "You Have Shown Me My End": Attitudes Toward Presymptomatic Testing for Familial Amyotrophic Lateral Sclerosis, 129A Am. J. Med. Genetics 248–253 (2004). Another group of commentators recommended that community input be obtained before establishing policies on offering genetic testing and screening for clinical and public health purposes. See Sarah E. Gollust et al., Community Involvement in Developing Policies for Genetic Testing: Assessing the Interests and Experiences of Individuals Affected by Genetic Conditions, 95 Am. J. Public Health 35–41 (2005).

5.   A 2005 study of the children of Alzheimer patients who underwent genetic testing for a genetic mutation, APOE4, associated with a higher risk of developing Alzheimer disease, found that persons whose test results were positive had no increase in anxiety or depression compared with those whose test results were negative. The study was part of a large-scale series of investigations known as REVEAL (Risk Evaluation and Education for Alzheimer's Disease). See Robert C. Green et al., The REVEAL Study: The Impact of Genetic Risk Assessment with APOE Disclosure for Alzaheimer's Disease, 1 Alzheimer's & Dementia s101 (2005).

TAMAR LEWIN, BOOM IN GENETIC TESTING RAISES QUESTIONS ON SHARING RESULTS

The New York Times, July 21, 2000, at A1.

As genetic testing becomes increasingly common, those who choose to learn their genetic risks, and the health professionals who treat them, are facing difficult decisions about how—and whether—to share the results with family members who share their genes.

And the new genetic information is creating new kinds of rifts, when one family member finds out what another family member does not want to know, or when family members react differently to the same knowledge.

"One woman who'd had ovarian cancer was tested for the breast cancer gene mutations mostly for the sake of her two adult daughters," said Katherine Schneider, senior genetics counselor at the Dana Farber Cancer Institute in Boston. "But when she told them she had it, they were so devastated that they didn't talk with her for two years. They didn't want to know."

"I tell that story a lot. There's nothing easy about any of this. But before testing, it's important to talk not only about what the information will mean for you, but what it might mean to your sisters, your children, your cousins."

Genetic tests are now commonplace, what with prenatal tests diagnosing hundreds of syndromes, midlife tests for mutations linked to breast and ovarian cancer, and—with the human genome newly mapped—more and more familial disorders.

The scientific advances have created debate about public policy on genetic discrimination. But the private effects on family dynamics are just as complex, as patients and health professionals adjust to thinking about family not just as flesh and blood, but flesh and blood and genes.

Usually, patients are happy to share health information with family members for whom it may be important, often asking the doctor or genetic counselor for a written explanation to pass along.

But when patients want to keep the information to themselves, health professionals may encounter situations that mix social problem and soap opera, and be ethically and legally pulled into uncharted waters.

A young man in Washington State called his genetics counselor to confess a guilty conscience: Several months earlier, he told her, he had made a sperm donation. And while he knew his test results had shown that he had an inheritable syndrome that causes heart trouble and, often, early death, he did not mention it to the sperm bank. Troubled, the counselor called the sperm bank and found that there had, indeed, been successful pregnancies with the man's sperm. She offered to counsel those families but does not know whether the sperm bank even passed on the information.

In a New York family with three adult daughters, the two married daughters know that their mother, who had breast cancer as a young woman, has been tested and found to carry a gene mutation associated with a high risk of breast and ovarian cancer. The mother has forbidden them to tell their unmarried sister, who has always felt herself to be the least attractive, for fear that it might make her less marriageable. They have obeyed, but want the family doctor to make sure she has frequent mammograms and screenings.

Two sisters who know their mother had genetic testing before she died of ovarian cancer want to find out her test results. But the Pennsylvania medical center that did the testing will not release the results to the young women without the consent of their stepfather, who has a dismal relationship with them. The sisters could, of course, have had their own genetic tests, but they had hoped by learning more about their family's history to avoid the process. The center's ethics committee is now revising its consent forms to require all patients tested to specify which family members should have access to the results after their death.

* * *

Often, the decision to pass on information is a delicate one, depending not only on such factors as the relatives' closeness, ages and emotional health, but also the nature of the disease and the severity of the risk. Where there is no treatment, or the risk is small, the case for sharing painful knowledge becomes less compelling. And the need to share information may be temporary, experts say, as the era approaches when complete genetic profiles become a routine part of individual health records. Meanwhile, the cost of testing even a single gene can run from several hundred to several thousand dollars.

Still, Josephine Wagner Costalas, a genetic counselor at Fox Chase Cancer Center in Philadelphia, has an unspoken worry whenever she counsels a patient who has tested positive for the breast cancer gene mutations.

"My worst nightmare is the scenario where I might have a patient who tests positive and doesn't tell her relatives," Ms. Costalas said, "and a few years later her sister will discover she has metastatic cancer, with a bad prognosis, and she'll find out that there was this information showing she was at risk. And maybe she'll sue me, saying I should have picked up the phone and told her, 'Your sister's positive, you should get tested.' This is all so new, and there are no clear guidelines, so I worry."

Still, Ms. Costalas does not pressure her patients to share their results. "If people aren't sure about sharing the information, I ask them to think about what it would be like if the situation were reversed," she said. "Would they want to know? But I do believe patients need to decide for themselves what they want to do."

And when several family members come in together, there are other issues. "What if they have different results?" Ms. Costalas said. "Who do you tell first? What if they have different reactions?"

* * *

Two years ago, the American Society of Human Genetics adopted a position recognizing the conflict between the health professions' duty to maintain confidentiality and the duty to warn about serious health risks. Health professionals should tell patients about potential genetic risks to their relatives, the statement said, and in some cases, they may be allowed to breach confidentiality to warn relatives at risk if the harm is "serious, imminent and likely" and prevention or treatment is available.

But there is little consensus on where to draw those lines. Generally, genetic counselors are more concerned about confidentiality and not pressuring patients, while physicians specializing in genetics are more concerned about the duty to warn, according to research by Dorothy C. Wertz, senior scientist at the Shriver Center in Waltham, Mass. As a practical matter, though, most health professionals cannot warn relatives.

"In the end it's up to the patient, because in real life, we don't have relatives' names and phone numbers," said Helen Hixon, a genetic counselor in cardiology at Cedars Sinai hospital in Los Angeles. "We do tell people pretty strongly that they should warn their relatives, that they may have a legal duty to do so."

NOTES AND QUESTIONS

What legitimate interests do family members have in the results of an individual's genetic testing? What is the proper way to satisfy these interests? What is the obligation of clinicians—primary care physicians, geneticists, genetic counselors, and so on—toward family members? The American Medical Association urges physicians to discuss with patients when the physician would deem it appropriate to convey genetic information to family members so that the patient can decline testing from a physician whose views seem unacceptable. Sara Taub et al., for the Council on Ethical and Judicial Affairs of the American Medical Association, Managing Familial Risk in Genetic Testing, 8 Genetic Testing 356–359 (2004). The AMA notes, however, that a physician would be entitled to breach the patient's confidentiality against the patient's wishes only in rare circumstances, which it does not specify.

A. LIABILITY ISSUES

PATE V. THRELKEL
661 So.2d 278 (Fla.1995).

WELLS, J.

We have for review the following question certified to be of great public importance:

DOES A PHYSICIAN OWE A DUTY OF CARE TO THE CHILDREN OF A PATIENT TO WARN THE PATIENT OF THE GENETICALLY TRANSFERABLE NATURE OF THE CONDITION FOR WHICH THE PHYSICIAN IS TREATING THE PATIENT?

We have jurisdiction. Art. V, § 3(b)(4), Fla. Const. We answer the question in the affirmative provided the children of the patient first establish that pursuant to the prevailing standard of care set forth in section 766.102, Florida Statutes (1989), a reasonably prudent physician would give such warning to his or her patient in light of all relevant circumstances.

In March 1987, Marianne New received treatment for medullary thyroid carcinoma, a genetically transferable disease. In 1990, Heidi Pate, New's adult daughter, learned that she also had medullary thyroid carcinoma. Consequently, Pate and her husband filed a complaint against the physicians who initially treated New for the disease as well as the physicians' respective employers. Pate and her husband alleged that the physicians knew or should have known of the likelihood that New's children would have inherited the condition genetically; that the physicians were under a duty to warn New that her children should be tested for the disease; that had New been warned in 1987, she would have had her children tested at that time; and if Pate had been tested in 1987, she would have taken preventative action, and her condition, more likely than not, would have been curable. Pate claimed that as a direct and proximate cause of the physicians' negligence, she suffers from advanced medullary thyroid carcinoma and its various damaging effects.

The respondent health care providers moved to dismiss the complaint for failure to state a cause of action. Specifically, the respondents alleged that Pate did not demonstrate the existence of a professional relationship between her and respondents and thus failed to establish that respondents owed her a duty of care. The trial court granted the motion and dismissed the Pates' complaint with prejudice, finding that the plaintiffs were not patients of the respondents and that they did not fit within any exception to the requirement that there be a physician-patient relationship between the parties as a condition precedent to bringing a medical malpractice action.

The district court affirmed the trial court's dismissal. The court rejected the Pates' argument that it should, based upon past decisions recognizing a doctor's duty to inform others of a patient's contagious disease, extend a physician's duty to cover the child of a patient who suffers from an inheritable disease. The court also rejected the Pates' reliance on Schroeder v. Perkel, 432 A.2d 834 (N.J.1981), in which the parents of a four-year-old child brought suit against the child's pediatricians for failing to diagnose the child with cystic fibrosis early enough to prevent the parents from having a second diseased child. The New Jersey court in Schroeder recognized that due to the special nature of the family relationship, a physician's duty may extend beyond a patient to members of the patient's immediate family.

* * *

We conclude that to answer the certified question we must consider two questions related to duty. First, we must determine whether New's physicians had a duty to warn New of the genetically transferable nature of her disease. We find that to make this determination we must apply section 766.102, Florida Statutes (1989), which defines the legal duty owed by a health care provider in a medical malpractice case. That section provides in part:

> (1) In any action for recovery of damages based on the death or personal injury of any person in which it is alleged that such death or injury resulted from the negligence of a health care provider as defined in s. 768.50(2)(b), the claimant shall have the burden of proving by the greater weight of evidence that the alleged actions of the health care provider represented a breach of the prevailing professional standard of care for that health care provider. The prevailing professional standard of care for a given health care provider shall be that level of care, skill, and treatment which, in light of all relevant surrounding circumstances, is recognized as acceptable and appropriate by reasonably prudent similar health care providers.

§ 766.102, Fla. Stat. (1989). In applying this statute to the instant case, we conclude that a duty exists if the statutory standard of care requires a reasonably prudent health care provider to warn a patient of the genetically transferable nature of the condition for which the physician was treating the patient.

In medical malpractice cases, the standard of care is determined by a consideration of expert testimony. Because this case comes to us on appeal from an order granting the physicians' motion to dismiss, the record has yet to be developed in respect to such testimony. However, the court's dismissal requires us to assume that the factual allegations in the complaint are true. * * * Accordingly, we must accept as true the Pates' allegations that pursuant to the prevailing standard of care, the health care providers were under a duty to warn New of the importance of testing her children for medullary thyroid carcinoma. Whether these allegations are supported by the statutorily required expert medical authority will have to be determined as the action progresses. We do note, however, that the plaintiffs have pled good-faith compliance with section 766.104, Florida Statutes (1989).

The second question we must address in answering the certified question is to whom does the alleged duty to warn New of the nature of her disease run? The duty obviously runs to the patient who is in privity with the physician. * * * In other professional relationships, however, we have recognized the rights of identified third party beneficiaries to recover from a professional because that party was the intended beneficiary of the prevailing standard of care. In such cases, we have determined that an absence of privity does not necessarily foreclose liability.

* * *

Here, the alleged prevailing standard of care was obviously developed for the benefit of the patient's children as well as the patient. We conclude that when the prevailing standard of care creates a duty that is obviously for the benefit of certain identified third parties and the physician knows of the existence of those third parties, then the physician's duty runs to those third parties. Therefore, in accord with our decision in Baskerville-Donovan Engineers, we hold that privity does not bar Heidi Pate's pursuit of a medical malpractice action. Our holding is likewise in accord with McCain because under the duty alleged in this case, a patient's children fall within the zone of foreseeable risk.

Though not encompassed by the certified question, there is another issue which should be addressed in light of our holding. If there is a duty to warn, to whom must the physician convey the warning? Our holding should not be read to require the physician to warn the patient's children of the disease. In most instances the physician is prohibited from disclosing the patient's medical condition to others except with the patient's permission. See § 255.241(2), Fla. Stat. (1989). Moreover, the patient ordinarily can be expected to pass on the warning. To require the physician to seek out and warn various members of the patient's family would often be difficult or impractical and would place too heavy a burden upon the physician. Thus, we emphasize that in any circumstances in which the physician has a duty to warn of a genetically transferable disease, that duty will be satisfied by warning the patient.

Accordingly, we conclude that the trial court erred by dismissing the complaint with prejudice. Whether the Pates can recover for medical malpractice depends upon the prevailing standard of care pursuant to section 766.102. The pleadings were prematurely terminated based upon the trial court's conclusion that a lack of privity prevented the Pates from stating a cause of action. We therefore quash the decision of the district court affirming the dismissal of the complaint with prejudice and remand for further proceedings in accord with this opinion.

It is so ordered.

SAFER V. PACK

677 A.2d 1188 (N.J. Super. Ct. App. Div. 1996).

KESTIN, J.

Plaintiffs appeal from the trial court's order dismissing their complaint and denying their cross-motion for partial summary judgment as to liability only. We reverse that portion of the order dismissing the complaint and affirm the denial of plaintiffs' motion.

Donna Safer's claim arises from the patient-physician relationship in the 1950s and 1960s between her father, Robert Batkin, a resident of New Jersey, and Dr. George T. Pack, also a resident of New Jersey, who practiced medicine and surgery in New York City and treated Mr. Batkin there. It is alleged that Dr. Pack specialized in the treatment and removal of cancerous tumors and growths.

In November 1956, Mr. Batkin was admitted to the hospital with a pre-operative diagnosis of retroperitoneal cancer. A week later, Dr. Pack performed a total colectomy and an ileosigmoidectomy for multiple polyposis of the colon with malignant degeneration in one area. The discharge summary noted the finding in a pathology report of the existence of adenocarcinoma developing in an intestinal polyp, and diffuse intestinal polyposis "from one end of the colon to the other." Dr. Pack continued to treat Mr. Batkin postoperatively.

In October 1961, Mr. Batkin was again hospitalized. Dr. Pack performed an ileoabdominal perineal resection with an ileostomy. The discharge summary reported pathology findings of "ulcerative adenocarcinoma of colon Grade II with metastases to Levels II and III" and "adenomatous polyps." Dr. Pack again continued to treat Mr. Batkin postoperatively. He also developed a physician-patient relationship with Mrs. Batkin relative to the diagnosis and treatment of a vaginal ulcer.

In December 1963, Mr. Batkin was hospitalized once again at Dr. Pack's direction. The carcinoma of the colon had metastasized to the liver with secondary jaundice and probable retroperitoneal disease causing pressure on the sciatic nerve plexus. After some treatment, Mr. Batkin died on January 3, 1964, at forty-five years of age. Donna was ten years old at the time of her father's death. Her sister was seventeen.

In February 1990, Donna Safer, then thirty-six years of age and newly married, residing in Connecticut, began to experience lower abdominal pain. Examinations and tests revealed a cancerous blockage of the colon and multiple polyposis. In March, Ms. Safer underwent a total abdominal colectomy with ileorectal anastamosis. A primary carcinoma in the sigmoid colon was found to extend through the serosa of the bowel and multiple polyps were seen throughout the entire bowel. Because of the detection of additional metastatic adenocarcinoma and carcinoma, plaintiff's left ovary was also removed. Between April 1990 and mid-1991, Ms. Safer underwent chemotherapy treatment.

In September 1991, plaintiffs obtained Robert Batkin's medical records, from which they learned that he had suffered from polyposis. Their complaint was filed in March 1992, alleging a violation of duty (professional negligence) on the part of Dr. Pack in his failure to warn of the risk to Donna Safer's health.

Plaintiffs contend that multiple polyposis is a hereditary condition that, if undiscovered and untreated, invariably leads to metastatic colorectal cancer. They contend, further, that the hereditary nature of the disease was known at the time Dr. Pack was treating Mr. Batkin and that the physician was required, by medical standards then prevailing, to warn those at risk so that they might have the benefits of early examination, monitoring, detection and treatment, that would provide opportunity to avoid the most baneful consequences of the condition.

* * *

In dismissing, the trial court held that a physician had no "legal duty to warn a child of a patient of a genetic risk[.]" In the absence of any evidence whether Dr. Pack had warned Mr. Batkin to provide information concerning his disease for the benefit of his children, the motion judge "assumed that Dr. Pack did not tell Robert Batkin of the genetic disease."

The motion judge's reasoning proceeded from the following legal premise: "in order for a doctor to have a duty to warn, there must be a patient/physician relationship or circumstances requiring the protection of the public health or the community [at] large." Finding no physician-patient relationship between Dr. Pack and his patient's daughter Donna, the court then held genetically transmissible diseases to differ from contagious or infectious diseases or threats of harm in respect of the duty to warn, because "the harm is already present within the non-patient child, as opposed to being introduced, by a patient who was not warned to stay away. The patient is taking no action in which to cause the child harm."

The motion judge relied on Pate v. Threlkel, 640 So. 2d 183 (Fla.Dist.Ct.App.1994), as the only "on point" authority respecting genetically transmissible disease.

* * *

Because the issue before us arose on a motion for summary judgment, we, too, are obliged to accept plaintiffs' proffer through their medical expert that the prevailing standard of care at the time Dr. Pack treated Mr. Batkin required the physician to warn of the known genetic threat.

* * *

We see no impediment, legal or otherwise, to recognizing a physician's duty to warn those known to be at risk of avoidable harm from a genetically transmissible condition. In terms of foreseeability especially, there is no essential difference between the type of genetic threat at issue here and the menace of infection, contagion or a threat of physical harm. See generally, e.g., McIntosh v. Milano, 168 N.J. Super. 466, 483–85, 403 A.2d 500 (Law Div.1979); Tarasoff v. Regents of Univ. of Cal., 17 Cal. 3d 425, 551 P.2d 334, 344, 131 Cal. Rptr. 14 (Cal. 1976); Restatement (Second) of Torts §§ 314, 314A (1965); T.A. Bateman, Annotation, Liability of Doctor or Other Health Practitioner to Third Party Contracting Contagious Disease from Doctor's Patient, 3 A.L.R. 5th 370 (1992). The individual or group at risk is easily identified, and substantial future harm may be averted or minimized by a timely and effective warning.

The motion judge's view of this case as one involving an unavoidable genetic condition gave too little significance to the proffered expert view that early monitoring of those at risk can effectively avert some of the more serious consequences a person with multiple polyposis might otherwise experience. We cannot conclude either, as the trial court did, that Dr. Pack breached no duty because avoidable harm to Donna was not foreseeable, i.e., "that Dr. Pack's conduct did not create a 'foreseeable zone of risk.'" Such a determination would ignore the presumed state of medical knowledge at the time.

* * *

Although an overly broad and general application of the physician's duty to warn might lead to confusion, conflict or unfairness in many types of circumstances, we are confident that the duty to warn of avertable risk from genetic causes, by definition a matter of familial concern, is sufficiently narrow to serve the interests of justice. Further, it is appropriate, for reasons already expressed by our Supreme Court, that the duty be seen as owed not only to the patient himself but that it also "extends beyond the interests of a patient to members of the immediate family of the patient who may be adversely affected by a breach of that duty."

* * *

We need not decide, in the present posture of this case, how, precisely, that duty is to be discharged, especially with respect to young children who may be at risk, except to require that reasonable steps be taken to assure that the information reaches those likely to be affected or is made available for their benefit. We are aware of no direct evidence that has been developed concerning the nature of the communications between physician and patient regarding Mr. Batkin's disease: what Dr. Pack did or did not disclose; the advice he gave to Mr. Batkin, if any, concerning genetic factors and what ought to have been done in respect of those at risk; and the conduct or expressed preferences of Mr. Batkin in response thereto. There may be enough from Mrs. Batkin's testimony and other evidence for inferences to be drawn, however.

We decline to hold as the Florida Supreme Court did in Pate v. Thelkel, supra, that, in all circumstances, the duty to warn will be satisfied by informing the patient. It may be necessary, at some stage, to resolve a conflict between the physician's broader duty to warn and his fidelity to an expressed preference of the patient that nothing be said to family members about the details of the disease. We cannot know presently, however, whether there is any likelihood that such a conflict may be shown to have existed in this matter or, if it did, what its qualities might have been. As the matter is currently constituted, it is as likely as not that no such conflict will be shown to have existed and that the only evidence on the issue will be Mrs. Batkin's testimony, including that she received no information, despite specific inquiry, that her children were at risk. We note, in addition, the possible existence of some offsetting evidence that Donna was rectally examined as a young child, suggesting that the risk to her had been disclosed.

This case implicates serious and conflicting medical, social and legal policies, many aptly identified in Sonia M. Suter, Whose Genes Are These Anyway? Familial Conflicts Over Access to Genetic Information, 91 Mich. L. Rev. 1854 (1993) and in other sources, including some referred to by the motion judge. Some such policy considerations may need to be addressed in ultimately resolving this case. For example, if evidence is produced that will permit the jury to find that Dr. Pack received instructions from his patient not to disclose details of the illness or the fact of genetic risk, the court will be required to determine whether, as a matter of law, there are or ought to be any limits on physician-patient confidentiality, especially after the patient's death where a risk of harm survives the patient, as in the case of genetic consequences. See generally Janet A. Kobrin, Confidentiality of Genetic Information, 30 UCLA L. Rev. 1283 (1983).

Issues of fact remain to be resolved, as well. What was the extent of Donna's risk, for instance? We are led to understand from the experts' reports that the risk of multiple polyposis was significant and that, upon detection, an early full colectomy, i.e., an excision of her entire colon, may well have been the treatment of choice to avoid resultant cancer—including metastasis, the loss of other organs and the rigors of chemotherapy. Full factual development may, however, cast a different light on these issues of fact and others.

Difficult damage issues portend also. Not the least of these will involve distinguishing between the costs of the medical surveillance that would have followed a timely and effective warning, and the costs of medical care attributable to any breach of duty that may be found to have occurred.

Because of the necessarily limited scope of our consideration, we have highlighted only a few of the potentially troublesome issues presented by this case. Such questions are best conceived and considered in the light of a fully developed record rather than in the abstract.

* * *

The order of the trial court dismissing the complaint is reversed. For similar reasons, the trial court's order denying plaintiffs' motion for summary judgment on liability is affirmed. The matter is remanded to the trial court for further proceedings.

NOTES AND QUESTIONS

1.   Both of the conditions that the physicians in *Pate* and *Safer* allegedly failed to warn the plaintiffs about, medullary thyroid carcinoma and familial adenomatous polyposis, are autosomal dominant disorders with nearly complete penetrance. Each child of an affected parent has a 50 percent chance of inheriting the mutation, and unless treated, has an extremely high probability of becoming ill. Does the physician's duty depend on the probability of inheriting the disorder? On its severity?

2.   What harms might be caused by disclosing genetic test results to family members at risk?

3.   If the genetic disorder is not treatable, does the health care professional still have a duty to warn third parties at risk? What benefits, if any, would disclosure provide? See Carol McCrehan Parker, Camping Trips and Family Trees: Must Tennessee Physicians Warn Their Patients' Relatives of Genetic Risks?, 65 Tenn. L. Rev. 585, 601–02 (1998).

4.   The classic case addressing the duty of a health care professional to warn third parties of a risk of harm created by a patient is Tarasoff vs. Regents of the University of California, 551 P.2d 334 (Cal. 1976). In that case, the Supreme Court of California held that a psychotherapist had a duty to take reasonable care to warn a foreseeable victim of a threat of a serious danger of violence created by a patient. (The patient allegedly told the psychotherapist that he planned to kill a female acquaintance, and later did so.) In what ways do the facts alleged in *Pate* and *Safer* resemble the facts

alleged in *Tarasoff*? Should the physician's duty to warn only extend to cases where the patient actively creates the harm? See Michelle R. King, Physician Duty to Warn a Patient's Offspring of Hereditary Genetic Defects: Balancing the Patient's Right to Confidentiality Against the Family Member's Right to Know—Can Or Should Tarasoff Apply?, 4 Quinnipiac Health L. J. 1 (2000).

The physician's duty to warn third parties has been extended to contagious and even non-contagious diseases. On the latter, see Bradshaw v. Daniel, 854 S.W.2d 865 (Tenn. 1993) (duty to warn husband that wife had Rocky Mountain Spotted Fever). Are genetic disorders "contagious"?

5.   Under the rule adopted by the court in *Safer*, what if the patient instructs the physician not to disclose the information to anyone? New Jersey enacted a statute in response to the *Safer* case that reads as follows:

N.J. STAT. ANN. § 10:5–47 (2001)

Conditions for disclosure of genetic information

a.   Regardless of the manner of receipt or the source of genetic information, including information received from an individual, a person may not disclose or be compelled, by subpoena or any other means, to disclose the identity of an individual upon whom a genetic test has been performed or to disclose genetic information about the individual in a manner that permits identification of the individual, unless:

(1)   Disclosure is necessary for the purposes of a criminal or death investigation or a criminal or juvenile proceeding;

(2)   Disclosure is necessary to determine paternity in accordance with the provisions of section 11 of P.L.1983, c.17 (C.9:17–48);

(3)   Disclosure is authorized by order of a court of competent jurisdiction;

(4)   Disclosure is made pursuant to the provisions of the "DNA Database and Databank Act of 1994," P.L.1994, c.136 (C.53:1–20.17 et seq.);

(5)   Disclosure is authorized by the tested individual or the tested individual's representative by signing a consent which complies with the requirements of the Department of Health and Senior Services;

(6)   Disclosure is for the purpose of furnishing genetic information relating to a decedent for medical diagnosis of blood relatives of the decedent;

(7)   Disclosure is for the purpose of identifying bodies;

(8) Disclosure is pursuant to newborn screening requirements established by State or federal law;

(9) Disclosure is authorized by federal law for the identification of persons; or

(10) Disclosure is by an insurer pursuant to the requirements of P.L.1985, c.179 (C.17:23A–1 et seq.).

b.   The provisions of this section apply to any subsequent disclosure by any person after another person has disclosed genetic information or the identity of an individual upon whom a genetic test has been performed.

In some states, the law immunizes health care professionals from civil or criminal liability in certain circumstances. Title 410, section 513/30 of the Illinois Compiled Statutes, part of that state's Genetic Information Privacy Act, states: "No civil or criminal sanction under this Act shall be imposed for any disclosure or nondisclosure of a test result to a spouse by a physician acting in good faith under this paragraph." Would this protect a physician who disclosed test results to a spouse without the consent of the person who was tested? Would the protection of the statute extend to disclosure to children?

6.   The Health Insurance Portability and Accountability Act (HIPAA) Privacy Rule prohibits the disclosure of individually identifiable health information without the authorization of the individual. 45 C.F.R. Parts 160, 164. One of the exceptions permits disclosures "required by law," and this includes common law as well as statutes. 45 C.F.R. § 164.512(a). Another exception permits disclosures "to prevent or lessen a serious and imminent threat to the health or safety of a person or the public." 45 C.F.R. § 164.512(j) Therefore, the Privacy Rule would not be a bar to *Tarasoff*-required disclosures. In theory, the Privacy Rule would not prohibit a state without a genetic privacy statute from judicially recognizing a duty to warn as suggested by *Safer*. On the other hand, the combination of widespread legislative action to protect genetic privacy and the spirit—if not the letter— of the Privacy Rule, would likely deter a court from imposing such a requirement.

7.   In *Safer*, the patient's wife asked the physician if his condition could affect their children and was "told not to worry." Does the patient or the patient's family have a duty to inquire? If they fail to inquire, should that discharge the physician's duty to warn? If the patient fails to ask the right questions, should she be deemed contributorily negligent? In Brown v. Dibbell, 595 N.W.2d 358 (Wis. 1999), the court stated:

A patient's duty to exercise ordinary care in an informed consent action generally does not impose on the patient an affirmative duty to ascertain the truth or completeness of the information presented by the doctor; to ask questions of the doctor; or to independently seek information when a reasonable person would want such information. * * * We do not conclude, however, that a patient may never be contributorily negligent for failing to take such steps. We merely conclude that it would require a very extraordinary fact situation * * *.

Can you think of such a fact situation in regard to information about an inherited disorder?

8.   The court in *Pate* states: "Thus, we emphasize that in any circumstances in which the physician has a duty to warn of a genetically transferable disease, that duty will be satisfied by warning the patient." Do you agree? Can you think of a situation in which warning the patient would not be sufficient to discharge the physician's duty? (See Chapter 6, *Molloy v. Meier*, for one example.) What if the patient said that she did not intend to disclose the information to members of her family who might be affected?

9.   The decision in *Safer* requires the physician to take "reasonable steps" to see that warning information reaches the person to whom the physician owes a duty to warn. What steps might be "unreasonable"? The plaintiff was a child when her father was diagnosed. Dr. Pack died before she reached maturity. What effect should this have on the duty to warn?

10.   A 2003 literature review identified 12 studies that found a lack of knowledge about genetics on the part of physicians. See Sandy Suther & Patricia Goodson, Barriers to the Provision of Genetic Services By Primary Care Physicians: A Systematic Review of the Literature, 5 Genetics in Med. 70–76 (2003). One survey found that only 13 percent of internists, 21 percent of OB/GYNs, and 40 percent of oncologists correctly answered questions about the genetic aspects of breast cancer and breast cancer testing. See Teresa Doksum, Barbara A. Bernhardt & Neil A. Holtzman, Does Knowledge About the Genetics of Breast Cancer Differ Between Nongeneticist Physicians Who Do or Do Not Discuss or Order BRCA1 Testing?, 5 Genetics in Med. 99–105 (2003). Harold Varmus, former director of NIH, commented in 2002 that the pace of the transformation to gene-based medicine "will be limited not only by the pace of discovery, but also by the need to educate practicing physicians, their coworkers, and their patients about the uses and shortcomings of genetic information." Harold Varmus, Getting Ready for Gene-Based Medicine, 347 New Eng. J. Med. 1526 (2002). Varmus noted that most medical schools had not anticipated the impact of molecular genetics, and that, as a result, "many physicians struggle with the new biology." Id. Physicians' knowledge of genetics does not seem to have improved much in the subsequent years. In a 2013 survey of academic family physicians, for example, a majority reported they did not feel knowledgeable about available genetic tests. Arch G. Mainous III et al., Academic Family Physicians' Perception of Genetic Testing and Integration Into Practice: A CERA Study, 45 Fam. Med. 257 (2013).

B. GENETIC COUNSELING

Individuals and families concerned about genetic disorders may obtain information and advice from a variety of health care professionals, including primary care physicians, physicians specializing in clinical genetics, and nurses. In addition, masters degrees are offered in genetic counseling. Masters-level genetic counselors are not licensed in an overwhelming number of states (California being a notable exception), but they may be certified by the American Board of Genetic Counseling. The National Society of Genetic Counselors (NSGC) had 3,033 members as of 2014. Roles may overlap, but a basic distinction is that, while any of these professionals may provide information and counseling, only physicians can make diagnoses and order genetic testing.

A major issue for health care professionals in general, and for those providing genetic counseling services in particular, is whether their interactions with patients and families should be directive or non-directive.

ANNE L. MATTHEWS, GENETIC COUNSELING, IN
ENCYCLOPEDIA OF ETHICAL, LEGAL, AND
POLICY ISSUES IN BIOTECHNOLOGY
349–350 (Thomas H. Murray & Maxwell J. Mehlman eds. 2000).

* * *

From Sheldon Reed's first publication defining genetic counseling as "a kind of social work done for the benefit of the whole family entirely without eugenic connotations," genetic counseling has been equated with the concept of nondirectiveness. Nondirectiveness appealed to the genetics community as a way to distance itself from the eugenics movement associated with Nazi Germany. Genetic counseling embraced Carl Rogers's client-centered counseling approach. Rogers felt that counselors need to provide a warm, accepting environment free from pressure or coercion for clients to reach a successful self-acceptance and self-understanding. Nondirectiveness is understood to mean nonprescriptive. Fine defines nondirectiveness as a genetic counseling strategy that supports autonomous decision making by clients. NSGC Code of Ethics states, "Therefore, genetic counselors strive to: * * * Enable their clients to make informed independent decisions, free of coercion, by providing or illuminating the necessary facts and clarifying the alternatives and anticipated consequences." Genetic counselors therefore are facilitators and advocates of informed decision making, with the goal of having the counselee make a decision based solely on his or her own values and beliefs.

However, consensus regarding the terms directiveness and nondirectiveness is difficult to find among genetics professionals and in the literature. Kessler notes that depending on how one defines the term nondirective will determine whether or not it can be achieved. White notes that nondirectiveness is often equated with value neutrality, which may "either imply that the counseling approach as a whole does not represent any values or moral positions, or it may refer to value-free communication, representing an ideal in which concepts and facts are expressed in impartial terms." A number of authors have argued that counseling is never value-neutral. The types of information provided or not provided, the tone of voice, body language, all convey counselor values. Singer elaborates on this theme by noting that many of the decisions that patients make take place in an atmosphere of crisis and that the issues are often highly emotional. Counselors relay information that is often highly technical, while most counselees are likely to have limited knowledge of the biological and statistical issues that arise; they are a vulnerable population. Thus a counselor, who has a duty to provide all the information that clients need in order to make informed decisions, must decide what information the counselee needs and how to present the information. In this sense the genetic counselor utilizes her expertise to decide what and how much information the counselee needs to make the best possible decision for her. Brunger and Lippman would agree. They conclude that genetic counseling is not a "one-size-fits-all" endeavor; rather, it is information that is tailored to specific counselees in specific situations. For some, this would be considered a directive approach. However, authors such as Kessler or Singer would suggest that the counselor is facilitating the goal of genetic counseling by providing information upon which counselees can make autonomous, independent, and informed decisions.

One of the often quoted mechanisms for deciding whether or not a counselor is being directive is to ask whether or not counselors answer questions such as "What would you do in my situation?"

* * *

While the literature regarding nondirective counseling remains unsettled, research suggests that nondirectiveness is not the only guiding principle employed by genetic counselors. In their efforts to provide and facilitate autonomous, independent, and informed decision making by counselees, genetic counselors strive to maintain a delicate balance between a nondirective stance and enhanced counselee understanding.

NOTES AND QUESTIONS

1.   Is the use of genetic counselors in addition to physicians a solution to the latters' lack of knowledge about genetics? One problem is the lack of

sufficient numbers of counselors. In 2011, for example, there were at least 15 U.S. states with less than five reported genetic counselors in the entire state, including several, such as Wyoming and the Dakotas, in which there were one or no reported counselors. Alice K. Hawkins & Michael R. Hayden, A Grand Challenge: Providing Benefits of Clinical Genetics To Those In Need, 13 Genetics in Med. 197 (2011).

2.   One approach Matthews describes for identifying whether counseling is directive or non-directive is whether the counselor answers the question "What would you do in my situation?" One reason people may consult health care professionals is to obtain the professional's expert opinion on what to do. How appropriate is it for professionals to refuse to provide this advice? Is there a way to provide advice in a non-directive manner? If not, is the goal of non-directiveness misguided?

3.   Although, in theory, genetic counseling is non-directive, the reality is somewhat different. See Barbara A. Bernhardt, Empirical Evidence That Genetic Counseling Is Directive: Where Do We Go From Here?, 60 Am. J. Human Genetics 17 (1997). It is also clear from consumer surveys that clients do not want complete non-directiveness.

4.   For a discussion of privacy issues in genetic counseling, see Barbara Bowles Biesecker, Privacy in Genetic Counseling, in Genetic Secrets: Protecting Privacy and Confidentiality in the Genetic Era 108–125 (Mark A. Rothstein ed. 1997). For a discussion of the role of genetic counselors in prenatal screening, see Sonia Suter, The Routinization of Prenatal Testing, 28 Am. J. L. & Med. 233 (2002).

C. GENETIC TESTING OF CHILDREN AND ADOLESCENTS

Genetic testing of minors creates special problems. For example, when, if ever, is it appropriate to test children and adolescents? Is it ever appropriate to test them without their knowledge and consent? Without the assent of their parents? What if the minor and parents disagree? Who should have access to the test results?

AMERICAN SOCIETY OF HUMAN GENETICS AND AMERICAN
COLLEGE OF MEDICAL GENETICS, POINTS TO CONSIDER:
ETHICAL, LEGAL, AND PSYCHOSOCIAL IMPLICATIONS OF
GENETIC TESTING IN CHILDREN AND ADOLESCENTS
57 Am. J. Human Gen. 1233 (1995).

Rapid developments in genetic knowledge and technologies increase the ability to test asymptomatic children for late-onset diseases, disease susceptibilities, and carrier status. These developments raise ethical and legal issues that focus on the interests of children and their parents. Although parents are presumed to promote the well-being of their children, a request for a genetic test may have negative implications for children, and the health-care provider must be prepared to acknowledge and discuss such issues with families.

This report is grounded in several social concepts: First, the primary goal of genetic testing should be to promote the well-being of the child. Second, the recognition that children are part of a network of family relationships supports an approach to potential conflicts that is not adversarial but, rather, emphasizes a deliberative process that seeks to promote the child's well-being within this context. Third, as children grow through successive stages of cognitive and moral development, parents and professionals should be attentive to the child's increasing interest and ability to participate in decisions about his or her own welfare.

Counseling and communication with the child and family about genetic testing should include the following components: (1) assessment of the significance of the potential benefits and harms of the test, (2) determination of the decision-making capacity of the child, and (3) advocacy on behalf of the interests of the child. The following points should be considered:

I.   POINTS TO CONSIDER

A.   *The Impact of Potential Benefits and Harms on Decisions about Testing*

1.   *Timely medical benefit to the child should be the primary justification for genetic testing in children and adolescents.* Under this condition, genetic testing is similar to other medical diagnostic evaluations. Medical benefits include preventive measures and therapies, as well as diagnostic information about symptomatic children. If the medical benefits are uncertain or will be deferred to a later time, this justification for testing is less compelling.

2.   *Substantial psychosocial benefits to the competent adolescent also may be a justification for genetic testing.* The benefits and harms of many genetic tests are psychosocial rather than physical. Relevant issues include anxiety, self-image, uncertainty, and the impact on decisions relating to reproduction, education, career, insurance, and lifestyle.

3.   *If the medical or psychosocial benefits of a genetic test will not accrue until adulthood, as in the case of carrier status or adult-onset diseases, genetic testing generally should be deferred.* Exceptions to this principle might occur when the adolescent meets conditions of competence, voluntariness, and adequate understanding of information. Further consultation with other genetic services providers, pediatricians, psychologists, and

ethics committees may be appropriate to evaluate these conditions.

4. *If the balance of benefits and harms is uncertain, the provider should respect the decision of competent adolescents and their families.* These decisions should be based on the unique circumstances of each family. The provider should enter into a thorough discussion about the potential benefits and harms and should assess the family's understanding of these issues.

5. *Testing should be discouraged when the provider determines that potential harms of genetic testing in children and adolescents outweigh the potential benefits.* A health-care provider has no obligation to provide a medical service for a child or adolescent that is not in the best interest of the child or adolescent.

B. *The Family's Involvement in Decision Making*

1. *Education and counseling for parents and the child, commensurate on maturity, should precede genetic testing.* Follow-up genetic counseling and psychological counseling also should be readily available. Providers of genetic testing should be prepared to educate, counsel, and refer, as appropriate.

2. *The provider should obtain the permission of the parents and, as appropriate, the assent of the child or consent of the adolescent.* Decisions about competence should not depend arbitrarily on the child's age but should be based on an evaluation of the child's cognitive and moral development. The provider should also attempt to establish that the child's decision is voluntary.

3. *The provider is obligated to advocate on behalf of the child when he or she considers a genetic test to be—or not to be— in the best interest of the child.* Continued discussion about the potential benefits and harms—and about the interests of the child—may be helpful in reaching a consensus.

4. *A request by a competent adolescent for the results of a genetic test should be given priority over parents' requests to conceal information.* When possible, these issues should be explored prior to testing. When a younger child is tested and the parents request that the provider not reveal results, the provider should engage the parents in an ongoing discussion about the benefits and harms of the nondisclosure, the child's interest in the information, and when and in what manner the results should be disclosed.

NOTES AND QUESTIONS

1. Minors of the same age differ in terms of their maturity. Do all of the foregoing sets of recommendations take this into consideration? How should maturity and mental competence be measured? For an overview, see Leonard H. Glantz, Research with Children, 24 Am. J. L. & Med. 213 (1998).

Typically, age restrictions under the law, such as minimum ages for driving or voting, are irrebuttable presumptions; minors are not permitted to argue that they should qualify for the privilege despite being under-age. Which of the foregoing recommendations advocate irrebuttable presumptions with regard to genetic testing of minors? Which advocate rebuttable presumptions? Should the approach for rules regarding genetic testing be different than for rules for, say, driving or voting? Why?

In some cases, the recommendations state that the rules for genetic testing of children and adolescents should be the same as the general rules for medical treatment or for medical research using children and adolescents as subjects. What are those rules? Are they different for treatment and research? For example, are children given the power to veto medical treatment? What about vetoing their participation in research? If the rules differ for the research and treatment contexts, which rules should apply to genetic testing?

2. What benefits might accrue from genetic testing of minors and adolescents? Which of these benefits do the foregoing recommendations recognize? Which harms? How do the recommendations balance benefit and harm? Do you agree with the result?

One issue is the impact of genetic test information on the child or adolescent. A number of studies suggest that disclosing test results to children is preferable to postponing the disclosure until they are adults. Do the recommendations agree?

3. The Huntington Disease Society of America recommends against testing asymptomatic minors for Huntington disease, a nontreatable, adult-onset disease. Nevertheless, 53 percent of health professionals stated that they would perform the testing at the request of parents. In a survey of genetic testing laboratories, 22 percent reported that they performed tests for Huntington disease in children under the age of 12. Is it desirable that there be a single, uniform national policy on genetic testing of children and adolescents? Who should administer such a policy?

D. ACCESS TO GENETIC SERVICES

Genetic testing can provide valuable information to aid in the diagnosis and treatment of genetic disease. As with any new medical technology, however, it may not be readily accessible to the public. A number of factors may limit access. The person may not know he or she is ill or at risk, and not seek professional services. Alternatively, the individual's primary care physician may not be familiar with the genetic basis of the condition in question; as noted earlier in this chapter in the excerpt from the 1997 Report of the Task Force on Genetic Testing, many physicians are not adequately informed about genetics or genetic testing. As a result, the primary care physician may not suggest testing to the patient, or refer the patient to a clinical geneticist or genetic counselor for additional information. Even if the patient is aware of the possibility of testing, health care professionals for ethical reasons may decline to provide testing. Many health care professionals reject parental requests for certain types of predictive testing for children.

As discussed in Chapters 15 and 16, even if health care professionals recommend testing, individuals may decline because of fears of discrimination.

Finally, genetic testing may not be covered by the person's health insurance, and depending on how expensive it is, the person may not be able to afford to pay for it out-of-pocket. Some genetic tests can be obtained for little more than $100 (for hereditary hemochromatosis at some laboratories, with free genetic counseling). But other tests, together with counseling, cost several thousand dollars.

MAXWELL J. MEHLMAN, ACCESS TO THE GENOME AND FEDERAL ENTITLEMENT PROGRAMS, IN THE HUMAN GENOME PROJECT AND THE FUTURE OF HEALTH CARE
119–123 (Thomas H. Murray et al. eds. 1997).

TRENDS IN ACCESS

To predict how FEPs [federal entitlement programs] are likely to cope with the demand for genetic services that will result from the HGP [Human Genome Project], we can examine how these programs are reacting to pressures to increase access, on the one hand, and to reduce health care spending on the other.

One way or another, limits on access due to the inability to meet eligibility criteria are bound to disappear. Whether the approach that eventually is taken will be to expand eligibility under the FEPs themselves, or to create new governmental entitlement programs, or to mandate that individuals be covered under private insurance, is unclear.
* * *

At the same time that it faces pressures to expand eligibility, however, the government also is being called upon to reduce national health care expenditures. The movement to expand third-party payment programs removes a common method of reducing spending: limiting access by restricting eligibility. To stem budget increases, for example, state Medicaid programs traditionally have lowered income thresholds in order to exclude persons who would otherwise be eligible. Prior to the increase in eligibility to cover all persons with incomes below the federal poverty level, or FPL, for example, the Oregon Medicaid program only provided benefits to persons who qualified for AFDC [Aid to Families with Dependent Children] if their incomes fell below 58 percent of the FPL.

Even if the federal government mandates universal health insurance, it might impose eligibility restrictions under future FEPs. For example, if Medicare and Medicaid were retained and government-subsidized private health insurance were provided for those who were not covered by FEPs or insured by their employers, a means test might be added to the eligibility criteria for Medicare, with those persons over 65 who had incomes or assets above the means threshold relegated to purchasing private insurance with their own funds. So long as the nation remained committed to providing universal access to health care, however, this would merely shift costs from government to private programs rather than lowering overall spending. Therefore, the government will need to pursue other methods in order to curtail health care costs.

Undoubtedly; the federal government will attempt to reduce prices for health care, and it will be aided in doing so by the increased leverage it will have as a result of the expansion of eligibility under government programs. However, price controls alone are unlikely to be able to curtail spending in the face of increased demand for services, particularly for genetic services stemming from the HGP. The government will continue to feel strong pressure to restrict access to health care generally, and to new, expensive genetic services in particular. Having lost the ability to restrict access by limiting eligibility, the government will be left instead with the options of co-payment, and restrictions on coverage and/or availability.

Maintaining or increasing the amounts that individuals pay for health care under government programs might be one way of limiting access to the genetic services that will emerge from the HGP. Those persons who could not afford the co-payments would not receive services, even though they were technically "eligible" for benefits. Medicare in particular has increased co-payments as a means to help control program costs. * * * Furthermore, the most recent effort to *reduce* co-payments under Medicare—the Medicare Catastrophic Coverage Act—failed miserably when Congress repealed the law under pressure from those elderly persons who would have footed the bill.

Co-payments represent fairly obvious limitations on access, however. In a nation committed to universal access, they are likely to be increasingly unacceptable as a cost-containment approach.

The same is true of overt restrictions on availability, or supply, particularly those that affect specific geographic areas or minority populations. For example, the government is likely to be under political pressure to increase the number of physicians and facilities for rural and inner-city residents. Yet shortages are likely to be an inevitable result of efforts to control costs, particularly if prices for health care are forced down substantially. Hospitals may be unwilling to purchase new technologies if their revenues are reduced, and health care professionals may refuse to treat patients who cannot supplement third-party reimbursement from their own resources. The government might try to force unwilling providers to treat patients, but it is unclear if it could do so successfully; or what the effect would be, for example, on the number of physicians entering or remaining in the market.

Furthermore, the government may be tempted to foster shortages deliberately as a method to contain costs, particularly if it can rationalize its behavior as something other than overt rationing. For example, the government might assert that it was merely encouraging "regionalization" or volume-based "centers of excellence" for certain high-technology services. This technique appears to be employed by national health systems such as Canada's, for example, where widespread queuing, at least for elective services, is reported. Whether deliberate or not, therefore, limitations on access as a result of the unavailability of services are likely to persist.

The final approach to limiting access is to restrict coverage. Faced with budget shortfalls, the government might well insist that it is unable to provide access under FEPs to specific services, particularly to the new, cost-increasing technologies emerging from the HGP.

While Medicare law precludes coverage for certain categories of services such as dental, eye, and nursing home care, as noted earlier, the Medicare program historically has defined the scope of covered services very broadly: The law itself stipulates that, with the exception of the categorical exclusions, beneficiaries are entitled to all items and services that are "reasonable and necessary for the diagnosis or treatment of illness or injury or to improve the functioning of a malformed body part." This has been interpreted to preclude the government from refusing to pay for care on the ground that it is too expensive. In 1989 the Health Care Financing Administration (HCFA) proposed to allow Medicare to refuse to cover a technology if it was not "cost effective"—that is, if it yielded no greater net benefit than a cheaper alternative. This proposal has triggered intense opposition, and was never finalized. In any-event, such a regulation would have little impact on new, cost-increasing technologies for which there were no alternatives, which is likely to be characteristic of many genetic services emerging from the HGP.

As a result of the scope of coverage embodied in the statutory language, it has been difficult for the government to limit coverage of specific technologies under Medicare in order to achieve cost savings. The government has had some success in controlling cost by limiting the amount of time patients can remain in the hospital. * * * Restrictions on length of stay alone do not discourage access to specific technologies, however, and would be of little use in restricting access to new genetic services.

The primary method by which the government has limited access to new technologies under Medicare has been to deem them "experimental." For many years, for example, Medicare refused to pay for heart transplants on the ground that their safety and efficacy had not been adequately demonstrated, and that therefore they had not been shown to be "reasonable and necessary." Medicare finally agreed to cover the transplants in 1979, but only if they were performed at the Stanford Medical Center. This policy lasted only nine months, at which time the HCFA revoked Stanford's authorization on the basis that the government lacked adequate data on the success and long-term implications of transplant technology. It was not until 1990 that Medicare once again agreed to reimburse for heart transplants, but then only under strict criteria limiting both the hospitals that could perform the procedure and the patients who could be selected.

The technologies emerging from the HGP initially will be experimental, and it will be some time before Medicare can be expected to reimburse providers for them. How much time it will take will depend on the significance of the expected benefit from the technology; the ratio of benefits to risks, and the degree of demand from both patients and health care professionals. Recent experience with AIDS drugs suggests that the government can be forced to accelerate the transition from experimental to therapeutic (and reimbursable) status given enough public clamor. This is likely to be the pattern for genetic services that promise to prevent or ameliorate serious genetic disorders.

Even after the safety and efficacy of a technology has been demonstrated, the government may delay paying for it on the basis that it remains experimental when the real reason is to hold down costs. For example, it is widely believed that the government has continued to maintain that heart transplants and certain other new technologies are experimental in large part in order to contain program costs. The government might be expected to resist paying for expensive, new genetic services under Medicare for the same reason.

Coverage restrictions under Medicare that limited access to genetic services on the basis of cost are not likely to survive for long, however. The elder lobby is too powerful, and its political power is growing as the population continues to age. Coincidentally, the post-World War II baby boom generation will become eligible for Medicare at approximately the same time that the HGP is expected to be completed. Even if younger voters somehow acquired the ability to thwart the interests of the elderly, they may be unwilling to restrict access to services that they may someday need themselves.

In contrast to Medicare, the Medicaid program is much more likely to restrict coverage of expensive, new technologies. A trend in this direction already is apparent. Until 1988 federal law required state Medicaid programs to provide liver transplants in order to receive federal matching funds. Coverage for these procedures became optional in 1988, and many states have since refused to reimburse for them. The Oregon demonstration project is even more far-ranging. * * * It has created a list of health services ranked on the basis of importance, and denies coverage for all services below an arbitrary cutoff chosen by the state legislature on the basis of budgetary constraints.

* * *

Several factors explain why the trend for Medicaid is so different from Medicare. First, the law underlying the Medicaid program is less clear-cut than the Medicare statute in terms of what services must be provided. There is no statutory language for Medicaid comparable to the "reasonable and necessary" standard under Medicare. Although courts generally have engrafted the Medicare standard onto Medicaid, they have shown some willingness to allow states to deny coverage for services because of their cost.

A second reason that Medicaid is likely to restrict overage is the growth of the program as a proportion of state budgets. * * * State budgetary woes have convinced the middle class that the only alternative to increasing taxes is to decrease the scope of benefits provided under Medicaid and other programs for the poor.

In contrast to the growing political dominance of elder Americans, the political power of the poor is weak. While everyone eventually hopes to be eligible for Medicare, most middle-and upper-class taxpayers never expect to be eligible for Medicaid, and therefore have no incentive to retain a generous coverage policy many consider to be contrary to their own self-interest.

Finally, coverage restrictions under Medicaid have been rationalized on the basis that they forestall cuts in eligibility. As noted earlier, the customary method for trimming Medicaid budgets has been to disqualify individuals from being entitled to any benefits, such as by lowering income thresholds. Limited coverage would seem preferable to none at all. Going a step farther, the Oregon project has justified its coverage limits on the basis that they allow the state to *expand* Medicaid eligibility, and to provide benefits, albeit incomplete, to all persons whose incomes are below the federal poverty level.

In summary, if current trends continue eligibility under FEPs is likely to increase, with more individuals entitled to receive benefits. To hold down costs, the government may try to increase the proportion that individuals must pay for their own care, and to promote "health planning" measures that limit the availability of services in certain geographic areas, but these efforts will be constrained by political pressures aimed at assuring access to some level of health care for all citizens. The most promising approach for limiting health care spending at the same time that eligibility restrictions are relaxed is to deny coverage under FEPs for certain technologies, particularly those that are new and expensive, and particularly for politically weak patient populations such as the poor.

MARK A. ROTHSTEIN & SHARONA HOFFMAN, GENETIC TESTING, GENETIC MEDICINE, AND MANAGED CARE
34 Wake Forest L. Rev. 849, 875–876 (1999).

Managed care organizations vary widely in their coverage and provision of genetic tests. According to a 1997 survey, of 197 responding HMOs, 45% covered predictive tests for breast cancer. In addition, 42% covered tests for colon cancer for some of their subscribers.

Managed care organizations first must decide whether a particular genetic test should be offered at all to their patient population and then whether it is appropriate for any particular individual.

* * *

A few general principles can be articulated. Managed care entities should not adopt a per se rule of refusing predictive testing in the absence of an effective intervention, because, at times, knowledge itself provides tremendous psychological comfort or invaluable opportunities for life planning in light of a known future. Individuals at-risk should neither be coerced into testing nor discouraged from undergoing appropriate genetic testing. Furthermore, genetic testing must be accompanied by suitable genetic counseling both before and after the testing. Currently, genetic counseling is often not covered by insurance and genetic counselors cannot bill separately for their services. Counseling, however, should be covered by the insurer to ensure its availability to all patients, regardless of their financial resources.

RACHEL REBOUCHÉ & KAREN ROTHENBERG, MIXED MESSAGES: THE INTERSECTION OF PRENATAL GENETIC TESTING AND ABORTION
55 How. L.J. 983, 993–996 (2012).

Medicaid programs cover the costs of prenatal genetic screenings in thirty-six states and the District of Columbia and testing in forty-seven states for particular categories of women. In addition, Medicaid programs in twenty-four states cover the costs of genetic counseling. Although state Medicaid programs vary, Congress has made clear that testing and abortion are not synonymous. No Medicaid programs may cover abortion costs unless the mother's life is in danger or the pregnancy arises from rape or incest.

The ACA will expand testing and screening services by increasing Medicaid coverage. The ACA promises to provide new health insurance coverage to approximately thirteen million women of childbearing age through extending Medicaid eligibility or through state-based exchanges. The expansion of Medicaid will be of significant value to pregnant women: over forty percent of U.S. women rely on Medicaid for prenatal care. By introducing higher incomes caps for Medicaid eligibility, even more women will qualify for low-cost or free testing and screening.

The ACA also outlines requirements of what "essential benefits" health insurance plans must offer without cost-sharing (co-payments, co-insurance, or deductibles, for example). Maternity and newborn care is an essential health care benefit, although the ACA does not explicitly reference prenatal genetic testing or screening. In December, the Obama Administration decided that each state, rather than the Secretary of HHS, would determine the definition and scope of essential benefits, leaving the inclusion of testing and screening as prenatal care for states to determine.

Prenatal genetic testing and screening might also be part of the preventive services that qualified health plans must cover. The definitions and scope of preventative services were set out in guidelines issued by the Health Resources and Services Administration (HRSA). In August 2011, the Secretary of HHS approved the guidelines submitted by the HRSA. Among other important features, the regulations include a well-woman visit, which incorporates prenatal care, in the definition of preventative treatment. Although neither the guidelines nor the recommendations spell out what prenatal care involves, an Institute of Medicine (IOM) report, on which the HRSA relied, suggests that screening and testing are part of prenatal care. In describing the routine coverage of private plans and public programs, the IOM report stated: "Pregnant women should receive . . . prenatal screening and testing for neural tube defects (for all women at elevated risk) and chromosomal abnormalities (for all women age 35 years and older), including, but not limited to amniocentesis, chorionic villus sampling, and ultrasound."

These recommendations represent the present consensus among health care professionals about which women should have testing or screening (women of advanced maternal age) and for what conditions (disorders that traditional technologies can recognize). Because the IOM

Committee on Preventative Services for Women is tasked with "regularly updating the preventative screenings and services to be considered," recommendations on genetic testing and screening can change over time and may create a forum in which new technology will influence revisions of HHS policy.

NOTES AND QUESTIONS

1.   You are the medical director of a large health plan. What process should the plan use to decide whether to provide coverage of genetic testing? What criteria should it employ?

2.   In April 2005, the Secretary's Advisory Committee on Genetics, Health, and Society issued a draft report entitled "Coverage and Reimbursement of Genetic Tests and Services." Among its "potential" recommendations was that the Secretary of Health and Human Services should "task an appropriate group or body to develop a set of principles to guide coverage decision making for genetic tests."

3.   For a further discussion of health insurance coverage, see Chapter 15.

E. INCIDENTAL FINDINGS

PRESIDENTIAL COMMISSION FOR THE STUDY OF BIOETHICAL ISSUES, ANTICIPATE AND COMMUNICATE: ETHICAL MANAGEMENT OF INCIDENTAL AND SECONDARY FINDINGS IN THE CLINICAL, RESEARCH, AND DIRECT-TO-CONSUMER CONTEXTS
(2013).

* * *

Incidental findings—traditionally defined as results that arise that are outside the original purpose for which the test or procedure was conducted—can create a range of practical, legal, and ethical challenges for recipients and practitioners. Discovering an incidental finding can be lifesaving, but it also can lead to uncertainty and distress without any corresponding improvement in health or wellbeing. For incidental findings of unknown significance, conducting additional follow-up tests or procedures can be risky and costly. Moreover, there is tremendous variation among potential recipients about whether, when, and how they would choose to have incidental findings disclosed. Information that one recipient regards as an unnecessary cause of anxiety could lead another recipient to feel empowered in making health-related decisions.

* * *

For clinicians and patients, one of the most challenging aspects of an incidental finding is determining what should be done in response. In some cases, clinical investigation of such a finding can lead to a diagnosis and beneficial, perhaps even lifesaving, treatment. In many other cases, however, further testing reveals that the incidental finding would have had no health consequences if left untreated. Pursuing an incidental finding might require conducting additional diagnostic tests or procedures that expose patients to additional risk, anxiety, or other psychological ramifications. If the finding turns out to have no medical significance, patients undertake these additional risks, including the risk of further incidental findings, without corresponding benefit.

For a variety of reasons, clinicians might be motivated to pursue diagnostic workups of incidental findings even when a clinician's professional judgment suggests that such workup is unnecessary. This motivation could stem, in part, from the prevailing notion that learning more information necessarily means providing better care. Both clinicians and patients can have difficulty accepting this uncertainty, even if certainty is unlikely to be obtained through additional testing. And ignoring an incidental finding or pursuing a "wait and see" course of action, often referred to as "watchful waiting," might be questioned if this decision results in a poor outcome. Clinicians might be motivated by patients and their families who prefer to be "better safe than sorry," without fully understanding that pursuing incidental findings often entails additional risks. Clinicians also might be motivated to err on the side of investigating incidental findings for fear of legal action, even though data on the motivations and rates of litigation do not substantiate these fears. In addition, clinicians might choose to seek secondary findings when suggested by professional guidance, such as the recent recommendations by the American College of Genetics and Genomics (ACMG) that laboratories seek and report a list of actionable genetic variants whenever clinical genomic sequencing is conducted.

* * *

To date, few reported U.S. medical malpractice cases (as opposed to those settled out of court) have addressed clinician liability for failure to identify or disclose incidental findings. A recent study evaluating this limited body of case law concluded that it is possible that clinicians could face liability for failure to identify or appreciate the significance of an incidental finding, or failure to disclose an incidental finding to the patient or other clinicians, if recognition and disclosure would have prevented or altered the course of future disease. In the 2006 case of Riley v. Stone, however, a Rhode Island court found that the defendant neurologist did not breach the standard of care when he failed to further assess an incidental finding that he deemed not to pose a danger to the patient.

* * *

Clinicians should make patients aware that incidental and secondary findings are a possible, or likely, result of the tests or procedures being conducted. Clinicians should engage in shared decision making with patients about the scope of findings that will be communicated and the steps to be taken upon discovery of incidental findings. Clinicians should respect a patient's preference not to know about incidental or secondary findings to the extent consistent with the clinician's fiduciary duty.

* * *

Professional and public health organizations should produce evidence-based standards for proposed screening programs that take into account the likelihood that incidental findings will arise. Professional organizations should provide guidance to clinicians on how to manage these incidental findings.

ACMG POLICY STATEMENT: UPDATED RECOMMENDATIONS REGARDING ANALYSIS AND REPORTING OF SECONDARY FINDINGS IN CLINICAL GENOME-SCALE SEQUENCING

Genetics in Medicine, Nov. 13, 2014,
http://www.nature.com/gim/journal/v16/n4/pdf/gim201415a.pdf.

As genome-scale sequencing is increasingly applied in clinical medicine, complex issues arise regarding the extent to which primary data should be analyzed and reported. At the present time, the most common clinical application of massively parallel sequencing lies in its use as a powerful new diagnostic tool in selected patients. When such sequencing is performed, primary data files consisting of a vast number of genomic variants are generated for each individual, with that information varying greatly with regard to relevance to the specific diagnostic question. What to do with these large numbers of "secondary" or "incidental" variants (nomenclature has varied with regard to such findings; the American College of Medical Genetics and Genomics (ACMG) has now adopted "secondary findings" as standard nomenclature, as recommended by the Presidential Commission on Bioethical Issues) has been a matter of considerable debate and discussion. Challenges include how extensively the primary data should be routinely analyzed and which of the many variants discovered should be reported to patients. These questions are especially challenging because although many of these variants are not clinically relevant or are uninterpretable, a minority may have important medical implications for the individual sequenced as well as for other family members.

In March 2013, the ACMG issued a set of recommendations regarding the use of clinical-scale sequencing. One recommendation advised laboratories performing whole-exome sequencing or whole-genome sequencing for any clinical indication to specifically analyze the sequence of 57 (later revised to 56) genes. These genes were selected based on substantial clinical evidence that pathogenic variants result in a high likelihood of severe disease that is preventable if identified before symptoms occur.

The release of this set of recommendations resulted in considerable discussion, much of it focused on whether the analysis of these 56 genes should be "mandatory" when whole-exome/whole-genome sequencing is pursued clinically, or whether patients should be able to "opt out" of such secondary analysis and reporting. This discussion was informed by a report by the Presidential Commission on Bioethical Issues regarding secondary findings and a survey administered by the ACMG to its membership in January 2014. In March 2014, the ACMG updated its recommendations, prompted in part by what appeared to be a general consensus among ACMG members and other relevant stakeholders that patients should be able to opt out of the analysis of genes unrelated to the indication for testing, and that the decision should be made during the process of informed consent before testing.

In this issue of *Genetics in Medicine*, we publish the results of this survey and articulate the current recommendations of the ACMG with regard to the analysis and return of secondary findings when clinical genome-scale analysis is pursued.

- When clinical genome-scale (e.g., whole-exome sequencing, whole-genome sequencing) sequencing is performed, written informed consent should be obtained by a qualified genetics health-care professional describing the nature of the test and addressing points such as interpretive uncertainty, privacy, possible impact on other family members, and the inevitable generation of data not immediately relevant to the clinical indication for sequencing. At the time of testing, the patient should be made aware that, regardless of the specific indication for testing, laboratories will routinely analyze the sequence of a set of genes deemed to be highly medically actionable so as to detect pathogenic variants that may predispose to a severe but preventable outcome.

- Patients should be informed during the consent process that, if desired, they may opt out of such analysis. However, they should also be made aware at that time of the ramifications of doing so.

- In accordance with the recent recommendations of the Presidential Commission for the Study of Bioethical Issues, as well as a lack of clear consensus in the ACMG membership survey administered in January 2014, the board recommends that the same policy should be adhered to in children as in adults; i.e., analysis of a set of selected genes to identify pathogenic variants associated with severe but preventable disease should be routinely performed. Parents should have the option during the consent process to opt out of such analysis.

• At this time, given the practical concerns and inherent difficulty of counseling patients about the features of each disorder and every gene on an ever-changing list, it is not feasible for patients to be offered the option of choosing a subset of medically actionable genes for analysis. Thus, the decision regarding routine analysis should apply to the entire set of genes deemed actionable by the ACMG.

The ACMG recognizes the complex nature of policies surrounding genome-scale testing and that positions will continue to evolve and change in response to new knowledge, new technologies, and ongoing input and discussion with our membership and the broader medical community. The ACMG will continue to explore these issues in the best interest of patients. A multidisciplinary working group has been formed to develop a process for updating and maintaining the list of genes to be routinely analyzed for secondary findings.

NOTES AND QUESTIONS

1.   To say, as the preceding publication states, that the original ACMG Policy Statement "resulted in considerable discussion" is a huge understatement. The original statement promulgated a list of 57 mutations that must be tested for any time that clinical gene sequencing occured and required that the test results be reported to the clinician who ordered the sequencing, without offering the patient a choice. This provoked widespread condemnation as a violation of patients' rights. See, e.g., Lainie Friedman Ross, Mark A. Rothstein, & Ellen Wright Clayton, Mandatory Extended Searches in All Genome Sequencing: "Incidental Findings," Patient Autonomy, and Shared Decision Making, 310 JAMA 367 (2013); Robert Klitzman, Paul S. Appelbaum & Wendy Chung, Return of Secondary Genomic Findings vs. Patient Autonomy: Implications for Medical Care, 310 J. L. Biosciences 369 (2013). For additional information about the controversy, see Anastasia Richardson, Incidental Findings and Future Testing Methodologies: Potential Application of the ACMG 2013 Recommendations, 1 J. Law & Biosciences 378 (2014).

2.   Under the Health Insurance Portability and Accountability Act (HIPAA), individuals have the right to access genetic information in their medical records. However, HIPAA exempted information possessed by clinical laboratories certified under the Clinical Laboratories Improvement Act (CLIA)—the type of laboratory that typically handles genetic tests for

clinical (as opposed to purely research) purposes. (See the discussion of the regulation of genetic testing in Chapter 12.) In 2014, federal regulations under HIPAA were amended to remove the exemption for CLIA labs. Under HIPAA, therefore, patients potentially now have a right to request their genetic test results directly from the lab, bypassing the physician who ordered the test. See 79 Fed. Reg. 7289 (Feb. 6, 2014). However, the amended regulation contains the following exception: "A licensed health care professional has determined, in the exercise of professional judgment, that the access requested is reasonably likely to endanger the life or physical safety of the individual or another person." 45 C.F.R. §164.524(a)(3)(i). In the Federal Register notice accompanying the amended regulations, the Department of Health and Human Services explained this exception as follows: "We do not believe that this rule will eliminate or interfere with the role or obligation of the treating or ordering provider to report and counsel patients on laboratory test results. The rule provides ample time to ensure providers receive sensitive test reports before the patient and to allow providers to counsel individuals on the test reports. In addition, as indicated above, we believe the rule will further encourage providers, at the time the test is ordered, to counsel patients on the potential outcomes of a test and what they may mean for the patient, given his or her medical history." The regulations give the patient the right to request a review of a lab's refusal to provide access to test results; the review is to be conducted by a "licensed health care professional who is designated by the covered entity to act as a reviewing official and who did not participate in the original decision to deny." 45 C.F.R. §164.524(a)(4). What effect do you expect the amended regulation to have on the practice of clinical genetic testing?

3.   Genetic testing can be used intentionally to establish whether a man is the biological father of a child. This is discussed more fully in Chapter 11. However, genetic tests for therapeutic purposes sometimes reveal that the presumed father of a child is not the biological father. Since the purpose of the test was to aid in the diagnosis or treatment of the child, rather than to establish biological parenthood, this finding is termed "unanticipated non-paternity" or misattributed paternity. Health care professionals providing the testing face difficult questions about what to do with this information. As one expert points out, routine disclosure may disrupt the family unit and cause physical, psychological, social, or economic harm to women, especially those in abusive relationships or those who are economically disadvantaged. An alternative is to only disclose the information to the woman and let her decide whether to reveal it to the man, which was the approach recommended by the Institute of Medicine's Committee on Assessing Genetic Risks in 1994, but this approach violates the principal that the genetic counselor owes equal ethical and legal obligations to both partners. Another approach is to address the issue before testing takes place as part of the informed consent process. However, raising the question of paternity may produce anxiety and lead women to reject genetic testing that may be of benefit to themselves and their families. Jean McEwen, Genetic Information, Ethics, and Information Relating to Biological Parenthood In Encyclopedia of Ethical, Legal, and

Policy Issues in Biotechnology 356, 359–362 (Thomas H. Murray & Maxwell J. Mehlman eds. 2000). Which of the approaches described by McEwen is the best and why? Can intentional nondisclosure or misrepresentation of paternity ever be justified?

V.   CANCER GENOMICS

Worldwide, cancer kills approximately eight million people each year. Recent developments in genomics have had a profound effect on the risk assessment, prevention, diagnosis, and treatment of a wide range of cancers. Indeed, genome sequencing of tumors is quickly becoming the standard of care in oncology. Two major initiatives are attempting to increase the scale of discovery in cancer genomics.

The Cancer Genome Atlas is a joint research program of the National Cancer Institute and the National Human Genome Research Institute at NIH. Its goal is to compile an atlas of the genomic structures of the 200 or more types of cancer. Understanding the genomic structure of the various types of cancer will aid in cancer prevention, early detection, and treatment. For further information, see cancergenome.nih.gov.

The International Cancer Genome Consortium is an international collaboration to obtain comprehensive descriptions of genomic, transcriptomic, and epigenomic changes in multiple tumor types and subtypes. For further information, see icgc.org.

The following excerpts review some of the recent advances and consider the next steps in cancer genomics.

LEVI A. GARRAWAY, GENOMICS DRIVEN ONCOLOGY: FRAMEWORK FOR AN EMERGING PARADIGM
31 J. Clinical Oncology 1806, 1806–1813 (2013).

Over the past decade, the oncology field has witnessed the advent of versatile means to test the hypothesis that comprehensive genomic information will enable rational therapeutic choices and improve outcomes for patients with cancer. The coming decade should produce the first wave of clinical studies that evaluate key tenets of genomics-driven cancer medicine. This accelerating pace of research invites consideration (albeit highly speculative) of what the world might ultimately look like on completion of the precision medicine experiment in oncology.

It should be emphasized that the genomics-driven paradigm is complementary to other frameworks currently shaping oncology therapeutic development (such as immunotherapy, targeting of the tumor microenvironment, or stem cell-based treatments). From the early observations of Sakurai and Sandberg to the present day, investigators have recognized that tumor genomic features must be evaluated as part of a larger clinical context that includes age, performance status, disease burden, cancer cell lineage, and histologic/molecular features when pondering treatment decisions. As with all medical advances, the emerging genomic framework must eventually become fully integrated within the existing spectrum of clinical knowledge leveraged by the oncologist to produce an optimal management plan.

Although knowledge of genomics may conceivably effect a profound transformation in the management of aggressive or advanced cancer, this prospect hardly represents a foregone conclusion. It is equally possible that the impact of genomics will prove more limited, particularly if clinical actionability is constrained by drug toxicity, tumor heterogeneity, or the overall complexity of tumor genomic information. Alternatively, the impact may prove substantive but not transformative; for example, genomic profiling may become relevant to some but not all cancer subtypes. Whatever the final outcome, the precision oncology hypothesis has certainly proved itself worthy of detailed interrogation during the coming years. In the words of Theodore Roosevelt, navigating the triumphs and challenges of genomics-driven cancer medicine will offer many oncologists "the chance to work hard at work worth doing."

BERT VOGELSTEIN ET AL., CANCER GENOME LANDSCAPES
339 Science 1546 (2013).

* * *

When we think about eradicating cancer, we generally think about curing advanced cases—those that cannot be cured by surgery alone because they have already metastasized. This is a curious way of thinking about this disease. When we think of cardiovascular or infectious diseases, we first consider ways to prevent them rather than drugs to cure their most advanced forms. Today, we are in no better position to cure polio or massive myocardial infarctions than we were a thousand years ago. But we can prevent these diseases entirely (vaccines), reduce incidence (dietary changes, statins), or mitigate severity (stents, thrombolytic agents) and thereby make a major impact on morbidity and mortality.

This focus on curing advanced cancers might have been reasonable 50 years ago, when the molecular pathogenesis of cancers was mysterious and when chemotherapeutic agents against advanced cancers were showing promise. But this mindset is no longer acceptable. We now know precisely what causes cancer: a sequential series of alterations in well-defined genes that alter the function of a limited number of pathways. Moreover, we know that this process takes decades to develop and that the incurable stage, metastasis, occurs only a few years before death. In other words, of the one million people that will die from cancer this year, the vast majority will die only because their cancers were not detected in the first 90% of the cancers' lifetimes, when they were amenable to the surgeons' scalpel.

This new knowledge of cancer has reinvigorated the search for cures for advanced cancers, but has not yet permeated other fields of applied cancer research. A common and limited set of driver genes and pathways is responsible for most common forms of cancer; these genes and pathways offer distinct potential for early diagnosis. The genes themselves, the proteins encoded by these genes, and the end products of their pathways are, in principle, detectable in many ways, including analyses of relevant body fluids, such as urine for genitourinary cancers, sputum for lung cancers, and stool for gastrointestinal cancers. Equally exciting are the possibilities afforded by molecular imaging, which not only indicate the presence of a cancer but also reveal its precise location and extent. Additionally, research into the relationship between particular environmental influences (diet and lifestyle) and the genetic alterations in cancer is sparse, despite its potential for preventative measures.

The reasons that society invests so much more in research on cures for advanced cancers than on prevention or early detection are complex. Economic issues play a part: New drugs are far more lucrative for industry than new tests, and large individual costs for treating patients with advanced disease have become acceptable, even in developing countries. From a technical standpoint, the development of new and improved methods for early detection and prevention will not be easy, but there is no reason to assume that it will be more difficult than the development of new therapies aimed at treating widely metastatic disease.

Our point is not that strenuous efforts to develop new therapies for advanced cancer patients should be abandoned. These will always be required, no matter our arsenal of early detection or preventative measures. Instead, we are suggesting that "plan A" should be prevention and early detection, and "plan B" (therapy for advanced cancers) should be necessary only when plan A fails. To make plan A viable, government and philanthropic organizations must dedicate a much greater fraction of their resources to this cause, with long-term considerations in mind. We believe that cancer deaths can be reduced by more than 75% in the coming decades, but that this reduction will only come about if greater efforts are made toward early detection and prevention.

NOTE AND QUESTIONS

1. One of the key insights of cancer genomics is that the genomic makeup of a tumor is often more important to therapy than the site of the

tumor. Thus, a treatment regimen previously approved for one cancer site might be valuable to use at another site. Although such "off label" use of therapeutics is permissible, there are some questions, including the following. First, without using random controlled trials, will it be possible to prove that the new therapy works? Second, will public and private payers pay for this "unapproved" therapy?

For further discussion, see Michael S. Lawrence, Discovery and Saturation Analysis of Cancer Genes Across 21 Tumor Types, 505 Nature 495 (2014); Richard Simon & Sameek Roychowdhury, Implementing Personalized Cancer Genomics in Clinical Trials, 12 Nature Reviews Drug Discovery 358 (2013); Michael R. Stratton, Peter J. Campbell & P. Andrew Futreal, The Cancer Genome, 458 Nature 719 (2009).

VI. DIRECT-TO-CONSUMER GENETIC TESTING

MAXWELL J. MEHLMAN, DIRECT-TO-CONSUMER GENETIC TESTING
Cyberounds® (2009).

More than a dozen companies now sell direct-to-consumer (DTC) or, as it is sometimes called, "home" genetic testing, purporting to reveal information relevant to health and lifestyle. Other companies offer only ancestry or paternity testing (e.g., www.familytreedna.com/, www.dnaancestryproject.com/, www.oxfordancestors.com, www.dna-world wide.com/). One company, Identigene (www.dnatesting.com/), sells its paternity testing both by mail and as kits that can be purchased in drugstores. Still other companies provide nutritional guidance purportedly based on the results of genetic tests (e.g., http://www.inherenthealth.com/).

POTENTIAL BENEFITS FROM DTC GENETIC TESTING

Like patent medicines in the 19th century and modern over-the-counter drugs, DTC genetic testing offers certain advantages to consumers. It is generally cheaper than genetic testing obtained through a physician, in part because DTC testing dispenses for the most part with the services of physicians and genetic counselors. Mail-order genetic testing may be more accessible for people in rural or medically-underserved communities and those with mobility constraints. DTC testing also may provide a greater sense of privacy. Unlike genetic testing by one's physician, the fact that someone has sought or obtained DTC genetic testing, as well as the test results themselves, do not become part of the patient's medical record unless the patient shares them with his or her physician. For persons concerned about the risk of social stigma and genetic discrimination in insurance and employment, DTC genetic testing thus offers many of the same advantages as anonymous testing, which colleagues and I described as follows in 1996 in an article in the *American Journal of Human Genetics*:

> It would encourage individuals to acquire important personal information at the same time that it safeguarded the information against disclosure. Anonymous testing would promote patient autonomy by making the proband the only person who could reveal identifiable test results to third parties. It would effectively eliminate concerns over unauthorized disclosure by the test provider. By avoiding automatic or unauthorized disclosure to insurers and employers, anonymous testing would reduce the potential for discrimination. It would be up to the proband to decide whether to reveal the fact that he or she had been counseled and tested, and the test results, to insurers, employers, physicians, and family members.

Arguably, concerns about discrimination have been lessened as a result of the enactment of the federal Genetic Information Nondiscrimination Act. [See the discussion in Chapters 15 and 16]. But people still may be concerned about the confidentiality of information from genetic tests performed by their physicians and placed in their medical records. Under the Health Insurance Portability and Accountability Act (HIPAA), medical records may be shared among an individual's clinicians and given to health insurers for claims administration purposes. Indeed, a major impetus for shifting the health care system to electronic medical records is the ease with which individual health care information in electronic form can be accessed by care givers. Individuals may blanch at the possibility that genetic information that becomes part of their medical record may be available to virtually anyone who works in a health care system where they obtain care, and they may turn to DTC companies in an effort to maintain greater control over the information.

How confidential is information from DTC genetic tests? The testing companies have privacy policies in which they state their intention not to let anyone outside the company see test information linked to a specific individual without the individual's permission, and although DTC genetic testing companies do not appear to be covered by the privacy protections of HIPAA, such as they are, some companies claim to be "HIPAA-compliant." It is unclear how easy is it for an outsider to discover the identity of the person who was tested, and how well the security systems employed by the companies work.

Ironically, despite all of the concern over genetic privacy, some DTC genetic testing companies are touting the ability of their customers to share their genetic information with others. 23andMe, for example, states: "Seeing your own genetics is just the beginning of the 23andMe experience. Our features also give you the ability to share and compare yourself to family, friends and people around the world." The company website goes on to urge people to "add some excitement at your family reunion" by "track[ing] the inheritance of specific genes in your family," having siblings "see which parts of their parents' DNA they share, and which they don't," and letting grandchildren "find out which genes they inherited from each grandparent." As a publicity stunt, 23andMe even hosted a "spit party" in Manhattan attended by such celebrities as Rupert Murdoch, film executive Harvey Weinstein, and fashion designer Diane von Furstenberg. As reported by the *New York Times*, participants spit into sample collection bottles and looked forward to using their genomes "as a basis for social networking."

CONCERNS ABOUT DTC GENETIC TESTING

Despite the possible benefits from DTC genetic testing, the practice has come in for substantial criticism. Aside from concerns about the confidentiality of identifiable information, critics complain about the validity of the tests and the difficulties of interpreting the results. 23andMe, for example, offers tests for 107 conditions and traits. * * * The company calls 28 of the tests "clinical reports," which refers to "conditions and traits for which there are genetic associations supported by multiple, large, peer-reviewed studies," and that also have "a substantial influence on a person's chances of developing the disease or having the trait." These tests include BRCA cancer mutations, Crohn's disease, cystic fibrosis, hemochromatosis, prostate cancer, Parkinson's disease, and type 1 and 2 diabetes. The company calls the remaining 79 tests "research reports," and describes them as "information from research that has not yet gained enough scientific consensus to be included in our Clinical Reports. This research is generally based on high-quality but limited scientific evidence." The company also classifies as research reports "scientifically accepted, established research that does not have a dramatic influence on a person's risk for a disease." The conditions covered by these tests include such non-disease traits as "avoidance of errors," "breastfeeding and IQ," "measures of intelligence," and "memory," as well as diseases such as asthma, brain aneurysm, lung cancer, ands ulcerative colitis. Some companies, such as Navigenics, only test for conditions which, they claim, bear directly on health.

Clearly there are different views on the validity and utility of various genetic tests. One would think that the government would play some role in assuring that only appropriate genetic tests were sold to consumers. The Food and Drug Administration (FDA) does require manufacturers of some home tests to obtain agency approval before the tests can be marketed, but this only applies to what are called "home test kits," which enable the user to obtain test results without sending a biological sample to a laboratory. (Examples of FDA-approved home test kits are tests for cholesterol, illicit drugs, fecal occult blood, glucose, hepatitis, HIV, menopause, ovulation, pregnancy, prothrombin time, and vaginal pH.) When the test sample must be sent to a laboratory for analysis, however, there may be no requirement of FDA approval for the test itself. The FDA has reviewed and approved only a handful of genetic tests, and purchasers of DTC tests are not likely to know which ones. [See the discussion in Chapter 7].

The Federal Trade Commission (FTC) is another government agency that is supposed to protect consumers from businesses that make false or misleading claims. In 2006, the FTC issued a warning to consumers about DTC genetic tests. In addition to explaining the limited ability of genetic testing in general to determine an individual's susceptibility to disease, the FTC advised consumers to be especially wary of claims about at-home testing. According to the commission, the FDA and the Centers for Disease Control and Prevention (CDC), which also plays a role in regulating medical tests, are not aware "of any valid studies that prove these tests give accurate results," and these agencies advise that, "because of the complexities involved in both the testing and the interpretation of the results, genetic tests should be performed in a specialized laboratory, and the results should be interpreted by a doctor or trained counselor who understands the value of genetic testing for a particular situation."

Some states also attempt to regulate DTC genetic testing. A 2007 survey by the Genetics and Public Policy Center at Johns Hopkins University reported that only 25 states and the District of Columbia allowed the marketing of DTC genetic testing; 13 states prohibit it explicitly; and the remaining 12 may prohibit it indirectly. In April 2008, the New York State Department of Health sent cease-and-desist letters to Navigenics, 23andMe, and 21 other DTC testing companies, ordering them to stop selling their tests in New York unless they obtained a permit from the state. In June 2008, the California Department of Public Health followed suit, issuing cease-and-desist orders to 13 companies. In addition to requiring the companies to obtain a state license to furnish clinical laboratory services, the state regulators warned that state law required residents to obtain genetic tests through a physician. At least one DTC genetic testing company, DNA Direct, was notified by the California Department of Public Health that it was in compliance with state law.

One of the main concerns about DTC genetic testing is the difficulty consumers may have in interpreting the test results. The companies issue results on-line, in the form of charts and tables purporting to explain whether, compared with the general population, the individual is at increased or decreased risk for the conditions and traits for which they have been tested. Making sense of a large number of these comparisons is challenging, to say the least. The problem may be exacerbated if the results do not include information about the prevalence of the condition in the wider population. It is one thing to learn that, due to your genes, you have a 25% higher risk of suffering from a certain disease than others; it is another matter if the disease only affects only 1 out of a million people, rather than 1 out of 100. Moreover, the tests invariably reveal increased and decreased risks for different disorders. Assuming there is something individuals can do to reduce their risk, which risks should they focus on? All of them? And what preventive steps are warranted? Should someone who is told that they have a 10 percent greater risk of breast cancer obtain a prophylactic mastectomy? On the other hand, should someone told that they have a reduced risk of lung cancer start smoking?

Consumers of DTC genetic testing might have it somewhat easier if they received expert guidance in interpreting their test results. But none of the on-line testing companies requires the test results to be delivered by a physician, geneticist, or genetic counselor, although at least one company (DNA Direct), requires customers to speak with a counselor before ordering tests and gives them access to an on-line genetic specialist at no extra cost after they receive their test results. Another company, LabSafe, permits its customers to consult a staff physician by telephone at a cost of $75 for 15 minutes. Commentators also worry that company counselors who discuss testing with consumers before the tests are ordered may steer them towards making especially expensive purchases.

How do the testing companies justify the risk of confusing and misleading consumers? The answer is that they all disclaim that they are giving health advice. 23andMe, for example, states in its online consent document that "accessing your genetic information through 23andMe does not translate into a personal prediction"; that the information "should not be used to estimate your overall risk of future disease"; that its services are "not a test or kit designed to diagnose disease or medical conditions," "nor are they intended to be medical advice"; and that "you should not change your health behaviors on the basis of this information." But if customers took all these disclaimers seriously, what would be the point of spending between $300 and $1200 to obtain DTC genetic testing?

In 2006, the U.S. Government Accountability Office (GAO) issued a report on DTC sites that provided "nutragenetic" testing, that is, genetic tests that supposedly yield recommendations about nutrition and lifestyle. Like 23andMe, the four websites that were investigated all stressed that they do not provide information intended to diagnose or treat any disease or disorder. Yet all of the test results obtained by the investigators contained "predictions that a consumer may interpret as a diagnosis," including that the consumers were at risk for osteoporosis, high blood pressure, type 2 diabetes, heart disease, a reduced ability to clear toxins, brain aging, and cancer. Furthermore, the nutrition and lifestyle recommendations that supposedly were based on the results of the genetic tests were in fact based on the results of fictitious information provided by the investigators on questionnaires that were submitted as part of the testing process. To add insult to injury, two of the four sites recommended that the consumer buy expensive, "personalized" dietary supplements from them, at a cost of $1200 a year in one case and $1880 a year in the other. The investigators purchased and analyzed some of the supplements, and found that their ingredients essentially were multivitamins that could be purchased in a supermarket for about $35 a year. Far from being "personalized," moreover, each of the three fictitious consumers that the investigators created for each of the websites were told to purchase the same product, despite that the fact that the DNA samples that were sent to the companies came from two different donors, and each had a different lifestyle profile described in their questionnaires.

Some DTC genetic testing companies require consumers to agree to allow them to use test results for research purposes. As noted earlier, although the companies promise that, unless the consumer agrees otherwise, researchers will be given access only to de-identified information, consumers must take the company's word that their coding and security systems would withstand an attempt to link test results to specific individuals. In addition, consumers may be told that the company is entitled to use the research to develop commercial products and services, and that they should not expect to receive any financial benefit.

PROFESSIONAL ACCEPTANCE OF DTC GENETIC TESTING

All of these criticisms of DTC genetic testing have led some professional medical groups to declare their opposition to the practice. In 2004, the American College of Medical Genetics issued a policy statement describing DTC genetic testing as "potentially harmful" and declaring that "genetic testing should be provided to the public only through the services of an appropriately qualified health care professional." In June 2008, the House of Delegates of the American Medical Association adopted a similar policy statement that also called for the Federal Trade Commission to increase its oversight of DTC genetic testing companies.

The position of the American Society for Human Genetics, however, is more nuanced, and considers the benefits as well as the risks of DTC genetic testing:

> Potential benefits of DTC testing include increased consumer awareness of and access to testing. In the current environment, consumers are at risk of harm from DTC testing if testing is performed by laboratories that are not of high quality, if tests lack adequate analytic or clinical validity, if claims made about tests are false or misleading, and if inadequate information and counseling are provided to permit the consumer to make an

informed decision about whether testing is appropriate and about what actions to take on the basis of test results.

In the same way that historic objections to patent medicines might be seen, at least in part, as an effort by physicians to avoid competition from unlicensed salespersons and commercial drug manufacturers, so too condemnations of DTC genetic testing by physicians, geneticists, and genetic counselors may strike some as self-serving attempts by medical professionals to protect their turf. This view is reinforced by studies showing that primary care physicians are not well-informed about genetics and genetic testing. If this holds true, it is unclear how much better off patients would be if they obtained genetic testing through their primary care physicians, unless the physician had specialized training in genetics.

JAMES D. KEROUAC, THE REGULATION OF HOME DIAGNOSTIC TESTS FOR GENETIC DISORDERS: CAN THE FDA DENY PREMARKET APPLICATION ON THE BASIS OF THE DEVICE'S SOCIAL IMPACTS?
5 J. Biolaw & Business 34–43 (2002).

* * *

Psychological Effects

The availability of over-the-counter (OTC) diagnostics for genetic disorders may lead to serious psychological difficulties for the users of these devices and their family and friends. Genetic information revealed through OTC diagnostics may provide the test subject with devastating information about his or her prospects of fixture health or disease. The psychological effects may be particularly acute for subjects using OTC tests for late-onset genetic disorders that are presently untreatable.

For example, Huntington's Disease is a late-onset degenerative neurological disorder. Huntington's Disease causes degenerative effects on the patient's ability to walk, talk, and reason, eventually causing complete dependence on others for daily needs. The ultimate result is death due to complications from the disease, such as "choking, infection or heart failure." The current genetic test for this disorder, not available over-the-counter, provides a conclusive determination of the subject's status. Thus, if the test subject receives a positive test result, they are effectively receiving a death sentence, condemning the subject to a long, slow death. "For those whose results are positive, the suicide rate is approximately thirty-five percent higher than among the general population." It is also noted that even those who receive a negative test result for this disorder may likewise suffer psychological effects.

Genetic tests are currently available for the BRCA breast cancer genes; which are related to other late-onset genetic disorders. These genes pose a more complex situation than that of the Huntington's Disease gene. In this case, the [BRCA] genes may confer a lifetime risk of eighty percent for developing breast cancer and fifty percent for developing ovarian cancer. This situation is further complicated by speculation that women with no family history of breast cancer who possess this gene sequence may have only a forty percent or less chance of developing the disease. Clearly, women who test positive for genetic mutations in the BRCA genes are faced with an uncertain fate and may feel psychologically pressed to make a radical decision to prevent the potential, but not certain, onset of breast or ovarian cancer. Given the uncertainty of the correlation between the detection of BRCA mutations and the eventual onset of breast and ovarian cancer and the dearth of available treatments for these diseases, women who test positive for these mutations are faced with a psychologically disturbing choice to have preventive surgery or to do nothing and be faced with the constant uncertainty that they may eventually contract the disease. Both choices are likely to result in psychological trauma.

A third type of late-onset disorder may not pose such a psychological risk: late-onset genetic disorders for which adequate treatment or non-intrusive preventive measures can be taken to avoid the disease exist. [sic] For example, a genetic test for the genetic mutations relating to adult onset diabetes would not pose significant risk of psychological trauma to the test subject.

While this discussion clearly is not a comprehensive analysis of all the potential psychological effects resulting from genetic test results, it illustrates a few important points relevant to the overall position advocated by this paper. (1) The results of genetic tests for some disorders, particularly those for which adequate treatment does not exist and those for which there is not a one-to-one correlation between the mutation and the disease, may have almost certain devastating psychological effects on the test subjects. (2) The balance between the psychological and social impacts of home diagnostic genetic tests and the benefits of those tests is delicate and is intimately entwined with the current technology available to treat the disease relating to that mutation. (3) The psychological effects of genetic test results are not uniform in the context of different genetic mutations, and thus the regulation of tests for these disorders should not reflect a per se reluctance to approve genetic tests for home use. A case-by-case approach is supported by the different impacts expected in the different contexts. (4) The availability of adequate counseling may counterbalance these psychological impacts in certain cases.

* * *

Overtreatment & Misdiagnosis Causing Unnecessary, Risky or Painful Treatment

Home use genetic testing devices could potentially lead to overtreatment or to the application of unnecessary treatments if the patient receives a false positive test result. The term "overtreatment" refers to the tendency to provide treatment for a disease when there is a less than one-to-one correlation between the genotype of the test subject and the expression of that genotype. For example, [mutations in] the BRCA genes are believed to confer an 85% to 90% lifetime risk of breast cancer. If all women who tested positive had preventive surgery then there would be a 10% to 15% rate of overtreatment due to the genetic test results.

Similarly, if a particular OTC genetic test leads to many false positive results, the test subjects may be forced to undergo unnecessary and risky treatments. For example, one commentator cites such risky and unnecessary treatment of children who falsely tested positive for phenylketonuria (PKU) in mass screening for the genetic disorder.

These potential harms may easily fit into the PMA [Pre Market Application] calculus as probable risks of injury under the safety analysis. However, they do also constitute social harms because of their potentially detrimental effects on public health.

Selective Abortion

The potential availability of prenatal OTC genetic tests for certain conditions may raise serious social risks about selective abortion and eugenics. * * * Specifically, the selective termination of a fetus because the fetus tests positive for ALS may be socially unwarranted because a person afflicted with ALS does not suffer from the disease until relatively late in life and perhaps later in that potential individual's life science would find a cure for the disease. Selective termination also raises concerns about false positive test results.

The possibility of temptation to selectively abort due to uninformed decisions made by parents based on home use genetic tests supports a high level of FDA wariness about approving such devices. These devices would require, at the very least, professional consultation to aid parents in understanding the implications of the tests as well as the implications of their choices based on the tests. Also, the risk of selective termination illustrates that the FDA must use caution to examine the context in which OTC genetic tests will be used. The social risks of using prenatal diagnostics in the home are relatively graver than those of testing for some treatable late onset disease by the test subject herself.

THE FDA'S PAST EXPERIENCE IN REGULATING
HOME USE DIAGNOSTIC TESTS

This section will discuss how the FDA dealt with home use diagnostic tests for HIV and drugs of abuse in the recent past. While neither case actually resulted in the denial of a PMA on the basis of social impacts, they do illustrate that the FDA takes social impacts very seriously as risks of home use devices. * * * For example, in the case of HIV, there is a strong public policy in favor of early detection to avoid further transmission of the disease, while in the case of Huntington's Disease early detection will result in primarily negative social impacts and there are no treatment options available—the positive result is merely a death sentence. In the latter case, therefore, the social impacts will outweigh the benefits to health.

The Saga of Regulating Home Use Diagnostics for HIV

The approval of home tests for diagnosis of HIV is illustrative of FDA's use of social risk information in the PMA process and in determining what restrictions are appropriate for devices raising significant social risks to assure that the devices are safe. As in the case of genetic home tests, many commentators believed OTC HIV tests raised serious social risks. Prior to the FDA's approval of HIV home test kits, many commentators cited psychological risks as one of the risks associated with the use of home HIV diagnostics. The standard argument that home testing for HIV posed psychological risks for patients receiving a positive test result is as follows: (1) A positive HIV test result amounts to a death sentence due to the lack of effective treatments for the disease. (2) Studies indicate that persons testing positive for HIV are more likely to commit suicide. This increased risk of suicide and the desperation accompanying a positive test result is clearly a psychological risk of HIV testing. (3) The only way to mitigate this risk is face-to-face counseling about the condition. The arguments about psychological risks of HIV home test kits clearly tracks those made above in the OTC genetic test kit context.

Similarly, the arguments against home HIV testing also track those against OTC genetic test kits regarding the social risks of insurance and employment discrimination. Some argued prior to the approval of home HIV test kits that marketing home HIV test kits would allow employers to screen potential employees "quickly, easily, secretly, and *without resort to any necessary intervention* of *health care professionals*. This faculty would enhance an employer's ability to fire or refuse to hire persons who are HIV-positive, with *reduced risk of liability for illegal discrimination*." Concerns about the removal of health care professionals from the HIV testing process also gave rise to similar fears of insurance discrimination.

* * *

The Lessons of the HIV Home Testing Saga

The FDA's history of institutional reluctance to grant PMA applications for home use HIV diagnostics, coupled with the counseling restrictions the agency placed on such test systems is instructive for the purposes of this paper for a number of reasons. First, the FDA's HIV home diagnostic PMA history indicates that the agency believes social risks are cognizable in the PMA approval process for home use diagnostic tests for certain conditions. Second, the agency's cost-benefit analysis in the PMA process for home use diagnostic systems includes such factors as the availability of therapies for the condition for which the home use diagnostic test is indicated. Third, when the public health benefits of a home use diagnostic test (e.g., the increased screening of high risk minorities due to the widespread availability of home use diagnostics) outweigh the risks (e.g., social risks such as the risk of suicide due to the serious nature of the diagnosis), the agency will approve the PMA application. This lesson would appear especially true when the test subject will be empowered to take precautions to prevent the further spread of a serious public health threat like HIV Finally, the FDA is likely to engage in some brand of social engineering to avoid certain social risks when those risks are serious, though they do not outweigh the potential benefits of the home use diagnostic system.

These lessons can and should be applied to any future PMA applications for OTC genetic tests.

REGULATION OF HOME USE DIAGNOSTICS FOR DRUGS OF ABUSE

The Social Risks of Home Testing for Drugs of Abuse

As in the context of genetic home diagnostics and HIV home diagnostics, home testing for drugs of abuse raises certain social risks that may or may not be cognizable in the PMA process. These risks, however, it is urged, do not rise to the same level as those in those contrasting contexts. The FDA's approach to regulating home tests for drugs of abuse should therefore reflect the lower level of social risks.

One social impact that was widely noted in relation to OTC tests for drugs of abuse was the potential for "family discord" resulting from parents' ability to handle drugs tests they administer themselves to their children. This social risk is clearly of a lower magnitude than those cited above in relation to genetic testing and HIV antibody testing. The congressional committee charged with oversight of the FDA reacted to claims regarding the threat of familial discord caused by drugs of abuse home test kits with little enthusiasm. Another possible risk of home use drugs of abuse testing systems is the risk of a consumer receiving a false positive being labeled a social pariah. Similarly, the receipt of a false negative result of a test for drugs of abuse would "cause the individual requesting the testing to miss the opportunity to obtain treatment for the problem."

* * *

The Lessons of the FDA's Drugs of Abuse Home Test Regulations

The FDA's regulatory history of test systems for drugs of abuse provides a number of lessons that are instructive in the context of home use genetic diagnostic test regulation. First, political pressure from Congress and the President can affect the FDA's reading of its statutory authority to recognize social risks in the regulatory calculus. Second, the agency can engage in significant social engineering to avoid certain social risks through device restrictions, even when the FDA has not classed the diagnostic device in Class III. These restrictions on the marketing of diagnostic devices are powerful tools to avoid certain social risks, even though the agency never explicitly expresses that it is attempting to address those social risks. The social risks in the context of home testing for drugs of abuse are incomparable to those in the HIV and genetic testing settings and do not warrant stringent regulation. This final lesson should be considered when the agency is poised to consider a PMA for a home diagnostic test for a genetic condition and the agency should thus avoid drawing analogies to the drugs of abuse situation in regulating home use genetic tests.

The FDA Has Authority to Consider Social Impacts in the PMA Process

The FDA's history regulating home use HIV test systems and drugs of abuse test collection systems indicates that social risks of medical devices may play a role in the regulatory calculus. This role may be explicit or it may subtly underlie the restrictions placed on the device. The consideration of social risks of a new home use diagnostic system is warranted by the unique context of each particular device, including the treatment options available for the disorder tested for and the ability to reduce the spread of disease.

Thus, when the agency considers social risks as part of its regulatory calculus in the PMA process for new home use genetic diagnostic systems, the agency should consider the availability of therapies for the condition and the reliability of the testing technology available. For example, in the case of a home use diagnostic test for Huntington's disease or Alzheimer disease, the agency should, consider the high risk of social harms, such as psychological risk to the patient and the risk of insurance and employment discrimination. If there are no available treatment options, then it is likely that the social costs of the device will outweigh the benefits to health and safety of such devices. However, where there are adequate options for treatment or disease prevention, the benefits to health and safety of home use genetic diagnostic kits will likely outweigh the social risks. Thus, for conditions like adult onset diabetes approving home use diagnostic kits may likely create incentives for at risk individuals to undergo testing and, if they receive a positive test result, alter their habits that contribute to the onset of the disease.

In Less Severe Cases FDA May Impose Restrictions on Devices Based on Social Impacts

In cases where the benefits associated with the availability of home use genetic diagnostics outweigh the risks of such technology, the agency will still need to engineer some protections into its device regulations to ensure safety and effectiveness of the devices. Given the power of genetic information to result in discrimination and cause significant psychological angst, the FDA will likely engage in some form of social engineering when it approves PMA applications for OTC genetic testing devices. The restrictions placed on such devices will likely be of the same nature as those placed on home use HIV diagnostics and drugs of abuse home collection systems, including requiring counseling with the provision of a positive test result.

CONCLUSION

The FDA appears to have authority to consider social impacts of OTC genetic testing technology in the PMA process. This is clearly indicated by the historical analysis of the FDA's regulation of home use HIV diagnostics and home use collection systems for drugs of abuse test kits. The consideration of social impacts, however, should be dictated by the particular technology available to screen and treat the condition tested for. Social impacts, at the extreme, may justify the denial of a PMA application when there is no available treatment for the disorder. However, the normal situation will likely be that the social impacts can be mitigated through the use of restrictions of the marketing of the devices. Such restrictions can include the provision of counseling services with the product and are well within the purview of the FDA's medical device regulatory authority.

LETTER TO ANN WOJCICKI, CEO OF 23ANDME, INC., FROM FOOD AND DRUG ADMINISTRATION
Nov. 22, 2013.

Dear Ms. Wojcicki,

The Food and Drug Administration (FDA) is sending you this letter because you are marketing the 23andMe Saliva Collection Kit and Personal Genome Service (PGS) without marketing clearance or approval in violation of the Federal Food, Drug and Cosmetic Act (the FD&C Act).

This product is a device within the meaning of section 201(h) of the FD&C Act, 21 U.S.C. 321(h), because it is intended for use in the diagnosis of disease or other conditions or in the cure, mitigation, treatment, or prevention of disease, or is intended to affect the structure or function of the body. For example, your company's website at www.23andme.com/health (most recently viewed on November 6, 2013) markets the PGS for providing "health reports on 254 diseases and conditions," including categories such as "carrier status," "health risks," and "drug response," and specifically as a "first step in prevention" that enables users to "take steps toward mitigating serious diseases" such as diabetes, coronary heart disease, and breast cancer. Most of the intended uses for PGS listed on your website, a list that has grown over time, are medical device uses under section 201(h) of the FD&C Act. Most of these uses have not been classified and thus require premarket approval or de novo classification, as FDA has explained to you on numerous occasions.

Some of the uses for which PGS is intended are particularly concerning, such as assessments for BRCA-related genetic risk and drug responses (e.g., warfarin sensitivity, clopidogrel response, and 5-fluorouracil toxicity) because of the potential health consequences that could result from false positive or false negative assessments for high-risk indications such as these. For instance, if the BRCA-related risk assessment for breast or ovarian cancer reports a false positive, it could lead a patient to undergo prophylactic surgery, chemoprevention, intensive screening, or other morbidity-inducing actions, while a false negative could result in a failure to recognize an actual risk that may exist. Assessments for drug responses carry the risks that patients relying on such tests may begin to self-manage their treatments through dose changes or even abandon certain therapies depending on the outcome of the assessment. For example, false genotype results for your warfarin drug response test could have significant unreasonable risk of illness, injury, or death to the patient due to thrombosis or bleeding events that occur from treatment with a drug at a dose that does not provide the appropriately calibrated anticoagulant effect. These risks are typically mitigated by International Normalized Ratio (INR) management under a physician's care. The risk of serious injury or death is known to be high when patients are either non-compliant or not properly dosed; combined with the risk that a direct-to-consumer test result may be used by a patient to self-manage, serious concerns are raised if test results are not adequately understood by patients or if incorrect test results are reported.

Your company submitted 510(k)s for PGS on July 2, 2012 and September 4, 2012, for several of these indications for use. However, to date, your company has failed to address the issues described during previous interactions with the Agency or provide the additional information identified in our September 13, 2012 letter for (b)(4) and in our November 20, 2012 letter for (b)(4), as required under 21 CFR 807.87(1). Consequently, the 510(k)s are considered withdrawn, *see* 21

C.F.R. 807.87(1), as we explained in our letters to you on March 12, 2013 and May 21, 2013. To date, 23andMe has failed to provide adequate information to support a determination that the PGS is substantially equivalent to a legally marketed predicate for any of the uses for which you are marketing it; no other submission for the PGS device that you are marketing has been provided under section 510(k) of the Act, 21 U.S.C. § 360(k).

The Office of In Vitro Diagnostics and Radiological Health (OIR) has a long history of working with companies to help them come into compliance with the FD&C Act. Since July of 2009, we have been diligently working to help you comply with regulatory requirements regarding safety and effectiveness and obtain marketing authorization for your PGS device. FDA has spent significant time evaluating the intended uses of the PGS to determine whether certain uses might be appropriately classified into class II, thus requiring only 510(k) clearance or de novo classification and not PMA approval, and we have proposed modifications to the device's labeling that could mitigate risks and render certain intended uses appropriate for de novo classification. Further, we provided ample detailed feedback to 23andMe regarding the types of data it needs to submit for the intended uses of the PGS. As part of our interactions with you, including more than 14 face-to-face and teleconference meetings, hundreds of email exchanges, and dozens of written communications, we provided you with specific feedback on study protocols and clinical and analytical validation requirements, discussed potential classifications and regulatory pathways (including reasonable submission timelines), provided statistical advice, and discussed potential risk mitigation strategies. As discussed above, FDA is concerned about the public health consequences of inaccurate results from the PGS device; the main purpose of compliance with FDA's regulatory requirements is to ensure that the tests work.

However, even after these many interactions with 23andMe, we still do not have any assurance that the firm has analytically or clinically validated the PGS for its intended uses, which have expanded from the uses that the firm identified in its submissions. In your letter dated January 9, 2013, you stated that the firm is "completing the additional analytical and clinical validations for the tests that have been submitted" and is "planning extensive labeling studies that will take several months to complete." Thus, months after you submitted your 510(k)s and more than 5 years after you began marketing, you still had not completed some of the studies and had not even started other studies necessary to support a marketing submission for the PGS. It is now eleven months later, and you have yet to provide FDA with any new information about these tests. You have not worked with us toward de novo classification, did not provide the additional information we requested necessary to complete review of your 510(k)s, and FDA has not received any communication from 23andMe since May. Instead, we have become aware that you have initiated new marketing campaigns, including television commercials that, together with an increasing list of indications, show that you plan to expand the PGS's uses and consumer base without obtaining marketing authorization from FDA.

Therefore, 23andMe must immediately discontinue marketing the PGS until such time as it receives FDA marketing authorization for the device. The PGS is in class III under section 513(f) of the FD&C Act, 21 U.S.C. 360c(f). Because there is no approved application for premarket approval in effect pursuant to section 515(a) of the FD&C Act, 21 U.S.C. 360e(a), or an approved application for an investigational device exemption (IDE) under section 520(g) of the FD&C Act, 21 U.S.C. 360j(g), the PGS is adulterated under section 501(f)(1)(B) of the FD&C Act, 21 U.S.C. 351(f)(1)(B). Additionally, the PGS is misbranded under section 502(o) of the Act, 21 U.S.C. § 352(o), because notice or other information respecting the device was not provided to FDA as required by section 510(k) of the Act, 21 U.S.C. § 360(k).

Please notify this office in writing within fifteen (15) working days from the date you receive this letter of the specific actions you have taken to address all issues noted above. Include documentation of the corrective actions you have taken. If your actions will occur over time, please include a timetable for implementation of those actions. If corrective actions cannot be completed within 15 working days, state the reason for the delay and the time within which the actions will be completed. Failure to take adequate corrective action may result in regulatory action being initiated by the Food and Drug Administration without further notice. These actions include, but are not limited to, seizure, injunction, and civil money penalties.

We have assigned a unique document number that is cited above. The requested information should reference this document number and should be submitted to:

James L. Woods, WO66-5688
Deputy Director
Patient Safety and Product Quality
Office of In vitro Diagnostics and Radiological Health
10903 New Hampshire Avenue
Silver Spring, MD 20993

[In March 2014, the FDA found that 23andMe had adequately addressed these concerns. www.fda.gov/ICECI/EnforcementActions/WarningLetters/ucm391016.htm.]

FRED LEDLEY, A CONSUMER CHARTER
FOR GENOMIC SERVICES
20 Nature Biotechnology 767 (2002).

Direct access to testing. Every individual has a fundamental right to obtain genetic information about himself or herself in a confidential manner by having genetic tests performed privately and receiving the test results directly from a testing laboratory. The consumer-focused model empowers consumers with direct and private access to genetic tests and services. To ensure quality, direct consumer services should be coupled to a valid informed consent process and sources of counseling, follow-up, and referrals to specialty healthcare providers.

NOTES AND QUESTIONS

1.   Home testing is available for both HIV and drug abuse. Is genetic testing different? If so, how, and what do these differences mean in terms of how home genetic testing should be regulated?

2.   For a discussion of the reasons for limiting home genetic testing, see Gail H. Javitt, Erica Stanley & Kathy Hudson, Direct-to-Consumer Genetic Tests, Government Oversight, and the First Amendment: What the Government Can (and Can't) Do to Protect the Public's Health, 57 Okla. L. Rev. 251, 264–267 (2004).

3.   One option is for the government to ban home genetic testing. Another is to permit testing as long as it meets certain requirements. What should these requirements be?

4.   In January 2015, 23andMe entered into deals with Genentech and Pfizer to use its customers' data for research. If you were the corporate counsel for 23andMe, what provisions would you want in 23andMe's contracts with the people submitting their DNA for analysis?

5.   One type of direct-to-consumer testing that has spawned litigation is testing that purports to tell pregnant women the sex of their child. According to Lori Andrews,

> the pregnant woman pricks her finger, then collects three drops of blood on a test card and sends it to the company for testing. For $275, Acu-Gen Biolab, Inc. offers pregnant women such a test which analyzes fetal cells circulating in maternal blood to make the assessment. The company claims that their Baby Gender Mentor Test is "highly accurate." However, the lawyer for a group of women suing Acu-Gen Biolab alleges that the company officials admit that 10 to 20 percent of customers have asked for refunds because of incorrect results. In addition to a class action for fraud filed in 2007, mothers in New York filed suit last month charging negligence and fraud against Acu-gen. One of the plaintiffs underwent testing because she wanted a boy and Acu-gen allegedly told her she would

have a boy. She didn't, and she blames the company for her marriage breaking up. * * * Some of the women who have used on-line genetic testing for fetal sex and had the sex misdiagnosed allege that they were told by the company not that the test was inaccurate but that their fetus was abnormal. The distraught mothers then sought costly chromosomal testing through the medical system to find the source of this "abnormality."

Lori Andrews, Lawsuits in Pink and Blue: Sex Selection Cases Hit the Courts, July 21, 2009, http://blogs.kentlaw.edu/islat/2009/07/lawsuits-in-pink-and-blue-sex-selection-cases-hit-the-courts.html.

CHAPTER 8

CLINICAL APPLICATIONS OF GENETICS IN TREATMENT

■ ■ ■

I. INTRODUCTION

This chapter begins with a discussion of pharmacogenomics—the use of genetic and genomic information to individualize drug prescribing. It then discusses gene therapy, beginning with an overview of its history and the underlying science, followed by an explanation of the main regulatory mechanisms: professional self-regulation, the Recombinant DNA Advisory Committee at the National Institutes of Health (NIH), and the Food and Drug Administration (FDA). It then discusses germline gene therapy and personalized genomic medicine.

II. PHARMACOGENOMICS

ALLEN D. ROSES, PHARMACOGENETICS AND THE
PRACTICE OF MEDICINE
405 Nature 857 (2000).

Every individual is a product of the interaction of their genes and the environment. Pharmacogenetics is the study of how genetic differences influence the variability in patients' responses to drugs. Through the use of pharmacogenetics, we will soon be able to profile variations between individuals' DNA to predict responses to a particular medicine. The medical significance and economic value of a simple, predictive medicine response profile, which will provide information on the likelihood of efficacy and safety of a drug for an individual patient, will change the practice and economics of medicine. The ability to rapidly profile patients who are likely to benefit from a particular medicine will also streamline drug development and provide opportunities to develop discrete medicines concurrently for different patients with similar disease phenotypes. Other than relatively rare and highly penetrant diseases related to mutations of a single gene inherited in families, science has never before had the tools to characterize the nuances of inherited metabolic variations that interact over time and lead to common diseases. Powerful pharmacogenetic research tools are now becoming available to classify the heterogeneity of disease as well as individual responses to medicines.

* * *

TARGET SELECTION

Target validation that will predict a well-tolerated and effective medicine for a clinical indication in humans is a widely perceived problem; but the real challenge is target selection. A limited number of molecular target families have been identified, including receptors and enzymes, for which high-throughput screening is currently possible. A good target is one against which many compounds can be screened rapidly to identify active molecules (hits). These hits can be developed into optimized molecules (leads), which have the properties of well-tolerated and effective medicines. Selection of targets that can be validated for a disease or clinical symptom is a major problem faced by the pharmaceutical industry. The best-validated targets are those that have already produced well-tolerated and effective medicines in humans (precedented targets). Many targets are chosen on the basis of scientific hypotheses and do not lead to effective medicines because the initial hypotheses are often subsequently disproved.

Two broad strategies are being used to identify genes and express their protein products for use as high-throughput targets. These approaches of genomics and genetics share technologies but represent distinct scientific tactics and investments. Discovery genetics uses human disease populations to identify disease-related susceptibility genes. Discovery genomics uses the increasing number of databases of DNA sequence information to identify genes and families of genes for tractable or screenable targets that are not known to be genetically related to disease.

The advantage of information on disease-susceptibility genes derived from patients is that, by definition, these genes are relevant to the patients' genetic contributions to the disease. However, most susceptibility genes will not be tractable targets or amenable to high-throughput screening methods to identify active compounds. The differential metabolism related to the relevant gene variants can be studied using focused functional genomic and proteomic technologies to discover mechanisms of disease development or progression. Critical enzymes or receptors associated with the altered metabolism can then be used as targets. Gene-to-function-to-target strategies that focus on the role of the specific susceptibility gene variants on appropriate cellular metabolism become important.

* * *

The difference between the genomic approach and the genetic approach is that the former creates a need to functionally validate the tissue distribution and other aspects of each identified gene and find a relevant disease or clinical indication. In contrast, once the disease-related variants of susceptibility disease genes are identified, a single susceptibility gene is automatically validated in human disease. The major distinction between the genomic and genetic approaches is target selection, with genetically defined genes and variant-specific targets already known to be involved in the disease process. The current vogue of discovery genomics for nonspecific, wholesale gene identification, with each gene in search of a relationship to a disease, creates great opportunities for development of medicines. However, there are also enormous economical costs associated with searching huge lists of genes for 'the right disease for the available gene.' It is correct to state that target validation is a major challenge to the pharmaceutical industry, but it is also critical to realize that the core problem for drug development is poor target selection. The screening use of unproven technologies to imply disease-related validation, and the huge investment necessary to progress each selected gene to proof of concept in humans, is based on an unproven and cavalier use of the word 'validation.' Each failure is very expensive in lost time and money.

* * *

PHARMACOGENETICS AND MEDICAL PRACTICE

Diagnosis

When we go to see our doctor, our symptoms and physical signs are evaluated, and appropriate tests (for example, blood, urine, X-ray and magnetic resonance imaging) are undertaken. To the non-physician, this process of disease diagnosis seems straightforward. However, for a patient to have all the classical symptoms and signs of a particular disease is the exception rather than the rule. How these diagnoses relate to the underlying mechanism of disease is often unknown. For example, patients with mutations in different genes may present as clinically identical. Mutations of APP, presenilin 1 and presenilin 2 lead to clinically indistinguishable forms of Alzheimer's disease. It is also important to note that mutations at different sites along the *APP* gene can lead to two distinct diseases, early-onset Alzheimer's disease and recurrent intracerebral hemorrhages. For many common diseases, the situation may be assumed to be even more complicated, with many contributing molecular variants of several interacting susceptibility genes leading to multiple clinical effects over varying time frames. Thus many of the diseases that we classify clinically may be syndromes with several distinct contributing pathogenic mechanisms. With all this clinical and genetic heterogeneity we should not lose sight of the fact that the major objective is to treat, cure or prevent disease. It is significant that a medicine works; does it matter whether it is effective in patients who may have different diagnoses? The goal of medicine is to relieve pain and suffering. Similar mechanisms may exist for quite diverse clinical diseases. As the targets and mechanisms are validated in humans, additional clinical indications may become more obvious because of shared mechanisms rather than similar clinical presentations.

How does your doctor know when making the diagnosis that medicines that are effective for you have not been precluded? Pharmacogenetics will enable individuals to be classified according to their likely response to a medicine. This is not a new concept as clinical subtypes are often classified by drug responsiveness (for example, steroid-sensitive and steroid-resistant asthma). Application of pharmacogenetics will expand the population to those who can be helped but might have otherwise been missed because their clinical syndrome did not fit neatly into a traditional disease category. Alosetron is a recently approved medicine in the United States for the treatment of female patients with diarrhoea-predominant [sic] irritable bowel syndrome (IBS). Most physicians will acknowledge that the diagnosis of IBS can be imprecise—in fact, the 'disease' is truly a syndrome. The value of a diagnostic test to sub-classify IBS into different types may be limited, but a simple medicine response profile to determine whether the patient's symptoms will be alleviated by alosetron could have considerable value. Pharmacogenetic approaches will no doubt confirm what clinicians already know—disease diagnosis is not easy nor necessarily homogeneous and accurate.

Apparently distinct diseases may have similar underlying mechanisms. A medicine developed for a specific indication could have value in treating other related or non-related conditions. This is also not a new concept. There are many medicines that were initially registered with a single indication, which have then been expanded as more clinical research is conducted. For example, carbamazepine was initially registered as a treatment for trigeminal neuralgia, a syndrome with intermittent severe lightning-like bursts of facial pain, but was later extended to treat various forms of epilepsy. By understanding the genetic basis of patient responses to medicines, and perhaps also by having a better understanding of how the medicine works, we will be able to identify additional clinical indications more quickly.

Treatment

How does a physician know if the medicine and the dose prescribed will be effective and whether or not the patient will experience adverse effects? Information is available from clinical trials in the medicine's data sheet/label in which similar patients were included and the physician may use experience of treating previous patients. On many occasions, the prescribed medicine will be effective and not cause serious side effects. Other patients may not respond or suffer adverse reactions. By applying the results of pharmacogenetic research to clinical practice, physicians will be able to use information from patients' DNA to determine how patients are likely to respond to a particular medicine. The clinical fact that the drug dose for some patients must be individualized has been accepted for years. Polymorphisms in genes encoding P450 enzymes, *N*-acetyltransferase and other key enzymes in drug metabolism account for the concentration variation of certain drugs in patients' blood. It is also well established that some patients can be slow in activating drugs and respond inadequately to some prodrugs, or exhibit reduced clearance and increased effects from some pharmacologically active agents. Enzyme tests that measure those variants have, in some cases, already been replaced with genetic variants on chips. In the future, metabolic screens of genetic variants will be standardized so that automated read-outs of each person's predicted response to each medicine could be generated. These DNA-based screens will not provide disease-specific diagnosis, but useful information to aid in individual dosing of medications or avoidance of side effects.

* * *

PHARMACOGENETICS AND DRUG DEVELOPMENT

More efficient clinical trials and enhanced drug surveillance

Application of SNP mapping technologies will enable effective medicines to be developed and made available for clinical use more rapidly. Using abbreviated SNP linkage disequilibrium mapping, medicine response profiles could be identified during phase II clinical trials. These could be used in the selection of patient groups enriched for efficacy in phase III studies. This is likely to make these trials smaller, faster and more efficient.

Regulatory agencies would correctly be concerned that there were not enough patients in these streamlined phase III trials to evaluate adverse events, although larger clinical trials that do not select "efficacy" patients are also unlikely to detect rare adverse events (less than 1 in 1,000). Regulatory authorities would also be apprehensive that, when the drug is marketed, patients who did not meet the pharmacogenetic criteria for prescription may be prescribed the drug without study of their potential benefits or adverse events. However, the risk-benefit ratio for patients with poor efficacy predictions may exclude them from phase III studies on ethical grounds as they would now knowingly be included solely to experience potential adverse events. Furthermore, in clinical practice, access to the medicine could be determined by prescriptions based on pharmacogenetic profiles.

In fact, pharmacogenetic technology may enable a significantly enhanced post-approval surveillance system to be established for approved medicines. Regulatory agencies, pharmaceutical companies and the public recognize the need to improve strategies for drug surveillance. In this proposed concept of regulated surveillance, hundreds of thousands of patients who receive the medicine would have blood spots taken and stored on filter papers in an approved location using the original blood sample screened for the initial medicine response profile for efficacy. As rare, serious adverse events are documented and characterized, DNA from patients who experienced the adverse event could be extracted and compared with DNA from control patients who received the drug but did not experience the adverse event. This would enable abbreviated SNP profiles for patients susceptible to the adverse event to be determined. These adverse event profiles would be combined with efficacy profiles to produce a comprehensive medicine response profile. This would allow selection of patients for both efficacy and lower complications of therapy.

A predictive pharmacogenetic adverse event profile derived from hundreds of thousands of patients taking the drug would be a major advance on the present system of documenting reported serious adverse events during the use of the medicine in clinical practice, as this current system often obtains little or no predictive information to help subsequent patients, other than broad warnings.

Over the next few years, as we approach the ability to differentiate patients by their therapeutic responses, regulatory agencies and pharmaceutical companies will need to work together to pilot and examine methods to evaluate fewer total patients in faster, more efficient clinical trials while enhancing drug surveillance systems. Initial studies using medicine response profiles would no doubt use nested populations of patients within trials designed to meet current guidelines and regulations in order to demonstrate proof of concept.

Medicines for all

The application of pharmacogenetics will not diminish the population in whom a drug is effective, but simply allow prediction of patient response rather than prolonged and expensive prescribing by trial and error. Just as it will be possible to identify patients with drug efficacy, it will also be possible to identify those patients who do not respond early in the process of drug development. The ability to target heterogeneous groups of patients for parallel drug development early, rather than waiting years for non-responsive populations to emerge after extensive clinical use of the medicine, will be a significant benefit. For example, SNP profiling of different medicine-responsive association groups during phase II trials will enable identification of the location of genes contributing to heterogeneous forms of the disease, leading to the discovery of new medicines and additional susceptibility targets.

By focusing clinical trials on patients who are most likely to respond, drug development resources could be targeted to those patients with continued unmet medical need. In particular, molecules that show less than a 30% response rate in a large population, but have clear efficacy in an identifiable smaller population of patients, would become viable as they could be readily identified for development and clinical practice.

As a result of disease heterogeneity, there may be large, definable sub-groups of patients suffering with a common phenotype, for example Alzheimer's disease, which represent only 10–15% of patients with that diagnosis. Focusing drug development on sub-groups of patients selected by either a disease-specific diagnostic or a medicine response profile will provide opportunities to develop more medicines for a larger proportion of patients with heterogeneous diseases. Similarly, patient groups who have vaguely defined phenotypes that are more difficult to categorize by objective criteria, such as depression, could be studied more efficiently using medicine response profiles as selection variables.

VALUE OF PHARMACOGENETICS TO HEALTH-CARE DELIVERY

The cost-effectiveness of new medicines (which are the product of considerable investment in research and development) is a significant concern to patients, funding bodies and governments. The application of pharmacogenetics to the delivery of medicines will maximize the value of each medicine. Medicines would be prescribed to only those patients where a high probability of efficacy without significant adverse events is expected. This is a much-preferred scenario than the problems facing funding agencies and governments at the present time. Medicines that might be prescribed to 100 patients to achieve an effect in 20 are becoming more difficult for sponsors of medical care to consider. However, selection of predicted responders offers a more efficient and economical solution to a growing problem that is leading governments and health-care providers to deny effective medicines to the few, because a proportion of patients do not respond to the treatment. The economy of predictable efficacy, limited adverse events, lower complications owing to targeted delivery, and increased cost-effectiveness of medicines will improve health-care delivery and eliminate the need for rationing. Effective and well-tolerated medicines with predictive medicine response profiles will obviate the need for formulary restrictions on prescribing and new policies to mandate cost-effectiveness to be proved in a broad population of patients.

Pharmacogenetics will impact medical care at multiple levels. As well-tolerated and effective medicines that treat, cure or prevent common diseases become a greater proportion of the medical care bill, the costs of chronic debilitating illnesses will be significantly reduced. As treatment and prevention of chronic and common diseases improves, a significant proportion of money saved by reducing hospitalization and long-term care costs could be transferred to well-tolerated and effective medicines.

FOOD AND DRUG ADMINISTRATION, GUIDANCE FOR INDUSTRY: PHARMACOGENOMIC DATA SUBMISSIONS

(2005).

Background

The promise of pharmacogenomics lies in its potential to help identify sources of inter-individual variability in drug response (both effectiveness and toxicity); this information will make it possible to individualize therapy with the intent of maximizing effectiveness and minimizing risk. However, the field of pharmacogenomics is currently in early developmental stages, and such promise has not yet been realized. The Agency has heard that pharmaceutical sponsors have been reluctant to embark on programs of pharmacogenomic testing during FDA-regulated phases of drug development because of uncertainties in how the data will be used by FDA in the drug application review process. This guidance is intended to help clarify FDA policy in this area.

Sponsors submitting or holding INDs [Investigational New Drug applications], NDAs [New Drug Applications], or BLAs [Biologics License Applications] are subject to FDA requirements for submitting to the Agency data relevant to drug safety and effectiveness (including 21 CFR 312.22, 312.23, 312.31, 312.33, 314.50, 314.81, 601.2, and 601.12). Because these regulations were developed before the advent of widespread animal or human genetic or gene expression testing, they do not specifically address when such data must be submitted. The FDA has received numerous inquiries about what these regulations require of sponsors who are conducting such testing.

From a public policy perspective, a number of factors should be considered when interpreting how these regulations apply to the developing field of pharmacogenomics. Because the field of pharmacogenomics is rapidly evolving, in many circumstances, the experimental results may not be well enough established scientifically to be suitable for regulatory decision making. For example:

- Laboratory techniques and test procedures may not be well validated. In addition, test systems may vary so that results may not be consistent or generalizable across different platforms. A move to standardize assays is underway, and much more information should be available within the next several years.

- The scientific framework for interpreting the physiologic, toxicologic, pharmacologic, or clinical significance of certain experimental results may not yet be well understood.

- The findings from a specific study often cannot be extrapolated across species or to different study populations (e.g., various human subpopulations with different genetic backgrounds).

- The standards for transmission, processing, and storage of the large amounts of highly dimensional data generated from microarray technology have neither been well defined nor widely tested.

Despite these concerns, some pharmacogenetic tests—primarily those related to drug metabolism—have well-accepted mechanistic and clinical significance and are currently being integrated into drug development decision making and clinical practice.

It is important for FDA to have a role in the evaluation of pharmacogenomic tests, both to ensure that evolving FDA policies are based on the best science and to provide public confidence in the field. The FDA developed this guidance to facilitate the use of pharmacogenomic tests during drug development and encourage open and public sharing of data and information on pharmacogenomic test results.

To this end, the Agency has undertaken a process for obtaining input from the scientific community and the public. On May 16 and 17, 2002, the Agency held a workshop, cosponsored by pharmaceutical industry groups, to identify key issues associated with the application of pharmacogenetics and pharmacogenomics to drug development. Subsequently, on April 8, 2003, a public presentation was made to the FDA Science Board. This presentation contained a proposal for developing guidance on the submission of information on pharmacogenomic tests and a potential algorithm for deciding whether submission of such data is voluntary or required. The Science Board endorsed moving forward with both of these proposals. In November 2003, FDA published a draft version of this guidance and received public comment on the draft guidance. The Agency also has developed internal policy related to pharmacogenomics and voluntary submissions.

The policies and processes outlined in this final guidance are intended to take the above factors into account and to assist in advancing the field in a manner that will benefit both drug development programs and the public health.

SUBMISSION POLICY

General Principles

The FDA recognizes that its pharmacogenomic data submission policies must be consistent with the relevant codified regulatory submission requirements for investigational and marketing application submitters and holders. At present, many pharmacogenomic results are not well enough established scientifically to be appropriate for regulatory decision making. This guidance interprets FDA's regulations for investigational and marketing submissions, with the goal of clarifying FDA's current thinking about when the regulations require pharmacogenomic data to be submitted and when the submission of such data would be welcome on a voluntary basis. In some cases, complete reports of pharmacogenomic studies suffice, while in others, an abbreviated report or synopsis should or must be submitted.

Because FDA regulations establish different requirements for investigational applications, unapproved marketing applications, and approved marketing applications, this guidance sets out different submission algorithms for each of these categories. The guidance also clarifies how the Agency currently intends to use such data in regulatory decision making—that is, when the data will be considered sufficiently reliable to serve as the basis for regulatory decision making; when it will be considered only supportive to a decision; and when the data will not be used in regulatory decision making.

This guidance also makes a distinction between pharmacogenomic tests that may be considered either probable or known *valid biomarkers,* which may be appropriate for regulatory decision making, and other less well-developed tests that are either observational or exploratory biomarkers that, alone, are insufficient for making regulatory decisions. Although, currently, most pharmacogenomic measurements are not considered valid biomarkers, certain markers (e.g., for drug metabolism) are well established biomarkers with clear clinical significance. Undoubtedly, the distinction between what tests are appropriate for regulatory decision making and those that are not will change over time as the science evolves. Throughout the development of these tests, as appropriate, FDA will continue to seek public comment as we evaluate whether a biomarker is a *valid biomarker* (e.g., via discussions at Advisory Committee meetings).

For the purposes of this guidance, a pharmacogenomic test result may be considered a *valid biomarker* if (1) it is measured in an analytical test system with well-established performance characteristics and (2) there is an established scientific framework or body of evidence that elucidates the physiologic, pharmacologic, toxicologic, or clinical significance of the test results. For example, the consequences for drug metabolism of genetic variation in the human enzymes CYP2D6 and thiopurine methyltransferase are well understood in the scientific community and are reflected in certain approved drug labels. The results of genetic tests that distinguish allelic variants of these enzymes are considered to be well established and, therefore, valid biomarkers.

This guidance makes an additional distinction between known valid biomarkers that have been accepted in the broad scientific community and probable valid biomarkers that appear to have predictive value for clinical outcomes, but may not yet be widely accepted or independently verified by other investigators or institutions. When a sponsor generates, or possesses, data sufficient to establish a significant association between a pharmacogenomic test result and clinical outcomes, the test result represents a probable valid biomarker. It would be expected that this biomarker would meet criteria (1) and (2) above, and its association with a meaningful outcome would have been demonstrated in more than one experiment.

The algorithms described below for investigational and marketing application holders describe when to submit to FDA data on known valid biomarkers. Data on probable valid biomarkers need not be submitted to the IND unless they are used by a sponsor to make decisions regarding specific animal safety studies or clinical trials (e.g., using biomarker data as inclusion or exclusion criteria, assessment of treatment-related prognosis, or stratifying patients by dose) or are a probable valid biomarker in human safety studies. However, we recommend that sponsors or applicants submit reports on all probable valid biomarkers to new (i.e., unapproved) NDAs or BLAs according to the algorithm in section IV.B.

Many pharmacogenomic testing programs implemented by pharmaceutical sponsors or by scientific organizations are intended to develop the knowledge base necessary to establish the validity of new genomic biomarkers. During such a period of scientific exploration, test results are not useful in making regulatory judgments pertaining to the safety or effectiveness of a drug and are not considered known or probable valid biomarkers. However, scientific development of this sort is highly desirable for advancing the understanding of relationships between genotype or gene expression and responses to drugs and, therefore, should be encouraged and facilitated. For these reasons, although submission of exploratory pharmacogenomic data is not required under the regulations, FDA is encouraging *voluntary submission* of such data, as described below.

Specific Uses of Pharmacogenomic Data in Drug Development and Labeling

As the field of pharmacogenomics advances, it is likely (and desirable) that sponsors will begin to use pharmacogenomic tests to support drug development and/or to guide therapy. Sponsors may choose to submit pharmacogenomic data that have not achieved the status of a valid biomarker to an investigational or marketing application to support scientific contentions related to dosing and dosing schedule, safety, or effectiveness. For example, a sponsor may wish to provide supportive data demonstrating that changes in drug-induced gene expression differ between species that have different toxicologic responses to a drug, thus correlating changes in certain gene expression patterns with a specific toxicity. Or, a pharmacogenomic test result might also be used to stratify patients in a clinical trial or to identify patients at higher risk for an adverse event to correlate test results with clinical outcome.

If a pharmacogenomic test shows promise for enhancing the dose selection, safety, or effectiveness of a drug, a sponsor may wish to fully integrate pharmacogenomic data into the drug development program. This integration could occur in two ways:

1.   The pharmacogenomic data may be intended to be included in the drug labeling in an informational manner. For example, such data might be used to describe the potential for dose adjustment by drug metabolism genotype (e.g., CYP2D6*5) or to mention the possibility of a side effect of greater severity or frequency in individuals of a certain genotype or gene expression profile. In such cases, the pharmacogenomic test result would be considered a known valid biomarker. However, an FDA-approved pharmacogenomic test may not be available or required to be available, or a commercial pharmacogenomic test may not be widely available. Given this level of complexity, at the current time, sponsors should consult the relevant FDA review division for advice on how to proceed in a specific case. However, whenever a sponsor intends to include pharmacogenomic data in the drug label, complete information on the test and results must be submitted to the Agency as described under §§ 314.50 and 601.2.

2.   The pharmacogenomic data and resulting test or tests may be intended to be included in the drug labeling to choose a dose and dose schedule, to identify patients at risk, or to identify patient responders. Inclusion of a pharmacogenomic test in the labeling would be contingent upon its performance characteristics. For example:

- Patients will be tested for drug metabolism genotype and dosed according to the test results.

- Patients will be selected as potential responders for an efficacy trial (or deselected because of a high risk) based on genotype (e.g., of either the patient or the patient's tumor) or gene expression profile.

- Patients will be excluded from a clinical trial based on genotype or gene expression profile (e.g., biomarker for risk of an adverse event).

In all of these cases, FDA recommends co-development of the drug and the pharmacogenomic tests, if they are not currently available, and submission of complete information on the test/drug combination to the Agency. The FDA plans to issue further guidance on co-development of pharmacogenomic tests and drugs.

The Office of In Vitro Diagnostics in CDRH, appropriate review divisions in CBER, and the Clinical and Clinical Pharmacology Review divisions in CBER or CDER are willing to meet jointly with sponsors to discuss both scientific and regulatory issues with regard to new pharmacogenomic tests. The CDRH has both formal (IDE) and informal (pre-IDE) processes to evaluate protocols for pharmacogenomic test development.

NOTES AND QUESTIONS

1. The terms "pharmacogenetics" and "pharmacogenomics" are often used inaccurately and interchangeably. As Roses explains, the difference lies in the starting point. With pharmacogenetics, the starting point is a human population with a genetic disease, and the task is to identify the genes that are associated with the disease. With pharmacogenomics, the starting point is the genome, the sequence of human DNA, and the task is to identify the diseases that are associated with differences in the genome, or polymorphisms. Pharmacogenetics is the older technique; pharmacogenomics was not feasible until stretches of the human genome were sequenced and the technology was available to rapidly identify single nucleotide polymorphisms, or "SNPs."

In both cases, the goals are the same: to improve the diagnosis of genetic disease; to develop drugs to fight genetic disease; to make clinical testing of drugs more efficient by identifying populations in which the drugs are likely to be especially efficacious (and presumably for whom they would be indicated on the labeling); and, using genetic information about patients, to maximize therapeutic benefit and minimize harmful side effects by prescribing drugs to targeted patient populations.

A related field is "proteomics," which focuses on the proteins that genes code for and the association of the proteins with disease.

2.   The fields of pharmacogenetics, pharmacogenomics, and proteomics are still in their early stages. However, some findings are beginning to be commercialized and used clinically. For example, a cytochrome P450 2D6 gene test was approved by the FDA in 2004 to help identify genetic mutations that affect how patients metabolize a number of drugs. Other applications include the use of a test for a gene known as TPMT that makes some patients highly sensitive to the chemotherapy agent used to treat acute lymphoblastic leukemia, the most common form of childhood cancer. The test reportedly can tell if a patient should get only five percent of the standard dosage to avoid serious side effects without significant loss of effectiveness. Another test can reveal if congestive heart failure will be responsive to drug therapy, or if a heart transplant will be necessary.

Warfarin (also known as Coumadin) is the most widely-used oral anticoagulant, which is used in patients with cardiovascular disease to prevent the formation of blood clots that can cause strokes. The dosage of the drug must be carefully calibrated for each patient to avoid catastrophic side-effects. Traditionally this was done on a risky trial-and-error basis, but pharmacogenomic research demonstrated that people with a variant of the genes CYP2C9 or VKORC1 break down the drug more slowly, which means that it stays in the body longer and causes bleeding. In 2007, the FDA announced that a new label was being prepared for Warfarin, which states under "precautions": "Certain variations in two key genes may increase the need for more frequent monitoring and the use of lower doses." Genetic tests for the two key genes cost $300–$500 and the turnaround time for test results means that initial dosing and titration of Warfarin levels must begin before the results are available. In 2009, the Centers for Medicare and Medicaid Services announced it will not pay for the genetic tests because of a lack of clinical utility. In 2010, the FDA revised the Warfarin label to lower the starting dose from 5 mg per day: "If the patients CYP2C9 and VKORC1 are not known, the initial dose of Coumadin is usually 2–5 mg per day."

3.   Not everyone is optimistic that positive developments will occur rapidly. See, e.g., Leslie Roberts, SNP Mappers Confront Reality and Find It Daunting, 287 Science 1898 (2000). In an article in the New Eng. J. Med., two respected genetics experts stated:

> [T]he new genetics will not revolutionize the way in which common diseases are identified or prevented. Mapping and sequencing the human genome will lead to the identification of more genes causing mendelian disorders and to the development of diagnostic and predictive tests for them. The development of safe and effective treatments, however, will usually lag behind, although occasionally a treatment does precede the discovery of the disease-causing allele, as was the case for hemochromatosis. Furthermore, only a small proportion of the population has mendelian disorders, and this will limit the ultimate impact of the Human Genome Project.

Our doubts stem from the incomplete penetrance of genotypes for common diseases, the limited ability to tailor treatment to genotypes, and the low magnitude of risks conferred by various genotypes for the population at large.

Neil A. Holtzman & Theresa M. Marteau, Will Genetics Revolutionize Medicine?, 343 New Eng. J. Med. 141 (2000).

Andrew Pollack in an article in The New York Times describes some of the problems encountered in using pharmacogenetic testing to refine the prescribing of the drugs Herceptin and tamoxifen:

> * * * The hurdles include drug makers, which can be reluctant to develop or encourage tests that may limit the use of their drugs. Insurers may not pay for tests, which can cost up to a few thousand dollars. For makers of the tests, which hope their business becomes one of health care's next big growth industries, a major obstacle is proving that their products are accurate and useful. While drugs must prove themselves in clinical trials before they can be sold, there is no generally recognized process for evaluating genetic tests, many of which can be marketed by laboratories without F.D.A. approval.
>
> Genentech, a developer of cancer drugs, petitioned the F.D.A. this month to regulate such tests. It warned of "safety risks for patients, as more treatment decisions are based in whole or in part on the claims made by such test makers."
>
> A cautionary case is Herceptin, a Genentech breast cancer drug that is considered the archetype of personalized medicine because it works only for women whose tumors have a particular genetic characteristic. But now, 10 years after Herceptin reached the market, scientists are finding that the various tests—some approved by the F.D.A., some not—can be inaccurate.
>
> Moreover, doctors do not always conduct the tests or follow the results. The big insurer UnitedHealthcare found in 2005 that 8 percent of the women getting the drug had tested negative for the required genetic characteristic. An additional 4 percent had not been tested at all, or their test results could not be found.
>
> Tamoxifen, * * * illustrates the promise and current limitations of genetic testing. In 2003, more than 25 years after tamoxifen was introduced, researchers led by Dr. David A. Flockhart at Indiana University School of Medicine figured out that the body converts tamoxifen into another substance called endoxifen. It is endoxifen that actually exerts the cancer-fighting effect. The conversion is done by an enzyme in the body called CYP2D6, or 2D6 for short.
>
> But variations in people's 2D6 genes mean the enzymes have different levels of activity. Up to 7 percent of people, depending on their ethnic group, have an inactive enzyme, Dr. Flockhart said,

while another 20 to 40 percent have an only modestly active enzyme.

The implications were "scary," Dr. Flockhart said. Many women were apparently not being protected against cancer's return because they could not convert tamoxifen to endoxifen.

The economic implications could be just as scary to big pharmaceutical companies.

Tamoxifen, now a generic drug, costs as little as $500 for the typical five-year treatment. But most patients in the United States are currently treated with a newer, much more expensive class of drugs, called aromatase inhibitors, that cost about $18,000 over five years. Those drugs—made by AstraZeneca, Novartis and Pfizer—performed better than tamoxifen in clinical trials before the role of 2D6 was generally understood.

If only women with active 2D6 had been assessed, tamoxifen might have worked as well or better than the newer drugs, according to researchers at the Dana-Farber Cancer Institute in Boston.

But proving these suppositions and having them incorporated into medical practice have not been easy.

The F.D.A., in its meeting this month, said clinical trials were the ideal way to validate a test. But many test developers argue that trials would be too costly and time-consuming, so many tests are validated by reanalyzing patient data from old trials.

In the case of tamoxifen, Dr. Matthew P. Goetz of the Mayo Clinic and colleagues went back to an old trial and used stored tumor samples to test the 2D6 genes of each patient. The researchers reported in 2005 that 32 percent of the women with inactive 2D6 enzyme had relapsed or died within two years, in contrast to only 2 percent of the other women.

But while some subsequent studies have backed those conclusions, two had contradictory results. That leaves many experts hesitant to use the test, which costs about $300.

There are other complications. Dozens of variants of the 2D6 gene exist, and laboratories can differ in their interpretation of test results. And it is not always clear how to act upon the information the test provides.

* * *

Such complexities are not confined to tamoxifen testing. The labels of about 200 drugs now contain some information relating genes to drug response, said Lawrence J. Lesko, the F.D.A.'s head of clinical pharmacology. But in many cases, he said, doctors are not told specifically enough what to do with the test results, such as how much to change the dose.

Andrew Pollack, Patient's DNA May Be Signal to Tailor Drugs, The New York Times, Dec. 30, 2008, at A1.

4.   Nutrigenomics is the study of the way dietary nutrients interact with individual genetic makeup to affect health outcomes. Scientifically, nutrigenomics is still in its infancy, and experts believe it will take years, if not decades, before research will support its widespread application to the human diet. Nevertheless, marketers are already touting genetic testing for nutrition-related genetic factors and selling customized vitamin supplements and food based on personalized genetic factors. The assessments and products run from $249.95 to $595.00. See Rhonda L. Rundle, Can Genetic Tests Aid in Nutrition? The Wall Street Journal, Mar. 1, 2005, at D6. How, if at all, should the law regulate these practices?

MARK A. ROTHSTEIN & PHYLLIS GRIFFIN EPPS, ETHICAL AND LEGAL IMPLICATIONS OF PHARMACOGENOMICS
2 Nature Reviews Genetics 228 (2001).

Pharmacogenomics is changing the way that drugs are developed, approved, marketed and prescribed. The objective of pharmacogenomics is to define the pharmacological significance of genetic variation among individuals and to use this information in drug discovery, thereby decreasing the number of adverse drug responses that injure and kill thousands each year. By determining which genetic variations are likely to affect a person's ability to metabolize a drug, drug manufacturers intend to develop more predictable and effective therapeutic agents. Towards this end, pharmaceutical companies are investing huge amounts of capital in the technologies that will revolutionize both how researchers identify drug targets and the amount of time needed to move a drug through development and approval. Pharmacogenomics promises to streamline the clinical trial phase of drug development. Researchers hope to use knowledge gained from high-throughput screening and other technologies to construct clinical trial groups that are composed of people most likely to benefit from a particular drug. The ability to streamline clinical trials by genotyping will enable researchers to "rescue" drugs that could not be approved under conventional models of research trials. In other words, drugs that were previously rejected after giving unacceptable rates of adverse responses in traditionally constructed trials will yield lower adverse-response rates after testing under the new model, thereby becoming acceptable candidates for approval. Pharmacogenomics will not only produce better drugs but also yield greater efficiency in the allocation of resources in drug development.

Other changes attributable to pharmacogenomics will be less welcome. Notwithstanding the increasingly efficient research and development process, pharmacogenomic-based drugs will be expensive, because of, for example, the need to recoup the cost of investment in new technologies. The ability to develop specialized drugs that are ultimately approved for smaller populations rather than for general use will fragment the market for pharmaceuticals. Will a pharmaceutical manufacturer react to this economic reality in a way that better suits profit margins than health, and is that socially acceptable? The use of groups in clinical trials that are increasingly similar genotypically raises several important ethical issues regarding social inclusion and the adequacy of current regulatory frameworks. Because polymorphisms of pharmacological interest might vary in frequency among different population subgroups, important social issues arise in multi-ethnic countries, such as the United States. Finally, pharmacogenomics will change the standard of care for pharmaceutical companies and health professionals, including physicians and pharmacists.

This article provides an overview of some ethical and social concerns that arise with the integration of pharmacogenomics into the discovery of drugs and the practice of preventive and therapeutic medicine. Specifically, the article addresses issues associated with the design of clinical trials, the relatively higher cost of pharmaceuticals developed using pharmacogenomics, and the allocation of ethical and legal responsibility. The objective is to highlight a few of the questions and challenges that will require further attention in the near future.

A NEW MODEL OF CLINICAL TRIALS

Pharmacogenomics promises to reduce the time and money required to develop a drug. The ability to predict drug efficacy by genotyping participants during the early stages of clinical trials for a drug would enable researchers to recruit for later trials only those patients who, according to their genotype, are likely to benefit from the drug. As a result, clinical trials could become smaller, cheaper and faster to run.

The prospect of clinical trials that are composed of smaller groups with the same polymorphisms at one or more loci of interest poses some risks, however. A group that reflects the diversity of the population yields information on how a drug will behave in a greater number of people. If the clinical trial group is smaller, or is less genotypically diverse, there is a greater risk that some side effects will go undetected. So, the trials will yield a greater quantity and quality of information, but on a smaller segment of the population. Whereas the conventional model yielded information about harmful side effects in a greater proportion of the population, the concentration of individuals pre-selected for a favourable response under the newer model might not produce the same information. Compared with traditionally designed human clinical trials, genotype-specific human clinical studies might be subject to equal or greater limitations in that the relatively short duration of the study, combined with the narrower subject population and smaller size, would hinder the ability of the studies to identify rare or delayed adverse reactions or drug interactions. A drug could reach the market with less information about the side effects or risk of harm from its non-prescribed uses. An unresolved issue is whether the ethical principles of beneficence and non-maleficence (that is, not causing harm to others) would preclude the deliberate inclusion of anyone who is not likely to respond favourably to treatment. With the advent of genotype-specific clinical trials, manufacturers and regulators must be ready to carefully evaluate post-market data by strengthening the existing guidelines for phase IV, or post-approval, clinical trials.

As in other areas of genetic research that involve human subjects, the likely effect of pharmacogenomics on clinical trials raises important questions regarding informed consent, which might include considerations of privacy and confidentiality. Current ideas regarding patient autonomy and informed consent require that patients agree to enter into research on the basis of adequate information regarding the risks and consequences of participation. Genotyping that is appropriate to pharmacogenomic research might not produce information regarding susceptibility to disease or early death, but it might reveal evidence of genetic variation that could lead to individuals being classified as "difficult to treat," "less profitable to treat," or "more expensive to treat." The fear of being so classified could act as a barrier to the recruitment of research participants.

Fear of stigmatization might prove to be a significant barrier to participation in clinical trials among members of population subgroups. Genetic variations of pharmacological significance are known to occur in varying frequency in groups categorized by their ethnicity. For example, different variants of glucose-6-phosphate dehydrogenase (G6PD—an enzyme critical for NADPH (nicotinamide-adenine dinucleotide phosphate reduced) generation in mature red blood cells) are found at a high frequency in African, Mediterranean and Asiatic populations, some of which disrupt the function of the enzyme. A deficiency of G6PD can predispose individuals from these populations to haemolytic anaemia, both in individuals with loss-of-function G6PD mutations and in response to some drugs, such as the malarial drug primaquine. Isoniazid is an anti-tuberculosis drug that is inactivated by acetylation; its impaired metabolism by slow acetylation causes it to accumulate to toxic levels. Variation in the N-acetyl transferase 2 (NAT2) gene accounts for whether individuals are rapid or slow acetylators of isoniazid, as well as of other therapeutic and carcinogenic compounds. About 50% of individuals in many Caucasian populations are genotypically slow acetylators of isoniazid, but more than 80% of individuals in certain Middle Eastern populations and fewer than 20% in the Japanese population have the slow acetylator phenotype.

The significance of data that imply a role for ethnicity in research has been a source of considerable debate among the research ethics community. One issue is how to advise potential research participants about the possibility of social harms from group-based findings even where the research is conducted without using the names of participants. Another matter of considerable debate in the literature is whether it is necessary or feasible to engage in community consultation when genetic research focuses on socially or politically distinct population subgroups.

COST AS A BARRIER TO ACCESS

Pharmacogenomic drugs will be expensive, cheaper clinical trials notwithstanding. Collectively, the pharmaceutical industry is investing huge amounts of time and money in the development of new technologies that will yield drugs that are more effective than those already available. Without the opportunity to recoup their investment, drug companies will not continue their efforts. At the same time, insurance systems and consumers are struggling to absorb the rising costs of pharmaceutical products.

Pharmacogenomics is based on the idea that pharmaceutical consumers will be better served by drug therapy once they have been subdivided by genotype and matched with the most suitable drug. From the industry perspective, the subdivision of a market into smaller markets is hardly ideal. Incentives for pharmaceutical companies to invest time, effort and resources into the development of drugs to treat limited populations are few compared with the development of drugs to treat more prevalent genotypes in the context of pharmacogenomics. Most drug companies might be expected to direct their resources towards the development of drugs to treat the more prevalent genotypes.

Those groups characterized by less-profitable genotypes are at risk of becoming therapeutic "orphans". At present, pharmaceuticals for rare diseases are termed "orphan drugs." The United States and Japan have enacted legislation to stimulate research and the development of orphan drugs through market mechanisms, such as tax-based cost incentives and time-limited monopolies, with varying degrees of governmental intervention. Canada, Sweden, France, the United Kingdom and other countries rely on broader national drug policies based on more substantial governmental intervention. The European Union has entertained initiatives to stimulate legislative action on orphan drugs, and the European Agency for the Evaluation of Medicinal Products has a provision that exempts drug companies from having to pay application fees to develop a drug if it is an orphan drug. Despite allegations of overpricing of orphan drugs under the American model, nearly all efforts have been followed by a measurable increase in the number of drugs that have been developed and approved for the treatment of rare diseases. As clinical trials increasingly consist of genetically non-diverse groups, policy makers will need to consider whether to expand the concepts underlying orphan drug policies to stimulate research into and the development of drugs for populations who, by virtue of their genetic make-up, face inequities in drug development efforts.

Cost might act as a barrier to access to pharmacogenomics in that the cost of participating in clinical trials or of the resulting drug therapy might be excluded from insurance coverage. Particularly in the United States, where managed care systems attempt to contain costs by rationing medical services, public and private third-party payers have refused or been reluctant to pay for treatments that they deem "experimental" or not "medically necessary." Increasingly, these terms have more political than legal or medical significance. There is some evidence that the insurers' disinclination to cover expenses that are associated with new drug therapies can be countered by high physician or consumer demand for the new drug. If consumers must absorb rising pharmaceutical costs, pharmacogenomics will not introduce new questions so much as it will intensify existing ones about equitable access to medical care.

PROFESSIONAL STANDARDS OF CARE

As pharmacogenomic-based drugs enter into the marketplace, physicians will encounter alternatives to conventional drug therapy and prescription practices. Although the evaluation of genetic variation among patients to determine proper medication and dosage during the course of treatment is not the standard of care at present, ethical concerns, economic considerations and the threat of malpractice liability are likely to encourage physicians to begin testing for and prescribing medications designed for use by specific, smaller groups of individuals. Moral and ethical proscriptions against causing harm might require a physician to integrate pharmacogenetics into clinical practice where necessary to minimize risk to a patient. By contrast, budgetary constraints imposed by insurers could slow the acceptance of drugs developed through pharmacogenomics by limiting their use by physicians and their availability to patients. The issues raised are not unique to pharmacogenomics but do require new applications of ethical principles and legal doctrine.

In countries where the legal systems are based on common law (that is, the English tradition of law-making based on the court decisions of judges), physicians and pharmacists are subject to liability under theories of negligence, which involve the violation of a duty based on a "reasonableness" standard or a standard of reasonable care. The standard of care is defined by how a similarly qualified practitioner would act in treating a patient under the same or similar circumstances. The literature, which includes professional scholarship and guidelines published by professional societies, and clinical experience establish the standard of care. In cases based on negligence in the form of medical malpractice, the standard of care is defined through the testimony of witnesses regarding what constitutes conventional practice within the medical community.

As pharmacogenomic-based drugs increase in prevalence over the next several years, the use of genotyping or genetic testing as a diagnostic tool and the prescription of medications based on genotypic information will become the standard of care for physicians. Physicians and pharmacists might be subject to liability if they lack sufficient knowledge of genetics to adequately interpret diagnostic tests, prescribe appropriate pharmacogenomic-based drug therapy in proper dosages, consider pharmacogenomic-based drug interactions, or properly dispense pharmacogenomic-based prescriptions. With greater knowledge comes greater responsibility. Pharmacogenomics might provide greater information about the likelihood of a drug being effective or causing adverse reactions in persons possessing a particular genetic characteristic, and will certainly yield drugs that are more likely to be suitable for smaller, specific groups of individuals. By increasing the information available for consideration in drug therapy and the importance of matching the right drug to the right person, pharmacogenomics will raise the standard of care applicable to all involved in the safe prescription and distribution of pharmaceuticals.

Pharmacists are primarily charged with the dispensation of prescriptions as administered by physicians, but the scope of their responsibilities has expanded over time to include ensuring that prescriptions and patient directions are correct and appropriate. Pharmacists also have a duty to warn their customers of the potential adverse effects or other problems associated with a prescribed drug therapy. Even if a pharmacist has dispensed a prescription according to a physician's instructions, some jurisdictions have imposed liability on pharmacists for the harm that resulted from a drug that was properly dispensed in accordance with an improper or harmful prescription. As information regarding the genotype of an individual becomes increasingly important to safe prescription and dosage, pharmacists might be charged with greater knowledge of their customers' genetic information than they now require. The increased amount of genetic information in pharmacies raises privacy and confidentiality concerns, especially where pharmacists belong to large pharmacy chains or corporations with widely accessible, centralized records. For physicians and pharmacists, the issue of continuing professional education and record maintenance will become more important, not only for improving competence but also for preventing liability.

Pharmacogenomics is likely to increase the burden shared by the pharmaceutical industry to provide adequate warnings of the limitations and dangers of their products. In the United States, for example, pharmaceutical manufacturers have a duty to warn physicians about any known or knowable risks, or dangers, of the use of a manufactured drug. Many states in the US will impose strict liability on a drug company for harm caused by the failure to adequately warn against the dangerous propensities of a drug that it has manufactured. Unlike negligence theory, the rules of strict liability are not concerned with the standard of care nor the reasonableness of the manufacturer's conduct; and an aggrieved party need only prove that the manufacturer did not adequately warn of a particular risk that was knowable in the light of generally recognized and prevailing best scientific and medical knowledge available at the time of manufacture and distribution. Pharmaceutical companies must consider the potential for liability if patients are harmed because they were excluded from the subgroup for which a pharmacogenomic-based drug is deemed safe and efficacious, particularly if the exclusion leads to a failure to yield information on possible side effects or alternative therapies. Not all adverse side effects are predictable, owing to the number of genes relevant to drug responsiveness, as well as environmental factors. The question is how to allocate responsibility for taking the greatest advantage of drugs specialized to suit relatively smaller segments of the population.

In June 2000, four individuals filed a class action lawsuit against SmithKline Beecham, alleging that the manufacturer of a vaccine for Lyme disease knew that some individuals would be susceptible to arthritis on exposure to the vaccine because of their genotype, but failed to warn about this by labeling. The case is still pending. Similar cases involve malpractice actions by the patient against the prescribing physician, who in turn seeks to recover against the manufacturer for failure to provide adequate information. Put simply, pharmacogenomics will raise the legal stakes for all involved whenever a patient suffers adverse reactions from the use of a drug that might have been contraindicated based on his or her genotype.

CONCLUSION

By lessening the uncertainty associated with the selection of drug targets and the design of human clinical studies in the development of new drugs, pharmacogenomics will result in the production of safer, more effective drugs for use in therapeutic medicine. The integration of pharmacogenomic technology into the drug development process and the practice of medicine will require consideration of ethical, social and legal questions. Answers to these questions might well determine the level of social acceptance and realization of the benefits of pharmacogenomic technology.

NOTES AND QUESTIONS

1.   Both pharmacogenetics and pharmacogenomics raise questions of the privacy and confidentiality of individually-identifiable genetic information and the potential for discrimination. Pharmacogenetics, which involves genetic testing of individuals and families, could cause individuals and lineages to be classified as expensive or "hard to treat," making it difficult for them to get health care or health insurance, as Rothstein and Epps point out. In theory, pharmacogenetic testing is restricted to narrow tests for pharmacologic responsiveness:

> "Genetic testing" needs to be defined carefully. The magnitude of the ethical, legal and social implications of genetic testing is dependent on the information derived from the test. Genetic tests for mutations in single genes that are causally related to rare diseases and are inherited in a simple mendelian fashion can have profound implications for the individual and family members. Genetic tests for disease-susceptibility gene polymorphisms—which are risk factors for the disease—have the added complication of uncertainty. In both cases the lack of effective intervention drives many of the issues. Pharmacogenetic profiles, on the other hand, will predict if an individual patient is likely to benefit from a medicine and be free of serious side effects. These profiles will not be designed to provide any other information, as the profile data are derived from the patients who respond with efficacy or adverse event when taking the drug, compared with patients who did not respond. It does not differentiate disease. Should a polymorphism that is found to be related to disease association be included in a profile, it can be removed and replaced by another SNP that is in linkage disequilibrium, thus avoiding any disease-specific association, even if inadvertent. This would be similar to replacing the *ApoE4* SNP by one or more of the others in linkage disequilibrium with *ApoE4* but not specifically associated with Alzheimer's disease. The ethical, legal and social implications of pharmacogenetic profiles are therefore of a lower magnitude of societal concern compared with specific genetic tests for disease.

Allen D. Roses, Pharmacogenetics and the Practice of Medicine, 405 Nature 857 (legend for Fig. 5) (2000). To what extent do Roses' expectations depend on the care with which genetic testing is performed? Should the law require potentially revealing information in a genetic profile to be replaced with less sensitive information, as Roses suggests? Who would impose such a legal requirement and on whom?

Pharmacogenomics, on the other hand, involves the analysis of DNA from random persons. The DNA can be stored and analyzed anonymously, as Roses assures is the case with the data bank maintained by his employer, GlaxoSmithKline. See Gina Kolata, Tailor-Made Medicine, The New York Times, Dec. 20, 1999, at A1.

2.   The prospect of drug variants for small patient populations whose genetic profile makes the variant especially safe and effective raises questions about how safety and efficacy would be determined. To meet FDA requirements, sponsors typically must conduct clinical trials in large numbers of subjects. It may be difficult to enroll enough subjects in studies of drug variants for small populations. Should the FDA relax its safety and efficacy requirements to facilitate pharmacogenetic testing? Should it proceed on a case-by-case basis for specific drugs? What factors should the agency consider in deciding what requirements to impose? Does the new FDA guidance document adequately answer these questions?

3.   As indicated by the class action suit against SmithKline Beecham mentioned in the article by Rothstein and Epps, Cassidy v. SmithKline Beecham, 1999 WL 33645128 (Pa. Com. Pl. 1999), drug manufacturers face products liability actions for failing to warn patients about small group susceptibilities to adverse drug reactions. The suit charged that 30 percent of the general population has the gene HLA–DR4+, which produces an autoimmune arthritic reaction triggered by an outer surface protein, Osp A, contained in the manufacturer's LYMErix vaccine. The suit charged that the manufacturer was aware of the connection because of its documentation in the literature, but did not advise physicians to recommend genetic testing for HLA–DR4+ prior to prescribing the vaccine. The suit was settled in 2003.

4.   The "Learned Intermediary Doctrine" makes health professionals such as physicians and pharmacists rather than the manufacturer responsible for providing safety warnings to patients, but the manufacturer can still be liable if in product labeling it does not make health professionals aware of safety information of which the manufacturer is aware (see, e.g., Schenebeck v. Sterling Drug, Inc., 423 F.2d 919, 923 (8th Cir. 1970)) or if it directs advertising to patients and omits warnings about serious side effects (see Perez v. Wyeth Laboratories, Inc., 734 A.2d 1245 (N.J. 1999)).

Would manufacturers be liable for marketing a drug with a design defect if the drug harmed a subgroup of patients but was safe for others? See Margaret Gilhooley, When Drugs Are Safe for Some But Not Others: The FDA Experience and Alternatives for Products Liability, 36 Hous. L. Rev. 927 (1999). As Gilhooley notes, the newly-adopted Restatement (Third) of Torts provides that a prescription drug is defective only if it is unsafe "for any class of patients." Restatement (Third) of Torts: Products Liability § 6 (c) (1998), and a comment by the authors of the Restatement explains that "a prescription drug * * * that has usefulness to any class of patients is not defective in design even if it is harmful to other patients." (Comment b).

5.   Note that, as Rothstein and Epps point out, not only manufacturers but physicians, pharmacists, and other health professionals also may be liable if they fail to meet the applicable standard of care in regard to the use of pharmacogenetic information in treating their patients.

6.   The FDA has begun approving pharmacogenetic tests as medical devices. In 2002, the FDA approved an HIV genotyping test. The test helps determine if a patient is infected with strains of the HIV virus that are resistant to certain antiretroviral drugs so that a different drug combination can be prescribed. In 2004, the agency approved a P450 genotyping test, the first DNA test to use a microarray chip to help determine whether a patient is more or less likely to suffer side effects from several commonly-prescribed drugs. A microarray chip permits a large number of polymorphisms to be tested simultaneously. The P450 test analyzes one of the genes from a family of genes called cytochrome P450, which affect the ability of the liver to metabolize certain drugs and other compounds, including those found in certain antidepressants, anti-psychotics, beta-blockers, and some chemotherapy drugs. In 2005, the FDA approved a test to detect a gene called UGT1A1, which affects the ability of the liver to metabolize drugs used in treating colorectal cancer.

III. GENE THERAPY

A. HISTORY OF GENE THERAPY

The first attempt at human gene therapy is said to have occurred in 1970, when Stanfield Rogers, a biochemist and physician, attempted to insert into three German girls a virus carrying a gene to combat an inherited liver disease. None of the girls improved.

In 1980, Martin Cline, a UCLA researcher and Chief of Hematology/Oncology at the UCLA Medical Center, attempted to insert DNA into the bone marrow of two patients, one in Italy and the other in Israel, suffering from beta thalassemia, a hereditary blood disorder. Cline submitted a protocol to the UCLA Institutional Review Board (IRB), but went ahead with the experiment before receiving IRB approval. The IRB later rejected Cline's protocol because of insufficient studies in animals. Cline's experiments were uncovered by a newspaper reporter for the L.A. Times. As a result, Cline lost his department chair and his funding from the NIH. The Cline incident raises issues of research ethics, such as the following: What is the reach of a research protocol? Should a protocol from a U.S. university extend to a professor's work abroad?

Ten years later, in 1990, the third attempt at gene therapy occurred at the NIH in Bethesda, Maryland. The patient, Ashanti DeSilva, was a four year-old suffering from SCID (severe combined immune deficiency). As a result of a genetic error inherited from both parents, patients with this disease do not manufacture the enzyme adenosine deaminase, required for proper functioning of the immune system. DeSilva led a cloistered, endangered existence, being vulnerable to severe infections. A team of physicians removed some of her white blood cells, inserted normal copies of the gene into the cells, and returned the cells into her bloodstream. After four infusions over four months, she improved. She continues to receive infusions every few months, however, because the cells with the normal gene do not continue to work indefinitely. Moreover, she continues to receive traditional drug therapy (PEGADA, a form of the missing enzyme) to supplement the effect of the gene therapy. Nevertheless, many regard DeSilva's experiment to be the first partially successful use of gene therapy.

Ten years after that, in 2000, French scientists announced that they had used gene therapy to successfully treat several infants suffering from a form of SCID (SCID–X1). Unlike in the case of DeSilva, the French researchers claimed to have inserted correctly-functioning genes in the babies' bone marrow, where they can continue to proliferate, thereby avoiding the need for repeat infusions. Moreover, the babies' immune systems have become normal, and they do not receive traditional drug therapy.

Three years later, however, the French scientists announced that, although nine of the 10 babies developed normal immune systems, two of them developed T-cell leukemia, a form of cancer. The FDA placed a hold on three U.S. gene therapy trials that used the same retroviral vector, as did France and Germany. Subsequently, researchers determined that the leukemia resulted from the coincidental insertion of the retrovirus near a cancer gene that it activated. It was hoped that improved vectors could alleviate the problem. But in 2004, one of the two babies died, and in 2005, a third child in the French experiment developed leukemia.

The events in France followed years of unsuccessful efforts to use gene therapy to treat diseases such as cystic fibrosis, familial hypercholesterolemia, Gaucher's disease, and cancer. They also followed the death in October 1999, of Jesse Gelsinger.

Gelsinger, 18 years old, enrolled in an experiment at the University of Pennsylvania to develop a gene therapy for OTC (ornithine transcarbamylase) deficiency, an x-linked, dominant, single-gene liver disorder whose sufferers, numbering about one out of every 40,000 births, are unable to metabolize ammonia, which is a by-product of the breakdown of protein in the body. The disease is especially severe in newborns. Affected babies slip into a coma within 72 hours of birth and suffer severe brain damage. Half die within one month, and half of the survivors die before they reach six months of age.

Interestingly, Gelsinger himself did not inherit the disease. Instead, it resulted from a de novo genetic mutation. Furthermore, Gelsinger had what is called mosaicism—the genetic makeup of his cells was not all the same and some of his liver cells were producing the missing enzyme, enough so that he did not become comatose after birth and was able to control the illness with a combination of a non-protein diet and enzyme pills. However, by the time he reached eighteen, he was taking 35 pills a day, and was likely to have had to increase the dosage as time went on. He was eager to help find a cure—both for himself and for the more severely-affected infants.

The study Gelsinger enrolled in was not intended to treat OTC. Instead, it was what is called a "Phase I" trial. The plan was to use an adenovirus as a vector; the DNA in the nucleus of the virus would be altered by recombinant DNA techniques to carry the correct gene, and an infusion of the adenovirus vector would be inserted into the subjects' livers. The purpose of the Phase I trial was to determine if, once inserted, the corrected genes would proceed to produce the missing enzyme, and to determine the "maximum tolerated dose" of the infusion—that is, the highest dose that would produce the desired effect without serious side effects.

At first, the Penn researchers proposed to conduct the experiment on a group of severely affected newborns, since their form of the disease was the ultimate target of the therapy. But Arthur Caplan, a leading bioethicist then at Penn, objected that the parents of these infants could not give valid informed consent, since parents of dying babies were subject to too much "emotional coercion." Sheryl Gay Stolberg, The Biotech Death of Jesse Gelsinger, The New York Times Sunday Magazine, Nov. 28, 1999, at 137. Consequently, the Penn researchers decided to do the Phase I study on adults, both female carriers and persons like Gelsinger with only partial enzyme deficiencies.

The Penn research was funded by the NIH. Therefore, the researchers submitted their protocol, or plan for the design of the study, to NIH for review. (The review was conducted by the Recombinant DNA Advisory Committee, known as the "RAC," discussed later in this chapter.) The NIH reviewers were concerned about imposing the risks of the experiment on asymptomatic volunteers like Gelsinger, but Caplan's position prevailed and the NIH gave Penn the go-ahead. The researchers also submitted their protocol to the FDA, as required by federal law, and the agency approved it. Finally, the protocol was reviewed and approved by Penn's own Institutional Review Board (IRB), a group made up primarily of Penn researchers.

There were 18 subjects in all, divided into three groups, with each group getting a different dose. Gelsinger was in the highest dosage group. Everything seemed to be going fine. A story in The New York Times tells what happened next:

The treatment began on Monday, Sept. 13. Jesse would receive the highest dose. Seventeen patients had already been treated, including one woman who had been given the same dose that Jesse would get, albeit from a different lot, and had done "quite well," Raper [the surgeon who administered the infusion] says. That morning, Jesse was taken to the interventional-radiology suite, where he was sedated and strapped to a table while a team of radiologists threaded two catheters into his groin. At 10:30 a.m., Raper drew 30 milliliters of the vector and injected it slowly. At half past noon, he was done.

That night, Jesse was sick to his stomach and spiked a fever, 104.5 degrees. Raper was not particularly surprised: other patients had experienced the same reaction. Paul Gelsinger [the patient's father] called; he and Jesse talked briefly, exchanging I love yous. Those were the last words they ever spoke.

Early Tuesday morning a nurse called Raper at home; Jesse seemed disoriented. When Raper got to the hospital, about 6:15 a.m., he noticed that the whites of Jesse's eyes were yellow. That meant jaundice, not a good sign. "It was not something we had seen before," Raper says. A test confirmed that Jesse's bilirubin, a breakdown product of red blood cells, was four times the normal level. Raper called Gelsinger, and Batshaw [a physician who proposed the experiment] in Washington, who said he would get on a train and be there in two hours.

Both doctors knew that the high bilirubin meant one of two things: either Jesse's liver was failing or he was suffering a clotting disorder in which his red blood cells were breaking down faster than the liver could metabolize them. This was the same disorder the scientists had seen in the monkeys that had been given the stronger vector. The condition is life-threatening for anyone, but particularly dangerous for someone with Jesse's disease, because red blood cells liberate protein when they break down.

By midafternoon Tuesday, a little more than 24 hours after the injection, the clotting disorder had pushed Jesse into a coma. By 11:30 p.m., his ammonia level was 393 micromoles per liter of blood. Normal is 35. The doctors began dialysis.

Paul Gelsinger had booked a red-eye flight. When he arrived in the surgical intensive care unit at 8 Wednesday morning, Raper and Batshaw told him that dialysis had brought Jesse's ammonia level down to 72 but that other complications were developing. He was hyperventilating, which would increase the level of ammonia in his brain. They wanted to paralyze his muscles and induce a deeper coma, so that a ventilator could breathe for him. Gelsinger gave consent. Then he put on scrubs, gloves and a mask and went in to see his son.

By Wednesday afternoon, Jesse seemed to be stabilizing. Batshaw went back to Washington. Paul felt comfortable enough to meet his brother for dinner. But later that night Jesse worsened again. His lungs grew stiff; the doctors were giving him 100 percent oxygen, but not enough of it was getting to his bloodstream. They consulted a liver-transplant team and learned that Jesse was not a good candidate. Raper was beside himself. He consulted with Batshaw and Wilson, and they decided to take an extraordinary step, a procedure known as ECMO, for extracorporeal membrane oxygenation, essentially an external lung that filters the blood, removing carbon dioxide and adding oxygen. It had been tried on only 1,000 people before, Raper says. Only half had survived.

"If we could just buy his lungs a day or two," Raper said later, they thought "maybe he would go ahead and heal up."

The next day, Thursday, Sept. 16, Hurricane Floyd slammed into the East Coast. Mickie Gelsinger [the patient's stepmother] flew in from Tucson just before the airport closed. (Pattie Gelsinger, Jesse's mother, was being treated in a psychiatric facility and was unable to leave.) Batshaw spent the day trapped outside Baltimore on an Amtrak train. He ran down his cell phone calling Raper; when it went dead, he persuaded another passenger to lend him his. The ECMO, Raper reported, appeared to be working. But then another problem cropped up: Jesse's kidneys stopped making urine. "He was sliding into multiple-organ-system failure," Raper says.

That night, at his hotel, Paul Gelsinger couldn't sleep. He left his wife a note and walked the half mile to the Penn medical center to see Jesse. The boy was bloated beyond recognition; even his ears were swollen shut. Gelsinger noticed blood in Jesse's urine, an indication, he knew, that the kidneys were shutting down. How can anybody, he thought, survive this?

On the morning of Friday the 17th, a test showed that Jesse was brain dead. Paul Gelsinger didn't need to be told: "I knew it already." He called for a chaplain to hold a bedside service, with prayers for the removal of life support.

The room was crowded with equipment and people: 7 of Paul's 15 siblings came in, plus an array of doctors and nurses. Raper and Batshaw, shellshocked and exhausted, stood in the back. The chaplain anointed Jesse's forehead with oil, then read the Lord's

Prayer. The doctors fought back tears. When the intensive-care specialist flipped two toggle switches, one to turn off the ventilator and the other to turn off the ECMO machine, Raper stepped forward. He checked the heart-rate monitor, watched the line go flat and noted the time: 2:30 p.m. He put his stethoscope to Jesse's chest, more out of habit than necessity, and pronounced the death official. "Goodbye, Jesse," he said. "We'll figure this out."

Sheryl Gay Stolberg, The Biotech Death of Jesse Gelsinger, The New York Times Sunday Magazine, Nov. 28, 1999, at 137.

Gelsinger was believed to be the first patient to die in the course of a gene therapy experiment. In the aftermath of Gelsinger's death, it was discovered that there had been a number of adverse events associated with gene therapy experiments that had never been made public. Many of them had been reported to the FDA, as required by FDA regulations. See 21 C.F.R. § 312.32 (requiring IND safety reports within 15 days of any serious or unexpected adverse events, and immediate notification of fatal or life-threatening adverse events). In accordance with long-standing FDA policy, however, these reports were considered trade secrets and not disclosed to the public. Even the fact that a sponsor had filed an IND (or IDE) was kept secret.

NIH also required that it be notified of serious adverse events occurring in gene therapy studies that it funded or that were conducted at an institution that received NIH funding. See Appendix M–VII–C, Points to Consider in the Design and Submission of Protocols for the Transfer of Recombinant DNA Molecules into One or More Human Subjects (www4. od.nih.gov/oba/rac/guidelines_02/Appendix_M.htm). In contrast to the FDA, however, the NIH made these reports public. Sponsors therefore were reluctant to make the reports. After Gelsinger's death, the NIH received reports of 691 serious adverse events; only 39 had been reported when they occurred, as required by the NIH rules.

The lack of public awareness of safety problems with gene therapy trials not only impaired the ability of researchers to inform subjects of potential risks in obtaining informed consent; it hampered the researcher's ability to design and conduct safe studies. In reviewing gene therapy research INDs, the FDA was not always able to consider the full implications of the adverse event reports it received for other investigations, and researchers would only hear about these events if their occurrence was "leaked" by their colleagues, for example, at science conferences or in private conversations.

Gelsinger's death and the resulting disclosures of the lack of awareness of adverse events prompted several government reactions. In March 2000, the Department of Health and Human Services announced a new Gene Therapy Trial Monitoring Plan whereby the FDA would more closely review the procedures employed by a sponsor to monitor gene therapy trials, and established a program of Gene Transfer Safety Symposia which would bring researchers together 4 times a year to review safety results from gene therapy experiments. See Food and Drug Administration, New Initiatives to Protect Participants in Gene Therapy Trials, March 7, 2000 (www.fda.gov/bbs/topics/NEWS/NEW00717.html). The Secretary of Health and Human Services proposed to ask Congress for new authority to levy $250,000 fines against investigators who violated human subjects protection rules, and $1 million fines against their institutions.

Finally, the FDA published proposed regulations which would provide for the public disclosure of IND safety reports for two types of experiments: gene therapy and xenotransplantation (the transplantation into humans of non-human organs or tissue). The proposal can be found at 66 Fed. Reg. 4688 (2001). This marked the first time that the FDA proposed to adopt formal regulations specifically dealing with gene therapy; all previous FDA pronouncements had been in the form of policy statements.

If adopted, the regulations would mark a significant change in the agency's attitude toward gene therapy and biotechnology more generally. As noted earlier, until now, the FDA has taken the position that biotechnology products should be subject to the same regulatory requirements as any other products. The proposed regulations, by pertaining only to gene therapy and xenotransplantation would signal that the agency had abandoned this viewpoint. This might lead to a broader shift in the government's regulatory policy toward biotechnology, with repercussions for areas such as genetically engineered foods and plants.

In March 2004, the NIH and FDA announced the creation of a new web data base, the Genetic Modification Clinical Research Information System (GeMCRIS). Information reported to the NIH about adverse events that occur in gene therapy trials will be posted on the data base and be available to researchers and to the public.

Two months after Gelsinger's death, the FDA inspected the research operation at Penn and, after finding a number of deficiencies, suspended all gene therapy experiments. The deficiencies included problems with the informed consent process in the OTC trial. The FDA also determined that Gelsinger was not a proper subject for enrollment into the study, since his liver was not functioning well-enough at the time he received the adenovirus infusion.

One of the most troubling revelations involved the significant financial conflicts of interest of the lead researchers who owned stock in a biotech company trying to monetize the gene therapy. The experiment in which Jesse Gelsinger died was part of a large-scale gene therapy research program at the University of Pennsylvania's Institute of Gene Therapy, headed by James M. Wilson. At the time, the institute had 250 employees and an annual budget of $25 million, and was considered the largest academic gene therapy research program in the country. Wilson was also the founder and a stockholder, along with the university, in a company called Genovo. Genovo did not fund the Gelsinger study, but it did provide twenty percent of the institute's budget, and had the exclusive right to commercialize any institute discoveries. According to the university's general counsel, the relationship between Wilson, Genovo, and Penn was so complicated that the university set up two committees to oversee it. When Genova was sold in 2000 to a company called Targeted Genetics Corp., Wilson was due to receive stock worth $13.5 million.

In May 2000, the FDA criticized researchers at the St. Elizabeth's Medical Center in Boston for failing to report a death in an experiment designed to determine if patients with blocked blood vessels of the heart could be improved by injecting them with genes that produce a substance that promotes revascularization. It turned out that the patient was not appropriate for the study because he had a lung tumor and was a heavy smoker, raising the concern that the inserted genes would promote tumor growth. The chief researcher was a founder of and major stockholder in the company sponsoring the experiment.

A great deal of attention has been given to the problems created by researchers' financial stake in the outcome of their experiments. See Catherine D. DeAngelis, Conflict of Interest and the Public Trust, 284 JAMA 2237 (2000); David Korn, Commentary: Conflicts of Interest in Biomedical Research, 284 JAMA 2234 (2000); Bernard Lo et al., Conflict-of-Interest Policies for Investigators in Clinical Trials, 343 New Eng. J. Med. 1616 (2000); S. Van McCrary et al., A National Survey of Policies on Disclosure of Conflicts of Interest in Biomedical Research, 343 New Eng. J. Med. 1621 (2000).

In 2005, the Justice Department settled a lawsuit against the Gelsinger researchers that had accused them of making false statements to the FDA, including misrepresentations that would have resulted in the FDA shutting down the experiment. Under the terms of the settlement, the University of Pennsylvania agreed to pay $517,000 in fines and the Children's National Medical Center (where Batshaw worked) $514,622. This was twice the amount of NIH funding for the experiment. The agreement also barred Wilson until 2010 from conducting clinical research under FDA jurisdiction, and imposed a 3-year ban on clinical research by Raper and Batshaw.

After several months during which he defended the researchers at Penn, Gelsinger's father filed a lawsuit for wrongful death. Arthur Caplan was initially named as a defendant, in what is regarded as the first suit against a biomedical ethicist for advice in connection with the design of a clinical trial. Caplan was subsequently dismissed as a defendant, however, and the suit eventually settled for an undisclosed amount.

For a poignant account of these events written by the father of Jesse Gelsinger, see Paul L. Gelsinger, Uninformed Consent: The Case of Jesse Gelsinger, Law and Ethics in Biomedical Research: Regulations, Conflict of Interest, and Liability (Trudo Lemmens & Duff R. Waring eds. 2006).

B. SCIENCE OF GENE THERAPY

The concept of gene therapy is broad and encompasses a number of different techniques that share a common approach: the administration of DNA to combat disease. This can occur in several ways, including replacing flawed genetic material in chromosomes; adding cells with properly-functioning DNA to an organism; altering the function of existing defective genes (such as by blocking messenger RNA, which in turn produces proteins); interrupting the aberrant functioning of mutant proteins (for example, by creating other proteins that block or destroy them); or creating "gene factories" that manufacture therapeutic substances in the body. In the experiment in which Jesse Gelsinger died, for example, the second technique was being used: infusing his liver with virus cells containing genes that would produce a missing enzyme. Moreover, gene therapy can be "somatic," meaning that it does not affect reproductive cells and therefore the altered DNA is not passed on to the patient's offspring, or it can be germline therapy, in which the altered DNA intentionally or unintentionally changes the genetic endowment of future generations. Finally, the same techniques of genetic modification might be aimed at altering normal, non-disease traits, in which case they would not be considered gene therapy but "genetic enhancement." For a fuller description of gene therapy techniques, see Stuart H. Orkin & Arno G. Motulsky, Report and Recommendations of the Panel to Assess the NIH Investment in Research on Gene Therapy, December 7, 1995; Theodore Friedmann, Overcoming the Obstacles to Gene Therapy, Scientific American, June 1997, 96–101. Genetic enhancement is discussed in Chapter 10.

Gene therapy faces a number of technical hurdles. First, the DNA has to get into the patient. There are a variety of ways this might be accomplished, including the use of artificial chromosomes and "naked DNA." The most common technique in gene therapy experiments is to insert the desired DNA into an organism, such as a virus, and then insert the organism either into the patient directly, or into cells in the laboratory that are then inserted into the patient. In the Gelsinger experiment, for example, DNA that produces the enzyme that metabolizes ammonia was inserted into an adenovirus—the type of virus associated with the common cold—and infused into the study subjects. An organism such as a virus that delivers DNA into a patient or into a cell is called a "vector." The two most common vectors are viruses, such as the adenovirus used in the Gelsinger experiment, and retroviruses, which contain RNA rather than DNA. It is important that the pathological or disease-causing elements of the viral vector be deleted as much as possible before the vector is used.

Once a suitable vector is chosen to deliver the DNA (or RNA), the next problem is making sure that the genetic material gets to the correct site. The site in the Gelsinger experiment was the liver, so the vector was inserted into the hepatic artery. Some vectors may not need to be so site-specific. A treatment for hemophilia (a clotting disorder) might only need to be introduced into the circulatory system. But other treatments, such as those for cancer, might fail, or be accompanied by unacceptably serious side effects, if they cannot be delivered directly to tumors.

Even if therapeutic genes reach the appropriate site, it is necessary that they function, or are expressed, rather than remain dormant. Every cell nucleus contains essentially a complete set of a person's DNA, but only some of the genes are "turned on"; otherwise, the genes in the nuclei of liver cells, for example, would produce not only liver enzymes but biochemicals that were supposed to be manufactured in the pancreas or the gall bladder, and so on. The therapeutic genetic material must not only function, but function correctly. It must produce the correct amount of an enzyme, for example, and not cause problems such as cell death, sterility, or uncontrolled cell division (cancer).

Finally, the gene therapy must continue to function for the amount of time necessary to achieve the desired therapeutic effect. The body discards cells after a certain amount of time; even the oldest tissues in our bodies, our bones, are completely regenerated within approximately three years. Yet the target condition may persist throughout the patient's lifetime, or for longer than the corrected genes would remain functional. One approach is to replace the therapeutic genes as they wear out or are discarded. DeSilva continues to receive infusions of corrected genes every few months. An alternative is to insert the genetic material in such a way that it is replicated as cells divide. This is one advantage of using retroviruses, which integrate the therapeutic genetic material into the host genome, over viruses, like the adenovirus used in the experiment in which Gelsinger died, which only have short-term effects. In the Gelsinger experiment, the researchers believed that a short-acting viral vector would be sufficient; their aim was to ward off the comas that produce devastating neurological effects in newborns with OTC within 72 hours of their birth.

Another gene therapy approach that is attracting significant interest is RNA interference (RNAi). Recall from Chapter 2 that during the process of transcription, the DNA double helix breaks apart and each strand combines with adenine, guanine, cytosine, and, instead of thymine, a nucleotide called uracil, to create messenger RNA. If the messenger RNA exits the cell nucleus and encounters a structure in the cytoplasm called a ribosome, the ribosome reads the information in the messenger RNA and constructs proteins, the process known as translation.

While messenger RNA usually consists of single strands, some forms of RNA come in double strands. This is often the case with RNA from viruses. When the cell detects double-stranded RNA, it regards it as an invader and destroys it. It turns out that cells use the same basic method to deactivate portions of DNA so that there is no translation—that is, the protein that the DNA codes for is not produced. This method of preventing translation is called RNA interference. In the context of gene therapy, the idea is to use RNAi to silence disease genes—that is, to deactivate stretches of DNA that, if active, would produce proteins that caused illness. The FDA has approved clinical trials of RNAi to prevent macular degeneration and respiratory syncytial virus, a disease that can cause pneumonia and other respiratory problems in infants and the elderly.

The great advantage of RNAi therapy is that it does not alter the DNA itself. One problem is that RNA degrades relatively quickly in the bloodstream, so that methods must be found to deliver the RNAi to the target cells quickly and accurately. For a discussion of regulatory issues raised by RNAi, see Reese McKnight, RNA Interference: A Critical Analysis of the Regulatory and Ethical Issues Encountered in the Development of a Novel Therapy, 15 Albany L.J. Sci. & Tech. 73–108 (2004).

C. REGULATION OF GENE THERAPY

1. The Recombinant DNA Advisory Committee (RAC)

PAUL BERG ET AL., LETTER
185 Science 303 (1974).

POTENTIAL BIOHAZARDS OF RECOMBINANT DNA MOLECULES

Recent advances in techniques for the isolation and rejoining of segments of DNA now permit construction of biologically active recombinant DNA molecules in vitro. For example, DNA restriction endonucleases, which generate DNA fragments containing cohesive ends especially suitable for rejoining, have been used to create new types of biologically functional bacterial plasmids carrying antibiotic resistance markers and to link *Xenopus laevis* ribosomal DNA to DNA from a bacterial plasmid. This latter recombinant plasmid has been shown to replicate stably in *Escherichia coli* where it synthesizes RNA that is complementary to X. laevis ribosomal DNA. Similarly, segments of *Drosophila* chromosomal DNA have been incorporated into both plasmid and bacteriaphage DNA's to yield hybrid molecules that can infect and replicate in *E. coli.*

Several groups of scientists are now planning to use this technology to create recombinant DNAs from a variety of other viral, animal, and bacterial sources. Although such experiments are likely to facilitate the solution of important theoretical and practical biological problems, they would also result in the creation of novel types of infectious DNA elements whose biological properties cannot be completely predicted in advance.

There is serious concern that some of these artificial recombinant DNA molecules could prove biologically hazardous. One potential hazard in current experiments derives from the need to use a bacterium like *E. coli* to clone the recombinant DNA molecules and to amplify their number. Strains of *E. coli* commonly reside in the human intestinal tract, and they are capable of exchanging genetic information with other types of bacteria, some of which are pathogenic to man. Thus, new DNA elements introduced into *E. coli.* might possibly become widely disseminated among human, bacterial, plant, or animal populations with unpredictable effects.

Concern for these emerging capabilities was raised by scientists attending the 1973 Gordon Research Conference on Nucleic Acids, who requested that the National Academy of Sciences give consideration to these matters. The undersigned members of a committee, acting on behalf of and with the endorsement of the Assembly of Life Sciences of the National Research Council on this matter, propose the following recommendations.

First, and most important, that until the potential hazards of such recombinant DNA molecules have been better evaluated or until adequate methods are developed for preventing their spread, scientists throughout the world join with the members of this committee in voluntarily deferring the following types of experiments.

Type I: Construction of new, autonomously replicating bacterial plasmids that might result in the introduction of genetic determinants for antibiotic resistance or bacterial toxin formation into bacterial strains that do not at present carry such determinants; or construction of new bacterial plasmids containing combinations of resistance to clinically useful antibiotics unless plasmids containing such combinations of antibiotic resistance determinants already exist in nature.

Type II: Linkage of all or segments of the DNA's from oncogenic or other animal viruses to autonomously replicating DNA elements such as bacterial plasmids or other viral DNA's. Such recombinant DNA molecules might be more easily disseminated to bacterial populations in humans and other species, and thus possibly increase the incidence of cancer or other diseases.

Second, plans to link fragments of animal DNA's to bacterial plasmid DNA or bacteriophage DNA should be carefully weighed in light of the fact that many types of animal cell DNA's contain sequences common to RNA tumor viruses. Since joining of any foreign DNA to a DNA replication system creates new recombinant DNA molecules whose biological properties cannot be predicted with certainty, such experiments should not be undertaken lightly.

Third, the director of the National Institutes of Health is requested to give immediate consideration to establishing an advisory committee charged with (i) overseeing an experimental program to evaluate the potential biological and ecological hazards of the above types of recombinant DNA molecules; (ii) developing procedures which will minimize the spread of such molecules within human and other populations; and (iii) devising guidelines to be followed by investigators working with potentially hazardous recombinant DNA molecules.

Fourth, an international meeting of involved scientists from all over the world should be convened early in the coming year to review scientific progress in this area and to further discuss appropriate ways to deal with the potential biohazards of recombinant DNA molecules.

The above recommendations are made with the realization (i) that our concern is based on judgments of potential rather than demonstrated risk since there are few available experimental data on the hazards of such DNA molecules and (ii) that adherence to our major recommendations will entail postponement or possibly abandonment of certain types of scientifically worthwhile experiments. Moreover, we are aware of many theoretical and practical difficulties involved in evaluating the human hazards of such recombinant DNA molecules. Nonetheless, our concern for the possible unfortunate consequences of indiscriminate application of these techniques motivates us to urge all scientists working in this area to join us in agreeing not to initiate experiments of types I and II above until attempts have been made to evaluate the hazards and some resolution of the outstanding questions has been achieved.

Paul Berg, *Chairman,* David Baltimore, Herbert W. Boyer, Stanley N. Cohen, Ronald W. Davis, David S. Hogness, Daniel Nathans, Richard

Roblin, James D. Watson, Sherman Weissman, Norton D. Zinder, Committee on Recombinant DNA Molecules, Assembly of Life Sciences, National Research Council, National Academy of Sciences

NOTES AND QUESTIONS

The Berg letter called on scientists to adopt a voluntary, world-wide moratorium on rDNA experiments until further deliberations could determine whether rDNA could be performed safely. A voluntary moratorium is a form of self-regulation, an alternative to external restraints, such as legal prohibitions. Is voluntary action a viable method of regulating gene therapy? What are its strengths and weaknesses as a regulatory approach? For an early discussion of these issues, see Barry Furrow, Governing Science: Public Risks and Private Remedies, 131 U. Pa. L. Rev. 1403 (1983).

Professional self-regulation may take the form of individual choices about behavior, such as when a physician refuses to perform procedures that violate the physician's moral or religious beliefs. It also may be embodied in the views of professional organizations, such as the ethical codes of physician groups or official positions adopted by scientific bodies.

AMERICAN MEDICAL ASSOCIATION COUNCIL ON ETHICAL AND JUDICIAL AFFAIRS
Current Opinion E–2.11. Gene Therapy (Updated 1996).

Gene therapy involves the replacement or modification of a genetic variant to restore or enhance cellular function or to improve the reaction of non-genetic therapies.

Two types of gene therapy have been identified: (1) somatic cell therapy, in which human cells other than germ cells are genetically altered, and (2) germ line therapy, in which a replacement gene is integrated into the genome of human gametes or their precursors, resulting in expression of the new gene in the patient's offspring and subsequent generations. The fundamental difference between germ line therapy and somatic cell therapy is that germ line therapy affects the welfare of subsequent generations and may be associated with increased risk and the potential for unpredictable and irreversible results. Because of the far-reaching implications of germ line therapy, it is appropriate to limit genetic intervention to somatic cells at this time.

The goal of both somatic cell and germ line therapy is to alleviate human suffering and disease by remedying disorders for which available therapies are not satisfactory. This goal should be pursued only within the ethical tradition of medicine, which gives primacy to the welfare of the patient whose safety and well-being must be vigorously protected. To the extent possible, experience with animal studies must be sufficient to assure the effectiveness and safety of the techniques used, and the predictability of the results.

* * *

As gene therapy becomes feasible for a variety of human disorders, there are several practical factors to consider to ensure safe application of this technology in society. First, any gene therapy research should meet the Council's guidelines on clinical investigation (Opinion 2.07) and investigators must adhere to the standards of medical practice and professional responsibility. The proposed procedure must be fully discussed with the patient and the written informed consent of the patient or the patient's legal representative must be voluntary.

Investigators must be thorough in their attempts to eliminate any unwanted viral agents from the viral vector containing the corrective gene. The potential for adverse effects of the viral delivery system must be disclosed to the patient. The effectiveness of gene therapy must be evaluated fully, including the determination of the natural history of the disease and follow-up examination of subsequent generations. Gene therapy should be pursued only after the availability or effectiveness of other possible therapies is found to be insufficient. These considerations should be reviewed, as appropriate, as procedures and scientific information develop.

QUESTIONS

Is the AMA's approach, which relies on investigators adhering to the organization's ethical standards, a suitable one for regulating gene therapy? What are the consequences if a physician-researcher violates these provisions? See generally David Orentlicher, The Influence of a Professional Organization on Physician Behavior, 57 Alb. L. Rev. 583 (1994). Do these provisions apply to non-physicians?

———————

Following publication of the Berg letter, another conference was held at the Asilomar Conference Center in California. The meeting was attended by 150 scientists, four lawyers, and 16 journalists. The focus was on how rDNA experiments could be conducted safely. As one attendee observed:

> The recombinant DNA issue was defined as a technical problem to be solved by technical means. Larger ethical issues regarding the purposes and the long-term goals of the research were excluded, despite the rich discussion that had occurred among geneticists and other biologists in the 1960s about where to draw the line when it became possible to do genetic engineering. * * *

Instead of these longer-term issues, the focus at Asilomar in 1975 was on safety of newly-developed technical tools for genetic engineering, on the means not the ends.

Charles Weiner, Recombinant DNA Policy: Asilomar Conference, in 2 Encyclopedia of Ethical, Legal and Policy Issues in Biotechnology 909, 910–911 (Thomas H. Murray & Maxwell J. Mehlman eds. 2000). For a description of the conference by one of the lawyers who attended, see Roger B. Dworkin, Science, Society, and the Expert Town Meeting: Some Comments on Asilomar, 51 S. Cal. L. Rev. 1471 (1978).

Shortly before the Asilomar Conference, the director of NIH established an advisory committee called the Recombinant DNA Advisory Committee, the "RAC." The RAC originally had 12 members, all scientists. It met for the first time immediately after the conference, and began to draft safety guidelines for recombinant DNA research based on the conference proceedings. The guidelines, published at 41 Fed. Reg. 27902 (1976), required all large-scale NIH-funded rDNA experiments to be approved by the RAC.

In 1978, the RAC was expanded to 25 members, one-third of whom were "public" members, including lawyers and bioethicists, and the RAC issued revised guidelines (42 Fed. Reg. 49596) which, recognizing that rDNA experiments were less risky than originally had been thought, relaxed some of the restrictions on rDNA research. For a history of the early RAC, see Sheldon Krimsky, Genetic Alchemy: The Social History of the Recombinant DNA Controversy (1982).

In 1982, a report entitled *Splicing Life* was issued by the President's Commission for the Study of Ethical Problems in Medicine and Biomedical and Behavioral Research. The President's Commission, best known for the 1979 *Belmont Report*, which laid out the ethical ground rules for human subjects research, called for expanded consideration of the ethical and social implications of gene therapy. However, the report was broadly supportive of the technology.

In response to the President's Commission report and to congressional hearings (Human Genetic Engineering, Hearing Before the Subcommittee on Investigations and Oversight, House Committee on Science and Technology, 97th Cong. 2nd Sess., November 16–18, 1982), the RAC and NIH began to consider whether the RAC, which hitherto had focused on laboratory and animal experiments using rDNA techniques, should review proposals for human gene therapy experiments. In 1984, the RAC established a Human Gene Therapy Working Group (later called the Human Gene Therapy Subcommittee). The Working Group, chaired by a bioethicist, LeRoy Walters, and comprising three laboratory scientists, three clinicians, three lawyers, three ethicists, two public policy specialists and a representative of the public, issued a 4,000-word document called "Points to Consider" to guide researchers seeking RAC approval for federally-funded human gene therapy trials.

DEPARTMENT OF HEALTH AND HUMAN SERVICES,
RECOMBINANT DNA RESEARCH: REQUEST FOR
PUBLIC COMMENT ON "POINTS TO CONSIDER
IN THE DESIGN AND SUBMISSION OF HUMAN
SOMATIC-CELL GENE THERAPY PROTOCOLS"

National Institutes of Health, 50 Fed. Reg. 2940 (1985).

Experiments in which recombinant DNA * * * is introduced into cells of a human subject with the intent of stably modifying the subject's genome are covered by Section III–A–4 of the National Institutes of Health (NIH) Guidelines for Research Involving Recombinant DNA Molecules (49 FR 46266). Section III–A–4 requires such experiments to be reviewed by the NIH Recombinant DNA Advisory Committee (RAC) and approved by the NIH. RAC consideration of each proposal will follow publication of a precis of the proposal in the Federal Register, an opportunity for public comment, and review of the proposal by a working group of the RAC. RAC recommendations on each proposal will be forwarded to the NIH Director for a decision, which will then be published in the Federal Register. In accordance with Section IV–C–1–B of the NIH Guidelines, the NIH Director may approve proposals only if he finds that they present "no significant risk to health or the environment."

In general, it is expected that somatic-cell gene therapy protocols will not present a risk to the environment as the recombinant DNA is expected to be confined to the human subject. Nevertheless, item I–B–4–b of the "Points to Consider" document asks the researchers to address specifically this point.

This document is intended to provide guidance in preparing proposals for NIH consideration under Section III–A–4. Not every point mentioned in the document will necessarily require attention in every proposal. It is expected that the document will be considered for revision at least annually as experience in evaluating proposals accumulates.

A proposal will be considered by the RAC only after the protocol has been approved by the local Institutional Biosafety Committee (IBC) and by the local Institutional Review Board (IRB) in accordance with Department of Health and Human Service regulations for the protection of human subjects (45 CFR, Part 46). If a proposal involves children, special attention should be paid to Subpart D of these regulations. The IRB and IBC may, at their discretion, condition their approval on further specific deliberation by the RAC and its working group. Consideration of gene therapy proposals by the RAC may proceed simultaneously with review by any other involved federal agencies (e.g., the Food and Drug Administration) provided that the RAC is notified of the simultaneous review. The committee expects that the first proposals submitted for RAC review will contain no proprietary information on trade secrets; therefore, the review will be open to the public. The public review of these protocols will serve to educate the public not only on the technical aspects of the proposals but also on the meaning and significance of the research.

The clinical application of recombinant DNA techniques to human gene therapy raises two general kinds of questions. Part I of this document deals with the short-term risks and benefits of the proposed research to the patient and to other people as well as with issues of equity in the selection of subjects, informed consent, and privacy and confidentiality. In Part II, investigators are requested to address broader ethical and social issues pertaining to the research and its longer-term implications. These broader questions go beyond the usual purview of IRBs and reflect the kinds of public concerns discussed by a recent presidential commission in its report entitled Splicing Life: The Social and Ethical Issues of Genetic Engineering with Human Beings. Responses to the questions raised in these "Points to Consider" should be in the form of either written answers or references to specific sections of the protocol or other documentation which accompanies the proposal. In addition, Part III of the "Points to Consider" summarizes other documentation that will assist the RAC and its working group in their review of gene therapy proposals.

I.   DESCRIPTION OF PROPOSAL

A.   Objectives and rationale of the proposed research. State concisely the overall objectives and rationale of the proposed study. Please provide information on the following specific points:

    1.   Why is the disease selected for treatment by means of gene therapy a good candidate for such treatment?

    2.   Describe the natural history and range of expression of the disease selected for treatment. In your view, are the usual effects of the disease predictable enough to allow for meaningful assessment of the results of gene therapy?

    3.   Is the protocol designed to prevent all manifestations of the disease, to halt the progression of the disease after symptoms have begun to appear, or to reverse manifestations of the disease in seriously ill victims?

    4.   What alternative therapies exist? In what groups of patients are these therapies effective? What are their relative advantages and disadvantages as compared with the proposed gene therapy?

B.   Research design, anticipated risks and benefits.

* * *

3.   Clinical procedures, including patient monitoring. Describe the treatment that will be administered to patients and the diagnostic methods that will be used to monitor the success or failure of the treatment.

a.   Will cells (e.g., bone marrow cells) be removed from patients and treated in vitro in preparation for gene therapy? If so, what kinds of cells will be removed from the patients, how many, how often, and at what intervals?

b.   Will patients be treated to eliminate or reduce the number of cells containing malfunctioning genes (e.g., through radiation or chemotherapy) prior to gene therapy?

c.   What treated cells (or vector/DNA combination) will be given to patients in the attempt to administer gene therapy? How will the treated cells be administered? What volume of cells will be used? Will there be single or multiple treatments? If so, over what period of time?

d.   What are the clinical endpoints of the study? How will patients be monitored to assess specific effects of the treatment on the disease? What is the sensitivity of the analyses? How frequently will follow-up studies be done? How long will patient follow-up continue?

e.   What are the major potential beneficial and adverse effects of treatment that you anticipate? What measures will be taken in an attempt to control or reverse these adverse effects if they occur? Compare the probability and magnitude of potential adverse effects on patients with the probability and magnitude of deleterious consequences from the disease if gene therapy is not performed.

f.   Serious adverse effects of treatment should be reported immediately to both your local IRB and the NIH Office for Protection from Research Risks (phone: 301-496-7005).

g.   Reports regarding the general progress of patients should be filed at six-month intervals with both your local IRB and the NIH Office of Recombinant DNA Activities (phone: 301-496-6051). These twice-yearly reports should continue for a sufficient period of time to allow observation of all major effects (at least three to five years).

h.   If a treated patient dies, will an autopsy be requested? If so, please indicate what special studies, if any, will be performed.

4.   Public health considerations. Describe the potential benefits and hazards of the proposed therapy to persons other than the patients being treated.

a.   What potential benefits or hazards are postulated?

b.   Is there any expectation that the recombinant DNA will spread from the patient to others or to the environment?

c.   What precautions will be taken, if any, to protect others (e.g., patients sharing a room, health-care workers, or family members) from such potential hazards?

5.   Qualifications of investigators, adequacy of laboratory and clinical facilities. Indicate the relevant training and experience of the personnel who will be involved in the preclinical studies and clinical administration of gene therapy. In addition, please describe the laboratory and clinical facilities where the proposed study will be performed.

a.   What professional personnel (medical and nonmedical) will be involved in the proposed study? What are their specific qualifications and experience with respect to the disease to be treated and with respect to the techniques employed in molecular biology? Please provide curricula vitae.

b.   At what hospital or clinic will the treatment be given? Which facilities of the hospital or clinic will be especially important for the proposed study? Will patients occupy regular hospital beds or clinical research center beds?

C.   Selection of subjects. Estimate the number of patients to be involved in the proposed study of gene therapy. Describe recruitment procedures and patient eligibility requirements. Indicate how equity consideration in the selection of subjects will be handled.

* * *

2.   How many eligible patients do you anticipate being able to identify each year?

3.   What recruitment procedures do you plan to use?

4.   What selection criteria do you plan to employ? What are the exclusion and inclusion criteria for the study?

5.   What equity issues, if any, are likely to arise in the selection of patients? How will these issues be addressed?

D.   Informed consent. Indicate how patients will be informed about the proposed study and how their consent will be solicited. If the study involves pediatric or mentally handicapped patients, describe procedures for seeking the permission of parents or guardians and, where applicable, the assent of each patient. Areas of special concern include potential adverse effects, financial costs, privacy, and the right to withdraw from further participation in the study.

1.   Will the major points covered in IA–IC of this document be disclosed to potential participants in this study and/or parents or guardians in language that is understandable to them? (Include a copy of the patient contest form as part of the documentation requested in Part II below).

2.   Will the innovative character and the theoretically-possible adverse effects of gene therapy be discussed with patients and/or parents or guardians? Will the potential adverse effects be compared with the consequences of the disease? What will be said to convey that some of these adverse effects, if they occur, could be irreversible?

3.   Will the financial costs of gene therapy and any available alternative therapies be explained to patients and/or parents or guardians?

4.   Will patients and/or parents or guardians be informed that the innovative character of gene therapy may lead to great interest by the media in the research and in treated patients? What special procedures, if any, will be followed to protect the privacy of patients and their families?

5.   Will patients and/or their parents or guardians be informed of their right to withdraw at any time from the proposed study and of the consequences of withdrawal at the various stages of the experiment? State the extent to which subjects will be specifically advised of the reversibility or irreversibility of procedures that are performed during the course of the experiment.

E.   Privacy and confidentiality. Indicate what measures will be taken to protect the privacy of gene therapy patients and their families as well as to maintain the confidentiality of research data.

1.   What provisions will be made to honor the wishes of individual patients (and the parents or guardians of pediatric or mentally handicapped patients) as to whether, when, or how the identity of patients is publicly disclosed?

2. What provision will be made to maintain the confidentiality of research data, at least in cases where data could be linked to individual patients?

II. SOCIAL ISSUES

The following issues are beyond the normal purview of local IRBs. However, since these issues have arisen in public debates about human gene therapy and the potential future applications of genetic techniques, the RAC and its working group request that investigators respond to questions A and B below and discuss, at their discretion, the general issues enumerated in point C.

A. What steps will be taken to ensure that accurate information is made available to the public with respect to such public concerns as may arise from the proposed study?

B. Do you or your funding sources intend to protect under patent or trade secret laws either the products or the procedures developed in the proposed study? If so, what steps will be taken to permit as full communication as possible among investigators and clinicians concerning research methods and results?

C. The following issues will also be considered by the RAC and its working group in reviewing each gene therapy proposal:

1. How strong is the evidence that the proposed somatic-cell gene therapy will not affect the reproductive cells of patients?

2. Is the proposed somatic-cell gene therapy an extension of existing methods of health care, or does it represent a distinct departure from present treatments of disease?

3. Is it likely that somatic-cell therapy for human genetic disease will lead to: (a) germ-line gene therapy, (b) the enhancement of human capabilities through genetic means, or (c) eugenic programs encouraged or even mandated by governments?

NOTES AND QUESTIONS

1. Do the "Points to Consider" adequately address the ethical, legal, and social issues that might be raised by gene therapy experiments? Which issues does it mention, and which, if any, does it neglect? For a critique, see Eric Juengst, The NIH "Points to Consider" and the Limits of Human Gene Therapy, 1 Human Gene Therapy 425 (1990).

2. The institution where the research is conducted is required to have an Institutional Review Board (IRB) and an Institutional Biosafety Committee (IBC) to approve and oversee the research. IBCs were required by

the NIH's first guidelines for rDNA research, 41 Fed. Reg. 27,902 (1976). According to the guidelines, institutional biohazards committees, as they were then called, are required to (1) advise the institution on policies regarding containment of rDNA organisms; (2) create a reference resource; (3) develop a procedures manual; and (4) certify to NIH that they have reviewed and approved the safety of rDNA experiments.

3.   The first protocol for a human experiment was received by the RAC in 1988. It was not an actual treatment experiment but a "gene marking" study in which the researcher, Steven Rosenberg, proposed to use cells (specifically, tumor-infiltrating lymphocytes) "marked" with an inserted bacterial gene to track the path of the tumor-fighting cells in cancer patients. The RAC approved the experiment, and after settlement of a lawsuit filed by the Foundation on Economic Trends, a group headed by Jeremy Rifkin, complaining of procedural irregularities in the RAC review process, the experiment took place. For a description of the suit and its aftermath, see Joseph M. Rainsbury, Biotechnology on the RAC: FDA/NIH Regulation of Human Gene Therapy, 55 Food & Drug L.J. 575, 584 (2000); Foundation on Economic Trends, Petition to Amend the National Institutes of Health Guidelines for Research Involving Recombinant DNA Molecules to Establish a Public Policy Advisory Committee, 2 Human Gene Therapy 131 (1991).

4.   Rosenberg's experiment was followed by W. French Anderson's trial involving Ashanti DeSilva, described earlier.

5.   In 1993, the director of NIH, Bernadine Healey, approved an exception to the normal RAC review process for "compassionate use"—in this case, for a patient suffering from Stage IV glioblastoma, a highly aggressive form of brain cancer. "Compassionate use" is an approach used by physicians to obtain supplies of experimental drugs for specific patients before the drugs are approved by the FDA. See 21 U.S.C. § 360bbb. The approval, which followed a letter to Healy from Senator Tom Harkin, sparked considerable debate within the RAC, and led to the adoption of the following amendment to the Points to Consider providing for "expedited review":

Recombinant DNA Research: Actions Under the Guidelines

IV.   Procedures to be Followed for Expedited Review

1.   An investigator submitting a request to the NIH for expedited review of a gene transfer protocol must provide detailed information regarding the necessity of expedited review.

2.   No protocol shall be considered without Institutional Biosafety Committee (IBC) and Institutional Review Board (IRB) approval.

3.   At this time, all gene transfer protocols must be considered experimental.

4.   Regardless of the method of review, the Points to Consider must be the standard of review for all gene transfer protocols.

5. Review of such protocols may include intramural NIH experts but must include extramural experts.

6. Among other factors to be considered by the reviewers, is the similarity of the new protocol to previously approved protocols.

7. The NIH will report to the RAC following expedited review and will include all of the materials on which the decision was based. The RAC will formally review the protocol at its next scheduled meeting. Patient privacy will be maintained.

8. Protocols that are deferred or not approved by the RAC in its normal review process are not eligible for expedited review. No protocol shall have more than one patient approved under expedited review.

9. As requested in the context of non-expedited review, none of the costs of the experimental protocol should be borne by the patient or the patient's family.

10. Data on all patients undergoing gene transfer shall be provided to the RAC within six months of the procedure.

58 Fed. Reg. 21,737 (1993). The idea behind the compassionate use exemption in general is to make experimental products available to patients who are not enrolled in clinical trials. When, if ever, is it appropriate to make an exception to established procedures designed to protect human subjects? Is this appropriate for gene therapy? Do these provisions provide adequate protection? How do these provisions compare to the Points to Consider? Which regime is stricter?

6. In 1985, the RAC issued a revised version of its "Points to Consider." 50 Fed. Reg. 33,462. The revision contained the following new language:

> The acceptability of human somatic-cell gene therapy has been addressed in several recent documents as well as in numerous academic studies.

* * *

> Civic, religious, scientific, and medical groups have all accepted, in principle, the appropriateness of gene therapy of somatic cells in humans for specific genetic diseases. Somatic cell gene therapy is seen as an extension of present methods of therapy that might be preferable to other technologies.

> Concurring with this judgment, the RAC and its working group are prepared to consider for approval somatic-cell therapy protocols, provided that the design of such experiments offers adequate assurance that their consequences will not go beyond their purpose, which is the same as the traditional purpose of all clinical investigations, namely, to benefit the health and well-being of the

individual being treated while at the same time gathering generalizable knowledge.

The two possible undesirable consequences of somatic-cell therapy would be unintentional (1) vertical transmission of genetic changes from an individual to his or her offspring or (2) horizontal transmission of viral infection to other persons with whom the individual comes in contact. Accordingly, this document requests information that will enable the RAC and its working group to assess the likelihood that the proposed somatic-cell gene therapy will inadvertently affect reproductive cells or lead to infection of other people (e.g., treatment personnel or relatives).

In recognition of the social concern that surrounds the general discussion of human gene therapy, the working group will continue to consider the possible long-range effects of applying knowledge gained from these and related experiments. While research in molecular biology could lead to the development of techniques for germ line intervention or for the use of genetic means to enhance human capabilities rather than to correct defects in patients, the working group does not believe that these effects will follow immediately or inevitably from experiments with somatic-cell gene therapy. The working group will cooperate with other groups in assessing the possible long-term consequences of somatic-cell gene therapy and related laboratory and animal experiments in order to define appropriate human applications of this emerging technology.

Note that the RAC for the first time declared its willingness to consider protocols for human gene therapy experiments.

2.   Food and Drug Administration

The Food and Drug Administration within the federal Department of Health and Human Services regulates drugs, medical devices, and a class of products called "biologics." Three weeks before the RAC issued its "Points to Consider" in 1985, the FDA issued a policy statement declaring its intention to assert regulatory authority over biotechnology products, including gene therapies, and describing the sources of its regulatory authority.

FOOD AND DRUG ADMINISTRATION, STATEMENT OF POLICY
FOR REGULATING BIOTECHNOLOGY PRODUCTS
49 Fed. Reg. 50,878 (1984).

INTRODUCTION

A small but important and expanding fraction of the products the Food and Drug Administration (FDA) regulates represents the fruits of new technological achievements. These achievements are in areas as diverse as polymer chemistry, molecular biology, and micro-miniaturization. It is also noteworthy that technological advancement in a given area may give rise to very diverse product classes, some or all of which may be under FDA's regulatory jurisdiction. For example, new developments in recombinant DNA research can yield products as divergent as food additives, drugs, biologics, and medical devices.

Although there are no statutory provisions or regulations that address biotechnology directly, the laws and regulations under which the Agency operates place the burden of proof of safety as well as effectiveness of products on the manufacturer, except for traditional foods and cosmetics. The administrative review of products using biotechnology is based on the intended use of each product on a case-by-case basis.

This notice describes the regulatory policy of the FDA applicable to biotechnology in general. The manner in which regulations for biotechnology are implemented in the United States could have a direct impact on the competitiveness of U.S. producers in both domestic and world markets. Inconsistent or duplicative domestic regulation will put U.S. producers at a competitive disadvantage. In addition, certification systems which favor domestic products, if adopted by our trading partners, could create substantial nontariff barriers to trade and block market access. Therefore during the development of the U.S. regulatory procedures for biotechnology products, attention is being paid to the need for achieving consistency in national regulation and international harmonization. With respect to international harmonization the U.S. is seeking to promote scientific cooperation, mutual understanding of regulatory approaches, international agreement on a range of common technical problems such as the development of consistent test guidelines, laboratory practices and principles for assessing potential risks. In achieving national consistency and international harmonization, regulatory decisions can be made in a socially responsible manner, protecting human health and the environment, while allowing U.S. producers to remain competitive.

The Agency possesses extensive experience with the administrative and regulatory regimens described as applied to the products of biotechnological processes, new and old, and proposes no new procedures or requirements for regulated industry or individuals. Public comment is requested on scientific and regulatory policy issues raised by this notice.

The marketing of new drugs and biologics for human use, and new animal drugs, requires prior approval of an appropriate new drug application (NDA), license, or new animal drug application (NADA). For new medical devices, including diagnostic devices for human use either a premarket approval application or reclassification petition is required. If the device is determined to be equivalent to an already marketed device, a premarket notification under section 510(k) of the Federal Food, Drug, and Cosmetic Act (the act) is required. For food products, section 409 of the act requires FDA preclearance of food additives including those prepared using biotechnology. Section 706 of the act requires preclearance of color additives. The implementing regulations for food and color additive petitions and for affirming generally recognized as safe (GRAS) food substances are sufficiently comprehensive to apply to those involving new biotechnology.

Genetic manipulations of plants or animals may enter FDA's jurisdiction in other ways; for example, the introduction into a plant of a gene coding for a pesticide or growth factor may constitute adulteration of the foodstuff derived from the plant, or the use of a new microorganism found in a food such as yogurt could be considered a food additive. Such situations will be evaluated case-by-case, and with cooperation with the U.S. Department of Agriculture (USDA), where appropriate.

THE REGULATORY PROCESS

Congress has provided FDA authority under the act and the Public Health Service (PHS) Act to regulate products regardless of how they are manufactured.

GENERAL REQUIREMENTS FOR HUMAN DRUGS AND BIOLOGICS

A new drug is, in general terms, a drug not generally recognized by qualified scientific experts as safe and effective for the proposed use. New drugs may not be marketed unless they have been approved as safe and effective, and clinical investigations on human subjects by qualified experts are a prerequisite for determination of safety and effectiveness. Sponsors of investigations of new drugs or new drug uses of approved drugs file an Investigational New Drug Application (IND) to conduct clinical investigations on human subjects. The IND must contain information needed to demonstrate the safety of proceeding to test the drug in human subjects, including, for example, drug composition, manufacturing and controls data, results of animal testing, training and experience of investigators, and a plan for clinical investigation. In addition, assurance of informed consent and protection of the rights and safety of human subjects is required. FDA evaluates IND submissions and reviews ongoing clinical investigations. Significant changes in the conditions of the study, including changes in study design, drug manufacture or formulation, or proposals for additional studies, must be submitted to FDA as amendment to the IND.

FDA approval of a New Drug Application (NDA) or an abbreviated New Drug Application (ANDA) is required before the new drug can be marketed. The NDA must contain:

— Full reports of investigations, including the results of clinical investigations, that show whether or not the drug is safe and effective;

— A list of components of the drug and a statement of the drug's quantitative composition;

— A description of the methods used in, and the facilities and controls used for, the manufacturing, processing, and packaging of the drug;

— Samples of the drug and drug components as may be required; and

— Specimens of the proposed labeling.

NDA holders who intend to market an approved drug under conditions other than those approved in the NDA must submit a supplemental NDA containing clinical evidence of the drug's safety and effectiveness for the added indications. Extensive changes such as a changed formula, manufacturing process, or method of testing differing from the conditions of approval outlined in the NDA may also require additional clinical testing.

Section 351 of the PHS Act defines a "biological product" as "any virus, therapeutic serum, toxin, antitoxin, vaccine, blood, blood component or derivative, allergenic product, or analogous product * * * applicable to the prevention, treatment, or cure of diseases or injuries of man * * *." Biologics are regulated similarly to new drugs during the IND phase; approval for marketing is granted by license, which is only issued upon demonstration that both the manufacturing establishment and the product meet standards designed to ensure safety, purity, potency, and efficacy. All biologics are subject to general provisions in the regulations that assure potency, general safety, sterility, and purity. In addition, specific tests and standards are established for particular products. To obtain a license, the manufacturer must submit information demonstrating that the manufacturing facility and the product meet FDA standards, and the facility must pass a prelicensing inspection. Licensed products are subject to specific requirements for lot release by FDA.

Manufacturers of new drugs and biologics must operate in conformance with current good manufacturing practice (CGMP) regulations, which address: adequately equipped manufacturing facilities; adequately trained personnel; stringent control over the manufacturing process; and appropriate finished product examination. CGMP's are designed to protect the integrity and purity of the product. Approval of the product application is also approval of the sponsor's process techniques.

* * *

GENERAL REQUIREMENTS FOR MEDICAL DEVICES

Medical devices for human use are regulated by requirements of the act as amended by the Medical Device Amendments of 1976. In general terms, a device is defined in the act as any health care product that does not achieve any of its principal intended purposes by chemical action in or on the body or by being metabolized. Devices include diagnostic aids such as reagents, antibiotic sensitivity discs, and test kits for in vitro diagnosis of disease. Veterinary medical devices are subject to the act but are not subject to preclearance requirements.

Regulations promulgated under the Medical Device Amendments control introduction of medical devices into commerce. In May 1976 when these device amendments were enacted, expert advisory committees recommended classifications for all medical devices of the types marketed at that time. The law segregates medical devices into three classes:

Class I devices are subject to the minimum level of control; general controls include the CGMP's.

Class II devices have been declared to require performance standards to assure their safety and/or effectiveness. They must also meet the controls of class I.

Class III devices require formal FDA approval of a Premarket Approval Application (PMAA) for each make and model of the device to assure its safety and effectiveness. The controls of class I are also required.

Before a manufacturer may introduce into commerce any medical device not previously marketed, the manufacturer must formally declare that intent to FDA and proceed along one of two legal avenues. The manufacturer can file a premarket notification to FDA seeking a determination that the device is substantially equivalent to a preamendment device and proceed to market the device subject to whatever controls apply to the older versions of the device depending on its classification. This is the so-called "510(k)" process, which takes its name from a paragraph in the act.

A new device—that is, one not substantially equivalent to a preenactment device—is automatically a class III device requiring FDA approval of a PMAA unless FDA reclassifies it into class I or class II. In the premarket approval process, the manufacturer must establish that the device is safe and effective. This is typically accomplished by scientific analysis by the Agency of product performance and data from clinical trials, submitted by the manufacturer in the PMAA.

For a "significant risk device," as defined in FDA's regulations, the sponsor must submit an application to FDA for approval to conduct the investigation. This application is known as the Investigational Device

Exemption (IDE). When the manufacturer believes there are sufficient data to establish the safety and effectiveness of its device, the manufacturer may file a premarket approval application, or PMAA. The law requires that FDA act on such an application within 180 days.

REGULATION OF SPECIFIC PRODUCTS

Within the framework of FDA's statutes and regulations, strategies have been developed for the evaluation of various kinds of "biotechnological" or "genetically engineered" products, as well as for other products. These strategies are product-specific rather than technology-specific. For example, review of the production of human viral vaccines routinely involves a number of considerations including the purity of the media and the serum used to grow the cell substrate, the nature of the cell substrate, and the characterization of the virus. In the case of a live viral vaccine, the final product is biologically active and is intended to replicate in the recipient. Therefore, the composition, concentration, subtype, immunogenicity, reactivity, and nonpathogenicity of the vaccine preparation are all considerations in the final review, whatever the techniques employed in "engineering" the virus.

Scientific considerations may dictate areas of generic concerns or the use of certain tests for specific situations. For example, a hepatitis B vaccine produced in yeast (via recombinant DNA techniques) would be monitored for yeast cell contaminants, while distinctly different contaminants would be of concern in a similar vaccine produced from the plasma of infected patients.

In order to provide guidance to current or prospective manufacturers of drugs and biological products, the FDA has developed a series of documents describing points that manufacturers might wish to consider in the production of interferon, monoclonal antibodies, and products of recombinant DNA technology, as well as in the use of new cell substrates. These documents, called "Points to Consider . . . ", are available from the Agency upon request.

Administrative jurisdiction within FDA's various organizational units are the same for a given product, whatever the processes employed in its production.

Nucleic acids used for human gene therapy trials will be subject to the same requirements as other biological drugs. It is possible that there will be some redundancy between the scientific reviews of these products performed by the National Institutes of Health and FDA.

* * *

SCIENTIFIC ISSUES SURROUNDING SPECIFIC PRODUCTS

There are some scientific issues raised by specific products manufactured with recombinant DNA technology. First, the molecular structure of some products is different from that of the active molecule in nature. For example, the "human growth hormone" from recombinant microorganisms has an extra amino acid, an amino-terminal methionine; hence, it is an analogue of the native hormone. Such differences may affect the drug's activity or immunogenicity and these considerations, among others, may affect the amount of clinical testing required. However, FDA possesses extensive experience with evaluation of analogues of native human polypeptides, a number of which have been approved for marketing.

Second, approval of the product application for pharmaceuticals is also approval of the sponsor's processing techniques, and FDA must determine whether the quality assurance within the manufacturing process is adequate to detect deviations that might occur, such as the occurrence of mutations in the coding sequence of the cloned gene during fermentation. Such mutations could, in theory, give rise to a subpopulation of molecules with an anomalous primary structure and altered activity. This is a potential problem inherent in the production of polypeptides in any fermentation process. One way FDA has dealt with these situations in existing IND's is to require batch-by-batch testing with appropriate techniques to ensure that the active drug substance is homogenous and has the correct identity.

SUMMARY

FDA's administrative review of products, including those that employ specialized biotechnological techniques such as recombinant DNA in their manufacture, is based on the intended use of product on a case-by-case basis. Although scientific considerations may dictate areas of generic concerns for certain techniques, e.g., the possibility of contamination with adventitious agents or oncogenes when cultured mammalian cells are the source of a drug, the use of a given biotechnological technique does not require a different administrative process. Regulation by FDA must be based on the rational and scientific evaluation of products, and not on a priori assumptions about certain processes.

NOTES AND QUESTIONS

1.   In its policy statement, the FDA states: "The Agency possesses extensive experience with the administrative and regulatory regimens described as applied to the products of biotechnological processes, new and old, and proposes no new procedures or requirements for regulated industry or individuals. * * * Nucleic acids used for human gene therapy trials will be subject to the same requirements as other biological drugs." This represents

the core of the FDA's approach to biotechnology: Biotechnology products and processes, including gene therapy, are subject to the same regulatory requirements as any other product or process, no more and no less. This position is noteworthy because it heralded the agency's long-standing approach to the whole range of biotechnology products, including genetically-engineered foods, that they would not be subject to any special review for safety. This approach has unraveled to some extent. Following Jesse Gelsinger's death, the FDA also announced its intent to impose special regulatory requirements on human gene therapy experiments, discussed below.

The FDA's position in the 1984 policy statement that the agency will apply its existing regulatory requirements to gene therapy is also noteworthy because it indicates the agency's willingness to regulate practices that might be regarded as the practice of medicine rather than the marketing of a product. Historically, the FDA has been deemed to lack the authority to regulate the practice of medicine. See, e.g., Chaney v. Heckler, 718 F.2d 1174, 1179 (D.C. Cir. 1983) (noting that legislative history of the Federal Food, Drug, and Cosmetic Act reflects congressional intent to prohibit FDA from regulating the practice of medicine), rev'd on other grounds, 470 U.S. 821 (1985); David A. Kessler, The Regulation of Investigational Drugs, 320 New Eng. J. Med. 281, 285 (1989). The agency itself has traditionally accepted this view. See 37 Fed. Reg. 16,503, 16,504 (1972) (concluding that "it is clear that Congress did not intend the [FDA] to regulate or interfere with the practice of medicine"); Online Pharmacies FAQs, Jan. 28, 2000, http://www.fda.gov/ForConsumers/ProtectYourself/index.htm (FDA will "continue to defer to states to regulate the practice of medicine and pharmacy"). The agency's lack of authority over the practice of medicine is what allows physicians to prescribe drugs for uses which the agency has not approved—a practice known as "off-label use"—without violating federal law. The FDA's lack of authority to regulate off-label use is discussed infra in Chapter 10 concerning the regulation of genetic enhancement. (The agency's lack of authority is cited by some commentators as a reason why it does not have jurisdiction to regulate human cloning, despite its claims to the contrary. See Elizabeth C. Price, Does the FDA Have Authority to Regulate Human Cloning?, 11 Harv. J. L. & Tech. 619 (1998).)

2.   The FDA policy statement observes: "It is possible that there will be some redundancy between the scientific reviews of these products performed by the National Institutes of Health and FDA." How do the procedures set forth in the FDA policy statement compare with the procedures established in the RAC's "Points to Consider"? Is the FDA's regulatory scheme truly "redundant"? Does the RAC consider issues that the FDA does not? For a history of the early interaction between the FDA and the RAC, see Richard A. Merrill & Gail H. Javitt, Gene Therapy: Law and FDA Role in Regulation, in 1 Encyclopedia of Ethical, Legal and Policy Issues in Biotechnology 321, 323–324 (Thomas H. Murray & Maxwell J. Mehlman eds. 2000).

3. In 1985, the RAC issued a revised version of its "Points to Consider." 50 Fed. Reg. 33,462. The revision contained the following new language:

> "Applicability: These 'Points to Consider' apply only to research conducted at or sponsored by an institution that receives any support for recombinant DNA research from the National Institutes of Health (NIH). This includes research performed by NIH directly."

The revision also contained a footnote stating: "The Food and Drug Administration (FDA) has jurisdiction over drug products intended for use in clinical trials of human somatic-cell gene therapy." Yet in 1987, the RAC issued a statement reiterating that gene therapy trials had to be reviewed and approved by the RAC even if they were approved by another agency.

4. Following the gene therapy trial with Ashanti DeSilva in 1990, the FDA intensified its efforts to regulate human gene therapy experimentation. In 1991, it issued its own "Points to Consider" document: Center for Biologics Evaluation and Research, Food and Drug Administration, Points to Consider in Human Somatic Cell Therapy and Gene Therapy (1991). In 1992, the FDA clarified that regulation of human gene therapy experiments would be coordinated by a new Division of Cellular and Gene Therapies in a new Office of Therapeutics Research and Review, housed in the agency's Center for Biologics Evaluation and Research (CBER). The new division was headed by Phillip Noguchi.

5. Toward the middle of the 1990s, gene therapy researchers and the biotechnology industry became increasingly frustrated at what many of them viewed as a duplication of regulatory oversight by the RAC and the FDA. Efforts were made to streamline the review process and eliminate the need to submit protocols using two different formats, one for FDA and the other for the RAC. In 1995, a committee headed by Inder Verma recommended to the director of the NIH, Harold Varmus, that the FDA take over the responsibility for reviewing most gene therapy protocols; the RAC would only review proposals that raised novel questions. Varmus decided to go even further. In 1996, he announced his intention to cede all regulatory authority to the FDA. His position was described in a publication in the Federal Register in July 1996 (61 Fed. Reg. 35,774) and formally set forth in a Federal Register publication in 1997 (62 Fed. Reg. 59,032, October 31, 1997). The size of the RAC was reduced to 15 members, and its functions reduced to three: (1) identifying "novel human gene transfer experiments deserving of public discussion" by the committee and transmitting its comments to the investigators, the sponsor, and the FDA; (2) identifying "novel scientific, safety, social, and ethical issues" and recommending revisions to the NIH's Points to Consider; and (3) recommending topics for "Gene Therapy Policy Conferences"—public discussions on "broad overarching policy and scientific issues related to gene therapy research." 62 Fed. Reg. 59,032. (The first Gene Therapy Policy Conference was held on September 11, 1997. The topic was the regulation of genetic enhancement.)

An article in The New York Times stated that part of Varmus' motivation was his concern over the quality of the research proposals the RAC was being asked to review, and his disapproval of the way that biotechnology companies touted a favorable RAC review for business purposes. See Sheryl Gay Stolberg, The Biotech Death of Jesse Gelsinger, The New York Times Sunday Magazine, Nov. 28, 1999, at 137. Varmus' concern over the quality of research was no doubt influenced by the 1995 Report and Recommendations of the Panel to Assess the NIH Investment in Research on Gene Therapy, headed by Stuart Orkin and Arno Motulsky. (http://osp.od.nih.gov/sites/default/files/resources/Orkin_Motulsky_Report.pdf) The report concluded that "significant problems remain in all basic aspects of gene therapy. Major difficulties at the basic level include shortcomings in all current gene transfer vectors and inadequate understanding of the biological interaction of these vectors with the host." The panel made a number of recommendations for changes in the direction of NIH-sponsored gene therapy research.

As noted in Chapter 7, the Secretary's Advisory Committee on Genetic Testing concluded that the FDA may not possess the capacity to assess the ethical and social implications of a genetic test, and that the Secretary therefore "should consider the development of a mechanism to ensure the identification and appropriate review of tests that raise major social and ethical concerns." What does this suggest regarding the FDA's ability to regulate gene therapy and genetic technologies in general?

6. As noted in its 1984 Statement of Policy, the FDA has basic regulatory authority over drugs, medical devices, and biologics (as well as foods and cosmetics). The FDA regulates drugs, devices and biologics somewhat differently, but all three regulatory schemes share common features. The manufacturer of the product, called the "sponsor," must demonstrate that the product is safe and efficacious[1] in order to be permitted to ship the product across state lines.

Under the Commerce Clause of the Constitution, federal regulatory authority is limited to interstate commerce. As in other areas, however, the courts have interpreted the scope of the FDA's authority over "interstate commerce" broadly. See, e.g., Baker v. United States, 932 F.2d 813 (9th Cir.

---

[1] "Efficacious" is a term of art that relates to the performance of a product in human experiments. The term "effectiveness" is reserved for the performance of a product in actual use. For a variety of reasons, a product may be efficacious, meaning that it performs satisfactorily in clinical trials, but turn out to be ineffective when marketed for widespread use. For example, the types of patients enrolled in clinical trials are usually carefully controlled to produce the maximum effects, effects that may not be seen when physicians use the product in broader patient populations. In addition, the physicians who treat the experimental subjects may be more expert at using the product than the physicians who provide the product after it is approved. The efficacy-effectiveness distinction was dramatically illustrated by the drug chymopapain, which was efficacious in clinical trials when injected into patient's spines to treat slipped lumbar discs without surgery but which proved lethal when used by less well-trained physicians following FDA approval. See Drug for Slipped Disks is Linked to 5 Deaths, 28 Serious Disorders, The Wall Street Journal, June 7, 1984, at 7.

1991) (ingredients shipped in interstate commerce). In terms of gene therapies, the FDA states:

> The interstate commerce nexus needed to require premarket approval under the statutory provisions governing biologics and drugs may be created in various ways in addition to shipment of the finished product by the manufacturer. For example, even if a biological drug product is manufactured entirely with materials that have not crossed State lines, transport of the product into another State by an individual patient creates the interstate commerce nexus. If a component used in the manufacture of the product moves interstate, the interstate commerce prerequisite for the prohibition against drug misbranding is also satisfied even when the finished product stays within the State.

Food and Drug Administration, Application of Current Statutory Authorities to Human Somatic Cell Therapy Products and Gene Therapy Products, 58 Fed. Reg. 53,248, 53,249 (1993).

FDA approval to ship across state lines is required for experimental products as well as for products that have received marketing approval. Before an experimental gene therapy can be given to human subjects in a clinical investigation, the sponsor must have submitted an application to the FDA describing the experiment, and the FDA must have given its approval. The process differs slightly for drugs, devices, and biologics. As described in the 1984 statement, sponsors of drug trials must submit an Investigational New Drug application, called an "IND." The agency then has 30 days in which to object to the study going forward, or the application is deemed approved. See 21 C.F.R. § 312.42. The same application is used for biologics. See 21 C.F.R. § 312.2. In the case of a medical device, the application is called an Investigational Device Exemption application, or "IDE." See 21 C.F.R. § 812 1(a). Once clinical trials are satisfactorily completed, the sponsor must file an application for marketing approval. For drugs, this is a New Drug Application or "NDA," described in 21 C.F.R. Part 314. Following passage of the FDA Modernization Act of 1997, 21 U.S.C. §§ 355–397, biologics manufacturers are required to obtain an approved Biologics License Application or "BLA." (Previously they had to obtain separate product and establishment licenses.)

The system for medical devices is more complicated. As described in the 1984 Statement of Policy, medical devices are divided into three classes; only Class III devices must have the equivalent of an approved NDA or BLA, called, in the case of medical devices, an approved Premarket Approval Application or "PMA." Most gene therapies that would be regarded as medical devices would be considered Class III or "significant risk devices," requiring an approved PMA.

Given the different regulatory processes for drugs, devices, and biologics, it is important for sponsors of gene therapy products to know which route to follow, that is, whether their gene therapy is a drug, device, or biologic. A device, by definition, does not achieve its effect by chemical or metabolic action in the body. See 21 U.S.C. § 321(h). Genetic test kits and the reagents used by testing laboratories therefore were medical devices, but not most gene therapies. The distinction between a drug and a biologic was more troublesome. The 1984 Statement of Policy provided little guidance. A subsequent policy statement, Center for Biologics Evaluation and Research, Points to Consider in Human Somatic Cell Therapy and Gene Therapy (1991), defined the term "gene therapy" ("a medical intervention based on modification of the genetic material of living cells"), but did not clarify whether a gene therapy was a drug or biologic. Finally, in 1993, the FDA issued a document entitled Application of Current Statutory Authorities to Human Somatic Cell Therapy Products and Gene Therapy Products (58 Fed. Reg. 53248), in which the agency explained that "synthetic products" (including "a synthetic polynucleotide sequence intended to alter a specific genetic sequence in human somatic cells after systemic administration") were drugs and required INDs and NDAs, while viral and retroviral vectors inserting natural DNA were biologics. 58 Fed. Reg. at 53251. Consequently, the experiments on Ashanti DeSilva and Jesse Gelsinger, as well as virtually all of the other gene therapy trials to date, fall into the regulatory category of biologics.

3.   Protecting Human Subjects

LARRY R. CHURCHILL ET AL., GENETIC RESEARCH AS THERAPY: IMPLICATIONS OF "GENE THERAPY" FOR INFORMED CONSENT
26 J. L. Med. & Ethics 38 (1998).

In March 1996, the General Accounting Office (GAO) issued the report Scientific Research: Continued Vigilance Critical to Protecting Human Subjects. It stated that "an inherent conflict of interest exists when physician-researchers include their patients in research protocols. If the physicians do not clearly distinguish between research and treatment in their attempt to inform subjects, the possible benefits of a study can be overemphasized and the risks minimized." The report also acknowledged that "the line between research and treatment is not always clear to clinicians. Controversy exists regarding whether certain medical procedures should be categorized as research."

This problem currently plagues gene transfer research. A few months prior to the GAO report, an ad hoc committee appointed by National Institutes of Health (NIH) Director Harold Varmus expressed similar concerns in its assessment of NIH investment in research on gene therapy. The committee's report stated:

> Expectations of current gene therapy have been oversold. Overzealous representation of clinical gene therapy has obscured

the exploratory nature of the initial studies, colored the manner in which findings are portrayed to the scientific press and public, and led to the widely held, but mistaken, perception that clinical gene therapy is already highly successful.

In mid 1996, the Recombinant DNA Advisory Committee's (RAC) five-year status report of gene therapy described the situation this way:

> It is clearly too early ... to assess the therapeutic efficacy of gene therapy or even to predict its promise. Numerous studies have reported the ability to express recombinant DNA in vivo, but few have reported clinical efficacy. ... The few "dramatic" successes claimed are not dissimilar to those that were reported with a variety of other therapeutic techniques for which enthusiasm ultimately dampened over time.

Yet despite this cautionary report, and despite the fact that no therapeutic benefit has been clearly demonstrated for the more than 2,100 subjects enrolled in gene transfer research worldwide, enthusiasm for gene therapy persists unabated.

* * *

At present, gene transfer research amplifies the already existing confusions between research and therapy and intensifies extant problems of informed consent.

* * *

Consider, for instance, the following excerpt from the minutes of 1991 meetings of RAC and its Human Gene Therapy Subcommittee. In the subcommittee's 1991 review of a protocol for gene therapy for familial hypercholesterolemia, not only is the research described by some discussants as treatment, but some subcommittee members also considered it "discriminatory" to "treat" adults before children were entered in the protocol. This is not an isolated example of the conflation of research and therapy. Indeed, the basis of this ambiguity is built into the ethical guidelines that RAC uses to review protocols for gene transfer research. The most recent version of RAC's "Points to Consider" document refers to research participants as "patients" in some places and "subjects" in others, and sometimes refers to clinical studies as "treatments." This oscillation in language cannot be helpful for the process of informed consent.

* * *

Yet although gene therapy is conceived as revolutionary, its administration is viewed as routine. For example, many advocates describe gene therapy as merely "a novel form of drug delivery," where this description does not refer to the practice of manufacturing traditional drugs with recombinant DNA techniques, but to gene transfer. Almost everyone agrees that germ-line intervention—affecting future generations and involving a host of unknowable consequences—presents major new ethical issues, but the accepted wisdom is that somatic cell gene transfer is simply a part of the therapeutic continuum, presenting no novel ethical dilemmas.

* * *

The revolutionary rhetoric about addressing the essence of disease in scientific research is fueled, of course, by the agendas of those with major social and economic investments in the gene therapy enterprise. Physicians and researchers working on gene transfer techniques have substantial interests in promoting this nascent field of medical science. Biotechnology companies, moreover, have an interest in turning out numerous products related to the so-called genetic revolution—for example, diagnostic tests and DNA-based medicines. The cluster of scientific, economic, and cultural hopes swirling around our genes seems to intensify and sustain the future promise of gene therapy at the same time that it frames this revolutionary concept in traditional garb—as merely the next wave of therapeutic options. The failure to discuss these factors candidly leads regulators, professionals, and the public to perpetuate confusion, misrepresentation, and disappointment in the sometimes appropriate, and occasionally misguided, pursuit of medical advancement.

* * *

CONCLUSION

Informed consent is fundamentally about language, about how doctors and patients, researchers, and subjects communicate. As a practice, informed consent is intended to foster genuinely collaborative decision making in both the research and patient care settings. But in the current milieu of therapeutic enthusiasm for research, informed consent has become a way of not talking, or more precisely, a way of not talking with sufficient candor. By failing to dispel confusion about the therapeutic intentions of gene transfer research, the consent process often perpetuates a false promise to subjects. To promote conversation, researchers must earn the trust of their subjects through communication that avoids the false appeal of a beneficence warranted only by compassionate intent and devoid of evidence of benefit. In promoting an ethically sound genetic research enterprise involving human subjects, policy-makers should craft institutional opportunities for meaningful informed consent discussions in which the nuances can be sorted out.

To achieve these goals, the minimum requirement is conceptual clarity. We argue that rectifying the language of the regulatory bodies is essential for restoring informed consent for research to its original role as a collaboration-oriented process that promotes appropriate access and yet fully informs and protects subjects from inflated promises of benefit.

Specifically, with regard to gene therapy, we suggest the following.

First, RAC, FDA, and the Office for Protection from Research Risks should delete the terms gene therapy and gene therapy research and any language that would imply that a gene therapy already exists from the informed consent process and committee deliberation. This conceptual clarity is essential in those oversight institutions that set the tone for researcher-subject discussions. The term gene transfer research more accurately conveys the experimental practice that is currently at issue.

Second, RAC should rewrite its "Points to Consider" to differentiate clearly patients from subjects and research from treatment where those references are misleading. In this regard, the recent diminution of RAC's oversight role is troubling. Over the past few years, RAC has received an abundance of criticism, including charges that it has exceeded its authority, delayed approval of protocols, and functioned in a "purely cosmetic" way. Members of RAC have seen their role differently, recognizing that they are charged with reviewing a "new form of medical experimentation." In many cases, RAC has changed the language of consent forms to delete terms like therapy and often challenged what it has perceived as overestimates of potential benefit from participation in gene transfer protocols, similar to the concerns we have discussed here. If the confusions about gene therapy are to be dispelled, we believe a more robust role for RAC is required, rather than a diminished one.

Third, all institutions [and investigators] charged with responsibility for protecting human subjects and ensuring their informed participation in research should critically rethink the ethical norms that currently shape the language of informed consent in areas like human gene transfer research. The meaning of the principle of beneficence as direct benefit to the patient-subject should be clearly distinguished from beneficence as a possible benefit to future patients. The use of beneficence to refer to motivations of compassionate intent or desperate use in research contexts is misleading, especially to patient-subjects, and should be eliminated. The appropriate place for beneficence in genetic research is almost always as a long-range, aggregate good stemming from research results, and not as an immediate benefit resulting directly from research participation. The goal of genetic research is generalizable knowledge to benefit future patients, not current subjects. This is especially relevant to the Phase I and II protocols for gene transfer now extant. Subjects are treated ethically only when a robust exercise of consent is combined with a commitment to eliminate or reduce harms. Beneficence is too often translated into false promises of therapy for subjects, and this compromises the consent process.

Fourth, consent forms should state clearly and explicitly that there is no expected benefit to the individual patient who becomes a subject in current gene transfer research. Moreover, researchers should work to minimize the unwarranted therapeutic assumptions that inevitably result when research is conducted in the physical environment and moral context of ongoing patient care. One way to achieve this would be for each protocol and informed consent document to provide a separate section entitled "Evidence of Benefit," thereby calling attention to whatever evidence for individual benefit exists and laying it open to critical scrutiny by federal oversight bodies, IRBs, investigators, and subjects.

Finally, the NIH training program in research ethics should make a significant investment in educating investigators to view informed consent as conversation, in the service of subject autonomy and professional self-scrutiny, and aimed ultimately at an improved, collaborative decision-making process in research.

NOTES AND QUESTIONS

1.   What are the differences between research and therapy? Are there differences between research subjects and patients undergoing treatment in terms of protections to prevent harm? Review the earlier discussion of the ethics of genetic research. Is the informed consent process the same in the cases of research and therapy? If not, how do they differ? Under federal law and the terms of NIH grants, all proposals for human subjects research involving the administration of a drug, device, or biologic must be reviewed by institutional review boards (IRBs), groups of individuals at the institution conducting the study. Is there an equivalent entity or function in the case of therapy?

2.   Especially troublesome problems arise when a patient's physician is also a researcher. As George Annas states: "When physician and researcher are merged into one person, it is unlikely that patients can ever draw the distinction between these two conflicting roles because most patients simply do not believe that their physician would knowingly harm them or would knowingly use them as a means for their own ends." George J. Annas, Questing for Grails: Duplicity, Betrayal and Self-Deception in Postmodern Medical Research, 12 J. Contemp. Health L. & Pol'y 297, 311–312 (1996). Do the recommendations suggested by Churchill et al. respond to this concern?

3.   Is the conflation of research and therapy a particular problem in gene therapy experimentation, or a general problem with medical research? Does the article by Churchill make a persuasive argument that gene therapy research is special?

4.   Will the recommendations in the article solve the problem? If not, what other approaches can you think of?

D. GERMLINE THERAPY

The foregoing discussion of gene therapy focused on "somatic cell therapy," that is, therapeutic interventions that do not affect reproductive cells. The infusions of genes that Ashanti DeSilva received, for example, did not alter her oocytes, or eggs. Another approach, however, is "germline therapy"—therapeutic genetic interventions that, intentionally or not, affect the genetic material of reproductive cells. As a result, the modifications directly alter the genetic endowment of the person's offspring, and their progeny in turn.

The distinction between somatic cell and germline therapy is not always clear. Somatic cell treatments that enabled people to have children, whether by repairing their reproductive systems or simply by saving their lives while they were still capable of reproducing, would affect the genes of offspring by making the lives of the offspring possible. Similarly, abortions performed because of fetal health problems or health-based decisions about which embryos to implant following IVF might be considered germline therapy because they affect the genes of a person's children, precluding the aborted fetuses or discarded embryos from passing on their genes via reproduction. But these interventions all involve naturally inherited genes; therapeutic abortions and embryo selection for implantation merely select among offspring on the basis of their natural genetic endowment. Most commentators reserve the term "germline therapy" for interventions that actually change the genes of surviving offspring.

Some commentators also distinguish somatic and germline therapy in terms of the target of the intervention. The goal of somatic cell therapy, they say, is to treat the person who is the subject of the procedure, while the goal of germline therapy is to treat that person's children. This distinction is blurred as well, however. As discussed below, one therapeutic approach might be to insert genes into an early stage embryo or fetus with the intent of correcting an abnormality or preventing a disease. If the insertion is made at an early-enough stage of development, the altered genes will be incorporated not only into the somatic cells of a surviving individual but into that person's reproductive cells.

Germline therapy refers to genetic manipulation of germ cells or "gametes": the egg and the sperm. In practice, it also refers to genetic alteration of the fertilized egg and genetic alteration of the cells of an early embryo (or embryonic stem (ES) cells), because these alterations will be incorporated in all the cells of the resultant child, including his or her germ cells. Therefore, the altered gene will pass down the generations. Currently, the following techniques show the most potential:

1.   Gene addition or "non-homologous recombination."

This technique is similar to the one currently used in somatic gene therapy, where cells are injected that contain copies of the normal gene. But in germline therapy, the genes are introduced into a fertilized egg where they get incorporated into the genome of the offspring and result in the correction or prevention of genetic disease in the progeny of the treated individual.

There has been success using this method in mice, where it produces the so-called "transgenic" animals. Diseases that have been successfully prevented include pituitary dwarfism and Lesch-Nyhan disease. However, there are several problems with this technique that make it particularly unsuitable for human germline therapy. First, it is inefficient. Only a minority of cells seem to take up the gene, and even when they do, the gene often is expressed at sub-optimal levels. Animals that demonstrate inadequate distribution or incorrect expression of the added gene, or that are damaged by the procedure, are destroyed, but this is problematic for humans. Furthermore, this technique may have unpredictable side effects. This is because chromosomes have two types of genetic elements along their DNA: genes themselves, each of which codes for a functional protein that contributes in some way to the functioning of the organism, and regulatory sequences, which control when and where particular genes are expressed. For an "added" gene to be effective, it must be expressed in the right place in the body, at the right time, and in the right amount. If only a gene sequence is added to the cell DNA, without its accompanying regulatory sequences, its expression will be unknown; it may become over-expressed, under-expressed, or not expressed at all. Another problem with this type of manipulation is that the added gene may become incorporated in the wrong location. This will result, at best, in perturbation of the added gene's activity, or in no gene activity at all. But at worst, it can have an effect on other genes in the cell, altering their expression and leading to cell death or other serious problems such as cancer.

2.   Gene replacement or "targeting" or "homologous recombination."

In this procedure, the defective gene is replaced with a corrected gene. This technique overcomes a number of problems associated with "gene addition," since it ensures that the replaced gene will be in its normal chromosomal location, and since its sequences and genes will not be changed. As a result, it will function in the right cells, at the right time, and at the right level.

Gene replacement appears to be the preferred technique for germline therapy. In particular, the advent of cloning or nuclear transfer has made this technique feasible in the near future. A possible scenario is as follows: IVF would be used to generate an embryo from the sperm and eggs donated by each parent. The embryos would be permitted to progress to a four-cell stage. Then three of these embryonic stem (ES) cells would be frozen for future use and the fourth cell grown in culture. After about twenty cell divisions, a million cells would be generated. The cells would then be genetically manipulated and those cells that have taken up the genes would be isolated and carefully examined to ensure that the genetic modification was accurate. At this point, the nucleus of one of the mother's eggs, or one of the three frozen ES cells, would be removed and replaced with the nucleus from a cell containing the prescribed genetic modification. The cell would then be allowed to divide in culture once or twice, and the resultant embryo would be implanted into the mother's womb. A child reproduced in this way will be a clone of the original embryo, with a single gene difference, and the genetic modifications would be incorporated in all of his or her cells, including the germ cells. Many of these techniques are being done now in animals. However, cloning humans presents a number of technical and moral problems that would have to be addressed before gene replacement could be used safely and ethically in humans. Another drawback is that, in animals, this technique is usually used for only one genetic modification at a time, while combating genetic diseases may require simultaneous manipulation of multiple genes. However, progress in solving this problem has been made recently by the addition of large numbers of genes through "artificial chromosomes," described below.

3.   Artificial chromosomes.

A new technique has been developed where an artificial chromosome, consisting of large numbers of modified genes together with their appropriate regulatory sequences, is introduced into a human cell. This procedure not only ensures proper gene expression, but also allows the introduction of large numbers of genes in order to alter characteristics that result from complex genetic combinations. So far, it has been shown that such a chromosome is stable and can persist through repeated divisions of the cell. However, potential problems with this technique may occur in the second generation. The side-effects of having an additional chromosome are not known. For example, the additional chromosome may cause sterility.

Although the ethical issues associated with human germline gene therapy are more complex than those of somatic gene therapy, some of the technical hurdles are actually less complex. Three major obstacles encountered in somatic gene therapy do not pose a problem in germline therapy, namely, gene delivery, gene expression, and immunological reactions. The delivery problem is solved since the gene will be automatically delivered to all cells in the body. The gene will be incorporated in the correct location to ensure proper expression. Finally, since the gene is expressed during fetal development, the altered gene product will be recognized as "self" and will not elicit an immune response.

In its Revised Points to Consider, the FDA stated that it would not approve any protocols for germline therapy:

> A distinction should be drawn between making genetic changes in somatic cells and in germ line cells. The purpose of somatic cell gene therapy is to treat an individual patient, e.g., by inserting a properly functioning gene into a patient's bone marrow cells in vitro and then reintroducing the cells into the patient's body. In germ line alterations, a specific attempt is made to introduce genetic changes into the germ (reproductive) cells of an individual, with the aim of changing the set of genes passed on to the individual's offspring. The RAC and its working group will not at present entertain proposals for germ line alterations but will consider for approval protocols involving somatic-cell gene therapy.

50 Fed Reg. 33,462, 33,464 (1985).

So far as is known, there have been no attempts yet to deliberately alter genes in a person's reproductive cells. However, there has been at least one successful inadvertent germline intervention. This involves a technique called "ooplasmic transfer" to treat a type of female infertility in which embryos do not properly grow and develop in the womb because of deficiencies, often related to age, in the portion of the egg, called the cytoplasm, that surrounds the nucleus. To correct the deficiencies, doctors remove the nucleus and insert it into an egg from another woman that has had its nucleus removed, leaving only the other woman's healthier cytoplasm. Using standard IVF techniques, the egg then is fertilized in the laboratory and implanted. Researchers using this approach reported the first successful birth in 1997.

Although most of a person's genetic material is found in the cell nucleus, a very small amount is contained in organelles or structures in the cytoplasm called mitochondria, which produce energy. Therefore, when an infertile woman's nucleus is implanted in the cytoplasm from another woman's donor egg, the resulting egg contains not only the mother's nuclear genetic material, but the donor's mitochondrial DNA, and as the fertilized egg divides, this mitochondrial DNA will be incorporated in the cells of the resulting child, including its reproductive cells, and passed on to its children. In short, a germline modification has been introduced, as confirmed by researchers in New Jersey who examined the resulting mitochondrial DNA in two children born as the result of ooplasmic transfer.

Given the RAC's de facto ban on germline alterations as reflected in its 1985 revised Points to Consider, how could any of these ooplasmic transfers have been lawfully conducted in the United States? In an editorial in Science, Eric Juengst and Erik Parens give the following answer:

> First, their intervention did not use recombinant DNA (rDNA). When RAC's guidelines, which apply only to interventions using rDNA, were articulated in the late 1980's, no one was thinking about transplanting ooplasm to treat a form of infertility. Insofar as the ooplasmic transfer technique does not involve rDNA, it falls outside of RAC's purview. However, as a recent American Association for the Advancement of Science (AAAS) report suggested, RAC's purview is unduly restricted to a consideration of techniques that now are more than two decades old. The AAAS working group (of which we were a part) argued that if new techniques raise the same ethical concerns as those raised by "traditional" germline gene transfer techniques, then either RAC's purview should be expanded to encompass them, or a new, RAC-like body should be created to oversee them. The working group argued that even though some inheritable genetic modifications (IGMs) might not involve rDNA, might not alter single genes, and might not alter nuclear DNA (nDNA), they should be subject to the same public scrutiny if they raise the same ethical questions as the traditional germline interventions. Examples of IGMs in the report included the introduction of artificial chromosomes, the use of oligonucleotides to repair genes in situ—and the transfer of mtDNA [mitochondrial DNA].

> Second, federal funds did not support this ooplasmic transfer experiment. RAC guidelines are binding only on those who receive federal funds. If, however, their protocol had aimed at achieving traditional germline interventions, they probably would have felt compelled to approach RAC, as do other privately funded researchers whose work raises novel issues. Given their recognition that they were engaged in "germline modification," it is unfortunate—though perfectly legitimate— that they did not bring their protocol before RAC.

> Third, gene transfer was an inadvertent effect of their intervention. Since the creation of the RAC guidelines, however, researchers have had to demonstrate that the chances of inadvertent germline gene transfer are miniscule. When an in utero gene transfer pre-protocol was recently put before RAC, the idea was rejected largely because the chances of inadvertent germline effects were too great. If the ooplasmic transplantation protocol had been within RAC's official purview, it probably would not have received RAC's blessing. We will never know.

Erik Parens & Eric Juengst, Inadvertently Crossing the Germ Line, 292 Science 397 (2001). Note that at least some attempts at ooplasmic transfer were being made before the RAC's authority to review gene transfer protocols was ceded to the FDA.

In June 2001, the FDA sent a letter to six fertility clinics warning them that ooplasmic transfer was a clinical experiment for which an approved Investigational New Drug application was required.

In 1998, W. French Anderson and Esmail D. Zanjani proposed a study in which corrected genes would be inserted by viral vectors into fetuses affected with the same immune deficiency disorder as Ashanti DeSilva, as well as fetuses with alpha thalassemia, a severe form of anemia. The idea was that by intervening at such an early stage of development, the corrected genes would become incorporated into virtually all of the child's cells and be perpetuated along with the child's natural DNA by means of normal cell division. The researchers were aware, however, that since the experiment would be performed before all of the fetal cells had differentiated, some of the inserted DNA might become incorporated into the child's reproductive cells. The corrected DNA then would be passed on to the child's offspring, creating another instance of germline alteration.

Mindful of the RAC's position on germline therapy, Anderson and Zanjani took the unusual step of submitting a preliminary plan for their experiments to the RAC for discussion. (See Minutes of the RAC Meeting, September 24–25, 1998, www4.od.nih.gov/oba/rac/minutes/9–98rac.htm). This generated considerable discussion in the media (see, e.g., Robert Cooke, Pushing a Human Limit, Gene Therapy That Could Affect Future Generations, Too, Newsday, Aug. 30, 1998, at A6; Rick Weiss, Scientists Seek Panel's Advice on In-Womb Genetic Tests, Wash. Post, Sept. 25, 1998, at A2; Rick Weiss, Science on the Ethical Frontier: Engineering the Unborn, Wash. Post, Mar. 22, 1998, at A1) and in the scholarly literature (see, e.g., see Emily Marden & Dorothy Nelkin, Displaced Agendas: Current Regulatory Strategies for Germline Gene Therapy, 45 McGill L. J. 461 (2000)).

In September 2000, the American Association for the Advancement of Science issued a report, Human Inheritable Genetic Modifications, which recommended that, in light of the potential for genetic harms, "any somatic genetic therapy applications where there is a reasonably foreseeable possibility of [germline modifications] should not proceed at this time." The AAAS stated that before any germline modifications are attempted, there should be evidence that they can be accomplished safely and effectively, including, when new genetic material is added, data from multiple generations. For a more permissive view, see John A. Robertson,

Oocyte Cytoplasm Transfers and the Ethics of Germ-Line Intervention, 26 J. L., Med. & Ethics 211 (1998).

In 2015, separate groups of scientists published commentaries calling for voluntary moratoria on human germ line engineering. Edward Lanphier et al., Don't Edit the Human Germ Line, 519 Nature 410-411 (2015); David Baltimore et al., A Prudent path forward for Genmoic Engiheering and Germline Gene Modification, 348 Science 36-38 (2015). The commentaries were inspired by the recent development of highly-effective techniques for editing DNA, including CRISPR-Cas9, zinc fingers, and TALENS.

The FDA has not issued any guidance on whether it will entertain INDs for germline therapy, nor what criteria it will apply in its review. Are there any impediments to that agency's ability to review research plans involving deliberate or inadvertent germline alterations? One potential issue is whether the FDA has authority to regulate germline therapy insofar as it consists of the practice of medicine.

NOTES AND QUESTIONS

1.   Should intentional germline therapy be regulated differently than somatic cell therapy? Should it be banned? Does it raise special health or ethical concerns? If so which ones?

2.   Under what circumstances, if any, would it be appropriate to initiate an experiment deliberately intended to alter the human germline? What safety information from laboratory and animal experiments should be required first? What kinds of conditions should the researchers target? Should the experiment be tried in subjects who are so severely ill that they will die unless the experiment succeeds? Or should it be tried in subjects who are less ill and therefore better able to withstand the physical rigors of the experiment? What special issues might be raised if the subjects are children, fetuses, or embryos?

In view of the safety concerns voiced in the AAAS Report, would it ever be ethical to initiate a deliberate germline therapy experiment? In this regard, the report states:

> For the reasons outlined above, many members of the working group, including several of the scientists, question whether we will ever have enough confidence in the safety of IGM to proceed to clinical use. This assessment led some to conclude that it would never be scientifically and ethically appropriate to begin human applications until we can surmount this problem.

AAAS Report at 26.

3.   All biomedical interventions are accompanied by some degree of risk. The question is whether the risks are outweighed by the benefits. What

are the potential benefits from germline therapy? The AAAS Report did not regard the potential benefits as significant, stating (at 13):

> The working group could identify few instances where IGM would be needed. There are currently several alternative approaches available that will help parents avoid passing on defective genes to their offspring. These include genetic screening and counseling, prenatal diagnosis, and abortion, pre-implantation diagnosis and embryo selection, gamete donation, and adoption. In the future, *in utero* somatic gene therapy and gene therapy on patients after birth are likely to offer effective means for correcting defects.

Is the AAAS Report correct? If there were no significant benefits from germline therapy, why would researchers want to try doing it?

Although they too are mindful of the need to proceed with caution, other commentators are more supportive of germline therapy in view of its potential benefits.

BURKE K. ZIMMERMAN, HUMAN GERM-LINE THERAPY: THE CASE FOR ITS DEVELOPMENT AND USE
16 J. Med. & Philosophy 593 (1991).

So-called genetic diseases afflict approximately two percent of all live births. Some of these are so severe that the victim faces only a few short years of painful existence. Others, such as cystic fibrosis or sickle-cell disease, can be managed with treatment which often becomes more heroic with increasing age. Although at present the afflicted face almost certain premature death, the outlook that such treatments may soon include somatic-cell gene therapy is quite promising. The first human experiments involving the implantation of a genetic marker in tumor-infiltrating lymphocytes have been carried out at the U.S. National Institutes of Health and clinical trials to treat patients with severely debilitating afflictions, such as ADA deficiency, have begun. Such trials have been approved in the United States by the Subcommittee on Human Gene Therapy of NIH's Recombinant DNA Advisory Committee.

While these trials represent milestone achievements in the development of molecular genetics as an important tool in human medicine, somatic-cell gene therapy is a treatment of existing pathology. But somatic-cell gene therapy cannot prevent genetic disease. In fact, should it become widely successful, it will increase the number of homozygous disease gene carriers, who will face the certainty of passing problem genes to their children. Moreover, somatic cell therapy is a strategy that is only appropriate for the treatment of a subset of the wide scope of clinical disorders that have a clearly established genetic component. Disorders involving developmental abnormalities may not be adequately reversible, even if diagnosed during early pregnancy. Those problems involving organ or tissue structure and function may not be correctable at all, if intervention is not made early in development. The bone marrow stem cells are easily accessible and may be replaced by new populations, making them ideal targets for somatic cell therapy. But disorders involving solid tissues or a function intimately dependent on structure (e.g., the brain) may be forever inaccessible to somatic cell therapy.

Clearly, if technically feasible, a strategy that can correct genetic anomalies before or during conception, or at the zygote stage, is one that would achieve true prevention. Even if such a strategy is complex and costly initially, the suffering and the costs in treating (even by somatic cell therapy) and caring for a severely handicapped individual is many times greater.

* * *

THE CASE FOR THE DEVELOPMENT AND USE OF METHODS FOR DIRECT GENETIC MODIFICATION OF PRE-IMPLANTATION EMBRYOS

The case for the development and eventual use of germ-line gene therapy (GLGT) rests on the following arguments.

A.   It is the moral obligation of the medical profession to use the best available methods and technology to prevent genetic pathology. It has long been the acknowledged responsibility of the medical profession and public health practitioners in Western society to treat and, if possible, prevent infectious diseases and non-infectious diseases (such as cancer and atherosclerosis), using techniques proven to be efficacious and safe. Conversely, it is considered to be unethical to withhold medical intervention that is known to be effective in the treatment or prevention of pathology. Should not a similar responsibility apply to genetic disease? In fact, the borderline between the major non-infectious diseases and the overtly genetic disorders is not a clearly defined one. We know, for example, that severe hyperlipidemia, leading to heart attacks at an early age, is in large part due to genetic factors. Recently, genetic defects leading to a high incidence of breast and other specific types of cancer have been reported. Moreover, susceptibility to many infectious diseases, and the severity of possible sequelae such as the auto-immune destruction of vital tissue, have a very strong genetic bias.

The application of the principle that the medical profession must act primarily in the interests of the patient clearly extends to the welfare of prospective parents carrying a genetic disability who seek restoration of reproductive health. A direct corollary of this responsibility is a broadening of the definition of 'patient' to include the genetic health of their baby, and the ensuing future generations. The criterion that must govern any strategies to be used is that the procedure must promise to help the patient more than it may harm him. In this case, that criterion must apply to the entire genetic legacy that may result from intervention in the germ-line, which imposes rather stringent requirements on the degree of uncertainty acceptable in any such procedure.

B.   Direct intervention in the germ-line is medically necessary to prevent certain classes of disorders or situations where screening and selection procedures will not work. While the most often discussed targets of genetic counseling and somatic cell therapy are the severe homozygous recessive disorders, the number of medical problems that are known to be genetically determined or predisposed continue to increase. Those involving complex genetics, cases with more than one genetic locus, will not be readily able to screening and selection. Parents, who may have been treated by somatic cell therapy and are homozygous for the trait in question, can, at best, have a child who will at least carry the trait. GLGT will allow genetically normal children to result in all such cases.

C.   The principle of parental autonomy should permit parents to choose to use GLGT to ensure a normal child. At least in Western societies, parents are generally considered to have the right to have their own child, and to choose to use whatever means, consistent with established norms of medical ethics, that will ensure a normal pregnancy and a healthy baby. While the concept of state paternalism has in some instances prevailed over maternal autonomy with respect to the right to terminate a pregnancy, or in preventing a parental choice to withhold necessary medical care, the right of parental autonomy to nurture a pregnancy has been upheld overwhelmingly; any public policies that would deny parental autonomy in such cases would be grossly inconsistent with prevailing practices. Just as parents with reproductive disabilities are free to choose *in vitro* fertilization procedures, they should also be accorded the right to subject their viable embryos to screening and selection, or to direct genetic intervention, in order to guarantee the genetic health of their children.

D.   Germ-line therapy is more efficient than the repeated use of somatic cell therapy in successive generations. Although many genetic disorders are not amenable to treatment through somatic cell therapy, an increasing number are, enabling the afflicted to reach reproductive age themselves. By comparison, the somatic cell treatments now contemplated are heroic in dimension and accompanied by substantial risk. Why subject each generation to having to undergo major, invasive intervention, when elimination of the culprit genes from the germ-line is possible? It is far more efficient, in terms of suffering and discomfort, risk, and cost, and technically, to correct such disorders at the beginning of life.

E.   The prevailing ethic of science and medicine is that knowledge has intrinsic value, and that its pursuit should not be impeded except under extraordinary circumstances. Knowledge, the result of basic research into the nature of things, is the foundation upon which any technology must be built. The process from principle to practice, however, first requires an intermediate stage, in which new techniques and methods are developed. Moreover, since the results of basic research are often unforeseen, the opportunities for application will expand in unpredictable directions, as long as the enterprise of research remains healthy. But the development of the needed methodology and, hence, the useful applications, will generally not come about before the underlying phenomena are understood. Thus, major programs to direct research toward specific goals before the basic knowledge was in place have generally not succeeded (e.g., the 'War on Cancer'), just so attempts to suppress the freedom of inquiry have failed. Yet the question of whether or not the concept of "forbidden knowledge" should be considered with respect to human germ-line therapy has received recent discussion.

NOTES AND QUESTIONS

1.   One concern that is sometimes voiced against germline therapy is that it could adversely affect the human gene pool, perhaps by eliminating genes that might have enabled future generations to respond to new environmental challenges. The AAAS Report disagreed, stating (at 34):

> It is also doubtful that IGM would have a serious impact on the gene pool. The number of carriers of recessive alleles related to monogenic impairments is far greater than the number of homozygotes with the diseases. Therefore, if we treat the latter with IGM, we would eliminate only a miniscule percentage of the carriers and would not have a major effect on the gene pool.

2.   Another objection to germline therapy is that it is "playing God." For a discussion of religious views, see AAAS Report at 27–32.

3.   For European views on regulating germline interventions, see Emily Marden & Dorothy Nelkin, Displaced Agendas: Current Regulatory Strategies for Germline Gene Therapy, 45 McGill L. J. 461, 479–480 (2000).

4.   In 2009, Japanese researchers reported that they had produced marmoset babies that glowed green under ultraviolet light, just like their genetically engineered parents, who had had fluorescent jellyfish genes inserted into their DNA when they were embryos. This was the first successful germline gene transfer in primates. See Marmoset Model Takes Centre Stage, 459 Nature 515–516 (2009).

5.   For a fuller discussion of the ethical, legal, and social implications of human germ line genetic engineering, see Maxwell J. Mehlman, Transhumanist Dreams and Dystopian Nightmares: The Promise and Peril of Genetic Engineering (2012).

CHAPTER 9

PUBLIC HEALTH

■ ■ ■

I.   INTRODUCTION

Although many of the ethical, legal, and policy challenges raised by human genetics concern private relationships, such as the relationship between patients and physicians or between employers and employees, a number of issues arise when government actions affect individuals' rights and interests. A number of government actions that relate to genetics involve the government's interest in promoting public health. This chapter covers several of these public initiatives, including the role of genetics in public health emergencies and newborn screening.

II.   PUBLIC HEALTH GENETICS

MUIN J. KHOURY ET AL., WILL GENOMICS WIDEN OR HELP
HEAL THE SCHISM BETWEEN MEDICINE AND PUBLIC HEALTH?
33 Am. J. Prev. Med. 310, 313 (2007).

* * *

Focus on Prevention

Advances in genomics could provide new opportunities for prevention—the main focus of public health—at the individual level or through population-wide interventions. Understanding genetic effects and gene-environment interactions in disease processes could produce recommendations that certain subgroups avoid defined exposures or receive targeted interventions. Stratification by genotype or family history already provides a means for tailoring screening tests for early disease detection (e.g., colorectal cancer screening in genetically susceptible persons), and this paradigm is likely to be extended to early detection of other conditions.

A review of the public health implications of genomic research related to asthma illustrates the potential opportunities and challenges for translating new knowledge into improved prevention and treatment of a common disease. Asthma is a chronic lung condition characterized by inflammation, hyper-reactivity, and reversible obstruction of the airways. Strong evidence supports a causal role for both genetic and

445

environmental factors. Genomics research has identified numerous gene loci associated with asthma, and further studies of biological pathways associated with asthma are likely to yield new approaches to prevention and therapy. The earliest clinical applications will be in pharmacogenomics, using genetic information to optimize therapy and to prevent adverse events.

Translating results of genomic research to population-level interventions will not always require genetic testing and knowledge of individual genotypes. For example, a study in Mexico of children with asthma found that supplementation with the antioxidant vitamins C and E improved lung function in children with a common polymorphism of glutathione S-transferase M1 (GSTM1) who are exposed to ozone. If confirmed by other studies, this finding might suggest a simple intervention—antioxidant vitamin supplementation—for children with asthma who are exposed to ozone. Without genotype-specific analysis, a potentially important population-level intervention could have been overlooked.

* * *

Once a genetic variant is discovered, producing a molecular test to detect it is theoretically straightforward. However, the clinical validity of such a test is highly dependent on population characteristics; these include not only prevalence of the genetic variant and the strength of its association with disease, but prevalence of the disease and interactions between this genetic variant and many other risk factors. Clinical utility is even more difficult to establish because it depends on the availability of a specific, effective intervention that adds value to existing practice. Although most gene discoveries for common diseases are not ready for prevention applications, they have, nevertheless, initiated a common interest in medical and public health to develop a common framework for how such discoveries can be evaluated for their potential applications for disease prevention.

WAYNE D. HALL, REBECCA MATHEWS & KATHERINE I. MORLEY, BEING MORE REALISTIC ABOUT THE PUBLIC HEALTH IMPACT OF GENOMIC MEDICINE
7 PLoS Med. No. 10, e1000347 (2010).

* * *

COMPETING POPULATION HEALTH STRATEGIES

Predictive genomic medicine adopts a "high risk" strategy that targets interventions at individuals who are at the highest risk of developing a disease. Public health professionals are concerned that an uncritical embrace of "high risk" strategies will displace more effective strategies that aim to shift population distributions of risk exposures, for example by reducing the population prevalence of cigarette smoking, per capita alcohol consumption, average blood pressure, or the consumption of energy-dense foods.

Population-based tobacco control strategies, such as taxing cigarettes and reducing opportunities to smoke, have halved cigarette smoking rates in Australia and the US over the past three decades. These population-based strategies are more efficient than high-risk strategies because fewer resources are needed to increase taxes on tobacco products, ban cigarette advertising, and restrict opportunities to smoke than are needed to screen whole populations in order to identify and intervene with the minority at high genetic risk of becoming nicotine dependent or developing tobacco-related diseases, if they smoke tobacco.

There are similar arguments for the greater efficiency of population-based strategies in reducing risky alcohol use, obesity, and diabetes. These strategies aim to reduce population access to cheap energy-dense foods and increase opportunities to exercise. Based on the successful experiences in tobacco control, such strategies will probably include: increased taxes on, reductions in the promotion of, and decreased availability of, energy-dense foods; and redesigning urban environments to reduce sedentary behaviour and increase opportunities for incidental exercise in everyday life.

SUBVERSIVE USES OF GENOMIC RISK INFORMATION

Public health professionals are also concerned about the potential misuse of genetic risk information by industries that wish to promote harmful forms of consumption (tobacco, alcohol, energy dense foods, and gambling). These industries are likely to advocate for population-wide genetic screening in order to undermine public health policies that will reduce the use of their products in the population.

Analyses of industry documents demonstrate that this is why the tobacco industry funded behavioural and molecular genetic research on smoking and tobacco-related disease in the 1970s and 1980s. A strategic decision was taken to promote genetic explanations of tobacco-related disease (initially promoted by the geneticist R.A. Fisher). By locating the risks of smoking in the genome of the individual smokers, this research could be used to exonerate tobacco smoking as a cause of disease.

The alcohol industry has also promoted the idea that alcohol-related problems only occur in a minority of genetically vulnerable drinkers. The policy implication favoured by the industry is that alcohol problems are better addressed by identifying and intervening with problem drinkers rather than adopting effective strategies for reducing population-level alcohol consumption, such as increased taxation and reduced availability of alcohol. The gambling industry has recently funded research into the genetics and neurobiology of problem gambling for presumably similar strategic reasons. The food industries will find genetic explanations of obesity similarly useful in undermining population-wide strategies to reduce obesity by modifying obesogenic environments.

THE NECESSITY FOR TECHNOLOGY EVALUATION

The major public health challenge in formulating a policy toward population-wide genomic screening will be in discovering how to obtain whatever public health benefits genomic medicine delivers for common diseases without undermining effective population health policies that reduce exposure to the common risk factors responsible for the high prevalence of these diseases in developed countries.

* * *

Until we have a much stronger evidence base, and more data on interactions between genotypes and common environmental exposures, advocates of genomic medicine should be much more modest than some have been in the claims they make about its likely impacts upon population health.

MARK A. ROTHSTEIN, PRIVACY ISSUES IN PUBLIC HEALTH GENOMICS, IN GENOMICS AND PUBLIC HEALTH: LEGAL AND SOCIO-ETHICAL PERSPECTIVES
152–154, 161 (Bartha Maria Knoppers ed. 2007).

It is important to note that the integration of genomics (and genetics) into public health interventions must be done carefully and with discretion because the values underlying public health are quite different from those underlying genomics and genetics. The exercise of public health authority not only involves governmental action, but it also means the possible use of coercive powers to enforce governmental objectives. Public health action is based on utilitarian and communitarian ethics, under which societal interests take precedence over individual interests. An example is the imposition of quarantine to fight the spread of an epidemic. By contrast, the dominant social values of genomics and genetics are autonomy, privacy, and reproductive freedom. Politically, it is more libertarian than communitarian. An example is the traditional client-centered, nondirective approach that has become a hallmark of genetic counselling. The role of the genetic counselor or medical geneticist is to educate the individual and to provide options, but the ultimate decision rests with the individual.

The inherent conflict between the values underlying public health and those underlying genetics and genomics strongly suggests that any undertaking in the field of public health genomics should be approached with great care. This need for caution is underscored by the history of eugenics, which represented a failed and discredited attempt at reproductive, public health genetics. Today, members of the public overwhelmingly are concerned about the applications to individuals of genetic technologies (especially with regard to reproduction) to achieve social goals. Eugenics continues to be a dark cloud over public health genomics, and we ignore this fact at our peril.

* * *

Because the purpose of public health is to advance the well-being of the population, sometimes at the expense of individual interests, public health may conflict with the ethical tradition of autonomy that has become ingrained in genetics. Only by carefully limiting the scope of public health activities in genetics can the public be assured that the government is not unreasonably encroaching into some of the most sensitive and private realms of individual health.

New genomic and bioinformatics technologies also will substantially increase the amount of genetic and genomic information contained in health records. Stringently enforced confidentiality and security safeguards must apply to the protection of this information. At the same time, public officials should be required to present a compelling justification before individual genetic or genomic information is mandated to be disclosed for public health purposes, including for use in biosurveillance. Even then, such disclosures should be the minimum necessary to achieve the purpose of the disclosure and in the least identifiable form. As with other types of sensitive health information, vigilance in protecting the privacy of genetic and genomic information is especially warranted where, as is the case with public health genomics, the ostensible purpose for the disclosure is benign.

NOTES AND QUESTIONS

1.   Khoury et al. are hopeful; Hall et al. are skeptical about the likely benefits of public health genomics. What will determine which of these visions of public health genomics will be realized in the years and decades ahead?

2.   Do you agree with the following statement in the Rothstein excerpt: "Eugenics continues to be a dark cloud over public health genomics, and we ignore this fact at our peril."

3.   Other aspects of public health genetics are discussed elsewhere in this book, including pharmacogenomics and toxicogenomics.

4.   For a further discussion, see generally Daniel W. Belsky, Terrie E. Moffitt & Avshalom Caspi, Genetics in Population Health Science: Strategies and Opportunities, 103 Am. J. Pub. Health No. S1 (2013); Wylie Burke et al., Extending the Reach of Public Health Genomics: What Should Be the Agenda for Public Health in an Era of Genome-Based and "Personalized" Medicine?,

12 Genetics in Med. 785 (2010); James P. Evans et al., We Screen Newborns, Don't We?: Realizing the Promise of Public Health Genomics, 15 Genetics in Med. 332 (2013); and Grace Wang & Carolyn Watts, The Role of Genetics in the Provision of Essential Public Health Services, 97 Am. J. Pub. Health 620 (2007).

III.   PUBLIC HEALTH EMERGENCIES AND GENOMICS

New technologies, especially those based on genomics, are likely to play an increasingly important role in attempts to prevent or respond to public health emergencies involving infectious diseases or other biological sources (e.g., anthrax spores). To begin with, genomic analysis of the infectious agent can indicate the strain of the pathogen, its source and precise transmission patterns, its virulence, and the possible bases for vaccines or treatment measures. Along these lines, there has been a call to create an Infectious Disease Genomics Project. See Rajesh Gupta, Mark H. Michalski & Frank R. Rijsberman, Can an Infectious Disease Genomics Project Predict and Prevent the Next Pandemic?, 7 PLoS Biology No. 10, e10000219 (2009), www.plosbiology.org. The Ebola outbreak in 2014 could increase the international interest in establishing such a coordinated research program.

The other role for genomics in a public health emergency involves a focus on the at-risk or already-infected population. Genomic information on individuals might identify individual susceptibility (or immunity) to particular infections, likely positive or adverse responses to vaccines, severity of illness, likelihood of infecting others, and optimal pharmaceutical product and proper dose. These measures essentially apply principles of personalized medicine to infectious disease outbreaks. Genomics already has proven to be valuable in public health responses to "established" diseases, such as tuberculosis, malaria, and HIV/AIDS. See Janet M. McNicholl et al., Public Health Assessment of Genetic Susceptibility to Infectious Diseases: Malaria, Tuberculosis, and HIV, in Genetics and Public Health in the 21st Century: Using Genetic Information to Improve Health and Prevent Disease (Muin J. Khoury, Wylie Burke & Elizabeth J. Thomson eds. 2000).

IV. NEWBORN SCREENING PROGRAMS

AMERICAN ACADEMY OF PEDIATRICS, REPORT OF THE TASK
FORCE ON NEWBORN SCREENING, PUBLISHED AS A CALL
FOR A NATIONAL AGENDA ON STATE NEWBORN
SCREENING PROGRAMS
106 Pediatrics 389 (Supp.) (2000).

Newborn screening in the United States is a public health program
aimed at the early identification of conditions for which early and timely
interventions can lead to the elimination or reduction of associated
mortality, morbidity, and disabilities. This screening takes place within
the context of a newborn screening system, and involves the following
components: screening,   short-term   follow-up,   diagnosis,
treatment/management, and evaluation. Inherent to each of these
components is an education process.

* * *

THE HISTORY OF NEWBORN SCREENING

Newborn screening programs began in the early 1960s with the
original work of Dr Robert Guthrie, who developed a screening test for
phenylketonuria (PKU) and a system for collection and transportation of
blood samples on filter paper. By 1962, Massachusetts launched a
voluntary newborn PKU screening program that demonstrated the
feasibility of mass genetic screening.

Initially, newborn screening for PKU was not a health department
role or a legislated activity. Health professionals were slow to adopt the
practice of screening for PKU, and the responsibility for screening was
not defined (e.g., should it be the responsibility of the hospital in which
the infant was born, the mother's obstetrician, or the infant's pediatrician
or primary care health professional). The American Academy of
Pediatrics (AAP), acting as the professional association that develops
policy for the care of children, raised concerns about the sensitivity and
specificity of PKU screening tests, as well as the efficacy of early
intervention for PKU. Out of these concerns, the need for further research
about this testing was recognized, and the federal Children's Bureau (now
the federal Maternal and Child Health Bureau [MCHB]) funded a
collaborative study to address questions and concerns about the
effectiveness of the PKU screening test.

At the same time, advocates for children remained concerned that
children with undetected PKU were at high risk for mental retardation.
The National Association for Retarded Citizens (now the ARC) proposed
model legislation for creation of public programs to address low detection
rates, and also conducted an extensive grass-roots lobbying effort to

support passage of mandatory PKU screening legislation. Many state health departments supported the adoption of such legislation. The Kennedy Administration, with the guidance of the Presidential Advisory Commission on Mental Retardation, was also supportive. The Commission hired the Advertising Council, which mounted a public campaign for mandatory PKU screening. Other advocacy groups, such as the March of Dimes Birth Defects Foundation, mobilized volunteers to lobby for passage of legislation at the state level. As a result of this multidimensional advocacy campaign, most states passed laws in the early 1960s that mandated newborn screening for PKU. Forty-three states had formal statutes by 1973. State health departments, particularly their maternal and child health (MCH) programs (funded by Title V of the Social Security Act of 1935), assumed the central role in implementation of these new laws.

As a response to this mandate, some states set up screening laboratories or added phenylalanine analysis to their state laboratory's repertoire of tests. In other states, private laboratories played a major role. Quality control was difficult because of the number of and the variability among testing sites; and became even more difficult as states added other genetic tests to their newborn screening batteries. Early in the 1970s, the need to improve quality assurance through systematic proficiency testing was recognized. In an early proficiency-testing study, the Centers for Disease Control and Prevention (CDC) found marked variability among health department laboratories. As a result, the Newborn Screening Quality Assurance Program was begun at the CDC, with additional funding from the Health Resources and Services Administration (HRSA).

In 1976, federal legislation to support screening for genetic diseases was adopted, and in fiscal years 1979 and 1980, 34 state genetic service programs received federal funding. This support was welcomed by the states, as the cost of screening tests and the health departments' coordination of screening activities had not been completely covered by many state budgets.

As a result of the laws mandating PKU testing, and the establishment of health department newborn screening units that occurred in the 1960s and 1970s:

- Every newborn had an opportunity to be screened for PKU when laws were properly implemented; consequently, most were screened.
- Financial barriers to screening and diagnosis were removed, but families often had to pay for the special formula, special foods, and other related treatments.

- State newborn screening programs evolved, with the goal of providing safe screening tests and appropriate follow-up to every newborn.

During the 1980s, further systems development took place at the state and regional level. Newborn screening systems were set up by public health agencies to ensure coordination between the hospitals from which most specimens were received, the public health laboratory, the infant's pediatrician or primary care health professional to whom positive results were reported, and pediatric subspecialists to whom infants were referred for diagnosis and treatment. Together these entities comprised the backbone of newborn screening systems. Some state newborn screening systems also played a role coordinating follow-up; depending on their public health structure, medical care structure, and available resources. In many states, the Title V Children With Special Health Care Needs (CSHCN) programs performed this role.

In 1985, the Council of Regional Networks for Genetic Services (CORN) was developed in response to the need for an organization to facilitate state genetic program efforts through coordination and special initiatives. The CORN published newborn screening system guidelines that defined a 5-part system of screening, follow-up, diagnosis, treatment/management, and evaluation. These guidelines were not treatment guidelines or standards of care, but provided public health agencies with a detailed framework for a systems approach to newborn screening.

By 1985, 12 states had laws allowing charges or fees for screening tests. Today, a majority of the states have established newborn screening fees to be collected from the health care professional, birthing facility, third-party payer, or the parent of the newborn. Although newborn screening fees are collected in most states, financing the treatment of children identified with genetic conditions through newborn screening remains problematic. Eligible families in many states are ensured access to therapy (e.g., low phenylalanine diet for PKU), particularly when the special formula is deemed a prescription drug. Families deemed ineligible financially may be burdened by the cost of necessary treatments. However, when special PKU formula is classified as a food, many health insurers refuse to cover it at all; creating a problem for both eligible and ineligible families.

Now, after 30 years of experience with PKU, it is clear that knowledge regarding PKU and the approach to newborn screening were rudimentary when the programs were first launched. Studies to validate the screening test, and to assess the safety and effectiveness of a special diet to prevent mental retardation, were completed after laws were implemented. However, the history of these efforts has set the context for the role of public health in newborn screening and genetics.

ELLEN WRIGHT CLAYTON, SCREENING AND TREATMENT OF NEWBORNS
29 Hous. L. Rev. 85, 103–134 (1992).

Even assuming that the identified disorder causes substantial morbidity and that effective treatment is available and accessible, accurately labelling a child as deviant may nonetheless be harmful in other ways. In American society, a substantial number of children are born to single women or into marriages that are under stress. A number of commentators have expressed concern that labelling a baby as "ill," particularly in the newborn period, may cause the dissolution of the family or cause the father to flee a relationship in which he otherwise would have remained. These authors are particularly fearful that the fathers fleeing will occur when further testing reveals nonpaternity.

Another set of problems arises because newborn screening, like any medical test, is not completely accurate. Even under the most ideal testing conditions, some children who actually have disease will be missed, and some healthy children will inappropriately be labelled as "ill." From one perspective, "false negative" tests that fail to detect affected children should not seem particularly troubling. After all, the argument goes, the disease surely would have gone undetected had there been no program at all, so children are not harmed when the program fails to work.

Things, however, are not that simple. To begin with, the existence of newborn screening programs can create a false sense of reassurance in physicians, possibly causing them to fail to make a diagnosis as quickly as they would have were there no screening in place once symptoms begin to appear.

The most common reason that affected children are missed, however, is not because of the inherent inaccuracy of testing but because the tests were not properly administered, if at all. Screening programs have encountered many problems, ranging from difficulties in getting adequate samples, to lab errors, to problems in recording and reporting results. For a significant number of children, blood samples simply do not reach the state departments of health at all. Although the move toward centralization of testing and emphasis on proficiency testing and quality assurance has improved procedures, some states still do not keep statistics on lapses in screening. Given all these problems with newborn screening programs, it is hardly surprising that litigation often results when a child's PKU or congenital hypothyroidism are not detected by screening tests.

Not only are some affected children missed, but some unaffected children are mislabelled as ill. Sometimes the screening test is diagnostic: the child with an abnormal result, in fact, has the disease being tested. In most instances, however, screening programs are set up as multistep processes in which, is order to capture all the true positives, the first step also yields abnormal results for some unaffected children who will later be distinguished by more sophisticated testing. Hence, mislabelling is inherent in the early stages of the screening process. The number of unaffected children, the "false positives," who are identified as potentially ill in the initial screening depends on the nature of the illness and the test. The presence of false negatives is troubling because labelling any child as ill in the newborn period, even if only for a few weeks or months, can disrupt the developing parent-child relationship, sometimes with long-term adverse consequences for the child.

Inadequate medical knowledge also causes mislabelling. For example, when screening for PKU began, it was not known that some children with high levels of phenylalanine did not in fact have PKU, but rather had hyperphenylalaninemia, which does not cause significant mental retardation. Until this fact was understood, children with this latter, benign condition were inappropriately thought to be ill and subjected to the restrictions and expense of treatment. Ironically, the treatment actually harmed some of these children, causing the very mental retardation that screening was supposed to avoid. The increased understanding of human variation that has emerged from this experience is desirable in itself, but this example and the problems described earlier demonstrate that screening is not an entirely benign procedure for children. Those who engage in traditional legal analysis or who advocate widespread testing often seem to forget, or at least give inadequate weight to, these very real harms.

Legal implications of screening for children. The effects of newborn screening on children have a wide range of legal consequences as well. Some are relatively straightforward. For those affected children whose diagnoses were missed as "false negatives," the question is usually whether some institution involved in the screening process failed to exercise due care. Traditional rules of negligence govern this issue but reflect the continuing erosion of charitable and governmental immunity. Even when an affected child who was missed can show negligence, he still must shoulder the burden of proving that he would have received adequate, effective therapy had the diagnosis been made in a timely fashion. For the "false positives," those healthy children who are inappropriately diagnosed as ill, the existence of a private legal remedy is more doubtful and raises such questions as whether a child can receive damages for interference with her relationship with her parents.

A larger problem is how the law can be used to limit the social consequences of labelling. For many years, this country has been engaged in a struggle involving how to deal with perceived or real differences between individuals—differences based upon race, gender, and disability. Federal legislation, such as Title VII of the Civil Rights Act of 1964, the Education for All Handicapped Children Act of 1975, and the Americans with Disabilities Act of 1990, embodies efforts to alleviate the problem of discrimination. State legislatures have enacted similar statutes. Despite this legislation, the ongoing debate about such strategies as affirmative action and accommodation demonstrates that there is no consensus about what to do.

In addition, these laws are only partial responses to the problem of discrimination. As a result, some children identified as different by newborn screening will not be covered by these laws. Some children, to be sure, will be protected because they will develop a dysfunction that allows them to qualify as disabled and will suffer at the hands of entities that are covered by the acts. Others, however, will not be officially disabled either because the manifestations of their diseases are effectively controlled by treatment or because their "disorders" have no clinical manifestations. One could hope that medical norms of confidentiality would protect such children; if no one knows that they have a particular condition, they cannot be the victims of discrimination on the basis of being affected. Such information, however, is hard to keep completely private. One need only remember the way that schoolmates are aware of and tease peers who take medicine or eat a special diet. Even when a condition requires no intervention, mere entry of the diagnosis into medical records makes it available to a wide array of people and institutions. Other children will be symptomatic but will be discriminated against by institutions or individuals not governed by these laws. These children who fall between the legislative cracks may nonetheless suffer real injury by virtue of being identified as different.

* * *

Legal implications of newborn screening for parents. Newborn screening affects parents' relationships with their children as well as parents' own decision making about future childbearing in a variety of ways. Regardless of whether the effects of such screening appear to the outside observer to be beneficial or harmful, these consequences have legal implications because they represent intrusions into matters that society has generally concluded the family, and not the state, is to decide. Newborn screening can alter what parents know and do about their children's health care. While most families may well value this knowledge, some will not, especially when they understand the broader implications of being informed.

* * *

The state has been the primary provider of newborn screening since shortly after such tests were developed. In some ways, having the state in this role should confer advantages. At the most mundane level, the existence of a state-run program usually means that the testing is paid for, thus avoiding the inequities inherent in the piecemeal health insurance that exists in this country. The involvement of the state should also mean that all children are tested, especially in states where screening is mandatory. In reality, the states vary widely in the percentage of children who are tested. Finally, given the fact that families move and change health care providers frequently, the state has more tools at its disposal with which to find children who are diagnosed with serious conditions at birth and to ensure that they receive continuity of care. Here as well, the success of states in the context of finding and tracking children varies widely.

Limits upon state action in the name of health. * * * The state has two sources of power with which to protect the public health, each applying in different circumstances and having different limits. The more commonly invoked and broader power is the police power-the state's authority to prevent one person from harming another. * * * The second and narrower power is that of the state as *parens patriae,* the authority to intervene to prevent a person at risk from the self-infliction of serious harm.

* * *

[I]f the affected child is the target, the state cannot justify screening as an exercise of the police power. Because genetic disorders are not "catching," the child does not pose a health risk to others. One might argue that the parents could "harm" future children by passing on the genetic disorder and that the state can appropriately intervene to prevent this injury. The problem with this argument is that the only way to protect the child from getting the genetic disorder is to prevent the child from being born. Even if one concedes that some conditions may make a child's life not worth living, the disorders for which newborn screening is currently performed do not qualify. Nor is it likely that the diseases sought in newborn screening will ever be the basis for wrongful life claims because newborn screening is most appropriate when effective treatment is available.

The state, then, is far more likely to invoke its role as *parens patriae* as the source of its authority to conduct newborn screening. At first, the analogy between the state as parent and parents as parents seems compelling, but further analysis reveals two problems with viewing the state as "parent." First, these children have "real" parents, whether by biological or other social connections, who have far-reaching authority to make important decisions regarding their children. The state is not completely free to override the parents' choices.

Second, concern for children does not seem to be the state's primary motivation for participation in newborn screening. The fact that the state bases its decisions about which diseases to seek on cost-benefit analyses makes clear that avoiding burdens on the public fisc is a major reason for screening. Further, the cost-benefit analyses that have been done are fundamentally flawed because they are based on the invalid premise that affected children receive care. This assumption is invalid because many states neither provide treatment nor require insurers to pay for it and many families have trouble meeting the demands of dietary and other therapeutic regimens necessary to provide care for affected children.

To be fair, the state must engage in a balancing process in deciding how to spend its money because money spent for one program is then not available for others. Even so, it is one thing to decide whether a particular expenditure is an effective way to help people and another to establish a program in order to avoid future burdens. One simply cannot assume that the state will have the child's interest primarily at heart.

How newborn screening became a function of the state. The political process that led to the adoption of newborn screening laws reveals another reason to scrutinize the state's motives. As Katherine Acuff and Ruth Faden recently pointed out, there is real reason to question why the issue of newborn screening ever entered into the public health and legislative/regulatory arenas at all. The process by which PKU screening came to be required by law is illustrative.

Some suggest that states enacted PKU screening laws to overcome the reluctance of individual physicians to test newborns. Although many practitioners were already incorporating these tests into their routine neonatal care, institutions such as the American Academy of Pediatrics initially opposed legislatively mandated screening. Yet the perception of medical foot-dragging regarding newborn screening does not suffice to explain the state's virtually complete occupation of this field. After all, legislators usually do not intervene merely because they believe that changes in medical practice are coming too slowly.

To say that states enacted newborn screening laws because of lobbying by individual practitioners and political interest groups is closer to the truth. For example, early PKU laws were put into place largely in response to the pressure exerted by Dr. Robert Guthrie, the developer of the test for PKU, and the National Association for Retarded Children (NARC). Although the legislative process typically moves in response to the voices of individual and institutional advocates, this response still does not resolve the question of whether the state may justifiably involve itself in newborn screening.

* * *

Moreover, while the states' approaches to screening vary widely, most of the approaches taken present some serious problems. In some states, the legislature defines which diseases are to be sought. In New York, for example, the legislature directs the state department of health to test for PKU, sickle cell anemia, congenital hypothyroidism, branched chain ketonuria (maple syrup urine disease), galactosemia, and homocystinuria. While one may applaud this "laundry-list" as permitting more accountability, such an approach presents some difficulties. If, for example, the state were to mandate testing for a disorder such as histidinemia that was later determined to be a benign condition, it is hard to imagine who would push for amendment of the statute to stop testing for the condition. Certainly, the families of the few children with the particular inborn error of metabolism are unlikely to have the political clout to do so. Furthermore, the companies that make the test and the laboratories that perform it might lobby against change.

Other state legislatures delegate authority to agencies to establish programs and to decide what to treat for. One might expect this approach to lead to better choices because it not only permits greater flexibility but also ensures that individuals who have greater expertise than legislators will make the decisions. The requirement in many states of public hearings prior to administrative action makes it even more likely that there is some public input into the process. Yet administrative agencies have less direct accountability to the public than do legislators. The possibility that regulators will be subject to less restraint is of some importance because they may not be even-handed in their actions, if for no other reason than their need to respond to the pressures of the bottom line and the implications of cost-benefit analyses. Moreover, evidence suggests that eugenic or other concerns that are publicly unacceptable motivate some administrators consciously or subconsciously. Consequently, there is reason to question whether the state will necessarily make better decisions about screening than the medical profession.

Thus, the state's role in newborn screening is complex and problematic. One can ask whether the states exceed their constitutional authority in establishing such programs. Certainly, the powers that generally justify state intervention into matters of health do not fit comfortably here, and the state's interest, no matter how well conceived, is hardly compelling. Even assuming that the states are acting within the limits of their power, it is not obvious that these programs should be in the public domain at all, particularly since similar screening efforts are undertaken as a matter of course in the context of routine medical care. No reasons suggest that the state is a particularly dispassionate or wise decision-maker in this area, for the state is subject to cost constraints that can oppose the interests of the children being screened and their families. In addition, history reveals that political advocacy by individual practitioners and special interest groups greatly influenced the development of newborn screening programs. Finally, although one can argue that the involvement of the state can lead to more uniform access, this potential has only been partially met.

NOTES AND QUESTIONS

1. For a table of the disorders included in mandatory newborn screening policies by states, see the website of the National Newborn Screening and Genetics Resource Center at genes-r-us.uthscsa.edu/nbsdisorders.pdf. This center was established by the Health Resources and Services Administration (HRSA) in the Department of Health and Human Services as a joint project of HRSA's Maternal and Child Health Bureau and the University of Texas Health Sciences Center at the San Antonio Department of Pediatrics. (As an indication of the center's enthusiasm for genetic testing, its website is GeNeS–R–US). The center appears to serve primarily as a clearinghouse for information about newborn screening and genetic testing programs, rather than as a source of testing standards or guidelines.

2. What genetic conditions should be the subject of newborn screening tests and how should they be selected? Over the years, several groups of experts have addressed these questions. In 1975, the National Academy of Sciences issued a report setting forth a number of criteria for newborn screening tests:

1. acceptance by healthcare professionals;

2. previous feasibility studies;

3. satisfactory test methodology;

4. appropriate laboratory facilities and quality control;

5. adequate resources for counseling, treatment, and follow-up;

6. acceptable costs;

7. effective education;

8. informed consent; and

9. adequate means of evaluation.

Another NAS report in 1994 focused on three criteria:

1. clear indication of benefit to the newborn;

2. a system in place to confirm the diagnosis; and

3. available treatment and follow-up.

The Task Force on Newborn Screening of the American Academy of Pediatrics emphasized:

1. screening should be of primary benefit to the infant;

2. the test should have analytical and clinical validity and utility; and

3. interventions to improve outcomes for the infant should be safe and effective.

What are the differences between these approaches? What values do they share?

A 2005 report by the American College of Medical Genetics (ACMG) commissioned by the U.S. Department of Health and Human Services identified the following 29 conditions as a "core panel" that should be included in every state newborn screening program: isovaleric isodemia, glutaric acidemia type I, 3–hydroxy 3–methyl glutaric aciduria, multiple carboxylase deficiency, mutase deficiency, 3–Methylcrotonyl-CoA carboxylase deficiency, methylmalonic acidemia, proprionic acidemia, beta-Ketothiolase deficiency, medium-chain acyl-CoA dehydrogenase deficiency, very long-chain acyl-CoA dehydrogenase deficiency, long-chain L–3–OH acyl-CoA dehydrogenase deficiency, trifunctional protein deficiency, carnitine uptake deficiency, PKU, maple syrup disease, homocystinuria, citrullinemia, argininosuccinic acidemia, tyrosinemia type I, sickle cell anemia, beta-thalassemia, Hb S/C disease, congenital hypothyroidism, biotinase deficiency, congenital adrenal hyperplasia, galactosemia, hearing loss, and cystic fibrosis. The ACMG selected the core panel of tests based on the availability of specific and sensitive test methods, a well-understood history of the condition, and the existence of available and efficacious treatments.

The March of Dimes, an organization focused on preventing birth defects and infant mortality, criticized the Task Force report for not calling for screening for an unlimited number of diseases: "We believe that a test (even for a rare disease)—as long as its early discovery makes a difference to the child—must be conducted for every newborn." Mike Mitka, Neonatal Screening Varies by State of Birth, 284 JAMA 2044 (2000). What kinds of "differences to the child" should count?

The National Academy of Sciences recommends that newborns not be screened for disorders for which no beneficial treatment is available. What if there is beneficial treatment, but it is equally effective if it is delayed until symptoms occur, rather than initiated as the result of newborn screening? Some studies suggest that this is the case with newborn screening for galactosemia, one of the standard newborn screening tests. There is also controversy over whether detecting cystic fibrosis in newborns improves patient health. The GAO expects controversy over testing for non-treatable disorders to increase with the spread of new tandem mass spectrometry (MS/MS) screening technology, which can screen for multiple disorders in a single analysis, including disorders for which treatment is not currently available.

Is treatment the only benefit that might derive from screening? What about research needs? What about information to aid the child and its family in planning for the future? At least one state has screened infants for Duchenne muscular dystrophy in order to provide reproductive information for the parents. (See also the discussion in Chapter 2 of newborn screening in the context of eugenics.)

What reasons might there be for not including as many tests as possible in a newborn screening program—even tests for extremely rare disorders as the March of Dimes suggests? The National Academy of Sciences (NAS) 1994 report includes the following observations:

> Newborn screening is not a trivial intervention and may raise important health and social issues. For example, detection of an affected child can disrupt the relationship between the parents and the newborn. Parents often experience guilt at having passed on a genetic disorder to their child. In addition, there may be social stigma, and such stigma may be increased if a reliable carrier screening test was available *before* pregnancy or birth.

Lori Andrews et al., Assessing Genetic Risks: Implications for Health and Social Policy 162 (1994).

3.   The 1994 NAS report recommends that screening be done only for conditions for which there is "available treatment and follow-up." What is meant by "available"? Suppose there is a treatment for the condition, but it is not readily available? Consider the following from the 2000 report of the Task Force on Newborn Screening:

> Funding for comprehensive medical care and treatment is challenging, and treatment of some conditions identified through newborn screening is costly. Not all children have health coverage or the means to purchase needed treatment. Managed care plans and other third-party payers often do not cover items such as special formulas, special foods, neurodevelopmental assessments, and therapies. Important psychosocial services and other support services for families are also less likely to be funded through health plans. Many managed care plans restrict access to specialized services or require that in-network health professionals who lack appropriate expertise deliver care. For children with complex conditions, treatment may best be delivered by a multidisciplinary team with specialized expertise; however, development and support of such teams requires financing beyond that provided through any form of insurance. Thus, many children with the disorders identified by neonatal screening do not receive optimal care because they have inadequate insurance coverage and/or lack access to qualified health professionals. For many, the situation is exacerbated when they reach adulthood and no longer qualify for public programs such as Medicaid.

4.   In 2003, a jury awarded a brain-damaged boy more than $70 million in damages in a suit claiming that the Stanford Hospital and the Palo Alto Medical Clinic where he was treated had failed to diagnose the boy's phenylketonuria (PKU) disease. The hospitals were held liable in part because the boy had been given newborn screening for PKU too soon after he was born, resulting in a false negative result.

According to the GAO, states reported that they spent over $120 million on newborn screening in state fiscal year 2001, with individual states' expenditures ranging from $87,000 to about $27 million. Seventy-four percent of these expenditures supported laboratory activities. The primary funding source for most states' newborn screening expenditures was newborn screening fees. The fees are generally paid by health care providers submitting specimens; they in turn may receive payments from Medicaid and other third-party payers, including private insurers. Other funding sources that states identified included the Maternal and Child Health Services Block Grant, direct payments from Medicaid, and other state and federal funds. Approximately four million babies are screened each year for genetic conditions. Approximately 3,000 cases of severe genetic disease are detected. In the late 1980s, the congressional Office of Technology Assessment calculated that, for every 100,000 babies screened for PKU and congenital hypothyroidism, the nation saved $3.2 million (in 1986 dollars), and that the net savings per detected and treated case was $93,000.

MARY ANN BAILY AND THOMAS H. MURRAY, ETHICS, EVIDENCE, AND COST IN NEWBORN SCREENING
38 Hastings Center Report 23, 27–28 (May/June 2008).

Could greater benefits or a fairer distribution of benefits be achieved by reallocating newborn screening resources to another use? In answering this question, all costs should be considered, and costs are often understated in newborn screening policy debates. A common error is to consider only the cost of the individual test. Advocates may say: "If Baby A had only had a fifty-dollar screening test for MCADD [medium chain acyl-coenzyme A dehydrogenase deficiency], his life could have been saved. Surely a child's life is worth fifty dollars!" That would indeed be a small price to pay to save an infant's life. But newborn screening programs must test many newborns in order to identify the few with MCADD, Thus, even if only the cost of testing itself is counted—ignoring for a moment many other activities that must accompany the testing—saving one life costs much more than the price of a single test.

Cost is also understated when advocates claim that the cost of testing all newborns for an additional condition is low because the blood sample is already being collected and the infrastructure is in place. For example, if tandem mass spectrometry is already used for PKU and MCADD, then adding one more metabolic disorder seems to add only a little to the cost. The real cost is more than the cost of testing, however. After we factor in the full costs of parental education, follow-up of all positives to a definitive diagnosis, treatment of affected children, and ongoing data collection and evaluation, adding a new disorder to an existing panel can be very expensive. Moreover, if the natural history of the condition is poorly understood and plainly effective treatments are lacking, children may receive no benefit, or may even be harmed by unnecessary interventions.

Another way to understate the cost of newborn screening is to count only the net cost of state budget appropriations earmarked for the program. In fact, adding a test to a mandatory newborn screening panel automatically imposes costs on private insurance (which is expected to pay for the screening test, follow-up, and treatment for insured infants) and on both the state and the federal government (which through the Medicaid program cover about a third of births in the United States). Other costs fall directly on families. These include the cost in time and money that families of children who test positive must bear to obtain a definitive diagnosis, and the unnecessary worry and anxiety experienced by families whose children turn out either not to have the disorder or to have a clinically insignificant form of it.

Finally, the full cost of newborn screening includes the cost of program-related research and quality improvement. The ACMG report concludes that the development and evaluation of evidence before and after introducing a test is an essential part of a national screening system, and it makes recommendations for incorporating ongoing research and quality improvement activities into newborn screening programs. It does not attempt to estimate the cost of all this work, however, and thus inevitably underestimates the total cost of newborn screening.

Once the full costs of newborn screening are understood, the benefits must be assessed and compared to the benefits that could be achieved from other ways of using the resources. The framework for equitable allocation of health care resources we used in our project starts from the premise that society has a moral obligation to ensure that every child has access to adequate health care and to distribute the cost of achieving this outcome fairly. The adequate level of care should be determined by considering the relative merits of different health services in the light of the reasons for the special importance of health care. This means that the resources devoted to newborn screening and treatment for genetic disorders should be established in the context of determining the entire adequate level of health care and the importance of health care relative to other important social goods. Unfortunately, the policy process is biased against doing this. The American health care system is not really a system. It has no institutional structure to take responsibility for stewardship of collective resources and force consideration of opportunity costs of decisions about public health programs or additions to standard clinical care. In newborn screening, this system-level problem has been made worse because each state makes its own decisions on newborn screening; furthermore, program financing is plagued by a lack of transparency. Advocacy by health professional groups, makers of screening technologies, and consumer groups such as the March of Dimes and associations supporting parents of children with genetic conditions also affects policy development. These advocates provide important perspectives, but often no one steps up to advocate for the programs that will not be undertaken and the people who will not be helped because health care resources have been directed elsewhere. Think again of Mississippi: a state expands newborn screening at the same time that it cuts support for prenatal care for poor women. The advocates for those women, and the children they were carrying, were either silent or ineffective.

RUTH R. FADEN ET AL., PARENTAL RIGHTS, CHILD WELFARE, AND PUBLIC HEALTH: THE CASE OF PKU SCREENING

72 Am. J. Pub. Health 1396, 1397–98 (1982).

THE FUNCTION OF PARENTAL CONSENT

Until recently, there has been little analysis of the function of a parental consent requirement when several competing interests are involved. Although case law links parental consent with the protection of parental self-interest and prerogatives, parental consent is generally not viewed as a mechanism for protecting the *autonomy* of parents or of parents' rights in medicine and biomedical research. Rather, parental consent is defended as a mechanism for protecting the welfare of children, on the theory that parents are their children's most conscientious advocates and have their children's best interest most accurately in focus. This analysis of the primary function of a parental consent requirement presupposes, but does not argue for, a well entrenched view in the literature of biomedical ethics, viz, that third-party consent is grounded in the principle of beneficence rather than the principle of autonomy. Even such starkly different positions as those defended by Paul Ramsey and the National Commission for the Protection of Human Subjects of Biomedical and Behavioral Research converge on this point.

Even if we consider general theories of proxy consent that allegedly are rooted in the principle of autonomy, such as the theory of substituted judgment, the focus of the obligation is not to respect the autonomy of the proxy but rather to honor the proxy's ability to infer, based on prior knowledge of the compromised person's values and preferences, what the individual would choose, if he or she had been competent. It is very doubtful, however, whether substituted judgment can be made an adequate theory for justifying policies of parental consent, particularly in the case of newborns.

If the primary function of a parental consent requirement is to protect the welfare of children, how does this apply to the case of PKU screening? In this form of screening, the intervention poses minimal risk of harm to normal infants and holds promise of the remote but important benefit of preventing mental retardation, which threatens not only the general well-being of infants, but also their future abilities to develop as autonomous agents. Thus, there appears to be no reasonable question or issue of judgment as to what is in the best interest of infants.

Under these conditions, is a public policy that grants parents the right to consign their children to a state of irreversible mental retardation morally acceptable? We think not, and it is for this reason that we question the moral justification for requiring parental consent for PKU screening. To require parental consent entails an obligation to respect parental refusal, and it is the validity of such refusals that we question. If the principle consideration is the welfare of children, their welfare is best served in this case by a program of compulsory and exceptionless screening.

CHILD WELFARE AND THE HARM PRINCIPLE

By making child welfare the overriding consideration in policy determinations about participation in child health programs, we are taking the position that in this context, any right of parents independent of their role as advocates for their children's welfare is subservient. The general outlines of this position in contemporary ethical theory can be traced historically to John Stuart Mill's *On Liberty,* where he discusses what is now popularly referred to as the harm principle. This principle states that a person's liberty may justifiably be restricted if the person's (e.g., a parent's) action or negligence poses significant risk of harm to another (e.g., the parent's child). The point of this appeal for our purposes is that parental refusal of PKU screening unjustifiably poses a risk of harm to the child.

Central to this argument for compulsory newborn screening for PKU is the absence of any reasonable question as to the welfare of children. To the extent that potential benefits to *individual* children may be present, a justification for a parental consent requirement is enhanced. Thus, from the perspective of a general policy on parental consent in public health programs, a central issue is whether risk/benefit judgments for individual children may sometimes differ from judgments about risks and benefits for children in general. If some children would be better off without the program, then parental consent may be required as a safeguard to protect the interests of those children. However, only if there is a reasonable possibility that some children would be better off should a policy permitting parental refusal be adopted.

It is important to clarify our position, which is based on the position that there is no *reasonable* question or issue of judgment as to the net beneficial character of the policy we propose. We do not mean that there can be no doubt in any parent's mind about the net benefit of the intervention. In the case of PKU, one could imagine parents opposing screening based on bizarre views about child welfare. For example, parents might believe that the screening test condemns children to eternal damnation. We would not interpret such metaphysical beliefs about damnation as providing a *reasonable* judgment as to the best interests of infants.

NORMAN FOST, GENETIC DIAGNOSIS AND TREATMENT: ETHICAL CONSIDERATIONS
147 Am. J. Diseases of Children 1190 (1993).

An important breach in the rule of informed consent occurred when newborn screening for phenylketonuria (PKU) was mandated by law in most states beginning in the 1960s. The origin of this mandate was the strong belief by advocates that the test was accurate, sensitive, and specific and that safe and effective treatment was available. Furthermore, given the rarity of the disease, there was concern that physicians left to their own devices would fail to perform the test on many infants, resulting in preventable harm. Finally, some believed that the benefits of testing and treatment were so clear and the risks of nontesting were so high that parents should not be allowed to refuse testing anyway, because to do so would constitute a form of medical neglect.

These presumptions all were later shown to be flawed. The Guthrie screening test turned out to be a remarkably nonspecific test, with a false-positive rate of between 15 and 20 to 1. As a result, many infants who, in fact, had benign forms of hyperphenylalaninemia were falsely labeled as having PKU. Confidence in the safety of the diet was also premature, resulting in brain damage and death in some infants who suffered from excessive restriction of an essential amino acid. The combination of these errors resulted in serious harm to an uncertain number of normal children.

Apart from disagreements about the practicality of informed consent in the setting of routine clinical care, there is stronger consensus, and clearer laws stating, that experimental treatments require stricter attention to explicit standards of informed consent. As an added precaution, approval by an institutional review board is required for experimental interventions. These strict standards for experimentation have been commonly ignored in genetic testing. The original PKU trials were begun before contemporary standards for institutional review were established, and consent from parents, to this day, is rarely obtained. Those who do not study history are doomed to repeat it, and the errors of the PKU program are repeated on a regular basis. Once the difficulties with PKU testing and treatment were resolved, it became common to add tests to the program, typically without institutional review or informed consent. In some cases, such as screening for hypothyroidism, there was a clearly positive outcome. In others, such as urine testing for iminoglycinuria or blood testing for CF [cystic fibrosis], the benefits were absent, as in the former case, or controversial, as in the latter. A positive outcome, of course, is not sufficient to justify bypassing the rules of experimentation; ends do not justify means.

The success of the PKU program also led to the widespread feeling that parental consent was now irrelevant because it would be unethical and possibly illegal for a parent to refuse permission for testing and treatment. It was also argued that it was inefficient to obtain consent for a simple test obtained from every newborn. These assumptions have also been shown to be flawed. Many states do allow parents to refuse testing for PKU, but they are seldom given the opportunity to do so. The notion that parents commit neglect when they expose a child to a 1:10,000 risk of serious harm is inconsistent with our general tolerance for refusal of circumcision, which is associated with comparable risks, and with decisions to allow a child to ride a bicycle or compete in gymnastics, activities with a higher risk than that of refusal of PKU testing. Finally, the claim that high standards for consent are impractical and inefficient are inconsistent with a study by Faden et al. showing that high standards for consent can result in higher compliance rates than those in states that mandate testing without consent.

These are the simple questions. The success of the PKU program is now clear if measured by the benefits and risks of preventing retardation in affected individuals. But treatments can have late effects that complicate assessment of benefits, risks, and costs. A pregnant woman who was successfully treated for PKU in childhood exposes her fetus to the most potent human teratogen, high maternal serum phenylalanine. Over 90% of such fetuses will be seriously damaged. Prevention of such damage requires strict adherence to a difficult diet throughout pregnancy, possibly from the moment of conception. It is not yet known how many children will be injured from such exposure. Because such women generally would not have borne children in the prescreening era, the net costs and benefits of screening cannot be assessed accurately. This high risk to exposed fetuses has also raised complex questions of law and ethics regarding forced treatment of women who cannot or do not consent to treatment.

NOTES AND QUESTIONS

1. What are the arguments in favor of and against obtaining parental consent for newborn screening tests? Which arguments do you find most persuasive?

In addition to the points made in the excerpt by Faden et al. in support of mandatory testing without parental consent, consider the following:

> Those who oppose the informed consent model contend that the logistical constraints of newborn-screening protocols make meaningful informed consent an unrealistic goal. The perceived limitations on time available to discuss complex screening issues prior to discharge, the logistical realities of varied birth settings, and the massive numbers of neonates to be screened can present genuine challenges to the implementation of the informed consent model. * * * In addition, some fear that it would be disruptive to established programs and might have a negative impact on both efficacy and cost-effectiveness. * * *

Elaine H. Hiller et al., Public Participation in Medical Policy-Making and the Status of Consumer Autonomy: The Example of Newborn-Screening Programs in the United States, 87 Am. J. Pub. Health 1280, 1286 (1997).

2. Only three states, Maryland, Minnesota, and Wyoming, currently seek parental consent for newborn screening. (Massachusetts recently has begun doing so in a pilot program.) In Maryland, the consent is for the total screening package; parents are not asked to consent to each test. Thirty-three states provide an exemption from screening if contrary to parents' religious beliefs, but, except in Maryland, Minnesota, and Wyoming, it is up to the parents to assert the objection without being asked.

DOUGLAS COUNTY V. ANAYA
694 N.W.2d 601 (Neb. 2005).

WRIGHT, J.

NATURE OF CASE

The Douglas County District Court ordered Josue Anaya and Mary Anaya to submit their daughter to testing for metabolic diseases as required by Neb.Rev.Stat. § 71–519 (Cum.Supp.2002). The Anayas appeal, asserting that § 71–519 violates their rights guaranteed under the 1st and 14th Amendments to the U.S. Constitution and that the issue is moot.

* * *

FACTS

Rosa Ariel Anaya was born in the Anayas' home, without a physician present, on July 11, 2003. The birth was reported to the Department of Health and Human Services (DHHS) on July 17.

In August 2003, a DHHS employee received Rosa Anaya's birth certificate, checked DHHS' database, and determined that the testing for metabolic diseases required by § 71–519 had not been performed. A certified letter was sent to the Anayas explaining the statute's requirements. Enclosed with the letter was a brochure detailing the screening process, which included drawing a small amount of blood from the heel of the infant to be tested. The Anayas declined to submit Rosa Anaya for the screening, stating that it was in direct conflict with their sincerely held religious beliefs that life is taken from the body if blood is removed from it and that a person's lifespan may be shortened if blood is drawn.

Douglas County brought an action seeking to compel the Anayas to comply with § 71–519. At a hearing on September 26, 2003, Mary Anaya testified as to the Anayas' religious beliefs.

The Anayas subsequently filed a motion for judicial exemption from prosecution and dismissal of the petition. They alleged that it was impossible for them to comply with § 71–519 because 70 days had passed since the birth was registered and DHHS regulations required that the testing be completed within 48 hours of the registration of the birth if the birth was not attended by a physician. They also claimed the statute violated the 14th Amendment to the U.S. Constitution.

The district court found that the State has a compelling state interest in the screening of infants for metabolic diseases and that the Anayas' religious beliefs did not outweigh the State's compelling interest that "these children can grow and develop to be free of a metabolic disease particularly in light of the minimal invasion of the blood test administration which is merely a pinprick to the child's heel." The court rejected the Anayas' claim that the issue was moot due to Rosa Anaya's age. Although testing procedures are most effective when administered shortly after birth, the court found that it was not too late to administer the test even if Rosa Anaya was 6 months of age or older. The court ordered the Anayas to comply with § 71–519 by submitting Rosa Anaya for metabolic screening forthwith.

* * *

The Anayas argue that § 71–519 infringes upon their First Amendment right to freely exercise their religion and that the district court erred in concluding that the State had shown a compelling interest which justifies the infringement.

"The free exercise of religion means, first and foremost, the right to believe and profess whatever religious doctrine one desires." Employment Div., Ore. Dept. of Human Res. v. Smith, 494 U.S. 872, 877, 110 S.Ct. 1595, 108 L.Ed.2d 876 (1990). The "'exercise of religion'" involves "not only belief and profession but the performance of (or abstention from) physical acts * * *." Smith, 494 U.S. at 877, 110 S.Ct. 1595. The statute which the Anayas challenged provides:

(1)   All infants born in the State of Nebraska shall be screened for phenylketonuria, primary hypothyroidism, biotinidase deficiency, galactosemia, hemoglobinopathies, medium-chain acyl co-a dehydrogenase (MCAD) deficiency, and such other metabolic diseases as [DHHS] may from time to time specify * * *.

(2)   * * * If a birth is not attended by a physician and the infant does not have a physician, the person registering the birth shall cause such tests to be performed within the period and in the manner prescribed by [DHHS].

§ 71–519. When Rosa Anaya was born, regulations prescribed by DHHS provided that if a birth was not attended by a physician and "the tests have not been performed within 48 hours of birth as otherwise required by these regulations, the person registering the birth must cause newborn screening tests for metabolic diseases to be performed within 48 hours of registration of the birth." 181 Neb. Admin. Code, ch. 2, § 008 (2002).

* * *

The Anayas argue that because they have raised a free exercise of religion claim along with a parental substantive due process claim, they have a hybrid constitutional rights claim, which requires strict scrutiny review. Under a strict scrutiny review, the law must be justified by a compelling governmental interest and must be narrowly tailored to advance that interest. See Church of Lukumi Babalu Aye, Inc. v. Hialeah, 508 U.S. 520, 113 S.Ct. 2217, 124 L.Ed.2d 472 (1993). The Anayas claim Smith held that strict scrutiny is required in cases in which a free exercise claim has been raised along with a claim of violation of another constitutional right.

In Smith, the claimants ingested peyote during a religious ceremony and were subsequently dismissed from their employment because Oregon law prohibited use of the drug. The question was whether the state's prohibition was permissible under the Free Exercise Clause. In upholding the Oregon law, the Court stated that it had never held that an individual's religious beliefs excused him from compliance with an otherwise valid law prohibiting conduct that a state is free to regulate. "[T]he right of free exercise does not relieve an individual of the obligation to comply with a 'valid and neutral law of general applicability on the ground that the law proscribes * * * conduct that his religion prescribes * * *.'" Smith, 494 U.S. at 879, 110 S.Ct. 1595 citing United States v. Lee, 455 U.S. 252, 102 S.Ct. 1051, 71 L.Ed.2d 127 (1982) (Stevens, J., concurring in judgment). * * *

We do not read Smith as supporting the Anayas' claim concerning strict scrutiny. Although Smith discussed prior decisions that involved not only the Free Exercise Clause but other constitutional provisions, the Court did not hold that a strict scrutiny review is required simply because more than one constitutional right might be implicated.

In Hialeah, the Court again held that to be found constitutional, a neutral law of general applicability does not require demonstration of a compelling governmental interest. "In addressing the constitutional protection for free exercise of religion, our cases establish the general proposition that a law that is neutral and of general applicability need not be justified by a compelling governmental interest even if the law has the incidental effect of burdening a particular religious practice." Hialeah, 508 U.S. at 531, 113 S.Ct. 2217.

Federal courts have also discussed hybrid rights claims. In Swanson By and Through Swanson v. Guthrie ISD I–L, 135 F.3d 694 (10th Cir.1998), the federal court addressed an argument that a school policy violated a home-schooled student's free exercise rights and the parents' right to direct her education. The court stated: "[W]e believe that simply raising such a claim is not a talisman that automatically leads to the application of the compelling-interest test." Id. at 699. "[I]t cannot be true that a plaintiff can simply invoke the parental rights doctrine, combine it with a claimed free-exercise right, and thereby force the government to demonstrate the presence of a compelling state interest." Id. at 700.

* * *

In Miller v. Reed, 176 F.3d 1202, 1207 (9th Cir.1999), the court stated, "[W]e recently held that, to assert a hybrid-rights claim, 'a free exercise plaintiff must make out a "colorable claim" that a companion right has been violated—that is, a "fair probability" or a "likelihood," but not a certitude, of success on the merits.'" The court further stated that "a plaintiff does not allege a hybrid-rights claim entitled to strict scrutiny analysis merely by combining a free exercise claim with an utterly meritless claim of the violation of another alleged fundamental right or a claim of an alleged violation of a non-fundamental or non-existent right." Id. at 1208. See, also, Boone v. Boozman, 217 F.Supp.2d 938 (E.D.Ark.2002) (court found that case did not present hybrid rights theory).

In rejecting the idea of strict scrutiny analysis for hybrid rights claims, the U.S. Court of Appeals for the Sixth Circuit has stated:

> Such an outcome is completely illogical; therefore, at least until the Supreme Court holds that legal standards under the Free Exercise Clause vary depending on whether other constitutional rights are implicated, we will not use a stricter legal standard than that used in *Smith* to evaluate generally applicable, exceptionless state regulations under the Free Exercise Clause.

Kissinger v. Board of Trustees, 5 F.3d 177, 180 (6th Cir.1993).

We conclude that the Anayas' assertion of a hybrid rights claim does not implicate a strict scrutiny review of § 71–519. A party may not force the government to meet the strict scrutiny standard by merely asserting claims of violations of more than one constitutional right.

The second constitutional rights violation asserted by the Anayas seems to suggest that § 71–519 violates their rights as parents to make decisions concerning the upbringing of their children. They rely upon Pierce v. Society of Sisters, 268 U.S. 510, 45 S.Ct. 571, 69 L.Ed. 1070 (1925), and Wisconsin v. Yoder, 406 U.S. 205, 92 S.Ct. 1526, 32 L.Ed.2d 15 (1972).

In *Pierce,* the Court held that a compulsory education law deprived parents of the right to select a school for their children. It held that the Oregon compulsory education statute "unreasonably interfere[d] with the liberty of parents and guardians to direct the upbringing and education of children under their control." Pierce, 268 U.S. at 534–35, 45 S.Ct. 571. The Court concluded that the challenged law served no state interest and therefore had no reasonable relation to any state purpose.

In *Yoder,* the Court held that a state could not compel Amish parents to require their children to attend formal high school and that the compulsory education law violated the 1st and 14th Amendments. The Court noted that no harm to the physical or mental health of the child was inferred but that when the health and safety of a child was involved, different considerations applied.

> To be sure, the power of the parent, even when linked to a free exercise claim, may be subject to limitation under Prince [v. Massachusetts, 321 U.S. 158, 64 S.Ct. 438, 88 L.Ed. 645 (1944),] if it appears that parental decisions will jeopardize the health or safety of the child, or have a potential for significant social burdens.

Yoder, 406 U.S. at 233–34, 92 S.Ct. 1526. The Court did not conclude that strict scrutiny was required.

It is true that "the custody, care and nurture of the child reside first in the parents." Prince v. Massachusetts, 321 U.S. 158, 166, 64 S.Ct. 438, 88 L.Ed. 645 (1944). However, the Court has never held that parental rights to childrearing as guaranteed under the Due Process Clause of the 14th Amendment must be subjected to a strict scrutiny analysis.* * *. See Troxel v. Granville, 530 U.S. 57, 120 S.Ct. 2054, 147 L.Ed.2d 49 (2000). "[T]he Supreme Court has yet to decide whether the right to direct the upbringing and education of one's children is among those fundamental rights whose infringement merits heightened scrutiny." Brown v. Hot, Sexy and Safer Productions, Inc., 68 F.3d 525, 533 (1st Cir.1995). *Pierce* and *Yoder* do not support an inference that parental decisionmaking requires a strict scrutiny analysis.

The question is not whether the Anayas have set forth a hybrid rights claim but whether the law they have challenged is neutral and has general application.

This case is analogous to cases in which courts have upheld the State's right to require immunization of children. In Boone v. Boozman, 217 F.Supp.2d 938 (E.D.Ark.2002), the court upheld the constitutionality of an immunization statute, finding that the free exercise claim challenged a neutral law of general applicability. The law applied to all school children except those whose health would be endangered by immunization. Because the law was neutral, heightened scrutiny was not required even though compulsory immunization might burden a plaintiff's right to free exercise.

The court stated, "It is well established that the State may enact reasonable regulations to protect the public health and the public safety, and it cannot be questioned that compulsory immunization is a permissible exercise of the State's police power." Id. at 954. Society's interest in protecting against the spread of disease takes precedence over parental rights and the right to free exercise of religion. *Id.*

In Prince, 321 U.S. at 166–67, 64 S.Ct. 438 the Court held that neither rights of religion nor rights of parenthood are beyond limitation. Acting to guard the general interest in youth's well being, the state as *parens patriae* may restrict the parent's control by requiring school attendance, regulating or prohibiting the child's labor and in many other ways. Its authority is not nullified merely because the parent grounds his claim to control the child's course of conduct on religion or conscience. Thus, he cannot claim freedom from compulsory vaccination for the child more than for himself on religious grounds. The right to practice religion freely does not include liberty to expose the community or the child to communicable disease or the latter to ill health or death * * *. [T]he state has a wide range of power for limiting parental freedom and authority in things affecting the child's welfare; and * * * this includes, to some extent, matters of conscience and religious conviction.

A law is neutral and of general applicability "if it does not aim to 'infringe upon or restrict practices because of their religious motivation,' and if it does not 'in a selective manner impose burdens only on conduct motivated by religious belief[.]' " San Jose Christian College v. Morgan Hill, 360 F.3d 1024, 1031 (9th Cir.2004), quoting Church of Lukumi Babalu Aye, Inc. v. Hialeah, 508 U.S. 520, 113 S.Ct. 2217, 124 L.Ed.2d 472 (1993). Section 71–519 is a neutral law of general applicability. It is generally applicable to all babies born in the state and does not discriminate as to which babies must be tested. Its purpose is not directed at religious practices or beliefs. Pursuant to Employment Div., Dept. of Human Res. v. Smith, 494 U.S. 872, 110 S.Ct. 1595, 108 L.Ed.2d 876 (1990), and its progeny, a neutral law of general applicability need not be supported by a compelling governmental interest even though it may have an incidental effect of burdening religion. * * *

Section 71–519 does not contain a system of particularized exemptions that allow some children to be excused from testing. See Kissinger v. Board of Trustees, 5 F.3d 177 (6th Cir.1993). The statute does not unlawfully burden the Anayas' right to freely exercise their religion, nor does it unlawfully burden their parental rights. Section 71–519 cannot be construed as directly regulating religious-based conduct. See Cornerstone Bible Church v. City of Hastings, 948 F.2d 464 (8th Cir.1991). There is no evidence that the State had an anti-religious purpose in enforcing the law. See id.

Whether a statute is constitutional is a question of law; accordingly, the Nebraska Supreme Court is obligated to reach a conclusion independent of the decision reached by the court below. Slansky v. Nebraska State Patrol, 268 Neb. 360, 685 N.W.2d 335 (2004). A statute is presumed to be constitutional, and all reasonable doubts will be resolved in favor of its constitutionality. Id.

* * *

We conclude that the effect of § 71–519 upon the constitutional claims the Anayas have asserted is properly analyzed under a rational basis review. Evidence was presented concerning the effects of the diseases that are tested for under the statute. Early diagnosis allows for prevention of death and disability in children. The State has determined that it is appropriate to test for these diseases soon after a child is born in order to address treatment options. The health and safety of the child are of particular concern, as are the potential social burdens created by children who are not identified and treated.

The State has an interest in the health and welfare of all children born in Nebraska, and the purpose of § 71–519 is to protect such health and welfare. This is a rational basis for the law, and it is constitutional.

[The discussion of mootness is omitted.]

NOTES AND QUESTIONS

1. A 1982 study in Maryland reported that only 27 out of approximately 50,000 mothers (0.05 percent) refused to consent to newborn screening when given the opportunity.

2. The report of the Task Force on Newborn Screening, American Academy of Pediatrics, recommends that "parents should always * * * have the opportunity to refuse testing." The 1994 report of the National Academy of Sciences recommended that screening be voluntary, but added that mandatory screening would be justified if there was "evidence that—without mandatory screening—newborns will not be screened for treatable illnesses in time to institute effective treatments (e.g., in PKU or congenital hypothyroidism)." The NAS went on to observe: "There is no evidence that a serious harm will result if autonomy is recognized, just as there is no evidence that mandating newborn screening is necessary to ensure that the vast majority of newborns are screened." Lori Andrews et al., Assessing Genetic Risks: Implications for Health and Social Policy 276 (1994). If parental consent is only permitted so long as parents give their consent, is the consent requirement meaningful?

What should a health professional do if parents refuse to consent to screening, especially for a disease that can be treated or prevented if it is detected early enough? Consider the following definition of child abuse and neglect under the federal Child Abuse Prevention and Treatment Act (CAPTA), under which states must require health professionals to report to child protective services agencies in order to receive federal grants: "Any recent act or failure to act on the part of a parent or caretaker, which results in death, serious physical or emotional harm, sexual abuse, or exploitation, or an act or failure to act which presents an imminent risk of serious harm." 42 U.S.C. § 5106g(2). Would a parental refusal to permit newborn screening fall under these provisions?

3. Is newborn screening analogous to vaccination, as the court in *Anaya* suggests? Vaccination is seen as a proper exercise of the police power because it protects third parties with whom the child might come into contact. Newborn screening will only affect that child and, with a 1 in 15,000 incidence of PKU, the child is unlikely to be "harmed" by the parents' refusal to test. (In fact, parents consent all the time to more risky activities of their children, such as participating in football.) Since the court views parents' refusal to consent to screening as creating a risk to the child, would the outcome be different for screening for one of the many other disorders that some states screen for in which there either is no treatment or the screening

is just done for carrier status, to aid in the parents' future reproductive choices?

AMERICAN ACADEMY OF PEDIATRICS, REPORT OF THE TASK FORCE ON NEWBORN SCREENING (PUBLISHED AS A CALL FOR A NATIONAL AGENDA ON STATE NEWBORN SCREENING PROGRAMS)

106 Pediatrics 389, 389–415 (Supp.) (2000).

Almost all infants screened have residual blood samples retained by the state programs. Enough blood is obtained when performing heelstick newborn screening to permit programs to repeat tests when necessary. However, because repeat tests are not always necessary, and a repeat test may not use up the blood sample, the vast majority of infants screened (in excess of 95%) will have residual blood samples retained by the state programs. Currently, state programs hold these samples for variable lengths of time: 10 programs save samples for 21 years or more; 6 programs for 5 to 7 years; 2 programs for 1 to 3 years; 6 programs for 6 to 12 months; 21 programs for 1 to 6 months; and 5 programs for 1 to 4 weeks. Only 1 program is known to save the samples under optimal conditions for later use in biochemical analyses. Optimal storage conditions are much less critical for genetic analyses, and samples stored in many states are adequate for genetic analyses. The lack of uniformity between programs reflects uncertainty and debate over whether residual blood samples should be retained and, if so, for how long and under what conditions.

* * *

Residual blood samples may be used for several purposes including:

- *Research related to new or existing newborn screening modalities.* As technology advances for newborn screening programs, new testing modalities will be developed for conditions included in current programs, and new tests will be added for other health conditions. Residual heelstick blood samples can be used to ascertain the validity of new testing modalities for existing conditions and of tests for new conditions. Identifiers are sometimes retained to enable follow-up contact with an infant's family if an effective intervention is available for children diagnosed with the condition.

- *Epidemiologic research relevant to clinical medicine and public health.* Public health officials need population-based data to determine the appropriate allocation of resources to care for children with specific conditions. A thorough understanding of many health conditions requires epidemiologic data on the prevalence of specific genetic or biochemical attributes in the general population. Residual newborn screening samples constitute a specimen bank of a large cohort of the population of states. As genetic technology advances, such a comprehensive bank, linked to basic demographic information, may be useful for certain types of research. The potential utility of such a resource will need to be carefully evaluated because residual blood samples in this context will not be linked to clinical data on the children.

- *Clinical or forensic testing.* For children who have moved and cannot be located, the heelstick blood sample may represent the only source of a biological specimen from a given child. The sample may be useful for forensic purposes. Testing of residual blood samples may be essential in the postmortem identification of a genetic condition that may have contributed to a child's death. At least 1 state has decided to store newborn blood spots indefinitely to permit identification of children who have been kidnapped.

ETHICAL CONCERNS RELATED TO USE OF RESIDUAL BLOOD SAMPLES

Storage and use of residual newborn screening blood samples raise a number of practical and ethical challenges. Ethical challenges include the development of guidance regarding the use of residual blood spots for purposes other than those for which they were originally obtained. The protection of privacy and confidentiality among children and families is a serious concern. In the case of newborn screening, when blood samples are collected from infants as a matter of law, there is additional reason to ensure appropriate storage and use.

At the same time, residual newborn screening samples have been used to address important public health issues. The prevalence of in utero exposure to drugs and environmental agents; the allele frequency of genes associated with significant morbidity, mortality, or disability in infancy or childhood; and the prevalence of serious maternal or intrauterine infections have been determined in various populations by anonymous use of residual blood spots. Samples linked to outcome have been used to assess the feasibility of screening for various diseases of the newborn and infant, and to determine risk factors for birth defects and developmental disabilities. To date, there have been no published reports of misuse of residual newborn screening samples in research projects; however, the potential for use and misuse is expanding.

NOTES AND QUESTIONS

1.   How does the storage and retention of these newborn blood samples compare with the practices of other DNA or tissue banks discussed in Chapter 3?

2.   What policies should govern the storage and retention of these blood samples? The Task Force on Newborn Screening of the American Academy of Pediatrics states that "[c]urrent national standards stipulate that epidemiological research may be conducted without consent, so long as identifiers are removed." In regard to identifiable samples, the report states:

> The Task Force concluded that parental permission should be sought for the use of identifiable samples in research to validate tests for additional diseases, or for epidemiologic research. Identifiable samples from newborns should be used for research only if: 1) IRB approval is obtained for the proposed research, 2) consent is obtained from the child's parent(s) or guardian for the proposed research, 3) newborn samples represent the optimal source of available tissue for the research, 4) unlinked samples will not suffice, and 5) acceptable samples from consenting adults are not available.

Are these recommendations appropriate?

3.   In 2009, parents in Texas sued to block the state from giving researchers access to newborn screening bloodspots. Pursuant to a settlement agreement, the state in 2011 destroyed 5.3 stored bloodspots, and the legislature passed a law requiring the state to obtain parental permission to use residual bloodspots for research purposes. In 2011, the Minnesota Supreme Court held that stored bloodspots were covered by the state's Genetic Privacy Act, which required parental consent for residual uses, including research. Bearder v. State, 806 N.W.2d 766 (Minn. 2011). The state eventually destroyed all bloodspots collected between the date of the court's decision and a subsequent hearing of the case on remand one year later. For a description of state laws governing retention and use of newborn screening bloodspots, see Michelle Lewis et al., State Laws Regarding the Retention and Use of Residual Newborn Screening Blood Samples, 127 Pediatrics 703–712 (2011).

CHAPTER 10

GENETIC ENHANCEMENT

■ ■ ■

I.   INTRODUCTION

As the human genome is more completely deciphered and the techniques of genetic testing, gene therapy, and pharmacogenetics and pharmacogenomics are perfected, the possibility arises that these technologies might be targeted at non-therapeutic or "enhancement" objectives. As an American Association for the Advancement of Science (AAAS) Report notes, "[t]he technology for therapy and enhancement procedures is basically the same." AAAS Report, Human Inheritable Genetic Modifications at 43 (2000).

II.   PROCEDURES

Distinguishing between "therapy" and "enhancement" is not easy. If "enhancement" is defined in terms of making improvements beyond what is "natural," does it include preventive measures like vaccines which confer an immunity beyond what people naturally would enjoy? The NIH has approved the use of gene transfer technology to boost the functioning of low density lipoprotein receptors above the normal range in persons suffering from hypercholesterolemia (an inherited inability to clear cholesterol from the blood). According to one expert, the result was to give these patients a "super-cleansing ability." Yet both of these interventions are aimed at preventing, or reducing the severity of, disease, and therefore seem therapeutic rather than enhancing in their objective.

Another approach might be that therapy is aimed at preserving or restoring "normal" function, while the goal of enhancement is to make a person more than "normal." This conceptualization is endorsed by Norman Daniels, who conceives of the "normal" in terms of the typical functioning of the species. See Norman Daniels, Just Health Care (1986); Allen Buchanan et al., From Chance to Choice: Genetics and Justice (2000). But it has been strongly criticized by Eric Juengst, who points out that it rests on questionable assumptions about what is "normal." See Eric Juengst, What Does Enhancement Mean?, in Enhancing Human Traits 29 (Erik Parens ed. 1998).

Perhaps the clearest distinction is between having a therapeutic or non-therapeutic goal. After all, this is the distinction that health insurance companies must make when presented with a claim for surgery that may be "cosmetic," and therefore not covered by the policy. But even this distinction is problematic on the ground that it depends on how we define "disease" or "disability," or on what we regard as "normal" appearance and functionality.

Depending on how "genetic enhancement" is defined, it could be achieved by a number of different types of techniques. For example, it could include drugs that affected non-disease traits and that were made with recombinant DNA manufacturing methods or using knowledge gained from decoding the genome. One example is human growth hormone (HGH), which is used by athletes to enhance performance, and by the general public to retard aging. Another hormone made using recombinant DNA engineering that is attractive to athletes is erythropoietin (EPO). This is a naturally-occurring hormone that influences how many of a person's blood cells are red, since the more red blood cells, the more oxygen is carried to the tissues. Recombinant DNA technology clones the human EPO gene and implants it into hamster ovary cells, which then act as genetically-programmed factories to make the protein. A third hormone with potential value to athletes and that is synthesized using recombinant DNA is Insulin-like Growth Factor-1 (IGF-1).

Not only can genetic factories produce synthetic versions of naturally-occurring substances, but the factories themselves can be inserted into organisms and programmed to turn on and off. A company called Oxford bioMedica has created a product called Repoxygen®. This is an EPO gene under the control of a gene which, when inserted into muscle cells, acts as a switch to turn the gene on to produce EPO in the presence of low amounts of oxygen. The company developed the product for the treatment of anemia, but it holds obvious interest for athletes, since they can obtain the benefit of EPO only when they need it, and more importantly, they may be able to avoid detection by anti-doping testing when the gene is turned off.

As genetic tests become available for non-disease traits, people can test themselves and prospective mates and use the results to decide whether or not to go ahead and have children. Or they could test a set of fertilized embryos in vitro to decide which ones to implant, or even use the results of prenatal testing to decide whether to abort a fetus. The use of genetic testing to make reproductive decisions based on non-disease traits might be termed "passive genetic enhancement," since it merely selects from naturally occurring genetic endowments. But genetic enhancement also might take the form of somatic or germline gene transfer, using the basic techniques of gene therapy to produce enhancement rather than therapeutic effects.

NIH funding is not available for research on genetic enhancement in human subjects. But in May 2007, NIH scientists announced that they had identified a genetic mutation in racing dogs that helps explain why some dogs run faster than others. The mutation is in the gene that codes for a muscle protein called myostatin. The researchers found that whippets with one mutated copy of the gene were the fastest racers, while dogs with two mutated copies had oversized muscles that slowed them down. Although the research was in dogs, Elaine A. Ostrander, the leader of the research team, acknowledged that it "could have implications for competitive sports in dogs, horses and possibly even humans." Medical researchers are seeking ways to turn off or counteract the production of myostatin in order to treat muscle-wasting diseases such as muscular dystrophy. They have developed an antibody that blocks myostatin in adult mice. The same techniques could enable healthy individuals to grow bigger muscles.

Another field of genetic research being watched closely by athletes involves genes that code for fast- and slow-twitch muscles. Fast-twitch muscles are associated with sports that require short bursts of energy, such as sprinting and weightlifting. People with more slow-twitch muscles are better at endurance sports, such as long-distance running. The discovery of genetic variations associated with the two different types of muscles already is impacting the sports world. Researchers have identified one variant of the ACTN3 gene in humans that codes for a protein called α-actinin–3, which helps to produce slow-twitch muscles. People who do not have this variant, called R577X, have more fast-twitch muscles. An Australian company is selling a genetic test that detects the variant for $93. The ACTN3 test is likely to be followed by many more performance-associated genetic indicators. For a critique of the science behind the test, see Lori Andrews, Testing Children for Sports Genes, blogs.kentlaw.iit.edu/islat/2009/01/06/testing-children-for-sports-genes/.
In 2006, one group of researchers published a human gene map for "performance and health-related fitness phenotypes," or traits. It contained over 100 entries.

Pharmacogenetics, discussed in Chapter 8, also has important implications for athletes. The same knowledge that explains why certain people respond better than others to specific drugs can be applied to the use of performance-enhancing substances by athletes. Because of their genes, some athletes are likely to respond better to certain of these substances than to others. Not only might this increase the impact of the substance on performance, but athletes may be able to avoid many, if not most, of the side effects.

Genetic enhancement research is targeting traits besides athletic ability. Parents are reported to seek human growth hormone, which is now made using rDNA manufacturing techniques, to increase the height of children of normal or even greater-than-normal height. Scientists at McGill University in Montreal have discovered a gene that codes for a memory-blocking protein, eIF2α. Mice with a mutation that blocks production of the protein performed better than normal mice at remembering how to swim to a hidden platform, and did better on a "fear-conditioning" test that measures their recall of a stimulus that precedes a mild foot shock. One researcher observed that "[i]f a person were reading a page of a textbook, it might take several times to memorize it. A human equivalent of these mice would get the information right away." The NIH itself sponsored a study to determine if a drug for Parkinson disease called tolcapone improved memory in schizophrenics. The subjects included a number of normal individuals acting as controls who were grouped based on differences in a particular gene, catecholamine-O-methyltransferase (COMT). The investigators reported that the drug significantly improved executive function and verbal episodic memory in subjects with one variant of the gene, while it impaired these abilities in subjects with another variant.

Genetic enhancement by actually inserting or deleting DNA remains a more distant prospect, since it faces the same hurdles described in Chapter 7 that beset gene therapy. Yet in 2004, a team of U.S. and South Korean researchers, led by Ronald Evans at the Salk Institute, announced the creation of a "marathon mouse" that can run twice as far as a normal mouse. The researchers were able to increase the activity of a "master regulator" called the PPARdelta gene, which decreased the production of fast-twitch muscles in favor of slow-twitch muscles. One key question was whether the genetic manipulation would disrupt the animals' reproductive capacity, but the mice remained fertile and the mutation was inherited by offspring. Researchers at the University of Pennsylvania also claim to have genetically engineered a strain of "smart" mice by boosting their production of a protein called NR2B that controls the brain's ability to associate one event with another, and Boston University scientists report that the mice maintain their superior learning and memory function into old age.

No type of biomedical enhancement generates more concern than human germ line genetic enhancement, whereby changes in an individual's DNA would be passed on to their offspring. So far as is known, the direct manipulation of DNA to produce germ line enhancement has not yet occurred in humans, although as illustrated by the preceding discussion of the marathon mouse, it has been accomplished in animals. As discussed in Chapter 7, however, human germ line genetic manipulation for medical purposes occasionally does occur inadvertently.

JON W. GORDON, GENETIC ENHANCEMENT IN HUMANS
283 Science 2023 (1999).

Dramatic advances in gene transfer technology since the early 1980s have prompted consideration of its use in humans to enhance phenotypic traits. The notion that genetic modification could confer special advantages on an individual has generated excitement. Controversial issues surround this prospect, however. A practical concern is determining how to ensure equal access to such advanced medical technologies. There has also been speculation that genetic enhancement might affect human evolution, and philosophical objections have been raised, based on the belief that to intervene in such fundamental biological processes is to "play God." Although such philosophical questions cannot be resolved through data analysis, we nevertheless have the tools in hand to objectively assess our state of progress. We can also assess the impact that promulgation of such technology might have on human evolution and formulate sensible guidelines for developing policies governing human genetic enhancements.

DEFINING GENETIC ENHANCEMENT

Some experts have argued that "enhancement" can have different meanings depending on the circumstances. For example, when a disease is common, the risk for developing the disorder may be considered the norm, and genetic alleviation of that risk might be regarded as a form of enhancement. This kind of semantic gamesmanship is misleading. The obvious public concern does not relate to improvement of traits for alleviation of deficiencies or reduction of disease risk, but to augmentation of functions that without intervention would be considered entirely normal. To raise the athletic capabilities of a schoolyard basketball player to those of a professional or to confer the talents of Chopin on a typical college music professor is the sort of genetic enhancement that many find troublesome. The experts in the gene transfer field should acknowledge the distinction in order to avoid causing public distrust and undermining the deliberative process.

Another important distinction is that between genetic changes that are heritable and those that cannot be genetically transmitted. At the present time, gene transfer approaches that involve the early embryo are far more effective than somatic cell gene therapy methodologies. Embryo gene transfer affords the opportunity to transform most or all cells of the organism and thus overcomes the inefficient transformation that plagues somatic cell gene transfer protocols. Moreover, the commonly used approaches to embryo gene insertion—pronuclear microinjection and transfection of embryonic stem cells—are associated with stable, high expression of donor DNA. Typically, however, genetic changes introduced into the embryo extend to the gametes and are heritable.

Scenarios can be constructed wherein introduced genes could be deleted from germ cells or early embryos derived from the treated individual. For example, transferred genes could reside on artificial chromosomes that could be deleted by activating a recombinase that induced recombination of the chromosome ends. Such approaches, however, are currently only speculative. Germline gene transfer has already succeeded in several animal species. Because of this and the general belief that voluntary abstention from germline modification in humans is unlikely, a candid discussion of genetic enhancement must include the possibility that changes introduced will be transmitted to offspring.

THE STATE OF THE ART

Animal experiments thus far have attempted to improve what are intuitively regarded as "simple" traits such as growth rate or muscle mass. Efforts to genetically improve the growth of swine have involved insertion of transgenes encoding growth hormone. Nevertheless, despite the fact that growth hormone transgenes are expressed well in swine, increased growth does not occur. Although the transgenic animals fortuitously have less body fat, these unexpected benefits cannot be extrapolated to human clinical protocols. Before a human embryo is treated with recombinant DNA, we must know exactly what we are doing.

Another spectacular failed attempt at enhancement resulted from efforts to increase muscle mass in cattle. When expressed in mice, the avian c-*ski* gene, the cellular counterpart of the retroviral *v-ski* oncogene, induced massive muscle hypertrophy. This prompted efforts to produce cattle expressing a c-*ski* transgene. When gene transfer was accomplished, the transgenic calf initially exhibited muscle hypertrophy, but muscle degeneration and wasting soon followed. Unable to stand, the debilitated animal was killed.

Why did these enhancement experiments fail? For clues, it is useful to compare modern-day gene transfer technology with the more traditional approach to genetic engineering: selective breeding. Selective breeding maximizes the reproductive efficiency of individuals that exhibit desired characteristics. The selection strategy is oblivious to the number of genes responsible for generating the phenotype. Swine selected for rapid growth may consume more food, produce more growth hormone, respond more briskly to endogenous growth hormone, divert proteins toward somatic growth, and possess skeletal anatomy that allows the animal to tolerate increased weight. Dozens or perhaps hundreds of genes may influence these traits, but in selective breeding, favorable alleles at all loci can simultaneously be selected. In contrast, gene transfer selects one relevant locus and attempts to improve it in isolation. It is little wonder that this approach, albeit potentially powerful and efficient, is more chancy, and has, despite more than 10 years of effort, failed to yield even one unequivocal success. Greater success has been achieved in genetic enhancement of plants, which are more easily manipulated genetically and reproductively.

Given the inherent limitations of the gene transfer approach to enhancement, discussion of extending such procedures to humans is scientifically unjustified. We clearly do not yet understand how to accomplish controlled genetic modification of even simple phenotypes. Where more complex traits such as intelligence are concerned, we have no idea what to do, and in fact we may never be able to use gene transfer for enhancement of such phenotypes. A useful way to appreciate the daunting task of manipulating intelligence through gene transfer is by considering the fact that a single cerebellar Purkinje cell may possess more synapses than the total number of genes in the human genome. There are tens of millions of Purkinje cells in the cerebellum, and these cells are involved in only one aspect of brain function: motor coordination. The genome only provides a blueprint for formation of the brain; the finer details of assembly and intellectual development are beyond direct genetic control and must perforce be subject to innumerable stochastic and environmental influences.

GENETIC ENGINEERING AND HUMAN EVOLUTION

Some have suggested that genetic enhancement and related reproductive technologies now give us the power to control human evolution. This solemn pronouncement is totally without scientific foundation. The evolution of the human species may be understood as a nonrandom change in allelic frequencies resulting from selective pressure. The change progresses over generations because individuals with specific patterns of alleles are favored reproductively. If new alleles were introduced by gene transfer, the impact on the species would be negligible. Every month worldwide approximately 11 million babies are born. The addition of one genetically modified individual could not significantly affect gene frequencies. Moreover, if the "enhanced" individual had his or her first child at the age of 20, then 2,640,000,000 unengineered children would be born during the interval between the birth and procreation of the gene recipient. Even if 1000 successful gene transfers were performed per year, a number not likely to be achieved in the foreseeable future, those newborns would constitute only 1/132,000 of all live births. Thus, any effort to enhance the human species experimentally would be swamped by the random attempts of Mother Nature.

Finally, there is no certainty that genetically enhanced individuals would have greater biological fitness, as measured by reproductive success. A genius or great athlete who has no children has no biological fitness as defined in evolutionary theory. For these reasons, neither gene transfer nor any of the other emerging reproductive technologies will ever have a significant impact on human evolution.

DEVELOPING POLICY

If we accept the notion that genetic enhancement is not practicable in the near future, what policies should we develop concerning the use of such technology? The decision to undertake any form of invasive medical intervention immediately renders the treatment subject a patient who has a right to informed consent as well as to protection from unjustifiably dangerous medical manipulation. Our inability to predict the consequences of an attempt at genetic enhancement makes informed consent impossible, and current knowledge from animal experiments tells us that embryo gene transfer is unsafe: The common approach of pronuclear microinjection is characterized by random integration of donor DNA, a lack of control of the number of gene copies inserted, significant rearrangements of host genetic material, and a 5 to 10% frequency of insertional mutagenesis. Homologous recombination in embryonic stem cells overcomes many of these shortcomings, but human embryonic stem cell transfection would necessarily be followed by nuclear transfer into enucleated oocytes. Because nuclear transfer in at least two animal models is associated with a low birth rate and a very high rate of late pregnancy loss or newborn death, this procedure is also unsafe. The risks are so high and the documented efficacy is so low for gene transfer that it could not compare favorably to straightforward prenatal diagnosis even when a compelling need for therapy exists, as in cases of genetic disease. The use of gene transfer for elective purposes such as enhancement would stray far beyond the limits of acceptable medical intervention.

To attempt genetic enhancement with extant methods would clearly be medically unacceptable, but attempts to ban gene transfer legally could be a cumbersome approach to limiting its clinical use. Verification of compliance would be difficult. The diverse resources required for gene transfer necessitate that the procedure be carried out in facilities equipped for in vitro fertilization. Direct inspection would be required to uncover gene transfer procedures in such facilities. This would impose on the privacy of patients undergoing accepted assisted reproduction procedures such as sperm injection. Moreover, gene transfer can be easily concealed; in the case of pronuclear microinjection, only a few seconds are needed to complete the process. Legal restrictions can also be easily avoided by performing the procedure outside the area of jurisdiction.

Finally, and perhaps most important, broad legal restrictions incur the risk of limiting invaluable research. Exemplifying this problem is the current overly broad ban on federal funding for experiments with human embryos. The recent derivation of human embryonic stem cells from preimplantation embryos has created important new research opportunities, accompanied by pressure to provide federal funds for the work. This pressure has led to the odd situation in which federal funds will likely be allowed for research with embryonic stem cells but not for manipulating human embryos to produce embryonic stem cell lines. If, as a society, we feel compelled to make a statement against genetic enhancement, we need not enact anticipatory legislation. Instead we can evaluate such manipulations as we would any other invasive clinical procedure. If we require that gene transfer be accompanied by informed consent, that it have a reasonable possibility of succeeding, that its cost not be excessive, that it have acceptable side effects and toxicities, that it not be accompanied by a burdensome requirement for long-term follow-up evaluation, and that it compare favorably with other treatment options, we will currently reject the procedure on all counts as medically unethical. Were entities such as the National Bioethics Advisory Commission or Congress to make such statements formally, no responsible physician would attempt genetic enhancement. Irresponsible use of technology can never be stopped, even by legislation.

Fear of genetic manipulation may encourage proposals to limit basic investigations that might ultimately lead to effective human gene transfer. History has shown that effort is far better spent in preparing society to cope with scientific advances than in attempting to restrict basic research. Gene transfer studies may never lead to successful genetic enhancement, but they are certain to provide new treatment and prevention strategies for a variety of devastating diseases. No less significant is the potential for this research to improve our understanding of the most complex and compelling phenomenon ever observed—the life process. We cannot be expected to deny ourselves this knowledge.

NOTES AND QUESTIONS

1. Is Gordon correct that "genetic enhancement is not practicable in the near future"? It may depend on how genetic enhancement is defined. If it includes drugs made with genetic knowledge or rDNA techniques, then as shown earlier, examples already exist.

On September 11, 1997, the National Institutes of Health convened the first of its "Gene Therapy Policy Conferences." The meeting was prompted by a request to NIH to approve a protocol for conducting a gene therapy experiment in healthy volunteers, rather than in patients. Although the experiment was part of an effort to develop treatments for cystic fibrosis, the proposed use of healthy subjects raised for the first time the question of whether and in what circumstances it was appropriate to use gene insertion technology in "normal" individuals. Officials at NIH realized that it was but a short step from preliminary testing in healthy subjects of a genetic treatment for disease to experiments the goal of which was to genetically enhance a normal person's physical or mental characteristics. As the President's Council on Bioethics observed in its report, Beyond Therapy: Biotechnology and the Pursuit of Happiness: "We have every reason to expect exponential increases in biotechnologies and, therefore, in their potential uses in all aspects of human life." President's Council on Bioethics, Beyond Therapy: Biotechnology and the Pursuit of Happiness 303 (2003).

As discussed in Chapter 6, some parents already base reproductive decisions on non-disease characteristics detected with genetic (and other) testing—namely, tests that reveal gender. See Dorothy C. Wertz & John C. Fletcher, Fatal Knowledge? Prenatal Diagnosis and Sex Selection, 19 Hastings Center Rep. 21 (1989) (discussing the common use of prenatal diagnosis for sex screening); Lynne Marie Kohm, Sex Selection Abortion and the Boomerang Effect of a Woman's Right to Choose: A Paradox of the Skeptics, 4 Wm. & Mary J. Women & L. 91, 92 (1997) (discussing how sex selection results in an unbalanced sex ratio). For an expansive view of genetic selection of offspring characteristics, including gender, see John A. Robertson, Genetic Selection of Offspring Characteristics, 76 B.U.L. Rev. 421, 479 (1996) (arguing that "commitment to procreative liberty necessarily leaves parents wide prebirth discretion to select or not the characteristics of their offspring").

Gene transfer for enhancement purposes may indeed be very far down the road, as Gordon suggests. But the potential demand may be so great that private companies may soon begin making a substantial commitment toward enhancement research and development.

2.   Why is Gordon so skeptical (and he is not alone)? What difference does it make to him if some people want to speculate about genetic enhancement? The answer is found in the policy discussion of his article. Does this suggest that he may be slanting the scientific prospects in order to protect what he regards as more worthwhile forms of genetic research? If so, is this appropriate?

MAXWELL J. MEHLMAN ET AL., ETHICAL AND LEGAL ISSUES IN ENHANCEMENT RESEARCH ON HUMAN SUBJECTS

20 Cambridge Q. Healthcare Ethics 30, 32–34 (2011).

* * *

The United States, along with other nations and international organizations, has developed an elaborate system of ethical norms and legal rules to govern biomedical research using human subjects. These policies govern research which might provide direct health benefits to participants, and research in which there is no prospect for participant health benefits. There has been little discussion, however, about how well these rules would apply to research designed to improve participants' capabilities or characteristics beyond the goal of good health. When mentioned at all in the literature, this so-called "enhancement research," as opposed to research aimed at diagnosing, preventing, curing, or treating illnesses or medical conditions, is usually dismissed without explanation.

* * *

One concern raised by enhancement research is how to decide if the risks from an experiment would be outweighed by the potential benefits. The degree of potential benefit depends on the nature of the benefit as well as its amount: The more important or valuable the potential benefit, the greater the risks that researchers ethically can impose on subjects.

It might be wondered, therefore, whether the benefit from an enhancement was inherently of so much less value than health-oriented research that it would be unethical to conduct an enhancement study unless it offered a much better ratio of benefits to risks. Suppose there was a drug used to increase muscle mass in people with muscle-wasting diseases, and that was known to cause liver damage in a small number of patients. Should an IRB [Institutional Review Board] approve a study to see if the drug increased muscle mass in normal individuals? Should an IRB approve a study to measure patient satisfaction with a new surgical technique for facelifts, given that any surgical procedure carries with it a certain risk of scarring? Would a risk of scarring that was acceptable in a study of plastic surgery to correct a facial deformity be acceptable in a study of cosmetic use? The answer is that the value of a benefit clearly depends on the nature of the benefit. It is reasonable to expect that some health-oriented benefits would be regarded as more valuable than some enhancement benefits. On the other hand, some enhancement benefits may be perceived to be more valuable than medical benefits. An enhancement that potentially increased cognitive function substantially, for example, might be deemed more valuable than a substance to treat a minor skin irritation. * * *

A second question is how much to defer to the subjects in assessing potential enhancement benefits. The Common Rule [For the Protection of Human Subjects] takes a highly paternalistic approach, allowing investigators to approach potential subjects to seek their informed consent to participate only after experts, in the form of institutional review boards, government sponsors, government regulators, and the investigators themselves, are satisfied that the potential benefits outweigh the risks. This may be justified in the case of health-oriented research on the ground that physicians and other medical experts are best suited to gauge medical benefits and risks. But it is not clear that these experts possess any particular advantage when it comes to assessing enhancement benefits. It will be difficult to measure many enhancement benefits against an objectively agreed upon standard since there is no baseline "normal" point of reference. And even in cases where there is some agreed upon standard of comparison, the perception of actual benefit may be highly subjective. This suggests that subjects in enhancement studies should be given more leeway than subjects in health-oriented research in accepting risks in return for potential benefits.

But it is important to recognize that experts continue to play a crucial role in protecting subjects even in enhancement experiments. Experts may be necessary to evaluate and explain medical risks of enhancement interventions. Moreover, only experts are likely to possess the ability to determine if a proposed study was properly designed, so that the risks to subjects can be justified in light of valid and reproducible results; or if the investigators had misrepresented the potential benefits, deemphasized risks, failed to disclose information necessary for informed consent, devalued subjects' welfare, or possessed an unacceptable conflict of interest. Experts also can prevent subjects from falling prey to the enhancement equivalent of the therapeutic misconception—what we might call the "melioristic misconception"—in which subjects mistakenly assume that they will derive some direct enhancement benefit from participating in a study, without realizing that they may be randomly assigned to a group of subjects that receives a placebo instead of the experimental enhancement, or that the experimental intervention may turn out to provide no enhancement benefits to the subjects who actually receive it.

IRB review also plays an important role in ensuring public support for the general research enterprise by limiting the types of research in which human subjects may be enrolled. In part this determination is made based on analysis of the risk-benefit ratio. But another question is whether the mechanisms relied upon by the Common Rule to prevent unethical experimentation are adequate to protect against the potential adverse *social* impacts of biomedical enhancements? One common concern, for example is that widespread use of enhancement interventions would exacerbate the divide between the "haves" and "have nots" by allowing those that could afford the interventions to gain biological advantages over those that could not, creating separate social classes of genetic haves and have-nots. It is not clear, however, that IRBs have the authority to consider this and similar social concerns, whether in enhancement or health-oriented research. On the one hand, the Common Rule says that an IRB may approve a study only if it concludes that the risks are reasonable in relation to the anticipated benefits, including benefits to subjects and the importance of the knowledge to be gained. Hence, the knowledge to be gained from a study of an enhancement that would increase inequality might not be deemed important enough to justify imposing any substantial risks on the subjects. But another section of the federal regulations specifically prohibits IRBs from considering these risks at all, saying:

> The IRB should not consider possible long-range effects of applying knowledge gained in the research (for example, the possible effects of the research on public policy) as among those research risks that fall within the purview of its responsibility. (45 C.F.R. § 46.111)

This category of risk was interpreted explicitly by the architects of this prohibition—the members of the National Commission for the Protection for Human Subjects in Biomedical and Behavioral Research—as including just the sort of speculative group harms raised by enhancement research. If social inequality is deemed to be a public policy concern, the rules may preclude IRBs from taking it into account in evaluating proposed human experiments. Additional guidance on this issue of long-term risks may be important both in the context of enhancement research and for more traditional health-oriented research.

NOTES AND QUESTIONS

1.   Are special rules needed to govern enhancement research in humans? If so, what should the rules be?

2.   A special set of concerns arises in connection with research on so-called vulnerable populations. The federal research regulations establish special protections for pregnant women, fetuses and newborns, prisoners, and children, and adds that other populations may be "vulnerable to coercion or undue influence, such as * * * mentally disabled persons, or economically or educationally disadvantaged persons." (45 C.F.R. § 46.111(b)) These same populations may be vulnerable in the context of enhancement research, raising the question of whether the current protections, which were aimed at health-oriented research, provide adequate protections when the goal of the research is enhancement. A second question is whether the nature of enhancements, particularly their ability to confer a competitive advantage, requires that other distinct groups receive special protection.

In connection with enhancement research in children, consider the following:

> Children have already served as subjects in some biomedical enhancement research. For example, there have been at least seven studies on the effects of caffeine in normal children. Some ethicists might think that it is unethical for parents to enroll their children in any enhancement trials, on the ground that biomedical enhancement is contrary to a child's best interest. Parents might be deemed to be sacrificing the children's welfare in order to further the parents' own ambitions or social status, or to be valuing the children too much in terms of their capabilities, that is, "commodifying" them. But there is little objection to parents placing

their children in experimental educational settings in order to try to make them better learners. Why should parents be prohibited from enrolling their children in a study simply because it involves a biomedical rather than an educational enhancement?

The regulatory protections relating to children focus on risk-benefit assessments. Few if any experiments in which children were given biomedical enhancements would be likely to qualify as minimal risk under section 404 [45 CFR § 404]. It is less clear whether enhancement studies could fall under section 406 of the regulations, which pertains to research that presents only a "minor increase over minimal risk." Although this term is not defined in the regulations, most biomedical enhancements probably would be deemed to create a greater risk than this, and besides, section 406 requires the study to yield "generalizeable knowledge about the subjects' disorder or condition which is of vital importance for the understanding or amelioration of the subjects' disorder or condition," and an enhancement by definition does not address a disorder or condition. However, an NIH panel that reviewed a study in which normal-but-short children were to be given HGH concluded that the study could proceed under section 406. The implications of this decision for enhancement research troubled bioethicist Carol Tauer, who worried that:

> Such an application of 46.406 creates a precedent for approving greater than minimal risk research with healthy children in order to study any condition researchers or clinicians would like to be able to modify.

An "enhancement" modification is designed to alter a condition that is considered undesirable, either absolutely or relatively. Given the precedent in the NIH committee report, section 46.406 could be used to approve greater-than-minimal-risk enhancement research on children

Section 405 of the regulations allows an IRB to approve research with children that entails greater than minimal risk as long as there is a prospect of direct benefit to the individual subjects from the intervention in question, and the IRB determines that the risks are balanced by the potential benefits to the subjects, and that the ratio of risks to benefits is at least as favorable as that which would be provided by alternative treatments. The question is whether a direct enhancement benefit would count as a "direct benefit." The regulations fail to define the term, and a survey of the heads of IRBs showed that they were unclear about what it means. The regulation does not speak in terms of a "direct *medical* benefit," but the focus of the Common Rule is on health-oriented research, and the regulation does require the potential benefit to be compared to the benefit from alternative "treatments." Still, since the regulation on its face does not rule out enhancement research, it might allow enhancement research presenting more than minimal risk to be conducted on children if an IRB were convinced that the risks were outweighed by the potential benefits.

The final section of the regulations, 407, is a catch-all that applies to research on children that does not fall under one of the other three sections. It allows children to participate as subjects if a special review panel appointed by the NIH's Office of Human Research Protections finds that "the research presents a reasonable opportunity to further the understanding, prevention, or alleviation of a serious problem affecting the health or welfare of children." (45 C.F.R. § 46.407) If an enhancement study would be deemed to address "a serious problem affecting the health or welfare of children," a 407 panel might be willing to approve even relatively risky enhancement research on children.

While no 407 panels have been convened to review enhancement research, one study that did receive approval through the 407 process, although it was never carried out, involved administering to normal children methylphenidate and dextroamphetamine, which are controlled substances approved for treating ADHD but which are also used off-label to enhance cognition. The purpose of the study was to see whether magnetic resonance imaging could be useful as a means of diagnosing children with ADHD. To find this out, the researchers needed to determine if children with ADHD who were taking the drugs exhibited different brain images than siblings who did not have ADHD but who were given the drugs.

Similar to the regulations for children, federal regulations currently permit research to take place on fetuses if the research holds out the prospect of "direct benefit" to subjects. (45 C.F.R. § 46.204(b)) Since the regulations do not define the term "direct benefit," there is no obvious reason why research that presented the prospect of a direct enhancement rather than a health benefit would be prohibited. Examples of enhancement research with fetuses may include manipulation of embryonic and fetal DNA to produce enhancement effects, and the administration of enhancement drugs in utero. The regulations permit research on fetuses that does not offer the prospect of direct benefit only if the risk is minimal and the purpose of the research is to develop important medical knowledge that cannot be otherwise obtained. (45 C.F.R. § 46.204(b)) But since it is unlikely that a study of a biomedical enhancement effect on fetuses would be regarded as presenting no more than minimal risk, enhancement research involving fetuses would have to entail a direct benefit either to the fetus or to the pregnant woman to be permissible under the current guidelines.

One concern is that, in their eagerness to give their offspring every advantage (and societal pressures to do so), parents may agree to participate in experiments that expose children (or fetuses) to undue risk. The parents also may fall prey to the melioristic misconception—mistakenly thinking that the trial will provide actual enhancement benefits to all subjects. This suggests that IRBs and other external sources need to protect children and fetuses from research risks even when the parents would give their consent. On the other hand, parents traditionally are accorded considerable discretion in exposing their children to risks; the law only steps in when parental actions amount to "abuse or neglect." Assuming that the parents are not operating under a type of melioristic misconception, this would seem to call for deferring to parental decisions about participating in enhancement research. Under such an approach, oversight bodies such as IRBs would be entitled to limit parental decision making only when the oversight body was convinced that reasonable parents, having paramount regard for the welfare of the child or fetus, would not subject the child or fetus to such risks.

Note that this is not necessarily the same as the standard that the federal regulations establish for IRB review in general: that the IRB must determine, among other things, that the risks to subjects are reasonable in relation to the anticipated benefits. (45 C.F.R. § 46.111(a)(2)) The general standard would seem to allow an IRB to refuse to approve a study when the IRB members felt that, from their perspective, the risks would be unreasonable. The standard suggested above would require the IRB to assess a research protocol from the viewpoint of a parent, rather than from the members' own perspectives.

Maxwell J. Mehlman et al., Ethical and Legal Issues in Enhancement Research on Human Subjects, 20 Cambridge Q. Healthcare Ethics 30, 35–37 (2011).

Other study populations that are especially vulnerable in the context of enhancement research are workers, students, athletes, and members of the military. What special protections are provided for these groups in the current regulations? Are they adequate? See Maxwell J. Mehlman et al., Ethical and Legal Issues in Enhancement Research on Human Subjects, 20 Cambridge Q. Healthcare Ethics 30 (2011).

3. Valid and reliable efficacy data for genetic enhancement technologies are likely to be extremely scarce not only because of ethical questions about how to conduct enhancement research on humans, but because of gaps in the current legal system for regulating drugs. Depending on how genetic enhancement is achieved, providers and suppliers may not be required to submit safety and efficacy data to the government and obtain government approval before marketing enhancement technologies. To the

extent that genetic enhancement is deemed a surgical or medical procedure, as opposed to the administration of a drug, biological, or medical device, it will not require prior approval by the FDA, with the attendant requirement that this approval be based on adequate and well-controlled clinical investigations. Without being required to submit these data, it is unlikely that anyone would go to the enormous expense of creating them. Furthermore, even if regulators regard genetic enhancements as drugs, biologicals, or medical devices, these technologies are likely to emerge first as unapproved or "off-label" uses of therapeutic technologies—that is, uses for which the manufacturers are not labeling or promoting the technologies—and manufacturers are not required to conduct clinical investigations to support these uses. The experience with HGH, mentioned earlier, is a good example. The drug was approved by the FDA for use in individuals who were deficient in growth hormone. But pediatric endocrynologists began prescribing it for other individuals with short stature, and as noted earlier, there are reports that parents are seeking the drug—and no doubt obtaining it—for use in children who are of normal height and even for use in some who are tall. Efficacy data exist for the approved use of HGH, but there are likely to be only unconfirmed reports from uncontrolled case studies for the off-label uses.

MICHAEL SANDEL, THE CASE AGAINST PERFECTION: WHAT'S WRONG WITH DESIGNER CHILDREN, BIONIC ATHLETES, AND GENETIC ENGINEERING
Atlantic Monthly, Apr. 2004.

Breakthroughs in genetics present us with a promise and a predicament. The promise is that we may soon be able to treat and prevent a host of debilitating diseases. The predicament is that our newfound genetic knowledge may also enable us to manipulate our own nature—to enhance our muscles, memories, and moods; to choose the sex, height, and other genetic traits of our children; to make ourselves "better than well." When science moves faster than moral understanding, as it does today, men and women struggle to articulate their unease. In liberal societies they reach first for the language of autonomy, fairness, and individual rights. But this part of our moral vocabulary is ill equipped to address the hardest questions posed by genetic engineering. The genomic revolution has induced a kind of moral vertigo.

* * *

Though some maintain that genetic enhancement erodes human agency by overriding effort, the real problem is the explosion, not the erosion, of responsibility. As humility gives way, responsibility expands to daunting proportions. We attribute less to chance and more to choice. Parents become responsible for choosing, or failing to choose, the right traits for their children. Athletes become responsible for acquiring, or failing to acquire, the talents that will help their teams win.

One of the blessings of seeing ourselves as creatures of nature, God, or fortune is that we are not wholly responsible for the way we are. The more we become masters of our genetic endowments, the greater the burden we bear for the talents we have and the way we perform. Today when a basketball player misses a rebound, his coach can blame him for being out of position. Tomorrow the coach may blame him for being too short. Even now the use of performance-enhancing drugs in professional sports is subtly transforming the expectations players have for one another; on some teams players who take the field free from amphetamines or other stimulants are criticized for "playing naked."

The more alive we are to the chanced nature of our lot, the more reason we have to share our fate with others. Consider insurance. Since people do not know whether or when various ills will befall them, they pool their risk by buying health insurance and life insurance. As life plays itself out, the healthy wind up subsidizing the unhealthy, and those who live to a ripe old age wind up subsidizing the families of those who die before their time. Even without a sense of mutual obligation, people pool their risks and resources and share one another's fate.

But insurance markets mimic solidarity only insofar as people do not know or control their own risk factors. Suppose genetic testing advanced to the point where it could reliably predict each person's medical future and life expectancy. Those confident of good health and long life would opt out of the pool, causing other people's premiums to skyrocket. The solidarity of insurance would disappear as those with good genes fled the actuarial company of those with bad ones.

The fear that insurance companies would use genetic data to assess risks and set premiums recently led the Senate to vote to prohibit genetic discrimination in health insurance. But the bigger danger, admittedly more speculative, is that genetic enhancement, if routinely practiced, would make it harder to foster the moral sentiments that social solidarity requires.

Why, after all, do the successful owe anything to the least-advantaged members of society? The best answer to this question leans heavily on the notion of giftedness. The natural talents that enable the successful to flourish are not their own doing but, rather, their good fortune—a result of the genetic lottery. If our genetic endowments are gifts, rather than achievements for which we can claim credit, it is a mistake and a conceit to assume that we are entitled to the full measure of the bounty they reap in a market economy. We therefore have an obligation to share this bounty with those who, through no fault of their own, lack comparable gifts.

A lively sense of the contingency of our gifts—a consciousness that none of us is wholly responsible for his or her success—saves a meritocratic society from sliding into the smug assumption that the rich are rich because they are more deserving than the poor. Without this, the successful would become even more likely than they are now to view themselves as self-made and self-sufficient, and hence wholly responsible for their success. Those at the bottom of society would be viewed not as disadvantaged, and thus worthy of a measure of compensation, but as simply unfit, and thus worthy of eugenic repair. The meritocracy, less chastened by chance, would become harder, less forgiving. As perfect genetic knowledge would end the simulacrum of solidarity in insurance markets, so perfect genetic control would erode the actual solidarity that arises when men and women reflect on the contingency of their talents and fortunes.

Thirty-five years ago Robert L. Sinsheimer, a molecular biologist at the California Institute of Technology, glimpsed the shape of things to come. In an article titled "The Prospect of Designed Genetic Change" he argued that freedom of choice would vindicate the new genetics, and set it apart from the discredited eugenics of old.

> To implement the older eugenics . . . would have required a massive social programme carried out over many generations. Such a programme could not have been initiated without the consent and co-operation of major fraction of the population, and would have been continuously subject to social control. In contrast, the new eugenics could, at least in principle, be implemented on a quite individual basis, in one generation, and subject to no existing restrictions.

According to Sinsheimer, the new eugenics would be voluntary rather than coerced, and also more humane. Rather than segregating and eliminating the unfit, it would improve them. "The old eugenics would have required a continual selection for breeding of the fit, and a culling of the unfit," he wrote. "The new eugenics would permit in principle the conversion of all the unfit to the highest genetic level."

Sinsheimer's paean to genetic engineering caught the heady, Promethean self-image of the age. He wrote hopefully of rescuing "the losers in that chromosomal lottery that so firmly channels our human destinies," including not only those born with genetic defects but also "the 50,000,000 'normal' Americans with an IQ of less than 90." But he also saw that something bigger than improving on nature's "mindless, age-old throw of dice" was at stake. Implicit in technologies of genetic intervention was a more exalted place for human beings in the cosmos. "As we enlarge man's freedom, we diminish his constraints and that which he must accept as given," he wrote. Copernicus and Darwin had "demoted man from his bright glory at the focal point of the universe," but the new biology would restore his central role. In the mirror of our genetic knowledge we would see ourselves as more than a link in the chain of evolution: "We can be the agent of transition to a whole new pitch of evolution. This is a cosmic event."

There is something appealing, even intoxicating, about a vision of human freedom unfettered by the given. It may even be the case that the allure of that vision played a part in summoning the genomic age into being. It is often assumed that the powers of enhancement we now possess arose as an inadvertent by-product of biomedical progress—the genetic revolution came, so to speak, to cure disease, and stayed to tempt us with the prospect of enhancing our performance, designing our children, and perfecting our nature. That may have the story backwards. It is more plausible to view genetic engineering as the ultimate expression of our resolve to see ourselves astride the world, the masters of our nature. But that promise of mastery is flawed. It threatens to banish our appreciation of life as a gift, and to leave us with nothing to affirm or behold outside our own.

GREGORY STOCK, REDESIGNING HUMANS: OUR INEVITABLE GENETIC FUTURE
1–5 (2002).

* * *

We know that *Homo sapiens* is not the final word in primate evolution, but few have yet grasped that we are on the cusp of profound biological change, poised to transcend our current form and character on a journey to destinations of new imagination.

At first glance, the very notion that we might become more than "human" seems preposterous. After all, we are still biologically identical in virtually every respect to our cave-dwelling ancestors. But this lack of change is deceptive. Never before have we had the power to manipulate human genetics to alter our biology in meaningful, predictable ways.

Bioethicists and scientists alike worry about the consequences of coming genetic technologies, but few have thought through the larger implications of the wave of new developments arriving in reproductive biology. Today in vitro fertilization is responsible for fewer than 1 percent of births in the United States; embryo selection numbers only in the hundreds of cases; cloning and human genetic modification still lie ahead. But give these emerging technologies a decade and they will be the cutting edge of human biological change.

These developments will write a new page in the history of life, allowing us to seize control of our evolutionary future. Our coming ability to choose our children's genes will have immense social impact and raise difficult ethical dilemmas. Biological enhancement will lead us into unexplored realms, eventually challenging our basic ideas about what it means to be human.

Some imagine we will see the perils, come to our senses, and turn away from such possibilities. But when we imagine Prometheus stealing fire from the gods, we are not incredulous or shocked by his act. It is too characteristically human. To forgo the powerful technologies that genomics and molecular biology are bringing would be as out of character for humanity as it would be to use them without concern for the dangers they pose. We will do neither. The question is no longer whether we will manipulate embryos, but when, where, and how.

We have already felt the impact of previous advances in reproductive technology. Without the broad access to birth control that we take so for granted, the populations of Italy, Japan, and Germany would not be shrinking; birth rates in the developing world would not be falling. These are major shifts, yet unlike the public response to today's high-tech developments, no impassioned voices protest birth control as an immense and dangerous experiment with our genetic future. Those opposing family planning seem more worried about the immorality of recreational sex than about human evolution.

* * *

The emerging reproductive technologies for selecting and altering human embryos * * * culminating in germline engineering—the manipulation of the genetics of egg or sperm (our "germinal" cells) to modify future generations—will have large consequences. Already, procedures that influence the germline are routine in labs working on fruit flies and mice, and researchers have done early procedures on nonhuman primates. Direct human germline manipulations may still be a decade or two away, but methods of choosing specific genes in an embryo are in use today to prevent disease, and sophisticated methods for making broader choices are arriving every year, bringing with them a taste of the ethical and social questions that will accompany comprehensive germline engineering.

The arrival of safe, reliable germline technology will signal the beginning of human self-design. We do not know where this development will ultimately take us, but it will transform the evolutionary process by drawing reproduction into a highly selective social process that is far more rapid and effective at spreading successful genes than traditional sexual competition and mate selection.

Considering the barrage of press reports about the project, we naturally wonder how much is hype. Extravagant metaphor has not been lacking. We are deciphering the "code of codes," "reading the book of life," "looking at the holy grail of human biology." It is reminiscent of the enthusiasm that attended Neil Armstrong's 1969 walk on the moon.

Humanity seemed poised to march toward the stars, but 2001 has come and gone, and there has been no sentient computer like HAL, no odyssey to the moons of Jupiter. Thirty years from now, however, I do not think we will look back at the Human Genome Project with a similar wistful disappointment. Unlike outer space, genetics is at our core, and as we learn to manipulate it, we are learning to manipulate ourselves.

Well before this new millennium's close, we will almost certainly change ourselves enough to become much more than simply human.

* * *

Many bioethicists do not share my perspective on where we are heading. They imagine that our technology might become potent enough to alter us, but that we will turn away from it and reject human enhancement. But the reshaping of human genetics and biology does not hinge on some cadre of demonic researchers hidden away in a lab in Argentina trying to pick up where Hitler left off. The coming possibilities will be the inadvertent spinoff of mainstream research that virtually everyone supports. Infertility, for example, is a source of deep pain for millions of couples. Researchers and clinicians working on in vitro fertilization (IVF) don't think much about future human evolution, but nonetheless are building a foundation of expertise in conceiving, handling, testing, and implanting human embryos, and this will one day be the basis for the manipulation of the human species. Already, we are seeing attempts to apply this knowledge in highly controversial ways: as premature as today's efforts to clone humans may be, they would be the flimsiest of fantasies if they could not draw on decades of work on human IVF.

Similarly, in early 2001 more than five hundred gene-therapy trials were under way or in review throughout the world. The researchers are trying to cure real people suffering from real diseases and are no more interested in the future of human evolution than the IVF researchers. But their progress toward inserting genes into adult cells will be one more piece of the foundation for manipulating human embryos.

Not everything that can be done should or will be done, of course, but once a relatively inexpensive technology becomes feasible in thousands of laboratories around the world and a sizable fraction of the population sees it as beneficial, it will be used.

ERIK PARENS, AUTHENTICITY AND AMBIVALENCE:
TOWARD UNDERSTANDING THE ENHANCEMENT DEBATE
35 Hastings Center Report 34, 37–38 (May/June 2005).

Although there are important disagreements among both critics and proponents, I want briefly to describe what I take to be an important difference between critics and proponents.

I have come to think that these different understandings of authenticity grow out of what I will call two different ethical frameworks. By "frameworks," I mean a constellation of commitments that support and shape our responses to questions about, among many other things, new enhancement technologies. When I refer to those different frameworks as "ethical," I use that term in its broadest possible sense, as designating habits of thought and being. Were it a more felicitous neologism, I would refer to "psycho-ethical frameworks," to emphasize that these frameworks have an important psychological (and perhaps aesthetic) dimension. Instead, I will say simply that I believe these different conceptions of authenticity grow, at least in part, out of different prerational experiences and understandings of our selves and of our proper relationships to the world.

These frameworks are built of answers to questions that do not have only one good answer. In another place I have described some of those questions at length, but for now I will merely mention some: Can we meaningfully distinguish between "natural" and "artificial" human interventions into nature? Should we conceive of technology as morally neutral or morally loaded? What do we mean when we claim that we are free, and to what extent are we free? And so forth.

To emphasize that these two frameworks are intimately related even as they are importantly different, I will dare to remind you of a single figure in an oft-cited book. In the book of Genesis, Jacob's wife Rachel, who was unable to bear children, begs him: "Give me children, or I shall die." Jacob famously responded to Rachel's injunction with a question, "Am I in the place of God?" With this question, Jacob expresses one of the book's central and best-known ideas: that we human beings are not the creators of life; we are creatures, whose job is to remember that life is a gift. It is our responsibility to express our gratitude for the mysterious whole, which we have not made.

This sort of attitude does not require a commitment to any particular religious tradition, indeed to any religion at all. Many a pagan environmentalist (like Bill McKibben, author of The End of Nature and Enough: Genetic Engineering and the End of Human Nature) adopts such an attitude. Many a left-leaning critic of corporatization (like Rich Hayes, who directs the Center for Genetics and Society) adopts it. Michael Sandel invokes the secular version of this idea when he writes, "If bioengineering made the myth of the 'selfmade man' come true, it would be difficult to view our talents as gifts for which we are indebted, rather than as achievements for which we are responsible. This would transform three key features of our moral landscape: humility, responsibility, and solidarity." Leaving aside whether Sandel's predictions are accurate, we can discern in his words the sort of view symbolized by Jacob's question: if we forget that life is a gift—albeit from an unknown giver—we will make a mistake about the sort of creatures we really are and the way the world really is.

But this very same Jacob, who exhibits a kind of gratitude that many today associate with "religion," also exhibits a radically different stance, which Genesis also celebrates. After all, as has been noted more than once, Jacob, the very one whose name would become Israel, was "the first genetic engineer"; he was the one with the creativity to fashion a device ("rods of poplar and almond, into which he peeled white streaks" [Gen. 30:38]) with which he induced his uncle's goats to produce only the valuable "speckled and spotted" (Gen. 30:39) young. According to Genesis, and it seems to me much of Judaism, our responsibility is not merely to be grateful and remember that we are not the creators of the whole. It is also our responsibility to use our creativity to mend and transform ourselves and the world. As far as I can tell, Genesis and Judaism do not exhort us to choose between gratitude and creativity. Rather, or so it seems to this pagan, it is our job to figure out how to maintain that fertile tension, making sure that neither stance gets more than its share.

When we observe scholars and others debate about "enhancement technologies," I believe that we often see people who have at least for the moment adopted either the gratitude or creativity framework, as I am calling them. As one side emphasizes our obligation to remember that life is a gift and that we need to learn to let things be, the other emphasizes our obligation to transform that gift and to exhibit our creativity. As one framework emphasizes the danger of allowing ourselves to become, in Heidegger's famous formulation, "standing reserve," the other emphasizes the danger of failing to summon the courage to, as Nietzsche put it, "create" ourselves, to "become who we are."

Indeed, sometimes the same scholar moves between frameworks in the same talk. I believe I saw my friend Eric Juengst, a philosopher who has thought deeply about human enhancement, do just that during a lecture at Hiram College in the summer of 2004; he operated out of the creativity framework when he criticized those who would oppose all efforts at extending life, and he operated out of the gratitude framework when he criticized efforts that would bring normal aging under the control of medical science. Again, most of us can be comfortable in both frameworks, even if most of us are considerably more comfortable in one framework than in the other. I should hurry to add: moving between frameworks, being ambivalent, seems to me to be a sign of openness and thoughtfulness, not confusion.

It's not only because I love that we find both attitudes in one figure that I invoke Jacob. Yes, it is essential to remember that none of us who is thoughtful inhabits only one of those frameworks. But it is also useful to remember that the figure of Jacob appears in a book that is "religious." In fact, one might tell a creation story about bioethics that has the field grow out of a battle between two titans, both of whom were theologians: Paul Ramsey, the Ur-critic of biotechnology, and Joseph Fletcher, the Ur-proponent. If one looked to the history of presidential commissions that broached the enhancement question, one would notice that each of them has brought out theologians from both the gratitude and creativity frameworks: one side reminds us of the importance of letting things be, eschewing arrogance, and so on, while the other reminds us with equal passion of our obligation to find the courage to become creative in our efforts to ameliorate human suffering.

Suggesting that we find religious soil at the roots of the critical and the enthusiastic stances toward enhancement helps me bring to the fore concerns I have about both sides of the enhancement debate. Beginning with the side I feel most comfortable on: the critics. Sometimes, when we critics speak, we sound as if we have forgotten or don't even fully appreciate that, in principle, the creativity framework is as worthy as the gratitude framework. When we try to make the case "against perfection" or when we raise problems with the "ethic of willfulness," we risk forgetting that at the core of that ethic is the noble impulse to be creative, to mend and transform ourselves and the world. Were we to speak, instead, of "the ethic of creativity," we might be more prone to give the other side its due.

By calling attention to the religious element of the commitments on both sides, I am trying to emphasize what I take to be an obvious but under-appreciated fact: the proponent is not as neutral as she sometimes seems to believe. She has no more than anyone else escaped the maw of extra-rational commitments.

Having identified these two ethical frameworks, I need to emphasize several caveats. First, I've tried to make abundantly clear that I don't think the difference between critics and proponents is the same as the difference between people who are religious and those who are secular. You find both kinds in both camps. Second, the distinction between the gratitude and creativity frameworks is not the same as that between political conservatism and liberalism; conservatives and liberals operate out of each.

Finally, I do not for a moment forget that distinguishing between the gratitude framework of the critics and the creativity framework of the proponents is a very crude heuristic. The outlines of the gratitude and creativity frameworks are neat only in speech. Nonetheless, I think that when we engage in debates about enhancement technologies, it can help to recognize that people on both sides are speaking out of the framework in which they feel most comfortable. And I think it is crucial to recognize that none of us, if we are reflective, feels comfortable only in one of these frameworks. Even if we settle in one for the sake of debating each other, in our day-to-day lives we shuttle between them. One might say that in our day-to-day lives we are often more prone to allow ourselves such thoughtfulness—and ambivalence—than when we sit down to engage in scholarship.

NOTES AND QUESTIONS

1.   The debate over the ethical, legal and social implications of genetic enhancement is part of a larger conversation about the use of biomedical enhancement in general. Within the world of sports, for example, a war against the use of performance-enhancing drugs has been waged since the late 1960s. Beginning in the late 1980s, however, the use of drugs in sports, generally referred to as "doping," began to attract the attention of the government. After a series of hearings in 1988, 1989, and 1990, Congress placed anabolic steroids on the list of controlled substances, making it a felony to distribute them for non-medical purposes, and amended the Federal Food, Drug, and Cosmetic Act to make it a felony to distribute, or possess with the intent to distribute, human growth hormone other than to treat disease. When the dietary supplement manufacturer Balco was accused of concocting and distributing steroid analogues, known as "designer steroids," that could not be detected by existing tests and that technically were not covered by the Controlled Substances Act, Congress amended the act in 2004 to close this loophole. In the winter of 2005, the U.S. Senate investigated the use of steroids in baseball, firing off subpoenas at players and executives. Senator John McCain threatened to revoke baseball's exemption from federal antitrust laws if it did not clean up its players. Later hearings targeted professional basketball and football. And in his first State of the Union message since the invasion of Iraq, President Bush declared:

> To help children make right choices, they need good examples. Athletics play such an important role in our society, but, unfortunately, some in professional sports are not setting much of an example. The use of performance-enhancing drugs like steroids in baseball, football, and other sports is dangerous, and it sends the wrong message—that there are shortcuts to accomplishment, and that performance is more important than character. So tonight I call on team owners, union representatives, coaches, and players to take the lead, to send the right signal, to get tough, and to get rid of steroids now.

States have not directly addressed doping in competitive athletics. However, most states have updated their controlled substance acts to reflect the federal stance against anabolic steroids. They have also made additional efforts to regulate steroids in schools and to disseminate information about the dangers of anabolic steroids.

2.   What accounts for this intrusion of government into the private world of sports? By what authority does it act? And most importantly, what does this bode for the legal status of biomedical enhancement use outside of sports?

3.   What are the distinctions between the use of biomedical enhancements for performance enhancement in sports and other uses? Are there significant differences between genetic enhancement and biomedical enhancement in general?

4.   The readings by Sandel and Parens deal with the use of enhancements for purposes of self-fulfillment. Whose argument seems more persuasive? Another important purpose for using genetic enhancements is to obtain a competitive advantage. Depending on the nature of the enhancement, this could be an advantage in a sports competition (e.g., a performance enhancing intervention), or in school or at work (e.g., a cognition enhancing intervention). If third-party payers, such as health insurers, treat genetic enhancements like cosmetic surgery, they will not pay for them, and only persons who can afford them out-of-pocket will obtain them. Depending on how expensive they are, only relatively well-off individuals and families may gain access, since the cost may make government subsidies too expensive. If genetic enhancements are highly effective at conferring advantages, this may erode the belief in equality of opportunity that is a fundamental tenet of western liberal democracies.

5.   An article in the September 2009 issues of The Chronicle of Higher Education notes the use of cognition-enhancing drugs by college students and quotes an Australian researcher predicting that they may soon face doping tests at exam time. Would this be appropriate? Paul Basken, At Exam Time, Students May Face a Separate Test—for "Smart Drugs," The Chronicle of Higher Education, Sept. 30, 2009.

MAXWELL J. MEHLMAN, THE LAW OF ABOVE AVERAGES: LEVELING THE NEW GENETIC ENHANCEMENT PLAYING FIELD
85 Iowa L. Rev. 517, 541–544 (2000).

* * *

Is it fair for some people to have greater genetic advantages than others? This is an age-old question, forming the crux of the problem of "natural inequality" that has plagued philosophers and social theorists for centuries. If it is unfair, then presumably society should do what it can to mitigate the consequences. Yet, what forms of intervention should society take, and how feasible would they be?

* * *

Maintaining a liberal democratic form of government is an important social goal. This goal is directly threatened by wealth-based genetic enhancement: The inequality of social opportunity that results may be so great that a liberal democratic form of government becomes unsustainable, and our political system instead becomes autocratic or oligarchic. This follows from the assumption that a minimum degree of equality is necessary for the existence of a modern liberal democracy. If social inequality becomes too pronounced, liberal democratic political systems, and the capitalist economic system upon which they rest, become unstable. As one sociologist states:

> Inequality in the distribution of rewards is always a potential source of political and social instability. Because upper, relatively advantaged strata are generally fewer in number than disadvantaged lower strata, the former are faced with crucial problems of social control over the latter. One way of approaching this issue is to ask not why the disprivileged often rebel against the privileged but why they do not rebel more often than they do.

The characteristics of genetic enhancement that threaten to destabilize liberal democratic government are the features that distinguish genetic enhancement from other forms of self-improvement: its high cost, which may place it beyond the reach of all but the very wealthy; the broad and fundamental nature of the traits that it could enhance; the magnitude of its effects; their multiplicity; the resulting ability to gain advantages in multiple spheres of social activity; and the possibility—created by germ line enhancement—that these advantages would be passed on to successive generations.

These characteristics not only give rise to social inequality; more insidiously, they undermine the belief in equality of opportunity. A widespread belief in equality of opportunity is the method by which liberal democracies accommodate the reality of capitalist inequality—that everyone is not equally endowed with equally beneficial natural assets or blessed with the same luck. Sociologists point out that "whereas most Americans are willing to tolerate sizeable inequalities in the distribution of resources, they typically insist that individuals from all backgrounds should have an equal opportunity to secure these resources." John Schaar notes that the belief in equal opportunity is instrumental in maintaining the prevailing social order, stating that "no policy formula is better designed to fortify the dominant institutions, values, and ends of the

American social order than the formula of equality of opportunity, for it offers *everyone* a fair and equal chance to find a place within that order."

Assuming, as discussed earlier, that the price of genetic enhancements prohibits people of ordinary means from acquiring them, genetic enhancement would create profound differences in ability that would endow the wealthy with opportunities utterly and irrevocably beyond the reach of the majority of the citizens. World history is filled with examples of societies similar to those that would result from wealth-based genetic enhancement. In medieval Europe, for example, individuals were born with a social status, and barring the infrequent case in which peasants were able to obtain education in religious institutions or became apprenticed and eventually esquired to knights, individuals remained members of the class into which they were born. Similarly, in slave-owning societies, people were born into bondage and could be freed only by escape (self-exile) or at the pleasure of their masters. The most obvious surviving example of such a society is the caste system in India. The caste system remains a constant threat to that nation's democratic institutions.

Genetic social stratification thus would undermine our current social system, but it is not certain how seriously. Perhaps society will adapt to the social artifacts of the genetic revolution and the result, while markedly different from present arrangements, will be relatively stable. The genetic underclass might cede power to their genetic superiors in return for enjoying the material benefits made possible by genetic advances. In this scenario, the underclass would accept the division between social strata, and be content with being upwardly mobile only within the confines of their own class. The genobility, in turn, would rule according to enlightened principles of noblesse oblige, taking care to permit sufficient benefits to trickle down to maintain political and social equilibrium. A democracy of sorts might even persist, with the underclass electing representatives who either belonged to the upper class or who were committed to preserving its privileges. In essence, such a system might not look very different from our own, given the extent to which we increasingly elect representatives who are considerably more privileged than their constituents.

This system, however, seems highly unstable. For one thing, the members of the genetic upper class would require great self-control to avoid over-reaching. At minimum, they would need to maintain effective means of monitoring and regulating the behavior of their peers to prevent antisocial excesses of greed. The system also would be vulnerable to demagogues who achieved power by promising to redistribute genetic endowments more evenly. Assuming that the principle of one-person/one-vote persisted, a numerically inferior genetic upper class could be out-voted by the underclass and Congress could become dominated by elected officials pledged to employ the full force of government to rectify genetic imbalances.

The genobility might respond with reprisals in an effort to preserve its privileged status. At one extreme these could range from threats to withhold the fruits of genetic medicine from non-privileged segments of society, to overt interference with the democratic process. At the other, the genetic upper class is liable to amass sufficient wealth and influence to enable it to control the media, which would in turn permit it to affect the outcome of elections in a manner quite out of proportion to its numbers. Efforts by the underclass to preserve its hegemony might prove no more successful than current efforts to reform campaign finance laws in order to dilute the power of special interests.

In the end, we might embark on an era of social chaos as the system swung in ever-widening arcs between rule by underclass demagogues and by the genetic aristocracy. Eventually, this could degenerate into mob rule and, then, anarchy. To rid itself of its status as the class of the genetically disadvantaged, the mob might even destroy the scientific foundations of the genetic revolution, perhaps by physically dismantling research centers and erasing mapping and sequencing data.

Alternatively, post-genorevolutionary society could devolve into totalitarian rule by a genetic autocracy. The genetic upper class would employ whatever repressive techniques were necessary in order to obtain power and to keep the underclass in check. Advances in genetic science might even enable the genobility to genetically manipulate the underclass in ways that make it more docile.

While it is impossible to predict with certainty what effect wealth-based genetic enhancement will have on society, what is clear is that it creates not only a moral challenge but a political threat. From a moral standpoint, those who obtain enhancement may not have done anything to deserve it. Adults may have obtained the means necessary to purchase enhancement in objectionable or morally irrelevant ways—through exploitation or the brute luck of inheritance. Moreover, it is difficult to argue that children earned their new-found advantages. Yet genetic enhancement poses more than an ethical quandary. Even if the resources necessary to purchase genetic enhancement are earned in a moral sense, wealth-based enhancement is likely to have a severe societal impact. Somatic enhancement alone could dramatically widen the gap between the haves and have-nots, and crippling class warfare would ensue. Germ line enhancement could create, quite literally, a master race. A future as bleak as this is not perhaps inevitable, but it is unquestionably within the realm of possibility. The question then becomes whether there is any practical way to prevent this.

NOTES AND QUESTIONS

1.   Is there a solution to the equality problem? See Mehlman, supra at 570–574 (suggesting licensing the use of genetic enhancements for public benefit and a national lottery in which everyone was enrolled). The high cost of enhancements also would create unfairness problems when the enhanced competed with the unenhanced for scarce societal resources, whether Olympic gold medals or admission to Harvard Law School. For possible ways of leveling the playing field, see Mehlman, supra 576–592.

2.   A particular concern is the prospect of germline genetic enhancement. A September 2000 report by the American Association for the Advancement of Science entitled "Human Inheritable Genetic Modifications" stated:

> In theory, genetic enhancement could be accomplished through either somatic or germ line intervention. Whether or not the latter will start us down a slippery slope toward enhancements, the desire to undertake enhancements will most likely favor IGM over somatic technology. Genetic enhancements are likely to require altering several genes that work in concert with each other. Such genetic interventions are likely to be more effective when conducted early in the development of the embryo or on the fetus *in utero,* although this remains to be demonstrated. In many, perhaps most instances, such early intervention would result in alteration of the germ line whether or not it was intended. The very considerable expense involved might incline parents to try to get the most for their investment, again favoring the IGM option.

AAAS Report, Human Inheritable Genetic Modifications 43 (2000).

3.   As with any germline modification, there may be latent risks that do not materialize for several generations. Moreover, if only the well-off can afford genetic enhancement, then highly effective germline modifications threaten to create a genetic aristocracy or "genobility" that passes genetic advantages on to their offspring. See Maxwell J. Mehlman & Jeffrey Botkin, Access to the Genome: The Challenge to Equality, 98–109 (1998). Should this risk prevent the development of therapeutic germline interventions? LeRoy Walters, former chair of the RAC, states: "Think about confronting a person in the future with a genetic disease that you could have prevented and telling them that even though you knew how to fix it, you stopped because you thought society might abuse this thing." Rick Weiss, Scientists Seek Panel's Advice on In-Womb Genetic Tests, Wash. Post, March 22, 1998, at A2. At what point, if any, would the risks from germline genetic enhancement outweigh this benefit? Which risks should count?

4.   To the extent that genetic enhancement products seek to alter the structure or function of the human body, the FDA has regulatory authority over them as drugs or devices. (A "biologic" comprises only products "applicable to the prevention or cure of diseases or injuries of man." 42 USC

§ 262(a)). Is the FDA well-suited to regulate enhancement products, however? See Maxwell J. Mehlman, How Will We Regulate Genetic Enhancement?, 34 Wake Forest L. Rev. 671, 701–703 (1999).

5. Given concerns about the adverse impact of genetic enhancement in general or germline genetic enhancement in particular, one alternative might be to attempt to prohibit it by law. In that case, the agency with regulatory authority might not be the FDA, but the Drug Enforcement Administration, acting pursuant to its authority under the Controlled Substances Act. See Maxwell J. Mehlman, How Will We Regulate Genetic Enhancement?, 34 Wake Forest L. Rev. 671, 704–705 (1999). This may seem far-fetched, but anabolic steroids are now classified as controlled substances in an effort to restrict their use by athletes, and the Federal Food, Drug, and Cosmetic Act contains a little known provision, added by Congress in 1991, that makes it a federal felony to distribute or possess human growth hormone "for any use in humans other than the treatment of disease or other recognized medical condition." 21 U.S.C. § 333(e)(1). How successful would a ban be? Would a black market arise similar to the current black market in illegal substances? Could the government stop citizens from traveling abroad to obtain enhancements that were illegal in the US? See Maxwell J. Mehlman & Kristen Rabe, Any DNA to Declare? Regulating Offshore Access to Genetic Enhancement, 28 Am. J. L. & Med. 179 (2002).

6. Since some forms of genetic enhancement, including in particular methods that altered the germline, would be likely to require the expertise of health professionals, one regulatory approach would be professional self-regulation. The American Medical Association's Council on Ethical and Judicial Affairs, for example, has issued an ethics opinion stating that "[e]fforts to enhance 'desirable' characteristics through the insertion of a modified or additional gene, or efforts to 'improve' complex human traits—the eugenic development of offspring—are contrary not only to the ethical tradition of medicine but also to the egalitarian values of our society." The statement goes on to assert that "genetic interventions to enhance traits should be considered permissible only in severely restricted situations: (1) clear and meaningful benefits to the fetus or child; (2) no trade-off with other characteristics or traits; and (3) equal access * * * irrespective of income or other socioeconomic characteristics." AMA Council on Ethical and Judicial Affairs, Report on Ethical Issues Related to Prenatal Genetic Tests, 3 Archives Fam. Med. 633, 637–639 (1994). Presumably, a physician who failed to comply with these conditions would be violating the physician's code of professional ethics.

Do these conditions make sense? How is a single physician supposed to ensure "equal access"? Why should a parent be prohibited from deciding that an enhancement is worth a certain price in terms of a trade-off of other characteristics or traits?

7. "Transhumanism" is a movement whose adherents believe that humans should employ genetic engineering to improve the future of

humanity. For a discussion of transhumanism and the potential impact of genetic engineering on the future of human evolution, see Maxwell J. Mehlman, Transhumanist Dreams and Dystopian Nightmares: The Promise and Peril of Genetic Engineering (2012).

8.   For a more thorough discussion of these and other issues relating to biomedical enhancement, see Maxwell J. Mehlman, The Price of Perfection: Individualism and Society in the Era of Biomedical Enhancement (2009).

CHAPTER 11

PARENTAGE AND FAMILY LAW

■ ■ ■

I.   INTRODUCTION

Throughout human history, the delicate relations among family members have engendered complex legal disputes. In particular, courts have faced questions about how to characterize the relationship between children and parents. What is the legal status of children? How should parentage be determined, and what rights and responsibilities does it entail? What happens when parents separate or divorce?

Beginning in medieval times and even until the start of the twentieth century, children were viewed as the property of their parents. Under English common law, fathers had primary decision-making authority over children if parents separated. It was not until the last half of the nineteenth century that courts developed the "tender years" doctrine, creating a presumption that young children were better off being reared by their mothers. The "tender years" doctrine was completely abolished by the 1970s when ideas of equality influenced courts to give equal weight to each parent's interests, with the goal being to determine the "best interests of the child."

The legal assignment of parental rights and responsibilities over children has combined both biological and social criteria. For countless generations, maternal rights over children were easy to assign. The woman who gave birth to the child was the legal mother. This concept still prevails in the language of the paternity laws of many states. For example, California has a statutory provision which states that a parent and child relationship may be established "between a child and the natural mother . . . by proof of her having given birth to the child."

With respect to fathers, determination of paternity has been more complicated. In large measure, paternity has been based on social, rather than biological, factors. Paternity statutes generally provide that, if a woman is married, her husband is the father of her child, unless the husband proves he was sterile or had no access to the wife at the time of conception (for example, he was away at sea for months). Now, though, DNA paternity tests can demonstrate to a high degree of certainty (99+%) who the biological father is, thereby generating questions about whether a biological assignment of fatherhood should replace the social one within marriage. Should the husband be able to authorize DNA testing on the child without the mother's consent in order to determine if he is the biological father? Should such DNA testing only be done by court order? If the couple divorces, should the ex-husband be able to sever ties with a child he reared for years, simply on the grounds that he was not the sperm provider? What about the ex-husband who wants custody of a child with whom he has a loving bond, but who is told by the ex-wife that he should have no rights because he is not actually the child's biological father? Does the social approach to parenthood serve important goals, such as protecting marriages and assuring support for children?

DNA Testing Van in New York City

And what about the lover of a married woman, who wants to use DNA testing to gain rights to the child? Should a man be able to gain visitation rights to visit a five year old with whom he has had no social relationship just because a DNA test says he is the father? Generally, when an unmarried biological father is trying to gain rights to a child, he must show that he has some social relation with that child. In Lehr v. Robertson, 463 U.S. 248 (1983), for example, an unmarried father petitioned to vacate the order of adoption of his two-year-old child by the mother's husband. The biological father, however, had never supported the child nor entered his name into a putative father registry. The Court held that the biological father's due process and equal protection rights were not violated when he was not given notice and an opportunity to be heard before his child was adopted, since the father had never had any significant custodial, personal, or financial relationship with the child.

The matter is entirely different if the issue is not rights, but responsibilities. If a mother is not married, a biological paternity determination is used to establish that a man owes child support to the child. Over the years, paternity testing has evolved to be more accurate. In many early cases, the baby was held in the air in the courtroom and the jury had to assess whether the baby resembled the putative father. Obviously, DNA testing is a more precise way to determine paternity.

DNA testing can play other roles in establishing family relationships. In some countries, it is used to provide evidence of family bonds in the context of immigration. Genetic testing could be used in the adoption setting to determine the fitness of parents—or the potential future health of the children available for adoption. In any of these settings, as with more traditional legal decisions about maternity and paternity, social values will be as important as biological predictions in determining the appropriate legal policies.

II.   REASSESSING TRADITIONAL PRESUMPTIONS OF PATERNITY IN THE DNA ERA

MICHAEL H. v. GERALD D.
491 U.S. 110 (1989).

SCALIA, J.

* * *

Under California law, a child born to a married woman living with her husband is presumed to be a child of the marriage. Cal. Evid. Code Ann. § 621 (West Supp. 1989). The presumption of legitimacy may be rebutted only by the husband or wife, and then only in limited circumstances. The instant appeal presents the claim that this presumption infringes upon the due process rights of a man who wishes to establish his paternity of a child born to the wife of another man, and the claim that it infringes upon the constitutional right of the child to maintain a relationship with her natural father.

I.

The facts of this case are, we must hope, extraordinary. On May 9, 1976, in Las Vegas, Nevada, Carole D., an international model, and Gerald D., a top executive in a French oil company, were married. The couple established a home in Playa del Rey, California, in which they resided as husband and wife when one or the other was not out of the country on business. In the summer of 1978, Carole became involved in an adulterous affair with a neighbor, Michael H. In September 1980, she conceived a child, Victoria D., who was born on May 11, 1981. Gerald was listed as father on the birth certificate and has always held Victoria out to the world as his daughter. Soon after delivery of the child, however, Carole informed Michael that she believed he might be the father.

In the first three years of her life, Victoria remained always with Carole, but found herself within a variety of quasifamily units. In October 1981, Gerald moved to New York City to pursue his business interests, but Carole chose to remain in California. At the end of that month, Carole and Michael had blood tests of themselves and Victoria, which showed a 98.07% probability that Michael was Victoria's father. In January 1982, Carole visited Michael in St. Thomas, where his primary business interests were based. There Michael held Victoria out as his child. In March, however, Carole left Michael and returned to California, where she took up residence with yet another man, Scott K. Later that spring, and again in the summer, Carole and Victoria spent time with Gerald in New York City, as well as on vacation in Europe. In the fall, they returned to Scott in California.

In November 1982, rebuffed in his attempts to visit Victoria, Michael filed a filiation action in California Superior Court to establish his paternity and right to visitation.

* * *

On October 19, 1984, Gerald, who had intervened in the action, moved for summary judgment on the ground that under Cal. Evid. Code § 621 there were no triable issues of fact as to Victoria's paternity. This law provides that "the issue of a wife cohabiting with her husband, who is not impotent or sterile, is conclusively presumed to be a child of the marriage." The presumption may be rebutted by blood tests, but only if a motion for such tests is made, within two years from the date of the child's birth, either by the husband or, if the natural father has filed an affidavit acknowledging paternity, by the wife.

On January 28, 1985, having found that affidavits submitted by Carole and Gerald sufficed to demonstrate that the two were cohabiting at conception and birth and that Gerald was neither sterile nor impotent, the Superior Court granted Gerald's motion for summary judgment, rejecting Michael's and Victoria's challenges to the constitutionality of § 621. The court also denied their motions for continued visitation pending the appeal under Cal. Civ. Code § 4601, which provides that a court may, in its discretion, grant "reasonable visitation rights . . . to any . . . person having an interest in the welfare of the child." It found that allowing such visitation would "violat[e] the intention of the Legislature by impugning the integrity of the family unit."

On appeal, Michael asserted, inter alia, that the Superior Court's application of § 621 had violated his procedural and substantive due process rights. Victoria also raised a due process challenge to the statute, seeking to preserve her de facto relationship with Michael as well as with Gerald. She contended, in addition, that as § 621 allows the husband and, at least to a limited extent, the mother, but not the child, to rebut the presumption of legitimacy, it violates the child's right to equal protection. Finally, she asserted a right to continued visitation with Michael under § 4601. After submission of briefs and a hearing, the California Court of

Appeal affirmed the judgment of the Superior Court and upheld the constitutionality of the statute.

* * *

III.

* * *

Michael raises two related challenges to the constitutionality of § 621. First, he asserts that requirements of procedural due process prevent the State from terminating his liberty interest in his relationship with his child without affording him an opportunity to demonstrate his paternity in an evidentiary hearing. We believe this claim derives from a fundamental misconception of the nature of the California statute. While § 621 is phrased in terms of a presumption, that rule of evidence is the implementation of a substantive rule of law. California declares it to be, except in limited circumstances, *irrelevant* for paternity purposes whether a child conceived during, and born into, an existing marriage was begotten by someone other than the husband and had a prior relationship with him. As the Court of Appeal phrased it:

> " 'The conclusive presumption is actually a substantive rule of law based upon a determination by the Legislature as a matter of overriding social policy, that given a certain relationship between the husband and wife, the husband is to be held responsible for the child, and that the integrity of the family unit should not be impugned.' "

Of course the conclusive presumption not only expresses the State's substantive policy but also furthers it, excluding inquiries into the child's paternity that would be destructive of family integrity and privacy.

* * *

Michael contends as a matter of substantive due process that, because he has established a parental relationship with Victoria, protection of Gerald's and Carole's marital union is an insufficient state interest to support termination of that relationship. This argument is, of course, predicated on the assertion that Michael has a constitutionally protected liberty interest in his relationship with Victoria.

It is an established part of our constitutional jurisprudence that the term "liberty" in the Due Process Clause extends beyond freedom from physical restraint * * *. Without that core textual meaning as a limitation, defining the scope of the Due Process Clause "has at times been a treacherous field for this Court," giving "reason for concern lest the only limits to . . . judicial intervention become the predilections of those who happen at the time to be Members of this Court." * * *

In an attempt to limit and guide interpretation of the Clause, we have insisted not merely that the interest denominated as a "liberty" be "fundamental" (a concept that, in isolation, is hard to objectify), but also that it be an interest traditionally protected by our society. As we have put it, the Due Process Clause affords only those protections "so rooted in the traditions and conscience of our people as to be ranked as fundamental." * * * Our cases reflect "continual insistence upon respect for the teachings of history [and] solid recognition of the basic values that underlie our society. . . ."

* * *

It is a question of legislative policy and not constitutional law whether California will allow the presumed parenthood of a couple desiring to retain a child conceived within and born into their marriage to be rebutted.

We do not accept Justice Brennan's criticism [in his dissenting opinion in this case] that this result "squashes" the liberty that consists of "the freedom not to conform." It seems to us that reflects the erroneous view that there is only one side to this controversy—that one disposition can expand a "liberty" of sorts without contracting an equivalent "liberty" on the other side. Such a happy choice is rarely available. Here, to *provide* protection to an adulterous natural father is to *deny* protection to a marital father, and vice versa. If Michael has a "freedom not to conform" (whatever that means), Gerald must equivalently have a "freedom to conform." One of them will pay a price for asserting that "freedom"— Michael by being unable to act as father of the child he has adulterously begotten, or Gerald by being unable to preserve the integrity of the traditional family unit he and Victoria have established. Our disposition does not choose between these two "freedoms," but leaves that to the people of California. Justice Brennan's approach chooses one of them as the constitutional imperative, on no apparent basis except that the unconventional is to be preferred.

IV.

We have never had occasion to decide whether a child has a liberty interest, symmetrical with that of her parent, in maintaining her filial relationship. We need not do so here because, even assuming that such a right exists, Victoria's claim must fail. Victoria's due process challenge is, if anything, weaker than Michael's. Her basic claim is not that California has erred in preventing her from establishing that Michael, not Gerald, should stand as her legal father. Rather, she claims a due process right to maintain filial relationships with both Michael and Gerald. This assertion merits little discussion, for, whatever the merits of the guardian ad litem's belief that such an arrangement can be of great psychological benefit to a child, the claim that a State must recognize multiple fatherhood has no support in the history or traditions of this country. Moreover, even if we were to construe Victoria's argument as forwarding the lesser proposition that, whatever her status vis-à-vis Gerald, she has a liberty interest in maintaining a filial relationship with her natural father, Michael, we find that, at best, her claim is the obverse of Michael's and fails for the same reasons.

Victoria claims in addition that her equal protection rights have been violated because, unlike her mother and presumed father, she had no opportunity to rebut the presumption of her legitimacy. We find this argument wholly without merit. We reject, at the outset, Victoria's suggestion that her equal protection challenge must be assessed under a standard of strict scrutiny because, in denying her the right to maintain a filial relationship with Michael, the State is discriminating against her on the basis of her illegitimacy. Illegitimacy is a legal construct, not a natural trait. Under California law, Victoria is not illegitimate, and she is treated in the same manner as all other legitimate children: she is entitled to maintain a filial relationship with her legal parents.

We apply, therefore, the ordinary "rational relationship" test to Victoria's equal protection challenge. The primary rationale underlying § 621's limitation on those who may rebut the presumption of legitimacy is a concern that allowing persons other than the husband or wife to do so may undermine the integrity of the marital union. When the husband or wife contests the legitimacy of their child, the stability of the marriage has already been shaken. In contrast, allowing a claim of illegitimacy to be pressed by the child—or, more accurately, by a court-appointed guardian ad litem—may well disrupt an otherwise peaceful union. Since it pursues a legitimate end by rational means, California's decision to treat Victoria differently from her parents is not a denial of equal protection.

The judgment of the California Court of Appeal is

Affirmed.

RICHARD WILLING, DNA AND DADDY
USA Today, July 29, 1999, at 1A.

From a billboard above a Baltimore expressway, a very pregnant version of Leonardo da Vinci's Mona Lisa soon will aim her enigmatic smile at motorists.

"Who's The Daddy?" the billboard asks. The ad supplies the phone number of a Baltimore laboratory that uses DNA tests to determine paternity.

These days, not everyone is smiling about using DNA for paternity testing. For men such as Gerald Miscovich, who discovered through a

DNA-based paternity test that he had not fathered the boy born during his marriage, the tests are serious business.

"I've spent the last seven years of my life trying to get this sorted out fairly," says Miscovich, 36, a computer programmer who lives near Philadelphia. "The test is just a beginning. You've got to be able to deal with what comes with it."

DNA-based paternity testing is booming, thanks to expanding technology and to laws that require women to name their child's father when applying for public assistance. Aggressive marketing, such as the Mona Lisa campaign that Baltimore's BRT Laboratories has used before and will mount again in October, helps drive the trend.

The tests, which are based on the same DNA technology that police use to catch criminals, are faster, cheaper and more accurate than the old-fashioned blood typing that was state-of-the-art until the late 1980s. DNA-based paternity testing has more than tripled during the past 10 years, to an estimated 247,000 cases in 1998. The new technology is clearing up inheritance controversies, fueling a $100 million annual business and even resolving age-old historical disputes like whether Thomas Jefferson fathered a child with the slave Sally Hemings. The DNA says he probably did.

"When you think of where we are and where we were just a short time ago, it's nothing short of a revolution," says Howard Coleman, founder of the GeneLex Corp., a Seattle test laboratory. "You want to catch your breath and say, 'What's next?'"

But experts in psychology and in family law are discovering that the phenomenon has a down side.

They say divorces have become more contentious and family ties strained as parents seek to avoid child support payments by testing children. Increasingly, laboratory technicians say, they must offer comfort and counsel to customers who are emotionally devastated by the test results.

Perhaps most significantly, the time-honored legal concept of parenthood, put in place centuries ago to protect children, is being re-evaluated in courtrooms across the country in light of the new testing.

'SIMPLE' TEST HAS SERIOUS REPERCUSSIONS

The old doctrine states that children born to a married woman are deemed to have been fathered by her husband. It makes no allowances for modern tests such as DNA.

"People say that we have a simple test and we ought to let technology decide for us, but there's a real human cost we haven't focused on," says Joan Entmacher, who directs the Family Economic Security Project at the

National Women's Law Center in Washington, D.C., a nonprofit organization that represents women in cases involving child support and other issues.

"The technology is a tool, and we should use it when it's useful but take care to see that it's appropriate."

Paternity testing is possible because when a child is conceived, he or she receives two pieces of genetic material, one from the mother and one from the father. If a gene is present that cannot be traced to the mother, it must be the father's. For years, scientists used red blood cells and blood antigens to exclude potential fathers and to identify the correct gene donor.

But blood typing was expensive—about $800 to $1,200 for a family—as well as slow and limited. It required blood to be drawn from mother, child and potential father, and the blood needed to be used quickly. And the accuracy was open to challenge.

The development of DNA analysis in the 1980s moved the science forward in a quantum jump. DNA, the cellular acid that contains an individual's genetic code, could now be examined directly, and fatherhood could be determined with a better than 99% probability. The tests, which cost $450 to $600 a family, can be completed within days and can use samples collected by mouth swabs as well as blood samples.

* * *

AN EXPLOSION IN DNA SUCCESS STORIES

Business has taken off. In 1988, the nation's labs performed 75,716 paternity tests, according to the American Association of Blood Banks, the national accrediting group. Most of those tests were blood tests. Last year's estimated 247,000 tests almost exclusively relied on DNA.

The success stories came quickly: The number of fathers acknowledging paternity tripled, from 512,000 in 1992 to 1.5 million last year, according to the U.S. Department of Health and Human Services. It is not known exactly how many of those cases were resolved through paternity testing, though the labs say the number rises every year.

"Men want to do the right thing, but they don't want to be fooled," says Neal Hurowitz of Philadelphia, who specializes in marital law. "Nowadays, you can get tested, know where you stand and make arrangements for the child, all without the adversarial situation of being pulled into court. And men are doing just that."

DNA testing has helped resolve inheritance disputes and clear up family mix-ups, including some celebrated cases:

Last year, DNA testing helped a Virginia couple show that the University of Virginia Medical Center had sent them home with another family's baby. The mother who had the DNA test, Paula Johnson, is now suing for custody of both children.

The children of four Filipino, Vietnamese and Micronesian bar girls have begun to share in the $500 million estate of air freight mogul Larry Hillblom, who died without marrying any of the mothers.

Using a variation of the standard paternity test, descendants of a slave owned by George Washington's half-brother are attempting to verify an old family tale: that the Father of Our Country was their literal ancestor, too.

* * *

But not all the stories are happy ones. In about a third of the welfare cases and 10% of other cases, lab directors say that the father named by the mother turns out not to be the biological parent.

Caskey, of Houston's Identigene lab, prepares test candidates by warning them of the possibility that the results could be disturbing, particularly because the science of DNA is considered so accurate. "I want to make sure they want to go through with it," she says.

At Baltimore's BRT Laboratories, which sponsors the Mona Lisa billboard, molecular biologist Frank Chiafari recently found himself counseling a civil servant who learned that his teen-age son had been fathered by another man.

"He broke down and cried; it was pretty awful," Chiafari recalls.

"His wife, like people do sometimes, had dropped a reference to it in anger, so he decided to check it out. (Before DNA-based testing,) he probably would have let it go."

* * *

'DOUBLE BLOW' FOR A DIVORCED FATHER

Gerald Miscovich's experience with DNA testing is especially compelling. During a visit with Gerald Jr. in 1992, two years after his marriage ended, Miscovich noted that the boy, then 4, had brown eyes. Both Miscovich and his former wife had blue eyes, making a brown-eyed child nearly impossible. A DNA-based paternity test confirmed that another man was Gerald Jr.'s father.

"It was a double blow," Miscovich says. "That my wife had stepped outside the marriage, and that my son wasn't my son."

To Miscovich's surprise, a Pennsylvania court nevertheless ordered him to pay his ex-wife $537 a month in child support. The court relied on a 500-year-old English common-law doctrine that presumes a child born in a marriage is the offspring of the spouses, unless the husband is impotent or can show he was abroad at the time of conception.

"The law is designed for the economic protection of children," says Jane Mattes, a New York psychotherapist and specialist in single mothers. In medieval England, "a child shown to be illegitimate would have virtually no rights."

Miscovich fought an unsuccessful seven-year battle to have the court order revoked. He gave up in May when the U.S. Supreme Court declined to hear his appeal.

"Certainly protect the child, but do it by requiring the man who produced him to pay," Miscovich says.

STATES BEGINNING TO CHANGE THEIR LAWS

Miscovich's ex-wife has remarried, and he has had no contact with Gerald Jr. for the past seven years. He says he would have liked to have played "some part" in the boy's life but was advised that to do so would have undercut his case. Telephone calls to a lawyer for Miscovich's former wife were not returned.

"This was good law for centuries, but that was before DNA and trans-Atlantic travel and other things that can make mockery out of the idea that a woman can only be pregnant by her husband," says Miscovich's lawyer, Neal Hurowitz. "The law has got to catch up."

THAT PROCESS IS UNDER WAY

In about two-thirds of the states, judges now allow DNA-based paternity testing to be admitted as evidence in child custody cases, though they are not bound to let deceived husbands off the hook for payments. Massachusetts permits husbands to file affidavits stating that a child was fathered by another man. And an Oregon judge recently granted a rare order excusing an ex-husband from child support payments after DNA tests excluded him as the father of his former wife's young son.

NOT EVERYONE LIKES THE TREND

"Are we saying that if you cared for a child for 15 years, (a test) is then going to make you walk away?" Entmacher says. "It does force you to think what it means to be a parent."

LACH V. WELCH

1997 WL 536330 (Conn. Super. Ct. 1997).

Memorandum of Decision Re: Motion to Cite in Party Defendant and Motion for Genetic Testing

DRANGINIS, J.

On October 21, 1993, the plaintiff, Shannon Lach, commenced this paternity action against the defendant, Richard J. Welch, as administrator of the estate of Michael R. Welch. Pursuant to General Statutes 46b–160, the plaintiff seeks an adjudication of paternity of Kaitlyn Ruddy, her minor child. Kaitlyn was born out of wedlock on November 12, 1990. In her petition, the plaintiff alleges that Kaitlyn was fathered by Michael Welch, who lived with the plaintiff from January 1990, through and including April 1990. On June 1, 1991, prior to the commencement of any paternity proceedings, Michael Welch died as the result of an automobile accident.

Presently before the court are two motions. The first is a motion to cite in Patricia Welch, Michael's mother, claiming that she is a necessary party to a determination of paternity and estate distribution. The second motion seeks genetic testing of Patricia Welch, Richard Welch, the plaintiff and the minor child to determine whether Michael is Kaitlyn's father. The plaintiff filed memoranda of law in support of both motions.

The attorney for the minor child filed a brief in support of both motions requesting that the court grant both motions and consider adding the defendant, Richard J. Welch, in his individual capacity. In the alternative, or in addition to DNA testing of the putative grandparents, counsel for the minor child seeks an order of exhumation of the body of the deceased putative father for purposes of genetic testing.

The defendant filed objections to both the motion to cite in Patricia Welch and the motion for genetic testing along with supporting memoranda. The defendant, however, did not object to the request for exhumation of the body of the deceased putative father for purposes of genetic testing beyond claiming that the court lacks subject matter jurisdiction to determine paternity after the death of the putative father.

I.   MOTION TO CITE IN PARTY DEFENDANT

* * *

The defendant argues that Patricia Welch has no interest in the present case in controversy whereas the plaintiff argues that Patricia Welch, as an heir to her deceased son's estate, does have an interest in the paternity determination because any disposition of the intestate estate will be affected if Kaitlyn is Michael's child.

This court finds that Patricia Welch is an indispensable party to this paternity action * * *. Although the question of the decedent's estate is not at issue in the present case, Patricia Welch's interest in the paternity action is that her share in the intestate succession of her deceased son's estate will be affected if Kaitlyn is found to be the daughter of Michael Welch.

* * *

Additionally, the defendant argues that Patricia Welch has no legal duty nor suffers any penalty in her capacity as the putative grandmother, and is thus immune from liability. Under General Statutes 52–102, "no person who is immune from liability shall be made a defendant in the controversy." Aside from setting forth the language of the statute and a definition of immunity as taken from Black's Law Dictionary, the defendant offers no authority to support the immunity argument. This court was not able to uncover any authority one way or the other on the issue of possible immunity under the circumstances of this case.

Lastly, the defendant argues that her presence is not necessary for a complete determination of any question involved in this action because DNA testing is not the only method possible to resolve plaintiff's claims equitably. Thus, Patricia Welch is not necessary within the meaning of General Statutes 52–102. As stated above, this court finds Patricia Welch to be, not only necessary, but indispensable to this paternity action. Although this court recognizes that exhumation of the deceased putative father provides an alternate to DNA testing on Richard and Patricia Welch, it also recognizes the inherent proof problems of posthumous DNA testing and in fairness to all parties grants the motion to cite in Patricia Welch as a party defendant and adds Richard J. Welch in his individual capacity as requested by counsel for the minor child.

II.   MOTION FOR GENETIC TESTING

* * *

When both parents of the child are tested, the possibility of paternity, as expressed in a percentage, will either approach one hundred percent or zero percent.

When one parent is unavailable, as in the present case, DNA fingerprinting may also be utilized to effectively establish a "probability" of paternity by testing relatives of the unavailable parent. The DNA "print" of a father, mother, or other relative of the deceased putative father can be compared to the DNA prints of the child and the available mother to determine whether the parties are related. Although the process can not be deemed conclusive, it has been recognized by the scientific community as quite valuable.

* * *

Furthermore, other courts, including one state Supreme Court has recognized the reliability of testing relatives for purposes of establishing paternity. In Sudwischer v. Estate of Hoffpauir, 589 So. 2d 474 (La.1991), cert. denied sub nom., Estate of Hoffpauir v. Sudwisher, 504 U.S. 909 (1992), the Supreme Court of Louisiana affirmed an order that the legitimate daughter of a deceased father provide a blood test to determine the paternity of an illegitimate daughter. The court reasoned that the DNA fingerprinting of the legitimate daughter would produce relevant evidence which could establish the probability of a relationship between the deceased legitimate daughter and the illegitimate daughter. The DNA expert testified that the probability of the relationship could be as low as one in five or as high as one in a hundred thousand.

* * *

In consideration of the scientific techniques available to determine paternity, this court will not deny Kaitlyn the right to prove her paternity so that she may equitably share in her father's estate. The plaintiff's motion for genetic testing is granted. The plaintiff, minor child, Patricia and Richard Welch are hereby ordered to submit to DNA testing. In addition, the court orders exhumation of the body of Michael Welch for purposes of conducting DNA testing.

NOTES AND QUESTIONS

1.   What was the social policy behind a statute providing that the husband of a woman is presumed to be the father of her child? Is assignment of paternity based on DNA testing a preferable approach?

2.   In certain rare instances, DNA testing for paternity purposes might go awry. When Lydia Fairchild applied for public assistance for her two children, the children underwent paternity testing to determine who the father was. Unfortunately, the tests showed that Lydia was not the mother. State officials assumed she was committing fraud. But when she gave birth to a third child, the same thing happened. It was later determined that Lydia was a chimera. Just as one embryo can split apart to create twins, two embryos can join together to create one person. Half of Lydia's cells had one DNA profile, while the other half had another. Lydia's parenthood of all three children was ultimately established by a DNA test using cervical cells rather than one based on a cheek swab. Lauren Friedman, The Stranger-Than-Fiction Story Of A Woman Who Was Her Own Twin, Business Insider, Feb. 2, 2014, www.businessinsider.com/lydia-fairchild-is-her-own-twin-2014-2.

3.   Over 400,000 paternity tests are conducted each year by accredited laboratories. Additional tests are conducted by people (generally putative fathers) who use over-the-counter paternity tests. Should fathers be able to test a child without the mother's permission? Should people be required to have a court order before having a child tested? Does testing a child without the mother's consent invade the mother's privacy? In Identigene, Inc. v. Goff,

774 So.2d 48 (Fla. App. 2000), a mother sued a DNA testing company for various intentional torts for taking a saliva sample from her minor son without her consent. The case was dismissed for lack of personal jurisdiction over the company.

4.   In Evelyn H. v. David H., 729 N.Y.S.2d 570 (N.Y.Sup.2000), a divorce proceeding, a mother and her children were ordered by the court to submit to DNA testing to establish paternity even though the court recognized that the testing was not in the best interests of the children. Should courts issue such orders?

5.   What is the proper statute of limitations for challenges to paternity? Under the Uniform Parentage Act § 607, the presumed father has a two-year period after birth in which to use DNA testing to challenge his paternity. Ohio has lengthened the period in which putative fathers can use DNA tests to disavow paternity, even in instances where a man has held out the child as his own. Ohio allows a putative father to challenge paternity at any time by using the results of a DNA test administered no more than six months prior to the filing of a motion for relief. Unless the father adopted the child or the child was conceived through artificial insemination, the man can use the DNA test even if he signed a birth certificate, supported the child, was presumed to be the father, or acknowledged the child, unless it was proved by a preponderance of the evidence he knew he was not the father and maintained a paternal relationship with the child. Ohio Rev. Code § 3119.962 (A).

Some states set a different statute of limitations for actions by the children. In Rushford v. Caines, 2001 WL 310006 (Ohio App. 2001), a woman in her 40s learned through an anonymous note that a man who died testate might be her biological father. She brought an action in probate court to release the decedent's DNA for testing, but the court applied a provision of the Ohio paternity statute that bars an action brought by a child more than five years after the child reaches age 18. The court was unpersuaded by her argument that the statute of limitations should have been tolled during the period she did not know that the decedent might be her biological father.

6.   Should the state require DNA tests before an acknowledgment of paternity? A Massachusetts court suggested in dicta that, "Where the State requires an unmarried woman to name her child's putative father, the department should require that the parties submit to genetic testing prior to the execution of any acknowledgment of paternity or child support agreement." The court reasoned that requiring genetic testing would save both children and potential putative fathers the heartache and uncertainty of relying solely on the mother's assertion of paternity. In re Paternity of Cheryl, 746 N.E.2d 488 (Mass. 2001).

7.   What if a woman's husband wants custody of the children despite learning through DNA testing that he is not the biological father? In Moss v. Moss, 2000 WL 1349242 (Ark. App. 2000), an ex-husband won custody in such a situation under a best interests analysis. In In re Marriage of Slayton,

685 N.E.2d 1038 (Ill. App. 1997) an ex-husband was granted visitation rights for a child he had previously believed to be his son based on the best interests of the child. In Karen P. v. Christopher J.B., 878 A.2d 646 (Md. Ct. Spec. App. 2005), a man was awarded custody of his biological son and non-biological daughter even though he had not been married to the children's mother. The mother took both children from school and moved from Maryland to New Jersey when their relationship ended, and the man did not learn that he might not be the daughter's father until the custody proceedings. The court determined that granting the father custody, with visitation from the mother, was in the best interests of the children. But, in Killingbeck v. Killingbeck, 711 N.W.2d 759 (Mich. Ct. App. 2005), the court did not award parental rights to the father. In that case, a man married a woman with whom he thought he had fathered a child. After their divorce, DNA paternity testing revealed that he was not the biological father of the child. The court refused to apply an equitable parent doctrine to grant rights to the man because he had not been married to the child's mother at the time of the child's conception.

8. A man who thinks he is the father of a child may learn through genetic disease testing that he is not. In one case, a seven-year-old boy was diagnosed with cystic fibrosis. Since he was not a carrier of the cystic fibrosis gene, the boy's "father" realized that his "son" was not his biological child. However, the court did not let him reopen his earlier divorce case because even though he knew his wife had been unfaithful, he had not sought paternity testing at the time of the divorce. Wise v. Fryar, 49 S.W.3d 450 (Tex. App. 2001).

9. Was it appropriate to undertake DNA testing to determine the likelihood that Thomas Jefferson fathered a child with his slave Sally Hemings? See Eugene A. Foster et al., Jefferson Fathered Slave's Last Child, 396 Nature 27 (1998). What are the potential issues with conducting such studies? The authors of the study published in *Nature* quickly came under criticism for failing to fully consider the possible paternity of other male relatives of Thomas Jefferson who lived in the area and could have had a relationship with Sally Hemings. See Eugene A. Foster et al., Reply: The Thomas Jefferson Paternity Case, 397 Nature 32 (1999). Was such criticism justified?

10. Should genetic analysis be done on deceased individuals' tissue to determine if they fathered existing children? In Anne R. v. Estate of Francis C., 634 N.Y.S.2d 339 (N.Y. Fam. Ct. 1995), the court ordered DNA testing on a deceased individual's frozen blood sample. In Malone ex rel. Randolph v. Barnhart, 2004 WL 1794912 (N.D. Ill. 2004), an administrative law judge in the Social Security Administration did not admit a DNA test using a one-year-old sample from the decedent's autopsied organs to establish paternity because of concerns about scientific validity, but a federal magistrate reversed the decision.

11. Should genetic testing be done only if a sample of the putative father's DNA is available short of disinterment of his corpse (for example, through analysis of a hair follicle from a comb or a blood sample at a hospital)? Should disinterment be allowed only if the child is still alive and needs financial support? Consider the case of In re Estate of Nasert, 748 N.Y.S.2d 654 (N.Y. Sur. Ct. 2002), in which DNA testing was performed on the decedent's willing identical twin to establish whether the decedent had fathered a child.

12. What are the arguments for and against a court ordering DNA testing on a deceased putative father's parents or legitimate children in order to assess paternity? Should the answer depend on the accuracy of the test? Should testing only be allowed if the parents or legitimate child will inherit from the estate and therefore might be reluctant to volunteer for such testing due to a financial conflict of interest?

13. With over 1,600,000 children born outside of marriage each year in the United States, questions arise as to how those children should be treated for inheritance purposes. By writing a will, a man can determine whether or not a genetic child or any other person will inherit from him. But in the absence of a will, nonmarital children can only inherit from a father if he has been adjudicated to be the father, has acknowledged paternity in writing, or has "openly and notoriously" held himself out as the father. Should genetic testing replace other ways of establishing paternity for intestacy purposes? Should it be used as an additional way to claim a share of the estate? In cases where the man has held himself out as the father and the child claims a share of the estate, should other relatives be able to demand a DNA test to attempt to prevent the child from inheriting? Are there different policy considerations in establishing paternity when the putative father is deceased than when he is still alive? Paula A. Monopoli, Nonmarital Children and Post-Death Parentage: A Different Path for Inheritance Law?, 48 Santa Clara L. Rev. 857 (2008).

14. The use of DNA testing to learn about family relationships goes beyond establishing legal parenthood. Direct-to-consumer testing companies provide services that allow people to learn of distant cousins or other relatives. Some additionally purport to trace family lines back to countries of origin generations earlier. Rachel L. Swarns, "With DNA Testing, Suddenly They Are Family," The New York Times, January 24, 2012, at A1.

15. For information on the ethical, legal, and social implications of DNA-based paternity testing, see Mark A. Rothstein et al., Genetic Ties and the Family (2005).

III. GENETICS AND SWITCHED BABIES

MAYS V. TWIGG

543 So.2d 241 (Fla. Dist. Ct. App. 1989).

PATTERSON, J.

The facts surrounding this case are exceptionally delicate and unique. The respondents, Ernest and Regina Twigg, have alleged that some ten years ago staff personnel at Hardee Memorial Hospital, Wauchula, switched their healthy newborn daughter with one born on approximately the same date to Robert Mays' late wife, Barbara, and that both couples went on to raise children not actually their own natural offspring. The child raised by the Twiggs, Arlena Beatrice, later died from a congenital heart condition. Shortly before Arlena's death the Twiggs learned, based on the child's blood type, that neither of them could have been her biological parent. Kimberly Mays was the only other white female in occupancy at Hardee Memorial Hospital at the time of Arlena's birth.

* * *

We hold that in cases such as this, before a putative father may obtain discovery relating to the paternity of the child, he must first prove the requisite standing to go forward with the suit * * *. Admittedly, natural parents have certain presumptive rights of custody as to their offspring. Those rights, however, are not absolute. Children are not property, but individuals whose needs and physical and mental well-being find protection in the law. The cases dealing with custody contests between a natural parent and a third party are replete with declarations that the privilege of custody of the natural parent must yield if such custody will be detrimental to the welfare of the child.

* * * If the trial court finds that the ultimate relief sought should not be granted because of probable detrimental effects upon the child, no additional discovery on the issue of paternity should be allowed.

* * *

The amended complaint stands dismissed with leave to amend. Upon the resumption of the action, we direct the circuit court to permit no further discovery except as in accord with this opinion.

QUESTION

1.   Under what circumstances should hospitals be considered negligent when babies are switched shortly after birth? In 1995, two baby girls were switched at the University of Virginia Medical Center. Photographs and medical records of the girls showed their identification bands were loose at

times and absent at others. Subsequently, the hospital began to use identification tags clamped on newborns' umbilical cords rather than identification bracelets. When sued, the hospital offered a $2 million settlement to each family. See Michael D. Shear, Mother of Switched Baby Sues for $31M, Washington Post, May 25, 1999, at B1.

IV. GENETICS AND IMMIGRATION

Great Britain uses DNA paternity testing in the country of origin on immigration applicants attempting to prove they are related to their sponsors in Great Britain; Canada has a similar system. Although the applicants have a right to refuse such testing, most are afraid to do so for fear that officials will become suspicious. Immigrant organizations, though, claim that such testing is expensive and is required only of certain ethnic groups and thus is designed to discourage immigration of people from certain "undesirable" countries. For further discussion see Lori Andrews & Dorothy Nelkin, Body Bazaar: The Market for Human Tissue in the Biotechnology Age 115–116 (2001).

Under United States law, a child born abroad out of wedlock to a U.S. citizen mother and non-citizen father is automatically granted U.S. citizenship. If the father is a citizen and the mother is not, though, the child can only become a citizen if, before the child reaches 18, the child is legitimated under the law of the father's domicile; the father acknowledges paternity in a writing under oath; or paternity is established by a court. 8 U.S.C. § 1409. In 2001, the U.S. Supreme Court addressed the question of whether, in light of the existence of DNA paternity testing which establishes paternity to a high degree, this statutory scheme violates the equal protection guarantee embedded in the Fifth Amendment's Due Process Clause. Tuan Anh Nguyen v. Immigration & Naturalization Service, 533 U.S. 53 (2001).

In that case, a child born out of wedlock in Vietnam to a Vietnamese mother and an American father was taken to the U.S. when he was six years old and raised by the father as a permanent U.S. resident. However, when the child was 22 years old, he pled guilty to two counts of sexual assault on a child whereupon the INS began deportation proceedings. His father then took a paternity test to establish his parenthood in order to keep his son in the country by establishing citizenship. The U.S. Supreme Court, in a 5–4 decision, ruled that because the father did not meet the statutory requirements of 8 U.S.C. § 1409 while his son was under the age of 18, the son was ineligible for citizenship.

The Court upheld the differential classification between children born abroad to U.S. mothers and those born to U.S. fathers on the grounds that "fathers and mothers are not similarly situated with respect to proof of biological parenthood." The majority opined that the woman demonstrates her biological connection by giving birth. The Court assumed that birth ensures a mother-child relationship. For fathers, the justices required proof not only of a biological tie but a father-child bond. "That interest's importance is too profound to be satisfied by a DNA test because scientific proof of biological paternity does not, by itself, ensure father-child contact during a child's minority."

The majority totally ignored the fact that the father had, by the time the case reached the U.S. Supreme Court, spent 32 years caring for his son. Rather than acknowledge this very real bond, the majority expressed fear about opening the floodgates to a vast number of children claiming U.S. citizenship based on DNA tests. The Court provided figures about how many American military personnel were stationed abroad in 1969, the year Nguyen was born (1,041,094) and in 1999 (252,763). The Court stated that modern travel (with 25 million trips abroad in 1999) provided "even more substantial grounds to justify the statutory distinction." The Court expressed concerns: "The fact of paternity can be established even without the father's knowledge, not to say his presence. Paternity can be established by taking DNA samples even from a few strands of hair, even after birth. Yet scientific proof of biological paternity does nothing by itself, to ensure contact between father and child during the child's minority."

Four dissenting justices (Justices O'Connor, Souter, Ginsburg and Breyer) opined that the statute violated equal protection, noting, "Sex-based statutes, even when accurately reflecting the way most men or women behave, deny individuals opportunity." The dissenters stated that the differential clarification failed to relate substantially to the achievement of important governmental objectives.

NOTES AND QUESTIONS

1. What are the implications of determining family ties in the immigration context based on DNA testing?

2. Isaac Owusu emigrated from Ghana to the United States with the hope that he would one day be reunited with his sons. Fourteen years after immigrating, he became an American citizen and had the opportunity to bring his sons to the United States, provided that paternity could be proved through genetic testing. But when DNA results came back, only one of the four sons was biologically related—calling into question the relationship that he had had with his deceased wife. While Isaac Owusu was able to bring the one biologically related son to the United States, the other three sons that he has cared for and loved cannot leave Ghana. Is this just? How should paternity or fatherhood be defined in the immigration context? While Isaac Owusu will not be able to bring the other three boys to the United States based on paternity, he may be able to challenge the decision, claiming status

as a stepfather. See Rachel L. Swarns, DNA Tests Offer Immigrants Hope or Despair, The New York Times, Apr. 10, 2007, at A1.

3. Section 212 (a)(4) of the United States Immigration and Nationality Act of 1952 provided:

(a) Except as otherwise provided in this Act, the following classes of aliens shall be ineligible to receive visas and shall be excluded from admission into the United States:

* * *

(4) Aliens afflicted with psychopathic personality, epilepsy, or a mental defect * * *.

Several cases used this statute as a basis to deport homosexuals. See, e.g., Boutilier v. Immigration & Naturalization Service, 387 U.S. 118 (1967); see also Quiroz v. Neelly, 291 F.2d 906 (5th Cir. 1961) (adhering to the Congressional rather than the psychiatric interpretation of "psychopathic personality" in including homosexuals within the meaning of the term).

The current version of this statute, 8 U.S.C. § 1182(a)(1), provides:

(a) * * * Except as otherwise provided in this Act, aliens who are inadmissible under the following paragraphs are ineligible to receive visas and ineligible to be admitted to the United States:

(1) Health-related grounds.

(A) In general. Any alien—

(i) who is determined (in accordance with regulations prescribed by the Secretary of Health and Human Services) to have a communicable disease of public health significance, which shall include infection with the etiologic agent for acquired immune deficiency syndrome,

* * *

(iii) who is determined (in accordance with regulations prescribed by the Secretary of Health and Human Services in consultation with the Attorney General)—

(I) to have a physical or mental disorder and behavior associated with the disorder that may pose, or has posed, a threat to the property, safety, or welfare of the alien or others, or

(II) to have had a physical or mental disorder and a history of behavior associated with the disorder, which behavior has posed a threat to the property, safety, or welfare of the alien or others and which behavior is likely to recur or to lead to other harmful behavior, or

(iv) who is determined (in accordance with regulations prescribed by the Secretary of Health and Human Services) to be a drug abuser or addict, is inadmissible.

Could this statute be used to exclude individuals with a genetic propensity for violent behavior or to exclude people with costly-to-treat genetic diseases?

V.   GENETICS, ADOPTION, AND DISABILITY

Genetic testing has been used in family law to assign legal rights and responsibilities. Such testing looks for genetic similarities between a putative parent and child. However, other types of genetic testing may enter the family law realm. In adoption, genetic testing could be undertaken to identify a predisposition to a genetic disease—to screen children genetically prior to adoption or to screen parents to determine current or future fitness to adopt. In order to assess whether such uses would be legal or ethical, it is useful to review how courts have dealt with genetic disability and other types of disability in the adoption realm.

AMANDA TREFETHEN, THE EMERGING TORT OF
WRONGFUL ADOPTION

11 J. Contemp. Legal Issues 620, 620–624 (2000).

Betty and Russell Burr were elated when the county social worker called to say that a "nice big, healthy, baby boy" had recently become available for adoption. According to the social worker, the mother was a healthy unwed 18-year-old who was financially unable to care for him. The Russells decided to adopt the 17-month-old, named him Patrick, and devoted their lives to caring and providing for him.

Soon the Burrs discovered that Patrick was mildly mentally retarded. A little while later he began to suffer from twitching, speech impediments, and poor motor skills; and later on, hallucinations. When he turned 20, Patrick was diagnosed with Huntington's disease, a genetically inherited, fatal disorder that destroys the nervous system.

The Burrs then obtained a court order to unseal the records concerning Patrick's history prior to adoption, and discovered that his mother was not an unwed teenager. Instead, she was a 31-year-old institutionalized mental patient with a history of psychotic reactions; and Patrick's unknown father was presumably also a mental patient at the same hospital. The Burrs also learned that Patrick had been in foster homes since birth; and that the county knew he was learning impaired and his medical background, which put him at risk for Huntington's disease, at the time of the adoption.

The Burrs filed a civil action against the adoption agency alleging false misrepresentation and fraudulent concealment of material information with the intent to deceive. In affirming the trial court's award of $125,000 in their favor, the Ohio Supreme Court [in Burr v. Bd. of County Com'rs, 491 N.E.2d 1101 (Ohio 1986)] concluded that the Burrs had established every element of fraud, and held:

> It would be a travesty of justice and a distortion of the truth to conclude that deceitful placement of this infant, known by appellants to be at risk, was not actionable when the tragic but hidden realities of the child's infirmities finally came to light.

The Burr decision ushered an erratic stream of cases premised on an emerging tort that came to be known as "Wrongful Adoption." Commentators as well as courts recognize that each of these cases requires a delicate balancing of the interests of prospective parents to whom pertinent family-history information is critical in making an informed decision and the interests of the adoption agency, concerned that disclosure requirements will require it to become the guarantor of children put up for adoption.

Inevitably difficult issues arise. Are adoptive parents entitled to a greater guarantee of health and well-being in their children than natural parents have in theirs? Does an adoption agency act in the child's best interests when it discloses, or instead intentionally withholds, pertinent negative medical history and background information in the hopes of finding the child a home? Can an adoption agency ever state that a child is "healthy" without inviting liability? Must adoptive parents prove, in order to establish their claim, that if they had known the risks involved they would not have adopted the child?

Responses to these questions have varied from state to state. Every state has adoption disclosure statutes that either require or permit access by adoptive parents to the medical records and relevant history of the adoptee. Nevertheless, adoptive parents are seeking remedies for an assortment of "wrongful adoption" tort claims ranging from intentional misrepresentation and fraud, to negligent misrepresentation, and on to intentional and negligent infliction of emotional distress. Courts diverge in the treatment of these tort claims arising from misinformation or failure to disclose in the adoption process.

The most successful of the potential wrongful adoption actions have been like *Burr*; they allege deliberate acts of misconduct such as fraud and intentional misinformation. The common law fraud claim requires that adoptive parents allege and prove (1) a material misrepresentation or omission was made to them in the course of the adoption, (2) made either with the intent of misleading them or with reckless disregard for the truth, (3) upon which they justifiably relied, and (4) in relying they were injured. Courts following *Burr* have upheld complaints or judgments that compensate adoptive parents for reasonable damages sustained as a result of the fraud perpetrated by the adoption agency. These decisions represent nothing more than the natural extension into the adoption arena of longstanding common law principles, the application of which has very little to do with adoption procedures per se.

But what of the duties of adoption agencies to disclose all known information? Increasingly the torts of negligent misrepresentation, negligent nondisclosure, and failure to investigate are finding application in the adoption context. A growing number of courts have held adoption agencies liable for negligently failing to disclose information or negligently misrepresenting the mental and physical background of the child. In holding an agency has a duty to disclose all known information about prospective adoptees, the Massachusetts Supreme Court reasoned that the duty is demanded by the notion of good faith and fair dealing. The court found that the burden on adoption agencies to disclose was substantially outweighed by the adoptive parents' need to for full disclosure. Other courts have shown reluctance to extend liability in negligence beyond this point. For example, no court as yet has held that an adoption agency has a duty to investigate, and several have specifically rejected such a claim.

Most wrongful adoption cases include claims for intentional or negligent infliction of emotional distress. Few courts have recognized the claim in the adoption context; and those that have set a difficult standard to meet, requiring that the adoptive parents show the defendant's reckless conduct was "outrageous and extreme." Other courts hold that unless the adoptive parent manifests symptoms of physical injury, he or she must show the defendant's conduct was "willful, wanton, or malicious."

Adopting a child is a permanent choice, much like the choice of those who have their own children. Natural parents have the information in front of them—their own medical histories and family backgrounds—and thus have the opportunity to weigh the risks and to make informed choices. Should not adoptive parents be permitted these same liberties? Absent a specific duty to investigate and disclose, adoption agencies will continue to choose silence and, in doing so, avoid any potential liability. But gone are the days in which quiet discretion and secrecy surrounded adoption. Advances in medical technology and the social sciences make knowledge, awareness, and early detection too critical to permit medial and historical information to be swept carelessly under an adoption agency's carpet. The interests of adopted children and their parents are best served when full disclosure is forthcoming.

MERACLE V. CHILDREN'S SERVICE SOCIETY OF WISCONSIN
437 N.W.2d 532 (Wis. 1989).

CALLOW, J.

* * *

We address two issues in this case. First, is the cause of action of Quentin and Nancy Meracle (the Meracles) barred by the statute of limitations? Second, is the Meracles' cause of action barred by public policy? We conclude that the Meracles' claim for future, extraordinary medical expenses is not barred by either the statute of limitations or by public policy. We also hold, however, that the Meracles' claim for emotional distress must be dismissed because the alleged emotional distress was not manifested by physical injury.

In 1977, the Meracles contacted Children's Service Society of Wisconsin (CSS), an adoption agency, about adopting a child. They told CSS they wanted a "normal, healthy child," which they defined as a child without a "disabilitating" or terminal disease, who is not deformed and who is of average or above average intelligence.

On October 10, 1979, the Meracles met with Josephine Braden (Braden), a social worker at CSS, to discuss the foster placement and adoption of Erin, a twenty-three month-old child. According to the Meracles' deposition testimony, Braden told them the following at the meeting: that Erin's paternal grandmother had died of Huntington's Disease; that Huntington's was a degenerative brain disease which is genetically transmitted between generations; that if one generation was free of the disease, the next generation would be free of it; that each child of a Huntington's Disease victim had a fifty-fifty chance of developing the disease; and that the disease was always fatal. According to the Meracles, Braden also told them that Erin's father had tested negative for the disease and that, therefore, Erin had no more chance of developing the disease than did any other child.

In her deposition, Braden recalled discussing Huntington's Disease with the Meracles at this meeting. However, she did not recall telling the Meracles there was no chance of Erin developing the disease, and could not believe she had done so.

On October 18, 1979, CSS placed Erin with the Meracles, and on November 12, 1980, the adoption was completed.

On February 8, 1981, Nancy Meracle saw a segment of the television program 60 Minutes which dealt with Huntington's Disease. The show stated that a child of a Huntington's Disease victim has a fifty percent chance of developing the disease. It also stated that there was no reliable test for someone at risk to determine whether he or she had inherited the disease.

"Alarmed" and "frightened," Nancy told her husband about the program. The Meracles obtained a pamphlet about Huntington's Disease from a library the next day which confirmed there was no test for the disease. They took no further action at this time.

On September 27, 1984, a neurologist diagnosed Erin as having Huntington's Disease. On September 25, 1985, the Meracles filed a complaint against CSS in the Milwaukee County Circuit Court. They subsequently amended the complaint twice to include two insurance companies as co-defendants: American Home Assurance Company (American Home) and St. Paul Fire & Marine Insurance Company.

* * *

[The trial court granted summary judgment for the defendants and the Meracles appealed.]

We first turn to CSS's contention that the Meracles' claim is barred by the three-year statute of limitations for negligence. CSS notes that Borello v. U.S. Oil Co., 388 N.W.2d 140 (Wis.1986), set forth the following rule for when a cause of action accrues:

> [U]nder Wisconsin law, a cause of action will not accrue until the plaintiff discovers, or in the exercise of reasonable diligence should have discovered, not only the fact of injury but also that the injury was probably caused by the defendant's conduct or product.

It insists that the Meracles' cause of action accrued in 1981 when the Meracles first learned of the negligent misrepresentation.

We find that in 1981, while the Meracles had learned of CSS's negligence, they had suffered no injury which would support a cause of action * * *. CSS contends that the Meracles could have stated a claim for the $1000 adoption fee and for the cost of raising Erin between the time of her adoption and the discovery of the disease in 1981. This is incorrect. These are costs which would have been incurred in any case during the adoption of a child. The Meracles wanted to adopt a child. These were ordinary expenses pursuant to that end. It is only the extraordinary expenses, the unexpected expenses resulting from Erin's special needs, which are actionable.

CSS also contends that the Meracles could have stated a claim for Erin's future medical expenses in 1981. This also is incorrect. In order to sue for future medical expenses in 1981, while Erin had not yet contracted the disease, the Meracles would have had to base their claim on the mere possibility that Erin would develop the disease. To recover for future expenses due to an injury, a plaintiff must demonstrate that the anticipated expenses are reasonably certain to occur. "[R]ecovery may be had for *reasonably certain* injurious consequences of the tortfeasor's negligent conduct, not for merely possible injurious consequences."

* * *

There was no reasonable medical certainty in 1981 that the Meracles would incur any future medical expenses because Erin had not developed Huntington's Disease. At the time, the Meracles only knew that Erin's paternal grandmother had developed the disease. They did not know whether her father would develop it. While Erin's father was not known to have developed the disease, there is a fifty percent chance that a Huntington's victim will genetically transmit the disease to his or her off-spring. The Meracles only knew that Erin's grandmother had the disease and her father had a fifty percent chance of developing Huntington's, and therefore Erin had only a twenty-five percent chance of developing the disease.

Further, Erin's chances of developing the disease within her first eighteen years, when the Meracles would have been responsible for medical payments, was even smaller. Deposition testimony revealed that only four to five percent of the people who develop Huntington's Disease do so while they are juveniles. In sum, even assuming that Erin would develop the disease at some point in her life, in 1981 there was only a four to five percent chance that the Meracles would incur future medical expenses for Erin. This risk constitutes a "mere possibility" and it was not an injury for which the Meracles could have recovered in 1981. They could not have shown with a reasonable medical certainty in 1981 that they would incur any future medical expenses. Thus, they did not suffer a pecuniary injury which would support a cause of action.

The Meracles likewise did not have a compensable claim for emotional distress in 1981. The general rule in Wisconsin is that, to recover for the negligent infliction of emotional distress, the "plaintiff's emotional distress must be manifested by physical injury." In Garrett [v. City of New Berlin, 362 N.W.2d 137 (Wis.1985)], we held that hysteria is a physical injury which can form the basis of a claim for negligent infliction of emotional distress. This rule exists because of the "fear of flooding the courts with fraudulent claims and exposing defendants to potentially unlimited liability for every type of mental disturbance." The existence of physical injury makes the genuineness of the claim much more likely.

CSS correctly points out that an exception to this rule exists. In La Fleur [v. Mosher, 325 N.W.2d 314 (Wis.1982)], we allowed a fourteen-year-old girl to recover damages for emotional distress when she was negligently confined in a police department cell for thirteen hours with no food, water or blankets. We stated that, "under the unique facts presented in this case," the nature of the confinement itself guaranteed the genuineness of the claim. We emphasized the fact that the tort involved "a substantial and unwarranted deprivation of liberty," which itself was "a sufficient guarantee that the claim is not frivolous."

CSS contends that the Meracles' claim in 1981 was such that we should make another exception to the requirement that a claim for the negligent infliction of emotional distress be accompanied by physical injury. We disagree. *La Fleur* involved unique facts and the decision emphasized the narrowness of its holding. The Meracles were not deprived of liberty or any other constitutional right in 1981 nor does the nature of their claim present a similar guarantee of the genuineness and severity of the injury.

We find, therefore, that the Meracles suffered no injury, pecuniary or emotional, which would support a compensable claim in 1981.

The Meracles did suffer an injury which could form the basis for a cause of action in 1984 when they learned that Erin had developed Huntington's Disease. The Meracles had a cause of action for pecuniary damages at this time. They could then demonstrate with reasonable medical certainty that Erin would need extensive future medical care. They were now certain to incur future expenses because of the adoption which they allege was induced by the affirmative misrepresentation that Erin's father had tested negative for the disease and therefore that Erin would not contract it. In 1984, the Meracles had "a claim capable of present enforcement."

* * *

Under the discovery rule of *Borello*, the Meracles' cause of action for medical expenses accrued on September 27, 1984, when Erin was diagnosed with the disease. They filed their first complaint on September 25, 1985, well within the three-year limitations period. Therefore, their claim for future medical expenses is not time-barred and should be remanded for trial.

CSS also contends that, even if the Meracles' suit is not barred by the statute of limitations, it should be barred because it violates public policy. CSS, citing Rieck [v. Medical Protective Co., 219 N.W.2d 242 (Wis.1974)], notes that:

> Even where the chain of causation is complete and direct, recovery may sometimes be denied on grounds of public policy because: (1) The injury is too remote from the negligence; or (2) the injury is too wholly out of proportion to the culpability of the negligent tort-feasor; or (3) in retrospect it appears too highly extraordinary that the negligence should have brought about the harm; or (4) because allowance of recovery would place too unreasonable a burden (in the case before us, upon physicians

and obstetricians); or (5) because allowance of recovery would be too likely to open the way for fraudulent claims; or (6) allowance of recovery would enter a field that has no sensible or just stopping point.

In support of its position CSS cites two California decisions which discuss the policy implications of wrongful adoption actions. In Richard P. v. Vista Del Mar Child Care Service, 165 Cal.Rptr. 370 (Cal.App.1980), the California Court of Appeals held that it would violate public policy to allow the adoptive parents of a child to sue an adoption agency which stated that the child, who later developed severe neurological damage, was healthy. The court feared that allowing such a suit to proceed would make adoption agencies the guarantors of the health of the children they place. In Michael J. v. Los Angeles County Department of Adoptions, 247 Cal.Rptr. 504 (Cal.App.1988), the California Court of Appeals held that public policy did not bar a suit based on intentional misrepresentation by an adoption agency. However, the court reaffirmed its decision in *Richard P.* that adoption agencies were not liable for negligence in placing adoptive children. CSS likewise contends that allowing this suit to proceed would place an unreasonable burden on adoption agencies, exposing them to potentially unlimited liability and making them guarantors of the health of the children they place.

Before determining whether we should bar this cause of action on public policy grounds, we feel it necessary to emphasize the uniqueness of this case. This is not a case in which an adoption agency placed a child without discovering and informing the prospective parents about the child's health problems. Therefore we need not and do not address the question of whether adoption agencies have a duty to discover and disclose health information about children they place for adoption. In this case, accepting the alleged facts as true for purposes of this summary judgment motion, CSS affirmatively misrepresented Erin's risk of developing Huntington's Disease. The agency assumed the duty of informing the Meracles about Huntington's Disease and about Erin's chances of developing the disease. Having voluntarily assumed this duty, the complaint alleges, CSS negligently breached it.

Given these unique circumstances, we hold that the Meracles' claim is not barred by public policy. Such a conclusion does not expose adoption agencies to potentially unlimited liability nor does it make such agencies guarantors of the health of adopted children. To avoid liability, agencies simply must refrain from making affirmative misrepresentations about a child's health. We do not hold that agencies have any duty to disclose health information. Further, our decision will not inhibit adoption. Indeed, it will give potential parents more confidence in the adoption process and in the accuracy of the information they receive. Such confidence would be eroded if we were to immunize agencies from liability for false statements made during the adoption process.

We also emphasize that we do not create liability which is remote from or out of proportion to the negligence because, as we discussed above, we only allow recovery for the *extraordinary* medical expenses which will be incurred by the Meracles as a result of the negligent misrepresentation. This case is very different from *Rieck*, in which we determined based upon public policy that parents could not maintain a wrongful birth action to recover ordinary expenses of raising a normal child against a doctor who failed to diagnosis a pregnancy. Finally, this decision does not open the way for fraudulent claims to be brought. There is no greater chance of fraud in a case like this than in any case in which the dispute centers over what words were spoken during a particular conversation. Based upon the unique factors in this case we conclude this suit is not barred by public policy.

AMERICAN SOCIETY OF HUMAN GENETICS SOCIAL ISSUES COMMITTEE AND AMERICAN COLLEGE OF MEDICAL GENETICS SOCIAL, ETHICAL, AND LEGAL ISSUES COMMITTEE, GENETIC TESTING IN ADOPTION

66 Am. J. Human Genetics 761–767 (2000).

Reports from geneticists have stated that prospective adoptive parents and adoption agencies are requesting a wider range of genetic tests before, during, or immediately after the adoption process. It is possible that certain children who are determined to have various harmful or undesirable genetic predispositions or characteristics will have a difficult time being adopted or, if adopted, will be treated differently by adoptive parents. Although these reports must be considered anecdotal or preliminary at the present time, it is clear that the pressure for genetic testing in adoption will increase as the range of available genetic tests increases.

The American Society of Human Genetics (ASHG) and the American College of Medical Genetics (ACMG) recommend the following:

1.   All genetic testing of newborns and children in the adoption process should be consistent with the tests performed on all children of a similar age for the purposes of diagnosis or of identifying appropriate prevention strategies.

2.   Because the primary justification for genetic testing of any child is a timely medical benefit to the child, genetic testing of newborns and children in the adoption process should be limited to testing for conditions that manifest themselves during childhood or for which preventive measures or therapies may be undertaken during childhood.

3.   In the adoption process, newborns and children should not be tested for the purpose of detecting genetic variations of or predispositions to physical, mental, or behavioral traits within the normal range.

* * *

The welfare of children affected by genetic conditions should be the first concern in the practice of medical genetics. In assessing which genetic tests are appropriate for all children, including adopted children, the nature of the tests is an important consideration. Among the types of tests currently available are (1) tests for diseases that can be prevented or the health consequences of which can be reduced through early treatment; (2) tests for serious childhood diseases; (3) tests for conditions that do not manifest themselves until adulthood and for which no treatment or preventive action is available in childhood; (4) tests indicating a predisposition to a common adult-onset disorder for which some general preventive measures may be taken in childhood; (5) tests for behavioral traits; (6) tests for carrier state and other conditions that may impact the child's future reproductive decisions; (7) tests that parents request without any direct relation to treatment or reproductive options for the child; and (8) tests performed solely for the benefit of another family member. Additional classifications or smaller subsets of available tests are possible and some of the categories may overlap when the same test is performed for more than one reason, but the eight types of tests described provide a good starting point for discussion of the appropriateness of genetic testing.

Of the eight categories of tests, only the first two categories should be viewed with unqualified approval. The immediate availability of medical benefits for a child who has or may soon develop a genetic condition provides the strongest reason for genetic testing. An often-cited example of the first type of test is newborn screening for phenylketonuria (PKU). Such tests serve the interests of the child directly, are medically indicated, and comply with the standards set forth in the 1995 ASHG/ACMG report and the statements of other medical groups and organizations. The test for PKU is used to screen newborns for a genetic condition that, left untreated, will result in severe mental and motor retardation. Where the condition is identified through testing, effective dietary therapy is available. Such screening is also frequently required by law. All states either mandate or offer testing for PKU.

The second type of test, which screens for serious childhood conditions, should also be supported when there is some health-related indication of the need to test. Such indications include symptoms and family history. An example would be a child with a birth sibling who was already diagnosed with cystic fibrosis (CF).

* * *

The issue of testing is further complicated by the ambiguity associated with predictive testing. Genetic tests usually do not predict when or to what degree a genetic disease or condition will manifest itself. More importantly, the mere presence of a gene coding for a genetic disease or condition does not mean that a child will invariably develop the disease or condition. Such test results supply only "probabilities, not certainties." At best, predictive genetic tests can only provide a range of risk. To subject a child to the potential for stigmatization, discrimination, and poor self-image based on ambiguous information is especially problematic. When the disadvantages of testing are weighed against the advantages of testing, the balance favors not testing, except in cases where genetic conditions manifest themselves during childhood or where effective, preventive measures may be undertaken during childhood.

IN RE MARRIAGE OF CARNEY
598 P.2d 36 (Cal. 1979).

MOSK, J.

Appellant father (William) appeals from that portion of an interlocutory decree of dissolution which transfers custody of the two minor children of the marriage from himself to respondent mother (Ellen).

In this case of first impression we are called upon to resolve an apparent conflict between two strong public policies: the requirement that a custody award serve the best interests of the child, and the moral and legal obligation of society to respect the civil rights of its physically handicapped members, including their right not to be deprived of their children because of their disability. As will appear, we hold that upon a realistic appraisal of the present-day capabilities of the physically handicapped, these policies can both be accommodated. The trial court herein failed to make such an appraisal, and instead premised its ruling on outdated stereotypes of both the parental role and the ability of the handicapped to fill that role. Such stereotypes have no place in our law. Accordingly, the order changing custody on this ground must be set aside as an abuse of discretion.

* * *

In August 1976, while serving in the military reserve, William was injured in a jeep accident. The accident left him a quadriplegic, i.e., with paralyzed legs and impaired use of his arms and hands. He spent the next year recuperating in a veterans' hospital; his children visited him several times each week, and he came home nearly every weekend. He also bought a van, and it was being fitted with a wheelchair lift and hand controls to permit him to drive.

In May 1977 William filed the present action for dissolution of his marriage. Ellen moved for an order awarding her immediate custody of both boys. It was undisputed that from the date of separation (Nov. 1972) until a few days before the hearing (Aug. 1977) Ellen did not once visit her young sons or make any contribution to their support. Throughout this period of almost five years her sole contact with the boys consisted of some telephone calls and a few letters and packages. Nevertheless the court ordered that the boys be taken from the custody of their father, and that Ellen be allowed to remove them forthwith to New York State. Pursuant to stipulation of the parties, an interlocutory judgment of dissolution was entered at the same time. William appeals from that portion of the decree transferring custody of the children to Ellen.

William contends the trial court abused its discretion in making the award of custody. Several principles are here applicable. First, since it was amended in 1972 the code no longer requires or permits the trial courts to favor the mother in determining proper custody of a child "of tender years". Civil Code section 4600 now declares that custody should be awarded "To either parent according to the best interests of the child." Regardless of the age of the minor, therefore, fathers now have equal custody rights with mothers; the sole concern, as it should be, is "the best interests of the child."

* * *

Ellen first raised the issue in her declaration accompanying her request for a change of custody, asserting that because of William's handicap "it is almost impossible for [him] to actually care for the minor children," and "since [he] is confined to a hospital bed, he is never with the minor children and thus can no longer effectively care for the minor children or see to their physical and emotional needs." When asked at the hearing why she believed she should be given custody, she replied inter alia, "Bill's physical condition." Thereafter she testified that according to her observations William is not capable of feeding himself or helping the boys prepare meals or get dressed; and she summed up by agreeing that he is not able to do "anything" for himself.

The trial judge echoed this line of reasoning throughout the proceedings. Virtually the only questions he asked of any witness revolved around William's handicap and its physical consequences, real or imagined. Thus although William testified at length about his present family life and his future plans, the judge inquired only where he sat when he got out of his wheelchair, whether he had lost the use of his arms, and what his medical prognosis was.

* * *

The final witness was Dr. Jack Share, a licensed clinical psychologist specializing in child development, who had visited William's home and studied his family. Dr. Share testified that William had an IQ of 127, was a man of superior intelligence, excellent judgment and ability to plan, and had adapted well to his handicap. He observed good interaction between William and his boys, and described the latter as self-disciplined, sociable, and outgoing. On the basis of his tests and observations, Dr. Share gave as his professional opinion that neither of the children appeared threatened by William's physical condition; the condition did not in any way hinder William's ability to be a father to them, and would not be a detriment to them if they remained in his home; the present family situation in his home was a healthy environment for the children * * *.

Ellen made no effort on cross-examination to dispute any of the foregoing observations or conclusions, and offered no expert testimony to the contrary. The judge then took up the questioning, however, and focused on what appears to have been one of his main concerns in the case—i.e., that because of the handicap William would not be able to participate with his sons in sports and other physical activities. Thus the court asked Dr. Share, "It's very unfortunate that he's in this condition, but when these boys get another two, three years older, would it be better, in your opinion, if they had a parent that was able to actively go places with them, take them places, play Little League baseball, go fishing? Wouldn't that be advantageous to two young boys?" Dr. Share replied that "the commitment, the long-range planning, the dedication" of William to his sons were more important, and stated that from his observations William was "the more consistent, stable part of this family regardless of his physical condition at this point." The judge nevertheless persisted in stressing that William "is limited in what he can do for the boys," and demanded an answer to his question as to "the other activities that two growing boys should have with a natural parent." Dr. Share acknowledged William's obvious physical limitations, but once more asserted that "On the side dealing with what I have called the stability of the youngsters, which I put personally higher value on, I would say the father is very strong in this area." Finally, when asked on redirect examination what effect William's ability to drive will have, Dr. Share explained, "this opens up more vistas, greater alternatives when he's more mobile such as having his own van to take them places. . . ."

* * *

More importantly, the judge conceded that Dr. Share "saw a nice, loving relationship, and that's absolutely true. There's a great relationship between [William] and the boys. . . ." Yet despite this relationship the judge concluded "I think it would be detrimental to the boys to grow up until age 18 in the custody of their father. *It wouldn't be a normal relationship between father and boys*." And what he meant by "normal" was quickly revealed: "It's unfortunate [William] has to have help bathing and dressing and undressing. *He can't do anything for the boys himself except maybe talk to them and teach them, be a tutor, which is good, but it's not enough.* I feel that it's in the best interests of the two boys to be with the mother even though she hasn't had them for five years." (Italics added.)

* * *

[I]f a person has a physical handicap it is impermissible for the court simply to rely on that condition as prima facie evidence of the person's unfitness as a parent or of probable detriment to the child; rather, in all cases the court must view the handicapped person as an individual and the family as a whole. To achieve this, the court should inquire into the person's actual and potential physical capabilities, learn how he or she has adapted to the disability and manages its problems, consider how the other members of the household have adjusted thereto, and take into account the special contributions the person may make to the family despite—or even because of—the handicap. Weighing these and all other relevant factors together, the court should then carefully determine whether the parent's condition will in fact have a substantial and lasting adverse effect on the best interests of the child.

The record shows the contrary occurred in the case at bar. To begin with, the court's belief that there could be no "normal relationship between father and boys" unless William engaged in vigorous sporting activities with his sons is a further example of the conventional sex-stereotypical thinking that we condemned in another context. For some, the court's emphasis on the importance of a father's "playing baseball" or "going fishing" with his sons may evoke nostalgic memories of a Norman Rockwell cover on the old Saturday Evening Post. But it has at last been understood that a boy need not prove his masculinity on the playing fields of Eton, nor must a man compete with his son in athletics in order to be a good father: their relationship is no less "normal" if it is built on shared experiences in such fields of interest as science, music, arts and crafts, history or travel, or in pursuing such classic hobbies as stamp or coin collecting. In short, an afternoon that a father and son spend together at a museum or the zoo is surely no less enriching than an equivalent amount of time spent catching either balls or fish.

Even more damaging is the fact that the court's preconception herein, wholly apart from its outdated presumption of proper gender roles, also stereotypes William as a person deemed forever unable to be a good parent simply because he is physically handicapped. Like most stereotypes, this is both false and demeaning. On one level it is false because it assumes that William will never make any significant recovery from his disability. There was no evidence whatever to this effect. On the contrary, it did appear that the hearing was being held only one year after the accident, that William had not yet begun the process of rehabilitation in a home environment, and that he was still a young man in his twenties. In these circumstances the court could not presume that modern medicine, helped by time, patience, and determination, would be powerless to restore at least some of William's former capabilities for active life.

Even if William's prognosis were poor, however, the stereotype indulged in by the court is false for an additional reason: it mistakenly assumes that the parent's handicap inevitably handicaps the child. But children are more adaptable than the court gives them credit for; if one path to their enjoyment of physical activities is closed, they will soon find another. Indeed, having a handicapped parent often stimulates the growth of a child's imagination, independence, and self-reliance. Today's urban youngster, moreover, has many more opportunities for formal and informal instruction than his isolated rural predecessor. It is true that William may not be able to play tennis or swim, ride a bicycle or do gymnastics; but it does not follow that his children cannot learn and enjoy such skills, with the guidance not only of family and friends but also the professional instructors available through schools, church groups, playgrounds, camps, the Red Cross, the YMCA, the Boy Scouts, and numerous service organizations. As Dr. Share pointed out in his testimony, ample community resources now supplement the home in these circumstances.

* * *

We agree, and conclude that a physical handicap that affects a parent's ability to participate with his children in purely physical activities is not a changed circumstance of sufficient relevance and materiality to render it either "essential or expedient" for their welfare that they be taken from his custody. This conclusion would be obvious if the handicap were heart dysfunction, emphysema, arthritis, hernia, or slipped disc; it should be no less obvious when it is the natural consequence of an impaired nervous system. Accordingly, pursuant to the authorities cited above the order changing the custody of the minor children herein from William to Ellen must be set aside as an abuse of discretion.

Both the state and federal governments now pursue the commendable goal of total integration of handicapped persons into the mainstream of society: the Legislature declares that "It is the policy of this state to encourage and enable disabled persons to participate fully in the social and economic life of the state. . . ." Thus far these efforts have focused primarily on such critical areas as employment, housing, education, transportation, and public access. No less important to this policy is the integration of the handicapped into the responsibilities and satisfactions of family life, cornerstone of our social system. Yet as more and more physically disabled persons marry and bear or adopt children— or, as in the case at bar, previously nonhandicapped parents become disabled through accident or illness—custody disputes similar to that now before us may well recur. In discharging their admittedly difficult duty in such proceedings, the trial courts must avoid impairing or defeating the foregoing public policy. With the assistance of the considerations discussed herein, we are confident of their ability to do so.

NOTES AND QUESTIONS

1. What are the duties of an adoption agency to inquire into genetic predisposition to disease in the biological parents' families? Should an adoption agency be required to order genetic testing of the infant? Should prospective parents be able to ask that the infant be tested genetically—for example, for the genetic mutation for Huntington disease? See Dorothy C. Wertz et al., Genetic Testing for Children and Adolescents: Who Decides?, 272 JAMA 875 (1994) for the recommendation that children, including children given up for adoption, not be tested genetically for late-onset disorders. For a more extensive discussion of genetic testing of children, see Chapter 7.

2. The Trefethen article advocates "full disclosure" of medical information about a child who is available for adoption. Would this include information about a family history of breast cancer? What about criminality? The director of a sperm bank once asked one of the casebook authors whether he had a duty to inform women who used a particular donor's sperm that the donor had been arrested for murder. Lori B. Andrews & Nanette Elster, Adoption, Reproductive Technologies and Genetic Information, 8 Health Matrix: Journal of Law-Medicine 125 (1998).

3. What is the standard for determining custody of a child when parents divorce?

4. When may a parent's disability, illness, or mental condition be taken into consideration when determining custody?

5. In a South Carolina case, a judge ordered a woman to be tested for Huntington disease (at the instigation of her ex-husband) in order to terminate her parental rights. This precedent may foreshadow genetic battles in all custody cases, creating situations in which divorcing spouses each seek genetic testing of the other in order to find out which one is less likely to get cancer or heart disease and is thus likely to live longer. Such an evidentiary quest may put quantity of time with the child above quality, since the quality of a parental relationship is tougher to measure and prove than the presence or absence of a gene. With this approach, then, the child may not actually end up with the "better" parent. And the genetic predictions themselves may turn

out to be wrong. Lori B. Andrews, Future Perfect: Confronting Decisions About Genetics 142–143 (2001).

6.   In 1990, Congress enacted the Americans with Disabilities Act (ADA) to ensure persons with disabilities "equality of opportunity, full participation, independent living, and economic self-sufficiency." 42 U.S.C. § 12101(a)(8). To accomplish these goals, Title II of the ADA prohibits a public entity from excluding or denying participation in public services, programs, or activities on the basis of a person's disability. 42 U.S.C. § 12132(a). Some disabled parents have tried using the ADA to challenge the termination of their parental rights, but nearly all have failed. Susan Stefan, Accommodating Families: Using the Americans with Disabilities Act to Keep Families Together, 2 J. Health L. & Pol'y 135 (2008).

7.   In the Interest of B.K.F., 704 So.2d 314 (La. App. 1997), a Louisiana appellate court case, affirmed a lower court decision that a mother with schizophrenia could not raise a violation of the ADA as a defense against the State's petition for termination of parental rights. The mother, who was diagnosed with severe chronic undifferentiated schizophrenia, gave birth to the minor child B.K.F. while she was hospitalized for her mental illness. The child was taken into the custody of the State at birth and placed in foster care. It was intended that the child remain in foster care until such time as the child could be freed for adoption or a parent experienced a sufficient change in mental condition that reunification was possible. However, despite the mother's enrollment in rehabilitation and parenting classes, an evaluation revealed that she was unlikely to develop the skills necessary to care for her child and it was recommended that the best interests of the child would be served by not returning the child to the mother. The mother brought suit alleging, *inter alia*, that the State failed to make appropriate modifications in its policy, practice, or procedure to accommodate her disability and comply with the ADA. The court held, however, that "termination of parental rights proceedings are not 'services, programs, or activities' within the meaning of the ADA" and thus the ADA may not be used as a defense in such proceedings. The decision of the Louisiana appellate court is not unique in this regard. Other courts have reached similar conclusions. See Stone v. Daviess County Div. of Children & Family Services, 656 N.E.2d 824 (Ind. Ct. App. 1995); In re Torrance P., 522 N.W.2d 243 (Wis. App. 1994); In re B.S., Juvenile, 693 A.2d 716 (Vt. 1997); In re Antony B., 735 A.2d 893 (Conn. App. 1999).

8.   Various other cases have determined that custody of a child may be denied to a parent manifesting schizophrenia. See, e.g., D.W. v. State Department of Human Resources, 595 So.2d 502 (Ala. Civ. App. 1992). The court in In re Juvenile 2006-833, 937 A.2d 297 (N.H. 2007), held that a mother who failed to take psychotropic medications she could not afford could have her parental rights terminated. Should custody be taken away from a parent prospectively if he or she has a gene mutation predisposing to schizophrenia?

CHAPTER 12

FORENSICS: GENETIC TESTING FOR IDENTIFICATION

■ ■ ■

I.   INTRODUCTION

Since 1985, law enforcement officials have increasingly used DNA testing in solving crimes. Genetic analyses have been used to help identify perpetrators by assessing the similarity of their DNA to that of semen, blood or other tissue from the crime scene. Since these comparisons provide a statistical probability that a given individual was present at the crime scene, courts face questions about whether an evolving series of DNA tests are admissible and what weight to give a DNA match. Law enforcement officials face questions about the circumstances under which they can compel suspects—or even the relatives of suspects—to provide blood, saliva, or other tissue for DNA testing.

In 1989, states began passing laws to require the collection of DNA samples from convicted violent offenders before their release from prison so their DNA could be compared to DNA collected from crime scenes. Law enforcement officials heralded the possibility of solving crimes with "the flick of a computer switch." All 50 states have passed laws to mandate the collection of DNA from offenders, but the collection of DNA in forensic banks raises constitutional, policy, and practical issues. Does the collection of DNA from convicted offenders violate the Fourth Amendment of the U.S. Constitution? Should DNA be banked, as it is in many states, from people convicted of lesser offenses, such as non-violent crimes, misdemeanors, juvenile offenses, or even from arrestees? Should DNA from all citizens be put in a DNA bank for law enforcement purposes?

As discussed in Chapter 13, Mental and Behavioral Genetics, DNA may also enter the criminal justice system at the behest of defendants who wish to claim that their genetic profile should exculpate them from conviction or mitigate their punishment. In the future, law enforcement officials may wish to use genetic information to attempt to predict the likelihood that someone might commit a crime (even though it is highly unlikely that such predictions will actually be valid).

The use of forensic DNA identification techniques goes beyond the criminal justice system, however. A military DNA bank has been established for future use to identify the remains of any soldiers killed in battle. In civil cases, including divorce, DNA testing has also been used for identification—for example, to prove adultery. In the future, DNA testing might be used to identify individuals as members of particular ethnic groups in order to provide social benefits.

II.   ADMISSIBILITY OF DNA EVIDENCE IN CRIMINAL CASES

Forensic DNA Profile.

A. THE SCIENCE OF FORENSIC DNA TESTING

THE NATIONAL COMMISSION ON THE FUTURE OF DNA
EVIDENCE, THE FUTURE OF FORENSIC DNA TESTING:
PREDICTIONS OF THE RESEARCH AND
DEVELOPMENT WORKING GROUP
13–20, 46–61 (U.S. Department of Justice, Washington, D.C., Nov. 2000).

The first genetic markers that were useful for human identification were the ABO blood groups discovered in the same year (1900) that Mendel's rules of inheritance were rediscovered. Nineteenth century scientists, investigating the causes of blood-transfusion reactions, mixed the bloods from different individuals in the laboratory. They soon discovered that when the bloods were incompatible, a clumping or precipitation of the red blood cells occurred. This allowed the scientists to identify the cell surface elements (called antigens) responsible for the reaction. They noted that human blood cells fell into four antigenic groups which Landsteiner (1900) designated A, B, AB, and O. It was quickly realized that the blood groups were inherited, but despite the seeming simplicity of the system, the genetic basis remained unclear. It was not until 1925 that the mode of inheritance was inferred from the population frequencies of the four groups * * *.

Different human populations were found to differ in the frequencies of the four types. For example, about 10 percent of Caucasian Americans are group B. If one of two blood samples was group A and the other group B, they must have come from different persons (in the absence of laboratory or other errors). On the other hand, if both were group B they could have come from the same person, but they could also have come from two different persons, each of whom happened to be group B. Over the years, several more independently inherited red blood cell systems were discovered. By 1960 there were some 17 systems, but not all were useful for identification. The most useful was the so-called HLA [human leukocyte antigen] system because it was highly polymorphic (i.e., with many alleles). Along with this battery of serological tests some laboratories included a few serum proteins and enzymes. Although it was quite probable that two blood samples from different persons would agree for one blood group or enzyme, it was less and less probable that two unrelated persons would agree for all loci as more tests were added.

The frequencies of a combination of such markers were typically one in a few hundred or less, although in some instances, when samples contained rare types, the probability of matching of samples could be much smaller. By the mid-1970s, analysis of evidence samples and calculations of random matches could be calculated. A combination of blood groups and serum proteins were sometimes used for identification in criminal investigations. Much more often, such probabilities were used in paternity testing and accepted as evidence of parentage, where civil criterion "preponderance of evidence," rather than the criminal criterion "beyond reasonable doubt," prevailed.

* * *

The nature of forensic identification changed abruptly in 1985. That year Alec Jeffreys and colleagues in England first demonstrated the use of DNA in a criminal investigation. He made use of DNA regions in which short segments are repeated a number of times [VNTRs—variable number of tandem repeats]. This number of repeats varies greatly from person to person. Jeffreys used such variable-length segments of DNA, first to exonerate one suspect in two rape homicides of young girls and later to show that another man had a DNA profile matching that of the sperm in the evidence samples from both girls. Soon after, some commercial laboratories made use of this "fingerprinting" procedure, and in 1988 the FBI implemented the techniques, after improving their robustness and sensitivity and collecting extensive data on the frequency of different repeat lengths in different populations.

* * *

After a first flush of immediate acceptance by the courts, the molecular methodology and the results of evidence analysis were challenged as unreliable. Although the majority of courts admitted the DNA evidence, a few highly publicized cases were overturned by higher courts, citing failure of sufficient DNA testing to meet the *Frye* or other standards for admissibility of scientific evidence as the reason.

* * *

During the decade 1985–1995, a revolutionary technical innovation became more and more widely used in molecular biology, so that by now it is almost universal. This is the polymerase chain reaction (PCR), a technique for amplifying a tiny quantity of DNA into almost any desired amount. It uses essentially the same principle as that by which DNA is normally copied in the cell, except that instead of a whole chromosome being copied only a short chosen segment of the DNA in a chromosome is amplified. This has made it possible to process the very tiny amounts of DNA often left behind as evidence of a crime and has greatly increased the sensitivity of the forensic systems available to the criminal justice system. Thanks to PCR, minute amounts of DNA extracted from hairs, postage stamps, cigarette butts, coffee cups, and similar evidence sources can often be successfully analyzed.

* * *

STRs (short tandem repeats) are similar to VNTRs in that they are based on repeated sequences dispersed throughout the chromosomes. While methods of interpretation for STRs and VNTRs are similar, STRs have smaller repeat units (usually 3 to 5 base pairs) and fewer of them (usually 7 to 15 alleles per locus). The small size makes them amenable to PCR amplification so that much smaller quantities of DNA are needed for analysis.

* * *

The FBI has selected 13 STR loci to serve as a standard battery of core loci, and increasingly laboratories are developing the capability to process these loci. As laboratories throughout the Nation employ the same loci, comparisons and cooperation between laboratories are facilitated * * *. The FBI and others are actively involved in getting frequency data from a number of populations of different population groups and subgroups. These populations are being continuously subdivided. For example, there are data from Japanese, Chinese, Koreans, and Vietnamese. In the Western Hemisphere, there are data for Bahamians, Jamaicans, and Trinidadians. With the 13 core loci the most common profile has an estimated frequency less than 1 in 10 billion. Of the 10 STR loci that the British system now uses, 8 are included in the 13 core loci, so international comparisons are feasible.

* * *

Techniques for using mitochondrial DNA (mtDNA) have been available for some years, but application to problems of forensic identification began in 1990. Several laboratories now have the necessary equipment and techniques to use this system. Mitochondria are intracellular particles (organelles) outside the nucleus in the cytoplasm of the cell. They contain their own small DNA genomes; circular molecules of 16,569 base pairs and the variants are identified by sequence determination. Each cell contains hundreds to thousands of mitochondria. For this reason, a single hair shaft, old bones, or charred remains, which are generally unsuitable for chromosomal DNA, sometimes provide enough intact material for mtDNA analysis. Mitochondria are transmitted by the egg but not by the sperm, so mtDNA is uniquely suited for tracing ancestry through the female line. It was used recently to identify some of the bodies of the Russian royal family, the Romanovs. Limitations of mtDNA include its relatively low discriminatory power and the dependence for that power on the creation of large databases of mtDNA sequences.

NOTES AND QUESTIONS

1.   The STR technique, like other DNA forensic techniques, has been promoted based on the idea that the section of DNA analyzed is "junk DNA" from the non-coding regions of the genome and thus provides only identifying information and not information about the individual's health. However, as Chapter 2 made clear, the DNA in these regions turns out to have many important functions and may reveal health information about the individual.

Even if all the STR loci chosen for analysis are in non-coding regions, their analyses could provide health information. An STR variation could identify disease susceptibility when (1) the STR variation occurs in a regulatory region, e.g., promoter or intron splice site, and thereby alters gene activity; or (2) the STR variation occurs in an intron or outside a gene and is positioned close enough (typically within 200,000 base pairs) to a functional mutation that it is almost always inherited with the mutation. See Jennifer M. Kwon & Alison M. Goate, Genes and Mutations, 24 Alcohol Research & Health 167 (2000). See also, William E. Evans & Mary V. Relling,

Pharmacogenetics: Translating Functional Genomics into Rational Therapeutics, 286 Science 487 (1999).

2.   What privacy concerns are raised when forensic DNA testing also provides potential health information? Should care be taken to choose STR sites that are not likely to be in gene regulatory regions or near known disease mutations? Should laws be adopted to prevent third parties from gaining access to information and samples in forensic DNA banks? Should relatives of offenders have a right to prevent a criminal's DNA from being stored on the grounds that the DNA reveals health information about them as well?

EMERGING TECHNOLOGIES: YSTR, LOW COPY NUMBERS AND SNPS

Standard STR DNA tests sometimes produce inconclusive results when the sample size is small or when there is a mixture of DNA, such as that of the rape victim and the rapist. New technologies are being developed to circumvent those problems. But, as each new technology is applied by forensic laboratories, the question of admissibility needs to be reconsidered.

As an alternative to the STR DNA test when there is an admixture of DNA, a method known as YSTR was developed which is specific to male DNA only. YSTR tests for short tandem repeats only on the Y chromosome. YSTR was held to be admissible under the *Frye* standard in Arizona v. Sanders, CR-2000 2900 (December 16, 2003) and in Shabazz v. State, 592 SE2d 876 (Ga. Ct. App. 2004).

The low copy number (LCN) DNA test was designed to deal with the problem of having just a small amount of DNA. However, because it multiplies the DNA in the sample by using more PCR cycles than traditional forensic DNA typing, there is more possibility of contamination. For example, the DNA of someone in the lab might be introduced into the sample. Courts have disagreed about the reliability and admissibility of LCN DNA tests. In People v. Megnath, a New York trial court found that LCN DNA testing was both "generally accepted as reliable in the forensic scientific community" and also was *"not a novel* scientific procedure within the scope of the *Frye* doctrine." 898 N.Y.S.2d 408, 415 (Sup.Ct. 2010). In U.S. v. McCluskey, the court did not allow the government to introduce LCN DNA testing, finding that they had not met the burden of proof to show it was "reliable and admissible under Daubert and Rule 702." 954 F.Supp.2d 1224, 1288 (D.N.M. 2013).

Another emerging forensic technology is based on SNPs. A single nucleotide polymorphism (SNP) represents a single base difference in the more than three billion bases of DNA in the human genome. SNPs are considered the most common form of genetic variation with each person carrying his or her own distinctive set of SNPs. SNP analysis purportedly can generate accurate matches using much shorter segments of DNA than other approaches. Although no public forensic DNA laboratory in the U.S. routinely analyzes forensic evidence for SNPs, the technique has been used for identification of human remains, as in the World Trade Center bombing. SNPs are not likely to replace STRs for most forensic applications, but SNPs may help solve special problems in forensic genetics. For example, SNPs might help identify male DNA by measuring polymorphisms on the Y chromosome (found only in men) from degraded samples. This approach is expected to be particularly useful in constructing the male profile in samples that contain mixtures of DNA from both a man and a woman.

NOTES AND QUESTIONS

1.   Identical twins have long presented a problem in forensic DNA testing, as traditional testing cannot distinguish between their DNA. When a female student was raped and assaulted in Grand Rapids, Michigan, the police obtained a DNA match to Jerome Cooper. However, Cooper had an identical twin brother Tyrone. Both men had records for sexual assault and both denied involvement. Police were unable to convict either since they could not prove through DNA testing which brother was responsible. In Malaysia, a man was arrested after he was stopped driving a car carrying 366 pounds of cannabis and 3.7 pounds of raw opium. His twin brother was arrested at the house where the car was headed. A DNA test could not be used to verify which man had been in the car and thus both men were set free. The judge remarked, "I can't be sending the wrong person to the gallows." Alison Gee, Twin DNA Test: Why Identical Criminals May No Longer Be Safe, BBC World Service, BBC.com, January 14, 2014, www.bbc.com/news/magazine-25371014.

By undertaking analyses of large portions of two twins' genomes—or even their whole genomes—scientists can determine which twin's DNA was left at the crime scene. Jacqueline Weber-Lehmann et al., Finding the Needle in the Haystack: Differentiating "Identical" Twins in Paternity Testing and Forensics by Ultra-Deep Next Generation Sequencing, 9 Forensic Science International: Genetics 42 (2014). Despite the utility of such testing, its high price tag may be prohibitive. Law enforcement officials in France estimated that they would have to pay about $1.3 million in testing costs to determine which of two identical twins was responsible for a series of rapes in Marseille. Ron Dicker, Identical Twins' DNA Evidence in Serial Rape Case Confounds Police in Marseille, France, Huffington Post, Feb. 11, 2013, www.huffington post.com/2013/02/11/identical-twins-dna-evidence-rape-france_n_2662896 .html.

2.   As of 2013, only two jurisdictions, Maryland and the District of Columbia, had laws that address familial and partial match analysis. Both prohibit these searches. However, California, Colorado, Texas and Virginia

have administratively developed procedures guiding the use of these techniques. These procedures all instruct that partial match analysis and familial searches "may only be used once all other leads have been exhausted." National Conference of State Legislatures, Emerging Issues, (2013), www.ncsl.org/Documents/cj/EmergingIssues.pdf. What additional privacy concerns are raised by the use of these techniques? Do these concerns outweigh the investigative efficiencies?

3.   IntegenX markets a product called RapidHIT 200 that can "generate a DNA profile, check it against a database, and report on whether it found a match" in a mere 90 minutes. Police have already used this technology in Arizona, Florida, and South Carolina. As rapid DNA testing becomes less expensive and more widely available, how should it be regulated? Are critics right to be concerned that this will spur law enforcement to "coop up and store ever more DNA profiles"? See Shane Bauer, The FBI is Very Excited About This Machine That Can Scan Your DNA in 90 Minutes, Motherjones.com, Nov. 20, 2014, www.motherjones.com/politics/2014/11/rapid-dna-profiles-database-fbi-police.

B.   THE LEGAL STANDARDS FOR ADMISSIBILITY

NATIONAL RESEARCH COUNCIL (NRC), THE EVALUATION OF FORENSIC DNA EVIDENCE
171–173 (1996).

GENERAL ACCEPTANCE AND SOUND METHODOLOGY

The technology used to examine VNTRs, STRs, or other loci must satisfy the standard required of scientific evidence. In the United States, two major standards exist for deciding whether scientific findings will be admitted into evidence: the "general-acceptance" test and the "sound-methodology" standard. In addition, some jurisdictions have adopted special statutes that provide for the admissibility of genetic testing in general or of DNA analyses in particular in criminal or civil cases. If a timely objection is raised, the judge must determine whether the applicable standard has been met.

The general-acceptance standard was first articulated in an influential 1923 federal case, Frye v. United States, 293 F. 1013 (D.C.Cir. 1923). In jurisdictions that follow *Frye*, the proponent of the scientific evidence must establish that the underlying theory and methodology are generally accepted within the relevant portions of the scientific community.

* * *

The sound-methodology standard is derived from phrases in the Federal Rules of Evidence. In Daubert v. Merrell Dow Pharmaceuticals [509 U.S. 579 (1993)], the Supreme Court held that these rules implicitly jettison general acceptance as an absolute prerequisite to the admissibility of scientific evidence. Instead of the *Frye* test, the Court prescribed a broader framework for deciding whether proposed testimony has sufficient scientific validity and reliability to be admitted as relevant "scientific knowledge" that would "assist the trier of fact." In that framework, the lack of general acceptance weighs against admissibility but is not invariably fatal. The Court discussed other factors that might be considered. Its nonexhaustive list includes the extent to which the theory and technology have been tested, the existence of a body of peer-reviewed studies, and the known error rates of the procedure.

C. ASSESSING THE RELIABILITY OF DNA EVIDENCE

ERIC E. LANDER, DNA FINGERPRINTING: SCIENCE, LAW, AND THE ULTIMATE IDENTIFIER IN THE CODE OF CODES: SCIENTIFIC AND SOCIAL ISSUES IN THE HUMAN GENOME PROJECT
191–210 (Daniel J. Kevles & Leroy Hood eds. 1993).

The rapidity with which the courts accepted DNA fingerprinting is understandable. In theory, the procedure is flawless: if enough sites of genetic variation are examined, it is certainly possible to determine whether two samples come from the same source.

In practice, however, DNA fingerprinting can be quite problematic. The difficulties become readily apparent from a comparison of DNA forensics with DNA medical diagnostics. DNA diagnostics can be conducted under optimal laboratory conditions: the samples are fresh, clean, and from a single individual. If uncertainty arises in the results, new samples can be taken and the test can be redone, which makes for a high standard of accuracy in the procedure. By contrast, DNA forensics compels the biologist to work with whatever samples happen to be found at the scene of a crime. Samples may have been exposed to numerous environmental insults: they may be degraded; they may be mixtures of samples from different individuals, as happens in a multiple rape. The forensic biologist often has only a microgram or less of sample DNA, enough to do perhaps only one test. If the test has ambiguous results, it often cannot be repeated because the sample will have been used up.

Moreover, DNA diagnostics usually asks only a simple question: which of two alternative * * * alleles has a parent passed on to his child? Because there are only two possible alternatives, there are natural consistency checks to guard against errors. By contrast, DNA forensics resembles analytical biochemistry. Given two samples about which we know nothing in advance, we wish to determine whether or not they are identical. We first need to determine if the band patterns match, a decision which requires us to make fine judgments about whether small differences between patterns are meaningful. If we decide that the patterns match at a few sites of variation, we must then assess the probability that the match might have occurred by chance. For this purpose, we must know the distribution of band patterns in the general population.

For these reasons, DNA forensics is considerably more challenging than DNA diagnostics. At the time that DNA fingerprinting was first introduced as evidence, however, the courts were not troubled by these potential problems—and neither were many other people, myself included. These issues have become obvious only in retrospect, as the result of experience.

* * *

Even if two samples show matching DNA patterns, it remains to determine the probability that the match might have occurred just by chance—that is, the probability expressed by the frequency of the pattern in the population. The most straightforward approach would be to compare the DNA pattern to a previously assembled data base containing the DNA patterns of a randomly selected population sample. If the DNA pattern in question matched no pattern in a data base of, say, 1,000 people, one would conclude that its frequency was probably less than 1 in 1,000. Such a conclusion would be completely defensible, provided that the sampling had been random. (In fact, the sampling schemes used by testing laboratories leave much to be desired in this regard: the FBI's original Caucasian data bases consist of samples from FBI agents, which hardly is a random sample with regard to ethnicity.)

DNA typing laboratories, however, claim much more extreme probabilities. They cite odds that range from 1 in 100,000, to 1 in 100 million, to 1 in 739 trillion in one case. How are such probabilities calculated? The explanation is simple: the laboratory assumes that each allele (that is, each band) in the DNA pattern is statistically independent and then multiplies the population frequencies of the alleles to produce the sometimes astronomical odds reported. Of course, the key is whether the assumption of statistical independence is correct.

The law has confronted the issue of statistical independence in the past. In a famous case called California v. Collins [438 P.2d 33 (Cal.1968)], an eyewitness reported seeing an interracial couple, the woman being a blonde, the man being black, leaving the scene of a crime in a yellow automobile. The police subsequently picked up such a couple. At the trial, a mathematician testified about the probability of finding a couple that matched this description. As part of his calculation, he multiplied (a) the frequency of blonde women in the population times (b) the frequency of black men times (c) the frequency of interracial couples. Using arithmetic of this sort, he reached the conclusion that the frequency of such couples was about 1 in 12,000,000; the jury convicted the defendants. The California Supreme Court overturned the conviction, because of this improper statistical testimony. Among several problems, the court noted that the three categories described in (a), (b), and (c) are certainly not statistically independent and so their frequencies cannot be multiplied.

In population genetics, the question of statistical independence comes down to whether the general population is randomly mixed or whether it contains genetically differentiated subgroups. If the latter is the case, then bands will not be statistically independent: if a band common among southern Italians is found at one locus, for example, it is more likely that the suspect has southern Italian heritage and thus it is more likely that a band common among southern Italians will be found at another locus.

* * *

The occurrence of false matches should come as no surprise: clinical laboratory errors occur in all areas at rates estimated at between 1 percent and 5 percent. Mistakes inevitably get made. Proficiency testing compels us to find our errors and confront their causes—with the result that procedures improve. It should also remind us that it makes no sense to report DNA fingerprinting results as accurate to one part in a hundred million, if the rate of laboratory errors is on the order of even 1 percent.

D. CONCERNS ABOUT DNA EVIDENCE

The Florida Supreme Court in Brim v. State, 695 So.2d 268, 271 (Fla. 1997) pointed out that "The fact that a match is found in the first step of the DNA testing process may be 'meaningless' without qualitative or quantitative estimates demonstrating the significance of the match." The DNA analysis assesses whether the accused's sample is similar to that from a crime scene. But a statistical analysis must be done to calculate the likelihood that such a match could occur by chance. The most common method of calculating these statistics is the multiplication or product rule. The product rule requires an expert to determine the frequency of certain genetic markers and then multiply those frequencies together.

Under the product rule, the probability of the joint occurrence of mutually independent events is equal to the product of the individual probabilities that each of the events will occur. If a person is rolling a die, there is a 1 in 6 chance that he or she will roll the number two. The chance that he or she will roll the number two twice in a row is $1/6 \times 1/6$—a 1 in 36 chance. But if the chance of a man having a beard is 1 in 6 and the chance of a man having a mustache is 1 in 6, these probabilities cannot be multiplied together to produce an estimate of 1 in 36, because the factors are not independent. (Many men with beards also have mustaches). So if a victim describes her assailant as a man with a beard and mustache and police arrest a man matching that description, it cannot be said that the probability that they have the wrong man is 1 in 36; the probability of a random match is higher.

Individual frequencies must be trustworthy for this rule to produce accurate results, but sometimes they are not because of the limited size of DNA databases. These limited databases, established for calculating population frequencies for broad racial categories, may not be representative of isolated subpopulations where intermarriage and inbreeding occur. The product rule also presents potential problems because it is based on an assumption that the genetic markers used for matching are independent (that is, not close enough to each other on chromosomes so that they are likely to be inherited together), but this is not always the case. See Paul C. Giannelli & Edward J. Imwinkelried, Scientific Evidence § 18 (3d ed. 1999). For instance, the admission of DNA evidence can be misleading in cases where the potential suspects are related and share common genetic markers.

E. ADMISSION OF DNA EVIDENCE THROUGH EXPERT TESTIMONY

WILLIAMS V. ILLINOIS
132 S.Ct. 2221 (2012).

JUSTICE ALITO announced the judgment of the Court and delivered an opinion, in which THE CHIEF JUSTICE, JUSTICE KENNEDY, and JUSTICE BREYER join.

In this case, we decide whether Crawford v. Washington, 541 U.S. 36 (2004), precludes an expert witness from testifying in a manner that has long been allowed under the law of evidence. Specifically, does *Crawford* bar an expert from expressing an opinion based on facts about a case that have been made known to the expert but about which the expert is not competent to testify? We also decide whether *Crawford* substantially impedes the ability of prosecutors to introduce DNA evidence and thus may effectively relegate the prosecution in some cases to reliance on older, less reliable forms of proof.

In petitioner's bench trial for rape, the prosecution called an expert who testified that a DNA profile produced by an outside laboratory, Cellmark, matched a profile produced by the state police lab using a sample of petitioner's blood. On direct examination, the expert testified that Cellmark was an accredited laboratory and that Cellmark provided the police with a DNA profile. The expert also explained the notations on documents admitted as business records, stating that, according to the records, vaginal swabs taken from the victim were sent to and received back from Cellmark. The expert made no other statement that was offered for the purpose of identifying the sample of biological material used in deriving the profile or for the purpose of establishing how Cellmark handled or tested the sample. Nor did the expert vouch for the accuracy of the profile that Cellmark produced. Nevertheless, petitioner contends that the expert's testimony violated the Confrontation Clause as interpreted in *Crawford*.

Petitioner's main argument is that the expert went astray when she referred to the DNA profile provided by Cellmark as having been produced from semen found on the victim's vaginal swabs. But both the Illinois Appellate Court and the Illinois Supreme Court found that this statement was not admitted for the truth of the matter asserted, and it is settled that the Confrontation Clause [of the Sixth Amendment] does not bar the admission of such statements. For more than 200 years, the law of evidence has permitted the sort of testimony that was given by the expert in this case. Under settled evidence law, an expert may express an opinion that is based on facts that the expert assumes, but does not know, to be true. It is then up to the party who calls the expert to introduce other evidence establishing the facts assumed by the expert. While it was once the practice for an expert who based an opinion on assumed facts to testify in the form of an answer to a hypothetical question, modern practice does not demand this formality and, in appropriate cases, permits an expert to explain the facts on which his or her opinion is based without testifying to the truth of those facts. See Fed. Rule Evid. 703. That is precisely what occurred in this case, and we should not lightly "swee[p] away an accepted rule governing the admission of scientific evidence."

We now conclude that this form of expert testimony does not violate the Confrontation Clause because that provision has no application to out-of-court statements that are not offered to prove the truth of the matter asserted. When an expert testifies for the prosecution in a criminal case, the defendant has the opportunity to cross-examine the expert about any statements that are offered for their truth. Out-of-court statements that are related by the expert solely for the purpose of explaining the assumptions on which that opinion rests are not offered for their truth and thus fall outside the scope of the Confrontation Clause. Applying this rule to the present case, we conclude that the expert's testimony did not violate the Sixth Amendment.

As a second, independent basis for our decision, we also conclude that even if the report produced by Cellmark had been admitted into evidence, there would have been no Confrontation Clause violation. The Cellmark report is very different from the sort of extrajudicial statements, such as affidavits, depositions, prior testimony, and confessions, that the Confrontation Clause was originally understood to reach. The report was produced before any suspect was identified. The report was sought not for the purpose of obtaining evidence to be used against petitioner, who was not even under suspicion at the time, but for the purpose of finding a rapist who was on the loose. And the profile that Cellmark provided was not inherently inculpatory. On the contrary, a DNA profile is evidence that tends to exculpate all but one of the more than 7 billion people in the world today. The use of DNA evidence to exonerate persons who have been wrongfully accused or convicted is well known. If DNA profiles could not be introduced without calling the technicians who participated in the preparation of the profile, economic pressures would encourage prosecutors to forgo DNA testing and rely instead on older forms of evidence, such as eyewitness identification, that are less reliable. The Confrontation Clause does not mandate such an undesirable development. This conclusion will not prejudice any defendant who really wishes to probe the reliability of the DNA testing done in a particular case because those who participated in the testing may always be subpoenaed by the defense and questioned at trial.

* * *

[JUSTICE THOMAS, concurring in the judgment, found only that Cellmark's statements were not testimonial because they were not of sufficient "formality and solemnity."]

* * *

Justice KAGAN, with whom Justice SCALIA, Justice GINSBURG, and Justice SOTOMAYOR join, dissenting.

Some years ago, the State of California prosecuted a man named John Kocak for rape. At a preliminary hearing, the State presented testimony from an analyst at the Cellmark Diagnostics Laboratory—the same facility used to generate DNA evidence in this case. The analyst had extracted DNA from a bloody sweatshirt found at the crime scene and then compared it to two control samples—one from Kocak and one from the victim. The analyst's report identified a single match: As she explained on direct examination, the DNA found on the sweatshirt belonged to Kocak. But after undergoing cross-examination, the analyst realized she had made a mortifying error. She took the stand again, but this time to admit that the report listed the victim's control sample as coming from Kocak, and Kocak's as coming from the victim. So the DNA on the sweatshirt matched not Kocak, but the victim herself. See Tr. in No. SCD110465 (Super. Ct. San Diego Cty., Cal., Nov. 17, 1995), pp. 3–4 ("I'm a little hysterical right now, but I think . . . the two names should be switched"). In trying Kocak, the State would have to look elsewhere for its evidence.

Our Constitution contains a mechanism for catching such errors—the Sixth Amendment's Confrontation Clause. That Clause, and the Court's recent cases interpreting it, require that testimony against a criminal defendant be subject to cross-examination. And that command applies with full force to forensic evidence of the kind involved in both the Kocak case and this one. In two decisions issued in the last three years, this Court held that if a prosecutor wants to introduce the results of forensic testing into evidence, he must afford the defendant an opportunity to cross-examine an analyst responsible for the test. Forensic evidence is reliable only when properly produced, and the Confrontation Clause prescribes a particular method for determining whether that has happened. The Kocak incident illustrates how the Clause is designed to work: Once confronted, the analyst discovered and disclosed the error she had made. That error would probably not have come to light if the prosecutor had merely admitted the report into evidence or asked a third party to present its findings. Hence the genius of an 18th-century device as applied to 21st-century evidence: Cross-examination of the analyst is especially likely to reveal whether vials have been switched, samples contaminated, tests incompetently run, or results inaccurately recorded.

Under our Confrontation Clause precedents, this is an open-and-shut case. The State of Illinois prosecuted Sandy Williams for rape based in part on a DNA profile created in Cellmark's laboratory. Yet the State did not give Williams a chance to question the analyst who produced that evidence. Instead, the prosecution introduced the results of Cellmark's testing through an expert witness who had no idea how they were generated. That approach—no less (perhaps more) than the confrontation-free methods of presenting forensic evidence we have formerly banned—deprived Williams of his Sixth Amendment right to "confron[t] . . . the witnesses against him."

* * *

IV

Before today's decision, a prosecutor wishing to admit the results of forensic testing had to produce the technician responsible for the analysis. That was the result of not one, but two decisions this Court issued in the last three years. But that clear rule is clear no longer. The five Justices who control the outcome of today's case agree on very little. Among them, though, they can boast of two accomplishments. First, they have approved the introduction of testimony at Williams's trial that the Confrontation Clause, rightly understood, clearly prohibits. Second, they have left significant confusion in their wake. What comes out of four Justices' desire to limit Melendez-Diaz v. Massachusetts [557 U.S. 305 (2008)] and Bullcoming v. New Mexico [564 U.S. ____ (2011)] in whatever way possible, combined with one Justice's one-justice view of those holdings, is—to be frank—who knows what. Those decisions apparently no longer mean all that they say. Yet no one can tell in what way or to what extent they are altered because no proposed limitation commands the support of a majority.

The better course in this case would have been simply to follow *Melendez-Diaz* and *Bullcoming*. Precedent-based decisionmaking provides guidance to lower court judges and predictability to litigating parties. Today's plurality and concurring opinions, and the uncertainty they sow, bring into relief that judicial method's virtues. I would decide this case consistently with, and for the reasons stated by, *Melendez-Diaz* and *Bullcoming*. And until a majority of this Court reverses or confines those decisions, I would understand them as continuing to govern, in every particular, the admission of forensic evidence.

I respectfully dissent.

NOTES AND QUESTIONS

1.   What are some of the distinctions between the *Frye* and *Daubert* standards for admissibility? Which seems more lenient?

2.   Some form of forensic DNA testing is admissible in every state. As new DNA technologies are introduced, however, new *Frye* or *Daubert* analyses must be undertaken to determine whether it is appropriate to admit them. Sometimes the biotechnology companies have developed forensic DNA testing kits and marketed them to crime labs. This approach has led to difficulties in admissibility. For example, the Florida Supreme Court refused to admit evidence of a DNA match when the expert witness from the police lab, who had used a DNA testing kit, could not describe the underlying methodology. Murray v. State, 692 So.2d 157 (Fla. 1997). In a 2000 unpublished Vermont district court decision, State v. Pfenning, No. 57-4-96 GiCr (Apr. 6, 2000), scientific.org/distribution/archive/pfenning.pdf, the trial court refused to admit a new type of DNA forensic test that assessed six genetic loci. The test was marketed as a kit, and the manufacturer had refused to publish the genetic sequences used in the PCR technique, claiming they were trade secrets. This prevented others from assessing the reliability of the technique and led to a decision in a *Daubert*-style hearing not to admit the match evidence. The *Pfenning* court stated, "[T]he failure of the manufacturers of DNA testing systems to disclose the primer sequences they have created to permit amplification of DNA is problematic from the perspective of scientific knowledge and, consequently, validation. It is more than problematic, it is anti-scientific in that it inhibits the ability of scientists in the field (including defense experts) to test the manufacturers' claims * * *. The manufacturer's proprietary concerns * * * cannot trump Defendant's right to a fair trial, which includes the right to have only scientifically validated evidence admitted for the jury to consider in the State's case against him. Especially, with a new test, which has not been validated by long use in a variety of settings with a variety of sample types, it is unacceptable to deny independent scientists (including defense experts)

access to primer sequences, which could allow the scientists to properly investigate the purported reliability and validity of the new technique." After courts in two other states made similar rulings, the manufacturer published the primer sequences.

3.   Courts have grappled with the issues raised by Eric Lander regarding the difficulties of determining the probability of a random match when the accused individual is a member of a minority ethnic group and that group is not adequately represented in the genetic database to which the sample from the crime scene is being compared. In United States v. Chischilly, 30 F.3d 1144 (9th Cir. 1994), a Navajo man accused of murder argued that the FBI's database of Native American DNA was too small and contained too few Navajos to determine accurately the odds of a random match between the suspect's DNA and crime scene DNA. The defendant also raised questions about "substructuring"—the fact that there is less genetic variability among ethnically homogeneous, non-randomly mating populations and consequently "the probability of a random match between two of its members is greater than the likelihood of such a match between two members of the population at large." The Ninth Circuit acknowledged that the defendant had raised legitimate concerns that may warrant review by the FBI and revision of its procedures. But the court held that these concerns went to the weight of the evidence, and not its admissibility.

4.   Other challenges to the weight of DNA evidence have focused on the probability of matches between the genetic profile of DNA evidence found at a crime scene and the genetic profiles stored in DNA databases, such as CODIS. The FBI estimates that a match between a crime scene sample and DNA in CODIS has the odds of occurring only one in 113 billion times. But a technician working in the Arizona Department of Public Safety Crime Laboratory, Kathryn Troyer, found 122 men in the Arizona database that matched at 9 loci, 20 at 10 loci, one match at 11 loci, and one match at 12 loci. Other laboratory workers claimed to have seen similar matches in their own crime labs. Jason Felch & Maura Dolan, The Verdict is Out on DNA Profiles, Los Angeles Times, July 20, 2008, articles.latimes.com/2008/jul/20/local/me-dna20.

5.   Scientists have developed a way to create blood or saliva samples containing anyone's DNA they choose. The process is simple—in fact, according to the author of a study in Forensic Science International, "any undergraduate in biology" can do it. First a small sample of a person's DNA is taken from a drinking cup or a hair follicle. Next, scientists use a process called "whole genome amplification" to make multiple copies of the persons DNA. This amplified DNA can be inserted into a fake saliva sample or a blood sample stripped of endogenous DNA. Considering that "DNA is a lot easier to plant at a crime scene than fingerprints," do you think law enforcement officials place too much faith in DNA evidence? Andrew Pollack, DNA Evidence Can Be Fabricated, Scientists Show, The New York Times, Aug. 18, 2009, at D3.

6. As part of the Dallas cold-case project, Sgt. Welsh tested 289 rape kits that were collected between 1983 and 1986 and identified matches in 23 of the cases. According to a Texas law, both prosecutors and parole boards will now have access to view DNA evidence, like evidence found by Sgt. Welsh, which connects suspects to sexual assault cases where the statute of limitations has expired. The law, Tex. Gov't Code § 411.0601 et seq., allows the DNA records to be attached to the suspect's criminal files and the information can then be used, among other things, to influence the terms of an inmate's parole. Troy Fox, administrator for the parole board stated that "this law could have an impact on an inmate's term of parole * * *. The board considers all input for conditions it might want to impose on a parolee to protect society." Ann Zimmerman, Links to Sex Crimes to Follow Texas Suspects Law Will Let Prosecutors, Parole Boards See DNA Evidence Even When Statute of Limitations has Expired; Due Process Concerns, The Wall Street Journal, Aug. 31, 2009, at A3. Does the use of DNA related to other crimes at sentencing or parole violate the defendant's Sixth Amendment right? Does it violate the individual's due process rights? See Katherine C. Lester, The Affects of Apprendi v. New Jersey on the Use of DNA Alone Convict of Unadjudicated Prior Acts?, 17 Wash. & Lee J. Civil Rts. & Soc. Just. 267 (2010).

7. Hundreds of thousands of DNA analyses are conducted annually in the United States at more than 200 forensic laboratories, of which more than 175 are publicly funded and approximately 30 are privately funded. In 2005, Congress authorized the National Academy of Sciences (NAS) to conduct a study on forensics science, including DNA analysis, in the Science, State, Justice, Commerce, and Related Agencies Appropriations Act of 2006. The NAS report notes that DNA analysis has been subjected to rigorous experimentation and validation prior to its use in forensic investigations, more so than any other forensic science discipline. The report ultimately concludes that DNA analysis is scientifically sound and has a high probative power for the following five reasons: "(1) there are biological explanations for individual-specific findings; (2) the 13 STR loci used to compare DNA samples were selected so that the chance of two different people matching on all of them would be extremely small; (3) the probabilities of false positives have been explored and quantified in some settings (even if only approximately); (4) the laboratory procedures are well specified and subject to validation and proficiency testing; and (5) there are clear and repeatable standards for analysis, interpretation, and reporting." National Research Council of the National Academies, Descriptions of Some Forensic Science Disciplines, Strengthening Forensic Science in the United States: A Path Forward, 130–131 (2009), books.nap.edu/catalog.php?record_id=12589.

The report further states that "DNA typing is now universally recognized as the standard against which many other forensic individualization techniques are judged." DNA has attained this position because of its reliability and the fact that probabilities for false positives are quantifiable and often miniscule. However, the report does caution that even a very small, but nonzero, probability of false positives can affect the odds that a suspect is the source of a matching DNA profile. When errors occur, they usually involve one of three situations: where interpretational ambiguities occur, where samples are inappropriately processed or contaminated by the laboratory, or where only a limited amount of DNA is available, which limits the amount of test information and increases the chance of misinterpretation. National Research Council of the National Academies, Descriptions of Some Forensic Science Disciplines, Strengthening Forensic Science in the United States: A Path Forward, 129–131 (2009), books.nap.edu/catalog.php?record_id=12589.

Although the NAS report confirmed the validity of DNA analysis in forensic testing, the report also indicated that the field of forensic science generally needs reform. "Problems [include] poor documentation, serious analytical and interpretative errors, the absence of quality assurance programs, inadequately trained personnel, erroneous reporting, the use of inaccurate and misleading statistics, and even 'drylabbing' (the falsification of laboratory results)." The NAS report recommends that serious study be undertaken to raise the standards of forensic science and also recommends that forensic labs be made independent of law enforcement agencies; knowledge of an ongoing investigation and the desired result can unduly influence scientific interpretation. National Research Council of the National Academies, Introduction, Strengthening Forensic Science in the United States: A Path Forward, 188, 193 (2009), books.nap.edu/catalog.php?record_id=12589. Do the reports of poor laboratory procedure undermine the probative value of DNA testing?

8.   Based on the claims of increased efficacy in solving crimes, one might expect that the percentage of crimes being solved or "cleared" would have increased as DNA databases expanded. However, while the crime rate has dropped, clearance rates have changed very little during that period. Moreover, the clearance rates for crimes typically associated with the availability of perpetrator DNA, homicide and forcible rape, were actually lower in 2013 than in 1995, meaning that law enforcement actually solved fewer of the reported crimes than it did when DNA databases were still in their infancy. FBI, Crime in the United States (1995) & (2013), www.fbi.gov/about-us/cjis/ucr/crime-in-the-u.s/1995/95sec3.pdf; www.fbi.gov/about-us/cjis/ucr/crime-in-the-u.s/2013/crime-in-the-u.s.-2013/offenses-known-to-law-enforcement/clearances/clearancetopic_final.

9.   When prosecutors have not yet identified a suspect, but have the suspect's DNA profile, they have obtained DNA arrest warrants and indictments that contain the profile. These are used to toll the statute of limitations until the offender is identified. A New York appellate court held that the use of a DNA profile in a criminal indictment did not violate a defendant's Sixth Amendment or state constitutional right to notice of the charges brought against him. The court reasoned that the charges read against the defendant at his arraignment provided him with sufficient notice. Therefore, the use of a DNA profile in the indicting document did not deprive

the defendant of any constitutional rights. The court also noted that the use of DNA profiles for this purpose was increasingly popular due to the ability of DNA to accurately identify an individual and was therefore appropriate for use in an indicting document. People v. Martinez, 855 N.Y.S.2d 522 (N.Y. App. Div. 2008). See also Wisconsin v. Dabney, 663 N.W.2d 366 (Wis. Ct. App. 2003)

10. Statutes of limitations promote the security and stability of society; "the defendant will not be asked to defend against acts committed in the distant past, the innocent and unsure will be free from erroneous prosecution, the witnesses and victims will be provided the peace of mind that the ordeal has reached an end and is past, and the police are free to conclude investigation of the old case and redirect their attention to more recent affairs." Corey E. Delaney, Seeking John Doe: The Provision and Propriety of DNA-Based Warrants in the Wake of Wisconsin v. Dabney, 33 Hofstra L. Rev. 1091 (2005). What purposes does a statute of limitations serve? Are DNA warrants consistent with those purposes?

F. OBTAINING DNA SAMPLES FOR A MATCH

LORI ANDREWS & DOROTHY NELKIN, BODY BAZAAR: THE MARKET FOR HUMAN TISSUE IN THE BIOTECHNOLOGY AGE
102–103 (2001).

Blair Shelton wept when the technician drew blood for a DNA test. The day before, police had come to Shelton's workplace, a T.J. Maxx, and quizzed the manager about him. They told his boss that a woman had been raped by a black male who stood between five foot seven and six foot two and was between twenty-five and thirty-five years old, implying that Shelton could be that man. Shelton, a thirty-seven-year-old African-American, owned his own home and held down two janitorial jobs, one at the T.J. Maxx and another at a local school. He lost the first job after the police questioned his boss about him.

Shelton was innocent, but the police would not take his word for it. Instead, they pressured him to submit a blood sample for testing by threatening to obtain a search warrant to extract the blood if he did not. Inexperienced in dealing with the police, Shelton was humiliated, intimidated, and reduced to tears when the sample was taken.

Shelton was just one of hundreds of African-Americans in Ann Arbor, Michigan, who were caught in this DNA dragnet operation. Based on the vague description of the rapist, Ann Arbor police stopped more than seven hundred men and took samples for DNA testing from 160 of them.

Shelton's DNA did not match the DNA from the rapist's samples, but that did not end the police intimidation of him. Over the next few weeks, police officers stopped him while he was waiting in line outside a theater, boarding a bus, buying bagels, and jogging around a baseball field. Each time he was required to show a receipt proving that his blood had already been tested. Once an officer held him at gunpoint until he could "prove" his genetic innocence. The receipt in effect became his "passport" to avoid further questioning. Once the rapist was found, Shelton sued the police to have his blood sample returned. In 1997 a court honored his request. Now, says Shelton, he keeps the two tubes in his refrigerator to "remind me how angry this whole thing makes me."

EDWARD IMWINKELRIED & D. H. KAYE, DNA TYPING: EMERGING OR NEGLECTED ISSUES
76 Wash. L. Rev. 413, 416–445 (2001).

Traditionally, DNA has been employed to link a suspect to a crime. Finding that a suspect's DNA matches the DNA left at a crime scene, for example, tends to incriminate the suspect. Inversely, when the DNA does not match, the suspect usually can be excluded as the source of the crime-scene DNA. If trace evidence is to be used in these ways, the police must secure samples of DNA from individuals who might have committed the crime under investigation. Officials can secure such samples in many ways. They can seek a court order to compel an individual to submit to sampling; they can turn to a preexisting collection of DNA samples; they can take a sample with the consent of the individual; or they can try to locate a sample that the suspect has abandoned.

As a matter of constitutional law, the principal constraint on such government action is the Search and Seizure Clause of the Fourth Amendment to the U.S. Constitution, which states:

> The right of the people to be secure in their persons, houses, papers, and effects, against unreasonable searches and seizures, shall not be violated, and no Warrants shall issue, but upon probable cause, supported by Oath or affirmation, and particularly describing the place to be searched, and the persons or things to be seized.

* * *

Because Schmerber [v. California, 384 U.S. 757 (1966)] established that the Fourth Amendment applies to removing material from a suspect's body, as a general rule, police must persuade a judge or magistrate that there is probable cause to believe that the desired DNA sample will produce evidence linking the suspect to the crime. With judicial authorization, police can use necessary force to extract the biological material. Furthermore, once the authorities legally have acquired a suspect's profile, they are permitted to compare it to profiles from unrelated, unsolved crime-scene stains. The current state of the law appears to allow evidence legitimately acquired for one purpose to be used for another purpose, at least if the additional use entails no further search or seizure of the person.

* * *

It also is likely that an order compelling a person to give a sample could be issued on something less than probable cause. In Davis v. Mississippi [394 U.S. 721, 727 (1969)], the Supreme Court suggested in dictum such a procedure. A woman in Meridian, Mississippi, reported that "a Negro youth" broke into her home and raped her. Police, "without warrants, took at least 24 Negro youths," including Davis, "to police headquarters where they were questioned briefly, fingerprinted, and released without charge." After Davis's fingerprints were discovered to match those lifted from the windowsill, he was indicted, tried, and convicted. His objection to the admission of the fingerprint evidence was overruled, and the Mississippi Supreme Court affirmed the conviction on the theory that fingerprint evidence is so reliable that the Fourth Amendment exclusionary rule does not apply to this evidence. The U.S. Supreme Court reversed. The Court held that the Fourth Amendment requires the exclusion of evidence that is the fruit of an unreasonable search or seizure, regardless of how reliable that evidence may be. Reasoning that Davis was detained without a warrant and without probable cause, and that he was not merely fingerprinted but interrogated, the Court concluded that the resulting fingerprints were inadmissible. However, the Court's response to the state's argument that an arrest made solely for the purpose of obtaining fingerprints should be allowed without probable cause was less definitive. Although Justice Brennan, writing for the majority of the Court, emphasized that "detentions for the sole purpose of obtaining fingerprints are * * * subject to the constraints of the Fourth Amendment," he added that:

> It is arguable, however, that, because of the unique nature of the fingerprinting process, such detentions might, under narrowly defined circumstances, be found to comply with the Fourth Amendment even though there is no probable cause in the traditional sense * * *. Detention for fingerprinting may constitute a much less serious intrusion upon personal security than other types of police searches and detentions. Fingerprinting involves none of the probing into an individual's private life and thoughts that marks an interrogation or search. Nor can fingerprint detention be employed repeatedly to harass an individual, since the police need only one set of each person's prints. Furthermore, fingerprinting is an inherently more reliable and effective crime solving tool than eyewitness identifications or confessions * * *. Finally, because there is no danger of destruction of fingerprints, the limited detention need not come unexpectedly or at an inconvenient time.

The Court opened the door to the possibility that "the requirements of the Fourth Amendment could be met by narrowly circumscribed procedures for obtaining, during the course of a criminal investigation, the fingerprints of individuals for whom there is no probable cause to arrest." The Court virtually invited states to devise procedures to obtain evidence of identifying characteristics on the basis of something less than probable cause.

Many states seized on this invitation by adopting statutes or court rules permitting the police to obtain evidence of identifying physical characteristics after a showing of founded or reasonable suspicion. For instance, Arizona authorizes magistrates to issue "an order authorizing * * * temporary detention, for the purpose of obtaining evidence of identifying physical characteristics" on a showing of "reasonable cause for belief that a felony has been committed" and proof that the "physical characteristics * * * may contribute to the identification of the individual who committed such offense." As in this instance, the language of many of these statutes and court rules is broad enough to apply to DNA samples.

One might argue that these statutes or rules are too broad—that unlike the fingerprints in *Davis*, blood, urine, or hair samples should be treated differently because they have the potential to reveal information that is more significant than the pattern of whorls and ridges in a fingerprint. Some support for this distinction can be found in Skinner v. Railway Labor Executives' Ass'n [489 U.S. 602 (1989)], which involved drug testing of railway employees. The Court observed that "chemical analysis of urine, like that of blood, can reveal a host of private medical facts about an employee, including whether he or she is epileptic, pregnant, or diabetic." The same concern with "private medical facts" arises with any samples that can be subjected to DNA analysis. To this extent, it would be facile to say that DNA typing, like the fingerprinting in *Davis*, "involves none of the probing into an individual's private life and thoughts that marks an interrogation or search." Certain parts of one's genome—those that are related to otherwise nonobvious disease states or behavioral characteristics—are as much, if not more, a part of "an individual's private life" as are the hormones or other chemicals found in one's urine.

However, all the other factors listed in the *Davis* dictum apply to DNA sampling. Detention to obtain the sample cannot "be employed repeatedly to harass an individual, since the police need only one set of each person's [DNA types]." DNA analysis "is an inherently more reliable and effective crime-solving tool than eyewitness identifications or confessions." And, "the limited detention need not come unexpectedly or at an inconvenient time." Moreover, in describing these features of fingerprinting, the *Davis* Court recognized the possibility that the police might abuse even fingerprinting to harass or inconvenience a suspect.

The suggestion of relaxing the probable cause requirement presupposes the police will conform to the court order and the judiciary will issue orders that avoid these problems. This premise applies as well to the informational privacy concern voiced in *Skinner*. Just as there is no need to detain an individual repeatedly or to detain a person in the middle of the night, there is no reason for the police to probe parts of the genome that conceivably could be used to indicate disease states, susceptibilities, or the like. Because the judicial order can limit the search to loci that are of strictly biometric interest, the analogy to *Davis* is apt. Detention for DNA typing, as much as detention for fingerprinting, "may constitute a much less serious intrusion upon personal security than other types of police searches and detentions." If a person can be compelled to submit to fingerprinting on reasonable suspicion rather than probable cause, he or she can be required to submit to DNA sampling on the same showing.

* * *

The police also might obtain a suspect's DNA sample surreptitiously, without detaining the person. Saliva deposited on a coffee cup at a restaurant, for example, can be collected and analyzed. Police unsuccessfully chasing a wounded felon might find sufficient blood has dripped onto the sidewalk for DNA profiling to be conducted. It could be argued that such activity is not a search (and hence requires neither probable cause nor a warrant) because the individual, having abandoned the material in a public place, retains no reasonable expectation of privacy in it. The Supreme Court used this reasoning in California v. Greenwood [486 U.S. 35 (1988)] in holding that the Fourth Amendment does not prohibit "the warrantless search and seizure of garbage left for collection outside the curtilage of a home." The Court commented:

> It is common knowledge that plastic garbage bags left on or at the side of a public street are readily accessible to animals, children, scavengers, snoops, and other members of the public * * *. Moreover, respondents placed their refuse at the curb for the express purpose of conveying it to a third party, the trash collector, who might himself have sorted through respondents' trash or permitted others, such as the police, to do so.

However, depositing DNA in the ordinary course of life when drinking, sneezing, or shedding hair, dandruff, or other cells differs from placing private papers in a container on the street to be collected as garbage. Depositing paper in the trash is generally a volitional act. Someone intent on preserving the secrecy of the papers can shred the papers or dispose of them in other ways that would defeat normal police surveillance. Leaving a trail of DNA, however, is not a conscious activity. The deposition of DNA in public places cannot be avoided unless one is a hermit or is fanatical in using extraordinary containment measures. In this setting, the inference of intent to abandon is markedly weaker.

If the police collection of inadvertently deposited DNA cannot be justified solely on an abandonment theory, under Katz [v. United States, 389 U.S. 347 (1967), a case about the application of the Fourth Amendment to electronic eavesdropping on public phone booth calls], the question becomes whether society does or should recognize as reasonable the expectation that government agents will not follow one about to obtain and analyze DNA that almost inevitably is left in public places. A case can be constructed that such an expectation exists. The public is extremely concerned with preserving genetic privacy.

* * *

It seems clear that, in a public restaurant after a suspect departed, the police could pick up a coffee cup used by the suspect and, consistent with the Fourth Amendment, examine it for fingerprints. Courts may find it a small step to conclude that the warrantless collection of inadvertently abandoned DNA does not violate the Fourth Amendment.

Before taking this step, however, courts should consider the extent to which meaningful, personal information that would not be available to private citizens will fall into the hands of government agents interested in accessing this information. When society enters an era in which DNA analyzers are as accessible as home pregnancy-test kits, the argument for an expectation of privacy will be weak. But in a world still at the threshold of an age of molecular biology, what expectation is reasonable is less obvious. Privacy expectations should turn on the incentives and disincentives for the government to acquire DNA information that is truly sensitive as well as the risk that this information will be used to harm individuals.

* * *

NOTES AND QUESTIONS

1. Was Blair Shelton's provision of a blood sample sufficiently coerced so as not to be considered "voluntary"? Under what circumstances should the police be able to request blood samples from individuals to match to a crime scene?

2. The Fourth Amendment protects individuals who have a reasonable expectation of privacy. Imwinkelried and Kaye state, "When society enters an era in which DNA analyzers are as accessible as home pregnancy-test kits, the argument for an expectation of privacy will be weak." How persuasive is their argument? Should the mere fact that technology makes certain invasions of privacy easier to accomplish override an individual's beliefs and social expectations that such information should be private? Just because a

woman can readily learn whether she is pregnant or not through a home kit does not mean she expects that information to be publicly available.

In Kyllo v. United States, 533 U.S. 27 (2001), police used novel thermal imaging technology to scan an individual's home to obtain evidence that he probably was using high-intensity lamps that aided the indoor growth of marijuana. The trial court and the Ninth Circuit did not find the scanning to be a search in violation of the Fourth Amendment. The appellate court held that the defendant had shown no expectation of privacy because he had not attempted to conceal the heat emanating from his home. Plus, the imagery did not expose intimate details of his life.

The Supreme Court reversed, holding "Where, as here, the Government uses a device that is not in general public use, to explore details of the home that would previously have been unknowable without physical intrusion, the surveillance is a 'search' and is presumptively unreasonable without a warrant."

3.   States are free to find that their state constitutions provide greater protection for privacy than the U.S. Constitution. In State v. Goss, 834 A.2d 316 (N.H. 2003), police executed a warrant to search the defendant's residence for marijuana and items used in marijuana cultivation. The warrant was based, in part, on a previous, warrantless search of the defendant's garbage, which had been left on the defendant's driveway in black plastic bags on the normal trash pick-up day. The defendant contended that he had an expectation of privacy in his garbage, and the search of his garbage did not fall within any of the recognized exceptions to the warrant requirement. The Supreme Court of New Hampshire agreed, saying, "Clues to people's most private traits and affairs can be found in their garbage. Almost every human activity ultimately manifests itself in waste products and any individual may understandably wish to maintain the confidentiality of his refuse." In reaching its decision, the court acknowledged that the U.S. Supreme Court had reached the opposite conclusion with regard to an expectation of privacy in garbage, but interpreted the New Hampshire Constitution as providing for greater protection than that found in the Federal Constitution.

4.   Under what circumstances may law enforcement officials obtain genetic information (or even DNA samples) from physicians when their patients are suspected of committing a crime? The U.S. Department of Health and Human Services has promulgated health privacy regulations pursuant to the Health Insurance Portability and Accountability Act of 1996 (HIPAA). A section of these regulations deal with the standards for disclosure for law enforcement purposes. See 45 C.F.R. § 164.512(f). Under the HIPAA privacy regulations, a health care provider or institution may disclose otherwise-protected health care information to law enforcement officials pursuant to a court order. Even if there is no court order, law enforcement officials may obtain certain protected health information (such as the type of injury, ABO blood type, and a description of distinguishing physical

characteristics) for purposes of "identifying or locating a suspect, fugitive, material witness or missing person." However, without a court order, the police may *not* obtain "information related to the individual's DNA or DNA analysis, dental records, or typing, samples or analysis of body fluids or tissue." Note that the covered entity is not required to disclose the information without court order.

5.   Under what circumstances may law enforcement officials obtain genetic information from a suspect's blood-relative (such as a child) for use as a comparison to genetic evidence found at a crime scene? In Reno, Nevada, ten months after 19-year-old Brianna Denison was raped and murdered, police arrested a suspect based on an anonymous tip and DNA collected from the suspect's four-year-old son. The mother of the child gave police permission to test the child's DNA to see if his father could be a potential match to the evidence found at the scene. The DNA not only matched evidence from the rape and murder of Brianna Denison, but it also matched evidence from another sexual assault that occurred in 2007. See Mallory Simon, Tip, DNA Lead to Arrest in Student's Slaying, CNN.com, Nov. 27, 2008, www.cnn.com/2008/CRIME/11/26/brianna.denison.arrest/index.html.

6.   John Paul Phillips had a fatal heart attack while on Death Row. Police sought to have his body exhumed and DNA testing undertaken to determine if he raped and murdered five additional women before his initial trial. Phillips was exhumed, and a DNA sample was extracted from his femur. The DNA sample matched skin samples found underneath the fingernails of one victim murdered in 1976 and also ruled Phillips out as a suspect in another murder case from 1981. Should the exhumation and testing have been allowed? See Brett Nauman, Police Want Dead Man's DNA, Chicago Sun-Times, Oct. 5, 2001, at 14; Blackwell Thomas, DNA Helps Solve Two Cold Case Murders, The Southern Illinoisan, Sept. 18, 2008, murderpedia.org/male.P/p/phillips-john-paul.htm; and Phil Beckman, DNA Testing Rules Out Suspect in 20-Year-Old Southern Illinois U. Murder, Daily Egyptian, Sept. 26, 2002, murderpedia.org/male.P/p/phillips-john-paul.htm.

7.   Items abandoned in public lack Fourth Amendment protection against unreasonable search and seizure by law enforcement agents because the act of abandonment destroys any expectation of privacy that the owner might have previously possessed. But is DNA abandoned in the same way that garbage is left out on the street? The law surrounding this issue is currently in flux. For example, a New York court accepted that the DNA on a piece of gum that a suspect gave to police officers was abandoned. The suspect gave the gum to the officers while participating in a staged Pepsi taste-test that the police department had designed to acquire DNA evidence from the suspect. People v. LaGuerre, 815 N.Y.S.2d 211, 213 (N.Y. App. Div. 2006). But where the DNA was "abandoned" may make a difference. The North Carolina Court of Appeals prevented DNA from being used as evidence in a criminal trial because it had been collected from a cigarette butt found on the defendant's patio. The court concluded that the cigarette butt and the DNA on it were not abandoned because a reasonable expectation of privacy

still attached to the cigarette butt, as it was seized on a private piece of property rather than in a public place. State v. Reed, 641 S.E.2d 320, 322–323 (N.C. Ct. App. 2007). See Laura A. Matejik, DNA Sampling: Privacy and Police Investigation in a Suspect Society, 61 Ark. L. Rev. 53 (2008) for a discussion of this issue.

8.   After Christa Worthington was murdered on Cape Cod, DNA samples from suspects were collected, but it took over a year for the state crime lab to analyze the results and identify her killer. Pam Belluck, Slow DNA Trail Leads to Suspect in Cape Cod Case, The New York Times, Apr. 16, 2005, at A1. Other women were outraged that her alleged killer had been allowed to remain free, perhaps to kill again during that time period. But such delays are common. In fact, a poll of U.S. law enforcement officials found a reluctance to collect DNA evidence, especially in cases involving non-violent offenses, because of a belief that due to cost, backlogs and storage problems, the evidence will never be sent to the lab and therefore never result in an arrest. See Nicholas P. Lovrich et al., National Forensic DNA Study Report, December 12, 2003, www.ncjrs.gov/pdffiles1/nij/grants/203970.pdf.

9.   Some police departments have demonstrated a reluctance to submit rape kits for DNA testing. For example, as of February 2009, there were at least 12,669 untested rape kits in Los Angeles County. And of the 4,727 kits in the Los Angeles Sheriff's Department's storage facility, over 300 were beyond the ten-year statute of limitations and another 100 were within six months of that deadline. Sarah Tofte, Testing Justice: The Rape Kit Backlog in Los Angeles City and County, (Human Rights Watch: New York 2009). Considering that rape is often a serial crime, this backlog allows for the possibility that thousands of assailants have gone unpunished or have committed additional sexual assaults. Solomon Moore, Progress is Minimal in Clearing DNA Cases, The New York Times, Oct. 24, 2008, at A9.

Despite being booked into evidence, the kits sit in evidence storage facilities because DNA testing and analysis has not been requested by a detective. One officer revealed that he did not request DNA testing in cases where the alleged perpetrator was known or where he thought the case was unfounded. Another officer did not request DNA testing unless he believed the kit would help to further the investigation. Sarah Tofte, Testing Justice: The Rape Kit Backlog in Los Angeles City and County, (Human Rights Watch: New York 2009). Are these valid exceptions to the policy of requiring every rape kit to be tested? Is an officer correct in believing that "[m]ost rape cases are 'he said/she said,' and a rape kit isn't going to help you figure out who is telling the truth"?

Contrast Los Angeles with New York City, where a 16,000 DNA sample backlog from sexual assault and homicide cases in 1999 was eliminated by 2003 by sending every untested kit to a private crime lab. As of January, 2009, testing on the backlogged kits returned 2,000 cold hits, which resulted in 200 active investigations, arrests, or prosecutions. Amy Goodwin, Rape Kits in Cold Storage, Ms. Magazine, Winter 2009, at 16. Additionally, testing the kits exonerated a wrongfully convicted defendant, and the arrest rate for rape has increased from 40 percent to 70 percent. Prosecutions and convictions for rape have also increased. Sarah Tofte, Testing Justice: The Rape Kit Backlog in Los Angeles City and County, (Human Rights Watch: New York 2009). Do these figures demonstrate that testing rape kits is an important tool in stopping these crimes?

Nationwide, despite an increase in DNA processing, the backlogs have increased due to an increase in demand for testing. The National Institute of Justice undertook a study to determine the length of time between the collection of DNA at a crime scene and its analysis. As of January 1, 2011, there were 83,603 untested DNA samples from crime scenes that were more than 30 days old, and that number rose to 91,323 samples by December 31, 2011. The average turnaround time for violent crimes was 106 days and it was 154 days for property crimes. The National Institute of Justice was awarded $117 million in fiscal year 2012 "for a DNA analysis and capacity enhancement program" and other forensic activities; it distributed this funding in three areas: building lab capacity and reducing waiting samples; research and development; and training and technical assistance. See Mark Nelson et al., Making Sense of DNA Backlogs, 2012—Myths vs. Reality, National Institute of Justice Special Report, U.S. Department of Justice (December 2013).

10. Given the backlog in the processing of DNA evidence, should law enforcement agencies reopen cold cases that, because of older technologies, were not solvable in the past, but have a chance of being solved now? Should statutes of limitations be extended so that perpetrators of a crime can be brought to justice at some point in the future? Scott Turow fears "that the growing capacity of today's forensics to reach farther and farther into the past seems likely to undermine the law's time-ingrained notions, embodied in statutes of limitations, about how long people should be liable to criminal prosecutions." Do you agree with this sentiment? Scott Turow, Still Guilty After All These Years, The New York Times, Apr. 8, 2007, at C11.

G. POST-CONVICTION DNA TESTING

SETH AXELRAD & JULIANA RUSSO, SURVEY OF POST-CONVICTION DNA TESTING STATUTES
American Society of Law, Medicine & Ethics, 2005.

Thirty-eight states and the federal government have passed statutes specifically providing for post-conviction DNA testing of biological evidence relating to a crime for which an offender has been convicted * * *.

* * *

- Who May Apply for Post-Conviction DNA Testing?

* * *

With respect to the severity of the offense, more than half of the state statutes limit eligible convicts to felons or a subset of felons. Kentucky and Nevada represent the extreme cases, limiting applicability to capital offenders. Less than half of the states, and the federal government, include those who have been convicted for any crime. The second criterion, [requiring that the individual be in] state custody, provides a means of restricting the potential postconviction remedy to those who need it to escape or reduce their imprisonment.

* * *

- What Evidence Can Be Tested? / What Criteria Must the Evidence Meet?

All of the state statutes place some restriction on the evidence that can be subjected to the requested DNA testing. The restrictions may be minimal, as in the case of Washington (requiring only that the evidence still exists); more common, however, are requirements that the evidence was secured in relation to the crime, was maintained or stored in a manner to ensure that the evidence has not degraded or been tampered with, and/or either was not previously tested, or was previously tested, but there exists good reason for retesting.

- Is the Prosecutor Involved in the Process?

The American criminal justice system is an adversarial system; accordingly, all of the post-conviction statutes except for North Carolina and Oregon explicitly provide for prosecutorial involvement. At the minimum is the requirement of notice to the prosecution of the motion for post-conviction DNA testing, and at the maximum is Washington's requirement for prosecutorial approval of the request. A typical statute will require notice to the prosecution and afford the prosecution an opportunity to respond to the motion.

* * *

- What Are the Review Criteria for the Petition?

This section lists the criteria that the decision-maker (usually the judge) will use in reviewing the defendant's motion for post-conviction DNA testing. Thus, this section identifies the barriers that the defendant must overcome in order to persuade a court to grant his or her post-conviction motion. In general, the courts require a showing that: the identity of the perpetrator (or accomplice) was an issue at trial; the evidence to be tested is relevant to the identity of the perpetrator; the evidentiary criteria have been met; and/or exculpatory DNA results, had they been introduced at trial, likely would have resulted in a different outcome at trial.

* * *

- Who Pays for the Costs of Testing?

This section identifies the allocation of the costs of DNA testing, if present in the statutory provision. The federal Justice for All Act of 2004 exemplifies a typical provision. The statute allocates the costs of testing to the applicant, except in cases where the applicant is indigent.

* * *

- What are the Consequences if the Results Do Not Favor the Petitioner?

* * * Some statutes, like Maryland, simply deny the petition for post-conviction relief upon unfavorable test results. Others penalize the petitioner in some manner, e.g., by requiring inclusion of the petitioner's DNA profile into the DNA database. The federal statute's punitive consequences arise as a result of its requirement that the petition for post-conviction DNA test contain an assertion of actual innocence under penalty of perjury; thus, upon the receipt of unfavorable test results, the petitioner can be held in contempt, or potentially prosecuted for making false assertions.

- What are the Consequences if the Results Do Favor the Petitioner?

In the event that the test results exclude the petitioner as the source of DNA evidence, the state and federal statutes specify the subsequent procedural steps a petitioner may take to challenge his conviction. The federal statute requires the petitioner to file a motion for a new trial, which the court shall grant upon a showing of compelling evidence that the new trial would result in an acquittal. The state statutes either similarly require a motion for a new trial, or provide the court more procedural flexibility upon reception of the favorable test results. North Carolina, for example, allows the court to enter any order "that serves the interests of justice," which may include an order setting a new trial or an order vacating and setting aside the petitioner's conviction.

* * *

- Will Compensation Be Awarded if the Petitioner is Exonerated?

Missouri, Montana, and Federal Government have statutes providing for restitution for wrongfully imprisoned persons exonerated through DNA testing. The Montana statute provides educational aid to exonerated petitioners, whereas the Missouri and Federal statutes provide direct financial restitution. [There are also other state laws, such as Mass. Gen. Laws Ann. Ch. 444 § 1, that provide compensation for certain exonerated individuals regardless of the nature of the evidence used to convict them.]

NOTES AND QUESTIONS

1.   Since 1989, DNA testing has led to the exoneration of 311 persons who were wrongfully convicted. All 50 states and the District of Columbia now have laws that allow inmates to apply for postconviction DNA testing. States differ on the types of convictions for which testing is allowed: 21 states allow testing for any crime; Iowa allows testing for all felonies and some misdemeanors; 16 states allow testing for any felony; and 10 states limit testing to enumerated felonies. Alabama allows testing only for capital offenses, the District of Columbia for any crime of violence, and Maine allows testing for crimes with a minimum of a one-year sentence. National Conference of State Legislatures, Post Conviction DNA Testing, 50 State Survey, (2013), www.ncsl.org/Documents/cj/PostConvictionDNATesting.pdf. Should there be limitations on the types of convictions for which a person may seek postconviction DNA testing?

2.   Should courts require a person to raise an identity defense at trial in order to preserve a right to postconviction DNA testing? Should postconviction testing be available to those who have confessed or pled guilty? See Justin Brooks & Alexander Simpson, Blood Sugar Sex Magik: A Review of Postconviction DNA Testing Statutes and Legislative Recommendations, 59 Drake L. Rev. 799, 818 (2010–2011).

3.   Exonerations have provided insight into the potential problems in the criminal justice system. An Innocence Project study of the first 225 cases of DNA exonerations revealed that "77% involved eyewitness misidentification, 52% involved improper forensics, 16% involved informants and snitches, and 23%—almost one in four—involved false confessions or admissions." Justin Brooks & Alexander Simpson, Blood Sugar Sex Magik: A Review of Postconviction DNA Testing Statutes and Legislative Recommendations, 59 Drake L. Rev. 799, 818 (2010–2011).

DISTRICT ATTORNEY'S OFFICE FOR THE THIRD JUDICIAL DISTRICT V. OSBORNE

557 U.S. 52 (2009).

CHIEF JUSTICE ROBERTS delivered the opinion of the Court.

* * *

This lawsuit arose out of a violent crime committed 16 years ago, which has resulted in a long string of litigation in the state and federal courts. On the evening of March 22, 1993, two men driving through Anchorage, Alaska, solicited sex from a female prostitute, K. G. She agreed to perform fellatio on both men for $100 and got in their car. The three spent some time looking for a place to stop and ended up in a deserted area near Earthquake Park. When K. G. demanded payment in advance, the two men pulled out a gun and forced her to perform fellatio on the driver while the passenger penetrated her vaginally, using a blue condom she had brought. The passenger then ordered K. G. out of the car and told her to lie face-down in the snow. Fearing for her life, she refused, and the two men choked her and beat her with the gun. When K. G. tried to flee, the passenger beat her with a wooden axe handle and shot her in the head while she lay on the ground. They kicked some snow on top of her and left her for dead.

* * *

Six days later, two military police officers at Fort Richardson pulled over Dexter Jackson for flashing his headlights at another vehicle. In his car they discovered a gun (which matched the shell casing), as well as several items K. G. had been carrying the night of the attack. The car also matched the description K. G. had given to the police. Jackson admitted that he had been the driver during the rape and assault, and told the police that William Osborne had been his passenger. Other evidence also implicated Osborne. K. G. picked out his photograph (with some uncertainty) and at trial she identified Osborne as her attacker. Other witnesses testified that shortly before the crime, Osborne had called Jackson from an arcade, and then driven off with him. An axe handle similar to the one at the scene of the crime was found in Osborne's room on the military base where he lived.

The State also performed DQ Alpha testing on sperm found in the blue condom. DQ Alpha testing is a relatively inexact form of DNA testing that can clear some wrongly accused individuals, but generally cannot narrow the perpetrator down to less than 5% of the population. The semen found on the condom had a genotype that matched a blood sample taken from Osborne, but not ones from Jackson, K. G., or a third suspect named James Hunter. Osborne is black, and approximately 16% of black individuals have such a genotype. In other words, the testing ruled out Jackson and Hunter as possible sources of the semen, and also ruled out over 80% of other black individuals. The State also examined some pubic hairs found at the scene of the crime, which were not susceptible to DQ Alpha testing, but which state witnesses attested to be similar to Osborne's.

Osborne and Jackson were convicted by an Alaska jury of kidna[p]ping, assault, and sexual assault. They were acquitted of an additional count of sexual assault and of attempted murder. Finding it " 'nearly miraculous' " that K. G. had survived, the trial judge sentenced Osborne to 26 years in prison, with 5 suspended. His conviction and sentence were affirmed on appeal.

Osborne then sought postconviction relief in Alaska state court. He claimed that he had asked his attorney, Sidney Billingslea, to seek more discriminating restriction-fragment-length-polymorphism (RFLP) DNA testing during trial, and argued that she was constitutionally ineffective for not doing so. Billingslea testified that after investigation, she had concluded that further testing would do more harm than good. She planned to mount a defense of mistaken identity, and thought that the imprecision of the DQ Alpha test gave her " 'very good numbers in a mistaken identity, cross-racial identification case, where the victim was in the dark and had bad eyesight.' " [Osborne v. State, 110 P. 3d 986, 990 (Alaska App. 2005) (Osborne I)] Because she believed Osborne was guilty, " 'insisting on a more advanced . . . DNA test would have served to prove that Osborne committed the alleged crimes.' " The Alaska Court of Appeals concluded that Billingslea's decision had been strategic and rejected Osborne's claim.

[The Alaska Court of Appeals subsequently rejected Osborne's claims of both a federal and state constitutional right to post-conviction DNA testing.]

* * *

Meanwhile, Osborne had also been active in federal court, suing state officials under 42 U.S.C. § 1983. He claimed that the Due Process Clause and other constitutional provisions gave him a constitutional right to access the DNA evidence for what is known as short-tandem-repeat (STR) testing (at his own expense). * * *

On cross-motions for summary judgment after remand, the District Court concluded that "there does exist, under the unique and specific facts presented, a very limited constitutional right to the testing sought." The court relied on several factors: that the testing Osborne sought had been unavailable at trial, that the testing could be accomplished at almost no cost to the State, and that the results were likely to be material. It therefore granted summary judgment in favor of Osborne.

The Court of Appeals affirmed, relying on the prosecutorial duty to disclose exculpatory evidence recognized in Pennsylvania v. Ritchie, 480 U.S. 39 (1987), and Brady v. Maryland, 373 U.S. 83 (1963). While acknowledging that our precedents "involved only the right to pre-trial disclosure," the court concluded that the Due Process Clause also "extends the government's duty to disclose (or the defendant's right of access) to post-conviction proceedings." [Osborne v. Dist. Attorney's Office, 521 F.3d 1118, 1128 (9th Cir. Alaska, 2006).] * * *

* * *

"No State shall . . . deprive any person of life, liberty, or property, without due process of law." U.S. Const., Amdt. 14, § 1. This *Clause* imposes procedural limitations on a State's power to take away protected entitlements. Osborne argues that access to the State's evidence is a "process" needed to vindicate his right to prove himself innocent and get out of jail. Process is not an end in itself, so a necessary premise of this argument is that he has an entitlement (what our precedents call a "liberty interest") to prove his innocence even after a fair trial has proved otherwise. We must first examine this asserted liberty interest to determine what process (if any) is due.

* * *

Osborne seeks to defend the judgment on the basis of substantive due process * * *. He asks that we recognize a freestanding right to DNA evidence untethered from the liberty interests he hopes to vindicate with it. We reject the invitation and conclude, in the circumstances of this case, that there is no such substantive due process right. "As a general matter, the Court has always been reluctant to expand the concept of substantive due process because guideposts for responsible decisionmaking in this unchartered area are scarce and open-ended." Collins v. Harker Heights, 503 U.S. 115, 125 (1992). Osborne seeks access to state evidence so that he can apply new DNA-testing technology that might prove him innocent. There is no long history of such a right, and "[t]he mere novelty of such a claim is reason enough to doubt that 'substantive due process' sustains it." Reno v. Flores, 507 U.S. 292, 303 (1993).

And there are further reasons to doubt. The elected governments of the States are actively confronting the challenges DNA technology poses to our criminal justice systems and our traditional notions of finality, as well as the opportunities it affords. To suddenly constitutionalize this area would short-circuit what looks to be a prompt and considered legislative response.

* * *

Establishing a freestanding right to access DNA evidence for testing would force us to act as policymakers, and our substantive-due-process rulemaking authority would not only have to cover the right of access but a myriad of other issues. We would soon have to decide if there is a constitutional obligation to preserve forensic evidence that might later be tested. If so, for how long? Would it be different for different types of evidence? Would the State also have some obligation to gather such evidence in the first place? How much, and when? No doubt there would be a miscellany of other minor directives.

In this case, the evidence has already been gathered and preserved, but if we extend substantive due process to this area, these questions would be before us in short order, and it is hard to imagine what tools federal courts would use to answer them. At the end of the day, there is no reason to suppose that their answers to these questions would be any better than those of state courts and legislatures, and good reason to suspect the opposite. * * *

* * *

The judgment of the Court of Appeals is reversed, and the case is remanded for further proceedings consistent with this opinion.

It is so ordered.

[JUSTICE ALITO'S concurring opinion is omitted.]

JUSTICE STEVENS, with whom JUSTICE GINSBURG and JUSTICE BREYER join, and with whom JUSTICE SOUTER joins as to Part I, dissenting.

The State of Alaska possesses physical evidence that, if tested, will conclusively establish whether respondent William Osborne committed rape and attempted murder. If he did, justice has been served by his conviction and sentence. If not, Osborne has needlessly spent decades behind bars while the true culprit has not been brought to justice. The DNA test Osborne seeks is a simple one, its cost modest, and its results uniquely precise. Yet for reasons the State has been unable or unwilling to articulate, it refuses to allow Osborne to test the evidence at his own expense and to thereby ascertain the truth once and for all.

* * *

The Fourteenth Amendment provides that "[n]o State shall . . . deprive any person of life, liberty, or property, without due process of law." § 1. Our cases have frequently recognized that protected liberty interests may arise "from the Constitution itself, by reason of guarantees implicit in the word 'liberty,' . . . or it may arise from an expectation or interest created by state laws or policies." Wilkinson v. Austin, 545 U.S. 209, 221(2005). Osborne contends that he possesses a right to access DNA evidence arising from both these sources.

* * *

Osborne asserts a right to access the State's evidence that derives from the Due Process Clause itself. Whether framed as a "substantive liberty interest . . . protected through a procedural due process right" to have evidence made available for testing, or as a substantive due process right to be free of arbitrary government action, see Harvey v. Horan, 285 F.3d 298, 315, 319 (CA4 2002) (LUTTIG, J., respecting denial of rehearing en banc), the result is the same: On the record now before us, Osborne has established his entitlement to test the State's evidence.

The liberty protected by the Due Process Clause is not a creation of the Bill of Rights. The "most elemental" of the liberties protected by the Due Process Clause is "the interest in being free from physical detention by one's own government." Hamdi v. Rumsfeld, 542 U.S. 507, 529 (2004) (plurality opinion).

[JUSTICE STEVENS notes that a prisoner retains some measure of constitutionally protected liberty interests while in prison, including the "fundamental liberty of freedom from physical restraint."]

Recognition of this right draws strength from the fact that 46 States and the Federal Government have passed statutes providing access to evidence for DNA testing, and 3 additional states (including Alaska) provide similar access through court-made rules alone, see Brief for State of California et al. as Amici Curiae 3–4, n. 1, and 2; ante, at 9. These legislative developments are consistent with recent trends in legal ethics recognizing that prosecutors are obliged to disclose all forms of exculpatory evidence that come into their possession following conviction. The fact that nearly all the States have now recognized some postconviction right to DNA evidence makes it more, not less, appropriate to recognize a limited federal right to such evidence in cases where litigants are unfairly barred from obtaining relief in state court.

* * *

The majority denies that Osborne possesses a cognizable substantive due process right "under the circumstances of this case," and offers two meager reasons for its decision. First, citing a general reluctance to " 'expand the concept of substantive due process,' " ante, at 19 (quoting [Collins, 503 U.S. at 125]), the Court observes that there is no long history of postconviction access to DNA evidence. " 'The mere novelty of such a claim,' " the Court asserts, " 'is reason enough to doubt that "substantive due process" sustains it,' " ante, at 19 (quoting Reno v. Flores, 507 U.S. 292, 303 (1993)). The flaw is in the framing. Of course courts have not historically granted convicted persons access to physical evidence for STR and mtDNA testing. But, as discussed above, courts have recognized a residual substantive interest in both physical liberty and in freedom from arbitrary government action. It is Osborne's interest in those well-established liberties that justifies the Court of Appeals' decision to grant him access to the State's evidence for purposes of previously unavailable DNA testing.

The majority also asserts that this Court's recognition of a limited federal right of access to DNA evidence would be ill advised because it would "short circuit what looks to be a prompt and considered legislative response" by the States and Federal Government to the issue of access to DNA evidence. Such a decision, the majority warns, would embroil the Court in myriad policy questions best left to other branches of government. Ante, at 19–20. The majority's arguments in this respect bear close resemblance to the manner in which the Court once approached the now-venerable right to counsel for indigent defendants. Before our decision in Powell v. Alabama, 287 U.S. 45 (1932), state law alone governed the manner in which counsel was appointed for indigent

defendants. * * * When at last this Court recognized the Sixth
Amendment right to counsel for all indigent criminal defendants in
Gideon v. Wainwright, 372 U.S. 335 (1963) our decision did not impede
the ability of States to tailor their appointment processes to local needs,
nor did it unnecessarily interfere with their sovereignty. It did, however,
ensure that criminal defendants were provided with the counsel to which
they were constitutionally entitled. In the same way, a decision to
recognize a limited right of postconviction access to DNA testing would
not prevent the States from creating procedures by which litigants
request and obtain such access; it would merely ensure that States do so
in a manner that is nonarbitrary.

* * *

Osborne has demonstrated a constitutionally protected right to due
process which the State of Alaska thus far has not vindicated and which
this Court is both empowered and obliged to safeguard. On the record
before us, there is no reason to deny access to the evidence and there are
many reasons to provide it, not least of which is a fundamental concern in
ensuring that justice has been done in this case. I would affirm the
judgment of the Court of Appeals, and respectfully dissent from the
Court's refusal to do so.

[JUSTICE SOUTER'S dissenting opinion is omitted.]

NOTES AND QUESTIONS

1.   Is a right to have DNA testing postconviction analogous to the
prosecutor's duty to disclose exculpatory evidence when it is not clear that
the results of the DNA test will indeed exculpate the individual?

2.   Should there be a duty to store evidentiary items that might have
DNA on them? With the advent of DNA technologies, forensic officials who
had been pack rats were able to convict people of decades-old crimes by
applying the new techniques to stored evidence from the original crime scene
evidence. Such evidence has also been retested through efforts like the
Innocence Project, letting many innocent men go free. In fact, in 2009,
volunteer lawyers in Virginia were trained on how to contact the 881 Virginia
felons whose old cases included evidence ripe for potentially-exculpatory
genetic testing.

With such technological miracles at hand, forensic specialists became
reluctant to throw anything away. Beds, cars, clothes—who knew what new
technologies would be developed in the future to allow the crime scene
investigators to coax clues out of evidence?

The storage situation worsened in Colorado in 2008 when, after an
innocent murder suspect was freed after nine years' imprisonment, a broad
law was adopted requiring storage of every piece of evidence that might
contain DNA. It required storage for the life of the defendant of "all

reasonable and relevant evidence that may contain DNA." A recent amendment, Colorado Statutes Section 18–1–1104, made clear that an entire large item, such as a car, need not be stored if the DNA can be lifted off the item. The new law does not require retention "if DNA evidence is of such a size, bulk, or physical character as to render retention impracticable." What policies would you suggest for the storage of evidence?

III. DNA BANKS

A. CONSTITUTIONALITY OF FORENSIC DNA BANKS

JONES V. MURRAY
962 F.2d 302 (4th Cir. 1992).

NIEMEYER, J.

Section 19.2–310.2 of the Virginia Code, effective July 1, 1990, requires convicted felons to submit blood samples for DNA analysis "to determine identification characteristics specific to the person" and provides for the creation of a data bank of the information for future law enforcement purposes. Six inmates have challenged the statute's constitutionality, contending that it authorizes the involuntary extraction of blood in violation of the Fourth Amendment prohibition against unreasonable searches and seizures.

* * *

II.

The principal argument advanced by the inmates is grounded on the contention that Virginia's blood testing program violates the inmates' Fourth Amendment rights against unreasonable searches and seizures by authorizing the search of their bodies in the absence of any individualized suspicion. They argue that the general purpose of enforcing the law by improving methods of identification is not sufficient to justify testing an entire class of people merely because the recidivism rate is higher for them. They note that several classifications of persons, for example, those affected by mental disease or environmental factors, who have never before been convicted of a crime, might statistically be equally likely to commit future crimes. They contend that the district court's ruling sustaining the Virginia program is "the first instance . . . that a pure law enforcement search has ever been sustained in the absence of any individualized suspicion."

The Commonwealth of Virginia observes that if individualized suspicion must exist before any felon can be required to submit to a blood test, any meaningful DNA identification bank will be impossible. The very idea of establishing a data bank refutes the possibility of establishing individualized suspicion because the collection of the blood samples is designed to solve future cases for which no present suspicion can exist. It argues that the special needs of the government warrant application of the balancing test identified in Skinner v. Railway Labor Executives' Ass'n, 489 U.S. 602 [(1989)] and National Treasury Employees Union v. Von Raab, 489 U.S. 656 [(1989)]. When considering the minimal level of intrusion, the Commonwealth argues, demonstrably higher rates of recidivism among felons and the improved methods of identification provided by DNA analysis justify the search. They refer to studies, including one which concluded:

> Of the 108,580 persons released from prisons in 11 states in 1983, representing more than half of all released State prisoners that year, an estimated 62.5% were arrested for a felony or serious misdemeanor within 3 years. . . . Before their release from prison, the prisoners had been arrested and charged with an average of more than 12 offenses each; nearly two-thirds had been arrested at least once in the past for a violent offense; and two-thirds had previously been in jail or prison. . . . An estimated 22.7% of all prisoners were rearrested for a violent offense within 3 years of their release.

* * *

It appears to be established, at least with respect to free persons, that the bodily intrusion resulting from taking a blood sample constitutes a search within the scope of the Fourth Amendment. And in the view of the inmates, all governmental searches conducted in the context of criminal law enforcement require individualized suspicion to satisfy the Fourth Amendment's requirement of reasonableness.

We have not been made aware of any case, however, establishing a per se Fourth Amendment requirement of probable cause, or even a lesser degree of individualized suspicion, when government officials conduct a limited search for the purpose of ascertaining and recording the identity of a person who is lawfully confined to prison. This is not surprising when we consider that probable cause had already supplied the basis for bringing the person within the criminal justice system. With the person's loss of liberty upon arrest comes the loss of at least some, if not all, rights to personal privacy otherwise protected by the Fourth Amendment. Thus, persons lawfully arrested on probable cause and detained lose a right of privacy from routine searches of the cavities of their bodies and their jail cells as do convicted felons. Even probationers lose the protection of the Fourth Amendment with respect to their right to privacy against searches of their homes pursuant to an established program to ensure rehabilitation and security.

Similarly, when a suspect is arrested upon probable cause, his identification becomes a matter of legitimate state interest and he can hardly claim privacy in it. We accept this proposition because the identification of suspects is relevant not only to solving the crime for which the suspect is arrested, but also for maintaining a permanent record to solve other past and future crimes. This becomes readily apparent when we consider the universal approbation of "booking" procedures that are followed for every suspect arrested for a felony, whether or not the proof of a particular suspect's crime will involve the use of fingerprint identification. Thus a tax evader is fingerprinted just the same as is a burglar. While we do not accept even this small level of intrusion for free persons without Fourth Amendment constraint, the same protections do not hold true for those lawfully confined to the custody of the state. As with fingerprinting, therefore, we find that the Fourth Amendment does not require an additional finding of individualized suspicion before blood can be taken from incarcerated felons for the purpose of identifying them.[2]

In the absence of a requirement for individualized suspicion, assuming that the Fourth Amendment continues to apply to lawfully confined prisoners, we must nevertheless determine the reasonableness of any search. We recognize that the search effected by the taking of blood samples may be considered a greater intrusion than fingerprinting. Yet blood tests are commonplace, and the intrusion occasioned by them is "not significant." The procedure "involves virtually no risk, trauma, or pain." In *Skinner*, the Supreme Court upheld a program which required mandatory blood testing of an entire class of railway employees, albeit not for law enforcement purposes. In a similar vein, mandatory blood testing of all prisoners to detect the presence of the Human Immunodeficiency Virus, which causes Acquired Immune Deficiency Syndrome (AIDS), has been justified by the governmental interests in controlling AIDS in prison. These decisions instruct that blood testing can be reasonable under the Fourth Amendment, even with respect to free persons, where the slight intrusion is outweighed by the governmental interest advanced by the intrusion.

---

[2] Because we consider the cases which involve the Fourth Amendment rights of prison inmates to comprise a separate category of cases to which the usual per se requirement of probable cause does not apply, there is no cause to address whether the so-called "special needs" exception, relied on by the district court, applies in this case. We do, however, find support for our holding in the fact that the Supreme Court has not categorically required individualized suspicion in the case of every search which advances a law enforcement objective. Only recently it concluded that a "slight" or "minimal" intrusion caused by the short stop of an automobile at a checkpoint, although directed at a class of people without individualized suspicion, may be justified as reasonable under the Fourth Amendment by a weightier interest advanced by the search. See Michigan Dep't Of State Police v. Sitz, 496 U.S. 444 (1990) (approving use of sobriety checkpoint to deter drunk driving).

Against the minor intrusion, therefore, we weigh the government's interest in preserving a permanent identification record of convicted felons for resolving past and future crimes. It is a well recognized aspect of criminal conduct that the perpetrator will take unusual steps to conceal not only his conduct, but also his identity. Disguises used while committing a crime may be supplemented or replaced by changed names, and even changed physical features. Traditional methods of identification by photographs, historical records, and fingerprints often prove inadequate. The DNA, however, is claimed to be unique to each individual and cannot, within current scientific knowledge, be altered. The individuality of the DNA provides a dramatic new tool for the law enforcement effort to match suspects and criminal conduct. Even a suspect with altered physical features cannot escape the match that his DNA might make with a sample contained in a DNA bank, or left at the scene of a crime within samples of blood, skin, semen or hair follicles. The governmental justification for this form of identification, therefore, relies on no argument different in kind from that traditionally advanced for taking fingerprints and photographs, but with additional force because of the potentially greater precision of DNA sampling and matching methods.

Thus, in the case of convicted felons who are in custody of the Commonwealth, we find that the minor intrusion caused by the taking of a blood sample is outweighed by Virginia's interest, as stated in the statute, in determining inmates' "identification characteristics specific to the person" for improved law enforcement.

The inmates argue that the usefulness of DNA as an identification technique is largely limited to violent crimes, based upon the unlikelihood of recovering from the scene of a nonviolent crime a DNA sample from the perpetrator that is sufficient for comparison with the suspect's DNA. According to statistics presented by the inmates, there is only a remote possibility that a nonviolent offender will commit a future violent crime which will produce sufficient DNA for an identification match. These statistics indicate that 97% of the cases in which DNA evidence was used to link a defendant with a crime involved murder or rape, and further, less than 1% of all nonviolent offenders are later arrested on murder or rape charges. They contend therefore that the DNA program cannot be justified with respect to the testing of nonviolent felons.

These numbers persuasively demonstrate, given the DNA technology that is currently available, that Virginia's interest in DNA testing is significantly more compelling with regard to those felons convicted of violent crimes than those not. However, we note that the fact that fingerprints are not found at a particular crime scene does not negate the Commonwealth's interest in fingerprinting the criminal suspect when caught. There may be uses for DNA technology other than merely verifying a suspect's presence at the scene of a crime. As we have noted, a

DNA print might be used to identify a criminal suspect who has attempted to alter or conceal his or her identity. Moreover, if DNA technology becomes more common (and particularly if it is established as a reliable and judicially accepted identification tool), then it is likely that law enforcement officials will become more aware of the technology and thus more likely to make use of the DNA clues that are left as a result of crimes other than murder or rape. The effectiveness of the Commonwealth's plan, in terms of percentage, need not be high where the objective is significant and the privacy intrusion limited.

It is not for us to weigh the advantages of one method of identification over another which is selected by the Commonwealth. While greater utility for use of DNA data can be supposed when the future crime is one of violence and those crimes can statistically be related more directly to inmates now incarcerated for crimes of violence, the utility of more exact identification in all cases still justifies the minor intrusion. We therefore agree with the district court's conclusion that § 19.2–310.2 does not violate the Fourth Amendment as applied by the Fourteenth Amendment to the Commonwealth of Virginia.

* * *

MURNAGHAN, J., concurring in part and dissenting in part:

To the extent that the majority opinion upholds the Virginia DNA testing procedure as applied to violent felons, and holds that the statute qualifies as an *ex post facto* law with respect to its effect on the mandatory release of prisoners convicted prior to its effective date, I concur in the decision. But I must respectfully dissent from the majority's determination of the constitutionality of the statute as applied to prisoners convicted of non-violent crimes. Prisoners do not lose an expectation of privacy with regard to blood testing, and the Commonwealth's articulated interest in the testing of non-violent felons does not counter-balance the privacy violation involved in the procedure.

I.

* * *

Prisoners most assuredly do give up specific aspects of their reasonable expectation of privacy because of practical concerns relating to living conditions, and because of the necessities involved in ensuring prison security. However, in the present case, appellants have not forfeited their expectation of privacy with respect to blood testing, and no practical penal concern justifies the departure involved in the DNA procedure. Accordingly, the Commonwealth's DNA testing procedure should be reviewed under the standard applied to a search of any individual when such a search is not based on individualized suspicion:

the privacy interest of the prisoner in remaining free of bodily invasion should be balanced against the state interest in carrying out the search.

The majority cites the Supreme Court's opinion in Bell v. Wolfish, 441 U.S. 520 (1979), to support its sweeping conclusion about the extent of prisoners' loss of privacy rights. Although *Bell* allows for certain invasive search procedures, *Bell* does not suggest that probable cause detainees have abrogated the entire panoply of privacy protections. To the contrary, the *Bell* Court reaffirms the conclusion that privacy interests of detainees or prison inmates remain, and that these privacy interests must be balanced against the "significant and legitimate security interest of the [penal] institution."

The majority today implicitly holds that, whether violent or nonviolent, a prisoner loses a reasonable expectation of privacy which justifies the search in the present case. Citing Hudson v. Palmer, 468 U.S. 517 (1984), which held that a prisoner has no reasonable expectation of privacy in his prison cell, the majority indicates that prisoners lose the aspect of their right to privacy that protects them from routine searches. However, the majority goes a step further by applying the *Hudson* standard to the Commonwealth's DNA procedure and implicitly holding that the lack of a reasonable expectation of privacy in a prison cell extends to permit unjustified searches of bodily fluids of every felon, violent and non-violent alike.

A prisoner certainly cannot stake a claim to the kind of sanctity of dominion to a cell that a non-incarcerated individual can to a home. Moreover, the Supreme Court has indicated that there are situations in which even a private citizen's expectation of privacy diminishes, or disappears altogether. It is apparent, however, that the search involved in the present case, blood testing, violates a privacy interest that even a prisoner, living in close quarters under constant security surveillance, reasonably can expect to enjoy.

No precedential justification exists for the majority's holding that convicted felons, violent or non-violent, solely because of past criminal activity, lose the expectation that their bodily fluids will be free of unjustified search. As the Supreme Court stated in Skinner v. Railway Labor Association, 489 U.S. 602 (1989), "it is obvious that this physical invasion [a blood test] penetrating beneath the skin, infringes an expectation of privacy that society is prepared to recognize as reasonable." Although *Skinner* involved the testing of free citizens, its determination that an individual has a reasonable expectation of privacy within one's own body applies equally to prisoners, unless the prisoner's privacy right is incompatible with the objectives of incarceration.

* * *

II.

The DNA testing of felons convicted of non-violent crimes is not justified, given the limited and non-compelling state interest in including them in the testing procedure. The only state interest offered by the Commonwealth for including non-violent felons is administrative ease. I cannot conclude that the government interest in administrative ease suffices to outweigh a prisoner's expectation of privacy in not having blood withdrawn from his body when that prisoner is not significantly more likely to commit a violent crime in the future than a member of the general population.

* * *

The record supports appellants' contention that there is an extremely tenuous link connecting persons convicted of non-violent felonies to the commission of future violent crime. It, therefore, contains nothing to substantiate a theory that DNA testing of non-violent felons would assist in solution of future crimes. United States Justice Department statistics provided in the record show that only 0.4% of non-violent felons are later arrested on rape charges, and only 0.8% are later arrested on murder charges. One might assume non-violent drug offenders would be more likely to commit violent crime subsequent to release than other non-violent felons; yet, only 0.4% of them are later arrested for rape, and 0.3% for murder.

The record does not provide similar percentage statistics for the general population. It can be readily inferred that the testing of all citizens, regardless of criminal record, would create a DNA data bank with a similar statistical likelihood of solving future crime as is provided by the testing of non-violent felons. Additionally, the testing of other discrete populations, e.g., racial minorities or residents of underprivileged areas, might produce significantly better statistics than 0.4%.[4]

Lacking a significant statistical likelihood to justify the inclusion of non-violent felons, the Commonwealth is forced to justify the inclusion of these individuals based on its amorphous concern for administrative efficiency * * *. Therefore, the majority opinion, by implicitly approving the Commonwealth's stated justification, leads me to a deep, disturbing, and overriding concern that, without a proper and compelling justification, the Commonwealth may be successful in taking significant strides towards the establishment of a future police state, in which broad

---

[4] An argument can be made that there is little likelihood that a state-sponsored program to create a DNA data bank of all racial minorities could survive an equal protection challenge, but it is clear that a similar program targeted at underprivileged citizens, having a disparate impact on these same minorities, would not be subject to equal protection analysis, given the non-"suspect" nature of wealth-based classifications. San Antonio Independent School Dist. v. Rodriguez, 411 U.S. 1 (1973).

and vague concerns for administrative efficiency will serve to support substantial intrusions into the privacy of citizens.

* * *

MARYLAND V. KING
133 S.Ct. 1958 (2013).

Justice KENNEDY delivered the opinion of the Court.

In 2003 a man concealing his face and armed with a gun broke into a woman's home in Salisbury, Maryland. He raped her. The police were unable to identify or apprehend the assailant based on any detailed description or other evidence they then had, but they did obtain from the victim a sample of the perpetrator's DNA.

In 2009 Alonzo King was arrested in Wicomico County, Maryland, and charged with first- and second-degree assault for menacing a group of people with a shotgun. As part of a routine booking procedure for serious offenses, his DNA sample was taken by applying a cotton swab or filter paper—known as a buccal swab—to the inside of his cheeks. The DNA was found to match the DNA taken from the Salisbury rape victim. King was tried and convicted for the rape. Additional DNA samples were taken from him and used in the rape trial, but there seems to be no doubt that it was the DNA from the cheek sample taken at the time he was booked in 2009 that led to his first having been linked to the rape and charged with its commission.

The Court of Appeals of Maryland, on review of King's rape conviction, ruled that the DNA taken when King was booked for the 2009 charge was an unlawful seizure because obtaining and using the cheek swab was an unreasonable search of the person. It set the rape conviction aside. This Court granted certiorari and now reverses the judgment of the Maryland court.

In a divided opinion, the Maryland Court of Appeals struck down the portions of the Act authorizing collection of DNA from felony arrestees as unconstitutional. The majority concluded that a DNA swab was an unreasonable search in violation of the Fourth Amendment because King's "expectation of privacy is greater than the State's purported interest in using King's DNA to identify him." In reaching that conclusion the Maryland Court relied on the decisions of various other courts that have concluded that DNA identification of arrestees is impermissible.

Both federal and state courts have reached differing conclusions as to whether the Fourth Amendment prohibits the collection and analysis of a DNA sample from persons arrested, but not yet convicted, on felony charges. This Court granted certiorari, 568 U.S. ____ (2012), to address the question. King is the respondent here.

Although the DNA swab procedure used here presents a question the Court has not yet addressed, the framework for deciding the issue is well established. The Fourth Amendment, binding on the States by the Fourteenth Amendment, provides that "[t]he right of the people to be secure in their persons, houses, papers, and effects, against unreasonable searches and seizures, shall not be violated." It can be agreed that using a buccal swab on the inner tissues of a person's cheek in order to obtain DNA samples is a search. Virtually any "intrusio[n] into the human body," Schmerber v. California, 384 U.S. 757 (1966), will work an invasion of "'cherished personal security' that is subject to constitutional scrutiny." The Court has applied the Fourth Amendment to police efforts to draw blood, see *Schmerber, supra*; Missouri v. McNeely, 569 U.S. ____ (2013), scraping an arrestee's fingernails to obtain trace evidence, see *Cupp, supra,* and even to "a breathalyzer test, which generally requires the production of alveolar or 'deep lung' breath for chemical analysis," Skinner v. Railway Labor Executives' Assn., 489 U.S. 602 (1989).

A buccal swab is a far more gentle process than a venipuncture to draw blood. It involves but a light touch on the inside of the cheek; and although it can be deemed a search within the body of the arrestee, it requires no "surgical intrusions beneath the skin." *Winston,* 470 U.S., at 760. The fact than an intrusion is negligible is of central relevance to determining reasonableness, although it is still a search as the law defines that term.

To say that the Fourth Amendment applies here is the beginning point, not the end of the analysis. "[T]he Fourth Amendment's proper function is to constrain, not against all intrusions as such, but against intrusions which are not justified in the circumstances, or which are made in an improper manner." "As the text of the Fourth Amendment indicates, the ultimate measure of the constitutionality of a governmental search is 'reasonableness.'" In giving content to the inquiry whether an intrusion is reasonable, the Court has preferred "some quantum of individualized suspicion . . . [as] a prerequisite to a constitutional search or seizure. But the Fourth Amendment imposes no irreducible requirement of such suspicion."

In some circumstances, such as "[w]hen faced with special law enforcement needs, diminished expectations of privacy, minimal intrusions, or the like, the Court has found that certain general, or individual, circumstances may render a warrantless search or seizure reasonable." Those circumstances diminish the need for a warrant, either because "the public interest is such that neither a warrant nor probable cause is required," or because an individual is already on notice, for instance because of his employment, or the conditions of his release from government custody, that some reasonable police intrusion on his privacy is to be expected. The need for a warrant is perhaps least when the search involves no discretion that could properly be limited by the "interpo[lation of] a neutral magistrate between the citizen and the law enforcement officer." Treasury Employees v. Von Raab, 489 U.S. 656 (1989).

The legitimate government interest served by the Maryland DNA Collection Act is one that is well established: the need for law enforcement officers in a safe and accurate way to process and identify the persons and possessions they must take into custody. It is beyond dispute that "probable cause provides legal justification for arresting a person suspected of crime, and for a brief period of detention to take the administrative steps incident to arrest. . . . The validity of the search of a person incident to a lawful arrest has been regarded as settled from its first enunciation, and has remained virtually unchallenged." Even in that context, the Court has been clear that individual suspicion is not necessary, because "[t]he constitutionality of a search incident to an arrest does not depend on whether there is any indication that the person arrested possesses weapons or evidence. The fact of a lawful arrest, standing alone, authorizes a search."

Perhaps the most direct historical analogue to the DNA technology used to identify respondent is the familiar practice of fingerprinting arrestees. From the advent of this technique, courts had no trouble determining that fingerprinting was a natural part of "the administrative steps incident to arrest."

DNA identification is an advanced technique superior to fingerprinting in many ways, so much so that to insist on fingerprints as the norm would make little sense to either the forensic expert or a layperson. * * * A suspect who has changed his facial features to evade photographic identification or even one who has undertaken the more arduous task of altering his fingerprints cannot escape the revealing power of his DNA.

In sum, there can be little reason to question "the legitimate interest of the government in knowing for an absolute certainty the identity of the person arrested, in knowing whether he is wanted elsewhere, and in ensuring his identification in the event he flees prosecution."

In light of the context of a valid arrest supported by probable cause respondent's expectations of privacy were not offended by the minor intrusion of a brief swab of his cheeks. By contrast, that same context of arrest gives rise to significant state interests in identifying respondent not only so that the proper name can be attached to his charges but also so that the criminal justice system can make informed decisions concerning pretrial custody. Upon these considerations the Court concludes that DNA identification of arrestees is a reasonable search that can be considered part of a routine booking procedure. When officers make an arrest supported by probable cause to hold for a serious offense and they bring the suspect to the station to be detained in custody, taking and analyzing a cheek swab of the arrestee's DNA is, like fingerprinting and photographing, a legitimate police booking procedure that is reasonable under the Fourth Amendment.

The judgment of the Court of Appeals of Maryland is reversed.

Justice SCALIA, with whom Justice GINSBURG, Justice SOTOMAYOR, and Justice KAGAN join, dissenting.

The Fourth Amendment forbids searching a person for evidence of a crime when there is no basis for believing the person is guilty of the crime or is in possession of incriminating evidence. That prohibition is categorical and without exception; it lies at the very heart of the Fourth Amendment. Whenever this Court has allowed a suspicionless search, it has insisted upon a justifying motive apart from the investigation of crime.

It is obvious that no such noninvestigative motive exists in this case. The Court's assertion that DNA is being taken, not to solve crimes, but to *identify* those in the State's custody, taxes the credulity of the credulous. And the Court's comparison of Maryland's DNA searches to other techniques, such as fingerprinting, can seem apt only to those who know no more than today's opinion has chosen to tell them about how those DNA searches actually work.

* * *

Although there is a "closely guarded category of constitutionally permissible suspicionless searches," that has never included searches designed to serve "the normal need for law enforcement." * * * Even the common name for suspicionless searches—"special needs" searches—itself reflects that they must be justified, *always,* by concerns "other than crime detection." We have approved random drug tests of railroad employees, yes—but only because the Government's need to "regulat[e] the conduct of railroad employees to ensure safety" is distinct from "normal law enforcement."

So while the Court is correct to note that there are instances in which we have permitted searches without individualized suspicion, "[i]n none of these cases . . . did we indicate approval of a [search] whose primary purpose was to detect evidence of ordinary criminal wrongdoing." That limitation is crucial. It is only when a governmental purpose aside from crime-solving is at stake that we engage in the free-form "reasonableness" inquiry that the Court indulges at length today. To put it another way, both the legitimacy of the Court's method and the correctness of its outcome hinge entirely on the truth of a single proposition: that the primary purpose of these DNA searches is something other than simply discovering evidence of criminal wrongdoing. That proposition is wrong.

It is on the fingerprinting of arrestees * * * that the Court relies most heavily. The Court does not actually say whether it believes that taking a person's fingerprints is a Fourth Amendment search, and our cases provide no ready answer to that question. Even assuming so, however, law enforcement's post-arrest use of fingerprints could not be more different from its post-arrest use of DNA. Fingerprints of arrestees are taken primarily to identify them (though that process sometimes solves crimes); the DNA of arrestees is taken to solve crimes (and nothing else). Contrast CODIS, the FBI's nationwide DNA database, with IAFIS, the FBI's Integrated Automated Fingerprint Identification System.

Fingerprints	DNA Samples
The "average response time for an electronic criminal fingerprint submission is about 27 minutes." *IAFIS*.	DNA analysis can take months—far too long to be useful for identifying someone.
IAFIS includes detailed identification information, including "criminal histories; mug shots; scars and tattoo photos; physical characteristics like height, weight, and hair and eye color."	CODIS contains "[n]o names or other personal identifiers of the offenders, arrestees, or detainees." See CODIS and NDIS Fact Sheet.
"Latent prints" recovered from crime scenes are not systematically compared against the database of known fingerprints, since that requires further forensic work.	The entire *point* of the DNA database is to check crime scene evidence against the profiles of arrestees and convicts as they come in.

* * *

Today, it can fairly be said that fingerprints really are used to identify people—so well, in fact, that there would be no need for the expense of a separate, wholly redundant DNA confirmation of the same information. What DNA adds—what makes it a valuable weapon in the law-enforcement arsenal—is the ability to solve unsolved crimes, by matching old crime-scene evidence against the profiles of people whose identities are already known. That is what was going on when King's DNA was taken, and we should not disguise the fact. Solving unsolved crimes is a noble objective, but it occupies a lower place in the American pantheon of noble objectives than the protection of our people from suspicionless law-enforcement searches. The Fourth Amendment must prevail.

* * *

The most regrettable aspect of the suspicionless search that occurred here is that it proved to be quite unnecessary. All parties concede that it would have been entirely permissible, as far as the Fourth Amendment is concerned, for Maryland to take a sample of King's DNA as a consequence of his conviction for second-degree assault. So the ironic result of the Court's error is this: The only arrestees to whom the outcome here will ever make a difference are those who *have been acquitted* of the crime of arrest (so that their DNA could not have been taken upon conviction). In other words, this Act manages to burden uniquely the sole group for whom the Fourth Amendment's protections ought to be most jealously guarded: people who are innocent of the State's accusations.

Today's judgment will, to be sure, have the beneficial effect of solving more crimes; then again, so would the taking of DNA samples from anyone who flies on an airplane (surely the Transportation Security Administration needs to know the "identity" of the flying public), applies for a driver's license, or attends a public school. Perhaps the construction of such a genetic panopticon is wise. But I doubt that the proud men who wrote the charter of our liberties would have been so eager to open their mouths for royal inspection.

I therefore dissent, and hope that today's incursion upon the Fourth Amendment, like an earlier one, will some day be repudiated.

* * *

STATE V. MEDINA
102 A.3d 661 (Vt. 2014).

DOOLEY, J.

1. Defendants in these consolidated cases challenge as unconstitutional a recent amendment to Vermont's DNA-database statute that, as of July 1, 2011, mandates warrantless, suspicionless DNA collection and analysis from anyone arraigned for a felony after a determination of probable cause. 20 V.S.A. § 1933(a)(2). All five of the trial courts in these cases found that the amendment authorizes unconstitutional searches and seizures, either under the Vermont Constitution, Chapter I, Article 11, or under the Fourth Amendment to the U.S. Constitution, or both. We affirm, addressing only the compliance of the statute with the requirements of Article 11 of the Vermont Constitution.

2. We repeat at the outset that our holding today pertains only to the Vermont Constitution and not to the U.S. Constitution. After the trial courts in these cases issued their opinions addressing both constitutions, the U.S. Supreme Court decided that a similar Maryland statute—one that authorized warrantless, suspicionless DNA collection from persons arrested for violent crimes or burglary—is constitutional under the Fourth Amendment. Maryland v. King, ___ U.S. ___, ___, 133 S.Ct. 1958, 1980, 186 L.Ed.2d 1 (2013). We delayed our ruling in these cases to consider the import of *King* and to allow additional briefing on the

matter. Having done so, we recognize that there are two possible bases to differentiate this case from *King:* (1) the Vermont statute sufficiently differs from the Maryland statute involved in *King* to produce a different result under the Fourth Amendment; and (2) the heightened standards and requirements of Article 11 of the Vermont Constitution compel a different result. * * *

I.

4. As an initial matter, Vermont's statutory scheme creates both a DNA data bank, which contains the DNA samples, and a DNA database, which contains the DNA records (also known as "profiles") derived from the DNA samples. 20 V.S.A. §§ 1932(10)–(11), 1938(c)–(d).

* * *

II.

12. Article 11 of the Vermont Constitution protects against unlawful searches and seizures. Vt. Const. ch. I, art. 11. We have previously determined that the DNA sampling mandated by § 1933 constitutes two distinct searches under Article 11: "The initial taking of the DNA sample, either by blood draw or by buccal swab, and the subsequent analysis, storage, and searching of the DNA profile are independent intrusions upon personal security that merit scrutiny under Article 11."

13. Article 11 states as follows:

That the people have a right to hold themselves, their houses, papers, and possessions, free from search or seizure; and therefore warrants, without oath or affirmation first made, affording sufficient foundation for them, and whereby by any officer or messenger may be commanded or required to search suspected places, or to seize any person or persons, his, her or their property, not particularly described, are contrary to that right, and ought not to be granted.

Vt. Const. ch. I, art. 11. Article 11 thus requires both a "warrant" and "oath or affirmation . . . affording sufficient foundation"—also known as probable cause. "The language of Article Eleven does not expressly limit its protection to 'unreasonable' searches and seizures as does the Fourth Amendment to the United States Constitution. This Court, however, has consistently interpreted Article Eleven as importing the 'reasonableness' criterion of the Fourth Amendment."

* * *

III.

* * *

33. The State urges us to deny the constitutional challenge based on the rationale of *King*—that the DNA sample requirement is part of a search incident to an arrest, and more particularly a booking search, and is constitutionally indistinguishable from a fingerprint requirement. Instead, for three main reasons, we reject that *King*'s analysis controls whether the Vermont statute complies with Article 11. The third reason—the difference between the requirements of Article 11 and the Fourth Amendment—is the fundamental one, but the first two provide important context for that analysis.

A.

34. First, the Maryland statute challenged and upheld in *King* is triggered by arrest, and the Court's rationale is based on the right of law enforcement officers to search incident to an arrest, particularly where the alleged criminal will be incarcerated pending trial. *King,* ___ U.S. at ___, 133 S.Ct. at 1970–71. Thus, the Court emphasizes the need to identify accurately the person who is being arrested and charged with a crime; to know that person's history; to know the risks the person presents for facility staff, other detainees and the arrested person; to ensure the arrestee will appear for trial; and to assess the danger the arrestee presents to the community. *Id.* at ___, 133 S.Ct. at 1971–73. The Vermont statute is triggered by the judicial finding of probable cause "at arraignment" for a felony, a determination that normally follows the defendant being brought to court and the preparation of an information. 20 V.S.A. § 1933(a)(2); see V.R.Cr.P. 5(c). The defendant may never be arrested, and even if arrested, may have been released from pretrial detention. Not surprisingly, identification of arrested persons is not included in the stated purposes for the Vermont DNA-collection law. See 20 V.S.A. § 1931. * * *

35. The mismatch between the triggers in the Maryland and Vermont laws means that the Supreme Court's rationale in *King* applies to only some of the defendants covered by Vermont's statute. Further, limitations contained in the Vermont law—the requirement of a judicial probable-cause determination, the limitation to felonies and the expungement of the DNA evidence where defendant is not convicted—are insignificant under the Supreme Court decision.

B.

36. Second, identification of the arrestee, even if the defendant is arrested and continued in pretrial detention, is tangentially accomplished by post-arraignment DNA collection and analysis. The current system of

photographs and fingerprints fully responds to the need for identification of the defendant.

* * *

C.

41. The third and most important reason to reject the *King* analysis is that it is inconsistent with precedents defining the underlying policies of Article 11.

* * *

44. We find a broad warrantless-search authorization, under the theory that it is a search incident to an arrest, to be inconsistent with the requirements of Article 11 as we have developed them. To the extent we have recognized the validity of a warrantless search incident to an arrest, it has been in cases where exigent circumstances were present. While it is possible that the fruits of a DNA search will produce information bearing on conditions of release or confinement with respect to a particular defendant, that possibility alone is insufficient to justify a warrantless DNA search of every defendant, with no distinction among those who will be searched.

45. In reaching this conclusion, we recognize that we have never held that a warrantless booking search of a detainee's person or property is inconsistent with Article 11 or that routine fingerprinting of arrestees is prohibited by Article 11. However we decide the validity of these routine practices under Article 11, they do not justify the DNA sample capture involved here. We do not equate a procedure that takes a visible image of the surface of the skin of a finger with the capture of intimate bodily fluids, even if the method of doing so is speedy and painless. More important, despite the occasional usefulness of DNA samples for ordinary identification as described in *King,* the real functionality, and statutory purpose, is to solve open criminal cases or ones that may occur in the future. While part of this functionality may respond to a special need as we held in *Martin,* it is far afield from the immediate concern for the protection of arresting officers or the destruction of evidence, the concerns underlying our search-incident-to-arrest doctrine. The real expansion of warrantless search power in *King* is "its reimagination of the idea of 'identity' to include criminal history and other information." E. Murphy, License, Registration, Cheek Swab: DNA Testing and the Divided Court, 127 Harv. L.Rev. 161, 177 (2013). Despite the assurances of the Court in *King,* it is difficult to see any limit on what information may be gathered about an arrestee and the effect of that information gathering on the decision whether to arrest.

* * *

63. The marginal weight of the State's interest in DNA collection at the point of arraignment, balanced against the weight of the privacy interest retained by arraignees prior to conviction, persuades us to hold that 20 V.S.A. § 1933(a)(2), and associated sections, which expand the DNA-sample requirement to defendants charged with qualifying crimes for which probable cause is found, violate Chapter I, Article 11 of the Vermont Constitution.

Affirmed.

KAEMMERLING V. LAPPIN
553 F.3d 669 (D.C. Cir. 2008).

SENTELLE, C.J.

Russell Kaemmerling, a federal prisoner, appeals from the district court's dismissal of his action seeking to enjoin application of the DNA Analysis Backlog Elimination Act of 2000 ("DNA Act" or "the Act"), 42 U.S.C. §§ 14135–14135e. Kaemmerling alleged that the Act violated his rights under the Religious Freedom Restoration Act ("RFRA"), 42 U.S.C. §§ 2000bb–2000bb–4, and the First, Fourth, and Fifth Amendments of the United States Constitution. * * * [W]e * * * affirm the dismissal of the case because his complaint fails to state a claim.

I

* * *

Kaemmerling was convicted of conspiring to commit wire fraud, a felony offense, and is currently incarcerated at the Federal Correctional Institution in Seagoville, Texas. Because he has committed a qualifying offense, the DNA Act requires the [Federal Bureau of Prisons (BOP)] to take a fluid or tissue sample from Kaemmerling for DNA analysis and inclusion in the CODIS. * * *

* * *

III

* * * Kaemmerling's complaint alleges violations of his rights under the RFRA and the First, Fourth, and Fifth Amendments. After thoroughly considering each of these challenges, we conclude that none of them state a claim upon which relief can be granted.

A

We begin with Kaemmerling's religious claim, which fails to allege a violation of the Free Exercise Clause. Kaemmerling contends that mandatory collection and analysis of his DNA under the DNA Act burdens the free exercise of his religious belief that "DNA sampling, collection and storage" "defile[s] God's temple." Even assuming this is true, it does not rise to the level of a constitutional violation. The right of free exercise protected by the First Amendment "does not relieve an individual of the obligation to comply with a valid and neutral law of general applicability on the ground that the law proscribes (or prescribes) conduct that his religion prescribes (or proscribes)." Kaemmerling does not suggest that the DNA Act is not, in theory or practice, a religion-neutral, generally applicable law, therefore he alleges no Free Exercise violation, even if the Act incidentally affects religiously motivated action.

B

But the First Amendment is not the only potential refuge for Kaemmerling's religious claim * * *. The RFRA prohibits the federal government from "substantially burden[ing]" a person's exercise of religion even if the burden results from a rule of general applicability unless the government can demonstrate that "application of the burden to the person—(1) is in furtherance of a compelling governmental interest; and (2) is the least restrictive means of furthering that compelling governmental interest." Congress instructs us that, in analyzing a claim under the RFRA, we must return to "the compelling interest test as set forth in Sherbert v. Verner and Wisconsin v. Yoder."

1

To apply this test, we first must determine if Kaemmerling alleges a substantial burden on his religious exercise. The RFRA defines "religious exercise" to include "any exercise of religion, whether or not compelled by, or central to, a system of religious belief." A litigant's claimed beliefs "must be sincere and the practice[ ] at issue must be of a religious nature." Because the burdened practice need not be compelled by the adherent's religion to merit statutory protection, we focus not on the centrality of the particular activity to the adherent's religion but rather on whether the adherent's sincere religious exercise is substantially burdened. A substantial burden exists when government action puts "substantial pressure on an adherent to modify his behavior and to violate his beliefs[.]" * * * An inconsequential or *de minimis* burden on religious practice does not rise to this level, nor does a burden on activity unimportant to the adherent's religious scheme.

In his complaint, Kaemmerling alleges that it is his sincere religious belief that DNA is "a foundational aspect . . . of God's creative work" and that "DNA sampling, collection and storage with no clear limitations of use, merely to satisfy the broadly overreaching efforts of secular authorities, politicians and their representatives" "defile[s] God's temple, as represented by one's mortal body, filled with the Holy Spirit." His complaint further alleges harms arising from government possession and storage of his DNA profile, including the potential that he could become an unwilling participant in future activities that violate his religious beliefs—including cloning experiments and stem-cell research—and use of his DNA profile by the anti-Christ, who according to Kaemmerling's religious beliefs will in the future rule the world and "make war against the saints," "forc[ing] everyone . . . to receive a mark . . . which is the . . . number of his name."

* * * Kaemmerling makes abundantly clear that he does not challenge the collection of any particular DNA carrier—such as blood, saliva, skin, or hair—but rather that, regardless of the medium by which the government acquires access to his DNA, he objects to the government collecting his DNA information from any fluid or tissue sample they may recover. At oral argument, counsel emphasized that Kaemmerling objects to any collection of his DNA profile at all, even collecting DNA information from hair and skin that he naturally shed onto his clothes then turned over to prison officials for washing. * * * His objection to "DNA sampling and collection," then, must be a more specific objection to collection of the DNA information contained within any sample. It is not penetrating the body or collecting bodily material that Kaemmerling alleges violates his beliefs but rather collecting the "building block of life" specifically. Given these representations, we understand Kaemmerling's objection to "DNA sampling and collection" not to be an objection to the BOP collecting any bodily specimen that contains DNA material such as blood, saliva, skin, or hair, but rather an objection to the government extracting DNA information from the specimen.

* * * [W]e conclude that Kaemmerling does not allege facts sufficient to state a substantial burden on his religious exercise because he cannot identify any "exercise" which is the subject of the burden to which he objects. The extraction and storage of DNA information are entirely activities of the FBI, in which Kaemmerling plays no role and which occur after the BOP has taken his fluid or tissue sample (to which he does not object). The government's extraction, analysis, and storage of Kaemmerling's DNA information does not call for Kaemmerling to modify his religious behavior in any way[.] * * *

Kaemmerling alleges no religious observance that the DNA Act impedes, or acts in violation of his religious beliefs that it pressures him to perform. Religious exercise necessarily involves an action or practice * * *. Kaemmerling * * * alleges that the DNA Act's requirement that the federal government collect and store his DNA information requires the government to act in ways that violate his religious beliefs, but he suggests no way in which these governmental acts pressure him to modify his own behavior in any way that would violate his beliefs.

Nor does the criminal penalty for "fail[ure] to cooperate[ ]" in the collection of "a tissue, fluid, or other bodily sample . . . on which a DNA analysis can be carried out[ ]" substantially burden Kaemmerling's exercise of religion. He objects only to the collection of the DNA information from his tissue or fluid sample, a process the criminal statute does not address, and he does not allege that his religion requires him not to cooperate with collection of a fluid or tissue sample. Moreover, he alleges that even "involuntary and/or forced collection" of his DNA would "violate[ ] [his] convictions." The criminal statute is therefore no inducement for Kaemmerling to cooperate and potentially violate his beliefs, because he alleges that collection of his DNA sample would violate his convictions whether or not he acquiesces in the process. Thus, Kaemmerling does not allege that he is put to a choice like the plaintiffs in *Yoder*, between criminal sanction and personally violating his own religious beliefs.

* * *

To the extent that Kaemmerling challenges storage of his DNA profile or retention of the DNA sample itself based on fear of specific future misuses that would conflict with his religious beliefs, we emphasize that we must consider the statute as it exists and is applied today, complete with its protections against misuse, and we cannot pass on hypothetical future harms.

2

Even if Kaemmerling did allege a substantial burden on his exercise of religion, his complaint would still fail to state a claim for relief because the burden "is in furtherance of a compelling governmental interest" and "is the least restrictive means of furthering that . . . interest," satisfying the RFRA exception.

The DNA Act serves the compelling governmental interest in accurately and expeditiously solving past and future crimes in order to protect the public and ensure conviction of the guilty and exoneration of the innocent.

Fundamental to the Act is the government's compelling interest in accurately identifying convicted offenders. DNA profiling furthers this interest in a way no other identifying feature can, because DNA is unique to each individual (excepting identical twins) and cannot, within current scientific knowledge, be altered or disguised.

* * *

C

Kaemmerling's complaint also alleges violations of his Fifth Amendment rights to equal protection and against self-incrimination and his Fourth Amendment right to be free from unreasonable searches and seizures. [The court held that collecting Kaemmerling's DNA did not violate his Fifth Amendment or Fourth Amendment rights.]

* * *

IV

For the foregoing reasons, we conclude that Kaemmerling's complaint fails to state a claim upon which relief can be granted and therefore should be dismissed. * * *

B. POLICY ISSUES IN FORENSIC DNA BANKS

MARK A. ROTHSTEIN & SANDRA CARNAHAN, LEGAL AND POLICY ISSUES IN EXPANDING THE SCOPE OF LAW ENFORCEMENT DNA DATA BANKS
67 Brooklyn L. Rev. 127 (2001).

The DNA data bank statutes have been challenged on several federal and state constitutional grounds. State constitutional arguments generally have tracked the federal arguments and neither have met with any success.

* * *

The most frequently raised argument, and the most substantial one, is that obtaining a DNA sample and using the genetic information derived from the sample constitutes an unreasonable search and seizure. The Fourth Amendment of the United States Constitution prohibits unreasonable searches and seizures, and applies to the states via the Fourteenth Amendment. Although nonconsensual searches conducted outside the judicial process are per se unreasonable, nothing in the Fourth Amendment expressly prohibits government searches without a warrant. The Fourth Amendment prohibits only searches that are unreasonable. The Supreme Court has interpreted the Fourth Amendment as establishing rules and presumptions that limit the government's ability to intrude upon matters of personal privacy.

* * *

Taking fingerprints or photographs upon arrest has not been held to violate the Fourth Amendment. Under the same reasoning, one could argue that taking DNA in a non-intrusive manner solely for identification purposes most likely would not violate the Fourth Amendment. Several courts bolster this point by focusing on the reduced expectation of privacy an offender has in his or her identity.

* * *

More recently, in Ferguson v. City of Charleston, [532 U.S. 67 (2001)] the Supreme Court applied the [City of Indianapolis v.] Edmond[, 531 U.S. 32 (2000)] "primary purpose test" to a case described by the lower court as a "special needs" case. In Ferguson, a state university hospital tested the urine of certain of its obstetrical patients suspected of drug use and notified police of positive drug screens. The hospital conducted the drug tests in accordance with a hospital policy developed in conjunction with law enforcement officials. Maternity patients arrested after testing positive for cocaine challenged the hospital's policy, claiming the drug tests were an unconstitutional search under the Fourth Amendment. The hospital policy provided for, among other things, a chain of custody for the urine sample so it could be used in later prosecutions, a range of possible criminal charges, and police notification and patient arrest after a positive test. The city argued that the hospital policy met the special needs exception to the Fourth Amendment's warrant requirement because the hospital had a need to facilitate the mother's drug treatment, and to protect the mother and unborn child—a need the hospital claimed was distinct from the normal needs of law enforcement.

The Supreme Court held that the hospital policy violated the Fourth Amendment. The Court noted the extensive involvement of police and prosecutors throughout the development of the policy and it held that, although the ultimate goal of the hospital policy may have been to get the women off drugs and into a substance abuse program for the benefit of both mother and baby, the policy was unconstitutional because "the immediate objective of the searches was to generate evidence for *law enforcement purposes. . . .*" The Court said that "virtually any nonconsensual suspicionless search could be immunized under the special needs doctrine by defining the search solely in terms of its ultimate, rather than immediate, purpose." The Court distinguished its other special needs cases, which had legitimate civil objectives, and did not involve the extensive entanglement of law enforcement as did this case.

* * *

A broad, fingerprint-like identification exception would ignore the fundamental differences between DNA and fingerprints. A fingerprint reveals only unique patterns of loops and whorls. In contrast, a DNA sample is the information-containing blueprint of human life, revealing one's genetic predisposition to disease, physical and mental characteristics, and a host of other private facts not evident to the public. Unlike fingerprint analysis, DNA analysis does not necessarily end with a DNA identification profile. Typical law enforcement practice today is to retain the subject's DNA sample indefinitely on the chance that technological advancements might require re-testing of the samples. Indefinite sample retention increases the opportunity for misuse or abuse of the samples, and the intrusion on the privacy of individuals providing the identifiable samples. Moreover, many state statutes allow access to the samples for undefined law enforcement purposes and humanitarian identification purposes, or authorize the use of samples for assisting medical research or to support identification research and protocol development. No statutes provide for the informed consent of the DNA donors prior to conducting such research. Unlike the laboratory analysis of fingerprints, the Supreme Court has recognized that a laboratory analysis of blood and other bodily fluids constitutes a "second search" subject to the Fourth Amendment's reasonableness requirement. Thus, any reasonableness determination ought to include an analysis of the use that law enforcement authorities intend to make of the DNA sample.

SETH AXELRAD, USE OF FORENSIC DNA DATABASE INFORMATION FOR MEDICAL OR GENETIC RESEARCH
American Society of Law, Medicine & Ethics (2005).

The state legislatures in all 50 states established DNA databases in order to aid and enhance law enforcement. Alabama's statute declares, "[T]he creation and establishment of a statewide DNA database is the most reasonable and certain method or means to rapidly identify repeat or habitually dangerous criminals." Ala. Code § 36–18–20(g). The state statutes also recognize, however, that the criminals' DNA information can be used for other purposes, including for medical and genetic research.

Eight states—Indiana, Rhode Island, South Dakota, Texas, Utah, Vermont, Washington, and Wyoming—expressly prohibit the use of the DNA database to obtain information on human physical traits, predisposition to disease, or medical or genetic disorders. Alabama, on the other hand, explicitly authorizes the use of DNA information for medical research, and is the only state to do so. Ala. Code §§ 36–18–20 and 36–18–31.

Michigan authorizes use of anonymous database information for an "academic" or "research" purpose, although it is unclear from the statutory language whether the state legislature meant to include medical or genetic research as an authorized use of database information. Mich. Comp. Laws Ann. § 28.176. The remaining 40 state statutes are either silent on this issue (4), or they neither expressly authorize nor prohibit such research (36).

Thus, with regard to most state DNA database statutes, the issue of the use of database information for medical or genetic research is not directly addressed. An indirect answer to the question of research uses may be gleaned from those statutes which provide a list of "authorized uses." For example, Alaska limits use of the DNA database "only for (1) providing DNA or other blood grouping tests for identification analysis; (2) criminal investigations, prosecutions, and identification analysis; (3) statistical blind analysis; (4) improving the operation of the system; or (5) exoneration of the innocent." Alaska Stat. § 41.41.035(f). This exclusive list does not include medical or genetic research and, presumably, such research uses would violate the statute. Therefore, by examining the "authorized uses" provisions of the statutes, one may get a clearer picture of how most US states regulate research use of database information. Furthermore, where the authorized uses apparently exclude research use, the states also may deter the dissemination of DNA information to researchers by criminalizing the disclosure of database information to unauthorized persons. Thirty states currently criminalize such disclosures.

NOTES AND QUESTIONS

1.   Should crime scene DNA be analyzed—and forensic DNA bank samples be analyzed—to attempt to ascertain the race of the perpetrator? What about analyzing the DNA for specific physical characteristics? "Determining that a DNA sample was left by a person with red hair, dark skin pigment, straight hair, baldness, or color blindness may be practical soon, if not already." National Commission on the Future of DNA Evidence, The Future of Forensic DNA Testing: Predictions of the Research and Development Working Group 13–20, 46–61 (U.S. Department of Justice, Washington, D.C., Nov. 2000).

In a 2011 study, researchers found that DNA analysis of only about 30–35 single nucleotide polymorphisms (SNPs) "can provide significant information on the pigmentation and ancestry of an individual." Katherine Butler et al., Molecular "Eyewitness": Forensic Prediction of Phenotype and Ancestry, 3 Forensic Science International: Genetics Supplement Series e498–e499 (2011). Butler's study of SNPs used self-reports from volunteers regarding their ancestry and phenotype. It also used spectrophotometry to measure skin pigmentation. How should the problems of quantifying race and ancestry affect the use of these analysis techniques in investigations? What precautions should be taken to address potential problems of standardization and accuracy?

In 2004, this type of DNA testing helped law enforcement solve a series of rapes and murders in Louisiana. The police were relying on witness testimony and were searching for a white male. But a product called "DNA Witness" predicted that the perpetrator was a light-skinned black man. This new information redirected the search and led to the capture and conviction of Derrick Todd Lee. Duana Fullwiley, Can DNA "Witness" Race?: Forensic Use of an Imperfect Ancestry Testing Technology, 21 Genewatch No. 3–4, 2008, at 12.

Various arguments are advanced for using race, ancestry, or phenotype information in the forensic context including that it can lead to a swifter and more efficient investigation. Race is already used ubiquitously in suspect descriptions. Testing can serve to confirm or contradict eyewitness accounts, which are often unreliable. Using a DNA-based description of a phenotype as a profile could help alleviate racial bias in the investigation by providing potentially more objective information to guide police searches. Proponents of the use of racial DNA profiling also say that we do not have a constitutional privacy interest in DNA abandoned at a crime scene; and further, the type of information needed to identify someone is not highly sensitive since it generally constitutes observable traits—eye, hair, and skin color. They argue that we can mitigate any privacy risks further by limiting testing and reporting to visible characteristics.

Despite its potential to aid in an investigation, serious issues arise regarding the use of this technology to predict race. Since race does not correlate to a gene or allele, any testing that purports to predict race necessarily incorporates assumptions, inferences, and cultural biases. It also reinforces the idea that race is a biological reality. Pilar Ossorio notes that even if testing proves sufficiently accurate, testing could be used to justify law enforcement's use of extreme and "intrusive search methods, such as DNA dragnets" when testing reveals a suspect who is a racial minority. Using genetics to bolster definitions of race inaccurately and inappropriately increases our cultural linkage of crime and race, regardless of the race of suspects. Pilar Ossorio, About Face: Forensic Genetic Testing for Race and Visible Traits, 34 J. L. Med. & Ethics 277 (2006).

Research suggests that race and crime are highly linked in people's minds; in particular, they show that mention of crime "can trigger images of black people in one's mind." There is also evidence that the linkage of a race to a suspect, even where the suspect is identified as white or Caucasian, will increase racist attitudes. A study of public health messages showed that racist attitudes increased where these messages mentioned a person's race, either white or black, in the messages, even if the content was not negative. Pilar Ossorio, About Face: Forensic Genetic Testing for Race and Visible Traits, 34 J. L. Med. & Ethics 277, 286 (2006). Given this potential to perpetuate racial bias, should these tests be used? Would the issue be resolved by reporting results of DNA analysis both to law enforcement and the public in terms of a specific, narrow phenotype rather than race?

2.   One-fifth of the genetic profiles in the DNA database in Britain are tied to individuals who have no criminal records. The House of Commons raised concerns about the fact that the genetic information of 42% of black males and 27% of the total population of black individuals in Britain are accounted for in a DNA database, while only 6% of white individuals are in the database. Are similar concerns appropriate in the U.S.? According to Hank Greely, 12% of the United States population is African American, while 40% of the genetic profiles in the federal database belong to African-American individuals. Solomon Moore, F.B.I. and States Vastly Expanding Databases of DNA, The New York Times, Apr. 19, 2009, at 1.

3.   Discuss each of the following policies that have been recommended by Rothstein and Carnahan:

a)   *DNA to be analyzed*—Only non-coding regions of DNA should be used for analysis, thereby ensuring that the only possible use of the DNA analysis is identification.

b) *Statistical and Reporting Issues*—All statistical methodologies used for determining a match between a crime scene or other sample and a DNA profile in the data bank should adhere to the latest scientific principles.

c) *Destruction of samples*—Law enforcement officials, including the FBI, favor retaining samples indefinitely for quality assurance and to re-type the samples in the event of changing technology. Twenty-nine state laws either authorize or require that agencies retain samples after analysis; only one state (Wisconsin) requires the destruction of samples, and no samples have actually been destroyed. The retention of samples, however, even under conditions of stringent security, raises concerns among the public that the samples could be re-analyzed for purposes other than identification. Therefore, samples should be destroyed immediately after analysis.

d) *Access to data bank*—Access to the data banks should be limited to law enforcement personnel, and data banks should not be used for any purpose other than identification, including research.

e) *Scope of data bank*—DNA data banks should be limited to DNA obtained from individuals convicted of violent sex offenses and other violent felonies.

What are the pros and cons of each recommendation? What are the pros and cons of retaining the printout of the DNA forensic tests instead of the samples themselves?

4. Should genetic databases be established in which all people are tested at birth? Will genetic identification someday be as common as fingerprint identification and Social Security cards? Some people argue that creating a population-wide database would be more fair than the current database in which people of color are overrepresented. In contrast, Rothstein and Talbott argue that a nationwide DNA database requiring submission by everyone, criminals and non-criminals alike, could pose a serious threat to fundamental civil liberties. They argue that once everyone's genetic information is in law enforcement's possession, it will be difficult to prevent other more dangerous uses of the information by the government. They reiterate Justice Douglas's concern in Osborn v. United States that "[t]aken individually, each step may be of little consequence. But when viewed as a whole, there begins to emerge a society quite unlike any we have seen—a society in which government may intrude into the secret regions of man's life at will."

For Rothstein and Talbott, the social costs outweigh the possibility that increasing the scope of DNA banks will increase law enforcement's ability to capture criminals and prevent future crime. "Our concern is not that expanded DNA databases would transform our country into a 'nation of suspects.' Our concern is that we would become a nation with unfettered police powers." Mark A. Rothstein & Meghan K. Talbott, The Expanding Use of DNA in Law Enforcement: What Role for Privacy?, 34 J. L. Med. & Ethics 153–164 (2006).

5.   If a suspect cannot be located, should police have the right to take DNA from the suspect's mother or sibling since the mitochondrial DNA from these individuals will be virtually identical to that of the suspect?

6.   Newborns are screened for a variety of diseases, and hospitals may keep samples of newborn blood for years. In 1997, Australian police obtained a search warrant allowing them to seize children's newborn screening cards from the hospital after the mother refused to let her children undergo blood tests in an incest case. The test results helped lead to a successful conviction. At the time, there were no laws protecting the database.

Public concern that participation in the newborn screening public health program would decrease if the samples were used for forensic purposes led the Western Australia Health Department to adopt a policy requiring the cards to be destroyed after two years. Other Australian states, including New South Wales and Victoria, have subsequently adopted policies that limit police access to newborn screening blood samples. The New South Wales policy limits access to samples suspected to come from a victim of a crime taken from a suspected crime scene. The police are required to make a reasonable effort to contact the next of kin or a parent to obtain consent except when doing so would be impracticable or would compromise an ongoing investigation. The Victoria policy requires specific court authority through a court order. Department of Human Services, Victoria, Australia Victorian Newborn Screening Review Committee Final Report for the Minister of Health—Supplementary Report of the Victorian Privacy Commissioner, (Aug. 2006). Should police have access to newborn blood for use in criminal investigations?

7.   In Friedman v. Boucher, the Ninth Circuit found that law enforcement agents violated a clearly established right against unreasonable search and seizure when they forcibly swabbed the inside of the mouth of a detainee to obtain a DNA sample. 580 F.3d 847 (9th Cir. 2009). Friedman was an ex-convict who had pled guilty to sexual intercourse without consent in 1980 and had completed his sentence in 2001. In March 2003, Detective Boucher asked Friedman, who was then detained pending prosecution for an unrelated charge, for a DNA sample to aid in the investigation of a cold case. Friedman refused and Boucher forcibly swabbed the inside of Friedman's mouth. The court found that "[t]he officer did not have a warrant or a court order authorizing the taking of the sample, nor was Freidman under any suspicion of a crime for which a DNA sample might be justified. The extraction occurred simply because the deputy district attorney wanted to put Friedman's DNA sample in a cold case data bank."

Boucher argued, among other things, that the search was "reasonable" because "pre-trial detainees have limited privacy rights that must yield to the desires of law enforcement to collect DNA samples for use in law enforcement databases." The court rejected this argument, finding that courts have traditionally limited administrative searches at detention facilities to those related to security concerns. Moreover, the court distinguished this search from previous cases that had upheld state laws requiring convicted felons that are currently under state supervision to submit DNA samples for use in a DNA bank. Friedman was not under state supervision and the detective's purpose of gathering human tissue for a law enforcement databank was in no way related to facility security. The court also concluded that "no reasonable detective or prosecutor could have thought that they could forcibly take a DNA sample from Friedman without violating his Fourth Amendment rights." Friedman v. Boucher, 580 F.3d 847 (9th Cir. 2009).

8.   Originally, state and federal databases were limited to DNA samples from sexual offenders and a few other violent felons, such as murderers. However, as of 2013, 48 states collect DNA for all felony convictions and 42 states now collect DNA for some misdemeanor convictions. Two states collect DNA only for some felony and misdemeanor convictions. National Conference of State Legislatures, Convicted Offender DNA Collection and Analysis Laws, (2013), www.ncsl.org/Documents/cj/Convicted OffendersDNALaws.pdf. Several courts have held that collection of DNA from convicted, non-violent felons as a term of release from prison before parole, probation or supervised release does not violate those felons' Fourth Amendment rights. See e.g. Banks v. U.S., 490 F.3d 1178 (10th Cir. 2007); U.S. v. Weikert, 504 F.3d 1 (1st Cir. 2007).

This expansion has resulted in increased laboratory backlogs for DNA testing. For example, California's expansion of DNA testing from violent felons to all felons resulted in a ten-fold increase in demand and a quadrupling of its backlog. Tania Simoncelli, Dangerous Excursions: The Case Against Expanding Forensic DNA Databases to Innocent Persons, 34 J.L. Med. & Ethics 390 (2006).

Additionally, 31 states collect DNA from convicted juveniles. In the Matter of Appeal in Maricopa County Juvenile Action Numbers JV–512600 and JV–512797, 930 P.2d 496 (Ariz. App. 1996), an Arizona appellate court held that DNA collected from convicted juveniles was not subject to expungement and could be used beyond the age of majority, including in adult prosecutions, because such testing was not punitive.

Thirty states collect DNA samples from individuals who have merely been arrested for certain offenses. National Conference of State Legislatures, Arrestee DNA Collection and Analysis, (2013), www.ncsl.org/Documents/cj/ ArresteeDNALaws.pdf.

What are the pros and cons of allowing DNA collection on arrestees? Supporters of arrestee DNA collection claim that the policy will help law enforcement solve crimes more quickly and efficiently. Opponents claim that the expected 1.2 million DNA samples to be collected and processed at the federal level each year would significantly increase the current workload and cost the country $45 million each year. Do you find the *King* or *Medina* case more persuasive with respect to whether DNA testing of arrestees is appropriate?

9.   Should a convicted felon have a say about whether medical studies are undertaken on his or her DNA?

10.   In 2008, the European Court of Human Rights found that the United Kingdom's policy of retaining DNA profiles, cellular tissues, and fingerprints from people charged with a crime but later acquitted violated Article 8 of the European Convention on Human Rights. Article 8 states, in relevant parts, "1. Everyone has the right to respect for his private and family life * * *. 2. There shall be no interference by a public authority with the exercise of this right except such as in accordance with the law and is necessary in a democratic society * * * for the prevention of disorder or crime * * *."

The Court found that:

In addition to the highly personal nature of cellular samples, the Court notes that they contain much sensitive information about an individual, including information about his or her health. Moreover, samples contain a unique genetic code of great relevance to both the individual and his relatives. In this respect the Court concurs with [the lower court's decision that "there could be little, if anything more private to the individual than the knowledge of his genetic make-up."]

Given the nature and amount of personal information contained in cellular samples, their retention *per se* must be regarded as interfering with the right to respect for private lives of the individuals concerned.

* * *

The Court observes * * * that the [DNA] profiles contain substantial amounts of unique personal data. * * * In the Court's view, the DNA profiles' capacity to provide a means of identifying genetic relationships between individuals is in itself sufficient to conclude that their retention interferes with the right to the private life of the individuals concerned. The frequency of familial searchers, the safeguards attached thereto and the likelihood of detriment in a particular case are immaterial in this respect. * * *

The Court also found "The possibility the DNA profiles create for inferences to be drawn as to ethnic origin makes their retention all the more sensitive and susceptible of affecting the right to private life." Additionally, in weighing the public interest of increasing the chances of capturing future offenders, the court concluded that:

[T]he blanket and indiscriminate nature of the powers of retention of the fingerprints, cellular samples and DNA profiles of persons suspected but not convicted of offences * * * fails to strike a fair balance between the competing public and private interests and that the respondent State has overstepped any acceptable margin of appreciation in this regard. Accordingly, the retention at issue constitutes a disproportionate interference with the applicants' right to respect for private life and cannot be regarded as necessary in a democratic society.

S. and Marper v. The United Kingdom, Nos. 30562/04 and 30566/04, 4 December 2008.

IV. DNA IDENTIFICATION OUTSIDE THE CRIMINAL SETTING

MAYFIELD V. DALTON

901 F.Supp. 300 (D. Haw. 1995), vacated as moot, 109 F.3d 1423 (9th Cir. 1997).

KING, J.

* * *

BACKGROUND

Beginning with Operation Desert Storm in 1991, the United States military has used DNA analysis to help with identification of soldiers' remains. Such analysis provides a means of identifying remains too badly damaged for identification through dental records or fingerprints. Identification is made by comparing DNA taken from the remains with a DNA sample previously taken from the decedent or his or her biological relatives.

Because of problems with obtaining reliable DNA samples during the Gulf War, the Department of Defense ("DOD") began a program to collect and store reference specimens of DNA from members of the active duty and reserve armed forces. That way, the reference samples would be available for use in identifying remains in future conflicts. The DOD DNA Registry, a program within the Armed Forces Institute of Pathology, was established pursuant to a December 16, 1991 memorandum of the deputy secretary of defense. Under this program, DNA specimens are collected from active duty and reserve military personnel upon their enlistment, reenlistment, or preparation for operational deployment. The military's goal is to obtain specimens from all active and reserve personnel by the year 2001.

The specimens consist of two small samples of dried blood stored on cards and a sample of epithelial cells taken from the inside of the subject's cheek using a cotton swab. One bloodstain card is sealed and stored in the service member's military health record, while the other bloodstain card and the swab sample are sent to the DOD DNA Repository. Once received by the repository, the bloodstain card is vacuum sealed, assigned a number and bar code, and stored in a refrigerated chamber. The swab sample is assigned an identical code and stored in alcohol. The specimens are to be stored in the repository for 75 years and then destroyed.

According to the military, except for a limited number of "quality assurance" tests in which the DNA is typed to ensure that the repository's storage and analytical mechanisms are working properly, DNA is not extracted from the samples unless and until there is a need for it to assist in the identification of human remains.

Also according to the military, access to the repository facility, computer system and the samples themselves is strictly limited. Specimens stored in the repository are not to be used for a purpose other than remains identification unless a request, routed through the civilian secretary of the appropriate military service, is approved by the assistant secretary of defense for health affairs. The Government notes that no such request from this program has ever been approved, though it is unclear how many, if any, such requests have been made.

Plaintiffs are members of the United States Marine Corps assigned to Company B, 1st Radio Battalion, Marine Forces Pacific. Scheduled to deploy in January 1995, the two were ordered to provide specimens for the DNA repository. Plaintiffs refused to do so, and each was charged with violation of an order from a superior commissioned officer. On May 23, 1995, the military judge in Plaintiffs' Court Martial dismissed the charges, holding that the regulations underlying the DNA Repository program were not punitive and thus no disciplinary action could be taken for refusal to provide the specimens. The Marine Corps has appealed the military judge's decision.

DISCUSSION

Plaintiffs' Constitutional Claims

Plaintiffs first allege that the collection, storage and use of DNA samples taken without their consent violates their "rights to freedom of expression, privacy, and due process under the First, Ninth, and Fifth Amendments to the United States Constitution, inter alia." In their moving papers and argument, however, Plaintiffs rely primarily on the Fourth Amendment to make their case for a constitutional violation.

The law is well-established that the Government's compulsory taking of blood and other bodily fluid or tissue samples constitutes a "seizure" subject to scrutiny under the Fourth Amendment. However, the Fourth Amendment prohibits only "unreasonable" seizures. The Court in Schmerber [v. California, 384 U.S. 757 (1966)] upheld a conviction for driving under the influence based in part on test results from a blood sample taken without the petitioner's consent. The court found the taking of the blood sample "reasonable" where there was probable cause that the petitioner was intoxicated and a delay to obtain a warrant might have resulted in a loss of evidence.

Plaintiffs herein suggest that *Schmerber* established a rule that the Government may not compel a subject to give a blood sample in the absence of a judicial warrant issued upon a showing of probable cause. The court made no such holding, however. What it did say was that it found nothing inherently unreasonable in the test chosen to measure the petitioner's blood alcohol level, noting that blood tests "are a commonplace in these days of periodic physical examination . . . and . . . for most people the procedure involves virtually no risk, trauma or pain."

In Skinner v. Railway Labor Executives Ass'n, 489 U.S. 602 (1989), the Supreme Court upheld a federally mandated drug and alcohol testing program for private railway workers. Citing *Schmerber*, the Court repeated its previous observation that the interference with privacy interests occasioned by a blood test is minimal. The Court weighed this minimal intrusion against the Government's compelling interest in testing railway employees whose jobs involved the safety of passengers and others and found the testing program to be reasonable. This was so even though the tests were conducted in the absence of probable cause or even any kind of individualized suspicion.

In National Treasury Employees Union v. Von Raab, 489 U.S. 656 (1989), the Court likewise upheld a U.S. Customs Service program requiring drug tests for employees entering positions involving drug interdiction or requiring the carrying of a firearm. The Court noted that certain public employees are necessarily subject to diminished expectations of privacy, and cited as an example members of the military and intelligence services, who "may not only be required to give what in other contexts might be viewed as extraordinary assurances of trustworthiness and probity, but also may expect intrusive inquiries into their physical fitness for those special positions."

The taking of blood samples and oral swabs for the purpose of remains identification presents, on its face, a far less intrusive infringement of Plaintiffs' Fourth Amendment privacy rights than the blood testing in either *Schmerber*, *Skinner* or *Von Raab*. The blood test at issue in *Schmerber* involved a seizure of evidence to be used in a possible criminal prosecution. In *Skinner* and *Von Raab*, blood, urine and breath tests were used to detect the illegal or illicit use of drugs or alcohol, the confirmation of which could be grounds for disciplinary action or criminal sanctions.

In the instant case, the blood and tissue samples at issue are not to be used as evidence against Plaintiffs, but only as a means of identifying their remains should they be killed in action with the Marine Corps.

Although the military itself undoubtedly has a significant interest in being able to confirm which of its members have fallen in battle, and which ones may have been taken prisoner or are otherwise unaccounted for, it is the next of kin of service members who will derive the greatest benefit, and solace, from the speedy and definite identification of the remains of their loved ones.

Plaintiffs concede that the military's stated purpose for the DNA registry—remains identification—is a benign one. But they argue that the military could, at some point in the future, use the DNA samples for some less innocuous purpose, such as the diagnosis of hereditary diseases or disorders and the use or dissemination of such diagnoses to potential employers, insurers and others with a possible interest in such information. Plaintiffs have presented no evidence that the military has used or disclosed, or has any plans to use or disclose, information gleaned from the DNA samples for any purpose other than remains identification. A challenge to such hypothetical future use, or misuse, as the case may be, of the samples in the DNA repository does not present a justiciable case or controversy.

The court finds that the military has demonstrated a compelling interest in both its need to account internally for the fate of its service members and in ensuring the peace of mind of their next of kin and dependents in time of war. The court further finds that when measured against this interest, the minimal intrusion presented by the taking of blood samples and oral swabs for the military's DNA registry, though undoubtedly a "seizure," is not an unreasonable seizure and is thus not prohibited by the Constitution.

Breach of Contract

Plaintiffs also contend that the DNA sampling program constitutes a breach of their enlistment contracts with the Marine Corps. They note that the enlistment contracts they signed do not specifically warn recruits that blood and tissue samples will be taken for the DNA registry. Plaintiffs also argue that because they enlisted before the registry was begun, they cannot be deemed to have given their implied consent to the blood and tissue sampling.

In fact, the enlistment documents that Plaintiffs concede they signed make amply clear that military enlistees may be subjected to a plethora of laws, regulations, and requirements that would not normally apply to civilian employees of the Government.

* * *

The enlistment documents promise no limits on the military's ability to take blood or tissue samples or perform other medical tests on enlistees, whether for purposes of assessing physical fitness, detecting the use of illegal drugs, or otherwise. Indeed, Plaintiffs were undoubtedly subjected to such tests in connection with their enlistment. The sampling performed in connection with the DNA registry is not so qualitatively different so as to require a separate, more specific form of consent than that required for other testing.

The court finds that the military's taking of blood samples and oral swabs for purposes of obtaining DNA samples for the DOD DNA Registry is not a violation of any enlistment contract between Plaintiffs and the military.

Regulations Governing Research on Human Subjects

Plaintiffs also rely on 32 C.F.R. Part 219, Protection of Human Subjects, which governs human research conducted, supported or regulated by the military or civilian branches of the federal government. They contend that the military has failed to comply with all of the requirements of the part, which is apparently intended to protect human research subjects and thus prevent a recurrence of past abuses, such as those connected with Government experiments involving exposure to radiation from nuclear blasts or the unwitting ingestion by service personnel of mind altering drugs.

The regulations in question define research as "a systematic investigation, including research development, testing and evaluation, designed to develop or contribute to generalizable knowledge." 32 C.F.R. § 219.102(d). Defendants argue, and the court agrees, that the DOD DNA Registry does not meet the regulatory definition of "research." The DNA samples in question are maintained for a particularized purpose, i.e., the identification of the remains of the samples' donors. According to the military, the only other purpose for which the samples are removed from their repository is for tests to ensure the integrity of the storage process. The registry does not have as its purpose the development of generalizable knowledge about DNA, the traits of service personnel, or anything else.

Moreover, and perhaps more importantly, there is no evidence that Plaintiffs or their fellow service members are being subjected to any kind of experimentation or research. Once a blood sample and oral swab are taken and stored, the individual service member's relationship with the registry becomes dormant. The sample is not retrieved and scrutinized unless and until the service member is believed to have died in action. Even then, the military's inquiry is limited to determining whether the DNA in the sample matches that in the remains believed to be those of the service member. The service members whose DNA samples are kept in the registry are no more human guinea pigs than are the millions of service members whose dental records were kept on hand by the military to provide for remains identification in past wars.

The court finds that the DOD DNA Registry and related blood and tissue sampling does not violate 32 C.F.R. Part 219.

* * *

CONCLUSION

For the foregoing reasons, Plaintiffs' Motion for Summary Judgment and Plaintiffs' Motion to Certify Class were DENIED and Defendants' Cross Motion for Summary Judgment was GRANTED.

NOTES AND QUESTIONS

1. Since the *Mayfield* case, other servicemen have refused to provide DNA to the Department of Defense (DOD) DNA bank. In April 1996, Sergeant Warren Sinclair, an Air Force medical equipment repairman, refused to submit blood and tissue samples for genetic testing. Sinclair, an African American, was convinced that DNA samples would be used to support racist claims. He said, "Would we ask Jews to give their genes to Germans? No * * *. Until the issue of racism is resolved, Afro-Americans should maintain possession of their genetic material." He was convicted by court-martial on May 10, 1996, and sentenced to fourteen days of hard labor and a two-grade reduction in rank.

Donald P. Power, a first class petty officer and navy nuclear technician on the U.S.S. Arkansas, refused to give a DNA specimen because it violated his religious principles as a member of a Native American lodge. Power lost a stripe and his nuclear classification as well as 40 percent of his income. He was reassigned to a shore unit during discharge proceedings. Subsequently he applied for a waiver on grounds of religious freedom. Eighteen months later, a religious waiver was accepted, his rank was restored, and his nuclear classification was reinstated. But few members of the armed services will be able to make use of the narrow religious exemption; moral objections alone are not enough to avoid military rules. See Lori Andrews & Dorothy Nelkin, Body Bazaar: The Market for Human Tissue in the Biotechnology Age 113–114 (2001).

2. Should the Department of Defense be allowed to use the DNA in its bank for any purposes other than identification of remains? Under what circumstances, if any, should law enforcement officials be able to gain access to the DOD DNA bank to see if a soldier's DNA matches DNA found at a crime scene? Under what circumstances, if any, should genetic researchers be able to gain access to samples in the DOD DNA bank? If identification is the only permissible use of the DOD DNA bank, should members of the military be able to direct that the DNA be held privately by the soldier's relatives rather than in the government DNA bank?

3. An amendment to Nanette Sexton's prenuptial agreement allowed her to collect millions in a divorce if her husband committed adultery. To prove that he had been unfaithful, Sexton authorized DNA testing from her husband's bed sheets, which identified his DNA and that of a woman other

than Sexton. The judge upheld a mediator's order that the DNA test was admissible. Mary McLachlin, Divorce Twist: Wife Says DNA Test Proves His Tryst, Palm Beach Post, December 26, 2000, at 1A.

CHAPTER 13

MENTAL AND BEHAVIORAL GENETICS

■ ■ ■

I.   INTRODUCTION

Anyone who has a canine companion knows about behavioral genetics. In the last few thousand years, through selective breeding hundreds of breeds of dogs have been bred from wolves. Besides their wide range of sizes, shapes, and colors, dogs have been bred for their temperament, including herding, hunting, retrieving, and contented sleeping on the couch next to their human companions.

Francis Galton

Experts agree that the temperament and behavior of other animals, including humans, also is affected by genetics. But, this is practically where the agreement ends. There is widespread disagreement about the range of behaviors influenced by genetics. Many experts consider mental illness, intelligence, addictive behavior, and sexual orientation to be influenced by genes. Others add to the list a genetic predisposition to rage, happiness, impulsivity, shyness, daydreaming, or suicide. Still others assert that contentment, spatial abilities, nurturing behavior, perfect pitch, and a sweet tooth are influenced by genes. One study claims to demonstrate that one's attitude toward reading books, abortion, playing organized sports, roller coaster rides, and the death penalty are influenced by genes, but not one's attitudes toward gender roles, easy access to birth control, being assertive, and playing bingo.

As important as the types of behaviors influenced by genes is their degree of heritability. Are genes responsible for 5% of intelligence or 50%? One of the most common ways of attempting to estimate the degree of heritability is the use of twin studies, a research method developed by Francis Galton in the 19th century. By comparing the behavioral traits of monozygotic (MZ) twins with dizygotic (DZ) twins and twins reared apart and reared together, association between heredity and environment ("nature and nurture" in Galton's words) can be estimated. Some twin studies have been criticized on methodological grounds, such as the similarities of twins raised apart are not necessarily attributable to

627

genetic influences when the environments are similar. Nevertheless, some of the similarities of twins reared apart are astounding.

In one celebrated example, MZ (identical) twins Jim Lewis and Jim Springer were adopted into different families in Western Ohio, about 100 miles apart. They were reunited after 39 years when they were part of a twin study conducted at the University of Minnesota. The investigators discovered several coincidences: each had been given the same name by their adoptive families, each had an adoptive brother named Larry and a dog named Toy. Other coincidences were more striking: each married and divorced a woman named Linda and remarried a woman named Betty; they named their first sons James Allan and James Alan. In school, both liked math and disliked spelling; both enjoyed carpentry and mechanical drawing; both became deputy sheriffs in different Ohio towns; both drove similar blue Chevrolets; both vacationed on the same beach in Florida; both had nearly identical patterns of chain smoking and drinking; both had a white bench around a tree in their backyard; both made miniature furniture in their wood shop; both had vasectomies; both followed stock car racing and hated baseball. The similarities went on and on. See Lawrence Wright, Twins and What They Tell Us About Who We Are 43–47 (1997). What, if anything, was gene-mediated? What similarities would they have with other men of the same age in the same part of the country of the same socio-economic background? In what ways were they different?

Behavioral genetics is a very complicated field, fraught with scientific and statistical obstacles to correlations that can be verified and replicated. Three of the leading problems are (1) defining the endpoint (e.g., accurately diagnosing mental illnesses or variations in personality traits); (2) accounting for the multiple genetic and environmental factors influencing behavior; and (3) excluding possible confounding factors. In fact, the difficulty in proving associations and the frequency with which research findings have been retracted have led to at least one area of inquiry, the genetics of schizophrenia, to be referred to as "the graveyard of molecular geneticists."

This chapter will explore the social and legal significance of behavioral genetics. In particular, it will consider the effect of behavioral genetics on criminal law and tort law. New discoveries in behavioral genetics challenge some of the basic assumptions of religion, philosophy, and the law involving free will and moral culpability. The law's response to behavioral genetic research will shape our law and society for years to come.

II.   HISTORY OF MENTAL AND BEHAVIORAL GENETICS

MARK A. ROTHSTEIN, BEHAVIORAL GENETIC DETERMINISM: ITS EFFECTS ON CULTURE AND LAW IN BEHAVIORAL GENETICS: THE CLASH OF CULTURE AND BIOLOGY
89–96 (Ronald A. Carson & Mark A. Rothstein eds. 1999).

* * *

The popularity of genetic determinism, like other beliefs about science, has been cyclical. The golden age of genetic determinism began in the second half of the nineteenth century. As Sir Francis Galton, the father of eugenics, phrased it, the debate centers on whether "nature or nurture" is more important to human development. In mid-nineteenth-century England there was little doubt that inherited explanations of behavior were gaining popularity. Lewontin et al. observe the influence of this theory in Charles Dickens' popular novel *Oliver Twist*, which was published serially between 1837 and 1839. When ten-year-old Oliver first meets Jack Dawkins, the "artful dodger," on his way to London, Oliver is described as having a genteel nature and speaking with perfect grammar, in stark contrast to the streetwise Dawkins. Oliver's mode of expression is inexplicable, inasmuch as he had lived virtually all of his life in a parish workhouse, with no mother and no education. What explains this phenomenon? Oliver's father was from a well-off and socially prominent family; his mother was the daughter of a naval officer. According to Lewontin et al., "Oliver's life is a constant affirmation of the power of nature over nurture."

At the turn of the century, Alfred Binet, director of the psychology laboratory at the Sorbonne, abandoned his work in the field of craniometry (using brain size and structure to measure intelligence) to develop a test that could directly measure inherited, native intelligence. The purpose of his first test, developed in 1905, was to identify Parisian children needing special education. In the second version of his test, published in 1908, he assigned an age level to each task in the test to establish a mental age for each child. In 1912, a year after Binet's death, German psychologist Wilhelm Stern divided mental age by chronological age to establish an intelligence quotient, and the IQ, the supposed expression of innate intelligence, was born. Stanford professor Lewis Terman created a paper-and-pencil version of the basic test, the Stanford-Binet Intelligence test.

In 1914, seventy-six years after *Oliver Twist*, George Bernard Shaw's *Pygmalion* was first performed. Shaw was a follower of Galton, and according to Shaw's vision, culture was not immutably fixed by biology, but nearly so. Only after six months of arduous work and the talent of phoneticist Professor Higgins could an ignorant flower girl overcome the deprivation of her station in life and appear to be a duchess. Liza Doolittle, of course, was a white English-woman. Were she nonwhite or from central or eastern Europe, the task surely would have been impossible. At this time, pauperism and shiftlessness—not to mention intelligence—were widely believed to be overwhelmingly or exclusively genetic.

English translations and American revisions of the basic intelligence test, primarily the Army Alpha Test, were used on a mass scale during World War I as a way to screen troops. The findings of the test were "startling." The test was given only in English, and immigrants from southern and eastern Europe scored much lower than either native-born Americans or immigrants from northern Europe. * * * [T]hese test results helped to sway Congress in 1924 to reduce immigration from southern and eastern Europe.

It is small wonder that genetic determinism is linked with eugenics. If genes determine the human condition (physical, psychological, behavioral, and social), then improving the gene pool will improve the human condition. The efforts at improvement take on two forms—negative eugenics, preventing the reproduction of the genetically "unfit"—and positive eugenics—encouraging the mating of those with "favored" genetic endowments.

* * *

In 1990, seventy-six years after Shaw's *Pygmalion*, the popular American film *Pretty Woman* was released. The premise, though hardly original, was simple. Even a lowly streetwalker in Los Angeles could become a member of high society literally overnight so long as she had good looks, a rich benefactor, and designer clothes. (Cinderella required supernatural intervention to accomplish a comparable, though morally pure, transformation.) In popular culture, the pendulum had swung completely from *Oliver Twist*.

The Human Genome Project officially began in 1990. It heralded a period in which claims for a genetic basis for homosexuality, aggression, impulsive behavior, nurturing, and numerous other behaviors was asserted. This has contributed to a resurgence of behavioral genetic determinism that is based on the misapprehension and misapplication of scientific discoveries and that threatens to have grievous social consequences.

* * *

Flawed scientific theories can be refuted by more rigorous science. A more perplexing social problem involves the permissible societal response to legitimate discoveries in behavioral genetics. Undoubtedly, there is *some* correlation between certain genes and behavioral traits. The only serious scientific dispute concerns the overall degree of correlation and the applicability of genetic factors in a range of specific behavioral traits. What, then, are the likely psychological, social, political, and legal consequences of such correlations?

As an example, take the case of alcoholism. Several past and ongoing studies have explored whether there is a genetic component to alcoholism. Assume there is such a component in some cases of alcoholism. Does that mean that, as a society, we will be more or less tolerant of alcoholics, more or less inclined to mandate genetic testing for such an allele or alleles, or more or less likely to embrace the disease model of alcoholism? On the one hand, it could be argued that the genetic component vitiates the moral taint from individuals with alcoholism. On the other hand, the genetic, heritable nature of the disorder may increase the stigma associated with alcoholism; it may increase the pressure for genetic screening for the mutation; it may contribute to individuals feeling a sense of resignation and a reluctance to enter treatment; and it may lead to disdain for individuals who, despite knowledge that they have the mutation, proceed to drink nonetheless. Research to find an association between genes and alcoholism is being conducted at the Ernest Gallo Clinic and Research Center at the University of California–San Francisco. If a genetic link to alcoholism were to be established, some of the social pressure against alcoholic beverages and their purveyors might be deflected onto "faulty" genes.

Similar issues are raised with regard to a possible genetic link to homosexuality. If we find a "gay gene," will it mean greater or lesser tolerance? My suspicion is that it will not change the way most people view homosexuals. For individuals who are tolerant of homosexuals, it will reaffirm that the behavior is physiologically based and does not represent moral depravity. On the other hand, for individuals who are intolerant of homosexuality, it will confirm their view that such individuals are "abnormal." It also could lead to proposals that those affected by the "disorder" should undergo treatment to be "cured" and that measures should be taken to prevent the birth of other individuals so afflicted.

III.   SCIENTIFIC ISSUES

Steven E. Hyman, Using Genetics to Understand
Human Behavior: Promises and Risks in Wrestling
With Behavioral Genetics: Science, Ethics,
and Public Conversation

113–116 (Erik Parens, Audrey R. Chapman & Nancy Press eds. 2006).

For both ethical and practical reasons, human genetics is an observational, not an experimental, science. Thus, the practice of human genetics differs markedly from study of other organisms in which breeding and environmental factors can be rigidly controlled, mutagenesis can be performed, and, in some cases, genes can be directly inserted or deleted. Before the advent of molecular genetics, human behavioral genetics was limited largely to analyses that attempted to quantify genetic versus nongenetic influences on behavioral phenotypes and to determine the modes of inheritance in cases in which genes proved relevant. Quantitative (or classical) genetic studies of behavior depended on observational designs in which genetic and environmental influences might be teased apart or in which patterns of segregation of genes might be inferred. These designs included multigenerational family studies, twin studies, and adoption studies. Multigenerational family designs permit the analysis of modes of inheritance across generations. Based on their relative convenience and analytic power, many behavioral genetic studies investigated phenotype concordance in twins, comparing identical twins versus fraternal twins raised together. That is, they investigated how similar identical twins raised together were with respect to some trait (e.g., height or schizophrenia or "IQ") and compared those observations with observations regarding how similar fraternal twins raised together were with respect to the same trait. On the assumption that identical twins are raised in the same environment and that fraternal twins are too, and given the fact that identical twins share 100 percent of their DNA and fraternal twins on average only 50 percent of theirs, researchers make inferences about the magnitude of the role of genes in the emergence of a particular trait. To be sure, the methodology of twin studies has the weakness that the 100 percent shared-DNA condition (identical twins) cannot truly be balanced by a 100 percent shared-environment condition in humans. Indeed, creating truly identical conditions even for lab rats has proved to be very difficult.

Studies of individuals who had been adopted away from their biological families early in life better distinguished the influences of heredity and environment, and studies of twins separated early in life provided an even more powerful design. But adoption studies are difficult to perform, since they depend on societies making both records and people available for examination and interview. Moreover, the selection of adoptive families by social service agencies and the phenomenon of gene-environment covariation (whereby the individual helps select or create his or her own experiential environment) have moved some observers to question the validity of the investigators' assumption that the environments of the adoptees are really so different.

Measures frequently used in thinking about disease phenotypes and other traits that can be derived from both twin and family studies are recurrence risk ratios (λ), which quantify the likelihood of sharing a phenotype with another person as a function of relatedness and therefore as a function of percentage of DNA shared. As I will discuss at greater length later, recurrence risk ratios, like heritability estimates can serve as a rough and ready measure to prioritize disease phenotypes for molecular investigation based on the notion that the greater the contribution of genes to a phenotype, the higher the likelihood of identifying the genetic loci that contribute risk. Both heritabilities and recurrence risk ratios are measures of the *aggregate* genetic contribution to a phenotype no matter how complex the genetic contribution; thus, a high recurrence risk ratio is not a guarantee of success in identifying *actual loci* contributing to a phenotype.

Extensive family and twin studies and a smaller number of adoption studies have led to the conclusion that genes contribute significantly to risk of autism, schizophrenia, bipolar disorder, major depression, anxiety disorders, alcoholism, and other disorders of brain and behavior. Recurrence risk ratios derived from many studies are consistent with a major role for genes in risk of mental illness. With the development of modern genomic and other molecular tools, we can now begin to address the extraordinary challenge of how genetic differences influence biochemical and cellular networks that affect the emergence of complex traits; thus, the traditional quantitative genetic analyses are no longer a goal in themselves, but a tool.

The goal of behavioral genetics in the twenty-first century is to identify the precise genetic variants that contribute to behavioral phenotypes. These discoveries, in turn, become tools of inquiry for neuroscience and for the neurobiology of disease. To provide just one kind of example of how gene identification provides tools for neuroscience, genes found to be associated with Alzheimer disease, Parkinson disease, or Rett syndrome in humans have been inserted into mice or used to replace the endogenous mouse gene, thus producing animal models for research and treatment development. Clearly, mouse models will never provide perfect replicas of human cognitive and behavioral disorders such as schizophrenia, but they can prove very useful as partial models. For example, a knock-in-mouse (i.e., a mouse in which the endrogenous gene was replaced by a gene of the investigator's choosing) made to express a human Rett disease mutation in the causative MEPC2 gene shows abnormalities in social behavior. This experiment was possible because Rett is a Mendelian (single-gene) disorder; what might not have been predicted is that human social deficits could be even partially modeled in a mouse. Overall there is growing evidence that useful, if imperfect mouse models can be constructed by inserting genes that confer disease risk in humans.

In sum, the importance of quantitative or classical genetic analyses of behavior now lies in helping to define phenotypes, suggesting paths of gene-environment interaction, and setting priorities for molecular analyses. The scientific future for behavioral genetics lies in providing tools to understand the brain in health and disease, and to point the way toward new therapies for brain disorders.

Robert Plomin, John C. DeFries, Ian W. Craig & Peter McGuffin, Behavioral Genetics in Behavioral Genetics in the Postgenomic Era
10–14 (Plomin et al. eds. 2003).

Quantitative Genetics: Beyond Heritability

Most of what is known today about the genetics of behavior comes from quantitative genetic research. During the past three decades, the behavioral sciences have emerged from an era of strict environmental explanations for differences in behavior to a more balanced view that recognizes the importance of nature (genetics) as well as nurture (environmental). This shift occurred first for behavioral disorders, including rare disorders such as autism (.001 incidence), more common disorders such as schizophrenia (.01), and very common disorders, such as reading disability (.05). More recently, it has become increasingly accepted that genetic variation contributes importantly to differences among individuals in the normal range of variability as well as for abnormal behavior. The most well-studied domains of behavior are cognitive abilities and disabilities, psychopharmacology, personality, and psychopathology.

Although twin and adoption studies of individual differences in previously neglected behavioral domains such as learning might yield important new insights into their etiology, asking only whether and how much genetic factors influence such domains would not fully capitalize on the strengths of quantitative genetic analysis. New quantitative genetic techniques make it possible to go beyond these rudimentary questions to investigate how genes and environment affect developmental change and continuity; *comorbidity* and *heterogeneity*, the links between disorders and normal variation; and interactions and correlations between genetic and environmental influences. Using these techniques, quantitative genetic research can lead to better diagnoses based in part on etiology rather than solely on symptomatology. They also can chart the course for molecular genetic studies by identifying the most heritable components and constellations of disorders as they develop and as genetic vulnerabilities correlate and interact with the environment. In this sense, quantitative genetics will be even more important in a post genomic era. The future of behavioral genetic research lies in identifying specific genes responsible for heritability, which will make it possible to address these same questions with much greater precision.

* * *

BEHAVIORAL GENOMICS

Despite the slower-than-expected progress to date in finding genes associated with behavior, the substantial heritability of behavioral dimensions and disorders means that DNA polymorphisms exist that affect behavior. We are confident that some of the genes responsible for this heritability will be found. Although attention is now focused on finding specific genes associated with complex traits, the greatest impact for behavioral science will come after genes have been identified. Few behavioral scientists are likely to join the hunt for genes because it is difficult and expensive, but once genes are found, it is relatively easy and inexpensive to use them. DNA can be obtained painlessly and inexpensively from cheek swabs—blood is not necessary. Cheek swabs yield enough DNA to genotype thousands of genes, and the cost of genotyping is surprisingly inexpensive.

It is crucial that the behavioral sciences be prepared to use DNA in research and eventually in clinics. What has happened in the area of dementia in the elderly population will be played out in many other areas of the behavioral sciences. The only known risk factor for late-onset Alzheimer's dementia (LOAD) is a gene, apolipoprotein E, involved in cholesterol transport. A form of the gene called allele 4 quadruples the risk for LOAD but is neither necessary nor sufficient to produce the disorder; hence, it is a QTL. Although the association between allele 4 and LOAD was reported less than a decade ago, it has already become a *de rigueur* in research on dementia to genotype subjects for apolipoprotein E in order to ascertain whether the results differ from individuals with and without this genetic risk factor. Genotyping apolipoprotein E will become routine clinically if this genetic risk factor is found to predict differential response to interventions or preventative treatments.

In terms of clinical work, DNA might eventually contribute to gene-based diagnoses and treatment programs. The most exciting potential for DNA research is to use DNA as an early warning system that facilitates the development of primary interventions that prevent or ameliorate disorders before they occur. These interventions for behavioral disorders, and even for single-gene disorders, are likely to be behavioral rather than biological, involving environmental rather than genetic engineering. For example, PKU, a metabolic disorder that results postnatally in severe mental retardation, is caused by a single gene on chromosome 12. This form of mental retardation has been largely prevented, not by high-tech solutions such as correcting the mutant DNA or by eugenic programs or by drugs, but rather by a change in diet that prevents the mutant DNA from having its damaging effects. Because this environmental intervention is so cost-effective, newborns have been screened for decades for PKU to identify those with the disorder so that their diet can be changed. The example of PKU serves as an antidote to the mistaken notion that genetics implies therapeutic nihilism, even for a single-gene disorder. This point is even more relevant to complex disorders that are influenced by many genes and by many environmental factors as well. With behavior-based interventions, psychotherapists eventually will be in the business of preventing the consequences of gene expression.

The search for genes involved in behavior has led to a number of ethical concerns. For example, there are fears that the results will be used to justify social inequality, to select individuals for education or employment, or to enable parents to pick and choose among their fetuses. These concerns are largely based on misunderstandings about how genes affect complex traits, but it is important that behavioral scientists knowledgeable about DNA continue to be involved in this debate. Students in the behavioral sciences must be taught about genetics to prepare them for this postgenomic future.

* * *

NOTES AND QUESTIONS

1.   Chapters 2 and 5 discussed the eugenics movement in the late-nineteenth and early-twentieth centuries. Although one of the ways of improving the "genetic stock" of the population was to decrease or eliminate individuals with physical disabilities, eugenics was even more concerned with eliminating people who were considered to be stupid and evil. Accordingly, eugenic measures were soon applied beyond individuals with disabilities to individuals and then entire groups of people who were allegedly intellectually and morally inferior. Often the two, intellect and morality, were tied together, as in Buck v. Bell, 274 U.S. 200 (1927), where the eugenic sterilization was precipitated by Carrie Buck's having a child out of wedlock. Thus, eugenics was closely linked with behavioral genetics.

2.   The controversy surrounding behavioral genetics has not been lessened by the contemporary rejection of eugenics. As long as certain behaviors are assigned values by society, studying those behaviors to find biological links will raise highly contentious issues, from whether the research should be attempted at all, to the methodology, to the findings, to

the implications of the findings. The possibility of group stigmatization from associations with behavioral traits such as violence, addictive behavior, and low intelligence makes behavioral genetics a lightning rod for genetic research.

3.   One of the main concerns surrounding behavioral genetics is that weak associations between genetic traits and behaviors will be incorrectly viewed in deterministic terms. According to biologist Steven Rose: "It is my argument that such naive neurogenetic determinism is based on a faulty reductive sequence whose steps include: reification, arbitrary agglomeration, improper quantification, belief in statistical 'normality', spurious localization, misplaced causality, and dichotomous partitioning between genetic and environmental causes." Steven Rose, The Rise of Neurogenetic Determinism, 373 Nature 380 (1995). For similar criticism, see Jonathan Michael Kaplan, The Limits and Lies of Human Genetic Research (2000); Richard C. Lewontin, Steven Rose & Leon J. Kamin, Not in Our Genes: Biology, Ideology, and Human Nature (1984). See also Kenneth S. Kendler, "A Gene for . . . ": The Nature of Gene Action in Psychiatric Disorders, 162 Am. J. Psychiatry 1243 (2005).

IV.   CRIMINAL LAW

A.   OVERVIEW

TROY DUSTER, BEHAVIORAL GENETICS AND EXPLANATIONS OF THE LINK BETWEEN CRIME, VIOLENCE, AND RACE IN WRESTLING WITH BEHAVIORAL GENETICS: SCIENCE, ETHICS, AND PUBLIC CONVERSATION
154–156 (Erik Parens, Audrey R. Chapman & Nancy Press eds. 2006).

While there is no single or simple answer to the question of why certain behaviors are subjected to a genetic explanation and others are not, there is a major avenue that is undertheorized, unexplored, and less appreciated for the rich potential for getting at the answer(s). Again, an impressive array of different kinds of data strongly suggests that the answer lies in what the Germans call the Zeitgeist, roughly translated as "the spirit of the times." If this begs the question of why "in these times," then that is precisely the point of entry for an explanation of what it is about "these times" that makes for the selection of particular behaviors as genetically explorable and explainable. Behavioral genetics has long been interested in "the genetics of criminality." At the same time the prospect of discerning a relationship between genes and violent behavior has been very contentious.

Critics have raised a variety of issues. One concern is whether violent behavior is a well-defined classification amenable to scientific analysis. Crime, by definition an act or the commission of activity that is forbidden, is socially constructed; that is, the very categorization of an act as criminal depends on social standards of behavior, the identity of the actor, and the environment in which it takes place. Criminal behavior can be a one-time phenomenon (impulsive homicide after discovery of adultery), or it can be a profession (the cat burglar—the professional thief, or the "hit-man" specialist for organized crime). The theoretical warrant for examining the impulsive homicide as having a completely different etiology than the professional thief is well developed. In the case of the latter, the empirical literature on both the professions and professional thievery is predictive of the manners and patterns of routinized behavior. That is in sharp contrast to the literature and conceptual framework with which one approaches an understanding of most homicides, where even if impulsivity sometimes gives way to planning, patterns of jealousy, shame, and rage predominate. Crime can be an occasional diversion from one's ordinary life, such as depicted in Cameron's classic study of shoplifting, or it can be a compulsive-neurotic habituation (sexual abuse of the young by adults); alternatively, crime can be a rational, calculated decision (stealing a loaf of bread to feed one's family), or a routine occupational imperative, as was the case with the price-fixing scandal among the largest electrical companies in the United States. Crime can be a bureaucratic response to turf invasion, such as with organized crime during Prohibition, or a violation of existing social stratifying practices, such as the crime of teaching a slave to read—or assisting a slave to run away.

In short, what is criminal is as variable, and as variably explained, as any wide range of human behaviors that are legal. To place in the same taxonomic system the theft of bread, exposing oneself in public, cat burglary, and euthanasia, as a single, examinable phenotype is to engage in a breathtaking mystification of the classification of crime. The theoretical warrant in each of these instances is both well articulated and highly differentiated in the best empirical work in criminology. As noted above, Cameron's research on shoplifting remains the standard and the classic—distinguishing and documenting how and why this form of crime is primarily performed by "amateurs." In so doing, Cameron explained why shoplifting has the lowest rate of recidivism when the perpetrator, almost always (over 90%) the "amateur," is confronted. At the other end of the continuum is the pickpocket, almost always a professional who works with groups of other professionals—where the rate of recidivism is, by contrast, extraordinarily high. The pickpocket regards arrest as an occupational hazard, and has strategies for minimizing its effect on his (usually) behavior. The arbitrary features of the social fabrication of the criminal law comes to us more clearly by looking back to a much earlier time. In late eighteenth-century England, for example, stealing linens from a linen factory was a crime punishable by death. With the hindsight of two centuries, we now see this more clearly as a narrow, politically and economically motivated specification of a "serious crime." But that is because we have a few centuries' hindsight. Today, we place in the same criminal category someone who leaves lethal nerve gas on a subway station (anonymous killings) and someone who shoots in the back a doctor working in an abortion clinic. Fifty years from now, if some researcher went through the police records to show whether adoptees had a similar "inclination to commit crime" as did those in then biological families, someone might point out the quite reasonable objection that the system of classification was constructed in such a way as to make any claims about a genetic basis for these crimes highly problematic. The search for a genetic explanation for such a demonstrably variegated "phenotype" (criminal) requires a theoretical warrant that has never been delivered. The closest that one can come is in the abstract notion of an "antisocial personality," but even for this abstracted version, the obstacles to linking phenotypes and genotypes are huge. That is, given this demonstrably high empirical variability (sometimes arbitrary, sometimes systemic reach of the criminal justice system) in what constitutes a crime, and even more demonstrably high empirical variability in what constitutes "antisocial behavior" across social time and space, how is it possible to search for a genotype? The answer, and the conclusion provide strong reasons for deep concern.

It is therefore not possible to study criminal behavior without taking the circumstances in which the behavior takes place into account. The very classification of criminals or criminal behavior as a biological category may also affect the way people understand a particular kind of behavior. The sheer knowledge of such categories can have a looping effect. That is, it may affect people's attitudes and behavior in a way that feeds back on the classification scheme itself.

MARK A. ROTHSTEIN, APPLICATIONS OF BEHAVIOURAL GENETICS: OUTPACING THE SCIENCE?
6 Nature Reviews Genetics 793, 795–796 (2005).

* * *

SPECIFIC APPLICATIONS

Criminal Law. Genetic explanations of anti-social behaviour represent an important area of research and one of the earliest applications of behavioural genetics. Behavioural genetics could potentially be used in several ways—from the earliest stages of a criminal investigation through to almost every aspect of the criminal justice system.

DNA forensic techniques are used by law-enforcement agencies around the world. In the absence of a match between the evidence from a crime scene and the profiles stored in forensic DNA databases, DNA forensic profiling can be used for several purposes—to identify the gender of and make predictions about the race or ethnicity, health status, age, or physical characteristics of the sample source. Behavioural genetic forensic profiling might be increasingly used in law enforcement to predict the perpetrator's behavioural traits and psychiatric conditions, such as learning disabilities and personality traits.

Once a suspect is arrested and charged with a crime, behavioural genetic information could be presented at a bail hearing. Prosecutors might urge that bail should not be granted or should be set at a high amount because of the defendant's genetic predisposition to impulsivity (for example, risk of flight) or aggression (for example, risk of committing further crimes).

At trial, evidence of behavioural genetic variations within the normal range is unlikely to establish an independent basis for acquittal. More extreme deviations might be part of the scientific evidence used to support an insanity defence. Behavioural genetic evidence might also be used to claim that the defendant lacked the mental capacity to form the intent necessary to commit the crime. For example, on this basis a defendant charged with premeditated murder might be convicted of a lesser offence, such as manslaughter.

In many states in the United States it is common for convicted defendants to introduce evidence that relatives across many generations have engaged in violent criminal activities, that the defendant has inexplicably engaged in antisocial activities from a young age, or that the individual has been diagnosed with a neurogenetic disorder. This is then used to assert that defendants who commit crimes caused at least in part by a genetic predisposition or compulsion are not as morally culpable and do not deserve the harshest sentences. It is difficult to determine whether such arguments have had an effect on the sentences imposed, but the willingness of some courts to consider such evidence leaves open the possibility that behavioural genetics could be afforded greater weight in the future.

Behavioural genetic information could also be introduced in parole hearings. Ironically, the positions of the government and the inmate with respect to the behavioural genetic evidence are likely to be the opposite of their arguments at the trial. At a parole hearing, the government might attempt to use genetic predisposition as a basis for denying parole; the inmate might use the absence of genetic predisposition as a basis for release under the theory that he or she is less likely to commit another crime in the future.

Finally, many states in the United States have enacted 'sexual predator laws', which permit the indefinite confinement of individuals who have been convicted of multiple sex crimes against children and who are considered likely to commit further crimes if released. In theory, behavioural genetic evidence might be used to predict the likelihood of the individual committing future sex crimes.

B. CULPABILITY

LORI B. ANDREWS, PREDICTING AND PUNISHING ANTISOCIAL
ACTS: HOW THE CRIMINAL JUSTICE SYSTEM MIGHT USE
BEHAVIORAL GENETICS IN BEHAVIORAL GENETICS:
THE CLASH OF CULTURE AND BIOLOGY
120–122 (Ronald A. Carson & Mark A. Rothstein eds. 1999).

Criminal law is viewed as a "choosing system" in that people are seen as having a choice about whether to engage in criminal behavior. People are seen as culpable when they *choose* to violate the law. This involves both a voluntary wrongful act (*actus rea*) and the mental state to know that the act was wrongful (*mens rea*). In situations in which the individual was not acting under free will, however, the law provides a variety of mechanisms to avoid traditional criminal penalties.

Evidence of one's genotype might be used to exculpate an individual or to mitigate punishment. A person may claim that his genes provoked involuntary actions that caused the inappropriate act (such as involuntarily physically harming someone during a seizure). Or he may argue that his genotype influenced his mental processes so as to prevent him from realizing his act was wrongful and controlling himself. Or he might argue that it is unjust to punish him because his actions are compelled by an illness rather than a "chosen" behavior.

With respect to the voluntary act requirement for criminal conviction, genetic defenses would be unlikely to be accepted if there was evidence that the individual could have ascertained his or her genetic status and done something about it. For example, a driver who unexpectedly blacks out and causes a fatal accident would not be criminally liable; however, a driver who knows he is prone to blackouts could be found guilty of manslaughter if he has a fatal traffic accident during a blackout. This is in keeping with the traditional legal approach, which holds that "the powerful influences exercised by one's hereditary make-up by his developmental and environmental background are not ignored, but the law takes the position 'that most men, in most of the relations of life, can act purposefully and can inhibit antisocial, illegal tendencies.'"

There is more potential to prove that a particular genotype influenced a defendant's mental status. If a person's genetic status causes him or her to be insane, the individual can be found not guilty by reason of insanity. There are a variety of legal tests for insanity, with twenty states applying a strict rule requiring proof that the defendant did not know the nature or the quality of the act he was committing, or if he did know it, that he did not know he was doing wrong. In twenty-seven states and the District of Columbia, a more liberal approach is taken, requiring the defendant to prove that he lacked substantial capacity to appreciate the criminality of his or her conduct or to control that conduct to the requirements of law.

At the federal level, the insanity test was changed significantly after John Hinckley was acquitted on the grounds that he could not conform his conduct to the requirements of the law. Now, under federal law, individuals can be found not guilty by reason of insanity only if they are unable to appreciate the nature and quality or wrongfulness of their acts. Merely not being able to conform their conduct is not enough.

Also in response to the Hinckley situation, the majority of states amended their criminal laws to create a verdict of guilty but mentally ill to avoid (except in rare instances) acquitting someone who had committed an antisocial act. This newer "guilty but mentally ill" verdict recognizes culpability but allows mitigation of the sentence in terms of its length or the type of facility in which the offender is institutionalized.

In traditional criminal law, several justifications are put forth for punishing people who have committed antisocial acts. People are institutionalized to deter them from committing future antisocial acts, to rehabilitate them, to deter others from committing antisocial acts, to incapacitate them, and to exact retribution (an institutionalized vengeance). If a genetic deterministic view is taken, the first two justifications may be eliminated on the ground that there would be nothing that could be done to change the individual. However, institutionalizing the offender might serve other purposes by deterring others from committing crimes (or from attempting to "game" the system by purporting to have a genetic defense), by preventing the offender (through incarceration) from having the opportunity to commit another crime, and by satisfying society's need for revenge.

Lawyer Maureen Coffey advocates that, "In light of increasing knowledge and understanding, traditional yet outdated notions of freedom and responsibility should be modified to square with a scientific view of human conduct." She argues that people with genetic susceptibilities for antisocial behavior are "innately different from the 'normal' person," but that their lessened free will should not make such individuals immune from punishment. Rather, punishment should be based, not on a subjective, moral culpability justification, but on "the legitimate objectives of social control and public welfare." Even though she acknowledges that "punishing an individual for crimes for which he is not responsible in the traditional sense seems to be morally offensive," she feels it can be outweighed by the greater social good.

Coffey's argument will probably be attractive to policymakers, who seem to have given up on a rehabilitative model of prison in favor of a punitive one. Thus, even in instances in which it is proven that the defendant acted in conformity with a genetic predisposition, people who argue that their genes caused them to commit an antisocial act may ultimately be incarcerated to prevent them from committing other acts, to deter others, or to satisfy society's need for vengeance.

STEPHEN J. MORSE, GENETICS AND CRIMINAL RESPONSIBILITY

15 Trends in Cognitive Sciences 378, 379 (2011).

* * *

TRANSLATING GENETIC RESEARCH FOR ASSESSING CRIMINAL RESPONSIBILITY

Genetics concerns mechanistic causation. Genes do not have mental states and do not commit crimes; people do. To make a useful internal contribution to criminal responsibility, the genetic data must be 'translated' into the law's folk psychological responsibility criteria. It must be shown how, precisely, the genetic data are relevant to whether a defendant acted, whether he or she possessed a particular mens rea, and whether the mental states relevant to defenses were present.

It is not sufficient to indicate that genetics played a causal role in explaining the criminal behavior, even if that causal role is very powerful. Causation and predictability are not excusing conditions in law and causation is not the equivalent of legal compulsion (most action is not the causal result of dire threats or uncontrollable desires). If they were, no one would be responsible because we inhabit a causal universe, but we nonetheless hold people responsible. A genetic predisposition to criminal conduct does not per se mitigate or excuse. Causation is relevant only if it tends to show the presence of a genuine excusing condition, but it is the latter that does the legal work. Believing that causation per se mitigates or excuses responsibility is the most pernicious confusion bedeviling the attempt to relate scientific findings to criminal responsibility. I have termed it the 'fundamental psycholegal error'. In the few legal cases in which genetic information has been used to mitigate responsibility, this error has been common.

We are reasonably confident that having a genetically induced MAO-A deficiency in interaction with childhood abuse causally increases the risk of criminal and antisocial behavior more than ninefold. Nonetheless, there is no reason to believe that offenders exposed to that interaction did not act or form the required mental states. If exposure to that interaction somehow diminished their rationality or produced some type of uncontrollable internal desire, then mitigation or excuse might be warranted. Such a diminished rationality or control problem would have to be demonstrated independently by evidence other than causation data.

MILLARD V. MARYLAND

261 A.2d 227 (Md. Ct. Spec. App. 1970).

MURPHY, J.

Charged with the offense of robbery with a deadly weapon, appellant filed a written plea that he was insane at the time of the commission of the crime under Maryland Code, Article 59, Section 9(a), which provides:

> "A defendant is not responsible for criminal conduct and shall be found insane at the time of the commission of the alleged crime if, at the time of such conduct as a result of mental disease or defect, he lacks substantial capacity either to appreciate the criminality of his conduct or to conform his conduct to the requirements of law. As used in this section, the terms 'mental disease or defect' do not include an abnormality manifested only by repeated criminal or otherwise antisocial conduct."

The basis for appellant's insanity plea, as later unfolded at the trial, was that he had an extra Y chromosome in the brain and other cells of his body which constituted, within the meaning of Section 9(a), a mental defect resulting in his lacking substantial capacity either to appreciate the criminality of his conduct or to conform his conduct to the requirements of law.

At the trial before a jury in the Circuit Court for Prince George's County, the State established the corpus delicti, adduced proof of appellant's criminal agency, and then rested its case. Thereafter, under the prescribed Maryland procedure, it became incumbent upon the appellant in undertaking to establish his insanity defense to first adduce sufficient competent proof in support thereof, out of the presence of the jury, from which the trial judge could properly find, as a preliminary matter of law, that the presumption of sanity had been rebutted and a doubt raised in the minds of reasonable men as to his sanity. To this end, and in conformity with the approved procedure, appellant adduced evidence through the testimony of a Lieutenant at the Prince George's County jail showing that while in confinement appellant was agitated, nervous, upset, and became so violent on occasions that he had to be handcuffed and shackled in leg irons; that appellant cut himself five or six times on his arm between the elbow and the wrist, resulting in severe bleeding, although no arteries were severed; that these cuts "ran the gamut from scratches to very severe cuts requiring quite a number of sutures"; and that as a result of his condition, appellant was sent to three different hospitals for treatment and evaluation.

Dr. Cecil Jacobson, the appellant's only medical witness, testified that he was an Assistant Professor in the Department of Obstetrics and Gynecology and Chief of the Reproduction Genetics Unit of the George Washington University School of Medicine; that he had obtained a degree in genetics from the University of Utah in 1960 and was "a research teacher teaching the full-time faculty" at the University; that he had published 42 articles in the field of genetics, had conducted extensive research in the field, supervised a number of genetics laboratories, and was a consultant in genetics to the Federal Government. He stated that in 1964 he also obtained a medical degree and was licensed to practice medicine in Maryland, Virginia and the District of Columbia; that he had interned for one year in 1964–1965 but did not serve a residency in medicine but "went directly into the academic program [at George Washington University] because he had an active teaching responsibility as a medical student." He testified that while he received formal training in psychiatry as a medical student, and had received clinical experience in the psychiatric wards during his medical internship, he was not a psychiatrist, had received no post-graduate training in psychiatry, was neither Board eligible nor Board certified, and had "no competence" in the field of psychiatry beyond that possessed by "the conventional physician."
* * *

Dr. Jacobson testified that on December 16, 1968, appellant was examined and his body cells found to contain an extra Y chromosome (XYY); that the presence of this extra chromosome constituted a "basic defect in the genetic complement of the cell" affecting not only the way the cells grow in the body, but also the physical growth of the body itself; that the presence of the extra Y chromosome caused "marked physical and mental problems" affecting the manner in which persons possessing the extra Y chromosome "will react to certain stimulus; certain physiological problems; certain behavioral characteristics." Dr. Jacobson then told of approximately 40 published reports indicating that persons possessed of an extra Y chromosome tended to be very tall, with limbs disproportionate to their body; that such persons had marked antisocial, aggressive and schizoid reactions and were in continual conflict with the law.

Dr. Jacobson stated that he had never previously testified in court. Asked whether he was familiar with the Maryland test of insanity, as defined in Section 9(a), he said that he had never read it, but believed it contained two parts—"One, whether there was a basic defect involved, and, secondly, whether or not the person is competent for his act." Section 9(a) was then read to Dr. Jacobson, and he was then asked whether appellant was insane. Dr. Jacobson responded with a professorial narrative of appellant's genetic make-up, after which he concluded that "if the definition of insanity has a mental defect, the answer is yes, he has a mental defect based upon his abnormal [chromosome] test." Asked whether the "defect" was such as to cause appellant to lack "substantial capacity either to appreciate the criminality of his conduct or to conform his conduct to the requirements of law," Dr. Jacobson answered:

> "I cannot say that because I have not examined him as a psychiatrist. I have no competence in that area."

Appellant's counsel then told the court that he intended to show through "case histories" that individuals having the extra Y chromosome have extremely aggressive personalities, "to the extent that most of them end up in jail for one reason or another because of their aggressive reactions." Dr. Jacobson was then asked to examine appellant's arms to determine whether the cuts thereon were "suicidal or merely attention cuts." Dr. Jacobson did so briefly and stated that based on his experience as a medical doctor, he believed the cuts constituted an actual attempt at suicide; that based on this fact, and his brief questioning of appellant during a five-minute court recess, he felt appellant's "reactions" were not normal; that appellant had a fear of "forceful activity with an attempt at extension of this regression and a lack of adequately controlling this;" that although he was "greatly restricted" by not knowing the "developmental history" of appellant, he believed, based upon the testimony of the jail lieutenant concerning appellant's conduct while in confinement, including the suicide attempts, coupled with appellant's genetic defect, that "this does not fall within the realm of sanity, as I understand it." Dr. Jacobson then testified that the extra Y chromosome in appellant's genetic make-up affected his behavioral patterns, as reported in other cases of persons similarly possessed of the extra Y chromosome. He conceded that persons having the extra Y chromosome may differ among themselves depending upon "what other physical effects are found in the body of the XYY," environment also being a factor accounting for differences between XYY individuals.

Under further questioning by the trial judge, the prosecutor, and defense counsel, Dr. Jacobson stated that appellant's genetic defect—which he characterized as a mental defect—influenced "his competence or ability to recognize the area of his crime;" that appellant had a "propensity" toward crime because of his genetic abnormality; that based upon the medical literature, the appellants' conduct and behavioral patterns, and his genetic defect, he was insane and not even competent to stand trial. The doctor defined insanity in terms of the "ability to comprehend reality" or the "inability to judge one's action as far as consequence." Dr. Jacobson next testified that he had "insufficient evidence" upon which to base a conclusion whether appellant appreciated the consequences of his action, but that because he had attempted to commit suicide, such an act constituted "an inability to comprehend the consequences of his act, the act of suicide, being death;" and that appellant's actions were "not consistent with sanity."

* * *

At the conclusion of Dr. Sauer's testimony, the trial judge ruled that he was not persuaded that reasonable minds could differ as to appellant's sanity; that the appellant's defect was physical and not mental; and that Dr. Jacobson's testimony did not, with reasonable medical certainty, overcome the presumption that appellant was sane. The trial judge thus declined to submit the issue of appellant's sanity to the jury. The jury subsequently found appellant guilty of robbery with a deadly weapon and he was sentenced to eighteen years under the jurisdiction of the Department of Correction.

We see no merit in appellant's contention on appeal that the trial judge erred in ruling that there had not been presented evidence of insanity under Article 59, Section 9(a) sufficient to overcome the presumption of sanity. Dr. Jacobson's testimony, if believed, clearly established that appellant possessed an extra Y chromosome (XYY) and that he was therefore genetically abnormal. It also tended to show in a general way that appellant's possession of the extra Y chromosome caused him to be antisocial, aggressive, in continual conflict with the law, and to have a "propensity" toward the commission of crime. But, * * * the test of responsibility for criminal conduct under Section 9(a) is predicated upon "mental disease or defect," the existence of which is "first and foremost a medical problem;" and that an opinion as to the ultimate fact whether an accused is insane under Section 9(a) should be reached "by a medical diagnosis," based on "reasonable medical certainty." The mere fact then that appellant had a genetic abnormality which Dr. Jacobson characterized as "a mental defect" would not, of itself, suffice to show that, under Section 9(a), he lacked, because of such defect, "substantial capacity either to appreciate the criminality of his conduct or to conform his conduct to the requirements of law." And to simply state that persons having the extra Y chromosome are prone to aggressiveness, are antisocial, and continually run afoul of the criminal laws, is hardly sufficient to rebut the presumption of sanity and show the requisite lack of "substantial capacity" under Section 9(a). Moreover, we think it entirely plain from the record that in testifying that appellant had a "mental defect," Dr. Jacobson did so only in a most general sense, without full appreciation for the meaning of the term as used in Section 9(a), and particularly without an understanding that such term expressly excludes "an abnormality manifested only by repeated criminal or otherwise antisocial conduct." But even if it were accepted that appellant had a "mental defect" within the contemplation of Section 9(a), Dr. Jacobson, by his own testimony, indicated an inability to meaningfully relate the effect of such defect to the "substantial capacity" requirements of the subsection. Not only did Dr. Jacobson candidly admit that he had "no competence" in the field of psychiatry, but he demonstrated that fact by showing that he had not theretofore familiarized himself with the substance of Section 9(a); indeed, his conception of the test of criminal responsibility in Maryland was shallow at best, at least until the test was read to him during his testimony. While Dr. Jacobson did ultimately testify in conclusory fashion that he thought appellant insane and even incompetent to stand trial, his testimony in this connection was obviously predicated on a definition of "insanity" different than that prescribed under Section 9(a)—a definition so general as to encompass as insane a person who would attempt suicide.

* * *

That Dr. Jacobson was a well qualified geneticist was clear beyond question. Equally clear is the fact that he was not a practicing physician, and his experience in mental illness was related essentially to his practice in the field of genetics. He conceded a lack of competence in the field of psychiatry, admitted having no prior familiarity with the provisions of Section 9(a), had not subjected appellant to any psychiatric examination, and defined "insanity" in terms different than those prescribed by the applicable law * * *. [T]o constitute proof of insanity sufficient to raise a doubt in the minds of reasonable men, competent medical evidence must be adduced to the positive effect that the accused, as a result of mental disease or defect, lacked substantial capacity either to appreciate the criminality of his conduct or to conform his conduct to the requirements of law; and evidence of some undefined mental disorder or instability is insufficient proof to overcome the presumption of sanity. On the record before us, we think Dr. Jacobson's opinion as to appellant's sanity under Section 9(a) was not competent in that it was not based on reasonable medical certainty, and that the trial judge, had he so concluded, would not have been in error.

NOTES AND QUESTIONS

1.   Based on the Andrews excerpt, what would a criminal defendant have to prove to make out a genetic defense to a crime? How, if at all, would it differ from an insanity defense? For a further discussion of these issues, see Jeffrey R. Botkin et al. eds., Genetics and Criminality: The Potential Misuse of Scientific Information in Court (1999).

2.   In 1965, a chromosomal study of 197 mentally subnormal males with dangerous, violent, or criminal tendencies in an institution in Scotland found that seven of the men had a karyotype of XYY. This was a surprisingly high percentage of 3.5%. In addition, the average height of the seven men was 6 feet, 1 inch, whereas the average height for the rest of the men was 5 feet, 7 inches. It was not long before an XYY genetic defense was asserted in

several criminal cases, based on the assumption that men with an extra Y chromosome were genetically programmed to commit violent acts for which they should not be responsible. The courts generally rejected the defense. See, e.g., People v. Tanner, 91 Cal.Rptr. 656 (Cal. Ct. App. 1970); People v. Yukl, 372 N.Y.S.2d 313 (N.Y.Sup.1975); State v. Roberts, 544 P.2d 754 (Wash.App.1976). Subsequent research indicated that men with an XYY karyotype tend to have lower intellectual functioning or even to be mildly retarded. Cognitive impairment, irrespective of genetic makeup, correlates with being institutionalized for crime.

3. The court in *Millard* adopted the majority view in rejecting the XYY defense. The expert witness for the defense, whose testimony was discredited by the court, became infamous several years later. In 1992, Dr. Cecil B. Jacobson was convicted of 52 felony counts for mail fraud, wire fraud, travel fraud, and perjury. Between 1976 and 1986, Dr. Jacobson, while owning and operating the Reproductive Genetics Center, Ltd., a fertility clinic, fraudulently injected his own sperm into patients instead of the promised sperm of the patient's husband or an anonymous donor during artificial insemination procedures at the clinic. As many as 75 children were born from these insemination procedures. Dr. Jacobson was sentenced to five years in prison, ordered to pay a $75,000 fine, and required to refund the $39,205 that patients had paid for his services. In addition to the federal criminal action, Dr. Jacobson was named in at least six civil suits brought by the parents of the children Jacobson allegedly fathered. The suits alleged various counts of fraud, battery, negligence, outrage, negligent infliction of emotional distress, medical malpractice, and child support.

4. Glenda Sue Caldwell was tried for the murder of her son and the aggravated assault of her daughter. She was found guilty but mentally ill and sentenced to life imprisonment. Her defense at trial was that she was insane, brought on by the fear of contracting Huntington disease and the stress of her separation from her husband. The psychiatrist who testified for the defense said that she was under stress and exhibited a borderline personality disorder, but she was not psychotic. Caldwell v. State, 354 S.E.2d 124 (Ga. 1987). After spending nine years in prison, Caldwell was granted a new trial and subsequently acquitted. By the time of the retrial, her Huntington disease symptoms had become more pronounced, which may have convinced the judge that she was not responsible for the shootings. Woman Wins Acquittal In Murder Case By Claiming Huntington's Disease, AP News Archive, Sept. 28, 1994. What effect, if any, should her later development of symptoms of Huntington disease have on her guilt or innocence? As predictive testing improves for various late-onset neurological disorders and dementias, what principles should the courts apply in determining the admissibility and effects of this evidence?

5. For a further discussion, see Paul S. Appelbaum, The Double Helix Takes the Witness Stand: Behavioral and Neuropsychiatric Genetics in Court, 82 Neuron 946 (2014); Nita A. Farahany & James E. Coleman, Jr., Genetics and Responsibility: To Know the Criminal from the Crime, 69 L. &

Contemp. Probs. 115 (2006); Karen H. Rothenberg & Alice Wang, The Scarlet Gene: Behavioral Genetics, Criminal Law, and Racial and Ethnic Stigma, 69 L. & Contemp. Probs. 343 (2006).

C. SENTENCING

HILL V. OZMINT
339 F.3d 187 (4th Cir. 2003).

KING, CIRCUIT JUDGE:

In October of 1995, David Hill was sentenced to death for the murder of Major Spencer Guerry, the Deputy Police Chief for the City of Georgetown, South Carolina. After the South Carolina courts denied relief on both direct appeal and collateral review, Hill sought habeas corpus relief in the District of South Carolina. The district court denied relief, and it declined to issue a certificate of appealability ("COA").

* * *

V.   THE IAC [INEFFECTIVE ASSISTANCE OF COUNSEL] CLAIM

In his IAC claim, Hill maintains that his defense lawyers were ineffective in calling Dr. Edward Burt to testify during the trial's sentencing phase. At sentencing, Hill's lawyers sought to show that Hill suffered from a genetically-based serotonin deficiency, which resulted in aggressive impulses. After his arrest and incarceration, Hill had been prescribed medication that they believed had successfully curbed these impulses. Thus, according to Hill's lawyers, the death penalty was not warranted because Hill's aggressive behavior was genetic (i.e., beyond his control) and treatable. To this end, Hill's lawyers presented the testimony of Dr. Emil Coccaro, who explained the role of serotonin in brain chemistry, as well as how genetics affects serotonin levels. Next, the defense called Dr. Bernard Albiniak, a forensic psychologist, who had performed a series of spinal taps on Hill to monitor his serotonin levels. Dr. Albiniak opined that Hill suffered from a chronic serotonin deficiency.

Finally, the defense called Hill's psychiatrist, Dr. Edward Burt. Dr. Burt was expected to testify that he has prescribed Prozac to treat Hill's serotonin deficiency, and that Hill had responded favorably to the medication. Dr. Burt's testimony sought to establish that Hill's serotonin deficiency caused his aggressive behavior, and that a long history of violence and suicide in his family indicated that his aggressive impulses resulted from a genetic condition. Dr. Burt, however, apparently suffered a breakdown while on the witness stand. Thus, while testifying during the trial's sentencing phase, Dr. Burt had difficulty responding to questions, particularly on cross-examination.

Hill contended * * * that his defense lawyers should have known that Dr. Burt was incapable of testifying effectively. According to Hill, his lawyers also knew that, approximately eight months before trial, Dr. Burt had been arrested for public intoxication. Hill maintained that, in light of his lawyers' knowledge of Dr. Burt's problems, the decision to call him as a witness fell below an objective standard of reasonableness. Further, the decision to present Dr. Burt's evidence, Hill maintained, prejudiced his defense because it undermined the compelling evidence of Drs. Coccaro and Albiniak.

The state court summarily rejected Hill's IAC claim. It concluded that, although Dr. Burt "was not as effective as [Hill] would have liked," Hill's lawyers were not constitutionally ineffective in calling him as a witness because they had properly investigated him and prepared him for trial. The district court also denied relief on the IAC claim, concluding that the state court's rulings were neither "contrary to" nor an "unreasonable application of" clearly established federal law. Hill now challenges the district court's ruling. Although we have issued a COA on this claim, we decline to award Hill any relief.

NOTES AND QUESTIONS

1.   Suppose Dr. Burt had been able to present his testimony as scheduled. Should it be used to mitigate the sentence of the defendant?

2.   Do you think that introducing genetic evidence at the sentencing stage is going to help or hurt the defendant? Although genetic propensity may explain the predisposition of the plaintiff (ostensibly militating toward a less harsh sentence), the determinist view of genes argued by the defendant may cause the court to think that a maximum sentence is necessary to keep the defendant off the streets as long as possible.

3.   In Mobley v. State, 455 S.E.2d 61 (Ga.), cert. denied, 516 U.S. 942 (1995), Stephen Mobley was convicted of murdering a Domino's Pizza store manager. Mobley's attorneys attempted to use his "genetic makeup" as a mitigating factor in sentencing. Based on his family history of violence, the defense requested expert and financial assistance to conduct a genetic analysis to determine whether Mobley had a genetic mutation associated with monoamine oxidase A (MAOA) deficiency, which some studies have linked with a predisposition to aggression and violence. The trial court denied the request based on an insufficient scientific evidence of correlation between MAOA deficiency and aggression. The Georgia Supreme Court affirmed. Mobley subsequently filed a habeas corpus petition in which he alleged ineffective assistance of counsel for attempting to present such an unorthodox mitigation defense, using genetic evidence. A trial judge vacated his sentence, but the Georgia Supreme Court reversed and held that Mobley's counsel had made a "reasonable strategic decision." Turpin v. Mobley, 502 S.E.2d 458 (Ga. 1998). The Eleventh Circuit agreed with the Georgia Supreme Court. Mobley

v. Head, 267 F.3d 1312 (11th Cir. 2001), cert. denied, 536 U.S. 968 (2002). For a further discussion, see generally Nita A. Farahany & James E. Coleman, Jr., Genetics and Responsibility: To Know the Criminal from the Crime, 69 Law & Contemp. Probs. 115 (2006); Dianne E. Hoffmann & Karen H. Rothenberg, Judging Genes: Implications of the Second Generation of Genetic Tests in the Courtroom, 66 Md. L. Rev. 858 (2007).

4.   Richard M. Ewanisyzk was an attorney who abused alcohol and misappropriated client funds. His disbarment was affirmed by the courts. In re Ewaniszyk, 788 P.2d 690 (Cal.1990). John David Baker was an attorney who abused alcohol and misappropriated client funds. The state bar and the courts considered it to be a mitigating factor that Baker conceded that he "had a genetic predisposition to addiction." He was suspended rather than disbarred. Baker v. State Bar of California, 781 P.2d 1344 (Cal.1989). To what degree, if any, should the genetic basis of the addictive behavior (assuming it could be established) affect the appropriate discipline in these cases or sentencing in criminal cases?

5.   Similar issues could arise at all stages of the criminal justice system, from bail to parole. As to bail, in United States v. Salerno, 481 U.S. 739 (1987), the Supreme Court upheld the use of predictions of future criminal conduct as a factor in deciding whether to grant bail and the proper amount. As to parole, a wide range of considerations may be used by parole boards, and the boards are given a wide range of discretion, subject to considerations of due process. See Greenholtz v. Inmates of Nebraska Penal & Correctional Complex, 442 U.S. 1 (1979).

6.   In general, a more lax evidentiary standard is used in bail, sentencing, and parole matters than is applied at trial. What standard should be applied to the introduction of proffered behavioral genetic evidence?

7.   In Roper v. Simmons, 543 U.S. 551 (2005), the Supreme Court held that it was unconstitutional to execute individuals who were under 18 years old at the time they committed their crime. The decision was based largely on "evolving national and international standards of decency" and the consensus that children lack the emotional and mental maturity necessary for the most culpable criminal intent. Amicus briefs submitted on behalf of the defendant emphasized, among other things, that teenagers have "an underdeveloped sense of responsibility." Studies using modern neuroscience imaging techniques were offered to show that the brain does not mature until the age of 20–25 and therefore teenagers do not have fully developed frontal lobes capable of impulse control. Based on this line of reasoning, how should the Supreme Court rule in a future case in which the defendant argues that it is cruel and unusual punishment to execute an adult who does not suffer from mental retardation, but whose impulse control has been compromised by a genetic mutation?

D. COMMITMENT PROCEEDINGS

KANSAS V. CRANE
534 U.S. 407 (2002).

JUSTICE BREYER delivered the opinion of the Court.

This case concerns the constitutional requirements substantively limiting the civil commitment of a dangerous sexual offender—a matter that this Court considered in Kansas v. Hendricks, 521 U.S. 346 (1997). The State of Kansas argues that the Kansas Supreme Court has interpreted our decision in *Hendricks* in an overly restrictive manner. We agree and vacate the Kansas court's judgment.

I

In *Hendricks,* this Court upheld the Kansas Sexually Violent Predator Act, Kan. Stat. Ann. § 59–29a01 *et seq.* (1994), against constitutional challenge. In doing so, the Court characterized the confinement at issue as civil, not criminal, confinement. And it held that the statutory criterion for confinement embodied in the statute's words "mental abnormality or personality disorder" satisfied "substantive due process requirements."

In reaching its conclusion, the Court's opinion pointed out that "States have in certain narrow circumstances provided for the forcible civil detainment of people who are unable to control their behavior and who thereby pose a danger to the public health and safety." It said that "[w]e have consistently upheld such involuntary commitment statutes" when (1) "the confinement takes place pursuant to proper procedures and evidentiary standards," (2) there is a finding of "dangerousness either to one's self or to others," and (3) proof of dangerousness is "coupled . . . with the proof of some additional factor, such as a 'mental illness' or 'mental abnormality.'" It noted that the Kansas "Act unambiguously requires a finding of dangerousness either to one's self or to others," and then "links that finding to the existence of a 'mental abnormality' or 'personality disorder' that makes it difficult, if not impossible, for the person to control his dangerous behavior." And the Court ultimately determined that the statute's "requirement of a 'mental abnormality' or 'personality disorder' is consistent with the requirements of . . . other statutes that we have upheld in that it narrows the class of persons eligible for confinement to those who are unable to control their dangerousness."

The Court went on to respond to Hendricks' claim that earlier cases had required a finding, not of "mental abnormality" or "personality disorder," but of "mental illness." In doing so, the Court pointed out that we "have traditionally left to legislators the task of defining [such] terms." It then held that, to "the extent that the civil commitment statutes we have considered set forth criteria relating to an individual's inability to control his dangerousness, the Kansas Act sets forth comparable criteria." It added that Hendricks' own condition "doubtless satisfies those criteria," for (1) he suffers from pedophilia, (2) "the psychiatric profession itself classifies" that condition "as a serious mental disorder," and (3) Hendricks conceded that he cannot " 'control the urge' " to molest children. And it concluded that this "admitted lack of volitional control, coupled with a prediction of future dangerousness, adequately distinguishes Hendricks from other dangerous persons who are perhaps more properly dealt with exclusively through criminal proceedings."

II

In the present case the State of Kansas asks us to review the Kansas Supreme Court's application of *Hendricks*. The State here seeks the civil commitment of Michael Crane, a previously convicted sexual offender who, according to a least one of the State's psychiatric witnesses, suffers from both exhibitionism and antisocial personality disorder. After a jury trial, the Kansas District Court ordered Crane's civil commitment. But the Kansas Supreme Court reversed. In that court's view, the Federal Constitution as interpreted in *Hendricks* insists upon "a finding that the defendant cannot control his dangerous behavior"—even if (as provided by Kansas law) problems or "emotional capacity" and not "volitional capacity" prove the "source of bad behavior" warranting commitment. And the trial court had made no such finding.

Kansas now argues that the Kansas Supreme Court wrongly read *Hendricks* as requiring the State *always* to prove that a dangerous individual is *completely* unable to control his behavior. That reading, says Kansas, is far too rigid.

III

We agree with Kansas insofar as it argues that *Hendricks* set forth no requirement of *total* or *complete* lack of control. *Hendricks* referred to the Kansas Act as requiring a "mental abnormality" or "personality disorder" that makes it *"difficult,* if not impossible, for the [dangerous] person to control his dangerous behavior." The word "difficult" indicates that the lack of control to which this Court referred was not absolute. Indeed, as different *amici* on opposite sides of this case agree, an absolutist approach is unworkable. Insistence upon absolute lack of control would risk barring civil commitment of highly dangerous persons suffering severe mental abnormalities.

We do not agree with the State, however, insofar as it seeks to claim that the Constitution permits commitment of the type of dangerous sexual offender considered in *Hendricks* without *any* lack-of-control determination. *Hendricks* underscored the constitutional importance of distinguishing a dangerous sexual offender subject to civil commitment "from other dangerous persons who are perhaps more properly dealt with exclusively through criminal proceedings." That distinction is necessary lest "civil commitment" become a "mechanism for retribution or general deterrence"—functions properly those of criminal law, not civil commitment. The presence of what the "psychiatric profession itself classifie[d] . . . as a serious mental disorder" there consisted of a special and serious lack of ability to control behavior.

In recognizing that fact, we did not give to the phrase "lack of control" a particularly narrow or technical meaning. And we recognize that in cases where lack of control is at issue, "inability to control behavior" will not be demonstrable with mathematical precision. It is enough to say that there must be proof of serious difficulty in controlling behavior. And this, when viewed in light of such features of the case as the nature of the psychiatric diagnosis, and the severity of the mental abnormality itself, must be sufficient to distinguish the dangerous sexual offender whose serious mental illness, abnormality, or disorder subjects him to civil commitment from the dangerous but typical recidivist convicted in an ordinary criminal case.

We recognize that *Hendricks* as so read provides a less precise constitutional standard than would those more definite rules for which the parties have argued. But the Constitution's safeguards of human liberty in the area of mental illness and the law are not always best enforced through precise bright-line rules. For one thing, the States retain considerable leeway in defining the mental abnormalities and personality disorders that make an individual eligible for commitment. For another, the science of psychiatry, which informs but does not control ultimate legal determinations, is an ever-advancing science, whose distinctions do not seek precisely to mirror those of the law. Consequently, we have sought to provide constitutional guidance in this area by proceeding deliberately and contextually, elaborating generally stated constitutional standards and objectives as specific circumstances require. *Hendricks* embodied that approach.

* * *

For these reasons, the judgment of the Kansas Supreme Court is vacated, and the case remanded for further proceedings not inconsistent with this opinion.

It is so ordered.

JUSTICE SCALIA, with whom JUSTICE THOMAS joins, dissenting.

Today the Court holds that the Kansas Sexually Violent Predator Act (SVPA) cannot, consistent with so-called substantive due process, be applied as written. It does so even though, less than five years ago, we upheld the very same petitioner (the State of Kansas) from the judgment of the very same court. Not only is the new law that the Court announces today wrong, but the Court's manner of promulgating it—snatching back from the State of Kansas a victory so recently awarded—cheapens the currency of our judgments. I would reverse, rather than vacate, the judgment of the Kansas Supreme Court.

NOTES AND QUESTIONS

1.   After remand of his case, doctors determined that Mr. Crane was no longer a threat, and he was released in January 2002. On October 14, 2003, Crane was found guilty of forcible rape, kidnapping, third-degree assault, and three counts of forcible sodomy that stemmed from the raping of a woman in an apartment complex parking lot in Kansas City, Missouri. He was sentenced to life in prison.

2.   About one-third of the states have laws similar to the Kansas law upheld in *Hendricks*, and new bills are introduced every year. See Ariz. Rev. Stat. Ann. § 36–3701; Cal. Welf. & Inst. Code § 6600; D.C. Code Ann. § 22–3808; Fla. Stat. Ann. § 394.910; 725 Ill. Comp. Stat. Ann. § 207/40; Iowa Code Ann. § 229A.1; Kan. Stat. Ann. § 59–29a01; Minn. Stat. Ann. § 253B.185; Mo. Rev. Stat. § 632.480; N.J. Stat. Ann. § 30:4–82.4; N.Y. Correctional Law § 402; N.D. Cent. Code § 25–03.3–13; S.C. Code Ann. § 44–48–20; Tex. Health & Safety Code Ann. § 841.081; Va. Code Ann. § 37.1–70.9; Wash. Rev. Code Ann. § 71.09.010; Wis. Stat. Ann. § 980.06. If you were a member of a state legislature, would you support such legislation? Why or why not?

3.   In United States v. Comstock, 560 U.S. 126 (2010), the Supreme Court held that a federal civil-commitment statute, that permits the Department of Justice to detain a mentally ill, sexually dangerous federal prisoner beyond the date of the prisoner's scheduled release does not violate due process. The Court held that the statute is a constitutional exercise under the Necessary and Proper clause, Article I, section 8, clause 18 of the Constitution.

4.   In Robinson v. California, 370 U.S. 660 (1962) (narcotic addiction) and Powell v. Texas, 392 U.S. 514 (1968) (alcohol addiction), the Supreme Court held that individuals may be convicted for unlawful acts, but it is unconstitutional to punish an individual for having the status of an addict. If an individual were found to have a genetic mutation linked to a predisposition to violence, would incarcerating the individual before he or she committed a crime be cruel and unusual punishment? Would it matter what degree of correlation there was between the mutation and the likelihood of committing the violent act? Would *Robinson* and *Powell* prohibit compelled treatment of an individual to prevent the commission of acts of violence, or to prevent the commission of additional acts of violence for an individual who already has been convicted?

V. EDUCATION

Assessing cognitive ability is the largest potential application of mental and behavioral genetics in educational settings. There are numerous scientific, technical, and moral concerns about whether to attempt to distinguish among individuals based on the genetics of cognitive ability. These concerns are heightened when dealing with children, who are often vulnerable to familial and peer-based stigmatization, self-fulfilling prophecies, and confusion about the deterministic effects of genetic predispositions. Nevertheless, it is likely that the use (or misuse) of genetics in educational settings will become increasingly important legal and social issues.

Potentially, there are two main types of genetic tests with relevance in educational settings. First, children might be tested for fragile X syndrome, autism, and various learning and behavioral disorders or predispositions. Second, children and young adults could be tested for the genetic component of cognitive ability, including "gifted" status and relative strengths and abilities in certain fields, such as musical ability and numeracy. Of course, the scientific research does not currently support such widespread uses, and ethical and legal considerations might even limit the use of scientifically valid testing.

MARK A. ROTHSTEIN, GENETICS AND THE WORK FORCE OF THE NEXT HUNDRED YEARS
2000 Colum. Bus. L. Rev. 371, 377–379 (2000).

The "channeling" or "tracking" of children based on their genetic endowment would be consistent with educational methods used in varying degrees for most of the twentieth century, which relied on IQ tests and standardized tests such as the SAT. It would also be consistent with elitist and even racist notions of worthiness of education and social advancement, which date back at least to the nineteenth century. For example, Herbert Spencer, the father of social Darwinism, opposed free public education in nineteenth century England on hereditarian grounds. In his view, parents who could not afford to pay for the education of their children, necessarily must lack the intellect, determination, and good character to succeed in life. Because he believed that these traits were heritable, it followed that the offspring of such individuals would possess similar defective traits and therefore public education would be a waste of public money.

* * *

The tracking of school children based on IQ has been criticized on a variety of grounds, including that it is inaccurate, unsound educationally and socially, discriminatory on the basis of race and ethnicity, stigmatizing, and a self-fulfilling prophecy. Perhaps the most important criticism, as we contemplate even more extensive tracking based on genetic predisposition, is that it is undemocratic. "The practice of sorting children into ability groups and providing them with a differentiated educational experience is inherently undemocratic and is contrary to the spirit of equality that is so important to Americans." Interestingly, the critics almost always focus on the asserted unfairness in the educational process rather than the larger effects on society of having an individual's future opportunities for the good life so severely limited at a young age and creating a *de facto* caste system.

GARY E. MARCHANT & JASON S. ROBERT, GENETIC TESTING
FOR AUTISM PREDISPOSITION: ETHICAL, LEGAL
AND SOCIAL CHALLENGES
9 Hous. J. Health L. & Pol'y 203, 221–222 (2009).

* * *

Accurate and timely diagnosis is critical for addressing autism in clinical settings. Establishing a diagnosis and understanding the underlying etiology may aid in predicting the prognosis, determining accurate recurrence risk, starting appropriate treatment and health maintenance planning, and offering family members considerable emotional relief. Children exhibiting symptoms or characteristics of autism might be genetically tested for autism predisposition genes to assist in diagnosing autism early in its development. The threshold question for this application is: how will the identification of a genetic marker in a child assist in the diagnosis or treatment of that child's condition? For example, will there be different treatment options based on the results of genetic testing? If not, will there be any other benefits for the child from identifying a genetic contributing cause? Will there be any benefits to the parents in terms of planning for future children? What are the risks that such testing might entail (e.g., in terms of parent-child relations, child's own self-image, and insurability)? How well characterized and validated must the genetic test be before it can be used for such purposes?

It is also important to understand how individuals perceive the genetic risk of their child developing autism given that genetic testing for complex diseases such as autism provides only the probability of developing the disease. It is unlikely that there will be a bright line between disease and non-disease status in people exhibiting autism traits, so how will genetic markers contribute to delineation of disease status from non-disease status? It has been shown that, regarding results from genetic testing, individuals often interpret probabilities as either presence or absence of the disease. The fact that mutations or polymorphisms are reported as either present or not present (despite the fact that the risk of developing the disease is probabilistic) may further exacerbate the problem. Knowledge that a young child and possibly other family members carry a genetic predisposition to autism may create a whole series of stigmas and negative perceptions related to being "at risk." There is some evidence associated with other genetically influenced diseases that the existence of a genetic explanation for a child's disease can provide emotional relief for the parents. However, a parent who is found to have contributed the genetic marker to an autistic child may have feelings of guilt and responsibility. Siblings of an individual with autism who are found to carry the same genetic marker but who did not develop autism may have misgivings and anxieties about becoming a parent and passing on such a trait to their children.

EMILY CHANG, IN CHINA, DNA TESTS ON KIDS ID GENETIC GIFTS, CAREERS

CNN.com (August 3, 2009), edition.cnn.com/2009/WORLD/asiapcf/08/03/china.dna.children.ability/index.html.

CHONGQING, China (CNN)—At the Chongqing Children's Palace, experts are hoping to revolutionize child-rearing with the help of science. About 30 children aged 3 to 12 years old and their parents are participating in a new program that uses DNA testing to identify genetic gifts and predict the future.

For about $880, Chinese parents can sign their kids up for the test and five days of camp.

When Director Zhao Mingyou first heard about the technology earlier this year, he instantly knew it could be a success in China.

"Nowadays, competition in the world is about who has the most talent," said Zhao. "We can give Chinese children an effective, scientific plan at an early age."

The test is conducted by the Shanghai Biochip Corporation. Scientists claim a simple saliva swab collects as many as 10,000 cells that enable them to isolate eleven different genes. By taking a closer look at the genetic codes, they say they can extract information about a child's IQ, emotional control, focus, memory, athletic ability and more.

"For basketball, we can test for height and other factors," said Dr. Huang Xinhua, a leading scientist on the project. "We also test listening ability so that can tell us if (the child) might be talented at music."

DNA testing has been used more widely to determine susceptibility to genetic disease. The test can identify mutations in the genetic code that lead to certain disorders, allow patients to assess risk levels and decide whether they want preventative treatment.

* * *

But according to Chinese scientists, this is the first time the test is being offered to children in China to help discover their natural talents.

For about $880, Chinese parents can sign their kids up for the test and five days of summer camp in Chongqing, where the children will be evaluated in various settings from sports to art. The scientific results, combined with observations by experts throughout the week, will be used to make recommendations to parents about what their child should pursue.

Dr. Huang said the testing can even help project careers down the road.

Examining one child's results, he told CNN: "This child is very thoughtful and focused, so I suggest she go into management."

Clinical psychologist Dr. Rob Blinn said the DNA test can be accurate but only "within a sort of limited field" and that results will not be "dramatic."

"You're not going to be able to predict that someone's going to be like the next Einstein. It's more like this person may have an IQ that's maybe 5 or 10 points greater than this other person because of the absence or presence of these particular genes," he said.

Still, parents are convinced it will help their child. It is no secret that China's one-child policy often produces anxious and ambitious parents with high expectations for their only child.

"China is different from Western countries," said Yang Yangqing, the lab's technical director. "There is only one child in our families so more and more parents focus on their children's education and they want to give them the best education."

Along with parents, the Chinese government is also interested in giving talented children an early start on their careers. Children as young as two are regularly hand-picked by the government to represent China on the international stage.

Future gymnasts, musicians, and basketball players are sent to rigorous training camps and specialized sports schools, and sometimes paid a government salary.

* * *

"It's better to develop her talents earlier rather than later," Chen Zhongyan said of her four-year-old daughter, who is attending the genetics camp. "Now we can find when she is young, and raise her based on what her natural gifts are."

Her daughter, Lai Hongni, has already shown a strong aptitude for dancing, while four-year-old twin boys Luo Lianzhao and Dong Liangtong appear to be good at drawing.

"This way we can really understand our kids," said the twins' father, Mr. Dong, referring to the program.

In the end, are these parents giving their kids a head start or taking a shortcut? Critics of the program said such analysis has frightening implications.

"Kids, especially at younger ages, they need to have fun, they need to enjoy themselves, they need to find meaning in life," Dr. Blinn said. "They need to have rich deep emotional interchange with their families and parents."

"Whether it's really good for a two- or three-year-old to be sent off to a camp to be genetically tested, you know, and put in this track so early in life, I have some real doubts about whether that's in the child's best interest," Blinn added. "It seems to be more in the parents' best interest."

LAURA F. ROTHSTEIN, GENETIC INFORMATION IN SCHOOLS IN GENETIC SECRETS: PROTECTING PRIVACY AND CONFIDENTIALITY IN THE GENETIC ERA
317–320 (Mark A. Rothstein ed. 1997).

Although little genetic information is being systematically collected or used in educational settings, this could change at any time. Well meaning but unthinking school officials could adopt programs of genetic screening or genetic classification of students. School officials also could acquiesce in commercial pressures by facilitating the collection of genetic information about students. The possibility of using genetic information in schools, obtained or maintained for any reason, raises a variety of important ethical, legal, and social issues that are poorly addressed by current policy.

WHY SCHOOLS WOULD ACQUIRE, HAVE, OR USE GENETIC INFORMATION

Educational purposes. A school could acquire, have, or use genetic information for four main reasons. If a school has genetic information about a condition such as dyslexia or fragile X syndrome, it may be able to provide appropriate educational programming for a particular child. If the school personnel believe that the basis for a child's weak academic performance is genetic, then the school may be able to intervene more appropriately in programming the child's education. Arguably, if problems are identified before a child begins school, difficulties can be anticipated and planned for. Diagnosing dyslexia through nongenetic means usually occurs only once a child is about eight years old. If diagnosis were to occur at a much earlier age through genetic testing, it is believed that interventions would be much more effective. Early speech and language therapy and physical therapy may be positive interventions for children with fragile X syndrome.

The second purpose for using genetic information is that where conditions relate to potential behavioral and disciplinary problems, the school can provide more appropriate behavior management or observe a particular child more closely in anticipation of problems. In most cases, behavior will also affect educational development because it will affect the child's ability to focus and understand. Children with fragile X syndrome have been shown to have positive behavior changes when treated with folic acid. Benefits also have been shown to derive from taking methylphenidate (Ritalin), dextroamphetamine (Dexedrine), and pemoline (Cylert). Identifying fragile X syndrome as the basis for certain behaviors also may ensure that appropriate behavior management techniques (e.g., "time outs") are used.

The third educational purpose relates to conditions that involve health impairments. The benefit of knowing such information is that the school can provide appropriate related services, such as diagnosis and physical therapy, for children whose health or physical ability has been adversely affected. If public health agencies were to provide population-wide information about the incidence of certain types of health impairment in a state based on genetic screening at birth, schools would be better able to budget and plan for related services in anticipation of the entry of these children into public schools.

The fourth reason relates to accountability. Schools must measure abilities and performance to meet the mandates of school excellence expectations as well as to obtain funds under special education laws. Having a genetic marker for certain conditions may in theory assist in better measuring students' eligibility for special education and for determining which students should and should not be held to certain performance expectations.

Noneducational purposes. Schools may in turn be able to provide genetic information to other social service agencies for public health services and planning. If public health officials were convinced that genetic screening of children promoted public health, then schools would be the ideal setting in which to conduct such screening. In almost every state schools already screen children for various public health purposes, including conducting screenings for tuberculosis and scoliosis, as well as dental, vision, and hearing tests.

Public health screening agencies could plan for appropriate interventions in response to the information they obtained through screening. It could be argued that schools are the logical screening and intervention point for many public health issues because (with the exception of children in home schooling) they are the one institution in which everyone is mandated by law to participate. Though not educational in nature, such programs as comprehensive vaccination efforts benefit society as a whole.

By screening all individuals of school age for certain conditions, public service providers could plan for future needs and requirements. For example, if children were screened for certain cancers, the medical community could plan for the required services. If there were comprehensive screening for various late-onset genetic disorders, such as Alzheimer's disease, society at large could make preparations for the number of individuals expected to develop the disorders. Not only could society at large make general preparations, but in some cases, individuals with the genetic marker could begin planning for services.

Schools might also facilitate genetic testing and screening by others for monetary reasons. It is not hard to imagine commercial enterprises providing financial and other incentives to schools to allow them to gain access to children or the names of children with certain genetic traits. In a case involving the Genentech Corporation, schools facilitated the acquisition of information about children who were unusually short for their age. The school board approved the school nurse's provision of information about children's heights, which Genentech then used in marketing its human growth hormone.

There are risks associated with commercial interests joining forces with the schools. Even assuming that the schools' motives are entirely benign, in most cases the administrators who grant permission to carry out such evaluations probably do not appreciate the consequences. One need only think of how television sets and commercial programming have found their way into many schools to realize that financially strapped schools are not averse to exploring opportunities for economic support. This in turn brings to mind the *Jurassic Park* problem: when commercial interests use science, they are unlikely to think through the moral and ethical implications of what they are doing.

DOE V. KNOX COUNTY BOARD OF EDUCATION
918 F.Supp. 181 (E.D. Ky. 1996).

COFFMAN, J.

This matter is before the Court upon the defendants' motion to dismiss.

BACKGROUND

The plaintiff, Jane Doe, files this action pursuant to 42 U.S.C. § 1983. She claims that the defendants violated her civil rights, in that they violated the Family Educational Rights and Privacy Act of 1974

("FERPA"), 20 U.S.C. § 1232(g); the right to academic privacy guaranteed by the Equal Protection Clause of the Fourteenth Amendment to the United States Constitution; and the Kentucky Family Education Rights and Privacy Act ("KFERPA"), K.R.S. 160.700, et seq. The plaintiff also asserts two tort claims: intentional infliction of emotional distress and invasion of privacy. The defendants' memorandum in support of their motion to dismiss addresses the plaintiff's federal and state FERPA claims and, indirectly, the tort claims. Their memorandum does not address the plaintiff's equal protection claim.

The plaintiff is a thirteen-year-old hermaphrodite. In 1994, a dispute arose between the plaintiff's mother, Mary Doe, and defendant Knox County Board of Education ("Board"). Mary was not satisfied with her daughter's educational plan and requested a due process hearing on the issue. A hearing officer held the hearing on August 18, 19 and 20, 1994. During the hearing, the hearing officer entered a protective order prohibiting the disclosure of the plaintiff's confidential records. The plaintiff alleges that the defendants discussed the plaintiff's educational placement, medical condition and disability with a newspaper reporter. The defendants allege that, in accordance with applicable law, the members of the Board discussed the reasons for emergency purchases made on behalf of the plaintiff and that discussions with the reporter were in that context. In any event, the following appeared in the *Mountain Advocate:*

> As an alternative to the residential placement, the emotional behavior disorder (EBD) unit was established at Lay Elementary at the beginning of the 1994–95 school year for the fifth through eighth grade.
>
> A written explanation in the board of education agenda from recent meeting stated that the EBD unit was created because of a 12-year-old female with severe emotional and behavioral problems, resulting primarily from a medical condition, hermaphroditism.
>
> Hermaphroditism is a person born having both male and female reproductive organs.

The plaintiff is suing the superintendent of the Knox County School District and several members of the Board in their individual and official capacities. The plaintiff is also suing the Board.

THE ELEVENTH AMENDMENT AND SOVEREIGN IMMUNITY

* * *

Therefore, sovereign immunity bars the plaintiff's state tort claims against the Board and against the superintendent and the members of the Board in their official capacities. Likewise, sovereign immunity bars the plaintiff's claim for damages against the Board and against the superintendent and the Board members in their official capacities for the defendant's alleged violation of KFERPA. Claims for injunctive or declaratory relief against those entities, however, may proceed.

FERPA

The plaintiff claims that the defendants violated her civil rights when they violated FERPA. The defendants argue that, even if they did violate FERPA, they are not liable to the plaintiffs because FERPA does not provide a private cause of action. The plaintiff does not dispute this but argues that a FERPA violation may be the basis for a claim under 42 U.S.C. § 1983. The defendants point out that all jurisdictions have not agreed on whether a plaintiff may recover under § 1983 for a violation of FERPA. However, the Sixth Circuit has addressed the issue. In an unpublished decision, the Sixth Circuit stated, "The district court correctly noted that FERPA itself does not give rise to a private cause of action, but does create an interest that may be vindicated in a § 1983 action." This holding is in accord with decisions in several other federal courts. The plaintiff's FERPA-based § 1983 claim may thus proceed.

Consequently, the Court must determine the applicability of FERPA to the plaintiff's claim. The plaintiff alleges that the defendants violated FERPA by releasing specific identifiable information without the consent or knowledge of the plaintiff. 20 U.S.C. § 1232(g)(b)(1) provides as follows:

> No funds shall be made available under any applicable program to any educational agency or institution which has a policy or practice of permitting the release of education records (or personally identifiable information contained therein other than directory information . . .) of students without the written consent of their parents to any individual, agency, or organization, other than to the following. . . .

The statute proceeds to list the exceptions, none of which includes newspapers or newspaper reporters.

Thus, the question becomes whether the information disclosed in the due process hearing and reported by the *Mountain Advocate* was personally identifiable. The defendants argue that the information was not identifiable and that one who did not already know this student would not have learned the identity of the student based on the information in the newspaper article. The defendants may be correct but that is an issue of fact that the jury must decide at trial.

KFERPA

The plaintiff's claim pursuant to KFERPA against the superintendent and Board members in their individual capacities for full relief and against the Board and the superintendent and Board members in their official capacities for declaratory and injunctive relief remains. K.R.S. 160.720(2) provides, "Educational institutions shall not permit the release or disclosure of records, reports, or identifiable information on students to third parties . . . without parental or eligible student consent. . . ." The statute proceeds to list several exceptions, none of which includes newspapers or newspaper reporters.

The defendants argue that the information was not identifiable. As discussed above, this is a question of fact for a jury to decide at trial. The defendants also argue that K.R.S. 160.990 provides the exclusive remedies available under this statute. The Court disagrees. K.R.S. 160.990 is not part of KFERPA, and its provisions apply to statutes that are not part of KFERPA. Accordingly, the defendants' motion to dismiss fails with regard to the individual-capacity KFERPA claims and any KFERPA claims for injunctive or declaratory relief against the Board or the Board members and the superintendent in their official capacities.

QUALIFIED IMMUNITY

The Board members and superintendent argue that they are entitled to qualified immunity with regard to the claims against them in their individual capacities. Government officials performing discretionary functions generally are immune from personal liability for civil damages so long as their conduct does not violate clearly established statutory or constitutional rights of which a reasonable person would have known. When analyzing whether a right is clearly established, a district court must carefully define the right at issue.

The issue in the present case is whether the plaintiff's right to avoid disclosure of the information printed in the *Mountain Advocate* was clearly established by federal statute or by the constitution. FERPA clearly establishes a right of freedom from a board of education's disclosure of personally identifiable information contained in education records. The defendants do not dispute that the information was contained in education records. Therefore, the question becomes whether the disclosed information was personally identifiable. The defendants argue that it was not. However, for purposes of a motion to dismiss, the Court must view the plaintiff's factual allegations in a light most favorable to the plaintiff. Viewed in this way, the information reported in the *Mountain Advocate* was personally identifiable. This is especially true within the context of a motion to dismiss, when the parties have had insufficient opportunity to develop the facts. Subsequent discovery will shed greater light on this issue, and the defendants may raise their qualified immunity argument in a motion for summary judgment or at trial if appropriate. The defendants have not raised directly the argument that the Board's members reasonably thought the disclosure complied with FERPA. However, the Court notes that if the information was identifiable, disclosing it to the press was not reasonable. For purposes of the motion to dismiss, the Court will not hold, at this stage, that the Board members had qualified immunity for purposes of the § 1983 claim that the Board members violated FERPA.

Because the parties have not addressed thoroughly the § 1983 claim that the Board members violated the plaintiff's Constitutional right to academic privacy, the Court will not rule on the Board members' qualified immunity argument as it applies to that claim.

CONCLUSION

Accordingly, the Court ORDERS that

1)   The defendants' motion to dismiss is GRANTED with respect to the plaintiff's state tort claims against the Board and the superintendent and Board members in their official capacities and the plaintiff's claim for damages under KFERPA against the Board and the superintendent and Board members in their official capacities.

2)   The defendants' motion to dismiss is DENIED on all other grounds and for all other claims.

NOTES AND QUESTIONS

1.   Which of the educational motivations of schools mentioned in the Rothstein excerpt do you think will be the most likely source of pressure to use genetic information in schools? What genetic disorders or traits do you think will be most relevant to schools?

2.   For a discussion of a likely application of genetics in educational settings, see Robert Plomin & John C. DeFries, The Genetics of Cognitive Abilities and Disabilities, Scientific Am., May 1998, at 62–69.

3.   In the *Doe* case, one of the defenses raised was that the name of the plaintiff never appeared in the newspaper article. How difficult do you think it would be for the readers of the *Mountain Advocate* to identify Jane Doe?

4.   There are currently no laws that directly address the issue of genetic information in schools. The Family Educational Rights and Privacy Act (FERPA), which safeguards the privacy of school records, applies only to recipients of federal financial assistance and provides for limited remedies. 20 U.S.C. § 1232g. In addition, it is not clear whether genetic information would be considered a "school record" subject to the Act. State school record laws are probably a better vehicle for protecting genetic privacy and confidentiality. These laws could be enacted or amended to limit the access of school personnel to genetic information in a student's record, grant parents a right to view and correct educational records, require that medical and other genetic information be stored in files separate from other educational records, and set time schedules and procedures for the destruction of the files.

VI. TORT LAW

CARLSEN V. WACKENHUT CORP.

868 P.2d 882 (Wash. Ct. App. 1994), review denied, 881 P.2d 255 (Wash. 1994).

ALEXANDER, J.

Ronda Carlsen appeals an order of the Pierce County Superior Court granting summary judgment to the Wackenhut Corporation, dismissing Carlsen's claims against Wackenhut for Wackenhut's alleged negligence in hiring and supervising an employee. We reverse.

On May 10, 1989, two 16-year-old girls, Ronda Carlsen and her friend, Heather, attended a rock concert at the Tacoma Dome with some acquaintances. The concert featured a group of musicians known as "Bon Jovi". During the course of the concert, Carlsen and Heather became separated from their companions. Consequently, they sought assistance from someone in authority to "help us find our friends". Toward that end, they approached a man who they believed was a "security guard".

The man, William Futi, indicated his willingness to help the two girls. After speaking with them for a short time, he asked them if they wanted to get closer to the stage and perhaps even meet the band members. The two girls were eager to meet the entertainers, so they accompanied Futi toward the stage of the Tacoma Dome. Their route required them to go under the bleachers. Carlsen indicated that "neither Heather or I wanted to go under the bleachers with him but since we were together and he was a security guard, we felt reasonably comfortable in proceeding." Part way to the stage, Futi mentioned that he could only take them one at a time. After Futi took Heather to the stage and returned, he told Carlsen that they would have to travel a different way back. As Futi led Carlsen under a set of bleachers, he threw her down and attempted to rape her. Carlsen screamed but she was not heard over the noise of the concert. Futi was eventually frightened away when the music ended and the lights came on.

Futi was charged in Pierce County Superior Court with second degree attempted rape. He later pleaded guilty to an amended charge of indecent liberties.

Carlsen brought suit against the Wackenhut Corporation, the company that had employed Futi at the Tacoma Dome. She claimed that Wackenhut had been negligent in its hiring of Futi in that it knew or should have known that Futi, who had a prior conviction for robbery, was unfit for employment with Wackenhut. She also claimed that Wackenhut was negligent in its supervision of Futi and that it was liable for Futi's actions under the theory of respondeat superior.

* * *

Although Futi's job was not high paying, the circumstances of his employment put him in a position of responsibility. A jury might well conclude that it was reasonable for concert patrons to look upon Futi as one authorized to perform security functions, and that, therefore, Wackenhut should have more extensively examined Futi's background before hiring him. The need for such a determination by a jury seems especially compelling in light of the limited information and inconsistencies in Futi's applications for employment. This additional investigation might well have disclosed Futi's prior juvenile record.

Wackenhut argues, finally, that even if it had performed a check of Futi's criminal record, nothing in that record indicated a propensity for sexual violence. Carlsen responds that robbery (only one of Futi's four convictions) involves the use of force or a threat of force which is indicative of a propensity toward violence. We agree with Carlsen that robbery is a crime of violence. Upon discovery of a prior robbery conviction, a prospective employer would be on notice that the prospective employee has a propensity for violent behavior. In short, we conclude that, although Wackenhut did not have actual knowledge that Futi was potentially dangerous, a trier of fact could find that the corporation breached its duty of ordinary care by not doing more to determine whether Futi was fit to work in the job he performed for Wackenhut.

NOTES AND QUESTIONS

1.   Tort liability is based on the employer's failure to determine the potential employee's dangerousness or propensity to engage in violent conduct. These actions are usually termed negligent hiring, negligent retention, or negligent supervision. See Mark A. Rothstein et al., Employment Law § 1.12 (5th ed. 2014).

2.   Can you think of other contexts in which third parties would be interested in learning about an individual's propensity to engage in violent conduct as a way of avoiding tort liability? Consider the following hypothetical.

> Suppose a young camper at summer camp unexpectedly and deliberately hit another camper in the head with a baseball bat, causing serious injury. Because the statutory liability of parents for the intentional torts of their children is quite limited, and because a child is unlikely to have adequate assets to satisfy a judgment, a negligence action might be brought against the camp. Assuming the boys were adequately supervised, the injured child's lawyer might assert that had the camp required behavioral genetic testing of all campers, it would have learned that the aggressor child was predisposed to violent behavior. It then could have refused to admit the child, thereby preventing the injury. If the injured child is able to obtain a judgment, or even a settlement, then the risk-averse

behavior for every other summer camp, boarding school, college dormitory, and other entities might be to require a review of behavioral genetic test results. Pressure to do so also could come from parents.

Mark A. Rothstein, Behavioral Genetic Determinism: Its Effects on Culture and Law, Behavioral Genetics in The Clash of Culture and Biology 107 (Ronald A. Carson & Mark A. Rothstein eds. 1999).

3.   Are there any negative consequences from screening individuals to make predictions about their genetic predisposition to violence? What are the most likely sources of legal protection against unreasonable conduct on the part of employers and other third parties?

4.   If there were "some" scientific basis for doing so, would you oppose the Navy's use of genetic testing for predisposition to claustrophobia before assigning sailors to serve on submarines? Would you oppose an auto insurance company's use of genetic testing for predisposition to risk taking behavior in basing insurance rates? If you oppose these uses, do you oppose *any* use of behavioral genetics or only certain kinds? Why?

CHAPTER 14

PRIVACY AND CONFIDENTIALITY

■ ■ ■

I.   INTRODUCTION

For experts and lay people alike, privacy is the defining issue in determining whether advances in genetics can be integrated into medical practice and other aspects of daily life without unacceptable social consequences. Virtually everyone is in favor of genetic privacy in the abstract, but agreement among individuals and interest groups on this issue rarely extends beyond the abstract.

On closer examination, it is extraordinarily difficult to: (1) reach consensus on the definition of privacy and the related concepts of confidentiality, security, and anonymity; (2) distinguish genetic privacy from more general notions of medical privacy; (3) differentiate among the tangible and intangible benefits and harms associated with the presence or absence of privacy, including the complex concept of genetic discrimination; (4) balance the interests in genetic privacy and confidentiality against other valid social interests, such as research, clinical care, public health, law enforcement, and cost; and (5) devise thoughtful, practical, and effective legislative and regulatory measures to protect genetic privacy.

This chapter challenges you to think critically about genetic privacy and confidentiality. There are few cases in the chapter because cases based on alleged invasions of privacy tend to be context-specific and therefore they are included in, for example, succeeding chapters on insurance and employment. Nevertheless, the readings and statutory materials are crucial because they explore the conceptual foundations on which all genetic privacy and confidentiality law, ethics, and policy are based.

SISSELA BOK, SECRETS: ON THE ETHICS OF CONCEALMENT AND REVELATION
20 (1983).

Control over secrecy provides a safety valve for individuals in the midst of communal life—some influence over transactions between the world of personal experience and the world shared with others. With no control over such exchanges, human beings would be unable to exercise choice about their lives. To restrain some secrets and to allow others freer play; to keep some hidden and to let others be known; to offer knowledge to some but not to all comers; to give and receive confidences and to guess at far more: these efforts at control permeate all human contact.

Those who lose all control over these relations cannot flourish in either the personal or the shared world, nor retain their sanity. If experience in the shared world becomes too overwhelming, the sense of identity suffers. Psychosis has been described as the breaking down of the delineation between the self and the outside world: the person going mad "flows out onto the world as through a broken dam." Conversely, experience limited to the inside world stunts the individual: at best it may lead to the aching self-exploration evoked by Nietzsche: "I am solitude become man.—That no word ever reached me forced me to reach myself."

In seeking some control over secrecy and openness, and the power it makes possible, human beings attempt to guard and to promote not only their autonomy but ultimately their sanity and survival itself. The claims in defense of this control, however, are not always articulated. Some take them to be so self-evident as to need no articulation; others subsume them under more general arguments about liberty or privacy. But it is important for the purposes of considering the ethics of secrecy to set forth these claims. Otherwise it will not be possible to ask, in particular cases, to what extent they should apply and what restraints they might require. Nor will it be possible to study the extrapolations made from them in support of collective practices of secrecy.

NOTES AND QUESTIONS

1.   There are many descriptions of the importance of privacy. Here is another one.

> Why we as Americans so cherish our privacy is not easy to explain. Privacy covers many things. It protects the solitude necessary for creative thought. It allows us the independence that is part of raising a family. It protects our right to be secure in our own homes and possessions, assured that the government cannot come barging in. Privacy also encompasses our right to self-determination and to define who we are. Although we live in a world of noisy self-confession, privacy allows us to keep certain facts to ourselves if we so choose. The right to privacy, it seems, is what makes us civilized.

Ellen Alderman & Caroline Kennedy, The Right to Privacy xiii (1995). How do you compare their view of privacy with Sissela Bok's?

2.   Is the right to privacy valued more or less today than in earlier times? Do we have more or less privacy today? What threats to privacy do you see in daily life? What, if anything, does the growth in social networking

websites indicate about public attitudes about privacy? Compared with other fields, such as consumer credit, educational records, and vital statistics, do we have more or less medical privacy?

II. GENETIC PRIVACY AND CONFIDENTIALITY

A. ANALYTICAL FRAMEWORK

ANITA L. ALLEN, GENETIC PRIVACY: EMERGING CONCEPTS
AND VALUES IN GENETIC SECRETS: PROTECTING PRIVACY AND
CONFIDENTIALITY IN THE GENETIC ERA
31, 33–34 (Mark A. Rothstein ed. 1997).

THE FOUR DIMENSIONS OF GENETIC PRIVACY

The word *privacy* has a wide range of meanings. It is used ambiguously in law and morals to describe and prescribe, denote and connote, praise and blame. "Genetic privacy" is no less rich with ambiguity than "privacy." Although the expression "genetic privacy" is a product of recent developments in science, it does not stand for a wholly new concept. "Genetic privacy" signifies applications of the familiar concept of privacy to genetic-related phenomena.

When used to label issues that arise in contemporary bioethics and public policy, "privacy" generally refers to one of four categories of concern. They are: (1) informational privacy concerns about access to personal information; (2) physical privacy concerns about access to persons and personal spaces; (3) decisional privacy concerns about governmental and other third-party interference with personal choices; and (4) proprietary privacy concerns about the appropriation and ownership of interests in human personality. "Genetic privacy" typically refers to one of these same four general categories.

"Genetic privacy" often denotes informational privacy, including the confidentiality, anonymity, or secrecy of the data that result from genetic testing and screening. Substantial limits on third-party access to confidential, anonymous, or secret genetic information are requirements of respect for informational privacy. However, family members may possess moral rights to undisclosed genetic data that patients and the professionals who serve them legitimately withhold from other third parties.

George Annas had informational privacy in mind when he warned that "control of and access to the information contained in an individual's genome gives others potential power over the personal life of the individual by providing a basis not only for counseling, but also for stigmatizing and discrimination." Likewise, Alan Westin was thinking of informational privacy when he defined "genetic privacy" by reference to what he called the "core concept of privacy"—namely, "the claim of an individual to determine what information about himself or herself should be known by others." Westin's definition captures well much of the informational dimension of genetic privacy and its connection to ideals of self-determination. Although it is adequate for purposes of a discussion of informational privacy, Westin's definition leaves important physical, decisional, and proprietary dimensions of genetic privacy in the shadows.

The genetic privacy concerns heard today range far beyond informational privacy to concerns about physical, decisional, and proprietary privacy. Briefly, issues of physical privacy underlie concerns about genetic testing, screening, or treatment without voluntary and informed consent. In the absence of consent, these practices constitute unwanted physical contact, compromising interests in bodily integrity and security. Decisional privacy concerns are heard in calls for autonomous decision making by individuals, couples, or families who use genetic services. A degree of choice with regard to genetic counseling, testing, and abortion are requirements of respect for decisional privacy. The fourth category of privacy concern, proprietary privacy, encompasses issues relating to the appropriation of individuals' possessory and economic interests in their genes and other putative bodily repositories of personality.

* * *

The human genome contains many mysteries that await scientific discovery. The air of mystery that shrouds gene science often shrouds discourse about genetic privacy, too. Yet genetic privacy is only an expansive concept, not an unfathomable one.

DAVID ORENTLICHER, GENETIC PRIVACY IN THE PATIENT-PHYSICIAN RELATIONSHIP IN GENETIC SECRETS: PROTECTING PRIVACY AND CONFIDENTIALITY IN THE GENETIC ERA
77, 78–81 (Mark A. Rothstein ed. 1997).

Privacy permits patients to retain control over the amount of intimate information they divulge about themselves and to whom they divulge it. Society demonstrates its respect for people when it gives them control over important aspects of their lives, including decisions about career, marriage, reproduction, and medical treatment. Control over personal information is of fundamental importance to individuals. It assures people that they can avoid the shame of having embarrassing intimate information disclosed publicly. It also assures individuals that they can pursue deeply held beliefs that are politically unpopular or engage in behavior that is unconventional without risk of opprobrium or retaliation. Privacy in personal information allows people the freedom of self-exploration as they shape their identity without the risk that, at some later date, they will be penalized for experiments with behavior or life-styles that they later rejected. Informational privacy is not only about shielding facts that might be viewed negatively by others, it is also about shielding facts that are generally viewed positively by others. For many people, for example, charity is noblest when given anonymously. Most fundamentally, informational privacy is valuable regardless of whether the information it shields is viewed positively or negatively by others. Informational privacy allows people to pursue their education, careers, friendships, romances, and medical care without the oversight, interference, or other unwelcome involvement of others. By controlling personal information, individuals can control the extent to which other people can participate in their lives.

* * *

Concerns about privacy in medical information are particularly present with genetic information. Genetic makeup is at the heart of personality. Genetics not only has a profound influence on such physical characteristics as height, weight, skin color, and eye color, but it almost certainly affects less tangible traits, such as shyness, altruism, sociableness, artistry, and intellectual skills. Indeed, a chief argument against the cloning of embryos has been the concern that the creation of genetically identical sibling embryos deprives those individuals who develop from the embryos of their unique identity. Individuals may not want to know whether they are at risk for a genetic disease, like Huntington disease, for which nothing can be done by way of prevention or treatment in advance. Such persons may conclude that they will be better off psychologically not knowing, and they may therefore decline medical testing to discover genetic information about themselves.

* * *

Privacy is especially important with genetic information also because an individual's genetic makeup reveals information not only about the individual but also about family members. If a person carries the gene mutation for Huntington disease, it follows that one of the person's parents also carries the mutation that each of the person's children has a 50% chance of carrying the mutation, and that each of the person's siblings also has a 50% chance of carrying the mutation. Violations of a patient's privacy with respect to genetic information may also mean that the privacy of many other persons has been violated.

NOTES AND QUESTIONS

1.   Genetic privacy has both a tangible and an intangible aspect. As David Orentlicher notes, people are concerned about protecting their genetic

privacy, regardless of whether there are any tangible, adverse consequences. Yet people are also concerned about how third parties may use "private" genetic information to the detriment of the individual. Which aspect of genetic privacy, tangible or intangible, is most important to people? See Mary R. Anderlik & Mark A. Rothstein, Privacy and Confidentiality of Genetic Information: What Rules for the New Science?, 2 Ann. Rev. Genomics & Human Genetics 401 (2001).

2.   As research shifts to gene function, it will become increasingly important to review the medical records of individuals to correlate genotype and phenotype. This "second stage genomics," going from identifying the location to learning the function of genes, raises additional privacy issues. See John A. Robertson, Privacy Issues in Second Stage Genomics, 40 Jurimetrics J. 59 (1999).

3.   Privacy is not the same as confidentiality. Confidentiality means that information disclosed in the course of a confidential relationship (e.g., physician-patient) will not be redisclosed outside of the relationship without the consent of the individual who supplied the information. It has been a core value of the medical profession ever since the time of the Hippocratic Oath, which provides, in pertinent part: "And whatsoever I shall see or hear in the course of my profession, as well as outside my profession in my intercourse with men, if it be what should not be published abroad, I will never divulge, holding such things to be holy secrets." The principle of confidentiality is also widely endorsed by the modern ethical codes of the medical profession. See Mark A. Rothstein, Privacy and Confidentiality, in Medical Ethics: Analysis of the Issues Raised by the Codes, Opinions and Statements (Baruch A. Brody et al. eds. 2001).

4.   The confidentiality of genetic information was addressed by the Institute of Medicine's Committee on Assessing Genetic Risks:

> Confidentiality as a principle implies that some body of information is sensitive, and hence, access to it must be controlled and limited to parties authorized to have such access. The information provided within the relationship is given in confidence, with the expectation that it will not be disclosed to others or will be disclosed to others only within limits. The state or condition of nondisclosure or limited disclosure may be protected by moral, social, or legal principles and rules, which can be expressed in terms of rights or obligations.

Committee on Assessing Genetic Risks, Institute of Medicine, Assessing Genetic Risks: Implications for Health and Social Policy 205 (Lori B. Andrews et al. eds. 1994). See also Eugene Pergament, A Clinical Geneticist Perspective of the Patient-Physician Relationship in Genetic Secrets: Protecting Privacy and Confidentiality in the Genetic Era 92 (Mark A. Rothstein ed. 1997); Madison Powers, Genetic Information, Ethics, Privacy and Confidentiality: Overview, in 1 Encyclopedia of Ethical, Legal, and Policy Issues in Biotechnology 405 (Thomas H. Murray & Maxwell J. Mehlman eds. 2000).

5.   Another important concept is security, which refers to the administrative, physical, and technical standards used to ensure that access to electronic personal health information is restricted to those with authorization. The HIPAA Security Rule appears at 45 C.F.R. Part 160, 164 subparts A and C. Among its many provisions are those dealing with access controls, user authentication, transmission security, and breach notification.

LORI B. ANDREWS, FUTURE PERFECT: CONFRONTING DECISIONS ABOUT GENETICS
140–141 (2001).

The problems of improper disclosure and misuse of genetic information are aggravated by the poor protections given to medical information in general. Secretary of Health and Human Services Donna Shalala says, "Every day, our private health information is being shared with fewer federal safeguards than our video store records."

Patient information is frequently disclosed. Dr. Mark Siegler describes a pulmonary patient who became concerned about the confidentiality of his medical record when he learned that the respiratory therapist had access to it. When the patient threatened to leave the hospital if confidentiality could not be guaranteed, Siegler inquired about the number of health care professionals and hospital personnel who had access to the patient's chart. When he revealed to the patient that seventy-five people had access to the chart in furtherance of his care, the patient stated, "I always believed that medical confidentiality was part of a doctor's code of ethics. Perhaps you should tell me just what you people mean by 'confidentiality'!"

In addition to the revelation of information to enhance patient care, the types of disclosures that a health care provider might be tempted to make range from pure gossip unrelated to the patient's well-being to disclosures to outside third parties that are thought to be in the best interest of the patient, another individual, or society. The individuals seeking disclosure from physicians might include law enforcement officials, public health authorities, relatives of the patient, employers, insurance companies, schools, and lawyers.

It is shocking how little protection exists for private medical information. In some states, laws protect only doctor-patient confidentiality and do not apply to other health care providers. Medical information collected in the workplace rather than the doctor's office is not protected in some states, so genetic screening and monitoring of employees is not covered. Even genetic information collected in a traditional health care setting may be unprotected, depending on *who* collects it. Some existing medical confidentiality statutes protect only medical information in the hands of *doctors* and will not cover genetic information in the hands of Ph.D. geneticists or genetic counselors.

Moreover, even states in which genetic information cannot be released without the individual's permission do not offer sufficient protection. As long as insurers and employers can continue to ask people to "consent" to the release of their genetic information, people will be discriminated against based on their genotype, no matter what the state's law is on medical confidentiality.

NOTES AND QUESTIONS

1.   Recent studies reveal significant public concerns about genetic privacy, and the belief that genetics is different from other conditions. One study involved 100 individuals from each of the following six disease groups at a major medical center: cystic fibrosis, sickle cell disease, diabetes, HIV infection, breast cancer, and colon cancer. When asked whether special privacy protections should be in place for certain medical conditions, the results produced the following table.

Abortion history	68.6%
Mental health history	60.1
HIV/AIDS	54.0
Genetic test results	46.5
Drug/Alcohol history	44.4
Sexually transmitted disease	44.0
Breast cancer	29.0
Colon cancer	23.5
Family history of cancer	20.4
Sickle cell disease	19.8
Cystic fibrosis	17.7
Huntington disease	15.5
Diabetes	12.0
Cholesterol level	10.7
Heart disease	10.3

Laura Plantinga et al., Disclosure, Confidentiality, and Families: Experiences and Attitudes of Those with Genetic versus Nongenetic Medical Conditions, 119 Am. J. Med. Genetics, Part C, 51 (2003).

2.   Another study sought to explore the concerns of at-risk relatives of colon cancer patients about genetic discrimination and their awareness of legislative protections. About half the respondents rated their concern about genetic discrimination as high. A significant majority (79%) learned about genetic discrimination from one of the following media sources: television, magazines, newspapers, or radio. Fewer than 5% said they had heard of laws dealing with genetic discrimination. Kira A. Apse et al., Perceptions of Genetic Discrimination Among At-Risk Relatives of Colorectal Cancer Patients, 6 Genetics in Med. 510 (2004).

3.   What, if anything, do these studies suggest about the need to protect genetic privacy, the preferred legislative or other method of protecting it, or the public and professional education needed about these issues? See generally Sheri Alpert, Privacy Issues in Clinical Genomic Medicine, or Marcus Welby, M.D., Meets the $1000 Genome, 17 Cambridge Q. Healthcare Ethics 373 (2008).

B. APPLICATIONS

1. Electronic Health Records and Networks

Amy L. McGuire et al., Confidentiality, Privacy, and Security of Genetic and Genomic Test Information in Electronic Health Records: Points to Consider

10 Genetics in Med. 495, 495, 499 (2009).

The clinical use of genetic/genomic information is becoming an increasingly important aspect of modern health care delivery. At the same time, the increasing role of health information technology platforms in organizing health information has led to the need to review the confidentiality, privacy, and security of electronic information. Electronic health records (EHRs) provide a useful way to manage complex medical information; as such, EHRs will become established in the future as the means to manage the large and complex datasets that accompany genetic/genomic tests and interpretations. The inclusion of genetic/genomic information in EHRs should inform the determination of disease risk, appropriate drug dosing to avoid adverse events, and the selection of effective treatment. However, electronic health information is portable and mobile; the ease with which information can be disseminated through EHRs raises concern about the potential for unauthorized access to and use of this information. A major policy question, then, is whether special protections should be created for genetic/genomic information that is stored in the EHR.

* * *

The inclusion of genetic/genomic information in the EHR will greatly impact personalized health care by informing disease risk determination, appropriate drug dosing, and the selection of effective treatment or preventive action. To realize the full potential of personalized medicine, however, policies must be implemented to protect the confidentiality, privacy, and security of genetic/genomic test information appropriately with regard to access and use. Genetic/genomic information features a series of attributes that must be carefully considered in the aggregate with regard to policy development. Genetic/genomic data should be afforded the same provisions as other sensitive health information with regard to potential restricted access in the EHR. Protection against potential discrimination based on genetic/genomic information must be ensured, and proper disclosures must also be made for the use of such data for research purposes. Attention to the issues raised by these discussions will help policy developers and health care professionals ensure that confidentiality, privacy, and security are appropriately maintained for genetic/genomic information contained in the EHR.

NOTES AND QUESTIONS

1.   The American Recovery and Reinvestment Act of 2009 (ARRA), Pub. L. 111–5, 123 Stat. 115 (2009), includes the Health Information Technology for Economic and Clinical Health Act (HITECH ACT), which commits the nation to shifting from paper to electronic health records (EHRs) in an attempt to make the practice of medicine safer, more effective, and more efficient. The ARRA provides substantial grants to develop new technologies and assist in their adoption and implementation. Similar efforts to shift from paper records are ongoing in much of the developed world.

2.   There are three essential attributes of EHRs and the networks designed to connect them. First, they are interoperable, meaning that they may be accessed and used from remote locations and utilize a standard system for transmitting and receiving information. Second, they are comprehensive, meaning that they compile information from all of an individual's health care encounters with various physicians, hospitals, pharmacies, laboratories, etc. Third, they are longitudinal, meaning that they contain an individual's records over an extended period of time. These three attributes enhance coordination of care, help avoid duplication of services, prevent errors, improve effectiveness of care, and facilitate outcomes and other research. They also challenge privacy, confidentiality, and security by providing easier access to a wider range of health information—sometimes when health care providers have no need to know the information. See generally Sharona Hoffman & Andy Podgurski, In Sickness, Health, and Cyberspace: Protecting the Security of Electronic Private Health Information, 48 B.C.L. Rev. 331 (2007): Mark A. Rothstein, Health Privacy in the Electronic Age, 28 J. Legal Med. 487 (2007); Nicolas P. Terry & Leslie P. Francis, Ensuring the Privacy and Confidentiality of Electronic Health Records, 2007 U. Ill. L. Rev. 681 (2007).

2. Compelled Disclosures

MARK A. ROTHSTEIN & MEGHAN K. TALBOTT, COMPELLED
DISCLOSURE OF HEALTH INFORMATION: PROTECTING AGAINST
THE GREATEST POTENTIAL THREAT TO PRIVACY
295 JAMA 2882–2883 (2006).

* * *

In the United States, laws to protect health information privacy and confidentiality are largely designed to protect against the unauthorized access to, use of, and disclosure of personal health information. A variety of state and federal laws attempt to make health information secure from snoops, hackers, and rogue health care employees. Some laws specify the form in which health records may be stored or transmitted; other laws attempt to punish unauthorized access through civil or criminal sanctions. Although these laws are valuable, they fail to address the compelled, authorized disclosure of personal health information.

As a condition of applying for employment, various types of insurance, and certain benefit programs such as Social Security Disability Insurance or workers' compensation, millions of Americans each year sign authorizations for the release of vast amounts of personal health information maintained in the files at their physicians' offices, hospitals, and other health care settings. There can be no effective protection of health privacy and confidentiality unless compelled, authorized disclosures of health information are regulated. Yet, legally and practically, this will be difficult to accomplish.

Few current laws place any restrictions on the scope or level of detail of information that third-parties may require individuals to release pursuant to an authorization. Even if there were legal restrictions, it would be practically impossible in most instances for the custodians of health records to limit the disclosure. Typical paper-based health records, such as most hospital and physician office records, are often a montage of disparate reports and clinical encounters involving wide-ranging conditions over a prolonged period of time. The records may intermingle routine clinical data with sensitive information, such as mental health, genetic test results, sexually transmitted diseases, human immunodeficiency virus (HIV) antibody status, sexual history, history of abortions and other reproductive matters, domestic violence, and drug and alcohol abuse. The disclosure of such sensitive health information to entities without a treatment relationship, without a need to know, and for non-medical purposes may lead to embarrassment and stigma. The mere possibility of such a disclosure also may lead individuals to forgo some potentially beneficial medical tests and procedures or even medical care altogether.

* * *

Disclosure of sensitive health information may result in the inability to obtain insurance or employment. In addition, individuals may experience embarrassment, humiliation, shame, anxiety, and depression if their health secrets are revealed. That is why many individuals withhold some sensitive health information from their loved ones, closest friends, and even their physicians. Yet, these individuals may not be able to withhold sensitive health information from other unknown third parties if they want to be considered for employment, other essential life activities, or insurance.

NOTES AND QUESTIONS

1.   The total number of compelled authorizations for disclosure of health records is unknown. The following table contains the only published estimates.

Annual Compelled Authorizations in the United States

Type of Authorization	Estimate
Employment entrance examinations	10,203,000
Individual health insurance applications	550,000
Individual life insurance applications	6,800,000
Individual long-term care insurance applications	200,000
Individual disability insurance applications	200,000
Disability insurance claims (individual and group)	1,500,000
Automobile insurance claims	1,360,000
Social Security Disability Insurance applications	1,700,000
Workers' compensation claims	1,560,000
Veterans' disability claims	632,000
Personal injury lawsuits	300,000
Total	25,005,000

Adapted from Mark A. Rothstein & Meghan K. Talbott, Compelled Authorizations for Disclosure of Health Records: Magnitude and Implications, 7 Am. J. Bioethics No. 3, at 38, 40 (2007).

2.   The privacy problem does not stem from the fact that health information is frequently disclosed to various third-parties with a legitimate need to access the information. It is based on the fact that there is no feasible method of restricting the amount of information disclosed and therefore it is commonplace for custodians of health records to respond to any request for health records by sending the entire record. As the use of comprehensive, longitudinal electronic health records expands, the quantity of information disclosed to third parties, such as employers and insurers, will increase dramatically. Without a way to limit the disclosures there could be serious public health consequences; for example, individuals might be reluctant to

seek care for sexually transmitted diseases, mental illness, domestic violence, or other stigmatizing conditions if the information will be disclosed in perpetuity. Would these same concerns affect the willingness of some individuals to undergo genetic testing?

III. LEGAL PROTECTIONS FOR MEDICAL AND GENETIC PRIVACY

A. CONSTITUTIONAL LAW

NASA v. NELSON
562 U.S. 134 (2011).

Justice ALITO delivered the opinion of the Court.

In two cases decided more than 30 years ago, this Court referred broadly to a constitutional privacy "interest in avoiding disclosure of personal matters." Whalen v. Roe, 429 U.S. 589, 599–600 (1977); Nixon v. Administrator of General Services, 433 U.S. 425, 457 (1977). Respondents in this case, federal contract employees at a Government laboratory, claim that two parts of a standard employment background investigation violate their rights under Whalen and Nixon. Respondents challenge a section of a form questionnaire that asks employees about treatment or counseling for recent illegal-drug use. They also object to certain open-ended questions on a form sent to employees' designated references.

We assume, without deciding, that the Constitution protects a privacy right of the sort mentioned in Whalen and Nixon. We hold, however, that the challenged portions of the Government's background check do not violate this right in the present case. The Government's interests as employer and proprietor in managing its internal operations, combined with the protections against public dissemination provided by the Privacy Act of 1974, 5 U.S.C. § 552a, satisfy any "interest in avoiding disclosure" that may "arguably ha[ve] its roots in the Constitution."

The National Aeronautics and Space Administration (NASA) is an independent federal agency charged with planning and conducting the Government's "space activities." NASA's workforce numbers in the tens of thousands of employees. While many of these workers are federal civil servants, a substantial majority are employed directly by Government contractors. Contract employees play an important role in NASA's mission, and their duties are functionally equivalent to those performed by civil servants.

One NASA facility, the Jet Propulsion Laboratory (JPL) in Pasadena, California, is staffed exclusively by contract employees. NASA owns JPL, but the California Institute of Technology (Cal Tech) operates the facility under a Government contract. JPL is the lead NASA center for deep-space robotics and communications.

* * *

Twenty-eight JPL employees are respondents here. Many of them have worked at the lab for decades, and none has ever been the subject of a Government background investigation. At the time when respondents were hired, background checks were standard only for federal civil servants.* * *

The Government has recently taken steps to eliminate this two-track approach to background investigations. In 2004, a recommendation by the 9/11 Commission prompted the President to order new, uniform identification standards for "[f]ederal employees," including "contractor employees." The Department of Commerce implemented this directive by mandating that contract employees with long-term access to federal facilities complete a standard background check, typically the National Agency Check with Inquiries (NACI).

* * *

As noted, respondents contend that portions of [the background check form] violate their "right to informational privacy." This Court considered a similar claim in *Whalen,* which concerned New York's practice of collecting "the names and addresses of all persons" prescribed dangerous drugs with both "legitimate and illegitimate uses." In discussing that claim, the Court said that "[t]he cases sometimes characterized as protecting 'privacy'" actually involved "at least two different kinds of interests": one, an "interest in avoiding disclosure of personal matters"; the other, an interest in "making certain kinds of important decisions" free from government interference. The patients who brought suit in *Whalen* argued that New York's statute "threaten[ed] to impair" both their "nondisclosure" interests and their interests in making healthcare decisions independently. The Court, however, upheld the statute as a "reasonable exercise of New York's broad police powers."

Whalen acknowledged that the disclosure of "private information" to the State was an "unpleasant invasion of privacy," but the Court pointed out that the New York statute contained "security provisions" that protected against "public disclosure" of patients' information, this sort of "statutory or regulatory duty to avoid unwarranted disclosures" of "accumulated private data" was sufficient, in the Court's view, to protect a privacy interest that "arguably ha[d] its roots in the Constitution." The Court thus concluded that the statute did not violate "any right or liberty protected by the Fourteenth Amendment."

* * *

As was our approach in *Whalen,* we will assume for present purposes that the Government's challenged inquiries implicate a privacy interest of constitutional significance. We hold, however, that, whatever the scope of this interest, it does not prevent the Government from asking reasonable questions of the sort included * * * in an employment background investigation that is subject to the Privacy Act's safeguards against public disclosure.

With these interests in view, we conclude that the challenged portions of both [forms] consist of reasonable, employment-related inquiries that further the Government's interests in managing its internal operations. As to SF–85, the only part of the form challenged here is its request for information about "any treatment or counseling received" for illegal-drug use within the previous year. The "treatment or counseling" question, however, must be considered in context. It is a follow-up to SF–85's inquiry into whether the employee has "used, possessed, supplied, or manufactured illegal drugs" during the past year. The Government has good reason to ask employees about their recent illegal-drug use. Like any employer, the Government is entitled to have its projects staffed by reliable, law-abiding persons who will " 'efficiently and effectively' " discharge their duties. Questions about illegal-drug use are a useful way of figuring out which persons have these characteristics.

In context, the follow-up question on "treatment or counseling" for recent illegal-drug use is also a reasonable, employment-related inquiry. The Government, recognizing that illegal-drug use is both a criminal and a medical issue, seeks to separate out those illegal-drug users who are taking steps to address and overcome their problems. The Government thus uses responses to the "treatment or counseling" question as a mitigating factor in determining whether to grant contract employees long-term access to federal facilities.

This is a reasonable, and indeed a humane, approach, and respondents do not dispute the legitimacy of the Government's decision to use drug treatment as a mitigating factor in its contractor credentialing decisions. Respondents' argument is that, if drug treatment is only used to mitigate, then the Government should change the mandatory phrasing of SF–85—"Include [in your answer] any treatment or counseling received"—so as to make a response optional. As it stands, the mandatory "treatment or counseling" question is unconstitutional, in respondents' view, because it is "more intrusive than necessary to satisfy the government's objective."

We reject the argument that the Government, when it requests job-related personal information in an employment background check, has a constitutional burden to demonstrate that its questions are "necessary" or the least restrictive means of furthering its interests. So exacting a standard runs directly contrary to *Whalen*. The patients in *Whalen*, much like respondents here, argued that New York's statute was unconstitutional because the State could not "demonstrate the necessity" of its program. The Court quickly rejected that argument, concluding that New York's collection of patients' prescription information could "not be held unconstitutional simply because" a court viewed it as "unnecessary, in whole or in part."

That analysis applies with even greater force where the Government acts, not as a regulator, but as the manager of its internal affairs. SF–85's "treatment or counseling" question reasonably seeks to identify a subset of acknowledged drug users who are attempting to overcome their problems. The Government's considered position is that phrasing the question in more permissive terms would result in a lower response rate, and the question's effectiveness in identifying illegal-drug users who are suitable for employment would be "materially reduced." That is a reasonable position, falling within the " 'wide latitude' " granted the Government in its dealings with employees.

* * *

Not only are SF–85 and Form 42 reasonable in light of the Government interests at stake, they are also subject to substantial protections against disclosure to the public. Both *Whalen* and *Nixon* recognized that government "accumulation" of "personal information" for "public purposes" may pose a threat to privacy. But both decisions also stated that a "statutory or regulatory duty to avoid unwarranted disclosures" generally allays these privacy concerns. The Court in *Whalen*, relying on New York's "security provisions" prohibiting public disclosure, turned aside a challenge to the collection of patients' prescription information. In *Nixon*, the Court rejected what it regarded as an even "weaker" claim by the former President because the Presidential Recordings and Materials Preservation Act "[n]ot only . . . mandate[d] regulations" against "undue dissemination," but also required immediate return of any "purely private" materials flagged by the Government's archivists.

Respondents in this case, like the patients in *Whalen* and former President Nixon, attack only the Government's *collection* of information on SF–85 and Form 42. And here, no less than in *Whalen* and *Nixon*, the information collected is shielded by statute from "unwarranted disclosur[e]." The Privacy Act, which covers all information collected during the background-check process, allows the Government to maintain records "about an individual" only to the extent the records are "relevant and necessary to accomplish" a purpose authorized by law. The Act requires written consent before the Government may disclose records pertaining to any individual. And the Act imposes criminal liability for willful violations of its nondisclosure obligations. These requirements, as we have noted, give "forceful recognition" to a Government employee's interest in maintaining the "confidentiality of sensitive information . . . in his personnel files." Like the protections against disclosure in Whalen and Nixon, they "evidence a proper concern" for individual privacy.

* * *

In light of the protection provided by the Privacy Act's nondisclosure requirement, and because the challenged portions of the forms consist of reasonable inquiries in an employment background check, we conclude that the Government's inquiries do not violate a constitutional right to informational privacy.

* * *

For these reasons, the judgment of the Court of Appeals is reversed, and the case is remanded for further proceedings consistent with this opinion.

It is so ordered.

Justice KAGAN took no part in the consideration or decision of this case.

Justice SCALIA, with whom Justice THOMAS joins, concurring in the judgment.

I agree with the Court, of course, that background checks of employees of government contractors do not offend the Constitution. But rather than reach this conclusion on the basis of the never-explained assumption that the Constitution requires courts to "balance" the Government's interests in data collection against its contractor employees' interest in privacy, I reach it on simpler grounds. Like many other desirable things not included in the Constitution, "informational privacy" seems like a good idea—wherefore the People have enacted laws at the federal level and in the states restricting the government's collection and use of information. But it is up to the People to enact those laws, to shape them, and, when they think it appropriate, to repeal them. A federal constitutional right to "informational privacy" does not exist.

* * *

NOTES AND QUESTIONS

1.   Based on *Whalen*, the Court assumed without deciding there was a constitutional right to informational privacy, but still found that the government action was reasonable. Two justices would hold there was no such constitutional right. Do you think there is much likelihood of success for plaintiffs to allege a constitutional privacy violation? See Mark A. Rothstein,

Constitutional Right to Informational Health Privacy in Critical Condition, 39 J.L. Med. & Ethics 280 (2011).

2.   In Matson v. Bd. of Educ., 631 F.3d 57 (2d Cir. 2011), the Second Circuit, relying on circuit precedent, held that there was a limited constitutional right to informational health privacy. It held that the privacy protection afforded medical information will vary with the medical condition. To be protected, the medical condition must be stigmatizing and lead to "discrimination and intolerance." Applying this test, the court held that disclosure of the plaintiff's fibromyalgia was not a constitutional violation. How would the disclosure of genetic information fare under this test? Would it matter what the genetic information revealed?

3.   Even claims involving stigmatizing conditions have not fared well in the courts. For example, in Doe v. Southeastern Pennsylvania Transp. Auth. (SEPTA), 72 F.3d 1133 (3d Cir.1995), cert. denied, 519 U.S. 808 (1996), the plaintiff was an employee who was the manager of his company's employee assistance program. Before he had a prescription filled under the company's drug plan he asked his supervisor, the head of the medical department, whether the company was able to identify what prescriptions individual employees had filled. When he was assured that the company did not get such information, the employee had his prescription for AZT, an antiviral drug used to treat AIDS, refilled under the company plan. When the pharmacy chain submitted its mandatory utilization report, which included a list of the names of all employees and the medications they were taking, the employer's medical department, including this particular employee's supervisors, learned that he was HIV-positive, a fact that they then indiscriminately shared. In an action for invasion of privacy, the jury awarded the plaintiff $125,000, but the Third Circuit reversed. The court held that the employer's "important interests" in the prescription information outweighed the "minimal intrusion" into the plaintiff's privacy. For a discussion of possible tort actions for invasion of genetic privacy, see June Mary Z. Makdisi, Genetic Privacy: New Intrusion a New Tort?, 34 Creighton L. Rev. 965 (2001).

4.   In what settings and in what ways do you think constitutional privacy issues could be raised with regard to genetics?

B. LEGISLATION

1.   Genetic Exceptionalism

THOMAS H. MURRAY, GENETIC EXCEPTIONALISM AND
"FUTURE DIARIES": IS GENETIC INFORMATION
DIFFERENT FROM OTHER MEDICAL INFORMATION?
IN GENETIC SECRETS: PROTECTING PRIVACY AND
CONFIDENTIALITY IN THE GENETIC ERA

60, 71 (Mark A. Rothstein ed. 1997).

The paths I have explored lead to one destination. Genetic information is special because we are inclined to treat it as mysterious, as having exceptional potency or significance, not because it differs in some fundamental way from all other sorts of information about us. Portions of that mystery and power come from the opaqueness of genetic information, the possibility that others will know things about the individual that he or she does not know, and how genetic information connects individuals to immediate family and more distant kin. The more genetic information is treated as special, the more special treatment will be necessary. Yet none of these factors is unique to genetic information.

I propose that genetic exceptionalism—the plea to treat genetic information as different from other health-related information—is an overly dramatic view of the significance of genetic information in our lives. It is a reflection of genetic determinism and genetic reductionism at least as much as the product of genuinely distinctive features of genetic information. There is a disturbing corollary to this thesis: there is a vicious circularity in insisting that genetic information is different and must be given special treatment. The more we repeat that genetic information is fundamentally unlike other kinds of medical information, the more support we implicitly provide for genetic determinism, for the notion that genetics exerts special power over our lives.

NOTE

George Annas, Leonard Glantz, and Patricia Roche drafted the Genetic Privacy Act and Commentary (1995), urging enactment of genetic-specific privacy legislation. Also supporting this position are Colin S. Diver & Jane Maslow Cohen, Genophobia: What Is Wrong with Genetic Discrimination?, 149 U. Pa. L. Rev. 1439 (2001) and Ronald M. Green & Mathew Thomas, DNA: Five Distinguishing Features for Policy Analysis, 11 Harv. J. L. & Tech. 571 (1998). Among the allegedly unique aspects of genetic information are (1) DNA's informational nature; (2) its longevity; (3) its use as an identifier; (4) the familial risks indicated by the information; and (5) the effects on communities. So far, genetic exceptionalism has been heavily criticized in the literature, but the approach has been adopted by legislatures, see Section B infra, where the laws have generally addressed genetics separately from other health issues. See generally Lawrence O. Gostin & James G. Hodge, Jr., Genetic Privacy and the Law: An End to Genetics Exceptionalism, 40 Jurimetrics J. 21 (1999); Deborah Hellman, What Makes Genetic Discrimination Exceptional?, 29 Am. J.L. & Med. 77 (2003); Trudo Lemmens, Selective Justice, Genetic Discrimination, and Insurance: Should We Single Out Genes in Our Laws?, 45 McGill L. J. 347 (2000).

MARK A. ROTHSTEIN, GENETIC EXCEPTIONALISM AND LEGISLATIVE PRAGMATISM
35 Hastings Center Report no. 4, at 27–33 (2005).

THE ALTERNATIVE TO GENETIC EXCEPTIONALISM

I have argued that genetic-specific laws have limited value in preventing or redressing harms caused by the uses and disclosures of genetic information. Genetic-specific laws also reinforce the stigma of genetic disorders (by treating them differently from nongenetic conditions) and ignore the underlying social problems that genetic privacy and discrimination exemplify. The fundamental issue raised by genetic discrimination in health insurance is the fairness of our system for allocating access to health care; the fundamental issue raised by genetic discrimination in employment is how to balance the rights of employers and employees in controlling access to employee health information and in deciding what role, if any, current or predictive health status should play in employment opportunities.

General legal standards are more effective in dealing with these problems than genetic-specific laws. As mentioned, genetic discrimination is not a concern for health care finance systems that are not based on individual medical underwriting. For example, genetic discrimination is irrelevant in government-sponsored programs, such as Medicare and Medicaid, and group-based health insurance. But individual underwriting in any insurance product is synonymous with "discrimination" (that is to say, with differentiation) since eligibility and rates are determined by risk classification. Thus, it will be virtually impossible to devise any effective measures to prevent genetic discrimination in a system based on discrimination.

* * *

WHEN IS HALF A LOAF BETTER THAN NOTHING?

Legislative champions for genetic-specific laws are easy to find, and they include sympathetic and persuasive advocates. Opponents are few, especially if the proposed legislation is narrow in scope. Only a small number of elected officials realize that genetic-specific laws are largely ineffective and may be counterproductive. To most lawmakers, it seems obvious that if there is a problem with genetic discrimination, then the solution is to enact legislation making genetic discrimination illegal.

More savvy lawmakers still may be reluctant to propose generic, rather than merely genetic, legislation, since generic legislation is extraordinarily difficult to enact. Support for logical, effective, and sweeping legislation is hard to find. The underlying issues—such as the right of access to health care, the relative rights of employers and employees to decide about health hazards in the workplace, and the principles to apply in medical underwriting for life and disability insurance—are extremely contentious. To date, efforts to address these issues have often been unsuccessful.

Because of the difficulty in enacting sweeping reforms, the policy question is whether it is a good idea to enact a genetic-specific law when there is insufficient support for broader legislation. In legislative circles it is often said that the perfect is the enemy of the good. In other words, many people would argue that it is better to have limited or even flawed protection against discrimination than no protection at all. On the other hand, enacting and then touting feel-good legislation with little or no substantive protection may mislead members of the public to rely on the law to their detriment. It may also encourage people to believe in genetic exceptionalism, thereby making it a self-fulfilling prophesy, and it may erroneously convince legislators that they have resolved the underlying issues, thereby delaying enactment of meaningful legislation.

In my view, four conditions need to be met before it is appropriate to support a genetic-specific law as a fallback position to more sweeping legislation. First, there must be some value to the law, both in the sense that there is a demonstrated need for legislative action and that the proposed legislation will help to resolve one or more aspects of the problem. Second, the law must be drafted carefully to avoid unintended consequences, such as interfering with clinical care or medical research, or unreasonably interfering with the economic interests of third parties such as insurers or employers. Third, enacting the law must not serve to delay the enactment of legislation better designed to promote public policies, such as not coercing individuals into genetic testing and not dissuading at-risk individuals from being tested for fear of the social consequences. And fourth, both legislators and the public must realize that the law is not ideal but merely the best that can be achieved at the moment.

* * *

It is difficult to assess whether enacting a weak or ineffective law delays the enactment of more meaningful legislation. On the one hand, the initial enactment may be viewed as "a foot in the door" or the first step to stronger legislation. Since 1995, every state to enact a law establishing a DNA forensic database for use in law enforcement has amended its law to add more categories of offenders who are required to provide DNA samples. This expansion reflects the continuing efforts of the law enforcement community and its legislative advocates to promote forensic DNA banks.

On the other hand, "legislative-fatigue" is sometimes used to describe the notion that having enacted *something,* legislators are ready to move on to the next issue and have no interest in reconsidering a problem they thought was resolved. For example, few amendments have been made to the privacy and antidiscrimination laws enacted in the last decade, especially to extend the privacy protections for individuals. Whether genetic legislation will be a precursor to stronger legislation or give way to legislative fatigue will depend on whether powerful legislative champions are satisfied with the initial version of the law.

My fourth condition is that legislators and the public realize that a genetic-specific law is not ideal. Unfortunately, in the press conferences and self-congratulation that usually follow enactment of legislation affording protection against genetic discrimination there is rarely any mention of the limitations of the new laws. Many people, including legislators, probably assume that the problem has been solved. Legislative sponsors and supporters would then view it as a sign of weakness or ineptitude to admit that the bill they advocated is flawed or ineffectual. If media descriptions of the new laws are based on press releases and interviews with advocates of the legislation, then the gaps in protection are unlikely to be noted.

NO SHORTCUTS

* * *

Genetic exceptionalism undercuts this essential reconsideration of the role of predictive health information in society. It allows elected officials to avoid difficult issues by enacting genetic-specific laws that seem to respond to a perceived new crisis, but in fact offer little or no protection and may even be counterproductive. It is not surprising that elected officials would want to avoid fundamental and controversial issues and focus instead on nominally protecting the public against the highly publicized evils of invidious genetic discrimination. For the time being, at least, it seems that the public is genetically predisposed to let them.

2. State Legislation

NEW MEXICO GENETIC INFORMATION PRIVACY ACT
(ENACTED 1998).

N.M. Stat. Ann.

§§ 24–21–2 Definitions.

As used in the Genetic Information Privacy Act [24–21–1 to 24–21–7 NMSA 1978]:

§§ 24–21–3 Genetic analysis prohibited without informed consent; exceptions.

A.   Except as provided in Subsection C of this section, no person shall obtain genetic information or samples for genetic analysis from a person without first obtaining informed and written consent from the person or the person's authorized representative.

B.   Except as provided in Subsection C of this section, genetic analysis of a person or collection, retention, transmission or use of genetic information without the informed and written consent of the person or the person's authorized representative is prohibited.

C.   A person's DNA, genetic information or the results of genetic analysis may be obtained, retained, transmitted or used without the person's written and informed consent pursuant to federal or state law or regulations only:

(1)   to identify a person in the course of a criminal investigation by a law enforcement agency;

(2)   if the person has been convicted of a felony, for purposes of maintaining a DNA database for law enforcement purposes;

(3)   to identify deceased persons;

(4)   to establish parental identity;

(5)   to screen newborns;

(6)   if the DNA, genetic information or results of genetic analysis are not identified with the person or person's family members;

(7)   by a court for determination of damage awards pursuant to the Genetic Information Privacy Act [24–21–1 to 24–21–7 NMSA 1978];

(8)   by medical repositories or registries;

(9)   for the purpose of medical or scientific research and education, including retention of gene products, genetic

information or genetic analysis if the identity of the person or person's family members is not disclosed; or

(10) for the purpose of emergency medical treatment consistent with applicable law.

D.   Actions of an insurer and third parties dealing with an insurer in the ordinary course of conducting and administering the business of life, disability income or long-term care insurance are exempt from the provisions of this section if the use of genetic analysis or genetic information for underwriting purposes is based on sound actuarial principles or related to actual or reasonably anticipated experience. However, before or at the time of collecting genetic information for use in conducting and administering the business of life, disability income or long-term care insurance, the insurer shall notify in writing an applicant for insurance or the insured that the information may be used, transmitted or retained solely for the purpose of conducting and administering the business of life, disability income or long-term care insurance, the insurer shall notify in writing an applicant for insurance or the insured that the information may be used, transmitted or retained solely for the purpose of conducting and administering the business of life, disability income or long-term care insurance.

E.   Nothing in Paragraph (5), (6), (8), (9) or (10) of Subsection C of Section 3 [24–21–3 NMSA 1978] of the Genetic Information Privacy Act authorizes obtaining, retaining, transmitting or using a person's DNA, genetic information or the results of genetic analysis if the person, his authorized representative or guardian, or the parent or guardian of a minor child, objects on the basis of religious tenets or practices.

* * *

§§ 24–21–5 Rights of retention.

A.   Unless otherwise authorized by Subsection C of Section 3 [24–21–3 NMSA 1978] of the Genetic Information Privacy Act, no person shall retain a person's genetic information, gene products or samples for genetic analysis without first obtaining informed and written consent from the person or the person's authorized representative. This subsection does not affect the status of original medical records of patients, and the rules of confidentiality and accessibility applicable to the records continue in force.

B.   A person's genetic information or samples for genetic analysis shall be destroyed promptly upon the specific request by that person or that person's authorized representative unless:

(1) retention is necessary for the purposes of a criminal or death investigation or a criminal or juvenile proceeding;

(2) retention is authorized by order of a court of competent jurisdiction;

(3) retention is authorized under a research protocol approved by an institution review board pursuant to federal law or a medical registry or repository authorized by state or federal law; or

(4) the genetic information or samples for genetic analysis have been obtained pursuant to Subsection C of Section 3 of the Genetic Information Privacy Act.

C. Actions of an insurer and third parties dealing with an insurer in the ordinary course of conducting and administering the business of life, disability income or long-term care insurance are exempt from the provisions of this section. However, before or at the time of collecting genetic information for use in conducting and administering the business of life, disability income or long-term care insurance, the insurer shall notify in writing an applicant for insurance or the insured that the information may be used, transmitted or retained solely for the purpose of conducting and administering the business of life, disability income or long-term care insurance.

D. Nothing in Paragraph (3) or (4) of Subsection B of Section 5 [24–21–5 NMSA 1978] of the Genetic Information Privacy Act authorizes retention of a person's authorized representative or guardian, or the parent or guardian of a minor child, objects on the basis of religious tenets or practices.

NOTES AND QUESTIONS

1. As of 2015, most states had enacted genetic privacy laws similar to the New Mexico law in at least some respects, although they may be limited to certain entities, such as employers or insurers. These laws typically contain one or more of the following provisions: (1) personal access to genetic information is required; (2) informed consent is required to perform a genetic test or obtain, retain, or disclose genetic information; (3) define as personal property genetic information or DNA samples; and (4) provide penalties for violations. State genetic privacy laws are collected and updated by the National Conference of State Legislatures on its website at http://www. ncsl.org/research/health/genetic-privacy-laws.aspx.

2. What are the benefits of enacting a law such as New Mexico's? Are there costs?

3. Health Insurance Portability and Accountability Act (HIPAA)

The Health Insurance Portability and Accountability Act (HIPAA), 42 U.S.C. §§ 300gg–300gg–2, enacted in 1996, contains a provision that required Congress to enact privacy legislation by August 21, 1999. If Congress failed to enact legislation by the deadline, the law directed the Secretary of Health and Human Services to promulgate regulations for the privacy of medical information. Following unsuccessful attempts to pass federal legislation, proposed regulations were issued in November 1999. After considering over 52,000 comments, the final regulations were issued on December 2000, and had a compliance date of April 2003. The regulations appear at 45 C.F.R. Parts 160 and 164. The key substantive provisions of HIPAA related to genetics and group health insurance are discussed in Chapter 15. The following excerpt describes in very basic terms the complicated and detailed HIPAA Privacy Rule.

OFFICE FOR CIVIL RIGHTS, DEPARTMENT OF HEALTH AND HUMAN SERVICES, SUMMARY OF THE HIPAA PRIVACY RULE

www.hhs.gov/ocr/privacy/hipaa/understanding/summary/privacysummary.pdf

WHO IS COVERED BY THE PRIVACY RULE

The Privacy Rule, as well as all the Administrative Simplification rules, apply to health plans, health care clearinghouses, and to any health care provider who transmits health information in electronic form in connection with transactions for which the Secretary of HHS has adopted standards under HIPAA (the "covered entities").

Health Plans.

Individual and group plans that provide or pay the cost of medical care are covered entities. Health plans include health, dental, vision, and prescription drug insurers, health maintenance organizations ("HMOs"), Medicare, Medicare+Choice and Medicare supplement insurers, and long-term care insurers (excluding nursing home fixed-indemnity policies). Health plans also include employer-sponsored group health plans, government and church-sponsored health plans, and multi-employer health plans.

Health Care Providers.

Every health care provider, regardless of size, who electronically transmits health information in connection with certain transactions, is a covered entity. These transactions include claims, benefit eligibility inquiries, referral authorization requests, or other transactions for which HHS has established standards under the HIPAA Transaction Rule.

Health Care Clearinghouses.

Health care clearinghouses are entities that process nonstandard information they receive from another entity into a standard (i.e., standard format or data content), or vice versa. In most instances, health care clearinghouses will receive individually identifiable health information only when they are providing these processing services to a health plan or health care provider as a business associate.

Business Associate.

In general, a business associate is a person or organization, other than a member of a covered entity's workforce, that performs certain functions or activities on behalf of, or provides certain services to, a covered entity that involve the use or disclosure of individually identifiable health information. Business associate functions or activities on behalf of a covered entity include claims processing, data analysis, utilization review, and billing. Business associate services to a covered entity are limited to legal, actuarial, accounting, consulting, data aggregation, management, administrative accreditation, or financial services. However, persons or organizations are not considered business associates if their functions or services do not involve the use or disclosure of protected health information, and where any access to protected health information by such persons would be incidental, if at all. A covered entity can be the business associate of another covered entity.

WHAT INFORMATION IS PROTECTED

Protected Health Information.

The Privacy Rule protects all *"individually identifiable health information"* held or transmitted by a covered entity or its business associate, in any form or media, whether electronic, paper, or oral. The Privacy Rule calls this information *"protected health information (PHI)."*

GENERAL PRINCIPLE FOR USES AND DISCLOSURES

Basic Principle.

A major purpose of the Privacy Rule is to define and limit the circumstances in which an individual's protected health information may be used or disclosed by covered entities. A covered entity may not use or disclose protected health information, except either: (1) as the Privacy Rule permits or (2) as the individual who is the subject of the information (or the individual's personal representative) authorizes in writing.

REQUIRED DISCLOSURES.

A covered entity must disclose protected health information in only two situations: (a) to individuals (or their personal representatives) specifically when they request access to, or an accounting of disclosures of, their protected health information; and (b) to HHS when it is undertaking a compliance investigation or review or enforcement action.

PERMITTED USES AND DISCLOSURES

Permitted uses and disclosures.

A covered entity is permitted, but not required, to use and disclose protected health information, without an individual's authorization, for the following purposes or situations: (1) To the Individual (unless required for access or accounting of disclosures); (2) Treatment, Payment, and Health Care Operations; (3) Opportunity to Agree or Object; (4) Incident to an otherwise permitted use and disclosure; (5) Public Interest and Benefit Activities; and (6) Limited Data Set for the purposes of research, public health or health care operations. Covered entities may rely on professional ethics and best judgments in deciding which of these permissive uses and disclosures to make.

AUTHORIZED USES AND DISCLOSURES

Authorization.

A covered entity must obtain the individual's written authorization for any use or disclosure of protected health information that is not for treatment, payment, or health care operations or otherwise permitted or required by the Privacy Rule. A covered entity may not condition treatment, payment, enrollment, or benefits eligibility on an individual granting an authorization, except in limited circumstances.

An authorization must be written in specific terms. It may allow use and disclosure of protected health information by the covered entity seeking the authorization, or by a third party. Examples of disclosures that would require an individual's authorization include disclosures to a life insurer for coverage purposes, disclosure to an employer of the results of a pre-employment physical or lab test, or disclosures to a pharmaceutical firm for their own marketing purposes.

All authorizations must be in plain language, and contain specific information regarding the information to be disclosed or used, the person(s) disclosing and receiving the information, expiration, right to revoke in writing, and other data.

LIMITING USES AND DISCLOSURES TO THE MINIMUM NECESSARY

Minimum Necessary.

A central aspect of the Privacy Rule is the principle of "minimum necessary" use and disclosure. A covered entity must make reasonable efforts to use, disclose, and request only the minimum amount of protected health information needed to accomplish the intended purpose of the use, disclosure or request. A covered entity must develop and implement policies and procedures to reasonably limit uses and disclosures to the minimum necessary. When the minimum necessary standard applies to a use or disclosure, a covered entity may not use, disclose, or request the entire medical record for a particular purpose, unless it can specifically justify the whole record as the amount reasonably needed for the purpose.

The minimum necessary requirement is not imposed in any of the following circumstances: (a) disclosure to or a request by a health care provider for treatment; (b) disclosure to an individual who is the subject of the information, or the individual's personal representative; (c) use or disclosure made pursuant to an authorization; (d) disclosure to HHS for complaint investigation, compliance review or enforcement; (e) use or disclosure that is required by law; or (f) use or disclosure required for compliance with the HIPAA Transaction Rule or other HIPAA Administrative Simplification Rules.

STATE LAW

Preemption.

In general, State laws that are contrary to the Privacy Rule are preempted by the federal requirements, which means that the federal requirements will apply. "Contrary" means that it would be impossible for a covered entity to comply with both State and federal requirements, or that the provision of State law is an obstacle to accomplishing the full purposes and objectives of the Administrative Simplification provisions of HIPAA. The Privacy Rule provides exceptions to the general rule of federal preemption for contrary State laws that (1) relate to the privacy of individually identifiable health information and provide greater privacy protections or privacy rights with respect to such information, (2) provide for the reporting of disease or injury, child abuse, birth, or death, or for public health surveillance, investigation, or intervention, or (3) require certain health plan reporting, such as for management or financial audits.

ENFORCEMENT AND PENALTIES FOR NONCOMPLIANCE

Compliance.

Consistent with the principles for achieving compliance provided in the Rule, HHS will seek the cooperation of covered entities and may provide technical assistance to help them comply voluntarily with the Rule. The Rule provides processes for persons to file complaints with HHS, describes the responsibilities of covered entities to provide records and compliance reports and to cooperate with, and permit access to information for, investigation and compliance reviews.

Civil Money Penalties.

HHS may impose civil money penalties on a covered entity of $100 per failure to comply with a Privacy Rule requirement. That penalty may not exceed $25,000 per year for multiple violations of the identical

Privacy Rule requirement in a calendar year. HHS may not impose a civil money penalty under specific circumstances, such as when a violation is due to reasonable cause and did not involve willful neglect and the covered entity corrected the violation within 30 days of when it knew or should have known of the violation.

Criminal Penalties.

A person who knowingly obtains or discloses individually identifiable health information in violation of HIPAA faces a fine of $50,000 and up to one-year imprisonment. The criminal penalties increase to $100,000 and up to five years imprisonment if the wrongful conduct involves false pretenses, and to $250,000 and ten years imprisonment if the wrongful conduct involves the intent to sell, transfer, or use individually identifiable health information for commercial advantage, personal gain, or malicious harm. Criminal sanctions will be enforced by the Department of Justice.

NOTE

Title XIII of the American Recovery and Reinvestment Act of 2009, P.L. No. 111–5, 111th Cong., 1st Sess. (2009), contains the Health Information Technology for Clinical Health Act (HITECH Act). Among the amendments to the HIPAA Privacy Rule contained in the Act are the following: (1) business associates of covered entities are subject to regulation and enforcement activities of the Department of Health and Human Services (HHS); (2) covered entities are required to notify the public in the event of a serious breach of security; (3) enforcement of the Privacy Rule by HHS is to increase; (4) additional restrictions are to be placed on the use of protected health information in marketing; and (5) public and professional educational programs of HHS are to be expanded.

On January 25, 2013, the final modifications to the HIPAA Privacy Rule were published, which included the provisions mandated by the HITECH Act and the Genetic Information Nondiscrimination Act (GINA). 78 Fed. Reg. 5566 (2013). See Mark A. Rothstein, HIPAA Privacy Rule 2.0, 41 J.L. Med. & Ethics 525 (2013).

C. COMMON LAW

MARK A. ROTHSTEIN, GENETIC STALKING AND VOYEURISM:
A NEW CHALLENGE TO PRIVACY
57 Kan. L. Rev. 539, 546–548 (2009).

* * *

In 1890, two young law partners from Boston, Samuel D. Warren and Louis D. Brandeis, published a seminal article on the right to privacy at common law. According to most historians, the impetus for the article was

Warren's great concern about the allegedly intrusive social reporting of the Boston press, but it is not clear what, if any, specific stories aroused his ire. Brandeis collaborated with Warren to write their seminal and legendary law review article, *The Right to Privacy*. Although it was inspired by perceived abuses by the press, Warren and Brandeis argued more broadly in favor of a comprehensive common law right of individuals to be free of unwanted and unreasonable intrusions of their "inviolate personality."

Louis D. Brandeis.

Warren and Brandeis expanded on Judge Thomas M. Cooley's notion of privacy as the right "to be let alone." They proposed a general legal principle of protecting "the privacy of private life" and urged creating a cause of action to redress "the more flagrant breaches of decency and propriety . . ." They concluded their article by observing the irony between the different standards used by the law in dealing with public and private interferences with peaceful habitation: "The common law has always recognized a man's house as his castle, impregnable, often, even to its own officers engaged in the execution of its commands. Shall the courts thus close the front entrance to constituted authority, and open wide the back door to idle or prurient curiosity?"

Despite its well-deserved acclaim in the academic literature, the Warren and Brandeis article did not immediately translate into a concrete common law doctrine that could be invoked to redress private wrongs. Beginning in the 1930s, courts in several states began to recognize a right of privacy, but the contours of the right were not well defined. The task of developing a cohesive doctrine fell to William L. Prosser who, in a famous law review article in 1960, proposed that the common law right to privacy was actionable in tort in four discrete situations: (1) intrusion upon the plaintiff's seclusion or solitude, or into his private affairs; (2) public disclosure of embarrassing private facts about the plaintiff; (3) publicity which places the plaintiff in a false light in the public eye; and (4) appropriation, for the defendant's advantage, of the plaintiff's name or likeness.

Some scholars have argued that, in carving out limited categories of protected interests, Prosser engaged in reductionism and oversimplification of the human dignity embodied in the right to privacy. Nevertheless, the *Restatement (Second) of Torts* adopted Prosser's classifications, and the limited, categorical approach to common law torts

for invasion of privacy steadily gained widespread acceptance in the
United States.

NOTES AND QUESTIONS

1.   Of the four common law torts for invasion of privacy, public
disclosure of private facts is the one most likely to be alleged in the context of
genetics. According to the *Restatement (Second) of Torts* § 652D, there are
four essential elements to the tort: (1) disclosure to the public or a large
number of persons; (2) of a fact that is private in nature; (3) which would be
highly offensive to a reasonable person; and (4) is not of a legitimate concern
to the public. This theory has been used when other types of health
information was unreasonably disclosed without consent. See, e.g., Urbaniak
v. Newton, 277 Cal.Rptr. 354 (Cal. Civ. App. 1991) (disclosure of HIV status);
Levias v. United Airlines, 500 N.E.2d 370 (Ohio App. 1985) (disclosure of
reproductive health).

2.   The other invasion of privacy tort of likely significance to genetics is
appropriation of name or likeness, where an individual's genetic information
or biological specimen has been used for private gain without consent. This
tort, and the related tort of conversion, is explored in Chapter 5.

3.   How valuable do you think common law actions are for invasion of
genetic privacy? What should the relationship be between statutory and
common law remedies?

IV.   DEALING WITH GENETIC DIFFERENCES

The first part of this chapter explored how the ability to maintain
some aspects of one's person, including genetic information, free from
access by or disclosure to others advances an individual's highly valued
interest in privacy. This aspect of the ability to protect one's genetic
privacy may be considered as a way of avoiding the intangible harm
associated with a loss of privacy. Another, sometimes overshadowing
concern, is the ability to avoid the adverse treatment that might flow
from a third party's access to one's genetic information, and this may be
considered a tangible harm. It is often equated with genetic
discrimination.

MARK A. ROTHSTEIN, LEGAL CONCEPTIONS OF
EQUALITY IN THE GENOMIC AGE
25 Law & Inequality 429, 455–460 (2007).

* * *

The genetic nondiscrimination and genetic privacy laws implicitly
attempt to advance the vision of a "genome-blind" society. It is
questionable whether genome-blind public policy is needed to assuage
public concerns about eugenics or whether such a strategy ever could be

successful. It is even more doubtful whether such an approach ought to be pursued.

The civil rights model of "sameness" and the fiction that all "difference is irrelevant" are inappropriate legal models for genetic diversity. Moreover, ignoring difference is not the only way to protect privacy and prevent invidious discrimination based on genetic variation.

* * *

Purging genetic information from all aspects of public and private life will become an increasingly untenable and counter-productive policy. As I have argued elsewhere, it is seemingly easier for legislators to enact laws prohibiting access to genetic information or outlawing genetic discrimination than it is to address the more fundamental and contentious underlying issues. For example, genetic discrimination in health insurance is really about access to health care, distributive justice, and health care finance, all of which most policy makers would prefer to avoid tackling. At the same time, separate legislative treatment of genetic information is certain to increase the level of stigmatization of individuals at risk for genetic disorders. Furthermore, protecting privacy and preventing discrimination are only two of the many public policies to be achieved with regard to obtaining, using, and disclosing genetic information.

In the pre-genomic age, legal conceptions of equality were based on the political ideal of equality of rights, the social goal of equality of opportunity, and the biological fiction of population homogeneity. In the genomic age, the political foundations and social aspirations remain the same, but the likelihood of achieving them will be enhanced by recognizing the biological reality of individual variation and, in appropriate situations, taking variation into account in formulating or revising various legal doctrines. Recognizing genotypic and phenotypic diversity of individuals is perfectly consistent with respecting and valuing every individual. It is also consistent with improving individual and population health, protecting health privacy, ensuring equal access to health care and other social goods, and guaranteeing civil rights.

NOTES AND QUESTIONS

1.   The Rothstein article argues that the nation's legislative policy on antidiscrimination, as exemplified by Title VII of the Civil Rights Act of 1964 (prohibiting employment discrimination based on race, color, religion, sex, and national origin), is based on the "sameness" model. That model assumes that all people are essentially the same and therefore they ought to be treated the same in all respects. By contrast, under the "difference" model, the law recognizes that people differ in important ways and therefore the law ought to take these differences into account. The Americans with Disabilities

Act, with its reasonable accommodation requirement, is presented as an example of the difference model. Is this conceptualization of discrimination instructive in thinking about genetic discrimination?

2.   How would a legal approach recognizing genetic differences differ from a "genome blind" approach?

3.   How difficult is it to obtain an individual's DNA sample without consent and to have it analyzed? Should such activity be prohibited? Is it feasible to do so? Consider the following article.

MARK A. ROTHSTEIN, GENETIC STALKING AND VOYEURISM: A NEW CHALLENGE TO PRIVACY
57 Kan. L. Rev. 539, 539–543, 576–578 (2009).

A new website has just been launched with the URL of celebritygenetics.com ("Celebrity Genetics").[1] Designed to appeal to the public's seemingly insatiable appetite for information about celebrities, Celebrity Genetics sells genetic information about hundreds of entertainers, politicians, athletes, and other public figures. For a fee ranging from twenty dollars to several hundred dollars, individuals and commercial publishers (such as blogs or tabloids) can purchase genetic information about selected celebrities, such as relatedness to other celebrities (e.g., paternity); ancestral place of origin; cognitive ability; behavioral genetic profile (e.g., genetic contribution to sexual orientation, propensity to addiction, and degree of risk-seeking behavior); and predisposition to various illnesses.

The analysis of celebrity DNA samples is merely the latest application of new genetic technologies to test individuals without consent and for purposes other than health care. In the late 1980s, law enforcement officials began matching DNA left at crime scenes with samples donated to police by suspects, often in "DNA dragnets," to identify serial murderers and rapists. Soon thereafter, law enforcement officers began obtaining DNA samples from suspects without consent and, in some cases, surreptitiously or by ruse from licked envelopes and stamps, soft drink cans, cigarette butts, chewing gum, and other objects.

At about the same time, fathers with child support obligations who were suspicious of their child's paternity were urged by billboard advertising and other mass marketing techniques to have DNA testing of themselves and their children (without the knowledge or consent of the child's mother) to confirm or rebut paternity. At first, the "doubtful dads" brought their children to genetic testing laboratories for the sample

---

[1]   The author owns the domain name, www.celebritygenetics.com, to prevent its use by others for commercial purposes. Of course, numerous similar names are available. Even if no commercial website is ever created, the genetic privacy issues, including the possibility of nonconsensual testing on a smaller, noncommercial scale, are important to consider.

collection. Soon, on-line entrepreneurs began advertising paternity testing services using home-collection kits involving cheek swabs, which captured buccal cells in saliva.

It was not long before an "anything goes" atmosphere permeated the internet world of DNA-based parentage testing, and the trend has continued unabated. For a fee, virtually any source of DNA that can be tested will be tested. For example, one web-based laboratory offers a list of items it will test and the cost for each, including the following: chewed chewing gum ($240—Wrigley Juicy Fruit© is claimed to work best); cigarette butts ($240—six should be sent); hard candy ($300—well-sucked lollipops are preferred); used condoms ($300); semen stains on clothing ($300); used tampons or feminine pads ($240); sweaty hats or ball caps ($300); "hocked loogies" ($300—best if uninfected); plucked hair ($240—three to ten strands); Q-tips with ear wax ($300—up to three swabs); snotty Kleenex ($300—best if full of mucus) and fecal matter ($360—must be frozen immediately).

Celebrity Genetics thus entered an already sleazy world of covert genetic analysis to offer yet another unsavory DNA testing service. Unlike testing for personal use, however, Celebrity Genetics assumes that the test results will generate more widespread and commercial interest. Celebrity Genetics' business depends on maintaining interest in the genetic information of celebrities and replenishing the supply of DNA for analysis, and the company uses an ingenious method to do both. Celebrity Genetics' website has a section called "DNA Wanted." Hundreds of celebrities are listed, each with a price or bounty for the first collector who submits a sample of the celebrity's DNA. As a result, Celebrity Genetics has created an army of thousands of amateur "gene-*arazzi*" from all over the world who hope to (and in some cases, do) make money and achieve fleeting notoriety by obtaining and selling the DNA of listed celebrities. The Celebrity Genetics website does not specify the method of sample collection; it merely lists some suitable items for DNA testing, such as used chewing gum and cigarette butts.

In attempting to verify that the DNA sample submitted is that of the celebrity claimed, the collector uses a cell phone or camera to obtain a digital image of the celebrity using a particular object (for example, a napkin in a restaurant). Then the collector places the object in a special mailing envelope sold by Celebrity Genetics to the DNA sleuths. Once received, the DNA is analyzed and the results are offered for sale on the Celebrity Genetics website. In their frenzy to obtain samples, DNA collectors in Hollywood, Cannes, Monte Carlo, Washington, Beijing, and other places have scavenged through the trash cans of political candidates, movie stars, judicial nominees, and Olympic athletes; pilfered napkins and utensils from chic restaurants; bribed bartenders and chambermaids for used glasses, towels, and linens; stolen dirty clothes from laundries and dry cleaners; and vandalized barber and beauty shops. Privacy advocates and various celebrities are concerned about the intrusions and disruptions in obtaining the DNA, and in publication of the test results.

Are Celebrity Genetics and its inevitable "copy-cat" websites merely the harmless, twenty-first century versions of gossip columns and tabloid photographs from an earlier era? Or, does this phenomenon represent an insidious infringement on the rights of individuals to be let alone and to prevent their intimate personal health information from being involuntarily generated, publicized, and exploited?

* * *

In the futuristic film *Gattaca*, the female lead, played by Uma Thurman, surreptitiously obtains a hair of her romantic interest, the film's protagonist, played by Ethan Hawke. She takes the hair to a laboratory that appears to specialize in the stealth genetic assessment of prospective mates. For a seemingly nominal fee, and in a matter of seconds, the laboratory presents her with the results of a full genome sequence analysis and an overall assessment of "9.3" which, she is told, makes the sample source "quite a catch." This aspect of the futuristic world portrayed in *Gattaca* is not science fiction; it is here today. The only differences are that today's genetic testing is not available "while you wait," only genome-wide association analyses rather than full sequence data are commercially available today, and the genetic testing of the future presumably would be more accurate than what is commercially touted today.

Genetic stalking and voyeurism involving celebrities serve to draw attention to the issue, but the underlying privacy concerns of surreptitious genetic testing are anything but frivolous and have population-wide applicability. Genetic information is among the most sensitive health and personal information about an individual. Without legislation prohibiting nonconsensual DNA analysis, human dignity and public civility will be irretrievably lost. Society will have succeeded in reaching a level of "zero" privacy and it will not be easy or desirable to "get over it."

* * *

Today, in the health care setting, a genetic test intended to benefit the patient may be ordered only by a licensed physician with informed consent from the patient, the testing must be performed by a certified clinical laboratory, and the confidentiality of the results must be maintained in accordance with the HIPAA Privacy Rule. Should strangers be permitted to acquire an individual's DNA sample on an inanimate object surreptitiously without any consent, arrange for an unregulated laboratory to perform genetic testing on the sample, and widely publish the results when the motivation is curiosity, commercial exploitation, or some other trivial, voyeuristic, or nefarious purpose?

NOTES AND QUESTIONS

1.   Do any of the legal remedies mentioned in the previous part of this chapter offer adequate protection against nonconsensual genetic testing and the exploitation of the results? If not, what would you recommend?

2.   Reports of plans to engage in the "genetic stalking" of England's Prince Harry was a prime motivation for the enactment of Section 45 of the United Kingdom's Human Tissue Act of 2004, which makes it unlawful for any individual, without proper consent, to possess any "bodily material" with the intent to have DNA testing performed. There are exceptions for medical treatment, law enforcement, research, and other uses. Violators are subject to fine and imprisonment.

3.   During the 2008 Presidential election campaign, someone placed for sale on eBay part of the uneaten breakfast and utensils used by Barack Obama, advertising that the buyer could perform genetic testing on the sample. Peter Aldhous & Michael Reilly, Who Is Testing Your DNA?, New Scientist, Apr. 24, 2009, at 8, 11. Should this be prohibited by U.S. law? Only a few states make it unlawful to perform nonconsensual genetic testing. On the other hand, Presidential candidates typically release their medical histories. Should they also release their genetic profiles? See Teneille R. Brown, Double Helix, Double Standards: Private Matters and Public People, 11 J. Health Care L. & Pol'y 295 (2008); Robert C. Green & George J. Annas, The Genetic Profile of Presidential Candidates, 359 New Eng. J. Med. 2192 (2009).

4.   Genetic information often is a powerful predictor of an individual's likely future health. Because there are frequently many other individuals and entities with an interest in learning the likelihood of any particular individual's future health, genetic privacy involves weighing the relative interests of the individual with those of the third parties. Insurance (Chapter 15) and Employment (Chapter 16) are examples explored in the following chapters, as is the use of genetic information in education, discussed in Chapter 13. Notes 5–7 discuss other less explored, but nonetheless important, possible uses of genetic information.

5.   Mortgage lenders make substantial investments in real estate based on the presumed ability of the borrower to make payments over a prolonged period of time—frequently up to 30 years. Although the mortgage companies have collateral in the form of the real estate itself, repossession and resale are a last resort for lenders. Along with the loan application and credit report, there is currently no law that would prevent a mortgage company from requiring a genetic test to predict the future health of the borrower. Some possible legal theories under which the practice could be challenged involve Title III of the Americans with Disabilities Act, the Fair Housing Act,

and state and federal consumer credit and banking laws. The applicability of any of these laws is unclear.

6. As baby boomers age, retirement communities are likely to experience a boom as well. Many retirement communities like to project the image of vigorous and active lifestyles, with golf, tennis, swimming, and other activities featured prominently in promotional materials. Residents sitting in the lobby in wheel chairs or with attendants caring for the basic needs of residents with dementia would not be good for business. Would it be lawful for a retirement community (either rental or sale properties) to require pre-approval genetic testing to determine the genetic risks of Alzheimer disease, Parkinson disease, or other debilitating conditions? Some of the legal theories challenging such practices would be similar to those mentioned in the prior note. What are the ethical and policy arguments that could be made for each side of the issue?

7. There are various possible government uses of genetic tests and genetic information. These include tests by government security agencies (e.g., concerns about genetic predisposition to mental instability); state motor vehicle licensing agencies (e.g., concerns about genetic predisposition to neurological impairments); and government benefits agencies (e.g., using genetic information to determine eligibility). Among the possible uses of genetic information by the military are to predict susceptibility to certain harmful environments, to assess the likelihood of developing post-traumatic stress disorder, to determine fitness for duty, and to establish the source of disability. See Susannah Baruch & Kathy Hudson, Civilian and Military Genetics: Nondiscrimination Policy in a Post-GINA World, 83 Am. J. Human Genetics 435 (2008).

CHAPTER 15

INSURANCE

■ ■ ■

I. INTRODUCTION

Insurance is a system for pooling resources against contingent risks. In the United States, the insurance market is a private, largely for-profit enterprise, and there are thousands of companies selling insurance. Many of the insurance products, such as homeowners insurance, auto insurance, fire and flood insurance, property and casualty insurance, and professional liability insurance attempt to protect against the harms caused by natural occurrences or human errors. Other product lines, including medical expense insurance (health insurance), life insurance, disability insurance, and long-term care insurance, attempt to provide expenses or replacement income in the event of unpredictable illness or death.

Risk classification lies at the heart of insurance. To use life insurance as an example, it is impossible to predict how long any particular individual will live. But, it is possible to predict how long the average member of a clearly defined group will live. Thus, if we know the individual's age, current health status, occupation, lifestyle (e.g. smoking, drinking), and other relevant factors, it is possible to predict the average life expectancy of a group of individuals with the same relevant characteristics. Underwriting is the process of assigning individuals to actuarially relevant groups for purposes of predicting risk and thus deciding the appropriate terms and rates for insurance coverage.

Predictive genetic assessments of individuals have a curious relationship with insurance. If insurance is based on coverage against unknown risks, to the extent that any individual's future illness or death becomes predictable, then insurance would be either (1) unnecessary (where there is little chance of serious illness or death within a given period of time) or (2) unavailable or unaffordable (where there is a virtual certainty of serious illness or death in a given period of time).

Genetic prognostications involving asymptomatic individuals have not yet reached the point where it is possible to make accurate estimates of future illness and death. This is true for monogenic disorders with high penetrance rates, and predictions are even more venturesome for complex disorders and disorders with lower rates of penetrance. Nevertheless, because risk classification is concerned with group experience rather than individual experience, it is clear that genetic information may well be relevant in risk classification.

The interests of consumers and insurers may be summarized in the following way. First, consumers are concerned that genetic information may be used inaccurately, such as during the early 1970s when some unaffected carriers of sickle cell trait were denied access to insurance despite a lack of scientific evidence of increased risk of morbidity or mortality. Second, they are concerned about the invasion of their privacy in insurance companies requiring that they undergo genetic tests they would prefer not to take or companies obtaining, retaining, and disclosing their genetic information. Third, consumers assert that even actuarially accurate insurance decisions may result in great unfairness in denying them access to essential services such as health care and long-term care.

On the other hand, insurers are extremely worried about adverse selection. This is the tendency of those who need insurance the most to purchase it and in the greatest amounts. Insurers argue that as more genetic tests are run in the clinical setting, greater numbers of individuals learn of their genetic risks. Those who learn that they are at greater risk of illness are more likely to seek insurance. Insurers assert that unless they have access to the same information as the individuals, then it is impossible to assign policy holders to the appropriate risk pool for purposes of underwriting. The result is that low-risk individuals are subsidizing the policies of high-risk individuals who have knowledge of their genetic risks, resulting in unfairness among policy holders as well as threatening the economic viability of the insurance companies.

Because of conflicts between the consumer and insurer positions, the use of genetic information in insurance is one of the most contentious social issues arising from the genetics revolution. Among the many questions raised are the following: First, when is the science sufficiently developed that it is appropriate to use genetic information in risk classification? Second, even if actuarially justified, are there social reasons why genetic information should not be used? Answering this question demands an inquiry into the social function of the particular insurance product; the harms associated with obtaining, storing, and using the information; and the existence of alternatives to a genetic-based risk classification scheme. Third, how should the insurance industry be regulated to accomplish social policy?

In this chapter we will consider the use of genetic information in four main contexts: health, life, disability, and long-term care insurance. Although this area has been a fertile ground for scholarship and legislative activity at all levels, there have been few cases thus far. As you consider these materials, try to determine the underlying social policies at issue and whether each proposal or enactment operates to further those policies.

II.   HEALTH INSURANCE

A.   BACKGROUND

The American system for payment of health care is incredibly complicated. It is public and private, commercial and noncommercial, federal and state, group and individual, premium-based and tax-supported. Efforts to make the system more effective, efficient, and equitable invariably succeed in making the system more complex.

According to the U.S. Census Bureau, in 2013, 64.2% of the U.S. population had private health insurance. Of that total, 53.9% was employment-based group coverage and 11% was individual coverage or "direct purchase." During 2013, 34.3% of the population had government health coverage under Medicare (15.6%), Medicaid (17.3%), or military and veterans insurance plans (4.5%). That left 13.4% of the population, 42 million people without any health insurance coverage. Note that multiple coverage and rounding errors account for the differential sums. U.S. Census Bureau, Health Insurance Coverage in the United States: 2013 (Sept. 2014), at 2–3.

Government-sponsored health coverage is not medically underwritten. If an individual satisfies the statutory criteria (e.g., age or permanent disability for Medicare; income limits for Medicaid), then the individual's health status is irrelevant. Non-government health coverage principally has been employer-sponsored group health plans and individual health insurance. Both of these private markets used to be relatively unregulated, but over the last 40 years a series of enactments have attempted to make health coverage more widely available and in accord with public notions of fairness.

Several federal laws dealing with private health coverage have had significant effects on genetic-based distinctions and genetic information in health coverage. The following are some of the key laws and some of their relevant provisions.

- The Employee Retirement Income Security Act of 1974 (ERISA), 29 U.S.C. §§ 1001–1046, regulates employer-sponsored pension and welfare plans—the latter includes health coverage. ERISA does not require employers to provide any benefits, but if they do the beneficiaries are given federal protections to enforce employer promises.

- The Health Insurance Portability and Accountability Act of 1996 (HIPAA), Pub. L. No. 104-191, 110 Stat. 1936, limits the ability of employer-sponsored group health plans (both commercially insured and self-insured) to apply preexisting condition exclusions to individuals moving from one job to another and prohibits the charging of differential premiums to individuals within a group plan.

- The Genetic Information Nondiscrimination Act of 2008 (GINA), 42 U.S.C. § 2000ff, prohibits health insurers in both the individual and group markets from discriminating on the basis of "genetic information," but the law does not protect adverse treatment based on an individual's health condition that has already manifested.

- The Affordable Care Act of 2010 (ACA), Pub. L. No. 111-148, 124 Stat. 119, prohibits medical underwriting in the individual health insurance market, and it attempts to guard against adverse selection by requiring large employers (those with 50 or more employees) to provide coverage for "essential health benefits." The ACA's "individual mandate" requires individuals without other coverage to purchase coverage, including by using health marketplaces and, if they have a limited income, with the use of government subsidies.

Traditionally, states have been responsible for regulating all forms of insurance sold in the state. Thus, it is not surprising that state genetic nondiscrimination in health insurance laws actually predate federal involvement. As of 2015, all but two states (Mississippi and Pennsylvania) have enacted legislation prohibiting at least some aspects genetic-based discrimination. With the increasingly significant role of federal legislation, however, state measures have become less important.

B. STATE LAWS

State genetic nondiscrimination laws were first enacted in the early 1970s to combat irrational sickle cell trait discrimination that arose from the federal government's poorly conceived and implemented sickle cell screening programs. Florida, Louisiana, and North Carolina enacted the first laws prohibiting discrimination in employment and health insurance. In 1981, New Jersey enacted a broader law that prohibited discrimination based on an individual's "atypical hereditary cellular or blood type," defined to include sickle cell trait, hemoglobin C trait, thalassemia trait, Tay-Sachs trait, or cystic fibrosis trait. Oregon, New York, Wisconsin, and other states followed suit. In the 1990s with the Human Genome Project serving as the impetus, numerous other states enacted laws prohibiting genetic discrimination in health insurance. Because ERISA preempts state regulation of employer-sponsored group health plans, these state laws applied only to individual health insurance and some small, non-employer group plans. As of 2014, 48 states and the

District of Columbia have laws prohibiting genetic discrimination in health insurance. For an updated list of the state laws, see http://www.genome.gov/27552194.

KAN. STAT. ANN. § 40–2259
(ENACTED 1997, amended 2010).

40–2259.   Genetic screening or testing; prohibiting the use of; exceptions. (a) As used in this section, "genetic screening or testing" means a laboratory test of a person's genes or chromosomes for abnormalities, defects or deficiencies, including carrier status, that are linked to physical or mental disorders or impairments, or that indicate a susceptibility to illness, disease or other disorders, whether physical or mental, which test is a direct test for abnormalities, defects or deficiencies, and not an indirect manifestation of genetic disorders.

(b) An insurance company, health maintenance organization, nonprofit medical and hospital, dental, optometric or pharmacy corporation, or a group subject to K.S.A. 12–2616 et seq., and amendments thereto, offering group policies providing hospital, medical or surgical expense benefits, shall not:

(1) Require or request directly or indirectly any individual or a member of the individual's family to obtain a genetic test;

(2) require or request directly or indirectly any individual to reveal whether the individual or a member of the individual's family has obtained a genetic test or the results of the test, if obtained by the individual or a member of the individual's family;

(3) condition the provision of insurance coverage or health care benefits on whether an individual or a member of the individual's family has obtained a genetic test or the results of the test, if obtained by the individual or a member of the individual's family; or

(4) consider in the determination of rates or any other aspect of insurance coverage or health care benefits provided to an individual whether an individual or a member of the individual's family has obtained a genetic test or the results of the test, if obtained by the individual or a member of the individual's family;

(5) require any individual, as a condition of enrollment or continued enrollment, to pay a premium or contribution which is greater than such premium or contribution for a similarly situated individual on the basis of whether the individual or a member of the individual's family has obtained a genetic test or the results of such test; or

(6) adjust premium or contribution amounts on the basis of whether the individual or a member of the individual's family has obtained a genetic test or the result of such test.

(c) Subsection (b) does not apply to an insurer writing life insurance, disability income insurance or long-term care insurance coverage.

(d) An insurer writing life insurance, disability income insurance or long-term care insurance coverage that obtains information under paragraphs (1) or (2) of subsection (b), shall not:

(1) Use the information contrary to paragraphs (3) or (4) of subsection (b) in writing a type of insurance coverage other than life for the individual or a member of the individual's family; or

(2) provide for rates or any other aspect of coverage that is not reasonably related to the risk involved.

NOTES AND QUESTIONS

1. The Kansas statute is typical of the state genetic nondiscrimination laws, although each one differs to some degree. Would the Kansas law prohibit discrimination in health insurance based on an individual's family history of genetic disease? Should insurers be prohibited from considering such information? Does the Kansas law prohibit an individual from voluntarily submitting favorable genetic information to an insurer to get a lower rate?

2. The exclusion in the Kansas law of life, disability, and long-term care insurance is typical of most of the state laws. These other forms of insurance are discussed later in this chapter.

3. Were these laws needed? Did they work? See below.

MARK A. HALL, LEGAL RULES AND INDUSTRY NORMS: THE IMPACT OF LAWS RESTRICTING HEALTH INSURERS' USE OF GENETIC INFORMATION
40 Jurimetrics 93, 94–99, 122 (1999).

Researchers and advocacy groups have reported cases of employers and health, life, and disability insurers using this new-found genetic information to deny coverage, raise rates, or limit the extent of coverage. Fear of genetic discrimination of this sort was shown to factor strongly into patients' and family members' decisions and concerns about undergoing genetic testing.

These laws are thus intended to achieve two kinds of social benefit: (1) to prevent unfair use of genetic information, however accurate that use might be as a source of underwriting information; and (2) to encourage more genetic testing for purposes of research, prevention, treatment, and family planning. This article reports on an extensive empirical study designed to assess what impact these laws have had, and why. This article focuses on only the first purpose of the legislation—preventing genetic discrimination. Other publications will explore the second purpose.

Several distinctive features of these laws must be considered in assessing their purpose and intended effects. First, they mostly target only comprehensive (or "major medical") health insurance, not life, disability, or long-term care insurance, and not employment discrimination. A few states address these other arenas, but the great majority so far have addressed only ordinary health insurance. This limitation results from two factors: health insurers put up less resistance to this legislation than do life insurers, and most people care more about maintaining health insurance than about other types of insurance.

The second crucial feature of these statutes is that they typically cover only certain types of genetic information: *presymptomatic* information derived from genetic *tests*. Most states still allow insurers to consider family history of disease, although an increasing number appear to prohibit this as well; however, almost every state allows health insurers to underwrite based on observed clinical signs and symptoms of medical conditions, regardless of their genetic status. The reasons are partly pragmatic, and partly central to the law's purpose. Since health insurers have always used symptoms of existing disease in medical underwriting, it would be infeasible and unjustified to distinguish between diseases with and without significant genetic components. One would either have to prohibit all medical underwriting, which cannot be done as long as the purchase of health insurance is voluntary, or to target only specific sources of information. Information from genetic tests is the sensible point of concern because that is where the fear of insurance discrimination has the greatest discernible impact.

* * *

For purposes of this study, genetic discrimination is defined as the denial, limitation, or increased price of health insurance based on the results of presymptomatic genetic information. In other words, genetic discrimination, as defined by these laws, means insurers using genetic information as part of medical underwriting to predict future health problems for people who currently do not have the genetic disease in question. A majority of states prohibit only information from genetic *tests*, but a substantial and growing minority also prohibit the use of family history information. However, almost no state defines genetic discrimination to include observed signs and symptoms of genetic disease, or medical tests other than genetic tests. Genetic discrimination could be defined more broadly, but then it would be impossible to distinguish it from other, non-genetic sources of information commonly used in medical underwriting. Presymptomatic genetic information is different because it results in branding someone as a high health risk who presently has no disease. However, we do not use "discrimination" necessarily as a pejorative term, but rather in the more neutral sense of differentiation. Thus, genetic discrimination includes insurers' use of genetic information regardless of whether that use might be considered fair or actuarially justified.

It appears from several independent sources that genetic discrimination by health insurers is very low or nonexistent, both before these laws were enacted and afterwards, and in states with and without these laws. Thus, these laws have had no discernible impact on actual genetic discrimination by health insurers. Although it is difficult to prove a negative assertion like this conclusively, strong confirmation exists if thorough examination of many reliable sources of information all point to the same conclusion. That is the case here. However, these laws have had an impact: they have discouraged health insurers from even considering the possibility of using genetic information.

* * *

Rather than criticizing these laws for responding to a problem that does not exist, one can maintain that the law has a legitimate function in simply expressing the social judgment that it is wrong to use genetic information in health underwriting. Even though insurers and agents do not have widespread and accurate knowledge of these laws, these laws have fortified their impression of social disapproval by creating a general climate of legal condemnation. Health insurers avoid the use of genetic information not so much because of the specific threat of law but because the law reinforces the instinct that doing otherwise would be socially wrong. To this extent, they have been effective. However, the expressive effect of the law can also have unintended negative consequences. It may be that, rather than calming fears about genetic discrimination and therefore encouraging more people to undergo beneficial genetic testing, these laws have heightened fears without substantial justification by calling undue attention to a problem that, in large measure, does not exist.

NOTES AND QUESTIONS

1. Hall's article is the first effort to study asserted discrimination in health insurance in a methodologically rigorous manner. Prior attempts to document anecdotal reports of discrimination relied on self-reports. See, e.g., Paul R. Billings et al., Discrimination as a Consequence of Genetic Testing, 50 Am. J. Human Genetics 476 (1992); E. Virginia Lapham et al., Genetic Discrimination: Perspectives of Consumers, 274 Science 621 (1996). The

problem with the case reports is that they often do not distinguish between asymptomatic and symptomatic individuals, and it is also difficult to verify self-reports of discrimination. Nevertheless, self-report studies are still widely cited in the media and elsewhere as evidence of health insurance discrimination. For a critical discussion of the popular literature on genetic discrimination, see Philip R. Reilly, Genetic Discrimination, in Genetic Testing and the Use of Information (Clarisa Long ed. 1999).

2.   Another common assumption is that individuals decline to undergo genetic testing because they are afraid of discrimination by health insurance companies. Hall and his colleague Stephen S. Rich attempted to study whether the enactment of state laws prohibiting genetic discrimination in health insurance had any effect on the willingness of at-risk individuals to undergo genetic testing. The study involved detailed interviews with genetic counselors and medical geneticists in selected states with and without antidiscrimination legislation. Hall and Rich found that the enactment of state laws had little effect on the willingness of individuals to undergo genetic testing:

> Although genetic counselors report that their patients have great concern about insurance discrimination, many counselors think that this concern does not rank so high as the psychological impact of learning one's genetic fate, or they believe this concern is important only when the need for the information is low. Thus, discrimination concerns are often overshadowed by other barriers to testing, or by the pressing need for the information.

> Where discrimination fears actually deter testing, there is little reason to believe that the legal protections so far have offered much reassurance or have altered any testing decisions. These laws provide little reassurance because counselors do not perceive them as significantly reducing the actual risk of discrimination, or counselors do not yet have sufficient confidence in these laws. These protections have not received nearly so much publicity as has the potential risk of discrimination, so patients' primary source of information about these laws is from genetic counselors. Although counselors mention these laws, they continue to place more stress on alerting patients to the potential risks than on reassuring them of the legal protections.

Mark A. Hall & Stephen S. Rich, Genetic Privacy Laws and Patients' Fear of Discrimination by Health Insurers: The View from Genetic Counselors, 28 J. L. Med. & Ethics 245, 254 (2000).

3.   If there is little genetic discrimination in health insurance today, to what do you attribute it? Antidiscrimination laws? The fact that most health insurance is group based? The desire of agents and companies to sell policies? The fact that adverse selection is less of a risk in health insurance? Other factors?

C. FEDERAL LAWS

HEALTH INSURANCE PORTABILITY AND ACCOUNTABILITY ACT

42 U.S.C. §§ 300gg–300gg–2.

(ALSO CODIFIED IN PART AT 26 U.S.C. § 9801, AND IN FULL AT 29 U.S.C. §§ 1181–1191c.)

PART A—GROUP MARKET REFORMS

Subpart 1—Portability, Access, and Renewability Requirements

§ 300gg. Increased portability through limitation on preexisting condition exclusions

(a) Limitation on preexisting condition exclusion period; crediting for periods of previous coverage

Subject to subsection (d) of this section, a group health plan, and a health insurance issuer offering group health insurance coverage, may, with respect to a participant or beneficiary, impose a preexisting condition exclusion only if—

(1) such exclusion relates to a condition (whether physical or mental), regardless of the cause of the condition, for which medical advice, diagnosis, care, or treatment was recommended or received within the 6-month period ending on the enrollment date;

(2) such exclusion extends for a period of not more than 12 months (or 18 months in the case of a late enrollee) after the enrollment date; and

(3) the period of any such preexisting condition exclusion is reduced by the aggregate of the periods of creditable coverage (if any, as defined in subsection (c)(1) of this section) applicable to the participant or beneficiary as of the enrollment date.

(b) Definitions

For purposes of this part—

(1) Preexisting condition exclusion

(A) In general

The term "preexisting condition exclusion" means, with respect to coverage, a limitation or exclusion of benefits relating to a condition based on the fact that the condition was present before the date of enrollment for such coverage, whether or not any medical advice, diagnosis, care, or treatment was recommended or received before such date.

(B) Treatment of genetic information

Genetic information shall not be treated as a condition described in subsection (a)(1) of this section in the absence of a diagnosis of the condition related-to such information.

* * *

§ 300gg–1.

(a) In eligibility to enroll

(1) In general

Subject to paragraph (2), a group health plan, and a health insurance issuer offering group health insurance coverage in connection with a group health plan, may not establish rules for eligibility (including continued eligibility) of any individual to enroll under the terms of the plan based on any of the following health status-related factors in relation to the individual or a dependent of the individual:

(A) Health status.

(B) Medical condition (including both physical and mental illnesses).

(C) Claims experience.

(D) Receipt of health care.

(E) Medical history.

(F) Genetic information.

(G) Evidence of insurability (including conditions arising out of acts of domestic violence).

(H) Disability.

(2) No application to benefits or exclusions

To the extent consistent with section 701, paragraph (1) shall not be construed—

(A) to require a group health plan, or group health insurance coverage, to provide particular benefits other than those provided under the terms of such plan or coverage, or

(B) to prevent such a plan or coverage from establishing limitations or restrictions on the amount, level, extent, or nature of the benefits or coverage for similarly situated individuals enrolled in the plan or coverage.

(3) Construction

For purposes of paragraph (1), rules for eligibility to enroll under a plan include rules defining any applicable waiting periods for such enrollment.

NOTES

1.   HIPAA was enacted in 1996, and the language applicable to genetic information was included late in the legislative process. HIPAA applies to employer-sponsored group health plans, the main avenue by which individuals obtain health care coverage in the private sector. According to HIPAA, genetic information may not be considered to be a preexisting condition and may not be used as a basis for denying coverage or setting rates.

2.   HIPAA does not require that any employer offer health benefits, it does not set a defined minimum benefits package, it does not limit the amount of money that employers charge employees to participate in the plan, and it does not prohibit an employer from dropping coverage altogether. HIPAA also does not apply to individual health insurance policies or non-employer group plans. The more comprehensive legislation was enacted later.

GENETIC INFORMATION NONDISCRIMINATION ACT (GINA)
P.L. 110–233 (2008).

* * *

SEC. 2. FINDINGS.

Congress makes the following findings:

* * *

(5) Federal law addressing genetic discrimination in health insurance and employment is incomplete in both the scope and depth of its protections. Moreover, while many States have enacted some type of genetic non-discrimination law, these laws vary widely with respect to their approach, application, and level of protection. Congress has collected substantial evidence that the American public and the medical community find the existing patchwork of State and Federal laws to be confusing and inadequate to protect them from discrimination. Therefore, Federal legislation establishing a national and uniform basic standard is necessary to fully protect the public from discrimination and allay their concerns about the potential for discrimination, thereby allowing individuals to take advantage of genetic testing, technologies, research, and new therapies.

TITLE I—GENETIC NONDISCRIMINATION IN HEALTH INSURANCE

SEC. 101. AMENDMENTS TO EMPLOYEE RETIREMENT INCOME SECURITY ACT OF 1974.

(a) NO DISCRIMINATION IN GROUP PREMIUMS BASED ON GENETIC INFORMATION.—Section 702(b) of the Employee Retirement Income Security Act of 1974 (29 U.S.C. 1182(b)) is amended—

* * *

(3) NO GROUP-BASED DISCRIMINATION ON BASIS OF GENETIC INFORMATION.—

(A) IN GENERAL.—For purposes of this section, a group health plan, and a health insurance issuer offering group health insurance coverage in connection with a group health plan, may not adjust premium or contribution amounts for the group covered under such plan on the basis of genetic information.

* * *

SEC. 102. AMENDMENTS TO THE PUBLIC HEALTH SERVICE ACT.

* * *

(b) AMENDMENT RELATING TO THE INDIVIDUAL MARKET.—

(1) IN GENERAL.—The first subpart 3 of part B of title XXVII of the Public Health Service Act (42 U.S.C. 300gg–51 et seq.) (relating to other requirements) is amended—

SEC. 2753. PROHIBITION OF HEALTH DISCRIMINATION ON THE BASIS OF GENETIC INFORMATION.

(a) PROHIBITION ON GENETIC INFORMATION AS A CONDITION OF ELIGIBILITY .—

(1) IN GENERAL.—A health insurance issuer offering health insurance coverage in the individual market may not establish rules for the eligibility (including continued eligibility) of any individual to enroll in individual health insurance coverage based on genetic information.

(2) RULE OF CONSTRUCTION.—Nothing in paragraph (1) or in paragraphs (1) and (2) of subsection (e) shall be construed to preclude a health insurance issuer from establishing rules for eligibility for an individual to enroll in individual health insurance coverage based on the manifestation of a disease or disorder in that individual, or in a family member of such

individual where such family member is covered under the policy that covers such individual.

(b) PROHIBITION ON GENETIC INFORMATION IN SETTING PREMIUM RATES.—

(1) IN GENERAL.—A health insurance issuer offering health insurance coverage in the individual market shall not adjust premium or contribution amounts for an individual on the basis of genetic information concerning the individual or a family member of the individual.

(2) RULE OF CONSTRUCTION.—Nothing in paragraph (1) or in paragraphs (1) and (2) of subsection (e) shall be construed to preclude a health insurance issuer from adjusting premium or contribution amounts for an individual on the basis of a manifestation of a disease or disorder in that individual, or in a family member of such individual where such family member is covered under the policy that covers such individual. In such case, the manifestation of a disease or disorder in one individual cannot also be used as genetic information about other individuals covered under the policy issued to such individual and to further increase premiums or contribution amounts.

(c) PROHIBITION ON GENETIC INFORMATION AS PREEXISTING CONDITION.—

(1) IN GENERAL.—A health insurance issuer offering health insurance coverage in the individual market may not, on the basis of genetic information, impose any preexisting condition exclusion (as defined in section 2701(b)(1)(A)) with respect to such coverage.

(2) RULE OF CONSTRUCTION.—Nothing in paragraph (1) or in paragraphs (1) and (2) of subsection (e) shall be construed to preclude a health insurance issuer from imposing any preexisting condition exclusion for an individual with respect to health insurance coverage on the basis of a manifestation of a disease or disorder in that individual.

(d) GENETIC TESTING.—

(1) LIMITATION ON REQUESTING OR REQUIRING GENETIC TESTING.—A health insurance issuer offering health insurance coverage in the individual market shall not request or require an individual or a family member of such individual to undergo a genetic test.

(2) RULE OF CONSTRUCTION.—Paragraph (1) shall not be construed to limit the authority of a health care professional who

is providing health care services to an individual to request that such individual undergo a genetic test.

MARK A. ROTHSTEIN, GINA'S BEAUTY IS ONLY SKIN DEEP
22 Gene Watch No. 2, at 9–10 (Apr.–May 2009).

* * *

GINA's prohibition on genetic discrimination in health insurance is largely a mirage. The Health Insurance Portability and Accountability Act (HIPAA) contains a little-known provision prohibiting employer-sponsored group health plans from denying individuals coverage, charging them higher rates, or varying their coverage based on "genetic information." Significantly, HIPAA prohibits discrimination by group health plans on the basis of any health information. Because HIPAA prohibits genetic discrimination for the largest source of private health coverage (group plans), GINA's main value is to cover people with individual health insurance policies in the few states that did not previously enact a state genetic nondiscrimination law.

Unfortunately, the protections afforded individuals under either state laws prohibiting genetic discrimination in health insurance or GINA are not particularly robust or valuable. (Because state laws and GINA are similar in substance, for simplicity, I'll merely refer to GINA.) The problem is that GINA only applies to asymptomatic individuals. There are few incentives for health insurers to discriminate against asymptomatic individuals and few laws to prohibit them from discriminating against symptomatic individuals.

An example will bring this problem more clearly into focus. Under GINA, it is unlawful for an individual health insurance company to refuse to offer coverage, charge higher rates, or exclude certain conditions on the basis of genetic information, including the results of a genetic test. For example, it would be unlawful to deny coverage to a woman with a positive test for one of the breast cancer mutations. Now, suppose some months or years later, the woman develops breast cancer. GINA simply does not apply. The insurance company's permissible response would depend on state insurance law. In virtually every state, the health insurance company could lawfully react to the changed health status of the individual by refusing to renew the policy (at its typically annual renewal date), increase the rates to reflect the increased risk (and the rates might be double or triple), or renew the policy but exclude coverage for breast cancer.

GINA does have some limited value in this scenario. Because of GINA, an at-risk woman is no worse off in terms of insurability due to having a genetic test, and there might be psychological or medical benefits from being tested, depending on the results. Yet, the overall picture in terms of health policy remains bleak. So long as individual health insurance is medically underwritten at the initial application and for renewals, individuals who are ill or more likely to become ill are extremely vulnerable. Many advocates and policy makers have concentrated on the issue of genetic discrimination in health insurance, but the issue is much broader and cannot be resolved by such a narrow focus. To state the obvious: Under any system of universal access to health care, the issue of genetic discrimination in health insurance disappears.

NOTES AND QUESTIONS

1. The express purpose of GINA is to allay fears of individuals that if they undergo genetic testing they will be subject to discrimination. GINA does not apply to life, disability, long-term care or other forms of insurance, and its health insurance provisions only apply to individuals who are asymptomatic. Do you think these limitations undermine the stated intent of GINA?

2. The essential problem of GINA is captured with the following example from Russell Korobkin & Rahul Rajkumar, The Genetic Information Nondiscrimination Act—A Half-Step Toward Risk Sharing, 359 New Eng. J. Med. 335, 335 (2008).

> Consider three Americans—one with an increased genetic risk for colon cancer, one with a family history of colon cancer, and one with colonoscopic finding of several large adenomatous polyps. Under the Genetic Information Nondiscrimination Act (GINA), which was recently signed into law by President George W. Bush, health insurance companies may not refuse to cover and may not raise premiums for the first two people, whose genetic information or family history puts them at higher risk for colon cancer. Insurers could, however, refuse to sell the third person an individual policy or quadruple his or her premiums.

3. The precursor bill of GINA was introduced in 1995, and it took 13 years before legislation was finally enacted. In the final vote, only one member of the House of Representatives and no member of the Senate voted against GINA. How can you explain this?

4. GINA can be fairly characterized as limited in scope and an example of genetic exceptionalism. Given these facts, if you were in Congress, would you have supported this bill? Reconsider the following article from Chapter 14, Mark A. Rothstein, Genetic Exceptionalism and Legislative Pragmatism.

5. Title II of GINA, dealing with genetic discrimination in employment, is discussed in Chapter 16.

AFFORDABLE CARE ACT OF 2010

On March 30, 2010, President Barack Obama signed the Health Care and Education Reconciliation Act, P.L. 111–152, also known as the Reconciliation Act, making changes to the Patient Protection and Affordable Care Act, P.L. 111–148, also known as the Affordable Care Act, or ACA, which passed one week earlier. The Acts collectively make numerous changes to existing laws and add a variety of new programs in an effort to expand access to health care, improve quality, prohibit discriminatory practices by insurers, and reduce costs. The legislation was designed to augment rather than supplant employer-based group health plans, and in several ways the new laws attempt to promote and support the role of employers in health care finance.

President Obama signing into law the Affordable Care Act, March 23, 2010.
Photo credit: Pete Souza

The health reform law is a notoriously long and complicated piece of legislation. The following discussion focuses on a selection of key issues.

EMPLOYER RESPONSIBILITIES

Large Employer Penalty. Under the ACA, employers are not required to provide health insurance coverage; however, beginning in 2014, certain large employers (those with 50 or more employees) that do not offer health insurance to their employees will be penalized. The ACA provides that "applicable large employers" that do not offer minimum essential health coverage under an eligible employer-sponsored plan, and that have at least one full-time employee who enrolls in a plan on the state health exchange using a federal premium tax credit or costsharing reduction, will be liable for a penalty. This penalty is also known as the "play-or-pay" mandate and the "free rider penalty." ACA § 1513 imposes a penalty in the amount of $2,000 on large employers that do not offer minimum essential health coverage each year (or $166.67 for each month the employer does not provide a plan), multiplied by the number of full-time employees. The first 30 employees do not count towards the penalty. The penalties for employers with 100 or more employees were postponed until January 1, 2015, and for employers with 50–99 employees they were postponed until January 1, 2016.

An "applicable large employer" is defined as an employer with at least 50 full-time employees on business days during the preceding calendar year. A "full-time employee" is defined as an employee who works an average of at least 30 hours per week. "Essential health benefits" includes the following non-comprehensive list of features:

(A) Ambulatory patient services;

(B) Emergency services;

(C) Hospitalization;

(D) Maternity and newborn care;

(E) Mental health and substance use disorder services, including behavioral health treatment;

(F) Prescription drugs;

(G) Rehabilitative and habilitative services and devices;

(H) Laboratory services;

(I) Preventive and wellness services and chronic disease management;

and

(J) Pediatric services, including oral and vision care.

Furthermore, large employers that offer coverage described above but whose coverage is not "affordable" or whose coverage does not provide a certain value must pay an additional penalty. To be "affordable" the premium of the employer-sponsored plan must cost less than 9.5% of the employee's household income. The plan must also provide a minimum value of at least 60% of the coverage (i.e., the employer's share must constitute 60% of the employee's covered medical expenses). If the large employer does not meet either of these minimum requirements of coverage, the employer will be liable for a penalty in the amount of $3,000 per year for each full-time employee (or $250 each month that the employer offers coverage below these levels). ACA § 1513(c)(2) provides a limitation on this penalty, which cannot exceed $2,000 per full-time employee per year (or $166.67 for each month), and the first 30 employees will not count towards the penalty.

Exempt from these penalties are large employers with seasonal workers and large employers that have over 50 full-time employees for only 120 days or less out of the calendar year, and the employees in excess of the 50 employees during that 120-day period are seasonal workers. A "seasonal worker" is defined as a "worker who performs labor or services on a seasonal basis as defined by the Secretary of Labor," and retail workers employed exclusively during holiday seasons.

Automatic Enrollment. The ACA amended the Fair Labor Standards Act (FLSA) to impose another duty on larger employers. Larger employers that have more than 200 full-time employees and offer group health plans are required to enroll automatically new full-time employees in a health benefits plan. They are also required to continue the enrollment of current employees. These employers must provide adequate notice to their employees of the automatic enrollment program, along with an opportunity for the employee to opt out of the program. Employees must affirmatively opt out of the program if they do not want coverage under their employer. The relevant provision is silent regarding the effective date of this mandate, but most experts have interpreted the provision to be effective in 2014.

Lifetime and Annual Limits. As of 2014, lifetime and annual limits are prohibited.

Rescissions. Rescissions of coverage for enrollees once they are covered are prohibited, except in cases of fraud or intentional misrepresentation of material fact (e.g., where employer has misstated its claims experience to obtain a group health policy). This provision took effect in 2010.

Coverage of Dependents. Individual and group health plans that provide coverage to dependents must continue to make coverage available to adult dependents up to age 26, regardless of marriage status (effective 2010).

Coverage of Individuals with Preexisting Conditions. Exclusions are prohibited for children up to age 18 with preexisting conditions (effective 2010). The prohibition with respect to preexisting conditions was extended to adults beginning in 2014.

Appeals Process. An internal and external appeals process must be established for appeals of coverage determinations and claims. The plan must allow an enrollee to review his or her file, present evidence and testimony, and receive continued coverage pending the outcome of the appeals process. Notice of the available internal and external processes must be given to enrollees (effective 2010). The internal process and external process both must meet requirements under certain state and/or federal law, and both processes must be updated with any new standards published by the Secretary of HHS.

Nondiscrimination. The ACA has a number of provisions designed to prohibit discrimination, shaping rules ranging from enrollment eligibility to marketing. Insurers are prohibited from having eligibility rules for enrollment based on health status, medical condition (including physical or mental illnesses) or medical history, claims experience, receipt of health care, genetic information, disability, evidence of insurability, or any factor determined appropriate by HHS (effective 2014). In addition, there is a prohibition on eligibility rules based on wages, or rules that otherwise have the effect of discriminating in favor of higher wage employees (effective six months after enactment). Insurers are also prohibited from utilizing discriminatory premium rates. Premium rates may only vary based only on the following factors: family composition, age, tobacco use, and geographic area. No rating variation is allowed based on health, race, or gender (effective 2014). Insurers may not employ marketing practices that have the effect of discouraging enrollment by individuals with significant health needs.

INDIVIDUAL RESPONSIBILITY

Concurrent with the employer's obligations under the ACA and the Reconciliation Act, supposedly beginning in 2014 (but postponed until 2015), individuals are required to maintain minimal essential health care coverage for themselves and their dependents. Individuals who fail to maintain such coverage will be subject to a penalty to be included in their tax return. The penalty will be either a percentage of the individual's household income, or a flat dollar amount for each year the individual fails to maintain coverage, whichever is greater.

The law exempts certain individuals from coverage, including individuals who object to health care coverage on religious grounds, who are not lawfully present in the United States, or who are incarcerated. The new law also provides exceptions from the penalty for certain low income individuals, including individuals who cannot afford coverage (defined as individuals whose required contribution for coverage would exceed 8% of household income for the taxable year) and individuals whose income is less than 100% of the federal poverty line, members of Indian tribes, and individuals who suffer hardship.

STATE HEALTH EXCHANGES

By January 1, 2014, states were required to establish an "American Health Benefit Exchange" or state health exchange, where individuals who do not have coverage under their employer can purchase qualified health plans. States are also required to establish a Small Business Health Options Program, or "SHOP Exchange," to assist small employers in enrolling their employees in qualified health plans. The state may establish only one exchange to serve both individuals and small employers; moreover, states may establish subsidiary exchanges for different geographical regions, and more than one state can coordinate to establish an interstate health exchange with the approval of the Secretary of HHS. The exchange will facilitate the purchase of health coverage by providing a website where individuals and small employers can compare different plans, which are assigned ratings by the exchange. The state health exchange must be a government agency or nonprofit entity established by the state. Only qualified health plans may be offered in the exchange.

As of 2015, only 16 states and the District of Columbia have chosen to have health exchanges. Individuals in other states use the federal health exchange.

NONDISCRIMINATION BASED ON GENETIC INFORMATION

The ACA contains only one provision on genetics in the entire act, but it is very important. Section 2705 of the ACA (42 U.S.C. § 300gg–4) provides: "A group health plan or health insurance issuer offering group or individual health insurance may not establish rules for new or continued eligibility based on several health status-related factors, including genetic information."

NOTES AND QUESTIONS

1. How does this provision differ from the relevant provisions under HIPAA and GINA?

2. Does the ACA strike the right balance between risk and responsibility? See Tom Baker, Health Insurance, Risk, and Responsibility after the Patient Protection and Affordable Care Act, 159 U. Pa. L. Rev. 1577 (2011).

3. If the ACA were repealed or significantly weakened, what do you think would happen to the genetic nondiscrimination provision or the protections for individuals with genetic conditions?

D. COVERAGE DECISIONS

KATSKEE v. BLUE CROSS/BLUE SHIELD
515 N.W.2d 645 (Neb. 1994).

WHITE, JUSTICE.

In January 1990, upon the recommendation of her gynecologist, Dr. Larry E. Roffman, appellant consulted with Dr. Henry T. Lynch regarding her family's history of breast and ovarian cancer, and particularly her health in relation to such a history. After examining appellant and investigating her family's medical history, Dr. Lynch diagnosed her as suffering from a genetic condition known as breast-ovarian carcinoma syndrome. Dr. Lynch then recommended that appellant have a total abdominal hysterectomy and bilateral salpingo-oophorectomy, which involves the removal of the uterus, the ovaries, and the fallopian tubes. Dr. Roffman concurred in Dr. Lynch's diagnosis and agreed that the recommended surgery was the most medically appropriate treatment available.

After considering the diagnosis and recommended treatment, appellant decided to have the surgery. In preparation for the surgery, appellant filed a claim with Blue Cross/Blue Shield. Both Drs. Lynch and Roffman wrote to Blue Cross/Blue Shield and explained the diagnosis and their basis for recommending the surgery. Initially, Blue Cross/Blue Shield sent a letter to appellant and indicated that it might pay for the surgery. Two weeks before the surgery, Dr. Roger Mason, the chief medical officer for Blue Cross/Blue Shield, wrote to appellant and stated that Blue Cross/Blue Shield would not cover the cost of the surgery. Nonetheless, appellant had the surgery in November 1990.

Appellant filed this action for breach of contract, seeking to recover $6,022.57 in costs associated with the surgery. Blue Cross/Blue Shield filed a motion for summary judgment. The district court granted the motion. It found that there was no genuine issue of material fact and that the policy did not cover appellant's surgery. Specifically, the court stated that (1) appellant did not suffer from cancer, and although her high-risk condition warranted the surgery, it was not covered by the policy; (2) appellant did not have a bodily illness or disease which was covered by the policy; and (3) under the terms of the policy, Blue Cross/Blue Shield reserved the right to determine what is medically necessary.

* * *

Blue Cross/Blue Shield contends that appellant's costs are not covered by the insurance policy. The policy provides coverage for services which are medically necessary. Blue Cross/Blue Shield denied coverage because it concluded that appellant's condition does not constitute an illness, and thus the treatment she received was not medically necessary. Blue Cross/Blue Shield has not raised any other basis for its denial, and we therefore will limit our consideration to whether appellant's condition constituted an illness within the meaning of the policy.

The policy broadly defines "illness" as a "bodily disorder or disease." The policy does not provide definitions for either bodily disorder or disease.

An insurance policy is to be construed as any other contract to give effect to the parties' intentions at the time the contract was made. When the terms of the contract are clear, a court may not resort to rules of construction, and the terms are to be accorded their plain and ordinary meaning as the ordinary or reasonable person would understand them. In such a case, a court shall seek to ascertain the intention of the parties from the plain language of the policy.

Whether a policy is ambiguous is a matter of law for the court to determine. If a court finds that the policy is ambiguous, then the court may employ rules of construction and look beyond the language of the policy to ascertain the intention of the parties. A general principle of construction, which we have applied to ambiguous insurance policies, holds that an ambiguous policy will be construed in favor of the insured. However, we will not read an ambiguity into policy language which is plain and unambiguous in order to construe it against the insurer.

* * *

We find that the language used in the policy at issue in the present case is not reasonably susceptible of differing interpretations and thus not ambiguous. The plain and ordinary meaning of the terms "bodily disorder" and "disease," as they are used in the policy to define illness, encompasses any abnormal condition of the body or its components of such a degree that in its natural progression would be expected to be problematic; a deviation from the healthy or normal state affecting the functions or tissues of the body; an inherent defect of the body; or a morbid physical or mental state which deviates from or interrupts the normal structure or function of any part, organ, or system of the body and which is manifested by a characteristic set of symptoms and signs.

The issue then becomes whether appellant's condition—breast-ovarian carcinoma syndrome—constitutes an illness.

Blue Cross/Blue Shield argues that appellant did not suffer from an illness because she did not have cancer. Blue Cross/Blue Shield characterizes appellant's condition only as a "predisposition to an illness (cancer)" and fails to address whether the condition itself constitutes an illness. This failure is traceable to Dr. Mason's denial of appellant's claim. Despite acknowledging his inexperience and lack of knowledge about this specialized area of cancer research, Dr. Mason denied appellant's claim without consulting any medical literature or research regarding breast-ovarian carcinoma syndrome. Moreover, Dr. Mason made the decision without submitting appellant's claim for consideration to a claim review committee. The only basis for the denial was the claim filed by appellant, the letters sent by Drs. Lynch and Roffman, and the insurance policy. Despite his lack of information regarding the nature and severity of appellant's condition, Dr. Mason felt qualified to decide that appellant did not suffer from an illness.

Appellant's condition was diagnosed as breast-ovarian carcinoma syndrome. To adequately determine whether the syndrome constitutes an illness, we must first understand the nature of the syndrome.

The record on summary judgment includes the depositions of Drs. Lynch, Roffman, and Mason. In his deposition, Dr. Lynch provided a thorough discussion of this syndrome. In light of Dr. Lynch's extensive research and clinical experience in this particular area of medicine, we consider his discussion extremely helpful in our understanding of the syndrome.

According to Dr. Lynch, some forms of cancer occur on a hereditary basis. Breast and ovarian cancer are such forms of cancer which may occur on a hereditary basis. It is our understanding that the hereditary occurrence of this form of cancer is related to the genetic makeup of the woman. In this regard, the genetic deviation has conferred changes which are manifest in the individual's body and at some time become capable of being diagnosed.

At the time that he gave his deposition, Dr. Lynch explained that the state of medical research was such that detecting and diagnosing the syndrome was achieved by tracing the occurrences of hereditary cancer throughout the patient's family. Dr. Lynch stated that at the time of appellant's diagnosis, no conclusive physical test existed which would demonstrate the presence of the condition. However, Dr. Lynch stated that this area of research is progressing toward the development of a more determinative method of identifying and tracing a particular gene throughout a particular family, thus providing a physical method of diagnosing the condition.

Women diagnosed with the syndrome have at least a 50-percent chance of developing breast and/or ovarian cancer, whereas unaffected women have only a 1.4-percent risk of developing breast or ovarian cancer. [sic] In addition to the genetic deviation, the family history, and the significant risks associated with this condition, the diagnosis also may encompass symptoms of anxiety and stress, which some women experience because of their knowledge of the substantial likelihood of developing cancer.

The procedures for detecting the onset of ovarian cancer are ineffective. Generally, by the time ovarian cancer is capable of being detected, it has already developed to a very advanced stage, making treatment relatively unsuccessful. Drs. Lynch and Roffman agreed that the standard of care for treating women with breast carcinoma syndrome ordinarily involves surveillance methods. However, for women at an inordinately high risk for ovarian cancer, such as appellant, the standard of care may require radical surgery which involves the removal of the uterus, ovaries, and fallopian tubes.

Dr. Lynch explained that the surgery is labeled "prophylactic" and that the surgery is prophylactic as to the prevention of the onset of cancer. Dr. Lynch also stated that appellant's condition itself is the result of a genetic deviation from the normal, healthy state and that the recommended surgery treats that condition by eliminating or significantly reducing the presence of the condition and its likely development.

Blue Cross/Blue Shield has not proffered any evidence disputing the premise that the origin of this condition is in the genetic makeup of the individual and that in its natural development it is likely to produce devastating results. Although handicapped by his limited knowledge of the syndrome, Dr. Mason did not dispute the nature of the syndrome as explained by Dr. Lynch and supported by Dr. Roffman, nor did Dr. Mason dispute the fact that the surgery falls within the standard of care for many women afflicted with this syndrome.

In light of the plain and ordinary meaning of the terms "illness," "bodily disorder," and "disease," we find that appellant's condition constitutes an illness within the meaning of the policy. Appellant's condition is a deviation from what is considered a normal, healthy physical state or structure. The abnormality or deviation from a normal state arises, in part, from the genetic makeup of the woman. The existence of this unhealthy state results in the woman's being at substantial risk of developing cancer. The recommended surgery is intended to correct that morbid state by reducing or eliminating that risk.

Although appellant's condition was not detectable by physical evidence or a physical examination, it does not necessarily follow that appellant does not suffer from an illness. The record establishes that a woman who suffers from breast-ovarian carcinoma syndrome does have a physical state which significantly deviates from the physical state of a normal, healthy woman. Specifically, appellant suffered from a different or abnormal genetic constitution which, when combined with a particular family history of hereditary cancer, significantly increases the risk of a devastating outcome.

* * *

In the present case, the medical evidence regarding the nature of breast-ovarian carcinoma syndrome persuades us that appellant suffered from a bodily disorder or disease and, thus, suffered from an illness as defined by the insurance policy. Blue Cross/Blue Shield, therefore, is not entitled to judgment as a matter of law. Moreover, we find that appellant's condition did constitute an illness within the meaning of the policy. We reverse the decision of the district court and remand the cause for further proceedings.

NOTES AND QUESTIONS

1.　A study published in 2001 demonstrates that prophylactic bilateral total mastectomy for women who have a BRCA1 or BRCA2 mutation substantially reduces the risk of breast cancer. Hanne Meijers-Heijboer et al.,

Breast Cancer After Prophylactic Bilateral Mastectomy in Women with a BRCA1 or BRCA2 Mutation, 345 New Eng. J. Med. 159 (2001). The decision whether to undergo such radical surgery is a difficult one, and it is not clear how many women will want to do so. It is virtually certain, however, that this study will increase the demand for prophylactic surgery. Will health insurers and health care plans have to pay for it? See generally Alexandra K. Glasier, Genetic Predispositions, Prophylactic Treatments and Private Health Insurance: Nothing Is Better Than a Good Pair of Genes, 23 Am. J.L. & Med. 45 (1997); Mark A. Rothstein & Sharona Hoffman, Genetic Testing, Genetic Medicine, and Managed Care, 34 Wake Forest L. Rev. 849 (1999).

2.   A woman discovered a lump in her breast, and a biopsy indicated stromal fibrosis and confirmed that the lump was noncancerous. After her consulting specialist included in her treatment options a prophylactic mastectomy, the woman elected the surgery. Her insurer's medical director denied coverage, stating that "breast removal is not an appropriate or recommended treatment for fibrocystic disease, for 'cancer phobia,' or for a patient with a family history which is positive for hereditary breast cancer." The woman sued to compel the health plan to pay. What result? See Anderson v. HMO Nebraska, Inc., 1993 WL 61839 (Neb. Ct. App. 1993)(health plan abused its discretion in refusing the surgery), rev'd on other grounds, 505 N.W.2d 700 (Neb. 1993).

3.   Physicians also need to be careful to provide patients with informed consent and a range of treatment options. In Brown v. Dibbell, 595 N.W.2d 358 (Wis. 1999), a malpractice action was brought against a physician in which the plaintiff successfully argued that her physician failed to provide her with treatment options or adequately discuss the risks and benefits prior to her electing to undergo a prophylactic mastectomy. See Mary R. Anderlik & Elaine A. Lisko, Medicolegal and Ethical Issues in Genetic Cancer Syndromes, 18 Seminars in Surgical Oncology 339 (2000).

4.   During the early 1990s a series of cases were brought challenging the denial of medical benefits under ERISA-qualified health plans for high-dose chemotherapy with autologous bone marrow transplants to treat advanced cases of breast cancer. The procedure costs in excess of $150,000, and most plans denied coverage on the ground that it was "experimental." Most of the cases upheld the denial of benefits. See, e.g., Harris v. Mutual of Omaha Companies, 992 F.2d 706 (7th Cir. 1993); Holder v. Prudential Insurance Co. of Am., 951 F.2d 89 (5th Cir. 1992). Some courts, however, held that the procedure was not experimental and ordered the plans to pay for the procedure. See, e.g., Kekis v. Blue Cross and Blue Shield of Utica-Watertown, Inc., 815 F.Supp. 571 (N.D.N.Y. 1993); Wilson v. Group Hospitalization & Medical Services, Inc., 791 F.Supp. 309 (D.D.C. 1992). Subsequently, scientific studies have shown that the procedure does not improve the survival of women with metastatic breast cancer. See Edward A. Stadtmauer et al., Conventional-Dose Chemotherapy Compared with High-Dose Chemotherapy Plus Autologous Hematopoietic Stem-Cell Transplantation for Metastatic Breast Cancer, 342 New Eng. J. Med. 1069 (2000). Do courts have

the expertise to decide cases involving the coverage of various medical procedures?

III.   LIFE INSURANCE

MARK A. ROTHSTEIN & YANN JOLY, GENETIC INFORMATION AND INSURANCE UNDERWRITING: CONTEMPORARY ISSUES AND APPROACHES IN THE GLOBAL ECONOMY IN HANDBOOK OF GENETICS AND SOCIETY: MAPPING THE NEW GENOMIC ERA
130–132 (Paul Atkinson, Peter Glasner & Margaret Lock eds. 2009).

LIFE INSURANCE

Unlike health insurance, which varies based on the health care finance system of each country, life insurance is more uniform internationally in its product line and social function. Also, unlike health insurance, most life insurance is individually underwritten, thereby increasing the concern that genetic predictions of mortality risk could be used in deciding an individual's insurability. In the United States, as evidenced by public opinion surveys and the degree of legislative attention, the use of genetic information in life insurance is of less concern than its use in health insurance. Nevertheless, the possible effect of genetics on life insurance is of substantial concern in the United States, Canada, Western Europe, and throughout the developed world. For example, according to one survey, all of the UK genetic centers reported that they had patients who refused to be tested for genetic susceptibility to breast cancer because of a fear of being unable to obtain insurance.

At the present time, genetic information is not widely used by life insurers. Also, the advent of more widespread genetic testing has not changed the percentage of policy applicants offered coverage. In the United States, 88% of applicants are offered coverage at preferred or standard rates, 6% are offered coverage at higher rates, and 6% are declined. Notwithstanding the current lack of use of genetic information, the situation could change. As the focus of genetic testing shifts from rare, monogenic disorders to more common, chronic, complex disorders (e.g., asthma, diabetes, epilepsy, hypertension), the amount of genetic information in the health records of individuals will expand. This information will be disclosed to insurers via individual authorizations in the process of medical underwriting. Furthermore, individual concerns about possible genetic discrimination already operate to discourage some at-risk individuals from undergoing genetic testing.

* * *

It is too soon to tell the effects of genetic information on consumer behavior. A source of great frustration for policy analysts and policy makers is the virtual absence of peer-reviewed research. One of the only empirical studies in the United States suggests that women who learn of their increased risk of breast cancer do not attempt to purchase additional life insurance. It is also too soon to tell the effect of legislative or voluntary industry practices on commercial activity. For example, it has been asserted that no British insurers "have endured financial hardship in the 3–5 years of the moratorium [on using genetic tests for life insurance for mortgage cover below £500,000]". It is often noted that life insurance in the United Kingdom is necessary to obtain a residential mortgage; therefore it is asserted to be a different product, presumably more immune from pressures of adverse selection. Nevertheless, it is the effect on insurers, not the reason for seeking coverage, that determines whether underwriting practices are undermined by individuals' knowledge of their mortality risks.

The ethical and policy issues depend on the social function or "moral mission" of life insurance. If life insurance is considered a purely commercial transaction or a type of investment for estate building purposes, then a strong case can be made that limitations should not be placed on any type of medical underwriting so long as it is actuarially sound and the confidentiality of personal health information is scrupulously maintained. On the other hand, if providing a death benefit to survivors or ensuring the availability of a residential mortgage is deemed an essential public policy, then the government would be justified in regulating the process and criteria for obtaining life insurance coverage.

J. ALEXANDER LOWDEN, GENETIC RISKS AND MORTALITY RATES, IN GENETICS AND LIFE INSURANCE: MEDICAL UNDERWRITING AND SOCIAL POLICY
95–98 (Mark A. Rothstein ed. 2004).

WHY WOULD LIFE INSURERS CONSIDER GENETIC TESTING?

Before offering coverage to an applicant, life insurers attempt to identify factors that may shorten the person's usual life expectancy at a given age. If identifiable risks exist, the underwriter uses actuarial and medical information to calculate life expectancy and determine an appropriate premium. Genetic tests may offer a means to identify future health risks and potentially could improve those calculations. At the present time most genetic tests for predisposition to disease lack valid actuarial information. The likelihood of developing a disease when a mutation in a particular gene is identified is often uncertain. More important, the risk may be greatly altered in the future as we learn how to use genetic knowledge to lower it.

There are many different types of life insurance products and their particular features play different roles in determining the price of each one. Whereas most of the cost of insurance can be determined from experience, actuarial tables, and corporate business practices, expected survival varies with the state of health of the applicant and consideration of future health risks. Because life expectancy is defined as the age at which half the insureds will have died, it is a moving target that increases with the age of the individual at the time of application. To estimate an individual's life expectancy, underwriters consider medical history, current health status, laboratory test results, family history, and lifestyle.

Risk is increased in applicants who have not experienced a clinical event, such as myocardial infarction, but who have evidence of risk in their medical status. Obesity and untreated hypertension trigger an added premium because they are associated with early mortality. Some laboratory tests may also indicate increased risk. Elevated cholesterol, indication of hepatitis C infection, or early evidence of diabetes can be uncovered in people who are otherwise in apparent good health but who, on the basis of a laboratory test showing such a disorder, can be expected to have a shortened life expectancy. Their insurance premiums must reflect the added risk.

The primary goal of medical underwriting is therefore to anticipate the impact of health history and current health status, including laboratory tests, on survival. Unanticipated events do occur. That is one of the reasons for purchasing insurance, but underwriters try to determine what is likely to happen to an applicant and price a policy accordingly. Genetic testing brings a somewhat different aspect to this picture. It potentially provides information about risks that are not anticipated and that may be unrelated to medical or family history.

Causes of death vary with age. Accidental death or trauma is a major factor in younger people, heart disease in middle and later life, and cancer in older people. Almost all mortality, however, has a genetic basis (table 5.1). Our knowledge about how mutations are linked to disease has escalated in a logarithmic fashion in the past few years. The HGP will provide many new insights into mechanisms of disease and will continue to identify genes associated with early mortality.

TABLE 5.1

Genetic basis	Number of deaths/100,000 lives
Chromosomal	380
Single gene defects	2,000
Somatic mutations	24,000
Multifactorial disease	64,600

Some genetic tests could possibly bring changes to underwriting decisions. In a person with no family history and no medical history, a series of tests might be able to predict an increased risk of unanticipated disease. Will, or should, insurers have the right to this information? How will they use it if they do acquire it? To approach the answers to these questions, let us consider knowledge of some common genetic diseases that may lead to early mortality in adults. People with many of these disorders can be underwritten and, for the most part, offered insurance at affordable rates. The secret to what might appear speculative underwriting practice is in knowing the risk and doing something to mitigate possible loss.

Making lifestyle changes or therapeutic decisions may not alter one's genetic risk today, but we live in a world in which scientific discoveries occur at an ever-increasing rate. If an individual has a fatal genetic mutation today, will developments lead to new methods of management or treatment in the next ten years? Will the mutation have been expressed before new therapy is available? The HGP was not devised to bring new genetic tests to market, but to use genetic information to improve health. In time, people who have genetic tests and know they have certain health risks will be better off than their untested peers for, with knowledge, will come the ability to prevent mutant gene expression. Thus, predicting future scientific developments as well as health risks based on new information makes medical underwriting extremely difficult.

NOTES AND QUESTIONS

1.   A leading study on the effect of BRCA mutations on life insurance purchasing behavior concluded that "if insurers continue to use family cancer history in their underwriting process, they have little need to worry about the impact that genetic tests for cancer-related gene mutations will have on consumer demand for life insurance." Cathleen D. Zick et al., Genetic Testing, Adverse Selection, and the Demand for Life Insurance, 93 Am. J. Med. Genetics 29, 38 (2000).

2.   Is there a difference between requiring that insurance companies have access to the results of genetic tests already performed and allowing insurers to require genetic testing as a condition of coverage? Should different rules apply for different coverage amounts? Should individuals be allowed to use their "good results" on genetic tests to obtain life insurance at lower rates?

3.   Would it be lawful for a life insurance company to tell an applicant that because she has tested positive for a BRCA1 mutation that she is not eligible for life insurance unless she has a prophylactic mastectomy?

4.   Lowden suggests that genetic tests are no different from other medical tests for underwriting purposes. Should the insurance company have to demonstrate the actuarial significance of any medical criteria used? In theory, state unfair trade practices laws already have such a requirement, but, in practice, insurers are given great deference by state insurance

commissioners and the courts. Should insurers be required to prove that adverse selection will occur if they are denied access to predictive health information or predictive genetic test results?

Vermont. Stat. Ann. Tit. 18, Ch. 217
(ENACTED 1997).

§ 9331. Definitions

For purposes of this chapter:

* * *

(2) "DNA" means deoxyribonucleic acid and "RNA" means ribonucleic acid.

* * *

(6) "Genetic information" means the results of "genetic testing" contained in any report, interpretation, evaluation, or other record thereof.

(7)(A)   "Genetic testing" means a test, examination or analysis that is diagnostic or predictive of a particular heritable disease or disorder and is of:

(i)   a human chromosome or gene;

(ii)   human DNA or RNA; or

(iii) a human genetically encoded protein.

(B) The test for human genetically encoded protein referred to in subdivision (A)(iii) of this subdivision shall be generally accepted in the scientific and medical communities as being specifically determinative for the presence or absence of a mutation, alteration, or deletion of a gene or chromosome.

(C) For the purposes of sections 9332 and 9333 of this title, as they apply to insurers, section 9334 of this title, and section 4727 of Title 8, and notwithstanding any language in this section to the contrary, "genetic testing" does not include:

(i)   a test, examination or analysis which reports on an individual's current condition unless such a test, examination or analysis is designed or intended to be specifically determinative for the presence or absence of a mutation, alteration, or deletion of a gene or chromosome; or

(ii) a test, examination or analysis of a human chromosome or gene, of human DNA or RNA, or of a human genetically encoded protein that is diagnostic or predictive of a particular heritable disease or disorder, if, in accordance with generally accepted standards in the medical community, the potential presence or absence of a mutation, alteration or deletion of a gene or chromosome has already manifested itself by causing a disease, disorder or medical condition or by symptoms highly predictive of the disease, disorder or medical condition.

(8) "Insurance" means a policy of insurance regulated under Title 8, offered or issued in this state, including health, life, disability and long-term care insurance policies, hospital and medical service corporation service contracts, and health maintenance organization benefit plans.

* * *

§ 9334. Genetic testing as a condition of insurance coverage

(a) No policy of insurance offered for delivery or issued in this state shall be underwritten or conditioned on the basis of:

(1) any requirement or agreement of the individual to undergo genetic testing; or

(2) the results of genetic testing of a member of the individual's family.

(b) A violation of this section shall be considered an unfair method of competition or unfair or deceptive act or practice in the business of insurance in violation of section 4724 of Title 8.

(c) In addition to other remedies available under the law, a person who violates this section shall be subject to the enforcement provisions available under Title 8.

§ 9335. Remedies

(a) Any person who intentionally violates section 9333 or subsection 9334(a) of this chapter shall be imprisoned not more than one year or fined not more than $10,000.00, or both.

(b) Any person aggrieved by a violation of this chapter may bring an action for civil damages, including punitive damages, equitable relief, including restraint of prohibited acts, restitution of wages or other benefits and reinstatement, costs, and reasonable attorney's fees and other appropriate relief.

NOTES AND QUESTIONS

1. Although most states have enacted legislation addressing genetic discrimination in health insurance, only a handful of states have enacted legislation dealing with other forms of insurance. In California, a life or disability insurance carrier may not refuse to sell or renew a policy "solely by reason of the fact that the person to be insured carries a gene which may, under some circumstances, be associated with disability in that person's

offspring, but which causes no adverse effects on the carrier." Cal. Ins. Code § 10143(a). Is this provision helpful? Note that another provision prohibits differentiation "because of a physical or mental impairment, except where the refusal, limitation or rate differential is based on sound actuarial principles or is related to actual and reasonably anticipated experience." Cal. Ins. Code § 10144.

2. What effects, if any, do you think the Vermont law will have on the availability of insurance in the state, the willingness of individuals to undergo genetic testing in the state, or the price structure of insurance in the state?

3. Do you think that criminal sanctions are appropriate for violations?

CHABNER V. UNITED OF OMAHA LIFE INSURANCE CO.
225 F.3d 1042 (9th Cir. 2000).

HUG, J.

* * *

Howard Chabner suffers from a progressive condition called facioscapulohumeral muscular dystrophy (FSH MD), a rare form of muscular dystrophy. The condition has confined Chabner to a wheelchair since 1991 and has caused "marked wasting" of his extremities. Chabner takes medication to help control the condition, and his doctor administers annual electrocardiograms to detect any cardiomyopathy that may arise.

On May 3, 1993, Chabner, who was 35 years old at the time, applied to United for whole life insurance. United forwarded Chabner's application to an underwriter who had experience in underwriting insurance policies for applicants with muscular dystrophy, but not with FSH MD. United possessed no internally developed actuarial data for people with FSH MD, and so its underwriter turned to external sources to estimate Chabner's mortality risk. The underwriter, who was not a doctor, arranged to have Chabner examined by a paramedic, reviewed Chabner's medical records, and consulted two underwriting source materials: the Cologne Life Reinsurance Company's "Life Underwriting Manual" ("Cologne manual"); and "Medical Selection of Life Risks" by R.D.C. Brackenridge and W. John Elder ("Brackenridge manual"). After reviewing these materials, the underwriter authorized a policy with a "Table 6" rating, which corresponded to a mortality rate of 150 percent above standard.

United offered Chabner a $100,000 whole life policy at a cost of $1,076 per year. Of the $1,076 annual premium, $305.44 was applied to the cost of insurance, and the remainder was invested in the policy's cash accumulation and surrender values. By contrast, even though the annual premium for a standard whole life policy (without an increased mortality rating) would have been the same $1,076, only $155.44 of that annual premium would have been applied to the cost of insurance, which would result in an additional $150 being invested in the policy's cash accumulation and surrender values each year.

Chabner accepted the policy, but inquired about the reason for his nonstandard premium. United's Vice President and Senior Medical Director of Underwriting sent Chabner a letter attempting to explain the nonstandard rating. In the letter, United acknowledged that FSH MD "has only a small effect on mortality" and stated that it reduced life expectancy by four years for a non-smoking man of his age. Unsatisfied, Chabner wrote United on two more occasions to inquire why his premium was 96.5% greater than standard if his condition had only a small effect on mortality. United did not respond, and Chabner filed this action.

Chabner filed his original complaint in California Superior Court on January 3, 1995, alleging violations of California's Insurance Code, its Business and Professions Code, its Unruh Civil Rights Act, and common law fraud. After United removed the case to federal court based on diversity jurisdiction, Chabner amended his complaint to add a claim under the ADA. Chabner sought class certification and moved for summary judgment on all but his fraud claim. The district court denied class certification, but granted Chabner's motion for summary judgment. The district court held that the ADA applies to insurance underwriting, that California law provides Chabner with a private cause of action for the alleged violation of the state insurance code, and that United's actions in this case violated the ADA, the California Insurance Code and the Business and Professions Code, and the Unruh Civil Rights Act.

* * *

I.   THE ADA

Chabner alleges that the nonstandard premium that United charged him for his insurance policy violated the ADA. Recently, however, we held that although Title III of the ADA requires an insurance office to be physically accessible to the disabled, it does not address the terms of the policies the insurance companies sell. See Weyer v. Twentieth Century Fox Film Corp., 198 F.3d 1104, 1115 (9th Cir.2000). We therefore hold that United did not violate the ADA by offering Chabner a nonstandard policy.

Title III of the ADA provides: "No individual shall be discriminated against on the basis of disability in the full and equal enjoyment of the goods, services, facilities, privileges, advantages, or accommodations of any place of public accommodation by any person who owns, leases (or leases to), or operates a place of public accommodation." 42 U.S.C. § 12181(a). The ADA also includes a "safe harbor" provision, which says that "[the ADA] shall not be construed to prohibit or restrict . . . an insurer . . . from underwriting risks, classifying risks, or administering such risks that are based on or not inconsistent with State law. . . ." 42 U.S.C. § 12201(c).

Weyer, which was handed down after the district court's order was issued, concerned the question of whether an insurance company that administers an employer-provided disability plan was a "place of public accommodation" under Title III of the Americans with Disabilities Act. We found that the term "place of public accommodation" required a connection between the good or service complained of and an actual physical place. As we explained: "[c]ertainly, an insurance office is a place where the public generally has access. But this case is not about such matters as ramps and elevators so that disabled people can get to the office. The dispute in this case, over terms of a contract that the insurer markets through an employer, is not what Congress addressed in the public accommodations provisions." In adopting this approach, we followed the Third and Sixth Circuits, each of which agreed that an insurance company that administered an employer-provided disability plan was not a "place of public accommodation" under the ADA because the employees received their benefits through employment, and not through a public accommodation. See Parker v. Metropolitan Life Ins. Co., 121 F.3d 1006, 1010–12 (6th Cir.1997) (en banc); Ford v. Schering-Plough Corp., 145 F.3d 601, 612–13 (3d Cir.1998). Taking these cases at face value, we are led to conclude that a similar distinction between "access" and "content" applies to this case. Here, we reiterate our observation, set forth in *Weyer*, that "an insurance office must be physically accessible to the disabled but need not provide insurance that treats the disabled equally with the non-disabled." Therefore, we do not uphold the district court's decision based upon the ADA.

II. CALIFORNIA LAW

A. Business and Professions Code section 17200 and Insurance Code section 10144

In his complaint Chabner alleged violations of California Insurance Code section 10144, and California Business and Professions Code section 17200. Insurance Code Section 10144 provides, in relevant part: "No insurer issuing [life insurance] shall refuse to insure, or refuse to continue to insure . . . or charge a different rate for the same coverage solely because of a physical or mental impairment, except where the refusal . . . or rate differential is based on sound actuarial principles or is related to actual and reasonably anticipated experience. . . ." Cal. Ins. Code § 10144. This statutory provision would have prohibited United from charging Chabner a nonstandard premium due to his FSH MD, unless the premium was based on sound actuarial principles or was related to actual and reasonably anticipated experience. However, it is unclear whether this insurance code section provides Chabner with a private cause of action. The parties did not address this issue in their briefs, and therefore we do not address it.

Chabner, however, also claimed violations of California Business and Professions Code section 17200. Section 17200 is part of the Unfair Competition Law, Cal. Bus. & Prof. Code §§ 17200–18209, and provides, in relevant part, that "unfair competition shall mean and include any unlawful, unfair or fraudulent business act or practice." Cal. Bus. & Prof. Code § 17200. Private causes of action for violations of Business and Professions Code section 17200 are authorized by Business and Professions Code section 17204. The district court held that Insurance Code section 10144 may be used to define the contours of a private cause of action under Business and Professions Code section 17200. We agree.

* * *

As applied to this case, the district court was correct in holding that Chabner could maintain a cause of action under section 17200 for United's alleged violation of section 10144. Setting the premium for a life insurance policy can quite "properly be called a business practice." Also, United's alleged misconduct (charging Chabner a discriminatory premium that is neither actuarially sound nor based on reasonably anticipated experience) would run afoul of section 10144, if proven. Accordingly, the prerequisites for "borrowing" a violation of section 10144 and treating it as a violation of section 17200 exist in this case.

* * *

B. The Unruh Civil Rights Act

Chabner also claims that United's actions violated California's Unruh Civil Rights Act. The Unruh Civil Rights Act provides, in relevant part, that "[a]ll persons within the jurisdiction of this state are free and equal, and no matter what their . . . disability are entitled to the full and equal accommodations, advantages, facilities, privileges, or services in all business establishments of every kind whatsoever." Cal. Civ. Code § 51. The Act also provides that a violation of the ADA is also a violation of the Unruh Act. Cal. Civ. Code § 51. The district court held that because United had violated the ADA, it also violated the Unruh Act. In light of our decision in Weyer v. Twentieth Century Fox Film Corp., 198 F.3d 1104 (9th Cir.2000), as discussed above, the district court's decision cannot be upheld on this basis.

We may, however, "affirm the district court on a ground not selected by the district judge so long as the record fairly supports such an alternative disposition." Chabner, and the State of California as amicus curiae, argue that United's actions violated the Unruh Act, regardless of whether they also violated the ADA. We agree that Chabner's allegations support an Unruh Civil Rights Act claim independently of the alleged ADA violation.

The Unruh Civil Rights Act works to ensure that all persons receive the full accommodations of any business within California, regardless of the person's disabilities. Cal. Civ. Code § 51. The insurance business is subject to the Unruh Civil Rights Act. Cal. Ins. Code § 1861.03 (a). Unruh prevents more than discrimination in access to a business or its services; it also prevents discrimination in the form of pricing differentials. However, disparities in treatment and pricing that are reasonable do not violate the Unruh Act. The critical question, therefore, is whether the nonstandard premium United charged Chabner was "reasonable."

To determine whether the nonstandard premium was reasonable, we are again informed by Insurance Code section 10144. Section 10144 prevents an insurer from charging "a different rate for the same coverage solely because of a physical or mental impairment," unless the "rate differential is based on sound actuarial principles or is related to actual and reasonably anticipated experience." Cal. Ins. Code § 10144. If Chabner's nonstandard premium was based on "sound actuarial principles" or "actual and reasonably anticipated experience," then it would certainly be reasonable for purposes of the Unruh Act because it would have been specifically allowed by statute. By contrast, if the premium was not based on one of the section 10144 prongs, then there would be no reasonable justification for it, and in that case we may consider the nonstandard premium to be arbitrary and a violation of the Unruh Act. Therefore, we hold that if United violated Insurance Code section 10144, it also violated the Unruh Act, but if section 10144 authorized United's actions, then Chabner's Unruh Act claim necessarily fails as well.

* * *

D.   *Summary Judgment*

* * *

The parties argue at length about the proper definitions of "sound actuarial principles" or "actual and reasonably anticipated experience." For example, they dispute whether an insurance company must base its rating decisions on "hard data" that is specific to each person, or whether it may take into account more generalized estimates of mortality when it lacks specific data. We need not resolve the debate about exactly what can justify a mortality decision as actuarially sound or related to actual and reasonably anticipated experience, for in this case there is no question that United's mortality rating was arbitrarily high.

The mortality rating United assigned to Chabner was not actuarially sound. United assigned Chabner a "Table 6" rating, which corresponds with a 150% mortality rating. The 150% mortality rating, in turn, reflects an estimate that Chabner's life expectancy is nine to eleven years less than that of a standard male non-smoker. United points to the Brackenridge manual, which recommended a mortality rating of 75%—150%, and the Cologne manual, which recommended a mortality rating of 300%, to argue that the 150% mortality rating was justified. However, United's own admissions subvert its reliance on these manuals. In his letter to Chabner, Dr. Robert Quinn, the Vice President and Senior Medical Director of Underwriting at United, admitted that FSH MD "has only a small effect on mortality." Moreover, Dr. Quinn estimated Chabner's life expectancy to be only four years less than standard. Even assuming that the estimate of a four year decrease in life expectancy is correct, it does not justify a rating that estimates a nine to eleven year decrease. Accordingly, by United's own admission, the 150% mortality rating (i.e., the estimate of a nine to eleven year decrease in life expectancy) was not actuarially sound.

Nor does the second prong of section 10144, which allows rate differentials if they are based on actual and reasonably anticipated experience, provide refuge for the 150% mortality rating. United's underwriter handling Chabner's application had experience with muscular dystrophy, but not with Chabner's rare fascioscapulohumeral muscular dystrophy. She thus had no "actual experience" with underwriting applicants with FSH MD. Moreover, she was not a doctor, she did not have a doctor examine Chabner, and she did not have a doctor review Chabner's medical records. Thus, the underwriter's basis for "reasonably anticipated experience" in evaluating an applicant with FSH MD was virtually nonexistent, especially considering that Dr. Quinn, who was a medical doctor and who was familiar with FSH MD, subsequently admitted that FSH MD has little effect on mortality. Therefore, viewing the evidence in the light most favorable to United, we hold that no reasonable jury could find that the 150% mortality rating was either based on sound actuarial principles or related to actual and reasonably anticipated experience. Section 10144 did not justify the discriminatory premium, and summary judgment on Chabner's Business and Professions Code section 17200 claim, and on his Unruh Civil Rights Act claim, was therefore proper.

* * *

CONCLUSION

For the foregoing reasons, the district court's grant of summary judgment for Appellee Chabner, and its judgment ordering Appellant United to modify the insurance policy, are AFFIRMED.

NOTES AND QUESTIONS

1.   The Ninth Circuit's holding that Title III of the ADA does not permit individuals to challenge the substantive provisions of insurance contracts is in accord with the weight of authority. See, e.g., Pallozzi v. Allstate Life Insurance Co., 198 F.3d 28 (2d Cir.1999). See generally Maxwell J. Mehlman et al., When Do Health Care Decisions Discriminate Against Persons with Disabilities?, 22 J. Health Pol., Pol'y & L. 1385 (1997).

2.   State unfair trade practice laws or other regulation of insurance practices exist in every state, although the remedies and the interpretation of the statutory provisions differ widely. Who should have the burden of proof with regard to underwriting decision making? What degree of deference, if any, should be given to the insurance company?

3.   The most commonly raised issue regarding genetics and life insurance is that actuarial fairness does not necessarily equate with moral fairness when allocating essential goods. *Chabner* raises a second concern, that the medical underwriting will not be based on sound actuarial principles. Which of the two issues is the more vexing problem? Why?

MARK A. ROTHSTEIN, POLICY RECOMMENDATIONS, GENETICS AND LIFE INSURANCE: MEDICAL UNDERWRITING AND SOCIAL POLICY

252–261 (Mark A. Rothstein ed. 2004).

1.   Establish a moratorium on requiring genetic testing and use of genetic information.

A moratorium could be imposed legislatively or voluntarily by individual insurers. There is no agreement on the length of time for the moratorium, although five years is frequently mentioned. Moratoria already have been adopted in some countries, including France, Germany, and the United Kingdom.

The theory behind a moratorium is that scientific and policy issues will be clarified in the next few years and appropriate policies can then be determined. From a scientific standpoint, this is wishful thinking. Although the relationship between some genotypes and mortality risks may be better established, the basic scientific issue—use of genetic information when its actuarial significance is not definitely established—will remain. As scientists accumulate better data on some associations, other associations will be suspected and investigated. Thus, the uncertainty simply will be shifted to a different group of genetic variations. With regard to policy, the question of the degree to which life insurance underwriting and pricing should be regulated to promote social considerations will remain the same.

* * *

2.   Prohibit genetic testing and using genetic information.

At first glance, prohibiting insurers from requiring genetic testing and using genetic information would appear to be the most effective way to "avoid the creation of an uninsurable underclass of individuals." By prohibiting use of genetic information, however, family health histories and other traditional measures of risk assessment also would be prohibited. As a result, major changes would be required in the way life insurance is underwritten and priced.

3.   Prohibit insurers from requiring genetic testing, but permit use of genetic information.

Under this option individuals would not be compelled to undergo insurer-ordered genetic testing as a condition of applying for life insurance. Insurers, however, could use the results of genetic tests already performed and in a person's medical record. This compromise option raises problems for both insurance companies and consumers. For insurers, individuals who were tested in research studies, anonymously, or off the record would be able to apply for life insurance without any way for underwriters to know of the results of the test. This is a recipe for adverse selection. Individuals, however, would not do well under this approach either. They would be deterred from having genetic testing in the health care setting, where it would be most beneficial, because the results would be placed in their medical record. Moreover, even without such test results, persons at increased risk because of family health history would still be subject to higher rates or denial of coverage.

Advocates of prohibiting life insurers from requiring genetic testing also must deal with another fundamental issue. If companies are permitted to require some medical tests (e.g., cholesterol, HIV, hepatitis B and C), on what basis should genetic tests be treated differently? Assuming the tests are predictive, is there something inherent in the fact that they are genetic suggest they should not be used?

* * *

4.   Establish a maximum amount of coverage that can be obtained without genetic testing or genetic information.

Establishment of maximum levels of coverage without genetic test results of other genetic information (sometimes referred to as a "safe harbor" or a "monetary threshold" approach) is popular in Western Europe, and some attempts have been made to introduce similar legislation in the United States. In Europe, however, life insurance has a different social role, because it is essential to have life insurance to obtain a mortgage. It is a different product with a different public interest at stake.

In European countries that adopted this approach, about $100,000 is the lowest level of life insurance coverage available without genetic testing or consideration of genetic information. With the average policy in the United States in 2000 of $134,800, a substantial percentage of the market would be included under a comparable proviso. In practice, establishing maximum levels of coverage without genetic information would be difficult. First, it would be necessary to define "genetic." Does the prohibition apply only to genetic testing or does it also apply to genetic information? As discussed previously, either definition raises serious problems. Second, it would be necessary to have some way of determining whether people had policies from more than one insurance company so that those at risk could not obtain a series of policies below the maximum. Third, some market adjustments in pricing would be necessary. For example, if companies could not consider information in underwriting policies of $100,000 or less, the rates for a $110,000 policy for a low-risk person (using genetic information) would likely be lower than for a $100,000 policy in the all-applicant (not using genetic information) pool. This would encourage individuals to undergo genetic testing and then apply for the higher amount if they tested negative and the lower amount if they tested positive. This would increase the price disparity between the genetically underwritten and nonunderwritten pools in a spiraling fashion. Thus, additional regulation or subsidies would be necessary to adjust the pricing structure.

5.   Prohibit insurance companies from offering preferred rates based on the results of genetic tests or genetic information.

One scenario in which life insurance companies may be compelled by market forces to require genetic testing or use of genetic information is the following. Company A begins to offer a "good gene" discount of 25% on its life insurance to individuals who voluntarily take ten selected genetic tests and are found not to have any deleterious mutations. Low-risk individuals will flock to company A for the discount. Company B, having lost some of its low-risk insureds, will then be forced either to raise rates for remaining policy holders and new applicants or also use genetic tests. This could quickly put pressure on other companies to do the same and, eventually, the rest of the industry would become segmented by whether genetic information was used.

Although it is not clear that the science would currently justify such an adjustment in the pricing structure merely based on the absence of ten deleterious mutations, the possibility of at least some companies attempting this approach cannot be dismissed. To prevent this from occurring, legislation could be enacted to prohibit life insurance companies from using the results of genetic tests or genetic information to sell policies at preferred rates (below standard). This is now expressly permitted under Indiana law, whereas Oregon prohibits the use of favorable genetic information to induce the sale of insurance.

* * *

6.   Permit individuals to use results of genetic tests to obtain coverage at regular rates.

An insurance company that is not permitted to use results of genetic tests would be forced to charge higher premiums to an individual who had a familial risk of a serious illness, but who had undergone genetic testing and learned that he or she did not inherit the lethal mutation. To prevent this from occurring, it has been suggested (and actually enacted in some states) that people should be allowed to use the results of genetic tests if they are favorable.

To prevent the assessment spiral from occurring, as well as coercing individuals into genetic testing, the individual should be permitted to obtain coverage at the regular rate he or she would be offered if genetic information were not considered. Thus, genetic information could not be the basis for a preferred rate, but a preferred rate could be offered to someone with a negative genetic test who would otherwise qualify for a preferred rate for other reasons, such as non-smoking and health lifestyle.

* * *

7.   Prohibit use of predictive testing or predictive information in group life insurance.

About one-third of all life insurance policies are purchased by employers or associations or as credit insurance under group policies. In theory, the group is underwritten, but individuals in the group are not. Nevertheless, there is some degree of medical underwriting in group life insurance, depending on the size and nature of the group.

Legislatures should prohibit use of predictive medical information in group health insurance as part of the federal Health Insurance Portability and Accountability Act of 1996. Such a measure might increase the price of group life insurance slightly, but only to the extent that underwriting takes place in group policies.

* * *

8.   Establish high-risk life insurance pools.

Previous options attempted to make adjustments to the current system of medical underwriting to prevent insurers from considering an individual's genetically increased risk of illness. If the ultimate goal of legislation dealing with genetic (or predictive) information is to provide an opportunity for high-risk individuals to purchase life insurance at affordable rates, it is better to confront the issue directly. The most likely way of ensuring access to life insurance is to create high-risk pools. These are already established in various other insurance product lines, including health, auto, and workers' compensation insurance. In the United States, if public policy supports taxpayer subsidization of flood insurance for beachfront vacation homes, some subsidies should be possible for life insurance for high-risk individuals.

NOTES AND QUESTIONS

1. Which, if any, of the proposals do you favor? Why? Are there any proposals that would be worse than the status quo? Which proposals do you think are the most and least politically viable? Which proposals are just? See Robert Klitzman, Paul S. Appelbaum & Wendy K. Chung, Should Life Insurers Have Access to Genetic Results?, 312 JAMA 1855 (2014).

2. In addition to these "substantive" proposals, Rothstein proposes the following procedural reforms: (1) regulate the use of predictive medical tests; (2) regulate testing laboratories; (3) regulate medical decision makers; (4) require informed consent for all medical examinations and tests; (5) require life insurers to disclose the medical basis of an adverse underwriting decision; and (6) prohibit use of medical information across insurance product lines or to underwrite family members. Which, if any, of these proposals do you think would be valuable?

IV. DISABILITY INSURANCE

Disability insurance policies pay a percentage of the wages of the insured individual (often about 70% to reflect after-tax income) in the event of short-term or long-term disability. Disability is tied to the ability to work in one's chosen profession and, not surprisingly, most disability policies are issued through employer-sponsored groups. Risk selection and pricing is done on a group basis, and the percentage of income replacement offered and premiums charged are influenced by the nature of the employment and the claims experience of the employer. Some employment-based group policies offer individuals a "buy up" option whereby they can purchase additional coverage. These supplements may be individually underwritten or they may be offered on a group-rate basis, where the pricing structure takes into account the likelihood for adverse selection.

Individual policies represent about 12 percent of all policies sold. Because of the cost, these policies are mostly bought by self-employed individuals and professionals such as lawyers and physicians. As with other individual policies (e.g. life, health), there is individual underwriting.

There are three main government disability insurance programs. Workers' compensation provides income replacement for workers who are injured or become ill from workplace exposures. Except for a few categories of workers, such as federal employees, employee eligibility, benefit levels, and administration are determined by the states. Social Security Disability Insurance (SSDI) provides disability payments to workers (and survivors of disabled workers) who qualify for Social Security but who become permanently and totally disabled before reaching retirement age. Supplemental Security Income (SSI) provides disability payments linked to financial need.

Disability insurance policies are regulated at the state level, but the policies adopted by the states on issues such as the use of predictive genetic information in underwriting may have an effect on both state and federal disability insurance programs.

As of 2015, about one-third of the states have enacted legislation regulating the use of genetic information by disability insurers. Most of these state statutes, however, only have limited applicability. The most common provisions prohibit discrimination that is not actuarially justified or require separate consent for an insurer to conduct genetic testing or use genetic information. A table of state genetic nondiscrimination laws appears at www.genome.gov/PolicyEthics/LegDatabase/.

Susan M. Wolf & Jeffrey P. Kahn, Genetic Testing and the Future of Disability Insurance: Ethics, Law, and Policy

35 J.L. Med. & Ethics (Supp. 2) 6, 11, 13 (2007).

Genetics may play a larger role in private disability insurance than private health insurance or life insurance. State and federal statutes place some limits on health insurers' use of such information, and very few limits on disability insurers. Further, in the realm of private individual life insurance, individual underwriting is less stringent than in disability insurance, as life insurers cover a single event—death. Because an individual may be disabled early in life precluding decades of income, disability insurers are exposed for longer periods of time than life insurers and for potentially much larger amounts of money. This exposure creates an incentive for disability insurers to use predictive medical information including genetic information, since genetics may help predict whether a disability precluding work will manifest at all, when, how, and for what duration.

To underwrite individual disability insurance, the insurer must carefully review the medical history of the applicant. On the basis of that information, the insurer may issue the coverage as applied for, charge additional premiums for the coverage, exclude specific conditions from coverage, change the benefit or elimination periods, or refuse to issue the coverage. As noted above, disability insurers providing individual policies generally rely less than group insurers on pre-existing conditions exclusions. The insurer is thus motivated to perform careful health research on an applicant. The insurer is also motivated by the requirement in most states that the policy include an incontestability clause. The incontestability clause provides that after two years, the insurer cannot deny benefits or cancel a policy if it discovers error in the information supplied by the applicant, so long as the insured did not intentionally defraud the insurer. Once this period has expired, the insurer thus loses the option to deny or cancel a contract due to pre-existing conditions that it failed to uncover. Incontestability clauses add to the insurer's incentives to discover as much as possible about an applicant's medical history—including genetic susceptibility to future disability—at the time of application, or at least within two years of it.

* * *

Given the importance of disability insurance, ideally legislators and regulators would impose the same restrictions on disability insurers as they do on health insurers. Norman Daniels analyzes the implications of setting up a disability insurance social safety net by eliminating medical underwriting (including consideration of genetics) while requiring that everyone have a minimum amount of disability insurance. Daniels does not go so far as to advocate this, but he recognizes it as an option to preserve equality of opportunity in the face of disability disrupting employment and income. For many individuals, this goal might be met through group insurance and public disability programs. When an individual can obtain the minimum amount of disability insurance needed through these other mechanisms, then individuals with a higher level of income can buy additional private individual insurance for additional income protection. Yet there will be some individuals without access to group insurance and unable to qualify for public programs who need access to a minimum safety net of individual disability insurance.

NOTES AND QUESTIONS

1. As with health insurance, public and private interests clearly intersect in the area of disability insurance. Disability income replacement is an important part of the Social Security system (SSDI), and private disability insurance provides supplemental protection for many workers. How might Social Security be affected by changes in the way that private disability insurance is regulated with regard to the use of genetic information?

2. Based on the legislative treatment of health insurance versus life insurance, at the moment, U.S. public policy seems to regard health insurance more as an entitlement or right to which all individuals have a claim, whereas life insurance is considered more of a commercial transaction to which actuarial principles should apply. Assuming this analysis is correct,

how should disability insurance be regarded, and how might this consideration affect public policy for disability insurance?

V. LONG-TERM CARE INSURANCE

MARK A. ROTHSTEIN, PREDICTIVE GENETIC TESTING FOR ALZHEIMER'S DISEASE IN LONG-TERM CARE INSURANCE
35 Ga. L. Rev. 707, 716–731 (2001).

* * *

Long-term care insurance is expensive; paying for the costs of long-term care out-of-pocket can be a catastrophic financial experience for individuals and their families. As long-term care for the elderly increases in expense and a larger portion of the population closes in on their twilight years, the number of insurance policies should be expected to grow. Nevertheless, private insurance is likely to have only a limited role in financing long-term care unless at least the following three things occur: First, long-term care insurance must become a more widely available employee benefit offered through "cafeteria plans" by employers and purchased by employees with pre-tax dollars. Second, because younger, working employees are unlikely to purchase a benefit that they probably will not need, if at all, until after they retire and are no longer paying the premiums needed to keep the policy in force, some "paid up" forms of long-term care insurance will be necessary.

* * *

On average, Alzheimer's disease patients live eight to ten years after they are diagnosed. Consequently, each additional patient with Alzheimer's disease represents a significant increase in the likely expenditures for long-term care. Insurance companies can easily identify symptomatic individuals, but identifying those asymptomatic individuals who are likely to get Alzheimer's disease is much more difficult. Any tests used today by insurers would be poor predictors of future cognitive impairment in asymptomatic and younger applicants. If new tests, including genetic tests, were developed that were better predictors of future dementia (or if they were believed to be better predictors), long-term care insurance companies would have a considerable economic interest in using them. If predictive testing were available, then insurers could learn of the individual's risk status, which may cause adverse selection. Testing by insurers would thus be merely "defensive" in nature.

* * *

In trying to discern the appropriate public policy for the use of predictive genetic information in long-term care insurance, it is valuable to contrast the public policy for health insurance with that for life insurance. For health insurance, restrictions on access due to genetic-based predictions of future health status are unacceptable. There are not clear indications of the specific reasons for this public policy. It may well be a combination of at least the following reasons: (1) the importance of private health insurance to well-being in a nation that does not provide for universal access to health care; (2) the lack of alternatives to health insurance as a way of spreading risk and, in the era of managed care, obtaining health services at negotiated rates; (3) the speculative nature of many types of predictive genetic information; (4) the asserted moral blamelessness of individuals with genetic predisposition to illness; and (5) successful lobbying by groups with an interest in genetic-specific health protections—genetic disease advocacy groups, public health officials, and pharmaceutical and biotechnology companies concerned that individuals will not take their genetic tests if they fear discrimination.

For life insurance, at least in the United States, restrictions on access or cost based on predictions of future health status currently are generally acceptable. The reasons for this policy are likely to include at least the following: (1) life insurance serves a valuable role in promoting peace of mind and in providing financial security for one's heirs, but it is not a necessity for the person who is insured; (2) there are various investment alternatives to some forms of life insurance; (3) medical underwriting based on predictions of mortality risk are commonly performed for various health and lifestyle measures, including smoking and drinking habits, diet, occupation, recreational activities, and various presymptomatic health measures ranging from weight to cholesterol levels; (4) unlike health insurance, where the benefits are largely defined, life insurance can be purchased in extremely large amounts, thereby increasing the incentives for adverse selection; and (5) life insurance has not yet been the subject of intense lobbying activity.

If the preceding arguments generally capture the current public sentiments with regard to health and life insurance, to determine the appropriate policy for long-term care insurance one must merely resolve the following question: As a policy matter, is long-term care insurance more like health insurance or life insurance? Arguing in favor of long-term care insurance being closer to health insurance is the fact that long-term care is a type of health care which is merely provided in a different setting, and even though there are different pricing levels among long-term care facilities, commercial policies are generally sold with certain defined benefits. Arguing in favor of long-term care insurance being closer to life insurance is the fact that there are alternatives to long-term care policies and the premium structure is based on mortality risk, much the way that life insurance (and disability insurance) is.

* * *

As with the use of genetic information in numerous other contexts, the issue of using genetic information in long-term care insurance cannot be resolved in isolation. If public policy prohibits long-term care insurers from requiring genetic testing or using the results of a genetic test, what about using predictive genetic information based on family history? If the use of *any* predictive genetic information should be prohibited, what about non-genetic health information predictive of dementia, such as a history of head trauma, smoking, or drinking? What about other non-health factors predictive of dementia, such as socio-economic status? What about underwriting based on medical and nonmedical factors predictive of other disabling conditions?

Ultimately, the question becomes who should have access to long-term care, or, at least, who should have access to long-term care insurance? The most logical, and defensible line of demarcation for risk classification may not be genetic versus nongenetic factors. It may be whether the applicant is asymptomatic or symptomatic, with only age as an underwriting factor for individuals who are asymptomatic and all actuarially relevant criteria permitted in underwriting symptomatic individuals.

CATHLEEN D. ZICK ET AL., GENETIC TESTING FOR ALZHEIMER'S DISEASE AND ITS IMPACT ON INSURANCE PURCHASING BEHAVIOR
24 Health Affairs 483, 484–488 (2005).

STUDY DATA AND METHODS

Study design.

The Risk Evaluation and Education for Alzheimer's Disease (REVEAL) Study is a recently completed randomized controlled trial (RCT) evaluating the impact of a genetic education and counseling program for adult children of Alzheimer's patients. As the largest study of its kind, it provides a rare opportunity to gain initial insights into the relationship between genetic testing for Alzheimer's disease and insurance purchasing behavior.

Participants in the REVEAL Study were either self-referred or systematically ascertained through their family's membership in existing Alzheimer's research registries in Boston, Cleveland, or New York City. Recruitment began in August 2000, and the last of the follow-up respondents surveys was completed in October 2003. A total of 162 participants were randomized into the clinical trial. All study participants were at higher-than-average risk for developing Alzheimer's because they have at least one parent affected by the disease.

In the control arm of the REVEAL Study, participants were informed of their risk of developing Alzheimer's based on sex and family history alone, with lifetime risk estimates ranging from 18 to 29 percent. Meanwhile, intervention-group participants learned their APOE genotype and were informed of their risk on the basis of sex, family history, and genotype, with lifetime risk estimates ranging from 13 to 57 percent.

Of the 162 people in the study, 148 were included in the analyses that follow. The remaining fourteen were excluded because they had missing data on one or more of the covariates. Among the 148 subjects, 46 were in the arm of the study where there was no APOE disclosure, 54 learned that they were a4 negative, and the remaining 48 learned that they were a4 positive (that is, had one or two a4 alleles).

Participants' characteristics.

Participants' sociodemographic information illustrates that the REVEAL sample, like all research volunteer samples, is not a representative sample of the population. People in this study were more likely to be white, female, and well educated than members of the general population. Participants were also typically older than the general population, since participants had to be an adult child of a diagnosed Alzheimer's patient. Before intervention, it was ascertained that 97 percent of the sample had health insurance, 78 percent had life insurance, and 19.8 had long-term care insurance. These high rates of insurance coverage likely reflect the age, education, and ethnic composition of the sample.

* * *

Adverse selection.

First, there was little evidence of adverse selection in the health, life, and disability insurance markets despite the fact that the sample consisted of highly motivated people (that is, all had a family history of Alzheimer's disease and were highly educated) who were participating in a closed research trial where confidentiality of genetic information was guaranteed. This finding might be expected, however, given the ages of the participants, the relatively short period of follow-up (one year), people's typical insurance buying patterns, and the unique attributes of various insurance products.

Long-term care insurance.

Second, the one insurance domain where we found suggestive evidence of adverse selection is long-term care. Almost 17 percent of those who tested positive subsequently changed their long-term care insurance coverage in the year after APOE disclosure, compared with approximately 2 percent of those who tested negative and 4 percent of those who did not receive APOE disclosure. The overall percentage with long-term care insurance rose from 19.8 percent at baseline to 27 percent just one year later. Roughly three quarters of this increase is attributable to study participants' having learned that they had tested positive for the a4 allele. Controlling for other insurance-related covariates, we found that participants who tested positive were 5.76 times more likely to change their long-term care insurance coverage during the subsequent year than were those who did not receive APOE disclosure (although this finding is not reinforced by the sensitivity analyses).

Potential for adverse selection.

Policymakers who are attempting to balance consumers' concerns regarding potential genetic discrimination against insurers' concerns that the withholding of genetic test results would make insurance markets unprofitable should proceed with caution. Our findings imply that the potential for adverse selection may vary considerably by insurance market, thus making it difficult to design a public policy that works well in all instances.

It may be that the natural history of Alzheimer's disease combines with APOE testing and the characteristics of the mostly private long-term care insurance market to create the "perfect storm" with regard to adverse selection. That is, (1) Alzheimer's is a condition that has a high probability of requiring formal, long-term care services; (2) APOE testing gives significant, albeit incomplete, predictive information for the at-risk population; and (3) long-term care insurance is generally a private insurance market where an information asymmetry can have serious consequences. Taken in combination, these conditions create a situation where adverse selection may occur and where its consequences for insurers and consumers may be significant. This premise is consistent with the fact that we observe a positive relationship between testing positive and changing one's long-term care insurance coverage even in our relatively small sample.

NOTES AND QUESTIONS

1.   Taken together, what do the Rothstein and Zick articles indicate about the nature and consequences of genetic information for long-term care insurance? According to another study, healthy people with an increased risk of illness based on predictive genetic tests were more likely to purchase long-term care insurance. Donald H. Taylor, Jr. et al., Genetic Testing for Alzheimer's and Long-Term Care Insurance 29 Health Affairs 102 (2010).

2.   If you favor laws prohibiting long-term care insurers from using genetic information in underwriting, would you do so through genetic-specific or more general laws? If the latter, how would you structure such a law?

3.   Genetic information may have an effect on a variety of other insurance products. Medical malpractice (for negligence in diagnosis or

treatment) and products liability (for pharmacogenomic medications) quickly come to mind. But there are other less obvious implications as well. For example, would it be permissible for an auto insurance company to test applicants to determine whether they were genetically predisposed to be risk takers? See Chapter 13 on Behavioral Genetics. In a claim filed under a homeowners or premises liability policy, can an insurer require genetic testing of an injured plaintiff to assess causation or determine life expectancy? See Chapter 17.

CHAPTER 16

EMPLOYMENT DISCRIMINATION

■ ■ ■

I. INTRODUCTION

Along with genetic discrimination in insurance, the topic of Chapter 15, genetic discrimination in employment is a topic of enormous concern to individuals and policy makers. Employment is not only a source of income but also the source of health insurance for the majority of Americans. Therefore, it is extremely important to resolve whether employers may get access to individuals' genetic information and, if so, what they may lawfully do with it. At the same time, it is necessary to consider the employers' interests in efficiency, employee health, and the health and safety of the public.

Employers have a keen interest in the health of their employees. A healthy work force is more stable, more productive, safer, and less costly in various ways than one composed of workers who are ill or likely to become ill in the future. Accordingly, medical screening of workers, the use of medical criteria in selecting and maintaining a work force, makes sense from a business standpoint and, if appropriately performed, from a health and policy standpoint as well. Medical screening of workers is not new; the only recent changes have been in the specific financial incentives for having healthier employees and the science used to make such determinations.

Medical screening became common in the United States at the beginning of the twentieth century. With industrialization, and the emergence of large manufacturing and other centralized employment facilities, employers attempted to ensure that their employees were free of tuberculosis and other communicable diseases. They also wanted to determine whether applicants and employees had the necessary vision, hearing, strength, stamina, dexterity, and other physical (and later mental) attributes necessary to perform the job safely and efficiently. Thus, "factory surgeons" were hired to screen out individuals who were deemed to be unacceptable. The nascent state of occupational medicine and the vulnerability of employer-paid physicians to making decisions for non-medical reasons, such as screening out union sympathizers for "medical reasons," sometimes compromised the integrity of the medical screening process during the first half of the twentieth century.

After World War II, there were new incentives to use more extensive medical screening. Besides workers' compensation and unemployment compensation liability for injuries and illnesses and employee turnover, employers began assuming a portion of employee (and later dependent) health insurance costs and, for some employers, disability insurance. In 1970, the Occupational Safety and Health Act subjected employers to civil penalties for safety and health violations, including those associated with occupational diseases or employee-caused accidents. The prospect of substantial tort liability for physical injuries and property damage sustained by the public resulting from employee-based mishaps further encouraged employers to select employees carefully based on medical criteria.

While pressures to increase medical screening were growing, civil rights legislation was enacted to limit employer prerogatives in employee selection. Title VII of the Civil Rights Act of 1964, as amended, and the Age Discrimination in Employment Act of 1967 (ADEA) prohibited discrimination based on race, color, religion, sex, pregnancy, national origin, or age. These laws had the effect of prohibiting employers from using stereotypical assumptions of individuals' abilities, thereby requiring an individualized determination of physical ability. In 1990, Congress enacted the Americans with Disabilities Act (ADA), which differed from Title VII and the ADEA in at least two important ways. First, Congress realized that it had to go beyond merely prohibiting discrimination based on disability; it was also necessary to address the previously unregulated process of selecting employees based on medical criteria. Thus, the ADA limits the timing and permissible scope of medical inquiries so that individuals with disabilities will not be excluded from consideration because of their disabilities before they have a chance to demonstrate their abilities. Second, the ADA requires that employers provide "reasonable accommodation" to enable individuals with disabilities to perform their jobs.

In 2008, Congress enacted the Genetic Information Nondiscrimination Act (GINA), Title II of which prohibits discrimination in employment on the basis of genetic information. Following the general framework of state laws enacted in the 1990s, GINA's main purpose is to reassure individuals that they can undergo genetic testing or genetic consultations without adverse consequences to their employment.

This chapter considers the broader context of genetic information and discrimination in the workplace. It explores what it means to "discriminate," whether genetic-specific or more general laws would be more effective in preventing discrimination, and the specifics of GINA and other legislation applicable to genetics in employment.

A. WHAT IS GENETIC DISCRIMINATION?

Matt Ridley, Nature Via Nurture
260–262 (2003).

Moral 4: Meritocracy

As the last candidate left the room, the chairman of the committee cleared his throat.

"Well, esteemed colleagues, we must choose one of those three people for the job of financial controller of the company: which is it to be?"

"Easy," said the red-haired woman. "The first one."

"Why?"

"Because she is a qualified woman and this company needs more women."

"Nonsense," said the portly man. "The best candidate was the second one. He has the best education. You can't beat Harvard's business school. Besides I knew his father at college. And he goes to church."

"Pah," scoffed the young woman with the thick glasses, "When I asked him what seven times eight is, he said 54! And he kept missing the point of my questions. What use is a good education if you haven't got a brain? I think the last candidate was by far the best. He was smooth, articulate, open, and quick. He didn't go to college, true, but he's got a natural grasp of numbers. Besides, he's got a real personality and the chemistry's right."

"Maybe," said the chairman. "But he's black."

Question: Who in this scene is guilty of genetic discrimination? The chairman, the red-haired woman, the portly man, or the woman with the glasses? Answer: All except the portly man. Only he is prepared to discriminate on the grounds of nurture. He is a true blank-slater, believing firmly that all human beings are born equal and stamped with their character by their upbringing. He is prepared to put his faith in the church, Harvard, and his college friend to create the right character whatever the raw material. The chairman's racism is based on the genetics of skin color. The red-haired woman's adherence to affirmative action for women is discrimination against people with Y chromosomes. The young woman in the glasses prefers to ignore qualifications and look for intrinsic talent and personality. Her discrimination is more subtle, but it certainly is genetic, at least in part: personality is strongly inherited, and her dismissal of the candidate from Harvard is based on the fact that his "nurture genes" have failed to take advantage of his education. She does not believe he is redeemable. I suggest that she is just as much of a genetic determinist as the chairman and the red-haired woman—and of course I hope her candidate got the job.

Every job interview is about genetic discrimination. Even if the interviews correctly ignore race, sex, disability, and physical appearance and discriminate on the grounds of ability alone, they are still discriminating, and unless they are prepared to decide on the basis of qualifications and background alone—in which case, why hold an interview?—then they are looking for some intrinsic, rather than acquired talent. The more they are prepared to make allowances for a deprived background, the more they are genetic determinists. Besides the other point of the interview is to take into consideration personality, and remember the lesson of twin studies: personality is even more strongly heritable in this society than intelligence.

MARK A. ROTHSTEIN & MARY R. ANDERLIK, WHAT IS GENETIC DISCRIMINATION AND WHEN AND HOW CAN IT BE PREVENTED?
3 Genetics in Med. 354, 354–355 (2001).

The two most common uses of the term discrimination differ dramatically in the degree of disapproval they connote. On the one hand, the term discrimination may be used to indicate a type of distinction that invariably is or should be socially unacceptable. We refer to this as the civil rights definition. For example, the Council for Responsible Genetics position paper on genetic discrimination does not define the term discrimination, but the negative connotation is clear from its use. Discrimination is linked to evaluating people based on "questionable stereotypes" rather than their individual merits and abilities, invading people's privacy, the morally and publicly unacceptable stratification of the community into "haves" and "have-nots," and the punishment of people for characteristics over which they have no control in violation of cherished beliefs in justice and equality. The proper response to discrimination is legal prohibition.

On the other hand, the term discrimination may be used as an all-purpose descriptor for the practice of making distinctions. Further, some individuals and entities link social unacceptability with irrationality, that is, they believe that only irrational distinctions should be socially unacceptable. We refer to this as the actuarial definition. For example, in the insurance industry, the term discrimination is considered neutral and simply refers to classification for purposes of underwriting. On the industry view, discrimination only becomes problematic where there is no sound actuarial basis for the manner in which risks are classified, or individuals with equivalent risks are treated differently. Often, in the business context, "irrational" means that the distinction cannot be defended in economic terms or, in the case of insurance, by reference to sound actuarial principles.

For both definitions, the term genetic discrimination also conveys that adverse treatment is based solely on the genotype of asymptomatic individuals. Differential treatment on the basis of phenotype is frequently rational and accepted as a social necessity, such as where an employer bases a hiring decision on a job-related need for visual acuity. Cases of adverse treatment based on the phenotypic expression of a genetic characteristic fit well within the analytical framework of laws dealing with disability-based or health status-based discrimination generally. The most important of these laws is the Americans with Disabilities Act. To the contrary, cases of adverse treatment of phenotypically "normal" individuals fit poorly within the disability discrimination framework. A large majority of the public considers discrimination against these individuals as unfair because current opportunities are being denied to seemingly unaffected individuals merely because a genetic test or assessment indicates an increased risk of future incapacity.

We define discrimination as drawing a distinction among individuals or groups plus an element of either irrationality or social unacceptability or both. Our definition draws upon elements of both the civil rights and actuarial definitions. When discrimination is defined in this way, the term clearly has a negative connotation, but it does not necessarily equate with a legal proscription of the classification. The appropriate legal and policy response to social unacceptability—a widely shared sense within a polity that some activity or state of affairs is "wrong"—will depend on the circumstances. In addition to or in lieu of legal prohibitions backed by criminal, civil, or administrative penalties are withdrawals of public funding, public condemnation, professional standards, and direct citizen action against the offending parties, for example, in the form of an economic boycott. Our definition recognizes that some forms of irrational discrimination are accepted, or at least tolerated, by society and some forms of discrimination are socially unacceptable despite the fact that they are rational.

Table 1 illustrates the application of our definition of discrimination by indicating how a sample of selection criteria for employment would be arrayed along dimensions of social acceptability and rationality. Note that standards for judging social acceptability will vary according to the context. While employers are generally not prohibited from basing hiring decisions on Zodiac signs, even though this is clearly irrational, an insurer would have to offer some actuarial basis for the distinction in order to meet the requirements of state insurance laws. One justification for differences in the law of employment and insurance is that, in our society, there is no history of systematic mistreatment of Virgos relative to Capricorns in employment, and the costs of policing idiosyncratic factors in isolated hiring decisions would be very high. On the other hand, risk classification in insurance involves assigning individuals to risk pools and hence insurance practices have the potential to create systematic mistreatment. Insurance underwriting policies also are more amenable to regulation than hiring decisions.

Table 1. Categories of Discrimination in Employment

	Rational	Irrational
Acceptable	• Choosing based on relative skill or other job-related criteria • Choosing based on medical assessment of ability to perform the job	• Choosing based on Zodiac sign • Choosing based on a coin toss
Unacceptable	• Excluding persons with cancer based on concerns about health care costs • Excluding pregnant women because they may shortly go on maternity leave	• Excluding based on religion (in a secular enterprise) • Excluding based on national origin

NOTES AND QUESTIONS

1. "Genetic discrimination" has long been an essential and accepted component of employee selection practices. For example, genes are a factor in height, vision, cognitive ability, and numerous other attributes of interest to employers. Thus, in a sense, it is "genetic discrimination" for a professional basketball team to select players based on their height. It is also "genetic discrimination" for an employer to refuse to hire an individual whose intellectual deficits preclude understanding key assignments or whose expressed genetic disorder precludes him or her from working. These forms of discrimination are generally considered legally and ethically permissible. Thus, "genetic discrimination" of a legally and ethically problematic nature, and as the term is commonly used, really means discrimination based on an unexpressed genotype. It is discrimination against presymptomatic or at-risk individuals.

2. Based on this definition, where would you place genetic discrimination on the preceding table?

3. Can you make an argument for including genetic discrimination in any of the other "boxes"?

4. What is the nature of the harm suffered by a victim of genetic discrimination? How does it compare with the harm suffered by the victims of other forms of discrimination in employment?

RICHARD A. EPSTEIN, THE LEGAL REGULATION OF GENETIC DISCRIMINATION: OLD RESPONSES TO NEW TECHNOLOGY
74 B.U. L. Rev. 1, 12–13 (1994).

* * *

At this point it is critical to note that the plea for privacy is often a plea for the right to misrepresent one's self to the rest of the world. In and of itself that may not be a bad thing. We are certainly not obligated to disclose all of our embarrassing past to persons in ordinary social conversations; and it is certainly acceptable to use long sleeves to cover an ugly scar. White lies are part of the glue that makes human interaction possible without shame and loss of face. Strictly speaking, people may be deceived, but they are rarely hurt, and they may even be relieved to be spared an awkward encounter. However, when a major change in personal or financial status is contemplated by another party, the white lies that make human interaction possible turn into frauds of a somewhat deeper dye. In order to see why this is the case, recall that the traditional tort of misrepresentation stressed the usual five fingers: a false statement, known to be false, material to the listener, and relied on, to the listener's detriment. There is little question, whether we deal with marriage or with business, that concealment of relevant genetic information satisfies each element. The only question, therefore, is whether one can justify what is a prima facie wrong.

I am hard pressed to see what that justification might be. No doubt the individual who engages in this type of deception has much to gain. But equally there can be no doubt that this gain exists in all garden variety cases of fraud as well. To show the advantage of the fraud to the party who commits it is hardly to excuse or to justify it, for the same can be said of all cases of successful wrongs. On the other side of the transaction, there is a pronounced loss from not knowing the information when key decisions have to be made. For example, a woman may choose the wrong husband; an employer may pass up a good employee with a strong medical record and a clear upward path in favor of a worker who will, in the end, be the source of enormous personal and financial costs. To show that the condition is one for which the speaker is not responsible hardly justifies concealment at all: Lying about one's age or about the place of one's birth is often fraud even though these facts are immutable—just ask the Immigration and Naturalization Service.

False statements about or deliberate concealment of genetic information is as much a fraud as false statements about or concealment of any other issue. The only possible justification for concealment, therefore, would be that it is unfair for the person with the pending disorder to deal alone with the suffering and financial loss. Yet, that loss is not sustained because of the wrong of another. Could the victim of a natural catastrophe keep it secret, and single out one other person to bear some substantial fraction of the loss? If not, then why give that same privilege to the victim of a genetic defect? Today, it is easy to find strong support for socializing losses. But why should a person laboring under a genetic defect be entitled to pick the person or group that has to pay the subsidy?

In sum, genetic discrimination raises problems no different from those associated with any other sort of misfortune, and calls for no different response. The greater knowledge that comes from testing increases the informational asymmetries that are always the bane of insurance markets. When testing is possible, dangers from strategic behavior are only enhanced. Accordingly, the case for insisting on standard insurance norms is greater than it was before. Full disclosure of material information in response to direct questions is an indispensable part of that system. If we have reason to suspect that a system of disclosure could prove unreliable, we should allow the employer or insurer to test in order to obtain the knowledge already available to the employee. The person who wants privacy need not apply for the position or the insurance coverage. But he should not be able to have it both ways, and at someone else's expense.

NOTES AND QUESTIONS

1. Do you agree that the desire for privacy should be equated with misrepresentation?

2. Epstein assumes that the individual has already undergone genetic testing and is withholding the results. Does an individual have an obligation to undergo genetic testing or to submit to genetic testing so that third parties can more accurately calculate the risk of future illness?

3. What scientific, economic, and social assumptions underlie Epstein's theory?

4. For a similar view, see Colin S. Diver & Jane Maslow Cohen, Genophobia: What is Wrong with Genetic Discrimination?, 149 U. Pa. L. Rev. 1439 (2001) (advocating "genetic transparency" in which all parties have access to genetic information).

B. THE WHY AND HOW OF EMPLOYER ACCESS
TO GENETIC INFORMATION

Employers have a considerable interest in the current and future health of their employees. The nature of the business and the work force will determine the specific interests, but in general, a healthy work force will be more productive; have less absenteeism and turnover; have fewer workers' compensation, disability insurance, and unemployment compensation claims; have fewer Family and Medical Leave Act requests for personal leave; require fewer accommodations under the Americans with Disabilities Act; and cause fewer OSHA violations.

The most important economic reason to have a healthy work force is to control health insurance costs. In the United States, about 85% of individuals who have privately financed health care coverage obtain their health benefits through their employer. The cost of health care coverage is the largest single non-salary compensation expense and, despite a moderating of increases in the 1990s attributable to managed care, the costs have begun increasing at a faster rate. In any given year, 5% of claimants represent 50% of expenditures, and therefore if the high-cost users could be excluded, dramatic savings (or cost-shifting to other, largely public payers) would be realized.

Employers attempting to limit their health insurance costs by selecting employees based on their health status may run afoul of the Americans with Disabilities Act as well as the Health Insurance Portability and Accountability Act of 1996 (HIPAA), the Affordable Care Act, and the Genetic Information Nondiscrimination Act. As a result, it might seem that employers have no lawful interest in the likely future health of individual employees and their dependents. Nevertheless, claims experience may be used in pricing the policy for an employer's group coverage and self-insured employers (mostly large employers) will have the solvency of their plan affected by the claims filed.

NOTE ON EMPLOYER ACCESS TO EMPLOYEE
HEALTH INFORMATION

Employers lawfully obtain medical information about employees in numerous ways. The following are 10 of the most common ways.

1. Application forms. Under the Americans with Disabilities Act (ADA), it is unlawful for an employer to make any medical inquiries of an applicant for employment until after there has been a conditional offer of employment. Therefore, it would be unlawful for an employer to require that the individual provide medical information on an application form. It is lawful, however, for an application form to ask an individual about previous jobs held and the reason why the individual left each prior job. The answer to one of these questions might be: "took time off work for cancer treatment."

2.   Interviews. It is unlawful for an employer to ask about health matters at the interview before a conditional offer of employment. But nothing would prevent an employer from asking, for example, why the individual is interested in working for a particular employer. The answer to such a question could be: "Your health benefits are excellent, and there is a good chance I will need a liver transplant in a few years."

3.   References. References sometimes disclose information about individuals that the individual would prefer not to have divulged to a potential employer. For example, a reference, trying to be helpful might say: "He has not let the fact that he tested positive for the Huntington disease mutation affect his positive outlook on life."

4.   Post-offer medical exams. Under the ADA, after a conditional offer of employment, the employer can require that the individual submit to a preplacement medical examination. These examinations may be unlimited in scope, regardless of the nature of the job or the individual's health history.

5.   Releases of medical records. Under the ADA, after a conditional offer of employment, an employer may require that an individual sign a blanket release authorizing disclosure to the employer of all of the individual's medical records. Under GINA, it is unlawful for an employer to request, require, or purchase genetic information about an employee or family member of an employee, but genetic information is generally interspersed with non-genetic information in medical records. Because there is no easy or low-cost method of separating this information in paper or electronic health records, the custodians of health records often send the entire files in response to a more limited request.

6.   FMLA requests. Under the Family and Medical Leave Act (FMLA), an employer of 50 or more employees is required to provide up to 12 weeks of unpaid leave for, among other things, the worker's own serious health condition that prevents him or her from working. The employer may require medical certification of the employee's need for leave, notwithstanding the ADA, which otherwise prohibits employers from requiring current employees to undergo non-job-related medical examinations. GINA, which prohibits employers from requesting genetic information from their employees, contains an exception for information related to an FMLA certification.

7.   Periodic medical exams. Employers often require that employees periodically undergo medical examinations. For jobs with certain workplace exposures, periodic examinations are required under the Occupational Safety and Health Act. Under the ADA, medical examinations of current employees must be job-related or voluntary.

8.   Workers' compensation claims. Employees sustaining work-related injuries and illnesses are eligible for workers' compensation. By submitting a claim, however, the employee places his or her medical condition at issue. The employer is therefore entitled to an independent medical examination of the claimant as well as access to the employee's medical records.

9.   Health insurance claims. Employers often have widespread access to claims information submitted under an employer-sponsored health benefits plan. With a self-insured, self-administered plan, the physicians' bills and fee explanations are sent directly to the employer for payment. Even when a third-party administrator is used, employers often have access to the information. Employers also gain access to the health claims of the employee's dependents.

10.   Voluntary disclosure. One of the most frequently used forms of disclosure of health information in the workplace occurs when employees voluntarily disclose their illnesses to co-workers and supervisors.

NOTES AND QUESTIONS

1.   Individuals fear workplace genetic discrimination and they *report* they have been subject to adverse treatment. See, e.g., E. Virginia Lapham et al., Genetic Discrimination: Perspectives of Consumers, 274 Science 621 (1996). Yet, there have been very few cases brought under the Americans with Disabilities Act or other laws. Why?

2.   To what extent do you think the lack of cases reflects the fact that genetic testing is an emerging technology and therefore few individuals' medical records contain the results of DNA based tests? Is it because individuals do not want to identify themselves as having a genetic predisposition? Is it because individuals often do not know the reason they are refused employment? Is it because discrimination based on future health risk is most likely to occur at the preplacement stage and applicants do not have such a financial or emotional interest in a job such that they are likely to sue? Other reasons?

3.   The public health concern underlying genetic discrimination in the workplace is that at-risk individuals who want to be tested for prevention or other health-related reasons will not do so if they are afraid they will be subject to discrimination, including in employment. Is allaying an irrational public fear an adequate reason for enacting antidiscrimination legislation, such as GINA?

4.   To what extent do you believe antidiscrimination legislation is encouraged by researchers and commercial interests concerned about the willingness of the public to undergo genetic testing in the absence of legislative assurances of nondiscrimination?

II.   GENETIC DISCRIMINATION UNDER THE AMERICANS WITH DISABILITIES ACT (ADA)

A.   COVERAGE

The Americans with Disabilities Act of 1990 (ADA), 42 U.S.C. §§ 12101–12213, was the first comprehensive federal law to prohibit discrimination in employment against the estimated 43 million

Americans with physical or mental disabilities. The ADA's five titles deal with employment (Title I), public services (Title II), public accommodations operated by private entities (Title III), telecommunications (Title IV), and miscellaneous issues (Title V). The ADA draws heavily upon Title VII of the Civil Rights Act of 1964, 42 U.S.C. § 2000e, and the Rehabilitation Act of 1973, 29 U.S.C. §§ 701–796i.

The ADA applies to employers with 15 or more employees. It also applies to state and local government employers and the United States Congress. Federal employees are not covered by the ADA, but they are covered by comparable provisions of section 501 of the Rehabilitation Act.

Section 102(a) of the ADA contains the general prohibition on employment discrimination. "No covered entity shall discriminate against a qualified individual with a disability because of the disability of such individual in regard to job application procedures, the hiring, advancement, or discharge of employees, employee compensation, job training, and other terms, conditions, and privileges of employment." There can be no liability if the employer did not know that the individual had a disability at the time it took the adverse action and therefore direct or circumstantial proof of employer motive is often determinative.

Besides the ADA, nearly every state has its own civil rights law prohibiting discrimination in employment on the basis of disability or handicap. Section 501(b) of the ADA provides that the ADA does not preempt any state or local law "that provides greater or equal protection for the rights of individuals with disabilities than are afforded by this [Act]." There are three main ways in which state laws are important to complement the protections of the ADA. First, the state law may apply to a wider class of employers. Twenty-five states and the District of Columbia have laws that apply to employers with fewer than 15 employees. Second, the state law may apply to a wider range of impairments than the ADA, such as individuals who are obese, who have substance abuse problems, or whose disabilities are not severe enough to meet the ADA definition. Third, the state law may more closely regulate certain medical or hiring procedures in employment. For example, in California and Minnesota preplacement medical examinations must be limited to assessing job-related health conditions. Medical examinations are discussed in Section IIB of this Chapter.

The ADA Amendments Act of 2008, P.L. 110–325, 110th Cong., 2d Sess. (2008), was signed into law on September 25, 2008. It was enacted to overturn Supreme Court decisions narrowly interpreting the definition of an individual with a disability. The essence of the new amendments is captured by the following rule of construction: "The definition of a disability in this Act shall be construed in favor of broad coverage of individuals under this Act, to the maximum extent permitted by the terms of this Act." ADA Amendments Act § 3(4). Among the Supreme Court decisions overturned were Sutton v. United Air Lines, Inc., 527 U.S. 471 (1999), and its companion cases. In *Sutton*, twin sisters with correctable vision problems were denied an opportunity to become airline pilots because their uncorrected vision did not meet the airline's medical standards. In the ADA action, however, the airline argued that they were not covered by the ADA because in their "mitigated" state they did not have a substantially limiting impairment. The Supreme Court, rejecting the EEOC's interpretation that impairments should be considered in their unmitigated state, held that the lower court was required to consider the effect of eyeglasses on their condition. The Court relied on the congressional finding that the ADA provided coverage to 43 million Americans with disabilities to conclude that the ADA was only intended to apply to individuals with substantially limiting impairments. Although Congress overturned *Sutton*, the ADA Amendments Act did not address the issue of genetic discrimination or discrimination based on the risk of future impairment. Perhaps Congress did not believe this was necessary in light of GINA (discussed below), which was signed into law four months earlier on May 21, 2008.

B. MEDICAL EXAMINATIONS

AMERICANS WITH DISABILITIES ACT
42 U.S.C. §§ 12101–12213.

SECTION 102. (§ 12112) DISCRIMINATION

(a) GENERAL RULE.—No covered entity shall discriminate against a qualified individual with a disability because of the disability of such individual in regard to job application procedures, the hiring, advancement, or discharge of employees, employee compensation, job training, and other terms, conditions, and privileges of employment.

* * *

(d) MEDICAL EXAMINATIONS AND INQUIRIES.—

(1) IN GENERAL.—The prohibition against discrimination as referred to in subsection (a) shall include medical examinations and inquiries.

(2) PREEMPLOYMENT—

(A) PROHIBITED EXAMINATION OR INQUIRY.—Except as provided in paragraph (3), a covered entity shall not conduct a medical examination or make inquiries of a job applicant as to whether such applicant is an individual with a disability or as to the nature or severity of such disability.

(B) ACCEPTABLE INQUIRY.—A covered entity may make preemployment inquiries into the ability of an applicant to perform job-related functions.

(3) EMPLOYMENT ENTRANCE EXAMINATION.—A covered entity may require a medical examination after an offer of employment has been made to a job applicant and prior to the commencement of the employment duties of such applicant, and may condition an offer of employment on the results of such examination, if—

(A) all entering employees are subjected to such an examination regardless of disability;

(B) information obtained regarding the medical condition or history of the applicant is collected and maintained on separate forms and in separate medical files and is treated as a confidential medical record, except that—

(i) supervisors and managers may be informed regarding necessary restrictions on the work or duties of the employee and necessary accommodations;

(ii) first aid and safety personnel may be informed, when appropriate, if the disability might require emergency treatment; and

(iii) government officials investigating compliance with this Act shall be provided relevant information on request; and

(C) the results of such examination are used only in accordance with this title.

(4) EXAMINATION AND INQUIRY.—

(A) PROHIBITED EXAMINATIONS AND INQUIRIES.—A covered entity shall not require a medical examination and shall not make inquiries of an employee as to whether such employee is an individual with a disability or as to the nature or severity of the disability, unless such examination or inquiry is shown to be job-related and consistent with business necessity.

(B) ACCEPTABLE EXAMINATIONS AND INQUIRIES.— A covered entity may conduct voluntary medical examinations, including voluntary medical histories, which are part of an employee health program available to employees at that work site. A covered entity may make inquiries into the ability of an employee to perform job-related functions.

(C) REQUIREMENT.—Information obtained under subparagraph (B) regarding the medical condition or history of any employee are subject to the requirements of subparagraphs (B) and (C) of paragraph (3).

NOTES AND QUESTIONS

1. Section 102(d) of the ADA has three different sets of rules for employee medical examinations and inquiries, depending on the stage of employment at which the examination or inquiry is conducted. Can you summarize the three different sets of rules? Are these privacy protection rules or antidiscrimination rules?

2. Even though post-offer medical examinations need not be job-related, an employer may not withdraw a conditional offer of employment based on a medical examination unless the withdrawal is based on the individual's inability to perform the essential functions of the job, § 102(b)(6), 42 U.S.C. § 12112(b)(6). Thus, it was held to be unlawful for a city to perform nonconsensual HIV testing at the post-offer stage and then withdraw conditional offers from those who tested positive. Doe v. City of Chicago, 883 F.Supp. 1126 (N.D.Ill.1994).

3. For a discussion of the legislative history of this section, see Chai Feldblum, Medical Examinations and Inquiries Under the Americans with Disabilities Act: A View From the Inside, 64 Temp. L. Rev. 521 (1991); Sharona Hoffman, Preplacement Examinations and Job-Relatedness: How to Enhance Privacy and Diminish Discrimination in the Workplace, 49 U. Kan. L. Rev. 517 (2001). For a discussion of the ADA and genetics, see Mark A. Rothstein, Genetic Discrimination in Employment and the Americans with Disabilities Act, 29 Hous. L. Rev. 23 (1992).

OTHER LAWS APPLICABLE TO GENETIC DISCRIMINATION IN EMPLOYMENT

Title VII of the Civil Rights Act of 1964 prohibits discrimination in employment on the basis of race, color, religion, sex, and national origin. 42 U.S.C. § 2000e–2(a)(1). Because genetic disorders often appear in higher frequencies in distinct population groups, discrimination against individuals with certain disorders or traits (e.g., sickle cell) might be alleged as disparate impact discrimination under Title VII. This was the theory used in Norman-Bloodsaw v. Lawrence Berkeley Laboratory, 135 F.3d 1260 (9th Cir. 1998). Without their knowledge or consent, blood and urine samples of certain employees obtained during their preplacement medical examinations were tested for pregnancy, syphilis, and sickle cell trait. Seven current and former employees sued under the U.S. and California Constitutions, Title VII, and the ADA. The Ninth Circuit, in reversing the district court's dismissal of all claims, held that the facts raised a valid constitutional claim. "One can think of few subject areas more personal and more likely to implicate privacy interests than that of one's health and genetic make-up." 135 F.3d at 1269. The court also held that a cognizable Title VII claim for sex discrimination was alleged by the pregnancy testing and a race discrimination claim because the sickle cell testing was limited to black employees. The dismissal of the ADA claims was affirmed, however, because, under the ADA, preplacement medical examinations can be of unlimited scope and need not be job-related.

The Employee Retirement Income Security Act (ERISA) makes it unlawful to discriminate against a participant or beneficiary "for the purpose of interfering with the attainment of any right to which such participant may become entitled under the plan * * *." 29 U.S.C. § 1140. However, ERISA applies only to current employees and therefore is inapplicable to a refusal to hire based on perceived future health insurance costs. The ADA and state genetic nondiscrimination laws would be the best recourse for discrimination before hiring.

III. GENETIC NONDISCRIMINATION LAWS

A. STATE LAWS

State laws prohibiting genetic discrimination in employment date back to the 1970s. At that time, widespread and ill-advised carrier testing for sickle cell trait caused confusion, resulting in discrimination against unaffected carriers. Florida, Louisiana, and North Carolina enacted laws prohibiting discrimination based on sickle cell trait. The first comprehensive genetic nondiscrimination law was enacted in Wisconsin in 1991. In the years since then, over half the states have enacted laws prohibiting genetic discrimination in employment, and new measures are introduced in more states every year.

The laws fall into two general categories. First, the laws in all but two of the states to enact genetic nondiscrimination legislation prohibit employers from requiring genetic testing as a condition of employment and prohibit discrimination based on genetic information. The definition of genetic information includes family health history in some states; in others it is limited to the results of a DNA-based genetic test. The laws do not prohibit employers from requiring that individuals sign a blanket release of their medical records after there has been a conditional offer of employment. The second category of laws, represented by only California and Minnesota, adopt a more generic approach, and prohibit employers from obtaining any non-job-related medical information at any time. Presumably, this also prohibits employers from requiring broad releases of medical information, which could include genetic information and family health history information from which genetic risks may be inferred.

B. FEDERAL LAWS

OVERVIEW OF THE GENETIC INFORMATION NONDISCRIMINATION ACT OF 2008 (GINA)

The Genetic Information Nondiscrimination Act of 2008 (GINA), was signed into law by President Bush on May 21, 2008, after a 13-year struggle in Congress. Previously, in 2000, President Clinton issued Executive Order 13145, which prohibited genetic discrimination in federal government employment. The executive order was designed to pave the way for legislation covering the private sector, but GINA was considered unnecessary or intrusive by some members of Congress until various objections were resolved.

Title II of GINA prohibits discrimination in employment. Specifically, it prohibits employers from requesting, requiring, or purchasing genetic information about employees or applicants. Genetic information is defined as information about the individual's genetic tests, the genetic tests of family members, or the manifestation of a disease or disorder in a family member. It does not apply to manifested diseases or disorders of the individual. Thus, as with Title I, applicable to health insurance (discussed in Chapter 15), Title II of GINA applies only to individuals who are asymptomatic.

Employers are prohibited from engaging in various unlawful employment practices, including refusing to hire, discharging, or discriminating in terms or conditions of employment, based on genetic information. There are several exceptions to the ban on acquiring genetic information, including inadvertent acquisition (e.g., disclosures by the employee), employer requests for health information in accordance with the Family and Medical Leave Act (FMLA), and optional genetic monitoring for the effects of occupational exposures.

For private sector employers, GINA has the same coverage and remedies as Title VII, except that disparate impact claims may not be brought. Title II took effect on November 21, 2009, 18 months after GINA was signed law. The Equal Employment Opportunity Commission (EEOC) has responsibility for issuing regulations and enforcement of GINA.

GENETIC INFORMATION NONDISCRIMINATION ACT OF 2008
(GINA)

P.L. 110–233, 122 Stat 881 (2008).

* * *

TITLE II—PROHIBITING EMPLOYMENT DISCRIMINATION ON THE BASIS OF GENETIC INFORMATION

§ 201.   DEFINITIONS

* * *

(4)   GENETIC INFORMATION—

(A) IN GENERAL—The term 'genetic information' means, with respect to any individual, information about—

(i)   such individual's genetic tests,

(ii) the genetic tests of family members of such individual, and

(iii) the manifestation of a disease or disorder in family members of such individual.

(B) INCLUSION OF GENETIC SERVICES AND PARTICIPATION IN GENETIC RESEARCH—Such term includes, with respect to any individual, any request for, or receipt of, genetic services, or participation in clinical research which includes genetic services, by such individual or any family member of such individual.

(C) EXCLUSIONS—The term 'genetic information' shall not include information about the sex or age of any individual.

(5) GENETIC MONITORING—The term 'genetic monitoring' means the periodic examination of employees to evaluate acquired modifications to their genetic material, such as chromosomal damage or evidence of increased occurrence of mutations, that may have developed in the course of employment due to exposure to toxic substances in the workplace, in order to identify, evaluate, and respond to the effects of or control adverse environmental exposures in the workplace.

(6) GENETIC SERVICES—The term 'genetic services' means—

(A) a genetic test;

(B) genetic   counseling   (including   obtaining, interpreting, or assessing genetic information); or

(C) genetic education.

(7) GENETIC TEST—

(A) IN GENERAL—The term 'genetic test' means an analysis of human DNA, RNA, chromosomes, proteins, or metabolites, that detects genotypes, mutations, or chromosomal changes.

(B) EXCEPTIONS—The term 'genetic test' does not mean an analysis of proteins or metabolites that does not detect genotypes, mutations, or chromosomal changes.

§ 202. EMPLOYER PRACTICES.

(a) Discrimination Based on Genetic Information—It shall be an unlawful employment practice for an employer—

(1) to fail or refuse to hire, or to discharge, any employee, or otherwise to discriminate against any employee with respect to the compensation, terms, conditions, or privileges of employment of the employee, because of genetic information with respect to the employee; or

(2) to limit, segregate, or classify the employees of the employer in any way that would deprive or tend to deprive any employee of employment opportunities or otherwise adversely affect the status of the employee as an employee, because of genetic information with respect to the employee.

(b) Acquisition of Genetic Information—It shall be an unlawful employment practice for an employer to request, require, or purchase genetic information with respect to an employee or a family member of the employee except—

(1) where an employer inadvertently requests or requires family medical history of the employee or family member of the employee;

(2) where—

(A) health or genetic services are offered by the employer, including such services offered as part of a wellness program;

(B) the employee provides prior, knowing, voluntary, and written authorization;

(C) only the employee (or family member if the family member is receiving genetic services) and the licensed health care professional or board certified genetic counselor involved in providing such services receive individually identifiable information concerning the results of such services; and

(D) any individually identifiable genetic information provided under subparagraph (C) in connection with the services provided under subparagraph (A) is only available for purposes of such services and shall not be disclosed to the employer except in aggregate terms that do not disclose the identity of specific employees;

(3) where an employer requests or requires family medical history from the employee to comply with the certification provisions of section 103 of the Family and Medical Leave Act of 1993 (29 U.S.C. 2613) or such requirements under State family and medical leave laws;

(4) where an employer purchases documents that are commercially and publicly available (including newspapers, magazines, periodicals, and books, but not including medical databases or court records) that include family medical history;

(5) where the information involved is to be used for genetic monitoring of the biological effects of toxic substances in the workplace, but only if—

(A) the employer provides written notice of the genetic monitoring to the employee;

(B)(i) the employee provides prior, knowing, voluntary, and written authorization; or

(ii) the genetic monitoring is required by Federal or State law;

(C) the employee is informed of individual monitoring results;

(D) the monitoring is in compliance with—

(i) any Federal genetic monitoring regulations, including any such regulations that may be promulgated by the Secretary of Labor pursuant to the Occupational Safety and Health Act of 1970 (29 U.S.C. 651 et seq.), the Federal Mine Safety and Health Act of 1977 (30 U.S.C. 801 et seq.), or the

Atomic Energy Act of 1954 (42 U.S.C. 2011 et seq.); or

(ii) State genetic monitoring regulations, in the case of a State that is implementing genetic monitoring regulations under the authority of the Occupational Safety and Health Act of 1970 (29 U.S.C. 651 et seq.); and

(E) the employer, excluding any licensed health care professional or board certified genetic counselor that is involved in the genetic monitoring program, receives the results of the monitoring only in aggregate terms that do not disclose the identity of specific employees; or

(6) where the employer conducts DNA analysis for law enforcement purposes as a forensic laboratory or for purposes of human remains identification, and requests or requires genetic information of such employer's employees, but only to the extent that such genetic information is used for analysis of DNA identification markers for quality control to detect sample contamination.

(c) Preservation of Protections-In the case of information to which any of paragraphs (1) through (6) of subsection (b) applies, such information may not be used in violation of paragraph (1) or (2) of subsection (a) or treated or disclosed in a manner that violates section 206.

* * *

§ 206. CONFIDENTIALITY OF GENETIC INFORMATION.

(a) Treatment of Information as Part of Confidential Medical Record—If an employer, employment agency, labor organization, or joint labor-management committee possesses genetic information about an employee or member, such information shall be maintained on separate forms and in separate medical files and be treated as a confidential medical record of the employee or member. An employer, employment agency, labor organization, or joint labor-management committee shall be considered to be in compliance with the maintenance of information requirements of this subsection with respect to genetic information subject to this subsection that is maintained with and treated as a confidential medical record under section 102(d)(3)(B) of the Americans With Disabilities Act (42 U.S.C. 12112(d)(3)(B)).

(b) Limitation on Disclosure—An employer, employment agency, labor organization, or joint labor-management committee shall not disclose genetic information concerning an employee or member except—

(1) to the employee or member of a labor organization (or family member if the family member is receiving the genetic services) at the written request of the employee or member of such organization;

(2) to an occupational or other health researcher if the research is conducted in compliance with the regulations and protections provided for under part 46 of title 45, Code of Federal Regulations;

(3) in response to an order of a court, except that—

(A) the employer, employment agency, labor organization, or joint labor-management committee may disclose only the genetic information expressly authorized by such order; and

(B) if the court order was secured without the knowledge of the employee or member to whom the information refers, the employer, employment agency, labor organization, or joint labor-management committee shall inform the employee or member of the court order and any genetic information that was disclosed pursuant to such order;

(4) to government officials who are investigating compliance with this title if the information is relevant to the investigation;

(5) to the extent that such disclosure is made in connection with the employee's compliance with the certification provisions of section 103 of the Family and Medical Leave Act of 1993 (29 U.S.C. 2613) or such requirements under State family and medical leave laws; or

(6) to a Federal, State, or local public health agency only with regard to information that is described in section 201(4)(A)(iii) and that concerns a contagious disease that presents an imminent hazard of death or life-threatening illness, and that the employee whose family member or family members is or are the subject of a disclosure under this paragraph is notified of such disclosure.

(c) Relationship to HIPAA Regulations—With respect to the regulations promulgated by the Secretary of Health and Human Services under part C of title XI of the Social Security Act (42 U.S.C. 1320d et seq.) and section 264 of the Health Insurance

Portability and Accountability Act of 1996 (42 U.S.C. 1320d–2 note), this title does not prohibit a covered entity under such regulations from any use or disclosure of health information that is authorized for the covered entity under such regulations. The previous sentence does not affect the authority of such Secretary to modify such regulations.

§ 207. REMEDIES AND ENFORCEMENT.

(a) Employees Covered by Title VII of the Civil Rights Act of 1964—

(1) IN GENERAL—The powers, procedures, and remedies provided in sections 705, 706, 707, 709, 710, and 711 of the Civil Rights Act of 1964 (42 U.S.C. 2000e–4 et seq.) to the Commission, the Attorney General, or any person, alleging a violation of title VII of that Act (42 U.S.C. 2000e et seq.) shall be the powers, procedures, and remedies this title provides to the Commission, the Attorney General, or any person, respectively, alleging an unlawful employment practice in violation of this title against an employee described in section 201(2)(A)(i), except as provided in paragraphs (2) and (3).

(2) COSTS AND FEES—The powers, remedies, and procedures provided in subsections (b) and (c) of section 722 of the Revised Statutes of the United States (42 U.S.C. 1988), shall be powers, remedies, and procedures this title provides to the Commission, the Attorney General, or any person, alleging such a practice.

(3) DAMAGES—The powers, remedies, and procedures provided in section 1977A of the Revised Statutes of the United States (42 U.S.C. 1981a), including the limitations contained in subsection (b)(3) of such section 1977A, shall be powers, remedies, and procedures this title provides to the Commission, the Attorney General, or any person, alleging such a practice (not an employment practice specifically excluded from coverage under section 1977A(a)(1) of the Revised Statutes of the United States).

* * *

(f) Prohibition Against Retaliation—No person shall discriminate against any individual because such individual has opposed any act or practice made unlawful by this title or because such individual made a charge, testified, assisted, or participated in any manner in an investigation, proceeding, or hearing under this title. The remedies and procedures otherwise provided for under this section shall be available to aggrieved individuals with respect to violations of this subsection.

(g) Definition—In this section, the term 'Commission' means the Equal Employment Opportunity Commission.

§ 208. DISPARATE IMPACT.

(a) General Rule—Notwithstanding any other provision of this Act, 'disparate impact', as that term is used in section 703(k) of the Civil Rights Act of 1964 (42 U.S.C. 2000e–2(k)), on the basis of genetic information does not establish a cause of action under this Act.

* * *

§ 209. CONSTRUCTION.

(a) In General—Nothing in this title shall be construed to—

(1) limit the rights or protections of an individual under any other Federal or State statute that provides equal or greater protection to an individual than the rights or protections provided for under this title, including the protections of an individual under the Americans with Disabilities Act of 1990 (42 U.S.C. 12101 et seq.) (including coverage afforded to individuals under section 102 of such Act (42 U.S.C. 12112)), or under the Rehabilitation Act of 1973 (29 U.S.C. 701 et seq.);

* * *

(4) limit or expand the protections, rights, or obligations of employees or employers under applicable workers' compensation laws;

(5) limit the authority of a Federal department or agency to conduct or sponsor occupational or other health research that is conducted in compliance with the regulations contained in part 46 of title 45, Code of Federal Regulations (or any corresponding or similar regulation or rule);

(6) limit the statutory or regulatory authority of the Occupational Safety and Health Administration or the Mine Safety and Health Administration to promulgate or enforce workplace safety and health laws and regulations; or

* * *

(1) with respect to such an individual or family member of an individual who is a pregnant woman, include genetic information of any fetus carried by such pregnant woman; and

(2) with respect to an individual or family member utilizing an assisted reproductive technology, include genetic information of any embryo legally held by the individual or family member.

(c) Relation to Authorities Under Title I—With respect to a group health plan, or a health insurance issuer offering group health insurance coverage in connection with a group health plan, this title does not prohibit any activity of such plan or issuer that is authorized for the plan or issuer under any provision of law referred to in clauses (i) through (iv) of subsection (a)(2)(B).

§ 210. MEDICAL INFORMATION THAT IS NOT GENETIC INFORMATION.

An employer, employment agency, labor organization, or joint labor-management committee shall not be considered to be in violation of this title based on the use, acquisition, or disclosure of medical information that is not genetic information about a manifested disease, disorder, or pathological condition of an employee or member, including a manifested disease, disorder, or pathological condition that has or may have a genetic basis.

§ 211. REGULATIONS.

Not later than 1 year after the date of enactment of this title, the Commission shall issue final regulations to carry out this title.

* * *

§ 213. EFFECTIVE DATE.

This title takes effect on the date that is 18 months after the date of enactment of this Act.

JESSICA L. ROBERTS, PREEMPTING DISCRIMINATION: LESSONS FROM THE GENETIC INFORMATION NONDISCRIMINATION ACT
63 Vand. L. Rev. 439, 440–41 (2010).

Historically, antidiscrimination law has been Janus-like, one face reflecting upon a legacy of discrimination with the other gazing forward to stop discrimination in the future. The four major employment discrimination statutes prior to GINA—Title VII of the Civil Rights Act, the Age Discrimination in Employment Act, the Rehabilitation Act, and the Americans with Disabilities Act—were all retrospective: each looked to discrimination in the past to justify protection in the present and the future.

Conversely, GINA has little upon which to reflect. GINA prohibits health insurers and employers from making decisions based on genetic information. While some examples do exist, both GINA's advocates and adversaries agreed that scant evidence indicated a significant history of genetic-information discrimination. Thus, whereas the preceding laws were retrospective, GINA is *preemptive*. It anticipates a form of discrimination that may pose a future threat. GINA's opponents cited the lack of existing genetic-information discrimination as evidence that the law was premature or unnecessary. Its proponents, however, presented GINA as a unique opportunity to stop discrimination before it starts. It is this preemptive nature, basing protection on future-rather than past or even present-discrimination, that truly makes GINA novel.

Novelty aside, preemptive antidiscrimination legislation has its benefits and its drawbacks. By passing GINA before genetic information discrimination could take hold, Congress may have effectively bypassed a new variety of discriminatory treatment. GINA's ability to preempt discrimination is perhaps its greatest strength. Yet the statute's preemptive qualities carry with them potentially serious hurdles regarding GINA's enforcement and effectiveness.

NOTES AND QUESTIONS

1.   Professor Roberts goes on to note that two main arguments in favor of the legislation were made by proponents of GINA: (1) that fear of discrimination has impeded the ability of researchers to recruit potential research subjects; and (2) the use of genetic information for discrimination is unjust, especially because it involves immutable characteristics over which the individual has no control. The congressional findings section of GINA (section 2(5)), concludes with the reasons for GINA's enactment: "Therefore Federal legislation establishing a national and uniform standard is necessary to fully protect the public from discrimination and allay their concerns about the potential for discrimination, thereby allowing individuals to take advantage of genetic testing, technologies, research, and new therapies."

2.   Is "preemptive" legislation necessary or a good idea? What do you think the major impetus was for enacting GINA?

3.   On the role of immutability, see Sharona Hoffman, The Importance of Immutability in Employment Discrimination Law, 52 Wm. & Mary L. Rev. 1483 (2010–2011).

4.   The implementing regulations promulgated by the EEOC appear at 29 C.F.R. Part 1635.

MARK A. ROTHSTEIN, GINA, THE ADA, AND GENETIC DISCRIMINATION IN EMPLOYMENT

36 J.L. Med. & Ethics 837, 838–839 (2008).

* * *

GINA

Both the health insurance and employment provisions of GINA expressly limit their protections to asymptomatic individuals who have been subjected to adverse treatment based on genetic information. GINA defines "genetic information" as information about an individual's genetic tests, the genetic tests of family members, and the manifestation of a disease or disorder in family members. Of critical importance, GINA provides that it is not unlawful to use, acquire, or disclose medical information "about a manifested disease, disorder, or pathological condition of an employee . . . , including a manifested disease, disorder, or pathological condition that has or may have a genetic basis."

Unfortunately, GINA does not define "a manifested disease, disorder, or pathological condition." GINA instead defines a "genetic test" as "an analysis of human DNA, RNA, chromosomes, proteins, or metabolites, that detects genotypes, mutations, or chromosomal changes." The definition does not include "(1) an analysis of proteins or metabolites that does not detect genotypes, mutations, or chromosomal changes; or (2) an analysis of proteins or metabolites that is directly related to a manifested disease, disorder, or pathological condition that could reasonably be detected by a health care professional with appropriate training and expertise in the field of medicine involved." These definitions do not provide much guidance as to the types of tests considered genetic, let alone when a disease, disorder, or pathological condition is "manifested."

READING THE ADA AND GINA TOGETHER

As illustrated in Figure 1, the coverage of the ADA and GINA are mirror images at the extremes. In the context of genetic discrimination in employment, asymptomatic individuals are unlikely to be covered by the ADA, but they are expressly covered by GINA. Conversely, severely affected individuals are covered by the ADA, but they are expressly not covered by GINA. The greatest uncertainty is in the middle. Under the ADA, an individual with a mild, temporary, or presymptomatic condition does not come within the statutory definition of an individual with a disability. Similarly, under GINA, an individual with a genetically based, biologically determinable difference beyond genotypic variation but short of phenotypic variation is unlikely to be protected.

FIGURE 1
COVERAGE OF GINA AND THE ADA

	ASYMPTOMATIC	BIOMARKERS, ENDOPHENOTYPES, MILD SYMPTOMS	MANIFESTATION OF DISEASE
GINA	Yes	?	No
ADA	No	No	Yes

The problems in interpreting GINA stem from the fact that the law is based on a scientifically dubious dichotomy between genetic and non-genetic information, tests, and disorders. It has been generally acknowledged by scientists for decades that virtually all human disease has both genetic and environmental components. New developments in proteomics, transcriptomics, metabonomics, epigenetics, and other fields have blurred the line between asymptomatic and symptomatic. The various biological processes by which a gene becomes expressed are still being elucidated. Increasingly sensitive biomarkers and sophisticated analyses of endophenotypes add further complexity to disease mechanisms. Regardless of the policy issues implicated by different definitions under GINA, the distinctions drawn in the statute are scientifically untenable today and are likely to be increasingly problematic.

CONCLUSION

The employment discrimination provisions of GINA take effect November 21, 2009, and the EEOC is charged with issuing regulations implementing GINA by May 21, 2009 [29 CFR §§ 1635.1–1635.12]. One of the most important tasks for the EEOC is to devise practical, understandable, and scientifically compelling rules for determining what degree of biological response or symptoms constitutes manifestation of a disease, thereby precluding an individual from coverage by GINA. Under any conceivable definition of "manifestation," however, an individual will be too affected to be covered under GINA long before having a substantial limitation of a major life activity necessary to be covered under the ADA.

NOTES AND QUESTIONS

1. On the issue of "manifestation," the EEOC's GINA regulations provide:

(g) *Manifestation or manifested* means, with respect to a disease, disorder, or pathological condition, that an individual has been or could reasonably be diagnosed with the disease, disorder, or pathological condition by a health care professional with appropriate training and expertise in the field of medicine involved. For purposes of this part, a disease, disorder, or pathological condition is not manifested if the diagnosis is based principally on genetic information.

29 C.F.R. § 1635(g).

2.   Does this definition resolve the "gap" between the ADA and GINA? Can the gap be eliminated through regulation? See Anya E.R. Prince & Benjamin E. Berkman, When Does an Illness Begin: Genetic Discrimination and Disease Manifestation, 40 J.L. Med. & Ethics 655 (2012). Will the need for protection against genetic discrimination lessen over time? See Robert C. Green, Denise Bautenbach & Amy L. McGuire, GINA Genetic Discrimination, and Genomic Medicine, 372 New Eng. J. Med. 397 (2015).

3.   Why do you think the "gap" involving manifestation exists in GINA? Hint: The answer lies in Chapter 15.

4.   Other possible gaps involve emerging technologies such as epigenetics and microbiomics. How should these gaps be resolved?

POORE V. PETERBILT OF VIRGINIA, LLC
852 F.Supp.2d 727 (W.D. Va. 2012).

JAMES P. JONES, District Judge.

In this civil case, the plaintiff alleges in his Complaint that his employer wrongfully terminated him on account of his age and in violation of the Genetic Information Nondiscrimination Act, as well as other claims. The employer has moved to dismiss the counts based on age and genetic information on the ground that the plaintiff fails to state claims upon which relief can be granted. For the following reasons, the motion will be granted in part and denied in part.

The facts, as alleged in the Complaint, and which are accepted for the purposes of the present motion, are as follows.

The plaintiff, Mark Poole, was employed by Peterbilt of Bristol, L.L.C. ("Peterbilt") beginning in May 2005. Throughout his employment, Peterbilt provided health insurance coverage for Poore and his family.

On December 18, 2009, Peterbilt was purchased by new owners. The following month, on January 23, 2010, Peterbilt's office manager asked Poore to complete a health insurance questionnaire regarding his family's general medical conditions and medications. In answering the questionnaire, Poore disclosed that his wife had been diagnosed with multiple sclerosis. On January 26, 2010, Peterbilt's office manager asked Poore when his wife had been diagnosed with multiple sclerosis and inquired about her prognosis. Three days later, Poore was terminated from his position without sufficient explanation. Prior to his termination, there were no complaints about Poore's work performance; in fact, Poore had been told by the new owners that he was doing an outstanding job.

Poore was 50 years old at the time of his termination. He was eventually replaced by a much younger individual with less experience.

As a result of his termination, Poore asserted claims against the defendants for discrimination due to (1) his association with his disabled wife, in violation of the Americans with Disabilities Act ("the ADA"); (2) genetic information collected by the defendants, in violation of the Genetic Information Nondiscrimination Act ("GINA"); (3) his age, in violation of the Age Discrimination in Employment Act ("the ADEA"); and (4) his participation in an employer-sponsored health insurance plan, in violation of the Employee Retirement Income Security Act ("ERISA").

* * *

A.   ADEA CLAIM.

["Poore has stated a valid claim for age discrimination."]

* * *

B.   GINA CLAIM.

Under GINA, it is unlawful for an employer "to fail or refuse to hire, or to discharge, any employee, or otherwise to discriminate against any employee . . . because of genetic information with respect to the employee." 42 U.S.C.A. § 2000ff–1(a) (West Supp.2011) (emphasis added). "Genetic information" is defined under GINA as information about (1) an individual's genetic tests; (2) the genetic tests of family members of an individual; or (3) the manifestation of a disease or disorder in family members of an individual. 42 U.S.C.A. § 2000ff(4) (West Supp.2011). The regulations issued by the Equal Employment Opportunity Commission clarify that the phrase "manifestation of a disease or disorder in family members" refers to an employee's "family medical history," interpreted in accordance with its normal understanding as used by medical providers. 29 C.F.R. § 1635.3(c)(iii) (2011).

The basic intent of GINA is to prohibit employers from making a "predictive assessment concerning an individual's propensity to get an inheritable genetic disease or disorder based on the occurrence of an inheritable disease or disorder in [a] family member." Congress included family medical history in the definition of "genetic information" because it understood that employers could potentially use family medical history "as a surrogate for genetic traits." For instance, a consistent history of an inheritable disease in an individual's family may be viewed to indicate that the individual himself is at an increased risk for that disease. However, the fact that an individual family member merely has been diagnosed with a disease or disorder is not considered "genetic information" if "such information is taken into account only with respect to the individual in which such disease or disorder occurs and not as genetic information with respect to any other individual."

Poore's Complaint fails to state a violation of GINA because the information Poore contends was obtained by Peterbilt does not constitute "genetic information with respect to the employee." Poore simply disclosed that his wife had been diagnosed with multiple sclerosis, and Peterbilt's office manager later inquired about the date of her diagnosis and her prognosis. The fact that Poore's wife was diagnosed with multiple sclerosis has no predictive value with respect to Poore's genetic propensity to acquire the disease. Furthermore, there is no allegation that Peterbilt used Poore's wife's diagnosis to forecast the tendency of any other individual to contract multiple sclerosis—Poore explicitly alleges that he was terminated as a result of "his wife's medical condition and [his] association with her." While he may have a claim for discrimination on the basis of a manifested condition under the ADA, Poore's termination does not constitute discrimination under GINA.

* * *

NOTES AND QUESTIONS

1.   The court in *Poore* relied on the legislative history for its decision, but it needed to look no further than GINA's interpretive regulations. The definition of "family member" excludes spouses, but covers dependents, including those that result from marriage or adoption (i.e., step and adopted children). 29 C.F.R. § 1635.3.

2.   By covering non-biological children the regulations are, seemingly, inconsistent with the refusal to cover spouses. The interpretation of the regulations explains this discrepancy as follows:

> [T]he acquisition of information about the occurrence of a disease or disorder in an applicant's or employee's adopted child could certainly result in the type of discrimination GINA was intended to prohibit. For example, an employer might use information it obtains about the current health status of an adopted child to discriminate against an employee because of concerns over potential health care costs including increased health insurance rates, associated with the family member's medical condition.

EEOC, Regulations under the Genetic Information Nondiscrimination Act of 2008; Final Rule, 75 Fed. Reg. 68912, 68915 (2010). If GINA's protection were to depend on heredity, it could open the door for court-mandated paternity testing or the differential legal treatment of biological and adoptive children.

3.   GINA has resulted in relatively few discrimination complaints. For example, in 2013, the EEOC received 333 GINA charges compared with over 90,000 charges for the other forms of discrimination. It also appears that

most of the GINA charges were "add ons" that followed investigations of other alleged forms of discrimination revealed that the employer inquired into family medical history. From 2010–2013 there were only 34 cases involving GINA; 15 of the cases involved the individual's own health history, which GINA does not cover. One case involved an individual's opinions about genetic information, and another alleged that sexual orientation information was genetic information. That leaves only 17 cases. Two of the cases alleged discrimination based on genetic testing. The other 15 alleged that the employer improperly requested family medical information. See Mark A. Rothstein, Jessica L. Roberts & Tee L. Guidotti, Limiting Occupational Medical Evaluations under the Americans with Disability Act and the Genetic Information Nondiscrimination Act, 41 Am. J.L. & Med. ___ (2015). How, if at all, do these data affect your answer to the earlier question about the utility of preemptive legislation?

4.   Because most of the GINA cases involve employer access to information, it is valuable to consider how the statute and regulations deal with the issue. Section 202(b) deals with an employer's acquisition of genetic information. "It shall be an unlawful employment practice for an employer to request, require or purchase genetic information with respect to an employee or a family member of the employee. . . ." There are several exceptions, including requests as part of the certification provisions of the Family and Medical Leave Act and disclosures in accordance with an employer-sponsored wellness program. Another exception applies "where an employer purchases documents that are commercially and publically available (including newspapers, magazines, periodicals, and books, but not including medical databases or court records) that include family medical history." The commentary in the regulations considers whether an employer's acquisition of genetic information via social media would violate this section. "The determining factor, then, in deciding whether a media source is commercially and publically available is whether access requires permission of an individual or is limited to individuals in a particular group, not whether the source is categorized as a social networking site, personal Web site, or blog." 75 Fed. Reg. at 68925.

CHAPTER 17

ENVIRONMENTAL AND OCCUPATIONAL REGULATION AND PERSONAL INJURY CASES

■ ■ ■

I. INTRODUCTION

Prior chapters have explored the relationship between genetic and environmental factors in human health and development in the context of clinical genetics (Chapters 6–8), pharmacogenomics (Chapter 8), and behavioral genetics (Chapter 13). Another interaction between genetics and the environment with important legal applications involves laws that protect the air, water, earth, wildlife, and food supply from pollutants. Similar issues are raised by laws that attempt to ensure that workers have safe and healthful workplaces. The overarching question is the degree to which human genetic variation should be considered in setting exposure limits and in prescribing other measures to prevent harm. One concern is that an overemphasis on genetic factors will shift the blame from polluters to the "faulty genes" of certain individuals. The regulatory consequences of adopting such an approach could include changing the focus from lowering exposures merely to warning at-risk individuals or, in the workplace setting, excluding them from employment. At the same time, it may simply not be technologically or economically feasible to lower all exposures to levels where the most vulnerable individuals can be exposed without any adverse health effects. It is difficult to decide what ethical and legal principles should be applied in these circumstances, especially when the scientific evidence is incomplete or inconclusive.

Regulatory agencies have begun considering genetic studies, and to a lesser extent epigenetic studies, in assessing the human health risks from environmental and occupational exposures. This chapter will consider the legal significance of developments in toxicogenomics and related avenues of scientific inquiry. In addition to discussing the applicable statutes, the chapter will also consider the admissibility and significance of genetic information proffered by either plaintiffs or defendants in personal injury litigation to prove or disprove exposure, causation, and damages. These legal actions could be based on negligence, strict liability, products liability, or other theories.

II. REGULATION

A. ENVIRONMENTAL

NATIONAL RESEARCH COUNCIL, APPLICATIONS OF
TOXICOGENOMIC TECHNOLOGIES TO PREDICTIVE
TOXICOLOGY AND RISK ASSESSMENT
186–189 (2007).

Toxicogenomic data have numerous potential applications in environmental, pharmaceutical, and occupational health regulation. Regulatory agencies such as the Environmental Protection Agency (EPA) and the [Food and Drug Administration (FDA)] have already produced guidance documents on the incorporation of genomic information into their regulatory programs. Some examples of potential regulatory applications of toxicogenomics and their implications are discussed below.

DEFINING NEW ADVERSE EFFECTS

Many regulatory requirements are based on a finding of "adverse effect." For example, national ambient air-quality standards set under the Clean Air Act are set at a level that protects against adverse effects in susceptible populations. Some subclinical effects (for example, changes in erythrocyte protoporphyrin concentration in blood) have been found to be adverse effects under this statutory provision and have required more stringent standards to prevent such effects from occurring in exposed populations. Furthermore, many EPA regulations for noncarcinogenic substances are based on the reference concentrations (RfC) or reference dose (RfD). Some gene expression or other changes measured with toxicogenomic technologies may constitute new adverse effects under these programs and thus lower RfDs and RfCs, resulting in more stringent regulations. Manufacturers of pesticides and toxic chemicals are required to notify the EPA of new scientific findings about adverse effects associated with their products. In pharmaceutical regulation, the detection of a biomarker that suggests an adverse effect may likewise trigger additional regulatory scrutiny or restrictions.

Therefore, a critical issue in the regulatory application of toxicogenomics will be determining whether and when a change constitutes an adverse effect. Many changes in gene expression, protein levels, and metabolite profiles will be adaptive responses to a stimulus that are not representative or predictive of a toxic response. Other toxicogenomic changes may be strongly indicative of a toxic response. Therefore, it will be important to distinguish true biomarkers of toxicity from reversible or adaptive responses and to do so in a way that is transparent, predictable, and consistent for the affected entities. At least initially, phenotypic anchoring of toxicogenomics changes to well-established toxicologic end points will likely be necessary to identify toxicologically significant markers.

REGULATORY DECISIONS BASED ON SCREENING ASSAYS

The availability of relatively inexpensive and quick toxicogenomics assays that can be used for hazard characterization of otherwise untested materials offers a number of potential regulatory opportunities. Full toxicologic characterization of the approximately 80,000 chemicals in commerce using a battery of traditional toxicology tests (for example, chronic rodent bioassay) is not economically or technologically feasible in the foreseeable future. Screening with a toxicogenomic assay, such as gene expression analysis that classifies agents based on transcript profiles, might be useful to quickly screen chemicals for prioritizing substances for further investigation and possible regulation. Another possibility is to require the manufacturer of a new chemical substance, or an existing substance that will be used in a new application, to include the results of a standardized toxicogenomics assay as part of a premanufacturing notice required under Section 5 of the Toxic Substances Control Act.

PROTECTION OF GENETICALLY SUSCEPTIBLE INDIVIDUALS

Many regulatory programs specifically require protection of susceptible individuals. For example, the Clean Air Act requires that national ambient air-quality standards be set at a level that protects the most susceptible subgroups within the population. Under this program, the EPA focuses its standard-setting activities on susceptible subgroups such as children with asthma. Recent studies indicate a significant genetic role in susceptibility to air pollution, which may lead to air-quality standards being based on the risks to genetically susceptible individuals. Regulations under other environmental statutes, such as pesticide regulations under the Food Quality Protection Act and drinking water standards under the Safe Drinking Water Act, may likewise focus on genetically susceptible individuals in the future, as might occupational exposure standards promulgated by the Occupational Safety and Health Administration. Likewise, pharmaceutical approvals may require considering and protecting individuals with genetic susceptibilities to a particular drug.

The identification of genetic susceptibilities to chemicals, consumer products, pharmaceuticals, and other materials raises a number of regulatory issues. One issue is the question of the feasibility of protecting genetically susceptible individuals. On the one hand, protecting the most susceptible individual in society may be extremely costly, and perhaps even infeasible without major, formidable changes in our industrial society. On the other hand, the concept of government regulators leaving the health of some individuals unprotected, who through no fault of their own are born with a susceptibility to a particular product or chemical, also seems politically and ethically infeasible. As more information on individual genetic susceptibility becomes available, regulators and society generally will confront difficult challenges in deciding whether and how to protect the most genetically vulnerable citizens in our midst.

GARY E. MARCHANT, TOXICOGENOMICS AND ENVIRONMENTAL REGULATION, IN GENOMICS AND ENVIRONMENTAL REGULATION: SCIENCE, ETHICS, AND LAW
11–14 (Richard R. Sharp, Gary E. Marchant & Jamie A. Grodsky eds. 2008).

Major uncertainties and data gaps limit the utility and credibility of risk assessment for informing regulatory decisions. These uncertainties include extrapolating results from animals to humans and from high-dose to more typical low-dose human exposures, understanding the mechanism of action of a toxicant and its implications for risk assessment, determining the shape of the dose-response curve, and estimating the exposure levels for actual human populations. Gene expression data have the potential to help address many of these unknowns.

Toxicogenomic data can improve risk assessment in several ways. First, gene expression data, by providing a characteristic "fingerprint" of different toxicological mechanisms, can be used to characterize the mechanism or mode of action of a toxicant. Regulatory agencies such as the U.S. Environmental Protection Agency (EPA) have recently focused on mode of action as a key factor in risk assessment, because this information is critical for addressing the issues raised above and for deciding whether an agent is likely to exhibit a threshold below which there is no significant toxicity. As noted in EPA's 2002 Interim Policy on Genomics, toxicogenomics will "likely provide a better understanding of the mechanism or mode of action of a stressor and thus assist in predictive toxicology, in the screening of stressors, and in the design of monitoring activities and exposure studies."

Second, gene expression will be useful in extrapolating results obtained in animal and epidemiology studies that typically involve higher dose levels than those more relevant for the general human population. Until now, low-dose effects have generally been refractory to empirical analysis, and risk assessors have had to rely on models to extrapolate results from high to low dose levels. A finding that gene expression changes characteristic of the carcinogenic response of a particular agent at high doses are also observed in low-dose groups, even though those low-dose animals may not develop tumors, may indicate that low-dose exposures present a carcinogenic risk in large populations. Alternatively, the absence of any characteristic gene expression response in low-dose animals may suggest that the carcinogenetic response occurs only at high doses.

Third, gene expression patterns may help to assess the relevance of animal studies for humans. Most toxicology data comes from animal studies, which are often but not always relevant to humans. By providing a quick and inexpensive test of whether a chemical is causing a similar response in rodents and humans, gene expression assays can help prevent false positives for chemicals that cause toxicity in rodents but not in humans and false negatives for chemicals that cause toxicity in humans but not rodents.

Fourth, gene expression data may also be beneficial for exposure assessment. Many types of environmental exposures lack adequate exposure data, which severely limits the ability to accurately determine the relationship between dose and response that underlies risk-assessment estimates. By characterizing gene expression patterns in exposed persons, microarrays have the potential to provide more precise quantitative estimates of exposure to specific toxic substances in contemporaneous and prospective human studies.

Fifth, gene expression profiling may be particularly useful for evaluating the toxicity of chemical mixtures, which is difficult to do with traditional chemical-by-chemical toxicological methods. DNA microarrays permit the simultaneous monitoring of all gene expression changes within a cell in a single experiment, thus they are "particularly suitable to evaluate any kind of combinational effect resulting from combined exposure to toxicants."

These potential applications of gene expression data may help reduce many of the most important uncertainties in risk assessment, although by no means eliminating such uncertainties altogether. The effect may be to give risk regulation greater credibility and certainty, which will allow environmental regulation to more directly target the most serious risks to human health and the environment.

HIGH-THROUGHPUT TOXICITY SCREENING OF CHEMICALS

The majority of chemicals in commercial use in the United States have not been comprehensively tested for human toxicity and carcinogenicity potential. EPA and the chemical industry have begun to address this data gap for chemical risk assessment with the high-production volume (HPV) chemical testing initiative. However, given that there are now some 80,000 chemicals in commerce, it is not feasible to conduct full toxicological testing for all or even most of these chemicals using existing methods. As the then-director of the National Institute of Environmental Health Sciences testified to Congress in 2002, many commercial products require additional testing, but "we can never satisfy this testing requirement using traditional technologies."

Gene expression assays have the potential to provide rapid, inexpensive, and high-throughput screening of chemicals for a wide range of genotoxic and nongenotoxic responses. Microarrays can be used to interrogate the gene expression of cells either in tissue culture or in living laboratory animals that have been treated with putative toxic agents. The resulting gene expression profiles can be used to classify those chemicals in specific toxicological categories to characterize likely risks. In addition to their relatively low cost and rapid results, microarrays offer possible advantages as a screening assay. Microassays can monitor changes in the expression of all genes within a cell, potentially permitting simultaneous evaluation of all toxicological endpoints in a single assay, something that is not possible with traditional toxicological technologies. In addition, microassays allow a more sensitive assay of potential toxicity, because they test for the initial molecular events in a toxic response. This is more sensitive than other assay methods that tend to monitor clinical effects that do not occur until much later in the disease process.

Initially, gene expression assays will need to be conducted in association with traditional toxicity testing until a sufficiently robust and validated data set has been accumulated to reliably correlate specific gene expression profiles with particular toxicological mechanisms and endpoints. Used in conjunction with traditional toxicology tests, gene expression data have the potential to improve the sensitivity and interoperability of the standard tests. After an adequate relational database has been established, gene expression assays might replace some or all of the current toxicological screening and testing assays or at least select the specific assays indicated by the observed gene expression pattern.

NOTES AND QUESTIONS

1.   Toxicogenomics is defined as the application of genomic technologies to study the adverse effects of environmental and pharmaceutical chemicals on human health and the environment. National Research Council, Applications of Toxicogenomic Technologies to Predictive Toxicology and Risk Assessment 12 (2007).

2.   There are thousands of commonly used industrial and consumer chemicals that could have toxicogenomic-mediated adverse effects on human health. A possible strategy to protect individuals is to issue warnings, perhaps because of regulatory requirements or the desire to limit tort liability. Imagine the shelves of the neighborhood grocery or hardware store, with numerous products containing genotype-specific warnings about exposures and harms. How helpful do you think this information would be? Might there be harms from such warnings?

3.   One likely effect of toxicogenomics is to increase the amount of individual genomic information. Refer back to Chapter 14. What risks to

privacy are raised by this additional information? How, if at all, would you protect against the adverse uses and effects?

MARK A. ROTHSTEIN, YU CAI & GARY E. MARCHANT, ETHICAL IMPLICATIONS OF EPIGENETICS RESEARCH
10 Nature Revs. Genetics 224 (2009).

* * *

First we consider environmental justice. Epigenetic effects have been associated with exposure to various toxic chemicals, airborne pollutants, pesticides and other harmful substances. Many of these exposures are linked with poverty, discriminatory land use, and substandard living and working conditions. At the same time, many individuals with these harmful exposures are considered medically vulnerable because of pre-existing health conditions that are frequently complicated by poor clinical management. Both the exposure to environmental hazards and the social, nutritional, medical and psychological stresses of low-income communities can separately and, perhaps even more importantly, cumulatively cause epigenetic changes that place exposed populations at increased risk. Epigenetics therefore provides a new window for understanding and possibly addressing the co-morbidities associated with disparate environmental exposures.

The second issue regards the intergenerational effects and equity of epigenetics research. A key implication of epigenetics research is that many environmental and hazardous exposures will affect not only the exposed individuals, but possibly their progeny and subsequent generations. This insight will create new challenges for environmental and health regulation, as well as for intergenerational equity. Intergenerational equity refers to the obligations of each generation to serve as a custodian or steward of the planet and its inhabitants for future generations. Thus, it could be asserted that each generation has an obligation to its decendants not to damage the genomes and epigenomes of future generations, such as through exposure to environmental hazards. It remains to be seen whether or how the possible transgenerational damage caused by environmentally induced epigenetic changes will affect environmental regulatory policies.

* * *

Some of the ethical concerns discussed above are similar to those already raised by genetics, but the role of environmental exposures in producing epigenetic effects adds new concerns. The use of epigenetics in environmental risk assessment will probably be among the first applications of the new research. Once epigenetic testing of individuals becomes available, concerns are likely to arise about possible privacy violations and epigenetic discrimination. The prospect of such non-genetic discrimination casts doubt on the wisdom and efficacy of current genetic-specific laws, and it suggests that broader laws are needed to prohibit adverse treatment on the basis of health status or biological markers.

Epigenetic research raises other profound issues, including individual and societal responsibilities to prevent hazardous exposures, monitor health status and provide treatment. Epigenetics also serves to highlight the effects of inequality in living and working conditions and adds a multigenerational dimension to environmentally caused adverse health effects.

NOTES AND QUESTIONS

1.   As discussed in Chapter 3, epigenetics literally means "above the genes." It refers to modifications of the genome that do not involve a change in the DNA sequence. The recent understanding of epigenetic processes stands in contrast to the traditional assumption that genetic variation was exclusively the result of changes in DNA sequence. Epigenetic changes or "marks" result from a wide range of environmental exposures, including diet, toxic substances, and environmental stressors. Epigenetic changes tend to occur at much higher rates than mutations in DNA sequences from similar exposures. Susceptibility is not only a function of dose, but also of the stage of development when exposure takes place, such as prenatal and neonatal exposure. Whereas genetic mutations tend to be irreversible, epigenetic changes can be reversed. How, if at all, should these factors influence legal regulation of substances causing epigenetic changes?

2.   A distinctive feature of epigenetics, especially changes resulting from the process of methylation, is that the effects may persist in future generations despite the lack of DNA sequence modification. Thus, parental exposures (e.g., to diesel exhaust fumes) may be expressed not only in the exposed generation in the form of respiratory disease, but in future generations as well. The issue of intergenerational equity raised in the article excerpt has been applied in the context of various environmental hazards, such as nuclear waste disposal, climate change, and extinction of species of plants and animals. Do you think the present generation is the steward of the genomes and epigenomes of future generations? If so, how can such an abstract concern be implemented in laws?

3.   There are many unresolved scientific questions surrounding epigenetics that will have significant effects on social policy. For example: How many substances and environmental conditions cause epigenetic effects, at what exposure levels, and at what time during human development? Are there predispositions that make certain individuals more susceptible to epigenetic changes? When will tests be commonly available to measure epigenetic effects? When will therapies be available to reverse epigenetic effects? Is it possible to regulate in the absence of answers to these questions?

4.   For further discussion, see Mark A. Rothstein, Yu Cai & Gary E. Marchant, The Ghost in Our Genes: Legal and Ethical Implications of Epigenetics, 19 Health Matrix 1 (2009).

B. OCCUPATIONAL

MARK A. ROTHSTEIN, OCCUPATIONAL HEALTH AND DISCRIMINATION ISSUES RAISED BY TOXICOGENOMICS IN THE WORKPLACE IN GENOMICS AND ENVIRONMENTAL REGULATION: SCIENCE, ETHICS, AND LAW
184–188 (Richard R. Sharp, Gary E. Marchant & Jamie A. Grodsky eds. 2008).

The Occupational Safety and Health Act of 1970 is the primary federal law regulating worker safety and health. The OSH Act covers employment in every state and territory—an estimated six million workplaces and ninety million employees. Unlike many labor and unemployment laws, there is no minimum number of employees or dollar volume of business needed for coverage. The OSH Act applies to all employers engaged in a business affecting interstate commerce—an easy standard to satisfy.

Among other requirements, each covered employer must comply with two provisions of the statute. First, section 5(a)(1) requires each covered employer to keep its workplace free from recognized hazards that are causing or likely to cause death or serious physical harm to its employees. Second, section 5(a)(2) requires each covered employer to comply with occupational safety and health standards promulgated by the Occupational Safety and Health Administration (OSHA) of the U.S. Department of Labor. The failure to comply with these requirements may result in the assessment of a range of civil penalties depending on the nature and gravity of the violation as well as on other factors.

STANDARD SETTING

Section 6 of the statute provides for the promulgation of standards in three ways. First, under section 6(a) the secretary of labor was authorized from 1971 to 1973 to adopt as OSHA standards, without rulemaking procedures, two types of existing standards—national consensus standards (developed by private organizations) and established federal standards (promulgated under other federal laws). This provision was designed to ensure the existence of OSHA standards soon after the effective date of the OSH Act in 1971, by adopting standards with which industry already was familiar. Second, under section 6(b), the secretary may modify, revoke, or issue new standards by complying with detailed rule-making procedures. This is the most important standards promulgation provision for new health standards. Third, under section 6(c), the secretary may issue emergency temporary standards in extraordinary circumstances, which may remain in effect for up to six months. Because standards promulgated under this provision have been difficult to sustain on judicial review, it has been rarely used.

Occupational safety and health standards generally have not been developed with an explicit concern for individual variability in response to toxic substances. Although such standards are designed to provide the maximum protection possible, OSHA has recognized that it may not be possible to protect workers with heightened sensitivity. For example, the preamble to the coke oven emissions standard provides: "Because of the variability of individual response to carcinogens and other factors, the concept of a 'threshold level' may have little applicability on the basis of existing knowledge. Some individuals may be more susceptible than others. Thus, while a 'threshold' exposure level, below which exposure does not cause cancer, may conceivably exist for an individual, susceptible individuals in the working population may have cancer induced by doses so low as to be effectively zero." New toxicogenomic studies will identify an increasing number of substances for which a particular genotype confers greater risk of illness based on occupational exposures. OSHA will need to decide if, or to what extent, individual variability should be incorporated into the agency's standards promulgation strategy.

As an initial matter, it is necessary to consider OSHA's statutory authority to promulgate health standards and the judicial construction of the exercise of that authority. Section 6(b)(5) of the OSH Act, which deals with the promulgation of standards for toxic substances and harmful physical agents, provides in part: "The Secretary of Labor shall set the standard which most adequately assures, to the extent feasible. . . . that no employee will suffer material impairment of health." This seemingly absolute language might be read as requiring OSHA to set standards at a level where even the most sensitive employee could work without ill effects. However, in *Industrial Union Department, AFL-CIO v. American Petroleum Institute* (1980)—also known as the *Benzene* decision—the Supreme Court rejected the notion that the OSH Act requires regulation at the level of zero risk.

The *Benzene* decision involved an industry challenge to OSHA rulemaking that lowered the permissible exposure limit for benzene from 10 parts per million to 1 part per million. In striking down the benzene standard, the Fifth Circuit held that, based on section 3(5) of the OSH Act, the secretary was required to prove that the benefits of the standard bear a reasonable relationship to the costs. The Supreme Court affirmed, but on different grounds. According to the plurality opinion, the secretary must initially demonstrate the need for a new standard by establishing that exposure at current levels poses a "significant risk" of harm. Because the secretary failed to make this finding, the benzene standard was struck down. The Court also cautioned that the duty imposed on employers by the statute was not absolute. "The statute was not designed to require employers to provide absolutely risk-free workplaces whenever it is technologically feasible to do so . . . [but] was intended to require the elimination, as far as feasible, of significant risks of harm."

Although the Supreme Court never explicitly stated whether the OSH Act requires employers to set exposure levels that would protect the most sensitive workers, *Benzene* implicitly holds that it does not. OSHA standards for toxic substances could be set to avoid requiring absolute levels of protection in two main ways: they could be limited to control measures that are economically and technologically feasible, or they could establish permissible exposure levels that would not protect the most sensitive workers. Although these appear to be distinct concepts, as a scientific and practical matter, they are closely related. Figure 11.1 plots a hypothetical linear dose-response curve.

As the dose increases (along the horizontal axis), the percentage of affected workers increases (along the vertical axis), and as the percentage of workers increases, even less sensitive individuals will exhibit the biological response. The lowest feasible level for reducing exposure is indicated by f. The intersection of f with the dose-response line, point 0, results in setting the susceptibility cutoff at s. Consequently, a standard lowering exposures only to the *Benzene* requirement of feasibility will necessarily result in a lack of protection for some of the most susceptible workers.

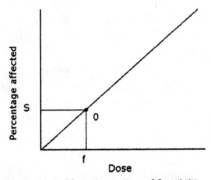

Figure 11.1. The intersection of feasibility
and susceptibility in dose-response analysis

NOTES AND QUESTIONS

1.   The *Benzene* case implicitly acknowledges it is impossible to protect the most sensitive workers from adverse health effects caused by occupational exposures. If Congress or the Supreme Court were to make this principle more explicit, what would it say? What would be the likely public reaction?

2.   The *Benzene* case fills 118 pages of the U.S. Reports—an indication of the complexity of the issues and the divisions within the Court. Toxicogenomics is likely to make the scientific issues even more complicated. Is judicial review of regulatory action now beyond the technical competence of the judiciary? Are there alternatives?

3.   In American Textile Mfrs. Institute, Inc. v. Donovan, 452 U.S. 490 (1981), the Supreme Court rejected the industry argument that the OSH Act requires the use of cost-benefit analysis. Relying on the plain meaning of the word "feasible" in § 6(b)(5) as "capable of being done," the Court held that imposing a cost-benefit requirement would be inconsistent with the mandate of Congress.

MARK A. ROTHSTEIN, GENETICS AND THE WORK FORCE OF THE NEXT HUNDRED YEARS
2000 Colum. Bus. L. Rev. 371, 393–95 (2000).

Autonomy and paternalism conflict in the area of genetic predisposition to occupational disease. Should workers be screened for polymorphic markers of varied sensitivity to toxic chemicals and other hazards in some workplaces? One view is that workers should not be screened; instead, the employer should be required to make the workplace safe and healthful for all workers. The problem is that reducing exposures to levels where even the most sensitive individual can work safely is neither technologically nor economically feasible because of the wide variability among individuals and because the difficulty and cost of reducing exposure levels increases exponentially as exposures are reduced to very low levels. The opposite view is that employers should be free to use genetic screening as a way of protecting the health of employees and their own financial interests. This approach, however, shifts the economic burden of working with dangerous substances from the employer to the worker, removes an important incentive to clean up workplaces for the benefit of even "low-risk" workers, and runs counter to the notion of autonomy embraced in *Johnson Controls* as well as the ADA.

[In International Union, UAW v. Johnson Controls, Inc., 499 U.S. 187 (1991), the Supreme Court held that the employer's rule prohibiting assignment of any fertile women to work with exposure to lead (which may cause in utero birth defects to the fetus of a pregnant woman employee) was sex discrimination because women have the right to decide which risks to their reproductive health are acceptable.]

A middle position is that a worker who is currently capable of performing the job should have the option of learning whether he or she is at increased risk of occupational disease based on genetic factors. This information should not be available to the employer, but should be used by the employee in deciding whether to accept or continue in the position. A threshold issue is whether a scientific test has sufficient analytical and clinical utility to be used as a screening device for individuals, as opposed to a research tool for population studies. Another issue is what criteria should be used in evaluating whether there is scientific justification for the individual to avoid a job with a certain exposure. Finally, other logistical questions include how individuals get referred for genetic testing, who pays for the testing, and who has access to test results.

In my view, where employers know or should know that research has identified genetic markers of increased risk based on exposure to substances in their workplace, they have a duty to inform applicants and employees. The applicants and employees then should have the option of undergoing genetic testing at the employer's expense, administered by a physician of the applicant's or employee's choosing, with the results available only to the individual. If the test is positive, the physician or a genetic counselor should discuss the risks of employment with the individual. The choice of whether to accept or continue in the job would rest with the individual. Only where employment of an individual would create a direct, immediate, and severe risk of harm to self, others, or property would the employer be justified in performing its own testing and excluding the individual from employment. These situations are likely to be rare.

NOTES AND QUESTIONS

1.   Section 202(b)(5) of GINA, provides that it is not unlawful for an employer to offer employees voluntary genetic monitoring to determine whether prior occupational exposures have caused genetic changes. GINA does not permit employers to offer new employees and those initially being assigned to work where there are certain exposures voluntary genetic screening to assess whether they are at increased risk from occupational exposures. Would you favor extending the exception to pre-exposure genetic screening?

2.   One of the first applications of toxicogenomic testing in the workplace involves occupational exposure to beryllium, a lightweight metal widely used in aircraft components, nuclear weapons, and a variety of industrial products. Exposure to beryllium can result in chronic beryllium disease (CBD), a serious respiratory condition. Individuals with a particular genetic marker, HLA–DPB1–Glu69, have been shown to be at an increased risk of CBD. At least two employers have used voluntary genetic screening for new workers, who could elect to undergo testing at no cost by an independent laboratory, with individual results not reported to the employer. Such efforts at genetic screening have raised a variety of scientific, ethical, and legal issues, many of them stemming from the low positive predictive value of the test. For a further discussion, see Ken Silver & Richard R. Sharp, Ethical Considerations in Testing Workers for the -Glu69 Marker of Genetic

Susceptibility to Chronic Beryllium Disease, 48 J. Occup. & Envtl. Med. 434 (2006).

GENETIC TESTING FOR SUSCEPTIBILITY TO CARPAL TUNNEL SYNDROME

Burlington Northern Santa Fe Railroad (BNSF) is the nation's second largest railroad company. The railroad operates 33,500 route miles of track covering 28 states and two Canadian provinces. In March 2000, BNSF began a pilot program that included genetic testing for employees who claimed work-related carpal tunnel disease. Rail industry safety rules and negotiated union contracts allow BNSF to require employees to undergo medical examinations to evaluate work-related injury claims. Since the initiation of the new policy, approximately 125 of its 40,000 active employees filed claims for carpal tunnel-related injuries. Of those 125, genetic testing was performed on 23 employees. None of the employees was told that the blood sample they were giving was being sent to a research laboratory for genetic analysis.

BNSF's practice of requiring genetic tests came to the attention of the Equal Employment Opportunity Commission (EEOC) when Janice Avary, a registered nurse and wife of a BNSF employee, began looking into the reason why BNSF was requiring her husband to submit seven vials of blood after he filed a claim for a carpal tunnel injury. Avary was concerned that her husband was asked to furnish such a large amount of blood and that he was not instructed to fast to ensure accurate results, as is typical when blood tests are taken. Two days before the scheduled exam, Avary called the company to ask for an explanation and to get a list of the lab tests that her husband would undergo. When the company's medical liaison mentioned possible genetic tests, Avary became alarmed. She called the railroad's headquarters to inform them that they could not subject her husband to a genetic test without his permission (under Iowa state law). According to Avary, BNSF told her that if her husband refused the exam, he could face an investigation for insubordination.

As a result of this experience, Gary Avary filed a complaint with the EEOC. Soon after, five more workers told the EEOC that they had given blood during the medical exams but were unaware of its ultimate use. While the union and the EEOC were investigating the claims against BNSF, Gary Avary received a disciplinary letter from BNSF as a result of his failure to comply with the examination. In response to this letter and to BNSF's practice of requiring genetic testing, on February 9, 2001, EEOC filed its first court action challenging genetic testing. EEOC v. Burlington Northern Santa Fe R.R. Co., No. C01–4013 (N.D. Iowa, filed Feb. 9, 2001). In its petition, the EEOC asked for a preliminary injunction against BNSF requiring the company to end genetic testing of employees who have filed claims for work-related injuries based on carpal tunnel syndrome. The EEOC alleged that the employees were unaware that they were submitting to a genetic test and further, that they were not asked to consent to such a test. The EEOC asked the court to order the railroad to end its nationwide policy of requiring employees who have submitted claims of work-related carpal tunnel syndrome to provide blood samples which are then used for a genetic DNA test for a chromosome 17 deletion associated with hereditary pressure palsy neuropathy, a rare condition which may predict some forms of carpal tunnel syndrome. For a discussion of the scientific basis of the genetic testing, see Paul A. Schulte & Geoffrey Lomax, Assessment of the Scientific Basis for Genetic Testing of Railroad Workers with Carpal Tunnel Syndrome, 45 J. Occup. & Envt'l Med. 592 (2003).

The EEOC also sought to halt any disciplinary action or termination of an employee who has refused to submit a blood sample. The EEOC claimed that the genetic testing violated the Americans with Disabilities Act (ADA) because it is not job-related or consistent with business necessity. Section 102 (d)(4) of the ADA provides that any medical examinations or inquiries of current employees must be either voluntary or job-related and consistent with business necessity, meaning that they measure the ability to perform the job safely and efficiently. EEOC's position was that the unproven test was not job-related. On February 12, 2001, BNSF announced that it would suspend its practice of requiring genetic testing, and a settlement agreement was approved by the court on April 18, 2001.

The *Burlington Northern* case generated a substantial amount of publicity. It was widely reported as the first action brought by the EEOC alleging genetic discrimination. Part of the publicity may be attributable to the fact that the case arose within days of the joint publication in *Nature* and *Science* of the completed draft sequence of the human genome. Thus, it provided the counterpoint for the scientific marvel—the possibility that genetics could result in discrimination. Yet, it is arguable that the case has little to do with genetics. What ADA and common law legal theories could be asserted by the EEOC and individual plaintiffs? How strong a case is this? What is the central ethical issue surrounding this incident?

Burlington Northern and Norman Bloodsaw v. Lawrence Berkeley Lab., 135 F.3d 1260 (9th Cir. 1998) (holding nonconsensual sickle cell testing violated Title VII) were the two genetic discrimination cases relied on by Congress to demonstrate the need to enact GINA. See Jessica L. Roberts, Preempting Discrimination: Lessons from the Genetic Information Nondiscrimination Act, 63 Vand. L. Rev. 439 (2010).

III. LITIGATION

A. INJURY

BRYSON V. PILLSBURY CO.

573 N.W.2d 718 (Minn.Ct.App.1998).

KALITOWSKI, J.

Appellant Nora Bryson challenges the district court's grant of summary judgment in favor of respondents Pillsbury Company, et al., arguing the district court erred because: (1) Bryson submitted evidence that raised a genuine issue of material fact as to whether she suffered a present injury; and (2) Bryson presented sufficient evidence to establish her claim for damages based on her alleged increased risk of developing cancer.

FACTS

Appellant Nora Bryson boarded her horse at the farm of an individual who, like Bryson, was an employee of respondent Pillsbury's subsidiary, Green Giant (company). On July 23, 1990, Bryson discovered that her horse had fallen into a pit filled with water from a storm. The pit, which was 20 feet by 20 feet with a 17-foot depth, had allegedly been used by the company to dispose of waste. Bryson entered the pit in an attempt to rescue the horse and, while in the pit, observed what she believed to be Captan-treated seeds floating in the water. Captan is a chemical treatment for seed that protects it from insects in the soil until germination.

Bryson and others succeeded in getting the horse out of the water. Later that day, Bryson broke out in a rash that covered her body. She presented evidence that she has subsequently developed additional rashes. Bryson, through her expert from the University of Minnesota, presented evidence that she suffered extensive chromosome breakage as a result of exposure to Captan and that, because of the chromosome breakage, she has an increased risk of developing cancer. The company made a motion for summary judgment arguing: (1) Bryson assumed the risk of harm by not leaving the pit when she saw the Captan-treated seeds; and (2) Bryson's alleged damages were too speculative. The district court denied the company's summary judgment motion on assumption of risk, but granted summary judgment in favor of the company stating that Bryson suffered no present injury and concluding that her claimed damages for future harm were too speculative as a matter of law.

ISSUES

1. Did Bryson present sufficient evidence to support her claim of a present injury?

2.   Did Bryson present sufficient evidence to support her claim for damages based on her alleged increased risk of developing cancer?

ANALYSIS

* * *

Bryson contends the district court erred in granting summary judgment, claiming she presented sufficient evidence to raise a genuine fact issue as to whether her chromosome damage constituted a present injury. The company asserts that because Bryson's claimed chromosome damage is asymptomatic, it does not constitute a legally compensable present injury. In a memorandum supporting its order for summary judgment, the district court, without reference to Bryson's allegations regarding present damages, stated: "In this matter there are no present injuries * * *." We conclude the district court erred by granting summary judgment where there is a genuine issue of disputed material fact regarding whether there was a present injury.

In Werlein v. United States, 746 F.Supp. 887, 901 (D.Minn.1990), vacated in part on other grounds, 793 F.Supp. 898 (D.Minn.1992), the United States District Court addressed a case in which the plaintiffs claimed that exposure to contaminated air and drinking water resulted in chromosome damage. The defendants argued that the plaintiffs did not suffer a present injury. In denying the defendants' summary judgment motion, the court in *Werlein* stated that it could not

> rule as a matter of law that plaintiffs' alleged injuries are not "real" simply because they are subcellular. The effect of volatile organic compounds on the human body is a subtle, complex matter. It is for the trier of fact, aided by expert testimony, to determine whether plaintiffs have suffered present harm.

The asymptomatic, subcellular damages claimed in *Werlein* are similar to the injury claimed by Bryson. Here Bryson's expert witness presented evidence that Bryson's exposure to Captan resulted in chromosome breakage, and that such breakage is a "real and present physical and biologic injury." This testimony was disputed by the company, whose expert testified that

> an elevated number of chromosome aberrations are not considered an "injury" per se because they do not in and of themselves result in any physical impairment.

Following the reasoning of *Werlein,* we conclude the trier of fact should resolve this fact dispute.

Further, like the plaintiffs in *Werlein,* Bryson claims emotional distress damages and medical monitoring expenses because of her alleged chromosome damage. The court in *Werlein* determined that the existence and extent of these alleged damages also presented fact questions for the jury. Again, following *Werlein*, we conclude that because there are genuine fact issues concerning the existence of Bryson's present injuries and damages, summary judgment on this claim is inappropriate.

Bryson next argues that because she has offered expert evidence that she has a present injury, she need only present evidence that is "fair comment" on the medical implications of chromosome breakage to establish future damages resulting from her increased risk of cancer. Alternatively, Bryson argues that she has presented sufficient evidence to a reasonable medical certainty that entitles her to compensation for future damages as a result of her increased risk of cancer. The district court concluded that because Bryson can neither prove that her increased risk of future harm is more likely than not to occur, nor quantify her increased risk of developing cancer, her claimed damages for increased risk of future harm are too speculative as a matter of law. We agree.

A plaintiff must prove every element of a claim by a preponderance of the evidence. For Bryson to establish her claim for future damages, she must show: (1) that the future harm is more likely than not to occur; and (2) that her future damages are not too speculative. Bryson failed to present evidence on both issues.

We disagree with Bryson's contention that she need only present evidence that is "fair comment" on the medical implications of chromosome breakage. The term "fair comment" has been used to characterize expert medical testimony for purposes of determining the admissibility of evidence, not to provide the standard for proving future injury. Here, Bryson's expert admitted that Bryson's increased risk of cancer could not be measured or quantified. Thus, the evidence presented by Bryson does not, as a matter of law, permit a factfinder to determine that Bryson is more likely than not to develop cancer.

Further, this court [has] affirmed the principle that plaintiffs may not recover damages that are too speculative. The determination of whether damages are too speculative or remote "should usually be left to the judgment of the trial court." Because Bryson has presented no evidence to quantify her risk of developing cancer, we conclude the district court properly granted summary judgment in favor of the company on Bryson's claim for future damages.

DECISION

The district court properly granted summary judgment in favor of the company on Bryson's claim for damages based on an alleged increased risk of future harm because: (1) Bryson has not presented evidence that it is more likely than not that she will develop cancer; and (2) Bryson's claimed damages for the increased risk of cancer are too speculative as a matter of law. We conclude, however, Bryson has presented sufficient evidence to establish a genuine issue of material fact concerning the existence of a present injury and damages as a result of the alleged injury. We, therefore, reverse and remand this claim for further proceedings.

Affirmed in part, reversed in part, and remanded; motion to strike denied.

SHORT, J. (concurring in part, dissenting in part).

I concur insofar as the majority concludes the trial court properly granted summary judgment in favor of Pillsbury Company on Bryson's "risk of cancer" claim. I respectfully dissent on the narrow remand concerning Bryson's "chromosome breakage" claim because there is no evidence supporting an award of damages for present physical injury. Mere allegations of emotional distress and possible medical monitoring expenses are insufficient to create a fact issue on whether Bryson now suffers from a present physical injury.

Even if an asymptomatic chromosome condition constitutes evidence of a present physical injury, Bryson also failed to offer any evidence that her alleged damages are capable of proof to a reasonable certainty. Under these circumstances, Bryson has no compensable injury and Pillsbury Company is entitled to judgment as a matter of law. I would affirm the trial court's grant of summary judgment.

NOTES AND QUESTIONS

1.   How can biomarkers of a genetic, unexpressed or preclinical "injury" help to prove causation and to establish a compensable harm?

The power of biomarkers to validate latent risk claims is demonstrated by the following hypothetical. A young woman is exposed to vinyl chloride emitted by a nearby factory. A blood test reveals the presence of DNA adducts in her lymphocytes that are consistent with a significant recent exposure to vinyl chloride. Two years later, the woman has a son with a mutation that inactivates ("knocks out") one of his two copies of the *p53* tumor suppressor gene. The mutation has the "genetic fingerprint" that is characteristic of vinyl chloride. Genetic testing of the mother reveals that most of her cells contain no such mutation, although a few of her cells have similar mutations. Moreover, other sequence variations in the mother's *p53* genes confirm that the son's defective copy of the gene came from the mother, thus indicating that the mutation must have arisen in the mother's germ cells. With only one functioning copy of the *p53* gene, the son is at a permanent, significantly increased risk of cancer. A mutation to the remaining functional copy of the *p53* gene, arising either spontaneously or from some other exposure later in life, would almost certainly result in cancer. By providing objective and specific evidence of an increased risk and the probable cause of such risk, the genetic biomarker strengthens the case for such a plaintiff to recover damages for his permanent and irreversible risk.

Gary E. Marchant, Genetic Susceptibility and Biomarkers in Toxic Injury Litigation, 41 Jurimetrics 67, 87 (2000). See also Jamie A. Grodsky, Genomics and Toxic Torts: Dismantling the Risk-Injury Divide, 59 Stan. L. Rev. 1671 (2007); Gary E. Marchant, Genetic Data in Toxic Tort Litigation, 14 J.L. & Pol'y 7 (2006).

2.   Is subclinical damage compensable, either by itself or because it signifies increased risk? In general, the courts have not been receptive to such claims based on products liability, see In re Rezulin Products Liability Litigation, 361 F. Supp.2d 268 (S.D.N.Y. 2005), or emotional distress, see Parker v. Wellman, 230 Fed. Appx. 878 (11th Cir. 2007). A physical injury or disabling sign or symptom is required.

3.   The measure of the damages for increased risk of future harms will, undoubtedly, be smaller than the damages for any harms that actually occur. Why not simply wait to see whether the injury manifests itself and then sue? What effect would statutes of limitation have in calculating whether to sue immediately after the injury or wait until the damage appears clinically? See Christopher H. Schroeder, Corrective Justice and Liability for Increasing Risks, 37 UCLA L. Rev. 439 (1990).

4.   Two other issues are also relevant: (1) the availability of damages for the psychological harm of worrying whether certain illnesses will become manifest, see James F. D'Entremont, Fear Factor: The Future of Cancerphobia and Fear of Future Disease Claims in the Toxicogenomic Age, 52 Loy. L. Rev. 807 (2006); and (2) the damages associated with increased medical monitoring to detect the early symptoms of disease at a time when treatment will be most effective, see James M. Garner et al., Medical Monitoring: The Evolution of a Cause of Action, 30 Envt'l L. Rep. 10,024 (2000).

B. CAUSATION

WINTZ V. NORTHROP CORP.
110 F.3d 508 (7th Cir.1997).

COFFEY, J.

Plaintiffs-appellants Van Wintz and Jill Wintz, both individually and on behalf of their daughter Jessica (the "Wintzes"), appeal the district court's order granting the jointly-filed motion for summary judgment of defendants-appellees Northrop Corporation ("Northrop") and Eastman Kodak Company ("Kodak"). The Wintzes sought damages for injuries allegedly suffered by Jessica as a result of her *in utero* exposure to the chemical bromide, allegedly contained in photographic developing material manufactured by Kodak and used by Jill Wintz in the course of her employment with Northrop. The questions presented are whether the district court erred in excluding the proffered testimony of a toxicologist hired by the Wintzes, and whether, absent that testimony, the Wintzes failed to establish a genuine issue of fact as to whether exposure to bromide caused injury to Jessica. We affirm.

I.   BACKGROUND

Prior to and during her pregnancy with Jessica, Jill Wintz was employed by Northrop as an Industrial Engineer Associate in Northrop's Defense Systems Division. Her employment with Northrop began in May 1979, and continued through March 1982. From March 1980 through October 1980, while she was pregnant, Jill's duties involved the mixing of certain chemicals manufactured by Kodak to develop photographic film used in the manufacturing process of the "black box" for jet fighter aircraft. One of these chemicals, Kodalith Developer B, contained bromide. The chemicals came in powdered form in paper-type bags, and Jill poured them from the bag into a container for mixing with water. During this process, the powder from the bags would create a dust in the air, and Jill alleges that she inhaled this dust while mixing the chemicals. According to Jill's affidavit, she was "never given or advised to use any type of protective breathing mask or other protective equipment during mixing or use of the chemical powders." Jill Wintz worked in this capacity for Northrop from March 1980 until she took a maternity leave of absence on October 31, 1980, approximately five weeks before giving birth to Jessica, and she mixed the chemicals on a daily basis during this period.

Jessica was born at Lutheran General Hospital in Park Ridge, Illinois on December 6, 1980, and shortly thereafter she began displaying a number of atypical symptoms for newborns. Most noticeably, according to the deposition of Dr. Henry Mangurten, a neonatologist who treated Jessica at that time, she displayed hypotonia (low muscle tone), poor sucking reflexes, and weak or infrequent cry, as well as abnormal facial features. When she was but four days old, the baby was placed in a neonatal intensive care unit and came under Dr. Mangurten's care. In an effort to determine the cause of these abnormal behavioral symptoms, Dr. Mangurten ordered a variety of tests but they came back inconclusive, at which time the specialist saw fit to interview and gain additional background information from Jill Wintz. Upon learning that Jill worked in an environment in which bromide was present, Dr. Mangurten, based on his previous experience in which he had treated a baby with elevated bromide levels and who had displayed symptoms similar to Jessica's, ordered a bromide test on the baby. A urine sample was obtained when she was 11 days old and prior to learning the results of this test, Jessica's condition showed signs of improvement and she was released from the neonatal intensive care unit when she was but 13 days old. Shortly thereafter, the test revealed elevated levels of bromide in Jessica's system. The doctor, at this time, ordered another urine sample taken when Jessica was 20 days old and this test again revealed the presence of bromide in her system but at a decreased level. This time, Dr. Mangurten also ordered a bromide test on her mother, Jill, which also revealed elevated bromide levels in her system as well.

Dr. Mangurten stated that Jessica's condition had improved somewhat, though not entirely, at the time she was released from the neonatal intensive care unit. According to Dr. Mangurten, Jessica's condition was tracked for roughly four years after she left Lutheran General pursuant to a follow-up program the hospital maintains for infants who have spent time in the neonatal intensive care unit. In an affidavit, Dr. Barbara Burton, Director for the Center of Medical and Reproductive Genetics at Michael Reese Hospital in Chicago, who reviewed Jessica's complete medical records, stated that Jessica has continued to display abnormal symptoms through the present, including strabismus (deviation of the eye), myopia, frequent upper respiratory infections, enamel defects in her teeth, and delayed development in mental and physical milestones. Dr. Burton, who is an expert in genetics and genetic disorders, opined in her affidavit that Jessica's symptoms are all "classical" symptoms of a person afflicted with a genetic disorder known as Prader-Willi Syndrome ("PWS").[1]

In the course of her follow-up care after being discharged, it was learned (and is not disputed by the Wintzes) that Jessica was in fact born with PWS. PWS is caused by a deletion of genetic material from the father's chromosomes. It is a purely genetic disorder which occurs prior to conception, and it cannot be caused by environmental exposure. As the Wintzes have acknowledged, all of the abnormal symptoms Jessica has experienced throughout her life are very similar, if not identical, to those experienced by children with PWS. During his deposition, Dr. Mangurten agreed with the statement that Jessica's developmental problems have "almost certainly" been caused by PWS.

In addition to Dr. Mangurten, the Wintzes listed Gilbert Elenbogen ("Elenbogen"), a toxicologist, as an expert witness. The Wintzes asserted that Elenbogen would testify that exposure to bromide caused Jessica's abnormalities. Elenbogen opined in an affidavit that Jill Wintz's exposure to bromide while mixing the photographic chemicals caused Jessica to be exposed to bromide, and that this exposure, as stated in Elenbogen's affidavit, "caused the child's symptoms at birth and her permanent

---

[1] Prader-Willi Syndrome is defined as "a congenital disorder characterized by rounded face, almond-shaped eyes, strabismus, low forehead, hypogonadism, hypotomia, insatiable appetite, early hypotonia, failure to thrive, and mental retardation." *Dorland's Illustrated Medical Dictionary* 1638 (28th ed. 1994).

developmental damage and problems." Elenbogen did acknowledge that Jessica had PWS, and that her symptoms which he attributed to her prenatal exposure to bromide were identical to those caused by PWS. No other expert testified for the Wintzes on the issue of causation.

Kodak and Northrop filed a combined motion for summary judgment after deposing Elenbogen and Mangurten. They argued that Elenbogen's testimony was inadmissible under rule 702 of the Federal Rules of Evidence as interpreted by the Supreme Court in Daubert v. Merrell Dow Pharmaceuticals, 509 U.S. 579 (1993). They argued that the toxicologist Elenbogen was not a licensed physician and surgeon and lacked sufficient experience with bromide or with PWS, and was thus not qualified to render an opinion as an expert as to the cause of Jessica's injuries. Northrop and Kodak further argued that, because Elenbogen's opinion that bromide caused Jessica's injuries was inadmissible due to his lack of qualifications, and because Dr. Mangurten agreed in his deposition testimony that PWS was the cause of Jessica's developmental problems, the Wintzes failed to establish a genuine issue of material fact as to whether bromide exposure was a proximate cause of any of Jessica's abnormalities. In a memorandum opinion dated December 21, 1995, the district judge agreed with Kodak and Northrop. The district court entered a summary judgment order in favor of Kodak and Northrop on December 21, and the Wintzes appealed.

* * *

In the present case, Dr. Mangurten's deposition established in clear and unequivocal language that, in his opinion, PWS caused Jessica's long-term developmental problems. It also established that he could not offer an opinion with any reasonable degree of medical certainty that Jessica's short-term problems at birth were caused by bromide, notwithstanding the observation that her symptoms decreased at the same time the bromide levels decreased. Whatever support the Wintzes hope to find in [Champion v. Knasiak, 323 N.E.2d 62 (Ill.App.Ct. 1974)], we do not agree that it can be read to suggest that they did not have the obligation to come forward with affirmative evidence to support their causation argument. Thus, the trial court did not err in concluding that Dr. Mangurten's testimony was insufficient to create a genuine issue of fact as to whether bromide caused any of Jessica's long-term or short-term symptoms.

The district court's decision excluding the proffered testimony of the Wintzes' toxicologist was not manifestly erroneous, and the evidence, when considered in its totality, fell short of raising a genuine issue of material fact as to the cause of Jessica's short-term or long-term symptoms. WE AFFIRM the grant of summary judgment in favor of Kodak and Northrop.

NOTES AND QUESTIONS

1.   As indicated in *Bryson* and *Wintz,* genetic information may be helpful to the plaintiff or the defendant.

2.   Genetic testing has been used by plaintiffs' lawyers to prove that a plaintiff's condition was *not* the result of a genetic disorder, thereby rebutting a defendant's claim to the contrary. See Lori B. Andrews, Future Perfect 143 (2001).

3.   The issue of causation has been one of the great conundrums of tort law. Toxic injuries and toxicogenomics add a layer of complexity to the issue of causation in fact. For example, scientists may demonstrate convincingly that if 1,000 people are exposed to substance A at B levels for C amount of time per day, over D number of years there will be E cases of cancer, which greatly exceeds the F number of cases for a similar group of unexposed people. Are these facts enough to establish that any particular individual's exposure to substance A caused his or her cancer? If not, what additional evidence is necessary? Genetic biomarkers may help to prove that the exposure actually caused a particular individual's cancer. If the science has not developed appropriate measures for the substance and disease at issue, what level of statistically increased risk should be required to prove causation in fact for legal purposes? See Daniel A. Farber, Toxic Causation, 71 Minn. L. Rev. 1219 (1987); Steve C. Gold, The More We Know, the Less Intelligent We Are?—How Genetic Information Should and Should not, Change Toxic Tort Causation Doctrine, 34 Harv. Envtl. L. Rev. 369; Sander Greenland & James M. Robins, Epidemiology, Justice, and the Probability of Causation, 40 Jurimetrics J. 321 (2000).

C. DAMAGES

MARK A. ROTHSTEIN, PREVENTING THE DISCOVERY OF PLAINTIFF GENETIC PROFILES BY DEFENDANTS SEEKING TO LIMIT DAMAGES IN PERSONAL INJURY LITIGATION
71 Ind. L.J. 877, 878–891 (1996).

Imagine the following situation: Dr. Jane Smith is a thirty-five year-old neurosurgeon who entered private practice three years ago upon completion of her training. She has an annual income of $200,000. One day, while crossing the street from the doctors' parking lot to the hospital, she is run over by a Zippy Express delivery truck, whose unlicensed, intoxicated driver was speeding to a delivery and failed to stop for a red light. As a result of the accident, Dr. Smith has become quadriplegic and will be unable to perform surgery again.

In a negligence action against Zippy Express, a key component of Dr. Smith's economic damages is her lost income. Assuming she would have been able to work for thirty more years, with an income of $200,000 per year, this would amount to six million in current dollars, exclusive of projected earnings increases, merely for lost income.

Suppose, however, that Dr. Smith is in the unaffected, presymptomatic stage of Huntington's disease, amyotrophic lateral sclerosis, or some other late-onset genetic disorder. Further suppose that experts will testify that, in all likelihood, irrespective of the accident, she would not have been able to practice medicine beyond age forty-five and that her life expectancy is fifty years. Applying traditional damages principles, this information would reduce her recovery for economic injury by at least four million dollars.

Zippy Express and its insurers therefore would have a great economic incentive to discover information about Dr. Smith's genetic profile and to introduce this information at trial. Should the defendants be able to discover this information by obtaining access to Dr. Smith's medical records? Should they be able to obtain a court order directing Dr. Smith to submit to genetic testing? Should it matter whether genetic testing previously had been performed on Dr. Smith or whether there was something in her family or medical history to suspect a genetic disorder? Should it matter whether Dr. Smith was suspected of having a genetic risk of a monogenic disorder, such as Huntington's disease, or a multifactorial disorder, such as cancer? What effect, if any, should be given to the penetrance, variable expressivity, and treatability of the disorder? Should it matter if Dr. Smith objects to genetic testing?

* * *

II.   DAMAGES FOR LOST FUTURE EARNINGS

In personal injury litigation, special damages for quantifiable losses are based on the increased expenses and lost income caused by the injury. The latter component, lost future earnings, is a function of income level and work life expectancy. A claim for lost future earnings or lost earning capacity is "an estimate of lost present ability to work in appropriate occupations, now and in the future." By contrast, a claim for lost earnings refers to the loss of income from the time of injury until the date of the trial. Ordinarily, damages for lost future earnings are only relevant after the plaintiff proves that he or she has suffered a permanent injury. Thereafter, the evidence focuses on two issues: (1) the plaintiff's expected rate of earnings, and (2) the plaintiff's expected number of lost years of earning capacity.

* * *

The first part, rate of earnings, is relatively easy to compute. It is based on the plaintiff's abilities, training, experience, and preinjury earnings. Prospects for wage increases and loss of fringe benefits also are considered. Loss of future earnings is not all-or-nothing; thus, reduction of future earnings as well as inability to generate any earnings at all are recoverable.

The second part, determining life expectancy, is already more difficult, and it is likely to become increasingly complicated in the new era of genetics and predictive medicine. Currently, life expectancy is based initially on standard mortality tables. These tables, however, are merely the starting point for making a determination of life expectancy or work expectancy.

* * *

The courts have permitted a wide range of information to be introduced by either party in attempting to ascertain the plaintiff's life expectancy and work expectancy with more precision than mortality tables. These additional factors include the plaintiff's work history, as well as past and current health, constitution, and habits. In a minority of jurisdictions, mortality tables proffered by the plaintiff are deemed inadmissible if the plaintiff had a preexisting condition, the theory being that mortality tables are based on the lives of "healthy people."

* * *

There are two types of evidence that could indicate that the plaintiff has a shorter life expectancy than the standard mortality tables. The first type of evidence involves previously diagnosed diseases. If the plaintiff already had been diagnosed with cancer, heart disease, or some other life-threatening illness at the time of the injury, this evidence would be admissible to show a reduced life expectancy. The second type of evidence involves factors that predict the likelihood of disease which would cause premature mortality. The courts have admitted a wide range of evidence of behavioral factors in attempting to prove that the plaintiff had a diminished life expectancy at the time of the injury. These factors include the plaintiff's use of drugs, alcohol, or cigarettes.

If evidence of cigarette smoking is admissible to show that the plaintiff's life expectancy is lessened because of the possibility of lung cancer, emphysema, or heart disease, then evidence that the plaintiff was genetically predisposed to such a disorder also would seem to be admissible. From the defendant's standpoint, the only issue is how to obtain access to such genetic information. The main ways include discovery of existing medical records, questioning the plaintiff at deposition, compelling a medical examination of the plaintiff, and questioning the plaintiff's physicians by interrogatories or depositions.

Although virtually all of the cases involve the defendant's attempt to introduce evidence of the plaintiff's shorter life expectancy, it is also possible for the plaintiff to introduce evidence of longevity.

* * *

With genetic prediction becoming increasingly sophisticated, it may be possible to estimate increased longevity. Nevertheless, for the foreseeable future, it is likely that decreased life expectancy will be the primary focus in personal injury litigation.

* * *

III. DISCOVERY OF MEDICAL RECORDS

The easiest way for a personal injury defendant to learn a plaintiff's prior medical history is to discover the plaintiff's medical records. Requests for the medical records of personal injury plaintiffs are considered routine and are rarely challenged.

Courts considering the issue of discovering a plaintiff's medical records have applied the general principle that discovery requests are liberally granted. In general, parties may discover any nonprivileged matter relevant to a claim or defense of any party to a lawsuit. If evidence of a plaintiff's preinjury health status is admissible on the issue of damages, then medical records indicating health status are presumptively discoverable. Thus, courts routinely order the discovery of medical records, including records relevant to the issue of damages for lost future earnings. Even sensitive information, such as psychiatric records, have been ordered disclosed.

* * *

IV. COMPELLED MEDICAL EXAMINATIONS

The most intrusive form of medical discovery is the compelled medical examination. Rule 35 of the Federal Rules of Civil Procedure provides that a mental or physical examination may be ordered by the court in an action in which the mental or physical condition of a party is "in controversy," upon a showing of "good cause." The rules of civil procedure of every state, except Mississippi, contain similar provisions.

In Schlagenhauf v. Holder, [379 U.S. 104 (1964)] the Supreme Court considered the meaning of the terms "in controversy" and "good cause."

* * *

Schlagenhauf has been interpreted by both federal and state courts to mean that any time a plaintiff seeks to recover for physical injuries, his or her physical condition is "in controversy." Although this may establish the discoverability of a plaintiff's medical records pursuant to Rule 26, it does not necessarily establish the existence of good cause for a medical examination. An important question is whether information in the plaintiff's medical records can establish good cause for a medical examination. This is crucial to the issue of genetics, because information in the plaintiff's medical record may cause the defendant to suspect an underlying genetic condition, and then seek to have a court-ordered medical examination that includes genetic testing.

* * *

Even when the "in controversy" and "good cause" requirements of Rule 35 are satisfied, the court has discretion in deciding whether to compel an examination. In general, the cases in which courts order a physical or mental examination fall into three categories.

First, the information must not be available elsewhere. The movant must show that other discovery procedures, such as the production of medical records, have been exhausted. Second, it must be established that useful information is likely to be gained from the examination. For example, repetitive examinations will not be permitted unless special circumstances justify an additional examination. Third, the examination must not create health risks to the examinee. Although most of the cases involving health risks are concerned with physical risks, there is some support for the view that the feelings, reputation, and psychological impact on the examinee also should be considered. For example, in Doe v. Roe, [139 Misc.2d 209, 526 N.Y.S.2d 718 (N.Y. Sup. Ct. 1988)] maternal grandparents attempted to gain custody of their grandchild from the allegedly unfit father. They sought an order requiring the child's father to have an HIV test. In rejecting the motion, the court noted that "the psychological impact of learning that one is [HIV-positive] has been compared to receiving a death sentence."

The potential psychological and social harm to the examinee is merely one factor to consider in the context of genetics. Public policy concerns about confidentiality and conservation of resources, discussed in the next section, also need to be weighed against the need for the information revealed by the testing. These issues are likely to arise in motions to compel genetic testing under Rule 35. The few cases that have been decided under this rule, however, have not developed the issues sufficiently to provide needed guidance to courts dealing with a genetics case of first impression.

NOTES AND QUESTIONS

1.   The argument has been made that advocating limitations on defendants' ability to obtain genetic information in medical records or require genetic testing of plaintiffs amounts to genetic exceptionalism (discussed in Chapter 14). Do you agree?

2.   Should the same rules apply to discovery of genetic information for proof of harm and causation as applied to estimations of life expectancy?

3.   If you think that limits should be placed on the compelled disclosure of genetic information to defendants for proof of damages, should the

limitation be judge-made through application of procedural rules or pursuant to legislative enactment?

4. For a further discussion of these issues, see Diane E. Hoffmann & Karen H. Rothenberg, Judging Genes: Implications of the Second Generation of Genetic Tests in the Courtroom, 66 Md. L. Rev. 858 (2007); Anthony S. Niedwiecki, Science Fact or Science Fiction? The Implications of Court-Ordered Genetic Testing Under Rule 35, 34 U.S.F.L. Rev. 295 (2000).

INDEX

References are to Pages

ABORTION
Amniocentesis based abortion decisions, 299
Embryonic and fetal research, abortion law restrictions, 118
Genetic counseling and wrongful birth litigation, 73
Home testing based abortion decisions, 359
Prenatal screening based abortion decisions, 232
Sex selection, 285

ACCESS TO GENETIC SERVICES
Generally, 334 et seq.
Federal entitlement programs, 335
Federal Funding, this index
Health Care Financing Administration policies, 337
Health insurance coverage, 335, 340
Human Genome Project, effects of, 336
Managed care organizations, 340
Medicaid policies, 339
Medicare policies, 337
Orphan drugs problem, 388
Pharmacogenomic drugs, 388
Primary care physician referrals, 335

ACHONDROPLASIA
Generally, 33

ADOLESCENTS
See Screening, this index

ADOPTION
Genetic disease risks of adoptees, 551
Genetic testing of adoptees, 551
Wrongful adoption, 536

ALLELE DISTRIBUTIONS
Race and ethnicity, 179

ALZHEIMER DISEASE
Long-term care insurance risks, 754, 757
Predictive testing, 314
Risk Evaluation and Education for Alzheimer's Disease (REVEAL) Study, 756

AMERICAN ACADEMY OF PEDIATRICS (AAP)
Newborn screening, 451, 476

AMERICAN COLLEGE OF MEDICAL GENETICS (ACMG)
Adoptees, genetic testing guideline, 544
Direct-to-consumer genetic testing, 356
Newborn screening, 461

AMERICAN MEDICAL ASSOCIATION (AMA)
Confidentiality policy, 317
Gene therapy opinion, 407

AMERICAN SOCIETY OF HUMAN GENETICS (ASHG)
Adoptees, genetic testing guideline, 544
Informed consent guidelines, 109

AMERICANS WITH DISABILITIES ACT (ADA)
Generally, 771
See also Discrimination, this index
Custody rights of disabled parents, 552
Genetic Information Nondiscrimination Act protections distinguished, 787
Life insurance discrimination, 741
Medical examinations requirements, 775
Parental rights, 552
Title VII distinguished, 762, 775
2008 Amendments, 772

AMNIOCENTESIS
Generally, 120
Abortion decisions based on, 299
Sex selection, 285
Test/experiment distinctions, 120
Testing risks, 218

ANCESTRY TRACING
See also Heredity, this index
Anonymous sperm donors, internet tracing of, 279
Direct-to-consumer genetic testing, 351, 353
Genealogy, group harms, 208
Immigration law, genetic testing to determine familial relationships, 533
Jefferson, Thomas, 522, 530
Mitochondrial DNA data, 557
Native American ancestry, DNA determinations, 214
Washington, George, 524

ANONYMITY
Direct-to-consumer genetic testing, 352

Research on anonymized samples, 109
Sperm donors, anonymous
        Generally, 250
        Internet tracing of, 279

ARRANGED MARRIAGES
Genetic disease risk considerations, 235

ARTIFICIAL INSEMINATION
See Reproductive Technology, this index

ASSISTED REPRODUCTION
See Reproductive Technology, this index

ATHLETES
Prowess enhancement
        Genetics, 482
        Pharmacogenetics, 483
Yao Ming, 77

AUTISM
Education testing, 657
Genetic markers for, 633, 659

BANKS
Biobanks, this index
Databanks, DNA, this index

BEHAVIOR
See Mental and Behavioral Genetics, this
    index

BIOBANKS
        Generally, 103
        See also Databanks, DNA, this index
Authorizations, 105
Informed consent, 105
Medical record linkages, 87, 104, 106
Ownership issues, 107
Population-based projects, 106
Privacy rights, 104
Prostate cancer project, 107
Risks of biobank research, 104

BIOLOGIC DETERMINISM
Race-based research and, 181

BLOOD SAMPLES
        See also Tissue Samples, this index
ABO groups, 554
Antigens, 555
Human leukocyte antigen (HLA) system,
    555

BREAST CANCER
Gene patents, 140
Gene therapy prospects, 38
Genetic testing for risk of, 301
Prophylactic mastectomies, 355, 733, 734,
    738
Screening and counseling, 316

CELEBRITY GENETICS
Privacy rights, 704

CELL DIVISION
Scientific overview, 29

CELL LINES
HapMap project, 42, 206
HeLa cell line, 177
Indigenous peoples', 202
Ownership rights, 158 et seq.
Patent rights, 166
Stem Cell Research, this index

CELL NUCLEI
Chromosome structure in, 26

**CENTERS FOR DISEASE CONTROL
    AND PREVENTION (CDC)**
Newborn screening program, 452
Research on existing tissue samples, 112

CHILDREN
Designer children policy concerns, 497
Genetic enhancement research, 493
Research subjects
        Federal regulations, 92, 493
        State regulation, 101
Screening of children and adolescents. See
    Screening, this index
Tort liabilities, child testing, 225

CHORIONIC VILLI SAMPLING
        Generally, 299
Test/experiment distinction, 120
Testing risks, 218

CHROMOSOMES
Abnormalities, 26
Artificial chromosomes, 436
Autosomes, 26
Breakage as compensable injury, 808
Discovery of, 22
Fluorescence in situ hybridization, 299
Fragile X Syndrome, this index
Karyotypes, 26
Meiosis and mitosis, 29
Sex determinative, 26
Structure of, 26
Toxic exposure causing chromosomal
    damage, 808
XYY criminal chromosome studies, 98, 645

CIVIL RIGHTS
ADA and Title VII distinguished, 762, 775
Employment discrimination, 764
Insurance underwriting practices, 740

CLINICAL GENETICS
        Generally, 297, 369
Enhancement, Genetic, this index
Gene Therapies, this index
Pharmacogenomics, this index
Public Health Genetics, this index

CLINICAL RESEARCH
        Generally, 86
        See also Experimentation, Human,
          this index; Research, this index
Conflicts of interest, 129 et seq.

Epidemiological research distinguished, 182
Genetic research leading to, 88
Patients' Rights, this index

CLONING
Generally, 280
Human cloning, 280
Neanderthal project, 284
Patent claims, 150
Procreative rights, 281
Restrictions on human cloning
Procreative rights conflicts, 281
Scientific overview, 280

COMMERCIALIZATION OF GENETIC RESEARCH
Generally, 129
AMA guidelines on commercial use of human tissue, 175
Fraudulent concealment of research goals, 172
Funded research and property rights, 130
Gene therapy conflicts of interest, 400
Human Genome Project, intellectual property aspects, 40
Indigenous peoples, exploitation concerns, 201
Intellectual Property Rights, this index
Licensing of patents, 169, 178
Patents, this index
Paternity testing industry, 521
Property Rights, this index
Protective strategies of researchers, 130
Technology Transfer Laws, this index
Tissue sample ownership issues, 107
Trade secret protection of genetic discoveries, 136

CONFIDENTIALITY
Generally, 671 et seq.
See also Privacy Rights, this index
Privacy and confidentiality distinguished, 676

CONFLICTS OF INTEREST
Gene therapy, 431
Research
Generally, 129
Therapy/research distinctions, 431

CONSENT
See Informed Consent, this index

CONSUMER TESTING
See Direct-to-Consumer Genetic Testing, this index

COUNCIL OF REGIONAL NETWORKS FOR GENETIC SERVICES
Newborn screening, 453

COUNSELING
Generally, 329

Abortion counseling and wrongful birth litigation, 73
Access to genetic services, 334 et seq.
AMA confidentiality policy, 317
American Board of Genetic Counseling, 329
Confidentiality, warning duty conflicts, 320
Directive and non-directive, 329
Direct-to-consumer genetic testing, 355
Eugenics activities distinguished, 329
Eugenics and, 73
Familial risk management, 317
Family members, testing disclosures among, 315
Federal funding for genetic services, 335
Huntington disease testing results, 96, 310
National Society of Genetic Counselors (NSGC), 329
Paternity, unanticipated misattributions, 347
Precounseling protocols, 310
Privacy issues, 331
Research subject counseling requirements, 96
Tarasoff duties, 325
Testing, follow-up counseling, 310
Third party warning duties, confidentiality conflicts, 316
Tort liabilities
Generally, 318 et seq.
Child testing, duties to parents, 225
Confidentiality, warning duty conflicts, 320
Warning duties, 318
Unanticipated misattributed paternity, 347
Warning duties
Confidentiality conflicts, 317
Tort liabilities, 318
Wrongful Birth, this index
Wrongful Life, this index

CRIMINAL LAW
Generally, 553 et seq.
Abandoned DNA collections, 579
Addictive status as crime, 656
Admissibility of DNA evidence
Generally, 554 et seq.
Civil litigation, 625
Emerging technologies, 568
Statistical evidence, 562
Arrest warrants, DNA, 571
Castration, surgical and chemical, 70, 80
Civil commitment of sexual offenders, 653
Cold-case projects, 570, 579
Court-ordered collection, 573
Crime scene sample collections, 561
Databanks, DNA, this index
Daubert challenges to DNA evidence, 560
Delays in testing, 580
DQ alpha testing, 585
Dragnets, DNA, 572
Expectations of privacy and Fourth Amendment protections, 577, 579
Faked DNA samples, dangers of, 569

Frye challenges to DNA evidence, 556, 560
Genetic defenses, effective assistance of
    counsel, 650
Genetic predisposition defenses, 640
Habitual criminal sterilization, 64
Huntington disease defense, 649
Identity Testing, this index
Indictments, DNA, 571, 574
Justice for All Act of 2004, 583
Mental and behavioral genetics
        Generally, 637 et seq.
      Culpability, 641
      Death penalty defense, 652
      Ineffective assistance claims, 650
Mixed DNA samples, 561
National Research Council admissibility
    standards, 570
PCR sample collections, 556
Physicians, obtaining of suspects' samples
    from, 578
Planted DNA, 569
Post-conviction DNA testing, 581
Privacy expectations and Fourth
    Amendment protections, 577, 579
Rape kit testing backlogs, 580
Recidivism, genetic predictions, 638
Relatives of suspects, collection of samples
    from, 579
Reliability of DNA fingerprinting, 561
Search and seizure challenges to collection
    efforts, 573
Sexual offenders, civil commitment of, 653
Short tandem repeat technique, 556
Statistical evidence, 562
Surreptitious DNA sample collection, 576
Testing delays, 580
Violence predictions, genetics based, 637
Warrants, DNA, 571
XYY chromosome carriers, 98, 645

CYSTIC FIBROSIS
    Generally, 29, 35, 36
Risk factors, 240

**DATA PROTECTION
    REQUIREMENTS**
Biobanks, this index
Databanks, DNA, this index

DATABANKS, DNA
    Generally, 591 et seq.
    See also Biobanks, this index
Admissibility of DNA evidence
    Criminal cases, 554 et seq.
    Statistical evidence, 562
British collection practices, 615
CODIS database, 569, 607
Cold-case projects, 570, 579
Collection torts, 572
Constitutionality challenges, 591
Constitutionality of collection
    requirements, 553
Department of Defense registry of soldiers'
    samples, 620

DNA Analysis Backlog Elimination Act,
    607
Dragnets, DNA, 572
European human rights law, 619
Expungement provisions, 618
FBI standards, 556
Fingerprint record analogy, 611
Forcible collections of samples, 617
Frequency data for populations and
    subpopulations
        Generally, 557
      Match probabilities, 569
Juveniles, collection from, 618
Liability for dragnet collection, 572
Match probabilities
        Generally, 569
      Frequency data for populations and
        subpopulations, 569
Misdemeanants, collection from, 618
Mitochondrial DNA data, 557
Non-forensic uses, 613
Non-violent felons, 594, 722
Policy considerations, 553, 611
Probable cause collection standards, 574
Racial discrimination in collection
    practices, 619
Rape kit testing backlogs, 580
Religious rights collection challenges, 607,
    625
Research uses, 613
Sample collections for, 553
Soldiers, DOD Registry, 620
Universal collection proposals, 616

DEFINITIONS AND ACRONYMS
AAP, 451
ACMG, 343
ADA, 552
ADEA, 762
AFDC, 336
Allele, 29
Amniocentesis, 120
Antigens, 555
ASHG, 109
Autosome, 26
BGI, 204
Biobank, 103
Biologic determinism, 182
Biological mother, 279
BLA, 428
CDC, 112
Centimorgan, 36
CF, 468
Chromosome, 22
Cloning, 23
Codon, 27
Confidentiality, 676
CORN, 453
CRADA, 154
Cytoplasm, 28
Deme, 208
DHHS, 470
Discrimination, 764

Dizygotic twins, 627
DNA, 23
DNA marker, 36
Dominant gene, 32
DTC, 351
DZ, 627
Effectiveness, 427
Efficaciousness, 427
EHR, 679
ELSI, 17
ENCODE, 28
EPA, 794
Epigenetics, 87, 800
EPO, 482
ERISA, 711
Eugenics, 45
FEP, 335
FERPA, 664
FISH, 299
FMLA, 770
FPL, 336
Gene, 5, 27
Genetic discrimination, 764
Genetic exceptionalism, 689
Genetic marker, 36
Genetic privacy, 673
Genetic screening, 302
Genetic testing, 302
Germline therapy, 297, 434
GINA, 700
GLGT, 442
GWAS, 86
Haplotype, 42
HCFA, 337
HD, 96
HGDP, 200
HGH, 482
HGP, 35, 40
HH, 301
HIPAA, 327
HITECH, 680
HLA, 555
Homozygous sequence, 32
HRSA, 341
HUGO, 40
IDE, 428
IGM, 438
IND, 376
Intron, 27
IRB, 84
IVF, 78
Karyotype, 26
LCN, 558
Marker, DNA, 36
Marker, genetic, 36
MCHB, 451
Meiosis, 29
Mendelian disorder, 248
Mitochondrial DNA, 27
Mitosis, 29
mRNA, 28
Monozygotic twins, 627
mtDNA, 557

MZ, 627
NDA, 428
NHANES, 112
NHGRI, 40
NIH, 40
NRC, 560
NSGC, 329
Nucleotide base, 27
Nutrigenomics, 385
Orphan drugs, 388
OTC, 395
Overtreatment, 359
PCR, 300
Penetrance, 34
PGD, 78
Pharmacogenetics, 369
Pharmacogenomics, 381
Phenotype, 29, 181
PKU, 451
PMA, 428
PMAA, 422
Polymorphic, 36
Polymorphic mutant type, 3
Privacy, 676
Protein, 27
Proteomics, 381
PWS, 814
RAC, 396
Race, 4
rDNA, 438
Reassortation, 21
Recessive gene, 32
Recombinant DNA, 22, 30
Ribosome, 28
RNA, 27
RNAi, 404
SNP, 42
Somatic cell gene therapy, 434
STR, 556
Surrogate mother, 279
TANF, 79
Toxicogenomics, 798
Triplet, 27
TRIPS, 151
UPA, 265
VNTR, 555

DEPARTMENT OF HEALTH AND HUMAN SERVICES (DHHS)
Gene therapy protocol proposals, 410
IRB regulations, 89, 493

DESIGNER CHILDREN
See Enhancement, Genetic, this index

DETERMINISM
Biologic, 182
Genetic
    Eugenics implications, 630
    Genetic exceptionalism and, 689
    Human Genome Project effects, 630
    Mental and behavioral genetics associations, 629, 637
    Popular beliefs, 283, 629

DIRECT-TO-CONSUMER GENETIC TESTING
Generally, 351
Abortion decisions based on, 359
Accuracy concerns, 354
American College of Medical Genetics, 356
Ancestry information, 351, 353
Anonymity advantages, 351
Confidentiality protections, 352
Counseling problems, 355
Discrimination concerns, 352
FDA approvals, 353, 360, 363
Health information, 351
HIV and drug testing, FDA policies, 360
Lifestyle information, 351
Overtreatment concerns, 359
Paternity testing, 351, 521
Policy concerns, 352
Privacy concerns, 705
Professional acceptance, 356
Psychological concerns, 357
Sex of fetus, 367
State regulation, 354
Tort liabilities, 367
Unanticipated misattributed paternity, 521

DISABILITIES
Americans with Disabilities Act, this index
Custody rights of disabled parents, 546, 551

DISABILITY INSURANCE
See Insurance, this index

DISCLOSURE
See also Privacy Rights, this index
Actuarially justified insurance requirements, 710
Children and adolescent screening, 333
Compelled disclosures of medical records, 681
Family and Medical Leave Act medical records disclosures, 770
Family members, testing disclosures among, 315
Fraudulent concealment of research goals, 172
Gene therapies, adverse events, 399
Genetic testing disclosure policies, 315
Insurance, actuarially justified requirements, 710
Medical records, compelled disclosures, 681
Prenatal screening decisions and risks, 236
Statutory, 326
Tissue research subjects, 102
Tissue sample research results, 110

DISCRIMINATION
Generally, 763
Americans with Disabilities Act, this index
Civil Rights, this index
Custody rights of disabled parents, 546, 551
Demic discrimination, 208

Employment Discrimination, this index
Genetic discrimination, 764
Genetic Information Nondiscrimination Act, this index
Health insurance protections, 498
Home testing anonymity, 351
Insurance, this index
Mental and behavioral genetic predictions, 635
Newborn screening discrimination problems, 456
Privacy rights breaches, 702
Sickle cell carriers, insurance discrimination, 710
State law protections, 776
Toxicogenomics, discrimination concerns, 798

DISEASES
Achondroplasia, 33
Adoptees, 551
Alzheimer Disease, this index
Arranged marriages, genetic disease risk considerations, 235
Assisted reproduction, screening in, 248
Autism, genetic markers for, 633, 358
Beryllium disease, genetic associations, 855
Breast Cancer, this index
Carpal tunnel susceptibility, genetic testing for, 806
Chromosomal abnormalities, 26
Clinical testing, 301
Cystic Fibrosis, this index
DNA, non-coding portions, 27
Eugenics implications of screening for genetic diseases, 79, 81
Family histories and testing decisions, 236
Fragile X Syndrome, this index
Genome Wide Association Studies (GWAS), 86
HapMap project, 42
Hereditary hemochromatosis (HH), 301
Human Genome Project discoveries, 134
Huntington Disease, this index
Incurable disorders, newborn screening for, 461
Linkage analysis, 36, 299
Mendelian disorders, 248
Non-coding portions of DNA, 27
Phenylketonuria, 35
Prader-Willi Syndrome, 814
Preimplantation genetic diagnosis, 240, 243
Public health based regulatory authority as to genetic diseases, 55, 81
Racial distinctions in disease incidence, 179
Risk prediction, 301
Schizophrenia, genetic associations, 628
Screening for genetic diseases, eugenics implications, 79, 81
Sickle Cell Disease, this index
Single-nucleotide polymorphism studies, 204

Tay-Sachs, this index
What genetic testing is appropriate, 236
XYY Chromosome Carriers, this index

DIVERSITY
See Human Genome Diversity Project, this
    index

DNA
Anonymous sperm donors, internet tracing
    of, 279
Band pattern matching, 561
Binding rules, 25
Codons, 27
Copyrighting proposals, 176
Cytoplasm, 28
Databanks, DNA, this index
Diagnostic studies, 88
Discovery of structure of, 23
Double helix structure, discovery of, 23
DQ alpha testing, 585
Emerging DNA technologies for identity
    testing, 558
Encyclopedia of DNA Elements (ENCODE),
    28
Fingerprinting, DNA
        Generally, 556
        See also Identity Testing, this index
Gel electrophoresis, 300
Haplotypes, 42
HapMap project, 42
Human Genome Diversity Project, this
    index
Human Genome Project, this index
Human species, history of, 2
Identity Testing, this index
Internet tracing of anonymous of sperm
    donors, 279
Introns, 27
Junk DNA, 27
Linkage analysis, 36, 299
Low copy number DNA tests, 558
Markers, 36
Markers, genetic, 36
Messenger RNA (mRNA), 28
Microarrays, 797
Mitochondrial DNA, 27, 557
Mixed DNA samples, 561
Non-coding portions, 27
Nucleotide base sequences, 27
Patents, this index
Paternity laws, effect of DNA testing, 515
Polymerase chain reaction (PCR), 300, 556
Polymorphic bases, 36
Recombinant DNA, development of, 23
Replication process, discovery of, 25
Reproduction, DNA testing, 215 et seq.
Ribosome structure, 28
RNA, 27
Sequences and Sequencing, this index
Short tandem repeat technique, 556
Single nucleotide polymorphism, 42
Species differentiation, 3

Testing, this index
Translation, 28
Triplets, 27
Variable number tandem repeats, 555

DO-IT-YOURSELF TESTING
See Direct-to-Consumer Genetic Testing,
    this index

**DONATION OF ORGANS AND
    TISSUES**
Conceiving a sibling to be a donor, 289
Reproductive Technology, this index
Testing, unanticipated misattributed
    paternity, 347

DRUGS
Manufacturers, learned intermediary
    doctrine, 393
Patents, this index
Pharmacogenomics, this index
Race and ethnicity, drug response
    connections, 185
Trials
        See also Food and Drug
            Administration, this index

EDUCATION
Channeling, testing based, 657
Family Educational Rights and Privacy
    Act, 663
Fragile X syndrome testing, 657, 661
Mental and behavioral genetics
    applications, 657
Testing and privacy concerns, 661

**ELECTRONIC HEALTH RECORDS
    (EHR)**
Privacy rights, 679

EMBRYONIC AND FETAL RESEARCH
        Generally, 117 et seq.
Abortion law restrictions, 118
Amniocentesis, 120, 189
Created-for-research fetuses, 118
Donations of embryos, 122
Excess embryo donations, 122
Federal funding, 118
Federal restrictions on embryo use, 118
Live and research-only embryos, 118
Regulation, 101
Reproductive privacy conflicts with
    regulations, 121
Tissue samples, 117

EMBRYOS
Cloning, this index
Pre-implantation embryos
        Genetic modification, 442
        Genetic selection, 482
Research on
        Generally, 83, 117
Stem Cell Research, this index
Transplantation. See Reproductive
        Technology, this index

EMPLOYEE RETIREMENT INCOME SECURITY ACT (ERISA)
Federal preemption of state laws, 711, 776

EMPLOYMENT DISCRIMINATION
Generally, 761 et seq.
See also Americans with Disabilities Act, this index; Genetic Information Nondiscrimination Act, this index
ADA and GINA protections distinguished, 787
ADA protections, 771
Age discrimination, 762
Benzene decision, 802
Carpal tunnel susceptibility, genetic testing for, 806
Civil rights discrimination, 764
Disability insurance, 751
Employer access to genetic information, 769
Family and Medical Leave Act requests for medical information, 770
Genetic discrimination, 763, 764
Genetic information discrimination, 762, 776, 777
GINA and ADA protections distinguished, 787
Health insurance access and employment
Generally, 761
Access to medical records, 770
Medical examinations, ADA requirements, 774
Medical records, employer access to, 770
Occupational Safety and Health Act, 762
Periodic medical exam requirements, 770
Safety-related health concerns, 762
Screening practices of employers, 761
State law protections, 776
Title VII and ADA rights, 772, 775
Toxicogenomics in the workplace, 801
Two types of discrimination, 764
Workers' Compensation, this index

ENCYCLOPEDIA OF DNA ELEMENTS (ENCODE)
Generally, 28

ENGINEERING, GENETIC
Future of, 6

ENHANCEMENT, GENETIC
Generally, 481 et seq.
Athletic prowess, 482
Children, research on, 493
Defining, 485
Designer children policy concerns, 497
Efficacy data, 497
Equality problem, 507, 511
Ethical issues, 493
Evolutionary impacts, 485, 500
Fairness concerns, 507
FDA regulatory authority, 511
Gene therapy enhancement objectives, 481

Germline genetic enhancement proposals, 484
Height preferences, 483
Human growth hormone
Generally, 482
Regulation, 506
IQ enhancement, 499
IRB oversight, 491
Legal issues, 490
Memory preferences, 484
Pre-implantation embryos, genetic selection, 482
Religious implications, 503
Research
Generally, 483
Athletic prowess, 482, 483
Child subjects, 493
NIH funding, 483
Therapy/enhancement distinctions, 481

ENVIRONMENTAL HEALTH
Generally, 793 et seq.
Adverse effects determinations, Clean Air Act, 794
Benzene decision, 802
Beryllium exposure, toxicogenomic testing, 805
Carpal tunnel susceptibility, genetic testing for, 806
Causation of exposure injuries, 812
Chromosomal damage, tort liability for, 808
Clean Air Act adverse effects determinations, 794
Damages, toxic exposures, 816
Environmental justice, epigenetics research, 799
EPA risk assessment standards, 794
Epigenetics Research, this index
Exposure risks, genetic variation in, 793
Genetic fingerprints of toxic chemicals, 811
Genetic variation in exposure risks, 793
High-throughput toxicity screening of chemicals, 797
Occupational Safety and Health Act protections, 801
Predictive toxicology and risk assessment, 794
Tort liability
Causation, 812
Chromosomal damage, 808
Toxic chemicals, genetic fingerprints of, 811
Toxicogenomics, this index

ENVIRONMENTAL JUSTICE
Epigenetics research, 799

ENVIRONMENTAL PROTECTION AGENCY (EPA)
Risk assessment standards, 794

EPIDEMIOLOGICAL RESEARCH
Clinical research distinguished, 182
Consent requirements, 479

EPIGENETICS RESEARCH
Generally, 85, 800
Definition, 800
Environmental justice, 799
Ethical concerns, 799
Regulatory implications, 793
Twin studies, 88

ETHICAL, LEGAL AND SOCIAL IMPLICATIONS (ELSI) PROGRAM
Generally, 17

ETHNICITY
See Race and Ethnicity, this index

EUGENICS MOVEMENTS
Generally, 43, 186 et seq.
Abortion counseling and tort law, 73
American Eugenics Society, 74
Animal husbandry model, 77
Athlete sperm banks, 76
Bounties, sterilization, 78
Castration, surgical and chemical, 70, 80
Contraception programs, 62, 63, 79
Criminal law sterilization, 63
Defective children and abortion counseling, 73
Determinism, eugenics implications, 631
Enhancement, Genetic, this index
Ethical, Legal and Social Implications (ELSI) program, 17
Federally funded family planning services, 62, 79
Fetal testing followed by abortion, 78
Gamete donation IVF practices, 77
Genetic counseling distinguished, 329
Genius sperm bank, 75
Health care rationing for the elderly, 74
Immigration laws, eugenic goals, 46, 80
Jukes family study, 45
Mendelism and, 5, 45
Mental and behavioral genetics relationships, 630, 636
Nazi philosophies, 52, 53, 73
Nazi programs, 74, 83
Neoeugenics, positive and negative, 78, 79
Newborn screening programs, 80
Origin of term, 45
Positive and negative, 72
Preimplantation genetic diagnosis (PGD), 78
Public health genetics movement, eugenics implications, 448
Race and class biases, 44, 56, 186
Screening for genetic diseases, 78, 81
Sickle-cell screening, 188
Social eugenics, 44
State-sponsored and private reproductive decisions, 76
Sterilization laws
Generally, 46
Constitutionality, 47, 48, 59

Federally funded family planning services, 62, 79
Nazi program, 57, 73
Sterilization programs
Bounty payments, 79
Criminal law penalties, 63
Vasectomy programs, 64
Wrongful birth damages questions, 70, 220
Wrongful birth litigation, eugenic implications, 70, 221, 232
Wrongful birth neoeugenics, 79
XYY criminal chromosome studies, 98
Yao Ming, 77

EVOLUTION
Generally, 2
Darwinism and Mendelism, 4
Genetic enhancement, evolutionary impacts, 485, 500
Genographic Project, 206
Human Genome Diversity Project studies, 200
Mutation, role in, 3
Neanderthals, 6, 284

EXCEPTIONALISM, GENETIC
Definition, 689
Genetic determinism and, 689
Litigation discovery rules, 816
Privacy rights, 693

EXPERIMENTATION, HUMAN
Generally, 83
See also Clinical Research, this index
Amniocentesis, test/experiment distinctions, 120
Chorionic villi sampling, test/experiment distinction, 120
Drugs trials
See also Food and Drug Administration, this index
Embryonic, 117
Federal regulations, 624
Gene Therapies, this index
Health insurance coverage for experimental treatments, 734
Legal distinctions, 119
Nuremberg Code, this index
rDNA experiments, moratorium proposals, 407
Routine vs experimental procedures, 120
Tuskegee syphilis study, 88

FAMILY AND MEDICAL LEAVE ACT (FMLA)
Employer requests for medical information, 769

FAMILY EDUCATIONAL RIGHTS AND PRIVACY ACT (FERPA)
Generally, 663

FAMILY LAW
Adoption, this index

Custody rights of disabled parents, 546, 552

Identity testing, adultery litigation, 625

Immigration rights based on familial relationships, 533

Parentage, this index

Parental rights terminations, adoptability determinations in, 536

Reproductive Technology, this index

FEDERAL FUNDING
See also Health Care Financing Administration (HCFA), this index

Access to genetic services, 335

Embryonic and fetal research, 117

Family planning services, 62, 79

Genetic enhancement research, NIH funding, 483

Genetic services, 335

Human Genome Diversity Project funding, 206

Newborn screening, 452, 462

Orphan drugs incentives programs, 388

Stem cell research funding restrictions, 118

Technology Transfer Laws, this index

FERTILITY CLINICS
See Reproductive Technology, this index

FETAL CELL SORTING
Generally, 243

FETAL DEVELOPMENT
Meiosis and mitosis, 29

FETAL RESEARCH
See Embryonic and Fetal Research, this index

FINGERPRINTING, DNA
Generally, 556, 561
See also Databanks, DNA, this index; Identity Testing, this index

FLUORESCENCE IN SITU HYBRIDIZATION
Chromosomes, 299

FOOD AND DRUG ADMINISTRATION (FDA)
Generally, 418

Biologics License Applications, 420, 428

Direct-to-consumer genetic test kits, 353, 363

Gene therapy authority, 418

Genetic enhancement products, regulatory authority as to, 511

Genetic testing product regulation, 303

HIV and drugs, home testing kits for, 360

Investigational Device Exemption applications, 366, 399, 428

Investigational New Drug Applications, 376, 420, 428

New Drug Applications, 376, 420, 428

Pharmacogenetic data submission guidance, 376

Premarket Approval Applications, 422, 428

Recombinant DNA Advisory Committee and, overlapping jurisdiction, 426

FORENSICS
Generally, 553 et seq.
Criminal Law, this index
Databanks, DNA, this index
Identity Testing, this index

FRAGILE X SYNDROME
Education testing, 657, 661
Failure to test for, 225
Testing indications, 226

FUNDING
See Federal Funding, this index

GAMETES
See Reproductive Technology, this index

GENDER
Inheritance rules of, 31
Selection. See Sex Selection, this index
XYY Chromosome Carriers, this index

GENE PATENTS
See Patents, this index

GENE POOL
Germline therapy risk, 444
Manipulation risks, 11

GENE THERAPIES
Generally, 488 et seq.
AMA opinion, 407
Artificial chromosomes, 436
Chemotherapy preceding, 412
Conflicts of interest, 401, 433
DHHS protocol proposals, 410
Disclosures of adverse events, 399, 401
Embryos, pre-implantation modification, 442
Enhancement, Genetic, this index
Enhancement objectives, 481
FDA authority, 418
Genetic research leading to, 88
Germline therapy
Generally, 434
Genetic enhancement proposals, 485
Policy considerations, 441
Scientific overview, 407, 434
Somatic cell therapies distinguished, 407, 434
Successive generations, impacts on, 444
History of, 394
Homologous recombination therapy, 435
Informed consent, 429
IRB approvals, 394
Modification of pre-implantation embryos, 442

Moratorium proposal for rDNA
experiments, 407
National Institutes of Health oversight
proposals, 406
Newborn treatment proposals, 396
Non-homologous recombination therapy,
435
Ooplasmic transfer, 437
Ornithine transcarbamylase deficiency
treatment, 395
Patients' Rights, this index
Personalized genomic medicine, 298
See also Personalized Medicine, this
index; Precision Medicine, this
index
Pharmacogenomics, this index
Pre-implantation embryos, modification of,
442
Protecting human subjects, 429
Public Health Genetics, this index
Radiation preceding, 412
Recombinant DNA Advisory Committee
approvals, 396, 404, 409
Recombinant DNA therapy hazards
Generally, 404
Moratorium proposal, 407
Oversight, 424
Regulation, 404 et seq.
Replacement therapy, 435
Research/therapy distinctions, 433
Risks, 395, 399
RNA interference (RNAi), 404
Scientific principles, 402
Somatic cell gene therapy, 407, 434
Successive generations, germline therapy
impacts on, 444
Targeting therapy, 435
Tort liabilities, 402

GENEALOGY
See also Ancestry Tracing, this index
Group harms of genetic genealogy, 208

GENES
Alleles, 29
Centimorgans, 5, 36
Definition, 5, 27
Dominant and recessive genetic effects, 32
Human genes, number of, 28
Multigene inheritance effects, 32
Protein relationships, 28
Race and ethnicity, 179
Recessive and dominant genetic effects, 32

GENETIC FINGERPRINTS
Toxic chemicals leaving, 811

GENETIC HOMOGENEITY
Human Genome Project, 6

**GENETIC INFORMATION
NONDISCRIMINATION ACT
(GINA)**
ADA compared, 787

Employment discrimination, 762, 777, 778
Enactment, 777
Health insurance discrimination, 720, 723
Medical record protections, 770
Voluntary genetic monitoring, 805

GENOGRAPHIC PROJECT
Evolution studies, 206

GENO-PHENOBANK
Generally, 87

**GENOME WIDE ASSOCIATION
STUDIES (GWAS)**
Generally, 86

GENOMES
Association studies (GWAS), 43, 86
Haplotype map of the human genome, 42
HapMap project, 42
Human Genome Project, this index
Neanderthal genome, 6, 284
Organism sequencing projects, 41
Sequencing projects, 41
Single nucleotide polymorphism (SNP), 42
1000 Genomes Project, 43, 204

GENOMICS
Behavioral, 635

GERMLINE THERAPY
See Gene Therapies, this index

HAPMAP PROJECT
Generally, 42, 206

HAVASUPAI TRIBE RESEARCH
Generally, 212

HAZARDOUS SUBSTANCES
See Environmental Health, this index

**HEALTH AND HUMAN SERVICES
DEPARTMENT**
See Department of Health and Human
Services, this index

**HEALTH CARE FINANCING
ADMINISTRATION (HCFA)**
See also Federal Funding, this index
Access to genetic services, 337
Laboratory certifications, 304

**HEALTH INFORMATION
TECHNOLOGY FOR ECONOMIC
AND CLINICAL HEALTH ACT
(HITECH ACT)**
Privacy rights, 680, 700

HEALTH INSURANCE
See Insurance, this index

**HEALTH INSURANCE PORTABILITY
AND ACCOUNTABILITY ACT
(HIPAA)**
Insurance portability rights, 718

Physicians, obtaining of suspects' samples
    from, 578
Privacy rights and disclosure duties, 327
Regulations implementing, 696

HEALTH RECORDS
See Medical Records, this index

HELA CELL LINE
Generally, 177

**HEREDITARY HEMOCHROMATOSIS
    (HH)**
Generally, 301

HEREDITY
Abortion counseling and tort law, 73
Eugenics Movements, this index
Mental and Behavioral Genetics, this index
Prenatal Screening, this index
Reproduction, DNA testing, 215 et seq., 299
    et seq.
Scientific overview, 2
Sickle-cell screening, 188, 217
Testing, this index

HISTORY OF GENETICS
        Generally, 1, 21
Darwinism, 4
DNA discovery, 21
DNA replication, 25
DNA sequencing, 41
Double helix structure, discovery of, 23
Employment health screening, 761
Eugenics Movements, this index
Evolution theory, 2, 4
Gene therapies, 395
Human Genome Diversity Project evolution
    and migration studies, 200
Mendelism, 4
Mental and behavioral genetics, 629
Newborn screening, 451
Paternity testing, 516
Sequencing of DNA, 41

HIV/AIDS
Genetic testing for, 301
Home testing kits for, 360

HOME TESTING
See Direct-to-Consumer Genetic Testing,
    this index

HOMOSEXUALITY
Genetic link questions, 631

**HUMAN GENOME DIVERSITY
    PROJECT (HGDP)**
        Generally, 200 et seq.
Chinese project, 205
Evolution studies, 200
Funding, 205
Genographic Project, 206
Group harms of genetic genealogy, 208
Indigenous peoples, exploitation concerns,
    201

Migration studies, 201
Model agreement for genetic research, 210
Political and policy concerns, 208
Race and deme, 208
Single-nucleotide polymorphism (SNP)
    studies, 204
Tissue sample misuse litigation, 214

**HUMAN GENOME ORGANIZATION
    (HUGO)**
Creation, 40

HUMAN GENOME PROJECT (HGP)
        Generally, 35 et seq.
Access to genetic services, HGP impacts,
    335
Commercial activities, 40
Costs of DNA sequencing, 42
Encyclopedia of DNA Elements (ENCODE),
    28
Ethical, Legal and Social Implications
    (ELSI) program, 17
Financing, 40
First phase completion, 35
Genetic homogeneity, 6
Genetic linkage maps, 35
Genome-wide association studies (GWAS),
    86
Goals, 35
Haplotype map of the human genome, 42
HapMap project, 42
Intellectual property aspects, 40
Mapping phase, 35
Markers, genetic, 36
Measurement conventions, 36
Mental and behavioral genetics studies,
    630
Nonhuman sequencing projects, 41
Phases of project, 35
Physical maps, 36
Private sector activities, 40
Sequencing, 41
Source subjects, 41
1000 Genomes Project, 43, 204
Unintended consequences, 15

HUMAN GROWTH HORMONE (HGH)
        Generally, 482
Regulation, 506

**HUMAN LEUKOCYTE ANTIGEN
    (HLA) SYSTEM**
Blood tests, 555
Typing, HLA, 203

HUNTINGTON DISEASE (HD)
        Generally, 29, 34, 334
Behavioral associations, 649
Criminal law defense, 649
Scientific overview, 29
Testing and counseling, 96, 310

IDENTITY TESTING
        Generally, 553 et seq.

See also Criminal Law, this index; Databanks, DNA, this index

Abandoned DNA collections, 579

Admissibility of DNA evidence
    Civil litigation, 625
    Criminal cases, 554 et seq.
    Emerging technologies, 568
    Statistical evidence, 563

Adultery litigation, 625

Ancestry Tracing, this index

Arrest warrants based on DNA information descriptions, 571

Band pattern matching, 561

Blood group markers, 554

Court-ordered collection, 577

Crime scene sample collections, 561, 568

Daubert challenges to DNA evidence, 560

DQ alpha testing, 585

Dragnets, DNA, 572

Emerging DNA technologies
    Generally, 558
    Admissibility challenges, 568
    Post-conviction challenges to earlier testing, 586

Faked DNA samples, dangers of, 569

False match rates, 563

FBI standards, 556

Fingerprinting, DNA
    Generally, 556
    Reliability standards, 561

Forcible collections of samples, 617

Frequency data for populations and subpopulations
    Generally, 556
    Match probabilities, 568

Frye challenges to DNA evidence, 556, 560

Genetic differences among individuals, 28

Health information disclosures during, 560

History of, 554

Immigration law, genetic testing to determine familial relationships, 533

Indictments of persons described by DNA, 571

Justice for All Act of 2004, 583

Laboratory contamination errors, 558, 571

Low copy number DNA tests, 558

Match probabilities
    Generally, 562
    Minority ethnic groups, 569

Matching error, 562

Mistakes and false match rates, 562

Mitochondrial DNA data, 556

Mixed DNA samples, 561

National Research Council admissibility standards, 560, 570

Native American ancestry determinations, 625

PCR sample collections, 556

Physicians, obtaining of suspects' samples from, 578

Planted DNA, 569

Polymerase chain reaction technique, 556

Post-conviction DNA testing, 581

Related persons, 564

Relatives of suspects, collection of samples from, 579

Reliability
    Generally, 561
    Challenging, 556

Scientific overview, 553

Search and seizure challenges to collection efforts, 573

Short tandem repeat technique, 556

Soldiers' remains, 620

Statistical independence assumptions, 562

Statistical match probabilities
    Generally, 562
    Minority ethnic groups, 569

Surreptitious DNA sample collection, 576

Tort liabilities, forcible collections of samples, 617

Variable number tandem repeats, 555

Warrants based on DNA information descriptions, 571

IMMIGRATION LAW

Eugenics era goals, 80, 81

Genetic testing to determine familial relationships, 533

IN VITRO FERTILIZATION

See Reproductive Technology, this index

INDIGENOUS PEOPLES

Cell line sources, 202

Exploitation concerns, 201

Havasupai Tribe research, 212

HLA typing, 203

Model agreement for genetic research, 210

INFORMED CONSENT

AMA guidelines on commercial use of human tissue, 175

ASHG guidelines, 109

Biobank research, 105

Cesarean section, right to refuse, 246

Children and adolescent screening, 333

Competency of minors to consent, 333

Donor conceptions, donor consent issues, 295

Gene therapies, 429

Genetic research projects, race and ethnic group consent to, 84

Genetic testing, 247

Invasive interventions, right to refuse, 246

Newborn screening, 465

Newborn treatment proposals, 396

Patients' rights as to research, 161, 170

Prenatal screening, 247

Prenatal screening and reproductive autonomy, 246

Research/therapy distinctions, 431

Tissue research, 102

Tortious failures to obtain, 127

INHERITANCE

Blending theories, 4

Chromosomes, role of, 22
Dominant and recessive genetic effects, 32
Enhancement, Genetic, this index
Gender, inheritance rules of, 31
Germline therapy impacts, 297, 434
Homozygous sequences, 32
Linkage analysis, 36
Markers, genetic, 36
Multigene effects, 32
Patterns of, 31
Penetrance of genetic characteristics, 34
Prenatal Screening, this index
Recessive and dominant genetic effects, 32

**INSTITUTIONAL REVIEW BOARDS
    (IRB)**
Development of, 84
Federal regulations applicable to, 89
Food and Drug Administration
    requirements, 89
Gene therapy proposals, 394
Genetic enhancement research, 491
HHS regulations, 89
Risk assessments, 99

INSURANCE
    Generally, 709 et seq.
Actuarially justified disclosures, 710
Adverse selection concerns of insurers
    Generally, 710
    Alzheimer risks, 756
Alzheimer disease predictions and long-
    term care insurance risks, 754
Americans with Disabilities Act, 741
Civil rights law challenges underwriting
    practices, 741
Coverage decisions, health insurance, 729
Disability insurance, 751
Disclosures, actuarially justified, 710
Discrimination challenges, life insurance,
    741
Employment and health insurance
    Generally, 761
    Access to medical records, 770
    ERISA preemption of state laws, 712
Employment Discrimination, this index
ERISA preemption of state laws, 712
Genetic Information Nondiscrimination
    Act, 720
Genetic screening laws
    Health insurance, 713
    Life insurance, 738
Health insurance
    Generally, 711 et seq.
    Access to genetic services, 335, 340
    Coverage decisions, 729
    Discrimination protections, 498
    Employment and health insurance
        access, 761
    ERISA preemption of state laws, 712
    Experimental treatments, 734
    Genetic Information
        Nondiscrimination Act, 720

Genetic screening laws, 713
Group policies, 711
HIPAA protections, 718
Pharmacogenetics influencing
    coverage determinations, 383
Refusals of coverage, 729
Underwriting practices, 716
Life insurance
    Generally, 735 et seq.
    Americans with Disabilities Act, 741
    Civil rights law challenges
        underwriting practices, 741
    Discrimination challenges, 741
    Genetic screening laws, 738
    Moral mission of, 736
    Policy considerations, 747
    Social function of, 736
    Underwriting practices, 736, 741
Long-term care insurance, 754
Moral mission of life insurance, 736
Predictive genetics assessments and risk
    determinations, 709
Privacy rights and applicant testing, 710
Risk classification basis of, 709
Risk Evaluation and Education for
    Alzheimer's Disease (REVEAL)
    Study, 756
Sickle cell carriers, discrimination, 710
Social function of life insurance, 736
Underwriting practices
    Civil rights law challenges, 741
    Health insurance, 716
    Life insurance, 736, 741
    Statutory regulation, 712

INTELLECTUAL PROPERTY RIGHTS
DNA copyrighting proposals, 176
Federal statutory protections, 129
Patents, this index
Technology Transfer Laws, this index
Trade secret protection of genetic
    discoveries, 136

INTELLIGENCE TESTING
Language biases, 630
Scientific overview, 629

**INVESTIGATIONAL DEVICE
    EXEMPTION (IDE)
    APPLICATIONS**
Generally, 399, 428

**INVESTIGATIONAL NEW DRUG (IND)
    APPLICATIONS**
Generally, 399, 420

LABORATORIES
    See also Testing, this index
Contamination errors affecting identity
    testing, 558
Identity testing, laboratory contamination
    errors, 558
Malpractice, 236

LANGUAGE BIASES
Intelligence testing, 630

LIABILITIES
See Tort Law, this index

LICENSING
See Patents, this index

LIFE INSURANCE
See Insurance, this index

LITIGATION
Discovery of medical records, 819

LONG-TERM CARE INSURANCE
See Insurance, this index

MALPRACTICE
See Tort Law, this index

MANAGED CARE ORGANIZATIONS
Access to genetic services, 340

MAPS, GENETIC
Haplotype map of the human genome, 42
HapMap project, 42, 206
Human Genome Project, this index

MARKERS, GENETIC
Generally, 36
Linkage analysis, 299

MATERNAL AND CHILD HEALTH BUREAU (MCHB)
Newborn screening, 451

MEDICAL RECORDS
See also Privacy Rights, this index
Biobanks, medical record linkages, 104
Constitutional protections, 683
Discovery in litigation, 819
Employer access to, 770
Family and Medical Leave Act disclosures, 770
Genetic Information Nondiscrimination Act protections, 770

MEDICAL REFERRALS
See Conflicts of Interest, this index

MEDICARE AND MEDICAID
Access to genetic services, 337

MENDELISM
Darwinism and, 4, 22
Eugenics movement, 45

MENTAL AND BEHAVIORAL GENETICS
Generally, 627 et seq.
Addictive tendencies, 656
Alcohol abuse predispositions, 651
Behavioral genomics, 635
Civil commitment of sexual offenders, 653
Criminal law
Generally, 637 et seq.
Culpability, 641

Death penalty defense, 652
Ineffective assistance claims, 650
Defenses to crimes based on genetic predisposition, 639
Determinism dangers, 629, 636
Discrimination concerns, 635
Dogs and wolves, 627
Education and, 657
Environment vs heredity influences, 627
Eugenics movement relationships, 630, 636
Fragile X syndrome testing, 662
Future of behavioral genetics, 633
Genomics, behavioral, 634
Historical development, 629
Homosexuality, genetic link questions, 631
Human and animal manifestations, 627
Human Genome Project effects on studies, 630
Huntington disease, behavioral associations, 649
Intelligence testing, 629
Language biases in intelligence testing, 630
Military applications, 669
Molecular genetics, 632
Obstacles to scientific investigation, 628
Predisposition defenses to crimes, 639
Privacy concerns in education testing, 661
Quantitative research, 633
Recidivist criminal behavior predictions, 638
Schizophrenia, genetic associations, 628
Scientific issues, 632
Sexual offenders, civil commitment of, 653
Tort law, 668
Twin studies, 627
Violence predictions, 637
XYY chromosome carriers, 98, 644

MINORITIES
See Race and Ethnicity, this index

MISATTRIBUTED PATERNITY
See Unanticipated Misattributed Paternity, this index

MITOCHONDRIAL DNA (MTDNA) DATA
Identity testing, 556

MOLECULAR GENETICS
Future of, 6, 11
Graveyard of molecular geneticists, 628
Mental and behavioral genetics, 631
Scientific overview, 148

MUTATIONS
Evolution and, 3
Polymorphic mutant types, 3

NATIONAL HEALTH AND NUTRITION EXAMINATION SURVEYS (NHANES)
Generally, 112

NATIONAL INSTITUTES OF HEALTH (NIH)
Gene therapy oversight proposals, 406
Technology Transfer Laws, this index

NATIONAL RESEARCH COUNCIL (NRC)
Admissibility of DNA evidence, 560, 570

NATIVE AMERICAN ANCESTRY
DNA determinations, 625

NEANDERTHALS
Gene sequencing and cloning, 284
Genome, 6

NEWBORN SCREENING
Generally, 451 et seq.
Accuracy concerns, 454
American Academy of Pediatrics
    recommendations, 451, 476
American College of Medical Genetics
    report, 461
CDC oversight, 452
Core panel of tests, 461
Cost/benefit considerations, 463
Costs and funding sources, 462
Council of Regional Networks for Genetic
    Services facilitation of state projects,
    453
Cystic fibrosis testing, 122
Discrimination problems, 456
Eugenics implications, 80
Federally-funded state programs, 452
Follow-up requirements, 453
Gene therapy treatment proposals,
    informed consent, 396
Harmful aspects of screening, 454
History of, 451
Incurable disorders, 461
Informed consent issues, 465
Labeling consequences, 456
Legal implications of screening for
    children, 455
Malpractice, 463
Mandated testing
    Constitutionality, 469
    Informed consent conflicts, 465
    PKU screening, 467
    Religious objections, 461
Mandatory screening laws
    Generally, 452, 460
    PKU screening, 458
Maternal and Child Health Bureau study,
    451
Maternal and child health (MCH) program
    requirements, 452
New tandem mass spectrometry (MS/MS)
    screening technology, 461
PKU screening
    Development, 451
    Malpractice, 463
    Mandated testing, 467
    Mandatory screening, 458

Policy concerns, 461
Public health genetics, 85, 454
Religious objections, 471
Research benefits, 462
Residual blood samples, 477
Therapeutic follow ups, 453
Treatable and nontreatable disorders, 81

NUREMBERG CODE
Adoption, 83
Voluntariness standard, 117

NUTRIGENOMICS
Generally, 385

**OCCUPATIONAL SAFETY AND
    HEALTH ACT (OSHA)**
Benzene decision, 802
Beryllium exposure, 805
Carpal tunnel susceptibility, genetic
    testing for, 806
Environmental protections for employees,
    801
Toxicogenomics in the workplace, 801

ORGAN DONATION
See Donation of Organs and Tissues, this
    index

OVARIAN CANCER
Genetic testing for risk of, 302

OVER THE COUNTER TESTING
See Direct-to-Consumer Genetic Testing,
    this index

OWNERSHIP QUESTIONS
See Property Rights, this index

PARENTAGE
Generally, 515 et seq.
Adoption model, 278
Assisted reproduction and paternity, 260
Biological mothers, 279
Blood testing, traditional, 522
Court-ordered testing
    Generally, 526
    Privacy rights conflicts, 528
Direct-to-consumer genetic testing, 351,
    526
Disabled parents, custody rights of, 546,
    551
DNA testing, effect on paternity laws, 515
History of paternal rights, 515
Immigration law, genetic testing to
    determine familial relationships, 533
Marriage presumptions, 515
Maternal rights, 515
One-parent and relatives testing, 527
Posthumous DNA testing, 527
Putative father registries, 516
Relatives of deceased parent, DNA testing
    of, 527
Semen donors, 263
Statutes of limitation, 529

Surrogacy
    Generally, 278
    Contracts, 268
Switched baby cases, 523, 532
Uniform Parentage Act (UPA), 265

PATENTS
Cell line patent rights, 166
Cloning patent claims, 150
Funded research and property rights, 130
Gene patents
    Generally, 129 et seq.
    International aspects, 149 et seq.
    Legal requirements, 133 et seq.
    Licensing agreements, 303
    Patentable subject matter, 137 et seq.
    Policy concerns, 135 et seq.
    Requirements of patentability, 133 et
      seq.
    Research-impeding patents, 136
    Tissue suppliers' rights, 131
    TRIPS, 151
Higher life forms, patentability, 145
International aspects of gene patents, 149
Inventorship and tissue ownership
    distinguished, 178
Licenses
    Genetic testing processes, 303
    March-in rights, 153
    Technology transfer laws, 151 et seq.
Patients vs researchers, 167
Requirements of patentability
    Gene patents, 133
Subject matter, patentable, 137 et seq.
Technology Transfer Laws, this index
Tissue ownership and inventorship
    distinguished, 178

PATERNITY
Parentage, this index
Presumptions, traditional, 517
Unanticipated Misattributed Paternity,
    this index

PATIENTS' RIGHTS
    See also Property Rights, this index
AMA guidelines on commercial use of
    human tissue, 175
Fiduciary duties of researchers, 161, 171
Informed consent as to research, 161, 170
Invasive interventions, right to refuse, 246
Newborn screening, 465
Prenatal screening and reproductive
    autonomy, 246
Researchers vs, 158
Tissue sample ownership rights, 158

PERSONALIZED MEDICINE
    Generally, 12 et seq.
    See also Precision Medicine, this
      index
ELSI implications, 12 et seq.
FDA, 190, 383
Limitations, 16, 356, 383

Public Health application, 450
Privacy considerations, 679
Regulatory considerations, 679
Testing, 383, 385

PHARMACOGENOMICS
    Generally, 369 et seq.
Access to pharmacogenomic drugs, 388
Athletic prowess, 483
Data submissions, FDA guidance, 376
Definition, 369
Drug manufacturers' interests, 388
Drugs, pharmacogenetic influences, 369
Enhancement objectives, 481
Ethical implications, 385
FDA authority, 418
Genomic and genetic approaches, 370
Health insurer coverage determinations,
    382
Legal implications, 385
Nutrigenomics, 385
Orphan drugs, 388
Pharmaceutical industry influences, 369
Pharmacogenetics distinguished, 381
Pharmacokinetic and pharmacodynamic
    variability, 191
Privacy rights, 392
Proteomics distinguished, 381
Race-based drugs
    Generally, 190
    Policy concerns, 194, 198
Recombinant human insulin, 298
Research, 369
Single nucleotide polymorphism (SNP)
    research, 373
Standard of care, developments affecting,
    389
Target validation, 370, 373
Warfarin dosage determinations, 382

PHENYLKETONURIA
Generally, 35

PHYSICIAN-PATIENT PRIVILEGE
Generally, 252

PHYSICIAN-PATIENT
    RELATIONSHIPS
Privacy rights, 674
Third parties, duties owed, 320

PKU SCREENING
See Newborn Screening, this index

POLLUTION
See Environmental Health, this index

POLYMERASE CHAIN REACTION
    (PCR)
Development of process, 300
Identity testing, 555

POST-CONVICTION DNA TESTING
    Generally, 581
Innocence Project, 590

Justice for All Act of 2004, 583

PRADER-WILLI SYNDROME
Generally, 814

PRECISION MEDICINE
Generally, 85, 105
See also Personalized Medicine, this
index
Oncology, applications to, 348
President Obama Initiative, 85, 106
Privacy considerations, 106

**PREIMPLANTATION GENETIC
DIAGNOSIS (PGD)**
Generally, 243
See also Reproductive Technology,
this index
Ethical considerations, 288
Eugenics aspects, 78
Malpractice, 240

PRENATAL SCREENING
Generally, 216 et seq.
Abortion decisions, 232
Amniocentesis, this index
Athletic prowess screening, 289
Blood testing, 215
Chorionic Villi Sampling, this index
Conceiving a sibling to be a donor, 289
Cystic fibrosis risks, 240
Disclosure duties as to risks and tests, 236
Ethnic groups, related fetal disorders, 218
Eugenics implications, 79, 81
Failure to warn liability, 232
False negative liabilities, 235
Family histories and testing decisions, 236
Fetal cell sorting, 243
Fetoscopy, 218
Fourth Amendment protections, 245
Informed consent, 247
Laboratory malpractice, 236
Mandatory, 243
Preimplantation genetic diagnosis, 240,
243
Reproductive autonomy conflicts, 246
Risks of, 218
Sex selection, 285
Tay-Sachs risks, 235
Techniques, 216
Ultrasound, this index
What testing is appropriate, 236
Wrongful adoption, 536
Wrongful Birth, this index
Wrongful Life, this index

PRESCRIPTION DRUGS
Drugs, this index

PRIMARY CARE PHYSICIANS
Testing referrals, 334
Tort liabilities, genetics-related, 325

PRIVACY RIGHTS
Generally, 671

See also Anonymity, this index;
Disclosures, this index
Anonymous testing, 351
Assisted reproduction donors, 250
Biobank research, 104
Celebrity genetics, 700
Certificates of Confidentiality for research
projects, 109
Children and adolescent screening, 551
Compelled disclosures, 681
Confidentiality and privacy distinguished,
675
Constitutional protections, 683
Controlled substance record laws, 683
Court-ordered paternity testing, 529
Dealing with genetic differences, 702
Dimensions of right, 673
Direct-to-consumer genetic testing,
anonymity advantages, 351, 705
Discrimination caused by breaches, 703
DNA databases, unauthorized uses, 614
Education testing and privacy concerns,
661
Electronic health records, 679
Embryonic and fetal research regulations,
reproductive privacy conflicts with,
121
Expectations of privacy and Fourth
Amendment protections, 577
Family Educational Rights and Privacy
Act, 663
Four aspects, 673
Genetic counseling privacy issues, 310
Genetic exceptionalism, 689
Genetic Privacy Act proposal, 689
Genetic privacy and confidentiality, 673 et
seq.
Genetic research stigmatization risk, 84
Health Information Technology for
Economic and Clinical Health Act
(HITECH ACT), 680, 700
Health Insurance Portability and
Accountability Act, this index
Home testing privacy concerns, 705
Identity testing, health information
disclosures during, 560
Insurance applicant testing, 710
Legal protections for medical and genetic
privacy, 683 et seq.
Misrepresentation and privacy
distinguished, 767
Paternity testing, court-ordered, 529
Pharmacogenetics research, 391
Physician-patient privilege, 252
Physician-patient relationships, 674
Prenatal screening, Fourth Amendment
protections, 245
Public concerns about genetic data, 678
Regulations implementing HIPAA, 695
Reproductive privacy conflicts with
embryonic and fetal research
regulations, 120
Reproductive technology, 250

Research publication, privacy rights
    conflicts, 100
Research stigmatization risk, 84
Research subjects, 95
State laws protecting genetic privacy, 694
Statutory disclosure duties, 326
Tissue research, 109
Tort law protections, 701
Toxicogenomics, privacy impacts, 798
Valuing privacy, 671
Warning duty conflicts, 320

PROBANDS
Definition, 95
Home testing anonymity, 351
Research recruitment through, 94

PROPERTY RIGHTS
    See also Intellectual Property Rights,
        this index; Patients' Rights,
        this index
AMA guidelines on commercial use of
    human tissue, 175
Conversion of tissue samples, 162, 172
Fraudulent concealment of research goals,
    172
Funded research and, 130
Havasupai Tribe research, 212
HeLa cell line, 177
Pre-embryos, ownership rights, 533
Prenatal screening and reproductive
    autonomy, 246
Protective strategies of researchers, 130
Screening conflicts, 246
Sperm and egg donors, compensation, 258
Technology transfer laws, 156
Tissue sample ownership rights, 158 et seq.
Unjust enrichment, 172

PROTEINS
Definition, 27
Gene relationships, 28

PUBLIC HEALTH GENETICS
    Generally, 445 et seq.
Eugenics implications, 449
Inherent value conflicts, 448
Newborn testing programs, 85, 454
Phenotypic prevention, 448
Regulatory authority as to genetic diseases,
    55, 81
Screening, this index
Toxicogenomics, 449

RACE AND ETHNICITY
    Generally, 179
Allele distributions, 179
Biologic determinism, danger of, 181
Biologic significance, 179
Census self-classifications, 184
Deme as alternative concept to race, 208
Demic discrimination, 209
DNA databanks

Frequency data for populations and
    subpopulations
        Generally, 556
        Match probabilities, 569
    Racial discrimination in collection
        practices, 618
DNA dragnets, race based, 572
Drug development, race-targeted
        Generally, 190
        Policy concerns, 194, 198
        Response connections, 185
Eugenics movement, race and class biases,
    45, 55
Fetal disorders, ethnic group-related, 218
Genetic disease incidence, 179
Genetic research stigmatization risk, 84
Genetic variation and, 3, 6, 179
Group consent to genetic research projects,
    84
Human Genome Diversity Project, this
    index
Medical histories, racial identifications in,
    182
Native American ancestry, DNA
    determinations, 625
Observable vs. biologic distinctions, 180
Pharmacogenetics, race-targeted drugs
        Generally, 190
        Policy concerns, 194, 198
Phenotype vs. biologic distinctions, 180
Research, race-based, 181
Sickle Cell Disease, this index
Social vs biologic distinctions, 179
Studies, measurements in, 183
Tuskegee syphilis study, 200

REASSORTATION OF GENES
Generally, 21

RECOMBINANT DNA (RDNA)
Advisory Committee (RAC)
        FDA and, overlapping jurisdiction,
            426
        Gene therapy approvals, 396, 404,
            410
Gene therapy hazards
        Generally, 404
        FDA oversight, 424
        Moratorium proposal, 407
Scientific overview, 23

RECOMBINATION EVENTS
Scientific overview, 23, 31

REPRODUCTIVE TECHNOLOGY
    Generally, 247 et seq.
Adoption model, parentage determination
    by, 278
Anonymous sperm donors
        Generally, 250, 272
        Internet tracing of, 279
Athlete sperm banks, 76
Biological mothers, 279

Children's identity determination rights, 279
Cloning, this index
Compensation of sperm and egg donors, 258
Conceiving a sibling to be a donor, 289
Designer children policy concerns, 497
Dizygotic twins, 627
DNA testing, 297 et seq.
Donors
    Anonymous sperm donors, 250, 279
    Compensation of sperm and egg donors, 258
    Conceptions, donor consent issues, 295
    Paternity status of semen donors, 263
    Reproductive technology donor mixups, 255
    Screening of donors, 248, 308
    Screening of gamete donors, 258
    Sperm mixups, 255
    Unknown genetic disorders of donors, 259
Embryonic and fetal research regulations, reproductive privacy conflicts with, 121
Emotional distress claims, 255
Enhancement, Genetic, this index
Excess embryo donations to research programs, 122
Gamete donation, 77
Genetic modification of pre-implantation embryos, 442
Genetic screening in assisted reproduction, 248
Genetic testing, 299 et seq.
Genius sperm bank, 75
In vitro fertilization (IVF)
    Generally, 77, 247
    Gamete donation selection practices, 77
Internet tracing of anonymous sperm donors, 279
Liabilities
    Generally, 250
    Switched baby cases, 272
Maternal rights and surrogacy, 515
Meiosis and mitosis, 29
Mixed sperm procedures, 255
Monozygotic twins, 627
Non-medical applications, 285
Parentage, this index
Paternity and assisted reproduction, 260
Preimplantation embryos
    Genetic modification of, 442
    Genetic selection, 482
Preimplantation Genetic Diagnosis, this index
Prenatal Screening, this index
Prenatal screening and, 245
Privacy rights, 250
Purposes, 247
Screening of donors, 248

Screening of gamete donors, 258
Semen donors, paternity status, 263
Sex selection, 285
Sperm and egg donors, compensation, 258
Surrogacy and maternal rights, 515
Surrogate brokers' responsibilities, 260
Surrogate mothers, 279
Surrogate parentage contracts, 268
Switched baby cases, 272
Unknown genetic disorders of donors, 259

RESEARCH
    Generally, 83 et seq.
Biobanks, this index
CDC research on existing tissue samples, 112
Certificates of Confidentiality, 109
Child subjects
    Generally, 331
    Federal regulations, 543
Clinical Research, this index
Commercialization of Genetic Research, this index
Conflicts of interest
    Generally, 108, 154, 400
    Therapy/research distinctions, 433
Control groups subjects, liabilities to, 122
Cooperative Research and Development Agreements (CRADA), 154
Counseling subjects, 96
Criminal chromosome studies, 98, 644
Cystic fibrosis testing, 122
Disclosures of tissue sample research results, 110
Disclosures to subjects, 96
Diseases, this index
Disposition of tissue samples, 110
DNA databases, research uses, 613
DNA diagnostic studies, 88
Drugs, this index
Embryonic and Fetal Research, this index
Enhancement, genetic, 490
Environmental Genome Project, this index
Epidemiological Research, this index
Epigenetics Research, this index
Experimentation, Human, this index
Federal regulation, 84, 88
Fetal research regulation, 101
Fetal research standards, 84
Fiduciary duties of researchers, 160, 171
Food and Drug Administration regulations, 89
Forensic DNA databases, research uses, 613
Funding
    Federal Funding, this index
    Property rights as to funded research, 130
    Technology Transfer Laws, this index
Gene patents, research impeding, 136
Gene therapy research following, 88
Genetic enhancement, 490
Genographic Project, 206

Genome Wide Association Studies (GWAS), 86
HapMap project, 92, 206
Havasupai Tribe research, 212
Human Genome Diversity Project, this index
Informed Consent, this index
Institutional Review Boards, this index
Law enforcement DNA databases, research uses, 613
Liabilities to research subjects, 122
Malpractice liabilities, 124, 127
Mental and behavioral genetics, quantitative research, 624, 632
Model agreement for genetic research, 210
National Health and Nutrition Examination Surveys (NHANES), 112
Nazi research atrocities, 83
Newborn screening, research benefits, 462
Nuremberg Code, this index
Office for Human Research Protections, 99
Ownership rights in tissue samples, 158 et seq.
Patient vs researcher ownership rights, 158 et seq.
Patients' Rights, this index
Pharmacogenetics, 369
Privacy of subjects, 96
Proband recruitment, 95
Property rights as to funded research, 130
Property rights protections in, 130
Proteomics, 381
Publication, privacy rights conflicts, 100
Publication of data, 97
Quantitative research, mental and behavioral genetics, 632, 634
Race-based, 181
Racial selection of subjects, 84
Recruitment of subjects, 94
Regulation
    Generally, 85 et seq.
    See also Institutional Review Boards, this index
    Embryonic research, 101
    Federal, 84, 88
    Food and Drug Administration, 89
    Office for Human Research Protections, 99
    Risk reduction, 94
    State regulation, 101
    Stem cell research, 117, 122
    Vulnerable population studies, 88, 92, 493
Retrospective studies of existing tissue samples, 111
Risk reduction regulations, 94
Selection of subjects, 83
Sequencing research regulation, 85
Single-nucleotide polymorphism (SNP) studies, 86, 204
Social implications, 15, 16
Stem Cell Research, this index

Stigmatization risk, 84
Technology Transfer Laws, this index
Therapy/research distinctions, 433
1000 Genomes Project, 43, 204
Tissue sample research, 102
Tuskegee syphilis study, regulatory response, 88
Vulnerable population studies, 88, 92, 101, 493

RIBONUCLEIC ACID (RNA)
Gene therapy, RNA interference (RNAi), 404
Scientific overview, 27

RISK EVALUATION AND EDUCATION FOR ALZHEIMER'S DISEASE (REVEAL) STUDY
Generally, 756

SCHIZOPHRENIA
Genetic associations, 628

SCIENTIFIC OVERVIEW
    Generally, 21 et seq.
Alleles, gene, 29
Cell division, 29
Cell nuclei, chromosome structure in, 26
Centimorgans, 36
Chromosomes
    Generally, 22
    Abnormalities, 26
    Structure, 26
Cloning, 280
Cystic fibrosis, 29
Cytoplasm, 28
DNA discoveries
    Generally, 23
    Double helix structure, 24
    Emerging DNA technologies for identity testing, 558
    Replication process, 25
    Sequencing, 300
Encyclopedia of DNA Elements (ENCODE), 28
Fetal cell sorting, 243
Forensics, 553
Fragile X syndrome, 226
Gene alleles, 29
Gene therapies, 402, 407
Gene/protein relationships, 28
Genes and proteins, 27
Genetic differences among individuals, 29
Genetic testing, 29
Genome-wide association studies (GWAS), 86
Germline therapy, 407, 434
Haplotype map of the human genome, 42
Heredity, 2
Human Genome Project, 35
Huntington disease, 29
Identical and fraternal twins, 627
Identity testing, 553
In vitro fertilization, 247

Intelligence testing, 629
Linkage analysis, 299
Markers, genetic, 36
Meiosis, 29
Mendelism, 5
Mitochondrial DNA, 27, 557
Mitosis, 29
Non-homologous recombination therapy, 435
Nucleotide base sequences, 24
Ooplasmic transfer, 437
Patterns of inheritance, 31
Penetrance of genetic characteristics, 38
Polymerase chain reaction (PCR), 300, 556
Preimplantation genetic diagnosis, 247
Protein/gene relationships, 28
Proteins, gene, 27
Race and Ethnicity, 179
rDNA experiments, 406
Reassortation of genes, 21
Recombinant DNA, 22
Recombination events, 22, 31
Ribonucleic acid, 27
Ribosome structure of DNA, 28
RNA interference (RNAi), 404
Sequencing, 83
Sex determinative chromosomes, 26
Short tandem repeat testing, 556
Single nucleotide polymorphism, 42
Somatic cell gene therapy, 407, 410
Testing, genetic, 29
Twin studies of behavioral genetics, 627

SCREENING
Generally, 302
See also Public Health Genetics, this index; Testing, this index
Assisted reproduction donors, 248
Children and adolescent
Generally, 331 et seq.
Competency of minors to consent, 333
Disclosure requests and restrictions, 333
Huntington disease, 334
Informed consent, 333
Late-onset diseases, 331
Legal implications of screening for children, 455
Parent/child conflicts, 332
Psychosocial issues associated with, 332
Results disclosures, 332
Competency of minors to consent, 333
Definition, 302
Disclosure requests and restrictions, 333
Employment Discrimination, this index
Entire population screening, 299
Gamete donors, 258
GINA voluntary genetic monitoring, 805
Harmful aspects of newborn screening, 454
High-throughput screening
Generally, 370, 385
Toxicity screening of chemicals, 797

Huntington disease, 334
Informed consent, children and adolescents, 333
Insurance, this index
Late-onset diseases, 331
Legal implications of screening for children, 455
Mandatory prenatal screening, 243
Megascreening, 298
New tandem mass spectrometry (MS/MS) screening technology, 461
Newborn Screening, this index
Parent-child conflicts, 332
Patients' Rights, this index
Prenatal Screening, this index
Property rights conflicts, 246
Psychosocial issues associated with screening, 332
Results disclosures, children and adolescents, 333
Sickle-cell screening, 17
Testing distinguished, 302
Toxicogenomics, 797

SEQUENCES AND SEQUENCING
Generally, 23
Costs, 42
Genome sequencing projects, 41
Genome-wide association studies (GWAS), 43
Heterozygous sequence, 32
Homozygous sequence, 32
Human Genome Project, this index
Neanderthals, gene sequencing and cloning, 284
Nucleotide base sequences, 27
Organism sequencing projects, 41
Regulation of sequencing research, 85
Scientific overview, 299

SEX SELECTION
Generally, 285
Home testing for baby gender, 367

SHORT TANDEM REPEAT (STR) TECHNIQUE
Identity testing, 556

SICKLE CELL DISEASE
Generally, 36
Carriers, insurance discrimination, 710
Screening, 17

SINGLE NUCLEOTIDE POLYMORPHISM (SNP)
Genetic research, 86
Pharmacogenetics research, 373
Research projects, 204
Scientific overview, 42

SOMATIC CELL THERAPY
See Gene Therapies, this index

SPECIES
See also Evolution, this index

DNA measures of differentiation, 3

STEM CELL RESEARCH
Generally, 117
Federal restrictions on embryo use, 117

STERILIZATION LAWS
See Eugenics Movements, this index

STUDIES
Race and ethnicity measurements in, 183

SURROGACY
See Reproductive Technology, this index

SWITCHED BABY CASES
Generally, 523, 532
Custody and visitation issues, 276, 532
Fertility clinic negligence, 272

TAY-SACHS
Generally, 36
Prenatal screening, 235

TECHNOLOGY TRANSFER LAWS
Generally, 151
Cooperative research and development
    agreements (CRADA), 154
Federal patent policy, 152
Licensing of patents, 153
March-in license rights, 153
NIH policies, 156
Privatization concerns, 156
Property right issues, 155

TEMPERAMENT
See Mental and Behavioral Genetics, this
    index

TESTING
Generally, 299 et seq.
See also Screening, this index
Access to genetic services, 334 et seq.
Adoption candidates
    Generally, 551
    ACMG and ASHG guideline, 544
Alzheimer disease, predictive testing, 314
Anonymous, 351
Arranged marriages, genetic disease risk
    considerations, 235
Breast cancer risk detection, 301
Carpal tunnel susceptibility, genetic
    testing for, 806
CDC, anlaysis of testing, 189, 452
CDC, laboratory regulation authority, 354
Clinical Laboratory Improvement Act
    regulation, 304
Clinical testing, 301
Complexity or regulatory oversight, 309
Confidentiality, warning duty conflicts, 320
Counseling, this index
Definition, 302
Direct-to-Consumer Genetic Testing, this
    index
Disclosure policies, 314
Disease risk prediction, 301

DNA sequencing, 300
Enhancement objectives, 481
Failure to test liability, 328
Familial risk management, 317
Family members, disclosures to, 314
FDA product regulation, 303
Federal funding for genetic services, 335
Federal regulatory agencies, 304
Fetal cell sorting, 243
Genetic counseling in conjunction with, 310
Genetic Information Nondiscrimination
    Act, 723
Health insurance coverage, 335, 342
Hereditary hemochromatosis (HH), 301
HIV infection detection through, 301
Huntington disease testing risks, 96, 310
Identity Testing, this index
Informed consent, 247
Insurance applicant testing, 710
Licensed testing processes, 303
Linkage analysis, 299
Managed care organization services, 340
Negative test results, misinterpreting, 302
Newborn Screening, this index
Ovarian cancer risk detection, 302
Overtreatment concerns, 359
Polymerase chain reaction process, 300
Predictive genetic testing
    Accuracy, 301
Preimplantation genetic diagnosis, 240,
    243
Prenatal Screening, this index
Primary care physician referrals
    Generally, 334
    Liability issues, 325
Privacy rights, insurance applicant testing,
    710
Product regulation, 303
Psychological and social risks, 244
Quality assurance programs, 305
Regulation, 303
Reproduction, 299 et seq.
Risk prediction, 301
Scientific overview, 35
Screening distinguished, 302
Sequencing, 300
Sex selection, 285
State regulation, 304
Tarasoff duties, 325
Third party warning duties, confidentiality
    conflicts, 316
Tort liabilities
    Generally, 318 et seq.
    Child testing, duties to parents, 328
    Confidentiality, warning duty
        conflicts, 320
    Failure to test, 328
    Primary care physician referrals for
        testing, 325
    Primary care physicians dealing with
        genetic testing issues, 325
    Warning duties, 318

Unanticipated Misattributed Paternity,
this index
Uses of, 301
Warning duties
Confidentiality conflicts, 316
Tort liabilities, 318

THERAPIES
See Gene Therapies, this index

TISSUE DONORS
See Donations of Organs and Tissues, this
index

TISSUE SAMPLES
See also Biobanks, this index
AMA guidelines on commercial use of
human tissue, 175
Amniocentesis, 120
Conversion, 162, 172
Databanks, DNA, this index
DNA patents, tissue suppliers' rights, 130
Embryonic and fetal research, 117
HeLa cell line, 177
HLA typing, 203
Human Genome Diversity Project, this
index
Misuse litigation, 213
Mixed DNA samples, 561
Newborn screening, residual blood
samples, 477
Ownership issues
Generally, 158 et seq.
See also Property Rights, this index
Patents, tissue suppliers' rights, 130
Physicians, obtaining of suspects' samples
from, 578
Research on tissue samples, 102

TORT LAW
Generally, 318 et seq.
Abortion counseling and wrongful birth
litigation, 73
Causation of environmental injuries, 812
Child testing, duties to parents, 328
Chromosomal damage, 808
Chromosomal damage, toxic exposure
causing, 808
Confidentiality, warning duty conflicts, 320
Damages for toxic exposures, 816
Direct-to-consumer genetic testing, 367
Discovery of medical records, 819
DNA dragnets, 572
Donor conception decisions, 289
Drug manufacturers, 393
Enhancement, genetic, 490
Environmental injuries
Generally, 808
Causation, 812
Damages, 816
Failure to conduct genetic testing, 328
Failure to warn, prenatal screening, 220
Forcible collections of samples for identity
testing, 617

Gene therapies, 402
Genetic testing, failure to conduct, 328
Havasupai Tribe research, 212
Identity testing, forcible collections of
samples, 617
Informed consent, failure to obtain, 107
Laboratories, 236
Learned intermediary doctrine, 393
Malpractice
Proximate cause, 293
Standard of care, 319
Tarasoff duties, 325
Third parties, duties owed, 319
Mental and behavioral genetics, 667
Newborn screening, 462
Pharmacogenetics developments affecting
standard of care, 389
Preimplantation genetic diagnosis, 240
Prenatal screening, 220
Primary care physician referrals for
testing, 328
Primary care physicians dealing with
genetic testing issues, 325
Privacy rights protections, 700
Reproductive technology
Generally, 250
Donor mixups, 255
Research malpractice, 122
Research subjects, liabilities to, 127
Switched baby cases, 532
Tarasoff duties, 325
Tissue samples, misuse, 213
Toxic exposures
Generally, 808
Chromosomal damage, 808
Damages, 816
Warning duties, 318
Wrongful adoption, 536
Wrongful Birth, this index
Wrongful Life, this index

TOXIC SUBSTANCES
See Environmental Health, this index

TOXICOGENOMICS
See also Environmental Health, this
index
Beryllium exposure testing, 805
Definition, 798
Discrimination concerns, 798
Privacy impacts, 798
Regulatory aspects, 794
Screening, 795
Technologies developments, 794
Testing, 806
Workplace issues, 801

**TRADE-RELATED ASPECTS OF
INTERNATIONAL PROPERTY
(TRIPS)**
Gene patents, 151

TUSKEGEE SYPHILIS STUDY
Regulatory response, 88

TWINS STUDIES
Behavioral genetic studies, 632
Behavioral genetics, 627
Epigenetics research, 87
Identical and fraternal twins, 627
Striking coincidences, 628

ULTRASOUND
Generally, 70
Sex selection, 285

UNANTICIPATED MISATTRIBUTED
PATERNITY
Generally, 255, 301
Counseling challenges, 301
Direct-to-consumer genetic testing, 351
Immigration rights testing, 533
Incidence of misattribution, 301
Non-paternity, unanticipated, 301
Research publication disclosures, 100

VARIABLE NUMBER TANDEM
REPEATS (VNTR)
Generally, 555

WARFARIN
Pharmacogenetics research, 382

WARNING DUTIES
Tort liabilities, 318

WORKERS' COMPENSATION
Generally, 752
Carpal tunnel susceptibility, genetic
testing for, 806
Medical examinations of claimants, 681,
769

WRONGFUL BIRTH
Generally, 220
Abortion counseling and tort law, 73
Damage awards and eugenics theory, 70
Damages issues, 233, 239
Eugenic implications, 232
Loss of consortium claims of parents, 241
Neoeugenics implications, 79
Policy considerations, 233
Pre-conception tort claims, 240, 241
Prenatal screening liability, 220
Statutory prohibitions, 231
Wrongful life claims distinguished, 237

WRONGFUL LIFE
Policy considerations, 242
Pre-conception tort claims distinguished,
240, 241
Statutory prohibitions, 231
Statutory restrictions, 243
Wrongful birth claims distinguished, 237

XYY CHROMOSOME CARRIERS
Generally, 98, 645